W9-BAC-373

to B. R. B.

PUBLIC FINANCE IN THEORY AND PRACTICE

PUBLIC FINANCE IN THEORY AND PRACTICE

Second Edition

Richard A. Musgrave
H. H. Burbank Professor of Political Economy
Harvard University

Peggy B. Musgrave
Professor of Economics
Northeastern University

McGraw-Hill Book Company
New York St. Louis San Francisco Auckland Düsseldorf Johannesburg Kuala Lumpur London Mexico Montreal New Delhi Panama Paris São Paulo Singapore Sydney Tokyo Toronto

Public Finance in Theory and Practice

1 2 3 4 5 6 7 8 9 0 KPKP 7 9 8 7 6 5

This book was set in Times Roman by Kingsport Press, Inc. The editors were J. S. Dietrich and Annette Hall; the cover was designed by Merrill Haber; the production supervisor was Dennis J. Conroy. New drawings were done by J & R Services, Inc. Kingsport Press, Inc., was printer and binder.

Library of Congress Cataloging in Publication Data

Musgrave, Richard Abel, date
Public finance in theory and practice.

Includes bibliographies and index.
1. Finance, Public—United States. I. Musgrave, Peggy B., joint author. II. Title.
HJ257.2.M87 1976 336.73 75–14139
ISBN 0–07–044121–9

Contents

PART FOUR FISCAL INCIDENCE

PART FIVE EFFECTS ON EFFICIENCY AND CAPACITY OUTPUT

Preface to the Second Edition

The early appearance of this second edition has been encouraged by a friendly reception of the first. It offers a welcome opportunity to update the quantitative and institutional materials which have been in rapid flux and to allow for many helpful suggestions from our readers. All these suggestions have been given careful consideration, and a good many have been adopted. Beyond this, significant additions and improvements have been made. The theory of social goods has been related more closely to that of efficient resource use in the private sector. A chapter on the optimal distribution of income has been added to provide a systematic treatment of the distribution function, similar to that of the allocation function in the chapter on social goods. Throughout, increased attention has been given to inflation, and a summary of major points has been added at the end of each chapter. To speed the flow of the argument, more technical or specialized materials have been placed in concluding sections or appendixes to various chapters. All this, we hope, will be helpful to our readers.

Courses in public finance vary in length and emphasis, and so will the uses of this book. Some courses may cover the material from beginning to end; others will emphasize certain sections and omit the rest. Part One offers a broadly based introduction to public finance and should be suitable for most uses, with less theoretical courses free to skip the concluding section of Chapter 3. Policy-oriented courses might then focus on the discussion of expenditure structure and analysis in Chapters 6–8, followed by that of tax policy in Chapters 9–16. Brief sections on tax incidence have been included in these chapters which, combined with the overview of incidence analysis in Chapter 16, will cover the major issues of tax policy. Theoretically inclined readers, however, will find the more thorough treatment of incidence and effects in Chapters 17–23 an important addition, but will keep in mind that there is little profit in theorizing about fiscal issues without knowing at least the rudiments of fiscal institutions. The material on fiscal stabilization and debt (Chapters 24–28) will fit the coverage of some courses but not of others, as will that on fiscal federalism (Chapters 29 and 30). The concluding chapters on current policy issues and applications, finally, may be added on a selective basis, depending upon the direction and length of the course. Our purpose has been to present the materials needed for thorough coverage over a fairly wide range of approaches, leaving further selection to consumer preferences.

Many people, colleagues and students, have contributed to this revision, and we are indebted to them. Particular thanks for extensive comments are due to Boris Bittker, Arnold Bockberg, Roger Brinner, Helen Ladd, Daniel Morgan, Alicia Munnell, Thomas Pogue, Ruth Shen, Ferdinand Schoettle, and Richard Tybout.

Richard A. Musgrave
Peggy B. Musgrave

Excerpt from the Preface to the First Edition

Choosing the title for a book is like naming a product. It must describe the basic service which it renders, yet one wishes to differentiate one's own brand. *Public Finance* does the former and *Theory and Practice* serves the latter purpose.

Public Finance is the term which has traditionally been applied to the package of those policy problems which involve the use of tax and expenditure measures. It is not a good term, since the basic problems are not financial but deal with the use of resources, the distribution of income, and the level of employment. Yet the term is familiar and it would be no less misleading to call this a study of public sector economics. While budgetary policy is an important part of that broader subject, it can hardly lay claim to the entire story. Important issues, such as antitrust and monetary policy, remain which fall outside the compass of this volume.

Theory and Practice is the flag under which this study is designed to sail. The subject matter derives its fascination precisely from the close interaction of theory and practice which it entails. On one side there is the vast array of fiscal institutions—tax systems, expenditure programs, budget procedures, stabilization instruments, debt issues, levels of government, Congress, the Executive, city halls, and the voters. On the other, there is the endless stream of issues arising in the operation of these institutions. How big a share of GNP should be included in the public sector and how should the choice of public expenditures be determined? What taxes are to be chosen and who really bears their burden? How should fiscal functions be divided among levels of government? How can a high level of employment be reconciled with stable prices? Pursuit of these issues leads from one end of economic analysis to the other. Thus the distinction between social and private goods lies at the heart of welfare economics while the incidence of taxation is one of the prime applications of microtheory. Public expenditure analysis leads into the nature of capital and how its returns should be measured. Fiscal relations among governmental units involve the rudiments of international economics. Stabilization policy has been central to the development of macroanalysis, and so forth.

Our study, therefore, must combine a thorough understanding of fiscal institutions with a careful analysis of the economic issues which underlie budget policy.

There is no way of doing the one without the other. As a result, the institutional material presented here may go a bit further than the theoretically inclined reader may wish and the analytical tools drawn upon may demand a bit more than the institutionalist would like. Though both are needed to understand the subject, the reader may adjust the material to his interest. Road signs are put up where sections of a more technical nature may be passed over by readers who have less interest in pursuing these aspects.

As a study in public policy, this volume deals with many of the central economic and social issues of the 1970s. They are issues which call for resolution by public policy because, like it or not, they cannot be handled adequately through a decentralized market. The existence of externalities, concern for adjustments in the distribution of income and wealth, as well as the maintenance of high employment and price level stability all pose issues which require political processes for their resolution. A public sector is needed to make society work and the problem is how to do this in a framework of individual freedom and justice. Given the central role of the political process in fiscal decisions, the study of public finance thus reaches beyond the sphere of economics narrowly defined and into what might otherwise be considered matters of political science and philosophy. Recognizing the importance of these overlaps, we have not shied away from such problems but have tried to meet them where they arise. *Making the fiscal system work is, after all, a large part of making democracy function.*

An enterprise of this sort, especially a conjugal one, leaves the authors with many debts to colleagues and students who at one time or another have commented on or contributed to various parts of the material. Our thanks to all of them, including William Andrews, Michael Boskin, Roger Brinner, Charlie Brown, Carl Case, Thomas Dernburg, David Harrison, Glenn Jenkins, Helen Ladd, Herman Leonard, James Medoff, Peter Mieszkowski, Alicia Munnell, Wallace Oates, Nancy Teeters, and Janet Yellen.

Richard A. Musgrave
Peggy B. Musgrave

PUBLIC FINANCE IN THEORY AND PRACTICE

Part 1

Introduction

Chapter 1

Fiscal Functions: An Overview*

A. Introduction: *Subject of Study; Modes of Analysis; Need for Public Sector; Major Functions.* **B. The Allocation Function:** *Social Goods and Market Failure; Public Provision for Social Goods; Public Provision versus Public Production.* **C. The Distribution Function:** *Determinants of Distribution; Optimal Distribution; Fiscal Instruments of Distribution Policy.* **D. The Stabilization Function:** *Need for Stabilization; Fiscal Instruments of Stabilization Policy; Monetary Instruments; Policy Mix.* **E. Coordination or Conflict of Functions:** *Coordination; Conflict.* **F. Fiscal Centralization versus Decentralization:** *Normative Aspects; Policy Issues.* **G. Summary.**

A. INTRODUCTION

In the United States economy of today, over 20 percent of total output is purchased by government budgets and one-third of total income is collected in taxes. This government participation falls short of that in other developed economies such as those of Canada and Western Europe, where the governmental share of budgetary activity is even larger. Beyond the budgetary function, public policy

**Reader's Guide to Chapter 1:* This chapter is designed to give the general setting to the fiscal problem, thereby taking a sweeping view of the issues to be considered in detail later on. You may therefore be left with many questions. But don't worry. They will be cleared up (it is hoped) as you proceed.

influences the course of economic activity through monetary, regulatory, and other devices. Public enterprise also plays a major role in most European countries, though it is of limited importance in the United States. The modern "capitalist" economy is thus a thoroughly mixed system in which public- and private-sector forces interact in an integral fashion. The economic system can be viewed as neither public nor private, but involves a mix of both sectors.

Subject of Study

This volume deals with the economics of the public sector, including not only its financing but its entire bearing on the level and allocation of resource use, as well as on the distribution of income among consumers. Although our subject matter is traditionally referred to as public finance, it thus deals with the real as well as the financial aspects of the problem. Moreover, it cannot be a matter of "public" economics only. Since the public sector operates in interaction with the private, both sectors enter the analysis. Not only do the effects of expenditure and tax policies depend upon the reaction of the private sector, but the need for fiscal measures is determined by how the private sector would perform in their absence.

Notwithstanding this broad view, we shall not deal with the entire range of economic policy but limit ourselves to that part which operates through the *revenue* and *expenditure* measures of the public budget. Other aspects, such as the regulation of competition through the courts, the operation of public enterprise, and the conduct of monetary policy, will be dealt with only where they are associated with the economics of budget policy.[1] The term "public sector" as used here thus refers to the *budgetary* sector of public policy only.

Modes of Analysis

In an analysis of the public sector, various types of questions may be asked. They include the following:

1. What criteria should be applied when one is judging the economic efficiency of various budget policies?
2. What are the responses of the private sector to various fiscal measures, such as tax and expenditure changes?
3. What are the social, political, and historical forces which have formed the shape of present fiscal institutions and which determine the formulation of contemporary fiscal policy?

Question 1 asks how the quality of fiscal institutions and policies can be evaluated and how their performance can be improved. The answer requires setting standards of "good" performance. Corresponding to the analysis of effi-

[1] The amount at which a particular activity is recorded in the budget does not indicate its significance for economic policy. The subsidy to the Postal Service, for instance, runs at about $1.5 billion for fiscal year 1974, while the Antitrust Division of the Justice Department costs a mere $13 million. Yet the latter is a vastly more important instrument of economic policy.

cient behavior of households and firms in the private sector, this calls for a type of economics which, in professional jargon, is referred to as "welfare economics." One may also refer to it as "normative economics." In considering the question of how fiscal measures may be designed better to serve the public purpose, one must also consider how fiscal objectives are determined. Because of this requirement, effective application of welfare economics to the public sector is even more difficult than its application to the private sector. But it must be undertaken, and Chapters 3 and 4 in particular will deal with these normative aspects.

Question 2 must be asked if the outcome of alternative policies is to be traced. If the merits of a corporation profits tax or of a sales tax are to be judged, one must know who will bear the final burden, the answer to which in turn depends on how the private sector responds to the imposition of such taxes. Or if aggregate demand is to be increased, one must know what the effects of the reduction in taxes or increase in public expenditures will be, effects which once more depend upon the magnitude and speed of responses by consumers and firms in the private sector. Analyzing the effects of fiscal measures thus involves what has been referred to as "positive" economics—i.e., the type of economic analysis which deals with predicting, on the basis of empirical analysis, how firms and consumers will respond to economic changes and with testing such predictions empirically. Much of our discussion, especially in Parts 4, 5, and 6, will involve this approach.

Question 3 likewise involves a "positive" approach, asking in this case why the fiscal behavior of governments is what it is. This not only is a matter of economics but also includes a wide range of historical, political, and social factors. How do interest groups try to affect the fiscal process, and how do legislators respond to pressures? How are the fiscal preferences of voters determined by their income and social and demographic characteristics, and how does the political process, in fact, serve to reflect their preferences? These are questions which will be examined in Chapter 5, where the politics of fiscal policy are taken up.

Need for Public Sector

From the normative view, why is it that a public sector is required? If one starts with the premises that (1) the composition of output should be in line with the preferences of individual consumers, and that (2) there is a preference for decentralized decision making, why may not the entire economy be left to the private sector? Or, putting it differently, why is it that in a supposedly private enterprise economy, a substantial part of the economy is subject to some form of government direction, rather than left to the "invisible hand" of market forces?

In part, the prevalence of government may reflect the presence of political and social ideologies which depart from the premises of consumer choice and decentralized decision making. But this is only a minor part of the story. More important, there is the fact that the market mechanism alone cannot perform all economic functions. Public policy is needed to guide, correct, and supplement it in certain respects. It is important to realize this fact since it implies that the proper size of the public sector is, to a significant degree, a technical rather than an ideological issue. A variety of reasons explain why this is the case, including the following:

1. The contractual arrangements and exchanges needed for the market operation cannot exist without the protection and enforcement of a governmentally provided legal structure.

2. The claim that the market mechanism leads to efficient resource use (i.e., produces what consumers want most and does so in the cheapest way) is based on the condition of competitive factor and product markets. This means that there must be no obstacles to free entry and that consumers and producers must have full market knowledge. Government regulation or other measures are needed to secure these conditions.

3. Even if all barriers to competition were removed, the production or consumption characteristics of certain goods are such that these goods cannot be provided for through the market. Problems of "externalities" arise which lead to "market failure" and require solution through the public sector.

4. The rate of discount used in the valuing of future (relative to present) consumption may differ as seen from a public and a private point of view.

5. The market system, especially in a highly developed financial economy, does not necessarily bring high employment, price level stability, and the socially desired rate of economic growth. Public policy is needed to secure these objectives.

6. Social values may require adjustments in the distribution of income and wealth which results from the market system and from the transmission of property rights through inheritance.

As we shall see later on, items 3 through 6 are of particular importance from the viewpoint of budget policy.

To argue that these limitations of the market mechanism call for corrective or compensating measures of public policy does not prove, of course, that any policy measure which is undertaken will in fact improve the performance of the economic system. Public policy, no less than private policy, can err and be inefficient; and the basic purpose of our study of public finance is precisely that of exploring how the effectiveness of policy formulation and application can be improved.

Major Functions

Although particular tax or expenditure measures affect the economy in many ways and may be designed to serve a variety of purposes, several more or less distinct policy objectives may be set forth. They include:

1. The provision for social goods, or the process by which total resource use is divided between private and social goods and by which the mix of social goods is chosen. This provision may be termed the *allocation function* of budgetary policy. Regulatory policies, which may also be considered a part of the allocation function, are not included here because they are not primarily a problem of budget policy.

2. Adjustment of the distribution of income and wealth to assure conformance with what society considers a "fair" or "just" state of distribution, here referred to as the *distribution function.*

3. The use of budget policy as a means of maintaining high employment, a reasonable degree of price level stability, and an appropriate rate of economic growth.

There is also the objective of stability in the balance of payments. We refer to all these objectives as the *stabilization function.*

B. THE ALLOCATION FUNCTION

We begin with the allocation function and the proposition that certain goods—referred to here as *social* as distinct from *private* goods—cannot be provided for through the market system, i.e., by transactions between individual consumers and producers. In some cases the market fails entirely, while in others it can function only in an inefficient way. Why is this the case?

Social Goods and Market Failure

The basic reason for market failure in the provision of social goods is not that the need for such goods is "felt" collectively, whereas that for private goods is felt individually. While people's preferences are influenced by their social environment, in the last resort wants and preferences are experienced by individuals and not by society as a whole. Moreover, both social and private goods are included in their preference maps. Just as I can rank my preferences among housing and backyard facilities, so I may also rank my preferences among private yards and public parks. Rather, the difference arises because the benefits to which social goods give rise are not limited to one particular consumer who purchases the good, as is the case for private goods, but become available to others as well.

If I consume a hamburger or wear a pair of shoes, these particular products will not be available to other individuals. My and their consumption stand in a rival relationship. This is the situation with private goods. But now consider measures to reduce air pollution. If a given air quality improvement is obtained, the resulting gain will be available to all who breathe. In other words, consumption of such products by various individuals is not "rival" in the sense that one's partaking of benefits does not reduce the benefits available to others. To put it differently, the benefits derived by anyone's consuming a social good are "externalized" in that they become available to all others. This is the situation with social goods. In the case of private goods, the benefits of consumption are "internalized" with a particular consumer, whose consumption excludes consumption by others.

The market mechanism is well suited for the provision of private goods. It is based on exchange, and exchange can occur only where there is an exclusive title to the property which is to be exchanged. In fact, the market system may be viewed as a giant auction where consumers bid for products and producers sell to the highest bidders. Thus the market furnishes a signaling system whereby producers are guided by consumer demands. For goods such as hamburgers or shoes this is an efficient mechanism. Nothing is lost and much is gained when consumers are excluded unless they pay. Application of the exclusion principle tends to be an efficient solution.

But not so in the case of social goods. For one thing, it would be inefficient to exclude any one consumer from partaking in the benefits, when such participation would not reduce consumption by anyone else. The application of exclusion would thus be undesirable, even if it were readily feasible. Furthermore, the application of exclusion is frequently impossible or prohibitively expensive.[2] Gains from air-cleansing measures cannot readily be withheld from particular consumers, streetlights shine upon all, and so forth. Given these conditions, the benefits from social goods are not vested in the property rights of certain individuals, and the market cannot function.

Since the benefits are available to all, consumers will not voluntarily offer payments to the suppliers of social goods. Each will benefit as much from the consumption of others as from his or her own, and with thousands or millions of other consumers present, the individual's payment is only an insignificant part of the total. Hence, no voluntary payment is made.[3] The linkage between producer and consumer is broken and the government must step in to provide for such goods.

Public Provision for Social Goods

The problem, then, is how the government should determine how much of such goods is to be provided. Refusal of voluntary payment is not the basic difficulty. The problem could be solved readily, at least from the theoretical point of view, if the task were merely one of sending the tax collector to those consumers to whom the benefits of social goods accrue. But matters are not this simple. The difficulty lies in deciding the type and quantity of a social good that should be supplied to begin with and how much a particular consumer should be asked to pay. It may be reasonable to rule that the individual should pay for the benefits he receives, as in the case of private goods, but this does not solve the problem; the fundamental difficulty lies in how these benefits are to be determined.

Just as individual consumers have no reason to offer voluntary payments to the private producer, so they have no reason to reveal to the government how highly they value the public service. Since each consumer is only one member in a large group, the total supply available to him is not affected significantly by his or her own contribution. Consumers have no reason to step forward and declare what the service is truly worth to them individually unless they are assured that others will do the same. Placing tax contributions on a voluntary basis would, therefore, be to no avail. People will prefer to enjoy as free riders what is provided by others. A different technique is needed by which the supply of social goods and the cost allocation thereof can be determined.

This is where the political process enters the picture and must substitute for the market mechanism. Voting by ballot must be resorted to in place of dollar voting. Since voters know that they will be subject to the voting decision (be it simple majority or some other voting rule), they will find it in their interest to vote so as to let the outcome fall closer to their own preferences. Thus decision making by voting becomes a substitute for preference revelation through the

[2] Situations may arise, however, in which exclusion is appropriate (because consumption is rival) but impossible. Here inapplicability of exclusion becomes *the* cause for market failure and *the* reason why budgetary provision is needed. See p. 51.

[3] Such at least is the case with large numbers of consumers. For the small-number case, see p. 61.

market. The results will not please everyone, but they will approximate—more or less perfectly, depending on the efficiency of the voting process and the homogeneity of preferences—the community's preferences in the matter. A more intensive exploration of this problem, which is perhaps the most fascinating aspect of public finance, is given in Chapter 3.[4]

Public Provision versus Public Production

Before considering how such public provision is to be arranged, a clear distinction must be drawn between public *provision* for social goods, as the term is used here, and public *production*. These are two distinct and indeed unrelated concepts which should not be confused with each other.

Private goods may be produced and sold to private buyers either by private firms, as is normally done, or by public enterprises, such as public power and transportation authorities or the nationalized British coal industry. Social goods, such as spaceships or military hardware, similarly may be produced by private firms and sold to government; or they may be produced directly under public management, as are services rendered by civil servants or municipal enterprises. If we say that social goods are provided publicly, we mean that they are financed through the budget and made available free of direct charge. How they are produced does not matter.

This distinction is brought out in the estimates of Table 1-1, where the total product of the United States economy is broken down according to (1) whether the goods and services are purchased privately or provided through the budget (corresponding roughly to our distinction between private and social goods), and (2) whether they have been produced publicly or by private firms. We find that only 12.7 percent of total production is in the public sector (line 4, column III), while 21.3 percent of output is provided through the budget (line 9, column II). We also note that 53.7 percent of social goods provided through the budget involves public production (line 4, column II), while this ratio is only 1.5 percent for private goods (line 4, column I). Finally, 90.5 percent of public production consists of social goods (line 7, column II) as against 11.3 percent of private production (line 8, column II). In short, production in the United States is undertaken almost entirely in the private sector, although social goods constitute a substantial part of total output; and such public production as exists is very largely for the provision of social goods. Public production for sale (public enterprise) plays only a very minor role.

A similar analysis for other countries[5] shows that the United States ranks

[4] This summary of the allocation function oversimplifies matters in various respects. Two major qualifications, to be noted in the later discussion, are:

(a) It is unrealistic to think of all goods as being divided into those which are private and those which are social. The existence of externalities and the social-goods problems to which they give rise are a matter of degree, and many goods carry both characteristics. Your education, for instance, will benefit not only you (we hope) but also others.

(b) In some instances, government decides to interfere with consumer preferences. Certain goods may be considered meritorious (milk), whereas others are considered harmful (liquor), so that one is subsidized while the other is taxed. This practice does not fit into the above framework and requires further explanation.

[5] See Richard A. Musgrave, *Fiscal Systems,* New Haven, Conn.: Yale, 1969, chap. 2.

TABLE 1-1
Forms of Production and Types of Goods
(United States Data for 1973)

	Privately Purchased Goods (Private Goods) (I)	*Goods Provided through Budgets (Social Goods) (II)*	*Total (III)*
1. Public production, billions of dollars	15.6	148.5	164.1
2. Private production, billions of dollars	1,002.9	127.9	1,130.8
3. Total, billions of dollars	1,018.5	276.4	1,294.9
4. Percentage publicly produced	1.5	53.7	12.7
5. Percentage privately produced	98.5	46.3	87.3
6. Percentage, both forms	100.0	100.0	100.0
7. Percentage of public production	9.5	90.5	100.0
8. Percentage of private production	88.7	11.3	100.0
9. Percentage of total production	78.7	21.3	100.0

Source: Based on *Survey of Current Business,* July 1974. Total social goods equal government purchases of goods and services of $276.4 billion; public production thereof equals income originating in general government of $148.5 billion as shown in table 1-13 of the *Survey.* Private production of $127.9 billion is residual. Total production of private goods equals GNP of $1,294.9 billion minus social goods of $276.4 billion. Public production of private goods equals value added by government enterprise of $15.6 billion, as given in table 1-13 also. Private production of private goods is residual.

low in the public production share, as does Canada. The share rises as we move to the United Kingdom and Sweden, where public enterprise is more important. It becomes much larger for the case of socialist economies such as the U.S.S.R., where the bulk of production is by public enterprise. But one also finds that the share of total output going into social goods differs much less. This is true even with regard to the U.S.S.R., provided that investment in public enterprise is excluded and that the comparison is limited to final goods. It is thus evident that the decision whether to allocate resources to social goods or to private goods is quite different from that whether to produce any good (private or social) in a public or a private enterprise. A socialist economy, in which most production is public, may produce largely private goods, while a capitalist economy, where all production is private, may produce a larger share of social goods. Moreover, provision for social goods poses much the same problem in the capitalist (private firm) as in the socialist (public enterprise) setting.[6]

C. THE DISTRIBUTION FUNCTION

The allocation function of securing an efficient provision of social goods poses the type of problem with which economic analysis has traditionally been concerned, but the problem of distribution is more difficult to handle. Yet, distributional issues are a major (frequently *the* major) point of controversy in the

[6] See p. 121.

determination of public policy. In particular, they play a key role in determining tax and transfer policies.

Determinants of Distribution

In the absence of policy measures to adjust the prevailing state of distribution, the distribution of income and wealth depends first of all on the distribution of factor endowments. Earnings abilities differ, as does the distribution of inherited wealth. The distribution of income, based on this distribution of factor endowments, is then determined by the process of factor pricing, which, in a competitive market, sets factor returns equal to the value of the marginal product. The distribution of income among individuals thus depends on their factor supplies and the prices which they fetch in the market.

This distribution of income may or may not be in line with what society considers a fair or just distribution. A distinction must be drawn between (1) the principle of effective factor use as based upon competitive factor pricing, and (2) the proposition that the distribution of income among families should be fixed by the market process. Principle 1 is an economic rule that must be observed if there is to be efficient use of resources. But conclusion 2 is a different matter. For one thing, factor prices as determined in the market may not correspond to the competitive norm. Monopoly profits are made and the return to personal services may also be set in imperfect markets. But even if all factor prices were determined competitively, the resulting pattern of distribution might not be acceptable. It involves a substantial degree of inequality, especially in the distribution of capital income; and though views on distribution differ, most would agree that some adjustments are required.

Optimal Distribution

This being the case, one must consider what constitutes a fair or just state of distribution. Modern economic analysis has steered shy of this problem. The essence of modern welfare economics has been to define economic efficiency in terms which exclude distributional considerations. A change in economic conditions is said to be efficient (i.e., to improve welfare) if, and only if, the position of some person, say A, is improved without that of anyone else, including B and C, being worsened. This criterion cannot be applied to a redistributional measure which by definition improves A's position at the expense of B's or C's. While the "someone gains, no one loses" definition of efficiency has served well in the assessment of the functioning of the market and in the evaluation of certain aspects of public policy, it contributes little to solving the basic social issues of distribution and redistribution.

The answer to the question of fair distribution involves considerations of social philosophy and value judgment. Philosophers have come up with a variety of answers, including the view that a person has the right to the fruits derived from his or her endowment, that distribution should be arranged so as to maximize total happiness or satisfaction, and that distribution should meet certain standards of equity, which, in a limiting case, may be egalitarian. The choice among these criteria is not simple, nor is it easy to translate any one criterion into the corresponding "correct" pattern of distribution. We shall encounter these difficulties in particular in interpreting the widely accepted proposition that people should be taxed in line with their "ability to pay."

There are two major problems involved in the translation of a justice rule into an actual state of income distribution. First, it is difficult or impossible to compare the levels of utility which various individuals derive from their income. There is no simple way of adding up utilities, so that criteria based on such comparisons are not operational. This limitation has led people to think in terms of social evaluation rather than subjective utility measurement. The other difficulty arises from the fact that the size of the pie which is available for distribution is not unrelated to how it is to be distributed. We shall find that redistribution policies may involve an efficiency cost which must be taken into account when one is deciding on the extent to which equity objectives should be pursued.

Notwithstanding these difficulties, however, distributional considerations have remained an important issue of public policy. Attention appears to be shifting from the traditional concern with relative income positions, with the overall state of equality, and with excessive income at the top of the scale, to adequacy of income at the lower end. Thus the current discussion emphasizes prevention of poverty, setting what is considered a tolerable cutoff line or floor at the lower end rather than putting a ceiling at the upper end, as was once the most popular view.

Fiscal Instruments of Distribution Policy

Among various fiscal devices, redistribution is implemented most directly by (1) a tax-transfer scheme, combining progressive income taxation of high-income households with a subsidy to low-income households.[7] Alternatively, redistribution may be implemented by (2) progressive income taxes used to finance public services, such as public housing, which particularly benefit low-income households, or (3) a combination of taxes on goods purchased largely by high-income consumers with subsidies of other goods which are used chiefly by low-income consumers.[8]

While no simple generalization can be made as to the best policy instrument, there is an assumption in favor of income taxes which, unlike selective measures, do not interfere with particular consumption or production choices. Although even this mechanism is not without its "efficiency cost," since the choice between income and leisure is affected, chances are that the distortion will be less than with more selective measures. Pending further discussion of this topic in Chapter 21, we shall think of the function of the distribution branch as being discharged by a set of direct income taxes and transfers, a process to be examined later under the heading of "negative income tax."

Where redistribution involves an "efficiency cost," this consequence is, in itself, no conclusive case against such policies. It merely tells us that (1) any given

[7] A progressive tax is defined as one in which the ratio of tax to income rises with income.

[8] We disregard here other nonfiscal approaches to distribution policy, such as manpower and education policies or policies designed to counteract discrimination. These measures, of course, also have an important part to play.

distributional change should be accomplished at least efficiency cost, and that (2) a need exists for balancing conflicting policy objectives. Efficiency in the broad sense, i.e., an optimally conducted policy, must allow for both concerns.

D. THE STABILIZATION FUNCTION

Having dealt with the bearing of budget policy on matters of allocation and distribution, we must examine its role as an instrument of macroeconomic policy. Fiscal policy must be designed to maintain or achieve the goals of high employment, a reasonable degree of price level stability, balance in the foreign accounts, and an acceptable rate of economic growth.

Need for Stabilization

Fiscal policy is needed for stabilization since full employment and price stability do not come about automatically in a market economy but require public policy guidance. Without it, the economy tends to be subject to substantial fluctuations, and/or it may suffer from sustained periods of unemployment or inflation. This eventuality, of course, does not preclude the possibility that public policy, if poorly conducted, may itself be a destabilizer. The purpose of our study, as noted before, is to see how policy can be shaped more effectively.

The overall level of employment and prices in the economy depends upon the level of aggregate demand, relative to potential or capacity output valued at prevailing prices. The level of demand is a function of the spending decisions of millions of consumers, corporate managers, financial investors, and unincorporated operators. These decisions in turn depend upon many factors, such as past and present income, wealth position, credit availability, and expectations. In any one period, the level of expenditures may be insufficient to secure full employment of labor and other resources. Because wages and prices are downward rigid and for other reasons, there is no ready mechanism by which such employment will restore itself automatically. Hence, expansion of policy measures to raise aggregate demand is needed. At other times, expenditures may exceed the available output under conditions of high employment and thus may cause inflation. In such situations, restrictive conditions are needed to reduce demand. Furthermore, just as deficient demand may generate further deficiency, so may an increase in prices generate further expectations of price rise, leading to renewed inflation. In neither case is there an adjustment process by which the economy is automatically returned to high employment and stability.

A wide range of models may be constructed on the drawing boards of economic theory, some of which are explosively unstable, while others are characterized by dampened oscillations or continuous, limited fluctuations. As we know from the world around us, the actual behavior of the economy is fortunately not explosive. Built-in stabilizers exist which limit fluctuations. There remains, however, a band of instability which is sufficiently serious to require stabilizing action.

This task is complicated by the fact that economies do not operate in isolation but are linked to one another by trade and capital flows. Again, there is no automatic mechanism by which external balance is maintained, especially in a world with fixed exchange rates and speculative capital movements. Domestic stabilization policy therefore must be conducted in a way which reconciles the requirements of both domestic and foreign balance and involves the complex problem of international policy coordination.

Whereas, in the thirties and forties, the problem of stabilization was mainly seen as one of reaching full employment with a given level of potential output, developments since the fifties have brought added concern about the rate of growth of potential output and the problem of inflation. After a high level of employment was reached in the mid-sixties, the problem became one of restraining inflation without losing the full-employment objective. As the experience of recent years has shown, policy may have to fight inflation and unemployment at the same time.

Injection of growth as a policy objective similarly changed the setting in which fiscal policy operates. Given the rate of increase in population and/or productivity, the level of aggregate expenditures must be adjusted to rise accordingly, so as to permit demand to expand in line with potential output. This objective will require periodic adjustments in fiscal policy. Furthermore, public policy may not accept the rate of growth of potential output as determined by market forces, but may wish to influence this rate. Since growth, among other things, depends upon the rate of capital formation, the rate of saving (or the division of output between consumption and capital formation) becomes of strategic importance.

Since the choice of a desirable rate of growth is essentially a question of present versus future consumption, it may be argued that this is a problem of resource allocation rather than of stabilization; and that policy decisions to affect the rate of growth are in fact allocation decisions. There is much to be said for this point of view, but the close link to other aspects of stabilization policy renders it convenient to treat growth in this macropolicy context.

Fiscal Instruments of Stabilization Policy

The very existence of the fiscal system has an immediate and inevitable influence on the level and structure of demand. First, even if fiscal policy was intended to be "neutral," it would be necessary to consider effects on aggregate demand to secure such neutrality. Second, changes in budget policy may be used as a positive means of obtaining or offsetting changes in demand.

Leverage Effects of a Given Budget Looking at the implications of a given budget for aggregate demand, it is evident that government purchases of products, like private purchases, constitute a component of final demand. Similarly, government purchases of factors (e.g., the hiring of civil servants) generate income leading to a further increase in private demand. Generally speaking, the effects on aggregate demand generated by the budget—the expansionary effect—will be the greater the larger the deficit or the smaller the surplus, as well as the larger the absolute size of government purchases.

Instead of looking at a given absolute *level* of receipts, we shall find it more instructive to think in terms of given tax *rates,* the yield of which changes with the level of national income. This is true because the level of income, profits, or sales to which tax rates apply varies with national income. Thus, the fiscal system possesses a "built-in flexibility" which responds to changes in the economic scene, even though no changes in policy (changes in tax rates or expenditure legislation) are made. As we shall see later, these built-in responses are helpful under some, and harmful under other, circumstances.

Changes in Budget Policy To supplement these built-in responses, discretionary policy measures may be taken to change tax statutes and expenditure programs, i.e., to raise or lower tax rates (hence to change the amount of revenue obtained from a given tax base) or to change the level of expenditures made at any given level of national income. Thereby an increase or a decrease in the level of aggregate demand can be achieved. Whereas monetary policy operates through changes in the cost and availability of credit and through adjustments of asset holders to a changing money supply, fiscal policy operates through the effects of taxes or transfers on disposable income and thence on private spending, or through the direct effects of changes in the level of public purchases.

Monetary Instruments

While the market mechanism, if it functions well, may be relied upon to determine the allocation of resources among private goods, economists agree that it cannot by itself regulate the proper money supply. As Walter Bagehot pointed out a century ago, "Money does not control itself." The banking system if left to its own devices will not generate just that money supply which is compatible with economic stability, but will—in response to the credit demands of the market—accentuate prevailing tendencies to fluctuation. Therefore, the money supply must be controlled by the central banking system and be adjusted to the needs of the economy in terms of both short-run stability and longer-run growth. Monetary policy—including the devices of reserve requirements, discount rates, open market policy, and selective credit controls—is thus an indispensable component of stabilization policy.

Policy Mix

Although monetary and fiscal measures supplement each other, they differ in their impact. By using them in proper combination, it is possible to achieve more objectives than would be possible with the use of one policy instrument alone.

In the context of domestic balance, we shall examine the proposition that a mix of easy money (permitting high expenditures, particularly investment) and a tight budget (reducing the level of aggregate expenditures, particularly consumption) is favorable to economic growth. In the context of foreign balance, we shall note that monetary policy has a special advantage (due to its effects on international capital movements) in securing balance-of-payments equilibrium, while fiscal policy is more effective in dealing with domestic needs. Monetary and fiscal policies, therefore, are linked by the need for obtaining a policy mix which will permit the pursuit of multiple policy objectives.

Moreover, there is a mechanical link between fiscal and monetary measures.

As we shall see, the generation of budgetary imbalance (surplus or deficit, depending on the needs of the situation) is an important tool of fiscal policy. But this means that the structure of claims, including money and public debt, is changed in the process. These "claim effects" are an inevitable by-product of budgetary imbalance, providing an important link between fiscal and monetary policy.

E. COORDINATION OR CONFLICT OF FUNCTIONS

It remains to consider how the three basic functions of fiscal policy—allocation, distribution, and stabilization—can be coordinated into an overall pattern of budget policy. Here in particular, our earlier distinction between a normative and a descriptive (or predictive) view of the fiscal process must be kept in mind. Although fully coordinated policy determination permits simultaneous achievement of the various objectives, actual practice gives rise to multiple conflicts.

Coordination

Consider first the coordinated approach as it would proceed under a normative or optimally conducted fiscal process. In dealing with the analysis of public policy, economists have shown that the number of available policy tools must match the number of policy targets. If the tools are insufficient, a conflict among targets must be accepted. Given our three targets—(1) provision for social goods, (2) adjustments in distribution, (3) stabilization—three policy instruments are needed to meet them.[9] Let us think of them as three separate subbudgets or fiscal branches, each designed for the implementation of its particular objective.

The manager of the distribution-branch budget will design a tax-transfer plan to secure the desired adjustment in distribution. For this purpose a full-employment level of income will be assumed. The manager also assumes that the allocation branch provides for public services financed by taxes imposed in line with consumer evaluation thereof. The subbudget of the distribution branch, by its very nature, will be balanced. The manager of the allocation branch in turn will provide for social goods and finance them by taxes imposed in line with consumer evaluation thereof. In so doing, this manager will assume that the distribution branch has secured the "proper" state of income distribution and that the stabilization branch has secured full employment. Again, this will involve a balanced budget.[10] The manager of the stabilization branch, finally, will provide for the necessary adjustment in aggregate demand, again proceeding on the assumption that the other two branches have met their tasks. By its nature this final budget will consist of either taxes or transfers and thus usually be in imbalance. Taxes and transfers used to accomplish the stabilization task may be designed so as not to interfere with the "proper" distribution as provided by the distribution branch, i.e., they will be proportional to the "proper" pattern of income distribution.

[9] To simplify, we think of target 3 merely in terms of full employment and price level stability, disregarding growth and foreign balance for the time being.

[10] Subject, however, to the qualification given in connection with considerations of intergeneration equity. See Chap. 28, Sec. E.

The reader may wonder how this can be done, since the respective plans of the three branches are closely interdependent. The answer is that the system may be solved by simultaneous determination.[11] When the three budgets have been determined in this fashion, it would then be cumbersome for administrative purposes to carry out each budget separately. Rather, it will be convenient to clear the taxes imposed by the allocation branch, the taxes and transfers of the distribution branch, and the taxes and transfers of the stabilization branch against each other and to implement only the resulting net transfers and taxes with regard to each consumer.

The combined or net budget may thus be viewed as a composite of the three subbudgets. It will have a deficit or surplus, depending on the position of the stabilization branch. Whether the net payment system will be progressive, proportional, or regressive is not obvious. The distribution branch component would tend to make it progressive, but it remains to be seen how the allocation component will look.[12] In addition to these net taxes and transfers, government must undertake the purchases of products or resources needed to provide for the services of the allocation branch.

This system has been spelled out not as a description of the actual budget process, but to show how the various objectives could be coordinated and pursued without interference with one another. We now turn to the real world of fiscal politics, where the situation is quite different.

Conflict

In the real world setting (be it Washington or the town meeting of a New England village), budget planning frequently does not permit evaluation of various objectives on their own merits. Rather, achievement of one objective is frequently accomplished at the cost of another. The history of fiscal politics abounds with illustrations of this sort.

Allocation and Distribution Consider first the relationship between allocation and redistribution measures. Although redistribution is accomplished to some extent through tax-transfer schemes, it is achieved largely by progressive tax finance of the provision for social goods. This is based on an "ability-to-pay approach," by which the distribution of the tax burden is determined by the ability of a taxpayer to sustain the sacrifice of income reduction, independent of the mix of social goods which is supplied and the benefits derived therefrom. Because of this, the degree of redistribution tends to depend on the levels of programs which are to be financed, thus associating extensive provision for social goods with extensive redistribution.

This approach furthered the cause of redistribution when budgets were small and the additional burden could be imposed on high-income recipients. But over time as budgets have increased relative to national income, additional finance had to be drawn more largely from the middle- and lower-income groups, thus revers-

[11] For further discussion see Richard A. Musgrave, *The Theory of Public Finance,* New York: McGraw-Hill, 1959, chap. 2.

[12] See p. 213.

ing this effect. However this may be, such a linkage between expenditure levels and redistribution does not make for efficiency from a normative point of view. People's attitudes toward redistribution need not coincide with their preferences for social goods. A person who wants public services should not have to oppose them because he dislikes redistribution, or vice versa. A better policy choice would be made, therefore, if each issue is taken up on its merits.

Allocation and Stabilization Now take the relationship between considerations of allocation and stabilization. In times of unemployment, when an expansion of aggregate demand is needed, an increase in government expenditures is often proposed as a remedy. Similarly, at times of inflation, when demand is to be restricted, a case is made for a reduction in such expenditure.

While it is proper for social goods to share in a general expansion or restriction of expenditures, there is no reason why they should account for the entire or major part of the change. As we have seen, the stabilizing adjustment can also be made through increase or reduction in taxes, or reduction or increase in transfers, while leaving the provision for social goods (appropriate at full-employment income levels) unaffected.

Mixing the issues leads to an oversupply of social goods or to wasteful public expenditures when expansion is needed; and to a no less wasteful undersupply when restriction is called for. Moreover, mixing the issues leads to opposition to expansionary fiscal measures by those who oppose high provision for such goods and to opposition to restrictive measures by those who favor high provision of social goods. If the issues are separated, reasonable people may agree on the need for stabilizing action while differing, in line with their preferences, on the appropriate scale at which social goods are to be provided.

Distribution and Stabilization Finally, consider the relationship between distribution and stabilization objectives. In the past it has been argued during periods of severe unemployment that lower-income groups should be given greater tax relief, since they are likely to spend more of their tax savings than higher-income recipients. The opposite case has been made in times of inflation, namely that taxes on low-income groups should be raised, since they are more potent in reducing demand than taxes on the higher incomes.

Again, proper stabilization action may be interfered with, or redistributional action may be biased, because the two objectives are linked. This is unnecessary since the stabilization adjustment can be made with distributionally neutral taxes—or, for that matter, any pattern of tax distribution—provided only that the overall level of taxation is raised or reduced by a sufficient amount.

Distribution and Growth Similar problems arise if the growth objective is introduced. A higher rate of growth may call for a higher rate of capital formation, which calls for increased saving and investment. Since the marginal propensity to save is higher among high-income recipients than among low-income groups, and since high-income taxpayers undertake most investment, it would seem that the tax structure should be such as to concentrate on lower incomes. Again the conclusion need not follow if we permit the possibility of public saving which, for any given tax-burden distribution, may be achieved through higher tax rates. But, as we shall see, the conflict may not be resolved as easily if effects of taxation on investment incentives are considered. Unless larger reliance on public investment is introduced, a higher rate of growth may be in conflict with redistribution objectives.

As we view these potential conflicts, it becomes evident that the normative view of neatly attuned subbudgets is not a realistic description of the fiscal process. Rather, it must be understood as a standard against which actual performance may be measured and the quality of existing fiscal institutions may be assessed.

F. FISCAL CENTRALIZATION VERSUS DECENTRALIZATION

So far, we have spoken of "the" fiscal structure or "the" public sector as if it were a single unit. Actually, a country's fiscal system consists of a number of units of varying size and importance. Apart from the central government, there are regional and local units. Depending on the political structure of the country, the fiscal system is more or less centralized, the United States pattern with its federal, state, and local governments being at the decentralized end of the scale.

Normative Aspects

The issue of fiscal centralization versus decentralization poses interesting normative as well as empirical problems. While actual fiscal institutions are the result of historical and political developments which have shaped existing units, our normative considerations point to a system in which fiscal functions are divided among numerous units. Although the stabilization and distribution function must be largely performed at the central or federal level, the allocation function, or provision for social goods, calls for a decentralized system.

This is the case because the benefit incidence of social goods is spatially limited—the illumination provided by streetlights only extends so far—and because the preferences of different communities regarding the supply of social goods may differ. Fiscal decentralization thus permits adaptation of budget patterns to the preferences of the residents of particular jurisdictions. Moreover, to some extent choice of residency may be determined by fiscal differentials among communities. Finally, economies of scale of various sorts enter into the determination of efficient community size.

Normative considerations thus point to fiscal jurisdictions of varying sizes with national services provided centrally on a nationwide basis, regional services provided for regionally, and local services accounted for locally. Indeed, much the larger part of social goods (excluding defense) is provided at the state and local levels rather than at the federal level.

Policy Issues

Actual institutions do not correspond closely to these norms. Fiscal jurisdictions as determined by historical development are frequently ill adapted to meet the task assigned to them. Spillovers of costs and benefits among jurisdictions introduce inefficiencies, and the distribution of fiscal capacities and needs among jurisdictions is frequently out of balance. Thus the problem arises of how these defects can be remedied through central measures aimed at coordination and at securing a better balance between needs and resources. Problems of this kind are among the most important United States fiscal issues of this decade.

G. SUMMARY

This chapter, being itself in the form of a summary, can hardly be summarized further. However, the main ideas presented are these:

1. Modern so-called capitalist economies are in fact "mixed" economies, with one-third or more of economic activity occurring in the public sector.

2. For purposes of this book, the term "public sector" is used to refer to those parts of governmental economic policy which find their expression in budgetary (expenditure and revenue) measures.

3. Three major types of budgetary activity are distinguished, namely, (1) the public provision of certain goods and services, referred to as "social goods"; (2) adjustments in the state of distribution of income and wealth; and (3) measures to stabilize the level of economic activity in the economy at large.

4. In discussing the provision of social goods (the allocation function), reference is made to payment for certain goods and services through budgetary finance. Whether the production of these goods is under public management, or whether the goods and services are purchased from private firms, is a different matter.

5. Provision for so-called social goods poses problems which differ from those which arise in connection with private goods. The main point of difference is that social goods tend to be nonrival in consumption and that consumer preferences with regard to such goods are not revealed by consumer bidding in the market. Therefore a political process is required.

6. The pattern of distribution which results from the existing pattern of factor endowments and from the sale of factor services in the market is not necessarily one which society considers as fair. Distributional adjustments may be called for, and tax and transfer policies offer an effective means of implementing them, thus calling for a distribution function in budget policy.

7. Tax and expenditure policies affect aggregate demand and the level of economic activity. They are also an important instrument in maintaining economic stability, including high employment and control of inflation. Hence, the stabilization function enters as the third budgetary function.

8. Fiscal policies may be conducted in centralized or decentralized fashion, with different budgetary functions being more or less appropriate at various levels of governmental activity.

Having posed these problems, we can now proceed to a closer examination of them, together with the fiscal institutions in the context of which they arise and in which policy measures must function.

FURTHER READINGS

Buchanan, J.: "Social Choice, Democracy and Free Markets," *Journal of Political Economy,* 1959, pp. 334–343.

Colm, G.: *Essays in Public Finance and Fiscal Policy,* Oxford: Oxford University Press, 1955, chap. 1.

Dalton, H.: *Principles of Public Finance,* 9th ed., London: Routledge, 1936, part I.

Houghton, R. W. (ed.): *Public Finance,* Penguin Modern Economics Readings, Baltimore: Penguin, 1970.

Musgrave, R. A.: *The Theory of Public Finance,* New York: McGraw-Hill, 1959, chaps. 1, 2.

Pigou, A. C.: *A Study in Public Finance,* London: Macmillan, 1928, part I.

Shoup, C. S.: *Public Finance,* book 1, Chicago: Aldine, 1970.

Chapter 2

Fiscal Institutions*

A. Survey of United States Fiscal Structure: *All Levels Combined; By Levels of Government; The Role of Intergovernmental Grants.* **B. The Constitutional Framework:** *Federal Powers and Limitations; State Powers under Federal Constitution; State Constitutions and Local Powers.* **C. Policy Implementation: (1) Expenditure Policy:** *History of Budget System; Budget Preparation; Form of Presentation; Congressional Budget Process; Presidential Approval; Execution of Program; Auditing.* **D. Policy Implementation: (2) Tax Policy:** *Executive Preparation; Legislation; Balance of Power; Administration; Reform Proposals.* **E. Overall Fiscal Policy. F. Trust Funds. G. Debt Management. H. Summary.**

The economic rationale for fiscal policy is one thing, and the existing set of fiscal institutions is another. These institutions, like other aspects of political and social organization, are the product of a multiplicity of historical forces, not necessarily well suited to perform the normative tasks set in the preceding discussion. Yet they must be drawn upon to do the job, and they must be adapted to its changing tasks.

* *Reader's Guide to Chapter 2:* Here we follow the preceding survey of fiscal issues with a similar sketch of fiscal institutions—federal, state, and local. The two chapters are equally important and provide the setting for what is to come.

TABLE 2-1
Expenditures to the Public by Function and Level of Government, Fiscal Year 1972
(In Billions of Dollars)

		Federal (I)	*State (II)*	*Local (III)*	*Total (IV)*
1.	Expenditure to the public, total	201.0	70.6	108.2	379.8
2.	National defense and international relations	79.3	—	—	79.3
3.	Veterans	6.9	—	—	6.9
4.	Interest	17.1	2.1	3.8	23.1
5.	General government	2.2	2.5	4.9	9.7
6.	Human resources	69.6	45.5	68.5	183.7
7.	Education	5.1	17.3	48.5	70.9
8.	Hospitals and health	4.2	6.0	6.9	17.0
9.	Housing and urban renewal	2.6	—	2.7	5.4
10.	Welfare	2.5	12.2	8.8	23.6
11.	Social insurance	55.2	10.0	1.6	66.9
12.	Development	20.9	15.6	15.5	51.9
13.	Natural resources and agriculture	11.1	2.5	7.7	21.2
14.	Transportation	4.6	13.1	7.8	25.4
15.	Postal Service	1.8	—	—	1.8
16.	Space research and technology	3.4	—	—	3.4
17.	Police and fire protection and correction	0.7	2.2	8.5	11.3
18.	Other	4.4	2.6	7.0	14.0

Notes: Includes net deficits of public enterprises (Postal Service, utilities, liquor stores).
Because of rounding, detail may not add to totals.
Line 3: Certain veterans' expenditures (amounting to $5.2 billion) are included in other expenditure categories.
Line 13: Includes local sanitation services and local parks and recreation.
Line 15: Includes deficit of Postal Service.
Source: *Governmental Finances in 1971–72,* U.S. Department of Commerce, Bureau of the Census.

A. SURVEY OF UNITED STATES FISCAL STRUCTURE

The fiscal structure of the United States for the fiscal year 1972 is set forth in Tables 2-1 to 2-3.[1] Since that year, total expenditures and receipts have shown a substantial further increase but the basic pattern has remained unchanged, and this is what matters for our present discussion.

All Levels Combined

We begin with the entire public sector, in which all levels of government—federal, state, and local—are included.

Expenditures As shown in Table 2-1, column IV, total expenditures to the public, including all levels of government (but leaving out intergovernmental transfers), amounted to $380 billion. Of the total, nearly $80 billion went for

[1] The federal fiscal year 1972 runs f m July 1, 1971, to June 30, 1972. The fiscal years for states vary somewhat, beginning in some st, es in May of the preceding year.

TABLE 2-2
Revenues from the Public by Sources and Level of Government, Fiscal Year 1972
(In Billions of Dollars)

	Federal (I)	*State (II)*	*Local (III)*	*Total (IV)*
1. Revenue from the public, total	215.8	82.4	66.0	364.2
2. Property	—	1.3	40.9	42.1
3. Individual income	94.7	13.0	2.2	110.0
4. Corporation income	32.2	4.4	—	36.6
5. Death and gift	5.4	1.3	—	6.7
6. General sales	—	17.6	2.7	20.3
7. Selective sales and excises	16.8	15.6	1.6	34.0
8. Customs duties	3.3	—	—	3.3
9. Other	1.3	6.7	1.6	9.5
10. Subtotal	153.7	59.9	48.9	262.5
11. Payroll	51.3	11.8	1.6	64.7
12. Total taxes	205.0	71.6	50.5	327.2
13. Charges and miscellaneous	10.8	10.8	15.5	37.1

Notes: Includes net surpluses of public enterprises (Postal Service, utilities, liquor stores). Because of rounding, detail may not add to totals.
Line 11: Includes all insurance trust revenue.
Line 13: Includes miscellaneous charges, assessments, interest earnings, and surpluses of public enterprises.
Source: *Governmental Finances in 1971–72,* U.S. Department of Commerce, Bureau of the Census.

national defense, or $86 billion if veterans' programs are included. Interest on public debt was $23 billion, leaving $270 billion for other purposes.[2]

Of this, the lion's share of $184 billion went into human resources or "people-oriented" programs, including $71 billion for education and $67 billion for social insurance. Next in importance are various items pertaining to economic development. The leading item is transportation with $25 billion, followed by natural resources development (including agriculture and recreation facilities) with $21 billion. Next, $11 billion was expended for internal protection, while "general government" claimed only $10 billion of the total.

The largest share, 48 percent, of government expenditures thus went to human resource programs, and the next largest, 21 percent, to national defense. Education took 18 percent, transportation absorbed 7 percent, and only a minor fraction, or 3 percent, went into general administration.

Revenues Total revenue from the public (with intergovernmental transfer payments excluded) as shown in Table 2-2, column IV, amounted to $364 billion. The difference between this figure and the preceding expenditure total of $380 billion was the deficit for that year.

Total revenue was divided between $327 billion of taxes and $37 billion of charges of various types. Looking at the tax structure (lines 2 through 12, column

[2] We are dealing here with the breakdown by expenditure functions, including in each function purchases as well as transfer payments. For a breakdown by national income categories, in which these two types of payment are distinguished, see Chapter 6.

IV), we find that the individual income tax is much the most important single source, accounting for 34 percent of tax revenue. It is followed by the payroll, property, and corporation income taxes, which provide 20, 13, and 11 percent of total tax revenue, respectively. The remainder of the tax revenue consists largely of sales and excise taxes, which amount to 10 percent. Death and gift taxes, as well as customs duties, are of quite minor importance in the total revenue picture. The overall tax structure is thus heavily income tax–oriented, the combined yield of the individual and corporation income taxes contributing nearly one-half the total, with payroll taxes next (and rising) in importance.

By Levels of Government

While it is important to keep this overall picture in mind, we must now turn to the way in which expenditures and revenues are divided among the various levels of government. This apportionment is of crucial importance because the United States is a federal, not a unitary, system. As distinct from such countries as the Netherlands and the United Kingdom with their highly centralized system of government, the United States—for better or worse—is a federation with a correspondingly decentralized fiscal system. Moreover, various levels of government specialize in particular expenditure functions, so that the changing role of various functions has brought with it changes in the distribution of expenditures among levels. Since the various levels of government also specialize in different taxes, these changes have also affected the changing composition of the overall tax structure.

Expenditures As shown in Table 2-1, the federal share in expenditures to the public (with intergovernmental transfers excluded) amounts to 53 percent of the total, with the local government share at 28 percent and the state share at 19 percent. If national defense is excluded and civilian programs only are considered, the federal share falls to 40 percent. If we go a step farther and exclude social security benefits, the federal share becomes 28 percent. The direct role of the federal government as a spending agent in civilian programs other than social security is thus less than one-third. Most of the business of providing for social goods is accounted for by the lower, and especially the local, level.

As we move down the columns, the table shows the two biggest items in the federal budget to be national defense and social insurance. These are followed by interest and veterans' payments. Human resource programs, other than social insurance, amount to 7 percent of the total and development expenditures account for 10 percent. The major items at the state level are education, transportation (mostly highways), and welfare, accounting for 25, 19, and 17 percent, respectively. By far the most important category at the local level is education with 45 percent, followed by welfare with 8 percent. Moving across the lines, we note that the national defense function is all federal, that education is mainly local, and that transportation is largely a state function. Welfare, finally, is of major importance at the state and local levels but less so at the federal level.

Revenue As we turn to the revenue side of the picture, Table 2-2 gives the distribution of revenue from the public (which excludes grant receipts) by levels of government. Of the total, 59 percent went to the federal, 23 percent to the state, and 18 percent to the local level. As shown in column I, the individual income tax furnished 44 percent of federal revenue and the corporation tax another 15 percent, making the federal tax structure highly income–tax intensive. Payroll taxes furnished 24 percent, while excises and customs duties contributed 9 percent.

At the state level, sales and excise taxes contributed 40 percent, with payroll and income taxes together amounting to about 35 percent. At the local level, tax revenue remains dominated, as it always has been, by the property tax, which still contributes over 80 percent of tax revenue and over 60 percent of total revenue. The role of charges, finally, is unimportant at the federal level but more significant at the lower levels, especially for local government, where the charges contribute nearly one-quarter of revenue.

The Role of Intergovernmental Grants

The preceding discussion, by focusing on expenditures to and revenues from the public, has bypassed the important problem of intergovernmental transfers. While netting out for the public sector as a whole, they are of major importance regarding the fiscal structure by levels of government.

This becomes evident as one compares line 1 of Tables 2-1 and 2-2. For the public sector as a whole, expenditures to and receipts from the public differ only by the amount of deficit or surplus, but the differences by level of government are much larger. Federal and state governments receive much more from the public than they spend, while local governments receive much less. The difference is made up by transfers. The two sides of the picture are reconciled in Table 2-3, which provides a bird's-eye view of our Federalist fiscal structure.

TABLE 2-3
Role of Intergovernmental Grants, Fiscal Year 1972
(In Billions of Dollars)

	Federal (I)	*State (II)*	*Local (III)*	*Total (IV)*
1. Expenditures to the public	201.0	70.6	108.2	379.8
Add: Grants to other levels				
2. States	27.5	—	0.6	28.1
3. Localities	6.1	36.8	—	42.9
4. Total	33.6	36.8	0.6	71.0
5. Total expenditures	234.6	107.4	108.8	450.8
Deduct: Grants from other levels				
6. Federal government	—	27.5	6.1	33.6
7. States	—	—	36.8	36.8
8. Localities	—	0.6	—	0.6
9. Total	—	28.1	42.9	71.0
10. Deficit (—), surplus (+†)	−18.8	+3.2	+0.1	−15.5
11. *Equals:* Revenue from the public	215.8	82.5	66.0	364.3

† Includes change in debt and cash balances.
Source: *Governmental Finances in 1971–72,* U.S. Department of Commerce, Bureau of the Census.

Beginning with column I, we find that the federal government makes substantial grants to states and lesser ones to local governments. Total federal expenditures are thus substantially above expenditures to the public. Since no grants are received, the total is paid for out of "own" revenue (i.e., revenue from the public) and deficit. Turning to column II, we find that states make large grants to local governments, with one-third of their total expenditures accounted for in this way. At the same time, receipt of federal grants is added to "own" revenue to defray the cost. At the local level, we find that no significant grants are made, so that total expenditures are accounted for by expenditures to the public only. At the same time, grants received (primarily from the states) constitute a substantial part of fiscal resources.

Viewing the expenditure side, we note that 14 percent of total federal, and 34 percent of total state, expenditures consist of grants. As a result, the distribution of expenditures as shown in line 1 of Table 2-3 is less concentrated at higher levels of government than is the case when expenditures are allocated on an origin basis, with grants imputed to the donor rather than the donee level. Whereas the shares in accordance with line 1 are 53, 19, and 28 percent for the three levels, respectively, shares on the origin basis are 59, 23, and 18 percent.[3]

On the revenue side of the ledger, the same pattern is observed. At the federal level, all revenue is drawn from the public since no grants are received. At the state level, 24 percent is obtained from grants, and at the local level the grant share amounts to 65 percent of total revenue, with only 35 percent derived from "own" sources.

Finally, it should be noted that the role of grants not only enters into the overall fiscal position of the various levels of government but also bears on the distribution of various expenditure functions. The reason is that grants are largely earmarked for the finance of particular expenditure functions. In particular, the role of state finance in education expenditures is much greater than appears on the basis of Table 2-1, in which only expenditures to the public were considered.[4]

B. THE CONSTITUTIONAL FRAMEWORK

The fiscal framework of the United States is deeply embedded in the Federalist spirit of its Constitution. Whereas a unitary government need not have its taxing and spending powers specified in the constitution, a federation by necessity must have them so specified. Indeed, fiscal arrangements—the assignment of taxing and spending powers—are at the very core of the contract between the constituent governments (the states in the United States, the provinces in Canada, or the *Länder* in the German Federal Republic) which combine to form the federation. While the central government necessarily must have fiscal powers, the composing units retain a sovereign right to conduct fiscal transactions of their own.

This is the spirit in which the fiscal provisions of the U.S. Constitution were

[3] To arrive at these ratios, the expenditure-to-the-public total is allocated so as to increase federal and state expenditures to the public by their intergovernmental grants made, while reducing state and local expenditures to the public by grant receipts.

[4] For further discussion of the grant problem, see Chap. 30, Sec. C.

written. Prior to the adoption of the Constitution, the Continental Congress was without taxing powers; the Revolutionary War was financed by the taxes of the Colonies and by borrowing. In no small part the Constitutional Convention of 1787 was called to deal with the financial aftermath of the war. The war debt had to be serviced and financial resources were needed to conduct the business of the future federal government. Fiscal arrangements were thus a major problem confronting the Convention.

Federal Powers and Limitations

The fiscal powers of the federal government were laid down in a series of specific constitutional provisions which came to be further defined by judicial interpretations given to certain other provisions not exclusively aimed at fiscal matters. The major provisions which are specifically fiscal include:

1. The granting of taxing powers
2. The uniformity rule
3. The apportionment rule
4. The prohibition of export taxes

What has been the significance of these provisions, and how have they been modified since their inception?

Taxing Powers and Expenditure Functions The general enabling statute for federal taxing powers is contained in Article 1, Section 8, of the Constitution, which provides that "the Congress shall have power to levy and collect Taxes, Duties, Imposts and Excises, to pay the Debts and provide for the common Defense and General Welfare of the United States." By including the "general welfare" as a legitimate objective of federal finance, the Constitution refrains from setting specific limits to the federal government's expenditure function. Interpretation of the term "general welfare" was left to the Congress and the courts, and it has come to be interpreted in an extremely broad sense. The general welfare is understood to cover not only general objectives, such as national defense or the administration of justice, but also highly selective programs aimed at particular regions or population groups, such as aid to Appalachia, grants-in-aid, and transfer payments. Thus, taxation for the finance of almost any type of expenditure program seems to be within the powers of the federal government.

Should the general welfare be understood to justify the use of taxation for regulatory purposes as well as for the financing of expenditures? The courts at times have disallowed such use, but the later trend has been toward permitting regulatory objectives. In all, the taxation and expenditure powers granted by Article 1, Section 8, of the Constitution are broad and general, subject only to certain specific limitations and judicial constraints.

Uniformity Rule The first specific limitation imposed by the Constitution is the uniformity rule of Article 1, Section 8. The rule requires that "all Duties,

Imposts and Excises shall be uniform throughout the United States." Thus, excises on tobacco or automotive products must be applied at the same rate in all states; but if this condition is satisfied, they are permissible, even though their revenue impact will differ greatly among the states, depending on where particular industries are located.[5] Uniformity, in other words, means uniform application of the statute, not of the amount of revenue collected from each state.

The uniformity rule, therefore, has imposed no significant limitation on the development of the federal tax structure on a nationwide basis. On the contrary, it has contributed to the development of an equal system by requiring equal treatment of taxpayers in equal position, independent of their place of residence. Similarly, it is also in accord with the efficiency rule that arbitrary interference with the location of industry—such as would be caused by regionally differentiated taxes—should be avoided. Nor does the uniformity rule interfere with the use of taxes as a tool of general stabilization policy, since tax rates may be raised and lowered on a nationwide basis as required.

The only respect in which the uniformity rule may interfere with the freedom of fiscal policy is in the use of the taxing power to deal with regional problems of economic development. Thus, a lower rate of manufacturer's tax on automobiles produced in West Virginia or Mississippi might serve to encourage automobile production in these states and help develop these particular regions. This could not be done under the uniformity rule.

While the Constitution relates the uniformity rule to "Duties, Imposts and Excises," thereby excluding "direct taxes," this was not meant to invite the use of direct taxes for regulatory purposes on a regionally differentiated basis.[6] Indeed, the framers of the Constitution did not visualize federal use of direct taxes, which at that time were thought of primarily in terms of the property tax. Nor is it likely that the courts would permit a regionally differentiated use of the income taxes under the Sixteenth Amendment.

Apportionment Rule and the Sixteenth Amendment Whereas the uniformity rule proved to be a generally sound constraint in the development of a rational nationwide tax structure, the apportionment rule imposed a barrier which later on was to prove unacceptable. By demanding that "no capitation, or other direct tax shall be levied, unless in Proportion to the Census or Enumeration herein before directed to be taken," Section 9 of Article 1 in effect required all such taxes to be head taxes. Thus, tax rates would vary among states in inverse proportion to their per capita tax base. The rates of property tax, for instance, would have to be twice as high in state A as in state B if the per capita property tax base in A were one-half that in B. Adopted initially as a tradeoff which offered the wealthier states a tax assurance in return for their willingness to accept a smaller number of representatives in the Congress, the need for such assurance

[5] Note we are speaking here of the initial impact or place of *collection,* and not of the place of *incidence.* Tobacco excises are collected in Virginia, and automotive excises in Michigan, while neither is collected in Nevada. Yet, the burden of both taxes will be spread among all three states, depending on their share in cigarette and automotive consumption.

[6] For a discussion of the economic distinction between direct and indirect taxes, see p. 227.

did not materialize for over a century, during which time federal revenue needs were met by the proceeds of indirect taxes, especially custom duties.

The apportionment clause did not bite until much later, when the federal government came to be confronted with the need for income taxation. The development of a national federal income tax was not possible if the apportionment rule were held by the courts to apply to such a tax. The rate schedule, even if proportional within states, would have had to differ between states, being higher for those states with lower per capita income. This would have been incompatible with the principle of equal treatment of taxpayers with equal capacity on a nationwide basis and would have imposed a regressive pattern of rates on an interstate basis. Under these conditions, a modern income tax could not have been developed, and though the original intent of the clause was to protect the wealthy against the poor *states,* its application in the modern setting would have been to prevent progressive (or even proportional) taxation at the federal level and thus to protect the wealthy against the poor *taxpayer.*

The question, therefore, was whether the income tax should be considered a "Duty, Impost or Excise" under the uniformity rule, or a "capitation or other direct tax" under the apportionment clause. When the first federal income tax was held valid in 1880, the court chose to interpret it as an excise, but the opposite view was taken in 1895, when the second attempt at income taxation was held unconstitutional as an unapportioned direct tax. While it seems evident, in economic terminology, that the income tax is a direct tax, it is less clear which interpretation was the correct one on constitutional grounds. However this may be, the die was cast in the 1895 decision. Given the rising revenue needs of the federal government, especially in response to the potential need for war finance, the problem was resolved in 1913 by the Sixteenth Amendment. It states that "Congress shall have power to levy and collect taxes on incomes, from whatever source derived, without apportionment among the several states, and without regard to census or enumeration," thus clearing the way for a uniform and nationwide income tax. Such a tax was introduced in 1913 and, as noted before, was destined to become the mainstay of the federal revenue structure.

But though federal *income* taxation has been totally freed from the shackles of the apportionment rule, the rule might retain some future significance were additional taxes, such as a federal net worth tax or property tax, to be considered. Such a tax could be held to be in the nature of an income tax and thus be validated under the Sixteenth Amendment, but until the matter is decided, the skeleton of the apportionment rule continues to haunt the tax lawyer's closet.

Export Taxes Article 1 of the Constitution prohibits the levying of export taxes. Reflecting the desire of the Southern states to protect their interest in cotton exports, this limitation did not prove a major factor in later years. However, it is interesting to note, in connection with the potential use of tax policy to affect the balance of payments, that there is no corresponding prohibition of export subsidies.[7]

[7] See Chap. 31, Sec. C.

Judicial Constraints In addition, certain other constitutional provisions have proved relevant to the federal taxing powers.

1. The Supreme Court once interpreted the federal system, with its "dual sovereignty" of federal and state governments, to imply that the federal government must not tax the instrumentalities of the states and local governments. Accordingly, interest on securities issued by such governments was held exempt from federal income tax and sales to such governments were held not to be subject to federal excise taxes. Though originally exempted on similar grounds, salaries of state and local government employees are generally subject to federal income tax. While the income tax statute continues to exempt interest on state and municipal bonds, chances are that the powers granted by the Sixteenth Amendment would now be interpreted by the Court as overruling the immunity doctrine as applied to the income tax.

2. Under the due process clause, provided in the Fifth Amendment to the Constitution, the federal government is constrained from depriving people of "life, liberty or property without due process of law." As applied to taxation, this means that taxes must not be arbitrary. While classification and differentiation are allowed, they must be "reasonable." The due process clause has not been interpreted, however, as placing an upper limit on permissible tax rates. At the same time, the taxpayer is protected by being given the right of judicial appeal.

Conclusion As this brief survey suggests, it can hardly be said that the development of the federal tax structure has been hampered greatly by constitutional provisions. The uniformity rule has been a wholesome constraint and the apportionment rule has been effectively overruled by the Sixteenth Amendment; and it has become increasingly apparent that taxation can be used for regulatory purposes. However, constitutional constraints still limit the feasibility of using taxation as an instrument of regional policy.

State Powers under Federal Constitution

Whereas the federal government has to be granted basic taxing powers by the Constitution, the states did not need this provision. Taxing power of the states is vested in their sovereign rights as constituent members of the federation and retained by them under the residual power doctrine. The Constitution, however, imposes certain restrictions on the taxing power of the states, partly through specific provisions and partly again through judicial application of other clauses of the Constitution to tax matters.

General Limitations Among various general limitations, the following three are of major importance:

1. In Article I, Section 10, of the Constitution, the states are prohibited specifically not only from imposing taxes on exports (which prohibition also applies to the federal government) but on imports as well. The purpose, of course, was to place the regulation of foreign commerce exclusively under the authority of the federal government.

2. The immunity doctrine, which forbids federal taxation of state and local instrumentalities, also applies in reverse. States may not tax the instrumentalities of

the federal government. Thus, interest on federal securities is exempted from state income taxes. State excises cannot be levied on sales to the federal government, and federally owned property cannot be subjected to property tax. Yet salaries paid by the federal government are subject to state income tax. As in the case of federal taxation, the question of what constitutes an "instrumentality" of state and local governments is not defined by the Constitution, and judicial interpretation remains in flux.

3. The due process clause of the Fourteenth Amendment has been interpreted to grant the taxpayer the right of appeal against arbitrary acts of state or local tax administration, similar to its application at the federal level.

4. The equal protection clause of the Fourteenth Amendment holds that a state must not "deny to any person within its jurisdiction the equal protection of the laws." This clause has been interpreted as a prohibition against "arbitrary" classification, and sets some limits (though loosely defined) on the extent to which states may discriminate among various categories of taxpayers.

Interstate Commerce Most significant and interesting to the economist are the provisions relating to interstate commerce and to the nondiscriminatory treatment of residents of other states. These provisions dealt, almost 200 years earlier, with essentially the same problems currently faced in the debate on fiscal integration of the Common Market countries. Among various provisions which are relevant in this connection, the following should be noted:

1. The due process clause is interpreted to limit a state's taxing power to its own jurisdiction.

2. The equal protection clause is interpreted as prohibiting discrimination against out-of-state citizens. Residents and nonresidents must be treated equally. This nondiscrimination rule, however, does not apply to out-of-state corporations not subject to process within the state.

3. Article VI, Section 8, delegates to the federal government the power "to regulate commerce with foreign nations, and among the several states. . . ." This clause has been interpreted as prohibiting states from using their taxing powers so as to interfere with the flow of foreign and interstate commerce. Imports from other states or exports to other states cannot be subject to discriminatory taxes. Thus, the character of the United States as a large area without internal trade barriers but common external tariffs is assured. At the same time, this does not assure neutrality of state taxation with regard to industrial location, as location may be influenced by differential rates of excise or profit taxes.[8]

4. The same clause is applied to regulate the taxation of businesses engaging in interstate commerce. Taxes on gross receipts or profits can be imposed by the various states involved, but the total tax base must be allocated among them on a reasonable basis. There has been considerable debate about what constitutes reasonable allocation, and the entire problem is currently under reconsideration by the Congress.[9]

Right to Education and School Finance Although, in general, the states have wide freedom in designing fiscal measures, a series of recent cases have

[8] See Chap. 27, Sec. D.
[9] See p. 312.

challenged the system for funding the public schools. The bulk of the funds for public elementary and secondary education comes from the local property tax. Since the property tax base varies among school districts, children in low-base districts may be disadvantaged. Starting in 1971 with the decision of California's supreme court in *Serrano v. Priest,*[10] a number of state courts and lower federal courts found the existing scheme for funding the public schools unconstitutional. The California supreme court in *Serrano v. Priest* held that the "right to an education in public schools is a fundamental interest which cannot be conditioned on wealth." Judicial opinions in these cases referred to both the equal protection clause of the United States Constitution and to the pertinent provisions of the relevant state constitution. However, primary emphasis in most of these early cases was placed upon the federal, not the state, constitution.

Those who hoped that the educational finance decisions would bring immediate change to the system of local government finance were disappointed by the United States Supreme Court's 1972 decision in *San Antonio Independent School District v. Rodriguez.*[11] In a 5-to-4 decision, the Supreme Court held that the Texas system for funding its public schools did not violate the equal protection clause of the Fourteenth Amendment to the United States Constitution. The basis of the Court's opinion seems sufficiently broad to validate the existing financial systems of most, if not all, of the states.

The *Rodriguez* decision did not foreclose arguments that the system of educational finance of a particular state violates the provisions of that state's constitution. Since *Rodriguez,* the Supreme Court of New Jersey has held that New Jersey's scheme of public school finance was unconstitutional under the New Jersey constitution.[12] At this point it is unclear (1) how many states will follow the Supreme Court of New Jersey, (2) whether these holdings as to education ultimately will be applied to other expenditures of local governments, and (3) what fiscal measures will be adopted to implement the holdings of those courts that find the existing scheme unconstitutional. The educational finance cases could ultimately have a substantial impact upon existing fiscal arrangements. However, most legal experts do not expect such change in the near future.[13]

Coordination This new perspective aside, we conclude that the constitutional framework (as amended) leaves almost complete freedom for development of the fiscal structure. There is no assignment of particular expenditure functions to the various levels, nor is there a prescription (apart from customs duties on foreign imports) about what taxes should be used by the various levels of government.

Although little or no coordination among the fiscal systems of the various levels of government is provided for, the Constitution has been successful in barring direct interference of state taxation with the development and functioning

[10] 5 Cal. 3d 584 (1971).

[11] 411 U.S. 1 (1972).

[12] 62 N.J. 473 (1973).

[13] For further discussion, see O. Oldman and F. P. Schoettle, *State and Local Taxes and Finance,* Mineola, N.Y.: The Foundation Press, 1974, pp. 944–1008.

of the United States economy over a large free-trade area. At the federal level, the uniformity rule prohibits regional discrimination for excise taxes. At the state level, interference with interstate trade through customs or export duties is prohibited.

In short, the constitutional framework assures the absence of trade barriers in the sense of internal import or export duties as well as uniform external duties; but it does not attempt to equalize the fiscal structures of the states, thereby precluding all tax-induced interference with internal commodity or capital flows. Since state and local tax rates have been relatively low, adverse effects on economic efficiency have not been serious and have received less attention than those encountered in the European Common Market, where the conflict is greater since it stems from much larger differentials in national tax structures. Yet, the basic problems are the same. While we shall find that fiscal decentralization has its attractions, it also has its efficiency costs.[14]

State Constitutions and Local Powers

State taxation operates under constraints imposed by state constitutions in addition to these federal constraints. These limitations differ in nature and in degree of detail. In some states, the tax structure is defined in detail, whereas in others, constitutional provisions deal with specific matters, such as debt limitations or prohibition of progressive tax rates. Also, the ease of amending state constitutions differs widely. The rigidity imposed by constitutional prescription of detailed tax matters has undoubtedly been a hampering factor in the development of state tax structures.

The fiscal powers of local government are granted by the states, since local government has no sovereign powers of its own. By the same token, the federal limitations on the taxing powers of the states also apply to the derived powers of the local governments. Although this is a correct description from a formal point of view, it can hardly be said that local governments are without political strength of their own. Their fiscal powers may only be "derived" in the constitutional sense, but in reality they have grown beyond this, and local government has become a full-fledged partner on the fiscal scene. The intergovernment problem of the United States, therefore, is very much a triangular, federal-state-local affair.

C. POLICY IMPLEMENTATION: (1) EXPENDITURE POLICY

We now turn to the governmental system by which the fiscal program is planned, legislated, and executed. Focus will be on the federal operation since it is much the largest, but more or less similar procedures are followed by states and localities. The three groups involved in the federal fiscal process are (1) the voters, (2) the President and his executive branch, and (3) the Congress. Our concern here is with the latter two, leaving the voters for later and more detailed consideration.[15]

The central instrument of expenditure policy is the budget. The four steps

[14] See Chap. 29, Sec. A.
[15] See Chap. 5.

involved in the "budget cycle" are (1) formulation of the President's budget by the executive branch; (2) appraisal of the President's budget by Congress and budget legislation; (3) the execution of this legislation by the executive branch; and (4) the auditing by the General Accounting Office. In this chapter, we briefly consider these four functions as parts of the decision-making and administrative process.

History of Budget System

The modern United States budget begins with the Budget and Accounting Act of 1921, some 100 years after Great Britain instituted an annual budget. Based on the earlier (1912) recommendations of President Taft's Commission on Economy and Efficiency, this act charged the President with the preparation of a comprehensive annual executive budget and its presentation to the Congress. The Bureau of the Budget was established as an agency in the Executive Department to assist the President in this task and to coordinate the budget requests of the various departments. Thus, presentation of a centrally coordinated program replaced the earlier practice, under which each department submitted direct requests to the appropriation committees of the Congress. Now called the Office of Management and Budget, the budget agency is subject to Presidential arrangement and has been modified and reorganized from one administration to another.

Given the great expansion of the executive departments and their programs over the previous fifty years, the creation of a centralized agency with an executive budget was imperative. Budgeting, by its very nature, requires that all expenditure items be weighed against one another. Consideration of departmental expenditure programs on an isolated basis is not enough. Preparation of the national budget calls for a large amount of coordinated staff work which cannot be done adequately in each department.

At the same time, it must be recognized that the struggle for a centralized and comprehensive budget, beginning with Alexander Hamilton's defeat in this quest, was not just a drive for efficient budget planning. More important, it was a struggle between executive and congressional control over expenditure policy. With the creation of an executive budget, the President's powers were greatly increased, though less than had been proposed. Thus, the 1921 Act did not follow the recommendations of the Taft Commission to allow the executive a greater degree of policy flexibility, but required the submission of detailed expenditure estimates and appropriations. Moreover, Congress continues to deal directly with the individual departments (such as Commerce, Labor, Agriculture, etc.) before, and again after, the budget has been submitted. The debate over the budget system continues and the historical conflict between executive planning and congressional control is still very much a part of the scene. The most recent development has been the Congressional Budget and Impoundment Act of 1974, designed to strengthen the congressional budget procedure and the weight of Congress in the budget process.

Budget Preparation

Beginning with October 1976, the fiscal year to which the budget applies runs from October 1 to September 30 of the following year, rather than July 1 to June

30, as in prior years. The period from October 1976 to September 1977 is known as fiscal year 1977. The executive preparation for the 1977 budget begins in early 1975; the budget is submitted to Congress in January 1976; and legislation is to be completed by the beginning of the fiscal year 1977 on October 1. Budget preparation and enactment thus extend over a period of about twenty months.

This lengthiness of the budget process should not be surprising. The federal budget contains the government's detailed expenditure plans, now running around $350 billion, and by its nature it is an enormously complex instrument. The central responsibility for its preparation rests with the Office of Management and Budget (OMB), prior to 1972 referred to as Bureau of the Budget. The function of the OMB is to coordinate the presentation of budget requests from the various governmental departments and agencies and to see that each department's plan is in line with the "President's program." Thus, during the early months of 1975, each department was asked to present its budget for the fiscal year 1977, including requirements under existing programs as well as recommended program changes. After an initial review of these plans, the OMB formulates a tentative budget. All this process begins immediately after the fiscal 1976 budget has been submitted to Congress.

The tentative budget is then considered by the President, who studies it together with appraisals of the economic outlook and of revenue projections as presented by the Council of Economic Advisers, the Treasury Department, and other agencies. On the basis of this preliminary picture, the President establishes general fiscal policy and budgetary guidelines. For example, it might be decided that expenditure increases from new programs should be held to $10 billion, or that economies in existing programs should yield an expenditure reduction of $5 billion and that this move is to be combined with tax changes raising revenue by $5 billion. As a result of these deliberations, preliminary expenditure ceilings are set for the various departments and agencies, which are then asked to prepare a second round of expenditure plans.

Beginning in summer, the Office of Management and Budget undertakes an intensive review of these programs. The examination division of the office conducts hearings in which the various agencies are called upon to defend their proposals. In late fall, the revised programs are brought together and presented to the President for his final approval. Remaining conflicts between departmental claims have to be resolved by him. At the same time, revenue prospects and the economic outlook are reviewed and both revenue and expenditure recommendations are evaluated from the point of view of stabilization policy. The final budget message is then drafted for submission in January, within fifteen days after Congress convenes.

Budget preparation is simplified by the fact that budgeting is a continuing process. The entire budget is not planned anew each year, but expenditures for any one year stem largely from programs which were legislated by Congress in earlier years. Thus, budget planning is a marginal rather than a total process. This fact simplifies matters but it also renders change more difficult. Thus, 72 percent of the expenditures submitted in the 1974 budget were said to be "uncontrollable" in the sense of being locked into the budget by previous congressional decision. Nevertheless, the task of budget preparation is enormous, and the Office of Management and Budget plays the key role.

Whereas the various departments and agencies are expected to represent the interests of their particular program areas, it is the function of the OMB, acting for the President, to weigh conflicting claims and to produce an overall budget which is in line with his policy judgments. The ability of the office to perform this task depends upon the authority lent to it by the President. This power is of crucial importance, especially in dealing with the large departments, such as Defense, which traditionally have preferred to deal with Congress directly. While the executive budget process as now operating is reasonably efficient, further improvements are in order. Among them is the development of program budgeting, which will be considered later when techniques of efficient expenditure planning are discussed.[16]

Form of Presentation

The form of budget presentation has changed over the years and is an important factor because it determines the level of understanding with which budgetary matters are discussed. As currently presented, the budget comprises three parts. The first part includes the President's budget message, in which the major policy outlines are set forth and the most important information is summarized. The second part includes a vast amount of detailed estimates, providing the basis for appraisal by the congressional appropriations committees. The third part includes special analyses of certain selected aspects of the total program. In all, the budget documents cover over 1,000 pages and deal with half a million items. Given the mass and detail of material to be evaluated, a clear and informative arrangement of the budget document is all-important. Basic requirements of good budgeting call for (1) comprehensiveness, (2) a meaningful presentation of the state of budgetary balance, and (3) an appropriate grouping of expenditure items.

Comprehensiveness Budgeting means the setting of expenditure priorities and the weighing of alternatives. For this purpose, it is essential that a comprehensive view of the government's expenditure programs be taken. Comprehensiveness is necessary also to assure congressional control and to assess the impact of budget operations upon economic activity. This objective has by now been fairly well accomplished. The transactions of trust accounts, which used to remain outside the budget, are now included and the scope for "backdoor financing" has been reduced.

Budgetary Balance In measuring the impact of the budget upon economic activity, the state of budgetary balance (the level of deficit or surplus) is of considerable importance. All expenditures and receipts must be included. Although some problems remain with regard to the treatment of lending and debt transactions, this objective is also met fairly well. Moreover, in recent years the state of budgetary balance has come to be presented in two ways, one being the estimated actual state of balance and the other being the so-called full-employ-

[16] See p. 198.

TABLE 2-4
Federal Expenditures by Functions and Departments
(Fiscal Year 1975 est., in Billions of Dollars)

	Budget Authority	*Budget Outlays*
By Departments		
Health, Education, and Welfare	114.0	109.9
Defense	88.6	85.4
Treasury	39.7	39.7
Labor	19.9	19.0
Transportation	19.1	9.1
Veterans' Administration	16.0	15.4
Agriculture	13.8	8.8
Housing and Urban Development	51.0	5.5
Other	33.0	20.6
Total	395.1	313.4
By Functions		
Income security	156.1	106.7
National defense	91.3	85.3
Interest	31.3	31.3
Health	28.4	26.5
Veterans benefits and services	16.0	15.5
Education, manpower, and social services	14.6	14.7
Commerce and transportation	28.9	11.8
Natural resources, enviroment, and energy	11.5	9.4
Other	17.0	12.2
Total	395.1	313.4

Source: The Budget of the United States Government, Fiscal Year 1976, pp. 322–323.

ment balance, i.e., the state of balance as it would be (with given expenditure programs and tax laws) if the economy were at full employment. More will be said about these various concepts when growth effects and stabilization policy are examined.[17]

Expenditure Categories The budget presents two sets of classifications, one by departments and agencies and the other by functions. The former grouping, as presented in the upper part of Table 2-4, is needed because the departments and agencies are the units to which congressional appropriations are made and which are responsible for the administration of expenditure programs. The functional classification in turn is needed to measure the costs and benefits of entire programs, even though more than one agency may participate therein. Although functional classification was already called for in the 1921 legislation, emphasis thereon is a relatively new development. The idea of "program and performance budgeting," which rests on the functional approach, has received much attention in recent years, together with the application of cost-benefit analysis to the

[17] See Chap. 26, Sec. B.

evaluation of expenditure programs. It will be given closer consideration when we examine program evaluation.[18]

Congressional Budget Process

Up to this point, the task of budget preparation is essentially similar to that under a parliamentary type of government. Indeed, it may be simpler since the various cabinet secretaries, in representing their departments, tend to have less independence than do ministers under the parliamentary system, as in the United Kingdom or in Canada. The situation is changed, however, when it comes to legislation. Under the parliamentary system, the government's budget is accepted as a whole without amendment. Thus a more or less unified budget plan is assured. Under the United States system, where executive and congressional powers are separated, Congress is free to change (add to, delete from, or substitute for) the President's budget proposals, and it deals with them not as a whole but department by department. That Congress is not subject to the kind of party discipline which controls most other parliaments adds to the difficulty.

The Old System Until recently, the congressional budget process was exceedingly cumbersome and lacking in coordination. After presentation, the President's budget message would be considered first in the House of Representatives. Examined initially by the Appropriations Committee, it would then be passed on to thirteen subcommittees dealing with appropriations for the various departments. After intensive hearings and consideration by these committees, the proposed bills would be returned to the Appropriations Committee which would report them to the floor of the House. After passage, they would then go to the Senate, where the entire procedure would be repeated by the Senate Appropriations Committee and its thirteen subcommittees. The Senate Appropriations Committee, holding its hearings while its House counterpart works on the bills, would report appropriation bills out very soon after receiving them from the House. After being voted upon on the floor of the Senate, the House and Senate bills would be reconciled in conference, prior to receiving their final vote by both houses.

This procedure involved serious shortcomings. Insufficient coordination among the subcommittees led decisions on the budget to be made in a piecemeal fashion, without reference to a common budget total. Failure to involve the House and Senate floors at an early stage reduced the authority of appropriation bills as reported out by the appropriations committees. No formal linkage existed between expenditure and tax legislation, nor between expenditure legislation and the broader implications of fiscal policy for economic stabilization. Lack of coordination between the efforts of the two houses of Congress resulted in excessive duplication. Finally, Congress did not have the staff support necessary to cope with the mass of detail and the technical problems involved. For these and other reasons, Congress increasingly felt that it had "lost control" over the budget.

Attempts had been made at various times to remedy these difficulties. Thus,

[18] See p. 198.

a single Appropriations Committee had been established in the House in 1921, thereby replacing eleven totally independent committees, but the resulting coordination had remained inadequate. Similarly, a so-called legislative budget had been introduced in 1947, aimed at setting a budget ceiling to be respected by both houses, but it had not been implemented effectively. A concerted effort to improve matters was made only recently under the Congressional Budget and Impoundment Control Act of 1974, which is now in the process of implementation. This legislation introduces a new congressional budget calendar and proposes a number of major innovations.

A New Approach A budget committee is established in each house in addition to the existing appropriations committees. In the House, the new committee is to include members from the Appropriations and Ways and Means Committees, the other standing committees, and the leadership of both parties. The Senate committee has a somewhat narrower membership. The two committees follow a common schedule, beginning with the preparation of a "concurrent resolution" on the budget. Each committee must report its version of the resolution to its house by April 15. This resolution is to set the overall level of expenditures for the coming fiscal year as well as to provide a breakdown among major functional categories and to determine the required level of revenue. By May 15, the legislative process on the resolution must be completed, including the conference to reconcile the difference between the two resolutions. Then, trying to stay within the limits set by the budget resolution, the Congress acts on the appropriation bills, finishing shortly after Labor Day. In the time remaining before the start of the new fiscal year on October 1, the Congress must pass a second concurrent resolution on the budget in which it reaffirms its earlier decisions or revises them. In the latter case, a reconciliation bill that carries out the dictates of the resolution —including cuts in appropriation bills already enacted—must be passed before the start of the new fiscal year. To help Congress to follow this expeditious and exacting budget schedule, a congressional budget office is to be established which will provide Congress with technical and staff assistance, in the hope of making it a more nearly equal partner in the budget discussion with the executive branch. The success of the new approach will depend on how well appropriations will stay within the framework of the resolution, and how well the skeleton budget, authorized in the resolution, will be planned.

Authorizations and Appropriations As we have seen, Congress does not legislate the budget as a whole, but deals with particular sections of it. The bills take two forms. First, Congress authorizes agencies to undertake particular programs, often with a limit on the amount that may be appropriated for the programs. This basic authorizing legislation may be for one or more years, or it may be unlimited. Subsequent to this basic authorizing legislation, Congress grants appropriations or authorizations to spend. From twelve to fifteen such appropriation bills are passed each year and these may be made on a year-to-year basis or for longer periods, with unused funds carried over to be used later for the originally determined purpose.

The legislative process thus involves both the determination of new programs and the financing of current outlays under previously determined programs. As shown in Table 2-4, there is no neat balance between new authority granted and outlays made. Unused authority granted in past years is drawn upon and the balance of unused authority is then carried over to the next year.

Presidential Approval

The President must sign or veto budget bills within ten days, but his hand may be forced. Congress may choose to include particular items in an appropriation bill which are unacceptable to the President even though the rest of the bill meets his approval, and passage cannot be postponed, because funds are needed for current operations. For this reason, budget experts have urged that the President be permitted to veto individual items, but the power to exercise such an item veto has not been granted by Congress.

Execution of Program

After an agency or department has received its appropriation or authorization to spend, it may proceed to do so, but the execution of the program remains under the supervision of the Office of Management and Budget to which periodic financial reports have to be made. The office apportions the amounts expendable in particular time periods and may establish reserves against appropriations.

While the basic task of the Executive is to administer the budget as legislated by the Congress, some flexibility remains. This is desirable, since changing circumstances may make it advisable to speed up or retard certain programs. At the same time, Congress has been concerned with limiting executive discretion in the matter. To forestall potential lack of congressional control because of executive use of previously authorized but unexpended funds, such funds may be rescinded by the Congress. More recently, primary concern has been with the opposite contingency, that of assuring that legislated programs will in fact be carried out. Thus, the recent 1974 legislation forestalls executive impoundment of appropriated funds by requiring the President to submit a rescission bill to Congress, without approval of which he must carry out the program. These difficulties arise because, under our executive system of government, the executive branch may not work in concert with Congress.

Auditing

The final stage in the budget cycle is the accounting and auditing function. According to the Budget and Accounting Act of 1921, this function is performed by the General Accounting Office, operating under the Comptroller General. This office is an independent agency, outside the Executive Office of the President and responsible directly to the Congress. Its task is to certify that funds have been expended for the purposes designated by Congress and to perform the auditor's function of certifying that the accounts truthfully reflect the underlying fiscal operations. Although many students of the budget process feel that the auditing function should be integrated with the Office of Management and Budget, Congress is not inclined to grant this request. The political issue is again one of congressional control over expenditure policy.

D. POLICY IMPLEMENTATION: (2) TAX POLICY

While expenditure legislation is required annually to provide appropriations, be if for new or existing programs, this need not be the case with tax policy. The existing tax structure provides a continuous if fluctuating flow of revenue, without further legislative action being taken. Action may be taken, however, to improve (or, for that matter, worsen) the equity of its burden distribution, to adjust overall revenue to changing expenditure requirements, and to adjust tax policy for stabilization purposes, where prompt measures to raise taxes (so as to curtail aggregate demand) or to reduce them (so as to increase demand) may be needed.

The major concern of tax reformers has been with the need to improve the equity of the tax structure so as to make it comply more nearly with prevailing views of what constitutes a fair distribution of the tax burden. Such standards change with the times and the political climate. Tax reform, therefore, is always a popular topic for discussion, but it tends to be handled in a discontinuous fashion. Major structural changes occur once or twice a decade, when political and other circumstances are ripe for "reform." Such changes occurred in 1954 and also in the periods 1962–64 and 1969–70. Typically, these were years following major changes in administration.

Executive Preparation

Tax policy proposals originate at both the executive and the congressional levels. At the executive level, a number of agencies are involved, depending on the nature of the proposal. Equity-oriented reforms of the tax structure are the primary responsibility of the Treasury Department. Administration proposals for such reform are prepared by the Office of Tax Analysis and the Office of the Tax Legislative Counsel. The work draws on a large staff of tax experts, economists, and lawyers, and it is a continuing process. Many tax economists, in and out of government, are consulted and participate in this work. Eventually, usually after a year or more of preparation, the program emerges and is presented to the President for his consideration. After the Presidential decisions are made, the final program is formulated and presented to the Congress in a tax message.

Proposals dealing with the short-run stabilization aspects of tax policy involve a wider range of agencies, including the Treasury, the Council of Economic Advisers, the Federal Reserve, and the Office of Management and Budget. The Treasury, moreover, must implement such changes in tax rates as have been decided upon, including prompt adjustments in withholding rates.

Legislation

The President's tax message is initially presented to the Ways and Means Committee of the House, not to the Senate. This is done because, according to Article 1, Section 7, of the Constitution, "All bills for revenue raising shall originate in the House of Representatives." After receiving the administration's recommendations or (at other times) on its own initiative, the Ways and Means Committee holds hearings. These typically begin with a presentation by the Secretary of the Treasury, followed by testimony from outside groups, such as industry representatives, unions, and other organizations. Apart from the Treasury, which is to represent the national interest, the bulk of the testimony is given by interest groups, with only occasional presentations by experts or individuals representing the public interest at large. After the hearings are completed, the bill is formulated in executive session. Frequently it bears little resemblance to the original administration plan. It is then reported out and, after limited discussion, usually subject only to amendments which are approved by the Ways and Means Committee, it is passed by the House.

The bill is then sent to the Finance Committee of the Senate where the same procedures, including a Treasury response to the House bill and extensive hearings, are repeated. Although the Senate legislation is based on the House bill, the Finance Committee is free to make changes or substitute its own proposals. The bill is then considered on the Senate floor and discussed extensively, without limitation on amendments. After being voted on by the Senate, it is sent to Conference Committee where differences between House and Senate versions are ironed out. The bill is then returned to both houses, passed, and sent to the President for signature.

Both the Ways and Means Committee and the Senate Finance Committee are assisted in their complex task by the staff of the Joint Committee on Internal Revenue Taxation, as well as by the staff of the Treasury Department. Many committee members—especially on the Ways and Means Committee—serve for lengthy periods and thus acquire considerable technical expertise. However, they are subject to a great deal of political pressure, and vested interests are built up which render action on reform exceedingly difficult to obtain.

Balance of Power

The President rarely vetoes a tax bill, and when vetoed, such bills have usually been sustained by a vote to override the veto. Indeed, the balance of power over tax policy lies very much on the congressional side and in particular with the Ways and Means Committee and its chairman. It is here that legislative action must originate, and the committee may or may not respond to administration recommendations. If it responds to the call for action, it may disregard the administration's wishes and substitute its own proposals. Moreover, the committee may act on its own, without administration initiative. Underlying a latent hostility between the Ways and Means Committee and the Treasury Department (independent of party lines) is the congressional feeling that revenue legislation is a constitutional prerogative of the Congress, and not really in the domain of the executive.

Administration

The tax laws, as defined by past revenue acts, are assembled in the Internal Revenue Code. This code is prepared by the legal staff of the Internal Revenue Service (IRS), and it interprets the revenue acts in their detailed application to a vast range of complex situations. Regulations are issued and codified on a continuous basis to guide both taxpayers and tax officials in the administration of the law. The IRS staff engaged in this task includes some 60,000 tax agents, operating in 60 district offices throughout the country. The annual budget for the IRS amounts to slightly over $1 billion, or less than one-half of 1 percent of revenue collected.

Although tax payments in the United States are based on the taxpayer's own declaration rather than on official assessment, the returns (about 120 million in all) must nevertheless be checked and audited. Procedures involved in examining and auditing tax returns are currently being revolutionized by the use of computers, but a large and highly trained staff remains necessary to assess the additional information.

A final function in the taxing process is performed by the tax courts, to which the taxpayer may turn with complaints. The prosecution staff of the Internal Revenue Service in turn may enforce the tax law through criminal charges in the regular system of the federal courts.

Reform Proposals

Many suggestions have been made to improve the operation of the tax policy mechanism. They relate primarily (1) to matters of flexibility and timing, (2) to establishing a closer linkage between tax and expenditure policies, and (3) to obtaining a better representation of the public interest in the committee hearings.

Flexibility The tax-legislative process is too slow and cumbersome to permit flexible use of tax policy for purposes of stabilization. The time lapse between the President's request for a change and the passage of the legislation may range from a speed record of one month (the Excise Tax Reduction Act of 1965), over fourteen months (the 1968 surcharge), to a marathon eighteen months (the Revenue Act of 1962). However, the tax reduction of Spring 1975 was legislated in a period of three months.

This delay in tax action reflects the difficult technical problems which must be dealt with in tax legislation, as well as the heavy political pressures which are brought to bear. While careful and even lengthy discussion is appropriate with regard to structural reforms of the equity type, the resulting delay constitutes a severe handicap when it comes to tax increase or reduction as called for by economic stabilization. For this reason, ways should be found to separate structural reform from such short-run stabilization changes.

To meet this problem, it has been suggested that the President be given the authority to make changes in the level of tax rates as needed for stabilization purposes. To protect congressional control, the Congress could in advance prescribe the pattern of such changes (such as equal percentage changes in income tax liabilities, limited to 10 percent) and could retain the privilege of terminating them. However, such proposals, as advanced in various forms by President Kennedy in 1962 and 1963, and by President Johnson in 1964 and 1966, have as yet been unsuccessful. Congress is adamant in its desire to preserve its control over the purse strings and has not been persuaded as yet that cyclical flexibility may be introduced without endangering this basic prerogative.[19]

Coordinated Tax-Expenditure Policy A closer linkage between tax and expenditure policies is desirable on two grounds. First, the net impact of fiscal policy on aggregate demand and economic activity depends on both the tax and

[19] See also Chap. 26, Sec. C.

the expenditure sides of the fiscal process. Thus, the proper levels of taxation and expenditures, as seen from the stabilization point of view, need be determined in relation to each other. Second, it is through decisions on tax policy that Congress is made aware of the cost of expenditure programs. The choice of expenditure programs must be traced in the last resort to the preferences of individual consumers, the taxing process being the instrument through which this tracing has to occur. By separating the two sides of the picture, the opportunity cost of public expenditures is obscured, thus inviting careless expenditure policy; at the same time, expenditure benefits come to be overlooked when tax decisions are made, thus establishing an undue presumption against taxes. A linkage between appropriation and tax committees is needed to bridge this gap.[20] As noted earlier, an attempt has been made in the Congressional Budget and Impoundment Act of 1974 to provide such a linkage, but it remains to be seen whether this will do the job.

Public Interest Finally, provision should be made for a more balanced presentation at tax committee hearings, involving a more equitable distribution of time between industry and other interest-group representatives on the one side, and tax experts or general representatives of the public on the other. Although industry and other group representatives have much to contribute, especially with regard to technical issues applied to particular industries or firms, their testimony on general policy approaches tends to be biased and should be balanced by other views.

E. OVERALL FISCAL POLICY

The role of expenditure and tax policies as instruments of economic stabilization has been mentioned in various connections. The Executive was charged with the responsibility for stabilization policy under the Employment Act of 1946, which called upon the President to "promote maximum employment, production and purchasing power," and, as added by the amendment of 1953, to promote "a dollar of stable value," to develop the policies needed for these objectives, and to report thereon to the Congress annually in his Economic Report. In this connection, the act established the Council of Economic Advisers to the Executive and the Joint Economic Committee at the congressional level.

The Council of Economic Advisers, including three council members and a staff, is to assist the President in the preparation of his Economic Report. Designed to play a key role in formulating the broader economic guidelines for stabilization policy as well as to deal with other aspects of the government's economic program, the actual role of the Council has differed with various administrations, each administration having, in the end, its own style of policy formulation.

At the congressional level, the Council of Economic Advisers is matched by the Joint Economic Committee. This committee receives the President's Eco-

[20] To reconcile both aspects of coordination, it has been proposed that the budget be balanced at the margin, so that incremental expenditure decisions must be reached by incremental financial decisions. See Chap. 25, Sec. E.

nomic Report submitted in late January, after the State of the Union and the Budget Messages have been submitted. The report is discussed in hearings and evaluated by the committee. The creation of this committee and its work have been of great value in promulgating an intelligent approach to economic policy in fiscal and other areas and in raising the level of congressional economic policy discussion. However, the committee has remained without direct legislative responsibility and has therefore been of limited influence on specific legislative measures. To increase its power and to secure better coordination, it has been suggested that the chairman and the ranking members from both houses might be made voting members of the Appropriations and Tax Committees.

F. TRUST FUNDS

While revenue and expenditure legislation are generally separated, with the bulk of tax revenue accruing to the government's General Fund, they are linked in the case of trust funds, which therefore carry a special role in the fiscal system. Total trust fund receipts in fiscal year 1975 amounted to $119 billion, with $62 billion going to federal old age, survivors, and disability insurance in the form of payroll taxes earmarked to this fund. Another $24 billion went to other insurance funds (including $11 billion for hospital insurance), leaving the Highway Trust Fund (with $4 billion financed largely by gasoline tax receipts) as the other major fund.[21]

The role of these trust funds and the merit of linking particular receipts and expenditures in this fashion will be considered later.[22] Here we only need to note that trust fund expenditures are not subject to annual appropriations but are made by each trust fund according to the rules set by Congress for its operations.

G. DEBT MANAGEMENT

Finally, the role of debt management should be noted. The responsibility for debt management is vested in the Treasury Department although, as we shall see later, it is closely related to monetary policy as determined by the Federal Reserve System.[23]

One function of debt management is to carry out the debt transactions necessitated by a current budget deficit or surplus, involving either an increase or a decrease in the total debt. Even though the budget may be balanced over the fiscal year as a whole, the flow of tax receipts and expenditures is not synchronized on a monthly basis, so that intermediate debt financing is required. A further function, and much more important in volume, takes the form of vast refunding operations. They must be undertaken as maturing debt instruments are replaced by new issues of varying maturities and other characteristics. This operation is carried out by the Debt Management Division of the Treasury, with the assistance of the Federal Reserve Bank of New York.

[21] See *Budget for the United States Government, Fiscal Year 1976*, p. 332.
[22] See p. 214.
[23] See Chap. 28, Sec. B.

The function of debt management is essentially an executive one and does not involve direct congressional participation. However, Congress has legislated certain restrictions with which debt managers must comply, including an interest ceiling and the provision that debt obligations may not be issued at a price below their maturing value. Also, Congress imposes a ceiling on the total debt which the Treasury is allowed to incur. This ceiling is used by Congress as an additional device to control the level of expenditures, even though expenditure programs have been authorized previously by congressional legislation. As will be seen later, this limitation has interfered with efficient conduct of public debt operations.[24]

H. SUMMARY

This review of federal fiscal institutions, sketchy though it is, suffices to show that the fiscal machinery is highly complex and slow-moving. Many functions appear in triplicate, at the executive, House, and Senate levels, and coordinating them is cumbersome and not readily responsive to changing situations. Yet, much of this is the reflection of our executive system of government and of the bicameral organization of Congress. The expenditure and taxing process, which is at the heart of the governmental operation, can hardly be exempted from the constraints which this system imposes. At the same time, better coordination could be obtained and a higher degree of flexibility should be possible, without disturbing the basic balance provided by our constitutional system.

Regarding the federalist nature of our fiscal system, the major factors to be kept in mind are these:

1. The United States fiscal structure is decentralized, with somewhat over 50 percent of expenditures originating at the federal level, nearly 30 percent at the local level, and below 20 percent at the state level.

2. The levels of government differ in their expenditure structures, with defense and transfer programs of major importance at the federal, highway expenditures at the state, and education expenditures at the local levels.

3. A similarly sharp difference exists in the composition of the revenue structure, with the federal level characterized by income, the state level by sales, and the local level by property taxes.

4. Transfers from the federal to the state and from the state to the local level have greatly increased in importance over the last decade.

Fiscal affairs are conducted within a framework provided by the United States Constitution. The major constitutional provisions are:

5. The Constitution requires federal taxes to be uniform in all states and originally called for direct taxes to be proportioned among states on a per capita basis. The uniformity requirement is still in effect but raises no problem with regard to national taxes; but the apportionment requirement has been largely eliminated by the Sixteenth, or Income Tax, Amendment.

6. The Constitution does not lay down explicit rules with regard to federal

[24] See Chap. 28, Sec. C.

expenditure policy, but authorizes the government to provide "for the common defense and general welfare of the United States."

7. The Constitution prohibits states from imposing export taxes and requires state taxation to comply with its "due process" and "equal protection" clauses.

8. Recently it has been argued that the "equal protection" clause requires states to provide equal service levels to all its citizens, a requirement which would cut across municipal differentials and which is still in process of adjudication.

9. Municipalities are the creatures of the states and their fiscal powers derive from the state constitutions.

Implementation of expenditure policy has been examined for the federal level. Both the executive and legislative branches have an important role to play:

10. The primary responsibility for budget preparation rests with the executive. The budget (fiscal) year runs from October 1 to September 30. The budget is presented to the Congress in January and legislation thereon is to be completed by October 1.

11. In presenting the budget, expenditures are shown on both a departmental and a functional basis and the major rules of good budgeting (in particular, the requirement of comprehensiveness) are reasonably well observed.

12. Congressional legislation in 1974 has provided for a streamlined and coordinated congressional budget procedure which is designed to strengthen the role of the Congress in the budget process.

The implementation of tax policy follows a similar pattern:

13. Proposals for tax legislation are made by the Treasury and are submitted to the Ways and Means Committee of the House, where all tax legislation must originate. After a vote by the House, they are passed on to the Senate Finance Committee and, after a vote on the Senate floor, the two bills are reconciled in Conference Committee.

14. Shortcomings of the existing tax policy process include a lack of flexibility with regard to the use of tax adjustments for purposes of stabilization policy. Moreover, deliberation of the tax committees suffers from inadequate exposure to the general interest as distinct from presentations on behalf of particular interest groups.

FURTHER READINGS

The Budget of the United States Government, Fiscal Year 1976.

Burkhead, Jesse, and Jerry Miner: *Public Expenditure,* Chicago: Aldine-Atherton, 1971.

Economic Report of the President, latest year.

Governmental Finances in 1971–72, U.S. Department of Commerce, Bureau of the Census.

Groves, Harold M.: *Financing Government,* 6th ed., New York: Holt, 1965. See chap. 19, The Power to Tax, for constitutional setting.

Pechman, Joseph A.: *Federal Tax Policy,* 2d ed., Washington: Brookings, 1971. See chap. 3.

Smithies, Arthur: *The Budgetary Process in the United States,* New York: McGraw-Hill, 1955.

Tax Foundation: *Facts and Figures on Government Finance,* New York: 1973.

Wildowsky, Aaron: *The Politics of the Budgetary Process,* Boston: Little, Brown, 1964.

Chapter 3

The Theory of Social Goods*

A. Social Goods and Market Failure: *Market for Private Goods; Market Failure due to Nonrival Consumption; Market Failure due to Nonexcludability; Combined Cause of Market Failure; Summary.* **B. Provision for Social Goods:** *Comparison with Private Goods; Need for Budgetary Provision.* **C. Mixed Goods:** *Benefit Externalities from Private Consumption; Spatial Limitation of Benefits and Local Finance; Congestion; Alternative Modes of Provision.* **D. Social Bads, External Costs, and Pollution. E. Bargaining in the Small Group:** *Bargaining for Social Benefits; Bargaining to Avoid Social Costs.* **F. Bases of Wants and the Role of Merit Goods:** *Individualistic versus Collective Evaluation; Merit Goods.* **G. Efficient Allocation Further Considered:** *Meaning of Efficiency; The General Model for Private Goods; Private-Goods Allocation through the Market; The General Model for Social Goods; Social-Goods Allocation through the Budget.* **H. Summary.**

**Reader's Guide to Chapter 3:* This chapter explores in some detail the complex problems underlying the theory of social goods. The central problem posed by the nature of "pure" social goods is discussed in sections A and B. Section C takes up the more realistic cases of mixed goods, and D deals with the parallel issue of social bads and pollution. Section E shows how externalities may be accounted for through bargaining if only small numbers are involved. In F we examine the nature of underlying wants and the rather different case of merit goods. The material through section F is essential to an understanding of the public sector problem. In section G we turn to a more rigorous view of the theoretical issues involved. This discussion assumes some acquaintance with intermediate microtheory. Though important for a more penetrating view of the problem, it may be passed over by the reader with no deep interest in theory.

The theory of social goods provides a rationale for the allocation function of budget policy. Although difficult to resolve, it is of central importance to the economics of the public sector, just as the theories of the consumer household and of the firm are at the core of private sector economics.

The central task is to extend the principles of efficient resource use to the public sector. Some believe this to be impossible and hold that the determination of budget policy is a matter of "politics" only and not amenable to economic analysis. This view is unduly pessimistic. While it may not be possible to find and implement the optimal solution, not all feasible policies are equally good. Efficiency of resource use, here as in the private sector, is a matter of degree, and economic analysis can help us in seeking the best answers. The task is to design a mechanism for the provision of social goods which will be as efficient as feasible; for this purpose, the underlying issues must be understood.

A. SOCIAL GOODS AND MARKET FAILURE

The market economy, provided certain conditions are met, serves to secure an efficient use of resources in providing for private goods. Consumers must bid for what they wish to buy, and they thus reveal their preferences to producers. Producers, in trying to maximize their profits, will produce what consumers want to buy and will do so at least cost. Competition will assure that the mix of goods produced corresponds to consumers' preferences. This view, of course, is a highly idealized picture of the market system. In reality, various difficulties arise. Markets may be imperfectly competitive, consumers may lack sufficient information, and so forth. For these reasons, the market mechanism is not as ideal a provider of private goods as it might be. But even so, it does a fairly satisfactory job.

At the same time, the market cannot solve the entire economic problem. For one thing, it cannot function effectively if there are "externalities," by which we mean situations where consumption benefits cannot be limited and charged to a particular consumer and those where economic activity results in social costs which need not be paid for by the producer or the consumer who causes them. For another thing, the market can respond only to the effective demand of consumers as determined by the prevailing state of income distribution, but society still must judge whether this is the distribution it wants. These are two of the major areas where budget policy comes into play, and this chapter deals with the former, or allocation, aspect.

Market for Private Goods[1]

The market can function only in a situation where the "exclusion principle" applies, i.e., where A's consumption is made contingent on his paying the price, while B, who does not pay, is excluded. Exchange cannot occur without property rights and property rights require exclusion. Given such exclusion, the market can function as an auction system. The consumer must bid for the product,

[1] Note that we are dealing here only with that type of market failure which results from the presence of externalities and social goods. Other types of market failure, such as imperfect market structures (monopoly, etc.) or misleading advertising, also exist but are not discussed here.

thereby revealing preferences to the producer, and the producer, under the pressures of competition, is guided by such signals to produce what consumers want. At least, such is the outcome with a well-functioning market.

This process can function in a market for private goods—for food, clothing, housing, automobiles, and millions of other marketable private goods—because the benefits derived therefrom flow to the particular consumer who pays for them. Thus, benefits are internalized and consumption is *rival.* A hamburger eaten by A cannot be eaten by B. At the same time, the nature of the goods is such that exclusion is readily feasible. The goods are handed over when the price is paid, but not before. But budgetary provision is needed if consumption is nonrival and/or if exclusion cannot be applied.

Market Failure due to Nonrival Consumption

Social goods are goods the consumption of which is *nonrival.* That is, they are goods where A's partaking of the consumption benefits does not reduce the benefits derived by all others. The same benefits are available to all and without mutual interference. Therefore it would be inefficient to apply exclusion even if this could readily be done. Since A's partaking in the consumption benefits does not hurt B, the exclusion of A would be inefficient. Efficient resource use requires that price equal marginal cost, but marginal cost in this case is zero, and so should be the price.

Consider, for example, the case of a bridge which is not crowded, so A's crossing will not interfere with that of B. Charging a toll would be quite feasible, but so long as the bridge is not heavily used, the charge would be inefficient since it would curtail use of the bridge, the marginal cost of which is zero.[2] Or consider the case of a broadcast, which (by jamming devices) can be made available only to those listeners who rent clearing devices. Again, the jamming would be inefficient since A's reception does not interfere with B's. These are situations where exclusion *can* be applied but *should not* be because consumption is nonrival. But without exclusion, provision through the market cannot function. Consumers will not bid to reveal their preferences, because, as free riders, they can enjoy the same benefits. Hence, a political process of budget determination becomes necessary.

Market Failure due to Nonexcludability

A second instance of market failure arises where consumption is rival but exclusion is not feasible. While most goods which are rival in consumption also lend themselves to exclusion, some rival goods may not do so. Consider, for example, travel on a crowded cross-Manhattan street during rush hours. The use of the available space is distinctly rival and exclusion (the auctioning off or sale of the available space) would be efficient and should be applied. The reason is that use of crowded space would then go to those who value it most and who are willing to offer the highest price. But such exclusion would be impossible or is too costly

[2] The reader might ask why the government has not avoided excess capacity by building a smaller bridge. The answer is that certain products are lumpy for technical reasons and are not available in small incremental units. In other instances, a given facility is needed to meet the demand in peak hours, while having excess capacity during slack periods. For further discussion, see p. 702.

at this time.[3] This is a situation where exclusion *should* but *cannot* be applied. Here the difficulty of applying exclusion is *the* cause of market failure. Public provision is required until techniques can be found to apply exclusion.

Think once more of why nonexcludability causes market failure. If partaking in consumption is not made contingent on payment, people are not forced to reveal their preferences in bidding for social goods. Such, at least, is the case if the number of participants is large.[4] Since the total level of provision will not be affected significantly by any one person, the individual consumer will find it in his or her interest to share as a free rider in the provision made by others. With all consumers acting in this fashion, there is no effective demand for the goods. The auction system of the market breaks down, and once more a different method of provision is needed.

Combined Cause of Market Failure

Although the features of nonrival consumption and nonexcludability need not go together, they frequently do. In these instances—for example, air purification, national defense, streetlights—exclusion both *cannot* and *should not* be applied. Since these are situations where both causes of market failure overlap, it may be futile to ask which is *the* basic cause. However, the nonrival nature of consumption might be considered as such, since it renders exclusion undesirable (inefficient) even if technically feasible.

Summary

The previous distinctions may be summarized as follows, classifying goods into four cases, according to their consumption and excludability characteristics:

	Exclusion	
Consumption	FEASIBLE	NOT FEASIBLE
Rival	1	2
Nonrival	3	4

Characteristics of case 1 depict the clear-cut, private-good case, combining rival consumption with excludability. This is where provision through the market is both feasible and efficient. In all other cases, market failure occurs. For the setting reflected in case 2, market failure is due to nonexcludability or high costs of exclusion, while for the setting of case 3 it is due to nonrival consumption. In the fourth case, both impediments are present. If we applied the term "social good" to all situations of market failure, cases 2, 3, and 4 would all be included. It is customary, however, to reserve the term for cases 3 and 4, i.e., situations

[3] As suggested by Prof. William Vickrey of Columbia University, electronic devices may eventually be developed which record the passage of vehicles through intersections and permit the imposition of corresponding charges, adjusted to differ for rush hours and slack periods. Such charges may then be billed to the vehicle owner via a computer, and the costs of crowding city streets may thus be internalized.

[4] See p. 61 for the small-number case.

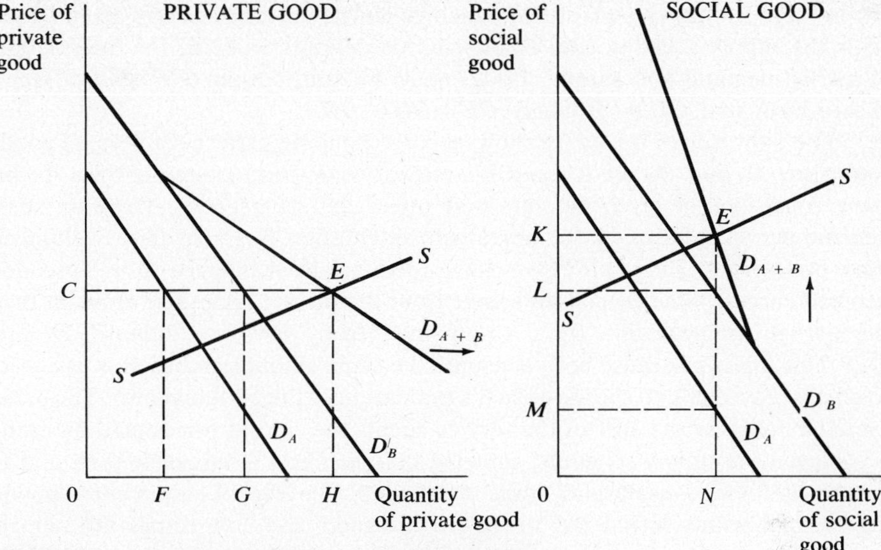

FIGURE 3-1 Demand for Private and Social Goods.

of nonrival consumption. These situations, to be sure, are similar to case 2 in that provision is made without exclusion and hence a budgetary process is called for. But they differ from case 2 in that the existence of nonrival consumption changes the conditions of efficient resource use from those applicable where consumption is rival as will be shown later in this chapter.

B. PROVISION FOR SOCIAL GOODS[5]

The nonrival nature of social-good consumption poses two important problems, including its implications for (1) what constitutes efficient resource allocation, i.e., allocation of resources to produce at least cost what consumers want most, and (2) decisions on how this allocation is to be achieved. These implications will now be examined more carefully.

Comparison with Private Goods

To explore problem 1, it is helpful to compare the familiar demand-and-supply diagram for private goods with a corresponding construction for social goods. The latter, as we shall note presently, is unrealistic, but it is nevertheless useful in noting essential differences between the two situations. The left side of Figure 3-1 shows the familiar market for a private good. D_A and D_B are A's and B's demand curves, based on a given distribution of income and prices for other goods. The market demand curve D_{A+B} is obtained by *horizontal* addition of

[5] As noted previously, the term "provision" as used here refers to the choice and payment process rather than to whether the products or services are *produced* by government (such as the services of civil servants) or by private firms (such as private construction companies which are contracted to build public roads). See p. 9.

D_A and D_B, adding the quantities which A and B purchase at any given price. *SS* is the supply schedule and equilibrium is determined at *E*, the intersection of market demand and supply. Price equals *OC* and output *OH*, with *OF* purchased by A and *OG* by B where $OF + OG = OH$.

The right side of the figure shows a corresponding pattern for a social good. As before, D_A and D_B are A's and B's respective demand curves, subject to the same conditions of given incomes and prices for other goods. Drawing such demand curves is based on the unrealistic assumption that consumers volunteer their preferences, and such curves have therefore been referred to as "pseudo-demand curves." The crucial difference from the private-good case arises in that the market demand curve D_{A+B} is now obtained by *vertical* addition of D_A and D_B.[6] This follows because both consume the same amount and each is assumed to offer a price equal to the individual's evaluation of the marginal unit. The price available to cover the cost of the service equals the sum of prices paid by each. *SS* is again the supply schedule, showing marginal cost (chargeable to A and B combined) for various outputs of the social good. The level of output corresponding to equilibrium output *OH* in the private-good case now equals *ON*, which is the quantity consumed by both A and B. The combined price equals *OK*, but the price paid by A is *OM* while that paid by B is *OL*, where $OM + OL = OK$.

Returning to the case of the private good, we see that the vertical distance under each individual's demand curve reflects the marginal benefit which derives from its consumption. At equilibrium *E*, both the marginal benefit derived by A in consuming *OF* and the marginal benefit derived by B in consuming *OG* equals marginal cost *HE*. This is an efficient solution because marginal benefit equals marginal cost for each consumer. If output falls short of *OH*, marginal benefit for each individual exceeds marginal cost and each will be willing to pay more than is needed to cover cost. Net benefits will be gained by expanding output so long as the marginal benefit exceeds the marginal cost of so doing, and net benefits are maximized therefore by producing *OH* units, at which point marginal benefit equals marginal cost. Welfare losses would occur were output expanded beyond *OH*, for marginal cost would thereby exceed marginal benefits.

Now compare this solution with that for social goods. The vertical distance under each individual's demand curve again reflects the marginal benefits obtained. Since both share in the consumption of the same supply, the marginal benefit generated by any given supply is obtained by vertical addition. Thus the equilibrium point *E* now reflects the equality between the *sum* of the marginal benefits and the marginal cost of the social good. If output falls short of *ON*, it will again be advantageous to expand because the sum of the marginal benefits exceeds cost, while an output in excess of *ON* would imply welfare losses, since marginal costs outweigh the summed marginal benefits.

Thus the two cases are analogous but with the important difference that for the private good, efficiency requires equality of marginal benefit derived by *each*

[6] This vertical addition of the demand curves for social goods was first presented by Howard R. Bowen in *Toward Social Economy*, New York: Rinehart, 1948, p. 177.

The demand curves are added vertically to show the sum of the prices which A and B are willing to pay for any given amount, the same amount being available to both since consumption is nonrival.

individual with marginal cost, whereas, in the case of the social good, the marginal benefits derived by the two consumers differ and it is the *sum* of the marginal benefits that should equal marginal cost. This is the rule established by Professor Samuelson in his pathbreaking articles of the late 1950s and which is explored further in section G of this chapter.[7]

Figure 3-1 also shows how, by applying the same pricing rule to both social and private goods—where the price payable by each consumer equals the individual's marginal benefit—different results are obtained in the two cases. Whereas in the private-good case, A and B pay the same price but purchase different amounts, in the social-good case, they purchase the same amount but pay different prices. Yet, in both cases, the same pricing rule is applied. Each consumer pays a single price for successive units of the good purchased, with the price equal to the marginal benefit the purchaser derives.[8]

Need for Budgetary Provision

While the presentation of Figure 3-1 is helpful in bringing out the change in efficiency conditions, it is misleading if taken to suggest that the provision of social goods might be implemented by a market mechanism of demand and supply, with equilibrium at E as in the case of the private good. This interpreta-

[7] See footnote 30, p. 72.

[8] A somewhat different way of presenting the case of the social good, first used by the Swedish economist Erik Lindahl, is as follows:

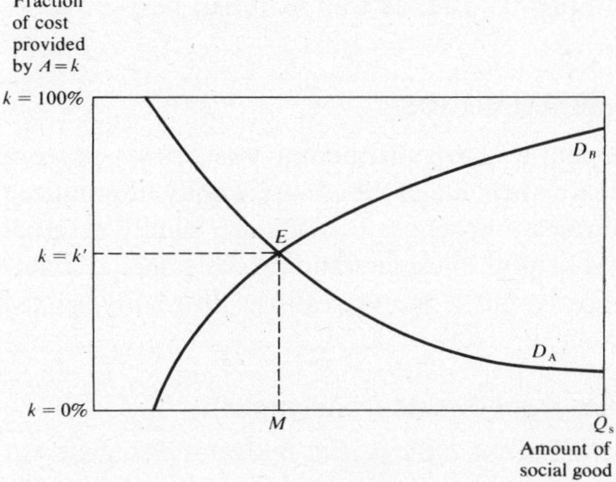

The vertical axis measures k or the fraction of unit cost contributed by A. Given the unit cost C and assuming it to be constant, kC is the price paid by A and D_A is his demand schedule for the social good S. Since B's price equals $(1 - k)C$, and since both share the same quantity of S, B's demand curve drawn with regard to k is given by D_B. Individual A may then look upon D_B as showing the price at which various quantities of S are available to him, i.e., as a supply schedule for the social good which confronts him. B similarly may regard D_A as his supply curve. The fraction of the price which both are willing to pay (k for A and $(1 - k)$ for B) adds to *1* at the intersection of D_A and D_B, at output OM. See Erik Lindahl, "Just Taxation: A Positive Solution," in Richard A. Musgrave and Alan Peacock (eds.), *Classics in the Theory of Public Finance,* International Economic Association, London: Macmillan, 1958, pp. 168–177. See also J. G. Head, "Lindahl's Theory of the Budget," *Finanzarchiv,* Band 23, Heft 3, October 1964, pp. 421–454; and H. Shibata, "A Bargaining Model of the Pure Theory of Public Expenditures," *Journal of Political Economy,* January 1971.

tion implies that consumers will bid as they do for private goods and thus overlooks the crucial fact that preferences for social goods (or willingness to bear shares of the cost in line with marginal benefits) will not be revealed voluntarily in the absence of exclusion. Where the number of participating consumers is large, it is in their interest to act as free riders, and the auction system of the market breaks down.[9] The demand schedules shown in the right half of Figure 3-1 do not come into play. They are pseudo-demand schedules only, based on the unrealistic assumption that preferences are revealed. A political (voting) approach must be taken to compel preference revelation. Individuals, knowing that they must comply with the decision made by the collective choice or voting process, will find it in their interest to vote for that solution which will move the outcome closer to their own desires, and in this way they will be forced to reveal their preferences. By serving as a mechanism of preference revelation, the voting process must link tax and expenditure decisions. The voter must be confronted with a choice among budget proposals which carry a price tag in terms of his or her own tax contribution. This price tag will depend on the total cost for the community as a whole as well as on the share to be contributed by others. The individual's choice is thus contingent on his own knowledge that others must also contribute in line with the adopted tax plan. It is this mandatory nature of the budget decision which induces preference revelation and permits the determination of social-good provision.

As will be seen in Chapter 5, the political mechanism is imperfect and can only approximate what would be the optimal budget choice. But it is the best (or only) available technique and must be used as well as it can be.

C. MIXED GOODS

Throughout the preceding discussion, a sharp distinction was drawn between private goods, such as hamburgers, the benefits of which are wholly internalized (rival), and others, such as air purification, whose benefits are wholly external (nonrival). This polarized view was helpful in understanding the essential difference between private and social goods, but it is not realistic. In reality, mixed situations of various kinds arise.

Benefit Externalities from Private Consumption

Problems of the social-good type arise not only in the budgetary context but wherever private consumption or production activities generate external benefits. Suppose, for instance, that A derives benefits from being inoculated against polio, but so do many others for whom the number of potential carriers, and hence the danger of infection, is reduced. Or, by obtaining education, A not only derives personal benefits but also makes it possible for others to enjoy association with a more educated community. Since numbers are large, bargaining does not work and a budgetary process will again be needed to secure preference revelation. But

[9] Where small numbers are involved, bidding will occur but the outcome will be determined by bargaining and may diverge from the competitive result. See p. 61.

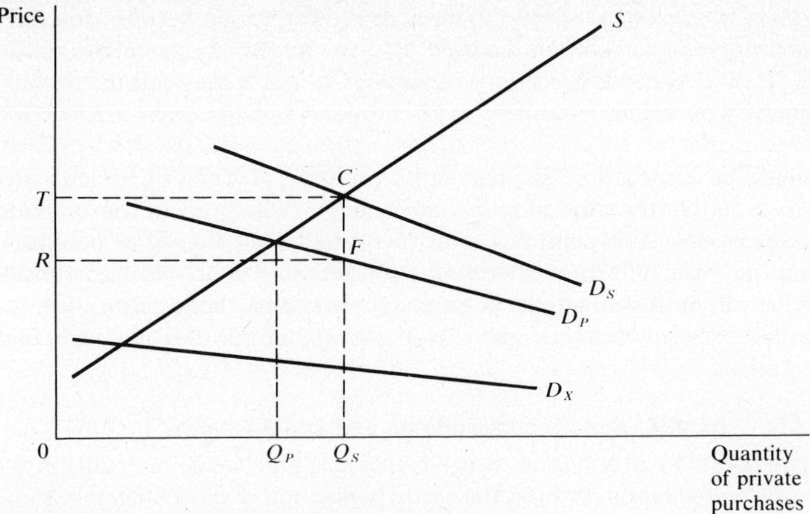

FIGURE 3-2 Adjustment for External Benefits.

the budgetary intervention in this case will not involve full budgetary provision; rather, it will take the form of subsidy to private purchases.

This is shown in Figure 3-2, where D_P represents the market demand schedule (obtained by *horizontal* addition of individual demand schedules) for a private good. Now let D_X be the supplementary schedule reflecting the further demand (or, as noted before in connection with Figure 3-1, pseudo-demand) for external benefits generated by private consumption and obtained by vertical addition of individual demand curves for such benefits. Adding D_P and D_X *vertically,* in a procedure similar to that followed in Figure 3-1, D_S is obtained to reflect total benefits and including both the D_P and D_X components. It is then evident that optimal output is at OQ_S while the private market will result in equilibrium output OQ_P only.

In order to expand output from OQ_P to OQ_S, the government should pay a subsidy equal to the difference between D_S and D_P. At output OQ_S, this difference equals *FC*. Given such a subsidy, output will be extended to OQ_S, with consumers paying a net price of *OR* and with the government subsidy contributing the difference *RT*. The total cost of the subsidy will equal *RFCT* and is contributed out of the budget. The evaluation of the external benefits—and the determination of the proper rate of subsidy—poses precisely the problems of preference revelation as arise with social goods and again calls for resolution through the political process.

The polar case of social goods, examined earlier, may thus be extended into a band of cases involving goods in which internal benefits to the individual consumer are increasingly supplemented by external benefits. At the one extreme of the purely private good, the distance *FC* in Figure 3-2 becomes zero, as D_S is the same as D_P and the subsidy becomes zero. At the other extreme of the purely social good, D_S becomes equal to D_X and the subsidy pays the entire price, i.e., the good is entirely provided for through the budget. In between, we have the cases of mixed goods, to be financed by a mix of private payments and of subsidies. The tax-expenditure theory of sections A and B may thus be restated more generally as a subsidy theory, with subsidies ranking from zero to 100 percent.

It might be argued that the externality problem dealt with here is in fact all-pervasive, so that the cases of purely internal (i.e., wholly rival) consumption become nonexistent. This point has some merit, but it should not be permitted to wipe out the basic difference between the consumption of private and of social goods. After all, most distinctions in economics are somewhat arbitrary (as, for instance, that between consumer and capital goods), but this does not mean that they are useless.

Spatial Limitation of Benefits and Local Finance

When speaking of social goods as "being available to all," we do not really mean that the world population, or even the entire population of one country, is to be included. The spatial benefit area is limited for most social goods and the members of the group are thus confined to the residents of that area. This restriction does not change the nature of the preceding argument. A group which is sufficiently large to require provision for social goods by political process need not be all-inclusive. At the same time, this feature of spatial limitation of benefits is central to the application of social-goods theory to local government. This being a major topic in its own right, consideration is postponed until the issues of fiscal federalism are examined.[10]

Congestion

Another case of mixed goods, also of special importance in relation to local finance, arises where goods, though consumed in equal amounts by all members of a particular group, are not truly nonrival in consumption. As more users are added, the quality of service received by all users from a given installation declines. Thus, the quality of instruction received by the individual student from a single teacher may decline as the size of the class increases. Demand schedules are still added vertically, but there is now the additional problem of determining how large the size of the group should be. We shall take up this problem later on when discussing local finance.[11]

Alternative Modes of Provision

Another obstacle to a clear-cut distinction between social and private goods arises because certain needs may be met in a variety of ways, some of which involve provision of private, and others provision of social, goods. Thus, the need for protection may be met by private locks for each house or by police protection for the entire city block. If the first route is taken, provision may be left to the market, whereas, in the second, budgetary provision is needed. In situations where this option exists, a choice must then be made between the two modes.

[10] See Chap. 29, Sec. A.
[11] See Chap. 29, Sec. A.

Since the private mode has the advantage of permitting individuals to consume different amounts, the social-goods mode, to be preferred, must more than outweigh this advantage by offering a lower cost per service unit.[12]

D. SOCIAL BADS, EXTERNAL COSTS, AND POLLUTION

The preceding discussion so far has been in terms of social *goods* and external *benefits.* It remains to note that there is another side to the picture, i.e., social *bads* and external *costs.* While budget policy does not address itself to the supply of social bads,[13] the problem of external costs, incidental to the production or consumption of other (private or social) goods, is pervasive and important. A free concert on the common is enjoyable to those who come to hear it but may be a disutility to a captive audience of nearby residents who would like to sleep. A manufacturing plant may emit smoke or odors which are a disutility to people in the neighborhood, and the noise of jet planes will disturb residents along the route. Such costs are external costs. They are real from a social point of view but they are not included as costs by the producer. The company does not have to pay for them, as it must for labor or materials. Such costs are not internalized and hence are disregarded. Social costs—which include both internalized (or private) *and* external costs—exceed private costs. Since the market accounts for the latter only, the price is too low and the good tends to be oversupplied. Similar problems arise where externalities are generated in the process of consumption (e.g., automobile pollution) rather than production. In either case, costs to society are disregarded. This is the problem of pollution, which will be discussed in more detail later on.[14] However, some general comments are in order here.

The case of externalities in the sense of social bads may be viewed as analogous to that of external benefits. Thus, Figure 3-3 restates the case of social bads in a way similar to that used in Figure 3-2 for external benefits or social goods. D_P is the market demand schedule for product X, and S_P is the industry supply schedule. It reflects only such costs as are internalized, i.e., those that involve outlays by the firm. Output is at OQ_P and price is at OP_P. Suppose now that the production of X generates an external cost, such as a smoke nuisance or river pollution through the effluence of chemicals. This effect is overlooked by the market, but proper allocation requires that the cost of such damage be allowed for. Let this cost be reflected by S_E. The pollution or external cost at output OQ_P thus equals Q_PF. Social cost (obtained by vertical addition of the two S schedules) is then given by S_S. To allow fully for social cost, a tax (equal at each level of output to S_E) should be imposed, thereby raising the supply schedule from S_P to S_S. As a result, price rises from OP_P to OP_S and output falls from OQ_P to OQ_S. The tax per unit at output OQ_S equals $HK = Q_SD$ and private cost equals

[12] See Carl S. Shoup and John Head, "Public Goods, Private Goods and Ambiguous Goods," *Economic Journal,* September 1969.

[13] It may be, however, that the minority not only values particular social goods less highly than the majority, but considers them a disutility. Pacifists may attach a negative value to defense, or people who like sun may object to cloud seeding.

[14] See Chap. 32, Sec. E.

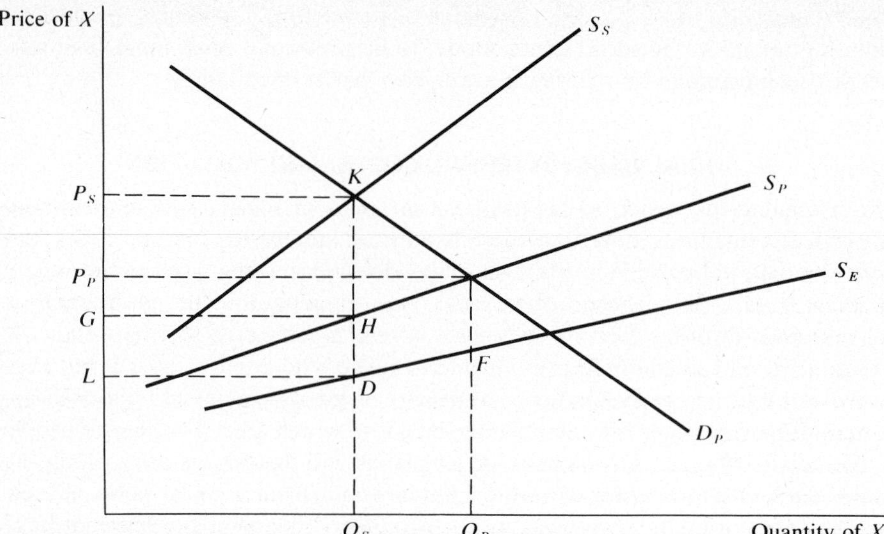

FIGURE 3-3 Adjustment for External Cost.

$Q_S H$. The role of tax in Figure 3-3, it will be noted, is analogous to that of the subsidy in Figure 3-2.

The tax correction will not wholly eliminate the polluting activity. Some degree of pollution cost $Q_S D$ remains, but it will be smaller than the pretax level $Q_P F$. The problem of pollution control, therefore, is not to eliminate pollution but to cut it back to its efficient level, i.e., the level at which the marginal cost of production (including the social cost of pollution) ceases to exceed the benefits derived by the consumers of the product.

In practice, the problem is complicated by the fact that production and pollution are not linked in a fixed relationship, as assumed in Figure 3-3, but that the level of pollution may be changed by adopting a different technology. Raising the height of chimneys may reduce pollution although it increases private costs. The problem, therefore, is one not only of adjusting the level of output for a given technology but also of adapting the technology to reduce pollution. Pollution-reducing changes should be made until the marginal private cost exceeds the marginal social benefit thereof. Public policy must thus be designed to encourage the choice of efficient pollution-reducing devices.

Moreover, the pollution problem always involves two parties, and prevention devices may be employed by either side. The remedy should be applied where it is cheapest, which may be where the damage is suffered rather than where it originates. Thus, it may be cheaper to relocate residents of a flood-prone area than to require upstream residents to build a dam.

A final difficulty in designing policy correctives is that the magnitude of external costs (the level of the S_E schedule) is not known but must be determined. As in the case of benefits, the true level of this cost is not readily revealed. Claims will be readily proffered, but they may be too high.[15] Except for the small-number

[15] In some instances, external costs may be registered in the market, e.g., the cost of noise pollution may be measured through its effects on real estate values close to airports.

case, a political process is again needed to determine true costs. Correction for pollution inefficiencies, though not difficult in theory, poses complex problems of implementation.[16]

E. BARGAINING IN THE SMALL GROUP

Our preceding argument has been that a political process is needed to provide for social goods because voluntary payments and preference revelation will not be forthcoming in the absence of exclusion. The reason is that any one individual will not consider it worth his while to pay because, with large numbers involved, his own contribution will not significantly affect the total supply. Instead, he will act as a free rider. This difficulty does not arise when few people are involved. They will find it worthwhile to contribute and to bargain, since each person's contribution now significantly affects the position of others. The market mechanism also fails to account for external costs or social bads where many persons are concerned, since the individual victim cannot effectively charge for the burden that is imposed on him. But bargaining may again result if few people are affected, thereby permitting "internalization" of external costs.

Bargaining for Social Benefits

While the problem of social goods arises primarily in the large-number context, there are important situations in which the small-number conditions apply. Neighbors, for example, may get together in a mutual effort at tree spraying; municipalities may join in building a common garbage-disposal plant; or national governments may cooperate in undertaking joint ventures. The small-number case is thus worth considering.

One way of looking at the bargaining process and its results is shown in Figure 3-4.[17] D_A and D_B are A's and B's demand schedules for the social good, and *SS* is the supply schedule (which, to simplify, is drawn horizontally). Suppose that, initially, both A and B purchase their own supply without considering the other. Thus A purchases Q_A while B purchases Q_B. They then note that this results in a full and two-directional spillover of benefits from A's consumption to B and from B's consumption to A. Now A finds that given B's provision of Q_B, his marginal evaluation of an additional unit is only Q_BG. Since he must pay a market price of *OS* for his own purchases, he will discontinue them. The initial position is thus one where B purchases Q_B at market price *OS*, with A purchasing nothing and acting as a free rider.

This is where the situation would remain if there were no bargaining. But bargaining is advantageous to both parties and will occur. A will be willing to purchase additional units at prices indicated along the *GC* range of his demand schedule. B will be willing to purchase more along the *ZD* range of his schedule. This will become possible if A contributes the difference between the *ZS* and *ZD* schedules. Plotting this difference as Q_BI, Q_BI becomes, from A's point of view,

[16] See Ralph Turvey, "On Divergence between Private and Social Costs," *American Economic Review*, August 1963. For further discussion of pollution, see Chap. 32, section E.

[17] Figure 3-4 follows that given in James M. Buchanan, *The Demand and Supply of Public Goods*, Chicago: Rand McNally, 1967, p. 30.

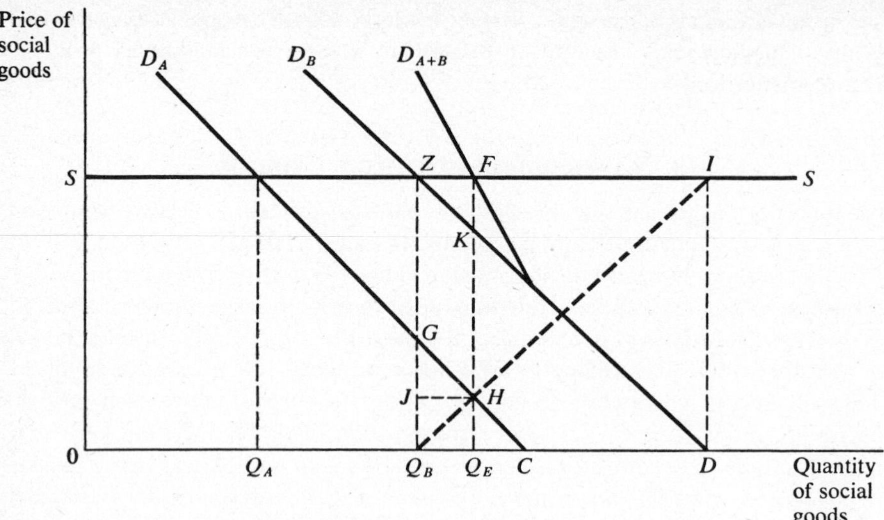

FIGURE 3-4 The Small-Number Case.

a supply schedule for additional units.[18] Equilibrium output is now equal to OQ_E, where Q_BI and GC intersect. The final position is thus one where OQ_E is purchased at the market price OS. For the amount OQ_B the full price OS is paid by B, while for the additional amount Q_BQ_E he pays only a net price HK, with Q_EH contributed by A. We thus find that bargaining leads to increased output and an efficient solution. Proceeding as in Figure 3-1, output OQ_E would be derived by vertical addition of demand curves. D_{A+B}, as shown in Figure 3-4, intersects the supply schedule at output OQ_E.[19]

Further complications may be introduced,[20] but this illustration shows what may happen in the bargaining process. However, these limitations must be noted:

1. A's contribution per unit of additional output Q_BQ_E may not equal Q_EH but may be larger. That is, B may drive a harder bargain and force A to pay

[18] Alternatively, we may move along B's demand schedule from Z to K and plot B's supply schedule as the difference between SS and GC. The latter schedule, anchored now at Q_A, will intersect ZD at K with equilibrium output again at Q_E. In this case, the purchase of additional units is made by A, with B the contributor.

[19] GC and Q_BI must intersect at output OQ_E since $Q_EH + Q_EK = Q_EF$ (by construction of D_{A+B}) and since $HF = Q_EK$ (by construction of Q_BI).

[20] We have assumed that the cost of the social good is the same for both A and B and that the spillover of benefits is reciprocal. But this may not be so. Suppose, for example, that A, by spraying his own lawn to eradicate dandelions, also benefits the adjacent lawn of B, but that B's spraying does not benefit A. B will then find it to his advantage to contribute to A's spraying. As a result of bargaining, A's spraying will be increased and B's will be reduced. Total consumption of spray protection is increased, although the total input of spray may be reduced. By moving the spraying from B, where it does not generate externalities, to A, where it does, the efficiency of the process is increased. Whereas, in the general case of social goods, the benefit flow is reciprocal, we deal now with a situation where it moves in one direction only. This being true, it now matters where the "own-input" occurs. See J. M. Buchanan and M. Z. Kafoglis, "A Note on Public Goods Supply," *American Economic Review,* June 1963.

higher prices for the earlier units of the additional output, thus taxing away A's entire consumer surplus thereon (equal to *JHG*). While the model leads to the same level of output as obtained by vertical addition of demand curves, it does not follow that our earlier pricing rule would apply.

2. We have assumed that, in the initial position, B purchases Q_B and that the bargaining relates to A's contribution to additional units only. But B may also demand that A contribute to the earlier units OQ_B and threaten to discontinue their purchase unless A contributes. Although B stands to lose more by this than A, it does not follow that some contribution may not be extracted from A.

3. Assuming a process of incremental bargaining, the efficient output OQ_E will be reached, but this need not be so if an "all or nothing" type of bargaining is followed. In this case, one of the parties may succeed in getting a better deal by settling on a level of output which falls short of the efficient amount.

Thus the assumption of small numbers renders bargaining possible, but the results are uncertain and there is no assurance that an efficient outcome will be reached. The same conclusion holds for bargaining over private goods where small numbers (and thus a noncompetitive situation) are involved. But whereas, in the private-goods case, increasing the number of participants leads to a competitive solution, such will not be the result where social goods are concerned. Although bargaining imperfections are reduced, individuals will have no further reason to reveal their preferences and make their contributions. A political process becomes necessary to solve the problem.

Bargaining to Avoid Social Costs

As with the case of external benefits, the problem differs depending on the numbers of participants. If the numbers are small on both sides, the polluter and the victims can get together and, by bargaining, achieve a more or less efficient solution. Thus, if there are only two people involved, the victim V and the polluter P, V will find it worthwhile to pay P to reduce pollution (either by curtailing the pollution-causing activity or by substituting other techniques) up to the point where the marginal cost of the side payment comes to equal the marginal benefit of pollution avoided. As before, a reasonably efficient bargaining solution will be reached, and there will be less need for tax or regulatory measures to internalize external cost. Because of this, it has been argued that market adjustments will tend to internalize what would seem to be external costs and benefits through mutual adjustment among the parties, thereby avoiding the need for regulatory measures. This proposition, which has come to be known as the Coase theorem, has some merit in a small-number setting but cannot be generalized to the large-number case.[21] Moreover, even for small numbers, the equity issue remains to be resolved. We shall return to this later on when the the problem of pollution is considered in more detail.[22]

[21] See R. H. Coase, "The Problem of Social Cost," *Journal of Law and Economics,* October 1960.

[22] See Chap. 37, Sec. E.

F. BASES OF WANTS AND THE ROLE OF MERIT GOODS

In concluding this survey of the social-good problem, we once more return to the basic nature of social goods, this time focusing on the way in which wants for such goods are generated and on the further problem of "merit goods."

Individualistic versus Collective Evaluation

Distinction between private and social goods was based on certain technical characteristics of social goods, i.e., the nonrival nature of consumption and the inapplicability of exclusion. It did not depend on a difference in psychological attitudes, or in social philosophy regarding the two types of goods. Indeed, the analysis in both cases was drawn in a framework in which all wants are experienced and evaluated by the individual consumer. This holds for benefits arising from the provision of social as well as private goods. In other words, the preference system of individuals includes social as well as private goods. It covers not only preferences as between oranges and apples (the textbook symbols of typically private goods), but also as between private backyards and public parks, where one facility is a private, and the other a social, good.

Our distinction between private and social goods, therefore, must not be confused with an alternative approach which would distinguish between individually and collectively experienced *wants.* According to the latter view, private goods are provided to satisfy private wants, experienced by the individual in his personal budget calculus and satisfied in his own interest; and social goods are provided to meet collective wants, experienced by the group as a whole and provided in its common interest. As will be noted later, this distinction does not stand up under close scrutiny. In the end, all wants are experienced by individuals.[23] A social group as a whole is not an entity which can experience wants.

This proposition is quite compatible with the notion that individuals do not live in isolation, but in association with others. Therefore, A's preferences will be affected by those of B and C. Dominant tastes and cultural values influence individual preferences and in turn are determined by them. Fashions are a pervasive factor in molding tastes and not only in regard to clothing. To say that wants are experienced individually, therefore, is not to deny the existence of social interaction.[24]

Moreover, our proposition does not imply that individual preferences relate only to the satisfaction which a person derives from his own consumption. Others will enter into a person's value scale. If A is a socially minded person, he will derive satisfaction not only from his own consumption but also from consumption by B; or, if he is selfish, he may enjoy his own consumption more if B cannot match it. Utilities are interdependent and, as we shall see later, this fact broadens

[23] See p. 121.

[24] Nor can it be argued that social goods differ from private goods because they satisfy the more noble aims of life. The wants to be satisfied may be noble or base in either case: social goods may carry high cultural or aesthetic values, such as music education or the protection of natural beauty, or they may relate to everyday needs, such as roads and fire protection. Similarly, private goods may satisfy cultural needs, such as harpsichord recordings, or everyday needs, such as bubblegum. Clearly, no distinction can be drawn on this basis.

the range over which the economics of social goods apply.[25] But, granting all this, what matters here is that satisfaction is experienced in the last resort by A and B individually and not by a mysterious third entity called A + B.

Merit Goods

The foregoing discussion seems reasonable enough and permits one to conduct the analysis of social goods within the usual economic framework shared by the analysis of private goods. Yet, observation of budget policy suggests many instances where the very intent of the decision maker appears to be to interfere with or override individual preferences. Thus, sumptuary taxes are imposed on liquor because the consumption thereof is held undesirable, or low-cost housing is subsidized because decent housing for the poor is held desirable. The consumption choices which are penalized or supported in some instances involve goods which, by our previous definition, are private (rival in consumption), and in others, goods which are social (nonrival). The issue now under consideration, therefore, must not be confused with the distinction between private and social goods itself.

Such policies cannot be explained in terms of our earlier approach to social-goods theory. Although that approach called for the compulsory acceptance of the voting decision and involved some interference with minority views, such interference was but the unfortunate by-product of a procedure designed to meet individual preferences as well as possible. In the situations now considered, such interference is not accidental but the very purpose of public policy. Certain goods are held meritorious (they are considered "merit goods") while others are held undesirable.

One explanation may simply be that even a democracy such as ours has aspects of an autocratic society, where it is considered proper that the elite (however defined) should impose its preferences. This seems in outright contradiction to free consumer choice. Alternatively, what appears to be a contradiction may turn out to be a correction for deficiencies in the prevailing exercise of consumer choice. Given incomplete consumer information, temporarily imposed consumption choice may be desirable as part of a learning process, so as to permit more intelligent free choice thereafter. Moreover, individuals may not not know the consequences of particular consumption choices and may need guidance. Children in particular are in need of protection. But, though reasonable to all but the most doctrinaire individualist if used as an informational device, these considerations can be readily subject to abuse and become the excuse for totalitarian indoctrination.

However this may be, such interpretations of merit goods hardly serve to explain away many budget items which imply imposed preferences, such as low-cost housing or school lunches. That provision for merit goods is frequently directed at the poor suggests paternalism as an explanation. If the purpose of such subsidies were merely redistributional, it could be served better by making cash transfers, allowing the recipients to use the cash in line with their own prefer-

[25] See p. 98.

ences. Donors, it appears, are willing to make gifts which are earmarked, but less willing to underwrite cash grants which may be used without the donor's control. Thus, the existence of merit goods is linked to voluntary redistribution.

Where does this leave the concept of merit goods? Interpreted as a device to provide consumer information, as a means of allowing for externalities, or as an expression of voluntary giving in kind, the merit-good concept falls within the framework of traditional analysis in which efficient allocation must in the end be related to individual choice. But, when interpreted as imposition of preferences of the ruling group or decision makers, allocation on a merit-good basis stands outside what has been dealt with here as the theory of social goods. In all these cases it is evident, however, that interference may apply with regard to private goods (e.g., pornography) no less than to what we have defined as social goods. The social- and merit-good problems must therefore be distinguished.

G. EFFICIENT ALLOCATION FURTHER CONSIDERED

In section A of this chapter, we have examined the efficient allocation of social goods and compared it with the allocation of private goods. This was done by comparing a market for private goods with a pseudo-market for social goods each viewed in a separate, partial-equilibrium setting. We now allow for the interdependence between the production and consumption of private and of social goods. We begin with a brief look at what is meant by efficient resource use. This is followed by a parallel view of the problem as applied first to private, and then to social, goods. The present section requires some understanding of intermediate microtheory and may be passed over by the reader who is disinterested in the theoretical aspects.[26]

Meaning of Efficiency

Economics, as one learns in the first college class on the subject, deals with the efficient use of resources in best satisfying consumer wants. If the economy consisted of one consumer only, the meaning of efficiency would be quite simple. Robinson Crusoe would survey the resources available to him and the technologies at his disposal in transforming these resources into goods. Given his preferences among goods, he would then proceed to produce in such a way and such a mix of output as would maximize his satisfaction. In so doing, he would act efficiently. But the real world problem is more difficult. The economic process must serve not one but many consumers; and various outcomes will differ in their distributional implications. This calls for a more careful definition of what is meant by "efficient" resource use.

To separate the problem of efficient allocation from that of distribution, economists have come up with a narrower concept of efficiency. Named *Pareto*

[26] For a compact statement and literature references, see Francis M. Bator, "The Simple Analytics of Welfare Maximization," *American Economic Review,* March 1957, pp. 22–59.

Introductory summary statements will also be found in microtheory texts, such as Donald S. Watson, *Price Theory and Its Uses,* 3d ed., Boston: Houghton Mifflin, 1972, chap. 15; and C. E. Ferguson and S. Charles Maurice, *Economic Analysis,* rev. ed., Homewood, Ill.: Irwin, 1974, chap. 12.

efficiency after the Italian economist who proposed it, the definition is as follows: A given economic arrangement is efficient if there can be no rearrangement which will leave someone better off without worsening the position of others. Thus, it is impossible in this situation to change the method of production, the mix of goods produced, or the size of the public sector which would help A without hurting B and C. If, on the other hand, such a change is possible, then the prevailing arrangement is inefficient and an efficiency gain can be had by making the change.[27] This definition, so far as it goes, is quite reasonable. Provided only that envy is ruled out or overlooked, most people would agree that a change which helps A without hurting B and C is efficient. Moreover, this approach permits one to separate the concept of efficient resource use from the more controversial problem of distribution, a topic to be dealt with in Chapter 4.

The General Model for Private Goods

In discussing efficient resource use, we shall begin with the more familiar case of private goods. This approach will also permit us to see just how the case of social goods differs. Suppose there exists an ominiscient planner who has all the relevant information, including knowledge of the stock of available resources, the state of technology, and the preferences of consumers. The planner is then asked to determine how resources are to be used efficiently, allowing for all possible states of distribution.

Efficiency Rules Economists have laid down certain conditions which must be met if the solution is to be efficient. To state the problem in simple terms, we shall consider an economy with two consumers, A and B, and two products, X and Y. These conditions must then be met:

1. Efficiency requires that any given amount of X should be produced in such a way as to permit the largest possible amount of Y to be produced at the same time. The best available technology should be used. If one technique permits production of 100 units of X and 80 units of Y, and another permits 100 units of X combined with only 50 units of Y, the former method is obviously to be preferred.

2. The "marginal rate of substitution" in consumption between goods X and Y must be the same for consumers A and B. By this we mean that the rate at which A and B will be willing to trade the last unit of X for additional units of Y should be the same. If A is willing to give 1 unit of X for 3 units of Y, while B will give 4 units of Y for 1 unit of X, it will be to the advantage of both to exchange, with A increasing his consumption of Y and B consuming more of X until equality of the marginal rates of substitution is restored.[28]

[27] As always happens, this principle has come to be qualified and has been made subject to various interpretations. The discussion has turned especially around the topic of compensation. Some say that for an arrangement to be efficient, compensation must be made, while others say that it is enough to conclude that compensation could be made. Consider a rearrangement under which a gain to A is worth $100, while the loss to B is valued at $90. If A compensates B, B's position is unchanged, while there remains a gain to A of $10. For purposes of our discussion, we assume that B is compensated.

[28] The underlying reasoning is that a consumer's marginal rate of substitution of X for Y declines as more X and less Y are consumed. Putting it differently, consumption of both X and Y is subject to decreasing marginal utility.

3. The marginal rate of substitution of X for Y in consumption should be the same as their marginal rate of transformation in production. The latter is defined as the additional units of X that can be produced if production of Y is reduced by one unit. Thus, if the marginal rate of substitution in consumption is 3 X for 2 Y while the marginal rate of transformation in production is 3 X for 1 Y, it will be desirable to increase the output of X and to reduce that of Y until the two ratios are equalized.

If these conditions are met (as well as some others not specified here), resource allocation will be efficient in the Pareto sense.

Finding the Set of Efficient Solutions The steps to be followed in tracing out the efficient solution may be summarized briefly. To facilitate matters, we consider again an economy with two private goods, X and Y, and two consumers, A and B. The first step is to construct the production possibility frontier *CD* in Figure 3-5. With output of private good X measured vertically and that of Y measured horizontally, *CD* shows the best possible combinations of both that can be produced. If all resources are put into X, the largest possible output of X equals *OC;* and if all resources are put into Y, the largest possible output equals *OD.* If *OE* of X is produced, the largest possible output of Y equals *OF* and so forth. As previously noted in condition 1, it is obviously desirable to produce any given output of X so as to supplement it by the largest possible output of Y, and vice

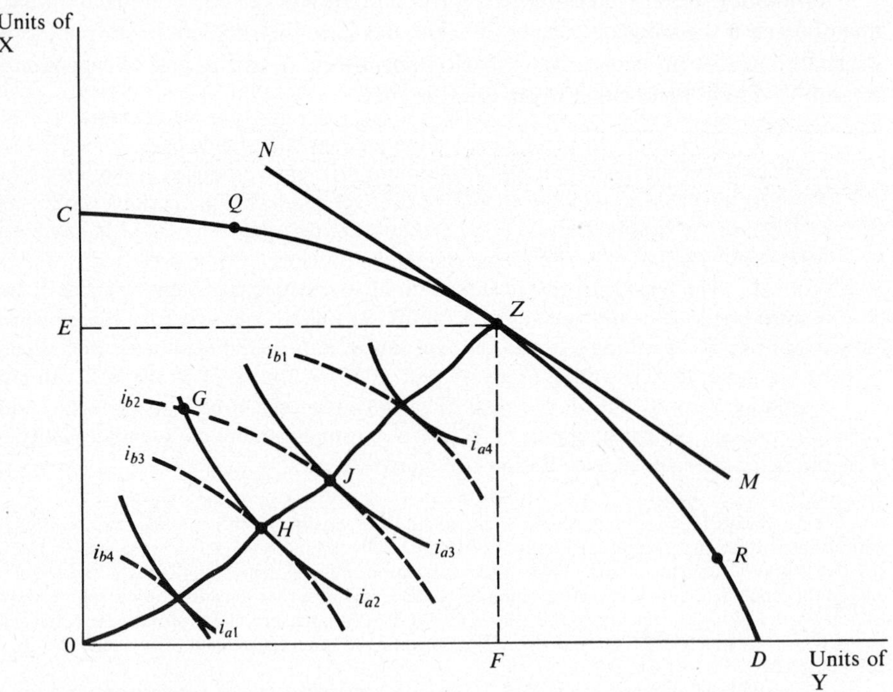

FIGURE 3-5 Efficient Output of Private Goods and Their Assignment.

versa. Just how this is done need not concern us here in detail, since this part of the problem is the same for both the private- and the social-good cases.[29]

The second step is to determine how the output at any one point on *CD* should be divided between A and B. Suppose that the output mix indicated by point *Z* is produced, involving *OE* of X and *OF* of Y. To show how this output may be divided between A and B, we consider the "box diagram" encompassed by *OFZE*. Beginning at *O* as origin, i_{a1}, i_{a2}, i_{a3}, etc., are consumer A's indifference curves, showing his preferences for X and Y. The curves are constructed so that while moving down any one curve, A remains equally well off, with more of Y being traded for less of X. At the same time, he will be better off when moving from a lower to a higher *i* (indifference) curve, say from i_{a1} to i_{a2}.

We next draw a similar pattern of indifference curves for B, but now we choose *Z* as the origin. That is to say, B's take of X is measured by moving left along *ZE* and his take of Y is measured by moving down along *ZF*. Various successively higher indifference curves for B are shown as i_{b1}, i_{b2}, etc. It can now be shown that the best possible solutions all lie along the "contract curve" *OZ*, which traces out the tangency points of the two sets of indifference curves. If the initial position is at *G*, movement to *J* will improve A's position without hurting B, just as movement to *H* will improve B's position without hurting A. By landing somewhere between *H* and *J*, the gain will be divided between the two. By following the rule that a gain to A without a loss to B (and vice versa) is an improvement, the efficient solutions must fall along *OZ*. Since these are the points at which the two sets of indifference curves are tangent, and since the slope of the indifference curves equals the MRS (marginal rate of substitution in consumption), it also follows that at each point on *OZ* the MRSs for A and B are equal. This reflects condition 2 above.

The next problem is to choose among the various points on *OZ*. The answer is that among all these points, *J* is the best solution. The reason is that at point *J*, the MRS of consumers, as indicated by the slope of the indifference curves or of *LK*, is equal to the MRT (marginal rate of transformation in production) or the slope of *NM*, thus meeting the previously noted condition 3. Having decided that the efficient allocation of output mix *Z* between A and B is given at *J*, the planner will now solve the same problem for all other points on *CD*, such as *Q* and *R*.

Choice of Optimum Having completed this job, our planner, acting as an omniscient technician, has derived an important set of solutions, but it remains for the policy makers to choose between these equally efficient alternatives. Each solution, corresponding to the various points on *CD*, carries its implications for the relative welfare positions of A and B. Thus, point *Z* in Figure 3-5 implies a utility level i_{a3} for A and of i_{b2} for B. Choosing among points on *CD* is thus a matter of judgment on distribution and, as noted earlier, cannot be made according to the efficiency rules by which Pareto optimality is defined. A tradeoff between the welfare levels of A and B is involved.

[29] Drawing the production possibility curve *CD* concave to the origin implies that both X and Y are produced under conditions of increasing cost.

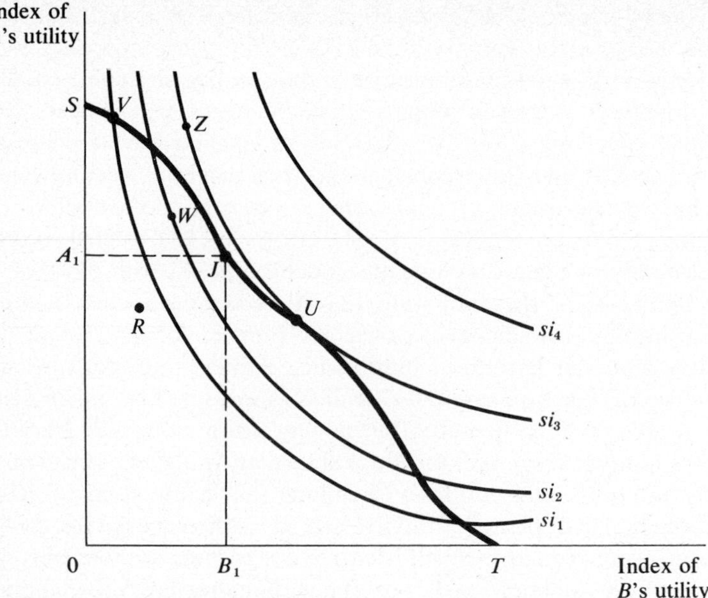

FIGURE 3-6 The Distribution Choice.

This is illustrated in Figure 3-6, where the vertical axis records a welfare or utility index for A, while the horizontal axis does so for B. We now take the best solutions for each output mix in Figure 3-5 (such as point *J* for mix *Z*) and record the corresponding utility levels for A and B. For example, OA_1 in Figure 3-6 corresponds to utility index i_{a3} for A, and OB_1 measures B's utility index i_{b2}, with these coordinates giving us point *J*. We may now trace out the utility positions of A and B for all other efficient solutions (corresponding to various product mixes along *CD*), and in this way we obtain a "utility frontier" such as *ST*, which shows for each level of utility allowed to A the largest possible level of utility obtainable for B. Each of these solutions involves a particular pattern of resource use between private goods X and Y and their distribution between consumers A and B. The best possible points lie on this utility frontier, with points north and/or east thereof unobtainable and points south and/or west inferior.

Although the rules of Pareto efficiency guide us to the frontier, the choice among the "best" points traced by this frontier involves a tradeoff between gains for A and losses for B, or vice versa. As we move from *S* to *T*, A's welfare declines and B's rises, and vice versa. The choice is one of distribution and must be made on the basis of a social welfare function, expressing an ordering by which society assigns relative values to levels of welfare experienced by A and B. Assuming these assignments to be known, they may be expressed by the social indifference curves si_1, si_2, etc., where each curve shows mixes of welfare derived by A and B that, from society's point of view, are equally "good." The gain to B which results when moving down any social indifference curve *si* is considered just offset by the resulting loss to A. The point of tangency of the utility frontier with the highest possible social indifference curve is at *U*. This is the so-called bliss point, the best of all possible solutions. It reflects a solution such as that indicated by output mix Z and goods assignment J in Figure 3-5; thus it meets both the requirements of Pareto efficiency as dealt with in Figure 3-5 and the broader equity considerations as reflected in Figure 3-6. Provided the social welfare function as reflected in the pattern of the *si* curves is also given to the planner, the solution at U thus involves a simultaneous determination of the efficient output mix and its distribution among consumers.

Private-Goods Allocation through the Market

Having stated the problem in terms of an omniscient planner to whom all information is given, we must now recognize that such a planner does not exist. It is fortunate, therefore, that the efficient solutions of Figure 3-5 can also be obtained by the functioning of a competitive market system. Producers, guided by their desire to maximize profits, will adopt the least-cost method of production, thus meeting condition 1. Moreover, they will produce those products which consumers want most as indicated by the price which they fetch in the market. Consumers, in turn, will allocate their respective budgets among products so as to equate their marginal rates of substitution with their price ratios, thus meeting condition 2. The consumer will do so because, if the price of X is twice the price of Y while his level of satisfaction would be unchanged by replacing consumption of 1 unit of X by less than 2 units of Y, he will choose to purchase and consume more Y and less X until the marginal rate of substitution of Y for X is equal to the price ratio. The same prices are paid by all consumers but, depending on their tastes and incomes, they consume different amounts. Sellers, in trying to maximize profits, equate marginal cost with marginal revenue, which, under conditions of competition, also equates marginal cost with price or average revenue. Thus condition 3 is met as well. Without spelling out the details, we can thus see that the market mechanism, acting as an auctioning system and functioning through competitive pricing, secures an efficient use of resources. Even a socialist planner (provided that he wishes to adapt his output mix to consumer wants) will find it helpful to play the competitive game or to advise his computers to do so, in order to obtain efficient results.

Viewing the problem in terms of a market mechanism has the great advantage of inducing consumers to reveal their preferences and of inducing producers to meet them, thus providing a solution without the use of a hypothetical and all-knowing planner. However, for the market mechanism to operate, we must take a distribution of income to be given. Returning to Figure 3-6, we note that each of the points on the utility frontier corresponds to the solution reached by the competitive market (and the pricing rule which it implies) on the basis of a given distribution of income. The quality of the solution, therefore, also depends on the appropriateness of the prevailing distribution. More about this will follow after the case of social goods is considered.

The General Model for Social Goods

We now reconsider the preceding problem in a situation where both social and private goods are produced. To simplify, we include only one social good S and one private good X. Proceeding as before, we again begin with a general model in which an omniscient planner, to whom all the information is given, is charged with determining the efficient set of solutions. The problem, as developed by Professor Samuelson,[30] is quite analogous to that previously developed for the study of private goods.

Efficiency Rules Returning to the efficiency rules previously stated in connection with private goods, we see no change with regard to condition 1. Construction of the production possibility frontier poses the same problem as before. But conditions 2 and 3 will change. Since consumers will now consume the same amount, their marginal rates of substitution of social for private goods may differ; and since they share in consuming the same units of social goods, efficiency now calls for equality between the marginal rate of transformation in production and the *sum* of their marginal rates of substitution in consumption. The solution may again be traced out in a number of steps.

Finding the Set of Efficient Solutions The solution is shown in Figure 3-7. The production possibility curve *CD* in the upper part of the figure again records the mixes of X and S that may be produced with available resources. The middle section of the figure shows the amounts of X and S consumed by A and the lower part gives the corresponding picture for B. Since both consume the same amount of S, both will be at the same point on the horizontal axis; but they may consume different amounts of X and be at different points on the vertical axis. These points are related, however, by the condition that the amounts of X consumed by A and B must equal the total output of X. To illustrate, suppose that A is at *G* in the middle panel, consuming *OF* of S and *FG* of X. We know from the upper panel that the efficient output mix which includes *OF* of S also includes *FE* of X. Since *FG* is consumed by A, the amount left for B equals $FE - FG = FH$, placing B at point *H* in the lower panel of the figure.

We now choose a particular level of welfare for A, say that indicated by the points on his indifference curve ai_1 which passes through *G*. We have seen that if A is at *G*, which is a point on this indifference curve, then B will be at *H*. Next, let us move A along ai_1 to such points as *P*, *T*, or *W*. Following the same reasoning, this places B at points *L*, *Z*, and *K*. As A travels from *W* to the left along ai_1, B travels to the left along *KHLZY*. Since all points on ai_1 are equally good for A, welfare is maximized by choosing the corresponding point which is best for B. This is at *L* where *YZLK* is tangent to B's highest indifference curve, leaving A at the corresponding position *P*. If A is to be at indifference level ai_1, the best solution is that where total output includes *ON* of S and *NM* of X, divided between A and B so that A receives *NP* and B receives *NL*.

We may now repeat the experiment by beginning with different welfare levels for A, say ai_0 or ai_2. For each of these, we arrive at a new locus of B's positions (corresponding to that marked by the points *M*, *P*, and *L* for ai_1). By this means

[30] See Paul A. Samuelson, "The Pure Theory of Public Expenditures," *Review of Economics and Statistics*, pp. 387–389, November 1954; and "Diagrammatic Exposition of a Theory of Public Expenditures," ibid., pp. 350–356, November 1955.

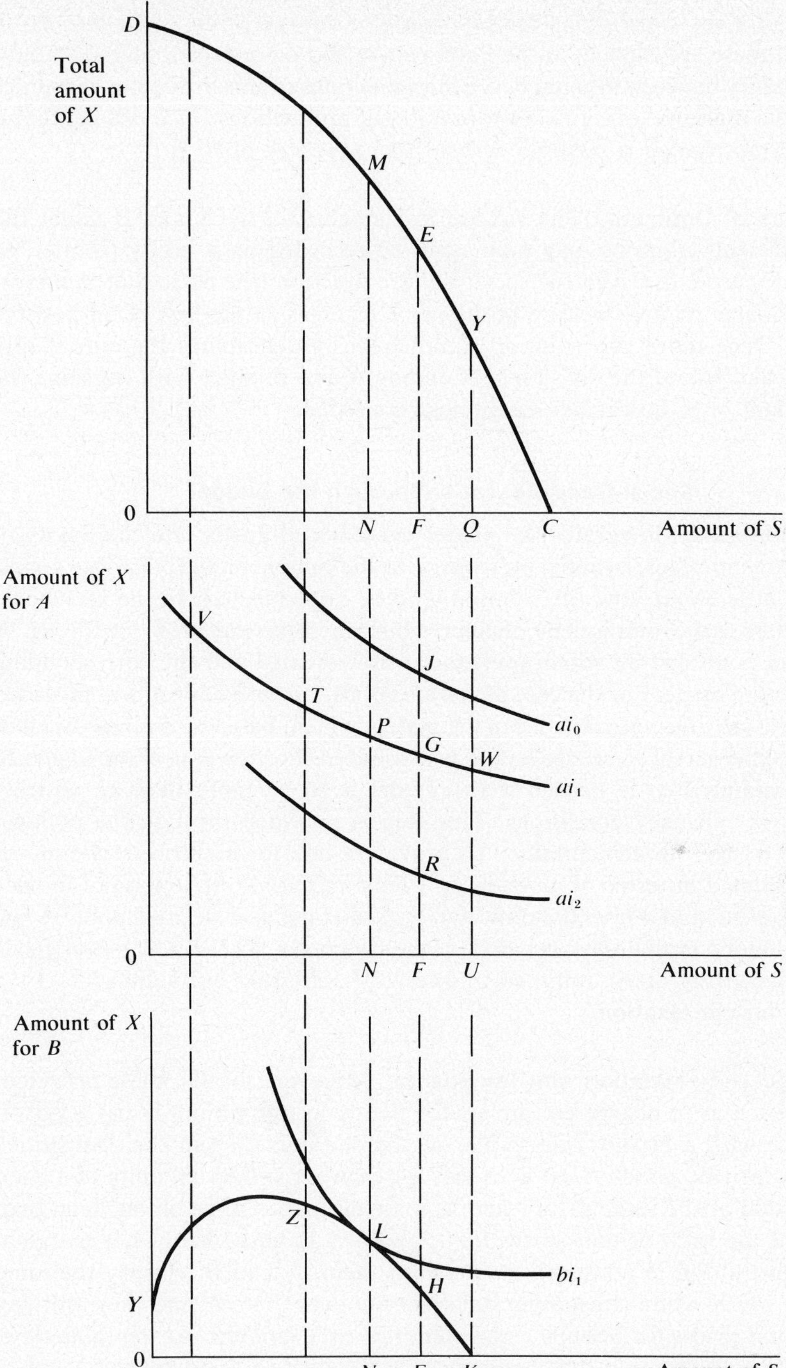

FIGURE 3-7 Social and Private Goods in General Equilibrium.

we arrive at a set of solutions corresponding to various levels of welfare for A and B. All these are efficient in the Pareto sense and meet the social-good condition of equality between the sum of the marginal rates of substitution in consumption and the marginal rate of transformation in production. Once this condition is reached, no change is possible without damage to A or to B.

Choice of Optimum The welfare levels achieved by A and B under the various efficient solutions may now again be recorded on a utility frontier, as shown in Figure 3-6. Given the social welfare function (the pattern of *si* curves) which evaluates relative welfare positions, *T* emerges as the best of all possible solutions. Once more this solution simultaneously determines the output mix between S and X and the division of X among A and B. Since both consume the same amount of S, no further assignment is needed.

Social-Good Allocation through the Budget

This general model integrates the properties of social goods into the theory of welfare economics but, as noted previously for the general model of private goods, it tells us little about how the solution is to be implemented. In the real world setting, there is no omniscient planner who can solve the problem for us. A mechanism is needed by which preferences are revealed and the corresponding allocations are made. For the case of private goods, this mechanism was provided through the use of a competitive pricing system which, based on a given distribution of income, serves to secure an efficient solution. For the case of social goods, a corresponding step is needed if the model is to be more than an abstract statement of efficiency conditions. This step is provided through the political process of budget implementation. To provide a link to the process, the model must be restated in terms of a system in which an initial distribution of income is taken to exist, and where the provision for social goods is decided upon in line with consumers' evaluations as based on their incomes. The cost of social goods is then covered by taxes, imposed in line with consumer evaluation, i.e., by a system of benefit taxation.

Budget Determination with Tax Shares More specifically, these tax prices are to be such as to charge consumers for their consumption of social goods in accordance with a pricing rule similar to the one operating in the competitive market for private goods. That is to say, for each consumer, all units of a good are to be sold at the same price (there is to be no higher price on intramarginal units), and the ratio of unit prices for X and S is to equal his or her marginal rate of substitution in consumption between them. A and B will pay the same unit price for X while consuming different amounts thereof; and they will pay different unit prices for S while consuming the same amount. At the same time, we retain the assumption that preferences are known to the planner.

The solution is illustrated in Figure 3-8. The production possibility line *CD* in the upper figure shows various mixes of S (the social good) and X (the private

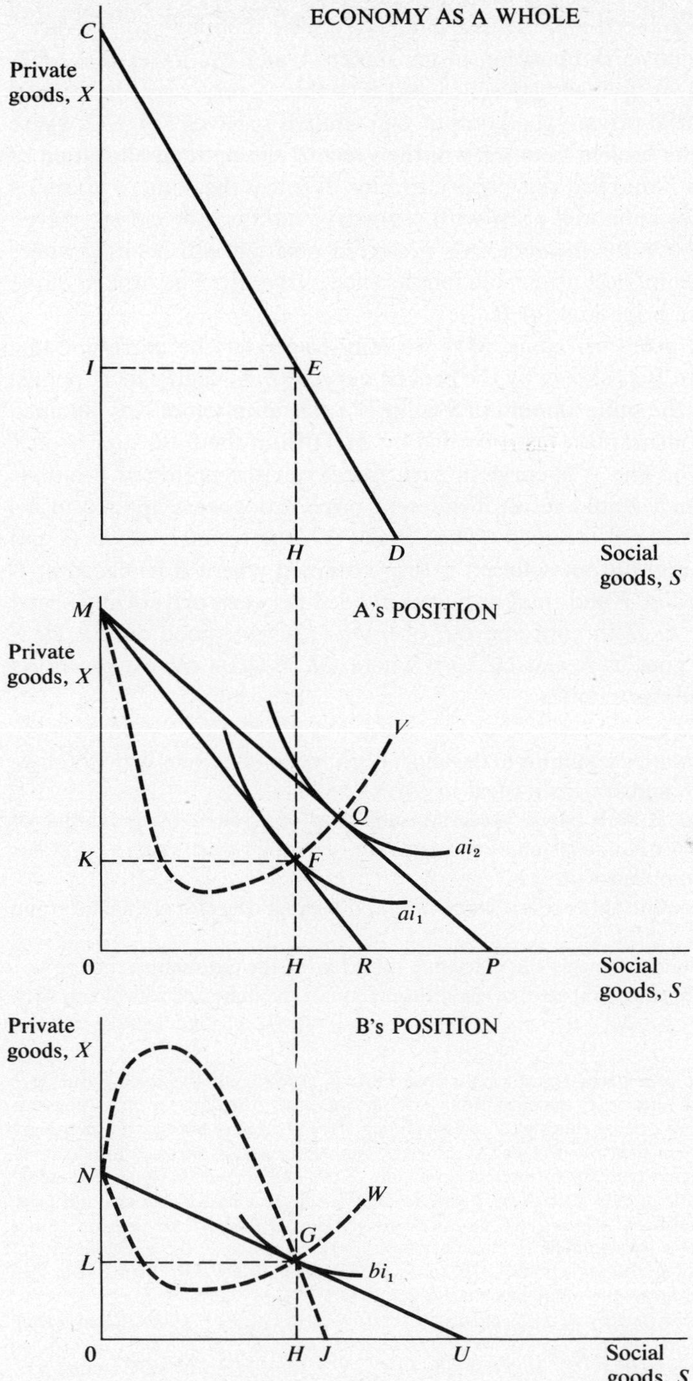

FIGURE 3-8 Social and Private Goods with Given Distribution.

good) that can be produced and that are available to the economy as a whole.[31] The middle figure shows the position of consumer A and the lower that of B. Suppose that income is divided between A and B so that A receives a share equal to OM/OC of potential private-good output OC, while B receives ON/OC, where $OM + ON = OC$. The broken line MV will then record the optimal allocation of A's income between X and S at varying price ratios. It traces the point of tangency of a set of price lines anchored at M with successive indifference curves. Given the price ratio OM/OP for instance, A's preferred position will be at Q where MP is tangent to the highest attainable indifference curve ai_2. The broken curve NW traces a similar price line for B.

Following A's positions along MV, we may trace out the corresponding positions available to B as shown by the broken curve NJ. At each pair of points, both must consume the same amount of S while B's consumption of X is obtained by deducting A's consumption (as recorded by MV) from the total supply of X (as recorded by CD). The NW curve in turn traces out the preferred positions for consumer B which would result if different price ratios were applied to his purchases of social and private goods. The NJ and NW curves intersect at G, and the correct pricing and output solution is thus obtained where B is placed at G while A is positioned at F and total output is divided between private and social goods as shown by E. Both consume OH of S while private-good output OI is divided so that OK goes to A and OL to B where $OK + OL = OI$. This solution has the following characteristics:

1. The solution conforms to the initial distribution of income, with A's share equal to OM/OC and B's share equal to ON/OC.

2. A and B both pay a tax price such that each one's marginal rate of substitution of S for X in consumption is equal to each one's price ratio, so that our pricing rule is complied with.[32]

3. The combined tax contribution of A and B equals the cost of S to the group as a whole.[33]

4. The solution meets the efficiency criterion of the Samuelson model, i.e., that the sum of the marginal rates of substitution equals the marginal rate of transfor-

[31] The assumption of a linear transformation schedule is necessary if the pricing rule here specified is to result in the necessary equality of tax revenue and cost. Allowing for increasing cost and a convex schedule, our pricing rule yields excess revenue. This is the case because intramarginal units of the social good can then be produced at a lower opportunity cost as measured in terms of private goods. Hence a more complex formula or a rebating of the excess revenue would be needed.

[32] The unit price for private good X or P_X is the same for both A and B, but the unit price for S differs. A's price ratio $P_S{}^A/P_X$ as given by price line MR equals OM/OR (Figure 3-8). Since the price line is tangent to the indifference curve at F, the price ratio equals the marginal rate of substitution in consumption. The same holds for B's ratio $P_S{}^B/P_X$ equal to ON/OU (Figure 3-8), with price line NU again tangent to the indifference curve bi_1 at G.

[33] The amount of tax paid by A or T_A equals $P_S{}^A \cdot OH$. Given $P_S{}^A/P_X = OM/OR$ and setting $P_X = 1$, we have $P_S{}^A = OM/OR$ and $T_A = (OM/OR)\ OH$. Since $OM/OR = KM/KF = KM/OH$, we obtain $T_A = KM$. Arguing similarly for B, we obtain $T_B = LN$. Since $OM + ON = OC$ and by construction of NW we know that $OL + OK = OI$, it follows that $T_A + T_B = IC$.

For the group as a whole, the price ratio is given by $P_S/P_X = OC/OD$. Setting $P_X = 1$, we have $P_S = OC/OD$, with the cost of supplying OH of S equal to $(OC/OD)\ OH$ which again reduces to IC. See, however, footnote 31 above.

mation.[34] The solution E thus reflects *a* point on the utility frontier of Figure 3-6, it being that point which corresponds to our given income distribution and specified pricing rule.

Extension to Voting This version of the model is helpful in providing a more realistic setting, where an initial distribution of money income is assumed to exist and tax shares are determined. This is in line with the approach of Chapter 1, where the allocation and distribution functions were viewed as distinct parts of the process, with the latter determining the proper distribution of money income and the former determining the provision (and finance) of social goods on that basis.

Nevertheless, the budget model remains unsatisfactory in that it leaves aside the crucial problem of securing preference revelation.

In the real world setting, there is no omniscient planner to whom the preference patterns of Figure 3-8 are known and who can derive a corresponding solution. Nor is the case of realism helped by substituting an assumption of voluntary bidding. As was noted earlier in our discussion of Figure 3-1, this solution breaks down once the large-number case is considered and the free-rider problem arises. To provide an operational view of the budget, the model must thus be extended to incorporate a theory of the voting process. More specifically, the task is to devise a voting system which is most effective in securing preference revelation and in designing a system of tax-expenditure determination which best approximates an efficient pricing rule, such as that shown in Figure 3-8.[35] Through the voting process, the pseudo-demand schedules of the earlier discussion tend to be revealed, the budget size determined, and the tax price applied. As we shall see in Chapter 5, the voting process by its very nature cannot bring about a perfect result. Except for a society where preferences are so homogeneous as to permit unanimity, some voters will remain dissatisfied. Yet some procedures will do better than others and the task is to find the best approximation.

Choosing the Optimum But once more, this approach falls short of dealing with the entire problem. Voting on the provision of social goods and assignment of their cost through taxes presumes the distribution of income to be given, just as did the solution of private-good allocation through the market. For the result to be optimal in the sense of Figure 3-6, this distribution must also be the correct one. The practical solution, in the social- as in the private-good case, involves two steps; namely, (1) determining the proper distribution of income, and (2) deriving the efficient allocation of resources based on that distribution. Although some eminent theorists hold that this is an artificial distinction, we believe it to be essential for an operational bridge between the theoretical model of social-

[34] This follows because $(OM/OR) + (ON/OU) = (KM/OH) + (LN/OH) = IC/OH$.

[35] To be efficient, the pricing rule used to solicit preference revelation must equate each consumer's rate of substitution with *his* or *her* price ratio at the *margin.* But it is not required that the intramarginal units be sold at the same price. By charging higher prices for intramarginal units of the social good, "consumer surplus" will be taxed away. Thus more than one efficient pricing rule is available. Among them, that one should be used which best permits implementation through the voting process.

goods allocation and its application to the practice of budget determination.[36] This, of course, leaves open the question of how the optimal state of distribution is to be determined, a puzzling problem to which we turn in the next chapter.

H. SUMMARY

This chapter deals with the efficient use of resources, in particular where the provision of social goods is concerned. The three basic concepts used in this discussion are:

1. *The concept of efficiency.* Efficient resource use occurs when there is no possibility to make a change which helps some without hurting anyone else. There are many efficient solutions to the allocation problem, each reflecting a different state of distribution among consumers.

2. *Private goods.* These are goods which are rival in consumption, so that consumption by A renders consumption by B impossible. If a particular good is consumed by A, B will be excluded from the benefits.

3. *Social goods.* These are typically goods which are nonrival in consumption, so that the same benefits can be enjoyed by all members of the group. In this case, exclusion is undesirable and in many instances not feasible.

Given these definitions, certain conditions may be laid down which must be met if resources are to be used efficiently, and the mechanism that can lead to efficient use may be considered. Thus:

4. In the case of private goods, the marginal rates of substitution in consumption must be the same for all consumers, and equal to the marginal rate of transformation in production.

[36] The case *against* separation of the two issues may be summarized as follows: Resource allocation, as determined by the budget model, is to be optimal. But the optimal distribution of money income cannot be determined without knowing relative prices and hence allocation. (This is so because the basic issue of distribution must be seen in terms of real, rather than of money, income.) It follows that the general model must be solved in any case, thus determining distribution and allocation simultaneously, and that nothing is gained by introducing the distribution of money income and of tax shares. The distribution and allocation aspects of the problem must thus be decided simultaneously, involving the reasoning of both Figs. 3-6 and 3-7.

The case *for* separation of the two issues may be summarized as follows: Although the introduction of an income distribution and of tax shares is indeed redundant in a model which assumes an omniscient planner, the situation differs in a more realistic model in which preferences are unknown and must be revealed. This requires a distribution of income on the basis of which consumers can express their evaluation, whether through bidding in the market, as in the case of private goods, or through voting, as in the case of social goods. While it is correct that the "proper" distribution must be defined in terms of welfare and not of income (or, putting it differently, that the proper distribution of income depends upon the pricing rule that applies), this fact does not render the concept of a "proper" distribution of money income circular or redundant. The pricing rule to be used is not arbitrary. In the case of private goods, the rule is that given by the competitive market (i.e., marginal cost pricing, with the same price charged to each consumer); in the case of social goods, it is that which can be implemented most effectively by the voting mechanism. In the above case, this was assumed to be the rule which, analogously to the private-goods case, equates the price ratios with the consumer's marginal rate of substitution between social and private goods.

For a further discussion of the separability of allocation and distribution aspects, see the contributions by Paul A. Samuelson and Richard A. Musgrave in J. Margolis and H. Guitton (eds.), *Public Economics,* New York: St. Martin's, 1969.

5. This result can be achieved through a competitive market where consumers reveal their preferences by bidding for goods.

6. In such a market, all consumers would pay the same price but consume different amounts, depending upon their income and their preferences. A market demand schedule is obtained by horizontal addition of individual demand schedules.

For the case of social goods, the solution to the problem differs for the following reasons:

7. Since such goods are nonrival in consumption, the same amount is consumed by all. Since consumers differ in incomes and tastes, the marginal rates of substitution are no longer the same and the market demand schedule is now obtained by vertical addition of individual schedules. The requirement now is that the *sum* of the marginal rates of substitution in consumption should equal the marginal rate of transformation in production.

8. Since the benefits from social goods are available to all, consumers will not reveal their preferences by bidding in the market but will act as free riders. Hence, a political process or voting system is needed to induce the revelation of preferences.

Although the essential problem may be seen best by dealing with the polar cases of purely private and social goods, the actual nature of goods in many instances falls between these extremes. Among various mixed situations, the following were considered:

9. The consumption or production of primarily private goods can give rise to external benefits. Such benefits are not accounted for in the market, and a subsidy is required to correct this defect.

10. The benefit incidence of social goods is frequently subject to spatial limitation.

11. While available to all members of the group, the level of benefits obtained from a given amount of social-good provision may decline as the number of members in the group increases, thus causing a "congestion" problem.

12. Externalities may involve not only benefits or social goods, but also costs or social bads. This is the problem of pollution. Again, market failure occurs since external costs are not allowed for by the firm. In this instance, a tax is required to internalize such costs.

Whereas the free-rider problem (and consequent market failure) arises in the case of large numbers, external benefits and costs may be accounted for through bargaining in the small-number case:

13. With small numbers, bargaining may permit a more or less complete accounting for external benefits and costs, thus reducing the need for public policy intervention. However, the equity implication of such bargaining solutions may not be satisfactory.

Finally, consideration was given to the nature of the wants underlying the provisions of private and of social goods:

14. Our concepts of social and private goods do not differ with regard to how the underlying wants are experienced. The demands for private and for social goods are both integral parts of the preference systems of individuals. While each person's preferences interact with those of others, all wants are basically experienced by the individual consumer and not by the collective entity.

15. There remains, however, the fact that budgetary provision frequently involves goods which are rival in consumption. This suggests interference with individual choice, and is here referred to as provision for "merit goods." Such provision may include private as well as social goods, and it poses quite a different problem.

FURTHER READINGS

Bator, F. M.: "The Simple Analytics of Welfare Maximization," *American Economic Review,* March 1957, pp. 22–59.

Buchanan, J. M.: *The Demand and Supply of Public Goods,* Chicago: Rand McNally, 1968.

Head, J. G.: "Public Goods and Public Policy," *Public Finance,* no. 3, 1962, pp. 197–221.

Johansen, L.: *Public Economics,* Amsterdam: North-Holland Publishing Company, 1965, chap. 6.

Mishan, E. J.: "The Postwar Literature on Externalities: An Interpretative Essay," *Journal of Economic Literature,* March 1971, pp. 1–35.

Samuelson, Paul A.: "Pure Theory of Public Expenditures and Taxation," in J. Margolis and H. Guitton (eds.), *Public Economics,* New York: St. Martin's, 1969.

______: "The Pure Theory of Public Expenditures," *Review of Economics and Statistics,* pp. 386–389, November 1954; and "Diagrammatic Exposition of a Theory of Public Expenditures," pp. 350–356, ibid., November 1955. Both articles reproduced in R. W. Houghton (ed.), *Public Finance,* Penguin Modern Economic Readings, Baltimore: Penguin, 1970.

Wicksell, K., and E. Lindahl: Excerpts of writings in R. A. Musgrave and A. Peacock (eds.), *Classics in the Theory of Public Finance,* New York: Macmillan, 1958.

Chapter 4

The Theory of Optimal Distribution*

A. Does Equity Belong in Economics? *Determinants of Distribution; Distribution as a Policy Issue.* **B. Approaches to Distributive Justice:** *Alternative Views; Endowment-based Criteria; Utilitarian Criteria; Equity Criteria; The Final Choice.* **C. The Problem of Utility Comparison:** *Are Subjective Comparisons Operational? Social Utility Approach.* **D. The Size of the Pie:** *Limits to Redistribution; Efficiency-Equity Tradeoff; The Leisure Problem; Optimal versus Feasible Solutions.* **E. Further Issues:** *Distribution Policy under Alternative Systems; Mandatory versus Voluntary Redistribution; Distribution as a Social Good; Distribution among Generations; Implementation Problems.* **F. Summary.**

Throughout the preceding chapter we have emphasized that the optimal use of scarce resources involves two basic issues. One is to secure efficiency and the other is to secure a state of just distribution. Defined in terms of Pareto efficiency, the proposition that there is a welfare gain when the position of any one individual can be improved without hurting that of another, the efficiency objective is noncontroversial. But, since there exists an efficient solution corresponding to

* *Reader's Guide to Chapter 4:* The theory of optimal distribution, considered in this chapter, poses problems not usually dealt with in the study of public finance. Yet the questions raised must be faced up to in designing budget policy. Moreover, criteria of distributive justice, though philosophically based, are constrained in application by economic considerations, so that the two perspectives must be joined.

each and every state of distribution, the question remains: which state should be chosen as equitable or just? Here the concept of Pareto efficiency helps little, if at all. The problem of distribution is one of evaluating a change in which someone gains while someone else loses. It is one of choosing among the points on the utility frontier of Figure 3-6.

As shown in that connection, the choice of the best or just solution might be found by postulating a "social welfare function," i.e., a set of rankings in which social weights are given to gains by some and to losses by others. Given such a function, the economist can grind out the answer, as illustrated by the tangency solution of Figure 3-6. But there remains the more basic problem of what shape this set of values (or the social welfare function) should take. In the end, one cannot avoid the question of what should be considered a fair or just state of distribution.

A. DOES EQUITY BELONG IN ECONOMICS?

Economists, over the last fifty years, have increasingly held that a theory of just or equitable distribution is not within the purview of economics but should be left to philosophers, poets, and politicians. Indeed, when talking about the "theory of distribution," economists have traditionally referred to the theory of factor pricing and the division of national income among returns to land, labor, and capital. This theory of factor shares plays an essential role in economic analysis, but its significance lies mainly in the area of efficient allocation. For resource use to be efficient, factors of production must be applied so as to equate the value of their marginal product in all uses, a condition which holds in a socialist, as well as a capitalist, society. But the theory of efficient factor use by itself is not a theory of distributive justice. For one thing, the proposition that factor allocation should be based on efficient factor pricing does not require that the final distribution of income among individuals be set equal to the proceeds from sales of their factor services in the market. The two can be separated by intervention of the distribution branch of the budget. For another thing, the ultimate concern of justice in distribution is with distribution among individuals or families and not among groups of factors. Factor shares are only loosely related to the inter-family distribution of income. While it is true that capital income accrues more largely to high-income families and wage income more largely to low-income families, there are important exceptions to the rule. The problem of distribution among individuals or families must thus be addressed directly.

Determinants of Distribution

In the market economy, the distribution of income is determined by the sale of factor services. It thus depends upon the distribution of factor endowments. With regard to labor income, this distribution involves the distribution of abilities to earn such income, as well as the desire to do so. With regard to capital income, it involves the distribution of wealth as determined by inheritance, marriage patterns, and lifetime saving. The distribution of labor and capital endowments is linked by investment in education, which in turn affects the wage rate which a person can command.

Given the distribution of endowments, the distribution of income depends further on factor prices. In a competitive market, these prices equal the value of the factor's marginal product. As such, they depend upon a wide set of variables, including factor supplies, technology, and the preferences of consumers. In many instances, however, returns are determined in imperfect markets where institutional factors, such as conventional salary structures, family connections, social status, sex, race, and so forth, play a significant role. As a result, the returns to various jobs may differ in line with status considerations rather than marginal product, and who gets the job may depend upon connections rather than innate endowment.

The distribution of income, as generated by the above forces, shows a substantial degree of inequality. This may be seen by comparing the percentage of income which accrues to various percentages of households as ranked by their income. Thus, 6 percent of personal income in the United States accrues to the 20 percent of families with the lowest incomes, while the income share received by the successively higher quintiles of family groups is 12, 18, 24, and 41 percent, respectively. As among various forms of income, the distribution of capital income is less equal than that of wage and salary income. Thus, if capital income only is considered, the corresponding income shares are 2, 4, 8, 12, and 74 percent.[1] How does this pattern, which is fairly similar in most advanced countries, relate to what might be considered a fair or just state of distribution?

Distribution as a Policy Issue

By posing this question, the focus shifts from distribution as a market outcome to distribution as a policy issue. However any one reader may view this issue, it is evident that distribution problems have been, are, and will continue to be a vital factor in politics and policy determination. Three aspects of the problem may be distinguished:

1. Even where distributional objectives are not the primary policy target, the distributional implications of various policies must be taken into account in setting the overall policy package.

2. If distributional changes are to be made, they should be done so as to be least costly in terms of efficiency loss.

3. To decide what distributional changes, if any, should be made, or to evaluate the distributional implications of other policies, there must be a basis for choosing among alternative distributions, i.e., a standard of distributive justice or fairness must be applied.

Beginning with aspect 1, it is evident that almost all policy measures, even those not immediately concerned with distributional objectives, have distributional repercussions. Thus, an inflationary situation may call for a restrictive policy so as to reduce aggregate demand. Its distributional effects will differ, depending on whether the demand reduction is obtained by increasing sales taxes or income taxes, by reducing various types of public expenditure programs, or

[1] See Table 14-2, p. 348.

by applying monetary restriction. Policies aimed at increasing the flow of international trade will have different distributional implications, depending on which tariffs are reduced. Antitrust measures designed to render markets more efficient will also affect the income of capital and labor in particular industries, as well as the real income of consumers of their products. Public investment programs, such as regional development or road construction, will affect the economic welfare of various population groups and hence the patterns of distribution. Public pricing policies, such as the pricing of publicly operated subways, similarly will affect the real income of subway riders, and so forth.

In all these cases, distributional effects result and, though their impact need not call for adjustments in the particular policy itself, it must be allowed for in the overall policy package. As we have seen in the introductory chapter, various policy instruments should be coordinated to achieve the desired combination of objectives.

When we turn to aspect 2, it is evident that such distributional changes as are made should be implemented in the most efficient manner. If a decision is reached to improve the position of low-income recipient L relative to that of high-income recipient H, this improvement should be designed so that for a given gain to L, H is hurt least; or that for any given loss to H, L will be benefited the most. This objective poses questions with regard to both sides of the transfer. Will it be more burdensome for H if the required revenue is obtained by an excise tax on luxuries rather than by a progressive income tax? As we shall see later, the burden imposed on H may not be the same under alternative tax measures. Similarly, will the benefits to L be greater if he is given a cash subsidy rather than if he is aided by services in kind, such as subsidized public housing or subsidized provision of private goods (for example, bread) which he can then purchase at a lower price?

Standard economic analysis may be utilized in providing guidance with regard to both aspects 1 and 2, but all this aid does not meet aspect 3. It does not tell us what state of distribution should be our goal, i.e., what the criteria for distributional justice and fairness should be. Traditionally, this final question has been considered as out of bounds for economists, whose job is taken to end with answers to factors 1 and 2. But, given the close bearing of distributional issues on questions of economic policy, the economist who is concerned with public policy can hardly detach his thinking from equity issues. He can be required only to distinguish them from efficiency considerations. This is especially true for the application of economics to the problems of public finance, an integral part of which is the function of our "distribution branch." The efficiency-based analysis of the preceding chapter must therefore be followed by at least a brief consideration of just or equitable distribution. Otherwise, our normative view of public sector theory cannot be complete.

B. APPROACHES TO DISTRIBUTIVE JUSTICE

A choice must be made between alternative criteria for just distribution, and their implications must be understood.

Alternative Views

Among possible criteria for what constitutes a just state of distribution, the following may be considered:

1. Endowment-based criteria
   a. Keep what you can earn in the market.
   b. Keep what you could earn in a competitive market.
   c. Keep labor (earned) income only.
   d. Keep what you could earn in a competitive market, given equal positions at start.
2. Utilitarian criteria
   a. Total welfare is maximized.
   b. Average welfare is maximized.
3. Equity criteria
   a. Welfare is maximized.
   b. Welfare floor is set with the endowment rule applicable above it.
   c. Welfare of the lowest group is maximized.

In choosing among these criteria, a high-income person will find 1*(a)* in his best interest, while he or she would have to be altruistic in supporting 3*(a)*. A low-income person would find himself in the opposite position. This, however, is not the only way of considering this choice. An alternative is offered by the philosopher's view of the problem as one of social contract,[2] where people, placed in what philosophers call the "state of nature," consider what should govern the relationship among persons in a just society, including the distribution of economic welfare. In the original position of people in this state of nature, they do not as yet know what their own position will be, so they can consider the problem in an impartial way. This assembly, moreover, must be viewed not as an initial historical occurrence but as a mental experiment which must be made when examining such issues. You may place yourself in this position right now. Given such a setting, your choice between, say, 1*(a)* and 3*(b)* is not a matter of selfishness versus altruism, but of deciding, in a personally disinterested way, the moral principles upon which the just society should be founded.

Endowment-based Criteria

Theorists of the social contract formulated the problem in terms of certain rights and duties to which all members of society are both entitled and committed, but they differed in their views on the content of the contract. Natural-law philosophers such as Hobbes and Locke, following what are here referred to as endowment-based criteria, postulated a person's innate right to the fruits of his efforts, thereby giving ethical support to distribution by factor endowment and the pricing of factors in the market. This proposition may be accepted without qualification, as in 1*(a)*, or it may be limited to such earnings as can be obtained in a competitive market, as in 1*(b)*. In the latter case, claims to monopoly profits would not be legitimate, nor would claims to wage or salary incomes in excess

[2] See Ernest Baker (ed.), *The Social Contract*, London: Oxford University Press, 1946.

of marginal product. Still another possibility, 1*(c)*, is to apply the endowment principle only to earned (wage or salary) income but not to capital income, presumably because the former involves disutility of work whereas the latter does not. Some such consideration was widely held by the classical British economists when they argued that "unearned" or capital income should be taxed more heavily than wage income. A modern version of the endowment approach, 1*(d)*, sanctions such inequality as would remain if all people were given an equal position at the start. This means acceptance of such inequality as results from innate differences in earning ability, application to income-earning activities, and thrift, with rejection of inequalities that arise from inheritance, different educational opportunities, family status, and so forth. Some would cite this view as reflecting the spirit of a pure "enterprise" system.[3]

Utilitarian Criteria

As distinct from supporters of these endowment-based criteria, other social philosophers rejected innate inequality in ability as a legitimate source of differences in economic well-being. The existence of such inequalities is recognized, but they should not be permitted to determine the state of distribution. To be born with a high- or low-ability level is not due to the will or action of the particular individual. Like social status, this accident of birth is considered as lacking ethical sanction as a basis for distribution. According to this view, some other principle of assignment must be sought.

One answer was given by the utilitarians, such as Bentham, who would have income distributed so as to achieve the greatest sum total of happiness, an objective which they thought appealing to all "reasonable men." According to this criterion, A should be given more income than B if his "utility level," or ability to derive happiness from personal income, is higher. Only if we assume that the marginal income utility schedules for all individuals are the same and are declining will an equal distribution of income be called for. The maximum satisfaction view, therefore, may or may not lead to an egalitarian solution.

This is illustrated in Figure 4-1. In each diagram, income is measured along the horizontal axis, while the vertical axis records the marginal utility of income, i.e., the increment in total utility which results as another dollar is added to income. The area under the curve thus measures the total utility derived at various income levels. To bypass the difficulty which arises because the utility of initial dollars may well be infinite, we consider the distribution of income above a certain minimum level *OM*. We assume, for the time being, that the utility of income can be measured in "utils" and that a utility comparison among various individuals is possible. The difficulties involved in these assumptions will be considered presently. We assume further that after providing each with *OM*, total income available for assignment between A and B is fixed at *MT*.

In the upper part of the figure, we postulate that two individuals, A and B, have the same marginal utility schedules. To maximize total satisfaction, this

[3] For an eloquent expression of this spirit, see Henry Simons, "A Positive Program for Laissez Faire: Some Proposals for a Liberal Economic Policy," *Public Policy Pamphlets*, no. 15, Chicago: The University of Chicago Press.

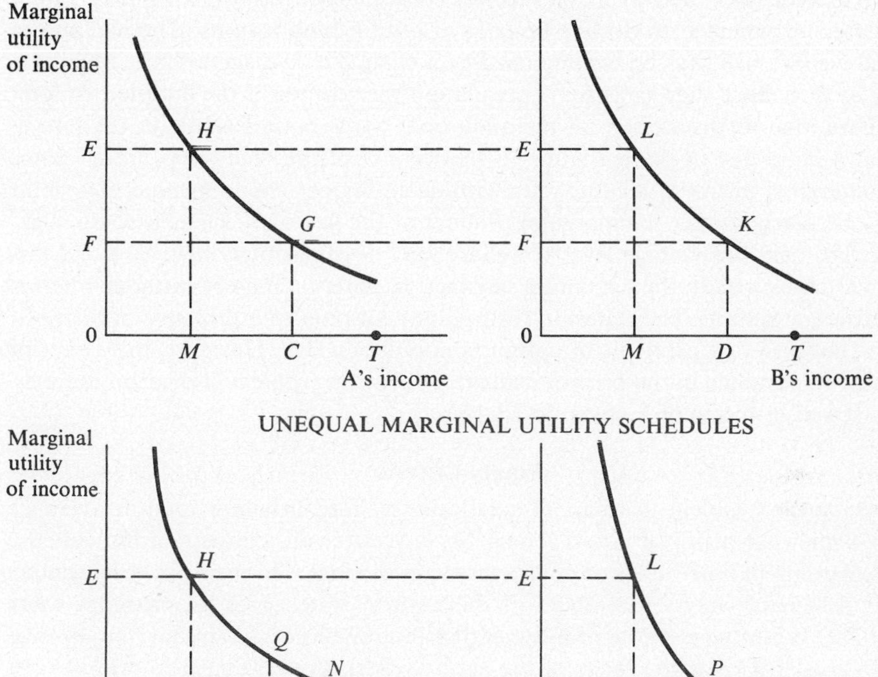

FIGURE 4-1 Patterns of Distribution.

income will then be divided equally between A and B so that A receives *MC* while B receives *MD*, with *MC* + *MD* = *MT*. The marginal utilities of A and B are set equal at *OF*, as are their total utilities, reflected by *MCGH* and *MDKL*, respectively.[4] In the lower part of the figure, we assume that A's marginal utility schedule, beyond the minimum income level *OM*, lies above B's. A, in other words, has a higher capacity to derive additional utility from income above *OM*. Assuming again a total income *MT* to be available for distribution, total utility is now maximized by assigning the larger amount *MK* to A and the smaller amount *MV* to B, where *MK* + *MV* = *MT*. Marginal utilities are equated at *OJ*, and A's total utility, or *MKNH*, now exceeds B's, or *MVPL*. Having a higher-lying utility schedule, A is better off for two reasons: he not only derives greater utility from the same income but, in addition, receives a larger income share.

The "maximum total welfare" criterion presents certain difficulties if popula-

[4] It is easy to see that the sum of utilities is maximized by equating marginal utilities. As long as more income is assigned to A than to B, A's marginal utility will be lower. Total utility, therefore, is increased by transferring income from A to B until marginal utilities and (given the same utility schedules) incomes are equalized.

tion changes are taken into consideration. As the size of population increases, total income rises. But, with other factors constant, per capita income may sooner or later be expected to decline because of diminishing returns. The increase in total welfare will thus be accompanied by a decline in average welfare. Maximizing total welfare then calls for a population increase until the addition to total welfare, due to the welfare of the additional workers, falls short of the loss in total welfare due to the reduction in the welfare of the "old" population. Since the marginal utility of income rises with declining per capita income, this point may be reached after the marginal product of the last worker has become negative. By then, the average level of welfare may be exceedingly low. To avoid this unreasonable result, the maximum satisfaction criterion may be restated in terms of average welfare. The criterion then points not only to a principle of distribution, but also to a principle of optimum population size. However, this is not of major importance in the present context, where the problem of distribution may be viewed in terms of a given population.

Equity Criteria

Viewing the problem in terms of maximum welfare (whether total or average) is a somewhat artificial construction. Society, after all, consists of individuals, not of a sum of individuals or of an average individual. This being so, why should "all reasonable men" assembled in the natural state agree to maximize total welfare? Is not the essential problem of distribution one of relative position *among* individuals? This is the focus of the equity-based formulations.

A first version [3*(a)*] postulates that equality of welfare is inherently desirable. Based on the humanistic view of the equal worth of each individual, this tenet underlines the egalitarian views of such writers as Rousseau and Marx. It is also in line with some current interpretations of Christian ethics, although in other times such ethics were interpreted more nearly in line with the endowment-based criteria, as reflected in the idea of the Protestant Ethic.[5] The implications of the equal-welfare rule for the distribution of income depend again on whether or not the utility schedules are the same. If they are, the upper part of Figure 4-1 applies and income is divided equally between A and B. The utilitarian (maximum total welfare) and egalitarian precepts both call for an equal distribution of income. But if utility levels differ, as assumed in the lower part of the figure, egalitarian distribution would assign MS to A and MR to B where $MS + MR = MT$ and $MSQH = MRUL$. The larger share of income now goes to the person whose utility scale is lower, and the pattern of income inequality becomes opposite to that achieved under the maximum total satisfaction rule.

It is doubtful, however, whether egalitarians such as Rousseau or Marx would have recognized differences in the level of utility schedules as legitimate reasons for income inequality. When Marx postulated, "From each according to his ability, to each according to his need,"[6] he referred to differences in need

[5] See Max Weber, *The Protestant Ethic and the Spirit of Capitalism* (trans., Talcott Parsons), New York: Scribner's, 1958.

[6] See Karl Marx, "Critique of the Gotha Program," in P. C. Tucker (ed.), *The Marx-Engels Reader*, New York: Norton, 1972, p. 388. In the same context Marx notes that incentive considerations do not permit application of this norm under socialism, it being attainable only in the final state of communism.

due to objective factors, such as family size or health, and not to subjective differentials in the capacity to enjoy income. Although enjoyment capacities may differ, the egalitarian philosophers would have interpreted the "equal worth" doctrine as calling for society to proceed as if utility schedules were the same, thereby arriving at an egalitarian distribution, qualified only by allowance for objective differentials.[7]

The variety of possible views is increased by combining equity and endowment-based considerations. Thus it may be held [criterion 3*(b)*] that equity calls for assuring the avoidance of the suffering of poverty, but that an endowment-based approach may be applied once this objective is met. It would seem that among the various criteria so far noted, this compromise view (combined perhaps with the equality-at-the-start interpretation of the endowment criteria) most nearly approximates emerging United States mores regarding the distribution problem.[8]

The Final Choice

Given this range of criteria to choose from, how is one to know which is the correct solution? Or, moving one step back, can it be argued that there *is* a correct solution? And if so, how can it be demonstrated to be correct? These, of course, are philosophical questions which cannot be resolved here. Some philosophers (from Plato on) have held that there exists a natural order of things in which a person's place in society is assigned by his station at birth. Others, such as Locke, have held that people may make use of their natural endowments. Still others, like Rousseau, believed that individuals are potentially equal and that their social relations must be derived from this premise. In some instances, thinkers like Kant and, more recently, Rawls have maintained that a set of moral imperatives points to a single positive solution, while in others, such principles are merely taken to prescribe the rules by which decisions are to be made. The basic question of whether the design of the good society can be derived by "reason" alone or whether "value judgment" is needed—and indeed, the question of the relationship between these two modes—remains unresolved, a matter to be rethought as civilization proceeds.

C. THE PROBLEM OF UTILITY COMPARISON

Much of the reasoning underlying the utility and equity criteria implies a comparison between the utility levels enjoyed by various individuals.[9] The difficulties involved in such a comparison, however, pose serious questions as to the meaning-

[7] Still another perspective is opened if one considers the possibility that inequalities in satisfaction derived from income may be used to offset inequalities in welfare deriving from other characteristics (in themselves unrelated to distribution), such as personal appearance, health, and musicality. While it may be impossible to allow for such features in practice, these inequalities should be noted at the more philosophical level if the full complexities of the problem are to be recognized.

[8] In a discussion of income distribution, the 1974 *Economic Report of the President* argues that "those who produce more should be rewarded more; and no individual or household should be forced to fall below some minimum standard of consumption regardless of production potential." *Economic Report of the President, February 1974,* p. 137.

[9] The same holds for the equal-sacrifice approaches to equity in taxation, which will be considered in a later chapter. See p. 216.

fulness of the entire approach. An alternative solution, based on social evaluation, may be needed.

Are Subjective Comparisons Operational?

Consider once more the information needed to implement the utilitarian (maximum welfare) and egalitarian rules demonstrated in Figure 4-1. Given the assumptions (1) that A and B have the same marginal utility of income schedules, and (2) that the schedule is a declining one, both rules call for equal distribution. This conclusion follows without our having to know the absolute level of utility that is experienced. An "ordinal" comparison or ranking suffices. Ranking A and B in terms of income also ranks them in terms of their marginal utility derived therefrom, so that total utility may be maximized and welfare equated by equating incomes. But if assumption 2 is not met and if schedules differ, neither rule can be implemented without knowing the absolute utilities which A and B obtain at various income levels. A "cardinal" utility comparison will be required. How can the necessary information be obtained, and in what units is "utility" to be measured? Unfortunately, economists have not been able to provide answers to these questions.

Assumption 1, that any one person's marginal utility of income schedule declines, is generally plausible,[10] but assumption 2 poses a more serious problem. While we may think it highly desirable, as a matter of value judgment, to treat people as if their income utility schedules were the same, it does not follow that in reality they are the same. People may differ in their ability to experience satisfaction from income; i.e., their income utility schedules may differ in slope and level. Assuming the schedule for each person to be known, the maximum- and equal-welfare rules could still be applied although the results would not be those of equal income. But the trouble is, the various schedules are, in fact, not known.

Attempts have been made to measure income utility, but the results are not applicable to implementing distribution rules. Thus, one may measure the rates at which people are willing to trade leisure for income.[11] These rates give interesting information on leisure-income preferences, but they do not provide an absolute measure of income utility, since the utility of leisure may also differ for various people. Or, one may observe people's behavior toward risk. Information regarding the slope of an individual's income utility schedule can be obtained by observing the person's willingness to gamble.[12] Since a dollar gained will be worth

[10] It may, however, be less evident than appears at first sight. Although it can be verified that a consumer's marginal rate of substitution (or tradeoff) of apples for oranges falls as more oranges are added to a constant supply of apples, it does not follow that the marginal utility of apples plus oranges (i.e., of all goods taken together, or of income) must fall as more of both are added. The hypothesis of declining marginal rates of substitution between goods is compatible with a constant or rising, as well as declining, marginal utility of all goods or income. This is the case especially if income is defined broadly enough to include leisure.

[11] See p. 483.

[12] See Milton Friedman and L. J. Savage, "The Utility Analysis of Choices Involving Risk," *Journal of Political Economy,* August 1948, reprinted in G. Stigler and K. Boulding (eds.), *Readings in Price Theory,* American Economic Association, Homewood, Ill.: Irwin, 1954, pp. 57–96; and Armen A. Alchian, "The Meaning of Utility Measurement," *American Economic Review,* March 1953.

less than a dollar lost (*if* the marginal utility of income schedule declines), the terms of the acceptable equal-odds bet (e.g., $1.25, $1.50, or $1.75 of gain as against an equally probable $1 of loss) reveal the slope of the utility schedule. This information, however, pertains to the *slope* of the schedule only and not to its *level,* as would be needed for sacrifice calculations which call for a comparison of utility levels between persons.

This being the case, the best one can do is to postulate (1) that marginal income utility schedules decline, and (2) that the slopes and levels of such schedules, though not identical for all individuals, will be distributed more or less normally, as are most characteristics (e.g., weight, height, or eyesight) of people living in a given society. Given these assumptions, which seem reasonable, a case can be made on probability grounds that an equal distribution will be called for under either the maximum welfare or the egalitarian rule.[13] But most economists do not accept this conjecture and feel that equity rules, if based on comparison of subjective utility levels, have little operational meaning.

Social Utility Approach

Nevertheless, it is evident that society does in fact engage in comparing the welfare experienced by different people. Distributional issues *are* dealt with, and people have ideas on how expenditure benefits should be valued and how tax burdens should vary with income. Views on these matters emerge through the political process and are reflected in legislative action. When all is said and done, society in fact postulates that people have similar utility functions and assigns social values to the utility derived from successive units of income. Considerations of this sort underlie discussions about welfare programs, the definition of poverty lines, the scale of tax progression and the evaluation of expenditure programs, and we shall return to the problem in these connections.[14] While there is no explicit legislation which sets social utility weights, such stipulation (which might be revised by succeeding administrations) might be helpful to assure consistency among various programs.

Pending a more satisfactory solution to the difficulties of subjective utility comparison, the social value approach is perhaps the best that one can take. If this view is adopted, a schedule of declining social marginal income utility again leads to an equal distribution, be it under the utilitarian or the egalitarian criteria. The rate at which utility declines need not be specified to obtain this result, as the same schedule is applied to all persons; but the rate of decline must be specified, once effects on the size of the pie are to be taken into account. It then becomes necessary to determine just how much is to be gained by successive moves toward more equal distribution (which depends on the level and slope of

[13] Dealing with two individuals, Abba P. Lerner has considered a situation where utility schedules are unequal but it is not known who has the higher or lower schedule. Redistribution toward equality is justified in this case under the maximum total welfare rule because probable gains (if a gain results) exceed probable losses (if a loss results). See A. P. Lerner, *The Economics of Control,* New York: Macmillan, 1944, p. 30. A similar conclusion holds for the equal welfare rule if a normal distribution of marginal utilities (at any given level of income) is assumed.

[14] For further discussion, see p. 168.

the schedule) so that a tradeoff can be made between equity gains and potential losses.

D. THE SIZE OF THE PIE

So far, we have discussed the problem of distribution under various criteria as if the total available for redistribution were given. But it is not. We must now allow for the fact that individuals can choose between income and leisure, so that the size of the pie may be affected by how it is distributed. This introduces three complications: (1) The feasibility of redistribution may be limited; (2) redistribution imposes an efficiency cost that must be allowed for; and (3) the "leisure problem" must be dealt with.

Limits to Redistribution

The fact that income redistribution will affect people's choices between income and leisure may limit the scope of feasible redistribution. Suppose that there are two individuals, H with high earnings capacity and L with low earnings capacity. To simplify, suppose that L's earnings capacity is, in fact, zero. In the absence of intervention, H has a substantial positive income, while L has none. Now a tax is imposed, and a transfer is paid to L. As a result of the tax, H finds that his net wage rate (the return in goods which he can obtain for selling his leisure) is reduced. This may induce him to retain more leisure, i.e., to work less.[15] As a result, the revenue obtained from a given rate of tax is reduced. As the tax rate is increased further, revenue will rise for some time until a point is reached beyond which further increases in the tax rate will result in declining revenue and hence reduced funds available for transfer to L. This point of diminishing revenue may be reached well before the point of equalization, with further attempts at income equalization resulting in income losses for L as well as for H.

Tax Rate, Percentage	*H's Hours, Worked*	*H's Pretax Income, Dollars*	*Tax Revenue, Dollars*	*H's Posttax Income, Dollars*	*L's Income, Dollars*
0	8	80	0	80	0
30	7	70	21	49	21
50	4	40	20	20	20
80	1	10	8	2	8
100	0	0	0	0	0

This is illustrated by the above schedule, showing H's response to various tax rates and assuming his hourly wage rate to be $10. Tax revenue in this illustration reaches a maximum at a rate of 30 percent. The result is plotted in Figure 4-2, where H's and L's net incomes are measured horizontally and vertically respectively, and the 45° line OZ measures equal distribution. In terms of

[15] As we shall see later (see p. 484), this need not be the outcome. The tax has both an income and a substitution effect which (as explained below) work in opposite directions.

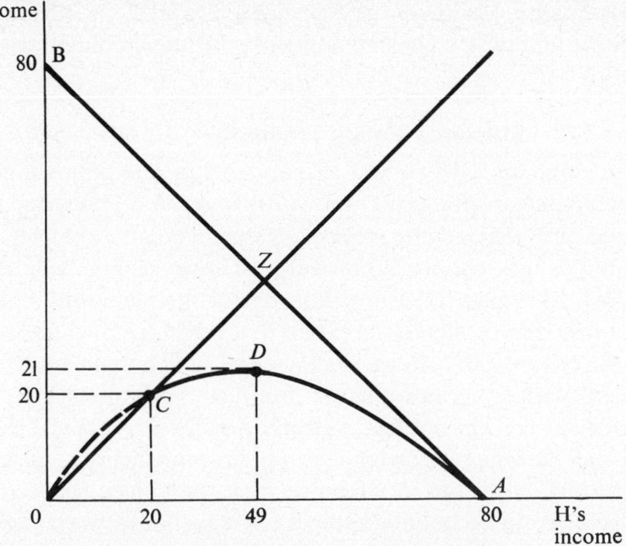

FIGURE 4-2 Income Redistribution with Variable Total.

our earlier discussion of Figure 4-1 where total income was fixed at, say, $80, the policy options lay along *AB*, with the egalitarian solution given at *Z*.[16] Since we have assumed L's earning ability to be zero, his work response need not be considered.[17] Now the set of options is given by the curve *OCDA*, reflecting the last two columns of the above schedule. If total income is to be maximized, the zero tax rate corresponding to point *A* is called for. Distribution is then determined by the endowment rule. If income is to be equalized, point *C* with a tax rate of 50 percent is chosen, but this leaves both H and L with lower incomes than they would have enjoyed at *D* where the tax rate is 30 percent and the income of L is maximized. An egalitarian who would be willing to settle on *Z* in the absence of the resulting change in income must now choose some point between *O* and *D*.

John Rawls in his *Theory of Justice* opts for stopping at *D*, where the income of L reaches a maximum. He thus holds that inequality, or retention of a higher income by H, is justified to the extent that it permits an increase in the level of welfare enjoyed by L.[18] Others, whose dislike for inequality is greater, may wish to go further and accept some decline in the lowest income in order to achieve

[16] Assuming income utility schedules to be the same.

[17] If we allow for the fact that L also works, though at a lower wage rate, her work effort will also be affected. As will be seen later in our discussion of welfare plans (see Chap. 31, Sec. B.), a redistribution scheme can hardly avoid the imposition of high marginal tax rates on L's earnings. Thus the problem of work response arises at both ends of the scale.

[18] Using the previously noted philosophical construct of an "original position," where individuals agree to consider the question of distribution in the abstract, Rawls concludes that the choice would call for (1) equality in the assignment of basic rights and duties, with (2) inequalities being "just only if they result in compensating benefits for everyone and in particular for the least advantaged members of society." Rational choice, he feels, calls for 2 because people do not wish to run the risk of being too badly off if caught at the bottom at the scale. An economist would take them to be extreme risk averters. John Rawls, *A Theory of Justice*, Cambridge, Mass: Harvard, 1972.

a higher degree of equality. However, no one will deny that the effects on the overall level of income and on L's absolute income position should be taken into account.

Efficiency-Equity Tradeoff

In the preceding section, we have viewed the tradeoff as one between equality and income loss due to detrimental effects on work incentives. This is too limited a view. If H is taxed and responds by working less, his income declines and so does national income as conventionally measured. However, his income loss is offset in part, at least, by a gain in leisure. The size of the pie consists of goods and leisure, and net loss results only to the extent that the loss of income is valued more highly than the leisure gain. As we shall see later, such a net loss (referred to as "excess burden") arises because the tax interferes with an efficient choice between goods and leisure.[19] The correct tradeoff, therefore, is between the gains from equality and the efficiency loss which results in implementing them. Such efficiency loss arises not only from interference with the choice between goods and leisure, but also with other economic choices, such as that between alternative forms of consumption or between consumption and saving.

The existence of an efficiency cost, of course, does not mean that there should be no distributional adjustments; it only follows that the tradeoff must be considered. The nature of this tradeoff may be illustrated by returning to Figure 3-6 in the previous chapter.[20] Suppose that with a given state of distribution of income and an efficient market system, a welfare position corresponding to point *V* is reached. Now it is desired to redistribute in favor of B by moving to point *U.* Since the tax-transfer system needed to redistribute imposes an efficiency cost (excess burden), this is not possible, the only available alternative being a move to, say, *W.* This move would be desirable even though it involves an efficiency loss (narrowly defined), i.e., a move to inside the utility frontier, because *W* lies on a higher social indifference *(si)* curve. If, however, the result is a move to *R,* the efficiency loss would outweigh the equity gain and the case would be against the adjustment. The choice thus depends on the magnitude of the efficiency cost and how society values it relative to equity gains.

But though society may well accept some efficiency loss to obtain an equity gain, distributional adjustments should be made so as to minimize this efficiency loss. In our initial sketch of distribution policy, as given in Chapter 1, we have suggested that a combination of income taxes and income transfers provides the most plausible mechanism to expedite distributional adjustments. This, we said, would have the advantage of permitting decisions on distribution policy to be made independent of policies aimed at the provision of social goods. The use of a general income tax most likely would interfere less with individual choices (i.e., impose a smaller excess burden) than would selective taxes on consumption or other uses of income. Similarly, the use of a general income transfer would leave the recipient with a greater benefit than would services in kind or subsidies to

[19] See p. 467.
[20] See p. 70.

particular forms of consumption that would distort his preferred consumption pattern. These conclusions remain plausible, but it must be noted that even income taxes and transfers are not free of distortions, since they affect economic choices. We shall have to consider more carefully, later on, what combination of tax and expenditure measures will involve the least burden.[21]

It remains to note that distributional adjustments need not involve an efficiency cost. They may, in fact, help to relieve inefficiencies which already exist in the market. Due to existing rigidities and patterns of discrimination, the distribution of human investment (whether in health or education) may not only be unequal but also inefficient, with a more equal distribution resulting in higher rates of return. In developing countries, a more equal distribution may generate a pattern of demand involving goods with a lower capital requirement so as to permit a more rapid rate of growth even though the savings rate falls. Viewed more broadly, redistributive measures create a social climate which reduces conflict and is more conducive to economic enterprise. Thus, a good case can be made that the rise of the welfare state, far from having been damaging to the decentralized market system, has been a precondition for the successful development of this form of economic order.

The Leisure Problem

Since a person's welfare depends on the consumption of both income and leisure, it is only just to define the distribution problem in terms of both these components. If income-leisure preferences were the same for all persons, the preceding discussion would not be greatly changed. But an additional difficulty arises once differences in income-leisure preferences are taken into account. It comes into being because income can be transferred, whereas leisure cannot. Consider four types of people—represented by A, who combines high earnings ability with a high-income preference, B, who combines high earnings ability with a high-leisure preference, C, who combines low earnings ability with high-income preferences, and D, who combines low earnings ability with a high degree of leisure preference. As a result, A has high income and D has low income, with B and C falling in between. If distribution is seen in income terms, A and B will be called upon to sustain C and D with A asked to make a larger contribution than B and D benefiting more than C. As a matter of distributional justice, such discrimination against A and C and in favor of B and D is unacceptable. The correct welfare measure and distribution criteria should allow for both income and leisure, leaving the mix between them to the individual's own choice.

Although this aspect of the problem has been bypassed in recent theoretical work on optimal distribution, it is a critical part of the problem and among the most controversial aspects of distributive justice. In many a situation, people may be willing to assist those whose income-earning capacity is low, but they are loath to support those who prefer leisure. This attitude does not imply that leisure is considered undesirable. High-leisure preference in this context means a high

[21] See p. 461.

preference for other than income-earning activities. They may include sleeping late, running the mile, improving one's music appreciation, or studying Sanskrit for one's own delight. The same attitude is involved when an academic economist, for love of research, forsakes the higher-paying position of a bank presidency (assuming it to be available to him). Substitution of psychic for monetary income in this context is equivalent to the choice of leisure. There is nothing wrong with taking one's welfare in leisure, as here defined, rather than in income. But this choice in the just system should not affect one's obligation to contribute to redistributive taxes (i.e., B should not be favored over A); and it should not affect one's claim to financial support (i.e., D should not be favored over C).

Low income, of course, is not proof of high-leisure preference, but may simply reflect low earnings capacities or opportunities. But, though the general assumption that the poor are poor because they prefer leisure is invalid, leisure preference—including discrimination against A as well as C—poses a central issue in distributive justice which cannot be overlooked.

Optimal versus Feasible Solutions

The optimal solution, which would resolve the three difficulties noted in this section, would be to make distributional adjustments through a set of taxes and transfers assessed in line with the individual's potential welfare, whether taken in income or in leisure. Since the tax liability would then be independent of the taxpayer's behavior, it would not call for defensive substitution of leisure for income. The same would hold with regard to the receipt of transfers. There would be no excess burden and no injustice due to differences in leisure preferences. Since there would be no change in the net wage rate of the taxpayer or transfer recipient, the policy maker (referring back to Figure 4-2) would be free to choose whatever solution on *AB* he or she desired.

But unfortunately this is not a practicable solution. While the efficiency loss of excess burden could be readily avoided by a head tax, this would not give a just solution. The simple reason is that all taxpayers have only one head each, whatever their earnings capacity. It has been suggested that both objectives of efficiency and equity could be served by imposing taxes (or giving transfers) which are geared to the individual's *potential* rather than *actual* earnings ability. This would have the quality of a lump-sum tax in that it would be independent of economic behavior and thus would avoid an efficiency cost; and it would also be fair, since it would be related to earnings capacity.

Once more, however, this prescription is not operational, since earnings capacities are not known independently of a person's actual earnings behavior. In short, redistributional taxes and transfers are bound to be related to economic performance (whether income, consumption, or wealth), so the difficulties noted in this section must be faced.

E. FURTHER ISSUES

In this concluding section, we note some additional aspects of the distribution problem which have particular significance for our subsequent discussion.

Distribution Policy under Alternative Systems

The types of expected economic response to distribution policy depend on the form of economic organization. Thus, effects on saving, investment, and risk taking are of special importance in the capitalist setting but less so for the socialist case, where these functions are carried out by the state. But the problem of work incentives is shared by both systems alike. Such at least is the case unless compulsory labor is required. If it is, gains in economic equality may be more than offset by losses of personal freedom with respect to the choice between work and leisure and to the option of selecting one's place of work. It follows that the problem of distribution in the end is not one of the distribution of economic welfare only. Different arrangements with regard to distribution also bear upon other aspects of the social condition, and they must be taken into consideration as well.

Mandatory versus Voluntary Redistribution

While it is interesting to philosophize about a *de novo* design of optimal distribution, society is an ongoing business, and the debate over distribution policy proceeds against the background of an existing distribution. The practical issue is one of *re*distribution, not of creating a *de novo* system. This is important, because in the latter case one might consider the state of distribution in the abstract, not knowing at just which point on the scale one would be. In the event of redistribution, any change is associated directly with gains or losses for particular individuals, and this is a different matter.

Mandatory Redistribution In a democratic setting, distributional changes will have to be decided by some form of majority vote. Suppose, first, that a person is concerned with his income only, without interest in the position of others. Those in the lower and middle thirds of the income scale might then form a coalition and vote a redistribution from the top third. Voters in the top third would oppose but (assuming majority rule) would lose. They might try to fend off the decision by making an equalizing offer to the middle group, which in turn might bargain further with the lowest, and so forth. An unstable bargaining solution is likely to result. Nevertheless, history shows that redistributive policies are in fact applied. Involuntary redistribution does occur, and it differs from expropriation only in that it operates through constitutional and democratic channels, i.e., through the budget process. Such adjustments have been a major factor in the changing structure of budget policy (e.g., the rise of the welfare state) during recent decades.

It would be incorrect, however, to assume that all individuals who lose in the redistribution process would have opposed such a vote, or that all who stood to gain would have favored it. That an equal distribution of votes coexists with a highly unequal distribution of income (coupled with the requirement of only a majority vote in fiscal matters) testifies to this point. The reasons are numerous. People in the lower half of the income scale may favor inequality because they hope to rise. This opinion may be annoying to the low-income–oriented reformer, but it is a fact nevertheless. Similarly, people in the upper brackets may favor equalizing measures, whether they believe this will protect their positions in the long run or they derive satisfaction from improving the position of others. This dichotomy poses the problem of voluntary redistribution which has received much attention in recent years.

Voluntary Redistribution Voluntary redistribution is readily explained if we allow for personal interdependence of utilities. Humans are social beings and their satisfactions are not derived in isolation. Thus A derives utility not only from his own consumption but also from the consumption of B and C. After A's own consumption has reached a relatively high level, he may derive greater satisfaction from giving income to B, whose consumption is low, than from adding to his own consumption. This will be a basis for voluntary redistribution from A to B and indeed offers the rationale for charitable giving.

A's preferences may be such that he derives utility from B's consumption independent of what products B consumes. In this case, he will wish to make a transfer to B in terms of money income. Or A may derive more satisfaction from B's consumption of milk than of beer; his giving will then take a paternalistic form and the transfer will be made in kind. Whatever policy is followed, such *voluntary* redistribution may be analyzed with the same tools used to determine efficiency in allocation economics. Since gains are obtained by both donor and donee, adjustments in distribution now improve efficiency under the "someone gains, no one loses" rule. This aspect of redistribution may then be handled in the context of Pareto optimality.[22] But note that the resulting state of distribution depends on the one that prevailed prior to the adjustment. This form of secondary redistribution thus differs from the more basic question of how the prior state of distribution should be determined.

Distribution as a Social Good

Giving of this sort may proceed on a person-to-person basis, but it may also arise in the budgetary context. High-income individuals may have little interest in sharing with their neighbors on a piecemeal basis but may desire to secure a higher degree of equality in the overall distribution, be it in the distribution at large or in the share received by, say, the lowest quarter of the population. A person knows that acting by himself to redistribute, he can make little dent in the overall situation. However, he will be ready to contribute to a redistribution if other high-income individuals do the same. In this way, provision for greater equality becomes a social-goods problem. A political process will be needed to induce the givers to reveal their valuation of obtaining a higher degree of equality and to implement the needed transfers through the budgetary process.

Distribution among Generations

It remains to note yet another aspect of the distribution problem—that of distribution between generations. Those now living may affect the welfare of future

[22] See H. H. Hochman and J. D. Rogers, "Pareto Optimal Redistribution," *American Economic Review*, September 1969.

generations in various ways. Thus, advances in science and technology made by this generation will be at the disposal of the next. Similarly, the capital stock accumulated by the present generation is bequeathed as a legacy to the next one. In many ways the present generation thus benefits the future one. On the other hand, exploitation of irreplaceable natural resources and destruction of the environment place a burden upon the future. All these relationships—the asymmetrical fact that the present can affect the future but not vice versa—pose questions of "intergeneration equity" to which we shall return later.[23] As we shall then see, they have special bearing on the choice of tax or loan finance and the distinction between current and capital expenditures of government. Now it need only be noted that introduction of a time dimension further adds to the complexities of the distribution problem.

Implementation Problems

Having dealt with mainly theoretical issues of distribution policy, in this concluding section we shall bring out some additional problems of implementation, problems which must be faced as specific tax and transfer measures are applied.

1. While dealing with the problem of distribution on an abstract level, it is possible to think of it in general terms, referring to the distribution of welfare at large. In practice, concern must be with a more concrete formulation involving the question of whether the distribution issue should be viewed in terms of income, consumption, or wealth. At a later point we shall have to consider this question when evaluating the case for or against reliance on particular tax bases.[24]

2. Assuming income to be chosen as the preferred base, one must then face the question of just how income should be defined for tax and transfer purposes. As we shall see when we discuss the income tax in detail, this is a thorny problem which reflects the complexities of economic and legal organization in modern society.

3. Another important question is whether the problem of distribution should be viewed in short- or long-run terms. Assuming again that distribution is viewed in terms of income, should reference be to annual, more extended or even lifetime income? Obviously, short-run income positions are subject to the impact of particular events and are less significant than are income positions over the longer run. Yet, administration of the tax system on a lifetime basis would hardly be feasible, and shorter-term positions have to be considered.

4. A further issue relates to defining the units among which the distribution problem should be applied. These definitions involve choice between individual earners and family units as the appropriate base for distribution analysis. If the family unit is chosen, further consideration has to be given to its definition, including such questions as the treatment of various types of dependents.[25] As one moves away from the broader philosophical issues of the distribution problem to its practical application, these and related issues advance into the foreground of the policy discussion. Yet the broader aspects must be kept in mind. Here, as in other connections, the details of policy implementation cannot be decided upon without knowing what the policy objectives are to be.

[23] See Chap. 28, Sec. E.
[24] See p. 220.
[25] See p. 271.

F. SUMMARY

The problem of just distribution, along with the problem of efficiency, is an essential part of the broader problem of optimal resource use:

1. The theory of factor shares as determined in a competitive market is important for efficient resource use, but it is not a theory of distributive justice.

2. The distribution of income as determined in the market depends on the distribution of factor endowments and the prices which the services of these factors will fetch.

3. The resulting distribution is also affected by the presence of market imperfections.

4. The distribution as determined by factor incomes need not coincide with what is considered socially desirable. The final distribution of income among families can be adjusted by fiscal measures.

Various approaches to distributive justice have been distinguished, and their implications for the distribution of income have been considered.

5. Endowment-based views sanction the distribution of income as determined by factor ownership and returns.

6. Utilitarian views call for a distribution of welfare so as to maximize total satisfaction. Here, an equal distribution of income is required only if the marginal utility schedules of all individuals are the same.

7. Egalitarian views would distribute welfare so as to equalize the position of all individuals. They again call for an equal distribution of income only if utility schedules are similar or differences are disregarded.

In implementing these rules, some major difficulties were noted:

8. The reasoning underlying the utilitarian and some egalitarian approaches involves interpersonal utility comparisons which, in the opinion of most economists, are nonoperational.

9. Instead, social utilities might be assigned to successive income increments and the resulting schedule be taken to apply to all individuals.

The problem is complicated further by the fact that individuals may choose between income and leisure:

10. The consumption of both income and leisure enters into a person's welfare, and both components should be evaluated in considering distributive justice.

11. As a person is taxed, he may substitute leisure for income, thus setting a limit to the feasible scope for income redistribution.

12. Redistribution policies involve an efficiency cost which must be taken into account. A tradeoff between efficiency and equity may arise.

13. Policies to secure redistribution of income tend to discriminate against people with low-leisure (high-income) preferences and to favor people with high-leisure (low-income) preferences. Such differences exist even among people with equal earnings ability.

14. These difficulties would be met by taxes and transfers relating to potential rather than to actual income. But this approach is hardly operational.

Among further aspects of the distribution problem, we have noted that:

15. Distributional adjustments need not involve an efficiency cost. In some situations they may result in an efficiency gain.

16. The efficiency cost of controlling distribution depends on the form of economic organization.

17. To some extent, distributional adjustments involve voluntary measures which may be viewed in efficiency terms.

18. Implementation of distributional measures requires definition of the income-receiving unit and the income base.

FURTHER READINGS

E. S. Phelps (ed.): *Economic Justice,* Penguin Modern Economic Readings, Baltimore: Penguin, 1973.

John Rawls: *A Theory of Justice,* Cambridge, Mass.: Harvard, 1972, part 1.

Chapter 5

Fiscal Politics*

A. Voting Systems and Individual Choice: *Voting Rules; Majority Rule and the Median Voter; Nonarbitrariness: (1) Voting Paradox; Nonarbitrariness: (2) Fiscal Choices; Representativeness of Outcome; Role of Strategy.* **B. The Theory of Representative Democracy:** *Vote Maximization; Political Change; Platforms and Coalitions; Logrolling; Range of Issues; Delegations and Numbers; Qualifications.* **C. Political Bias and the Size of the Public Sector:** *The Underexpansion Hypothesis; The Overexpansion Hypothesis; Conclusion.* **D. Interest Groups and Group Interest:** *The Marxist View; Interest Groups; The Community Interest; Quantitative Studies of Fiscal Policies.* **E. Summary.**

We have noted repeatedly that budget determination involves a political rather than a market process. The purpose of this chapter is to consider this political process more closely. How are the individual's views on fiscal matters expressed and how are they translated into political action? How are fiscal decisions related to political decisions in other areas? What is the role of the party system, of

* *Reader's Guide to Chapter 5:* Since the political process is at the heart of budget determination, fiscal theory must transgress the traditional bounds of economics and invade the adjacent domain of political theory. This is precisely what is done in this chapter, and some fascinating problems are encountered in the process. The more hidebound economics majors may skip this chapter. Others should enjoy it.

Congress, and of the executive? We begin with some basic analytical issues and then proceed to an empirical view of fiscal politics in the United States. Although traditionally these matters have been classified as political science rather than economics, both disciplines must be drawn upon in dealing with budget determination.

A. VOTING SYSTEMS AND INDIVIDUAL CHOICE

Once more our story begins with the individual consumer who is the final beneficiary of public services and whose consumption of private goods is reduced when resources are transferred to the public sector. The key question is how preferences on the matter can be expressed and implemented. As we have seen, decisions may be reached in the small group by a process of negotiation and bargaining. Each individual's contribution is sufficiently important to him and others for them to enter into a bargaining process. Negotiation among the parties may lead to an agreement on what supply of social goods should be provided and on who contributes how much. In the real world setting, this situation is approximated by the town meeting in a small village, or by compacts between nations, states, or municipalities designed to carry out common projects, be they a dump shared by various municipalities, the St. Lawrence Seaway undertaken jointly by the United States and Canada, or a peace-keeping mission financed by the United Nations.

But such bargaining solutions are not feasible for political units in which large numbers are involved. Here the contribution of any one individual is too small to make a difference if he acts on his own and numbers are so large as to make negotiation unmanageable. Individual preferences must now be translated into budgetary decision through a political process, involving the individual's preferences as recorded by his vote and the response of those political parties or leaders to whom he delegates the final decision.

Leaving the issue of delegation until later,[1] we begin with a simplified setting where fiscal decisions are made by direct referendum among individual voters. Each voter knows that the group decision reached by voting will be binding on him. Therefore, he will vote so as to move the decision in a direction more compatible with his own tastes.[2]

Voting Rules

The situation differs, depending on the voting rules which apply. They involve (1) the distribution of votes, and (2) the rules by which the winning vote is determined.

In the modern (post-eighteenth century) view of democracy, it is generally agreed that each person should be given one vote. As distinct from Plato's

[1] See p. 115.

[2] The cynic will agree that in the large-number case, the individual will not find it worthwhile to vote because a single vote will hardly make a difference to the outcome. Hence, why bother? Fortunately, many people do not take this view—either because they consider voting a civic duty, or because they are aware that their voting will set an example for others.

Republic, where decisions are made by the intellectual elite, the views of all citizens are to be given equal weight. Thus our mores combine a radically egalitarian standard of "one person, one vote" in politics with a nonegalitarian distribution of "dollar votes" in the economic sphere. But though the principle of uniform vote distribution is hardly debated, the specifics of voter eligibility are still in flux. Swiss women were allowed the right to vote for the Federal Assembly only recently, but some cantons still exclude them. Eighteen-year-olds are now eligible to vote in the United States, whereas previously they were not. In some countries extra voting rights are retained by special groups (e.g., British university representation up to 1948), and so forth.

Next, a particular voting rule must be chosen. The most commonly used rule is that of *simple majority.* Each individual has one vote, the yeas and nays are counted, and the simple majority wins. Where more than two alternatives are considered, they must be voted upon by successive elimination among surviving pairs. The United States Congress and other legislatures follow this rule of majority vote except in particular circumstances, such as a constitutional change or the overriding of a presidential veto or impeachment, where a *qualified majority* (usually two-thirds) is called for. Fiscal (tax and expenditure) decisions are generally made by simple majority vote.

Theoretically, many other voting systems may be designed. Under *plurality voting,* each voter ranks the issues in his order of preference. If there are ten issues, one point is assigned to the most, and ten to the least, desirable, and that issue wins which has received the lowest number of points. Or variants of this approach may be used, whereby the two top-ranking contenders in the first round are then rematched in a runoff, and so forth. The outcome is the same as under majority vote if there are only two issues, but it may well differ if more alternatives are involved.

Another possibility is a system of *point voting.* Here, the voter is given a number of points which he may allocate among the various alternatives as he wishes. Thus, he may give all points to his top choice, or distribute them among the alternatives as he desires. The alternative receiving the largest number of points wins. The result is the same as under the other systems if the choice is between two issues only, but it is likely to differ in a multi-issue case.

Majority Rule and the Median Voter

Under majority rule, the median voter will win. This is illustrated in Figure 5-1. Suppose that there are three levels of budget activity to choose from—high (A), medium (B), and low (C). To simplify exposition, assume that there are three voters only, X, Y, and Z, the same reasoning being applicable to the large-number case.[3] Finally, we assume that the cost will be spread equally among them.

Suppose, further, that X is a large-budget man who prefers A to B to C; Y is a small-budget man who prefers C to B to A; and Z is a moderate-budget man who prefers B to C to A. This pattern is plotted as Case I in Figure 5-1,

[3] In spirit, this analysis deals with the large-number setting, although negotiation would be superior to majority rule in the three-number case.

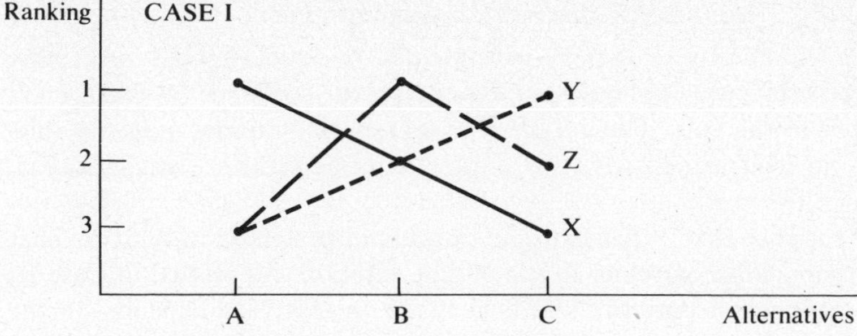

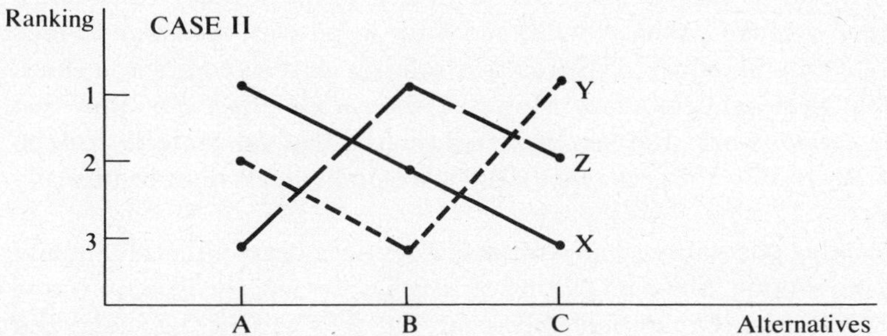

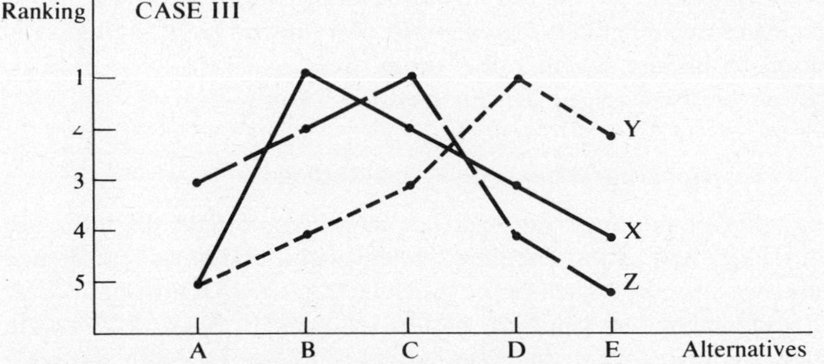

FIGURE 5-1 Preference Patterns and Majority Rule.
(Voters X, Y, and Z; Alternatives A, B, C, D, and E)

where 1 is the highest and 3 the lowest rank. Since more than two issues are involved, successive pairs must be voted upon. Beginning with A versus B, we find that B wins; and matching B with C, B is again the winner. The same holds if we begin with A versus C followed by C versus B, or with C versus B, followed by B versus A. In all instances B will win. As shown in the figure, all preferences, if plotted, show a single-peaked pattern, and the sequence of pairing does not matter. Voter Z, who prefers the median alternative and who is referred to as the "median voter," wins. This simple voting model is the one typically used in designing models of fiscal decision making.[4]

[4] See p. 107.

Nonarbitrariness: (1) Voting Paradox

In considering the quality of various voting rules, one requirement is that the outcome not be arbitrary. It should not depend on the sequence in which pairs of issues are put to the vote. This problem arises especially under majority rule. As just noted, no arbitrariness results if all preference patterns are single-peaked, as in Case I.

But now suppose that Y has extreme tastes, and prefers C to A to B. That is to say, he prefers both extremes to the middle solution. As plotted in Case II, his is a multiple-peaked pattern. The final result in this case depends on the sequence in which the issues are paired. Beginning with A versus B, we find that B wins over A, and in turn C wins over B; thus C is the winner. However, if we begin with B versus C, then A wins; and if we begin with A versus C, then B wins. This "voting paradox," explored by Professor Arrow, comes as a shock to one's faith in electoral democracy. However, the paradox does *not* imply that majority rule *cannot* work. Rather, the conclusion is that for majority rule to give nonarbitrary results, the preference structure of individuals must be typically single-peaked.[5]

Moreover, this possibility of arbitrariness does not occur in the situation of plurality or point voting. Since no pairing of issues is needed, the issue of voting sequence does not arise. Draws may still occur, but they narrow the choice and may be resolved by runoffs among the highest-ranking alternatives. But, as we shall see later, there are other disadvantages to plurality or point voting. It is useful, therefore, to inquire whether the voting paradox is likely to arise in majority decisions on fiscal issues. To this question we now turn.

Nonarbitrariness: (2) Fiscal Choices

The voting paradox of majority rule will not arise if preference patterns are single-peaked, i.e., if there is an absence of voters with "extremist" preference patterns. Preference structures such as those depicted in Case II must not occur. Single-peaked preferences may follow the pattern exhibited by X, Y, or Z in Case I, or all preferences may follow the cone patterns of Case III, with the peak reached at different points in the scale, and with the win going to the median peak. The question then is whether fiscal choices will tend to be of this single-peaked type.

Variable Size of Budget The answer depends on the type of choice under consideration. As the simplest case, suppose that the budget contains only one type of public expenditure, that successive units are provided at constant cost

[5] See Kenneth J. Arrow, *Social Choice and Individual Values,* New York: Wiley, 1951, where it is more generally argued that it is impossible to devise a social ordering which meets certain requirements of consistency. Among them Arrow includes the requirement that the outcome not be affected by the dropping out of a nonwinning alternative. This requirement is not met by plurality or point voting, but its validity for fiscal choices (as distinct from scoring athletic contests) is not evident. See also J. M. Buchanan and G. Tullock, *The Calculus of Consent,* Ann Arbor: The University of Michigan Press, 1962, pp. 323–340.

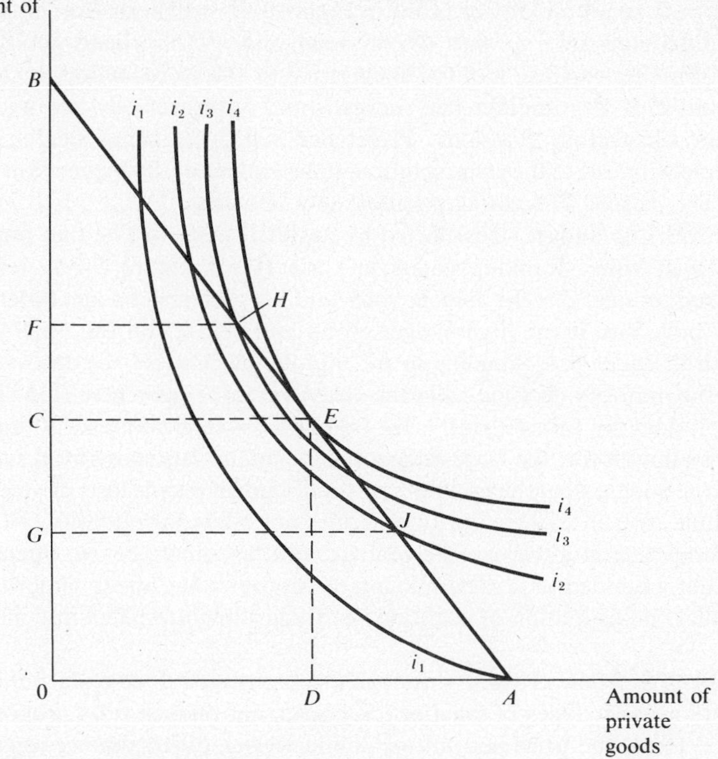

FIGURE 5-2 Choice of Private and Social Goods.

for the group,[6] and that the cost is to be spread equally among all. With three consumers, each bears a "head tax" equal to one-third of total cost. The problem is only to determine the desired amount.

In this situation, there is good reason to expect that preferences will be single-peaked and of the Case III variety. Provided the public good is useful to the consumer, he will prefer some budget size to both larger and smaller sizes. The principle is the same as with private goods. If apples cost 25 cents a pound, the consumer will choose to purchase a given number, say 5 pounds rather than 4 or 6.

This is shown in Figure 5-2, where private goods are measured on the horizontal axis and social goods on the vertical axis. Suppose that a certain consumer's intake of private goods in the absence of social goods equals *OA*. He is thus located at *A* on indifference curve i_1. Now the choice of a social good is offered, and the tax price charged to him is shown by the price line *AB,* the price ratio of social to private goods available to him being *OA/OB.* His preferred

[6] The following reasoning remains unchanged if we assume that conditions of increasing cost prevail. Preference patterns will then peak at a smaller budget, but they will still be single-peaked.

point—the peak of his ranking schedule in Figure 5-1—will be at *E* on his highest feasible indifference curve i_4, with *OC* of social, and *OD* of private, goods being consumed. Further expansion of the budget size to *OF*, or reduction to *OG*, will place him at *H* or *J* on indifference curves i_3 and i_2 respectively and will leave him in less satisfactory positions. Preference schedules being single-peaked, majority rule will lead to the same solution, independent of the sequence in which the issues are paired. The voting paradox does not arise.

Moreover, the budget size selected by majority vote will be that preferred by the median voter. Ranking voters in Case III of Figure 5-1 in terms of preferred budget size, Z is the median voter and his preferred budget (alternative C) wins. Above him is the high-budget group and below him the small-budget group, both of equal size. Standing in the middle, he can cast the decisive vote. Although the majority decision will thus please voters at the center of the preference scale, it does not follow that it is the best or most efficient choice. If intensity of feeling is allowed for, the large-budget people might gain more from substitution of a large budget than the middle- and small-budget people lose, or vice versa. In this simple case at least, majority rule does not allow for intensity of feeling, and this restriction is a major disadvantage. But, as shown below, intensity of feeling is not excluded as a determinant of the outcome under majority rule provided that the formation of coalitions and logrolling are taken into account.

Variable Tax Price How is this conclusion changed if we replace the head tax by more realistic types of taxation? Suppose that finance is by proportional income tax. Here, the price per unit of public service differs among consumers with different incomes. As the budget expands, the tax rate goes up, but the unit price of the public service to any one taxpayer remains unchanged.[7] The conclusion, therefore, is the same as under the head tax of the previous section.

If the income tax is progressive, the answer depends on how rates are increased as the budget expands. If all liabilities are raised by the same percent (i.e., all bracket rates go up by the same percentage), the price per unit of public service again remains unchanged for the individual taxpayer. The earlier conclusion still holds. But suppose that bracket rates are raised by equal percentage points. This increase will make the rate structure less progressive. The share contributed by people with lower incomes will rise. A 10 percent increase in the budget or quantity of public services will raise their taxes by more than 10 percent, and they will now have to pay a higher price per unit of public service. The reverse will apply to people with high incomes. For low-income people, preferences among budget sizes will remain single-peaked, although the peak will be at a smaller budget. High-income people will prefer a larger budget, but the impact on their preference structure is more complex.

More important, no general conclusion can be drawn if the change in tax shares changes directions as the budget expands. For instance, a rising budget may first raise and then lower the share of high-income taxpayers. As a result, they find that their unit cost for public services is highest for a medium-sized

[7] As before, we assume that the service is produced under constant cost.

budget. Consequently, a V-shaped or multiple-preference pattern may emerge similar to that of Y in Case II, thereby introducing the voting paradox and rendering majority rule arbitrary.

Variable Expenditure Mix While the level of expenditures on identical parks may be ranked numerically, the choice between types of parks, or between parks and fire protection, is a different matter. If we think of projects A to C in Figure 5-1 as a lineup among alternative outlays of a given amount on parks (A), fire protection (B), and roads (C), no presumption for single-peakedness can be derived from the preference function of the individual consumer. There is no obvious ordering (such as holds for the case of budget size), and all depends on how the choices are lined up. Only if tastes among consumers are highly homogeneous will there be an ordering for which all preference rankings are single-peaked.

In all, the nature of fiscal choices—especially choices among various budget mixes—is not such that single-peaked preferences may be readily assumed to exist. However, the contingency of arbitrariness may be reduced by combining issues which, as a bundle, permit decisions to be reached, even though this may not be possible over single issues. As we shall see presently, it is the function of the politician to identify and present such bundles or political programs.

Representativeness of Outcome

Even if we assume that majority rule can be made to work without arbitrary results, it still remains necessary to evaluate the "quality" of the outcome under the various voting rules. By this we mean how close the resulting solution, including the mix of goods provided for and the assignment of costs, comes to reflecting the actual preferences of the voters. We have noted before that decision by vote is not an ideal solution, since mandatory application of the outcome will leave some voters dissatisfied. Voters whose preferences diverge from that of the group may be left either with better terms than they would have been willing to accept or with worse terms. In the latter case, they must submit to a consumption pattern (mix of private and social goods) which is not to their liking. Nevertheless, not all solutions will be equally defective in these respects, and various voting rules must be compared from this point of view.

The obvious way to protect the minority, of course, would be to substitute the requirement of unanimous consent for majority rule. If only those expenditure-tax propositions are undertaken which command unanimous consent, no individual will be forced to accept projects which he or she does not value. But unanimity is not a realistic option, because the granting of a universal veto would tend to block provision for public goods entirely.[8] It is unlikely that any of the proposed expenditure-tax packages would receive unanimous consent, the more so as it is not feasible to consider an infinite number of combinations. A voting rule (be it majority, plurality, or point voting) with mandatory enforcement of

[8] Knut Wicksell [see excerpts in R. A. Musgrave and A. Peacock (eds.), *Classics in the Theory of Public Finance,* New York: Macmillan, 1958] therefore speaks of "approximate unanimity" or "qualified majority."

the outcome is needed to induce the revealing of preferences; and if some are hurt or benefit less while others benefit more in the process, this fact is a disadvantage which must be accepted and which follows from the nature of social goods, especially in the large-number case. The more closely bunched are the peaks of the individual preference patterns, the closer will the result approximate a unanimous vote, and the less will be the disadvantage which the minority must suffer.

In comparing the quality of the various voting rules, let us assume first that each voter records his or her true preferences, without regard for the attitude of others. In other words, let us suppose that no "voting strategy"—a concept to which we shall return presently—is applied. In this case, it is readily seen that point voting is the best approach, followed by plurality and majority voting in that order. Under majority rule, voters (in the absence of coalitions and logrolling) can only express their rankings between pairs of issues as they come up; they cannot give expression to their strengths of preference, nor can they relate issues appearing in different pairs. Under the plurality rule, they can relate all issues to one another, but this relation can again be expressed in terms of ranking only. Alternative B may be ranked first, A second, and C third, but the difference between B and A may be large while that between A and C is small, or vice versa.

Intensity of preferences is directly allowed for only under point voting.[9] In the extreme case, a voter may give all his points to B and none to A or C. Suppose, for instance, that each voter is allotted 10 points and that within the rankings of Case I above, the distribution of points is as follows:

	VOTER X		VOTER Y		VOTER Z	
Choice	*Rank*	*Points*	*Rank*	*Points*	*Rank*	*Points*
A	1	5	3	1	3	1
B	2	3	2	3	1	5
C	3	2	1	6	2	4

The majority rule would let B win. Under plurality, where the rankings are added, B receives the low score and is again the winner. Under point voting, the highest and winning score goes to C. This makes a prima facie case for some form of point voting.

Role of Strategy

Such is true, provided that voting strategy is not used. But in the real world, voting strategy *is* important. Because of this, B and C may not be the winners. Voters (like speculators in the stock market) will take into account how others will vote, and will not throw away their votes on issues which cannot win, even though they prefer them. They may rather settle for their second choice, so as to avoid ending up with the third. Voter X may thus overstate her preference for A, giving it all 10 points, thereby making A, which she prefers to C, the winner

[9] This conclusion will be amplified in the following discussion of coalitions.

under point voting. Others may use similar strategies, and the outcome then comes to depend on political skills.

Attempts to deal with these problems in an analytical way have not been very successful, and the outcome is hard to predict.[10] What matters here is that the scope for strategy differs with the various voting rules. While the outcome depends on the particular preference structure, this dilemma results: The better the rule in the absence of strategy (i.e., the more sensitive the voting rule to intensities of preference), the greater tends to be the scope which it leaves for the use of strategy. Thus, a compromise must be drawn between these various aspects, and in the end a cruder system less open to manipulation, such as majority voting, may be the better choice.

B. THE THEORY OF REPRESENTATIVE DEMOCRACY

Our discussion must now be made more realistic by discarding the assumption that individual voters participate directly in the decision process. While the degree of direct participation differs among countries, it is only at the local level that fiscal decisions are made in referendum style. Rather, they are delegated to congressmen, senators, or other legislative representatives who seek election as nominees of political parties. How does this affect the decision-making process, and to what extent will the preferences of individual voters be reflected in the final decisions?

One explanation, which is of particular interest to the economist, draws an analogy between the firm's competition for consumers in the market and the politician's competition for voters in the political arena. Just as economic competition, under certain assumptions, guides producers to supply in line with preferences of consumers, so does political competition under certain assumptions guide representatives to act in line with the interests of the voters.

Vote Maximization

This model, as sketched by the famous economist Joseph Schumpeter and developed in detail by Anthony Downs, offers an intriguing interpretation of the democratic process.[11] In analogy to the economist's precept of "homo economicus," it is assumed that political action is rational, with both politicians and voters acting in their self-interest. The politician's objective is to maximize votes so as to stay in power. The voter's objective is to maximize the net benefits which he derives from the fiscal operation, i.e., the excess of benefits derived from government expenditures over his tax costs. Voters will thus cast their votes for those who will best represent their interests, and politicians will offer programs and support legislation which best meet the interests of their constituents. Those

[10] The basic work in this area remains J. von Neumann and O. Morgenstern, *The Theory of Games and Economic Behavior,* Princeton, N.J.: Princeton, 1944.

[11] Joseph A. Schumpeter, *Capitalism, Socialism and Democracy,* New York: Harper, 1950, p. 282; and Anthony Downs, *An Economic Theory of Democracy,* New York: Harper & Row, 1956 (see especially chaps. 4, 10).

politicians who come closest to so doing will receive most votes and hence gain or retain political power.

Political Change

If this were the nature of the political process, why would there be more than one party, or one political program? If there is *a* most desired combination of positions on various issues, why is not this combination discovered and supported by all politicians, so that only one program is offered? A number of reasons may be offered to explain why competing parties arise and why governments may change in successive elections.

1. The party in power, even though it offers the winning program, may not do a good job in implementing it. Sooner or later, corruption and inefficiency set in and eventually they become apparent. The voting public then decides "to throw the rascals out" and to place their confidence in a new team. This, apart from policy differences, is a basic reason why more than one party is needed. It is also the rationale for the traditional view of the two-party system in the United States, in which both parties are needed even though they represent more or less similar cross-sections without deep ideological or program differences.

2. Preference patterns may be such that there is no single winning solution. The voting paradox may apply. The incumbent party may then lose to an opposition because of a changing sequence in the pairing of issues which come to the forefront. The position is an inherently unstable one.

3. Politicians do not operate in a world of certainty, where voter preferences are known and getting voter support is only a matter of designing the proper program. The issues involved are highly complex, and even though governments tend to make only marginal changes in budget plans, there are many possible combinations. One party may guess better than another.

4. Uncertainty is the greater since voter preferences may change. The winning program this year may be the losing one next year. The political reward thus goes to the most skillful politician, just as the financial reward goes to the most skillful entrepreneur. Parties rise and fall, depending on the astuteness of their leadership.

5. The politician's skill, finally, is directed not only at responding to the voter preferences but also at generating new preferences which he believes desirable. Voter support is gained not only by response to existing preferences but also by creation of new preference patterns and loyal adherence thereto. Political leadership introduces a dynamic element into party structures, thus making for further change.

For these and other reasons, competition for votes does not lead to a single position, and continuous change may result. At the same time, there is a tendency toward maintaining the status quo—e.g., keeping old expenditure programs unchanged and tax rates where they are—and a substantial change in preferences of leadership may be needed to introduce new policies.

Platforms and Coalitions

Successful political leadership must take a position on combinations of issues so as to obtain a program which is acceptable to a majority. Issues are not considered

TABLE 5-1
Preferences and Party Platforms

	CASE I			CASE II		
	VOTER			VOTER		
	X	*Y*	*Z*	*X*	*Y*	*Z*
Issue 1						
Option A	1	51	60	1	51	60
Option B	99	49	40	99	49	40
Issue 2						
Option C	51	52	45	51	52	20
Option D	49	48	55	49	48	80
Combinations						
Winners: A and C	52	103	105	52	103	80
Losers: B and D	148	97	95	148	97	120
Preferred	B, D	A, C	A, C	B, D	A, C	B, D

in isolation, but are typically combined in packages or party platforms. Coalitions are formed which combine voters with congenial views on a set of issues. Policies which would lose if considered separately may win if considered in combination.

In forming winning coalitions, intensity of preferences come to be accounted for, even though a majority rule applies. This is illustrated in Table 5-1. We assume that there are three voters and two issues presented as pairs of options. Issue 1 offers a choice between options A and B, while issue 2 offers a choice between options C and D. Decision is by majority vote, but to indicate the strength of consumer preferences, numbers are used to serve as an index of the relative value which the voter attributes to various options.[12] For issue 1, X considers option B 99 times as valuable as option A; for issue 2, he considers option C slightly more desirable than D; and so forth.

Beginning with the preferences as recorded in Case I, suppose that a majority-vote choice is to be made with regard to issue 1. It follows from the assigned numbers that both Y and Z prefer A, which therefore wins. When voters turn to issue 2, option C emerges as the winner, with X and Y joining in the majority. This much can be concluded without recording the intensity of preferences—namely, that two out of three voters rank A ahead of B and C ahead of D. But now let us consider a vote between combinations of issues. For instance, let the winners (A and C) be combined into one platform and the losers (B and D) into another.[13] Combining the numbers assigned to the two options in each platform, we find that X prefers the B-D combination while Y and Z prefer A-C. The A-C combination thus wins as a platform, just as A and C won in the separate votes.

[12] In the illustration, the voter is given 100 points to allocate between A and B, and 100 points between C and D. The choice of 100 is arbitrary, as we are concerned with relative weights only. Moreover, the results would be the same if different point totals were given to different voters. The argument implies no interpersonal ranking or utility comparison between voters.

[13] The problem differs if combinations of A with D and B with C are also considered, but given the points assigned in Case I, the A-C combination still wins over the A-D and B-C combinations.

The result seems as one might expect, but, as shown in Case II, the outcome might easily be reversed. Case II differs from Case I in that voter Z has a much stronger preference for option D over option C than in Case I, assigning 80 percent of his points to D. We again find that A wins over B in issue 1 and C wins over D in issue 2 if the issues are considered separately. But now we find that the B-D combination is preferred by both X and Z and beats the A-C combination. The winning platform combines options which would lose if considered separately. This result comes about because, in Case II, the minority voter Z feels more strongly about his position on issue 2 than in Case I. Strength of preferences thus matters even under majority voting, if the voting is on platforms rather than on isolated pairs of issues.

The successful politician (or statesman) is thus one who can find winning combinations, and for this he must consider the intensity of preferences. As voters' preferences change, he must keep abreast of such changes and spot the development of new groupings which make for potential winners. It is this ability which, at the political level, may be compared with the sense for profit possibilities which guides the successful entrepreneur in the economic sphere.[14] But here, as in the economic sphere, we shall find situations where such maximizing behavior does not lead to a solution which is in line with the public interest.[15]

Logrolling

The same example also serves to illustrate the role of "logrolling." Returning to Case II, the winners, in the absence of communication between voters, will be option A in issue 1 and option C in issue 2. X will be displeased with the first outcome; Y will be pleased with both; while Z will be satisfied with issue 1 but not with issue 2. Suppose now that the voters know one another's preferences. X will then suggest to Z that he is prepared to vote for D on issue 2 if Z will vote for B on issue 1. This will involve a net gain for both X and Z and the bargain will be made. Y loses as a result, but for the values shown in Case II, the gain obtained by X and Z exceeds Y's loss. The outcome is the same as that achieved previously by the winning platform. As in that case, intensity of feeling comes to be allowed for and results in a more efficient choice.[16]

This illustration, of course, oversimplifies matters but it shows that logrolling in the sense of vote trading on issues is a constructive factor in decision making, to be distinguished from the shady practice of "pork-barrel" deals, which suggests a disregard of the voter interest.

[14] More specific models may be developed by stipulating further rules of the game, e.g., that the incumbent party offers a set of majority options, while the opposition counters with a minority coalition, and so forth. In this way, Downs (op. cit., chap. 4) develops a dynamic theory of government change.

[15] See p. 116.

[16] This, however, is not a necessary result. The loss on Y's part may outweigh the gains of X and Z. Only if logrolling could operate through side payments among voters would the efficient outcome be assured by unanimous vote. This being impossible with large numbers, the outcome of majority voting has to be used. Chances are that the quality of the result can be improved by coalitions and logrolling.

Range of Issues

The linking of positions on a variety of issues, far from being disreputable, is thus an essential and useful part of the political process. Moreover, those issues entering the combination need not be confined to the fiscal sphere. The winning combination may encompass fiscal issues, such as highway construction or income tax rates, along with other issues, such as school prayers and busing. The fact that some of these issues are fiscal while others are not does not exclude the possibility that they may be related systematically within preference patterns. Thus, progressive taxation, restriction of billboards, and abolition of the death penalty might be joined in a platform, even though they are technically unrelated issues. Through this linkage of preferences, fiscal decisions are related to public policy determination at large. Thereby the complexity of the problem is increased, but so also is the scope for choosing combinations of issues on which determinate decisions, and decisions commanding a substantial majority, can be reached.

Delegations and Numbers

Throughout this discussion, we have considered the problem in two settings: (1) the small-number case where negotiation can occur, and (2) the large-number case where a political process is needed. Viewing the large-number case in referendum terms, the difference from the small-number setting is clear-cut. But once the electoral process is introduced, final decisions are delegated to a relatively small number of representatives, so that the final decisions are made in the small-number setting.

This means that both levels of analysis are involved. That final decisions are made in a small-number setting does not obviate consideration of the process by which the delegates are elected, i.e., the process by which the preferences of the large number of voters make themselves felt. At the same time, the "bargaining process" of the small-number case applies at the level of the legislature, with the bargaining of each representative being constrained, more or less narrowly, by the preferences of his large number of constituents.

Qualifications

The preceding model of the political process, like the economic model of markets, has its merits, but also its shortcomings. In either case, optimal results will be achieved only under certain assumptions.

For the market, these involve (1) a "proper" distribution of income, (2) the presence of competition, and (3) the absence of externalities. For the political process, the requirement of proper distribution is now seen in terms of votes, and though we have seen that the principle of equal voting power is accepted, marginal questions, such as voting age and literacy requirements, remain open. Also, the availability of registration and voting facilities may affect people's ability to exercise their voting rights.

The assumption of a competitive political system, involving many independent politicians (representatives) vying for the voter's favor, is once more unrealistic. Representatives operate within the framework of parties and are subject to party discipline. Such discipline is relatively mild in the United States, more severe in Canada and the United Kingdom, and quite strict in most continental systems. Given this situation, representatives may be unable to reflect the preferences of their constituents, or it may even be difficult for unrepresented groups to gain representation.

In the absence of proportional representation or central candidates to whom splinter votes are credited, an absolute majority must be obtained within the election district, a difficult task for new or minority groups. In some cases, the rise of minority parties is complicated further by a minimum requirement being set (for instance, in the West German Constitution) in terms of total votes on a nationwide basis. This aids political stability, but also interferes with popular representation.

Moreover, political campaigning is costly, both in obtaining information about voter preferences and in seeking voter support for particular positions or platforms. Campaign expenditures in presidential year 1972 ran around $300 million. The politician must therefore obtain financial support and, in so doing, is likely to accept constraints on particular issues. Voters, in turn, may not be given the option to vote for representatives who will reflect their position, or (to put it in less extreme form) representatives with financially supported positions may be able to launch stronger campaigns. The incumbent, for obvious reasons, disposes over resources which put him at an advantage relative to the opposition, and so forth.

Finally, it can hardly be assumed that political competition is always a rational process. Lack of information about the true cost of alternative programs or the incidence of the cost among individuals is a case in point. Media bias may stand in the way of correct information and the "charismatic personality" of candidates may persuade by emotional appeal. For these reasons, it would be surprising indeed if decisions by representatives were fully to reflect the considered preferences of the voters.

The perfection of the democratic process, like everything else in life, is a matter of degree. Its merits must be judged by comparison with the available alternatives. It will work the better, the more open and competitive the political process is, and the more homogeneous are the preference patterns of the voters. By the same token, the system may collapse or become a facade for dictatorial rule where the political process is not open and where deep-rooted cleavages prevail.

C. POLITICAL BIAS AND THE SIZE OF THE PUBLIC SECTOR

Given the imperfections and difficulties of the process by which individual preferences are translated into political decisions, there is every reason to expect that the final outcome will only approximate these preferences and that sizable distortions of one type or another will occur. Various writers have gone further and argued that there will be a systematic bias leading to underexpansion or overexpansion of the public sector.

The Underexpansion Hypothesis

The major arguments behind the underexpansion hypothesis are these:

1. A. C. Pigou, in his treatise *The Economics of Welfare,* argued that the market results in an undersupply of goods where marginal social benefits exceed marginal private benefits.[17] This is the case because the individual equates costs with private benefits, and thus fails to account for that part of total benefits which is external and accrues to others. By the same token, goods for which social cost exceeds private costs are oversupplied. This conclusion holds if there is no negotiation between the parties concerned. But individuals *can* negotiate with one another and the condition of undersupply or oversupply may be corrected if numbers are small.[18] However, the process of negotiation involves effort, so undersupply or oversupply will tend to be corrected only where it is substantial. More important, the negotiation process breaks down where a large number of consumers are included. A voting system, with compulsory application of the winning policy, is needed if social goods are to be provided for at all. Without such a mechanism, there is gross undersupply. Yet, the question remains whether the voting rule itself leads to an inadequate or excessive provision.

2. J. Kenneth Galbraith holds that the political process leaves a deficiency in the provision for social goods because the consumer-voter is subject to intensive advertising pressure from the producers of private goods, without corresponding praise for the attractions of social goods.[19] Thus, the voters' choices are distorted away from their true preference patterns. The question is whether the producers (if not the consumers) of social goods are not also capable of making themselves heard. Such is clearly the case with defense industries, highway lobbies, or (we are forced to add) teachers' associations. More of such pressures may develop in the future, especially for programs involving hardware purchases from the private sector. Moreover, social goods (such as highways or recreation facilities) are frequently complementary to private goods (cars or motorboats), and advertising for the one will also generate demand for the other.

Furthermore, a distinction must be drawn between the proposition that fewer social goods are provided than should be (given the public's true preferences in the matter) and the contention that voters have poor taste (as judged by the social critic's standards) in opting for too small a public sector. The remedy, in this case, is to improve information rather than to offset imperfections in the mechanism by which preferences are recorded.

3. Advertising aside, the individual may be biased toward expenditures on private goods because they involve a more visible link between his outlay and the benefits accruing to him. Tax legislation is not looked upon favorably because the linkage to expenditure legislation is not clearly in view. Moreover, the individual has greater flexibility in making expenditures on private goods, since individual action can be taken and one need not wait for budgetary or other group decisions.

[17] A. C. Pigou, *The Economics of Welfare,* 4th ed., London: Macmillan, 1932, chap. 9.

[18] See p. 61.

[19] See John Kenneth Galbraith, *The Affluent Society,* Boston: Houghton Mifflin, 1958, p. 261.

The Overexpansion Hypothesis

Others have argued that the system has a built-in tendency to overexpansion:

1. James M. Buchanan and Gordon Tullock hold that majority vote tends to produce an oversupply of public services.[20] Noting that public services usually benefit particular subgroups while tax costs are borne by all members of the group, they present the following argument: Any one voter will join in coalition with a majority of voters (say 51 out of 100) to gain support for their particular interests (e.g., an access road from *their* properties to a throughway). The marginal cost to the 51, however, will be only 51 percent of the total cost, since the 49 percent borne by the others (who have no interest in this road) is disregarded. Thus oversupply results because part of the cost is imposed on nonbeneficiaries. Given the provision of jointly-financed services which benefit particular groups only, this conclusion follows, but it does not apply where public services benefit all members of the contributing group, nor does it hold for differential tax burdens in line with the distribution of benefits.

2. The voter may favor expenditure legislation without being fully aware that an opportunity cost is involved, or he may assume that the cost will be borne by someone else. This will be the tendency particularly if taxes are invisible. Thus, an increase in income tax is felt more directly and therefore meets more opposition than does an increase in indirect taxes. Among the latter, in turn, retail sales taxes, which appear on the sales slip, are more visible than taxes which are added to cost at earlier stages of production. The less visible the taxes, the more likely it is that expenditures will be considered costless and therefore will tend to be overexpanded.

3. Just as failure to link expenditure benefits with tax legislation may impose undue restraint, so may the failure to link costs with expenditure legislation induce undue expansion. In periods when marginal expenditures are subject to deficit financing, the bias is apt to be in the direction of overexpansion, as additional projects appear costless to the voter. In periods of surplus finance, public services seem more costly than they are, and voters will be led to be too restrictive. These tendencies once more point to the distortions which arise if fiscal policy issues are not separated.[21]

4. Redistributional objectives may be related to the level of public services. The use of direct tax transfers for income redistribution purposes may be politically unacceptable, whereas progressive tax finance of generally shared public services is acceptable. As noted before, this has been a major factor making for a rising ratio of public expenditures to GNP up to World War II, but may have come to be a retarding factor since then.[22]

Conclusion

Combining these considerations, it is difficult to strike a balance among them. More likely than not, the public receives about the level of public services which

[20] See James M. Buchanan and Gordon Tullock, *The Calculus of Consent,* Ann Arbor: The University of Michigan Press, 1962, chap. 10.

[21] See p. 17.

[22] See p. 17.

it desires, and those who find this level deficient or excessive reflect departures from majority preferences rather than proof that the political process is itself grossly inadequate in giving expression to these preferences.

D. INTEREST GROUPS AND GROUP INTEREST

The preceding discussion views the democratic process as a mechanism by which individual preferences are translated into group decisions. There may be flaws in this process, but this is nevertheless taken to be its function. Brief consideration may now be given to alternative interpretations. Some of them constitute a modification only, while others differ more basically.

The Marxist View

In Marxist thinking, the state (prior to the revolution) is to be seen as an instrument by which the ruling (capitalist) class exploits the subjugated (working) class. Actions of the state must be interpreted as part of the class struggle, which transcends the political as well as the individual sphere of social relations.

While Marx himself had little to say on fiscal matters,[23] a historical view, as sketched by Goldscheid, throws an interesting perspective on the sociology of the fiscal process.[24] In the Middle Ages, the feudal lord extracted payments in cash or kind from his serfs to sustain his rule and the military establishment needed to maintain or improve his position. Thus it was in the interests of the ruling class to have as strong a state and as rich a state treasury as possible. With the rise of democratic government, the ruling class lost its tight control over the state, and power went increasingly to popular majorities who shifted the costs of maintaining the state to the hitherto ruling class. As a result, the ruling class changed its view of the state. Its interests were now served better by a weak state, and it thus came to favor small budgets, low taxes, and general noninterference with the private sector. A later view of "state capitalism" would modify this picture by introducing a dependence of the state on "monopoly industry" which may once more increase the public sector, especially as defense industries press for ever-rising military budgets.

This view of fiscal politics has its merits. If the social process is seen in terms of class struggle, tax and expenditure decisions will be a major instrument thereof. But, by the same token, the role of budgetary activity may change from a means of exploitation to a tool of social accommodation, once a less divisive view of society is taken. Budget policy then becomes an instrument of gradual reform

[23] However, two references may be noted. A call for steeply progressive taxation is found in the *Communist Manifesto.* (See *A Handbook of Marxism,* New York: International Publishers, 1935, p. 46.) Progressive taxation is not viewed as a device to redistribute income or as a means to expropriate the ruling class (or partly to do so) through majority action. Rather, the manifesto (like conservative business groups) views progressive taxation as a means of hastening the breakdown of the capitalist system. Contrary to this expectation, progressive taxation has in fact acted as a major safety valve and protection for that system.

A second reference to fiscal matters is contained in the discussion of the earlier stages of socialism where Marx suggests that the share of social goods in total output will rise. See footnote 6, p. 88.

[24] See Rudolf Goldscheid, "A Sociological Approach to Public Finance," translated from the German, 1925, in Richard A. Musgrave and Alan Peacock (eds.), *Classics in the Theory of Public Finance,* New York: Macmillan, 1958.

and cooperation. Looking back at the history of the last century, there can be little doubt that fiscal action played a key role in this growth of social cohesion. Indeed, the modern welfare state, with its emphasis on transfers and (theoretically at least) progressive taxation, places the public budget at the hub of the social system.

Interest Groups

If the fiscal process as an instrument of class struggle is too partial a view, fiscal decisions are nevertheless a means by which group interests are expressed. On the expenditure side, such pressures are generated by both consumers and producers of public services. Among consumer groups, automobile associations support highway construction, tenants favor low-cost public housing, parents press for larger school budgets, campers advocate public parks, welfare organizations call for higher benefits, and so forth. Among producer organizations, the weapons industry favors military outlays, the building lobby advocates housing programs, the construction and trucking lobbies press for highways, the electronics industry supports space exploration, educators' associations demand more teachers and higher pay, and so forth. Various groups maintain lobbies to exert these pressures and to advocate the particular interests which they represent.

While the term "special interest groups" has a somewhat evil flavor, the groups themselves may (like logrolling) serve to promote more efficient resource use by pointing out the benefits to be derived from various public services. But they may also distort decisions by giving exaggerated weight to particular items or by influencing legislative decisions through campaign support or more or less legitimate bribes.

A similar picture may be drawn with respect to taxation. Various taxpayer groups organize to represent their interests, and the congressional tax committees, as previously noted,[25] are under great pressure from such groups, whether it be the oil industry arguing for depletion allowances, the real estate lobby wanting faster depreciation, governors advocating exemption of interest, or university representatives calling for deductibility of tuition payments or unlimited deductibility of contributions. Where it is their objective to see that their own group is not overtaxed relative to others, such groups will contribute to the construction of a more equitable tax system. But if they seek, and succeed in securing, undertaxation for themselves, the opposite holds. The whole problem of "horizontal equity" and "loopholes" in the income tax base falls under this heading and will be considered in Chapter 11.

In all, a realistic view of the fiscal system cannot deny the important role of interest groups. The political structure does not consist merely of individual voters and their representatives structured in political parties; as a further element, other groupings are at work which attempt to influence voters and their representatives and thus exert an important influence on political behavior. Indeed, John R. Commons and his school have argued that such groups are more representative of the interests of their members than territorially selected dele-

[25] See p. 43.

gates and that, in fact, it would be better to have a parliament which is selected by representatives of such groups.[26] The same view is found in the theory of the corporate state and is rooted in the social philosophy of the Roman Catholic Church.[27]

While interest groups are here to stay and their influence in the political arena will continue, their role depends on the extent to which they provide for a balanced representation. Group interests are not represented with equal effectiveness in all cases, and the automatic development of a neatly balanced structure of countervailing powers cannot be relied upon. This imbalance is not only a matter of lethargy on the one side or of diabolical purpose on the other. For collective action to be undertaken, the individual must be assured that others will participate, since otherwise his action is not worthwhile; and mutual support can be developed more readily in some groups than in others.[28] Thus, effective organization of individuals into consumer and taxpayer groups is more difficult than is the organization of industry or union interests. To secure better balance in representation, public policy should assist consumer and taxpayer groups in attaining effective representation.

The Community Interest

According to the preceding views, social action reflects the interests of particular individuals or of subgroups of individuals with similar interests. The economic system is designed to maximize individual satisfactions. Although this maximization can largely be achieved through the market, a political process is needed when it comes to the provision of social goods and allowance for externalities. It is needed for distributional adjustments and stabilization. But, though group action through the political process is required in providing for social goods, this fact does not deny that this provision aims at the satisfaction of individually based preferences.

Consider now an alternative view of society as a group of individuals who cooperate to advance common goals rather than compete to achieve individual ends. Individual interests either coincide with group interests, or the latter are given priority where a conflict arises. This harmonious view of society may be found in many of the utopias which have adorned social philosophy from the Middle Ages to date, whether their sponsors be of religious persuasion (such as Thomas More) or of a secular school (such as Robert Owen).[29] This tradition continues among current writers of the New Left, and its implications for fiscal theory should be noted.[30]

[26] See John R. Commons, *Economics of Collective Action,* New York: Macmillan, 1940; and the discussion of group action in Mancur Olson, Jr., *The Logic of Collective Action,* Cambridge, Mass.: Harvard, 1965, especially chap. 5.

[27] Such views, going back to scholastic philosophers such as Thomas Aquinas, were developed in the encyclical *Rerum Novarum,* issued by Pope Leo XIII, May 15, 1891.

[28] See Olson, op. cit., chap. 1.

[29] See Sir Thomas More, *Utopia,* London: A. Vele, 1551; and Robert Owen, *A New View of Society,* London: 1817. For a general discussion of utopias, see Frank E. Manuel, *Utopias and Utopian Thought,* Boston: Houghton Mifflin, 1966.

[30] For a recent attempt at a systematic exposition of neo-Marxist thought, see Ernest Mandel, *Marxist Economic Theory,* New York: Monthly Review Press, 1968.

Consider first the proposition that there exists a community interest as such, an interest which is attributable to the community as a whole and which does not involve a "mere" addition of individual interests. To put it differently, the community is said to experience collective wants, wants which are generated by and pertain to the welfare of the group as a whole.[31] The concept of community interest thus defined can no longer be identified with the provision of social goods or the internalizing of externalities. Collective wants, if the concept is to be taken seriously, would exist also in a setting where all goods are nonrival in consumption, as this term has been used in the preceding chapter. The concept of collective wants thus comes close to that of merit goods in their unadulterated form. The basic question which must then be answered is, to whom is *the* true community interest revealed and how is it to be determined? Unless these points are made clear, "community interest" may be but a cover-up for special interests or for preferential treatment. Various interpretations of the concept may be offered.

1. The true structure of collective preferences is said to be revealed to a great teacher or political leader who, as in the Maoist pattern, then transmits this insight to the people. The public, after an initial period of compulsion, comes to accept these values as their own, thus removing the distinction between private and collective wants. This tenet is inconsistent with our view of democracy, and it cannot be justified by holding that, in the end, preferences are "always" socially conditioned.[32]

2. A more attractive interpretation of the collective-want concept is that, by virtue of sustained association, people come to develop common concerns. A group of people, for instance, share a historical experience with which they identify, thereby establishing a common bond. Individuals will join in defending the borders of "their" territory or to protect the beauty of "their" countryside. At the same time, it is difficult to extend this existence of common concern to the contention that resource allocation should, generally speaking, be based on consensus rather than on individual preference. X and Y may join in defending "their" territory even though each wishes to make an independent choice regarding his consumption of apples and oranges.

3. A further possibility is to view the idea of community interests as an attitude whereby each individual attributes as much value to the welfare of others as to his own.[33] This approach, however, is concerned with an issue in distribution rather than allocation, and it does not deny that allocation should be such as to meet individually experienced preferences.

These arguments do not leave one with a clear concept of collective wants or a convincing case against a fiscal theory based on the satisfaction of individual

[31] This view may be found among continental European writers, especially the German romanticists. For an illustration during the Nazi period, see Hans Ritschl, "Communal Economy and Market Economy," in Musgrave and Peacock, op. cit., p. 233. See also p. 64.

[32] Obviously, everyone's preferences are socially conditioned and affected by the environment, including not only the grosser influences of high-pressure advertising but also the more subtle effects of one's desire to be approved by one's peers. However, each individual retains a degree of freedom in responding to such environmental influences. To deny this is to rule out any vestige of free will.

[33] The "others" in question may be defined more or less broadly, e.g., the world, the nation, the village, or the family.

preferences. There remains, however, another dimension of the community approach. It consists of the view that relations among individuals in the good society should be based on cooperation rather than on competition.[34] This belief rests on the moral proposition—well founded in the tradition of humanist thought—that a cooperative system is more conducive to human dignity and fulfillment. In the economic sphere, it might thus be argued that a cooperative approach to economic activity is to be preferred even in the absence of externalities, and even if the mechanism were to prove inferior on economic efficiency grounds. Economic welfare narrowly defined, after all, is not the only objective in life; and efficiency (as a criterion for rational action) should be interpreted to include all objectives that matter. Once more we ask, what will be the implications of the cooperative approach for fiscal theory?

With regard to *production,* the cooperative approach might call for a more congenial organization of production establishments, but such cooperation would apply to the production of goods which are to be consumed privately as well as those which are to be provided for publicly. The problem, therefore, is not a public sector issue as we have defined the term. With regard to *consumption,* the cooperative approach might suggest a bias in favor of social, as against private, goods. The reason is that the former have to be consumed "in equal amounts by all." The question, however, remains as to whether this bias is based on the egalitarian aspect of social-good consumption[35] or on the notion that togetherness in consumption is desirable. The latter interpretation need not follow: People may sit together while eating hamburgers, yet a person may enjoy the beauty of a national park in solitude. Finally, it may be argued that the nature of the political *organization* needed to provide for social goods or to adjust distribution will change under the cooperative approach. The mandatory application of majority rule might be replaced by the consensus of a Quaker meeting. Perhaps so. But unless a very optimistic view is taken, the necessity remains for overriding a minority veto lest the provision of social goods be made impossible.[36]

When one assesses the potentials of the cooperative approach, its appeal as a form of social relations is evident. At the same time, care must be taken not to compare the shortcomings of actual systems with a utopian image of cooperation. In particular, it must be realized that in modern society, some central principle of organization has to be applied, whether it be of the market type or the planning type. While those who dislike the idea of competition may reject the former mode, they should not fail to allow for the potential shortcomings (with regard to individual freedom and other aspects of society) under the latter.

[34] The reader should be aware of the semantic difficulties of such a statement. The fathers of the liberal philosophy—such as John Locke, Jeremiah Bentham, and Adam Smith—would have argued that profit maximization and competition are the supreme form of cooperation. Therefore, the profit motive as a motivation is both in the social interest and morally valid. The critic, in this case, must reply either (1) that the facts are wrong and that certain costs of competition are overlooked, or (2) that the good society cannot be one in which self-interest and group interest coincide, since, in such a society, there would be no place for the ethical quality of self-sacrifice.

[35] See p. 51.

[36] See p. 55.

The Role of Bureaucracy In this context, it remains to note yet another view of the "public interest." This view centers on the contribution of the civil servant who sees it his or her function to administer policy in the public interest. This function is to analyze and present the implications of alternative policies as they may affect all groups in society and to administer policies, once they have been decided upon, in an impartial fashion. Contrary to what has become the popular connotation of "bureaucracy," the civil service performs a function which, as shown by Max Weber, plays a central role in society.[37]

Quantitative Studies of Fiscal Policies

Opening up a new line of research, recent studies have attempted to apply quantitative analysis to measuring the role of political variables in fiscal policy.

One set of studies has explored the effects on federal elections of changing business conditions, hypothesizing that the voter will hold the administration's stabilization policy responsible for such changes. These studies have been inconclusive to date. While some found little connection, others found a significant link with voters responding adversely to unemployment and inflation. Much depends on what response lags are allowed for and on how particular variables are specified.[38] Little work has been done as yet to link quantitative aspects of expenditure or tax structure to voting behavior.[39]

Another set of studies has dealt with fiscal behavior at the state and local levels. In particular, some studies have made use of the proposition that majority voting reflects the preferences of the median voter.[40] Others have attempted to introduce political variables, such as the party in power or the form of city government, into equations designed to predict state and local fiscal behavior.[41] Though still in its early stages, this empirical approach to the study of fiscal behavior opens up a new and promising perspective.

E. SUMMARY

Because preferences for social goods are not revealed except in the small-number case, budgetary determination based on a voting process is needed:

[37] This aspect of the public interest issue is emphasized by Gerhard Colm in *Essays in Public Finance and Fiscal Policy,* New York: Oxford University Press, 1955. Also see H. H. Gerth and C. Wright Mills, *From Max Weber,* New York: Oxford University Press, 1970, pp. 196–252.

[38] See G. H. Kramer, "Short-term Fluctuations in U.S. Voting Behavior," *American Political Science Review,* March 1971; George J. Stigler, "General Economic Conditions and National Elections," *American Economic Review,* Proceedings, December 1972; and Howard S. Bloom and H. Douglas Price, "Voter Response to Short-run Economic Conditions: The Asymmetric Effect of Prosperity and Depression." *American Journal of Political Science,*" December 1975.

[39] See, however, Gavin Wright, "The Political Economy of New Deal Spending: An Econometric Analysis," *The Review of Economics and Statistics,* February 1974.

[40] See T. E. Borcherding and R. T. Duncan, "The Demand for Services of Non-Federal Governments," *American Economic Review,* December 1972; and T. C. Bergstrom and R. R. Goodman, "Private Demand for Public Goods," *American Economic Review,* June 1973.

[41] See Otto H. Davis and George A. Haines, "A Political Approach to a Theory of Public Expenditures: The Case of Municipalities," *The National Tax Journal,* XIX, No. 3, September 1966.

1. Majority voting may lead to arbitrary decisions, which will depend on the sequence in which issues are paired.

2. This outcome, however, is less likely if preferences are homogeneous.

3. As applied to various fiscal choices, the voting process is simplest when deciding the size of the budget for a single social good and with a fixed tax assignment. The problem becomes more difficult if budget composition and tax structure are allowed to vary.

4. Plurality and point voting lead to more representative outcomes as intensity of preferences comes to be reflected. But use of voting strategy may interfere with efficient outcomes.

A system of representative democracy has been examined, and these features were noted:

5. Politicians may be thought of as maximizing votes by providing popular options.

6. By combining issues and platforms, majority voting may come to reflect intensity of preferences.

7. Similar considerations apply to logrolling, which may therefore be a constructive feature.

8. Delegation of decision making to elected representatives introduces small-number bargaining at the final level of decision making.

The political process, by not precisely reflecting the preferences of voters, may introduce biases into the size and composition of the budget:

9. Since individual voters do not allow for the part of the cost paid for by others, the size of the budget tends to be too large.

10. Since provision of social goods is not supported by consumer advertising and since the benefits are more remote, the size of the budget may be too small.

Alternative modes of fiscal behavior were considered, including the following:

11. The Marxist view of fiscal politics, which sees budget determination as a question of class conflict.

12. The fiscal process viewed as an interaction of interest groups, with such groups arranged according to a variety of characteristics.

13. The view that the fiscal process should be related to a concept of collective wants and cooperative organization.

FURTHER READINGS

Arrow, Kenneth: *Social Choice and Individual Values,* 2d ed., New York: Wiley, 1951.

Black, Duncan: *The Theory of Committees and Elections,* Cambridge, England: Cambridge, 1958.

Buchanan, J. M., and G. Tullock: *The Calculus of Consent,* Ann Arbor: The University of Michigan Press, 1962.

Downs, Anthony: *An Economic Theory of Democracy,* New York: Harper & Row, 1956.

Olson, Mancur, Jr.: *The Logic of Collective Action,* Cambridge, Mass.: Harvard, 1965.

Part Two

Expenditure Structure

Chapter 6

Public Expenditures: Structure and Growth*

A. Size of the Public Sector: *United States Public Sector Share; Comparison with Other Countries.* **B. Growth and Status of Public Expenditure Structure:** *Absolute Expenditure Growth; Expenditure Growth in Relation to GNP; Expenditure Elasticity; Changing Composition of Civilian Expenditures.* **C. A Cross-sectional View. D. The Causes of Expenditure Growth:** *Growth of Per Capita Income and Product Mix; Other Causes of Rising Share; Relative Costs of Public Services; Changing Scope of Transfers; Availability of Tax Handles; Threshold Effects and War Finance; Political and Social Factors.* **E. Summary. Appendix: Public Sector in the National Income Accounts:** *Public Sector in GNP; Public Sector in National Income; Public Sector in Personal Income; Public Sector in Disposable Income.*

We now turn to a series of chapters dealing with public expenditure structure and the policy issues arising in designing expenditure programs. To set the stage, this chapter examines the size of the public sector in the United States economy and surveys its growth. The concept of the public sector, as we have seen previ-

* *Reader's Guide to Chapter 6:* This chapter provides the background for the subsequent study of expenditure policy. We examine the size of the public sector as viewed from various perspectives and survey the United States expenditure structure at various government levels. This exploration is followed by a study of expenditure growth and its causes—easy reading, but important to understand where the public sector has been and where it is going. An appendix on the place of budget items in the national income accounts is added for those who wish to pursue this aspect further.

ously, may be interpreted in various ways. It may be conceived as reflecting budgetary transactions, public enterprise, public regulation, and similar concerns. All these policies are of significance, but our focus here is on budgetary activity.

A. SIZE OF THE PUBLIC SECTOR

Even if this narrower view is taken, the size of the public sector may be measured in different ways. Various ratios may be devised, relating budgetary activities to different components of the national income accounts, such as gross national product, national income, and personal income. The more precise relation of budget items to these accounts is considered in the appendix to this chapter, but the major ratios are examined here and are given in the first column of Table 6-1.

United States Public Sector Share

These ratios offer a convenient way of examining the relative importance of the public sector in the structure of the United States economy.

Relation to GNP The most comprehensive measure is given by the ratio of total government expenditures to GNP. This ratio, which stood at 33 percent in 1974, is, however, not a satisfactory measure. Government expenditures which go into the numerator include transfer payments, while GNP in the denominator includes expenditures for the purchase of goods and services only. If government expenditures are to be related to GNP, it would be more meaningful, therefore, to exclude transfer payments from government expenditures. This ratio, amounting to 22.1 percent in 1974, shows the share of total output which is purchased by government. As noted earlier, it reflects in a rough way the weight of social goods in total output.

Consideration of a global ratio is less objectionable if we deal with the ratio of tax revenue to GNP. This ratio, at 32.6 percent in 1974, is close to the overall expenditure ratio, the only difference being that nontax receipts and public borrowing are excluded. It measures the country's tax effort, or the share of gross income which is diverted from the private income stream into the public budget.

Relation to National Income National income measures the sum total of factor incomes (wages, profits, rent, interest, etc.) earned during a given period. In 1973, 13.8 percent of this total originated in general government, being dispensed in the form of wage and salary payments, and a further 2 percent originated in public enterprises. Viewing the role of earnings from government in a somewhat different way, we may also note that 19.3 percent of total employment was provided by the public sector.

Relation to Personal Income Personal income includes income received by households, and it contains three government components. One consists of transfer payments, which in 1974 amounted to 11.7 percent of personal income; another is made up of wage and salary earnings from public employment, accounting for 13.8 percent; and a third comprises interest receipts, which

TABLE 6-1
Relative Size of Public Sector in the United States and Other Countries
(All Levels of Government Included)

	United States,[a] 1974	1971[b]					
		United States	*Canada*	*United Kingdom*	*France*	*Germany*	*Sweden*
1. Total expenditures as percentage of GDP	33.0	32.6	36.2	36.9	36.6	36.7	44.8
2. Tax receipts as percentage of GDP	32.6	29.8	33.0	36.4	36.4	36.8	43.4
3. Tax receipts excluding payroll tax as percentage of GDP	26.2	23.6	30.2	31.2	21.3	24.9	35.1
4. Government purchases as percentage of GDP	22.1	22.3	22.4	22.2	15.4	20.9	27.6
5. Transfers to persons as percentage of personal income	11.7	9.8	11.8	10.8	22.4	15.8	15.6

Notes and Sources:
[a] *Economic Report of the President,* February 1975. Ratios refer to *GNP* rather than *GDP.*
[b] All ratios are derived from data presented in *National Accounts of OECD Countries, 1960–71,* Paris: OECD Department of Economics and Statistics. Since this source reports GDP (gross domestic product) rather than GNP (gross national product), GDP is used in the denominators. Otherwise, the underlying data are adapted to approximate so far as possible the concepts as defined in the United States national income accounts. For instance, GDP and government expenditure figures are reduced by consumption of fixed capital in the public sector to accord with the United States gross product concept.
Using United States national income accounts data *(Survey of Current Business, July 1974)* and GNP rather than GDP yields the following 1971 ratios for the United States: line 1, 32.2%; line 2, 30.5%; line 3, 24.4%; line 4, 22.2%; line 5, 10.3%.

amounted to about 1.5 percent. The government thus contributed 26 percent of total personal income. Of this contribution, 56 percent was returned to the public budget in the form of personal taxes.

Comparison with Other Countries

In short, the public sector in the United States absorbs 33 percent of GNP as tax revenue, purchases slightly over 22 percent of total output, and pays out some 14 percent of national income. Its contribution to personal income amounts to 26 percent, while personal taxes draw back some 18 percent. How do these magnitudes compare with those of other countries?

Turning again to Table 6-1, lines 1 and 2 show that the 1971 ratio of both expenditures and taxes to GNP is lower for the United States than for Canada, the United Kingdom, and other European countries; it is much below that for Sweden, where the public sector is largest. Line 3 shows that the United States ratio approximates those of Germany and France if social security taxes are excluded in the comparison, but that it falls much below the ratios for the U.K. and Sweden. As shown in line 4, the United States ratio of government purchases to GNP is on a par with that of other countries, with transfer payments being the main reason for the lower level shown in line 1. This is also brought out in line 5, which shows the higher share of transfer payments in personal income for the other countries. It appears that, although the welfare state is advancing in the United States, it has not moved so far as it has in other countries.

B. GROWTH AND STATUS OF PUBLIC EXPENDITURE STRUCTURE

Writing in the 1880s, the German economist Adolph Wagner advanced his "law of rising public expenditures." He felt, perhaps in anticipation of trends to be realized fifty to a hundred years later, that the development of modern industrial society would give rise to increasing political "pressure for social progress" and call for increased allowance for "social considerations" in the conduct of industry. In consequence, continuous expansion in the public sector should be expected.[1] Has this law been borne out over the years, and just how should it be defined?

Absolute Expenditure Growth

Obviously, public expenditures have risen in absolute terms. As shown in Table 6-2, line 1, expenditures (including all levels of government) have increased 400-fold in the United States over the last eighty years. But this is not a meaningful way of looking at expenditure growth. Prices over the same period (line 10) quintupled, so that the multiple in terms of constant dollars (line 2) was cut to 94. Also, population (line 9) more than tripled, so that the multiple, measured on a per capita basis (line 3), falls to 28.[2]

Expenditure Growth in Relation to GNP

These are obvious corrections, but they are not enough. One must also note that there has been a vast increase in productivity over the period, leading to a nearly sixfold rise in per capita income in constant dollars. There is every reason to expect that part of this gain should have been spent on the goods and services provided by the public sector. In other words, focus should be on the share of government in total expenditures, and the law of rising public expenditures should be defined in terms of a rising public sector *share.*

Total Expenditures Beginning with the most global measure, we find that the ratio of public expenditures (all forms of government) to GNP rose from 7 to 32 percent over our eighty-year period, a nearly fivefold increase in the relative size of the public sector.[3] This leaves us with a substantial increase, but by no means so drastic a rise as is suggested by the record of growth in absolute expenditures.

[1] See the relevant passages from A. Wagner in Richard A. Musgrave and Alan Peacock (eds.), *Classics in the Theory of Public Finance,* New York: Macmillan, 1958, pp. 1–16. Also see chap. 3 in Richard A. Musgrave, *Fiscal Systems,* New Haven, Conn.: Yale, 1969.

[2] The nature of social goods poses an interesting problem in the interpretation of growth in GNP as a measure of rising welfare. Regarding private goods, growth in welfare is approximated by the growth in per capita income. With regard to social goods, focus on rising per capita income understates the welfare gain. If consumption is truly nonrival, an increase in numbers (with GNP constant) should not reduce per capita income.

[3] By omitting price level adjustments, we assume that the same price index can be applied to both public and private expenditures. If, as has been argued, productivity gains for publicly provided goods lag behind those of private goods, failure to distinguish price changes in the two sectors will overstate the growth of the public sector share.

TABLE 6-2
Growth of Government Expenditures in the United States—Absolutes and Relatives

	1890	*1902*	*1913*	*1922*	*1929*	*1940*	*1950*	*1960*	*1970*	*1973*
Total Expenditures										
1. Current dollars (billions)	0.8	1.5	3.2	9.3	10.7	17.6	65.9	136.1	313.6	408.0
2. 1958 dollars (billions)	2.8	4.6	8.6	17.9	21.1	40.0	82.4	132.1	232.2	264.4
3. Per capita, 1958 dollars	45	58	89	163	173	303	542	730	1,133	1,260
4. As percentage of GNP	6.5	7.3	7.8	12.6	10.4	17.6	23.1	27.0	32.2	31.5
Civilian Expenditures										
5. Current dollars (billions)	0.7	1.2	2.8	7.9	9.5	15.5	42.2	84.4	225.1	328.0
6. 1958 dollars (billions)	2.3	3.6	7.6	15.2	18.6	35.2	52.8	81.9	166.7	212.6
7. Per capita, 1958 dollars	36	46	78	138	152	267	347	453	813	1,010
8. As percentage of GNP	5.0	5.8	6.8	10.7	9.2	15.5	14.8	16.7	23.1	25.3
Related Statistics										
9. Population (millions)	63	79	97	110	122	132	152	181	205	210
10. Price index (1958 = 100)	30	32	37	52	51	44	80	103	135	154
11. GNP, current dollars (billions)	13	20	41	74	103	100	285	504	974	1,294

Sources:

Lines 1 and 5: 1890–1929: Richard A. Musgrave and J. M. Culbertson, "The Growth of Public Expenditures in the United States," *National Tax Journal,* June 1953. 1940–1950: *Historical Statistics of the United States,* United States Bureau of the Census, 1960, pp. 723, 719. 1960–1974: *Survey of Current Business,* July 1974, and *National Income Accounts,* 1929–1965, U.S. Department of Commerce.

Line 9: 1890–1940: *Historical Statistics of the United States,* ibid., 1950–1970: *Economic Report of the President,* January 1974.

Line 10: 1890 and 1922 estimated by carrying implicit price deflation for GNP for 1929 back in line with the Bureau of Labor Statistics wholesale price index given in *Historical Statistics of the United States,* op. cit., p. 116. 1929–1970: *Economic Report of the President,* op. cit., p. 198.

Line 11: 1890–1902: *Historical Statistics of the United States,* op. cit., p. 139. 1929–1970: *Economic Report of the President,* op. cit.

The path of overall expenditure growth, as measured by the ratio of total public expenditures to GNP, is shown in line 4 of Table 6-2 and is further plotted in Figure 6-1, where comparable ratios for the United Kingdom and Germany are included as well. With years selected so as to avoid wartime peaks, we note a one percentage point growth in the United States ratio from 1890 to 1902, little change from 1902 to 1913, and a rise of 4.8 points from 1913 to 1922. This was followed by a decline in the 1920s and a sharp 7.2 point increase in the 1930s. The rise continued in the subsequent decades but at a declining rate, 5.5 points for the 1940s, 3.9 points for the 1950s, and 5.2 points for the 1960s. Another way of looking at the matter is in terms of elasticities and will be considered later.

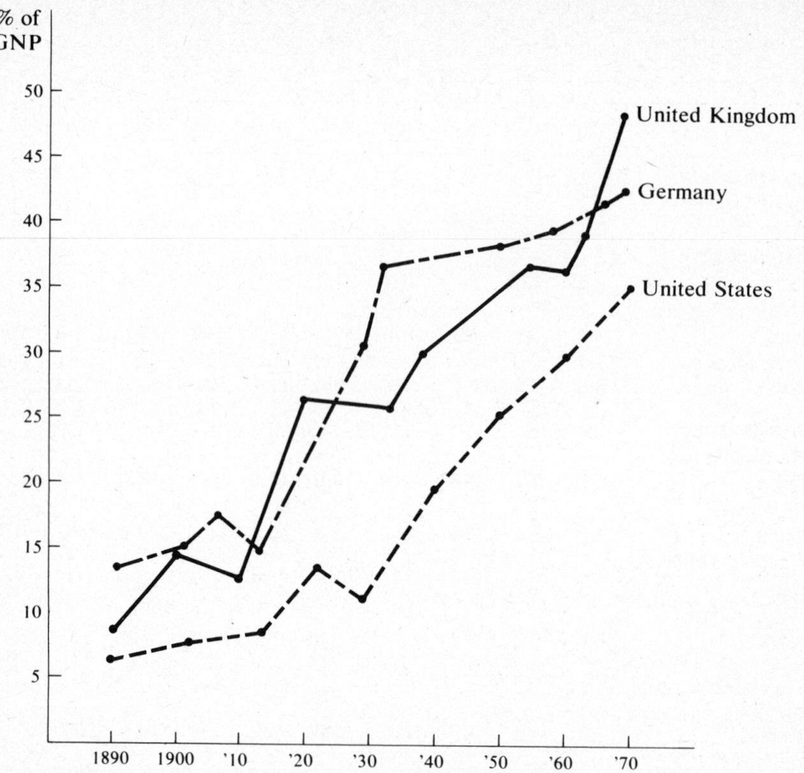

Notes: Includes all levels of government. GNP at factor cost. *Source:* Up to 1958: *Fiscal Systems,* op. cit., p. 100. For the United States, 1958–1970: *Survey of Current Business,* July 1971. For Germany and the United Kingdom: *National Accounts of OECD Countries,* 1953–1969, OECD, 1971.

FIGURE 6-1 Public Expenditures as Percentage of GNP.

However one may interpret the precise pattern by subperiods, it is evident that Wagner's law of rising public expenditures is borne out for the past eighty-year period. As shown in Figure 6-1, much the same picture holds for the United Kingdom and Germany, although their ratios have been higher throughout these years than those in the United States.

Defense versus Civilian Expenditures The reader will wonder whether this evidence of expenditure growth is to be explained in terms of expenditures for defense, or whether it applies to civilian expenditures as well. The ratio of civilian expenditures to GNP is shown in line 8 of Table 6-2 and both ratios are plotted in Figure 6-2. We find that for the eighty-year period as a whole, the defense expenditure ratio has increased somewhat faster than the civilian ratio, but both have risen substantially. However, the pattern by subperiods differs sharply. The increase in the defense ratio occurred primarily from 1940 to 1950, while the rise in the civilian ratio explained almost the entire increase for the 1890–1940 and 1950–1970 periods. From 1970 to 1973, finally, civilian expenditures (especially at the state and local levels) rose sharply while defense expenditures declined in absolute terms. Although such comparisons have their short-

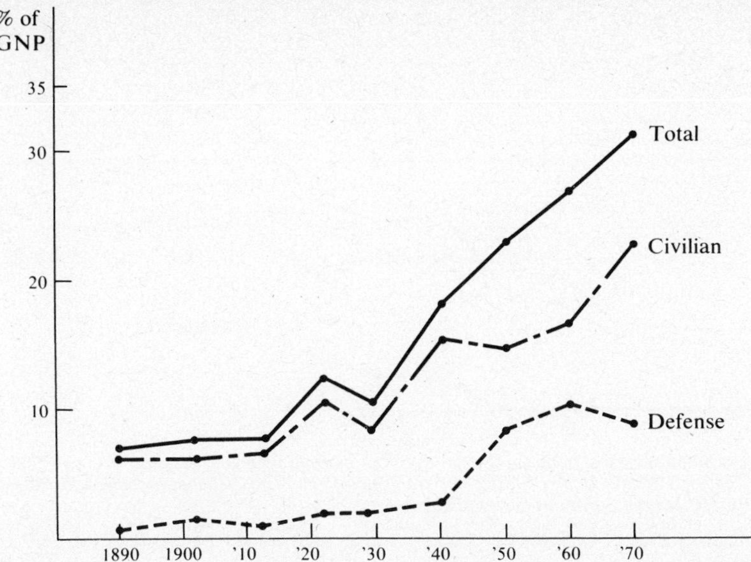

FIGURE 6-2 United States Civilian and Defense Expenditures as Percentage of GNP.

comings, it is evident that expenditure growth has not only been a matter of rising defense expenditures.[4] Viewed over the longer run, the civilian expenditure ratio has risen at a substantial rate. As against a ratio of 9 percent in the pre-Depression year 1929, it stood at about 23 percent of GNP in 1970 and had risen to 25.3 percent by 1973.

Purchases versus Transfer Payments Figure 6-3 shows a further breakdown of United States expenditure growth, this time between purchases and transfers (including interest). Since national defense expenditures are almost entirely purchases, the comparison is limited to civilian expenditures only. We find that both purchases and transfers have contributed to the rising expenditure share, but that the transfer share has been of increasing importance since the 1930s. Reflecting the rise of social security and the growing importance of welfare payments, transfer payments have accounted for about one-half the growth in the civilian expenditure ratio since that time.

Expenditure Elasticity

Another view of the same development is taken in Table 6-3 where the data of Table 6-2 are recast in terms of expenditure elasticities. The table shows the GNP elasticity of total and civilian expenditures over selected years. We note that both elasticities were substantially above unity throughout, reflecting the rising expenditure–GNP ratios. The table also shows the economy's marginal propen-

[4] One element of arbitrariness lies in the choice of the particular years which are taken for comparison and another rests with the definition of defense expenditures. Our choice of years was made such as to avoid wartime peaks, while the underlying definition of defense expenditures is comprehensive, including not only military expenditures, but military aid and all veteran outlays as well.

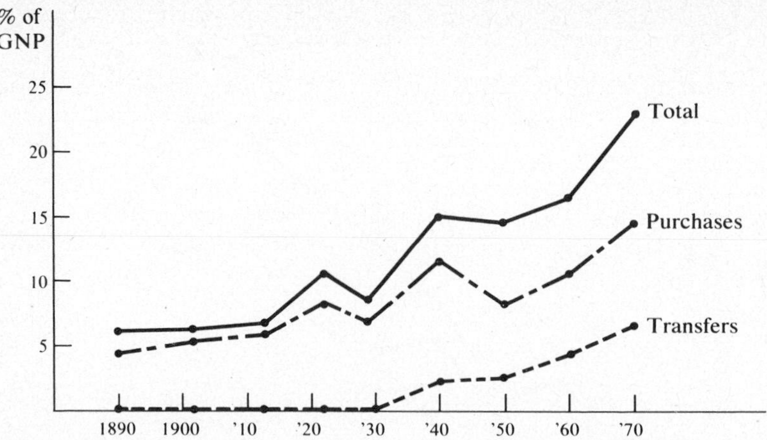

Notes: Defense includes veterans' benefits. Civilian transfers exclude veterans' benefits. *Source:* 1890–1922: *Historical Statistics of the United States,* op. cit., 1929–1970: *The National Income and Product Accounts of the United States, Survey of Current Business.*

FIGURE 6-3 United States Civilian Purchases and Transfers as Percentage of GNP.

sity to spend in the public sector. Defined as the increase in public expenditures as a percentage of the increase in GNP, the marginal propensity for public spending has moved up with regard to both total and civilian outlays.

Changing Composition of Civilian Expenditures

We now turn from the overall expenditure–GNP ratios to changes in the composition of expenditures and the growth of particular functions. We continue to combine all levels of government for purposes of this discussion. While changes in the composition of expenditures had important bearing on the division of total expenditures among the levels of government, their effect will be considered at a later point.[5] The broad outlines of this development are shown in Table 6-4. Lines 1 and 2 show the composition of total expenditures between defense-related and civilian outlays. As noted before, the rise in total expenditures (except for the 1940s) was fueled by the civilian component, leading to a rising share of

TABLE 6-3
Expenditure Elasticities and Propensities
(All Levels of Government)

	GNP ELASTICITY*		MARGINAL PROPENSITY†	
	Total	*Civilian*	*Total*	*Civilian*
1890–1929	1.7	1.8	10.9	9.0
1929–1950	2.9	2.2	30.4	18.4
1950–1970	1.6	1.8	35.9	26.5
1890–1970	5.0	4.7	32.4	23.4

* Ratio of percentage rise in public expenditures to percentage rise in GNP.
† Increase in public expenditures as percentage of increase in GNP.
Sources: Same as Table 6-2.

[5] See Chap. 30, Sec. A.

TABLE 6-4
Development of Government Expenditures in the United States
(All Levels of Government)

	1902	*1927*	*1940*	*1950*	*1960*	*1970*	*1973*
As Percentage of Total Expenditures							
1. Defense-related	20.8	11.8	11.8	36.0	38.0	28.2	22.9
2. Civilian	79.2	88.2	88.2	64.0	62.0	71.8	77.1
3. Total	100.0	100.0	100.0	100.0	100.0	100.0	100.0
As Percentage of Civilian Expenditures							
4. Social welfare	9.0	7.5	16.3	16.3	29.1	34.7	38.4
5. Education	22.4	25.5	18.2	22.9	22.3	24.8	23.7
6. Civil services	14.7	10.9	6.4	5.9	7.6	7.2	5.7
7. Economic development	18.9	26.3	34.2	23.9	19.6	14.8	11.3
8. Transportation	17.1	23.6	16.5	10.7	11.7	8.1	6.8
9. Other	1.8	2.7	17.7	13.2	7.9	6.7	4.5
10. General government	15.2	6.0	4.8	3.7	8.9	9.5	10.9
11. Interest	8.4	15.3	10.0	11.5	8.9	6.6	5.9
12. Foreign relations and aid	0.3	0.2	0.1	10.0	2.6	1.2	1.1
13. Miscellaneous	11.1	8.3	9.8	5.9	0.9	1.2	3.0
14. Total	100.0	100.0	100.0	100.0	100.0	100.0	100.0
As Percentage of GNP							
15. Defense-related	1.5	1.2	2.1	8.3	10.3	9.1	7.2
16. Civilian	5.8	9.2	15.5	14.8	16.7	23.1	24.3
17. Social welfare	0.5	0.7	2.5	2.4	4.9	8.0	9.3
18. Education	1.3	2.3	2.8	3.4	3.7	5.7	5.8
19. Civil services	0.9	1.0	1.0	0.9	1.3	1.7	1.4
20. Economic development	1.0	2.4	5.4	3.5	3.3	3.5	2.7
21. Transportation	1.0	2.2	2.6	1.6	2.0	1.9	1.7
22. Other	0.1	0.2	2.8	1.9	1.3	1.6	1.1
23. General government	0.9	0.5	0.7	0.5	1.5	2.2	2.6
24. Interest	0.5	1.4	1.6	1.7	1.5	1.5	1.4
25. Foreign relations and aid	*	*	*	1.5	0.4	0.3	0.3
26. Miscellaneous	0.6	0.8	1.5	0.9	*	0.3	0.7
27. Total	7.3	10.4	17.6	23.1	27.0	32.2	31.5

* Less than 0.05.
Notes:
Detail may not add to total because of rounding.
Defense-related: Includes military assistance abroad and veterans' benefits and services.
Social welfare: Includes social security and welfare, health and hospitals, housing and community development.
Civil services: Includes sanitation, fire and police, and recreation.
Transportation: For 1902–1950 excludes state and local nonhighway transportation which is included in miscellaneous.
Other economic development: Includes space, natural resources, agriculture, and net subsidy to Postal Service.
General government: For 1902–1950 this item is classified as "General Control."
Foreign relations and aid: Excludes military assistance which is included in "Defense-related."
Sources:
1902–1950: Calendar years, *Historical Statistics of the United States,* United States Bureau of the Census, p. 723.
1960: *National Income Accounts,* 1929–1965, United States Department of Commerce, 1970 and 1973: *Survey of Current Business,* July 1974, table 3.10, pp. 29–31.

civilian expenditures in the expenditure total up to 1940, a sharply declining share in the 1940s, and once more a rising share in the 1960s, with a sharp upturn in recent years.

Turning now to the changing composition of the civilian expenditure structure, we note that the most striking feature is the rising trend in the share of social welfare expenditures (line 4) and particularly the dramatic upturn in the 1950s and 1960s. Primarily, this reflects the expansion of social security but also includes other welfare payments. The share of education in total civilian expenditures (line 5) has remained more or less constant, with a temporary decline in the 1940s. The transportation share (line 8) showed a sharp rise in the 1920s, when the development of the automobile had its major impact on highway needs, but followed a downward trend since then. Development expenditures other than transportation (line 9) show a decline since 1940 but are not a very meaningful category since widely differing items such as farm support and the space program are included. Other categories, shown in lines 10 to 13, follow a fluctuating pattern.

The same picture is repeated in lines 15 to 26, giving this time the expenditure–GNP ratios for the various functions. Since the ratio of total civilian expenditures to GNP rose sharply (line 16), the expenditure to GNP ratio for particular functions (such as education) which maintained a constant expenditure share also showed a substantial increase relative to GNP.

C. A CROSS-SECTIONAL VIEW

The historical picture, as presented in Figure 6-1, shows a steady rise of the public expenditure share over time for the United States, the United Kingdom, and Germany. During the same period, these countries also experienced a substantial increase in per capita income. Putting the two developments together suggests an association between rise in per capita income and a rising share of public expenditures in GNP. But the rise in per capita income was only one among many factors of change during the period. The rising expenditure share may also have been due to changing social and political forces, so that it is difficult to isolate the influence of per capita income in the historical process.

As an alternative way of looking at the role of per capita income in explaining the rising expenditure share, we now compare the expenditure shares for countries with varying levels of per capita GNP but at the same point of time. Again, this approach does not neatly isolate the influence of per capita income, since low-income countries may operate under different social and political conditions than do high-income countries, but it should throw some light on the matter.

Such a comparison is shown in Figure 6-4. For lack of adequate expenditure data, the comparison is in terms of a tax to GNP ratio, but the results are essentially the same. A group of countries at widely differing levels of development are compared.[6] We find that if all are included, the ratio is related positively to per capita income, in line with the rising-share hypothesis.[7] This relationship,

[6] The data are averages for 1969–71. See R. J. Chelliah, H. J. Baas, and M. R. Kelly, "Tax Ratios and Tax Effort in Developing Countries, 1969–71," *IMF Staff Papers,* International Monetary Fund, 1975.

[7] Writing T for tax revenue and GNP_{pc} for per capita income, the regression equation (based on fifty-three countries) is

$$T/GNP = 14.64 + .006GNP_{pc}$$
$$(11.3) \quad (8.6)$$

where the figures in parentheses are the ratios of intercept and regression coefficient to their respective standard errors and the R^2 is 0.59.

If social security taxes are excluded, the equation (based on sixty-three countries) becomes

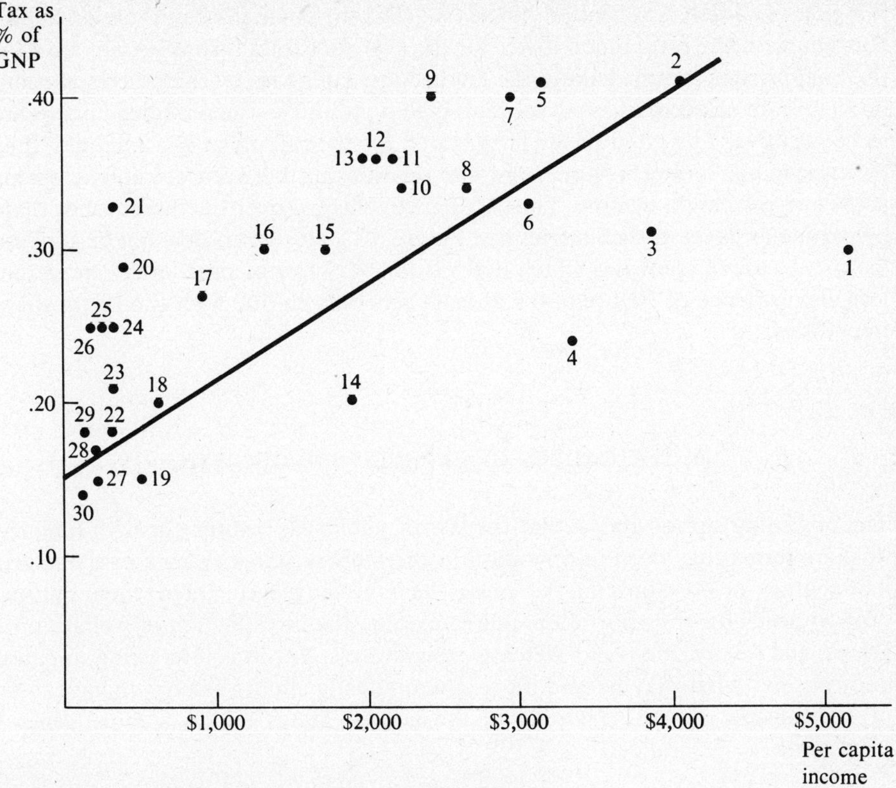

FIGURE 6-4 Tax–GNP Ratio and Per Capita Income.

Identification of Numbers

1. U.S.A.
2. Sweden
3. Canada
4. Switzerland
5. Denmark
6. Germany
7. Norway
8. Belgium
9. Netherlands
10. Finland
11. United Kingdom
12. Austria
13. France
14. Japan
15. Italy
16. Ireland
17. Chile
18. Jamaica
19. Costa Rica
20. Brazil
21. Zambia
22. Turkey
23. Malaysia
24. Guyana
25. Ecuador
26. Tunisia
27. South Korea
28. Ghana
29. Sri Lanka
30. Kenya

$$T/GNP = 14.11 + .004GNP_{pc}$$
$$(15.2) \quad (6.7)$$

with an R^2 of 0.41. Thus, per capita income has a high explanatory value in both cases and a good fit is obtained. This picture, however, deteriorates if developing and developed countries are grouped separately. Excluding social security, the equation for forty-seven developing countries is

$$T/GNP = 13.69 + .004GNP_{pc}$$
$$(10.5) \quad (1.3)$$

and that for sixteen developed countries is

$$T/GNP = 23.36 + .001GNP_{pc}$$
$$(4.7) \quad (0.5)$$

with R^2 values of 0.040 and 0.024, respectively. (For source, see preceding footnote.)

however, is largely a reflection of the fact that the countries are grouped in two clusters, with the ratio much lower for the low per capita income group than for the high-income group. Taking the low-income countries by themselves, we find no significant relationship, and for high-income countries the relationship appears to be negative. The good linear fit obtained for the sample as a whole may thus be misleading, hiding a more complex relationship between the public sector share and per capita income. The experience reflected over the last seventy years by particular developed countries (see Figure 6-1), moreover, may not be applicable to the case of countries which now exhibit very low income levels. Nevertheless, the evidence of Figure 6-4 is at least generally in line with the rising-share hypothesis.

D. THE CAUSES OF EXPENDITURE GROWTH

The preceding survey shows that the law of public expenditure growth (defined in share terms) has been in operation in the United States at least over the last half-century or so. Some of the causes have already been noted, including increased needs for transportation and education, the introduction of welfare programs, and finally, the rise of defense expenditures. Yet, it is interesting to pause and consider what may be said more systematically about the underlying causes of expenditure growth, not only in the United States but in a more general framework.

Growth of Per Capita Income and Product Mix

In dealing with the underlying causes of expenditure growth, consider first the proposition that the efficient product mix between private and social goods changes as per capita income rises, and that this change involves a rising share of social goods. If so, this would suggest that efficient budget policy calls for a rising ratio of government *purchases* (and civilian purchases in particular) to GNP, as noted in Figure 6-2.

The rise in per capita income, seen in the historical context, records the development of the economy from an agricultural and low-income state to an industrial and high-income state. It would be surprising if, in the course of this development, the output of social goods (assuming it to be determined efficiently) should remain constant. To put it differently, the demand for such goods can hardly be expected to have an income elasticity of zero. At the same time, there is no particular reason to expect that this elasticity should be just unity, thereby leaving the public purchase share unchanged as per capita income rises. As we have seen, this share has increased considerably. Including government purchases for civilian purposes only, the United States elasticity (ratio of percentage increase in per capita expenditures to percentage increase in per capita GNP) has been 1.4 for the period from 1890 to 1929 and 1.8 for the period from 1929 to 1969.

Consumer Goods and Services In trying to explain this result, it is well to distinguish between consumer goods and capital goods. We shall begin with the former. The German economist Ernst Engel pointed out over a century ago that the composition of the consumer budget changes as family income increases.[8] A smaller share comes to be spent on certain goods, such as work clothing, and a larger share on others, such as fur coats. As average income increases, similar changes in the consumption pattern for the economy as a whole may be expected to occur. Is there any reason to foresee that, in the dynamics of consumer budgeting, social consumer goods will exhibit a higher income elasticity than do private goods?

At first sight, the opposite may be expected. One thinks of government services as related to basic needs, such as safety, elementary education, and basic sanitation, which seem more like necessities than luxuries. Further consideration suggests, however, that there are other public services, such as higher education or improved health services, which move within reach as income rises above poverty levels. Also, there are items, such as parks, marinas, high-speed highways, and space exploration, which (at present levels of income) are of the luxury type. Some of these reflect the rising tendency for government to render services which are complementary to luxury-type private goods. In all, speculation on the point does not lead to any clear-cut hypothesis about what might be expected: the government share in consumption may well rise and fall over successive phases of income growth.

Capital Goods The relationship is more discernible with regard to public provision for capital goods. In the earlier stages of economic development, a particular need exists for the creation of overhead capital, such as roads, harbors, and power installations. Many of these items are such that the benefits are largely external, or they require large amounts of capital the returns on which are spread over a long time, and thus do not lend themselves readily to private provision. Hence, there is reason to expect that the public share in the provision for capital goods should be larger at the earlier stages of development. As these basic facilities are built up and capital markets are developed, the path is cleared for capital formation of the manufacturing type to go into place and for industrial development in the private sector to occur. Accordingly, one would expect the public share in capital formation to decline over time.

The law of expenditure growth thus seems to be reversed. But again there are countervailing trends. Industrial development generates problems of its own, such as urban blight and congestion, which then call for a rising level of public investment. Such investment, being of a more or less remedial sort, aims at meeting social diseconomies generated by the private sector. Moreover, as income rises, an increasing share of investment is directed at "human investment" and the finance of education has been primarily a public function. On balance, it is again difficult to forecast what the trend should be, and chances are that periods of rising and of declining share may alternate.

[8] His finding, which came to be known as Engel's Law, referred to the declining pcrtion of outlays on food.

Other Causes of Rising Share

While rising per capita income is of major importance, it is by no means the only factor to be considered.

Technical Change Certain other elements, such as technological or population change, may also alter the share of social goods in an efficient product mix. Technological change in particular has a major bearing on the development of the expenditure share. As technology changes, so do the processes of production and the product mix which it is efficient to produce. These changes in technology may be such that they increase or decrease the relative importance of goods whose benefits are largely external, and which must therefore be provided by government.

Consider the invention of the internal combustion engine and the resulting rise of the automobile industry. This development generated a vast increase in the demand for travel and for highways, making for a larger public sector operation than was called for in the horse-and-buggy and steam-engine eras. As we noted already, this consequence has been especially burdensome for state finances. Changes in weapons technology, similarly, greatly increased the cost of military outlays, an equipment-intensive military establishment being more costly than a manpower-intensive one, especially if soldiers are conscripted rather than paid going wages. As we have seen, this was the major factor of expansion at the federal level during the 1940–1960 period.

Future technological changes are difficult to predict, but chances are that the course of space technology—e.g., whether space stations will prove to be social or private goods—will be among the most important factors in determining the share of public purchases over the next century.

Population Change Population changes may also be a major determinant of the public expenditure share. Changes in the rate of population growth generate changes in age distribution, and this trend is reflected in expenditures for education as well as care for the aged. The baby boom of the postwar period has resulted in a vastly higher school and college enrollment, thus placing a major burden on state and local finances. If the more recent population trends continue, education needs will give way to demands for housing facilities; and as the population bulge moves up further in the age scale, the major fiscal problem forty or fifty years hence may well be that of support for the aged.

In addition to these conditions, the need for public services is influenced by factors such as population mobility, leading to the growth of new cities and resulting in demands for additional municipal facilities.

Relative Costs of Public Services

Another cause of a rising expenditure share may be found in the rising relative costs of public services. Expressed in current prices, the ratio of government purchases to GNP rose from 8.3 percent in 1929 to 22.1 percent in 1974. But the price index for government purchases rose more sharply. While the overall GNP price index rose by 236 percent, that for government purchases climbed by 448 percent.[9] If the 1974 levels of GNP and government purchases are deflated and expressed in their 1929 prices, the ratio for 1974 becomes 13.5 percent. Looked at this way, the share of government purchases in GNP showed a much smaller increase. This reflects both greater sensitivity of government purchases to inflation and the fact that many public services—such as education—are highly labor-intensive, a condition that may render them less open to cost reduction through technical progress.[10]

Changing Scope of Transfers

The preceding discussion has related to the share of public purchases or the role of social goods in the efficient product mix. It remains to consider the role of transfers. While transfers were relatively unimportant up to the thirties, since then about one-half the rise in the share of civilian expenditures in GNP has been due to the growth of transfers. The major factor in this development has been the rise of old-age insurance. This program developed, initially at least, not as a means of adjusting the distribution of income but rather as a means of providing old-age security on a self-financing basis. Although the system has moved away from this principle, it nevertheless remains more or less distinct from distributional measures—such as welfare payments—which are pointed directly at equalizing the size distribution of income. Moreover, distributional measures do not appear only in the transfer section of the expenditure budget but also are present in purchase programs aimed at the provision for social goods and services.

Nevertheless, is there reason to expect the role of redistributive transfers to increase with rising per capita income? As the level of per capita income rises, the need for, and scope of, redistributional measures may be affected in two ways.

For one thing, the need for redistribution (given society's views on the desirability of equality) depends on the prevailing state of distribution prior to adjustment. If income inequality decreases as per capita income rises, less extensive redistribution measures are needed. Actually, this change has not occurred to any considerable degree. The size distribution of income has been surprisingly stable over the years, with only a slight tendency toward greater equality.

For another thing, the case for redistribution may change as income rises, depending on how the objective of redistribution policy is defined. If the objective is to adjust family incomes so as to achieve a given relative income distribution, an increase in the average level of income leaves the need for redistribution unchanged. The situation differs if the objective is to set a tolerable minimum level determined in absolute terms, such as the cost of meeting minimum nutrition

[9] See *Economic Report of the President,* January 1975, p. 252.

[10] See D. F. Bradford, R. A. Malt, and W. E. Oates, "The Rising Cost of Local Public Services: Some Evidence and Reflections," *National Tax Journal,* June 1969, pp. 185–202; and W. Baumol, "Macroeconomics of Unbalanced Growth: The Anatomy of Urban Crisis," *American Economic Review,* June 1967, pp. 415–426.

TABLE 6-5
Redistribution Policies

	FAMILY			TRANSFER BUDGET	
	A	*B*	*C*	*Total*	*As Percentage of Earnings*
Low Level					
Earnings	1,000	4,000	10,000		
Transfers (+) and taxes (−)					
Policy I	+1,500	+1,000	−2,500	2,500	16.6
Policy II	+1,500	−428	−1,072	1,500	10.0
Policy III	+1,500	−428	−1,072	1,500	10.0
High Level					
Earnings	3,000	12,000	30,000		
Transfers (+) and taxes (−)					
Policy I	+4,500	+3,000	−7,500	7,500	16.6
Policy II	0	0	0	0	0
Policy III	+4,500	−1,284	−3,216	4,500	10.0

Note: For explanation, see text.

requirements. In this case, the need for redistribution falls as average income rises. But again, if the minimum level is defined as a function of average income, say one-third thereof, the need for redistribution once more remains unchanged as income rises. A reading of United States social philosophy would suggest that concern is with minimum levels, rather than a generalized state of relative shares, but it also appears that the minimum is set in relation to the average, rather than in absolute terms. Hence, one might expect the scope of redistribution (income transfers as a percentage of GNP) to remain constant.

This is illustrated in Table 6-5 for a simple three-family case. Policy I is to give an income to A (the poor family) equal to 50 percent of the average, to B (the middle family) equal to the average, and to leave C (the rich family) with 150 percent of the average. Policy II is to give A a minimum income of $2,500 as defined in absolute terms, while leaving the relative positions of B and C unchanged. Policy III provides A with an income equal to 50 percent of the average but again avoids redistribution between B and C. Thus the tax on B and C in policies II and III is assessed on a proportional basis. In the lower part of the table, the same policies are repeated for a higher level of earnings. We see that the scope of redistribution (the level of transfers in relation to the level of total earnings) does not change for policies I and III but declines for II as we move from the low-income to the high-income case.

A further change in the appropriate scope of redistribution may result from demographic factors. A declining rate of population growth is reflected in an aging population, thus calling for increased provision for the aged. But, though the growth of old-age security payments (OASI) in the United States began in a phase of aging population, it was followed by two decades of accelerated population growth. Now that the rate of population growth is on the decline, the turn of the twentieth century will bring a sharp increase in the ratio of retired to working-age population and, with it, a rise in the ratio of old-age benefit payments to GNP.

Although these factors are of interest, they do not adequately explain the phenomenon of sharply rising welfare and transfer payments both in the United States and in other countries. This development, it appears, must be explained primarily in terms of social and political change, including growing political pressures for "forced" redistribution ("taking") as well as use of the budgetary mechanism in providing for voluntary or semivoluntary redistributional measures ("giving").[11]

Availability of Tax Handles

So far, we have looked primarily at changing needs for public expenditures as the economy develops. Parallel to that, we also find a changing ability to finance such expenditures. In the typical low-income economy, it is much more difficult to impose and collect taxes than in the advanced economy. Not only are the skills and facilities of tax administration less developed, but the structure of the economy is such that it affords fewer and less adequate "handles" on which to attach taxes. The features of economic organization which lend themselves to income taxation are absent. Income is typically derived from self-employment and such wage income as exists is typically paid by small establishments. This makes income taxation much more difficult than in the modern economy, where earned income is largely in the form of wages and salaries and people work in large-scale establishments which readily permit the withholding of income taxes. To make matters worse for the less developed countries (and this is relevant for profit as well as income taxation), accounting practices are not adequately developed to permit effective determination of taxable income and efficient auditing procedures.

Nor are matters much better with regard to sales taxation. Retail taxes are made difficult by the existence of small and nonpermanent retail outlets, and even excises at the producer level are not readily applied in a situation where the market is divided among many small suppliers. One feasible source of revenue collection is imports and exports, explaining why the tax and expenditure ratio to GNP among low-income economies with high trade involvement is usually larger than in economies which do not have this convenient tax handle.[12]

These difficulties do not exist, or exist to a much smaller degree, in highly developed countries, where effective income, profit, and sales taxation is feasible. While taxation in such countries must adapt itself to a highly complex financial and industrial structure, these complications can usually be solved provided there is the necessary political determination to deal with them. The relative absence

[11] See Chap. 3, p. 97.

[12] See Richard A. Musgrave, *Fiscal Systems,* New Haven, Conn.: Yale, 1969.

of adequate tax handles in low-income countries, therefore, is a major factor in explaining why their tax to GNP ratios are lower, and this quite apart from sociological or cultural characteristics which are said to create an aversion to tax collection in low-income countries.

Threshold Effects and War Finance

A further hypothesis regarding the rising ratio of expenditures to GNP runs as follows: Voters have a basic resistance to raising taxes, but after taxes have been increased, they grow to accept them and do not insist on reducing them to their former level. National emergencies, particularly war, may cause a temporary but compelling increase in the need for public expenditures, for which voters are willing to overcome the old "tax threshold" and to accept an increase in the level of taxation which they otherwise would resist. After the emergency has passed, they are willing to retain the new level of taxation, or in any case a level substantially above that tolerated previously. Hence, new civilian public expenditures can be accommodated which otherwise would not have been provided for.

This fact is of particular importance in connection with war finance. War expenditures first displace private outlays and then are displaced by nonemergency public outlays. Since the aftermath of war is typically accompanied by social upheaval and change, the revenue windfall coincides with a change in preferences and political powers which raise the effectively desired level of civilian public expenditures. The resulting increase is thus attributable to both social and political change on one side and the availability of excess revenue at prevailing rates of tax on the other.[13]

Testing this theory for the United States, we find the pattern shown in Table 6-6. We note that the overall expenditure ratio rose sharply during both world wars, and fell off sharply thereafter. We also note that the ratio for defense-related expenditures remains above prewar levels. All these facts are in line with the threshold hypothesis. However, the pattern of civilian expenditures may also be taken to reflect the normal rise of the expenditure ratio—as shown in Figure 6-1—interrupted only by war periods. The threshold theory, while interesting, cannot be taken to give a conclusive explanation of the growth of the public expenditure ratio, at least in the United States. The table also shows that the Vietnam war did not result in a sharp increase in the expenditure ratio comparable to that of previous wars, the ratio of defense expenditures to GNP in general declining over the decade of the 1960s.

Political and Social Factors

It remains to note the importance of political and social change as determinants of expenditure growth. Over the last century, there have occurred vast changes in social philosophy, as well as shifts in the balance of political power among various sectors of the population. They all have had a deep effect not only on what individuals consider to be the desirable size of the public sector, but also

[13] This approach is developed in Alan T. Peacock and Jack Wiseman, *The Growth of Public Expenditures in the United Kingdom,* National Bureau of Economic Research, Princeton, N.J.: Princeton, 1961.

TABLE 6-6
United States Public Expenditures in War Years
(As Percentage of GNP; All Levels of Government)

	Fiscal Year	*Total*	*Defense-related*	*Civilian*
	1913	8.0	1.1	6.9
World War I	1919	29.4	17.7	11.7
	1922	12.1	1.9	10.2
	1938	19.1	1.8	17.3
World War II	1945	46.1	39.2	6.9
	1948	22.3	7.4	14.9
Korean war	1953	30.9	15.4	15.5
	1955	29.1	11.9	17.2
	1965	27.6	8.5	19.1
Vietnam war	1969	34.3	9.9	24.4
	1971	33.1	8.1	25.0
	1973	31.5	6.2	25.3

Notes: Military includes defense expenditures and veterans' benefits and services. Figures are based on budget and census rather than National Income Accounts data.

Sources:

1913–1969: *Facts and Figures on Government Finance,* 16th ed., New York: Tax Foundation, 1971.

1971 and 1973: Based on *Budget of the United States Government,* Fiscal Year 1974; and *Economic Report of the President,* January 1974.

on the force with which the views of various groups make themselves felt in the political decision process.

Quite possibly, the effect of these developments—particularly the rise of transfer payments as a by-product of the incipient welfare state—outweighed the economic and structural factors noted in the preceding discussion. But more likely, they combined with these factors in shaping the actual course of events. Whatever the influence of these particular forces, it is evident that their combined result was a substantial rise in the share of the public sector in GNP.

E. SUMMARY

The size of the public sector may be defined in relation to the major totals in the national income accounts, such as gross national product (GNP), national income, and personal income. The following ratios were noted:

1. Total public expenditures are somewhat over 31 percent of GNP, with the ratio of tax revenue to GNP generally slightly lower.

2. Government purchases are about 21 percent of GNP.

3. Income originating in the public sector is about 14 percent of national income.

4. Transfer payments from government are about 11 percent of personal income, and all receipts from government (including transfers, wages, and interest) constitute about 26 percent.

The public sector share in total economic activity has risen over the years:

5. Total expenditures as a percentage of GNP have shown a more or less steady upward trend since the end of the nineteenth century, and especially over the last forty years.

6. This process applies not only to public expenditures as a whole but also to the defense and nondefense components separately.

7. The increase in the civilian expenditure share has been fueled largely by the rise of social security and welfare programs.

8. The pattern of the rising expenditure share which may be observed historically on a time-series basis also holds for a cross-section comparison between high- and low-income countries.

Turning to the causes of the rising public sector share, various factors may have been of importance:

9. Consumer demand for public services may be income-elastic, so that public services are in the nature of luxury goods, claiming a rising proportion of expenditures as per capita income increases.

10. Depending on the stage of a country's economic development, the structure of capital formation may be such as to require more or less public investment.

11. Changing attitudes, social structures, and political forces may have been behind the rising share of transfers and redistribution-oriented programs.

12. The occurrence of periods of war finance, with a sharp rise in the budget share for war purposes, may have served to raise the threshold of what are considered acceptable levels of taxation.

FURTHER READINGS

Federal Expenditure Policy for Economic Growth and Stability, Joint Economic Committee, U.S. Congress, Nov. 5, 1957, Part I: Arnold M. Soloway, "Growth of Government over the Past 50 Years," and Paul B. Trescott, "Some Historical Aspects of Federal Fiscal Policy."

Kendrick, M. Slade: *A Century and a Half of Federal Expenditures,* Occasional Paper 48, New York: National Bureau of Economic Research, 1955.

Musgrave, Richard A.: *Fiscal Systems,* New Haven, Conn.: Yale, 1970, chaps. 3 and 4.

Peacock, Alan T., and Jack Wiseman: *The Growth of Public Expenditures in the United Kingdom,* National Bureau of Economic Research, Princeton, N.J.: Princeton, 1961, chap. 2.

Schultze, Charles: "Budget Alternatives after Vietnam," in K. Gordon (ed.), *Agenda for the Nation,* Washington: Brookings, 1968.

Wagner, Adolph: "Three Extracts on Public Finance," in Richard A. Musgrave and Alan Peacock (eds.), *Classics in the Theory of Public Finance,* New York: Macmillan, 1958, pp. 1–16.

APPENDIX: PUBLIC SECTOR IN THE NATIONAL INCOME ACCOUNTS

Since the national income accounts offer the most comprehensive frame of reference in which to view the economy, it is helpful to understand the role of

TABLE 6-A1
Composition and Uses of United States Gross National Product for 1973
(In Billions of Dollars)

Major Items	
1. Personal consumption expenditures	805.2
2. Gross private domestic investment	209.4
3. Net exports	3.9
4. GOVERNMENT PURCHASES	276.4
5. Gross national product	1,294.9
6. − Capital consumption allowances	110.8
7. Net national product	1,184.1
8. − INDIRECT BUSINESS TAXES	119.2
9. + SUBSIDIES LESS SURPLUS OF GOVERNMENT ENTERPRISE	0.6
10. − Business transfer payments	4.8
11. − Statistical discrepancy	−5.0
12. National income	1,065.6
13. − CORPORATION TAX	49.8
14. − Undistributed profits	43.3
15. − SOCIAL SECURITY CONTRIBUTIONS	91.2
16. − Inventory valuation adjustment	−17.6
17. + GOVERNMENT TRANSFER PAYMENTS TO PERSONS	113.0
18. + GOVERNMENT INTEREST PAYMENTS	15.4
19. + Business transfer payments	4.9
20. + Interest payments by consumers	22.9
21. Personal income	1,055.0
22. − PERSONAL TAXES	151.3
23. Disposable income	903.7
24. − Consumption	805.2
25. − Interest paid by consumers	22.9
26. − Personal transfers abroad	1.2
27. Personal savings	74.3

Note: Government items are shown in capital letters.
Source: *Survey of Current Business*, pp. 13–28, July 1973. Items 1–5, see table 1.1; items 6–12, 15, 17, 19, see table 1.9; items 13, 14, 16, see table 1.10; item 18, see tables 3.1, 3.3; items 20–27, see table 2.1. Note that the total of item 18 plus item 20 is also given in table 1.9. Components may not add to totals, owing to rounding.

government items in these accounts. This is shown in Table 6-A1 for 1973 data. For the time being, federal, state, and local governments are combined into one public sector.

PUBLIC SECTOR IN GNP

The gross national product may be looked upon as the aggregate of expenditures on currently produced output. Government contributes to these expenditures through its purchases of goods and services.

Total Share

As shown in item 4 of Table 6-A1, such purchases are a major component of GNP, with 21 percent of total output purchased by government.[14] Looked at from the other end, 21 percent of goods and services when received by users are not paid for directly but are provided free of direct charge and paid for indirectly through the government budget. While not all these goods can be strictly classified as "social goods" as defined in Chapter 3, we may nevertheless record the fact that over 20 percent of total output is based on budgetary provision.

In examining how this provision fits into the economic structure, we now inquire how government purchases are divided between (1) purchases of factors and purchases of products; (2) provision for consumption and provision for investment; and (3) provision to consumers and provision to firms.

Purchase of Factors versus Products

The first distinction does not appear directly in the national income accounts, but it can be approximated by equating governmental factor purchases with public sector wage payments. Not shown in the table, such compensation amounted to 53 percent of total government purchases, the remainder being the purchases of products from private firms. Thus government assumes the role of producer for about one-half the goods and services which it provides through the budget.

Provision for Consumption versus Investment

The second distinction is between consumption and capital formation. If we define capital formation by government as similar to that in the private sector, new structures, all durable equipment, and additions to inventory should be included. On this basis, 22 percent of government purchases go into capital formation.[15] This is slightly above the corresponding private sector ratio of 20 percent (private investment as a percentage of private purchases) for the same year.

It may be argued, however, that the concept of investment should be defined more broadly so as to include investment in human resources. This is especially important for the government sector. Here, expenditures for such functions as research, education, and health might be included. Using such a broad concept of capital formation, capital expenditures of the public sector come to comprise a much larger share of public purchases. According to this approach, about two-thirds of civilian government purchases (excluding defense) are of the capital formation type, thus raising the ratio of capital formation to consumption substantially above that in the private sector. Such remains true even if we apply an equally broad concept of investment to the latter. Capital formation, it appears, is a major function of the public sector, a fact to be kept in mind in our later discussion of fiscal policy effects on growth.

[14] The Department of Commerce concept of government purchases includes purchases by general government plus gross investment of government enterprises. The current output of government enterprises is excluded from government purchases and is reflected in private purchases.

[15] See *Survey of Current Business,* July 1974, table 3.16, p. 32.

Provision to Consumers versus Provision to Firms

The division of publicly provided goods and services between final goods supplied to consumers and "intermediate goods" supplied to firms does not lend itself readily to statistical determination. A substantial part of highway expenditures, of municipal services, and of developmental outlays are in the intermediate good category, i.e., they are grants which reduce the cost of production for private firms rather than go directly to the private consumer.[16] At least part of education outlays also belong in this category. Some intermediate goods are of the current service type (police protection for plants), whereas others are of the investment type (roads). Excluding defense, it may well be that one-third or more of total purchases are of the intermediate type.

PUBLIC SECTOR IN NATIONAL INCOME

In moving from GNP to *net national product,* depreciation or capital consumption allowances are deducted. These include (or should include) depreciation on government assets.[17] Moving on to *national income,* we deduct indirect business taxes (item 8 of Table 6-A1).[18] Indirect business taxes, such as sales taxes, are deducted because they reduce the amount available for disbursement to factors, with national income defined as the sum of factor incomes.

For similar reasons, subsidies to business firms are added, the impact being the same as that of negative taxes (item 9). Moreover, profits of public enterprise are deducted. If government enterprises make profits, such profits, unlike business profits, do not become available as income to the private sector. Similarly, if they record losses, factor earnings by the private sector exceed the value of the product as recorded in GNP. Therefore, the surplus must be deducted and the deficit must be added when moving from net national product to national income.[19]

Since national income reflects the total of private factor earnings, it may be broken down into income derived from, or "originating in," the government and the private sector. The bulk of income originating in government is in the form of wages and salaries paid by government; i.e., it is equal to the share of government purchases which are used for factor rather than product purchases. For 1973, such payments equaled $147 billion, or 14 percent of national income. If

[16] See Chap. 7, p. 163, for a further discussion of this distinction.

[17] To obtain a proper figure of net output, depreciation on government as well as on privately held assets should be deducted, but in fact the national income accounts do not allow for this.

[18] There are two difficulties with this treatment:

1. In the United States national income accounts as prepared by the Department of Commerce, indirect business taxes also include some $45 billion of property tax receipts, about half of which are derived from owner-occupied residences and should not be included in this part of the accounts. Rather, these taxes should be deducted along with income tax when moving from personal to disposable income.

2. While it is customary in the United States accounts to think of factor shares as shares in national income, it may be preferable to focus on net national product, thus including indirect taxes as part of gross factor earnings.

[19] Other items included in the transition from net national product to national income do not involve government. They are business transfer payments and the statistical discrepancy, which reconciles the estimation of the accounts from the product and the income sides.

current operations of government enterprise are included, the share is increased to 16 percent.

PUBLIC SECTOR IN PERSONAL INCOME

Moving from national to personal income, we again encounter a number of government items, of which some divert from, and others add to, income available at the personal level.

First, the corporation profits tax (item 13 of Table 6-A1) is deducted,[20] followed by social security contributions (item 15), including contributions by both employers and employees.[21] Government transfer payments are then added. They largely involve social security payments (somewhat in excess of contributions), while veterans' benefits and public assistance are the next most important items.

Finally, government interest payments to persons are added. This is necessary because interest paid by government is not included in GNP or in national income. The reason is that interest paid on government debt must be distinguished from earnings imputed to government-owned assets. Such imputation clearly should be a part of GNP, but interest on public debt cannot serve as proxy for it. This is evident when one considers that the bulk of public debt has been incurred in the cause of war finance, rather than in acquiring government assets. The service which is rendered by the bondholders, and for which they must be paid, is significant for stabilization policy,[22] but it does not enter into current output. Debt issued by private business, on the other hand, goes to finance capital used in the process of production, and interest on such debt reflects the factor earnings which accrue to the capital which this debt finances. It is thus included in the value of total output (GNP) as the factor payments which comprise national income.[23]

Personal income, finally, may again be broken down into the part received from payments by government, and the part received from private disbursements. For 1970, the government share (including earnings, net transfers, and interest) was 26 percent. Reflecting the important role of transfer payments, this is a substantially larger share than that of national income originating in the public sector.

PUBLIC SECTOR IN DISPOSABLE INCOME

In moving to disposable income, personal tax payments (item 22 of Table 6-A1) must be deducted. These amount to 15 percent of personal income. Of this, 10

[20] There is some question why indirect business taxes should be deducted when moving from net national product to national income, while the corporation profits tax is deducted when moving from the latter to personal income. See Richard A. Musgrave, *The Theory of Public Finance,* New York: McGraw-Hill, 1959, p. 198.

[21] It might be argued that the employee contribution part of the payroll tax should be included in personal income and be deducted (along with the income tax) only when moving from personal to disposable income.

[22] See Chap. 28, Sec. B.

[23] The exclusion of government interest from GNP is analogous, however, to the treatment of interest on consumer debt in the private sector, which is excluded for similar reasons.

percent is accounted for by the federal individual income tax and 4 percent by other taxes.

Proceeding to the uses of disposable income (items 24–27), no further budget items appear since all taxes have been deducted in advance and since public enterprise sales to consumers are included in consumption, along with private sales. Disposable income as defined in the accounts, however, falls short of a person's real income. In addition to the cash earnings reflected in an individual's disposable income, real income also includes the free provision of public services by government; and if such real income was included on the income side, public services would become an important item of income use.

Chapter 7

Expenditure Evaluation: Principles*

A. Some Basic Concepts: *Fixed Budget; Variable Budget.* **B. Measuring Benefits and Costs:** *Types of Benefits and Costs; Real versus Pecuniary; Direct versus Indirect; Tangible versus Intangible; Risk; Final versus Intermediate; Inside versus Outside.* **C. Project Selection:** *Objective Function; Multiple Objectives; Sectoral Allocation; Distributional Weights.* **D. Discounting and the Cost of Capital:** *Importance of Discounting; Private Rate; Social Rate; Rules of Thumb; Local Rate.* **E. Summary. Appendix: Further Problems of the Discount Rate:** *Adjustment for Income Tax; Social Rate of Discount.*

In our earlier discussion of social goods, we examined how the provision for such goods may be determined, how it might be related to consumer choice, and how the political process enters in solving the problem. We now turn to a more limited, if more practical, view of expenditure determination.

Suppose the voters have delegated expenditure decisions to their representatives. What information would they need to determine the worthiness of alterna-

* *Reader's Guide to Chapter 7:* Here we present the analytical framework of cost-benefit analysis, an aspect of public finance on which there has been the most lively discussion in recent years. Eminently practical in application, it nevertheless involves some knotty theoretical problems. As discussed in section D, they arise especially in connection with discounting. Some of the more technical aspects of this problem are raised in the chapter appendix and may be passed over by the less theoretically inclined reader.

tive projects, and how should they go about assessing them? We now explore the general methodology which has been developed to deal with this problem.

In recent years this analysis has become one of the most lively branches of fiscal economics at both the practical and the analytical levels. Actually, it has a long history, beginning with the evaluation of federal expenditures in the field of navigation undertaken by the Corps of Engineers. The Flood Control Act of 1936 lent further impetus to cost-benefit analysis in the realm of water resource projects, and in 1950 general principles and rules were set out by an interagency committee concerned with the evaluation of various river basin projects.[1] Following a period of rapidly developing interest and research in cost-benefit analysis, in 1965 a planning-programming-budgeting (PPB) system was introduced by executive order to apply to all federal departments and agencies. This system, as well as applications of cost-benefit analysis to particular situations, will be examined in the next chapter. First, certain basic concepts will be considered.

A. SOME BASIC CONCEPTS

Project evaluation, like all issues in allocation economics, involves determination of the ways in which the most efficient use can be made of scarce resources. In its simplest form, the issue is how to determine the *composition* of the budget of a given size and how to allocate a total of given funds among alternative projects. There is also the more complex question of determining the appropriate *size* of the budget. Further complications arise when various types of benefits and benefit mixes may be generated by one project and tradeoffs must be made among them. In taking a first look at these various situations, we assume that benefits and costs are known. The measurement of costs and benefits is considered in the next section.

Fixed Budget

Suppose the budget director is to advise the legislature—be it Congress or a city council—how best to allocate a given sum, say $1 billion, between two expenditure projects, X and Y. The problem may be likened to that of the head of a consumer household who has to allocate the family budget. First, the director must determine the cost C involved in providing each service and the benefit B to be derived therefrom. He must then allocate outlays between X and Y so as to derive the greatest total benefit from the budget, i.e., to maximize the excess of total benefits ΣB over costs ΣC. With ΣC given by the size of the budget, the task is simply to maximize ΣB.

Divisible Projects Assuming the project choices to be finely divisible, the task is simple. The opportunity cost of spending $1 on X is the benefit lost from not spending it on Y, and vice versa. To maximize total benefits the policy maker should allocate outlays so that total benefits minus total costs are at a maximum. Such is the case if $MB_x/MB_y = MC_x/MC_y$, where MB is marginal benefit and

[1] Inter-Agency River Basin Committee (Subcommittee on Costs and Budgets), *Proposed Practices for Economic Analysis of River Basin Projects,* Government Printing Office, 1950.

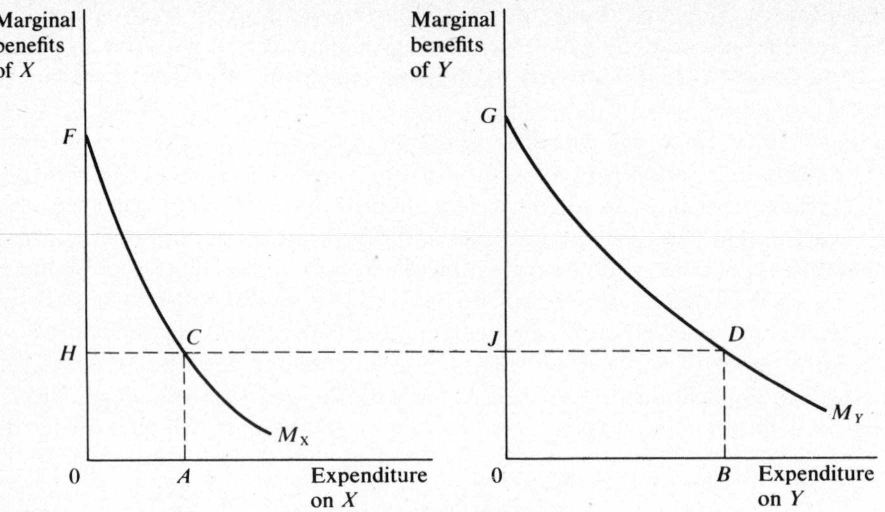

FIGURE 7-1 Expenditure Allocation with Fixed Budget.

MC is marginal cost. Given $MC = \$1$, the policy maker will equate MB_x and MB_y.

This is shown in Figure 7-1, where the M_x and M_y schedules show the value of the marginal benefit (additions to total benefits) derived from spending successive dollars on X and Y. Total expenditures E are distributed between X and Y so that the marginal benefit of expenditures on X or *AC* equals that on Y or *BD*. Thus *OA* is spent on X and *OB* on Y such that $OA + OB = \text{E}$ the assigned budget. If this is done, total benefits from X as measured by the area *OACF*, plus those from Y as measured by *OBDG*, are maximized.[2] Putting the matter in cost-benefit terms, we see that the two projects are pushed to the point where the ratios of marginal benefits to marginal costs are equal. Since marginal cost in both cases equals \$1, we again have $AC = BD$.

Lumpy Projects We have assumed so far that expenditures may be divided finely between projects X and Y, so that benefits may be equated for the marginal dollar spent on each. Where we deal with the allocation of funds between broad expenditure categories, this marginal approach is more or less applicable. But when it comes to specific allocation within departments, choices must be made

[2] If the marginal benefits *MB* obtained from various quantities *Q* are given by

$$MB_x = a - bQ_x$$
$$MB_y = c - dQ_y$$

we have the efficiency condition

$$MB_x = MB_y$$

and the budget constraint

$$Q_x\bar{P}_x + Q_y\bar{P}_y = \bar{E}$$

from which Q_x and Q_y may be found.

TABLE 7-1
Project Rankings with Fixed Budget

Project	Costs	Benefits	Benefits minus Costs	BENEFIT-COST RATIO $\frac{B}{C}$	$\frac{B-C}{C}$	Ranking
	(In Thousands of Dollars)					
A	200	400	200	2.0	1.0	2
B	150	195	45	1.3	0.3	4
C	100	120	20	1.2	0.2	5
D	50	125	75	2.5	1.5	1
E	300	450	150	1.5	0.5	3
F	125	125	0	1.0	0	6
G	300	270	−30	0.9	−0.1	7

between particular projects which are indivisible, involve lump-sum amounts, or are not smoothly expandable. If a choice has to be made between a road connecting cities X and Y and another connecting X and Z, where the X to Y distance is twice the Y to Z distance, no marginal adjustment is possible. Maximizing total benefits as nearly as possible now leads to unequal "marginal" benefits. Suppose that we have $700,000 to spend, say on alternative highway projects, and may choose among the projects A to G as shown in Table 7-1. The cost for each project is measured by the dollar outlay required. The benefit valuation gives the total benefit of each project. For instance, returning to Figure 7-1, the total benefit of project X, involving an outlay *OA*, corresponds to the area *OACF*.

To make the choice, we must compare the projects and choose those which are most profitable. The result should again be such that total benefits ΣB are maximized. How is this to be done? Since different amounts are involved, outlays on various projects cannot be ranked by absolute benefit levels (where E would lead) or by absolute benefit-cost differentials (where A would lead). Rather, we may determine the *ratio* of benefit to cost for each investment, and rank the projects in order of their B/C ratio. Alternatively, ranking may be in terms of their $(B - C)/C$ ratio, which gives a rate of return on cost analogous to measuring returns in the private sector. The rankings are the same under either ratio.

Moving down from the highest ranking, the budget will be exhausted after projects D, A, E, and B are included. Here ranking by cost-benefit ratios is a means of maximizing total benefit for a given outlay.[3] That the B/C ratio exceeds 1 at the margin suggests that the rate of return is higher in the public than in the private sector, but nothing can be done about this so long as we operate within a fixed budget constraint. Similarly, the fixed budget is too large and should be cut back if the B/C ratio falls short of 1 and private investment is more profitable.

[3] To simplify, the figures in Table 7-2 were chosen so that the cost of the highest-ranking four projects equals the budget constraint. Choosing the highest-ranking four projects therefore maximized total benefits within this constraint. But suppose that project B with a ratio of 1.2 costs $90,000 only, yielding benefits of only $108,000. Maximizing benefits now calls for inclusion of project C (with benefits of $120,000) while omitting B. Choice by ranking, as followed in the text, thus oversimplifies matters. The proper rule is to pick that bundle of projects which maximizes total benefits.

Variable Budget

Actually, the government does not consist of one unit, operating within a fixed budget. At each level, allocative decisions must be made in dividing resources within a small unit (say a section), as well as among sections within a branch, among branches within a division, among divisions within a department, and among departments within the government at large. Finally, government must decide how resources are to be divided between private and public use and it must decide the size of the total government budget itself. We must therefore drop the assumption of a fixed budget and reconsider project choices along with determining total budget outlays. Within the fixed budget, the opportunity cost of pursuing one public project consists of the benefit lost by not pursuing another public project. But in the open budget the opportunity cost of public projects must be redefined as the lost benefits from private projects which are foregone because resources are transferred to public use.[4]

Divisible Projects As before, we begin with the assumption of finely divisible outlays. The task is to maximize $\Sigma B - \Sigma C$, including benefits and costs of both public and private projects. This condition is met by equating marginal benefits for the last dollar spent on alternative public and private projects. Public projects are expanded and private projects are restricted until the benefit from the last dollar spent in either sector is the same. Interpreting X as "the" public project and Y as "the" private project, the solution of Figure 7-1 again applies. Given perfect markets, the marginal benefit from spending \$1 in the private sector equals \$1, and the same must hold on the public side. Thus public expenditures are extended until the last dollar spent yields a dollar's worth of benefits. The marginal B/C ratio will be 1 in both sectors.

Lumpy Projects Allowance must again be made for the fact that public investment may be lumpy. Suppose that a highway investment of \$1 million is to be considered. The total benefits derived are measured as the area under the marginal benefit curve, say $OACF$ in Figure 7-1. Benefits lost in the private sector in turn are measured by the resource cost of the private project foregone, i.e., as \$1 million.[5] The B/C ratio in the private sector is taken to equal 1 and the public project will be undertaken if the ratio exceeds 1; or, using a preferred criterion, if the absolute value of $B - C$ is positive.[6] Returning to Table 7-1, all projects except G would be undertaken if there were no budget constraint.

B. MEASURING BENEFITS AND COSTS

It is not enough to say that all "relevant" costs and benefits should be included. The problem is to decide which costs and benefits are relevant and how they

[4] The argument has to be qualified if unemployment is allowed for. See Chap. 26, Sec. C.

[5] For a fuller discussion of consumer and producer surplus, see E. J. Mishan, *Cross-Benefit Analysis,* Praeger, N.Y., 1973, chap. 7.

[6] The $B - C > 0$ criterion is preferred because it may be difficult to decide whether certain project characteristics (e.g., air pollution caused by use of a highway) should be entered as a reduced benefit or an increased cost. This decision will not affect the value of $B - C$, but it will affect B/C.

should be valued. In dealing with this issue, we first disregard the time dimension and assume that all costs and benefits will accrue at once. The discount problem which arises with the consideration of time patterns will be examined in section C.

Types of Benefits and Costs

In dealing with various types of benefits and costs, these major categories may be distinguished:

Benefits and costs may be real or pecuniary
Real benefits and costs may be:
- direct or indirect
- tangible or intangible
- final or intermediate
- inside or outside

Illustrations of various types of benefits and costs are given in Table 7-2.

Real versus Pecuniary

The most important distinction is that between real and pecuniary aspects. Real benefits are the benefits derived by the final consumers of the public project. They reflect an addition to the community's welfare, to be balanced against the real cost of resource withdrawal from other uses. Pecuniary benefits and costs come about because of changes in relative prices which occur as the economy adjusts itself to the provision of the public service. As a result, gains accrue to some individuals but are offset by losses which are experienced by others. They do not reflect gains to society as a whole.

Price Changes As labor is hired and a road is constructed, the wage rates for construction workers may rise because the relative scarcity of their skills is increased. This result is a gain to them, but it is offset by a decline in (relative) wage rates in some other employment where demand is reduced because of higher taxes. To count both the value of the road and the gain in wages would thus be double counting. Or, the construction of the road may lead to higher prices for tents (if it is an access road to camping grounds) or for trucks (if it is a trucking highway). Such gains are again relevant to people occupied in these particular industries, but they do not reflect a net gain to society, as they are offset by costs to others, i.e., the consumers of tents or trucks who must pay higher prices. Still another illustration would be rising land values on roadside property, or increased earnings of roadside restaurants.

Pecuniary changes are relevant if one examines the *distributional* consequences of the road project. But they do not reflect net gains to society and hence

TABLE 7-2
Illustrations of Project Benefits and Costs*

		Benefits	*Costs*
		IRRIGATION PROJECT	
Real			
Direct	tangible	Increased farm output	Cost of pipes
	intangible	Beautification of area	Loss of wilderness
Indirect	tangible	Reduced soil erosion	Diversion of water
	intangible	Preservation of rural society	Destruction of wildlife
Pecuniary		Relative improvement in position of farm equipment industry	
		MOON SHOT PROJECT	
Real			
Direct	tangible	As yet unknown	Cost of inputs
	intangible	Joy of exploration	Pollution of universe
Indirect	tangible	Technical progress generated	
	intangible	Gain in world prestige	
Pecuniary		Relative increase in land values at Cape Kennedy	
		EDUCATION PROJECT	
Real			
Direct	tangible	Increased future earnings	Loss of students' earnings, teachers' salaries, cost of buildings and books
	intangible	Enriched life	Forgone leisure time
Indirect	tangible	Reduced costs of crime prevention	
	intangible	More intelligent electorate	
Pecuniary		Relative increase in teachers' incomes	

* The benefits and costs noted in the table are merely illustrative for each project and not intended to be comprehensive.

do not enter into benefit evaluation unless distributional weights are to be attached to the particular benefit streams which accrue to various individuals.

Unemployed Resources Another aspect of this problem relates to the costing of otherwise unemployed resources. The cost to be accounted for in public resource use is the lost opportunity for putting these resources to alternative uses, be they other public projects (in the fixed budget context) or private projects (in the open budget setting). This reasoning breaks down if the resources are otherwise unemployed and the opportunity cost is zero. Thus, it may be argued that public works are costless in a period of unemployment, or may even be beneficial (beyond their own value) in that they create additional employment via multiplier effects.[7]

[7] See p. 520.

This argument is correct as far as it goes. Using unemployed resources poorly may indeed be better than not using them at all. But it is not as good as using them for a superior purpose. Unless there are political constraints which permit only one use, cost-benefit analysis should apply the concept of opportunity cost even where resources are otherwise unemployed. This applies with regard both to choices among rival public works projects and to choosing between higher public outlays and increased private spending through tax reduction.

But though unemployment is no excuse for failing to evaluate the merits of alternative uses, employment effects of particular projects become relevant to benefit evaluation if alternative policies to deal with unemployment are not available. The resulting gain in employment is then an additional benefit, or the opportunity cost of labor is zero. Project A may be preferred to project B even though its intrinsic merit is less, provided that the superior effect on employment outweighs the latter shortfall. Thus, building a road in location X may be superior to doing so in location Y if X has a high unemployment rate while Y does not, even though benefit calculus in the absence of employment effects would point to Y. Such is the case provided that alternative ways of dealing with unemployment in X are not available. This may be so because unemployment is of a regional nature and not amenable to reduction by stabilization policy on a national scale. If alternative approaches, such as relocation, are available, cost-benefit analysis should compare policy packages, e.g., road construction in Y plus relocation of manpower from X, with road construction in X. To put it differently, efficient policy planning has to be on a comprehensive basis and cannot be limited to an isolated consideration of specific policy tools or projects.

Direct versus Indirect

Real benefits and costs may be direct or indirect or, which is the same, primary or secondary. Direct benefits and costs are those related closely to the main project objective, while indirect benefits are in the nature of by-products. This distinction has a common-sense meaning but cannot be defined rigorously. The most useful interpretation is in terms of legislative intent. Thus, a river development program may have flood control as its immediate objective but may also have important bearing on the supply of power, on irrigation, or on soil erosion in adjacent areas. Development of defense technology, while aimed primarily at increased defense capacity, may have important side effects on improving technology in the private sector. The space program may be undertaken primarily to explore the moon, but it may also lead to gains in defense technology or technological improvements in the automobile industry. An education program may be directed primarily at raising the earning power of the student but it may also reduce the need to combat delinquency. In all these cases, indirect or secondary results may be distinguished from the direct or primary objective. Obviously, the former should be included along with the latter in assessing project benefits. Tracing of the more indirect benefits may be difficult, but they should be included.

Tangible versus Intangible

The term "tangible" is applied to benefits and costs which can be valued in the market, whereas others which cannot are referred to as "intangible." The distinction is thus synonymous with that between benefits from private and social goods or between costs which are internalized and costs which are external.

Measuring Tangible Costs and Benefits Assuming a perfect market, the social value of tangible benefits is measured by the price which the service would fetch in the market, just as the social cost is measured by the price that must be paid for the inputs needed to render the service. But if market imperfections exist, market prices and costs do not reflect true social values and costs, and they must be adjusted accordingly.

Such adjustments—referred to by economists as the use of "shadow prices" —may be called for where markets are noncompetitive, where relative prices are distorted by indirect taxes, or where externalities have to be taken into account. A much-discussed instance of shadow pricing, as we shall see presently, arises in choosing the appropriate rate of discount, but this is not the only example. Thus indirect taxes should be excluded since they do not reflect a true social cost. For similar reasons, rental incomes or monopoly profits should not be counted. Suppose that the market cost of a given factor of production is $1 million, but that in a competitive market it would have earned only $900,000. The opportunity cost in this case is $900,000, not $1 million, even though the factor supplier may be able to extract the higher price. This increased rent is a pecuniary gain, but not a real cost to society.[8]

Other important instances of shadow pricing arise in developing economies with large labor surpluses but extensive social legislation, including minimum wages. It may then be desirable to account for labor costs at a lower rate than applies in the market. Or, overvalued exchange rates may set too low a price on imported capital and induce wasteful investment unless higher shadow prices for such capital are applied.

Measuring Intangible Costs and Benefits Tangible benefits result where government operates a public enterprise which sells in the market. The Postal Service is such a case. In other operations, tangible benefits result from free provision of goods such as housing which could be provided by the market. In other instances, benefits are clearly intangible, as in the case of national defense. In still other situations, both tangible and intangible benefits may result. Thus, education yields intangible benefits via cultural enrichment and improved functioning of the democratic process. At the same time, there is a tangible benefit of increased earning power. Similarly, costs may be partly tangible (e.g., the cost of the resource input into the construction of a superhighway) and partly intangible (e.g., the resulting damage to the beauty of a wilderness area).

Wherever intangible benefits and costs are involved, measurement takes us back to the central problem of social-good evaluation. This, as we have seen, must be accomplished by budget determination through the political process. Cost-

[8] Another problem of shadow pricing occurs where the transfer of the factor to public use raises its price in private use, and the question arises as to the price (before and after reduction in private activity) at which the opportunity cost should be measured. As before, a midway value offers a reasonable approximation to the proper result.

benefit analysis is no substitute for this process; it is only a way of choosing among projects *after* the value of a benefit has been determined. Thus cost-benefit analysis is most easily applied in those areas where benefits are tangible and there is least need for public provision to begin with.

But even though evaluation of benefits may be difficult, analysts may be helpful in two respects. First, they can point out where benefits (gains in literacy, increases in offensive or defensive capability, reduction in number of accidents, etc.) result from particular projects. This at least gives a basis for valuing these end results in dollar terms. Second, they may determine how desired results may be maximized with given inputs. Thus, the analyst may compare the effectiveness (in achieving a certain objective) of spending a given amount, say $1 billion, in alternative ways. This approach, referred to as "cost-effectiveness" analysis, is helpful even though the valuation of the end product may be difficult.

Risk

Project benefits may not be readily predictable at the outset. Public project planning, no less than private investment, proceeds under uncertainty. Risk and uncertainty regarding future benefits reduce the present value of the income stream.[9] Thus, highway planning will involve forecasts of population growth, a weapons program will involve judgments regarding future technical developments and the resulting rate of obsolescence, and so forth. While it may be argued that in certain situations the social risk is less than the private risks involved in particular activities, it does not follow that risk is a minor matter in public project planning.[10]

Final versus Intermediate

The task of benefit evaluation is facilitated where the public facilities are in the nature of intermediate goods rather than final goods. In the case of final goods such as parks (and assuming there is no crowding problem), the social-good aspect must be faced head on. Since evaluation through toll pricing would require the inefficient device of exclusion, some other approach is needed. In the case of the trucking road, the benefits of the road may be evaluated in terms of the reduction in trucking cost to industry. Even though the road itself may be a social good (if we assume absence of crowding), it enters as an intermediate good into the production of a final output which is a private good (the transported product ready for sale), the value of which can be assessed in market terms. Flood control, irrigation, and many other projects may be evaluated in these terms. Even though irrigation water is not sold to individual farmers, its value may be computed as the value of the increased output of farm products minus the cost of the other inputs which the farmer needs to secure the increased output.

This is illustrated in Figure 7-2 where *JK* is the demand curve for a certain private good and *GS* is the firm's marginal (and, since constant, also average)

[9] Alternatively, a risk premium might be added in calculating project cost.

[10] See Kenneth Arrow, *Essays in the Theory of Risk-bearing,* Chicago: Markham, 1971, chap. 11.

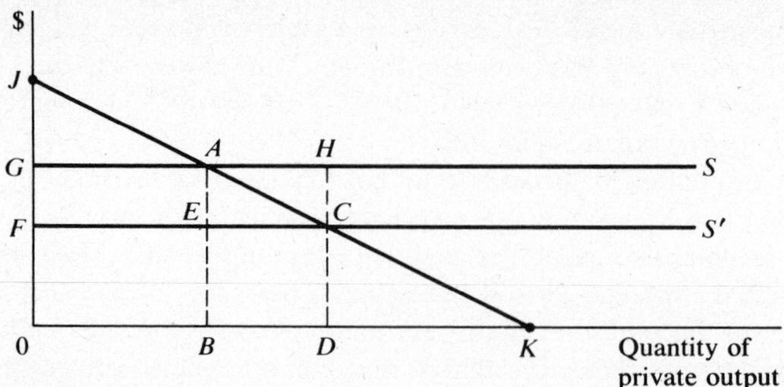

FIGURE 7-2 Measuring Benefits from Intermediate Public Goods.

cost prior to the project. As the project is introduced, the firm's cost curve falls to *FS′*. Output rises from *OB* to *OD* and price falls from *OG* to *OF*. Total benefits rise from *OBAJ* to *ODCJ*, while total costs to consumers change from *OBAG* to *ODCF*. Deducting the change in cost from the gain in benefits, we obtain *FCAG*.[11] This reflects the increase in consumer surplus (from *GAJ to FCJ*) that has resulted. The gain in this case may be measured with reference to the change in market price of the final private product, thus avoiding the difficulties of valuation which arise in the instance of products which constitute final social goods.[12]

Another situation which facilitates the task of benefit evaluation arises where provision of the public service relieves society of other costs which now become unnecessary. Thus, benefits of a program to reduce school dropouts may be measured in terms of savings in outlays on correctional institutions, or public health measures may be evaluated in terms of reduced hospital costs. The estimation of benefits in terms of costs saved provides an approximation by which to determine project selections.[13]

Inside versus Outside

Another distinction is between benefits and costs which accrue inside the jurisdiction in which the project is undertaken and others which accrue outside. Thus, flood-control measures undertaken on the Connecticut River by Vermont may

[11] The change in benefits equals

$$ODCJ - OBAJ = BDCA = BDCE + ECA$$

The change in the consumers' costs (which may be positive or negative) equals

$$ODCF - OBAG = OBEF + BDCE - (OBEF + FEAG) = BDCE - FEAG$$

The net increase in benefits equals

$$BDCE + ECA - BDCE + FEAG = ECA + FEAG = FCAG$$

[12] Thus in terms of Fig. 7-2, the gain *FCAG* equals *FEAG* + *ECA*. But *FEAG* = *FE* × *FG* = original quantity consumed *OB* times the reduction in price *FG*; and *ECA* equals one-half *(EC × EA)* or one-half the increase in quantity consumed *BD* times the reduction in price. The components of *FCAG* are thus all measurable quantities.

[13] The value thus set gives a lower limit, since the private activity which becomes unnecessary was valued at the margin without counting consumer surplus.

be helpful not only in Vermont but may also prevent floods farther down in the state of Connecticut. The former benefits are internal and the latter are external. They constitute a "spillover" from one jurisdiction to another. Both benefits should be included in assessing the project, but interstate cooperation is needed to do so. This is a matter which we shall pursue further when dealing with the economics of fiscal federalism.

C. PROJECT SELECTION

After benefits and costs are determined, further issues arise in the course of project selection.

Objective Function

Stated most generally, budget planners may base this process of project selection on an "objective function" which defines the social welfare, W_s, that is to be maximized. This may take the form

$$W_s = [W_{G1} + W_{G2} + \cdots + W_{Gn}] - [W_{L1} + W_{L2} + \cdots + W_{Ln}]$$

where W_{G1} *to* W_{Gn} are the real welfare gains that will result for individuals 1 to n from the public project, and W_{L1} *to* W_{Ln} are the losses which result to the same individuals if the resources were withdrawn from their best alternative uses.[14] If all gains are given equal weight, the objective function calls for maximizing the aggregate net gain as defined by $W_s = \sum_{i=1}^{z} (W_{Gi} - W_{Li})$.

Introducing distributional considerations, this becomes

$$W_s = \left[\alpha \sum_{j=1}^{m} (W_{Gj} - W_{Lj}) + \beta \sum_{k=n}^{z} (W_{Gk} - W_{Lk})\right]$$

where net income gains of individuals in groups 1 to m are given weight α while those of individuals in groups n to z are given weight β. These groups may refer to income brackets, regions, or whatever other characteristics are relevant.

Multiple Objectives

Frequently, an expenditure project does not yield one single type of benefit but serves a number of objectives. For instance, a particular weapon system may have various defensive and offensive uses, expenditures on education may serve both to reduce illiteracy and to stimulate scientific progress, projects differ in their distributional implications, and so forth. By redesigning the project, one or the other objective may be emphasized. In such cases, a comparison among projects involves attributing relative weights to the various benefits which result. Suppose, for instance, that \$3 billion is to be spent on schools, and to be distributed between elementary and higher education. Also, suppose that for each \$1 billion spent, outlays on elementary education contribute 4 times as much to literacy as do

[14] See Otto Eckstein, "A Survey of the Theory of Public Expenditure Criteria," as cited in the Further Readings at the end of this chapter.

outlays on secondary education, but that their contribution to advancing technology is only one-fifth that of higher education. For this purpose we may think of literacy units as measured by the number of students receiving a given test score and of technology units as the number of science majors that result. Using alternative expenditure allocations, we then have these options:

Expenditure Pattern	EXPENDITURES ON *Elementary Education* *(In Billions of Dollars)*	*Higher Education*	UNIT GAINS IN *Literacy*	*Technology*
I	3	0	12	3
II	2	1	9	7
III	1	2	6	11
IV	0	3	3	15

The figures showing unit gains in the literacy column tell us that expenditure pattern I yields a gain 4 times as large as pattern IV, and so forth, without expressing absolute values.[15] The same holds for the column showing gains in technology, where pattern I is one-fifth as effective as pattern IV. If a choice is to be made, a common measure of valuation for the two types of unit gains is needed. This may be in terms of resulting increase in GNP, or it may involve other considerations. For example, the gains in education may be valued on cultural grounds, quite apart from the resulting addition to GNP as measured by the official statistics, and a dollar value may be put on this gain.

When moving from pattern I toward pattern IV, 1⅓ technology units are gained for each literacy unit lost. Therefore, if one literacy unit is valued at less than 1⅓ technology units, pattern IV will be chosen; if it is valued at more than 1⅓, pattern I is preferred, while all plans are equally good if one literacy unit equals 1⅓ technology units. This view, of course, is too simple, since the rate of substitution in consumption between literacy and technology changes with the mix and level of total outlays. This is shown in Figure 7-3 where the lines i_1, i_2, i_3, etc., are the social indifference curves pertaining to literacy and technology. Moreover, the tradeoff between literacy and technology units in production may be variable, giving us a convex "project utility" frontier as illustrated by points I to IV in the figure. As shown, III is now the preferred pattern since it places us on the highest social indifference curve.

Sectoral Allocation

Another illustration is given by the problem of allocating police forces among sections of a city.[16] Suppose there is an uptown precinct X and a downtown precinct Y. Population size is the same in both but the crime rate is higher in Y. Assume further that crime prevention is subject to increasing cost in both

[15] For this presentation, see Arthur Smithies, "Programs, Objectives and Decision Making," in H. Hinrichs and G. T. Taylor (eds.), *Program Budgeting and Benefit-Cost Analysis,* Pacific Palisades, Calif.: Goodyear, 1969, p. 181.

[16] See Carl S. Shoup, "Standards for Distributing a Free Government Service: Crime Prevention," *Public Finance,* pp. 393–394, 1964; and Douglas Dosser's note on the same article, ibid., pp. 395–401.

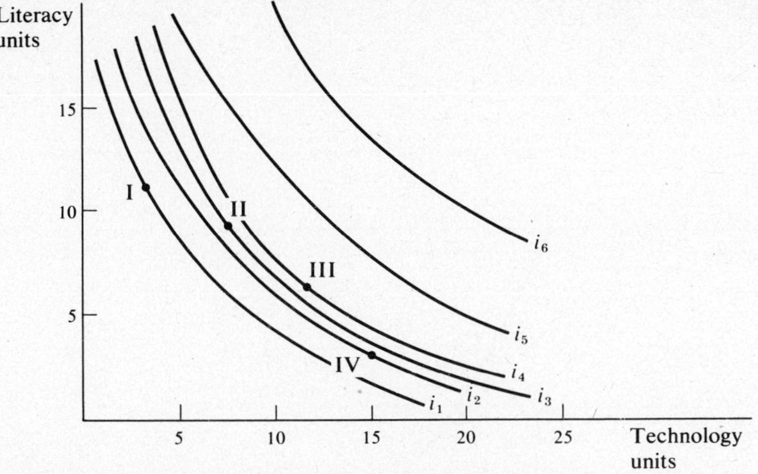

FIGURE 7-3 Multiple Objectives and Program Selection.

districts. The question is how a given police budget shall be allocated between X and Y. Among various targets, the following may be considered:

1. Equal number of crimes prevented in each sector
2. Equal protection, or equal number of crimes still committed in each sector
3. Maximum crime reduction for both sections combined
4. Equality of the marginal rate of transformation between crime reduction in the two districts and the marginal rate of substitution of utilities derived from crime reduction in the two districts

Which of these goals is preferable on equity and/or efficiency grounds?

The alternative solutions to the problem are illustrated in Figure 7-4, where the crime level in sector X is measured on the vertical axis and that in Y on the horizontal axis. *AB* is a transformation schedule showing what combinations of remaining crime levels can be obtained with a given budget.[17] If the entire police force is used in X, crime levels will be shown by *B;* if it is all allocated to Y, crime levels will be as shown by point *A.* If there is no protection for either, the location is at *C.*

To implement goal 1, the appropriate solution is at *D,* obtained by drawing a line through *C* at a 45° angle with the axes and taking its intersection with the transformation curve. To implement goal 2, the solution is at *E,* obtained by drawing a 45° line through the origin and again taking its intersection with *AB.* To implement goal 3, the marginal cost of crime prevention must be equal in both sectors. The solution is at *F* where the slope of the transformation function equals −1, it being tangent to the line *JK* where $OK = OJ$. Goals 1 to 3 cannot

[17] The slope of *AB* reflects the assumption of increasing cost of crime prevention in each sector. The function is concave from above rather than convex, since we plot "crime remaining" rather than "crime prevented." To simplify matters, we also assume equal population size for the two sectors and disregard spillover effects between them. On the latter point, see Chap. 26.

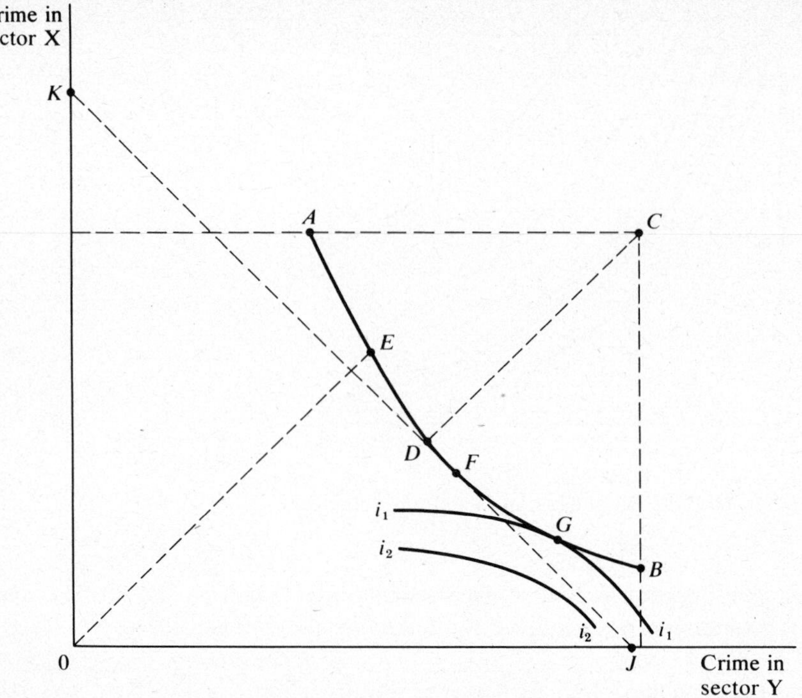

FIGURE 7-4 Police Allocation among Sectors of City.

be ranked without involving some distributional judgment, which judgment is made explicit in 4.

Goal 4 calls for a social welfare function which values crime prevention in X and Y as expressed by indifferent curves $i_1 i_1$ and $i_2 i_2$. The optimal solution is given at *G* where *AB* is tangent to the highest possible indifference curve.[18] This is where the marginal rate of transformation of crime reduction in X into crime reduction in Y equals the marginal rate of substitution of the social value assigned to crime reduction in Y for that in X. Since the social welfare function involves distributional judgments, the solution may fall anywhere on *AB*, including points *E*, *D*, and *F*, depending on the nature of the social welfare function (indifference curve pattern). To the extent that distributional objectives enter, the question again arises whether redistribution should be implemented in kind (i.e., by superior levels of police protection) or in cash.

Distributional Weights

Additional considerations arise where project benefits differ with regard to their distributional implications.[19] Thus the benefits from one project may accrue

[18] The indifference curves are convex from above because we plot remaining crime rather than absence of crime.

[19] See Burton Weisbrod, " Income Redistribution Effects and Benefit-Cost Analysis," in S. B. Chase (ed.), *Problems in Public Expenditure Analysis*, Washington: Brookings, 1968; and "Collective Action and the Distribution of Income: A Conceptual Approach," in Joint Economic Committee, *The Analysis Evaluation of Public Expenditures*, 91st Cong., 1969.

primarily to people in low-income groups, while those of another may accrue to higher-income consumers. Moreover, distributional differences may come about because factor payments made in the course of construction accrue primarily to high- or low-income earners. While pecuniary benefits and costs, as noted before, are not part of social benefits or costs, they may have important distributional implications.

Choosing Weights If distributional weights are to be introduced, their values (i.e., coefficients α and β in the objective function) must be specified. How these specifications are to be determined once more raises the problem encountered in our earlier discussion of the social welfare function. A table such as the following may be specified as an illustration:

Income	*Social Weights*
Under $2,000	10
$2,000– $5,000	5
$5,000–$10,000	2
Over $10,000	1

Benefits and costs of the project may be weighted accordingly, depending on the group on which they fall. As shown later, attempts have also been made to derive the schedule of weights which seems to be implicit in actual policies, but they are subject to change reflecting the policies of any particular administration.[20]

Should Distributional Weights Be Applied? Assuming the weights to have been determined, there remains the more general question of whether the use of distributional weights is appropriate for cost-benefit analysis. To illustrate, suppose that a project planner is to consider the location of a park facility in L or in H, where L is a low-income town and H is a high-income town. Suppose also that the same facility costs less in H and that the number of residents is the same in both places. In the absence of distributional considerations, cost-benefit analysis calls for installation in H, but allowance for distributional considerations may tip the scale in favor of L, where the benefits become available to a lower-income group. Or suppose that the question is whether to locate a shipyard in H or L. Suppose that H has better port facilities so that without distributional considerations, H is chosen. But location in L will give additional employment to lower-income residents, with distributional considerations once more tipping the balance toward L. What then is the correct solution?

The case for using distributional weights in the cost-benefit calculus depends on whether alternative measures for distributional adjustments—such as tax and transfer policies—are available. If so, project selection does not have to serve this function and H can be chosen. Once more the framework of cost-benefit analysis should be extended to cover a number of policy instruments, rather than be applied to a particular measure. This extended view is called for by the functional

[20] See also p. 220 for a derivation of weights from income tax legislation.

approach taken in Chapter 1, where it was argued that policy objectives can be reconciled by applying an appropriate combination of fiscal instruments.[21] This, however, may not be readily feasible in practice. The public works department, in which the instrument is planned, may have no influence on tax-transfer policy and there may be no coordinated policy which aligns the two departments. Consequently, use of distributional weights and the choice of L may be called for as a second-best solution.

Moreover, we must allow for the fact that alternative distributional adjustments, even if feasible, may involve an efficiency cost or excess burden which must be weighed against the advantages otherwise derived from location in H.[22] Only if this cost is less is there a clear case for choosing H. If the cost is larger, L may be the best choice.[23] The appropriateness of using distributional weights in cost-benefit analysis thus depends on the circumstances of the particular case. While there is an inclination for locating projects where the cost is least or the benefits are largest, situations arise where distributional weights are in order. The same holds for public purchases in general. While the rule should be to buy where the cost is least, exceptions based on distributional considerations may be appropriate.

D. DISCOUNTING AND THE COST OF CAPITAL

We must allow for the fact that benefits and costs do not accrue instantaneously, but over time. Some expenditures, such as current salaries for firemen, yield immediate benefits, while others, such as investments in river basin developments or turnpikes, yield a benefit stream over many years. To evaluate such benefit streams, future proceeds (or costs) must be translated into present values. They must be discounted, to allow for the fact that future benefits are less valuable than present ones. The same applies to the evaluation of costs. The opportunity cost of resources withdrawn from the private sector should now be measured in terms of the present value of private consumption forgone, where future consumption losses (due to forgone investments) are similarly discounted to their present value.

Importance of Discounting

The evaluation of projects and their ranking is highly sensitive to the discount rate which is used. This is illustrated in Table 7-3, where the present values of benefits and benefit-cost ratios for various investments are compared.[24]

[21] See p. 16.

[22] For a discussion of excess burden, see Chap. 21.

[23] Note, however, that adjustments by income taxes and transfers are not the only alternative. Distributional adjustments can also be made by taxing certain private goods while subsidizing others. If distributional adjustments are to be made by interfering with resource allocation, it is arbitrary to limit this option to *public* projects. In this sense, the use of distributional weights in cost-benefit analysis of public projects remains only second-best.

[24] The present value P of a sum R due in n years, discounted at the rate of interest i, is

$$P = \frac{R}{(1+i)^n}$$

The present value of an annual income stream R for n years equals

TABLE 7-3
Present Value and Discount Rates

Projects	*X*	*Y*	*Z*
Cost ($)	10,380	10,380	10,380
Number of years	5	15	25
Annual benefits ($)	2,397	1,000	736
Interest Rate (%)	PRESENT VALUE OF BENEFIT STREAM IN DOLLARS		
3	10,978	11,938	12,816
5	10,380	10,380	10,380
8	9,571	8,559	7,857
	BENEFIT-COST RATIO (*B/C*)		
3	1.057	1.150	1.235
5	1.000	1.000	1.000
8	0.922	0.825	0.757
	BENEFIT-COST DIFFERENTIAL (*B* − *C*) IN DOLLARS		
3	598	1,358	2,436
5	0	0	0
8	78	175	243

We consider three investments X, Y, and Z with equal cost and income flows extending over 5, 15, and 25 years, respectively. The annual incomes are chosen such that present values of benefits are the same at a 5 percent rate of discount. As we move from a 5 percent to a 3 percent rate, Z becomes the best and X the poorest choice. Reducing the discount rate will raise present value more if the period over which income accrues is longer. Moving to an 8 percent rate has the opposite effect. Project X now becomes most attractive and Z least. Raising the rate of discount favors the relatively short investment. While the present value of all investments rises as the discount rate is reduced and falls as it is raised, the ranking of the various investments changes in the process.

Based on these present value figures, we obtain the corresponding benefit-cost ratios (B/C) and differentials ($B - C$). With the initial cost of building the project assumed to be $10,380, the annual returns are chosen so that the ratio with a discount rate of 5 percent is equal to 1 for all investments.[25] The present value of benefits equals that of costs, and whether to invest or not is a matter of indifference. At the 3 percent rate, all three investments are profitable with B/C ratios greater than 1.0, but Z does best and X comes last. At the 8 percent rate, none of the three investments pays its way, but X is now best while Z has

---

$$P = \frac{R_1}{1+i} + \frac{R_2}{(1+i)^2} + \frac{R_3}{(1+i)^3} + \cdots + \frac{R_n}{(1+i)^n}$$

and may be obtained conveniently from annuity tables. For the case of a perpetual annuity, this expression becomes

$$P = \frac{R}{i}$$

[25] We assume for the time being that all costs are incurred in the first year, overlooking certain difficulties which arise when costs are spread out over longer periods.

become last. As will be seen from this illustration, the ranking of various investments and their acceptability depends greatly on which discount rate is used. Rates used by the federal government range from 3 percent to 15 percent and the lengths of the income stream cover an even wider range than shown in the table. Finding the "proper" rate is thus of major importance.[26] The problem is intricate and the general reader may pass over the following material proceeding directly to the more practical applications discussed under the heading "Rules of Thumb."

In choosing the discount rate, government may proceed on the premise that it is desirable to use a rate equal to the time preference of private consumers; or, it may substitute a social discount rate of its own. We begin with the former case.

Private Rate

The rationale for using the private or market rate of return is that this rate reflects consumer choice between present and future consumption.[27]

Perfect Markets Given an economy with wholly flexible prices and perfectly competitive capital markets, all households invest and borrow at the same rate, and all investments yield the same rate of return. The market in fact records a single rate of interest i. This reflects the consumers' marginal rate of substitution of future for present consumption, i.e., their rate of time preference. By accepting this rate for purposes of project evaluation, the government thus respects this preference. Moreover, the market rate also reflects the marginal rate of transformation in production, i.e., the marginal efficiency of investment. As saving and investment are pushed to the point where the two rates are equated, an efficient allocation between present and future consumption is achieved.

Government, in determining the present value of the benefit stream from public investments, will discount this stream at i. Moreover, it will value the social opportunity cost of resource withdrawal from the private sector at the actual dollar cost involved. Since the market is perfect, no "shadow prices" are needed. Public investments qualify if the present value of the benefit or income stream

[26] For instance, it has been estimated that use of a 6 percent rather than a 2⅝ percent discount rate would have disqualified 64 percent of the 1962 appropriations for federal water resource projects by reducing their benefit-cost ratios below 1.0. See Irving K. Fox and Orris C. Herfindahl, "Attainment of Efficiency in Satisfying Demands for Water Resources," *American Economic Review*, May 1964.

[27] This is a difficult problem which has been the subject of intensive discussion. Among various contributions are:

Martin S. Feldstein, "Net Social Benefit Calculation and the Public Investment Decision," *Oxford Economic Papers*, March 1964.

Otto Eckstein, "Interest Rate Policy for the Evaluation of Federal Programs," in *Economic Analysis of Public Investment Decisions: Interest Rate Policy and Discounting Analysis, Hearings before the Subcommittee on Economy in Government of the Joint Economic Committee*, 90th Cong., July 3, 1968, pp. 50–571.

Arnold Harberger, "On the Opportunity Cost of Public Borrowing," in *Economic Analysis of Public Investment Decisions*, ibid., pp. 57–65.

William J. Baumol, "On the Discount Rate for Public Projects," in *The Analysis and Evolution of Public Expenditures: The PPB System*, Compendium, vol. 1, Joint Economic Committee, 1969, pp. 489–503.

B exceeds cost C. The benefit-cost ratio B/C must be at least 1, or alternatively, $B - C$ must be positive. The result is the same whether resources are withdrawn from private consumption or investment.

Risk The simple assumption that there exists a single market rate of interest is invalidated by the presence of risk. Since some investments are riskier than others, gross rates of return differ by the presence of risk premiums. Risk may also apply regarding the return on public investment, so that it should be allowed for by adding an appropriate risk premium to the discount rate used in determining the present value of the benefit stream for a public investment.

Moreover, the presence of uncertainty regarding the future level of interest rates results in differentials between short- and long-term rates in the capital market. Therefore, the question arises as to which rate should be used in discounting the public benefit stream. Since the pattern of market yields may be taken to reflect the probable cost of capital in future years, a case can be made for choosing a yield which corresponds to the period over which the benefit stream of the public investment will extend.

Market Imperfections Markets are imperfect owing to monopolistic elements of various kinds. As a result, various consumers may be confronted with different borrowing rates and various investments may yield different returns. As a result, it is no longer obvious just which rate should be used in discounting the public investment stream or how the opportunity cost of resource withdrawal from the private sector should be measured. The latter now depends on just which investment is forgone, and it may not even be possible to identify it. In practice, the best that can be done is to apply an average rate for discounting the public investment while valuing the opportunity cost of private resource withdrawal at its actual or market price.

Adjustment for Profits Tax A further difficulty arises in dealing with the corporation profits tax and, for that matter, the income tax on capital income. Given perfect capital markets, only *the* market rate i has to be dealt with, but the tax now enters as a wedge between i_g, the gross or before-tax rate of return (reflecting the marginal rate of transformation of present for future consumption in production), and i_n, the net or after-tax rate of return (the rate of substitution of present for future consumption). Thus $i_n = (1 - t)i_g$, where t is the tax rate. Which of these rates should be used in discounting the benefits of the income stream from public investment? The i_n rate has the merit of properly reflecting the time preference of consumers, this being the rate which the consumer obtains and with which he equates his or her marginal rate of substitution of future for present consumption. At the same time, the i_g rate has the advantage of measuring the social rate of return on the investment forgone, since, from society's point of view, the tax revenue (which enters as a wedge between i_n and i_g) is not lost. As a pragmatic solution, it has been suggested that an average between i_g and i_n be used, but this is not a very convincing procedure. A more subtle solution is needed, which will be discussed further in the appendix to this chapter. As shown there, the solution differs depending on whether resources are withdrawn from private consumption or from investment, with more projects eligible in the former instance.

Social Rate

The difficulties of identifying "the" market rate are avoided if a social rate is used instead. Various reasons have been advanced for using this rate.

Rationale for Social Rate Advocates for using a social rate i_s usually propose that i_s be set below i. They argue that individuals suffer from "myopia" so that, in arranging their private affairs, they underestimate the importance of saving and overestimate that of present consumption. Such may be the case especially in low-income countries where the advantage of higher income levels has not been experienced and where aspiration levels are low. Hence, the consumers' time discount is too high and government should correct this error by applying a lower rate. Also, it is argued that people as members of society *should* care more about future generations than in fact they do, i.e., that future consumption should be considered a merit good. Furthermore, it is held that consumers underestimate the gain from postponing consumption because they overlook the fact that capital formation increases the future income of others as well and that they will derive satisfaction therefrom. Finally, investment, especially in developing countries, generates external benefits which are not reflected in the return to the individual investors. Thus the social return exceeds the private return and investment is not carried far enough. All these points call for a social rate of discount below the private rate.

Pointing in the other direction, analysts have noted that individuals do not foresee the rise in per capita income due to technological progress and thus overestimate the value of future consumption derived from present saving. Since the marginal utility of consumption tends to decline, the utility of additions to future consumption will be less if future income and consumption are already larger. This argument might then call for a social rate of discount above the private rate.

Another line of support for the use of a social rate stems from the difficulty inherent in determining "the" private rate. These difficulties, as noted before, arise in an imperfect capital market characterized by a complex rate structure and the role of profits taxes.

But there are more fundamental considerations as well. The very case for application of the market rate rests on the proposition that this rate can be taken to secure an efficient allocation of consumption over time. This rationale involves a model of national income determination such that planned saving is always matched by investment, with neither unemployment nor inflation occurring. Such is not the outcome in the real world. Rather, the setting is one where stabilization measures may be needed to maintain macrobalance, i.e., full employment and stability of the price level. Since these measures may be taken in various combinations of monetary and fiscal restraint or expansion—all of which result in different rates of interest—there is no "natural level" of interest rates. Hence, there is no obvious norm that can be counted on in the sense of efficient pricing rules.[28]

Application of Social Rate Suppose that for these reasons the government decides to use a social rate i_s. Let this rate be 5 percent while the market rate is 10 percent. The present value of the benefit stream from public investment, discounted at 5 percent, is higher than it would be with the 10 percent rate. At a given interest cost, more projects are thus made eligible. However, the social rate i_s must also be applied to measurement of the opportunity cost of private resource withdrawal. As shown in the chapter appendix, projects once more will qualify more readily if withdrawal is made from consumption rather than from investment.

Rules of Thumb

As is frequently true, actual practice falls short of these sophisticated considerations. If officials of the United States government were asked whether it was their intention to follow the market or to apply a social rate, their answer would be the former. But in so doing, rather crude rules of thumb are applied.

One such rule is to use the government's cost of borrowing for discounting the public benefit stream and to compare the present value thus obtained with project cost. This approach has a certain appeal because it reflects business thinking—that government, like a business firm, should carry on its investment to the point where its rate of return equals its borrowing cost.[29] If the government's rate is 6 percent, an investment costing $100,000 and yielding an annual income of $574 over twenty-five years will be on the margin of qualifying. If the income stream is less, or if the total proceeds of $143,500 accrue more slowly, it will not.

To implement this approach, a decision must be made on which yield (i.e., on short- or long-term government bonds) should be used. This choice is important because, until recently, yields have differed substantially by maturities. Over the last decade, the yield on short maturities has equaled or exceeded that on long issues, but for the preceding three decades long yields were higher. According to a congressional directive issued in 1962, investments in water and land resources are to be discounted at a rate payable by the Treasury on issues of fifteen years and more.[30] Presumably, this choice is based on the assumption that such yields are better predictors of future yields than are those on short-term issues.[31] The long-term rate in 1962 was 3 percent, but is now a multiple thereof. This

[28] The same holds in determining the "proper" growth rate for the economy. See Chap. 22, Sec. B.

[29] See Elmer Staats, "Survey of Use by Federal Agencies of the Discounting Technique in Evaluating Future Programs," in *Interest Rate Guidelines for Federal Decision Making, Hearings before the Subcommittee on Economy in Government, Joint Economic Committee,* 90th Cong., Jan. 29, 1968, pp. 3–33.

[30] Senate Document 97, *Policies, Standards, and Procedures in the Formulation, Evaluation and Review of Plans for Use and Development of Water and Related Land Resources,* 87th Cong., 2d Sess., 1962.

[31] It should not be based on the fact that most public investments have a long payoff period, since such investments may be refinanced during that period.

high level of interest rates is a reflection, in part, of an anticipated inflation. Since the same expected price rise should be allowed for in estimating the dollar value of the benefit stream, it does not follow that previously eligible investments have now become ineligible.

Given the long-term rate, it is further argued that the government, acting as a good businessman, should allow for the loss of tax revenue (mostly corporation tax) which results as private investment is replaced by the public project. This, after all, is a cost which the government will incur, a cost which may be estimated to raise the total borrowing cost to close to 13 percent. This is in line with the rates now applied by the Departments of Defense and Interior. Other departments, still using substantially lower rates, are encouraged to move in this direction.

How much sense does this approach make? As it not infrequently happens, the results are better than the underlying reasoning. The government, acting as the trustee of the social interest, should undertake a project if it is beneficial to society and not simply if it proves profitable to the Treasury, i.e., if the return exceeds its own borrowing cost. Moreover, though investment at the state and local levels tend to be loan-financed, federal investment (with revenue largely from taxation) is mostly tax-financed. Derivation of the discount rate must also be applicable to this case. It should reflect the social cost of capital, and the Treasury's own borrowing rate is relevant only if it can be taken as an indicator of that cost.

At the same time, the cost of borrowing may serve as a proxy. The rate of return on long-term bonds gives a fair reflection of the average return on relatively riskless capital.[32] Moreover, adding in the "loss of tax revenue" serves a purpose. Investors, in choosing between government bonds and corporate investment, equate the bond rate with corporate returns *net* of corporate tax; but it is the corporate return before tax which is indicative of the social return. It is appropriate, therefore, to gross up the bond rate to make it a better proxy for the social rate.

Local Rate

The preceding analysis was geared to investment decisions by the federal government. Turning now to project evaluation by state or local governments, the problem may be cast in simpler terms. Such governments are faced with a given rate at which they can borrow, and they should use this rate in evaluating their investments. The fact that this rate may reflect market imperfections or that the social return should be figured on a gross rather than a net basis is not relevant to their decision, the problem being one of efficient resource use within their region and not on a nationwide basis.

E. SUMMARY

In developing some basic concepts of project evaluation, we have distinguished between a fixed and a variable budget:

[32] If the public investment entails risk (see p. 163), the use of a riskless rate of discount calls for the addition of a risk premium to the investment cost.

1. If the budget is fixed, the choice is between alternative public projects only. Where such projects are freely divisible, the best solution will be reached by equating the marginal benefits from the last dollar on each project. Where projects are lumpy, they have to be ranked in terms of their benefit-cost ratio, with the highest-ratio projects implemented first.

2. If the budget size is flexible, the choice is not only between alternative public projects but also between private and public uses of resources.

In measuring the social benefits and social costs of public projects, certain rules have to be followed:

3. Only real costs and benefits should be included, while pecuniary costs and benefits should be excluded. A special problem arises in connection with the costing of otherwise unemployed resources.

4. Both direct and indirect costs and benefits should be included.

5. Where possible, intangible as well as tangible benefits and costs should be included.

6. Intermediate-type benefits can be valued more readily than benefits of the final type.

7. Interjurisdictional cooperation is needed to allow for benefits and costs accruing outside the initiating jurisdiction.

In selecting the particular projects to be undertaken, allowance must be made for the fact that multiple objectives may be involved:

8. Where the two alternative projects differ in their relative capacity to serve one or another objective, the two objectives must be valued so as to permit comparison.

9. Where the distributional implications of alternative projects differ, such differences may be allowed for by the introduction of distributional weights. The appropriateness of applying such weights depends on the availability of alternative means of securing distributional adjustments and on the efficiency cost of using them.

Where the benefit stream from a public project accrues over future years, present value must be determined by discounting. The same discounting procedure must be applied in determining the cost of resource withdrawal where such withdrawal is from private investment.

10. In choosing the discount rate, government may aim at a rate which corresponds to that used in the private sector or it may wish to apply a social rate of discount.

11. In the former case, determination of the proper market rate is complicated by risk differentials, market imperfections, and the corporation profits tax. The rate typically used is the long-term bond rate, increased to allow for loss of corporation tax revenue.

12. Choice of a social rate usually rests on the proposition that the private sector tends to underestimate the social value of future consumption and capital formation, thus calling for the use of a lower rate by the public sector.

FURTHER READINGS

Eckstein, Otto: "A Survey of the Theory of Public Expenditure Criteria," in James Buchanan (ed.), *Public Finances: Needs, Sources and Utilization,* Princeton, N.J.: Princeton, 1961.

Layard, Richard (ed.): *Cost-Benefit Analysis, Selected Readings,* Baltimore: Penguin, Modern Economics Readings, 1972.

Marglin, Stephen A.: *Public Investment Criteria,* Cambridge, Mass.: M.I.T., 1967.

Margolis, Julius: "Secondary Benefits, External Economies and the Justification of the Public Investment," *Review of Economics and Statistics,* August 1957.

Mishan, E. J.: *Cost-Benefit Analysis,* New Hyde Park, N.Y.: University Books, Inc., 1971.

Musgrave, Richard A.: "Cost-Benefit Analysis and the Theory of Public Finance," *Journal of Economic Literature,* September 1969.

Prest, A. R., and R. Turvey: "Cost-Benefit Analysis: A Survey," *Economic Journal,* pp. 683–735, December 1965.

APPENDIX: FURTHER PROBLEMS OF THE DISCOUNT RATE

Here we consider in more detail two previously noted difficulties arising in the application of discounting in cost-benefit analysis.

ADJUSTMENT FOR INCOME TAX

The private rate approach is simple if we assume a perfect market and no tax, in which case *the* market rate i is used for discounting purposes. But capital income is taxed, so we must distinguish between the gross or before-tax rate of return i_g and the net or after-tax rate of return i_n, where $i_n = (1 - t)\ i_g$ and t is the tax rate on capital income. We may think of t as the rate of corporation income tax.

We now compare project evaluation with and without tax. Beginning with a situation without tax, the benefit-cost ratio is given by B/C, where B is the present value of the benefit stream discounted by i and C is the cost of the investment. The private and social evaluations coincide and no further adjustment is needed. In a situation with tax, the present value of the public benefit stream, or B_t, is obtained by discounting with i_n. This is the rate which measures consumer time preference, i.e., the rate with which the consumer equates his or her marginal rate of substitution of future for present consumption. We thus have $B_t = (i_g/i_n)B$, so that $B_t > B$.[33]

Turning to the opportunity cost of resource withdrawal from private use, the solution differs depending on whether the withdrawal is from consumption or from investment. If withdrawal is from consumption, the social opportunity

[33] Such is the case for the simplifying assumption of a perpetual annuity R where $B = R/i_g$ and $B_t = (i_g/i_n)B$.

cost C_s is still measured by C, the cost of private consumption forgone. The benefit-cost ratio thus becomes B_t/C. Since $B_t/C > B/C$, some public investment projects which did not qualify in the absence of the income tax now qualify.

If, instead, the withdrawal is from private investment, the cost of the investment forgone, or C, is no longer a true measure of the social cost C_s. Reflecting the behavior of private investors, C equals the *net* income stream, discounted at i_n. This follows because private investment will be carried up to the point where no further investment is profitable. But the social cost, or C_s, equals the *gross* income stream, discounted at i_n. We thus have $C_s = (i_g/i_n)C$, with $C_s > C$. The correct benefit-cost ratio is now given by $B_t/C_s = (i_g/i_n)B \div (i_g/i_n)C$ which, in turn, equals B/C. Thus the tax does not affect the eligibility of public investment projects, provided the resource withdrawal is from private investment.

The upshot of the argument is that public investment will qualify more readily if financed so as to cause withdrawal from consumption rather than from investment. Tax finance (and especially finance from taxes on consumption) tends to be more favorable to public investment than does loan finance. Why should this be so? The reason is that the tax on capital income has caused the level of private investment to be deficient and that public investment (if based on consumption withdrawal) tends to correct for this by raising total investment.[34]

The question remains of whether cost-benefit analysis should be assigned to play this role. Two disadvantages may be noted. First, the procedure tends to distort the investment mix, introducing a bias toward public investment. Second, it favors consumption taxes as a source of finance, taxes which tend to be regressive. It may thus be better to rely on other measures to provide the necessary correction, i.e., a change in the fiscal–monetary policy mix which increases the level of private investment. Once more, the problem is one of choosing the proper combination of policies rather than of trying to achieve multiple objectives with a single policy instrument.

Social Rate of Discount

Similar considerations apply in connection with the social rate approach. In considering this aspect, the tax problem is now disregarded. Suppose the private rate of return i is 10 percent while the social rate i_s is 5 percent. Government will now apply a 5 percent rate in determining the present value of the benefit stream from public investment. This present value will now be higher, so that B_s exceeds B where B_s is based on discounting by i_s and B on discounting by i. But to determine how this affects the eligibility of public investment, we must again consider the implications for the social cost of capital. As in the case of the income tax adjustment, this cost differs depending on the nature of the resource withdrawal. If resources are withdrawn from consumption, the social cost of capital is properly measured by C and the benefit-cost ratio is increased. Previously ineligible investments now become eligible. If resource withdrawal is from investment, the benefit stream forgone must now be discounted at i_s to obtain

[34] Taxation thus enters the problem in two ways: (1) the existence of an income tax enters as a wedge between i_g and i_n, and (2) use of tax rather than loan finance places a larger part of the burden on consumption.

the social cost C_s. Since both numerator and denominator of the benefit-cost ratio are raised by applying a lower discount rate, the ratio remains unchanged.[35]

As in the preceding case of the tax adjustment, project evaluation again turns out to be more favorable if resource withdrawal is from consumption. Once more, this is so because project evaluation is to serve as an instrument for adjusting a prevailing distortion in the market. Now traceable to the differential between i and i_s, this distortion again results in a level of private investment which is deficient and a structure of investment which is too short. As before, the use of project evaluation as a corrective biases the investment mix and calls for the use of taxes which may carry an undesirable burden distribution. These difficulties would be avoided by adjusting the fiscal-monetary policy mix so as to align i with i_s, in which case no further adjustment through project evaluation is needed.

[35] By substituting i for i_g and i_s for i_n, the previous argument for the tax correction again applies.

Chapter 8

Expenditure Evaluation: Case Studies*

A. Highway Construction: *Rationale of Project Evaluation; An Illustration; Further Problems.* **B. Outdoor Recreation:** *Measuring Benefits to Users; Other Benefits.* **C. Education:** *Benefit-Cost Ratio Based on Earnings; Qualifications; Tax and Subsidy Aspects.* **D. The Planning-Programming-Budgeting System:** *Objectives and Procedures; Evaluation and Shortcomings.* **E. Summary.**

Application of the principles set forth in the preceding chapter is now being actively promoted in various areas of expenditure planning, and beyond this, attempts are being made to build such analysis systematically into the budget process. The problems and difficulties encountered differ with the type of expenditure, and ingenious approaches have been developed to deal with some of them. The purpose of this chapter is to illustrate these problems by considering a number of case studies.

**Reader's Guide to Chapter 8:* This chapter provides a set of illustrations examining the application of cost-benefit analysis to various areas of project evaluation. The discussion should be of particular interest to practically inclined readers. They may apply the analysis of Sec. C to their returns on the purchase of this book.

A. HIGHWAY CONSTRUCTION

Highway expenditure in 1972 amounted to $21.6 billion, $12 billion of which went for capital outlays, $5 billion for maintenance, and the remainder for interest and administrative services. Somewhat over one-half the total went into state highways, one-quarter into local roads, and the rest into unclassified roads.[1] Combining all levels of government, highways and roads are the second most important civilian expenditure function, surpassed in magnitude only by education. While highway expenditures enter at the federal level only as intergovernmental transfers, they are a dominant factor in state and local budgets.

Looked at from a broader point of view, planning of highway investment is part of the general problem of designing an efficient transport system. For distant transport, highways compete with rail and air facilities. In the metropolitan area, they compete with mass transit facilities such as trains or buses. The product to be furnished is transport and the most efficient facility should be chosen. This broader setting of the transportation problem is important, but will be excluded here. To illustrate the essential aspects of cost-benefit analysis, let us consider a quite specific and limited problem, i.e., the evaluation of a particular highway project.

Rationale of Project Evaluation

Our problem is that of a state highway department, which must decide whether to improve highway facilities between two cities. Is such an investment worthwhile and how extensive should the new facility be?[2]

To answer the question, we must evaluate the benefits and costs involved. Benefits are measured in terms of reduced travel cost to the user. This approach is possible because travel is an "intermediate good," entering into the final product, which is "being at the point of destination." Reduction in travel cost is a reduction in the price at which this final product can be purchased.[3] The better the available facilities, the lower will be the cost per trip for any given volume of traffic. Also, the greater the volume of traffic, the higher will be the per-trip cost.

This is shown in Figure 8-1*a*. The total number of trips is measured along the horizontal axis, and dollar costs and prices per trip are measured on the

[1] See *Facts and Figures on Government Finance,* New York: Tax Foundation, 1973, p. 162.

[2] The economics of highway investment has received considerable attention by economists. See, for instance:

Hans A. Adler, "Economic Evaluation of Transport Projects," in G. Fromm (ed.), *Transport Investment and Economic Development,* Washington: Brookings, 1965, pp. 170–194.

Robert W. Harbeson, "Some Allocation Problems in Highway Finance," in *Transportation Economics,* National Bureau of Economic Research, New York: Columbia, 1965, pp. 139–169.

Herbert Mohring, "Urban Highway Investments," in R. Dorfman (ed.), *Measuring Benefits of Government Investments,* Washington: Brookings, 1965, pp. 231–291.

James R. Nelson, "Policy Analysis in Transportation Programs," in *The Analysis and Evaluation of Public Expenditures: The PPB System,* A Compendium of Papers, Joint Economic Committee, 91st Cong., 1969, vol. 3, pp. 1102–1127.

[3] By the same token, this calculus does not apply to the pleasure driver, where the trip itself is the product. Benefit estimation in this case is more difficult, as shown in the following section on recreational facilities.

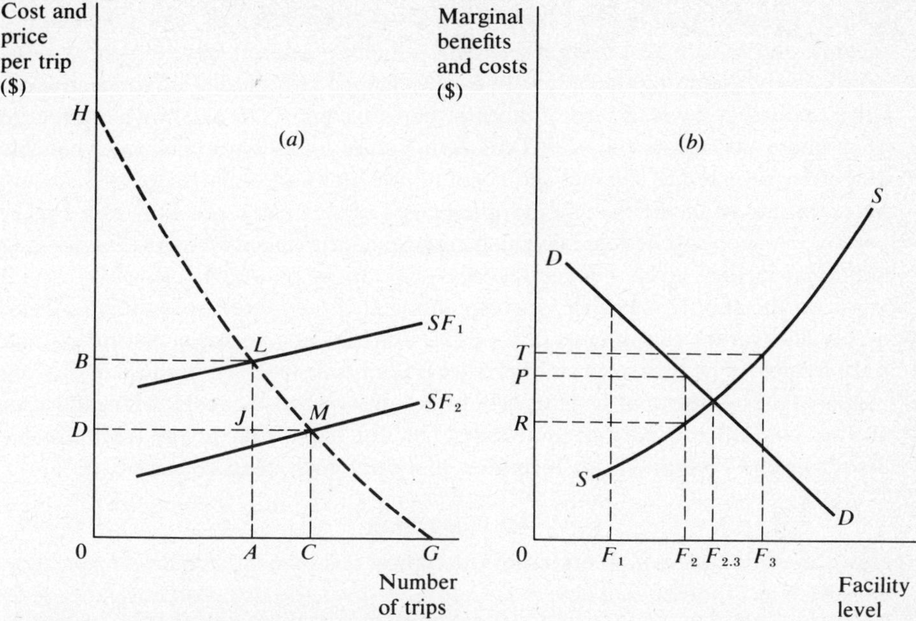

FIGURE 8-1 Highway Cost-Benefit Analysis.

vertical axis. Schedule SF_1 shows the cost per trip to the road user at which various traffic volumes can be accommodated with a given level of highway facilities F_1, while SF_2 shows the same for an expanded level of facilities F_2. With any given facility, the cost per trip rises with increasing traffic volume or number of trips, owing mainly to crowding and longer driving time. Schedules SF_1 and SF_2 thus represent travel supply schedules to the users, where their own travel cost is the "price" which they must pay to make a trip in terms of travel time, accident cost, automotive expenses, etc. Their demand schedules are not known, but we observe point *L* which shows that with existing facility F_1, the number of trips equals *OA*, with an average user cost per trip of *OB*. We estimate that if costs are reduced by expanding facilities to level F_2, users will move from *L* to *M*. The number of trips will increase to *OC* with a user cost of *OD*. This estimate may be based on observing the effects of expanding facilities in other locations. *LM* may then be regarded as the estimated demand curve over the relevant range. It is extended here to *G* and *H* to develop the subsequent analysis.

The gain from increasing the facility level from F_1 to F_2 may be measured as the area *DMH* minus *BLH*, or as *DMLB*.[4] *DMLB* is the gain in consumer surplus which results from introduction of the new facility. Of this, *DJLB* reflects the cost saving on the old number of trips *OA*, while *JML* reflects the gain on the additional trips *AC*. This latter gain on the new trips equals *JML*, not *ACML*, because *ACMJ* is offset by the additional user cost which results as the number of trips is expanded.

Turning now to Figure 8-1*b*, we see that levels of highway facility (measured

[4] For similar reasoning, see p. 467.

in terms of lanes, paving, etc.) are measured on the horizontal axis. The demand schedule *DD* reflects the marginal benefit which consumers derive from various facility levels, assuming the optimum use (as defined in Figure 8-1*a*) for each level. Thus, at facility level F_2, the marginal benefit equals *OP* as shown in Figure 8-1*b*, where *OP* equals the area *DMLB* in Figure 8-1*a*. These marginal benefits must then be assessed against the costs to the highway department of securing the expansion of facilities. The marginal costs of expansion are shown in Figure 8-1*b* by the supply schedule *SS* which represents the resource costs of supplying additional facility levels.[5] Since facilities are lumpy or indivisible, only certain points on the supply schedule, corresponding to F_1, F_2, etc., are possible. Thus, in this illustration the intersection of *DD* and *SS* falls between F_2 and F_3 and is not feasible. The best solution therefore is to choose level F_2, because in moving from F_2 to F_3 additional benefits would be outweighed by costs. Marginal user benefits *OP* still exceed marginal costs *OR*, for expansion to the next feasible facility level F_3 would result in higher marginal costs than benefits.

An Illustration

This is the principle which underlies the typical cost-benefit calculation for highways such as is shown in Table 8-1. Column I gives the situation at facility level F_1, column II after expansion to F_2, and column III after expansion to F_3.

Calculation of Net Benefits to Users Benefits, as noted previously, are to be measured in terms of savings in reduced travel time and other transport costs to the user. The first step, therefore, is to determine the reduction in travel cost which results from the expansion of facilities. Column I shows the computation of travel cost prior to project expansion. The first item is the cost of travel time. If we assume that the average trip takes thirty minutes (line 1) and that the average cost of travel time is $2 per hour, the money cost of travel time per trip prior to expansion is $1 (line 2, column I).

Figuring the average cost of travel time is far from simple. The required time, here assumed at thirty minutes, depends on the type of road as well as on traffic conditions. As any commuter well knows, travel time differs greatly between peak and slack hours, so that the average time requirement must be determined. Furthermore, the opportunity cost of time spent in travel, here assumed at $2 an hour, varies according to the type of traveler. Again the average cost must be found. In the case of a truck driver, the cost of travel time may be measured readily by his wage rate, but the estimate is difficult for the commuter, who could either sleep longer or get to work sooner. The cost of travel time per trip is thus a complex figure to estimate.

Next, certain other user costs must be allowed for. These are fuel costs (including taxes)[6] and wear of car, as well as accident costs. All these costs in

[5] To simplify, we may assume that all costs are capital costs incurred in the initial year of construction and that the highway department incurs no variable costs, such as increased maintenance or traffic control.

[6] The proper treatment of gasoline taxes depends on the governmental unit involved. Thus a state should not count its tax as a part of gasoline cost, while a locality which does not receive the revenue may include it.

TABLE 8-1
Profitability of Highway Construction

	Pre-expansion Level F_1 (I)	*After Expansion to F_2 (II)*	*After Expansion to F_3 (III)*
Estimation of Benefits to Users			
1. Time per trip (minutes)	30	18	16
2. Time cost of trip ($2 per hour)	$1.00	$0.57	$0.53
3. Other cost per trip	$1.75	$1.90	$1.85
4. Total variable cost per trip	$2.75	$2.47	$2.38
5. Number of trips per year	1,000,000	1,500,000	1,750,000
6. Total variable costs per year	$2,750,000	$3,705,000	$4,165,000
7. Cost savings per trip		$0.28	$0.09
8. Cost savings on previous number of trips		$280,000	$135,000
9. Cost savings on additional trips		$70,000	$11,250
10. Total benefits per year		$350,000	$146,250
11. Present value of benefits (8%, 25 years)		$3,736,172	$1,561,186
Estimation of Project Cost			
12. Capital cost		$2,000,000	$2,000,000
13. Annual maintenance cost	$20,000	$30,000	$50,000
14. Increase in maintenance cost		$10,000	$20,000
15. Present value of maintenance cost (8%, 25 years)		$106,748	$213,496
16. Total project cost, present value		$2,106,748	$2,213,496
Evaluation			
17. Benefit-cost ratio (line 11 ÷ line 16)		1.77	0.71

turn depend on the type of road as well as on the type of vehicle used. These additional costs are shown in line 3. Setting them at an average 15 cents per mile for the preexpansion case and taking our road to be 11.7 miles long, we find that such costs equal $1.75 (line 3).[7] We thus arrive at the total variable user cost per trip of $2.75 (line 4). Assuming 1 million trips to be made on the old facility, total variable costs are $2,750,000 per year (line 6). Assuming our preexpansion costs to correspond to facility level 1, we see that this total corresponds to area *OALB* in Figure 8-1*a*.[8]

Column II shows the situation after the facility level has been expanded to F_2. This may involve a widening of the existing road or the addition of a new one.[9] We note that the time per trip has gone down to 18 minutes, while other costs per trip have increased slightly to $1.90. More gasoline is used at the higher

[7] Cost estimates for various types of vehicles and roads are given in *Road User Benefit Analysis for Highway Improvements,* Washington: American Association for State Highway Officials, 1960.

[8] More precisely, the references to Fig. 8-1 should be in terms of discounted values of benefits and costs.

[9] The choice between these two techniques is a production problem. We assume that the cheaper technique is chosen.

speed and wear is increased. On balance, the total variable cost per trip has fallen by 28 cents. The number of trips has increased to 1,500,000 and total annual travel cost has gone up to $3,705,000. This corresponds to area *OCMD* in Figure 8-1.

We are now ready to compute the net user benefits from project expansion as reflected in the net savings in user cost. As shown in line 7 of the table, expansion to facility level F_2 reduces travel cost per trip from $2.75 to $2.47, or by 28 cents. Applying this to the old number of trips, we obtain a saving of $280,000 (line 8), corresponding to area *DJLB* in Figure 8-1*a*. Regarding the 500,000 additional trips, we count only one-half the saving, or 14 cents, thus obtaining a further gain of $70,000 (line 9) corresponding to the triangular area *JML* in the figure.[10] Total benefits, corresponding to the area *DMLB* in the figure, thus amount to the combined annual cost savings of $350,000 (line 10).

Since the benefits (cost savings) will occur in the future, the present value of the future stream of benefits must be obtained by discounting. Suppose that the planning horizon extends twenty-five years ahead and that a discount rate of 8 percent is applicable. As shown in line 11, this gives us a present value of $3,736,172 for the benefit stream generated by expanding facilities to F_2.

The same procedure is followed in column III of the table for raising facilities from F_2 to F_3. Travel time is reduced further and other costs fall slightly. The total saving in user cost is 9 cents per trip and the number of trips rises to 1,750,000. Following the same procedure as before, the present value of anticipated benefits (or cost savings to users) equals $1,561,186.

Calculation of Costs Turning now to the costs involved in the expansion of facilities, the main items to be considered are construction costs, site costs, and maintenance costs.

Construction costs are measured in terms of market price and need no further explanation. Site acquisition is by eminent domain and involves evaluation of the taken property, but this may again be based on fair market value, reflecting the opportunity cost of the land in alternative uses. As shown in line 12, total construction costs are assumed at $2 million for each project. These capital costs are undertaken at the outset, so that no discounting is needed.

Road maintenance costs are partly dependent on traffic volume and type and are partly independent thereof. The estimation of maintenance cost thus involves some of the same considerations which arise in estimating the savings in user cost. Maintenance costs are assumed to increase by $10,000 per year in raising the facility level from F_1 to F_2 and by $20,000 in going from F_2 to F_3. The present values of these maintenance-cost streams, accruing over a twenty-five-year period, are shown in line 15, and total costs (both construction and operating) in present-value terms are shown in line 16. These costs correspond to *OR* and

[10] Counting half the savings, or 7 cents, is a rough-and-ready procedure for measuring the gain in consumer surplus which results, since it assumes a linear demand schedule between traffic volumes A and C. In the absence of better information, this is the best that can be done. For an explanation of this technique, see p. 467.

OT for the F_2 and F_3 expansions respectively in the supply schedule of Figure 8-1*b*.

Comparison of Costs and Benefits We are now ready to compare the present value of costs and benefits.[11] For raising facilities from F_1 to F_2, benefits exceed costs and the benefit-cost ratio, as shown in line 17, is 1.77. For raising facilities from F_2 to F_3, the reverse holds and the ratio equals only 0.71. It follows that expansion to F_2 is profitable, while expansion to F_3 is not.[12] The high return to expansion to F_2 also suggests that a modified extension beyond it, but less ambitious than F_3, would be desirable. Provided that projects may be carried out in small units and that the budget is flexible, additional expansion to $F_{2.3}$ in Figure 8-1 would indeed be desirable until the incremental benefits and costs are the same and the benefit-cost ratio becomes 1 for the last unit of expanded facilities.

Alternative Choices The question posed here was whether and how far road facilities between two particular cities should be expanded. The same question, obviously, can be asked for facilities between any other pair of cities. If there is no budget constraint, all such facilities that are profitable (i.e., have a benefit-cost ratio above 1) should be undertaken. Provided that the proper rate of discount is used—a problem which we found to be rather tricky to solve—this resource use would then be more profitable than would have been the private use that is displaced.

Typically, budget choices are not made in this fashion, but within a given budget constraint. The highway budget is fixed and the question is where the funds should be spent. The problem, then, is to compare the return obtained by expanding facilities between alternative pairs of cities. If the projects are indivisible, the various benefit-cost ratios are computed, following the above procedure in each case, and the better project is chosen. If the improvements can be made in small amounts, a number of facilities may be improved in varying degrees, such

[11] Our procedure has been to reduce both cost and benefit streams to their present value. An alternative procedure is to compare the undiscounted annual benefit with a corresponding annual cost, defined to include amortization of capital as well as maintenance cost. If the amortization period is the same as the number of years over which benefits are estimated, and the annual benefits and costs accrue at constant rates, the two procedures give the same result.

In practice the alternative procedure is usually followed and the amortization period is estimated independently of the benefit period. The amortization period, estimated in accordance with the physical life of the asset, differs for various components of the project, such as surface and grading. The average amortization period for the project thus determined frequently exceeds the number of years over which benefits can be estimated. The analysis (see *Road User Benefit Analysis,* op. cit.) is then based on the shorter benefit period, comparing the annual benefits with the present-value annual cost computed to include only that part of amortization that occurs during this shorter period. This approach overestimates or underestimates profitability, depending on whether the remaining (not estimated) benefit stream falls short of or exceeds unamortized costs. Where the amortization period is shorter, only benefits for that period are included, thus understating profitability.

[12] Note that the analysis should not proceed by considering the benefit-cost ratio obtainable by immediate expansion from F_1 to F_3 without considering the partial expansion from F_1 to F_2. Although expansion from F_1 to F_3 appears profitable, with a benefit-cost ratio of 1.23, the incremental expansion from F_2 to F_3 is unprofitable. Since an incremental approach is possible, the expansion should stop at the expansion to F_2.

that the benefit-cost ratios for the marginal improvements will be the same in all cases.

Further Problems

The preceding illustration oversimplifies matters in various respects, some of which may be noted briefly.

Changing Environment We have noted that estimation of benefits involves considerable difficulties, even in a static setting, such as determining the value of travel time. But the complexities are increased greatly once economic change is allowed for. Highways have a long life span, say forty years, and the traffic volume is difficult to predict over such a period. Cost estimation should not be based on a comparison of user's cost before and after project expansion while holding "other factors" constant, but should make full allowance for changes in such factors. Thus, traffic volume will be affected by changes in population and per capita incomes, and by the pattern of regional development. Moreover, the project itself may have an important effect on these variables. All these factors must be allowed for in estimating cost savings and in calculating benefits on that basis. Thus a sizable task of economic forecasting is involved.

Project versus System Analysis As noted before, the individual transportation project is part of a broader transportation system and cannot be evaluated properly if considered in isolation. Expanding the direct road from town X to town Y may reduce traffic previously routed via Z, or expanding road facilities may divert traffic from other modes of transportation. Intelligent transport planning must thus relate to the entire transport system, linking individual highways with the road system, and the road system with the transport system at large. The profitability of expanding highway facilities in the metropolitan area in particular must be assessed in relation to that of other transport facilities, such as buses or commuter trains. As just noted, availability of transport facilities is itself an important factor in economic development, and transport systems no less than individual projects must be planned in that context.

Moreover, transport facilities by their very nature provide a linkage between regions and hence require cooperation between various governmental units, such as states and municipalities. This is an aspect to which we will return later, when problems of fiscal federalism are considered.[13]

Indirect Benefits and Costs Benefit measurement in the preceding illustration has allowed for benefits to direct highway users only. These "direct" benefits are relatively easy to measure, owing to the nature of transportation as an "intermediate" good. But in a fuller analysis, other benefits or costs must be considered as well.

Important indirect benefits may result from the repercussions of transport expansion on economic development. Thus expansion of facilities between two

[13] See Chap. 29, Sec. D.

cities may generate economic development of the region and permit a better division of labor between the two locations. The resulting benefit will exceed the gain as measured above since factor earnings in both locations will increase. In developing countries in particular, the opening of communication brings heretofore unutilized resources into use and establishes communication with the market. The early development of canals, the growth of the United States railroad system in the middle of the nineteenth century, or today's highway construction in Latin America are cases in point. The developmental gains to the economy resulting from such growth in transport facilities are more difficult to predict and cannot be formulated simply in terms of reduced travel cost.

On the cost side, social cost may exceed the direct construction cost in a variety of ways. Dwellings may have to be destroyed and their replacement cost must be included as an indirect though tangible cost. Beyond this, a throughway may disrupt established communities and force relocation, introducing a further indirect and, this time, intangible cost. The true social cost may, in fact, greatly exceed the replacement cost of housing. Moreover, the pecuniary losses and gains which result may have important distributional implications. The destruction of low-cost housing may not hurt the landlord, who is compensated, but nevertheless place a burden on the tenants if the supply of low-cost housing is reduced in the process.[14]

B. OUTDOOR RECREATION

As our next case, we consider the evaluation of projects for outdoor recreation, say a public park. The benefits which accrue include (1) benefits to the users, (2) benefits to the surrounding community, and (3) certain other benefits, such as preservation of the natural beauty of the environment, which are of a more or less intangible sort. As before, we focus first on user benefits which are considered the major component of the benefit calculation.

In contrast to highways, we now deal with a social good which is in the nature of a final or consumer good, rather than of an intermediate good. The problem is to evaluate the benefits which are derived from the park itself and not, as in the case of roads, from the reduced cost of obtaining other benefits, such as those of getting to a destination. The question "What is a visit to the park worth?" must be faced. Given the answer, we can then compare the present value of costs and benefits along much the same lines as in the preceding illustration.

Measuring Benefits to Users

Various techniques of benefit measurement have been suggested and used. They include direct pricing through user charges, estimation of willingness to pay hypothetical user charges, use of prices paid for similar private facilities, costs

[14] The present discussion has dealt with evaluating the profitability of alternative projects, not with how they are to be financed. For a discussion of toll finance and gasoline taxes as benefit taxation, see p. 214.

undertaken in using the facilities, and the construction of indices such as merit-weighted user days.

User Charges Let us assume our park to be such that "exclusion" can be readily applied, i.e., that the administrative cost of limiting admission to those who pay the price is insignificant. We have seen that, in the absence of crowding, exclusion is incompatible with efficient use of the particular park since consumption is nonrival.[15] However, individual parks are not planned in isolation. A park agency will be confronted with providing parks in different locations, and the experience gained from A may be used for planning the location of B. A case can thus be made for testing the profitability of park construction by charging fees in one initial park, even if marginal cost is zero, so as to obtain a measuring rod for further park construction.[16] If the present value of prospective fees from park A exceeds the project cost, similar facilities will be called for in other locations where demand conditions are expected to be similar. The inefficiency which results from underutilizing park A (or from having constructed a park which proves unprofitable) may be more than offset by the increased efficiency in planning other park construction made possible by the information gained.

Hypothetical User Charges Instead of experimenting with actual user charges, market survey techniques may be used in an attempt to obtain the same information. Potential users may be asked how much they would be willing to pay for various facilities, or how much use they would make of given facilities at various prices. By this means, an attempt can be made to construct a simulated demand schedule and to evaluate benefits without the inefficiency of exclusion. But the difficulty is that the respondents are not likely to tell the truth: they will give too high an evaluation if they wish to encourage the construction of the facility and too low a figure if they wish to discourage it. Nevertheless, this approach has proved to be of some use and has been strongly advocated by several experts.[17]

Prices for Private Facilities In some instances it may be possible to draw a parallel to prices paid for more or less similar private facilities. Thus, fees paid for membership in a private club providing similar facilities may be indicative of the consumption value obtained by the use of the public park. There are two weaknesses to this approach. First, it may well be that the price paid for the private facility is depressed because another public facility is available free of direct charge. Thus, use of the price paid for admission to the private facility understates the value of the additional public park. Second, a factor working in

[15] See Chap. 3, p. 51. Of course, charging of fees is appropriate to cover maintenance costs or where crowding occurs.

[16] For further discussion of pricing schemes, see Chap. 32, Sec. D.

[17] See Jack L. Knetsch and Robert R. Davis, "Comparison of Methods for Recreation Evaluation," in A. V. Kneese and S. C. Smith (eds.), *Water Research,* Washington: Resources for the Future, 1965, pp. 125–143.

the opposite direction is that the price paid for the private facility may include a premium for "exclusiveness" generated by membership in the private facility. Thus, the value of the public park would be overstated. For the method to be reliable, it would be necessary for the two facilities to be fairly comparable, a condition that will rarely be found.

Costs Incurred Approaching the estimation of the dollar value of recreation benefits indirectly, some studies have made use of the personal costs incurred by users in securing their outdoor recreation. The first question is how this cost should be estimated; the second is whether the procedure of using costs as a proxy for benefits is valid.

Pursuing this approach, it has been estimated that the average expenditure per person for all outdoor recreation in 1962 was $74.90, including travel cost and other outlays. It was also estimated that people spent an average of 258 hours for recreational purposes. This finding suggested an expenditure of roughly 30 cents for each hour spent in outdoor recreation, and the conclusion was drawn from this that, on the average, the value of services provided by recreation facilities was roughly 30 cents per hour.[18] Thus the benefit stream of a given park may be obtained by valuing visiting hours at 30 cents. The present value of this stream is then compared with the construction and maintenance costs of the facility. The same magic figure of 30 cents is obtained if one divides the widely used figure of a price of $2 per visit by an assumed average stay of six or seven hours.[19]

Allowing for price rise since 1962, the figure of 30 cents might now be raised to, say, 50 cents, but this is not the main problem. The entire procedure of estimating benefits from user costs is open to serious objection. At best, the recreationist's travel cost measures the marginal benefit derived from his or her last visit to the park. The product of travel cost and number of visits falls short of total benefits by the consumer surplus obtained from acquiring the earlier visits at the same cost. Yet, it is precisely this consumer surplus which constitutes the benefit that should be matched with the cost of providing the facility.[20] But to

[18] See Ruth P. Mack and Sumner Myers, "Outdoor Recreation," in Robert Dorfman (ed.), *Measuring Benefits of Government Investment,* Washington: Brookings, 1965, p. 87.

[19] In guidelines proposed by the federal government, the per-person value of a recreation day for the use of general facilities has been set at 50 cents to $1.50, while the value of specialized facilities is rated from $2 to $6. (See *Evaluation Standards for Primary Outdoor Recreation Benefits,* supplement no. 1, Washington: Ad Hoc Water Resources Council, June 4, 1964, p. 4.) Although the document does not give the basis on which these figures are reached, the reasoning was presumably similar to that given in the text. A point system by which to choose the appropriate value in the indicated range of 50 cents to $1.50 is given in *Methodology for Determining General Recreation Values,* Senate Doc. No. 97, Pacific Southwest Inter-Agency Committee, July 1969.

For further discussion of program evaluation, see also *Policies, Standards, and Procedures in the Formulation, Evaluation and Revenue of Plans for Use and Development of Water and Related Land Resources,* Senate Doc. No. 97, May 29, 1962; and Inter-Agency Committee on Water Resources, Subcommittee on Evaluation Standards, *Report of the Panel on Recreational Values on a Proposed Interim Schedule of Values for Recreational Aspects of Fish and Wildlife,* May 24, 1960.

[20] Let *OA* be the cost per trip and *OB* the observed number of trips, so that *C* is the observed point on the demand schedule. The product of cost and number of trips, or *OBCA,* falls short of total

estimate consumer surplus we would have to know the demand curve over various levels of output, and not only a single point thereon.[21]

A more meaningful role of travel cost is to consider the saving in cost which results as a new and closer facility is opened. This saving offers an approximation to the gain from the additional facility.[22] But, except in this context, travel cost is a poor basis on which to estimate benefits. Not only does it fail to estimate consumer surplus but it also constitutes a poor measure of total cost to the consumer. To determine the latter, the opportunity cost of time spent in the park should also be allowed for. The importance of travel cost in total user cost thus defined varies widely, depending on the travel time involved, and parks with little or no travel cost may be at least as useful as those with high travel cost. A park which involves no user cost except the opportunity cost of the time spent should be used up to the point where this opportunity cost comes to exceed the benefit derived. The gain as measured in terms of consumer surplus is increased, rather than reduced, by the absence of travel cost.

Merit-weighted User Days As an alternative procedure to estimating the value of user days, it has been proposed that certain weights be assigned to various user characteristics.[23] Thus, user days may be weighted according to the user's income, residence, age, or other characteristics. The weights are to be determined in terms of specified policy objectives, such as income redistribution or regional development, thus permitting the comparison of various projects where more than one policy objective is to be taken into account. The spirit is essentially that

---

benefits, or *OBCD*, by consumer surplus, or *ACD*. Since benefit component *OBCA* is paid for by travel cost, it is the *ACD* component which must be matched against the cost of the facility.

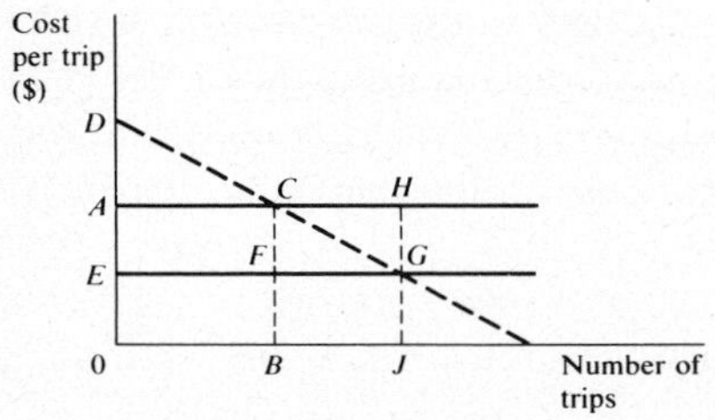

Instead of matching the benefit stream as measured by *ACD* with the facility cost, total benefits as measured by *OBCD* may be matched with facility plus travel cost. In maximizing the excess of benefits over cost or expanding output to the point where the two are equal, both procedures give the same result. However, different cost-benefit ratios are recorded, depending on which method is used, unless the ratios are equal to 1. This shows a certain arbitrariness of the ratio approach. See Chap. 7, p. 157, footnote 3.

[21] See Jack L. Knetsch, "Economics of Including Recreation as a Purpose of Water Resource Projects," *Journal of Farm Economics*, December 1964, pp. 1148–1157.

[22] Referring back to the figure in footnote 20, let provision of the new facility reduce travel cost from *OA* to *OE*. The gain is then given by area *EGCA* or, assuming a linear demand schedule by *EFCA* + ½ *FGHC*, the formula used in our earlier discussion of the highway case. This use of travel cost was pointed out to us by N. A. Back, Director, Center for Economic Studies, Institute for Water Resources, Corps of Engineers, Department of the Army.

[23] See Mack and Myers, op. cit.

of cost-effectiveness studies, where comparison is made between the efficiency of alternative uses of given funds in achieving a desired set of objectives and where the value weights to be attributed to these objectives are given in advance.

Other Benefits

So far, only benefits accruing to and valued by users have been allowed for. In addition, other benefits may enter. Outdoor recreation projects are frequently part of broader programs aimed at multiple objectives, e.g., water resource or regional development projects. Thus, a dam may be built to generate power, to control floods, to serve irrigation, *and* to yield recreational facilities. The benefits from the various products must then be evaluated in conjunction with one another so as to obtain the best product mix.

Outdoor recreation, moreover, may be considered a merit good, so that social valuation exceeds the value attributed by private users, resulting in a writing-up of the benefit evaluation similar to a subsidy to private-type merit goods. Similar considerations arise with regard to objectives such as conservation of natural beauty or of wildlife. These objectives involve social values which cannot be measured readily by market tests and thus tend to be set aside. Possible conflicts between social and private time preference are also involved, relating in this instance to the interests of future versus present generations. In recreation as elsewhere, it is natural for economic analysis to focus on those aspects of the problem which permit analogy to market pricing and which are therefore more feasible to deal with. These are by no means the only, or even in some cases the most important, aspects.

C. EDUCATION

The analysis of education expenditures has received a great deal of attention by economists in recent years.[24] Viewed as "investment in human resources," returns to education expenditures have been computed and the profitability of "human" investment relative to "plant and equipment" investment has been assessed.[25] By concentrating exclusively on the earning-generating effects of education while disregarding other aspects, this approach does less than justice to the role of education. These other aspects will be noted later on, but for the time being we address ourselves to the more tangible and readily measured earnings feature.

The importance of education in public sector policy is enormous. As shown in Table 8-2, public expenditures on education amounted to over $70 billion in fiscal 1972. With private expenditures of only $11 billion, 86 percent of the total outlay was in the public sector. Accounting for nearly 30 percent of total public expenditures other than defense, education is by far the most important civilian item. About two-thirds of the costs were at the local level, directed at the provi-

[24] We are here dealing with the cost-benefit aspects of education only. Other questions, such as how education should be financed and whether it should be public or private, are considered in a later chapter. See Chap. 30, Sec. C.

[25] For the basic work, see Gary S. Becker, *Human Capital,* New York: Columbia, 1964.

TABLE 8-2
Direct Public Expenditures on Education, Fiscal 1972*
(In Billions of Dollars)

	Federal	*State*	*Local*	*All*
Elementary and secondary	—	0.5	45.1	45.6
Higher	5.1	16.7	2.6	24.4
All	5.1	17.2	47.7	70.0

* See *Governmental Finances in 1971–72,* Department of Commerce, Bureau of the Census, p. 23. The table shows expenditures to the public, with grant-financed expenditures included at the recipient level.

sion of elementary and secondary education. Higher education is primarily financed at the state level, but federal money plays an increasingly important role. Evaluation of education programs is thus a vital factor at all levels of government.

Benefit-Cost Ratio Based on Earnings

The use of earnings effects in cost-benefit evaluation of education expenditures may be illustrated by considering the major steps in estimating the returns for various levels of education.

Benefits Benefit evaluation has concentrated on the increase in the student's lifetime earnings due to education. This gain in earnings has been estimated by observing earnings differentials among people with various levels of education and attributing these differentials to the influence of education. The earning increment is then projected over the student's working life and discounted to obtain a present value. The process is complicated by adjusting for such factors as productivity changes and lifetime earnings profiles. However, a set of illustrative figures is shown in Table 8-3 to bring out the basic nature of the problem.

Column I shows estimated annual lifetime earnings for male workers at various levels of education and column II shows the resulting differentials.[26] Column III shows the estimated number of earnings-years over which these gains

TABLE 8-3
Estimated Average Value of High School and College Education, 1972
(In Thousands of Dollars)

				PRESENT VALUE OF GAIN	
Education	*Mean Annual Earnings (I)*	*Gain (II)*	*Number of Years Applicable (III)*	*Discount Rate 8% (IV)*	*Discount Rate 4% (V)*
Below high school	8.0				
High school	12.0	4.0	45	48.4	82.9
College	18.0	6.0	41	71.8	120.0

[26] Figures based on *Economic Report of the President,* 1974, p. 146.

TABLE 8-4
Estimated Average Cost of Education, 1972
(In Dollars)

	AVERAGE COST PER STUDENT	
	High School (4 years)	*College (4 years)*
1. Operation of schools	4,000	16,000
2. Forgone earnings	7,000	15,000
3. Other incidental costs	500	6,000
4. Total	11,500	37,000
5. Present value, 8% discount	9,648	30,987
6. Present value, 4% discount	10,339	33,207

Notes: Lines 1 to 4 represent undiscounted average costs per pupil cumulated over four years. The earnings rate on line 2 falls short of that shown in Table 8-3 because the latter refers to lifetime earnings, while earnings at high school or college age are lower.

Source: Estimates in line 1 based on Elchanan Cohn, *The Economics of Education*, Toronto: Lexington Books, 1972, chap. 3.

will be realized. Column IV shows the present value of these gains using a discount rate of 8 percent, while column V shows the same for a rate of 4 percent. To simplify, it is assumed that the annual earnings gain is constant and extends up to age sixty-three. Since earnings, especially for college graduates, are typically higher in the later period of their earnings life, this overstates the present value of the gain, since insufficient discounting is applied. It will be noted that the present value of the gain from increased education depends greatly on the discount rate used. This is so because investment from education has a very long payoff period.

Costs Turning to the cost side, we include (1) the capital and operating cost of running schools, and (2) the costs incurred by the student. The latter include the opportunity cost of earnings forgone and outlays incurred, such as books, travel, and additional (not total!) living costs. These costs differ widely by type of school and region of the country, but, on the average, they may be estimated as shown in Table 8-4. It will be noted that for the college case, the cost of forgone earnings is an important item in the total picture.

Benefit-Cost Ratio We may now put the two sides together and obtain the benefit-cost ratios or differentials shown in Table 8-5.

Taking these results at face value, it seems that investment in education, especially high school education, is highly profitable. Benefit-cost ratios for college and high school education, even discounting at 8 percent, are 2.3 and 5.0, respectively.[27] Proceeding on the efficiency principle that the rate of return to

[27] Others have measured the return to education in terms of an internal rate of discount, i.e., that rate at which the present value of the income stream equals the investment cost. Thus the return to college education has been estimated by Gary Becker at 14 percent and by G. Hanoch at 9.6 percent. For a discussion of these and other estimates, see Elchanan Cohn, *The Economics of Education*, Toronto: Lexington Books, 1972, chap. 5.

TABLE 8-5
Benefit-Cost Patterns
(Present Values)

	High School	*College*
Benefit-cost ratio		
8 percent discount	5.0	2.3
4 percent discount	8.3	3.6
Benefit-cost differentials		
8 percent discount	$38,800	$40,813
4 percent discount	$72,561	$86,793

capital should be equalized in various uses, and since there is considerable slack in student input (only about 50 percent of all students complete high school and only one-third of high school graduates proceed through college), it appears that considerable scope for increased investment in higher education still exists.

Qualifications

The preceding type of calculation is interesting, but the implicit benefit measure is subject to serious qualifications.

1. Measuring the returns to education in terms of observed average earnings differentials of people with varying levels of education assumes that these differentials are caused entirely by education. Other factors may be present as well. Thus, differences in earnings may reflect differences in innate earnings capacity, whether due to differences in intelligence, drive, pecuniary motivation, or what not. Since innate earning ability may be positively related to the length of education, part of the difference in average earnings by education levels may be due to ability rather than training differentials. Attempts have been made to correct for this by comparing earnings of people with equal ability (as measured by test scores, IQ, etc.) but different schooling, but this is a much more difficult task.

2. Further overestimation of the social return to education may arise where wage rates are not closely related to the worker's marginal product, but higher-paying jobs are reserved for people with higher ranking in the educational hierarchy. "Prestige hiring" is not an unknown feature, and not all personal services are valued in a competitive market. In such cases, training differentials are relevant from the private point of view but resulting differentials in earnings reflect pecuniary rather than real benefits and therefore should not be allowed for in measuring social gains.

3. Reference to averages may be highly misleading if applied to subgroups or individuals. Thus, it has been shown that rates of return to education differ by social groups since the fruits of education are not always competitively priced. Furthermore, educational investment opportunities may be restricted rather than freely available.

4. While the preceding items suggested a possible overstatement of benefits, other considerations indicate that the earnings approach undervalues education. Such is the case because it disregards external benefits and fails to allow for the contribution to a fuller life which (one hopes) education renders. In other words, investment in education is looked upon purely as the creation of an income-earning asset, where income is defined as factor earnings in the market. It may also be considered an investment in a durable consumer good which generates a psychic income stream to the student throughout his life.[28]

For many forms of education, the latter is at least as important as the former. Preoccupation of economists with the earnings aspects not only leads one to underestimate the total value of education, but also contributes to distorted choices between types of education. The "earnings differential" approach to education economics, as developed over the last decade, has been most misleading in this respect.

5. A further source of underestimation of benefits arises because the earnings differential records only those gains which are internalized in the student's earning prospects. It does not capture external benefits which others may derive from this education. As noted earlier, education is a mixed good which generates both private and social gains.[29] The latter may be tangible gains which arise because the labor force can sustain a more advanced technology, or because of increased productivity stemming from innovations; or, they may be intangible benefits in the form of a more intelligent political process, or a culturally more rewarding environment.

Finally, education policy has a profound bearing on income distribution and social stratification. It can thus be a vital instrument of social policy. Inequalities in the distribution of income are strongly related to inequalities in educational investment. Unequal education thus perpetuates unequal income, and provision for more equally distributed educational inputs in turn helps to reduce inequality in the distribution of earnings. At the same time, discrimination (social and racial) must not be permitted to interfere with educational gains as reflected in earnings, lest education become ineffective as a source of social mobility and equalization.

Over a considerable range, this situation opens an opportunity for policy measures which are both efficient in the output-oriented sense of the economist, and which serve desirable social ends of reduced inequality. By extending human investment where it has been held back artificially through discrimination, rigidities, and inability to obtain the necessary funds, both these purposes are served. Moreover, where earnings are low because of discrimination, they are not the proper prices to be used in assessing social gain. Rather, use should be made of shadow prices which account for the return receivable without discrimination. Beyond this, there may be a case for "overinvestment" in education of underprivileged groups even though the earnings payoff will be less. This form of distributional adjustment may be preferable on social grounds to transfer payments and may offer a better chance for permanent escape from poverty.

Tax and Subsidy Aspects

In Tables 8-3 to 8-5 we have considered earnings gains and costs to society and thus have derived a benefit-cost ratio for college education of 2.3. This ratio, however, is not the same as the one which confronts the individual student who is concerned with his private benefits and costs only.

While benefits from a college education were estimated at $71,800 (present value), the net gains to the individual will be less because he must pay taxes thereon. Suppose that his average tax rate is 25 percent so his benefits are reduced to $53,850.

[28] In addition, the learning process (and what goes with it) may itself be enjoyable, thus giving consumption benefits during the student's school years.

[29] See p. 56.

On the cost side, private costs fall short of total costs because the operating cost of schools is only partly sustained by tuition, and because part of the student's missed earnings are offset by reduced tax liabilities. Suppose that one-third of the college costs are tuition-financed and that 5 percent of missed earnings are recouped in lower taxes. Total private costs then equal $19,220 and the private benefit-cost ratio rises to 2.9. The average college student, it appears, receives a high return even if additional future taxes are accounted for.

One further aspect of the tax treatment should be noted here. Earnings from private investment in education are taxed on a gross basis without provision for depreciation or expensing of capital cost, as applies to plant and equipment investment. This may be expected to lead to private underinvestment in education, a factor which tends to be compensated for by public investment therein.

D. THE PLANNING-PROGRAMMING-BUDGETING SYSTEM

During the 1960s, increasing efforts were made to expand the application of principles of cost-benefit analysis to government expenditure decisions. These efforts began with the application of cost-effectiveness analysis in the Defense Department and later centered on the introduction of the so-called planning-programming-budgeting (PPB) system to the entire federal government as well as to a number of state and local governments. At the same time, this development may be looked upon as the extension of long-standing efforts to improve the formulation of expenditure policy at the executive level. At the time the Bureau of the Budget was created in the Treasury Department by the Accounting Act of 1921, the emphasis was on operational control over expenditure programs.[30] When the bureau was separated from the Treasury and placed in the President's office in 1939, emphasis shifted to managerial efficiency. This tendency was supported by the report of the Hoover Commission in 1949 which called for the introduction of "performance budgeting." Improvements in accounting and cost data were introduced by the 1950 Budget and Accounting Act. As noted, a broader and more systematic approach to expenditure planning was developed in the Department of Defense in the early 1960s, and the extension of this methodology was pushed by various executive directives, beginning in 1965.

Objectives and Procedures

Three basic ideas underlie the concept of PPB:

1. Although, for purposes of legislative control, appropriations must be made to agencies, expenditure programs may overlap agencies, and there is need to look at the program and planning unit as a whole.

[30] Prior to that time, each department submitted its own appropriation requests directly to the Congress, but as early as 1912, President Taft had submitted to the Congress a model budget, involving classifications by functions and activity as well as by organization. For a discussion of this history, see Allen Schick, "The Road to PPB: The Stages of Budget Reform," *Public Administration Review,* p. 243, December 1966; and Charles Schultze, *The Politics and Economics of Public Spending,* Washington: Brookings, 1968.

2. A proper evaluation of an expenditure program requires scrutiny of more than one time period.

3. In the interests of applying standards of efficiency to the budget, cost-benefit analysis should be applied where feasible and expenditure programs should be evaluated in these terms.

Thus the objective of the PPBS has been described as "an approach to decision making designed to help make as explicit as possible the costs and consequences of major choices and to encourage the use of this information systematically in the making of public policy."[31] This approach involves the use of new tools of analysis, e.g., cost-benefit techniques, and, beyond this, an effort to assure the use of these tools in a systematic fashion.

The main responsibility for implementing the new approach was to rest with the various governmental departments and agencies, but the central responsibility for coordination and guidance remained with the Office of Management and Budget. As one of the major innovations, program structures were prescribed to secure the grouping of activities into objective-oriented classifications. The purpose was to obtain a view of the total costs and benefits involved in a program, components of which may appear in different parts of the organization and may be included in different appropriation categories. Given such total program evaluation, a better basis is provided for analyzing the comparative merits of alternative programs and the possible tradeoffs among them.

The budget for the fiscal year 1970 for the first time included a presentation of agency budgets by program as well as by appropriation categories and this approach has been expanded in subsequent budgets. The presentation for the Department of Health, Education, and Welfare, for instance, includes major program categories such as health, social and rehabilitation services, and income security. The education program category is divided into subcategories such as development of basic, occupational, and academic skills, etc., grouping together in each subcategory a number of program elements, such as education of the disadvantaged and the physically handicapped, otherwise included in separate appropriation categories. In recent years, the budget presentation has given increasing attention to presenting budget outlays by function as well as by agencies.

The PPB system as introduced in 1965 also prescribed various procedures by which to integrate the approach into step-by-step budget planning. Thus, the Office of Management and Budget, in negotiation with each agency, was to submit an "issue letter" to the agency, defining the major issues which should be analyzed in each budget cycle. The agencies were to prepare, along with the budget submission, brief program memoranda for selected major program categories. These were to incorporate the results of the underlying analysis, identify alternatives, and then serve as evidence in the program evaluation. As a final component of the PPB system, the agency was to submit a current program and financial

[31] See J. Carlson, "The Current Status of the Planning-Programming-Budgeting System," in *The Analysis and Evaluation of Public Expenditures: The PPB System,* Joint Economic Committee, 91st Cong., 1st Sess., 1969, vol. 2, p. 613; and Jesse Burkhead and Jerry Miner, *Public Expenditure,* Chicago: Aldine-Atherton, 1971, chap. 6.

plan covering the preceding two and the coming five years. This plan was to show the funds committed to various program areas by past decisions, as well as projected program outputs for the same period. It would then serve as a guide in relating annual budget allocations to longer-term plans and priorities.

Evaluation and Shortcomings

The objectives of the PPB system were clearly desirable, but the details proved too cumbersome and most of the specific requirements imposed upon the agencies were subsequently reduced or withdrawn in 1971. Some of the major difficulties were as follows:

1. The PPB system places the major responsibility for program evaluation on departments and agencies. This stipulation may allow the evaluation of whole programs, but only to the extent that such program categories can be confined to particular departments or agencies. Frequently this is not the case. The poverty program, for instance, covers many departments and agencies other than Health, Education, and Welfare. Comprehensive program evaluation must thus be interdepartmental, or components must be transferred out of present departments into a new unit.

A similar difficulty arises from the fact that federal programs in many instances operate through grants to state and local governments. Program evaluation therefore requires a joint effort, an effort that is not provided for in the federal budget process.

2. While program evaluation and planning along PPB lines is important, it is not the only function of the budget process. As we have seen in Chapter 2, the budget must also function as a framework for congressional appropriation and control, and as a tool of executive management. For appropriation and control purposes, expenditures have continued to be classified by traditional categories, but for management purposes, expenditure breakdown by executive units (departments, bureaus, and divisions within departments) is needed. Thus, the various objectives of budget policy (planning, control, and management) call for distinct expenditure classifications which inevitably give rise to complexity and potential confusion. In time, congressional appropriation categories should be made to coincide with planning (program) categories, thus eliminating the complex system of crosswalk required by the present practice, and the recent budget reforms which involve the Congress more actively in the budgetary process should be helpful in this respect.

3. PPB has been criticized for tying the implementation of expenditure analysis too closely into the budget process. The budget process, so this argument goes, must be directed essentially at preparing appropriations requests for Congress. In this task there is neither time nor the analytical frame of mind which is needed to apply rigorous program evaluation. Thus, it is suggested that the task of program evaluation be taken out of the Office of Management and Budget and put into a new executive agency, thereby limiting the role of the OMB. Moreover, there now arises the question whether the new congressional budget office should also engage in such analysis.

4. Finally, the efforts made in the late 1960s to introduce a comprehensive PPB system have been criticized for requiring too much too soon and for transplanting the Defense Department system, where cost-benefit analysis proved most readily applicable, to civilian agencies where it is less feasible. Weapons systems are easier to evaluate by cost-effectiveness analysis than are many civilian programs, where less readily measurable results must be identified and the required expert staff is not available. Sham figures may be reported to pacify the OMB. Indeed, so this criticism goes, project analysis should be decentralized and left to the initiative of the individual departments.

These criticisms have some merit and future experience will undoubtedly bring new developments in this area. These will include not only modifications in PPB and the governmental structure involved in its application, but perhaps more drastic departures from traditional practice.[32] However this may be, failure of the attempt to introduce a comprehensive PPB system all at once should not be permitted to condemn the basic merits of the PPB idea. The concept of program evaluation and the application of quantitative tools of evaluation are clearly a step forward and will receive continued consideration. The application of these tools will not solve all problems, particularly the identification and evaluation of intangible benefit streams, and no set formula can be applied in all situations. However, where the system can be applied, it will make for a more systematic and careful evaluation of such information as can be obtained. Thereby it will contribute to a more efficient conduct of the public sector. Moreover, the spirit of PPB as a framework for national budget planning is of importance not only to the federal government but also at the state and local levels.

E. SUMMARY

The application of cost-benefit analysis to the evaluation of highway projects was examined, with the following conclusions:

1. The measure of benefits involved the cost of travel time saved as well as other reductions in travel costs. The analysis involved determination of incremental cost savings from successive expansion of facilities.

2. On the cost side, construction costs, site costs, and maintenance costs were considered.

3. In addition, indirect benefits and costs were allowed for.

In dealing with outdoor recreation, the major difficulty was how to value the resulting benefits to users:

4. Benefits may be measured by user charges, but this method interferes with efficient utilization.

5. Market surveys may be used to measure potential demand.

6. Benefits may be measured in analogy to charges for comparable private facilities.

7. The personal cost incurred by users may be taken to measure their evaluation.

[32] See, for instance, Aaron Wildavsky, "Rescuing Policy Analysis from PPBS," *The Analysis and Evaluation of Public Expenditures: The PPB System,* vol. 3, Joint Economic Committee, U.S. Congress, 1969, where it is proposed that annual budget legislation be required only where fundamental changes in major expenditure programs are to be made, with the remaining programs continuing automatically.

8. In computing merit-weighted user days, various weights might be attached to different users.

Consideration was given to an application of cost-benefit analysis to education and to estimating a rate of return on investment in education:

9. Benefits were estimated as the discounted value of the resulting increase in expected earnings.

10. In estimating costs, the student's forgone earnings were included as well as the cost of operating schools.

11. Various qualifications were introduced and a distinction was drawn between the social and the private return to education.

Finally, the planning-programming-budgeting system (PPBS) was examined, including its objectives, procedures, merits, and shortcomings.

FURTHER READINGS

Chase, S. B. (ed.): *Problems in Public Expenditure Analysis,* Washington: Brookings, 1968.

Dorfman, R. (ed.): *Measuring Benefits of Government Investments,* Washington: Brookings, 1965.

Hinrichs, Harley H., and G. M. Taylor: *Program Budgeting and Benefit-Cost Analysis,* Pacific Palisades, Calif.: Goodyear Publishing Co., 1969.

———: *Systematic Analysis: A Primer on Benefit-Cost Analysis and Program Evaluation,* Pacific Palisades, Calif.: Goodyear Publishing Co., 1972.

Joint Economic Committee, 91st Cong.: *The Analysis and Evaluation of Public Expenditures: The PPB System,* 1969.

Part Three

Revenue Structure

Chapter 9

Introduction to Taxation*

A. Development of the United States Tax Structure: *Federal Level; State Level; Local Level; All Levels.* **B. Equity Rules and the "Good" Tax System:** *Requirements for a "Good" Tax Structure; Approaches to Equity.* **C. Application of Benefit Principle:** *A General Benefit Tax; Specific Benefit Taxes; Taxes in Lieu of Charges; A Note on Earmarking.* **D. Application of Ability-to-Pay Principle:** *Horizontal and Vertical Equity; Equal-Sacrifice Rules and the Issue of Progression; Critique of Assumptions; Social Value Approach.* **E. Measures of Ability to Pay:** *Income versus Consumption; Wealth; Timing; Conclusions on Ability Measures; Vertical Equity and the Base of Redistribution.* **F. Categories of Taxes:** *Taxes on Current Output and Income; Taxes on Holding and Transfer of Wealth.* **G. Further Distinctions:** *Personal versus In Rem Taxes; Direct versus Indirect Taxes.* **H. Conclusion. I. Summary.**

We now turn from the expenditure to the financing side of the fiscal structure. To provide public services, government must have the means to purchase the

* *Reader's Guide to Chapter 9:* This chapter lays the basis for the subsequent discussion of the tax structure. Before delving into the nitty-gritty of particular taxes and the technical provisions which make them what they are, a general view of the problem will be helpful. This includes a brief sketch of tax-structure development, an examination of tax equity—including the hot question of what basis there is for progressive taxation—and a look at where and how various taxes are inserted into the flow of income and expenditures in the economy—an essential chapter for the subsequent discussion.

necessary resources or products. The alternative would be direct conscription of resources or output, but this is used only to a limited degree, notably in the case of military draft. Similarly, revenue is needed to finance transfer payments. The necessary funds may be obtained in various ways, including (1) taxation, (2) borrowing, and (3) charges. We begin with tax finance, which accounts for well over 90 percent of total public revenue and thus deserves first consideration.[1]

A. DEVELOPMENT OF THE UNITED STATES TAX STRUCTURE

Paralleling the growth in public expenditures, the overall level of taxation as shown in Table 9-1 has risen substantially in recent decades. The picture (see line 4 of the table) is similar to that of Table 6-2 where expenditure growth was shown. As with expenditures, the growth of tax revenue must be seen in relation to that of GNP and not in absolute terms. Omitting the temporary wartime peaks, the ratio of tax revenue to GNP hovered around 6 percent in the first two decades of the century and around 10 percent during the twenties. By 1940, the level had risen to nearly 15 percent. In each of the following three decades the ratio was to rise by 5 percentage points, reaching 20 percent in 1950, 26 percent by 1960, and 30 percent by 1970. The causes of increase are similar to those underlying the development of the expenditure side and need not be restated. Instead, we now focus on the major changes in the composition of the tax structure which accompanied this overall growth. For this purpose, it is useful to begin with a separate view of the various levels of government before proceeding to the overall picture.

Federal Level

Beginning with the federal component (lines 5 to 12 of Table 9-1), we find an almost exclusive reliance on indirect taxes up to World War I, with revenue about equally divided between receipts from customs duties and domestic excises. The introduction of the Sixteenth Amendment in 1913 opened the way for income taxation, and by the early twenties income taxes had come to supply nearly 60 percent of federal revenue. Excises had declined in relative importance, and customs duties had become but a minor item. The increase in the total federal tax to GNP ratio (line 1) was met largely by the introduction of federal income taxes, with the corporation tax leading the individual income tax.

The relative importance of the income taxes continued to rise during the twenties while the excise tax share declined. This trend was reversed in the Depression years of the thirties, when excise rates were raised in a futile attempt to balance the budget, and revenue from the income taxes suffered from the decline in national income. The late thirties also brought the advent of payroll taxes associated with the creation of the social security system.

World War II finance brought the second major expansion of income taxation and of the individual income tax in particular. Over the decade of the 1940s, the individual income tax share rose from 17 to 49 percent of federal revenue,

[1] Loan finance is discussed in Chap. 28 and charges are taken up in Chap. 32.

TABLE 9-1
Development of United States Tax Structure

	1902	1913	1922	1927	1940	1950	1960	1970	1972
I. TAX REVENUE AS PERCENT OF GNP									
1. Federal	2.3	1.7	4.6	3.6	5.7	13.6	18.2	19.8	17.7
2. State	0.7	0.8	1.4	1.8	4.4	3.4	4.5	6.0	6.2
3. Local	3.2	3.3	4.2	4.7	4.5	2.9	3.8	4.2	4.3
4. Total	6.2	5.8	10.2	10.1	14.5	19.9	26.5	30.0	28.2
II. PERCENTAGE COMPOSITION OF TAX REVENUE									
Federal									
5. Individual income tax	—	—	} 56.8 (5 and 6)	25.6	16.9	40.7	45.4	48.1	46.2
6. Corporation income tax	—	5.3		36.6	19.8	27.1	24.0	17.5	15.7
7. Sales and excises	47.6	45.6	24.4	14.6	31.6	19.2	12.8	8.4	8.1
8. Customs duties	47.4	46.8	9.3	17.0	5.8	1.1	1.2	1.3	1.6
9. Death and gift	1.0	—	4.1	2.6	6.3	1.8	1.8	1.9	2.6
10. Payroll			1.2	2.1	14.2	9.0	14.2	22.3	25.0
11. Other	4.1	2.3	4.2	1.4	5.5	1.1	0.7	0.5	0.7
12. Total	100.0	100.0	100.0	100.0	100.0	100.0	100.0	100.0	100.0
State									
13. Individual income tax	—	—	4.1	4.0	4.7	7.4	9.9	16.0	18.2
14. Corporation income tax	—	—	5.5	5.3	3.5	6.0	5.3	6.5	6.2
15. Sales and excises	17.9	19.9	27.2	42.8	51.0	55.6	54.0	52.2	51.0
16. Property tax	52.6	46.5	33.0	21.2	5.9	3.1	2.7	1.9	1.8
17. Payroll	—	—	10.1	7.9	24.5	18.8	19.4	16.4	16.4
18. Death and gift	29.5	33.6	20.1	18.9	10.3	9.1	1.9	1.7	1.8
19. Other	—	—	—	—	—	—	6.9	5.2	4.6
20. Total	100.0	100.0	100.0	100.0	100.0	100.0	100.0	100.0	100.0
Local									
21. Individual income tax	—	—	—	—	} 0.4 (21 and 22)	0.8	} 1.3 (21 and 22)	} 4.1 (21 and 22)	} 4.4 (21 and 22)
22. Corporation income tax	—	—	—	—		0.1			
23. Sales and excises	—	0.2	0.6	0.6	2.8	5.9	7.7	8.1	8.7
24. Property		91.0	96.4	96.8	91.3	86.2	85.0	82.1	81.0
25. Payroll	—	0.2	0.5	0.6	1.5	2.3	2.9	3.2	3.2
26. Other	11.4	8.6	2.5	2.1	3.9	4.7	3.0	2.5	2.8
27. Total	100.0	100.0	100.0	100.0	100.0	100.0	100.0	100.0	100.0

TABLE 9-1 *(Continued)*

	1902	*1913*	*1922*	*1927*	*1940*	*1950*	*1960*	*1970*	*1972*
All Levels									
28. Individual income tax	—	—	}	9.8	8.1	29.3	33.0	35.4	33.5
29. Corporation income tax	—	1.5	} 27.0	13.9	8.7	19.6	17.3	12.8	11.2
30. Sales and excises	19.8	16.1	15.1	13.2	28.5	23.6	19.1	17.2	17.6
31. Customs duties	17.7	13.6	4.2	6.0	2.3	0.7	0.8	0.9	1.0
32. Property	51.4	58.6	44.0	48.8	30.3	13.0	12.7	11.9	12.8
33. Payroll	—	0.1	2.1	2.4	13.3	9.7	13.4	18.5	19.7
34. Death and gift	11.1	10.1	7.5	5.8	8.9	4.2	1.5	1.6	2.0
35. Other							2.1	1.7	2.1
36. Total	100.0	100.0	100.0	100.0	100.0	100.0	100.0	100.0	100.0
				III. LEVELS AS PERCENT OF TOTAL					
37. Federal	37.4	29.1	45.2	35.5	38.8	68.3	68.5	65.8	62.7
38. State	11.4	13.2	13.9	18.0	30.0	17.3	17.1	20.1	21.9
39. Local	51.3	57.6	40.9	46.5	31.2	14.4	14.5	14.1	15.4
40. Total	100.0	100.0	100.0	100.0	100.0	100.0	100.0	100.0	100.0

Notes:
Calendar years through 1950, fiscal years 1960, 1970, and 1972.
Detail may not add to total due to rounding.
Local motor vehicle and operator's licenses included in "other" to 1950 and in sales taxes thereafter.
Sources:
1902–1950: U.S. Bureau of the Census, *Historical Statistics for the United States; Colonial Times to 1957,* pp. 724, 727, 729.
1960, 1970, and 1972: U.S. Bureau of the Census, *Governmental Finances,* 1959–60, 1969–70, and 1971–72.

while the corporation income tax share increased from 20 to 27 percent. The ratio of federal tax revenue to GNP doubled in this period, and the individual income tax to GNP ratio rose from 1 to 6 percent. In the process, this tax was transformed from a tax on the rich, paid by a small fraction of high-income recipients, to a mass tax paid by almost all income earners. The number of income taxpayers rose from 7 million in 1939 to 50 million in 1945. The very process which produced this extensive shift from indirect to direct taxation at the same time served to render the income tax a less progressive instrument.[2] The number of income taxpayers is now close to 80 million, including 98 percent of all those employed.

The fifties brought a further sharp rise in the ratio of federal tax to GNP. Accounted for largely by increased payroll taxation, it resulted in a declining share of revenue from other taxes, with only the individual income tax showing further gain. The sixties, finally, saw the overall tax to GNP ratio rise a further

[2] A tax is said to be regressive, proportional, or progressive, depending on whether the tax to income ratio falls, remains constant, or rises as we move up the income scale. See p. 285.

three to four percentage points, accompanied by a further sharp increase in the payroll tax share. The payroll tax by this time had become the second most important tax in the system, while the corporation income tax and excises continued to decline in relative importance.

Notwithstanding these changes, the individual income tax has remained much the largest component, contributing 46 percent of the 1972 total. Payroll taxes are next with 25 percent, followed by the corporation income tax with 16 percent. Indirect taxes provide only 8 percent. This highly income-and-payroll tax-intensive revenue structure stands in sharp contrast to the earlier federal tax structure, which included indirect taxes only. Although the expansion of the income tax involved a vast downward extension of the taxable income base, it is still the most progressive major component of the tax structure. Its rise during the forties has been a significant factor in rendering the distributive impact of the overall federal tax structure more progressive. It is not surprising, then, that the predominance of the individual income tax continues to render income tax reform one of the most lively aspects of federal tax policy.

State Level

At the state level, the major development over the first half of the century (see lines 13 to 20 of Table 9-1) was the dwindling of the property tax share from 53 to 3 percent, and a rise in the importance of sales and gross receipt taxes, particularly retail sales and gasoline taxes. Owing to the preponderance of these taxes, state taxation, as we shall see later, is less progressive and may even be regressive in its distributional impact.[3] Although the data record a rise in the individual income tax share in recent decades, this increase has not been sufficient to change the highly sales tax–intensive nature of state taxation. The overall ratio of state tax revenue to GNP (line 2) rose slowly during the twenties and thirties; but thereafter, state taxation leveled out at about 4 percent.

Local Level

The local tax structure has always been, and continues to be, almost entirely a property tax system. As shown in lines 21 to 27 of Table 9-1, the property tax has provided over 80 percent of local revenue throughout the period. The use of sales and income taxes has increased in recent decades but remains a relatively minor factor. Since the distributional impact of the property tax is not assessed as readily as that of income or sales taxes, judgment on the incidence of local taxation is postponed to a later point.[4] The overall level of local taxation (total revenue as a percent of GNP) has remained fairly stable, ranging between 3 and 5 percent from the beginning of the century to World War II (line 3). The ratio declined during the forties, making room for war finance, and recovered the 4 percent level during the fifties. The ratio continued to rise slowly during the sixties, but its level is not above what it was half a century ago, in contrast to the state and federal ratios which rose to several times their earlier levels.[5]

[3] See p. 392.
[4] See pp. 394 and 430.
[5] See Chap. 30, Sec. A.

All Levels

The changing composition of the combined tax structure—which is what matters for overall tax policy—reflects both changes at each level and their changing weights in the total picture. As shown in lines 37 to 40, the federal share was relatively stable at 30 to 40 percent of the total from 1900 to 1940, but rose sharply during the forties, reaching 68 percent in 1950. It showed little change during the 1950s but by 1972 had turned down and fallen to 63 percent. For the first half of the century, the state share rose slowly, while the local share declined sharply; but thereafter, both shares evened out during the fifties and sixties. Whereas state and local taxation accounted for over two-thirds of the total prior to World War II, by 1960 it had dropped to little more than 30 percent. The overall picture was thus one of increasing centralization, with the federal share rising primarily at the cost of the local. Recent years, however, have shown a reversal of this trend, with the state-local tax share rising to 37 percent in 1972.[6]

This increasing centralization made for heavier reliance on income taxation in the overall tax structure (lines 28 to 36). Whereas income taxes (individual and corporate) provided only 17 percent of total revenue in 1940, they now furnish 45 percent. Over the same period the share of sales taxation fell from 31 to 19 percent, that of payroll taxes rose from 13 to 20 percent, and that of property taxes declined from 30 to 13 percent. These changes have left the United States with an overall tax structure which is highly income tax–intensive.[7]

B. EQUITY RULES AND THE "GOOD" TAX SYSTEM

The United States tax system, like that of any other country, has developed in response to many influences—economic, political, and social. It has not been constructed by a master architect in line with the optimal requirements for a "good tax structure." Yet, ideas as to what constitutes a "good" tax system have had their influence. Economists and social philosophers, from Adam Smith on, have propounded what such requirements should be.

Requirements for a "Good" Tax Structure

Among them, the following are of major importance, although they are not meant to be all-inclusive:

1. The distribution of the tax burden should be equitable. Everyone should be made to pay his "fair share."

2. Taxes should be chosen so as to minimize interference with economic decisions in otherwise efficient markets. Imposition of "excess burdens" should be minimized.

3. At the same time, taxes may be used to correct inefficiencies in the private sector, provided they are a suitable instrument for doing so.

[6] The reasons for this, as noted earlier, are to be found on the expenditure side and need not be repeated here. See Chap. 6, Sec. A, p. 134.

[7] For a comparison with the tax structures of other countries, see R. A. Musgrave, *Fiscal Systems,* New Haven, Conn.: Yale, 1969, chap. 7.

4. The tax structure should facilitate the use of fiscal policy for stabilization and growth objectives.

5. The tax system should permit efficient and nonarbitrary administration and it should be understandable to the taxpayer.

6. Administration and compliance cost should be as low as is compatible with the other objectives.

These and other requirements may be used as criteria to appraise the quality of a tax structure. The various objectives are not necessarily in agreement, and where they conflict, tradeoffs between them are needed. Thus, equity may require administrative complexity and may interfere with neutrality. Corrective use of tax policy may interfere with equity, and so forth. These conflicts will be considered as we proceed. Our present concern is with the requirement of a fair burden distribution.

Approaches to Equity

For the time being, our concern is with the equity objective only. While not always controlling, it is a basic criterion for tax-structure design. Everyone agrees that the tax system should be equitable, i.e., that each taxpayer should contribute his "fair share" to the cost of government. But there is no such agreement about how the term "fair share" should be defined. As noted in our earlier discussion of distributive justice, a variety of approaches may be taken. In particular, two strands of thought may be distinguished.

One approach rests on the so-called benefit principle. According to this theory, dating back to Adam Smith and earlier writers, an equitable tax system is one under which each taxpayer contributes in line with the benefits which he receives from public services.[8] According to this principle, the truly equitable tax system will differ, depending on the expenditure structure. The benefit criterion, therefore, is not one of tax policy only, but of tax-expenditure policy. This is in line with our approach in Chapter 3 where we viewed the economics of the public sector as involving a simultaneous solution to both its revenue and its expenditure aspects.

The other strand, also of distinguished ancestry, rests on the "ability-to-pay" principle. Under this approach, the tax problem is viewed by itself, independent of expenditure determination. A given total revenue is needed and each taxpayer is asked to contribute in line with his ability to pay.[9] This approach leaves the

[8] Historically, the benefit principle of taxation derives from the contract theory of the state as understood by the political theorists of the seventeenth century, such as Locke and Hobbes. Subsequently it was woven into the greatest-happiness principle of the utilitarians, such as Bentham. It appeared early in classical economics in Adam Smith's first canon of taxation, which in one sentence combines both the benefit and the ability-to-pay approaches: "The subject of every state ought to contribute towards the support of the government as nearly as possible in proportion to their respective abilities; that is, in proportion to the revenue which they respectively enjoy under the protection of the state." (Adam Smith, *The Wealth of Nations,* vol. 2, edited by E. Cannan, New York: Putnam, 1904, p. 310). Benefits are here viewed in terms of protection received and are thus related to income which, in turn, is also a measure of ability to pay.

[9] The origin of the ability-to-pay principle predates the benefit rule. It dates back to the sixteenth century and has found prominent supporters ever since. They include a wide range of thinkers such as Rousseau, Say, and John Stuart Mill. In the twentieth century, ability to pay has been emphasized primarily by redistribution-oriented writers.

expenditure side of the public sector dangling, and it is thus less satisfactory from the economist's point of view. Yet, actual tax policy is largely determined independently of the expenditure side and an equity rule is needed to provide guidance. The ability-to-pay principle is widely accepted as this guide.

Neither approach is easy to interpret or implement. For the benefit principle to be operational, expenditure benefits for particular taxpayers must be known. For the ability-to-pay approach to be applicable, we must know just how this ability is to be measured. These are formidable difficulties and neither approach wins on practicality grounds. Moreover, neither approach can be said to deal with the entire function of tax policy: the benefit approach, ideally, will allocate that part of the tax bill which defrays the cost of public services, but it cannot handle taxes needed to finance transfer payments and serve redistributional objectives. It assumes that a "proper" state of distribution exists to begin with.[10] This is a serious shortcoming especially since, in practice, there is no separation between the taxes used to finance public services and the taxes used to redistribute income.[11] The ability-to-pay approach better meets the redistribution problem, but it leaves the provision for public services undetermined.

Notwithstanding these shortcomings, both principles have important, if limited, application in designing an equitable tax structure, i.e., one which is acceptable to most people and preferable to alternative arrangements.

C. APPLICATION OF BENEFIT PRINCIPLE

As we have seen in Chapters 3 and 5, the political process involves determination of both tax and expenditure policy and, in a democratic framework, tends to approximate application of the benefit rule. People, or some majority thereof, would not be willing to sustain a fiscal program if, on balance, they did not benefit therefrom. We have also noted that, by relating particular tax to particular expenditure decisions, a more rational decision process may be achieved. Let us now see how the benefit principle may be applied as a guide to tax-structure design.

A General Benefit Tax

Under a strict regime of benefit taxation, each taxpayer would be taxed in line with his demand for public services.[12] Since preferences differ, no general tax formula could be applied to all people. Each taxpayer would be taxed in line with his evaluation. Still, some pattern might be expected to emerge. The typical mix of private goods purchased is known to vary with the income level of the consumer household, and similar patterns may be expected to prevail for social goods. But instead of noting how quantities bought (at the same price) will vary

[10] See Chap. 3, p. 77.

[11] As noted before, the distinction between an allocation and a redistribution function is a useful analytical device rather than a description of the real budget process. See Chap. 1, p. 17.

[12] As noted above (see Chap. 3, p. 74), various pricing rules may be used. Let us suppose here that the consumer is charged the same price per unit, i.e., consumer surplus is not taxed away by charging higher tax prices for intramarginal units.

with income, we now ask how much various consumers are willing to pay for the same amount. Unless the social good in question is what economists call an inferior good, consumer valuation may be expected to rise with income. To simplify, suppose that taxpayers have the same structure of tastes (i.e., pattern of indifference curves) so that persons with the same income value the same amount equally. People with incomes of $10,000 value a given level of public services at, say, $1,000. With 1,000 units of the service supplied, they would be willing to pay $1 per unit. Making the usual assumption that marginal utility of income falls with rising income, others with incomes of $20,000 would be willing to pay a higher unit price of, say, $2. In this case, a proportional rate schedule will apply. If they are not willing to pay as much as $2 but only, say, $1.50, the appropriate rate schedule will be regressive. If they will pay more, a progressive schedule will be in order.[13]

The appropriate tax formula thus depends upon the preference patterns. More specifically, it depends upon the income and price elasticity of demand for social goods. If income elasticity is high, the appropriate tax prices will rise rapidly with income; but if price elasticity is high, the increase will be dampened. More specifically, the required rate structure will be proportional, progressive, or regressive, depending on whether income elasticity equals, exceeds, or falls short of price elasticity.[14]

This finding is interesting, but it does not permit easy implementation. The relevant price and income elasticities are not known or readily derived from market observation as in the case of private goods. Moreover, they will differ among various types of public services. It is not at all obvious which elasticity (income or price) will be larger and by how much, especially if the entire budget is considered. The question of rate structure thus remains open. Nevertheless, this line of reasoning points up the fact that the rationale for or against progressive taxation may be discussed in terms of benefit taxation as well as in the usual ability-to-pay context. Even if the latter points to progression, the former need not do so.[15]

Specific Benefit Taxes

Whereas the general benefit tax is of interest mainly as a theoretical concept, practical applications of benefit taxation may be found in specific instances where particular services are provided on a benefit basis. This may be the case where

[13] This may also be stated in terms of our earlier illustration of social-goods policy in the benefit context. Returning to Fig. 3-8 (Chap. 3, p. 75), we noted that the taxes paid by A and B for OH units of social goods equal KM and LN respectively. If $KM/OM = LN/ON$, a proportional tax rate is required. Since $OM > ON$, a situation where $KM/OM > LN/ON$ calls for a progressive rate structure, while one where $KM/OM < LN/ON$ calls for regression.

[14] This relationship may be specified as follows: Let P be the appropriate unit price of public services to a taxpayer with income Y. Now suppose that the person's income rises. The required tax rate will be proportional, progressive, or regressive, depending on whether $(\Delta P/P) \div (\Delta Y/Y)$ equals, exceeds, or falls short of 1. Since income elasticity $E_y = (\Delta Q/Q) \div (\Delta Y/Y)$ and price elasticity $E_p = (\Delta Q/Q) \div (\Delta P/P)$, we have $(\Delta P/P) \div (\Delta Y/Y) = E_y/E_p$. Thus, the tax will be proportional, progressive, or regressive according to whether E_y is equal to, greater than, or less than E_p. See James M. Buchanan, "Fiscal Institutions and Collective Outlay," *American Economic Review*, pp. 227–235, May 1964.

[15] See also Chap. 1, p. 17.

direct financing is made via fees, user charges, or tolls. Or certain taxes may be applied indirectly in lieu of charges, as is done in the taxation of gasoline and other automotive products for purposes of highway finance.

Under what conditions is this technique feasible and desirable? The case for finance by direct charges to the user is clear-cut where the goods or services provided by government are in the nature of private goods, i.e., where consumption is wholly rival. Benefits can be imputed to a particular user who can be asked to pay. The issuance of licenses, the financing of municipal transportation, and the provision of airport facilities are more or less in this category. Where benefits are internalized, the government may act in a capacity similar to that of a private firm and the same principles of pricing are appropriate. As has been pointed out in recent years, a considerable range of public services might be placed on this basis, thereby easing the pressure on general revenue finance. By using a market mechanism, a more efficient determination of the appropriate level of supply becomes possible.[16]

Taxes in Lieu of Charges

In other instances, where imposition of direct charges is desirable but too costly, a tax on a complementary product may be used in lieu of charges. Gasoline or automobile taxes may be viewed in this light. The yield of automotive taxes (on gasoline and cars) in the United States, including all levels of government, roughly matches the cost of highway expenditures. In the case of the federal highway program, gasoline tax proceeds are earmarked for the Highway Trust Fund, and the income of the fund is used to defray the cost of a federal highway network. In the instance of state and local financing, such direct earmarking does not always exist, but proceeds from highway user taxes nevertheless go largely into road finance.

How effective an approach to benefit taxation does this offer? Although it may be true that such taxes place the total cost of highways on all drivers as a group, it is questionable whether the equity objective of benefit taxation for the individual driver is met. While gasoline use depends on distances driven, not each mile driven results in the same variable cost, nor does it require the same capital outlay in providing new road facilities. Driver X, using road A, may be called upon to support road B, used by driver Y. Gasoline taxes, therefore, are only a rough approximation to the benefit rule in highway finance. Nor will such taxes effectively enter into the determination of demand for new highway construction. Expenditure decisions are made for specific outlays, while taxes are paid independently of particular highways used, so that there is no direct linkage between the two at a disaggregated level. Moreover, there has been increasing support in recent years for legislation which will permit diversion of highway trust fund receipts into the financing of mass transportation. This is justified as a way of internalizing the external costs of highway use.

Another illustration is given by certain uses of the property tax. Special

[16] Other situations may be such that direct charges are technically possible (exclusion can be applied at a relatively low cost) but would not be an efficient mode of finance. For a fuller discussion of public enterprise pricing and user charges, see Chap. 32.

assessments may be used to charge dwellings in a certain block for the cost of improvements which service their particular location. At a more general level, the property tax has traditionally been viewed as a charge for services rendered by local government, it being assumed that the benefits which result are roughly proportional to property values. How well founded this belief is remains to be seen.[17]

Social security taxes may provide another instance of benefit taxation. Payroll tax contributions by the employee may be considered a strict benefit tax, provided that the later benefit payments stand in direct relation to the contribution and that the benefit formula is not redistributive.[18] The same cannot be said for the employer contributions unless they are passed on to the employee.

A Note on Earmarking

Finally, a word on earmarking in relation to benefit taxation. Fiscal experts have argued that earmarking is poor budgeting procedure, since it introduces rigidities and does not permit proper allocation of general revenue among competing uses. Thus, it is inefficient to freeze, say, 50 percent of sales tax revenue as the state contribution to the cost of elementary education. The appropriate allotment may be larger or smaller than this amount. Moreover, it may be desirable to use the sales tax for other purposes.

At the same time, other uses of earmarking may be appropriate and in line with the benefit approach. First, particular taxes may be linked to particular expenditures because tax payments are equivalent to (or are held to approximate) charges imposed on the consumer. As just noted, this holds to some extent for gasoline taxes. Such linkage may be both efficient (in charging for variable costs) and equitable (in distributing costs in line with benefits received). Second, linkage of voting on particular taxes with specified expenditure votes may be helpful in inducing preference revelation and thus contribute to better expenditure decisions. Depending on how it is used, earmarking may thus be an arbitrary procedure leading to budgetary rigidity, or it may be a helpful device for approximating benefit taxation.[19]

D. APPLICATION OF ABILITY-TO-PAY PRINCIPLE

While the benefit principle may be applied directly to the finance of certain governmental functions, it does not solve the general problem of tax-structure design. The range of expenditures to which specific benefit taxes may be applied is relatively limited and the bulk of tax revenue is not derived (nor derivable) on a specific benefit basis. While tax legislation should be related to expenditure legislation, application of the benefit rule in this broader sense does not obviate the need for tax formulas and a rule by which they are designed. Moreover, benefit taxation, even at its best, can relate only to the financing of public services and not to the redistributive function of the tax-transfer process.

[17] See p. 343.

[18] As noted in Chap. 29, these assumptions do not hold for the present United States system.

[19] See Chap. 3, and James M. Buchanan, "The Economics of Earmarked Taxes," *Journal of Political Economy*, October 1963.

Thus an alternative principle of equitable taxation must be applied. This is the rule that people should contribute to the cost of government in line with their "ability to pay." This calls for equal amounts of tax to be paid by taxpayers with equal abilities to pay and for different amounts of taxes when such capacities differ.

Horizontal and Vertical Equity

The requirement of equal taxes for people in equal positions is also referred to as "horizontal" equity, and the proper pattern of unequal taxes among people with unequal incomes is referred to as "vertical" equity. Both are part of the same principle of equal treatment.[20]

Since John Stuart Mill, the ability-to-pay rule has been viewed in terms of an equal-sacrifice prescription. Taxpayers are said to be treated equally if their tax payments involve an equal sacrifice or loss of welfare.[21] The loss of welfare in turn is related to the loss of income.[22] If the level of welfare as a function of income (i.e., the marginal utility of income schedule) is the same for all taxpayers, the equal-sacrifice rule calls for people with equal income (or ability to pay) to contribute equal amounts of tax. Further, people with different incomes should pay different amounts. The more difficult question is how these amounts should differ. To answer it, one must know the shape of the marginal utility of income schedule, and even then the answer differs, depending on how the term "equal" is interpreted.

Equal-Sacrifice Rules and the Issue of Progression

The traditional assumptions of sacrifice theory are that (1) income utility is measurable in cardinal (or absolute) terms, i.e., that we can go beyond saying that total utility derived rises with income and measure by how much; and (2) the income utility schedule is the same for all people. It then follows that people with equal incomes will give up the same utility—suffer the same sacrifice—if they pay equal taxes. The implementation of horizontal equity is thus readily met.

[20] Yet, it is sometimes said that the horizontal aspect is more basic and less controversial. Equal tax for equal incomes merely applies the basic principle of "equality" under the law, while the determination of tax differentials among unequal incomes seems arbitrary. What this argument overlooks is that equality of treatment calls for equal loss of utility, not for equal loss of income. Given equal income utility schedules as discussed in Chap. 4, equal treatment calls for unequal amounts of tax to be paid by taxpayers with unequal income no less than for equal amounts to be paid by those with equal incomes. Both equity rules, therefore, follow from the same principle of equal treatment and neither is more basic. If the purpose of horizontal equity were merely to allocate taxes without malicious discrimination, this goal could be achieved as well by distributing them on a lottery basis, which would hardly be a satisfactory solution. It is true, however, that horizontal equity is simpler in application. While implementation of horizontal equity depends only on the assumption of equal income utility schedules, implementing vertical equity requires further knowledge of the shape of the common schedule.

[21] See John Stuart Mill, *Principles of Political Economy,* edited by W. J. Ashley, London: Longmans, 1921, p. 804.

[22] Some writers (see A. C. Pigou, in Further Readings, p. 230) have argued that the disutility of earning income as well as the utility of receiving it should be allowed for. On this basis, equal treatment would call for a recipient of wage income to pay a lower tax than the recipient of an equal amount of capital income.

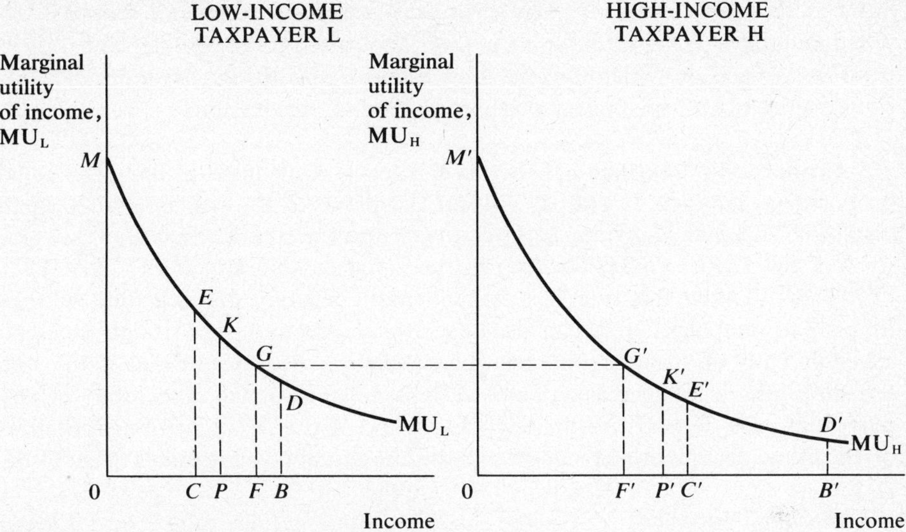

FIGURE 9-1 Measures of Equal Sacrifice.

But what about vertical equity and the pattern of taxation among people with unequal incomes? In particular, does equal sacrifice call for a progressive tax?

Alternative Rules The answer depends on both the shape of the income utility schedule and by what rule "equality of sacrifice" is defined. It may be interpreted to mean equal *absolute,* equal *proportional,* or equal *marginal* (least total) sacrifice. These concepts may be explained with the help of Figure 9-1, where the left diagram pertains to low-income taxpayer L and the right to high-income taxpayer H. MU_L and MU_H are the respective marginal utility of income schedules which are identical and assumed to decline at a decreasing rate. L's income before tax is OB while that for H is OB'. The total utilities derived by L and H are $OBDM$ and $OB'D'M'$, respectively. If a given revenue T is to be drawn from the two, how will it be allocated under the three rules?

Absolute Sacrifice Beginning with the equal absolute sacrifice rule, L, with income OB, pays CB, while H, with income OB', pays $C'B'$, where $CB + C'B'$ is the needed revenue T. The loss of utility or sacrifice incurred by L equals $CBDE$ while the loss to H equals $C'B'D'E'$, and T is distributed such that $CBDE = C'B'D'E'$.

If the MU schedule were constant (parallel to the horizontal axis), equal absolute sacrifice would require tax liabilities to be the same for all incomes. Equal sacrifice would call for a head tax. But with a declining MU schedule, tax liability must rise with income. This much is clear, but it does not follow that a progressive tax will be called for. As may be shown mathematically, the required tax distribution will be progressive, proportional, or regressive, depending on whether the elasticity of the marginal income utility with respect to income is greater than, equal to, or less than unity.[23] While it seems reasonable to assume that the *MU* schedule falls, there is no intuitive answer about its rate of decline. Thus, there is no ready basis on which to conclude whether equal absolute sacrifice calls for progression, not to speak of the proper degree of progression.

Proportional Sacrifice If the tax burden is distributed in line with equal proportional sacrifice, L will pay PB and H will pay $P'B'$, with $PB + P'B'$ again equal to T. The tax is divided between the two so that the fraction of pretax utility lost for L (or $PBDK/OBDM$) is the same as that for H (or $P'B'D'K'/O'B'D'M'$). Under this rule, it is evident that a constant *MU* schedule will call for proportional taxation. It can also be seen that a declining but straight-line *MU* schedule calls for progression, but generalizations become difficult if the *MU* schedule falls at a decreasing rate, as is usually assumed. The result in any particular case depends on the level and slope of the *MU* schedule, as well as on the initial distribution of income and the amount of revenue that is to be raised.

Marginal Sacrifice Under the equal marginal sacrifice rule, L pays FB and H pays $F'B'$, where $FB + F'B'$ is the required revenue T. The marginal sacrifice is the same, since $FG = F'G'$. At the same time, the total sacrifice for both (or $FBDG + F'B'D'G'$) is minimized. After-tax incomes are equalized at $OF = O'F'$.

If the marginal utility of income were constant, the distribution of the tax bill under *equal marginal* sacrifice would be indeterminate. Any distribution drawing at least some small amount from all taxpayers would meet the requirement. Given a declining *MU* schedule, equal marginal sacrifice calls for "maximum progression"; i.e., the leveling down of income from the top until the required revenue is obtained. The rate of decline does not matter in this case.

The principle of equal marginal sacrifice as applied in Figure 9-1 leaves both taxpayers with the same income. It also results in *least total* sacrifice (equal to $FBDG + F'B'D'G'$) for both H and L combined. The same result is obtained whether we use an equal marginal, or a least total, sacrifice rule. But suppose now that the revenue requirement is less than the excess of H's over L's income. Here, equal marginal sacrifice cannot be achieved and the result must be stated in terms of least total sacrifice. To achieve least total sacrifice, the tax is applied so as to lop off incomes from the top down, leaving all those who pay tax with equal marginal sacrifice, but not necessarily including all individuals in the taxpaying group.

The equal marginal sacrifice rule may thus be viewed as an efficiency rule (calling for total sacrifice to be at a minimum) rather than as an equity rule; and once this step is taken, the argument is readily extended beyond the amount of revenue that happens to be required. Instead of saying that the sacrifice due to taxation should be minimized, we can also say that the welfare derived from what is left over should be maximized, thus leading us to the previously examined

[23] See Richard A. Musgrave, *The Theory of Public Finance,* New York: McGraw-Hill, 1959, p. 100; or Paul A. Samuelson, *Foundations of Economic Analysis,* Cambridge, Mass.: Harvard, 1947, p. 227. As noted in Chap. 31, Sec. C, this does not hold for the present United States system.

utilitarian view of a just distribution.[24] After all, if maximum satisfaction from private income is called for, the adjustment should not be limited to the amount of revenue needed to finance public services.

Conclusion Comparing the results for H and L, we see that the marginal rule is worst for H and best for L. This will always be the situation so long as the utility schedule declines. Given the schedule as drawn in Figure 9-1, H also does better under the absolute than under the proportional rule, but this need not be so in all situations.

With the exception of equal marginal sacrifice, the case for progression (or the degree thereof) is thus quite inconclusive, and this is true even if the underlying assumptions of declining and identical utility schedules are accepted. Even with equal absolute sacrifice, which some consider the most reasonable of the three formulas, all that follows for sure is that tax liabilities should rise with income. Beyond this, there is no intuitive conclusion about whether progression is called for and, if so, what degree of progression should apply. Matters are even less predictable under the equal proportional sacrifice rule. In all, the ability-to-pay rule is doubly inconclusive as the answer depends on (1) what formulation of equal sacrifice is chosen, and (2) the precise shape of the *MU* schedules.

As noted in our earlier discussion of justice criteria, there are serious difficulties with this entire approach. While the assumption of a declining marginal utility schedule seems reasonable, the precise slope of the schedule is not known and schedules may differ among individuals. More basically, the entire proposition of interpersonal utility comparison is questionable.[25] It is more realistic, therefore, to view the problem in terms of a social utility schedule based on society's evaluation of successive units of income, rather than of one based on a measure of subjective utilities as actually experienced by each individual. Approaching the problem in this way, suppose that the income tax structure as enacted by Congress does in fact reflect its intention to implement a given sacrifice rule. Postulating a declining *MU* schedule, we know that the intent could not have been to implement equal marginal sacrifice. Although progression applies, it falls far short of leveling down incomes from the top. But suppose that the intent was to implement equal absolute sacrifice. One may then compute the social marginal income utility schedule which is implicit in the prevailing tax-liability distribution. If we set the marginal income utility at an income of $3,000 as equal to 1, the schedule shown in Table 9-2 emerges for a single person; and corresponding schedules may be derived for larger family units.

These results are based on the rather heroic assumption that the rate schedule reflects a rigorous application of congressional intent to apply an equal sacrifice rule. Nevertheless, this interpretation illustrates a potentially useful approach. Congress or the executive branch might stipulate an explicit social income utility schedule and then proceed to formulate its tax and expenditure policies accordingly.[26]

[24] See p. 86.

[25] See Chap. 4, p. 216.

[26] See our earlier discussion of income weights in cost-benefit analysis, p. 168.

TABLE 9-2
Index for Marginal Utility of Money Income Derived from Income Tax Schedule

Income (In Dollars)	*Marginal Utility Index*	*Income (In Dollars)*	*Marginal Utility Index*
1,000	8.51	20,000	0.05
2,000	1.83	30,000	0.03
3,000	1.00	50,000	0.01
4,000	0.64	70,000	0.009
5,000	0.45	100,000	0.007
10,000	0.15	200,000	0.003

Notes: The index is derived from liabilities computed by applying 1965 rates and standard deductions to adjusted gross income. An alternative computation based on reported tax liabilities gives a much lower degree of effective progression (see Chap. 10, p. 237) and hence implies a less rapidly falling marginal income utility schedule.

Source: From Koichi Mera, "Experimental Determination of Relative Marginal Utilities." *Quarterly Journal of Economics,* pp. 464–477, August 1969.

E. MEASURES OF ABILITY TO PAY

The traditional discussion of ability to pay has been in terms of income as the best index of fiscal position. While much may be said for income as the best measure of economic capacity, consumption and wealth offer alternative measures of economic position which deserve consideration.

Income versus Consumption

The major choice is between income and consumption. Which of these is the better measure of ability to pay or sacrifice incurred?[27]

The case for income lies in its comprehensiveness as a measure of capacity. The income base includes all sources of income (as seen from the sources side) or consumption plus saving (as seen from the uses side). Income is thus a more comprehensive base than consumption. A person with an income of $20,000 and consumption of $18,000 must be as well off as another with the same income and consumption of $20,000 simply because the first person also could have consumed the entire amount. Horizontal equity thus calls for the broader income base.

The case for consumption as the best tax base has been made in various ways. A traditional argument has been that capacity should be defined by what a person "takes out of the pot" (i.e., consumes) and not in terms of what he or she "puts into the pot" (i.e., saves and invests). This view, dating back to Hobbes, holds that saving and investment constitute social acts which are advantageous to others, while consumption is selfish and basically antisocial.[28] Therefore, taxation should be based on consumption only, be it out of current income or out of past accumulation. This interpretation of saving as an altruistic act is unconvincing.

[27] Another question—more in line with the benefit principle—is the following: Since a voting system must be used to induce the consumers of public services to reveal their preferences, and since a tax formula (rather than individual bids) is needed to implement this, which tax (an income-based or a consumption-based one) will be more likely to secure an efficient result?

[28] John Hobbes, *Leviathan,* part 2, New York: Dutton, 1924, chap. 30, p. 184.

Rather, it is a decision to postpone consumption, reached in line with the saver's preferences and the available rate of interest. Moreover, future consumption is not the only utility that can be derived from saving. The value of status and economic power inherent in accumulation must also be considered. On equity grounds, it is thus difficult to justify the exclusion of saving from the tax base. A person's capacity is measured by income, and taxation imposes a sacrifice whether the tax falls on consumption or on saving.

Another line of reasoning in favor of the consumption base considers the income tax as unfair because it involves "double taxation" of saving.[29] The income tax, so the argument goes, reduces the potential level of future consumption in two ways. First, it reduces the amount of income that is left for saving and then it again reduces the earnings on such reduced savings. This is true enough but the result is unfair only *if* one takes the consumption-base view. Taking the income-base view, it is the consumption tax that is unfair because it involves undertaxation of saving. Income which is consumed is taxed, but income used for saving enjoys tax postponement (if consumed later) or escapes tax altogether (if accumulation continues). This does not happen under the income tax where each initial gain is taxed once. If the recipient chooses to save or to invest, any earnings thereon constitute a new income, properly subject to new tax. The "double taxation" thesis, therefore, does not prove that consumption is the proper base. Rather, it follows if the presumption of the consumption base is accepted to begin with.[30]

In practice, the choice between an income base and a consumption base has another dimension. Income taxes are imposed on a personal basis with exemptions and progressive rates geared to the individual taxpayer's circumstances, whereas consumption taxes usually have flat rates. Therefore, the two differ sharply in their distributional implications.[31] Proponents of progression have thus found the income base preferable while opponents have preferred the consumption base.

Wealth

Instead of measuring taxable capacity in terms of flows, such as income or consumption, can a case also be made for using stocks in the form of wealth as a capacity measure?

Taxpaying capacity inherent in the holding of wealth may be viewed as the capacity to receive capital income therefrom.[32] If the yield of capital is 10 percent,

[29] This argument dates back to John Stuart Mill (op. cit., pp. 814–817), and has been advanced most vigorously by Irving Fisher in his *Constructive Income Taxation,* New York: Harper, 1942. Equity considerations aside, the "double taxation" argument is correct if interpreted to mean that a tax on income discriminates against future consumption, whereas a general tax on consumption does not, so that the consumption tax may be preferable on efficiency grounds.

[30] Such at least is the case if we view equity in taxation as referring to discrete periods of consumption or income receipt. If a lifetime view is taken, lifetime income may be defined as the present value of lifetime consumption, so that (apart from bequests) the two bases are the same.

[31] Moreover, since consumption falls as a percentage of income as income rises, a proportional tax on consumption is regressive, if related to the income base.

[32] Capital income only is involved since wealth, as conventionally defined, excludes the capitalized value of labor income.

the income derived from a \$1,000 asset is \$100. A 1 percent tax on this asset is thus equivalent to a 10 percent tax on its income. For a property tax rate t_p on a given asset to yield the same revenue as an income tax rate t_y on the income derived therefrom, we must have $t_p = t_y\ i$ where i is the rate of interest. Given this simplified formulation, the form in which revenue was collected would be a matter of indifference. A tax on wealth may be viewed simply as a tax on income therefrom. But if capital income is already taxed under a comprehensive income tax, why should such a supplementary income tax on capital income be applied? As we shall see in the next chapter, income is income whether in the form of wages or profits and should be treated equally as part of the global base.

But does not the ownership of wealth carry with it an element of economic capacity other than the income derived therefrom? Is not A, who receives \$10,000 of property income which (with an interest rate of 10 percent) reflects assets worth \$100,000, in a better position than B, who receives an equal amount of wage income? Certainly A can fall back on his property and dissave if he so desires, while B cannot. Moreover, wealth holding brings social status and power as well as economic security. It thus yields benefits distinct from the potential consumption power which might be realized by dissaving. These benefits may be considered a form of consumption inherent in the holding of wealth. For these reasons, is not an additional tax on capital income justified? Granted that these considerations place A in a better position, it does not follow that he should pay a supplementary income tax. Suppose that both started out with wage income, but A saved while B did not. Under the income tax philosophy, A is properly taxed on his interest income derived from his saving, but it would not be correct to add a further tax on his capital, since the same opportunity for accumulation was open to B. Taxable capacity was measured adequately when income was taxed to begin with.

Timing

Another difficulty arising in the definition of the tax base stems from the use of progressive rates. Under a system of progressive rates, tax liabilities will differ depending on whether bracket rates are applied to monthly, annual, or longer-period income. Thus, a person earning an income of \$40,000, \$10,000, and \$40,000 in three successive years will pay more over the three-year period than another who earns a steady \$30,000 each year. This fact poses the question of the appropriate time period (annually, five years, lifetime?) to which tax rates should be applied. As this problem is of particular importance in connection with the income tax, it will be considered further in that context.

Conclusions on Ability Measures

The preceding considerations led to the conclusion that income is the superior measure of taxable capacity. Given a truly comprehensive measure of income, no supplementary tax on consumption or wealth would be needed on ability-to-pay grounds. The equitable tax structure (in the ability-to-pay context) would be one in which all revenue was derived from this source.

At the same time, the argument is only as good as the existing income tax, or the possibility of improving it. Thus, in an agricultural society where most income is derived and consumed on farms, the income tax approach would be extremely difficult. A tax on property or cattle, as in colonial America, would offer a more feasible way of approximating taxable capacity. Similarly, developing countries find it usually very difficult to reach capital income under the income tax. In such situations, a tax on real property, which can be readily detected, offers a useful supplement.

Nor do these difficulties apply to developing countries only. The individual income tax, as applied in the United States, is far from comprehensive and it is even less so in most other nations. As we shall see in the following chapters, some forms of capital income are excluded from the tax base and others are given preferential treatment. Accretion by bequest or gift stays outside the income tax base. For these reasons, supplementary taxes on consumption and wealth may be called for, if only as the second-best means of approximating taxation in line with ability to pay, such as could be attained under a comprehensive income tax.

While choosing the proper index of economic capacity is important, it is only a first step in designing an equitable tax structure. The second step is to apply this index—be it income, consumption, or wealth—to the complexity of economic and legal institutions. In this process, a host of highly technical and difficult problems arise. How should corporations be taxed, how should capital gains be treated, how should depreciation be timed, how should the particular problems of financial institutions be dealt with, and so on? Since the economy itself is complex and the tax law must be tailored thereto, no single concept of tax base can be implemented to perfection. Moreover, an equitable tax system cannot be simple. An excessively complex tax structure, on the other hand, leads to lawful tax avoidance (some taxpayers adapt their activities to minimize liabilities) as well as illegal evasion, which in turn undermines equity. Tax policy, therefore, is an art no less than a science; and equity is to be sought as a matter of degree, rather than an absolute norm.

Vertical Equity and the Base of Redistribution

Given our earlier conclusion that income is the best measure of capacity, it follows (1) that horizontal equity calls for equal treatment of people with equal income, and (2) that vertical equity and the problem of progressive taxation should be related to relative income positions. This approach is in line with our earlier view of just distribution in terms of relative economic capacities, independent of the uses to which these capacities are put.[33]

There remains, however, the possibility that society's views on distribution are not related to general economic capacity but depend on the uses to which it is put. Thus, concern may be with two distinct types of inequalities, one relating to consumption and the other to wealth. In the first case, concern might be with minimum consumption standards or with the unpleasantness of conspicuous consumption. In the other case, concern might be with inequalities in social and political power which result from inequalities in wealth. Both deal with different

[33] See p. 95.

types of distribution, and what is considered an acceptable degree of inequality may differ for the two. If such is so, both a consumption and a wealth tax would be needed to accomplish the distributive objective, with different patterns of progression used in both cases. An income tax would not do. Such a system, of course, would be in conflict with horizontal equity as defined in terms of general economic capacity or income; and the attachment of social values to various levels of consumption or wealth would now be based on a different set of considerations.

F. CATEGORIES OF TAXES

The form in which taxes are imposed will determine the way in which they enter into the operation of the economy or the accounts of households and business firms, and how they enter will determine their economic effects. As a preliminary to the analysis of particular taxes, it is thus helpful to view our major taxes from this perspective. Most taxes may be divided into two groups, those imposed on purchases or sales made in the production of current output (or receipt of current income), and others imposed on the holding of property or its transfer.[34]

Taxes on Current Output and Income

The bulk of tax revenue (with the major exception of the property tax) is derived from taxes on current output or income.

Taxes in the Circular Flow Figure 9-2 presents a simplified picture of the circular flow of income and expenditures, together with the major points at which such taxes are inserted. We may think of the monetary flow of income and expenditures shown in the figure as proceeding in a clockwise direction, while the real flow of factor inputs and product outputs (not shown) moves in a counterclockwise direction. Thus, income is received by households and divided into consumer expenditures and household savings. Consumer expenditures flow into the market for consumer goods and become receipts of firms selling such goods. Savings are channeled into investment, become expenditures in the market for capital goods, and turn into receipts of firms producing such goods. Part of business receipts is set aside to cover depreciation and the remainder goes to purchase the services of labor, capital, and other inputs in the factor market, representing the factor shares in the national income. These shares are paid out to suppliers of factors—in the form of wages, dividends, interest, rent, and so on—and become income of households. Some profits, however, are withheld as retained earnings rather than paid out as dividends. Retained earnings, together with depreciation allowances, comprise business savings and combine with household savings to finance investment or the purchase of capital goods. Thus the circular flow of income and expenditures is closed.[35]

[34] In addition to taxes on transactions undertaken in the process of producing income, taxes may also be imposed on other types of transactions, such as secondhand sale of property, credit transactions, or the issuance of various forms of legal documents. Such taxes, referred to traditionally as "transaction taxes," are, however, of minor importance.

[35] Since the national income accounts take an ex post view, saving and investment must be equal as a matter of accounting identity. For a further discussion of this, see pp. 509 and 523.

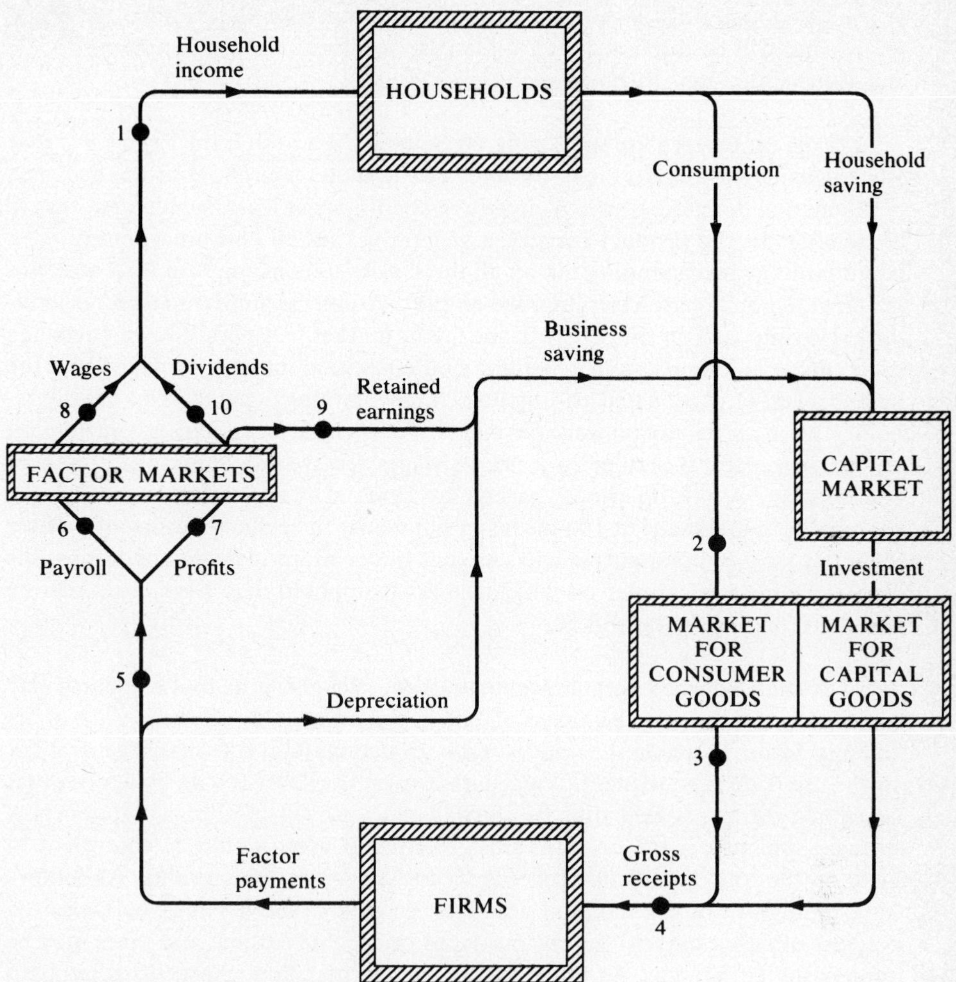

FIGURE 9-2 Points of Tax Impact in Circular Flow.

We may now locate the impact points of various taxes, as shown in Figure 9-2. Taxes may be imposed on household income at point 1, on consumer expenditures at 2, on business receipts from retail sales at 3, on total gross receipts of business at 4, on business receipts net of depreciation at 5, on payrolls at 6, on profits at 7, on wage receipts at 8, on retained earnings at 9, or on dividends at 10.[36] The major taxes in the United States system are readily identified with these various points of impact. The personal income tax is imposed at 1, the corporation income tax at 7, retail sales taxes at 3, the employer contribution to the payroll tax at 6, and the employee contribution to the payroll tax at 8. Taxes imposed

[36] To maintain the circular flow intact, Fig. 9-2 would have to be adjusted not only to show the various tax drains leading into the public budget, but also the expenditure flows from the budget back into the private sector.

at 2 and 5 do not exist in our tax structure, but are potential candidates for tax reform and will be discussed later under the headings of the expenditure tax (2) and value-added tax of the income type (5).

Taxes on Buyers versus Taxes on Sellers We note from Figure 9-2 that any particular transaction may be taxed at either the household or the firm side of the market counter. Under competitive conditions at least, such pairs of taxes are similar. In the product market, a general tax on all consumer outlays at 2 is similar to a corresponding tax on all retail sales to consumers at 3. A selective tax on automobile purchases imposed on the consumer is similar to a corresponding excise imposed on the seller. In the factor market, a general tax on payments to factors at 5 is similar to a general tax on household income, provided that the latter (point 1) is adjusted to impute retained earnings (point 9) to the shareholder. Or, a partial tax on wage payments at 6, such as the employer contribution to social security, is similar to a tax on wages received at 8, i.e., the employee contribution. A tax on profits earned by firms at 7 is similar to one on the shareholder's dividends at 10 plus his or her equity in retained profits at 9. These identities hold in competitive markets, but under more realistic conditions, the side of the market counter on which the tax is imposed may have some bearing on where the incidence will be.[37]

Taxes on Sources versus Taxes on Uses We also note that any particular household or firm may be taxed at either the sources or the uses side of its account. Since the account balances (total uses equal total sources), a general tax on the uses side is equivalent to a general tax on the sources side. A tax on total household income would thus be equivalent to one on total consumption plus savings. Similarly, a tax on total gross receipts of firms would be equivalent to a tax on the total use of its proceeds or cost payments plus profits. As follows from the nature of the national accounts, economic activity may be measured in terms of either current output produced or income earned, and taxes may be imposed on either side. As follows from the circular flow chart, taxes imposed on the uses side of the household's accounts have their counterpart in taxes on the sources side of the firm's accounts and vice versa.

Combining the buyer-seller and sources-uses distinctions, our major taxes may thus be arranged as follows:

	Uses	*Sources*
Households	Use taxes Expenditure tax	Income tax Employee payroll tax
Firms	Profits tax Employer payroll tax	Sales tax

[37] See Chap. 17, Sec. C, p. 410.

Keeping in mind how various taxes fit into the national income accounts will be helpful in viewing similarities or differences among them and in tracing taxpayer responses in our later discussion of incidence and effects of taxation.

Taxes on Holding and Transfer of Wealth

A second category of taxes may be imposed on the holding of wealth or stocks, rather than on transactions or flows generated in current production. The principal example is the property tax. If interpreted as a tax on capital income, it might be incorporated in Figure 9-2, but other wealth taxes, such as those imposed on the transfer of wealth by inheritance or gift, cannot be so included.

G. FURTHER DISTINCTIONS

Cutting across the preceding distinctions are those between personal and "in rem" taxes, and between direct versus indirect taxes.

Personal versus In Rem Taxes

Personal taxes are taxes which are adjusted to the taxpayer's personal ability to pay, while in rem taxes (taxes on "things") are imposed on activities or objects as such, i.e., on purchases, sales, or the holding of property, independently of the characteristics of the transactor or owner.

In rem taxes may be imposed on either the household or the firm side. But personal taxes, by their very nature, *must* be imposed on the household side of the transaction. Thus, if proceeds from the sale of factors of production are to be taxed in a personal fashion, the tax must be imposed on households as a personal income tax. Taxes imposed on factor payments of firms cannot distinguish the taxpaying ability of particular income recipients. While family size can be allowed for in the withholding schedule, the final settlement must be with the individual employee. Similarly, if consumption is to be taxed in a personal fashion, the tax must be placed on the household in the form of a personal expenditure tax. A sales tax imposed on firms is not responsive to the particular consumer, but gives the same treatment to all households which undertake the taxed transaction. The same again holds for the taxation of wealth under the property tax, as against a net worth tax relating to the wealth position of the owner.

It follows from our earlier discussion that the equity of the tax system must be evaluated in terms of the resulting burden distribution among people. Since the burden of all taxes, including those imposed on "things," must ultimately be borne by persons, their equity must be evaluated by the resulting burden distribution among persons. As such, in rem taxes are inferior to well-designed personal taxes imposed directly so as to allow for the particular taxpayer's ability to pay. Since personal taxes must be assessed on the household side, such taxes tend to be generally superior in equity to those imposed on the firm side.

Direct versus Indirect Taxes

Finally, brief attention should be given to the frequently used distinction between "direct" and "indirect" taxes. While this distinction is ambiguous, most writers define direct taxes as those which are imposed initially on the individual or household that is meant to bear the burden. Indirect taxes are taxes which are imposed at some other point in the system but are meant to be shifted (a concept which will be examined presently) to whomever is supposed to be the final bearer of the burden.

Personal taxes, such as the individual income tax, are thus "direct," and most in rem taxes, such as the sales tax, are "indirect." At the same time, the distinction between direct and indirect taxes does not always coincide with that between personal and in rem taxes. Thus the employee contribution to the payroll tax may be considered direct, yet it is not a personal tax since no allowance is made for the owner's ability to pay. Rather, it is an in rem tax, assessed on wage receipt as a transaction. Similarly, the property tax on owner-occupied residences is direct, but it is an in rem tax (being imposed on ownership as such) rather than a personal tax which would allow for the owner's individual circumstances.

The term "excise," finally, refers to a subcategory of indirect taxes and is applied to certain selective sales taxes imposed at the manufacturer level. A legal, rather than economic, category in nature, it appears in the constitutional provision that direct taxes must be imposed on a population basis, while others, such as "duties, imposts, and excises," need not be.[38]

H. CONCLUSION

In the preceding pages we have considered certain basic principles of tax policy and categories of taxes. These considerations are important when dealing with the "nuts and bolts" issues of practical tax policy. But they are far from the entire story. As noted before, taxes are applied in a complex economy and a host of specific issues must be faced in designing a good tax system. No matter how well particular taxes are meant to apply, they will be only as good as their actual operation. In the following chapters we will conclude the discussion of each tax with a brief evaluation of its place in the tax structure, including its burden distribution. As an introduction to the problem of burden distribution, the reader may wish to turn to sections C and D of Chapter 16 at this point.

I. SUMMARY

The development of the United States tax structure has been shaped by these trends:

1. A shift from indirect to direct taxes at the federal level, with increasing emphasis on the personal income tax, especially since World War II, and a sharp rise in the share of the payroll tax in recent years.

2. A declining role for the property tax at the state level, with rising importance of the sales tax.

3. Continued predominance of the property tax at the local level.

[38] See p. 28.

Various requirements have been developed to be met by a good tax structure. Among these is the need for an equitable distribution of the tax burden.

4. Two major approaches to tax equity involve the benefit and ability-to-pay principles.

5. The benefit principle, while linking the expenditure and tax sides of budget policy, is not readily implemented, since consumer evaluation of public services is not known to tax authorities but must be revealed through the political process. However, in some instances, benefit taxation can be applied.

6. The ability-to-pay principle calls for a distribution of the tax burden so as to secure horizontal and vertical equity. To obtain horizontal equity, taxpayers with equal ability to pay should contribute the same amount. For vertical equity, taxpayers with unequal ability to pay should contribute correspondingly different amounts.

7. The principle of vertical equity may be reformulated so as to call for equality of sacrifice. This may or may not require progressive taxation, depending on how "equal sacrifice" is defined and on the slope of the marginal utility of income schedules.

8. Since it is debatable whether and how such schedules can be measured and compared, implementation of the ability-to-pay principle has to make use of a socially determined income utility approach.

Implementation of equitable taxation in line with ability to pay further requires the definition of a specific index by which ability to pay is to be measured. These conclusions were reached:

9. A broadly defined concept of income, rather than of consumption, is superior since it provides a more comprehensive measure of capacity.

10. Taxation of wealth is not necessary if all income has already been subject to a comprehensive income tax; but since this condition is in practice not met, supplementary taxes on consumption and wealth may be called for on ability-to-pay grounds.

11. Separate taxes on consumption and wealth may be called for if society views the distribution problem in terms of the specific distribution of consumption and wealth, rather than in terms of the overall distribution of economic capacity as measured by income.

Various taxes were distinguished and their impact points in the circular flow of income expenditures have been traced. The major distinctions were between:

12. Taxes on factor transactions and taxes on product transactions.
13. Taxes on buyers and taxes on sellers.
14. Taxes on transactions and taxes on the holding of wealth.
15. Personal and in rem taxes.
16. Direct and indirect taxes.

FURTHER READINGS

Blum, Walter J., and Harry Kalven, Jr.: *The Uneasy Case for Progressive Taxation,* Chicago: The University of Chicago Press, 1953.

Fagan, E. D.: "Theories of Progressive Taxation," *Journal of Political Economy,* p. 457, August 1948; reprinted in Richard A. Musgrave and Carl Shoup (eds.), *Readings in the Economics of Taxation,* American Economic Association, Homewood, Ill.: Irwin, 1958.

Goode, Richard: *The Individual Income Tax,* Washington: Brookings, 1964, chap. 2.

Kaldor, N.: *An Expenditure Tax,* London: Allen, 1955, chap. 1 and app.

Mera, Koichi: "Experimental Determination of Relative Marginal Utilities," *Quarterly Journal of Economics,* pp. 464–477, August 1969.

Pigou, A. C.: *A Study in Public Finance,* 3d ed., London: Macmillan, 1951, part 2.

Thurow, Lester C.: *The Impact of Taxes in the American Economy,* New York: Praeger, 1971, chap. 7.

Chapter 10

Individual Income Tax: Defining Taxable Income*

A. Major Provisions: *Determining Taxable Income; Computing Tax; Declaration, Payments, and Withholding; Audit; Average and Marginal Rates; Effective Rates.* **B. Structure of the Tax Base:** *From GNP to Taxable Income; Size Distribution of Tax Base; Distribution of Tax Base by Income Source.* **C. Income Definition in Principle and Practice:** *Gross Income versus Net Income; Capital Income versus Labor Income; Capital Gains versus Other Income; Imputed Income; Earnings versus Transfers; Pension Plans; Exclusions; Allowance for Losses.* **D. Deductions:** *Types of Deductions; Rationale for Itemized Deductions; Evaluation of Itemized Deductions; Standard Deduction; Conclusion.* **E. Summary.**

The individual income tax is much the most important single tax and the kingpin of the federal, if not the entire United States, tax structure. It is therefore the first tax to be considered and one to be dealt with at greater length. While our concern is primarily with the federal tax, brief attention is also given to state and local income taxes.

* *Reader's Guide to Chapter 10:* This is the first in a series of chapters dealing with the particulars of various taxes. The practically inclined reader will find these chapters of particular interest. The theorist in turn is urged to take them seriously, since little good can come of theorizing about the principles of taxation and its economic effects unless one knows the statutes and how they work. While studying this discussion of the income tax, students are urged to examine the Individual Income Tax Return, Form 1040, and practice filling it out.

A. MAJOR PROVISIONS

The basic principle of the United States individual income tax is that the taxpayer's income from all sources be combined into a single or "global" measure of income. Total income is then reduced by certain deductions and exemptions to arrive at taxable income. This is the base to which tax rates are applied in computing the tax.

Determining Taxable Income

The derivation of taxable income begins with adjusted gross income (AGI), the base to which deductions and personal exemptions are applied.

Adjusted Gross Income Income from all sources is combined to determine AGI. This includes wages, interest, dividends, rent, royalties, profits from unincorporated business operations, and so forth. Although the resulting total is referred to as adjusted *gross* income, this is misleading since, in the economist's language, it reflects a *net* income concept, i.e., income net of costs incurred in earning that income. Unincorporated business income is included in AGI on a net basis, and adjustments are made for certain personal costs incurred in earning income (such as moving expenses and certain employee business expenses) before arriving at AGI. While AGI is meant to give a comprehensive measure of the taxpayer's income position, we shall find that in practice it is not as comprehensive as it should be. Noncash income (such as imputed rent and unrealized capital gains) is omitted and certain forms of cash income are specifically excluded.

Deductions From AGI thus defined, various deductions are made. At the taxpayer's option, they may be taken as itemized deductions, or by applying the so-called standard deduction.

Among allowed itemized deductions, the most important are interest paid on mortgages and other consumer loans, state and local taxes, and charitable contributions. Other deductible items include unusually high medical expenses, casualty losses, and child care expenses.

Under the Tax Reduction Act of 1975, the taxpayer who opts for the standard deduction may choose between deducting (1) a flat amount of $1,600 for a single return ($1,900 for a joint return) or (2) 16 percent of adjusted gross income, the deducted amount not to exceed $2,300 and $2,600 for single and joint returns respectively. Option 1, referred to as the "low-income allowance," puts a "floor" under the standard deduction. Taking the case of a joint return, the low-income allowance is more advantageous than the percentage standard deduction for AGIs up to $11,875 (16 percent of which equals $1,900) and will therefore be used over this range except for unusual situations where itemized deductions exceed $1,900.

Option 2 comes into play above this AGI level, but owing to the upper limit of $2,600 (joint return), the advantage derived from it declines when moving up the income scale. Up to an AGI of $16,250, taxpayers will use the standard deduction unless itemized deductions exceed 16 percent of AGI, which is unusual. With higher AGIs, itemizing becomes advantageous when such deductions exceed $2,600, even though they are less than 16 percent of AGI. Since deductions typically exceed $2,600, most taxpayers in the higher-income brackets itemize.

Personal Exemptions The remaining AGI is reduced by the allowable amount of personal exemptions. Under the Tax Reform Act of 1969, the personal exemption was raised from $600 to $750 per taxpayer, the spouse, and each dependent. The exemption for a single person thus equals $750, for a married couple $1,500, for a family of four $3,000, and so forth, rising with the number of dependents. Certain groups, including the blind and the aged, are allowed an additional exemption.

Computing Tax

Once taxable income has been obtained in this fashion, the tax is computed by application of the rate schedule. This schedule is legislated in the form of marginal or bracket rates. As shown in Table 10-1, these rates are applied to successive slabs of taxable income. For joint returns, the first $1,000 is taxed at a rate of 14 percent, the next $1,000 at a rate of 15 percent, and so forth until income in excess of $200,000 is reached, where a rate of 70 percent applies. As will be seen from the table, the brackets widen with rising income. Since the Tax Reform Act of 1969, so-called earned income (defined as income from wages, salaries, and professions) is subject to a top-bracket rate of 50 percent only, which rate is reached at a taxable income of $44,000 (joint returns). Special rates applicable to capital gains income are dealt with later in this chapter.

The Tax Reduction Act of 1975 introduced two further provisions. One of these gives a tax credit of $30 per exemption, i.e., reduces tax liability by this amount, but without refund. The other, referred to as the "earned-income tax credit," allows an additional credit against tax equal to 10 percent of earned income on the first $4,000 of earnings. As AGI rises above this amount, the credit diminishes and becomes zero when AGI reaches $8,000.[1] Where the credit thus computed exceeds tax liability, a refund or "negative tax" is due. This provision, however, applies only to taxpayers with dependents. This feature will be discussed further in the next chapter when dealing with the problem of exemptions and other devices by which the tax burden at the low end of the income scale may be relieved.[2]

A further provision, applicable to high-income taxpayers, is the so-called minimum tax, introduced under the Tax Reform Act of 1969. Having computed his tax along regular lines, the taxpayer must also compute his minimum tax, imposed at a 10 percent rate on his "preference income." He then pays both taxes. The provision is designed to limit the advantages gained by high-income taxpayers from various tax preferences, but we shall find that the minimum tax is far from stringent and applies to a small group of taxpayers only.

[1] The credit declines by 10 percent of the excess of AGI over $4,000, thus falling to $300 at an AGI of $5,000 and so forth until it vanishes at an AGI of $8,000.

[2] See p. 271.

TABLE 10-1
Structure of Tax Rates
(Married Taxpayers Filing Joint Returns or Surviving Spouse)

Joint Taxable Income (In Dollars) (I)	*Bracket or Marginal Rate (In Percent) (II)*	*Tax at Lower Bracket Limit (In Dollars) (III)*	*Average Rate (Tax as Percent of Taxable Income at Lower Bracket Limit) (IV)*
0– 1,000	14	0	0
1,000– 2,000	15	140	14.0
2,000– 3,000	16	290	14.5
3,000– 4,000	17	450	15.0
4,000– 8,000	19	620	15.5
8,000– 12,000	22	1,380	17.3
12,000– 16,000	25	2,260	18.8
16,000– 20,000	28	3,260	20.4
20,000– 24,000	32	4,380	21.9
24,000– 28,000	36	5,660	23.6
28,000– 32,000	39	7,100	25.4
32,000– 36,000	42	8,660	27.1
36,000– 40,000	45	10,340	28.7
40,000– 44,000	48	12,140	30.4
44,000– 52,000	50	14,060	32.0
52,000– 64,000	53	18,060	34.7
64,000– 76,000	55	24,420	38.2
76,000– 88,000	58	31,020	40.8
88,000–100,000	60	37,980	43.2
100,000–120,000	62	45,180	45.2
120,000–140,000	64	57,580	48.0
140,000–160,000	66	70,380	50.3
160,000–180,000	68	83,580	52.2
180,000–200,000	69	97,180	54.0
200,000 and over	70	110,980	55.5

Notes: Bracket rates above 50% apply to capital income only. For earned income, the marginal rate equals 50% for all income above \$44,000. The table shows liabilities prior to applying the \$35 credit and does not allow for the earned-income credit applicable to returns with dependents.

Sources:
Columns I and II: Internal Revenue Code as amended under Tax Reform Act of 1969.
Columns III and IV: Derived from Cols. I and II.

Declaration, Payments, and Withholding

Tax returns must be filed if earnings exceed the tax-free amount, as defined by exemptions plus the low-income allowance. Single taxpayers must file if their income is \$2,050, and married taxpayers (filing joint returns) must do so if the combined income is \$2,800, the level at which liability begins in the absence of dependents. Returns must be filed by April 15 for the preceding calendar year and the remaining tax is due at that time. Together with returns for the preceding year, the taxpayer also files an estimated return for the current year. The excess of estimated liability over estimated current-year withholding is payable in quarterly installments.

Over 80 percent of the tax liability is collected through withholding. This system was introduced in World War II and has great advantages. By linking tax payments to the current level of income, rather than by having them lag behind one year, the responsiveness of tax payments to changes in the level of personal income is greatly increased. This responsiveness is of vital importance for the effectiveness of stabilization policy.[3] The withholding system also assures fuller compliance since the declaration of income is not left entirely to the recipient. Indeed, certain forms of income (such as interest and dividends) which are not subject to withholding are subject to the requirement that the payer must file an information return.

At the same time, the withholding system has its costs. Taxpayers who underpay on the basis of their estimated returns must make a final payment and the Treasury must make refunds to those who overpaid. In 1972, for instance, 63 million out of 78 million taxpayers overpaid (on the average, by 30 percent) while 11 million underpaid (on the average, by 27 percent).[4]

Audit

The basic system underlying the United States income tax is one of self-assessment. Each taxpayer is responsible for declaring income and computing income tax thereon. While the Bureau of Internal Revenue checks the arithmetic of tax computations, it cannot carefully audit over 70 million returns. The cost of doing so would be excessive.[5] However, spot checks are made to keep taxpayers on their toes. Returns with unusual features (e.g., very high deductions or unusual sources of income) may be audited, and at various times particular groups of taxpayers, such as doctors or cattlemen, are singled out for special attention. Nevertheless, the extent of audit is relatively limited. This may change in time, when increasingly sophisticated use of computer facilities (involving not-as-yet feasible cross-checking between returns) should greatly extend the range of practicable audit and cross-checking.

Average and Marginal Rates

Tax liabilities are computed by applying the bracket rates as set in the tax law (column II of Table 10-1) to taxable income. These rates apply to slabs of income and are thus in the nature of *marginal* rates. Alternatively, the resulting tax liabilities may be expressed as a percentage of income, giving an *average* rate. Such rates, computed as ratios of tax to taxable income, are shown in column IV of Table 10-1.

The relationship between the bracket (marginal) and average rates shown in the table is a purely mechanical one. Both relate to taxable income as base. Bracket rates are used merely as a matter of legislative convenience.[6] As shown

[3] See Chap. 26, Sec. B.

[4] See *Individual Income Tax Returns, Statistics of Income for 1969,* U.S. Treasury Department, 1971, p. 124.

[5] In 1974 the total cost of the Internal Revenue Service amounted to $1.5 billion, or 87 cents per $100 of collections.

[6] Alternatively, Congress would have to legislate a set of average tax rates, but this would require a complex formula (of parabolic form) which would be difficult for both congressmen and taxpayers to interpret.

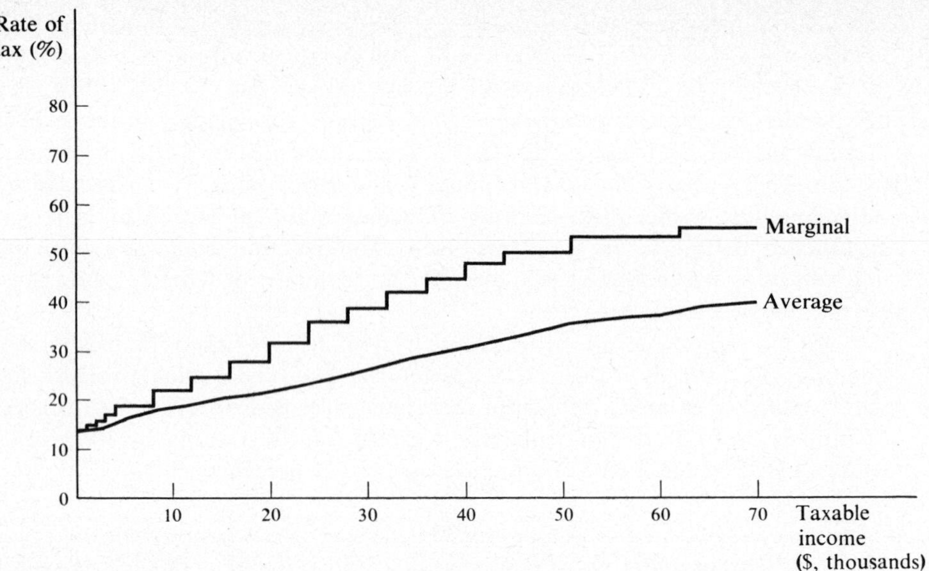

FIGURE 10-1 Ratio of Tax to Taxable Income, Marginal and Average Rates. (Married taxpayer, joint return, no dependents.)

in Figure 10-1, the bracket rate rises above the average rate, with the difference first widening and then narrowing as income rises.[7] At the bottom, the average and marginal rates are both 14 percent. At the highest, the marginal rate reaches a ceiling of 70 percent (or 50 percent for earned income) and the average rate approaches this level asymptotically. Whereas the marginal rate rises stepwise and by widening brackets, the average rate rises smoothly.

Effective Rates

A second set of average rates may be computed as the ratio of tax liabilities to AGI. This is shown in Table 10-2, where column IV gives the average rates using taxable income as base and column V gives the average rates using AGI as base. The latter rates depend upon the differential between AGI and taxable income (i.e., exemptions and deductions) as well as upon bracket rates. The pattern thus differs with family size and level of deductions. The rates using AGI as base, as shown in column V, are much the more meaningful indicators of tax-burden distribution. Since AGI exceeds taxable income, the AGI-based rates are below the taxable income–based rates for the corresponding levels of taxable income. This is the case especially for low incomes where the AGI-based ratio is held down by the weight of personal exemptions and the low-income allowance.

When examining the degree of income tax progression, we see that it is the *slope* of this average rate schedule—the so-called effective rate schedule—rather

[7] It is assumed for purposes of Fig. 10-1 that all income is from sources subject to the full bracket rates.

TABLE 10-2
Average Rates of Tax
(Joint Return without Dependents)

			AVERAGE RATES	
AGI *(I)*	*Taxable Income* *(II)*	*Tax* *(III)*	*Tax as Percentage of Taxable Income* *(IV)*	*Tax as Percentage of AGI* *(V)*
$ 3,829	$ 429	$ 0	0	0
3,836	436	1	0.2	0.03
5,000	1,600	170	10.6	3.4
10,000	6,600	1,054	16.0	10.5
20,000	15,100	2,975	19.7	14.9
50,000	40,000	12,080	30.2	24.2
100,000	81,500	34,150	41.9	34.2

Notes: Based on provisions applicable to 1975 income. The low-income allowance is applied to AGI levels up to $10,000; the percentage standard deduction applies to the $20,000 level, beyond which itemized deductions equal to 17 percent of AGI are assumed. For the $100,000 level, the rate applicable to unearned income is used. The tax liabilities shown allow for the credit of $30 per exemption, but not for the earned-income credit, since there are no dependents.

than that of the taxable income–based schedule, which must be considered.[8] The impact of exemptions and deductions, as well as bracket rates, must be allowed for.

Indeed, we shall presently find that the analysis of progression should relate to an average rate schedule based on an even more broadly defined income concept, so as to allow for imperfections in the definition of AGI. This relationship is of particular importance with regard to the treatment of capital gains and, as will be seen in Table 11-2, results in a more or less proportional pattern at the upper end of the income scale.

B. STRUCTURE OF THE TAX BASE

Having surveyed the major provisions of the income tax, we now turn to the size, composition, and distribution of its base.

From GNP to Taxable Income

As shown in Table 10-3, taxable income for 1972 amounted to $446 billion (line 25) as against a gross national product of $1,158 billion (line 1). Thus only 38 percent of GNP appeared in taxable income. For a tax which is reputed to be the most comprehensive measure of ability to pay, this may seem a rather poor performance. Closer consideration, however, shows that, say, two-thirds of the total is explained by justifiable adjustments. Nevertheless, this leaves a substantial shortfall of taxable income below what would be included under a full income concept.

[8] For a consideration of various measures of progression, see p. 285.

TABLE 10-3
Taxable Income in Relation to GNP, 1972
(In Billions of Dollars)

1.	Gross national product		1,158
2.	Deduct:	Capital consumption allowances	103
3.		Indirect business taxes	110
4.		Corporation income tax	41
5.		Retained earnings of corporations	30
6.		Social security contributions	73
7.	Add:	Government transfers to persons	99
8.		Interest paid by government	15
9.		Other, net	30
10.	Personal income		945
11.	Deduct:	Transfer payments	103
12.		Other labor income	42
13.		Imputed income	37
14.		Other exclusions	29
15.	Add:	Social security contributions, employee	35
16.		Net gain from sale of capital assets	17
17.		Other	12
18.	AGI estimated from personal income		798
19.	Deduct:	Nonreported AGI	51
20.	AGI on tax returns		747
21.	Deduct:	AGI on nontaxable returns	29
22.	AGI on taxable returns		718
23.	Deduct:	Deductions on taxable returns	143
24.		Exemptions on taxable returns	128
25.	Taxable income		446

Notes:

Line 12: Includes fringe benefits, employer pension contributions, etc.

Line 13: Of the total of $32 billion, $13 billion is accounted for by imputed rent.

Line 14: Includes sick pay, business expenses of employees, moving expenses, contributions to self-employed retirement plans, tax-exempt military pay, tax-exempt interest, and excluded dividends.

Line 19: A residual equal to line 18 minus line 20.

Sources:

Lines 1–13 and 15: See *Survey of Current Business,* July 1974.

Lines 16, 18–25: See *Individual Income Tax Returns, Preliminary Statistics of Income for 1972,* U.S. Treasury Department, 1974.

Lines 14, 17: Based on G. M. Brannon, *The Federal Revenue System,* New York: General Learning Press, 1971, p. 7.

GNP to AGI In moving from GNP to AGI, these major additions and subtractions are made:

1. Capital consumption or depreciation (line 2) is deducted. This is clearly appropriate since the income tax is to be a tax on net income.

2. Indirect business taxes (line 3) are deducted. Collected from business, they are not part of net earnings and they reduce business receipts available for income payments. We shall question, however, whether all such taxes should remain outside the base, especially those which are in fact paid by consumers of government services and which therefore may be viewed as benefit charges.

3. Interest payments by government which are not part of GNP are included when moving to personal income (line 8), and they properly remain in the tax base. However, interest paid by state and local governments is not taxable and is taken out subsequently (item 14). This exclusion is one of the least justifiable omissions.

4. Both corporation tax and retained earnings drop out when moving on to personal income (lines 4 and 5). As we shall see later, a good case can be made for including retained earnings in the base.

5. Government transfer payments are added to GNP when moving to personal income (line 7), but they are excluded when arriving at AGI (line 11). Like all other sources of income, they should be included in a comprehensive base.

6. To the extent that such transfer payments are in the nature of social security benefits, however, it may be argued that they should be excluded, provided that insurance contributions are not deductible. This provision is in effect with regard to employee contributions which, after being deducted in line 6, are added back in line 15, but not with regard to employer contributions, which appear in line 6 only.

7. Elements of income in kind and imputed income (line 13) which are included in the Department of Commerce concept of personal income are not included in AGI, thereby causing a substantial deficiency in the tax base. As shown below, this is significant especially with regard to imputed rent of owner-occupied residences.

8. Capital gains which are not included in the Department of Commerce concept of personal income, on the other hand, enter the tax base (line 16). But, as we shall see later, they do so only to a partial degree, thus posing the most important and controversial problem of income tax reform.

After these and other adjustments, an estimated AGI of $798 billion (line 18) is arrived at. This compares with an AGI recorded on tax returns of $747 billion. The difference of $51 billion includes income received by people whose income falls below the filing requirement and therefore does not appear in AGI. This factor might account for, say, $20 billion. The remainder of $31 billion is a net figure, reflecting failure to declare income and estimating errors in the national income accounts. Unless national income is substantially underestimated, it appears that over 90 percent of the "true" total is in fact recorded, which seems a surprisingly good result.

From AGI to Taxable Income Moving on from reported AGI of $747 billion, a loss of $29 billion is accounted for by nontaxable returns, $143 billion by deductions, and $128 billion by exemptions, leaving a taxable income of $446 billion. Together, these losses reduce reported AGI by 40 percent and are major determinants of the final level of taxable income.

Size Distribution of Tax Base

The distribution of the tax base by adjusted gross income brackets, shown in Table 10-4, is of great importance for tax policy because it shows where the money comes from. We note that both ends of the distribution are relatively unimportant, with the bulk of the returns, tax base, and revenue located in the middle-income range. For 1972, the 18 percent of returns with lowest income furnished only 2.2 percent of the revenue, and the 1 percent of returns at the top furnished

TABLE 10-4
Distribution of Income Tax Base, 1972
(Taxable Returns Only)

Adjusted Gross Income (In Dollars)	*Number of Returns (Millions)*	*AGI (Billions of Dollars)*	*Taxable Income (Billions of Dollars)*	*Tax (Billions of Dollars)*
Under 2,000	0.2	0.1	0.1	*
2,000– 5,000	11.0	40.1	13.8	2.1
5,000– 10,000	20.3	151.4	80.1	13.4
10,000– 15,000	15.3	188.0	113.1	20.0
15,000– 20,000	7.8	133.0	88.0	16.7
20,000– 50,000	5.7	152.1	109.5	24.7
50,000–100,000	0.5	31.8	24.4	8.5
Over 100,000	0.1	21.2	15.9	7.9
Total	60.9	717.7	444.8	93.6
		AS PERCENTAGE OF TOTAL		
Under 2,000	0.3	†	†	†
2,000– 5,000	18.1	5.6	3.1	2.2
5,000– 10,000	33.4	21.1	18.0	14.2
10,000– 15,000	25.2	26.2	25.4	21.5
15,000– 20,000	12.7	18.5	19.8	17.8
20,000– 50,000	9.4	21.2	24.6	26.5
50,000–100,000	0.8	4.4	5.5	9.1
Over 100,000	0.1	3.0	3.6	8.8
Total	100.0	100.0	100.0	100.0

* Less than 0.05.
† Less than 0.05 percent.
Source: Derived from *Individual Income Tax Returns, Statistics of Income for 1972,* Preliminary, U.S. Treasury Department, 1974, table 1.

18 percent.[9] Neither the poor nor the rich loomed large. The bulk of the revenue came from the in-between range. In 1972, for example, the low-middle range of $5,000 to $10,000 contributed 14 percent, the middle range of $10,000 to $20,000 contributed 39 percent, and the higher range of $20,000 to $50,000 furnished 27 percent. Incomes over $20,000 on the whole contributed 44 percent, while reporting 29 percent of AGI.

It is evident from the data that the extent to which revenue may be drawn from the very-high-income taxpayers is limited. The rich, unfortunately, are not numerous enough. In 1972 the over-$50,000 brackets, for example, included only 1 percent of returns; and though the ratio of tax to income was higher, its taxable income share was only 9 percent. At the same time, low-income families are also a relatively unimportant factor. No great revenue loss is involved by reducing their burden (if the relief can be limited to these low brackets) just as no great amount of revenue is gained by selective tax increases on the rich.

[9] The figures are for 1972, the latest available year, but the general pattern is not changed significantly for later years.

The distribution of the tax base in turn determines the addition to total yield obtained from successive bracket rates. The basic rate of 14 percent applies to the entire base. In 1972 it contributed 0.14 × $445 billion = $62 billion, or two-thirds of the total of $94 billion. The revenue obtained by including bracket rates up to 25 percent accounts for some 80 percent of the revenue total.[10] Putting it differently, the additional revenue obtained from permitting incremental rates to rise above 25 percent was only about $17 billion; and the gain from letting rates rise above 40 percent contributed only about $2 billion. The crucial contribution to revenue is thus highly dependent on the level of the lower bracket rates.

In evaluating this result, one must keep in mind that the tax base itself reflects the statutory definition of taxable income with all its imperfections. A more comprehensive definition of taxable income would raise the revenue potential of the higher brackets and thus increase their liabilities under present rates. But even if all preferences were to be eliminated, taxable income in the brackets above, say, $50,000 would still be far from dominating the revenue picture. Thus, even if liabilities in these brackets were doubled (as might be the case if all preferences were removed), their share in the total would be raised to only 30 percent. Moreover, adoption of a comprehensive base would also raise taxable income at the lower end of the scale. Our previous conclusion regarding the dominating importance of the base provided by the middle-income brackets would not be greatly changed.

To put it differently, the case for steeply rising marginal rates must be made on equity rather than revenue grounds. It is a fact of life that for a high-yield income tax, the bulk of revenue must be derived from the middle ranges since this is where most taxable income is received. Only if yield requirements are low relative to national income, can "soaking the rich" (as it was referred to in the New Deal years of the thirties) be a major revenue consideration. By the same token, tax relief at the bottom (if given so as to accrue entirely to low-income taxpayers) is relatively inexpensive.[11]

Distribution of Tax Base by Income Source

If the income tax were a truly global tax, the distribution of income by source would not affect the burden distribution. But even though our income tax is meant to be global rather than schedular, elements of differential treatment among income sources remain.[12] The distribution by income source is thus of considerable interest. As shown in the upper half of Table 10-5, the composition of AGI by source changes greatly as we move up the income scale. While low-bracket income is largely from wages and salaries, high-bracket income is largely in the form of capital income. Of special importance for our subsequent discussion is the sharp rise in the capital gains share at the high-income levels. But, though capital income is much more important as a share of total income in the high-

[10] Reference is to all those slabs of income (for all taxpayers) to which bracket rates up to and including 25 percent apply.

[11] See p. 273.

[12] The most important differences arise regarding (1) the upper rate limit on earned income, (2) the preferential treatment of capital gains, and (3) the taxation of corporate profits (or dividend) income.

TABLE 10-5
Distribution of Tax Base by Type of Income
(Taxable Returns, 1972)

Adjusted Gross Income Brackets	*Wages and Salaries (I)*	*Business, Professions, Farms, Partnerships (II)*	*Dividends, Interest, Rent, Royalties (III)*	*Sale of Capital Assets (IV)*	*All Other (V)*	*All Sources† (VI)*
PERCENTAGE OF AGI DERIVED FROM EACH SOURCE						
Under $5,000	86.3	2.3	7.2	0.9	3.3	100.0
$5,000– $10,000	88.9	3.8	5.0	0.7	1.5	100.0
$10,000– $20,000	91.1	4.1	3.5	0.8	0.5	100.0
$20,000– $50,000	76.4	12.0	7.8	2.6	1.2	100.0
$50,000– $100,000	47.3	25.8	15.7	7.7	3.5	100.0
$100,000– $500,000	32.9	16.1	25.8	19.4	5.8	100.0
$500,000–$1,000,000	14.3	3.1	33.0	43.7	5.9	100.0
$1,000,000 and over	6.5	0.5	31.7	58.1	3.2	100.0
Total	83.5	6.9	6.2	2.2	1.3	100.0
PERCENTAGE OF EACH SOURCE GOING TO VARIOUS BRACKETS OF AGI						
Under $5,000	5.8	1.9	6.6	2.8	14.8	5.6
$5,000– $10,000	22.5	11.7	16.9	6.7	25.3	21.1
$10,000– $20,000	48.8	27.0	25.7	16.4	15.0	44.7
$20,000– $50,000	19.4	37.0	26.7	25.3	20.0	21.2
$50,000– $100,000	2.5	16.7	11.3	15.5	12.1	4.4
$100,000– $500,000	0.9	5.7	10.0	21.2	11.1	2.4
$500,000–$1,000,000	*	*	1.3	4.9	1.1	0.2
$1,000,000 and over	*	*	1.5	7.8	0.7	0.3
Total†	100.0	100.0	100.0	100.0	100.0	100.0

* Less than 0.05 percent.
† Ratios need not add to 100 because of rounding.
Notes: Column I equals column 5 in *Statistics of Income,* table 4; column II includes columns 7, 9, 11, 13, 15, and 17; column III includes columns 31, 33, 37, 39, 41, and 43. Column IV includes columns 23 and 25, thus allowing for only one-half of long-term gains; column V includes the remainder of base.
Source: *Individual Income Tax Returns, Preliminary Statistics of Income for 1972.*

than in the lower-income brackets, it does not follow that the bulk of capital income accrues to the very rich. As shown in the lower part of the table, this is not so. About 23 percent of dividend, interest, rent, and royalty income goes to returns below $10,000 and nearly one-half goes to returns below $20,000. The below-$20,000 group similarly receives about 26 percent of capital gains income. In all, capital income weighs much more heavily in the upper-income groups, but a substantial share of total capital income also goes to the middle- and lower-income ranges. The importance of this distribution for income tax policy will become apparent as we move along.

C. INCOME DEFINITION IN PRINCIPLE AND PRACTICE

The basic income concept, upon which the determination of income tax liability in practice rests, is AGI, or adjusted gross income. How satisfactory a concept is AGI? Or, more precisely, how good a measure of taxable capacity does it furnish? In the preceding chapter we concluded that income and consumption are the prime candidates for a broadly based personal tax, with income having the edge as the more comprehensive measure of ability to pay. For this to be true, income, as an index of taxpaying capacity, should be defined broadly as total accretion to a person's wealth. Seen from the income uses side, this also equals the increase in the individual's net worth plus his or her consumption during the period. All accretion should be included whether it be regular or fluctuating, expected or unexpected, realized or unrealized. Income from all sources thus defined should be treated uniformly and be combined in a global income measure to which tax rates are applied. Without globality, the application of a progressive rate schedule cannot serve its purpose of adapting the tax to the taxpayer's ability to pay. This view of the income tax, as expounded by Henry Simons, has been widely accepted by students of taxation.[13] Appealing and simple enough in principle, the accretion concept must now be considered more closely for what it implies in practice and how well it is satisfied by the AGI definition.

Gross Income versus Net Income

Income under the accretion approach should be measured in terms of net income, i.e., income after the costs of earning it are deducted. The tax law in fact attempts to define adjusted gross income as a net income concept, since costs incurred in earning income are usually, though not always, deducted. For instance, the law permits deduction of certain work-related expenses, whereas there is no provision for tax-free recovery of costs incurred in educational investment, and a child care allowance for working wives has been added only recently. In other instances, items which are more nearly income are treated as costs, e.g., entertainment expenses charged on expense accounts. But these are exceptions rather than the rule, the statute being generally in line with the principle of *net* income.

Capital Income versus Labor Income

According to the accretion concept—with income measured as increase in net worth plus consumption during the period—it does not matter from what source income has been derived. Yet writers on taxation have at times distinguished between "earned" (or wage) and "unearned" (or capital) income, implying that the former should be taxed less heavily. This may be rationalized as allowing for disutility of work,[14] or as a convenient device to grant low-income relief. Neither argument is convincing. If disutility of work had to be allowed for, it would surely be necessary to distinguish among types of jobs; and if relief is to be granted to low incomes, it should be made available also to low-income families with capital (e.g., retirement) income.

Notwithstanding these considerations, the income tax favors earned income in two respects. At the lower end of the scale, the Tax Reduction Act of 1975 provided for the previously noted earned-income tax credit, while at the upper

[13] See the reference to Henry Simons, Chap. 11, Further Readings, p. 287.

[14] See footnote 22, p. 216.

end of the scale the Revenue Act of 1969 limited the top-bracket rate applicable to earned income to 50 percent.

Capital Gains versus Other Income

Turning now to the question of capital gains, we arrive at perhaps the most important and controversial issue in income definition.

Present Status Under current law, realized gains are taxed on a preferential basis while unrealized gains are not taxed at all. Realized capital gains are defined as gains which result from the sale of assets other than those held in the ordinary conduct of business. Inventory gains made by a department store, gains from appreciation in the value of securities held by a security dealer or in houses held by a real estate firm are treated as ordinary income. But gains from the sale of securities held by an investor or of a house by a homeowner are given capital gains treatment. While short-term gains (or gains from the sale of assets held for less than six months) are treated as ordinary income and included in AGI in full, long-term gains (from the sale of assets held over six months) are included only at one-half their value in adjusted gross income. The maximum rate on long-term gains is thus 35, or one-half of 70 percent.[15] Moreover, under the so-called alternative method, the first $50,000 of long-term gains are taxed a maximum of only 25 percent.

The partial taxation of capital gains is matched by a limited allowance for capital losses. One-half of net long-term losses may be charged against short-term gains, but the charging of losses (short- or long-term) against other income is limited to $1,000.

Implications for Equity Quite apart from the possibility of total tax avoidance through nonrealization, this preferential treatment of realized gains gives a strong incentive to receive capital income in the form of capital gains rather than as operating profits, dividends, or interest. This incentive rises with the taxpayer's bracket rate. It is not surprising, therefore, that the share of capital gains in AGI rises sharply as we move up the income scale. As was shown in Table 10-5, capital gains rise from 5 percent of AGI at the $50,000 level to 10 percent at $100,000, and to over 50 percent at the $1 million level. Capital gains as a percentage of capital income rise from about 25 percent in the $20,000 to $50,000 range to 65 percent above $1 million.

The damage to tax equity is far-reaching. Horizontal equity is damaged because of resulting differentials in tax liabilities at given levels of income; and vertical equity is interfered with because the capital gains preference goes far in offsetting the bite of progressive taxation on capital income. As will be seen in the next chapter, the capital gains issue dwarfs the importance of all other tax preferences for high incomes. At the same time, it does not follow that a move

[15] To this may be added a "minimum tax" of 1.5 percent, thus raising the total to 36.5 percent. See p. 270.

toward full taxation of capital gains would have to result in a much more progressive tax. While this would be the case if present rates (going up to 70 percent) were applied to such gains, the inclusion of capital gains could be accompanied by a reduction in bracket rates. The major result would then be an improvement in horizontal equity.

Are Capital Gains Income? The foregoing view of the matter is based on the hypothesis that capital gains are part of income and should be treated accordingly, along with full allowance for losses against all other income. Is this a valid assumption?

With regard to realized gains, most students of taxation hold that there is no good justification on equity grounds for preferential treatment. It should make no difference, in measuring taxable capacity, whether capital income is (1) paid out currently as dividends, or (2) permitted to accumulate and then realized by sale of the asset. Income is received in both cases and there is no basis on which to distinguish the two. Although a special problem arises in that capital gains are discontinuous and volatile, so that they would pay more under progressive rates than would an equal amount of income received in a steady flow, this difficulty can be met through adequate averaging provisions. Nor can it be argued convincingly that capital gains should be given special treatment because they frequently are not expected or "regular" income, but are windfalls which happen to accrue without intention. This may be the case for some gains though not for others; and even where gains are unexpected, they nevertheless add to the recipient's taxable capacity. There seems little doubt, on equity grounds, that realized capital gains should be treated as ordinary income.

But what about the treatment of unrealized gains? Since AGI is defined in cash terms and includes cash income only, unrealized gains are not taxed. This is clearly in contravention of the accretion principle. According to this principle, income as an index of taxpaying ability should be measured as accretion to wealth. All increments should be included, whether realized (turned into cash) or not. If Mr. Jones holds corporate shares which have appreciated in value by $100,000, this is the amount by which his net worth has risen and which he would have been able to turn into cash if he had so chosen. The fact that he has retained this particular asset shows that he preferred continued holding over the available alternatives, e.g., sale with consumption or reinvestment in some other asset. Whether the gain is realized or not is irrelevant to whether or not there has been an increase in economic capacity. Provided that realization is possible, the decision whether or not to realize is a problem in portfolio (asset) management and not in the creation of income.

Nevertheless, these conclusions have been subject to continuous debate, as shown by the following arguments:

1. "Unrealized gains should not be taxed because the owner has refrained from consumption."

While there has been no consumption, this is not relevant in defining the base of an *income* tax. Here the principle is that all income should be taxed, independently of how it is used; and even under a consumption tax, the distinction between realized and unrealized gains is not the decisive issue.[16]

2. "Unrealized gains should not be taxed because in the absence of realization we do not know whether they really exist."

Thus, in the early origins of bookkeeping, the Venetian merchant was well advised not to count his proceeds until his captain had returned to home port and delivered the treasure chest. Prudent accounting would call for "realization" in cash (or gold) before income was said to exist. But institutions change and the analogy is quite inappropriate for, say, a holder of AT&T shares which can be sold at once. As will be noted later, measurement of unrealized gains may be difficult, but this is not an insuperable obstacle.

3. "Taxation of unrealized gains requires the owner to pay a tax even though he or she has not obtained cash with which to pay it."

The observation is correct, but does it matter? As would be necessary with other debts that may come due, it is not unreasonable to ask the taxpayer to liquidate part of his or her assets to make the tax payment if needed. For situations in which partial liquidation is not possible (e.g., a family business), adequate time must be granted.

4. Finally, the following argument is occasionally made: For income to be received, it must be "separated" from the asset. This view, which had much legal support in the earlier stages of the income tax discussion, is hard to fathom from the economist's point of view. Separation is a matter of investment choice, whereas income accrues when the asset value is increased.

So far, it appears that, on equity grounds, unrealized gains should be considered taxable and included along with income from all other sources.

Inflationary Gains The equity case for full taxation of capital gains is tempered, however, by the impact of inflation. If capital gains are a reflection of an inflationary increase in nominal values only, they should not be taxed. To produce a meaningful index of taxable capacity, it is evident that income should be defined in real terms, i.e., that changes in the price level should be allowed for in determining taxable income. This is of special importance with regard to changes in asset value.[17] A rise in the money value of an asset which is matched by an increase in price level is an illusory capital gain and should not be considered income. But if an adjustment is made here, should not the same principle be extended also to allow for the real losses suffered by holders of claims, such as cash, savings bonds, or mortgages, and for real gains made by debtors of these instruments? Thus the problem of inflation adjustment is very much broader, extending beyond the case of capital gains arising from the sale of shares or real assets.

Economic Effects of Full Taxation While equity considerations on the whole point to the taxation of capital gains as regular income, objections to such

[16] Under a consumption tax, unrealized gains would be excluded and realized gains would be included *only if consumed.* Realized gains which are not consumed but are reinvested or held as cash would be excluded. On the other hand, consumption financed by drawing down balances would be subject to tax.

[17] Note that this problem arises quite apart from the structure of tax rates and applies even for a proportional tax. It thus differs from the effects of inflation on the application of progressive rates, as discussed later. See p. 379.

a step are also based on its potential economic effects. In particular, these two arguments are advanced:

1. It is argued that full taxation of realized gains would be detrimental to the capital market. Since transference of assets (selling and reinvesting) would occasion a tax, such shifts would be discouraged. The tax would tend to lock in investments, especially where the investor is subject to a high bracket rate.[18] This is a valid argument, although its force would be greatly reduced if a way could be found to tax unrealized gains.

2. It is argued that full taxation of realized gains, and especially the inclusion of unrealized gains into the tax base, would be detrimental to investment and economic growth. This question, which involves the comparative merits of preferential capital gains treatment and other investment incentives, is considered further on. The conclusion will be reached that superior forms of investment incentives may be found.[19] Moreover, it must be noted that full taxation of gains should also bring with it full allowance for losses, so that the change would also have its advantages to the taxpayer.[20]

Implementation Problems Suppose that fuller taxation of capital gains is to be applied; the question remains how it can be implemented. Problems of implementation involve (1) determining a feasible way of reaching unrealized gains, and (2) applying an inflation adjustment:

1. Full taxation of realized gains can be implemented without technical difficulties, but the situation is more difficult for unrealized gains. Yet realized gains cannot be taxed fully without taxing unrealized gains also, otherwise severe lock-in effects would result. However, taxation of unrealized gains on a current basis is not feasible owing to the impracticality of annual valuation of all assets. Some assets, such as traded securities, could be valued and taxed periodically, say every five years, but other assets (e.g., paintings or farms) may be more difficult to value. It has therefore been proposed that accrued gains be taxed at death or transfer (by gift) as if realized at that time. Referred to as "constructive realization," this would reduce the need for valuation to a single time, thus reducing this task to manageable proportions. By permitting averaging and the spreading of payments over a period of time, inequities which would arise from forced liquidation of assets may be avoided. Under such a procedure, all gains would be eventually taxed, thus reducing the lock-in effect. A constructive realization provision has recently been enacted in

[18] Suppose the investor has an asset with a market value M and a yield y, which gives him an income $I = yM$. If the asset was purchased at original cost C, his income after sale and reinvestment equals $I^* = y^*[M - t(M - C)]$, where y^* is the yield of the new asset and t is the investor's marginal rate of tax. Now let $\frac{M-C}{M} = \alpha$, the capital gain as a fraction of M. By substitution, $I^* = y^* M(1 - t\alpha)$. If the switch is to be worthwhile, we must have $I^* > I$ or $y^* > y(1 - t\alpha)$. Thus, if the yield on the old asset was 10 percent, α is 60 percent and t is 50 percent, the yield on the new investment would have to be over 14.3 percent. The level of y^* required to make the asset switch profitable will be the higher, the larger are t and α.

[19] See Chap. 22, Sec. C, p. 492. A case for the importance of saving to economic growth is made in C. Lowell Harriss, *Innovations in Tax Policy and Other Essays*, Hartford: John C. Lincoln Institute, 1972, p. 277.

[20] See p. 494.

Canada[21] and has been repeatedly proposed in the United States, but has not as yet been accepted by the Congress.[22]

While constructive realization would move unrealized gains into the tax base, it would still leave capital gains with some advantage. Whereas other income is taxed on a current basis, the tax on unrealized gains would be delayed until death, thus leaving the taxpayer with the possibility of earning income thereon in the meantime. Tax delay is equivalent to receiving an interest-free loan, the value of which may be substantial, especially for young investors.[23]

2. Making an inflation adjustment would call for application of a price index so as to deflate the sales value to the level of prices applicable when the asset was bought. This involves the choice of a proper index, but even an approximate adjustment could take care of the major part of the inequity which arises from disregard of inflation.[24]

Conclusion In conclusion, it appears that (1) the preferential treatment of capital gains is unsatisfactory on equity grounds, and (2) techniques can be found which permit the inclusion of unrealized gains at death or transfer as well as an allowance for inflation. In the meantime, it should be noted that incomplete taxation of capital gains is not confined to the United States tax. Some countries, such as the United Kingdom, until recently exempted altogether, even realized gains, and others—including most European countries—still do so for most types of gains.

Imputed Income

Some people hold earning assets that bring cash income; others hold durable consumer goods that earn imputed income. The most important example is the owner-occupied residence. The resident obtains an "imputed rent" equal to the return he or she could obtain by letting the house. Since accretion is defined as increase in net worth plus consumption, such imputed consumption values should be included in the tax base. AGI, by adhering to a cash income concept, does not include imputed income. This omission, as we shall find later on, causes inequities in the tax treatment of houseowners and renters.

Income received in kind, such as food grown on farms, the services of company cars, or gains from fringe benefits, are similarly omitted in AGI but

[21] Under the Canadian legislation of 1971, unrealized gains are taxed at death but gains accrued prior to enactment of the new provision are excluded. The earlier proposal for periodic taxation of accrued gains on shares was not enacted. See *Proposals for Tax Reform,* Ottawa: Queen's Printer for Canada, 1969, p. 36.

[22] Constructive realization was proposed by the Kennedy administration in 1964 but was rejected out of hand by Congress. A more modest substitute proposal (made in 1964 by the administration and again in 1969 by the Ways and Means Committee) was also rejected. This related to the computation of gains by the heir who sells an asset acquired from an estate. Under present provision, he may use the written-up asset value at the time of the estate as base, rather than the original cost incurred by the deceased. Thus, even realized gains escape taxation if the asset is passed through an estate. The proposal was to require the heir to use the original cost as the base when computing capital gains upon future realization, the rule now applicable to gains from assets acquired by gift.

[23] This consideration, it may be noted, runs counter to recent proposals for reducing the inclusion rate of long-term gains with the length of the holding period.

[24] For a proposal which would combine a correction for the interest gain due to delay and the inflation factor, see Roger Brinner, "Inflation, Deferral and the Neutral Taxation of Capital Gains," *National Tax Journal,* December 1973, pp. 565–574.

should be in the income concept. This is especially important where payments in kind may be substituted for cash payments to avoid income tax. At the same time, the inclusion of imputed income becomes unworkable if carried too far. Thus, a good case could be made conceptually for imputing earnings to housewives for the services which they render to the family. If this were done, the tax base might well be raised by, say, $250 billion, but part of this would be lost by the need for increased personal exemptions. An even more puzzling problem is posed by leisure. If a person chooses leisure, this is evidence (arguing in analogy to unrealized capital gains) that he values it by the income equivalent lost in not working. The pure logic of accretion would suggest that consumption in the form of leisure be included in the tax base, but implementation of such a rule, as noted earlier in our discussion of distributive justice, seems to be impracticable.

Earnings versus Transfers

From the economist's point of view, national income is the sum of factor earnings during the period, reflecting in turn the value of output which the factors have produced. Transfers received from government or private sources (such as gifts or bequests) are not components of income in the national income sense. But it does not follow that they should be excluded from taxable income. Choosing a suitable definition of taxable income is an issue in tax equity, not in national income accounting. A person's taxable income need not be the same as his share in national income; nor need total taxable income equal total national income.

Transfer receipts from government, such as welfare and veterans' benefits, are excluded from AGI, but there is no good reason for this exclusion. Indeed, $1,000 received in benefits adds no less to a person's economic capacity than does $1,000 received in wages. While the transfer recipient's income will frequently be too low to justify its taxation, this situation should be taken care of by devices such as exemptions and the low-income allowance, devices which apply equally to all recipients of low earnings. The treatment of social security benefits poses a special problem, to be discussed later in this chapter.

Private transfers, such as bequests and gifts, also remain outside the income tax. Such transfers are neither deducted by the donor, nor included by the donee. In terms of the accretion concept, the receipt of bequests or gifts constitutes an addition to economic capacity just as does accretion from other sources. Although such transfers are taxed separately under the estate and gift taxes, a good argument can be made for including them in the income tax base of the recipient.

Pension Plans

Contributory pension plans involve the setting aside of current income for future use. Proper tax treatment would call for disallowing deduction of contributions when made and excluding benefits when received later on, except for such part thereof as reflects interest earnings on earlier contributions. An alternative, allowing for deduction of contributions when made with full taxation of subsequent benefits, would not be so satisfactory since it would leave the taxpayer with two advantages not enjoyed by other savers. Since tax payments are postponed, the taxpayer would receive an interest gain. Moreover, as his future income is likely

TABLE 10-6
Tax Treatment of Pension Plans

Type	Contributions or Premiums	Benefits	Interest
OASI			
Employee	Not deductible	Not taxed	Not taxed
Employer	Deductible	Not taxed	Not taxed
Private Retirement Plans			
Employee	Not deductible	Not taxed	Not taxed
Employer	Deductible	Taxed	Taxed
*Self-Employed**	Deductible	Taxed	Taxed
Life Insurance	Not deductible	Not taxed	Not taxed†

* Limited to 10 percent of AGI with annual ceiling of $2,500.
† If distribution made prior to death, interest component is taxed.

to be smaller, a lower bracket rate would apply. As shown in Table 10-6, the actual treatment of pension and insurance plans varies and usually falls short of the proper solution.

Social Insurance Beginning with old age and survivors' insurance (OASI), note that employee contributions are not deducted from AGI but employer contributions are deducted. Benefits in turn are tax-free. Viewing OASI as a contributory system, the proper procedures would be to (1) disallow deduction of all contributions while including only such part of the benefits as reflect interest earnings, or (2) permit deduction of all contributions while fully taxing benefit receipts. Present procedure thus involves a highly preferential treatment regarding the employer-financed part where the insured remains entirely tax-free. If, instead, OASI is viewed in noninsurance terms, the proper solution would be to tax benefits. Since the federal income tax does not allow for deduction of other federal taxes, deduction of the employee's contribution would then seem inappropriate.

Private Retirement Plan The treatment of private retirement plans comes closer to inclusion of the full tax base. While treatment of contributions is the same as for OASI, benefits based on the employer contribution are now taxable. Thus, the only remaining preference due to noninclusion is failure to tax the interest component of the employee-financed benefit share.

More important, however, is the tax advantage which results because the deferred payment mechanism of pension plans works as an averaging device. Since averaging is generally desirable on equity grounds, this is not necessarily objectionable, except that the option to postpone is not always available. It has been of special importance for highly paid executives and has led to extensive use of deferred payment arrangements.[25] A similar but limited provision is now

[25] Other forms of deferred compensation involve the transfer of shares which until recently not only permitted tax postponement but also subsequent taxation at capital gains rates. These provisions have been tightened under the Tax Reform Act of 1969, and further legislation is expected.

available for self-employed persons, who may deduct 10 percent of earned income but not over $2,500.

Life Insurance Similar rules apply to the savings component of life insurance. Premiums are not deducted and benefits are not taxed, thus permitting interest on premiums to escape. However, interest is taxable if distribution is made prior to death. Forms of insurance which carry no savings component (such as term insurance) yield no interest earnings. Benefits are properly exempted, without allowing a deduction of premiums.

Exclusions

Not only does the law omit some income components from AGI because they are not cash income, but certain forms of cash income are taken out explicitly as so-called exclusions. One of them is the previously noted exclusion of one-half of realized long-term capital gains. The next most important item is that of interest on state and local securities.

State and Local Interest Interest on state and local securities is not taxable under the federal income tax. Although this exclusion was originally based on the constitutional provision that any one level of government should not tax the instrumentalities of another, most legal opinion now holds that the inclusion of such interest would be permissible under the Sixteenth Amendment. Inclusion can no longer be ruled out on constitutional grounds. On its merits, exclusion is undesirable because it undermines the equity of the income tax. Moreover, tax exemption is an inefficient means of supporting state and local government borrowing.

Beginning with equity aspects, exclusion gives the greatest advantage to high-income taxpayers with capital income. The gains from exemption rise with the investor's tax bracket. For an investor whose marginal rate is 50 percent, a tax-exempt security yielding 5 percent is equivalent in net yield to a taxable issue yielding 10 percent. For an investor whose marginal rate is 60 percent, the equivalent yield on a taxable issue is 12.5 percent, while for an investor with a bracket rate of 20 percent, it is only 6.25 percent. This explains why the great bulk of tax-exempts held outside banks are held by wealthy individuals. Of the $1.8 billion of estimated revenue loss from interest exemption (1968), over $1 billion involved individual returns, 75 percent of them from taxpayers with AGI above $100,000.[26] The remainder, which involves trust accounts and financial intermediaries, also largely benefits upper-income groups. While these tax savings are much less than those from the capital gains preference, they are nevertheless a major reason why so little tax is paid by many high-income taxpayers. Moreover, they are another major cause of horizontal inequity among upper-bracket taxpayers.

Apart from being inequitable, the exemption is an *inefficient* way of subsidiz-

[26] See Table 11-2 and *Tax Reform Studies and Proposals,* part 2, U.S. Treasury Department, Joint Publication, Committee on Ways and Means and Committee on Finance, Feb. 5, 1969, p. 83.

ing state and local governments.[27] More aid could be given at the same cost if the federal government were to subsidize state and local interest payments directly. Because interest on state and local securities is tax-exempt, such securities are worth more to investors. Therefore they will pay a higher price or, what amounts to the same, accept a lower before-tax yield. Because of this, the government can issue securities at a lower interest cost. However, less than the entire revenue loss is passed on to state and local governments in the form of lower borrowing costs.

Consider the following situation: Mr. H, who pays a high-bracket tax rate of 60 percent, has $800 to invest, while Mr. L, who pays a lower rate of 40 percent, invests $200. Both can invest in federal securities at 10 percent, giving them a net yield of 4 and 6 percent respectively. Neglecting risk differentials, they will purchase state and local securities yielding below this level. If $1,000 of such securities are to be placed, the yield must be at least 6 percent so that both will participate. The state and local governments then save $40 in interest cost since they now lend at 6 rather than 10 percent. The federal government loses income tax revenue of $56, which it would have obtained had H and L invested in taxable 10 percent issues. The net loss to governments of $16 accrues to Mr. H, whose earnings are $48 as against after-tax earnings (in the absence of the exclusion provision) of $32. Mr. L has $12 left, the same as from investing in taxable 10 percent issues.

In practice, matters are more complicated, but our illustration shows why the device is inefficient: the subsidy must be set sufficiently high to attract the marginal investor, while investors with higher-bracket rates could have been attracted for less. The same aid could be given to state and local governments through a direct subsidy of $40, leaving them with the same net interest cost of $60. Or, by giving a direct subsidy of $56, that gain could be raised by nearly 30 percent and damage to tax equity would be avoided. Moreover, by raising the yield, the market for state and local securities would be broadened as investment by savings institutions would be attracted.

Proposals to substitute a direct subsidy for tax exemption on new issues have been advanced but rejected by Congress. State and local governments, like other groups, prefer their subsidies in hidden form; and they fear that a direct subsidy would be less permanent in nature. For these reasons, the combined opposition of governors, mayors, and high-bracket taxpayers has, to date, been too strong to permit a sensible reform. Prospects are, however, that the support available through the traditional technique of tax exemption will become insufficient as the market becomes saturated with such securities. This in turn will render state and local governments more receptive to new techniques such as direct subsidy of state and local interest payments.

Dividend Exclusion The first $100 of dividends are excluded from AGI. Looked at from the point of view of the income tax alone, there is no justification for permitting a supplementary exemption on this particular form of income.

[27] In recent years there has been increasing pressure to include industrial development bonds (sponsored by state or municipal government but raising capital for private firms) under this privilege.

TABLE 10-7
Types and Amounts of Deduction, 1972

	Number of Returns (Millions)	*Dollar Amount (Billions of Dollars)*
Standard		
Low-income allowance	36.1	45.9
Percentage standard deduction	14.2	14.2
Total	50.3	60.1
Itemized	27.0	96.5
All	77.3	156.6

Source: *Individual Income Tax Returns, Preliminary Statistics of Income for 1972,* U.S. Treasury Department, 1974, p. 3.

Evaluation of this exclusion must, however, be made in a broader framework, involving the interaction of corporation and income tax liabilities. Since the $100 limit makes the provision insignificant for high-income taxpayers, it may be considered as a rough (but only a very rough) offset to the higher incremental tax burden which the corporation income tax imposes upon shareholders at the lower end of the income scale.[28]

Allowance for Losses

Since accretion is designed to measure consumption plus increase in net worth, operating losses should be deducted in arriving at the net income of a business. Losses reduce net worth just as gains increase it, and the government should be a partner in both cases. While the law does not go so far as to grant a refund in case of net losses, it does make substantial provision for the spreading of losses over a nine-year period, including three years past and five years ahead. As will be seen later, adequate allowance for losses is of key importance for the investment effects of an income tax.[29]

D. DEDUCTIONS

Deductions, no less than exclusions, may be used to make taxable income a better measure of economic capacity; but inappropriate use may again give rise to preferences and distortions.

Types of Deductions

Deductions in 1972 are shown in Table 10-7. We note that about two-thirds of all taxpayers used the standard deduction, while only one-third itemized. Over 70 percent of returns using the standard deduction claimed the low-income allowance. At the same time, only 38 percent of *deducted amounts* were claimed as standard deductions, while 62 percent were accounted for by itemized returns.

[28] See Chap. 12, Sec. C, p. 295.
[29] See p. 494.

TABLE 10-8
Deductions as Percent of AGI, 1968
(Taxable Returns Only)

		ITEMIZED DEDUCTIONS				
AGI Class	*Standard Deduction*	*Taxes*	*Interest*	*Contri-butions*	*Medical Expenses*	*All*
$4,000– $5,000	33.7	12.6	10.4	5.4	13.5	45.4
$9,000– $10,000	15.2	8.5	8.0	3.2	4.2	26.6
$10,000– $15,000	14.8	8.3	7.5	2.8	2.7	24.0
$15,000– $20,000	11.9	8.1	6.4	2.5	1.7	20.7
$30,000– $50,000	5.7	8.0	4.5	2.8	1.1	18.1
$50,000–$100,000	3.4	7.8	4.3	3.2	0.7	17.8
$100,000–$200,000	2.0	7.7	4.5	4.6	0.5	19.6
$1,000,000 and above	*	7.3	3.3	18.3	*	31.7

* Less than 0.05 percent.

Notes: Itemized deductions are shown as percent of AGI of returns using itemized deductions. Standard deduction includes low-income allowance and percentage deduction and is shown as percent of AGI of returns using standard deduction.

Source: Individual Income Tax Returns, Statistics of Income for 1968, U.S. Treasury Department, 1972, p. 65.

Low-bracket returns typically use the "low-income allowance" form of standard deduction, middle incomes use the percentage standard deduction, and high-bracket returns typically itemize. Thus the percentage of itemizers rose from 13 percent in the under-$5,000 bracket to 32 percent for those in the $5,000 to $10,000 bracket and 79 percent for those with income above $15,000.

Table 10-8 shows various itemized deductions as a percentage of AGI for returns with standard and itemized deductions. For the former group, deductions as a percentage of AGI are largest at the lower end of the scale and then decline, reflecting the nature of the low-income allowance, as well as the upper limit on the percentage form of standard deduction. For the itemizing group, the ratio is again highest at the bottom, reflecting the fact that such returns will use itemizing only in unusual cases, such as heavy medical expenses. The ratio then settles at 18 to 20 percent over the $15,000 to $100,000 range but rises again to 30 percent for incomes above $1 million.

Particular items vary in importance by income levels. Medical deductions are of primary significance at the lower end of the income scale, with interest deductions most important in the low-middle range. Charitable contributions are most vital at the upper end, with deduction of state and local taxes of importance throughout the income scale.

Rationale for Itemized Deductions

The principle of income taxation calls for a comprehensive tax base, including all forms of accretion. This approach establishes a prima facie case against deductions, yet some deductions may be justified.

Equity Aspects Equal income may not imply equal ability to pay if taxpayers are in otherwise different positions. This is recognized with regard to family size, but may apply also in other respects. Taxpayers with heavy emergency expenses, such as large medical bills, may be said to have less taxable capacity than others with equal income but no such emergencies. It is also reasonable to suggest that such situations will be of special importance for low-income taxpayers. This principle is reflected in the allowance for medical expenses which may be deducted if in excess of 3 percent of AGI. A similar argument can be made regarding casualty losses and losses from theft, such losses now being allowed up to $100. If designed properly, emergency deductions are not objectionable and may indeed be helpful in securing a more equitable tax base.[30] The objective, after all, is not to maximize the tax base but to secure a fair measure of taxable capacity.

Incentive Aspects Deductions may be viewed as a way of providing an incentive to use income in a "meritorious" form or to encourage expenditures on items which generate external benefits.[31] The deduction here acts as a matching grant by which the government reduces the cost of certain activities for the taxpayer, thereby inducing the individual to spend more on this activity. If the particular activity merits support and if tax deduction is the best technique of giving it, the resulting gain may outweigh the damage to tax equity. There is no law of nature which says that taxation must not be used for purposes other than revenue collection. Rather, the question is whether the supported activity merits a subsidy, and if so, whether the subsidy should be given in this form. More will be said about this when considering charitable contributions.

This rationale does, however, raise the question of whether allowance should be made as a deduction from AGI in arriving at taxable income or as a credit against tax. In the former case, the value of the benefit (in terms of tax reduction) rises with the bracket rate and hence with income, whereas in the latter case it is constant for all taxpayers. If allowance for emergency needs is viewed as a matter of income definition, the deduction approach is in order, but if considered in the nature of hardship relief, a credit (granted if total hardship items exceed a certain percentage of AGI) seems more appropriate.

A further case for deductions is based on the proposition that certain components of income are not available to the taxpayer for his or her own free use. This argument is usually made to support the deduction of state and local taxes but, as we shall see presently, is more appropriate for some such taxes than for others.

Evaluation of Itemized Deductions

The single most important itemized deduction is that for state and local taxes. In 1972, this accounted for a loss in taxable income of $35 billion. Next came interest deductions with $26 billion and charitable contributions with $13 billion.

[30] Similar considerations arise in connection with extra exemptions for the blind. To the extent that being blind calls for extra expenses, the equal treatment principle justifies an extra allowance. The same case cannot be made, however, with regard to the extra exemption for the aged.

[31] See p. 650.

Together, these accounted for 80 percent of total itemized deductions of $92 billion.[32]

State and Local Taxes Deduction of taxes is clearly appropriate where they enter as a cost of doing business, and such deduction is permitted for both federal and lower-level taxes. In addition, the law permits deduction of income, property, gasoline, and general sales taxes imposed by state and local governments even where they are nonbusiness taxes paid by households and consumers.

Here the case hinges on whether such tax payments are viewed as uses of income similar to other private uses, or whether they should be considered a forced reduction in the taxpayer's own income. In the first case, deduction is inappropriate, while in the second, it is proper. It follows from this that the case for deductibility is weakest where taxes are in the nature of benefit charges, such as gasoline taxes which may be considered payment for highway services. But, though the repeal of gasoline tax deductibility has been urged at various times, most recently in the 1969 reform, it has not been accepted by the Congress. By the same token, the case for deduction is strengthened with income taxes. Such taxes are general charges which reduce the taxpayer's disposable income, and the relationship of the person's own contribution to benefits received is less direct. Although the taxpayer receives the benefit of public services, the situation differs from that of private uses of his or her income. Taxpayers must pay the tax, and while they have a vote, they do not have a veto. For these reasons, deductibility of state and local income taxes is generally counted as valid.[33]

With regard to other taxes, the case remains controversial. While disallowance of the sales tax deduction has been argued on the grounds that the consumer is not forced to buy (so that tax payment is optional), this is hardly convincing, especially where the tax is general. Nor can disallowance of the property tax be justified simply by looking at the tax as a benefit tax, since most of property tax revenue is used to finance more or less general outlays. From a theoretical point of view, the best approach might be to allow the deduction of all taxes (including, for that matter, federal taxes) while including benefits from public services in the tax base, but this would not be a feasible procedure. Short of this approach, there does not appear to be a clear-cut solution.

Mortgage Interest and Housing Next in importance are deductions for interest payments. Such deductions comprise 25 percent of total itemized deductions, with mortgage interest accounting for 60 percent of interest deductions.[34] As with taxes, a distinction must be drawn between interest paid as a cost of doing business and interest paid on consumer debt. Deductibility of business interest is clearly appropriate for the simple reason that taxable income should be defined as net income. But deductibility of interest on consumer debt, such as mortgages, is a different matter. While both types of interest are cost payments or negative

[32] *Individual Income Tax Returns, Statistics of Income for 1972,* Preliminary, U.S. Treasury Department, 1974.

[33] For further discussion, see p. 281.

[34] See *Annual Report of the Secretary of the Treasury,* 1968, p. 340.

income streams, the treatment of the corresponding benefit streams differs. In the case of business borrowing, the benefit stream is included as taxable business income, while in the instance of mortgage or consumer debt, the benefit stream (in the form of imputed rent from house ownership) is not treated as part of the resident's taxable income.

Consider three people, each with $30,000 to invest and wishing to live in a $30,000 house. Also assume that the return on all capital is 5 percent. Mr. R decides to rent and invest his funds in shares. As shown in the table, he receives $1,500 in dividends. On this he pays a tax of 30 percent, or $450. Mr. O decides to own his house outright and pays $30,000 in cash. He buys no shares and receives no dividend income, but benefits from imputed rent of $1,500. Since this is not counted as taxable income, he pays no tax. Ms. M purchases a $30,000 residence by taking up a mortgage, while using her $30,000 to purchase shares. She derives $1,500 in dividends but pays $1,500 in interest. Since the latter can be deducted, she is again left without taxable income. Now compare the three as in line 5. They all have the same net worth and live in similar houses, but R pays $450 in tax while O and M are tax-free.

	Renter R	*Equity Owner O*	*Mortgage Owner M*
1. Owner's imputed rent	0	$1,500	$1,500
2. Interest paid	0	0	$1,500
3. Dividends	$1,500	0	$1,500
4. Taxable, present law	$1,500	0	0
5. Tax, present law	$ 450	0	0
6. Variant 1 tax	$ 450	0	$ 450
7. Variant 2 tax	$ 450	$ 450	$ 450
8. Variant 3 tax	0	0	0

How can the three be placed in an equal position? Removal of the interest deduction (variant 1) will not do. While M would lose her advantage and be placed in the same position as R, O would remain free of tax. In order to treat all alike, we must either make imputed rent taxable while continuing to allow deduction of interest (variant 2), or disregard imputed rent and deduct interest, but make rent payments deductible as well (variant 3). With variant 2, O and M must both pay the same tax as R, while with variant 3, R's liability is removed and no one pays. Both solutions are neutral as between the various types of housing arrangements, but variant 2 shows no preference for housing while 3 makes all housing expenditures tax-exempt. From the point of view of a global income tax, variant 2 is clearly the preferred solution. Equal treatment should apply not only among people who consume housing in different form, but also among those who consume housing and others who consume different items.[35]

[35] The question may be raised whether—from the point of view of the tax structure as a whole—preferential treatment of housing under the income tax might be considered an offset to the extra burden imposed on housing under the property tax, provided that its proceeds are used to finance general (rather than housing-oriented) expenditures. See p. 354.

The case for preferential treatment would thus have to be made on incentive grounds. The question then is whether the incentive should be given to ownership in particular or to housing expenditure in general. The present procedure, which gives preferential treatment to ownership, is difficult to defend, especially since low-income housing is more largely in rental form. But even generalized tax relief for housing (ownership or rental) is of dubious validity. Support for low-cost housing in particular may be desirable, calling for limitation of the tax preference to rental payments and interest deduction on such housing. But for this purpose, tax preferences are hardly the appropriate solution. Taxes paid by truly low-income families are too low (if the family is taxable at all) to make a substantial difference. Rental subsidies and direct provision for low-cost housing offer superior approaches.

However strong the case for inclusion of imputed rent may be in principle, it is politically unpopular and not in the cards.[36] Given this situation, would removal of the interest deduction (variant 1) be desirable as a second-best solution? As noted before, this would equalize the position between R and M, but leave O in a preferred position. Moreover, it would differentiate the treatment of O and M, who are now in similar positions. Nevertheless, there would be an equity gain in such a change. The Rs and Ms are more numerous than the Os, so that horizontal equity would be improved by equalizing their treatment.[37]

Similar reasoning applies to interest on other types of consumer debt such as automobile loans. Again interest is deductible but the imputed income derived from the car is not taxed. Here, renting is of only limited (though growing) importance, but the difference between outright purchases and debt finance remains. With low-income families in this case typically in the debtor position, the vertical equity aspect of the interest deduction is modified, the deduction now being beneficial at lower levels of income.

Charitable Contributions Charitable contributions account for close to 25 percent of itemized deductions. Taxpayers may deduct contributions to a wide range of nonprofit institutions up to 50 percent of AGI. Prior to the Tax Reform Act of 1969, taxpayers whose charitable contributions and tax liability together exceeded 90 percent of AGI were allowed to deduct without limit. This provision, which resulted in about 100 of the wealthiest taxpayers paying little or no tax, was repealed in 1969 and is scheduled to run out by 1975. Under the same act, capital gains–free gifts of appreciated property were limited to 30 percent of total contributions.

Since the revenue cost of deductions for charitable contributions is over $2 billion, Congress, in effect, allocates this amount as a public contribution to eleemosynary institutions. These contributions, however, are made as matching

[36] Great Britain, which has traditionally included imputed rent, has discontinued the practice in recent years.

[37] For further discussion of the tax treatment of housing, see H. Aaron, "Income Taxes and Housing," *American Economic Review,* December 1970.

For a study of horizontal inequality in the tax treatment of housing, see M. White and A. White, "Horizontal Inequality in the Federal Income Tax Treatment of Homeowners and Tenants," *National Tax Journal,* September 1965.

grants to private donors, leaving it to them to select the recipient. The matching rate equals the donor's marginal tax rate. A donor in the 70 percent bracket must put up only 30 cents to make a gift of $1, while a donor in the 20 percent bracket must put up 80 cents. A philosopher-economist might observe that the opportunity cost of virtue falls as one moves up the income scale.

The merit of charitable deductions is not easy to judge. On the pro side it is evident that, without the pincer effect of high marginal rates and deductibility, charitable contributions would be considerably less. Private educational institutions, foundations, the United Fund, churches, and other recipient organizations would suffer and some might not survive. Congress would hardly be willing to spend corresponding amounts for such purposes. Moreover, there may be an advantage in decentralizing the choice of supported projects. On the con side, it may be argued that some of the functions now supported by charity should be the responsibility of the state and that allocations made from public funds (whether as a direct appropriation or via special tax provision) should be subject to public direction and scrutiny. The issue carries broad social and cultural implications which go much beyond the realm of tax policy.

There is, however, a more technical issue to be considered. Assuming the incentive approach to be desirable, the question remains whether the present deduction technique is most efficient in encouraging contributions. The answer is hardly positive. For instance, the revenue cost might be reduced with little loss in incentive terms if a 3 percent floor were applied and deductions allowed only for contributions in excess of this floor. Such deductions in 1966 amounted to 78 percent of the total.[38]

Substitution of a credit for a deduction might also be considered.[39] This would increase the tax value of contributions for low-income taxpayers and lower them for high-income taxpayers. The matching rate would be equalized. The effect on total contributions would depend on the elasticities of the donation schedules at the two ends of the scale. Beyond this, the pattern of giving (the choice among different charities) would be affected. Substitution of a credit approach would tend to increase the share received by churches, which depend more largely on low-income contributions, while lowering that of foundations and educational institutions.

Child Care Deduction A new itemized deduction which has received increased attention in recent years is the deduction for child care expenses. This provision now permits deduction of such expenses up to $400 a month for working parents, provided that their joint AGI does not exceed $35,000. Above that level the deduction is reduced and vanishes at $44,600. Though called a deduction from AGI, this provision may be interpreted as an allowance for the

[38] See *Tax Reform Studies and Proposals,* op. cit., part 2, p. 200.

[39] With deducted contributions of, say, $13 billion and an estimated revenue loss from such deductions of $3.5 billion (1970), a credit against tax of 27 percent of contributions could be granted instead (assuming total giving unchanged). Whether or not this would be the case depends on the response of givers below the $16,000 level (joint returns) whose terms of giving would be improved as against that of higher-income givers whose terms would be worsened. It is interesting to note in this connection that in 1970 about half the total giving originated above the $16,000 bracket.

cost of earning income (e.g., similar to employee business expenses) and as such should properly be made an adjustment to income included in AGI.[40] If considered this way, it would be available not only to taxpayers using itemized deductions, as is the case now, but also to those using the standard deduction.

Education Costs Many proposals have been advanced to grant tax relief for expenditures on education, including a deduction from AGI and—as in more recent proposals—a credit against tax. The distributional results differ and the previously noted issues in the choice between credit and deduction again arise. Against such tax incentives, it is argued that assistance to education can be granted more equitably and efficiently via an expenditure program. Yet, there is one form of tax relief for education which would have particular merit as a tax device. Expenditures on education may, at least in substantial part, be considered as a form of investment in human resources undertaken to increase earnings in later life.[41] These earnings will be taxed, although they constitute a net income only to the extent that they exceed the capital cost. Therefore, the taxpayer should be allowed to recover his or her cost in computing net income; in other words, depreciation should be permitted against human as well as against physical investment. The appropriate solution—in line with charging depreciation over asset life[42]—would be to allow such charges against the student's income after the investment is made, rather than as a current deduction from parents' income while education costs are incurred.

Standard Deduction

Given these options to itemize, why should the taxpayer be given the alternative of a standard deduction? As noted earlier, the latter takes two forms: (1) the flat 16 percent deduction with a $2,600 upper limit, and (2) the flat deduction of $1,900, referred to as the "low-income allowance," both figures applicable to joint returns. Since the rationale for deductions is to deal with special circumstances, it makes little sense to grant them on an across-the-board basis.

There are, however, two pragmatic reasons for the standard deduction. The first is that itemizing is cumbersome for both the taxpayer and the Internal Revenue Service. Use of the standard deduction in lieu of itemizing facilitates matters for the bulk of taxpayers. While some taxpayers get more than they deserve (their itemized deductions would fall short of 16 percent), this tax loss may be worth the gain in simplification. Moreover, the benefit from the standard deduction decreases with rising income so that the standard deduction has served as an indirect way of giving relief to middle-income taxpayers. The low-income allowance form of the standard deduction, which has become the most widely

[40] While the adjustment removes a disadvantage otherwise imposed on the working wife, it does so in a rough fashion. The theoretically correct (though hardly practical) solution would be to include imputed income of housewives in the tax base, while granting an individual exemption (whether parents work or not) sufficiently large to compensate for child care. There would thus not only be an imputation of income of stay-home spouses but also of costs involved in meeting the social obligation of child care.

[41] See p. 194.

[42] See p. 302.

used form, does the same for low-income taxpayers. As noted later, it may, in fact, be viewed as a vanishing exemption.[43]

The second reason is that most itemized deductions are of dubious merit and give rise to horizontal inequities. Making the percentage standard deduction available improves the position of taxpayers with low itemized deductions and thus offsets the gain which itemizers derive. The 1969 and 1975 increases in the standard deduction thus reduced the relative advantage gained by homeowners in the middle-income ranges. This, of course, is a second-best solution only. The better procedure would be to eliminate unjustified deduction items.

Conclusion

The principle of accretion may be stated without too much difficulty, but implementation is troublesome and the actual definitions of AGI and of taxable income fall far short of full implementation. In some instances, this reflects the technical difficulties which permit only approximation to the correct solution. In others, however, the deficiencies reflect policy intent of granting preferential treatment. But, though implementation is imperfect, it remains crucial that the specific issues of income definition, as they arise in practice, be measured against the yardstick of an income concept which provides a meaningful and consistent criterion of equity. In the absence of such a norm, technical issues of taxable income definition applicable to particular cases cannot be settled in a consistent and equitable fashion and the ever-present pressures for loophole snatching cannot be resisted.

E. SUMMARY

Among the basic features of the income tax law by which liabilities are determined, we have noted the following:

1. Adjusted gross income (AGI) minus deductions minus personal exemptions equals taxable income.

2. Deductions may be itemized or a standard deduction may be used, the latter involving a choice between the percentage deduction and the low-income allowance.

3. The tax is computed by applying bracket or marginal rates.

4. The term "effective rate" refers to the ratio of tax to AGI.

Regarding the size and structure of the tax base, our findings were these:

5. Total AGI amounts to about two-thirds of GNP. It differs from GNP by some items which are added in and others which are excluded.

6. The bulk of income tax returns and of taxable income fall in the income range from $5,000 to $20,000.

7. Wage income is most important for low-income brackets, and capital income for high-income brackets.

[43] See p. 274.

The ideal definition of AGI is given by a broad-based or accretion concept of income. However, numerous difficulties arise in implementing it:

8. Costs of doing business should be excluded in arriving at net income, but they are not always easily defined.

9. Under present practice, realized capital gains are partly excluded from the tax base, and unrealized gains are fully excluded. Fuller taxation of gains is desirable in principle, but various problems of implementation arise.

10. Certain forms of imputed income should be accounted for in the tax base.

11. Transfer income should be included in the tax base, with special problems arising in the treatment of social security and private pension plans.

12. Interest from state and local securities is excluded but should not be.

13. Losses should be adequately allowed for.

Having determined AGI, certain deductions are made in moving to taxable income:

14. Nearly two-thirds of all taxpayers use a standard deduction, with only one-third itemizing. However, the revenue cost of itemizing is much larger.

15. The extent to which various itemizable deductions may be justified differs. Among the most important items are state and local taxes, mortgage interest, and charitable contributions.

16. The granting of a standard deduction is difficult to justify in principle. However, it is an expedient way of reducing compliance and administrative cost and is used to give relief to low-income taxpayers.

FURTHER READINGS

See references at end of Chapter 11.

Chapter 11

Individual Income Tax: Preferences, Exemptions, and Rates*

A. The Significance of Tax Preferences: *Revenue Loss; Tax Expenditures; Implications for Equity; Minimum Tax.* **B. Personal Exemptions and Low-Income Allowance:** *What Is the Proper Level of Exemption? Effects of Exemptions on Progression; Alternatives to Exemptions.* **C. Family Unit:** *Present Practice; Evaluation.* **D. Rate Structure:** *Pattern of Progression; Maximum Rate; Averaging; Negative Income Tax; Inflation Effects.* **E. State and Local Income Taxes:** *State Income Taxes; Local Income Taxes.* **F. Appraisal of Income Tax. G. Summary. Appendix: Measuring Progression.**

A. THE SIGNIFICANCE OF TAX PREFERENCES

We have seen that the statutory definition of taxable income, after allowing for exclusions and deductions, is by no means identical with the theoretical concept of accretion. Substantial differences exist and, in most cases, result in a taxable income below that called for by the accretion concept. Tax preferences (the polite term for loopholes) arise from the exclusion of certain items which should be included and the deduction of others which should not be deducted. Both have important implications for revenue yield and equity. Since it is not always obvious

* *Reader's Guide to Chapter 11:* More on the structure and workings of the individual income tax, including the implications of tax preferences, definition of the taxable unit, and the rate structure, as well as the effects of inflation thereon.

what constitutes a "tax preference," careful evaluation of particular provisions is needed. The same applies with regard to a "tax penalty" which results where the definition of taxable income is too inclusive.

Revenue Loss

While it is debatable just which provisions constitute "tax preferences," it is evident that the revenue cost of existing preferences is very substantial. The major items and their revenue implications for 1974 are listed in Table 11-1.[1] The combined revenue loss for 1974 is estimated at about $58 billion for the individual income tax and $14 billion for the corporation income tax. With an actual yield of $131 billion for the individual income tax, this meant a loss of 30 percent from the potential yield of $189 billion. Or putting it differently, the same revenue could be obtained from the comprehensive base while cutting rates across the board by 30 percent. As shown in the table, the revenue losses from preferential treatment of capital gains,[2] homeowner preferences, deduction of state and local taxes and transfer payment exclusions are among the most important items. Corresponding losses for the corporation tax are somewhat less, amounting in all to 22 percent of the whole yield.

Tax Expenditures

Seen from a different perspective, tax preferences may be viewed as subsidy payments to preferred taxpayers. Such implicit payments have recently been referred to as "tax expenditures" and the recent Budget Act requires that they be listed in the budget.[3] To illustrate, there is no basic difference between making outright expenditures for a low-cost housing program and forgoing revenue because of accelerated depreciation on such housing. The objective in both cases is to increase the supply of low-cost housing. Exclusion of interest from state-local securities, similarly, gives a subsidy to state and local borrowing; deduction of mortgage interest subsidizes mortgage-financed house ownership; charitable deductions give a budgetary subsidy to churches and educational institutions, and so forth. In all these cases, an expenditure program (subsidy or matching grant) can be constructed which is equivalent to the tax device.

If we grant that these provisions are not needed to secure a better measure of taxable capacity, the basic issues are (1) whether the particular expenditure objective merits support and, if so, (2) whether this support is best given by tax

[1] The revenue gains from particular items should be interpreted as *net* gains. Thus, taxation of interest from state and local securities might result in reduced investment in such securities, so that the gain (as measured on the new base) would be less than shown on the table. At the same time, such investment might be shifted into other taxable issues, raising revenue at that point. The amounts shown should be interpreted as the net effect of tax law changes designed to repeal such preferences.

[2] The estimated revenue loss due to only partial taxation of capital gains, as shown in the table, does not include that due to nontaxation of unrealized gains. The latter is an uncertain amount and may be substantially larger than that shown for realized gains. Thus, it has been estimated by Martin Bailey that taxation of unrealized gains might yield as much as or more than realized gains. See M. J. Bailey, "Capital Gains and Income Taxation," in A. C. Harberger and M. J. Bailey (eds.), *The Taxation of Income from Capital,* Washington: Brookings, 1969.

[3] See Stanley S. Surrey, *Pathways to Tax Reform,* Cambridge, Mass.: Harvard, 1973.

TABLE 11-1
Estimated Revenue Gain from Removal of Major Tax Preferences
(1974, In Billions of Dollars)

	Corporations	*Individuals*
1. Present revenue	49.1	131.2
2. Revenue gain from preference removal	14.1	57.5
3. One-half realized capital gains	0.7	6.2
4. State and local interest	2.8	1.1
5. Depletion	1.8	0.3
6. Investment credit, depreciation, DISC, etc.	6.0	1.6
7. Charitable contributions	0.4	4.2
8. Employer's medical contributions	—	2.9
9. Life insurance interest	—	1.4
10. Homeowner preferences	—	10.4
11. Medical expenses	—	2.1
12. Interest on consumer credit	—	2.4
13. State gasoline taxes	—	0.9
14. Other state and local taxes	—	7.0
15. Over–sixty-five exemption	—	1.2
16. Transfer payments and insurance benefits	—	12.0
17. Other	2.4	3.8
18. Revenue after adjustment	63.2	188.7

Notes:

Item 2: This total differs from that given in the Budget Analysis in that we do not include the corporate surtax exemption or the excess of percentage standard deduction over the minimum standard deduction; the revenue cost of homeowner preferences shown here also differs from that given in the Budget Analysis (see item 10 below).

Item 5: Largely eliminated under the Tax Reduction Act of 1975.

Item 6: Includes depreciation in excess of straight-line, deferral of tax on income of domestic international sales corporations, certain foreign income preferences, and expensing of R&D.

Item 7: Includes contributions to educational institutions.

Item 8: Includes exclusion of employer contributions to medical insurance premiums and medical care.

Item 9: Includes exclusion of interest on life insurance savings.

Item 10: Includes exclusion of imputed rental income of owner-occupied housing after deduction of depreciation; this figure differs somewhat from that given in the Budget Analysis which is based on the deduction of mortgage interest and property taxes on owner-occupied homes.

Item 13: Includes deduction of nonbusiness gasoline taxes.

Item 14: Includes deduction of nonbusiness state and local taxes (other than on owner-occupied homes and gasoline).

Item 16: Includes exclusion of social security benefits, railroad retirement, unemployment insurance, workmen's compensation and public assistance benefits, net exclusion of pension contributions and other employee benefits, and veterans benefits and services.

Source: Based on *Special Analyses, Budget of the United States, Fiscal Year 1976,* Washington, D.C.: U.S. Government Printing Office, pp. 108–109, with modifications as noted above. See also J. A. Pechman and B. A. Okner, "Individual Income Tax Erosion by Income Classes," table 3, in *The Economics of Federal Subsidy Programs,* part 1, Joint Economic Committee of the U.S. Congress, May 8, 1972.

relief or by outright subsidies. Point 1 should not be viewed as an issue in tax policy, but as a general matter of setting budget priorities. Even if the tax relief route is to be used, efficient program planning requires that the policy objectives be faced explicitly; and program budgeting calls for the inclusion of such outlays under their respective program headings. Chances are that expenditure planning will be more efficient if subsidy programs are voted on by the relevant appropriation committees rather than by the tax committees which have no particular expertise in specific expenditure areas and which should concentrate on designing an equitable tax system.

The revenue cost of tax expenditures, as given in the 1976 budget, provides for a functional grouping showing which program areas derive the benefits.[4] While these classifications are quite problematical, the most important items are shown to be "personal investment" defined to include homeowner benefits; "income security" defined to include preferential treatment of transfer payments; "state and local governments" defined to include interest exclusion and deduction of taxes; "international affairs" defined to include preferential treatment of foreign investment income; and "business investment" defined to include the investment credit, excess depreciation, and so forth. Although these classifications may be questioned in detail, they point to the crucial question of just what expenditure programs are in fact reflected in the granting of tax preferences.

Implications for Equity

The existence of preferences would be of little concern if base reductions due to tax preferences were a fixed proportion of the "full" base for all taxpayers. In this event, they could be readily neutralized by correspondingly higher rates. But in fact, the incidence of preferences varies widely. Preferences are important, not so much because they narrow the base and reduce tax yield with given rates—as is sometimes suggested—but because they are distributed unequally and thereby affect the distribution of liabilities.

Preferences cause the distribution of liabilities to differ from that intended by the pattern of tax rates, with resulting horizontal and vertical inequities. While the equity implications of the major preferences listed in Table 11-1 have already been dealt with in principle in Chapter 10, their joint impact on vertical and horizontal equity of the United States income tax is here considered in quantitative terms.

Vertical Equity The various preference items listed in Table 11-1 differ in their implications for vertical equity. For instance, tax savings from preferential treatment of capital gains and state-local interest (items 3 and 4) accrue primarily to the upper-income groups, of home ownership and life insurance interest (items 10 and 9) to the middle ranges, and that of transfer payments (item 16) pertains mostly to taxpayers in the lower brackets. The net effect on the progressivity of the tax structure thus depends on the weight of the various provisions and on just what is included as a preference.

Table 11-2, column 2, shows the existing pattern of progression under the income tax. It gives the effective rate of tax, i.e., the ratio of actual tax liabilities to AGI, the latter adjusted to include certain preference items.[5] We note that the tax is sharply progressive over the lower-middle range, but that the increase

[4] See *Special Analyses, Budget of the United States Government, Fiscal Year 1976,* op. cit.

[5] AGI is expanded to include income items which were previously excluded. Thus, the adjustment is reflected in the denominator as well as the numerator of the effective rate ratio. The expanded concept is also used in defining bracket limits in column 1. The pattern of effective rates shown here thus differs somewhat from that of Table 10-2, column 5, where AGI is used in the denominator.

TABLE 11-2
Effects of Tax-Base Erosion on Average Rates of Tax
(1972 Income Levels)

Selected Brackets of Expanded AGI (In Thousands of Dollars) (1)	AS PERCENTAGE OF EXPANDED AGI									Tax Savings as Percentage of Full Tax (Col. 8 as Percent of Col. 9) (10)
	Actual Tax (2)	TAX SAVINGS						Full Tax (Col. 2 plus Col. 8) (9)		
		Capital Gains (3)	Other Exclusions and Preference Income (4)	Home-owners (5)	Other Deduc-tions (6)	Transfer Payments (7)	Total (8)			
2– 3	0.5	—	—	0.1	—	0.3	0.4	0.9		44
5– 6	2.8	0.1	—	0.2	—	3.0	3.3	6.1		54
10– 11	7.6	0.1	0.2	0.7	1.7	1.8	4.5	12.1		35
17– 20	11.1	0.4	0.4	0.9	1.5	1.2	4.4	15.5		28
25– 50	14.5	1.7	0.7	1.8	1.7	1.3	7.2	21.7		33
50– 75	22.1	5.3	0.9	1.8	2.0	0.4	10.4	32.5		32
75– 100	26.8	6.9	1.0	1.6	2.2	0.1	11.8	38.6		31
100– 200	29.4	10.9	2.6	1.2	2.1	—	18.8	48.2		39
200– 500	29.6	18.3	3.3	0.9	1.9	—	24.4	54.0		45
500–1,000	30.4	22.8	3.3	0.6	1.6	—	28.3	58.7		48
1,000 and over	32.1	26.9	2.1	0.2	1.1	—	31.3	63.4		49
All brackets	5.8	1.5	0.6	1.0	1.2	1.5	4.3	10.1		43

Notes:

Column 1: AGI raised to include preference income rendered taxable under columns 3 to 7.

Column 2: Liability under 1971 Revenue Act for 1972 income year.

Column 3: Additional liability due to full taxation of gains when realized and at death or transfer.

Column 4: Additional liability due to taxation of interest on state-local bonds; disallowing excess of percentage over cost depletion and excess of accelerated over straight-line depreciation; removal of dividend exclusion; taxation of life insurance interest.

Column 5: Includes effect of disallowing personal deduction for mortgage interest and real estate taxes and taxing *net* imputed rent.

Column 6: Increased liability due to eliminating percentage standard deduction; curtailing itemized deductions other than those for homeowner interest allowed for under column 5; eliminating additional exemptions for aged and blind; eliminating retirement income credit.

Column 7: Increased liability due to inclusion of all transfer payments. If OASI is viewed as a contributory scheme, this amount should be reduced to allow for tax-free recovery of contributions.

Source: Based on table A-5 in J. A. Pechman and B. A. Okner, "Individual Income Tax Erosion by Income Classes," in *The Economics of Federal Subsidy Programs,* A. Compendium of Papers, Joint Economic Committee, U.S. Congress, 1972.

in the effective rate flattens out at higher income levels.[6] This, of course, is bound to be the pattern since, as we have noted earlier, the average rate tends to approach (though not reach) the top-bracket rate. However, it is surprising to note that the effective rate flattens out at slightly above 30 percent, which is much below the top marginal rate (on unearned income) of 70 percent. The explanation for this is to be found in the role of tax preferences.

In columns 3 to 7, we show the ratio of additional tax to income which would result if various preference provisions were removed. Column 3 gives the incremental rate due to full taxation of capital gains. Note that the increase is slight at the lower, and very substantial at the upper, end of the scale. In fact, at the top it accounts for nearly the entire increase in liabilities which would result from full taxation. Column 4 shows the additional liability due to inclusion of certain items, such as state and local interest, life insurance interest, and the first $100 of dividends which are presently excluded, as well as the repeal of accelerated depreciation. The major increase is again at the upper end of the scale, but its weight is slight relative to that of the capital gains preference. The next item, shown in column 5, gives the incremental burden from removing preferences now enjoyed by the homeowner, i.e., taxation of net imputed rent or of gross rent minus mortgage interest and property tax. Here a substantial increase in tax results for the middle-income range. The same holds for the next item (column 6), which shows what would happen if most itemized deductions and the percentage standard deduction were removed. The pattern is similar to that of the preceding column. Column 7, finally, shows the incremental liability which would ensue if all transfer payments were included. Note that this would result in a substantial increase in liabilities at the low end of the scale. However, as noted before, inclusion of OASI benefits would not be appropriate unless accompanied by deduction of the employee's social security contribution.

The additional tax ratios are aggregated in column 8. By adding them to the actual tax ratio (column 2) we obtain the hypothetical full-tax ratio shown in column 9. In column 10, we show the tax savings due to preferences as a percentage of the full tax. We find that these savings are relatively high at the bottom and top ends of the income scale but comprise a rather constant percentage of full tax over a broad middle and upper range from, say, $10,000 to $100,000 of AGI. Over this range, into which most taxpayers fall, the existence of preferences thus results in a more or less proportional tax reduction and hence does not carry great significance with regard to vertical equity. Nevertheless, preferences, as we shall see presently, are important in their bearing on horizontal equity, or the burden distribution *within* given AGI brackets.

Horizontal Equity The effects of tax preferences on horizontal equity are shown in Table 11-3. The table shows the percentage of returns in various AGI brackets which are subject to various average rates of tax.[7] We find that prefer-

[6] Various measures of progression are discussed in the appendix to this chapter.

[7] The rates are based on liabilities applicable to 1969 income, i.e., prior to the changes provided for by the 1969 and 1971 legislation. However, the picture would not be greatly changed if the study were repeated for current liabilities. The income concept used in the denominator equals AGI expanded to include 100 percent of realized gains as well as certain other preference income.

TABLE 11-3
Percentage of Returns Subject to Various Rate Levels, 1969

Average Tax Rates (Percentage)*	ADJUSTED GROSS INCOME (Thousands of Dollars)					
	$5–7	*$10–15*	*$15–20*	*$50–100*	*$500–1,000*	*$1,000+*
0–10	6	1	1	1	2	4
10–20	94	92	77	6	1	†
20–30	—	7	22	34	54	58
30–40	—	—	—	53	10	7
40–50	—	—	—	6	6	6
50–60	—	—	—	—	13	5
60–70	—	—	—	—	14	20
Total	100	100	100	100	100	100

* Liabilities applicable to 1969 income as a percentage of taxable income broadened to include excluded realized capital gains, excluded state and local interest, and depletion in excess of cost.

† Less than 0.5.

Source: Based on *Tax Reform Studies and Proposals,* part 1, U.S. Treasury Department, Joint Publication, Committee on Ways and Means and Committee on Finance, Feb. 5, 1969, p. 77.

ences result in a wide dispersion of average rates applicable at similar AGI levels. Moreover, the spread widens as we move up the income scale. Fifty-four percent of taxpayers in the $500,000 to $1 million bracket paid between 20 and 30 percent, 13 percent paid between 50 and 60 percent, and 14 percent paid over 60 percent. There is even greater dispersion of rates above the $1 million level, with 4 percent of taxpayers paying less than 10 percent, among whom were some who paid nothing. At the same time, 20 percent (who received income from taxable sources and had lower deductions) paid 60 percent or more.[8] It is thus evident that the income tax involves a high degree of horizontal inequity and especially at high-income levels.

Conclusion The conclusions to be drawn from this brief survey are that preferences have had these effects:

1. They have resulted in a substantial revenue loss, such that adoption of a full base would permit an average rate reduction by one-third or more while holding revenue constant.

2. They have given rise to substantial horizontal inequities over the entire scale, but mostly at the upper end.

3. With regard to vertical equity, they have resulted in sharp reductions in liabilities at both ends of the income scale, with more or less constant proportional reduction over a wide middle range.

Adoption of a broader base would thus permit improvement in horizontal equity as well as a reduction in bracket rates over the entire scale. At the lower end, it may be expected that substantial rate reductions would be applied to offset the

[8] Note also that the fraction of taxpayers paying over 30 percent actually declines as we move above the $500,000 to $1 million level.

increase in liabilities which would otherwise result from expansion of base. Few would wish to raise upper-end liabilities to levels resulting from application of present bracket rates to a full income base. But some increase in liabilities would remain even if the top marginal rate on full income were reduced to, say, 50 percent. Over the middle range, rate reductions of 10 to 15 percent would be possible to offset base expansion, the major result being a redistribution of liabilities between homeowners and others. In all, the gain would be primarily in improved horizontal equity and lessened distorting effects on taxpayer behavior. From the point of view of vertical equity, the major gain would be in the curtailment of tax avoidance in the high-income ranges.

Minimum Tax

The preceding survey of exclusions and deductions makes it amply evident that deficiencies in the definition of taxable income lead to a substantial difference between the apparent and the actual level of tax rates. The efforts of tax reformers over the last 30 years at improving the tax base by plugging specific loopholes (or eliminating specific preferences) have not been very successful. While students of taxation are widely agreed that it would be desirable to trade reduced rates for a fuller tax base, not much has been accomplished to date. This lack of progress had led to the view that reform might be achieved more effectively by certain general approaches to preference limitation, second-best though they may be in nature, than via item-by-item reform.

The minimum tax introduced by the Tax Reform Act of 1969 was such an innovation. This provision is designed to assure that at least some tax is paid by people who benefit heavily from the variety of available tax preferences, especially capital gains. To determine the minimum tax, the taxpayer must compute his so-called preference income. Preference income includes the excluded half of long-term capital gains, depletion in excess of cost, accelerated depreciation allowances, and certain other items, with interest on state and local securities notably absent. Preference income is then reduced by the ordinary tax plus $30,000, and a 10 percent rate is imposed on the remainder. The resulting "minimum tax" on preference income is then paid in addition to the regular tax.[9]

Although the minimum tax as enacted in 1969 accomplished but little, it suggests an interesting new approach. Whereas the efforts of tax reformers have been directed traditionally and not very successfully at removing preferences one by one, this approach discarded such specific efforts in favor of a cruder, but perhaps eventually more effective, strategy.

Prorating of Deductions Also to be noted in this category is the proposal (advanced in 1969 but not enacted) to "prorate" deductions between AGI and preference income (i.e., income excluded from AGI), with only the former share

[9] A more ambitious plan for an alternative tax was passed by the House in 1969 but rejected in the Senate. Under this plan, the taxpayer would have paid the larger of (1) the tax as computed on taxable income ordinarily defined, and (2) a tax computed at half rates on taxable income increased to include preference income. This would have disallowed preferences in excess of one-half of total (taxable plus preference) income.

allowed for deduction. Consider a taxpayer with an AGI of $100,000, including $60,000 of capital gains and $40,000 of salary income, who also obtains tax-exempt interest of $40,000. His taxable AGI of $100,000 then compares with a total (or "economic") income of $200,000. Suppose his deductions are $30,000. He would then be permitted to deduct only 50 percent, or $15,000, from his AGI of $100,000. Although this approach is somewhat unsatisfactory in that it uses disallowance of deductions as a correction for unjustified exclusions, it nevertheless offers a form of base correction which, though second-best, serves to compensate to some degree for base erosion.

B. PERSONAL EXEMPTIONS AND LOW-INCOME ALLOWANCE

Personal exemptions now equal $750 each for the taxpayer, the spouse, and their dependents. Their role is to set the point in the income scale where tax liability begins, but beyond this they are an important factor in determining the progressivity of the effective rate schedule over the lower-middle range. Moreover, the level of income at which a positive tax liability begins is affected by a number of other provisions, including the $30 credit per exemption and the earned-income credit.

What Is the Proper Level of Exemption?

One reason for leaving a minimum amount of income tax-free is that an initial slice of income needed for subsistence should not be taxed. Taxable income should be defined as AGI minus this basic allowance, to be granted independent of income. Another view is that people with inadequate ability to pay should not be taxed. To accomplish this, there is no need to grant a similar allowance to higher incomes. In either case, the so-called poverty line might be used as a level above which tax payment begins, but the former approach calls for the granting of such an allowance to all taxpayers, while the latter calls for it to vanish as income rises. As we shall see later, the present system (which combines a personal exemption with a low-income allowance and a tax credit) is a mixture of the two.

Since the poverty line differs with size of family, the level at which tax begins should vary accordingly. Combining the exemption of $750 per person with the low-income allowance, the earned-income tax credit and the $30 exemption credit, the relationship among family size, tax-free income, and poverty line is shown in Table 11-4.

As may be seen from Table 11-4, the minimum income at which a positive tax begins to apply increases with family size. For taxpayers with dependents, moreover, it is substantially higher for returns with earned as against unearned income. This reflects the earned-income credit provided for in the Tax Reduction Act, which applies to returns with dependents only. As can also be seen from the table, the tax-free limit was set substantially above the 1975 poverty line.

A good case can be made for setting the tax-free limit at a reasonably high level, but there is an important caveat: Nothing is gained if low-income groups are exempt from income tax, but the revenue loss is made up by relying on excise

Table 11-4
Levels of Tax-Free Income
(Applicable to 1975 Income, in Dollars)

Taxpaying Unit	*Level of AGI above Which Tax Liability Becomes Positive*		*Poverty Income**
	Earned Income	*Unearned Income*	
Single	2,564	2,564	2,694
Married	3,828	3,828	3,470
Married, one dependent	6,090 †	4,793	4,253
Married, two dependents	6,660 †	5,757	5,442
Married, four dependents	7,800 †	7,667	7,226

* Department of Health, Education, and Welfare.
† AGI levels below which refund is due.

and other taxes which burden them more heavily. Such taxes are frequently regressive at the lower end of the scale, whereas the income tax is highly progressive. The effective rate on AGI just above the exemption level is low, simply because exemptions are a large fraction of AGI. To the extent that low incomes are to be taxed, the income tax is therefore the best device. Prior to excluding low-income groups from the income tax, the regressive burden imposed by other taxes should be removed.

Effects of Exemptions on Progression

Exemptions are important in determining who should not pay tax, but they are also a significant factor in determining the amount of tax payable by people whose income exceeds the exemption and who are thus subject to tax. For them, exemptions act as a zero-rate bracket covering an initial slab of their income and are thus an integral part of the rate structure. By exempting $3,000 (joint return, two dependents) we in fact set a zero rate for the bracket from zero to $3,000. Instead of saying that a 14 percent rate applies to the first $1,000 of taxable income after exemptions, we may say that a zero rate applies to the first $3,000 of net income before exemptions, a 14 percent rate to the $3,000 to $4,000 bracket, and so forth.

Since the value of exemptions as a fraction of AGI declines when moving up the income scale, they result in a sharply rising effective rate (ratio of tax to AGI) over the $3,000 to $10,000 income range. They are the major factor behind the rising average rate curve (see Table 10-2, column 5) over the lower part of the income range. In fact, the rise in bracket rates does not become a major factor until a much higher income is reached. Over an income range up to, say, $10,000, progression in the average rate (ratio of tax to AGI) is dominated by the role of exemptions and the low-income allowance and not by rising bracket rates.[10]

[10] Under actual bracket rates, the effective rate (ratio of tax to AGI) rises from 0.3 percent at an AGI of $4,000 to 9.1 percent at an AGI of $10,000. Assuming a flat 14 percent rate, the ratios would be 0.3 percent and 7.7 percent, respectively, for a family of four.

Alternatives to Exemptions

The exemption device as now applied is appropriate if the intent is to exclude a cost-of-living allowance from AGI and to do so for all taxpayers. But difficulties arise if exemptions are viewed as an instrument of lower-end progression. In this case the double role of exemptions, in (1) determining the level of income below which no tax is due, and (2) determining tax liabilities above that level, has a disadvantage. If exemptions are raised in order to increase the tax-free limit, this increase implies a heavy revenue cost as it will reduce liabilities for all taxpayers and not only for the lowest group. Thus the present exemption of $750 per person reduces taxable income (taxable returns) by about $160 billion at a revenue cost of $35 billion. Raising exemptions by $50 reduces tax revenue by an additional $3.5 billion (1974 levels).[11] Raising exemptions is thus costly in terms of lost revenue. Moreover, as noted previously in connection with deductions, tax savings in dollar terms will rise with bracket rates and hence with income. This increase is in line with the subsistence-cost interpretation of exemptions but not with the taxable-capacity view. This suggests the use of alternative techniques which will permit adjustment in the level of tax-free income without affecting the liabilities (at given bracket rates) in the higher-income brackets.

Credit in Lieu of Exemption The Tax Reduction Act of 1975 introduces such a technique in the form of a tax credit of $30 per exemption claimed and in addition thereto. This amount is permitted as a credit against tax rather than as a deduction from taxable income. By permitting a credit of $30 per taxpayer and per dependent, the value of the credit (in terms of tax saving) becomes independent of the taxpayer's income. It differs in this respect from the exemption itself. The tax saving from exemptions for a family of four in the 14 percent bracket is $420, while a family of four in the 60 percent bracket gains $1,800. With the credit against tax used instead, all families are given the same dollar benefit. The credit technique could be expanded to replace the entire exemption system. With the average exemption dollar now benefiting at a marginal rate of about 25 percent, the $750 exemption per person could be replaced by a credit of $185 while holding revenue constant. This would raise the benefit for a low-income family of four from $420 to $740 while reducing that of a family in the 60 percent bracket from $1,800 to $740.

Low-Income Allowance The low-income allowance, though offered as an alternative to the percentage standard deduction, also fits into this pattern. It is, in fact, a supplementary exemption which vanishes as income rises. While it raises the level of AGI at which tax liability begins by $1,600 and $1,900 for a single and joint return respectively, the extra exemption gained declines with AGI. Since the taxpayer (joint return) may deduct either $1,900 or 16 percent of AGI under the percentage standard deduction, the extra exemption under the low-income allowance equals $1,900 minus 16 percent of AGI. Thus, a taxpayer with an AGI of $4,000 is given an extra exemption of $1,260; with an AGI of $6,000,

[11] The cost of successive increases in exemptions is less because of slippage, as lower-income taxpayers cannot use the entire addition when it exceeds their income.

TABLE 11-5
Positive and Negative Taxes on Earned Income
(In Dollars)

AGI	*Single (I)*	*Joint (II)*	*Joint, Two Dependents (III)*	*Joint, Four Dependents (IV)*
2,000	—	—	−200	−200
3,000	63	—	−300	−300
4,000	220	24	−400	−400
5,000	403	170	−300	−300
6,000	593	326	−165	−200
7,000	796	492	86	−100
8,000	1,006	674	347	50
9,000	1,230	864	519	206
10,000	1,452	1,054	709	372

Notes:
Col. I: Tax begins at AGI of $2,564.
Col. II: Tax begins at AGI of $3,828.
Col. III: Tax begins at AGI of $6,660.
Col. IV: Tax begins at AGI of $7,800.

the extra exemption falls to $940; and with an AGI of $11,875, it vanishes altogether. Because of this feature, the low-income allowance has been a most efficient device for giving tax relief to low-bracket taxpayers at a minimum cost since the entire relief accrues to this group. Thus the total revenue loss from the low-income allowance is less than $5 billion (1975 levels), although it gives a much higher extra exemption to most low-income taxpayers than would an equal-cost increase in present personal exemptions of around $150.

Earned-Income Tax Credit A major change in the treatment of low incomes was made in the form of the earned-income tax credit. Introduced in the Tax Reduction Act of 1975, this credit applies to earned income only with capital income excluded. Equal to 10 percent of earned income up to $4,000, the credit is reduced as AGI comes to exceed $4,000 and is wiped out at an AGI of $8,000.[12] The credit applies only to returns with dependents and, most important, is refundable in the form of a "negative tax," to the extent that it is in excess of the tax liability.

As shown in Table 11-5, the earned-income credit (together with the other provisions affecting low-income liabilities) results in a complex pattern. Returns with dependents and earned income fare much better than do others, since they enjoy a refund at the lower end as well as a substantially higher level of AGI at which positive tax liabilities apply. By providing for refunds, an important step toward introduction of a "negative income tax" has been taken; but, as noted below, the form in which this has been done is rather different.

[12] While unearned income is not subject to credit, total AGI (including unearned income) is counted for purposes of credit diminution as AGI exceeds $4,000. The maximum credit of $400 is reduced by 10 percent of the excess of AGI over $4,000 of earnings, thus disappearing at an AGI of $8,000.

C. FAMILY UNIT

With a single progressive rate structure, resulting liabilities will differ greatly, depending on how the taxpaying unit is defined, i.e., whether each earner is to be taxed singly or whether family incomes should be combined. The more comprehensive the combination is, the higher will be the tax liability of the unit if the same rate schedule is applied to the more comprehensive unit.

Present Practice

Prior to 1969, both single and married taxpayers paid according to the same rate schedule, but the latter were permitted to split their income, thus paying twice the tax applicable to one-half of their joint income, rather than a single tax on the total income. As a result, the tax paid by a single taxpayer was much higher than that paid by a couple with the same combined income. Such tax savings reached 30 percent of tax liability at a taxable income of $28,000, the relative tax advantage declining for lower and higher income levels. A bachelor earning $28,000 could reduce his tax liability from $10,000 to $7,100 upon marriage, an Internal Revenue dowry of $2,900 per annum.

The tax benefit of marriage (or cost of being single) has been narrowed and evened out under the Tax Reform Act of 1969. Under this act, income splitting was effectively abolished and different rate schedules were applied for single individuals and for spouses opting to file joint returns. Liabilities on single returns are now about 20 percent above those on joint returns for the larger part of the income range.[13] A bachelor earning $28,000 now finds his tax reduced from $8,490 to $7,470 upon marriage, the IRS dowry having been cut to $1,020 per annum. Is this too little or too much, and on what criteria is our judgment to be based?

Evaluation

In defining the taxpaying unit, two views may be taken. One is to hold that each person should pay tax on whatever income he or she earns. The other is that in order to measure taxpaying capacity, the incomes earned by various members of a family or spending unit should be pooled. Results under the two approaches will differ since, under a progressive rate schedule, the tax rate is higher if incomes are pooled.

Neither approach is easy to implement. Under the earnings approach, wage and salary earnings may be readily linked to a particular person, but difficulties arise with regard to capital income. Property may be distributed among various members of the family so as to spread out its income and thus incur a lower tax. Under the family-unit approach, there is the problem of how the unit should be defined. The prevailing definition includes taxpayer, spouse, and dependents, but it is not obvious just who is a dependent,[14] and an argument may be made for

[13] The Tax Reform Act of 1969 also provided two further schedules, applicable to heads of family and married taxpayers filing single returns respectively.

[14] Students may be claimed as dependents by their parents as long as they provide over half their support, independent of the student's own earnings.

including other earning members of the family unit.[15] Viewed from an equity point of view, the family-unit approach seems more meaningful, since the family's standard of living (and its ability to pay) will depend upon the joint income.

The key issues relate to the treatment of single as against married taxpayers, and the treatment of single-earner as against multiple-earner units. To bring out these problems, consider the following three situations:

1. Mr. A is single and earns $30,000.
2. Mr. B is married and earns $30,000, while Mrs. B has no income.
3. Mr. C is married and earns $15,000, while Mrs. C also earns $15,000.

Question 1 is whether the same tax should be paid by A and the B's. The answer is "no." The B's should pay less since a family receiving a joint income of a given amount has less ability to pay than a single person receiving the same amount. How much their liabilities differ should depend upon the differential in living costs, to be allowed for in the corresponding levels of exemptions or credits. Clearly, this cost adjustment does not justify the much larger benefits of income splitting. Question 2 is whether B and C should pay the same. Viewed as a matter of property rights, one might argue that Mr. and Mrs. C should each pay on *their* respective incomes. Under a progressive rate schedule, they would therefore pay less than the B household. But, as noted before, this makes little sense in the ability-to-pay context. For tax purposes, the C's constitute a family unit, as do the B's. Since costs are the same for both, they should pay the same tax, but less than A.

In order to have the B's and C's pay the same but somewhat less than A, the proper solution is to grant higher *exemptions* (to adjust for living costs) on married than on single returns,[16] combined with *mandatory joint returns* and (contrary to the present law) a *uniform rate schedule.* Such a solution encounters the objection that marriage between the C's would be discouraged since their combined tax liability (due largely to a shift into higher rate brackets) would be increased substantially. They would gain by joining without benefit of marriage while continuing to file single returns. A solution which is in line with ability-to-pay considerations thus appears to conflict with social values regarding marriage. Since the rate differentials between the single- and joint-return schedules are modest, the present approach offers a more or less reasonable compromise.[17]

[15] For a proposal to define taxable income as the joint incomes of the comprehensive family unit, see *Report of the Royal Commission on Taxation,* vol. 3, *Taxation of Income,* Ottawa: Queen's Printer, 1966, chap. 4.

[16] How much higher they should be (i.e., whether doubling is the appropriate rule) will not be considered here.

[17] However, permitting earning spouses to file single returns gives the C's preferential treatment. There is no marriage deterrent, but their liability is less than it would be if ability to pay is viewed in terms of the family unit. Moreover, there remains some advantage for capital income since this may be split between spouses filing single returns. A partial solution might be to require mandatory joint returns where capital income is of predominant importance.

D. RATE STRUCTURE

Given the definition of taxable income, setting the bracket rates is the instrument by which the desired distribution of tax liabilities (or pattern of average rates) is to be implemented.

Pattern of Progression

As we have seen in our earlier discussion of distributive justice and equal sacrifice, no absolute statement about the desirable degree of rate progression can be made. While the economic effects of alternative patterns must be examined and allowed for, the final answer is essentially one of social value judgment.[18] However, the following points may be noted:

1. The present system, under which some income recipients are subject to high marginal rates while others (with the same total income) pay much less, is unsatisfactory and in urgent need of revision. The principle should be that of defining taxable income comprehensively, taxing it globally at uniform rates, and then limiting bracket rates to such level as is considered appropriate and enforceable. This, clearly, would be much superior to the past practice of enacting highly progressive bracket rates which are then made ineffective by a deficient income definition.

2. Even high marginal rates, so long as they fall short of 100 percent, leave taxpayers better off as they move into a higher rate bracket. Yet the net return on additional work effort or risk taking is reduced. As we shall see later, it is this marginal-rate effect which constitutes a potential disincentive to effort and which imposes an "excess burden."[19] These considerations, as well as equity aspects, must be allowed for in setting progression. Unfortunately, average rates cannot be made to rise without bracket or marginal rates being in excess of average rates. A design to obtain substantial progression without accepting the disturbing effects of high bracket rates is an illusion. The two are linked by the simple mathematics of average and marginal rates. The average rate pattern shown in Table 10-1 cannot be obtained without the corresponding pattern of marginal rates.

3. Similar considerations apply to the extension of the income tax into a refund or negative tax range. As we shall see later, a declining average rate of negative tax is equivalent to a positive marginal rate of tax.[20]

Maximum Rate

While we have seen that top-bracket rates applicable to very high incomes carry little revenue importance, they involve major issues of social policy. Although the maximum rate on capital income continues at 70 percent, the Tax Reform Act of 1969 limited the maximum bracket rate on "earned" (i.e., wage, salary, and professional) income to 50 percent.[21] In joint returns, this benefits recipients

[18] Even the recent discussion of "optimal taxation" cannot avoid this judgment in arriving at the optimal tax schedule. See p. 471.

[19] See p. 471.

[20] See p. 676.

[21] The effect of the procedure is to tax earned income at a maximum rate of 50 percent while taxing unearned income at the bracket rates which would apply if all income were unearned. For details, see Individual Income Tax Return, Form 1040.

of earned income whose taxable income (from all sources) exceeds $52,000. Preferential treatment of "earned" as against "unearned" income has a long history, but, as we have seen before, the preference has traditionally been concentrated at the lower end of the income scale where it has served as a form of low-income relief. Applying the preference at the upper end has to be defended as an offset to preferences given to capital income or by incentive considerations.

Averaging

As noted before, the application of progressive rates to annual income discriminates against the taxpayer whose income fluctuates. To reduce this effect, the law permits some degree of averaging. The taxpayer may average such part of his or her income as exceeds 120 percent of average income for the four preceding years. Averageable income, to be eligible, must be at least $3,000, and net long-term capital gains may be included. The procedure is to add averageable income for the past four years to the current year's income and to compute the tax liability on one-fifth thereof.[22]

This procedure has the advantage that it does not involve adjustments of prior years' returns. It provides relief only where current income exceeds past income, but not where current income falls short of past income. In principle, averaging for income decline is equally justified. While averaging is most important at high-income levels (where, under the progressive rate structure, the spread in applicable rates is widest), it is not without importance for low-income taxpayers, where a temporary decline in income may permit less than full utilization of exemptions. Since the rate spread between taxable and exempt income is substantial (i.e., 14 percentage points,) a similar averaging provision allowing the recapture of unused exemptions would be helpful. However, the number of returns involved, and hence the administrative cost, would be much larger.

There remains the basic question of how long the averaging period should be. If extended to the limit, the averaging rule might apply to lifetime income. This would not be practicable, but if correct in principle, it would suggest that the longest feasible averaging period should be chosen.

Negative Income Tax

While the case for a "negative income tax" will be considered more fully later on,[23] brief reference should be made to it here since it is among the most important new ideas in the taxation of low incomes. As was shown in Table 10-2, column V, the effective rate of income tax is zero until a certain income is reached and then becomes positive. For a joint return (without dependents) this happens at an AGI of $3,828. This involves an implausible discontinuity. If it is proper for the effective rate to rise from $3,828 up to higher-income levels because taxable capacity increases, it should also be proper to apply differential treatment over the zero to $3,828 range. This calls for a falling subsidy rate (or negative rate of tax) over this income range. The income tax then becomes a tax-transfer

[22] For an explanation of the averaging procedure, see Individual Income Tax Return, Form 1040.

[23] See p. 678.

plan, where the \$3,828 level is merely the break-even point. Setting the break-even point takes the place of determining the exemption level. As was shown in Table 11-5, the refundability feature of the earned-income credit has resulted in the introduction of what in effect amounts to a negative income tax. However, that feature applies to earned income only and is limited to returns with dependents. Neither of these limitations would seem appropriate under a more direct approach to the negative income tax problem.[24]

Inflation Effects

A novel aspect of the income tax problem has arisen in recent years, because of the impact of inflation. As prices rise in the course of inflation, so does the level of money incomes. For families whose money income rises at the same rate as prices, real income remains unchanged. If the income tax were imposed at a proportional rate, there would also be no change in the real value of their after-tax income.[25] Under a progressive tax, however, the situation differs because the tax rate rises with money income. Thus, a household with constant real income finds itself sliding up the rate brackets and must pay a higher tax. This is an arbitrary and unintended tax increase, the magnitude of which depends on the slope of the effective rate schedule over the range of money income increase. If rate brackets were related to real income rather than to money income, this increase would not occur, since the tax rate applicable at a given level of money income would be reduced so as to hold constant for any given level of real income. An analogous situation applies to a family whose money income remains constant and whose real income therefore falls with inflation. For such a family, its tax in money terms remains unchanged even though its real income falls. With an appropriate adjustment, the tax in money terms would decline in proportion to the decline in real income.

The two cases are illustrated in Table 11-6 for the period from 1969 to 1974, with incomes assumed to rise in line with prices in the upper part of the table, and to remain unchanged in the lower part. It will be seen from line 7 that failure to adjust rate brackets is especially burdensome for low-income families and at the \$50,000 range. It is here that the slope of the effective rate schedule rises most sharply, so that the inflation-induced upward slide in bracket rates is sharpest.

To avoid this arbitrary rate change due to inflation, various countries are now giving consideration to linking bracket limits to price change. This approach has been used for some time in various Latin American countries where much sharper inflation rates have been experienced. Canada has recently introduced such legislation, and it is also being considered in some Western European countries. As we shall see later, there is some question whether such an adjustment

[24] The legislative intent was not to provide a negative income tax but rather to give a wage subsidy to low-income workers with dependents so as to correct for their exclusion from welfare benefits. Note that the subsidy rate is constant up to \$4,000 and then declines. See p. 675.

[25] Thus, disposable income before price rise equals $(1-t)Y_m$ where t is the tax rate and Y_m is income in money terms. As prices rise by, say, $100z$ percent, disposable money income becomes

$$\frac{(1-t)(1+z)Y_m}{1+z} = (1-t)Y_m$$

TABLE 11-6
Effects of Inflation on Individual Income Tax

	(I)	*(II)*	*(III)*	*(IV)*	*(V)*
1. AGI, 1969	$4,310	$5,000	$10,000	$25,000	$50,000
2. Tax, 1969	$ 1	$ 98	$ 905	$ 3,890	$11,915
			AGI rises with inflation		
3. AGI, 1974	$5,232	$6,070	$12,140	$30,350	$60,700
4. Tax, 1974	$ 172	$ 301	$ 1,255	$ 5,339	$16,398
5. 1974 tax, 1969 prices	$ 141	$ 247	$ 1,029	$ 4,378	$13,446
6. Additional tax, 1969 prices (5 − 2)	$ 140	$ 149	$ 124	$ 488	$ 1,531
7. Additional tax, as percentage of item 1	3.2%	3.0%	1.2%	2.0%	3.1%
			AGI remains constant		
8. AGI, 1974	$4,310	$5,000	$10,000	$25,000	$50,000
9. 1974 AGI, 1969 prices	$3,534	$4,100	$ 8,200	$20,500	$41,000
10. Tax on item 9	—	—	$ 658	$ 3,066	$ 8,676
11. Tax reduction forgone (2 − 10)	$ 1	$ 98	$ 247	$ 824	$ 3,239
12. Tax reduction forgone as percentage of item 8	.03%	2.4%	3.0%	4.0%	7.9%

Notes:
Lines 2, 4, and 10 computed under present law. See notes to Table 10-2.
Line 3 is derived by inflating line 1 by a factor of 1.214, corresponding to a rise of 21.4 percent in the consumer price index between 1969 and 1974.
Line 9 is obtained by deflating line 8 to allow for the above price rise.

is desirable from the point of view of stabilization policy, in which context the automatic increase in tax rates may be seen as providing a prompt and desirable check to inflation.[26]

E. STATE AND LOCAL INCOME TAXES

As noted before, the income tax is primarily a federal tax. In the 1969–1970 period, 89 percent of individual income tax revenue went to the federal government, 9 percent to the states, and 2 percent to local governments. As a percent of their total revenue, the three levels of government derived 59, 11, and 4 percent from this source, respectively. Nevertheless, the income tax is used by forty-one states and in recent years has also become increasingly important at the local level.

State Income Taxes

Structure of State Taxes Of the forty states which use a general income tax (applicable to both earned and unearned income), more than thirty apply it to AGI as defined under the federal income tax. Where the federal base is used,

[26] See pp. 540 and Chap. 26, Sec. B, p. 555.

TABLE 11-7
Effects of Tax Deductibility

		INCREMENTAL BURDEN FROM 10 PERCENT STATE TAX		
Taxable Income	*Federal Marginal Rate (I)*	*No Deductibility (II)*	*Deductibility of State Tax at Federal Level (III)*	*Mutual Deductibility (IV)*
$100	14.0%	10.0%	8.6%	7.5%
$20,000	32.0%	10.0%	6.8%	4.8%
$44,000	50.0%	10.0%	5.0%	2.6%
$200,000	70.0%	10.0%	3.0%	1.0%

certain adjustments are made, with interest on federal securities and frequently capital gains excluded.[27] Most states permit a 10 percent standard deduction. Personal exemptions are typically at the federal level or somewhat higher, with a few states using a credit in lieu of an exemption. Rates in all but four states are progressive, ranging typically from 2 to about 8 percent, but in some states reaching as high as 15 percent. While rate progression is moderate, the effective rate (even in states using a flat rate schedule) is strongly progressive, especially over the lower-income ranges, owing to generally high exemptions. Three states (Vermont, Nebraska, and Alaska) determine liability under the state tax as a percentage of federal tax. Some states tax capital income at a higher rate while others exempt wage income. Most states permit income tax paid to other states as a credit against their tax. We thus find considerable variety among the state income taxes, but the typical pattern is one of approximating federal AGI and exemptions and of progressive rates from 2 to 8 percent.

Deductibility State income taxes are deducted in computing taxable income under the federal income tax, and the federal income tax is deducted in some (though a decreasing number of) states in computing taxable income for purposes of the state tax. The deductibility provisions are important because they determine the *net* addition to the tax burden which results from the state tax.

Suppose first that only the federal government permits deductibility and that a 10 percent state tax is imposed. The net cost (increase in combined state and local tax) per dollar of state tax depends on the taxpayer's federal rate bracket. If this bracket is 70 percent, the net cost of each dollar of state tax equals 30 cents, with 70 cents recouped through the reduction in federal tax. If the bracket is 14 percent, the net cost equals 86 cents, since only 14 cents is recaptured in reduced federal tax. The incremental tax caused by a flat-rate state tax is thus regressive. As shown in column III, of Table 11-7, the incremental effective rate imposed by a 10 percent state tax falls from 8.6 percent at the bottom to 3 percent

[27] For these and other relevant facts, see *State and Local Finances, Significant Features,* 1973–74 ed., Advisory Commission on Intergovernmental Relations.

at the top of the income scale. Some might argue that this is not relevant, since the state should consider the liability which it imposes, without allowing for repercussions at the federal level.[28] Yet, to overlook repercussions is unrealistic since, in fact, a substantial part of the state tax is financed by recoupment of federal tax.

The situation becomes more complex if the state also allows deductibility of the federal tax.[29] As shown in column IV, this deduction further reduces the liability at the state level and adds to the regressivity of the net state tax. Furthermore, closer consideration shows that the net gain to the taxpayer from deducting the federal tax is but slight, while the revenue loss to the state is very substantial.[30] It is inadvisable, therefore, for states to permit deduction of the federal tax.

Limitations It is not a matter of accident that state income tax rates are relatively modest, as compared with federal rates. This reflects the fact that at higher rate levels, interstate rate differentials would come to have significant effects on economic location. Moreover, in dealing with capital income, the difficulties inherent in the treatment of income earned outside the jurisdiction would become substantial. Unless all jurisdictions were to use the same rate structure, the role of distributional adjustments through progressive taxation at the state and local level is quite limited; but with uniform rates, policy would in fact be a national one. The function of redistribution, as we shall see later, must be largely centralized.[31]

Local Income Taxes

While income taxes at the local level are relatively unimportant in overall magnitude, they are now imposed by over 3,000 local governments, including cities, counties, and over 1,000 school districts. The rate is typically at 1 percent and in most cases no exemptions are granted. Local earnings by nonresidents are included in the tax base. As we shall see in a later chapter, local income taxation of earnings by nonresidents may come to play a major role in restructuring urban finances.[32]

[28] The relationship is similar to that which will be observed in the next chapter when the interaction of corporation and individual income taxes at the federal level is considered.

[29] To apply mutual deductibility on a current basis, the taxpayer would have to be adept in solving simultaneous equations; and the process would be difficult because the appropriate rate brackets would be unknown. In practice, the problem is solved, however, by deducting last year's tax.

For further discussion of deductibility, see Pechman, *Federal Tax Policy*, pp. 221–234.

[30] Let the federal and state statutory tax rates be f and s. With federal deductibility, the effective federal rate becomes $f(1-s)$ and the combined rate is $f(1-s)+s$. With mutual deductibility, the effective federal rate is $f(1-s)/(1-fs)$ and the net state rate is $s(1-f)/(1-fs)$, the combined rate being $[f(1-s)+s(1-f)]/(1-fs)$.

Assuming $s=0.10$ and $f=0.7$, the combined rate prior to deduction of the federal tax at the state level is 0.73. With mutual deductibility, it becomes 0.71, giving a reduction in the net tax of 2 cents per dollar of income. At the same time, state revenue falls from 10 to 3 cents per dollar of income.

[31] See p. 623.

[32] See p. 650.

F. APPRAISAL OF INCOME TAX

The individual income tax has the great advantage of relating tax liability to a comprehensive measure of ability to pay and of permitting adaptation to the personal circumstances of the taxpayer. It is the personal tax *par excellence,* and, at its best, it is superior to all other taxes in implementing horizontal and vertical equity. Since it is a comprehensive tax, the taxpayer cannot avoid it by changing employment or investment from one occupation or industry to another. Such, at least, is the case for the federal tax; and, since factor supplies to the economy as a whole are relatively inelastic, it is generally assumed that the tax burden remains with the taxpayer. However, there may be situations in settings of imperfect markets where part of the burden is passed on to consumers.[33]

As will appear from our later discussion of the incidence of the United States tax structure (see Table 16-1, line 1), the individual income tax, owing to the use of exemptions and progressive rates, is by far the most important contributor to progressive taxation in the overall tax structure. This is so even though the degree of progression, especially over the upper-income ranges, is very much less than observation of the bracket rates would suggest. The debate over the share of the income tax in the tax structure, therefore, is to a considerable degree won on grounds of the desirability of progressive taxation.

But whatever the beauties of the income tax may be in principle, it must also be recognized that its implementation involves many difficulties and that the existing United States income tax is far from perfect. The definition of taxable income as accretion (i.e., increase in net worth plus consumption) provides us with a norm by which to resolve a host of specific problems pertaining to various forms of income and the institutional arrangements under which it is earned. Without such a norm, resolution of these problems would be impossible; yet application of the norm is frequently difficult. The existing income tax base falls far short of what it should be, with tax preferences of various kinds resulting in a substantial impairment of horizontal, as well as vertical, equity standards. There remains much scope for improvement, and income tax reform continues to provide the most lively topic in tax policy discussions. Yet, when all is said and done, the income tax is still the best instrument of taxation that is available, and the United States income tax structure compares favorably with that of most other countries.

G. SUMMARY

Tax preferences result in a deficient definition of taxable income and thereby weaken the equity of the income tax in both its horizontal and vertical aspects.

1. Preferences result in a loss of one-third of the revenue which would be obtained under a full tax base.

2. Preferences are especially important at the lower and upper ends of the income scale. Owing mostly to the preferential treatment of capital gains, the effective

[33] For further discussion of income tax incidence, see Chap. 17, p. 403.

rate flattens out at slightly above 30 percent, much below the level suggested by the nominal bracket rates.

3. Horizontal inequities result because the benefit of tax preferences is distributed unequally among taxpayers with the same income.

4. By using a "minimum tax," an attempt has been made to remedy the preference situation at the upper end of the income scale, but the present minimum tax is of only minor significance.

The level of personal exemptions and other low-income provisions are important, both in obtaining progression at the lower end of the income scale (where such allowances may be viewed as a zero bracket rate) and in differentiating among taxpayers by family size.

5. The levels of tax-free income as provided by personal exemptions and other low-income provisions lie somewhat above the so-called poverty line.

6. The personal exemption, as a deduction from taxable income, is now supplemented by a credit against tax.

7. The low-income provision, operating as a vanishing exemption, is especially effective in concentrating tax relief at the low end of the income scale. For returns with dependents this is accentuated further by the earned-income credit.

8. The earned-income credit, being refundable if in excess of tax liability, results in a limited form of negative income tax.

Definition of the taxable unit involves the treatment of single versus married taxpayers and the treatment of single versus multiple earners within the taxpaying unit.

9. The basic choice is between defining the taxable unit in terms of earners or in terms of family (spending) units. The latter is the more meaningful approach in an ability-to-pay context.

10. The best solution is provided by a uniform rate schedule, mandatory joint returns, and exemptions adjusted to family size.

The rate structure is defined in terms of bracket rates which, together with exemptions, determine the average or effective rates.

11. The present law is characterized by highly progressive bracket rates which, because of deficient definition of taxable income, are not reflected in a corresponding set of average or effective rates.

12. Progressive rates discriminate against fluctuating incomes unless adequate allowance is made for income averaging.

13. The principle of progressive taxation, extended into a tax-transfer system, would call for a negative income tax.

14. Inflation changes the real value of bracket rates, thereby resulting in an arbitrary increase in tax liabilities at given levels of real income.

While the income tax is largely used at the federal level, it also operates in most states, though at much lower rates. It is also used to a limited degree at the local level.

15. State income taxes may be simplified greatly by using the same income concept as applies under the federal tax.

16. State income taxes are deducted from taxable income under the federal tax, but a case may be made for using a tax credit instead.

FURTHER READINGS

Goode, Richard: *The Individual Income Tax,* Washington: Brookings, 1964.

Pechman, Joseph A.: *Federal Tax Policy,* 2d ed., Washington: Brookings, 1971.

Pechman, J. A., and B. A. Okner: "Individual Income Tax Erosion by Income Classes," in *The Economics of Federal Subsidy Programs,* part 1, A Compendium of Papers, Joint Economic Committee, U.S. Congress, 1972.

Simons, Henry: *Personal Income Taxation,* Chicago: The University of Chicago Press, 1938; and *Federal Tax Reform,* Chicago: The University of Chicago Press, 1950.

Surrey, Stanley: *Pathways to Tax Reform,* Cambridge, Mass.: Harvard, 1973. U.S. Treasury Department, Joint Publication, Committee on Ways and Means and Committee on Finance, *Tax Reform Studies and Proposals,* part 1, Feb. 5, 1969.

APPENDIX: MEASURING PROGRESSION

The distinction among progressive, proportional, and regressive taxes is readily drawn. A tax is progressive if the ratio of tax to income rises when moving up the income scale, proportional if the ratio is constant, and regressive if the ratio declines. This distinction is obvious, but the situation is more complex if we wish to measure the *degree* of progression or regression.

As was shown in Figure 10-1, the average rate curve (ratio of tax to taxable income) rises and is therefore progressive throughout the income scale, but the *degree* of progression varies between points in the scale. There is no single "correct" way by which to measure the degree of progression.

Various measures may be applied, including:[34]

[34] Applied to discrete income intervals, the corresponding formulas are:

1. $$\frac{T_1/Y_1 - T_0/Y_0}{Y_1 - Y_0}$$

2. $$\frac{T_1 - T_0}{T_0} \cdot \frac{Y_0}{Y_1 - Y_0}$$

3. $$\frac{(Y_1 - T_1) - (Y_0 - T_0)}{(Y_0 - T_0)} \cdot \frac{Y_0}{Y_1 - Y_0}$$

where Y_0 and Y_1 are the lower and higher levels of income and T_0 and T_1 are the corresponding tax liabilities.

These measures, as here written, relate to discrete income *spans.* Alternatively, one might consider the slope of the various curves at particular income *points.* In this case equation 2 becomes $(dT/T)/(dY/Y) = (dT/dY)/(T/Y)$ or the ratio of marginal to average rate of tax.

See Richard A. Musgrave and Tun Thin, "Income Tax Progression, 1929–48," *Journal of Political Economy,* December 1948.

TABLE 11-A1
Measure of Progression
(Joint Return for Family of Four)

	TAX		DEGREE OF PROGRESSION*		
AGI *$* *(I)*	*Liability* *$* *(II)*	*Average Rate* *%* *(III)*	*Average Rate Progression* *(IV)*	*Liability Progression* *(V)*	*Residual Income Progression* *(VI)*
5,000	98	1.96			
			1.42	8.23	0.86
10,000	905	9.05			
			0.43	2.20	0.88
25,000	3,890	15.56			
			0.33	2.06	1.80
50,000	11,915	23.83			
			0.21	1.90	1.72
100,000	34,500	34.50			
Coefficient for proportional tax			0	1	1
Coefficient for progressive tax			>0	>1	<1
Coefficient for regressive tax			<0	<1	>1

* Values computed from formulas in footnote 34, p. 285, reflecting progression over respective AGI ranges.

1. The ratio of change in effective rate to change in income
2. The ratio of percentage change in liability to percentage change in income
3. The ratio of percentage change in after-tax income to percentage change in before-tax income

Measure 1, which may be referred to as *average rate progression,* gives the slope of the curve obtained by plotting the effective rate against income, i.e., of the average rate curve plotted in Figure 10-1. The value of the coefficient is zero for a proportional tax and positive for progression. The effective rate curve tends to flatten out and progression tends to decline as we move up the income scale. Measure 2, which may be referred to as *liability progression,* records the elasticity of the tax liability with respect to income. The coefficient measures the slope of the curve obtained by plotting tax liability against income on a double-log chart. Proportionality is now reflected in a coefficient of 1 and progression in a coefficient above 1. Measure 3 or *residual income progression* records the elasticity of after-tax income with respect to income. It gives the slope of a curve obtained by plotting before- and after-tax income on a log chart. The coefficient again equals 1 for a proportional tax but progression is now indicated by a coefficient of less than 1. Progression under all indicators tends to decline as we move up the income scale, but may rise over particular income spans.

The coefficients are shown in columns IV to VI of Table 11-A1 as they apply to various income spans. We note that the degree of progression as measured by the various coefficients differs considerably, as does the change in the level of progression between various income spans. Not even the direction of change need be the same. Yet these measures are all correct and reflect the same basic pattern of tax liabilities, while describing them in different ways. To avoid confusion in comparing progression over different income ranges or for different tax structures, it is necessary therefore to specify just what measure is used.

This is of importance in considering what happens to progression when changes in rates are made. When taxes are increased or reduced, particularly for a temporary adjustment, Congress may consider it desirable to make the change in a "neutral" fashion, calling for an "across-the-board" change. But what is meant by "across-the-board"? If all liabilities (or rates) are increased by an *equal percent,* as was largely the case in the surcharge of 1968, liability progression is left unchanged. Average rate progression rises and residual-income progression falls. If all liabilities are raised by an *equal number of percentage points,* average rate progression remains constant, while liability and residual income progression fall. The first type of rate increase is preferable for low and the second for high incomes, with the reverse order holding for a rate reduction. The definition of neutrality is thus important for distributive reasons but there is no uniquely correct definition.

Another and more fundamental measure of progression relates to the overall reduction in inequality which results from a tax. "Effective progression" thus defined involves not only the pattern of effective rates (as for the above measures) but also the level of yield and the income distribution to which the rates are applied. This will be considered later when we examine the overall effects of taxation upon income distribution.[35]

[35] See Chap. 16, Sec. D, p. 389.

Chapter 12

Corporation Income Tax*

The corporation income tax, like the individual income tax, is primarily a federal tax. Over 90 percent of total revenue from this source accrues at the federal level,

* *Reader's Guide to Chapter 12:* The purpose of this chapter is to appraise the role of the corporation tax (Secs. A and B) and to examine its burden distribution (Sec. C). In Sec. D, the problem of integrating corporate source income into the individual income tax is explored, while Sec. E samples the problems of income definition under the corporation tax. Reflecting the great variety in the legal and economic structure of business, these complexities are the natural habitat of the tax lawyer and cannot be fully dealt with in this text. The final sections discuss the taxation of small business and the role of the corporation tax at the state level. In the chapter appendix, the derivation of burden ratios is examined in more detail.

where it now contributes 15 percent of total revenue, or only about one-half its share two decades ago. The corporation tax is also used by most states, though at much lower rates than at the federal level.

A. STRUCTURE OF FEDERAL CORPORATION INCOME TAX

The federal corporation tax is imposed at a rate of 20 percent on the first $25,000 of taxable profits, of 22 percent on the next $25,000, and of 48 percent on profits in excess thereof. Putting it differently, a surcharge of 26 percent applies to profits in excess of $50,000. While nearly 80 percent of all corporations are taxed at the lower rates only, over 90 percent of all profits are subject to the highest rate of tax. This reflects the fact that large corporations furnish the bulk of the tax base, the size distribution of corporate profits by profit brackets being more unequal than that of personal income by personal income brackets.

Determination of Taxable Income

The basic principle in determining taxable income is simple enough. Gross income of the corporation is reduced by costs incurred in doing business, and the rest is net income subject to tax. Certain problems posed by exclusions and deductions under the individual income tax again arise, such as capital gains, tax-exempt securities, and charitable contributions. Other issues are added, further complicating the design of an equitable corporation tax. This involves determining just what items should be deductible as business costs and what the timing of such charges should be. Different industries present different problems and it is difficult to design a uniform tax treatment for such divergent industries as, for instance, manufacturing and banking. Given the legal complexities of corporations and their interrelationships, it is evident that a fair corporation tax cannot be a simple tax.

Derivation of Tax Base

Whereas the individual income tax is a general tax (or at least aims at being so), the profits tax applies to capital income only. Moreover, it is limited to capital income which (1) accrues in the form of profits, and (2) originates in the corporate sector. Corporate profits as reported in the national income accounts for 1973 may be estimated to account for 85 percent of total profit income and for 55 percent of total capital income.[1] Thus the corporate tax is fairly general if viewed

[1] Based on the following figures for 1973:

	(In billions of dollars)
1. Corporation profits (including inventory valuation adjustment)	$105.1
2. Profits of unincorporated enterprise	20.3
3. Rental income	26.1
4. Net interest	52.3
Total	$203.8

Items 1, 3, and 4 from *Survey of Current Business,* July 1974, pp. 16 and 18. Item 2 is estimated by assuming that the ratio of profits to wages and salaries in the unincorporated sector is the same as that in the corporate sector. This ratio was then applied to proprietor's income to give estimated profits of unincorporated enterprise.

TABLE 12-1
Corporation Tax Returns by Size Groups
(Returns with Net Income, 1971)

Size of Total Assets (In Thousands of Dollars)	RETURNS		NET INCOME		TAX	
	Number (In Thousands)	*As Percentage of Total*	*In Billions of Dollars*	*As Percentage of Total*	*In Billions of Dollars*	*As Percentage of Total*
Under 100	914	56	.3	*	.2	*
100– 250	331	20	.5	*	.4	1
250– 500	173	11	4.0	5	1.8	5
500– 1,000	98	6	3.0	4	1.3	4
1,000– 25,000	99	6	12.7	16	6.6	18
25,000–100,000	6	*	6.0	8	2.9	8
100,000–250,000	1	*	5.5	7	2.7	7
250,000 and over	1	*	45.8	59	20.8	57
Total	623	100	77.5	100	36.6	100

* Less than .05 percent.
Notes: Components may not add to total because of rounding. Corporations with assets of zero or unreported are excluded.
Source: Corporation Income Tax Returns, Statistics of Income for 1971, Department of the Treasury, 1973, p. 9.

as a tax on profits, but less so if viewed as a tax on capital income. Moreover, it represents only 9 percent of total national income.

With corporate profits as defined in the national income accounts of $105 billion (1973), taxable income reported on tax returns was $93 billion. In moving from the former to the latter, various adjustments are made. They involve addition of certain items, including realized capital gains, inventory valuation gains (or losses), and foreign income, as well as deduction of others, such as depletion allowances and state income taxes. The items, however, are relatively minor and the difference between taxable profits and profits as defined in the national income accounts is much less than that between personal income and taxable income under the individual income tax. There is no counterpart to personal exemptions and the range of permissible deductions from net income is more limited.

Structure of Tax Base

The structure of the corporation tax base, as shown in Table 12-1, differs strikingly from that of the individual income tax. The total number of returns is much smaller and there is a much heavier concentration of returns at the lower end of the scale. In 1971, over 56 percent of the returns were from corporations with assets of less than $100,000, and over 76 percent had assets of under $250,000. Yet, these returns represent only 1 percent of total net income and contribute but 1 percent of the tax. Turning to the other end of the scale, corporations with assets of over $250 million comprise less than one-tenth of 1 percent of returns but contribute nearly 60 percent of total net income and tax paid. This simply reflects the predominating importance of large enterprises in the corporate sector. From the revenue point of view, then, only the large and giant corporations matter.

B. ROLE IN THE TAX SYSTEM

The role of the corporation tax in a good tax system is by no means obvious and requires careful examination. Some view the tax as a mere device for integrating corporate-source income with the individual income tax base; others see it as an additional, "absolute" tax applied to corporate-source income independent of that imposed under the individual income tax.

The Integrationist View

Those who take the integrationist position view the problem of taxation at the corporate level merely as a way of including all corporate-source income in the individual income tax base. Their basic proposition is that, in the end, all taxes must be borne by people, and that the concept of equitable taxation can be applied to people only. Moreover, they hold that income should be taxed as a whole under a global income concept, independently of its source. Proceeding on the assumption that the corporation income tax falls on profits, they criticize such a tax because (1) profits, if distributed, are taxed twice—first at the corporation level under the corporation tax and then at the personal level as dividends under the individual income tax; and (2) retained profits are taxed at the corporate rate, a rate which usually differs from that which would apply under the shareholder's individual income tax at the personal level. Thus, if a person has corporate-source income of $100, such income is first subject to a 48 percent corporation tax. If one-half of profits after tax is distributed, his dividends equal $26. Suppose that his marginal rate under the individual income tax is 40 percent. He then pays a further $10.40 in income tax. His total tax equals $58.40. If his personal income tax had applied to the entire profit income, it would have equaled $40. Thus he pays an "extra tax" of $18.40. "Integration" means adjustment of the system in such a manner that profits are taxed at the personal rate, neither higher nor lower, whether they are retained by the firm or distributed to the shareholder.

The integrationist's position can be brought out most clearly by asking this question: What would be your view on corporate taxation if in fact corporations made it a practice to distribute all profits as dividends and to retain no earnings? The integrationist would answer that, in this case, no corporation tax would be called for. All that would be needed would be source withholding of individual income tax on dividend income, just as is done with wages paid out by the corporation.

But in reality not all profit income is distributed as dividends. During the sixties, slightly less than one-half of corporate profits after taxes were paid out, while over one-half was retained. The corporation tax thus serves the useful purpose of bringing retained earnings into the tax base. Although the corporation tax does not do this at the proper rate (low-income shareholders in particular are overtaxed), it nevertheless plugs what would otherwise be an intolerable tax loophole. Integrationists, therefore, must find a way by which, in the absence of the corporation tax, this part can be included in taxable income under the individual income tax, just as they must find a way to avoid imposing an "extra tax" on such corporate income as is, in fact, distributed. The integrationists thus find the present arrangement unsatisfactory because it does not do a proper job of taxing retained earnings and because it imposes an extra tax on dividends. As shown below, they are prepared to suggest procedures by which a correct solution can be found, i.e., all corporate-source income can be taxed similarly to other income under the individual income tax. In the absence of a correct solution, they may find that the corporation tax as it stands does more good in reaching retained earnings than it does harm in imposing an extra tax on dividends, but they will accept it as a second-best solution only.

This view, of course, is based on the assumption that the tax on corporate profits will in fact be reflected in reduced corporate profits and, hence, in reduced corporate-source income of shareholders. As we shall see in Chapter 18, this is not necessarily the case. Part of the burden may well be passed on to consumers in higher prices or to wage earners in reduced wages, thus cushioning the impact of the tax on net profits.[2] To the extent that this is done, the tax neither imposes an extra tax on dividends nor acts as a proxy for income taxation on retained earnings. The implications of this for the integration problem will be noted later on.

[2] See Chap. 18, Sec. B, p. 419.

The Absolutist View

Those who take an opposing position believe that the integrationist approach rests on an unrealistic view of the corporation. The large, widely held corporation—which accounts for the great bulk of corporation tax revenue—is not a mere conduit for personal income. It is a legal entity with an existence of its own, a powerful factor in economic and social decision making, operated by a professional management subject to little control by the individual shareholder. From this it is concluded that, being a separate entity, the corporation also has a separate taxable capacity which is properly subject to a separate and absolute tax. Whether profits after tax are distributed or retained is irrelevant in this context.

This "absolute" view of the corporation tax is difficult to defend. Corporations do indeed act as distinct decision-making units, only more or less vaguely related to the wishes of the shareholders, thus calling for a regulatory policy at the corporate rather than the shareholder level. Moreover, tax devices may be useful under certain circumstances for such regulatory purposes. However, this is quite a different matter from proposing that a corporation has an ability to pay of its own and should be subject to a distinct tax.[3] Obviously, all taxes must in the end fall on somebody, i.e., on natural persons. Corporate profits are part of the income of the shareholders and, in the spirit of the accretion approach to the income tax, should be taxed as part of their income. There is no reason why they should either bear an extra tax or be given preferred treatment.

Once more, note that this view of the corporation tax rests on the assumption that the tax falls on profits and is not passed on to consumers or wage earners. To the extent that such shifting occurs, the intent of the absolutists to impose an extra tax on corporate source income is thwarted. The tax, in this case, becomes an inferior and arbitrary sales or wages tax, without a rational place in an equitable tax structure.[4]

Other Reasons for Corporation Tax

While there is no valid argument for an absolute corporation tax on ability-to-pay grounds, a number of other considerations might justify such a tax. However, it would hardly be of the same order of magnitude or structure as the federal profits tax.

Benefit Considerations Corporations may be called upon to pay a benefit tax. Government renders many services which benefit business operations by reducing costs, broadening markets, facilitating financial transactions, and so forth. Most of these services, however, do not accrue solely to corporations but to other forms of business organization as well. The rationale would therefore

[3] One may, of course, speak of the ability of a corporation to pay a certain tax without going bankrupt or without curtailing its operations. The concept of capacity to pay as used in this sense, however, relates to the economic effects of the tax rather than to ability to pay as used in the context of equity considerations.

[4] It is inferior because the implicit rates of sales or payroll taxation will vary arbitrarily with the profit-sales ratio (margin) or the profits-wage bill ratio of particular corporations.

be for a general tax on business operations, rather than for a tax on corporations only. While there are certain governmental costs incurred in connection with corporations in particular, these costs are a minor factor and hardly justify a tax.[5] The privilege of operation under limited liability is, of course, of tremendous value to corporations, but the institution of limited liability as such is practically costless to society and hence does not justify imposition of a benefit tax. The purpose of benefit taxes is to allocate the cost of public services rendered, not to charge for costless benefits.

To the extent that a benefit tax is appropriate, two further questions arise. One relates to the level at which such a tax should be imposed. Since most public services which accrue as benefits to business are rendered at the state and local levels, it is evident that such a tax would not be primarily a federal matter. The other relates to the appropriate tax base. This will differ with the service rendered, but in most cases it will not be profits. Thus, real property would best reflect the value of fire protection; employment would reflect the input of school expenditures; transportation would reflect road services; and so forth. If a general proxy is to be used, total costs incurred in the state or locality might be the best overall measure, with value added (which includes profits as well as other factor costs) a second possibility.

Regulatory Objectives A different case for an absolute corporation tax may be made if the tax is viewed as an instrument of control over corporate behavior. The appropriate form of corporation tax then depends on the particular policy objective that is to be accomplished.

1. The control of monopoly has been traditionally undertaken through regulatory devices, but a tax approach might be used. This, however, would not call for a general tax on profits, which would not be effective in correcting monopolistic behavior. Rather, it would call for a more complex tax, related to the degree of monopolistic restriction.

2. If it were desired to restrict the absolute size of firms or bigness (which is not the same as restricting monopoly or market shares), a tax might again be used for this purpose. Here, a progressive business tax would be called for. The reason for progression, however, would not be ability to pay, as in the individual income tax. Large firms might be owned by small investors and small firms might be owned by wealthy investors. Rather, progression would be used to discriminate against the large firm and curtail what are considered to be undesirable social effects of bigness. The question then arises whether such a tax should not be on asset size or sales, rather than on profits. Even if bigness is held undesirable, it is not a reason for penalizing the profitable big firm in particular.

While we have no full-fledged experience with such an approach (a progressive corporation tax was recommended by the Roosevelt administration in 1936 but rejected), a limited application is found in the two-rate schedule which applies a

[5] The combined costs of the Securities and Exchange Commission and of the Justice Department's Antitrust Division for fiscal year 1973 were $45 million, a minute fraction of corporation tax revenue of $35 billion.

lower 25 percent rate to small firms. This is a subject to which we shall return later on.[6]

3. An excess profits tax may be imposed in periods of emergency (such as wars) when direct controls over wages and prices are needed. Wage constraints under such conditions cannot be applied effectively without corresponding profit constraints, and a tax on excess profits is a helpful tool in this connection. The United States imposed such a tax in both world wars as well as during the Korean war. While sound in principle, the excess profits tax is difficult to administer since excess profits are not readily defined. Such profits may be measured by comparison with a base period, but inequities may result from differences in initial position; or, a standard rate of return may be used, in which case risk differentials can hardly be overlooked, thus posing the difficult problem of what rates are appropriate for what industries.

4. As a stimulus to capital formation and growth, it may be desirable to encourage corporate saving and to discourage dividend distribution. This objective may be accomplished by imposing a tax on dividends paid out while exempting earnings retained. Alternatively, it may be held desirable to encourage corporate distributions and to discourage retentions in order to improve the functioning of the capital market or to increase consumption expenditures. This goal may be achieved by imposing a tax on undistributed profits while exempting profits which are paid out as dividends. Such a tax was imposed in the late thirties with the intention of stimulating consumer spending.

5. Finally, the corporation tax may be used to provide incentives or disincentives to investment, as distinct from corporate savings. Devices like the investment credit or accelerated depreciation may be used for this purpose, and they may be applied on a cyclical or a secular basis. The effectiveness of such measures will be considered in more detail later on, but it should be noted here that such incentives are better given directly—i.e., in the form of investment subsidies or penalties—rather than as relief under the profits tax.

In all, these considerations suggest that tax instruments may be helpful devices in controlling corporate behavior but, in most cases, a form of taxation would be required which differs from the profits tax.

C. DISTRIBUTION OF BURDEN AMONG SHAREHOLDERS

In assessing the burden of the corporation profits tax, much depends on whether the tax falls on corporate profits or whether it is passed on to consumers or wage earners, a question to be discussed later.[7] Unless otherwise indicated, we assume here that the tax is not shifted, i.e., that it falls on corporate profits. On this basis, how is the burden distributed among income groups? The answer depends on how the burden concept is defined. Here a distinction will be drawn between *gross burden, net burden,* and a third concept which we shall refer to as *extra burden.*

Gross Burden Distribution

The gross burden is the amount of corporation tax which is imputed to the shareholder. For purposes of imputation, the corporation tax is assigned to

[6] See p. 309.

[7] See Chap. 18, p. 415.

TABLE 12-2
Alternative Concepts of Corporate Tax Burden*

	AGI ADJUSTED					
Tax Rates	*$5,000*	*$10,000*	*$30,000*	*$75,000*	*$150,000*	*$750,000*
1. Gross rate†	2.9%	2.0%	8.8%	13.0%	20.6%	26.2%
2. Net rate						
(a) 45% distribution	2.7	1.8	7.5	9.8	14.7	18.0
(b) Zero distribution	2.9	2.0	8.8	13.0	20.6	26.2
(c) Full distribution	2.5	1.6	6.0	5.9	6.9	7.9
3. Extra rate						
(a) 45% distribution	2.3	1.4	4.3	1.6	−0.4	−3.1
(b) Zero distribution	2.1	1.2	2.9	−1.2	−7.1	−12.0
(c) Full distribution	2.5	1.6	6.0	5.9	7.3	7.9

* For derivation, see appendix to this chapter.
† Gross rate is independent of distribution rate.

shareholders in line with their shares in corporate equity or corporate-source income (both retained and distributed). For purposes of Table 12-2, it is distributed in line with dividend income.[8] The gross rate is then obtained as the ratio of imputed corporation tax to AGI, the latter expanded to include total corporate-source income or share in corporation profits before tax. Since the ratio of dividend (or corporate-source) income to AGI rises when moving up the income scale, the gross burden rate also increases. This is shown in line 1 of Table 12-2. Apart from a regressive phase at the lower end of the scale which reflects the importance of retirement income at low-income levels, we find the gross rate to be progressive. This is the basis on which the corporation tax is held to be a progressive element of the tax structure and corresponds to the pattern shown later in Table 16-1, line 3.

Net Burden Distribution

The preceding way of looking at the matter is, however, somewhat misleading and overstates the progressivity of the corporation tax. The reason is that we have disregarded the effects on individual income tax liability which result as the corporation tax is introduced.

To observe the net or incremental burden, we must compare the combined corporate and individual tax now paid with the income tax on individuals paid without a corporation tax. The difference between the two is the net or incremental burden of the corporation tax. This net tax consists of two parts. One is the additional tax imposed by the corporation tax. The other is a tax saving which results because dividends and, hence, individual income tax on dividend income will be less if a corporation tax applies. This tax saving per dollar of dividends will be greater for high-income shareholders whose bracket rate under the individual income tax is higher. Therefore, the extra tax per dollar of dividends will be less for the high-income shareholder.

[8] This assumes that the pay-out ratio is the same whatever the shareholder's total income.

It does not follow, however, that the net burden of the corporation tax is regressive. Its impact must be measured by the ratio of the taxpayer's *total* net tax to *total* income. This ratio depends not only on the net tax per dollar of profit but also on the share of profits in total income. Since the profit share rises as we move up the income scale, we have two opposing forces: One is a declining net tax per dollar of profit income, which points to regressivity; the other is a rising profit share in adjusted AGI, which points to progression. The net result cannot be predicted on general grounds but depends on the variables involved.

As shown in lines 2*a,* 2*b,* and 2*c* of the table, it turns out that the net tax remains progressive on the whole, but less so than the gross tax. The result, moreover, now depends on the rate of dividend distribution. Since the saving in individual income tax occurs only with regard to distributions, the net burden falls with the distribution ratio. Assuming a 45 percent ratio, which corresponds to recent patterns, the level of the net rate (as shown in line 2*a*) is substantially lower than that of the gross rate and the degree of progression is less.[9] This result is accentuated if (as in line 2*c*) full distribution is assumed.

Extra Burden Distribution

Under the present system there are two reasons why corporate-source income is taxed differently from other income. Distributed profits are subject to both the corporation and personal tax while retained profits are subject to the corporation tax only and escape personal tax. As a result, the tax burden on corporate profit income differs from that on other income. How important is this difference, and how does it relate to the shareholder's income level?

To measure the difference or "extra tax," we compare the present combined tax (including corporation tax and individual income tax on dividends) with what the tax would be under an integrated system, i.e., a system without corporation tax but with application of individual income tax to retained as well as distributed earnings.

The extra tax thus contains two components. One is the net burden of the corporation tax and the other is the tax savings which arise because, under the present system, retained earnings are not subject to personal income tax. Component 1, as we just saw, is mildly progressive, at least for the 45 percent distribution case. Component 2 rises with AGI, not only because the ratio of retained earnings to AGI rises but also because a higher marginal rate comes to apply. The extra rate should thus be lower and less progressive than the net rate.

This is shown in the lower part of the table. With a 45 percent distribution assumption (line 3*a*), we find that the extra burden ceases to be progressive and "bounces" over the lower-middle income range, while turning regressive at the upper end. Indeed, for high incomes, the extra tax becomes negative, the additional tax which the present system imposes in the form of the net corporation

[9] The remaining degree of progressivity is dampened further if the capital gains tax is allowed for. Suppose that 40 percent of retained earnings (probably a high ratio) come to be included eventually in taxable income. Recomputing line 2*a* of Table 12-2 accordingly, the ratios become 2.7, 1.7, 6.9, 8.2, 11.8, and 13.9. The net burden is reduced, since the corporation tax now results in savings on the taxation of both dividends and capital gains. This is especially significant for high incomes where progression is sharply reduced.

tax being less than the tax savings which result by permitting retained earnings to escape the personal income tax. The corporation becomes a "tax shelter." This result, of course, becomes more pronounced for the zero distribution case (line 3*b*), while the extra burden equals the net burden for the case of full distribution (line 3*c*).

In choosing among these concepts of tax burden, one must decide what question is to be answered. Given the fact that the personal income tax is the centerpiece of the federal tax structure, it would seem that the contribution of the corporation tax to the progressivity of the tax structure should allow for its effects on personal income tax liabilities and thus be viewed in net, rather than in gross, terms. If, instead, the corporate tax burden is viewed by comparison with a horizontally equitable system, the extra burden concept is what matters. Seen this way, the corporation tax is not progressive, and at very high incomes, becomes regressive.

D. TECHNIQUES OF INTEGRATION

As noted before, there is much to be said for viewing the corporation as a conduit of income accruing to the individual shareholder and for integrating corporate-source income with the individual income tax. What adjustments in the tax structure would be called for to accomplish this objective? Complete integration may be accomplished either via the partnership method or through full taxation of capital gains.

Partnership Method

To secure complete integration, the adjustment must equalize the tax treatment for both retained earnings and dividend distributions. The obvious solution is to impute total profits to the shareholder and to tax them under the individual income tax. Where earnings are retained, the corporation would inform their shareholders that a specified amount had been retained on their behalf and added to their equity; the shareholders would then include this amount in computing their taxable income.

At the same time, it would still be desirable to apply source withholding to profit income. Just as the corporation acts as a withholding agent for the individual income tax on the wage income of its employees, so it will act as withholding agent for the profit income of shareholders. Suppose a certain shareholder receives a profit share of $1,000 and is notified accordingly. It does not matter for tax purposes whether cash dividends are paid out or the profits are retained. The corporation withholds at a rate of, say, 25 percent, leaving the shareholder a net income of $750, and pays $250 to the Treasury. The shareholder then "grosses up" his net share by the tax paid on his behalf, thus including the full $1,000 of profits in his taxable income. Suppose that his marginal tax rate is 40 percent, so that he owes a tax of $400. The amount of $250 withheld for him by the corporation is then credited against this liability, reducing the additional amount due to $150. By using this grossing-up procedure, the taxpayer will pay at his proper marginal rate. If the withholding rate exceeds his personal rate, a refund will be due to him.

Shareholders, in other words, are treated for tax purposes as if they were partners in an unincorporated business. Since their tax is paid when the profits accrue, capital gains which reflect an increase in share value caused by retention of profits must then be excluded from subsequent capital gains taxation. This is done by permitting shareholders to write up the base (add to the purchase cost of their shares) by an amount equal to their share in retentions.

This procedure seems eminently fair, and it has been among the standard proposals made by tax reformers for a long time. However, certain difficulties with the method have been pointed out. Thus, it has been argued that the taxpayer should not be required to pay a tax on income which he or she has not "received." Hence, it is "unfair" to impute retained earnings to the person's taxable income. This objection is essentially the same as that raised against the taxation of unrealized gains. It is not convincing. For one thing, a substantial part of the tax will be paid by source withholding, thus imposing no liquidity problem on the shareholder. The remainder, payable where the individual's marginal rate exceeds the withholding rate, may be financed by a sale of shares. This may not be possible in the case of closely held corporations which are not traded, but here the shareholder may obtain the necessary cash by raising his or her payout ratio. It is also argued that the partnership approach, while feasible for small and closely held corporations, would not be practicable for large and widely held firms. It is difficult, however, to see the reasons for this argument. Taxable profits, once determined, can be prorated by shares and shareholders can be notified accordingly, just as dividends can be assigned.[10] It is true, however, that integration by partnership method does not in any way bypass the problems involved in determining taxable income of corporations. This determination remains as important as it is under the absolute corporation tax. Integration by partnership method does not simplify tax administration.

Capital Gains Method

Administration would be simplified, however, if the other route were taken and integration were secured through full taxation of all (including unrealized) capital gains, combined with a repeal of the profits tax. The distributed part would then appear in the shareholder's income as dividends, while the retained part would appear as capital gains. No determination of taxable profits would be needed. Under this approach, periodic (say quintennial) taxation of unrealized gains on traded shares might be combined with taxation at death or transfer for other assets.[11]

Techniques of Partial Integration

A more limited approach would remove the differential tax for dividends only, while leaving an absolute tax on retained earnings. This may be done in two ways. One procedure is to apply the corporate rate to all profits, but to consider the

[10] For a careful analysis of the technical problems involved, see the *Report of the Royal Commission on Taxation,* vol. 4, Ottawa: Queen's Printer, 1969.

[11] As an objection to this approach, it is argued that retained earnings may not be reflected properly in share values. The adherent of the accretion principle must respond that if they are not thus reflected, no income has accrued.

part imputed to dividends as source withholding on the shareholder's individual income tax. As under the partnership method, the shareholder is then required to gross up. Shareholders will raise their dividends by the amount withheld thereon, compute their individual income tax on the grossed-up basis, and then credit the amount withheld against their tax.[12] Under this arrangement, called the withholding method or "dividends-received credit," differential treatment is eliminated for dividends but continues for retained earnings. Shareholders whose marginal rate exceeds the corporate rate benefit, while those whose marginal rate is less, lose.

An alternative approach, known as the "dividend-paid credit," is to exclude dividends paid from the corporation tax base, i.e., to apply the corporation tax to retained earnings only. In the absence of shifting and assuming no effects on payout ratios, the two methods give identical results.

Further Integration Problems

While the case for integration is a persuasive one, certain disadvantages and difficulties should be noted.

Revenue Cost The revenue cost of integration would be substantial. To illustrate, assume corporate profits before tax of $140 billion, corporation tax liability of $67 billion, dividend payments of $36 billion, and retentions of $37 billion. Assuming the average dividend dollar to be taxed at 30 percent under the individual income tax, the yield on dividend income is $11 billion. Total tax revenue from corporate-source income is thus $78 billion ($67 billion plus $11 billion). Under an integrated arrangement, the average applicable bracket rate under the individual income tax would be somewhat higher, say 35 percent. Applied to total taxable profits of $140 billion, it would yield a revenue of $49 billion. The revenue loss would thus be $78 billion minus $49 billion, or $29 billion. The corresponding tax relief of $29 billion would be distributed as shown by line 3*a* of Table 12-2. To make up for this loss, the yield of the individual income tax would have to be raised by about 20 percent. The net distributional impact would depend on how this increase was distributed.

Capitalization of Past Burden It may be argued that integration, by granting relief to shareholders, would not remove the inequity (differential taxation of corporate-source income) which was imposed when the corporation tax was originally introduced. The reason is that the additional tax has long been "capitalized" and has come to be reflected in reduced share prices.[13] Assets have changed

[12] The grossing up is an essential part of proper withholding. The 4 percent dividend credit, enacted in 1954 and repealed in 1969, did not provide for grossing up and was therefore highly inequitable. Since all shareholders received the same gain per dollar of dividends, the differential tax was cut by a larger percentage for the high-bracket shareholder. See J. A. Pechman, *Federal Tax Policy,* 2d ed., Washington: Brookings, 1971, p. 135.

[13] Before application of taxes and with an interest rate of 5 percent, asset A, bringing an annual income stream of $10,000, will sell for $200,000, while asset B, bringing an income stream of $20,000, will sell for $400,000. Now let income from asset A be taxed at 50 percent while B is exempted. Net income from A falls to $5,000 and the capitalized value falls to $100,000. The next owner of the asset buys it at $100,000 only and receives the same return obtained by the holders of the tax-free asset B. See also Chap. 18, Sec. A.

hands since imposition of the corporation tax, and most present shareholders bought at the lower price. Hence they have suffered no loss, and removal of the differential tax, by leading to a rise in share prices, would leave them with an unjustified capital gain.

This argument has merit so far as the taxation of "old" capital is concerned, especially if the resulting capital gain would not be subject to tax. But, carried too far, it means that old inequities, like original sin, can never be removed. Whatever the transition problem, this difficulty disappears as new capital comes to be formed and the system develops into a state of more neutral taxation.

Implications of Shifting The preceding discussion of integration was based on the assumption that the corporation tax falls on corporate profits. The picture changes if instead the tax is shifted (in the sense of being charged to the consumer or wage earner) so that net profits are not reduced.[14]

In this case, dividends pay no additional tax. The corporation tax comes to be in the nature of a sales tax and its crediting to the dividend recipient would be inappropriate, as it would result in deficient taxation of profit income under the individual income tax. If the tax is shifted in part, only partial crediting (for the nonshifted part) is in order.[15]

Moreover, the possibility of shifting bears on the problem of how retained earnings are best integrated into the income tax. If corporate management shifts an absolute tax, how will it react to source withholding of the shareholder's personal income tax? Given the possibility that shifting may apply to a source-withholding type of tax, the better part of wisdom would be either to approach integration via full taxation of capital gains or to collect the tax at the shareholder level. In the latter case, the corporation would be required to file information returns on the profits accruing to shareholders in order to prevent tax evasion. By the same token, if integration is to be partial and apply to dividends only, exclusion of dividends from corporation tax will be preferable to collection from the corporation with crediting at the shareholder level.

E. ISSUES OF INCOME DEFINITION

Whether one thinks in terms of an absolute corporation tax or of partnership-type integration, taxable income must be defined and the countless difficulties which this poses must be faced.[16] Only a few aspects of this complex problem will be noted here.

[14] For a discussion of shifting, see Chap. 18. If the tax is not shifted to consumers or workers but falls on all capital income rather than on corporate profits in particular, integration would call for crediting the corporation tax (at a correspondingly reduced rate) to the recipients of all capital income.

[15] Suppose that prior to tax, the profits of a firm equal $100,000. After a 50 percent tax is imposed, gross profits rise to $150,000 while net profits fall to $75,000. The amount of tax borne by the shareholder thus equals $25,000, or one-third of the total tax of $75,000. Thus, two-thirds of the tax is shifted and only one-third of the tax (or $25,000) should be credited.

[16] As noted above, the need for defining taxable income of the corporation is bypassed only if integration takes the form of full taxation of capital gains. But even then the need for defining such income will remain at the partnership and proprietor level.

Depreciation

Since the corporation tax is a tax on *net* income, recovery of the capital outlay must be permitted in computing taxable income. The question is how to time these costs and how to set the base.

Timing Certain outlays, like those for research and development, are expensed (i.e., are deducted in full as incurred) even though they are in the nature of capital formation. Physical capital assets used in the production process (i.e., plant and equipment) cannot be expensed but may be charged over a prescribed period of time. The timing of the recovery of capital cost is important because the present value of tax liability is reduced when depreciation is charged. Deduction of capital costs gives rise to tax savings to the investor, and these are the greater the earlier the capital costs are deducted. This is so because a time discount must be applied to future tax savings. The present value of the tax paid over the life of the investment may be thought of as containing two parts. One is the present value of the tax as it would be without depreciation. The other, which is subtracted, is the tax savings which are due to deducting depreciation.[17] Thus the reduction in earnings, brought about by a tax, depends not only on the tax rate, but also on the timing of depreciation deductions. These factors involve both the time span over which depreciation is charged and the speed at which it proceeds within this interval.

The time span is in practice set in line with the "useful service life" of the asset. The Internal Revenue Service has set "guideline" lives ranging from three years for automobiles to ten years for machinery and forty to sixty years for structures. These guidelines relate to about eighty fairly broadly defined classes of assets. The Revenue Act of 1971 introduced the so-called asset depreciation range (ADR) system, permitting the taxpayer to raise or lower the service lives by 20 percent.[18]

The rate of depreciation over this time span depends on which of several write-off methods are applied. Three methods are distinguished. Under the *straight-line* method, the same amount of c/n is written off each year, where c is the asset cost and n is the asset life. Thus, for a \$100,000 asset with a life of ten years, \$10,000 is deducted each year. Under the *double-declining balance method,* twice the straight-line percentage is deducted in the first year and this same percentage is then applied to the as yet undepreciated amount in each successive year. Thus, \$20,000 is deducted the first year, \$16,000 in the second

[17] For the straight-line case, the present value of the tax equals

$$t\left(RA_n - \frac{C}{d} A_d\right)$$

where t is the profits tax rate, R is the annual income for n years, C is the cost of investment, and d is the number of years over which depreciation extends. A_n and A_d are the present value of an annuity of \$1, discounted at the market interest rate i, for n and d years respectively.

[18] This act also repealed the so-called reserve-ratio test, introduced in 1965 and designed to hold service lives for tax purposes in line with the actual depreciation practice used by the firm. Unfortunately, the period of application was too short to give this method a fair test.

TABLE 12-3
Present Value of Depreciation
(In Dollars, Asset Cost $100,000)

Service Life (Years) (I)	*Straight Line (II)*	*Double-declining Balance (III)*	*Sum-of-Years Digits (IV)*
		6 PERCENT DISCOUNT	
5	86,750	87,811	87,515
10	75,787	78,716	79,997
20	59,055	64.661	67,680
50	32,460	40,935	44,756
		10 PERCENT DISCOUNT	
5	79,534	81,100	80,614
10	64,469	68,528	70,099
20	44,663	51,539	54,697
50	20,806	28,829	31,439

Source: Harold Bierman, Jr., and Seymour Smidt, *The Capital Budgeting Decision,* 2d ed., New York: Macmillan, 1966.

year, and so forth.[19] Under the *sum-of-years-digits method,* the fraction deducted each year equals the ratio of remaining years to the sum of the years over the service life. Thus, for a $100,000 asset with a ten-year useful life, the sum of the years is $10 + 9 + 8 + \cdots + 1 = 55$. The charge for the first year is 10/55ths of $100,000 = $18,111; for the second year the charge is 9/55ths of $100,000 = $16,374; and so forth.

As shown in Table 12-3, the present value of depreciation is higher under the double-declining balance than under the straight-line method, and the difference increases with the length of service life. The same holds if we compare the sum-of-years-digits method with the straight-line method. As between declining balance and sum-of-years digits, we note that the former is preferable for short, and the latter for long, investments.

The straight-line method is available for all depreciable assets, but various categories may be depreciated at a faster rate. Thus, depreciable property with a useful life of over three years, if newly acquired, may be depreciated at double-declining balance, years-digits, or other "consistent" methods. In the case of used property, the declining-balance method may be used but not at a rate exceeding 150 percent of the straight-line method. Special provisions apply for real estate. New real estate may be depreciated at 150 percent declining balance, except in the case of rental property where double-declining balance or years-digits may be applied. A 100 percent declining-balance method is available for used rental

[19] The taxpayer is also permitted to switch to straight-line when the amount deductible under straight-line becomes larger than that deductible under double-declining balance. Thereby, the total amount is depreciated within ten years. If double-declining balance is retained, a salvage value remains which is accounted for in the last year.

property, and rehabilitation outlays for low-cost housing may be depreciated over a five-year period. Certain pollution-control facilities, finally, may be depreciated over a thirty-month period. Depreciation schedules, once agreed upon, must be adhered to thereafter and cannot be changed without agreement from the Internal Revenue Service.

Given the advantage of more rapid depreciation, it is surprising that most corporations still use the straight-line method.[20] However, more than 50 percent of total depreciation is now taken under double-declining balance, which is coming into increasing use. The use of rapid depreciation rates for tax purposes (to reduce taxable profits) and slow depreciation for book purposes (to appear more profitable to the shareholder) is not looked upon with favor by the tax authorities, but is nevertheless often the practice.

There remains the basic question of what constitutes the "proper" rate of depreciation. If rapid write-offs are advantageous to the taxpayer, they are costly to the Treasury. With regard to any one investment, the same burden—defined as present value of tax—may be imposed by various combinations of tax rate and depreciation rate. A lower tax rate and slower depreciation rate will give the same present value of tax as a higher tax rate and a more rapid depreciation rate. If all investments were the same, it would make little difference which combination were chosen to provide the Treasury with a given revenue stream. The difficulty arises because investments differ in length and profitability and thus fare differently under the various policies. Yet they should be treated equally, as a matter of both equity (investors with the same income should pay the same tax) and neutrality (taxation should not distort the pattern of investment). What depreciation pattern is required to secure an equitable and neutral income definition?

The depreciable asset, as noted before, may be looked upon as generating two income streams. One is a positive income stream of earnings, arising from the use of the asset. The other is the negative income stream, or diminution of capital, which results as the asset is worn out and declines in value because of obsolescence. Netting out, the asset gives rise to a net income stream, the present value of which is the value of the asset. Assets with equal present value of net income streams should carry an equal burden as defined by the present value of the tax.

This might be done by charging depreciation in line with the actual diminution in asset value, thus taxing the true net income stream as it is received each year. If the current value at any one time equals the capitalized value of the future income stream generated by the asset, the decline in value equals the capitalized value of the reduction in the remaining income stream. This then is the capital cost which should be charged along with other costs in computing net income. This is the approach which, in line with the accretion concept, gives the correct definition of net income. But, though the principle is clear, it is not easily applied. Modern capital equipment does not wear out evenly and it frequently becomes obsolete before it has been "used up." Obsolescence rates will differ and cannot

[20] For an investment of $100,000 (fifty-year life), the present value of depreciation under years-digits exceeds that under straight-line by $12,326. At a 48 percent tax rate, the present value of the tax saving equals $5,560.

be predicted. Thus, the best that can be done is to gear service lives to actual business practice while relying on the assumption that the latter will tend to reflect the "true" service life and time path of the income stream. With this as the standard, more rapid rates of depreciation may be referred to as "accelerated" depreciation. Such depreciation has been used as an instrument to provide investment incentives, and its effectiveness for this purpose will be considered later on.[21]

Depreciable Base and Inflation We now turn to the amount that is to be depreciated. The law sets the depreciation base equal to original cost, but it is frequently argued that replacement cost should be used instead.[22] It is pointed out that, in times of inflation, original cost depreciation is insufficient to enable the firm to replace the asset, replacement-cost depreciation being needed for this purpose.[23] When we look at the problem in equity terms, we are returned to the previously noted distinction between money and real income. As the price level rises, the services of the asset generate a higher income in money terms, and the investor must pay tax thereon. But the tax savings from depreciation (if based on original cost) do not rise accordingly. The investor thus finds the real value of his or her after-tax return reduced. Ideally, this should be adjusted for, along with other instances where inflation distorts the net income position. As noted before, in an ideal system, net debtors would have imputed to them a gain in real income and creditors would be granted a loss. But given the difficulties of a general adjustment of this sort,[24] the case for allowing replacement depreciation is of questionable merit. Clearly, it should not be applied without also adjusting the remaining part of the corporate balance sheet, e.g., imputing a gain from declining real value of net indebtedness.

Depletion

A related problem arises in the case of the extractive industries. Such industries have been given preferential treatment in two respects. First, investors were permitted to expense (rather than depreciate) outlays for exploration cost. Second, they were permitted a percentage depletion allowance. This is a deduction over and above recovery of actual costs equal to a set percent of gross receipts.

The depletion allowance was granted initially because it was difficult to assess the original cost of developed wells when the tax was introduced, and depletion was to serve as a proxy for previously undertaken but not as yet depreciated costs. Later it came to be looked at as an allowance, justified in its own right, for the "using up" of the stock of mineral resources and the resulting reduction in asset value. At first sight, this seems a proper procedure, since the drawing out of oil resources reduces the remaining deposit and renders it less

[21] See pp. 492 and 497.

[22] Another aspect of the base problem arises in connection with investment incentives. If an investment credit is given, the taxpayer may be permitted to include the credit in the base, thus depreciating more than cost. See p. 498.

[23] Countries with chronic and rapid inflation have usually dealt with the problem by periodic revaluation of assets rather than by current adjustment.

[24] See p. 246.

valuable. Such diminution of value would appear to be deductible under the accretion concept. But this is only one side of the coin. The other is that the accretion or gain involved at discovery should be included in taxable income. Since this gain is in fact not included, its subsequent loss should also not be allowed for as a deduction. In short, deduction for actual cost (exploration and drilling) is appropriate, and expensing (rather than gradual deduction) of such costs may be an acceptable concession, since exploration costs are frequently undertaken in vain. But without initial taxation of the gain, there is no justification on equity or neutrality grounds for depletion allowances.

While the justification of percentage depletion as compensation for loss of asset value has come to be recognized as untenable, the defense has shifted to other grounds. One viewpoint is that since investment in natural resources is said to be especially risky, a lower rate of taxation is called for. Again, this is not a convincing argument. Another is that extractive industries may be of special importance to national policy, be it for purposes of defense or to assure the interests of future generations. There is no reason to believe, however, that the granting of depletion allowances serves the purposes of development and more efficient resource management over time. On the contrary, it tends to encourage more rapid exploitation, whether by attracting additional capital through offering a tax shelter or by increasing sales through lowering prices to consumers.

The Tax Reform Act of 1969 reduced the depletion allowance from 27.5 to 22 percent for oil and by 1 percentage point for other natural resources previously enjoying depletion allowances of 23 and 15 percent. The Tax Reduction Act of 1975 moved farther in this direction with elimination of percentage depletion on oil and gas industries, except for the small producers for whom depletion is to be gradually reduced to 15 percent.

Investment Credit

The law permits a credit against tax equal to a certain percentage of investment in plant and equipment. To be eligible, investments must have a useful life of at least three years. This credit, which is granted as an investment incentive, is set at 8 percent, but for 1975–76 it has been raised to 10 percent.[25]

Losses

The law provides for the carry-over of net operating losses to the two past and five subsequent years. Thus, a firm which has a net loss in any one year does not lose the opportunity to charge the loss against profits, provided its gains over these seven adjacent years are sufficient to absorb it. The loss carry-over is a form of averaging which protects the firm with occasional loss years but net gains over the eight-year period. The legislation does not take care of losses in all cases, but the bulk of losses is allowed for in this fashion. As noted in our previous discussion of the income tax, adequate allowance for losses—which makes the government a partner in both negative and positive gains—is of particular importance in cushioning the effects of taxation on investment incentives.[26]

[25] See p. 498.
[26] See p. 494.

Inventory Accounting

Increases in the value of inventories (i.e., stock-in-trade held as a normal part of conducting business over the taxable year) are included in the firm's operating profits. These changes may be measured on either a LIFO (last-in, first-out) or a FIFO (first-in, first-out) basis which, once selected, must continue to be used by the firm.[27] LIFO gives smaller profits in periods of rising prices and smaller losses when prices fall. It thus makes for a more stable tax base over the business cycle than does FIFO. Being used by most corporations, LIFO also makes for a continuously smaller tax base under conditions of sustained inflation, automatically excluding inflation gains from the tax. Moreover, the treatment of inventory profits and losses is an interesting application of taxing unrealized capital gains, just as depreciation is a case of allowing for unrealized capital losses.

Interest

Interest paid by corporations is properly deducted in computing taxable income. It is a cost of doing business, just as are wage payments. Since earnings derived from the investment of borrowed funds are included, the equity issue posed by the deduction of mortgage interest does not occur.

A problem does arise, however, because interest on borrowed funds may be deducted while deduction of imputed interest on equity capital is not permitted. This may bias management toward use of debt finance. To secure neutrality in the choice between debt and equity finance, corporations would have to be allowed to deduct imputed interest on invested capital. This deduction in turn would call for inclusion of such income in the shareholder's tax base, i.e., for integrated treatment under the partnership method. However this may be, the share of equity finance (mainly from internal sources) has increased rather than decreased in recent decades, and there is little evidence that the differential tax treatment has been a significant factor in retarding this increase.

Capital Gains

The corporation tax, like the individual income tax, gives preferential treatment to capital gains in the form of realized gains from the sale of assets which are not stock-in-trade. The capital gains rate for corporations is now at 22 percent for those with net income below $25,000 and 30 percent for those with net income above that level.

Real Estate Tax Shelters

Finally, we should take note of certain tax advantages which may arise from the interaction of depreciation and capital gains provisions. If accelerated depreciation is permitted, the early years of asset life may result in depreciation charges in excess of income, thus recording a loss for tax purposes. By offsetting this loss against other income, taxpayers will reduce their liability thereon. A loss of $100

[27] Suppose that at the end of 1969 an automobile dealer has a stock of ten cars, acquired at $2,000 each. In 1970 he acquires twenty additional cars at $2,500 and sells ten cars at $4,000 each. His stock at the end of 1970 is twenty cars. Under the LIFO method, profits for 1970 are 10 × ($4,000 − $2,500), or $15,000, while under the FIFO method, profits equal 10 × ($4,000 − $2,000), or $20,-000. Since prices have risen, FIFO profits are larger.

is worth $48 of tax reduction. When a given taxpayer decides to sell the asset, he will find that his remaining cost base is less because more depreciation was charged under the accelerated schedule. Thus, for each additional $100 of depreciation that was taken, his gain will be increased by $100. But the tax thereon at the 25 percent capital gains rate is only $25, thus leaving him with a net saving in tax of $23. In other words, income which otherwise would have been taxed at an ordinary rate of 48 percent is transferred into capital gains income taxable at 25 percent only. As a result, the net return on the investment subject to accelerated depreciation is greatly increased. This advantage, moreover, can be magnified if a relatively small amount of equity is given the leverage of a large amount of borrowed capital. In this case the investor may find that his total tax liability is reduced rather than increased by making an additional investment, so that the implicit rate of tax on the latter is negative.

Such was the mechanism which in the fifties and sixties led to the development of the so-called real estate tax shelter, when real estate investment was permitted to depreciate at a double-declining balance. Since then, the preference has been greatly curtailed, partly by limiting accelerated depreciation and partly through the so-called recapture clause. Under the latter, such part of capital gains as reflects depreciation in excess of the straight-line depreciation must be taxed as ordinary income, i.e., at the full rate. However, accelerated depreciation without the recapture clause continues to apply for rental housing. Support of such housing by a tax subsidy which bestows a large windfall on the developers (provided they subsequently sell) is hardly the best way of accomplishing this incentive objective. Similar problems arise in connection with depreciation rules for leasing of equipment.

Expense Accounts

Expense accounts and "expense-account living" have been a much discussed topic. By permitting entertainment expenses as deductible business costs, the net cost of such outlays is reduced by nearly one-half and activities which hardly deserve public subsidy are encouraged. Moreover, by making payments in kind rather than in cash, the corporation may help its employees to reduce their personal income tax. Thus, if a $4,000 car is furnished to the executive, the cost to the corporation is the same as if his or her salary were raised by this amount. But a salary gain would increase the individual's tax liability, whereas the car services do not.

This avenue of individual income tax avoidance may be closed either by including income in kind in the individual's taxable income, or by disallowing deduction of such costs at the corporation level. A modest effort was made in the Revenue Act of 1964 to limit deductibility and to reduce expense-account allowances. However, the effort met with heavy opposition and was not successful. Since making detailed distinctions between deductible and nondeductible items would cause serious administrative difficulties, the British practice of disallowing almost all entertainment expenses is perhaps the only feasible alternative.

Financial Institutions

Differences in the products or services supplied by various industries frequently lead to structural differences which generate tax problems specific to such industries. The previously mentioned depreciation problem is an illustration. The treatment of financial institutions is another. Given the nature of their assets, good accounting practice for such institutions requires that a "bad-debt" reserve be set aside. Charges to such a reserve are a legitimate cost of doing business and are appropriately allowed for as deductions under the tax law. The question is how high such charges should be. In the past, very high charges unrelated to actual bad-debt experience were permitted, but these have been cut back by the Tax Reform Act of 1969.

Under this act, additions to bad-debt reserves by commercial banks were reduced from 2.4 to 1.8 percent of outstanding loans, or they may be computed on the basis of actual bad-debt experience. This percentage will be reduced gradually over the years until such reserves will be based entirely on actual experience, using a six-year moving average.

Mutual savings banks and savings and loan associations previously were permitted to deduct 3 percent of real property loans or 60 percent of taxable income. The former method, which once resulted in complete tax exemption for most of such institutions, was repealed in 1969. The 60 percent deduction is to be reduced to 40 percent over a ten-year period.

Tax-exempt Organizations

Prior to 1969, nonprofit organizations such as churches, educational institutions, and foundations, though organized as corporations, were exempt from corporation tax. Since then, such corporations have become taxable on income obtained from the operation of an "unrelated business." In addition, a 4 percent tax is now imposed on their net investment income.[28] Moreover, various provisions were enacted to limit abuses of their tax-exempt status, such as profitable arrangements between foundation and donors ("self-dealing") and leaseback arrangements. Finally, foundations must now distribute 6 percent of their assets and are subject to a penalty tax of 15 percent on deficient distributions.

F. PROGRESSION AND SMALL-BUSINESS RELIEF

There are three corporate tax rates: 20 percent on the first $25,000 of income, 22 percent on the next $25,000, and 48 percent on the remainder. While 80 percent of corporations pay at the lower rate only, the bulk of taxable income is received by large corporations and subject to the 48 percent rate. The revenue cost of applying the lower rates is about $3 billion, or 6 percent of total profits tax revenue in 1975.

[28] Taxable corporations are permitted to deduct 95 percent of dividends received from other taxable corporations, and in the case of affiliates, 100 percent deduction is allowed. With a 48 percent corporate rate, the 95 percent deduction leaves a net tax of 2.4 percent.

Should Rates Be Progressive?

The rationale underlying progressive rates for the individual income tax cannot be applied to the corporate sector. The corporation does not have a taxpaying ability of its own in the sense in which individuals do, and all tax burdens are ultimately borne by individuals. Nor can it be said that progressive taxation of firms is a means to progressive taxation of shareholders. There is no positive relationship between the size of the corporation and the net income of its owners. Many small corporations are owned by high-income individuals and a substantial share of dividends (the bulk of which are paid by large corporations) are received by middle-income individuals.

If a case is to be made for a progressive rate structure, it must be based on other grounds, such as a desire to restrain "bigness" and to support small firms. As noted before, restraining bigness differs from restraining monopoly. The latter is a matter of market shares, the former of absolute size. If bigness is to be restrained, this may be done through a progressive tax, but such a tax would be related more appropriately to asset size than to profits. If it is bigness that is held undesirable, there is no reason to favor big firms that are unprofitable. The economic case for restraining bigness is, however, of questionable value. Middle-sized and large firms tend to be more efficient than small firms, although there is little evidence that giant size is needed to achieve efficiency. However this may be, the Jeffersonian ideal is not a viable alternative for modern society, and chances are that balance between large units is the more reasonable solution.

Nevertheless, tax relief for small firms has always been and continues to be a popular political cause. Partly, this may be justified to balance the superior ability of large firms to operate in imperfect capital markets and to benefit from restrictive practices. More important, however, is the persistent view that the maintenance of a small-business class is socially desirable even though it may be inefficient.

Aid to Small Business

For this and other reasons, preferential treatment of small business is an ever-present topic of tax reform. Assuming that such aid is to be given, the question is how it may be done most efficiently.

Partnership Option The law now permits corporations with no more than ten shareholders to elect taxation on a partnership basis. This option is especially advantageous to corporations with small shareholders who pay a low-bracket rate on dividends and plan to operate with a high payout ratio. This choice typically benefits small firms. Large corporations which are closely held are usually owned by wealthy people for whom corporate tax treatment is an advantage since they are subject to a high marginal personal tax rate which may be avoided by a low payout ratio. The partnership option is thus an effective method of relieving the corporate tax burden of small firms with low-income owners, without depriving them of the advantage of limited liability.

Low Initial Rate The benefit of the 20 and 22 percent initial rates of tax primarily accrues to small corporations. The effect of the low rate on the liability of large corporations is not very significant. The trouble with the low initial rate is that it can readily serve as a shelter from individual income tax. In effect, it increases the range over which the differential corporation tax is negative. With a corporate rate of only 20 percent and a shareholder individual income tax rate of 40 percent, the differential rate is negative (incorporation gives a tax advantage) provided the payout ratio is below 62 percent. This result might be avoided by disallowing the lower corporation rate to small but closely held corporations if the marginal rates of their shareholders are, on the average, above a certain level.

A further difficulty arises because larger corporations are induced to split up into multiple units (to spin off), so as to benefit from a number of surtax exemptions. Prior to 1969, corporations were permitted to split into a group of "controlled corporations" using multiple surtax exemptions at the penalty of an additional tax of only 6 percent. This practice was terminated under the Tax Reform Act of 1969, which largely eliminated the availability of multiple surtax exemptions by 1974.

Other Approaches Small corporations now enjoy certain other tax privileges, such as additional first-year depreciation allowances of 20 percent up to $10,000. This type of concession may well be preferable to the lower-rate technique since it lends itself less readily to tax-shelter abuse. Moreover, provisions may be designed which are of special value to new and expanding firms rather than based exclusively on the size criteria.

G. STATE CORPORATION TAXES

The role of the corporation tax, like that of the individual income tax, is of primary importance at the federal level. Even though a corporation tax is imposed by forty-five states, it provided only 6 percent of state tax revenue in 1970. Its contribution to local tax revenue is below 1 percent. State corporation tax rates range from 2 to 11 percent, with most states applying lower rates to small corporations. In some cases, alternative bases are provided and the highest tax is chosen. Thus, the New York 7 percent tax on net income is linked with two alternative taxes: (1) a 1¼-mill tax on invested capital, and (2) a 7 percent tax on 30 percent of net income plus compensation paid to officers.

Rates imposed by the major industrial states cluster around the 5 to 6 percent level, with fairly small differentials. This is necessary because capital is mobile and sharp rate differentials might cause capital to flow from high- to low-rate states. Even though slight rate differentials may be relatively unimportant as compared with other factors in location decisions, states tend to consider them a major factor and therefore engage in low-rate competition to attract capital. All these considerations produce a built-in tendency toward modest rates and a fair degree of uniformity.

Interesting problems arise in determining how the tax base of corporations engaging in interstate trade should be divided among the different states. Any one state may tax a corporation doing business within its jurisdiction, and various state laws use different formulas to determine what share of profits they should tax. Typically, this involves an apportionment formula, including property, payrolls, and sales within the state, with equal weight given to the three factors under the so-called Massachusetts formula. It is now widely believed that a uniform set of rules should be adopted, subject to the supervision of the Treasury, and that sales be eliminated from the formula.[29]

Choice of the appropriate formula depends on the philosophy of base allocation. If benefit considerations are controlling, the ideal solution would be to charge in accordance with the cost of public services rendered to the firm in its various locations. As a first approximation, it might be argued that all costs are reduced equally by the provision of public services, in which case an allocation by costs incurred would be appropriate. At the same time, it would not be very meaningful to allocate profits on this basis. The benefit approach, as noted before, does not call for a profits tax but for an ad valorem charge on costs incurred.

If the philosophy of an absolute profits tax is applied, the appropriate method of apportionment should be according to the source of profits. If we assume that the firm's return on capital is the same in all locations, profits should be allocated in line with the location of capital use. Sales would enter the formula, but only to the extent of capital invested in sales operations and not in the form of gross sales. The payroll factor would enter in line with the average capital requirement for payroll finance, but not total wages paid. Under such an approach, the sales and payroll factors would be weighted less heavily than in the conventional three-factor formula, while immovable capital would be included at its full value.

Until recently, it was felt that the inclusion of sales in the profits apportionment formula would be strongly in the interest of low-income states, while that of capital and payroll would be in the interest of high-income, manufacturing states. The Report of the Judiciary Committee, however, showed that the role of the sales factor had been misjudged.[30] The states which do most of the producing also offer the biggest markets and do most of the buying. While inclusion of the sales factor will affect the states to which a particular firm must pay its revenue, the effect on overall revenue allocation is but minor. Since the inclusion of the sales factor causes high compliance costs—to assure proper administration, a firm would have to file returns in all the states to which it sells—the Judiciary Committee's recommendation for a two-factor formula, including capital and payroll only, is justified on both pragmatic and theoretical grounds.

H. APPRAISAL OF THE CORPORATION INCOME TAX

While the corporation income tax has been a major and steady revenue producer in the federal tax structure, various objections to it may be raised.

[29] See *State Taxation of Interstate Commerce, Report of the Special Subcommittee on State Taxation of the Committee on the Judiciary,* 88th Cong., 2d Sess., House Report No. 1480, 1964. See also C. Lowell Harriss, "State-Local Taxation of Interstate Commerce: Progress and Problems," in *Innovations in Tax Policy,* Hartford: John C. Lincoln Institute, 1972.

[30] See ibid., vol. I, chap. 16.

1. Proceeding on the assumption that the tax is not passed on to consumers or wage earners but falls on profit income, it may be said to discriminate against corporate-source income since such income (to the extent that it is distributed) is already subject to personal income tax. At the same time, the corporation tax acts as an income tax substitute for retained earnings.

2. Equal treatment of all sources of income would call for integrating the taxation of corporate-source income (whether distributed or not) with the personal income tax. This integration would involve a substantial revenue loss which would have to be made up and would present certain administrative difficulties. However, it is difficult to defend the present type of corporation tax (as compared with an integrated system) if judged by the rule of equal treatment within the income tax structure.

3. Although the corporation tax is usually regarded as a highly progressive part of the tax structure, this view is questionable even if it is assumed that the burden falls on profits. The burden distribution differs, depending on how the burden concept is defined. While the gross burden distribution is strongly progressive, the net burden distribution is less so. The extra burden imposed by not granting equal treatment to corporate-source income, finally, is not progressive and becomes regressive for very high incomes.

4. It is questionable, moreover, whether it is correct to assume that the burden falls on shareholders. With competitive markets, it is likely to be shared by all capital income; and with imperfect markets, part of the burden may be passed on to consumers or workers. As shown in Table 16-2, the incidence of the corporation tax is highly dependent on the shifting pattern that results.[31]

5. Finally, the corporation tax (even in perfect markets) leads to distortions because it applies in the corporate sector only, thus inducing capital to move into other sectors of the economy. This drawback, as we shall see later, would not apply to an extra tax on capital income in all its uses.

Whatever the role of the corporation tax at the federal level, use of this tax at the state level presents additional problems. Decisions must be made on how the corporation tax base is to be divided among jurisdictions and allowance must be made for the tendency of capital to avoid high-rate jurisdictions, thus limiting the freedom of action for individual states to draw on this particular revenue source. It is not surprising, therefore, that the corporation tax at the state level is imposed at relatively low, and more or less uniform, rates.

I. SUMMARY

The corporation tax is an important source of federal revenue. With regard to the size and structure of the corporation tax base, we have noted that:

1. Corporate profits account for nearly 90 percent of total profits and 55 percent of all capital income.

2. Unlike the personal income tax base, the bulk of taxable profits is received by a small number of very large corporations.

[31] See Table 16–2, p. 393.

In assessing the role of the corporation tax in the "good" tax structure, we have distinguished between a view of this tax as an "absolute tax" on corporations as such and its role in integrating the taxation of corporate-source income under the individual income tax. As a basis for an absolute corporation tax, it might be argued that:

3. Corporations should be charged for benefits received from public services. Such a tax, however, would be smaller in amount than the present corporation tax and also different in form.

4. Various regulatory uses of taxation with regard to controlling size or monopoly power might be made but would also call for different forms of taxes.

The case for corporate taxation as a major revenue source has to be based on its role as an ability-to-pay tax. Here we have drawn these conclusions:

5. The equity of corporation tax must be assessed in terms of its burden impact among individuals, not firms. If we assume that the corporation tax is not to be passed on, its burden must be attributed to the shareholder.

6. On the premise that all sources of income should be treated equally, item 5 calls for integration of corporate-source income into the personal income tax.

7. Assuming the burden of the corporation tax to fall on the shareholder, its burden distribution differs, depending on how the burden ratio is defined:

- **a.** The *gross burden* is strongly progressive
- **b.** The *net burden* distribution is less progressive
- **c.** The distribution of the *extra burden* is not progressive and becomes regressive at the upper end of the income scale

Various techniques of integration were examined, including both full and partial integration:

8. Full integration may be obtained by the partnership or the capital gains method.

9. Partial integration may be obtained by the exclusion of dividends from corporation tax or by granting a dividend credit at the shareholder level.

Numerous problems arise in the appropriate definition of taxable income, among which the following were noted:

10. Proper treatment of depreciation allows for both the speed of depreciation and the size of the depreciation base.

11. Depletion allowances involve preferential treatment for natural resource industries.

12. Other items covered included the treatment of losses, inventory profits, tax shelters, expense accounts, and the investment credit.

Finally, the role of the corporation tax at the state level was considered. Various problems were noted which point to only a minor role for this tax at lower levels of government.

FURTHER READINGS

Goode, Richard: *The Corporation Income Tax,* New York: Wiley, 1951.
Holland, D. M.: *Dividends under the Income Tax,* New York: National Bureau of Economic Research, 1962.
Pechman, Joseph A.: *Federal Tax Policy,* 2d ed., Washington: Brookings, 1971, chap. 5.
Report of the Royal Commission on Taxation, vol. 4, *Taxation of Income,* part B, "Taxation of Income Flowing through Intermediaries," Ottawa: Queen's Printer, 1969.
U.S. Treasury Department, Joint Publication, Committee on Ways and Means and Committee on Finance, *Tax Reform Studies and Proposals,* Feb. 5, 1969, part 3.

APPENDIX: Derivation of Alternative Burden Ratios

In this appendix we derive the alternative burden ratios summarized previously in Table 12-2.

GROSS BURDEN

The derivation of the gross burden ratio is given in Table 12-A1. This involves the determination of average shares in retained earnings and corporation tax at various levels of AGI, based on the reported relationship of dividend income to AGI for 1969. By adding corporation tax and retained earnings imputations to AGI, AGI adjusted is obtained and the tax rate is then derived on that basis.

TABLE 12-A1
Gross Burden Impact of Corporation Income Tax

	TAXPAYER					
Item	*A*	*B*	*C*	*D*	*E*	*F*
1. AGI	$5,000	$10,000	$30,000	$75,000	$150,000	$750,000
2. Dividends as percentage of AGI	1.5%	1.0%	5.0%	8.0%	15.0%	22.0%
3. Dividends	$75	$100	$1,500	$6,000	$22,500	$165,000
4. Retained earnings	$92	$122	$1,833	$7,333	$27,500	$201,667
5. Corporation tax	$154	$205	$3,077	$12,308	$46,154	$338,461
6. Share in gross profits (3 + 4 + 5)	$321	$427	$6,410	$25,641	$96,154	$705,128
7. AGI adjusted (1 + 4 + 5)	$5,246	$10,327	$34,910	$94,641	$223,654	$1,290,130
8. Gross tax as percentage of AGI adjusted (5 ÷ 7) X 100	2.9%	2.0%	8.8%	13.0%	20.6%	26.2%

Notes:
Line 2: Based on *Statistics of Income, Individual Income Tax Returns* for 1969, 1971.
Line 4: Based on assumption that 45 percent of profits after tax are distributed, so that $R = .55(R + D)$, where R is retained earnings and D is dividends.
Line 5: Based on $T = .48(D + R + T)$, where T is tax.

TABLE 12-A2
Net Burden of Corporation Income Tax*

	TAXPAYER					
	A	*B*	*C*	*D*	*E*	*F*
1. AGI	$5,000	$10,000	$30,000	$75,000	$150,000	$750,000
2. AGI adjusted	$5,246	$10,327	$34,910	$94,641	$223,654	$1,290,130
3. Share in gross profits	$321	$427	$6,410	$25,641	$96,154	$705,128
4. Bracket rate	14%	19%	32%	55%	64%	70%
	45 PERCENT DISTRIBUTION					
Tax per $100 of profits						
Present law						
5. Corporation tax	$48.00	$48.00	$48.00	$48.00	$48.00	$48.00
6. Dividends	$23.40	$23.40	$23.40	$23.40	$23.40	$23.40
7. Individual income tax	$3.28	$4.45	$7.49	$12.87	$14.98	$16.38
8. Combined tax	$51.28	$52.45	$55.49	$60.87	$62.98	$64.38
Without corporation tax						
9. Dividends	$45.00	$45.00	$45.00	$45.00	$45.00	$45.00
10. Individual income tax	$6.30	$8.55	$14.40	$24.75	$28.80	$31.50
11. Net tax (8 — 10)	$44.98	$43.90	$41.09	$36.12	$34.18	$32.88
Tax on total profit share						
12. Net tax (11 × 3) ÷ 100	$144.39	$187.45	$2,633.87	$9,261.53	$32,855.44	$231,846.08
13. as percentage of AGI adjusted (12 ÷ 2) × 100	2.8%	1.8%	7.5%	9.8%	14.7%	18.0%

	II ZERO DISTRIBUTION†					
14. Net tax per $100 of profits	$48.00	$48.00	$48.00	$48.00	$48.00	$48.00
15. Total net tax (14 X 3) ÷ 100	$154.08	$204.96	$3,076.80	$12,307.68	$46,153.92	$338,461.44
16. as percentage of AGI adjusted (15 ÷ 2) X 100	2.9%	2.0%	8.8%	13.0%	20.6%	26.2%
	III FULL DISTRIBUTION†					
17. Net tax per $100 of profits	$41.28	$38.88	$32.64	$21.60	$17.28	$14.40
18. Total net tax (17 X 3) ÷ 100	$132.51	$166.02	$2,092.22	$5,538.46	$16,615.41	$101,538.43
19. as percentage of AGI adjusted (16 ÷ 2) X 100	2.5%	1.6%	6.0%	5.9%	7.4%	7.9%

* The net burden equals the difference between the combined corporation profits and individual income tax liabilities under the present law and the individual income tax liability which would apply under present law in the absence of corporation tax.

† In considering zero and full distribution, we assumed the gross profit share to be the same as in line 3.

Notes:

Line 2: Equals line 7 of Table 12-A1.

Line 3: Equals line 6 of Table 12-A1.

Lines 14 and 17: Derived by same method as shown for line 11.

NET BURDEN

Derivation of the net burden ratio is shown in Table 12-A2, for three different distribution assumptions.[32] Lines 1, 2, and 3 are repeated from lines 1, 7, and 6, respectively, of Table 12-A1, and line 4 gives the applicable bracket rates under the individual income tax at each AGI level.[33] Lines 5 to 11 show the derivation of the net tax under the assumption that 45 percent of after-tax profits is distributed as dividends. Consider taxpayer A, whose bracket rate is 14 percent. His total tax on $100 of profit income equals $48 of corporation tax plus a 14 percent individual income tax applied to a dividend income of $23.40 (45 percent of $52), or $3.28. His total tax is thus $51.28. In the absence of a corporation tax, dividends would equal $45 and his individual income tax would be $6.30. This would then be his total tax. The incremental or net tax thus equals $51.28 minus $6.30, or $44.98, as is shown on line 11. For taxpayer F, whose marginal rate is 70 percent, the present tax on $100 of profit income is $64.38, or $48 plus 70 percent of $23. His tax in the absence of the corporation tax would be $31.50 (or 70 percent of $45), and his net tax is therefore $32.88 ($64.38 minus $31.50). As will be seen in moving across line 11, the net tax per $100 of profits thus falls as we move up the income scale. But corporate-source income once more becomes an increasing share of total income which points to progression. The final result thus depends on the relative magnitudes of these two effects.

This is shown in line 12 of Table 12-A2, giving the total net tax, and in line 13, giving its ratio to total income. We find that the net burden is again regressive at the very lowest end of the scale and progressive thereafter. However, progression is less marked than for the gross burden distribution (line 8 of Table 12-A1). Yet it is this net burden pattern that matters when considering the distributional implications of changes in corporation tax.

In the lower part of the table, corresponding results are shown for assumptions of zero and full dividend distribution. For the case of zero distribution, the net tax per $100 of profits (line 14) is the same for all taxpayers since the personal

[32] The net tax T_n equals the joint tax T_j which now applies, minus the personal income tax T_p, which would apply if there were no corporation tax. We thus have

$$T_j = t_c P + t_p\, d(1 - t_c)P$$
$$T_p = t_p dP$$
$$T_n = T_j - T_p = t_c(1 - dt_p)P$$

where t_c is the corporate rate, t_p is the applicable personal bracket rate, d is the percentage of after-corporation tax profits which is paid out, and P is the taxpayer's share in before-tax profits.

If allowance is made for the capital gains tax on increases in the share value at the time of realization, the net tax becomes

$$T_n = t_c(1 - dt_p)P - gt_p(1 - d)t_c P$$

where g is the fraction of gains that comes to be included in the tax base.

[33] The discerning reader may criticize the analysis of Table 12-A2 by noting that the applicable bracket rates under the income tax are a function of AGI and not of AGI adjusted to include retained earnings and corporation tax. Since the level of AGI corresponding to a given level of AGI adjusted differs with the distribution ratio, the rates shown in line 3 may differ for our various assumptions regarding dividend distribution. This is overlooked here, assuming that the same bracket rates apply for all three cases. The error, however, does not affect the resulting pattern to a significant degree.

bracket rate does not come into play. The burden distribution of the net tax in relation to total income (line 15) is therefore more progressive. The opposite holds for the assumption of full distribution (line 19), where the regressive influence of the declining net rate receives increased weight. The progressivity of the net tax thus depends greatly on the pay-out ratio. Since this ratio tends to decline as the shareholder's income rises, line 13 may well overstate net progression.

EXTRA BURDEN

The burden derivation for the "extra tax" concept is shown in Table 12-A3. Lines 4 to 6 derive the extra tax per $100 of profit income, assuming a 45 percent pay-out ratio. The combined tax under present law, shown in line 5, is the same as line 8 of Table 12-A2. The tax under an integrated system is obtained by applying the personal tax rate (line 4 of Table 12-A2) to $100 of profits, as in line 4. The extra tax per $100 of profits is then simply the difference between the two and is given in line 6. This extra burden, as shown in lines 7 and 8, is seen to fall as the shareholder's income rises, for reasons similar to those noted in our discussion of the net tax. However, the extra tax is less than the net tax and becomes negative at the upper end of the scale.[34] If the personal bracket rate is very high, the additional gross burden imposed by the corporation tax (as compared with an integrated system) may be more than offset by the savings in personal income tax due to retention. Thus, the extra tax declines and turns into a tax shelter as we move up the scale. For a distribution rate of 45 percent, the extra tax becomes negative if the bracket rate exceeds 62.7 percent.[35]

As before, the outcome is not independent of the payout ratio. Under conditions of zero distribution (line 10 of Table 12-A3), the extra tax per $100 of dividends is less, and the point at which it becomes negative is reached at a lower income level. The same holds for the relation of extra tax to AGI (line 12). If there is full distribution, the extra tax is increased and remains positive throughout (lines 14 and 16). Thus, the burden of the extra tax is again least (and the resulting tax shelter most substantial) where a high bracket rate is combined with a low rate of distribution.

[34] The extra tax T_e equals the joint tax T_j minus the tax under integration T_i. Using the notations as in the preceding note, we have

$$T_j = t_c P + t_p d(1 - t_c)P$$
$$T_i = t_p P$$
$$T_e = T_j - T_i = [t_c + t_p d(1 - t_c) - t_p]P$$

It is thus seen that $T_e = T_n - t_p(1 - d)P$.

[35] The shelter situation arises if

$$t_p > t_c + t_p d(1 - t_c)$$

or

$$t_p > \frac{t_c}{1 - d(1 - t_c)}$$

With t_c equal to 0.48 and d equal to 0, 0.3, 0.5, and 1.0 respectively, the levels of t_p at which T_e becomes negative are 48, 57, 64, and 100 percent respectively.

TABLE 12-A3
Extra Burden of Corporation Income Tax*

	TAXPAYER					
	A	*B*	*C*	*D*	*E*	*F*
1. AGI	$5,000	$10,000	$30,000	$75,000	$150,000	$750,000
2. AGI adjusted	$5,246	$10,327	$34,910	$94,641	$223,654	$1,290,130
3. Share in gross profits	$321	$427	$6,410	$25,641	$96,154	$705,128
4. Tax under integration per $100 of profits	$14.00	$19.00	$32.00	$55.00	$64.00	$70.00
	I 45 PERCENT DISTRIBUTION					
5. Combined tax, present law, per $100 of profits	$51.28	$52.45	$55.49	$60.87	$62.98	$64.38
6. Extra tax per $100 of profits (5 − 4)	$37.28	$33.45	$23.49	$5.87	−$1.02	−$5.62
7. Total extra tax (6 × 3) ÷ 100	$119.67	$142.83	$1,505.07	$1,505.13	−$980.77	−$39,628.20
8. as percentage of AGI adjusted (7 ÷ 2)	2.3%	1.4%	4.3%	1.6%	−0.4%	−3.1%
	II ZERO DISTRIBUTION†					
9. Combined tax, present law, per $100 of profits	$48.00	$48.00	$48.00	$48.00	$48.00	$48.00
10. Extra tax per $100 of profits (9 − 4)	$34.00	$29.00	$16.00	−$7.00	−$16.00	−$22.00
11. Total extra tax (10 × 3) ÷ 100	$109.14	$123.83	$1,025.60	−$1,794.87	−$15,384.64	−$155,128.16
12. as percentage of AGI adjusted (11 ÷ 2) × 100	2.1%	1.2%	2.9%	−1.2%	−7.1%	−12.0%

	III FULL DISTRIBUTION†					
13. Combined tax, present law, per \$100 of profits	\$55.28	\$57.88	\$64.64	\$76.60	\$81.28	\$84.40
14. Extra tax per \$100 of profits (13 − 4)	\$41.28	\$38.88	\$32.64	\$21.64	\$16.28	\$14.40
15. Total extra tax (14 × 3) ÷ 100	\$132.51	\$166.02	\$2,092.22	\$5,548.71	\$15,653.87	\$101,538.43
16. as percentage of AGI adjusted (15 ÷ 2) × 100	2.5%	1.6%	6.0%	5.9%	7.3%	7.9%

* The extra burden equals the difference between the combined corporate income tax and individual income tax under present law and the liability which would prevail if the individual income tax only applied but retained earnings were included in the tax base.

† For the cases of zero and full distribution the same gross profit share is assumed to apply as in line 3.

Notes:

Line 3: Equals line 6 of Table 12-A1.

Line 4: Equals bracket rate (line 4, Table 12-A2) times \$100.

Line 5: Equals line 8, Table 12-A2.

Line 13: Equals corporation tax of \$48 plus individual income tax applied to dividends of \$52.

Chapter 13

Sales Taxes*

A. Sales Taxes in the United States Tax Structure: *Federal Taxes; State Taxes; Local Taxes.* **B. Types of Sales Taxation:** *Sales Tax Alternatives; Choice of Base; Stage of Imposition; Ad Valorem versus Unit Tax.* **C. Evaluation of Sales Tax:** *Burden Distribution; Credit.* **D. Personal Expenditure Tax:** *Determining Taxable Consumption; Evaluation.* **E. Summary. Appendix: Problems of Value-added Tax.**

Sales taxes are like income taxes in that they are imposed on flows generated in the production of current output. But they differ in other respects. Whereas income taxes are imposed on the sellers' side of *factor* transactions (i.e., on the net income received by households), sales taxes are imposed on the sellers' side of *product* transactions (i.e., on the gross receipts of business firms). The impact on the former is at point 1 in Figure 9-2, and that of the latter is at point 3 if on consumer goods or at 4 if on all goods.

Moreover, sales taxes on consumer goods—and as we shall see, most sales

* *Reader's Guide to Chapter 13:* In this chapter we discuss the conventional forms of sales taxation as well as some novel approaches to the taxation of consumption, including the value-added tax, which has received much attention in recent years, and a personalized approach referred to as the expenditure tax. Consumption taxation in these various forms promises to be an active area of tax reform discussion in the future. Techniques of value-added taxation are considered in more detail in the chapter appendix.

taxes are of this form—may be considered equivalent to taxes imposed on household purchases of the corresponding items, i.e., to taxes imposed at point 2 in Figure 9-2. They are thus based on the uses rather than the sources side of the household account. For the general consumption tax, income set aside for saving is omitted from the tax base.

Finally, and most important, sales taxes differ from the income tax in that they are *in rem* rather than *personal* taxes. As such, they do not allow for the personal circumstances of consumers as does the individual income tax with its exemptions, deductions, and progressive rates. Sales taxes are thus inferior on both horizontal and vertical equity grounds. But even though consumption taxes usually take this form, it is not a necessary feature of consumption taxation. As we shall see presently, a personal consumption or expenditure tax may be constructed which is not open to this objection.

A. SALES TAXES IN THE UNITED STATES TAX STRUCTURE

We begin with a brief look at the role of sales taxes in the United States tax structure. As was shown in Table 9-1, sales taxes are of only limited importance at the federal level, where they produce less than 10 percent of total revenue; but they are the major source of revenue at the state level, where over 50 percent of the total is derived from this source.

Federal Taxes

Federal excise and sales taxes are all of the selective type, being imposed on specific products. As may be seen in Table 13-1, the bulk of the revenue comes from a small group of products, including alcohol, tobacco, gasoline, and telephone services. Customs duties which once were very important are now a negligible factor in the overall revenue picture of the federal government. Federal excises are imposed largely at the manufacturer's level, the major exceptions being telephone services and air transportation which are, in effect, charged at retail. Most federal excises (including those on alcohol, tobacco, gasoline, and tires) are levied on a unit basis, while others (including telephone taxes) are of the ad valorem type.

State Taxes

Turning to the state level, the retail sales tax holds the center of the stage. Being a tax on retail sales, it corresponds to a more or less general tax on consumer expenditures. Such a tax is now imposed by all but four states. Rates range from 2 to over 6 percent, and the comprehensiveness of base varies. Moreover, the states also make substantial use of selective excises. As shown in Table 13-1, the primary objects of selective taxation are again liquor, tobacco, and gasoline. Most of these excises (including again gasoline taxes) are imposed on a unit basis, but ad valorem rates are also used. The general sales tax is imposed at the retail level, as are most selective taxes. However, manufacturer's taxes are used as well. As noted later, the choice between taxation at the retail level (involving taxation at

TABLE 13-1
Sales Taxes in the United States Tax System
(Fiscal Year 1971–72, in Billions of Dollars)

	Federal	*State*	*Local*	*Total*
General retail sales taxes	—	17.6	2.7	20.3
Alcoholic beverages				
Taxes	5.1	1.8	1.7	6.6
Liquor stores*	—	1.9	0.3	2.2
Tobacco	2.2	2.8	0.2	5.2
Manufacturers excises				
Cars and accessories	1.1	—	—	1.1
Motor fuel	4.2	7.2	0.1	11.5
Other	0.7	—	—	0.7
Miscellaneous excises				
Telephone	1.7	—	—	1.7
Utilities	—	1.2	0.9	2.1
Other	1.7	2.7	0.4	4.8
Motor vehicle and operators licenses	—	3.3	0.2	3.5
Customs duties	3.4	—	—	3.4
Total	20.1	38.5	4.5	63.1

* Net profit base of government liquor stores included though not listed as taxes in Census source.
Sources: U.S. Bureau of the Census, *Governmental Finances in 1971–72;* and *U.S. Commissioner of Internal Revenue, Annual Report,* 1972.

destination of the product) and taxation at the manufacturer level (involving taxation at the origin) has important bearing on the size of the tax base available to any jurisdiction as well as the distribution of the tax burden between jurisdictions.

Local Taxes

General retail sales taxes are also imposed by 300 municipalities, and this number is rapidly increasing. In addition, municipalities make substantial use of special assessments and service charges. Such charges, being in the nature of purchase payments by the consumer, may be included in the general category of sales taxation.

In 1972 sales taxes and charges provided 25 percent of the revenue of cities but were of special importance for smaller cities without ready access to taxes other than property tax. Special assessments are used to finance road and sewerage construction, and service charges may be applied to public facilities such as parking lots, airports, and hospitals. Being in the nature of benefit taxation, charges offer an important alternative to general taxation, especially at the local level where the type of expenditure is frequently such as to permit direct assignment of benefits to particular consumers.

TABLE 13-2
Types of Sales Taxes

	BASE			
	Consumer Goods			
Stage	*General (I)*	*Selective (II)*	*Consumer and Capital Goods (III)*	*Total Transactions (IV)*
Single				
Retail	(1)	(5)	(9)	—
Wholesale	(2)	(6)	(10)	—
Manufacturer	(3)	(7)	(11)	—
Multiple				
Value-added	(4)	(8)	(12)	—
Turnover	—	—	—	(13)

B. TYPES OF SALES TAXATION

As is apparent from the preceding view of sales taxation at the various levels, sales taxes may take a variety of forms. In some cases they reflect varying policy objectives, while in others they reflect differing administrative devices to accomplish the same objective.

Sales Tax Alternatives

Such taxes may differ with regard to scope of coverage or base, to points of collection, and to assessment on unit or ad valorem base. Leaving aside the latter distinction for the time being, the various approaches may be summarized as shown in Table 13-2.

Horizontally, Table 13-2 shows the distinction among various sales tax bases. These include a comprehensive consumption base (column I), a selective consumption base (column II), and a base in which both consumer and capital goods are included (column III). Whereas the base covered in I equals the consumption component of GNP, that covered in III equals total GNP. In column IV, the base is defined not in terms of final output (as in columns I through III) but includes all sales, thus covering a unit of output more than once as it moves through successive stages of production and trade.[1]

Vertically, the table shows the various stages at which the tax may be collected. Among single-stage taxes, these include retail, wholesale, or manufacturer's taxes. Under the multiple-stage group, we have the value-added tax, which, as we shall see below, differs from the single-stage approach only in matters of administration, as well as the turnover tax which is basically different in nature.

The various sales taxes may now be classified readily in terms of Table 13-2.

[1] The base will thus be larger even though included transactions are limited to those involved in the production of current output as it moves from one stage of production to another. Beyond this, the base may be made to include "secondhand" transactions among final users and even financial assets.

The retail sales taxes imposed at the state level correspond to (1), although they fall short of being truly general. Gasoline taxes illustrate case (5) while federal taxes on liquor illustrate case (7). The value-added taxes now imposed in European countries correspond to (4), while the turnover taxes which they replaced corresponded to (13).

Choice of Base

The choice of base is the crucial policy issue in sales tax design. Assuming that the tax is to be general, the question is whether it should include consumption only (type I), consumption plus investment or GNP (type III), or all turnover (type IV).

Inferiority of Total Transactions Base To begin with, the turnover tax which applies to the total of transactions may be eliminated as least desirable. Under this tax, a product is taxed repeatedly as it moves through the stages of production. Thus, the sale of iron ore is taxed when it moves from mine to steel mill; the sale of steel is taxed when it moves from the mill to a rolling plant; sheet metal is taxed when it is sold to an automobile body plant, and so on until the final tax is imposed on the retail sale of the car. As a result, the tax base is a multiple of GNP and high yields can be obtained at very low rates. With a GNP of $1,400 billion, a comprehensive 1 percent turnover tax could yield $50 billion, or nearly one-half the yield of the income tax. This has political appeal, and inclusion of total transactions would do no harm if each product went through the same number of transactions, so that the combined turnover tax liabilities as a percentage of value at final sale would be the same. But they are not. A turnover tax, therefore, imposes arbitrary discrimination against products which involve many stages of production and distribution. Moreover, in order to avoid tax, firms will attempt to join with their suppliers, thus encouraging vertical integration and reducing competition. Further inequities are introduced as the tax is "pyramided" from stage to stage, by entering into the base of each successive stage. For these reasons, the turnover tax is considered an inferior form of taxation, and the recent replacement of the turnover tax by the value-added tax in European countries reflects a belated recognition of this fact. The United States, fortunately, has never suffered from a turnover tax.

GNP Base versus Consumption Base Granted that such double-counting should be avoided, there remains a choice between a tax based on gross national product, net national product, or consumption. Most general sales taxes are, or at least aim to be, of the consumption-based type.

The GNP type would impose a sales tax on both consumer and capital goods. Thus, its base would be equivalent to that of a tax on gross income, i.e., an income tax which does not allow for depreciation. Such a tax would be objectionable on both equity and efficiency grounds. With regard to equity, it would offend the basic dictum of income taxation which says that income from all sources should be taxed fully, but on a net basis. With regard to efficiency, it would compound the discrimination against saving which even a tax on net income involves.[2]

[2] See p. 468.

TABLE 13-3
Estimated Base of Retail Sales Tax, 1973

	In Billions of Dollars	
Consumer expenditures	805.2	
Items generally excluded		
— Housing*	116.4	
— Domestic services	5.2	
— Food furnished employees	2.2	
— Medical supplies	8.6	
— Insurance premiums	9.7	
— Foreign travel	5.6	
— Other personal business	35.5	
= Remaining base	622.0	
As percentage of total consumption		77%
Items frequently excluded		
— Home-consumed food	125.5	
— Medical care expenses	54.1	
— Household utilities	32.7	
— Tobacco and gasoline	41.9	
— Private education	13.2	
— Miscellaneous	25.0	
= Remaining base	329.6	
As percentage of total consumption		41%

* Includes rental payments and imputed rent of owner-occupied housing.
Source: Survey of Current Business, U.S. Department of Commerce, July 1974, p. 24.

These objections do not apply if the tax is limited to a base which in fact equals net national product, or GNP minus depreciation. Such a tax would be similar in base to a general income tax and (as will be noted a little later) may be implemented via an income type of value-added tax.[3] Since the income base is already available under the income tax, this leaves the consumption base under which consumer goods only are subject to tax. This approach is the one most generally used and must now be considered more closely.

Comprehensive versus Narrow-based Consumption Tax The so-called general or retail sales tax, as imposed by the states, aims at a comprehensive coverage of consumption. Nevertheless, all these taxes exclude certain items, thereby reducing the base to one-half or one-third of the total available under a truly general consumption tax.

This is shown in Table 13-3. We note than even a broadly defined base,

[3] Imposed in single-stage form, this would call for a tax both on consumer and on capital goods, with the base defined as sales value minus the depreciation component of cost. Since the retailer does not have this information, such a tax would be impractical. For the value-added type of income tax, see p. 338.

estimated at $622 billion for 1973, falls 23 percent short of total consumer expenditures of $805 billion. The main single item of slippage is rent (imputed and cash), which accounts for over one-half of the loss. In addition, even broad-based-tax states, such as Michigan, exclude a variety of items such as food grown and consumed on farms, private education, prescription drugs, and foreign travel. Other states, for example, Massachusetts, use a much narrower base and exclude a wide variety of further items. Exclusion of food purchased for home consumption accounts for the largest base loss. Exclusion of products subject to selective excise taxes and utilities comes next in importance. Allowance for such items reduced the 1973 excise base to about $330 billion, or 41 percent of total consumption as measured in the national product accounts.

It is evident, therefore, that adoption of a narrow base requires a substantially higher tax rate if the same revenue is to be obtained. This requirement is not objectionable in itself if the base is improved thereby, but unless there are specific reasons for excluding certain items, the inclination is in favor of a broad-based tax. One reason for excluding items such as imputed rent and certain services may be that inclusion would be administratively difficult. Exclusion of such items as rent or home-consumed food may be designed to reduce the regressivity of the tax, although—as we shall note presently—other and more effective ways of doing this may be available. Finally, still other items, such as prescription drugs, may be excluded because their consumption is to be encouraged as a merit good, their exclusion from the general sales tax being equivalent to a subsidy in the absence of tax. But, as with the income tax, the admission of certain exclusions readily spreads and erodes the tax base.

Selective Sales Taxes As distinct from the more or less general type of sales tax, selective sales taxation is applied to particular products. This may be done for various reasons.

1. Selective sales taxes may be rationalized as substitutes for service charges. Thus, the gasoline tax may be considered an approximation, if an imperfect one, to a service charge for the use of roads.

2. Selective sales taxes may be imposed to implement progressivity. Thus, taxation of products which weigh heavily in high-income budgets results in a progressive burden distribution. In situations where a progressive income tax is difficult to implement—as is typically a problem in developing countries—selective excises on luxury goods, supported by corresponding taxes on imports, may offer a feasible approach.[4]

3. Particular products may be chosen for taxation in situations where tax administration is difficult, because such taxes are easier to administer. This approach is again useful in developing countries where products produced by a small number of manufacturing establishments may offer a readily available tax handle. The same advantage applies to the taxation of imports.

4. Selective taxes may be imposed to discourage the consumption of "de-merit" goods. This approach explains why, honoring the spirit of Carrie Nation, alcoholic beverages and tobacco account for nearly one-half of federal sales taxes.

[4] See p. 754.

Such taxes, though they tend to be highly regressive, are supported on "sumptuary" grounds, be it because the consumption of such products is considered immoral or unhealthy. Society decides to interfere with consumer choice, and to treat such items as demerit goods. Whatever the desirability of such interference, there is the further question of effectiveness. Consumption will be reduced only to the extent that demand is elastic. Since the demand for cigarettes and liquor is relatively inelastic, these taxes are not likely to have a major effect on consumption, as evidenced by the very fact that they produce such a large yield. For regulatory taxes to be effective, the activity in question must be greatly curtailed, resulting in little or no tax revenue.

5. A further use of regulatory taxes, likely to be expanded in the future, is as a deterrent to pollution.[5] Imposed to internalize the external costs generated by certain production or consumption activities, excises may be used to correct for inefficiencies in resource use.

6. Still another type of control objective underlies a set of federal taxes officially designated as regulatory taxes. Such taxes, including those on narcotics, adulterated butter, and wagers, are imposed to facilitate enforcement of other regulations or other taxes without a direct revenue objective.

Stage of Imposition

We now turn to the stage at which the tax is to be imposed. This decision involves the choice of the best stage for single-stage taxes, as well as the choice between a single- and a multiple-stage approach. Whereas setting the scope of coverage is a substantive issue in determining what kind of tax is to be applied, the choice of the appropriate stage or stages is essentially a matter of administrative efficiency in implementing a tax on the chosen base.

Manufacturer versus Retail Level In dealing with single-stage taxes, the question is whether the tax should be imposed at the manufacturer, the wholesaler, or the retail level.

If the tax is to be general, the retail base is preferable because it permits the imposition of a uniform ad valorem rate. Equal-rate ad valorem taxes imposed on various products at the manufacturing level result in dissimilar equivalent rates at the retail level. This occurs because the ratio of retail to manufacturer's prices differs among products. Imposition of differential rates to allow for this diversity would be a difficult and clumsy way to approximate what can be done better with a uniform tax at the retail level.

If the tax is to be selective, the answer is less evident. If the product is identified at the manufacturing stage, e.g., low- or high-priced cars or television sets, it will be advantageous to tax at that level, since selective retail taxation may be more difficult. In other situations (e.g., fabrics which may be made into low- or high-priced garments), this may not be possible. Differentiation here may have to be related to the nature of the final product at retail. Nevertheless, the general presumption in favor of retail, applicable to the case of the general tax, does not hold for the selective case.

In developing countries in particular, a good argument can be made for taxing at the manufacturer level. This approach reduces the number of taxpayers

[5] See p. 708.

from whom the tax has to be collected and thus facilitates administration. Moreover, manufacturing establishments tend to be larger than retail establishments, more permanent, and conducted on a more sophisticated basis, with better bookkeeping methods. These characteristics improve their quality for assessment purposes. Developing countries may do better with a set of manufacturers' taxes, where the number of collection points is smaller, even though this may result in differentials in the implicit retail rates.

Another aspect of the stages problem arises where goods are traded between jurisdictions. Taxation at the retail stage (the so-called destination principle) permits the inclusion of imported goods, thus making it possible for states to tax the use of gasoline and automobiles even though they do not produce these items. On the other hand, taxation at the manufacturing level (the so-called origin principle) permits inclusion of exported goods which are consumed abroad. Thus, Michigan may find it beneficial to tax automobiles at the manufacturer level rather than the retail level. But, as we shall see later, this may not be desirable from an interstate (or, seen more broadly, from an international) point of view. Resulting effects on trade and the division of revenue between governments must then be allowed for. In the international context, effects on the balance of payments also enter the picture.[6]

Retail Level versus Value Added The other question is whether the tax should be collected in one swoop and at the final point of sale only, or whether it should be collected in slabs as under the value-added procedure. With this approach, the value of the product is divided into slices or slabs (the value added at each stage) to which the tax is applied at successive stages in the production process. As we shall see later, the value-added tax of the consumption type resembles a retail sales tax; only the method of collection differs, and the choice has to be made in terms of administrative convenience. Use of the multiple-stage approach in the value-added context must thus be distinguished sharply from its previously noted use in connection with the turnover tax. Since the value-added tax has come to be the basic instrument of tax coordination among Common Market countries, it has also received increasing attention in the United States discussion. The old debate over whether there should be a retail sales tax has been revised in this form. A more detailed examination of the value-added approach is presented in the chapter appendix.

Ad Valorem versus Unit Tax

It remains to note the form in which the tax is imposed. The tax may be assessed as a percentage of sales price, when it is referred to as an *ad valorem tax.* Or, it may be assessed as a given amount per unit of product, in which case it is referred to as a *unit tax.* From an analytical point of view, there is an important distinction between the two since the former reduces the firm's revenue per unit sold and the latter raises variable unit costs. The one is a tax on the value of sales while the other is a tax on the quantity of sales.

While a unit tax may be translated into a corresponding ad valorem rate given the price of the product, the two techniques are not readily interchangeable.

[6] See p. 722.

A tax on a particular product may be applied in a unit or an ad valorem form, but a general sales tax (which is to be a uniform percentage of the price on all products) calls for an ad valorem approach. As shown later, this has certain efficiency advantages.[7] Use of the unit tax, moreover, may induce the producer to adjust the units in which the product is sold, e.g., to produce long cigarettes if the tax is imposed per package. Finally, the unit tax reduces the built-in revenue flexibility of the tax system with regard to inflation, as the tax per unit remains constant as prices rise. For these and other reasons, there is a strong case for transforming the existing unit taxes to an ad valorem basis.

C. EVALUATION OF SALES TAX

In our subsequent discussion of incidence, we shall conclude that the burden of a general sales tax on consumer goods tends to fall on the consumer. Despite some qualifications to this conclusion, we shall now proceed on this premise.

Burden Distribution

A general retail sales tax on consumer goods or a consumption-type value-added tax is equivalent in principle to a general flat-rate tax on consumption expenditures. From the point of view of *horizontal* equity, such a tax is equitable if the index of equality is defined in terms of consumption. By the same token, it is inequitable if the index is defined in terms of income. Families with similar incomes may have differing consumption (or saving) rates, whether due to age or other differences. Such families will pay different amounts of tax, thus violating horizontal equity. Regarded from the viewpoint of *vertical* equity, the general sales tax is proportional as related to the consumption, but regressive as related to the income, base. This is so because consumption as a percentage of income declines (savings as a percentage of income rises) as we move up the income scale. This is shown in line 4 of Table 16-1, where the sales tax appears as a regressive element in the tax structure.[8] The point is further illustrated in Table 13-4. Column I shows the burden distribution of $25 billion raised by a progressive income tax, while column II shows the estimated distribution for a broadly based 5 percent sales tax yielding a similar amount. We note that the effective rate (ratio of tax to income) of the income tax rises as we move up the income scale, while that of the sales tax falls.[9] Moreover, though not shown in the table, the sales tax burden at any given income tends to rise with family size. Since the savings rate at a given level of income falls with family size, expenditures, and hence the tax burden, rise. Thus, it is estimated that at an income level of $5,500, the Michigan sales tax paid by a family of four is $128, whereas a single person pays only $78.[10]

[7] See p. 465.

[8] See p. 391.

[9] Regressivity is more pronounced than shown in the table if the *net* burden of the tax is considered. This is the case as the sales tax is deducted from taxable income under the federal income tax (rather than credited against tax), so that savings from the deduction rise with bracket rates.

[10] Based on sales tax deductions permitted under the federal income tax. See Individual Income Tax Return, Form 1040, 1974.

TABLE 13-4
Burden Impact of Raising $25 Billion in Alternative Ways
(Tax as Percentage of AGI)

Adjusted Gross Income	*Income Tax (I)*	*Broadly Based Sales Tax, 5% (II)*	*Sales Tax with Food Exemptions, 7% (III)*	*Broadly Based Sales Tax, 6% with Credit (IV)*
$ 2,000	—	4.4	3.1	—
4,300	—	3.2	2.9	0.5
5,000	0.5	3.2	2.9	1.0
10,000	2.3	3.0	2.9	3.6
15,000	3.0	2.8	2.9	3.3
50,000	6.0	2.2	2.9	2.6
100,000	8.6	1.8	2.5	2.0

Notes:

Column I: Joint returns, four exemptions. Above $15,000 assumes 10 percent as deduction. All income fully taxable. Assuming the yield from present rates at $100 billion, the above equals one-quarter of present liabilities so as to yield $25 billion.

Columns II and III: Ratios estimated on basis of Tax Foundation, *Tax Burden and Benefit of Government Expenditures by Income Classes 1961 to 1965,* New York: 1967; and Joseph A. Pechman, *Federal Tax Policy,* 2d ed., Washington: Brookings, 1971, p. 157.

Column IV: A credit of $120 (equivalent to $2,000 of tax-free consumption) is given but declines by $24 for each $1,000 of income in excess of $5,000.

This regressive nature of the general sales tax remains but is reduced substantially if home-consumed food is exempted. Two-thirds of the sales tax states provide such exemptions. Since this practice results in a substantial reduction in tax base, the rate as shown in column III must be raised from 5 to 7 percent to maintain the yield. While the tax remains regressive at the very bottom and top ends of the income scale, it now becomes more or less proportional over the middle range. The regressive pattern is greatly dampened, but it is not removed.

Credit

A more effective way of dealing with regressivity is to tackle the problem directly by permitting a tax-free amount of expenditure. This may be done by permitting the taxpayer a corresponding credit against his or her state income tax. Such a credit is now used by seven states and the District of Columbia. In some states, the credit is given as a flat amount, while in others it is limited to taxpayers below a certain income level. In others, the credit declines as income rises. A credit of $4 given in Massachusetts, for example, capitalized at a tax rate of 3 percent, implies a tax-free expenditure of $133. As the credit is given per person, it allows for the number of dependents. Thus it reduces not only regressivity for a given family size, but also the burden for large, as against small, families. For all but low-income taxpayers, this allowance is readily made, since it may take the form of a credit against state income tax. For low-income taxpayers not subject to state income tax, the matter is more difficult, since a direct refund payment is required.

The potentialities of a credit arrangement are shown in column IV of Table 13-4, where it is assumed that a similar amount of $25 billion is obtained from a broadly based sales tax while a more substantial credit is granted. To make up for the resulting revenue loss, a 6 percent rate is now applied. We now find that the sales or value-added tax pattern is progressive over a substantial part of the income scale covering, say, 80 percent of all taxpayers. To hold down the revenue cost of the credit (here set at $120 for a family of four), we assume that the credit is to decline for levels of AGI above $5,000 and to disappear when $10,000 is reached.

As shown in the table, it is thus possible, by use of a credit, to remove regressivity and render the sales or value-added tax progressive over a large part of the income range. At the same time, two important qualifications remain: (1) The effectiveness of the credit device hinges on the feasibility of administering cash refunds at the lower end of the income scale; and (2) the device does not lend itself to achieving progressivity over the upper end of the income scale. There one must either rely on the income tax or, if a consumption base is to be used, apply a personal expenditure tax.

D. PERSONAL EXPENDITURE TAX

It is not surprising, therefore, that in the historical development, income taxation has been identified with progressive taxation and sales taxes with regressive taxation. Accordingly, the political support for income taxation has tended to come from proponents of progression, while that for consumption taxation has tended to come from its opponents. But there is nothing in the logic of the two tax bases which makes this necessarily so. This situation has arisen because the income tax has developed in the framework of *personal* taxation, while consumption taxes have been locked into the vise of the impersonal or in rem approach of sales taxation. This leaves a gap in tax policy choices, especially if society wishes to apply different distributional standards with regard to income and to consumption. This it may wish to do because the social implications of consumption distribution (e.g., differentials in welfare derived from different levels of consumption, resulting envy, etc.) differ from those of income and wealth distribution (e.g., economic and political power).

Resort to a personal type of consumption tax would break this bondage. Such a tax was proposed by the U.S. Treasury during World War II but was given little consideration. While it has been tried in a limited way in Ceylon and India, actual experience with such a tax under modern conditions has been absent to date. It is still a new and exciting idea.[11]

[11] Like most new ideas, it also has a long history behind it. A personalized expenditure tax was put forth as an ideal by Alfred Marshall and proposed in detail by Irving Fisher (*Constructive Income Taxation,* New York: Harper, 1942), who felt (going back to John Stuart Mill) that income taxation is unfair because it discriminates against the saver. While we have found this proposition to rest on a confusion between equity and efficiency considerations (see Chap. 9, p. 221), the expenditure tax is an interesting alternative. In modern form, the case for a personal expenditure tax has been made by N. Kaldor, *An Expenditure Tax,* London: G. Allen, 1955. Kaldor recommends such a tax as a supplement to an imperfectly functioning income tax, especially because of ineffective progression at high-income levels.

Determining Taxable Consumption

When consumption is taken as the index of taxpaying ability, all that has been said previously about the desirability of a global definition of the income tax base again applies.[12] All consumption should be included in the base and people's tax liabilities should be independent of the particular pattern of their consumption outlays. In analogy to the income tax, the taxpayer would determine his or her consumption for the year, subtract whatever personal exemptions or deductions were allowed, and apply a progressive rate schedule to the remaining amount of taxable consumption.

The idea sounds simple, but it remains to be seen how taxable consumption is to be determined. Addition of individual consumption items would not be feasible. One possibility would be to begin with income and deduct savings. To arrive at consumption, savings would have to be defined as *net* saving (saving minus dissaving) or increase in net worth. This would be a formidable task. The best and most feasible procedure would be to determine the taxpayer's annual consumption in line with the following schedule:

1. Bank balance at the beginning of the year
2. + receipts
3. + net borrowing (borrowing minus debt repayment or lending)
4. − net investment (costs of assets purchased minus proceeds from assets sold)
5. − bank balances at end of year
6. = consumption during the year

Consumption in this way would be derived from the change in bank balances and the flow of receipts and nonconsumption payments during the year. The tax return would call upon the taxpayer to declare the listed items (broken down in more detail) just as income is shown under the income tax.

The concept of receipts as used in the above schedule equals income as defined under the income tax, adjusted to exclude capital gains but to include imputed rent of owner-occupied housing as well as all bequests and gifts received. Net investment would be defined to include net purchases of all assets, including owner-occupied residences, but excluding other durable consumer goods. While housing consumption would be included via the imputed rent component of income, purchases of durable consumer goods, such as cars, would be treated as current consumption, with averaging permitted to avoid inequities.

In some respects, the approach would be simpler than under the income tax. The dilemma of how to deal with unrealized capital gains would disappear. If assets were sold, the proceeds would enter into the tax base unless offset by purchases of other assets or an increase in balances. Unrealized changes in the value of capital assets would be irrelevant. Also, there would be no need to determine corporate profits. Dividends would appear as receipts, and unrealized capital gains, obtained through retention of profits or otherwise, would be irrelevant until realization occurred and the proceeds were channeled into consump-

[12] See p. 243.

tion. The difficult problem of depreciation accounting, similarly, would disappear.

But an expenditure tax would also pose new and difficult problems. To begin with, it would be crucial that there be a complete recording of cash balances at the outset. Otherwise, tax-free consumption might be financed later by withdrawing such balances. Inclusion of imputed consumption—e.g., housing and home-grown food—might be needed to obtain a meaningful tax base, especially at the lower end of the scale, so that the imputation problem cannot be overlooked as readily as it is under the income tax. Borrowing must be accounted for. Individual lenders being subject to tax would find it desirable to report loans made so as to reduce their own base; but where lending was by institutions not subject to the expenditure tax, lenders would have to be required to file information returns on loans made.

A problem would arise in dealing with long-lived consumer goods such as housing. These might be taxed either as imputed consumption over their useful life, or at the time of initial outlay, with appropriate averaging permitted. A more serious difficulty would arise in drawing a line between consumption and investment. Certain investments (such as purchase of shares in a country club or a pleasure farm) carry consumption benefits and would be difficult to classify. Outlays on education would pose a similar problem, as they again involve both consumption and investment aspects. The expense-account problem, difficult enough under the income tax, would assume large proportions. Finally, the proper definition of the taxable unit would become of great importance. Unless a strict definition applied, a high-consumption taxpayer might commission a low-consumption taxpayer (under the guise of a gift or otherwise) to make purchases for him or her. Problems of averaging would arise as under the income tax, and administration would be more difficult in that less use could be made of source withholding.

On balance, the administrative difficulties for an expenditure tax may well equal or outweigh those of an income tax. For higher-income individuals at least, more or less complete balance-sheet accounting would be needed. Yet, this is precisely the income range over which effective administration would matter most. At low levels of income, there is relatively little difference between an income and an expenditure tax approach. The distinction becomes of major importance only as we move up the income scale and the savings rate rises.

Finally, it may be noted that the timing of tax liabilities over the taxpayer's life cycle would be more burdensome under the expenditure than under the income tax. Under the expenditure tax, the burden would tend to be heavier during those years of the taxpayer's life when personal obligations are highest and he or she is least able to pay. This might suggest the use of an expenditure tax as a limited supplement to, rather than a replacement of, the income tax.

Evaluation

Though the difficulties might be considerable, a personal expenditure tax along with the income tax would rank high on equity grounds. Use of a personal expenditure tax in lieu of a general sales tax would greatly change the burden distribution of consumption taxes. Effects on the overall tax system could then be tempered by adjustments of the income tax. Thus the expenditure tax could be used in partial substitution for the income tax as a vehicle of progression, leaving the system with a dual approach to personal taxation. In this fashion, distributional objectives might be achieved with less distorting effects.

E. SUMMARY

The role of sales taxation in the United States tax structure is characterized as follows:

1. About 60 percent of sales tax revenue accrues to the states and most of the remainder to the federal government.

2. About one-third of the total comes from general retail sales taxes imposed at the state level. The remainder comes from selective taxes, with nearly one-half thereof drawn from the taxation of tobacco, liquor, and gasoline.

There are various ways in which sales taxes may be imposed and administered. These are the major differences:

3. General sales taxes may be GNP- or consumption-based.

4. Consumption-based taxes may be comprehensive or more narrowly confined.

5. Selective taxes may be designed to serve as benefit taxes, to discriminate against demerit goods, or simply to be imposed on readily available transactions.

6. Sales taxes may be single- or multiple-staged.

7. Single-stage taxes may be imposed at the manufacturer, wholesale, or retail level.

8. Multiple-stage taxes may be of the turnover, or value-added, variety. Whereas the former is undesirable, the latter may serve as a helpful way of administering what, in its final result, is similar to a single-stage tax at the retail level.

Sales taxes have generally been considered as regressive, and have thus been contrasted with the progressive income tax.

9. The regressive nature of the sales tax arises because it falls on consumption, and consumption as a percentage of income declines when moving up the income scale.

10. Regressivity may be reduced considerably by the exemption of certain mass-consumption items or by the granting of a credit against income tax.

11. The linkage between regressivity and consumption taxation could be broken by the use of a personalized expenditure tax.

FURTHER READINGS

Due, John: *Sales Taxation,* London: Routledge, 1957.
Kaldor, N.: *An Expenditure Tax,* London: G. Allen, 1955.
Shoup, Carl S.: *Public Finance,* Chicago: Aldine, 1969, chap. 9.

Slitor, Richard V.: "Expenditure Tax," in Richard A. Musgrave (ed.), *Broad Based Taxes, New and Old,* New York: Committee for Economic Development, 1973.
Tax Foundation: *Special Assessments and Service Charges in Municipal Finance,* New York: 1970.
———: *State and Local Sales Taxes,* New York: 1970.

APPENDIX: Problems of Value-added Tax

As noted before, a sales tax may be imposed in either single- or multiple-stage form. If the latter is implemented in the value-added (rather than the turnover) sense, it is equivalent, from the economists' point of view, to a corresponding single-stage tax. Since the value-added approach has received recent attention, it deserves closer consideration.

FINAL VALUE AS AGGREGATE OF VALUE ADDED

Consider a finished product, such as shoes. Tracing it through the various stages of production, we begin with the rancher selling the hides to the tanner, the tanner selling the leather to the shoe manufacturer, the manufacturer selling the shoes to the wholesaler, the wholesaler selling them to the retailer, who finally sells to the customer. At each stage the value of the product is increased and the sales price rises accordingly. Each increment in price reflects the value added at that stage, with the value or price of the final product equal to the sum of the increments or values added at the various stages. A tax imposed on the increments is thus identical in its base to a tax imposed on the final value of the product.

TYPES OF VALUE-ADDED TAXES

Three major types of value-added taxes (corresponding to the gross national product, net national product, and consumption bases) may be distinguished, although only the consumption type is up for practical consideration.

GNP Type

Suppose now that *all* final goods and services produced and sold during a given period, i.e., the entire gross national product, were subject to a general sales tax. This tax would be applicable to both consumer and capital goods. It would be paid by the seller when the product was sold to its last purchaser, be it a consumer, a firm which adds to its inventory, or a firm which purchases capital goods. With a GNP of \$1.4 trillion, an all-inclusive 5 percent tax would yield \$70 billion. The same would be accomplished by using the value-added approach, taxing each seller at a rate of 5 percent rate on value-added, i.e., gross, receipts minus the cost of purchasing intermediate goods from prior producers in the production line. The tax base at each stage would thus equal depreciation, wages, interest, profits, and rent. This would be the most comprehensive form of value-added tax, and may be referred to as a value-added tax of the GNP type. As noted before, it is equivalent to a sales tax applicable to both consumer and capital goods, with its impact point (in terms of Figure 9-2) at 11 or, which is the same, at 4.

Income Type

The value-added approach, as previously noted, may also be used to implement a sales tax on *net* product. Suppose that the intent is to tax net national product, equal to GNP minus capital consumption allowances or depreciation. Such a tax may be imposed in multiple-stage form by taxing the *net* value added by each firm, with net value added defined as gross receipts minus purchases of intermediate goods and depreciation.[13] The same result may also be accomplished by a general income tax, since the bases of a net product and an income tax are in fact the same. The value-added tax of the income type thus differs from that of the consumption type in that the former permits the firm to deduct depreciation while the latter permits it to deduct gross investment, i.e., purchase of capital goods.[14]

Consumption Type

Next, consider a tax which is to be imposed on consumption only. This may be accomplished in any of three ways, namely, a flat-rate consumer expenditure tax inserted at point 2 in Figure 9-2; a retail sales tax inserted at point 3; or a tax on the incremental value added in the production of consumer goods. The last method is referred to as the consumption type of value-added tax.

The base of the value-added tax is now defined as the firm's gross receipts, minus the value of all its purchases of intermediate products (materials and goods in process) as well as its capital expenditures on plant and equipment. By permitting each firm to deduct its capital expenditures, we are left with the value of consumer goods output only. Such a tax, therefore, is equivalent to a general retail sales tax on consumer goods, the two differing in administrative procedure only.

[13] Such a tax could not be imposed as a tax on the total *net* value of the product when the last sale is made, since this procedure would require the recording of depreciation costs incurred by all producers further down the line. Thus, only the value-added approach is feasible if a sales tax is to be imposed on net product.

[14] The base of the income-type tax therefore exceeds that of the consumption-type tax by the difference between gross investment I_g and depreciation D, i.e., by net investment I_n. Disregarding governmental purchases, indirect business taxes, and net exports, this relationship is brought out by the following identities

$$\begin{aligned} \text{GNP} &= I_g + C \\ I_g &= D + I_n \\ \text{NNP} &= I_n + C \\ \text{NY} &= \text{NNP} \end{aligned}$$

where NNP is net national product, NY is national income, I_g is gross investment, I_n is net investment, D is depreciation, and C is consumption. Note that GNP $- D$, equal to NNP or NY, is the base of the income-type value-added tax; and that GNP $- I_g$, or GNP $-(I_n + D) = C$, is the base of the consumption-type value-added tax.

FEATURES OF CONSUMPTION-TYPE VALUE-ADDED TAX

As noted earlier in this chapter, there is nothing to be said for a value-added tax of the GNP type. The choice between the income and the consumption bases is less evident and, as we have pointed out, involves both efficiency and equity considerations. However, income is already taxed under the income tax which, as a personal tax, is superior to an income-type but in rem value-added tax. A good case can be made, therefore, for relating a possible value-added tax to the consumption base as is, in fact, done in the current European usage of this tax.

Size of Base

The size of the tax base for a consumption-type value-added tax is similar to that of a retail-type sales tax on consumer goods. As was shown in Table 13-3, the base depends greatly on the breadth of coverage, ranging from $622 billion for a broad-based tax (1973 data) to $329 billion for a narrowly defined base. Thus, the former falls short of consumer expenditures by one-quarter, while the latter falls short by 60 percent. Although the retail sales and value-added taxes tend to be thought of as general taxes, in reality they are far below this goal of complete generality.

An Illustration

An illustrative computation of the various types of value-added tax is given in Table 13-A1.

The consumption base, shown in line 10, is computed for each firm by taking total sales receipts (line 4) and deducting the purchase of intermediate and capital goods (lines 6 and 9).[15] The income base, shown in line 11, is computed for each firm as sales (line 4) minus the cost of intermediate goods and depreciation (lines 6 and 7). The GNP base, shown in line 12, finally equals total sales (line 4) minus the purchase of intermediate goods (line 6). Adding the bases for the three firms, we obtain the base for the entire economy. As shown in the last column, the total bases in turn equal the values of consumption, national income, and GNP as defined in the national income accounts.

Collection Method

Taking the consumption type of value-added tax, we have seen that each firm computes its tax base as sales minus purchases of intermediate and capital goods. When it has done so, there are two possibilities for collecting the tax. One, the so-called accounts method, is to ask each firm to pay its tax on the base thus determined. Another, the so-called invoice method, is to have the firm compute its gross tax by applying the tax rate to total sales, and then to credit against this

[15] The text shows derivation of the three bases in line with the so-called deduction method. Alternatively, an "addition method" may be used. For the income base, this simply involves the addition of various factor payments included in line 5. The GNP base is determined by adding factor payments and depreciation (lines 5 and 7). The consumption base is determined by adding factor payments and depreciation (lines 5 and 7) while deducting the purchase of capital goods (line 9). Thus, the addition method is readily applicable to the income type but clumsy for the consumption type of value-added tax.

TABLE 13-A1
Illustration of Value-added Tax Bases

	FIRMS			
	A	*B*	*C*	ECONOMY
Current Receipts				
1. Sale of consumer goods	—	70	151	221
2. Sale of intermediate goods	120	45	—	165
3. Sale of capital goods	—	100	—	100
4. Total	120	215	151	
Current Costs				
5. Wages, interest, profits, etc.	100	80	90	270
6. Purchase of intermediate goods	—	120	45	165
7. Depreciation	20	15	16	51
8. Total	120	215	151	
Capital Costs				
9. Purchase of capital goods	—	—	100	100
Tax Bases				
10. Consumption base (line 4 minus line 6 minus line 9)	120	95	6	221
11. Income base (line 4 minus line 6 minus line 7)	100	80	90	270
12. GNP base	120	95	106	321
National Accounts				
13. Consumption				221
14. Plus investment				100
15. GNP				321
16. Minus depreciation				51
17. National net product (NNP) or national income (NY)				270

tax an amount equal to the tax already paid by the suppliers from which the firm has purchased intermediate and capital goods.[16] By making the tax credit for each firm contingent on presentation of the tax receipt made out to the preceding supplier, the invoice method includes a self-enforcing element as each buyer will demand copy of such receipt. The invoice method is used generally in European countries and constitutes an advantage of the value-added approach, especially in countries where tax compliance is otherwise poor.

Retail Sales versus Value-added Tax

We have seen that the value-added tax of the consumption type has the same base as a retail sales tax with corresponding coverage. This being so, why should

[16] See section on value-added tax in *Broad Based Taxes: New Options and Sources,* R. A. Musgrave (ed.), A Supplementary Paper of the Committee for Economic Development, Baltimore: The Johns Hopkins Press, 1973, especially the contributions by John F. Due, Charles E. McClure, Jr., and Carl S. Shoup.

there be such a strong difference of opinion regarding which of the two taxes is preferable?

One difference relates to the politics of the matter. Proponents of the value-added tax feel that it "looks" different and thus may not share the traditional disrepute of a retail sales tax. This may or may not be the case. If the retailer's gross tax is shown as a separate part of the consumer's price, the consumer should be equally aware of his or her tax under either approach. Beyond this political consideration, there are some technical differences in implementation which are of importance.

Under the retail tax, the number of taxpayers is less than under the value-added tax. This facilitates administration provided that retailers can be reached effectively. In the United States setting, this would be feasible, but in other countries (especially in developing countries where retail establishments are small), it might not be. Under the value-added tax, on the other hand, exclusion of capital goods may be accomplished more effectively than under the retail sales tax, where it is difficult to trace the use of items purchased from the retailer. Furthermore, under the invoice method of collection, the value-added tax has an element of self-enforcement which the retail sales tax lacks.

These and other points may be cited in favor of one or the other approach, but most important is the question of how a federal consumption tax, if it were to be introduced, would relate to the existing consumption taxes at the state level. Since these taxes are in retail form, their integration with a federal consumption tax would be much easier if the latter were also imposed at the retail level. In this case, state taxes could be levied as supplements to the federal tax and the duplicative administrative costs of a federal value-added tax could be avoided. Just as, in the income tax field, we are now in the process of using the federal income tax as a base for state income tax collection, so an integrated system of consumption taxation would be preferable to a set of separate tax administrations. Since it would be exceedingly difficult to integrate a federal value-added tax with retail taxes at the state level, the conclusion is that a federal consumption tax, if it were to be imposed, should also take the retail form.

Chapter 14

Property and Wealth Taxes*

A. Rationale for Wealth Taxation: *Benefit Considerations; Ability-to-Pay Considerations; Social Control; Taxation of Land; Conclusions.* **B. Composition and Distribution of Wealth:** *Stock of Wealth; Distribution of Wealth Holdings.* **C. The Property Tax:** *History; Tax Base; Nominal Rates, Assessment Ratios, and Effective Rates; Market Value versus Income as Assessment Base; Land versus Improvement Components of Base; Burden Distribution; Circuit Breaker; Outlook.* **D. Net Worth Tax:** *Foreign Experience; Problems; Capital Levy; A Net Worth Tax for the United States?* **E. Death Duties:** *Rationale of Death Duties; The Federal Estate Tax; Federal Gift Tax; State Inheritance Taxes; Conclusion.* **F. Summary.**

Having considered the taxation of income and expenditure *flows,* we now turn to that of *stocks,* i.e., of wealth. Such taxes may be imposed on the holding of wealth, including taxes on property and net worth; or they may be imposed on

* *Reader's Guide to Chapter 14:* This chapter examines the role of wealth taxation in the tax system. The property tax, though the oldest tax in the United States tax structure, has always been controversial and is currently again in the center of tax debate. Both its weight in the overall tax structure and its role in local government finance are discussed. The role of death duties, while traditionally minor, is also slated for brief consideration.

the transfer of assets, including transfer by bequest (estate and inheritance taxes) and transfer by gift (gift taxes).[1]

Of all these taxes, only the property tax is of major importance in the fiscal structure of the United States. As previously noted in Table 9-1, this tax was much the most important single source in the United States tax structure up to the 1930s. Thereafter, its relative importance declined sharply because of the rise of income taxation. The property tax, nevertheless, continued to dominate the local tax scene and still furnishes over 80 percent of revenue at that level. Indeed, property taxation in recent decades has been almost entirely local, as the United States has no federal property tax and the property tax lost its former importance for state revenue prior to World War II. Nor does the United States fiscal structure include a net worth tax. Death duties and gift taxes are imposed at both the federal and the state levels, but their contribution to total revenue is only 1.5 and 1 percent at the two levels respectively.

A. RATIONALE FOR WEALTH TAXATION

Some argument for wealth taxation may be made on both benefit and ability-to-pay grounds, but neither suggests a tax such as the existing property tax, imposed more or less uniformly on real property only. Benefit considerations point to a set of in rem–type property taxes on real assets while ability-to-pay considerations point to a personal tax on net worth.

Benefit Considerations

The benefit rationale for wealth taxation is that public services increase the value of real properties and should therefore be paid for by the owners. In its most general form, the supporting argument may be derived from Locke's theory of the state as a protector of property, expounded toward the close of the seventeenth century. One of the basic functions of the state, as seen by the natural-law theorists, is the protection of property; and property owners should therefore pay for the state's expenses. Whatever the merits of the premise as a theory of state, its logic points to a comprehensive tax, including a person's entire property (intangible as well as real property) in the base. Better still, the base would be defined in terms of *net* worth, i.e., the taxpayer's property minus his or her liabilities. Also, in the spirit of this approach, revenue from this tax would be limited to cover the cost incurred in rendering protection services, such as the cost of law enforcement, legislation, and judicial administration. While the range of includable costs is debatable, certainly not all governmental functions would be covered. Use of the property tax for education finance, for instance, cannot be rationalized in this way.

A more specific application of the benefit rule, pertinent especially at the local level, suggests that property owners should pay for particular services which

[1] Taxes imposed on the sale of assets, such as stock-transfer taxes, are of minor importance in the modern tax system and will not be dealt with here.

go to raise property values. Building a sidewalk, for instance, increases the values of adjoining homes, as does the rendering of police protection in the precinct. In some cases, the specific benefit share derived by any one property may be measured by indices such as the length of its road frontage or its location. In others, benefit shares may have to be approximated by relative property values. This line of reasoning, however, does not point to a general tax on real property. Rather, it indicates special charges or assessments, imposed to finance particular services. Such assessments, which are a special form of user charge or of public pricing, are occasionally applied in local finance, but remain of only minor importance in the overall picture. As shown below, a good case can be made for wider use of such charges.[2]

To make a benefit case for the general property tax as now applied, one would have to maintain that all real property benefits equally from local public services and that the value of such benefits equals the property tax yield. Neither proposition holds. The bulk of property tax revenue goes to provide general public services such as education, the benefits from which need not be distributed in line with property ownership. A general tax on real property, therefore, is a poor instrument for charging for services rendered. Other indicators would be superior. Thus, income might be a better proxy than residences for general benefits received by individuals, and value added might be a better proxy than business structures for benefits to firms.

A more subtle benefit argument in support of a local property tax arises from differential service levels among communities. If the level of public services is higher in community A than in community B, this difference will be reflected in higher house values in A. Such will be the case provided that residence in A is prerequisite to the enjoyment of this higher service level. Thus, homeowners in A may be said to benefit, even though the services are not directly housing-related. A benefit link is established, via the capitalization of service benefits, between ownership and the service level. However, this link is a tenuous one and applies only to the extent that service levels in A exceed those in B. The argument does not give benefit-taxation status to the total property tax but only to the differential. If the service level were the same in both A and B (in other words, if the same services were rendered to capital everywhere), there would be no reason for its being reflected in the value of assets. Moreover, if pursued carefully the analysis points to a tax on ground rent rather than a tax on total property values. The reason is that capital will move, thus equalizing net (after-tax) returns, whereas land cannot move between jurisdictions.

Ability-to-Pay Considerations

Consider now the case for wealth taxation from the point of view of ability to pay. As noted previously, there is no single tax base, which is best under all circumstances. In the Colonial period, real estate and personal property (such cattle) were the most convenient index of "faculty," or ability to pay. A significant share of income was received in kind, so that money income as it is now defined would have been a misleading index. But under modern conditions, income is

[2] See p. 665.

received largely in money form and wealth is more difficult to measure than income. Under these circumstances, can property taxation still be justified on ability-to-pay grounds and, if so, in what form?

When considering the use of wealth as a measure of taxpaying ability, we concluded that a tax on wealth, being a supplementary tax on capital income, is not called for if capital income is already taxed under a comprehensive income tax.[3] But we also noted that a wealth tax may be useful in supplementing incomplete coverage of capital income under the income tax. While it may be difficult to reach capital income in developing countries, real property is readily visible to the tax collector and a real property tax, though only a crude substitute, may be used effectively where the income tax fails. Even where the income tax works fairly well, the base of wealth taxation is broader in some respects, as nonearning as well as earning assets are included. However, if wealth is to be taxed on ability-to-pay grounds, what is called for is not an in rem tax on real property but a personal tax on net worth.[4]

This has important implications. First of all, the tax should be imposed on individuals only, with business property being imputed to its owners. Second, the tax should be imposed on an individual's net worth, rather than on the gross value of his or her assets. Both sides of the balance sheet should be considered. Just as a determination of net income involves deduction of interest paid on business debt, so should a person's net worth be determined by deducting his or her liabilities from assets. Third, the tax should be imposed uniformly rather than through differential charges against particular pieces of property. All assets (tangible and intangible) should be included and all debts should be deducted. The principle of global assessment should apply as under the income tax, with exemptions and progressive rates related to the taxpayer's total net worth.

Social Control

Alternatively, the taxation of wealth may be approached not as a matter of charging for benefits received or of ability to pay, but as a form of social control. The social consequences of inequality in the distribution of wealth, as is easily seen, differ from those in the distribution of consumption, so that society may wish to deal with them separately. For this purpose, a progressive tax on wealth, rather than on income, is the proper instrument. As under the ability-to-pay approach, the indication is again for a personal tax and a global wealth definition.[5] But it might now be argued that the base should be defined in terms of gross rather than net wealth, since it is the former which determines the scope of economic control which the owner derives.

Taxation of Land

The singling out of land (as distinct from taxable property in general) has been advocated on both efficiency and equity grounds. Since the return to land is in

[3] See p. 222.

[4] For a development of this view and a plea for a net worth tax, see Lester C. Thurow, "Net Worth Taxes," *National Tax Journal,* September 1972; and Thurow, *The Impact of Taxes on the American Economy,* New York: Praeger, 1971, chap. 7.

[5] See p. 243.

the nature of economic rent (being a return to a factor of production in inelastic supply), it may be taxed without giving rise to an "excess burden." Indeed, land taxation may be used, especially in developing countries to encourage more intensive utilization. Moreover, gains derived from increases in land values may be considered unjust enrichment, as initially argued by Henry George.[6]

Conclusions

Wealth taxation may be advocated on various grounds, each calling for a different type of tax. While the benefit view points to differentiated taxes or charges on particular items of real property, the ability-to-pay approach points to a global and personal tax on net worth. The rationale for a uniform property tax based largely upon realty, as reflected in the existing property tax, is more difficult to establish. However, we should note that it is a convenient means of local taxation and one which is not likely to be dispensed with in the foreseeable future.

B. COMPOSITION AND DISTRIBUTION OF WEALTH

While ample data on the distribution of income are available, statistics on the composition and distribution of wealth are very imperfect. Nevertheless, some picture of the scope and nature of the tax base may be derived and is needed to assess the potential of wealth taxation.

Stock of Wealth

An estimate of total privately held wealth in the United States for 1970 is given in Table 14-1. Although no firm figures are available, we estimate real privately held wealth at about $2.5 trillion and total privately held wealth (net wealth) at $3.1 trillion. With a GNP of $974 billion in that year, wealth holdings are about 3 times GNP. The major categories are housing, fixed business capital (including plant and equipment), and consumer durables. Private debts and claims (such as mortgages, bonds, or shares) are excluded, but privately held public debt and outside money (claims against government) are included.[7] The resulting total equals the combined net worth of the private sector. It falls short of national wealth because wealth owned by government is excluded.[8] As shown below, it substantially exceeds assessed value under the property tax.

[6] Henry George, *Progress and Poverty,* New York; Appleton, 1882.

[7] Private debt is excluded because it enters as both an asset into the balance sheet of the creditor and as a liability into that of the debtor. The same holds for deposits or inside money which, though an asset to the holder, is canceled by debt owed to banks. Outside money (Federal Reserve credit and currency in circulation) is not offset by private debt and hence is included.

[8] It might be argued that inclusion of the public debt is inappropriate since the community "owes the debt to itself." The debt as an asset is offset by the capitalized value of tax liabilities required for debt service, and the rational taxpayer should allow for this. There is merit to this view, but taxpayers are not sufficiently sophisticated to consider the matter in this way. They are not aware of the liability created by capitalizing future tax payments. Moreover, the negative assets (capitalized tax liabilities) needed to service the debt are not distributed in the same way as are debt holdings nor are they deducted in computing net worth. Inclusion of public debt in the wealth tax base is thus justified. See p. 603.

TABLE 14-1
Estimated Value of Privately Held Wealth, 1970
(In Billions of Dollars)

1. Owner-occupied residences	870
2. Rental housing	178
3. Consumer durables	350
4. Fixed business capital	660
5. Inventories	220
6. Land	240
Total, real assets	2,518
7. Public debt, privately held	411
8. Outside money	122
Total, financial assets	533
Total	3,051

Sources:

Lines 1 and 2: Given an assessed value for residential housing for 1966 of $2.36 billion (U.S. Bureau of the Census, *Taxable Property Values,* 1967, p. 7) and assuming an average assessment ratio of 0.325 (same source, p. 11), we obtain an estimated market value of $726 billion. Raising this figure by 23 percent (the 1966–1970 increase in the GNP price deflator for structures), we obtain a total of $890 billion. Allowing for an annual increase at 3 percent, the estimate for 1970 is $1,048 billion. Of this total, 83 percent is allocated to owner-occupied residences (for 1966 ratio see ibid., p. 7) and the remainder to rental housing.

Line 3: Estimate of $190 billion for 1958 (see Dick Netzer, *Economics of the Property Tax,* Washington: Brookings, 1966, p. 144) is raised in line with the percentage increase in consumer expenditures on durables from 1958 to 1970.

Line 4: See *Survey of Current Business,* U.S. Department of Commerce, April 1970. Based on 1968 estimate of $506 billion of undepreciated asset cost.

Line 5: Corporate inventories of $190 billion (*Economic Report of the President, 1971,* p. 287) is raised by 17 percent to allow for noncorporate inventory in accordance with the average ratio of corporation to noncorporation inventory valuation adjustment. (See *Survey of Current Business,* U.S. Department of Commerce, July 1972, p. 38.)

Line 6: Assessed value for acreage, farms, and vacant lots (other than included in lines 1–4) in 1966 of $50 billion raised by assessment ratio of 0.25 gives a total of $200 billion, which in turn is raised by 20 percent to allow for price increase to 1970.

Line 7: Includes $230 billion of publicly held federal debt (see *Economic Report of the President, 1971,* p. 277) and $134 billion of state and local debt (ibid., p. 270).

Line 8: Includes Federal Reserve credit and currency in circulation. See *Federal Reserve Bulletin,* November 1971, tables A4 and A16.

Distribution of Wealth Holdings

While data on the distribution of income are ample, those on the distribution of wealth are very scarce. As noted previously (see Table 10-5), the distribution of capital income is much more unequal than that of wage and salary income. This is further brought out in Table 14-2, lines 1 and 2, where the distribution of total income may be compared with that of capital income. Whereas the upper 40 percent of income recipients obtain 65 percent of income from all sources, they obtain 86 percent of capital income. Capital income is distributed less equally than total income. Since capital income is derived from wealth, this suggests that

TABLE 14-2
Comparison of Estimated Distributions of Income and Wealth

	Lowest Quintile	*Second Quintile*	*Third Quintile*	*Fourth Quintile*	*Highest Quintile*	*All**
I. HOUSEHOLDS GROUPED BY INCOME†						
1. Percent of money income	6	12	18	24	41	100
2. Percent of capital income	2	4	8	12	74	100
3. Percent of gross wealth	7	10	11	16	56	100
4. Percent of indebtedness	4	6	16	28	46	100
5. Percent of net wealth	8	10	10	13	59	100
II. HOUSEHOLDS GROUPED BY NET WEALTH†						
6. Percent of net wealth	—	3	5	16	76	100

* Components may not add to total due to rounding.
† Households are defined as consumer units.
— Below 0.5 percent.
Sources:
Line 1: Income distribution by families and unrelated individuals for 1960, U.S. Bureau of the Census, *Statistical Abstract of the United States,* 1970, p. 323.
Line 2: From *Individual Income Tax Returns, Statistics of Income for 1967.* Same derivation as Table 9-5, column 3. The distribution of adjusted gross income in that source is very similar to that of line 1, so that comparison of lines 1 and 2 is permissible.
Line 3: Dorothy S. Projector and Gertrude S. Weiss, *Survey of Financial Characteristics of Consumers,* Board of Governors of the Federal Reserve System, March 1964, p. 10, chart 2. Data for 1960.
Line 4: Same source as line 3.
Line 5: Estimating the indebtedness of households at $530 billion (*Economic Report for 1971,* p. 270) and gross wealth held by households at $3 trillion (figures for 1970), the distribution of net worth is obtained from the distribution of wealth and debt.
Line 6: Based on Dorothy S. Projector, *Survey of Changes in Consumer Finances,* Board of Governors of the Federal Reserve System, 1968, pp. 318, 320.

the distribution of wealth by income brackets is also much less equal than that of total income. But, as shown in line 3 of the table, this is not the case. While the distribution of wealth is somewhat less equal, the difference is not drastic. The explanation is that wealth is distributed more equally than is capital income. This is true because the concept of capital income as used in line 2 includes cash income only, but not income received in imputed form, such as housing services from owner-occupied residences. At the same time, property yielding such income is held more largely by lower- and middle-income groups.

This finding is strengthened further if we consider the distribution of net worth (gross wealth minus indebtedness), shown in line 5. Since the lower groups owe a smaller share of debt than they own of wealth, the distribution of net worth is more equal than that of gross wealth and only slightly less equal than that of total income.

The pattern of wealth distribution changes strikingly, however, if we turn to the distribution of net worth among households arrayed by net worth rather than by income brackets. As shown in line 6, this distribution is much more unequal. The highest 20 percent of net worth holders are estimated to hold 76 percent of all net worth and the lowest 20 percent to hold practically nothing. The highest 1 percent alone holds an estimated 20 percent and the highest 2 percent holds nearly 30 percent of the total. Inequality in the distribution of wealth by wealth classes is more or less similar to the inequality of distribution of capital income by income classes.

C. THE PROPERTY TAX

We now take a closer look at the local property tax, which is *the* major representative of wealth taxation in our tax system. As previously noted, it is still the second most important tax in the United States and practically the sole source of local finance.

History

The American property tax has its origins in early American history. Initially, it was assessed on selected items of property such as land and cattle, with different rates imposed on various categories. This "classified" property tax was the main source of revenue to the Colonies. During the eighteenth and nineteenth centuries, a greater variety of property emerged, making it difficult to maintain such differentiation. Thus, the tax developed into a general and uniform rate tax. This uniform tax was applied to property independent of form, with total property viewed as a general measure of taxable capacity. Subsequently, this approach gave way under the increasing complexity of property forms. The growing importance of intangible property, in particular, made it increasingly difficult to apply a general tax on a comprehensive base. By the end of the century, the general property tax had been supplanted by a much narrower approach. It became a selective tax on real estate and business personalty (i.e., equipment and inventory) and has remained so ever since. Tangible property (other than real estate) held by persons now largely escapes tax, and no attempt is made to reach intangible property. While the share of the property tax in total tax revenue (including all levels) has declined from over 50 percent at the beginning of the century to around 10 percent at present, property tax revenue as a percentage of privately held wealth or as a percentage of GNP has not changed greatly over the last century. It is estimated that the revenue-wealth ratio has remained at about 1 percent.[9]

The property tax in the United States originated as a local tax and has continued as such. In 1972 it accounted for 83 percent of local tax revenue, its importance being greatest for school districts (98 percent), followed by townships (91 percent) and counties (86 percent). The share was lower, however, for municipalities (64 percent) which were able to develop additional revenue sources.[10] Not only does property tax revenue accrue almost entirely to local government but the tax is imposed locally. It thus differs greatly between localities in both rates and administrative procedure. While some guidance is provided by state legislation and certain types of property (such as railroads and utilities) are assessed by the state, assessment is still far from equalized. The United States property tax differs sharply in this respect from that of other countries, such as the United Kingdom, where the system of "rates" is administered as a national

[9] See Dick Netzer, *Economics of the Property Tax,* Washington: Brookings, 1966, p. 2.
[10] See U.S. Bureau of the Census, *Government Finances in 1971–72,* p. 30.

TABLE 14-3
Property Tax Revenue by Type of Base, 1972
(In Millions of Dollars)

Nonbusiness	
Nonfarm residential realty	19,023
Farm realty	817
Vacant lots	320
Personalty	770
Total	20,930
Business	
Farm realty	1,860
Vacant lots	480
Other realty	9,170
Personalty	4,741
Public utilities	3,019
Total	19,270
Total	40,200

Source: See Advisory Commission on Intergovernmental Relations, *Federal-State-Local Finances: Significant Features of Fiscal Federalism,* 1973–74 ed., Washington: p. 173.

tax although revenue goes to local governments. Among the larger countries, only Canada has a decentralized property tax of the United States type.

Tax Base

The distribution of property tax revenue by type of tax base is shown in Table 14-3 for 1972. The revenue was divided about equally between nonbusiness and business property. In the nonbusiness sector, almost the entire amount came from residential realty, with farm realty, vacant lots, and personalty (i.e., personal property other than real estate) contributing only 5 percent. In the business category, over one-half came from realty and one-quarter from personalty (including, in this case, inventory and part of business machinery).

Turning to the underlying tax base, we find that the total assessed value for 1971 was reported at $695 billion.[11] For 1972, the corresponding total may be estimated at close to $800 billion. The market value of included property, however, was substantially larger since property for tax purposes is assessed below market value. Assuming an average assessment ratio of one-third, the market value of included property for 1972 came close to $2.5 trillion. If we estimate the 1972 value of all privately held real property at $3 trillion (up 20 percent from the 1970 level), it appears that about 75 percent thereof was accounted for by the property tax base, with a good part of the remainder reflecting tax-exempt institutions whose holdings do not appear on the assessment rolls.

[11] U.S. Bureau of the Census, *Taxable Property Values and Assessment–Sales Price Ratios, Part 1, Taxable and Other Property Values,* 1972 Census of Governments, Washington: 1973, p. 4.

The breakdown of the tax base among types of property again shows residential real estate as the major component. Census data for 1971 show 36 percent of locally assessed values to have been from single-family homes, 23 percent from other residential property, 5 percent from vacant lots and acreage, and 37 percent from commercial and industrial property.[12]

Nominal Rates, Assessment Ratios, and Effective Rates

In judging the level of property taxation, it is important to distinguish between the nominal and the effective rate, the latter being the product of nominal rate and assessment ratio.[13] With an estimated assessed value of $800 billion and market value of $2.5 trillion, the 1972 revenue of $40.2 billion gives an effective rate of 1.6 percent and a nominal rate of 5 percent. The latter is usually expressed as $50 per $1,000 of assessed value, the so-called mill rate.

Since it is the effective rate that matters, it would seem to make little difference whether properties are assessed at full market value or less. Depending on the required revenue, a lower assessment ratio simply means that the nominal rate has to be correspondingly higher. Such indeed would be the case if all properties were subject to the same assessment ratio. Actually, assessment ratios differ between jurisdictions, and within any one jurisdiction among types of property, a condition that causes inequities to arise.

Differentials between Jurisdictions In comparing levels of property tax rates between jurisdictions, differences in nominal rates must not be taken to stand for differences in effective rates. Jurisdictions with high nominal rates tend to have low assessment ratios, and those with low nominal rates tend to have high assessment ratios. As a result, the dispersion of nominal rates is significantly greater than that of effective rates. Thus, nominal rates ranged from over 10 percent for the highest 10 percent to under 3 percent for the lowest 10 percent of cities. The corresponding range for effective rates was from over 3 percent to below 1.2 percent.[14]

Failure to apply a uniform assessment ratio across jurisdictions becomes exceedingly important when assessed values are used as a measure of fiscal capacity and considered in allocating state aid among local jurisdictions. To avoid this difficulty, an increasing number of states have introduced measures to secure uniform statewide assessment practices. Short of transferring the assessment function to the state level, full uniformity is difficult to bring about.

But even if assessment ratios were equalized, nominal rates and hence effective rates would still differ among jurisdictions. As a result, location decisions, whether by business or residents, may be affected by tax differentials, leading to inefficient location choices. This influence will be modified where higher rates of property taxation are indicative of higher service levels (rather than higher costs),

[12] Ibid.

[13] We have $T = t_n AV$ and $AV = rMV$, where T is the tax, t_n is the nominal rate, AV is the assessed value, r is the assessment ratio, and MV is the market value. Also, we have $t_e = T/MV$ where t_e is the effective rate. Thus we obtain $t_e = t_n r$.

[14] Approximate ratios, based on U.S. Bureau of the Census, *Taxable Property Values,* 1967, p. 15.

so that tax differentials are offset by benefit differentials. However, such is not always the case. Resulting inefficiencies are a cost of fiscal decentralization which can be eliminated only by equalizing effective rates, at least across neighboring jurisdictions, such as units within a metropolitan area. This equalization, however, involves moving toward a more centralized revenue system, with the likely result of reduced variety on the expenditure side.

Differentials within Jurisdictions While the same nominal rate applies to different types of property in any one jurisdiction, assessment ratios may differ. Thus it is estimated that the 1966 average assessment ratio was 35 percent for residential real estate, 36 percent for commercial and industrial real estate, 24 percent for vacant lots, and 19 percent for acreage and farms.[15] Moreover, differentiation exists even between specific properties within the same general category. In a census study for 1966, for example, 53 percent of the covered sample areas showed coefficients of dispersion in the assessment ratio for nonfarm houses of below 20 percent, 28 percent had ratios from 20 to 30 percent, and the remainder had ratios above 30 percent.[16] Or, to offer another illustration, effective rates of tax on residential houses within the city of Boston ranged from 2.4 percent in the lowest rate quartile to 4.0 percent in the third quartile, with a median ratio of 3.1 percent.[17] These are substantial divergencies, introducing a capricious element of differentiation into the property tax. Although complete conformity in effective rates is difficult to obtain, experts argue that the coefficient of dispersion for single-family houses should not exceed 20 percent.

Market Value versus Income as Assessment Base

In addition to the need for equalized assessment, there is the more basic question of how property values should be measured. Should property be assessed on sales or rental income values and should use be made of actual or potential values? The United States approach has been in terms of sales or market value, while the British tradition has been to assess on the basis of actual rental income derived from the asset. Assuming perfect markets and optimal utilization, this difference disappears since the sales value of property equals the capitalized value of actual income and the latter is equal to its income-earning potential. But under realistic conditions, this equality does not hold.

If property is underutilized, assessment on the income base yields a lower value. Such assessment, therefore, discriminates in favor of underutilization. This has adverse incentive effects, especially in developing countries. Little or no income may be received as land is held idle for speculative purposes or as potentially productive farmland is used for grazing only. In other instances, real estate, such as vacation homes, may be left idle or rented at nominal charges for part of the year. If assessment is based on market value, such understatement of assessed value is less likely to arise since market values are likely to reflect alternative and more profitable uses. However, where markets are imperfect, recorded sales values may also fall short of the potential. To assure full assess-

[15] *Taxable Property Values,* ibid., p. 42.
[16] Ibid., p. 75. The coefficient measures the average deviation from the median assessment ratio.
[17] Ibid., p. 152.

ment, determination of potential income or market value is required. This is feasible only if up-to-date and accurate cadastral surveys are available, a precondition which is usually not met in developing countries. As an alternative, it has been proposed that the determination of full value be obtained through a system of self-assessment, under which the property owner would be required to sell the property at a price equal to his or her declared value. This is an ingenious proposal, but its implementation would be difficult if at all feasible.[18]

Another difference between the market value and income approaches stems from differences in risk. One property with an annual income of $100,000 may have a market value of $500,000, while another property with the same income may have twice that market value. Incomes are capitalized at different rates of interest or, to put it differently, at gross rates which add different risk premiums to the market rate on safe investment. This is the case with regard to properties in urban slums which have high yields of income relative to market values. Such properties do better under the market value approach than under the income base of assessment. Where such differences exist, the market value offers the better base since the income base should be corrected to allow for differences in risk.

Short of a major effort to determine potential as distinct from actual income, market value is the preferable approach. At the same time, even the determination of true market value poses a difficult problem, especially in developing countries.

Land versus Improvement Components of Base

The property tax is imposed on the market value of a given piece of real estate without drawing a distinction between its land and improvement components. Yet, from an economic point of view, this is an important distinction which will be examined when dealing with the incidence of this tax.

Since the supply of land is given, taxing the rent of land or imposing a tax on the value of land (reflecting the capitalized value of its rent) has long been recognized as a form of taxation which is least likely to deter incentives to invest in improvements. Moreover, the windfalls which arise from rising land values due to population and income growth might be considered as socially unwarranted gains. This indeed was the main theme of Henry George's *Progress and Poverty* which swept the United States in the 1890s and gave rise to the single-tax movement, calling for exclusive reliance on land taxation.[19] Unfortunately, the exaggerated claims on behalf of the single tax have interfered with a continuing and strong case for taxing site values at a higher rate.

In the more recent discussion, it has been argued that the urban property tax, by placing a tax burden on improvements, has discouraged such investment, especially in low-income housing. A heavier tax on land value, combined with a lesser tax on improvements and reliance upon user charges, plus taxation of capital gains, might well be helpful to urban reconstruction; it has been advocated as the most desirable direction of property tax reform.[20]

[18] See John D. Strasma, "Market-enforced Self-Assessment for Real Estate Taxes," *Bulletin for International Fiscal Documentation,* September and October 1965.

[19] Henry George, *Progress and Poverty,* New York: Appleton, 1882.

[20] See Dick Netzer, "The Local Property Tax," in G. E. Peterson (ed.), *Property Tax Reform,* Washington: The Urban Institute, 1973, p. 23.

TABLE 14-4
Burden of Real Estate Tax on Low-Income Households and Elderly Single-Family Homeowners, 1970

	REAL ESTATE TAX AS PERCENTAGE OF FAMILY INCOME			PERCENTAGE OF HOMEOWNERS	
*Family Income**	*All (I)*	*Elderly† (II)*	*Nonelderly (III)*	*Elderly† (IV)*	*Nonelderly (V)*
Less than $2,000	16.6	15.8	18.9	74.5	25.5
$2,000– 2,999	9.7	9.5	10.1	70.3	29.7
$5,000– 5,999	5.5	6.2	5.1	32.0	68.0
$10,000– 14,999	3.7	3.9	3.7	6.4	93.6
$25,000 or more	2.9	2.7	2.9	9.8	90.2
All groups	4.9	8.1	4.1	20.2	79.8

* Census definition of income, which excludes imputed rent.
† Age sixty-five and over.
Source: Advisory Commission on Intergovernmental Relations, *Federal-State-Local Finances: Significant Features of Fiscal Federalism,* 1973–74 ed., Washington: p. 201.

Burden Distribution

The property tax in recent years has been the major source of complaint about excessive tax burdens. Yet, the rate of increase in this tax has been less rapid than that of other state and local taxes. Thus, over the decade from 1962 to 1972, property tax revenue increased by 128 percent, as against 160 percent for all other state and local taxes. Property tax revenue as a percentage of personal income has remained constant; and though the effective tax rate (ratio of tax to market values) has risen somewhat, the increase was less than the rise in revenue. The larger part of the revenue gain was explained by an increase in the base, due to both inflation and an increased stock of real property. The particular concern of taxpayers with what they feel to be their rising property tax burden therefore needs explanation. The property tax—or that part of it which is imposed on residents—is more visible than the sales tax; payments are usually due annually in one single installment; and tax liabilities are increased frequently as local fiscal needs require. Moreover, homeowners may not be aware of the rise in housing values due to inflation, a development which is not as apparent as in the case of rising money wages. This makes the property owner feel that taxes are increasing on "the same old house," not being aware that the value of the house has also risen.

Viewed as a tax on housing services, the property tax (at first sight at least) appears highly regressive. As shown in column I of Table 14-4, the tax on real estate as a percentage of family income declines sharply when moving up the income scale; and though the table applies to homeowners only, the burden of the property tax on rental housing (if imputed to tenants) may be expected to show a similar pattern. In interpreting this evidence of regressivity, various queries have to be raised. The income base, as used in the table, excludes imputed rent, and if it were redefined to include the latter, regressivity would be reduced.

Moreover, the table is based on cross-section data showing the relationship between family income and property tax payment for a particular year. If, instead, the comparison could be based on a similar relationship over a longer period, it has been argued that the degree of regressivity would be reduced and that the tax might even turn progressive.[21] The regressive pattern of the table may reflect high housing expenditures of the elderly with typically low income.

The burden distribution of the property tax as a tax on housing services is affected further by differences in assessment ratios and tax rates as applied to various types of property. Thus, it has been shown that effective property tax rates tend to be especially high in low-income neighborhoods, partially because property tax rates in central cities are apt to be high in general and partially because residential properties in low-income neighborhoods are often assessed at a higher portion of market value than are properties in higher-income surroundings.[22]

Our reasoning so far has been based on the hypothesis that the property tax is borne by the consumers of housing services. As we shall see later on, this is a controversial question. Recently it has been argued that the burden of a tax on real property will be spread to all property, so its incidence should be in line with that of a tax on property in general. As shown in line 7 of Table 16-2, this assumption would make it a progressive tax.[23] This reasoning, however, is compelling for perfect markets only. With imperfect market structures, other patterns may result. Thus, that part of the property tax (roughly one-half) which is derived from residential property may fall on the consumers of housing services, be it as owner-occupiers or as tenants. That part which is drawn from property other than residences may be passed on partially to the consumer of other products. As shown in lines 6 to 10 of Table 16-2 and discussed further in Chapter 19, the resulting burden distribution depends greatly on what particular assumptions are made.

Since the major complaint over the property tax has come from homeowners, it is interesting to compare their position as investors in housing services with that of investors in corporate shares, allowing in both cases not only for the property tax but also for the personal income tax and corporation tax. Although the investor in housing services is likely to pay more in property tax, the overall tax burden remains substantially less if all three taxes are combined.[24] This is

[21] The comparison depends on the income elasticity of housing expenditures with respect to "permanent," as against current, income. Estimates of income elasticity with regard to permanent income range from well above 1 percent, which would make for a progressive burden distribution (see Frank de Leeuw, "The Demand for Housing: A Review of Cross-Sectional Evidence," *Review of Economics and Statistics,* February 1971, p. 1) to much below 1 percent, which sustains regressivity (see Geoffrey Carliner, "Income Elasticity of Housing Demand," Institute for Research in Poverty, University of Wisconsin Discussion Paper 144–172, November 1972). For a similar point in connection with sales taxation, see p. 443. Note, however, that this view is not supported by columns II and III of Table 14-4 which show similar patterns for elderly and nonelderly homeowners.

[22] See George E. Peterson, "The Property Tax in Low-Income Housing Markets," in G. E. Peterson (ed.), *Property Tax Reform,* op. cit., p. 110. Peterson also notes that owing to higher risk, the ratio of market value to rent is lower in low-income neighborhoods, so that the tax per dollar of rent is less, thereby providing an offset to the higher assessment ratio.

[23] See p. 393.

[24] Consider a homeowner with a house valued at $35,000. Applying an average property tax rate of 1.8 percent of market value, his property tax is $630. Assuming a 40 percent mortgage at

partially due to the additional burden borne by the shareholder under the corporation income tax, and partially to the favorable treatment of the homeowner under the personal income tax.

Circuit Breaker

Property tax liabilities not only weigh relatively heavily in low-income budgets, but they are also thought to be especially burdensome for the aged. As shown in the last two columns of Table 14-4, a large number of low-income homeowners are elderly, so that the problem does pertain especially to this group. For this reason, measures have been developed in recent years to provide property tax relief for the aged and low-income families. Given mostly in the form of a credit against state income tax, practically all states now apply some such relief provisions, referred to as "circuit breakers." Various techniques are used to limit the credit to low-income families.[25] Most, but not all, states limit the relief to the aged, and all states extend it to renters by stipulating a presumptive property tax. Since vanishing or otherwise limited credits go primarily to low-income families and since exemptions under state income taxes are relatively high, most claimants are without income tax liabilities and the credits must consequently be paid as cash refunds. As in the case of sales tax credits, this provision raises the question of whether such refunds will in fact be claimed by low-income taxpayers.

Outlook

The property tax traditionally has been and still is almost entirely a local tax. This is not surprising since its ready visibility and relative immobility render real property a ready object for local taxation. With elementary and secondary education accounting for 45 percent of local expenditures in 1972, the property tax provides the bulk of educational finance. Since the property tax endowment differs widely among communities, there is substantial variation in the quality of education offered by various communities. Recent court decisions (with judicial interpretation still in flux) have held this variation to be unconstitutional and hence have instructed states and their municipalities to render school finance

---

5 percent, his interest payment will be $700, giving a total deduction from taxable income under the individual income tax of $1,330. With, say, a marginal tax rate of 23 percent, his savings in personal income tax equals $306 (23 percent of $1,330), and his net tax will be $324 ($630 minus $306). Assuming the rate of return on capital to be 5 percent (net of property tax), his imputed rent is $2,074 (5 percent of $35,000 plus $324), and his tax rate thereon is 16 percent ($324 as a percentage of $2,074).

Turning now to the corporate investor, let us assume that his property tax equals 15 percent of profits. His net corporate tax equals $.48\ (1 - .15) = .41$, or 41 percent. The personal tax, assuming a 50 percent dividend distribution, equals $.23 \times .5\ (1 - .15 - .41) = .05$, or 5 percent. His overall tax burden in turn is $.15 + .41 + .05 = .61$, or 61 percent. This is nearly 4 times that paid by the investor in housing services.

For further discussion, see Helen F. Ladd, "The Role of the Property Tax: A Reassessment," in R. A. Musgrave (ed.), *Broad Based Taxes, New and Old,* Committee for Economic Development, Baltimore: Johns Hopkins, 1973.

[25] For a discussion of such credits, see Advisory Commission on Intergovernmental Relations, *Significant Features of Fiscal Federalism,* 1973–74 ed., Washington: ACIR, pp. 172–193. For a critique of these provisions, especially their failure to allow for the taxpayer's wealth position, see Henry Aaron, "What Do Circuit-Breaker Laws Accomplish?" *Property Tax Reform,* op. cit., p. 53.

independent of the local tax base. As we shall discuss further in Chapter 30, this ruling need not mean reduced reliance on property taxation but may merely involve a transformation of the property tax from a local tax to a state tax, with subsequent redistribution of funds among municipalities on a need basis.

D. NET WORTH TAX

In discussing the rationale for property and wealth taxation, we have distinguished between a benefit argument pointing toward differential user charges on real property imposed on an *in rem* basis and an ability-to-pay argument pointing toward a tax on net wealth, imposed on a *personal* basis. The existing property tax—which applies more or less uniformly as an in rem tax to all real property within the jurisdiction—follows neither pattern. We now turn to a brief consideration of its theoretically more attractive though less widely used cousin, the net worth tax.

Foreign Experience

A net worth tax is used in about seventeen countries, including the Netherlands, West Germany, the Scandinavian countries, and Switzerland. India and various Latin American countries also make use of this tax. In most countries the tax is imposed on natural persons only, though in some (including West Germany and India), corporations are also taxable. The definition of taxable assets usually includes intangibles as well as tangibles, and in most cases, all debt obligations are deductible. However, some countries disallow obligations not related to the acquisition of taxable assets. Natural persons are granted exemptions and rates are either proportional (typically 1 percent or less) or progressive (ranging up to 2.5 percent).[26]

The net worth tax, except in the Swiss cantons, is imposed at the central level. Countries making use of this tax usually impose it in addition to the ordinary property tax, with net worth tax revenue typically only a small fraction (below 5 percent) of total revenue. Nevertheless, as noted at the outset of this chapter, a net worth tax is a potentially important component of the tax structure.

Problems

Some of the problems and difficulties posed by the implementation of a net worth tax may be noted briefly.

Tax Base The net worth tax relates to ability to pay. Hence it should be imposed on individuals and not on corporations. Corresponding to the partnership view of the corporation profits tax, the net worth of the corporation should be imputed to the owners. Similar to the case of the income tax, the base should be defined globally, so as to give equal treatment to all components of net worth. Moreover, the principle of uniformity should be applied to both the asset and the liability side of the balance sheet. Intangible as well as tangible and nonearn-

[26] See Roger W. Thomas, *Net Worth Taxation,* unpublished manuscript, Cambridge, Mass.: Harvard Law School, International Tax Program.

ing as well as earning assets should be included. Similarly, all debt obligations should be deductible.

Rates and Exemptions As always, imposition of a personal tax raises the question of exemptions and rate structure. If exemptions and progressive bracket rates are applied under the income tax, they would also seem in order for the surcharge on capital income implicit in a net worth tax. As noted before, the basic question is whether and why such a surcharge is called for. One use of the net worth tax (especially important for developing countries) is as substitute for ineffective taxation of capital income under the income tax. In the case of real property, at least, the property itself may be located more readily than the income derived therefrom, and the taxes in combination may be administered more effectively than either tax by itself can be.

Measuring Net Worth Administration of the net worth tax calls for identification of the taxable assets and for verification of debts claimed. In short, it calls for tax returns which include an annual balance sheet in which the taxpayer's assets and liabilities are listed.

With regard to accounting for assets, authorities must be assured that all assets have in fact been declared. Moreover, there is a problem of asset valuation. Difficulties inherent in current valuation of all assets have already been discussed in connection with capital gains taxation. Here, as there, approximations must be used. Thus, assets subject to property tax (especially if assessment is equalized) may be valued on that basis, while others, such as traded securities, may be valued by market quotation. For the remainder, rough approximations (such as cost of acquisition minus depreciation) have to be used. Similar difficulties arise with deductible debts.The difficulties of administering a bona fide net worth tax are considerable. It is not surprising, therefore, that in many instances it degenerates into a tax on real estate only. However, they are not insurmountable, especially if administration is integrated closely with that of the income tax. In the age of computerized tax administration, cross-checking between the net worth and income tax returns should permit the identification of most income-earning assets and allowable liabilities.

Capital Levy

Still another type of wealth taxation takes the form of a capital levy. Imposed on a once-and-for-all basis, such levies have been used by various countries in emergency situations such as wartime or postwar adjustments, but there is no record of such levies in United States fiscal history. If truly in the nature of a once-and-for-all tax, which is neither anticipated nor expected to be repeated, such a levy would differ from other forms of wealth taxation (imposed annually or at death) because it has no disincentive effects.[27]

A Net Worth Tax for the United States?

Speculation on the future of tax reform in the United States should allow for the possibility of a net worth tax. For various reasons, such a tax would have to be

[27] See p. 464.

applied at the federal level and it would have to be related to death duties and the property tax. Quite apart from concern with the distribution of wealth as distinct from that of income, a case might be made also for spreading the taxation of capital income more evenly between the taxation of capital income and the taxation of capital stock or wealth, an adjustment which need not imply an increase in the overall tax burden on capital. Also, an argument can well be made for transforming at least part of the in rem tax on real estate (which constitutes the present property tax) into a personal tax on net worth.

E. DEATH DUTIES

We turn now to the taxation of wealth, not on an annual basis but at the time of transfer by bequest or gift. Taxation of bequests is much the more important item. It may be in the form of taxes imposed on the estate under the federal type of estate tax or of inheritance taxes imposed on the heir by the states. As shown in Table 9-1, these taxes are not of major revenue importance and, even if expanded substantially, could not become such. But they are of considerable interest as a matter of social philosophy and as a policy instrument in adjusting the distribution of wealth. For this reason they are an important element of the tax structure.

Rationale of Death Duties

Death taxes may be imposed in various forms and for various reasons. Disregarding gifts for the time being, let us suppose that all transfers are made at death. The tax may then be imposed either on the estate (referred to as estate tax) or on the heir (referred to as inheritance tax) with or without allowance for family ties between testator and donee. Which is to be considered the proper approach depends on the objectives that are to be achieved. Various objectives and types of taxes may be distinguished.

1. Society may wish to limit a person's right to dispose of his or her property at death. Society says to individuals that they may use their property during their lifetime, but that their title ceases or is curtailed at death. In this case, an estate tax of the federal type is the appropriate approach. If society feels that small estates may be left but not large, progressive rates are in order. If society wishes to allow free bequests up to a certain amount, an exemption is in order. If it wishes to confiscate estates in excess of a certain limit, a 100 percent rate above that limit would apply.

2. Society may wish to limit a person's right to acquire wealth by way of bequests, i.e., without his or her "own effort." This objective is served by an inheritance tax, imposed on the heir. Again, society may wish to differentiate between small and large acquisitions, thus calling for progressive rates. Given this objective, it would in fact be more sensible to combine such accessions from all sources, i.e., to relate progression to total accessions from bequests over lifetime, rather than to each specific inheritance. This is referred to as an "accessions tax."

3. Society may have the more general objective of achieving a more equal distribution of wealth. Since the institution of inheritance is one of the major factors making for concentration of wealth, an inheritance tax or, better, an accessions duty is one of the more effective approaches to this problem. The logic of this approach, however, would call for rate progression relating to the heir's total net worth (including the bequest and his or her prebequest wealth) rather than on the size of the bequest only. Moreover, a supplementary measure might be a concentration-of-wealth tax, applicable to the combination of wealth through marriage.

4. Finally, the objective may not be one of imposing a separate tax on transfers at death, but simply to correct the income tax and fully implement the accretion view of income by including the receipt of bequests as part of the taxpayer's income under the income tax. This objective was previously noted as a possible rationale for a wealth tax. If implemented as a death duty instead, it would call for imposition of the tax on the heir, but the rates in this case would depend on the heir's other income. This approach would call for liberal averaging allowances so as to avoid the penalty of bunching under progressive income tax rates.

There is no reason, of course, why these four objectives should be mutually exclusive. Society may wish to integrate bequests into the income tax as suggested under 4, while at the same time pursuing both objectives 1 and 2. Thus, it may wish to impose both an estate tax, thereby limiting the testator's right to dispose, and an inheritance tax designed to limit the heir's right to receive and/or to compensate for noninclusion of bequests into taxable income. Choice among these objectives and selection of the appropriate tax device, it should be noted, is an issue which should be distinguished from the further question of how high rates should be and how far equalization should be pushed.

Moreover, the design of death duties must again address itself to the proper definition of the taxpaying unit, involving society's view of the family.[28] While people may agree that there should be some limit to the leaving or receiving of bequests, most people feel that this limitation should be less strict if the recipient is in a close family relationship to the deceased. This principle is reflected under the federal estate tax which exempts up to one-half the estate if left to the spouse. However, an inheritance tax approach is needed if finer differentiation is to be applied. This is done under the state inheritance taxes which apply differential rate structures depending on the closeness of the family relationship.

The Federal Estate Tax

We now turn to the federal estate tax and some of its problems. From a technical point of view, this tax and the closely related problem of gift taxation have been one of the most complex areas of the tax law.

Structure The filing requirement is set at gross estates of $60,000 or above. The gross estate includes all the property owned by the decedent[29] but is then reduced by certain items (see Table 14-5) to arrive at the net or economic estate. These deductions include funeral and administration expenses, debts owed, and charitable contributions. Also, up to one-half of the estate may be deducted for tax purposes if left to the spouse, as well as a general exemption of $60,000. As

[28] See also p. 275.

[29] Capital assets are valued according to their market value at time of death. As noted before, this base also comes to be used for determination of capital gains if the asset is sold by the heir to the capital. See p. 248, footnote 22.

TABLE 14-5
Reported Federal Estate Tax, 1969
(In Millions of Dollars)

Tax Base	
Total estates	27,445
Deductions	
Expenses	−1,309
Debts	−1,691
Charitable	−2,132
Marital	−5,527
Exemptions	−8,037
Additions	
Lifetime transfers	+2,262
= Taxable estates	11,011
Tax	
Tax before credits	3,416
− Credits	413
Tax after credits	3,003

Note: Items may not add to totals because of rounding.
Source: U.S. Department of the Treasury, *Estate Tax Returns, 1969, Statistics of Income.*

shown in the table, only 42 percent of the amount declared comes to be included in the tax base, with most of the loss due to the marital and personal exemptions. The taxable estate is then subject to progressive rates ranging from 3 percent on the first $5,000 to 30 percent on $110,000 to $250,000, 49 percent on $2 to $2.5 million, and 77 percent for estates above $10 million. As we shall note later, a limited credit for state inheritance taxes is permitted.

The number of estate tax returns filed in 1970 was 133,944, which corresponds to about 8 percent of the number of deaths. The distribution of returns is shown in Table 14-6. We note that the largest 8 percent of all taxable estates contributed 50 percent of the tax base and 61 percent of estate tax revenue. The estate tax in this respect has remained much like the income tax prior to the 1930s, when it was applied to the very small fraction of the highest recipients only. We also note that a large share of the smaller estates (those up to $500,000) are not subject to tax and that even some of the larger estates escape without tax liability. This points to the importance of exemptions, deductions, and related aspects, to which we now turn.

Estate Tax Issues Estate tax design raises a host of technical issues, only some of which are noted here.

1. To begin with, there is the problem of interfamily bequests. The estate tax permits up to one-half the property of the deceased to be transferred to the spouse tax-free. Suppose that Mr. D leaves a net estate of $300,000, after allowing for expenses and deducting debts. Of this, he leaves $150,000 to his wife tax-free. Deducting his exemptions of $60,000, a taxable estate of $90,000 remains. Mrs. D at the time of her death again has a personal exemption of $60,000, leaving a taxable estate of $90,000. The initial exemption of half the estate has two consequences. If Mrs. D decides to consume her bequest during her lifetime, her ability to do so is substantially increased by the marital exemption. But even if she maintains the estate intact, the allowable exemption has, in fact, been doubled from $60,000 to $120,000.

Alternative approaches to correct for this might be *(a)* to disallow the initial marital exemption, thus treating the spouse like any other heir or *(b)* to disallow the second $60,000 exemption, in which case the surviving spouse would be treated preferentially only for purposes of consumption of the estate. Which of these policies is preferable depends on how one sees the role of inheritance and the family in society. Most people would agree that the right to leave or receive inherited wealth is more clear-cut in the case of close relatives than in the case of strangers or distant relatives. On the basis of this argument, some such allowance as now applies to the spouse might in fact be extended to estates left to children. As we shall see presently, this principle is applied extensively under the inheritance taxes of the states.

2. Next, there is the use of trusts as a device of estate tax avoidance. The deceased may leave half his or her property to the surviving spouse tax-free, while leaving the other half not outright (in which case it is taxable) but in *trust,* provided *(a)* that the spouse receive the income therefrom during his or her lifetime (i.e., establishing the spouse as a life tenant), *(b)* that children of the deceased become life tenants after the death of the spouse, and *(c)* that at the death of the children, the estate becomes the property of a third person (the remainder man). An estate tax is paid initially when the estate is placed in trust, but the trust arrangement permits the skipping of the estate tax when the property passes from the surviving spouse to the children.[30] If the property had been left to the surviving spouse outright, such a tax would have been due at the time of the spouse's death.

Given these tax implications, trust arrangements are advantageous to wealthy decedents and wide use is made of them. While there is nothing wrong with trust arrangements as a way of designing bequests, the tax implications of such arrangements should be neutralized. While the revenue loss due to generation skipping is not very large—involving, say, $500 million—the equity implications are unfortunate and should be avoided. Thus the trust should be made taxable at the death of the life tenant as part of the estate, or it may be made taxable as received by the successive tenants. While certain legal difficulties are involved, they should not be insuperable.[31]

3. Finally, there is again the problem of charitable contributions. Under current law, there is no limit to the deduction of charitable contributions under the estate tax. In 1966, such contributions amounted to $1.3 billion, or about 6 percent of estates. Frequently, such contributions go to established foundations, the Rockefeller, Carnegie, and Ford Foundations having been created in this fashion. Also, bequests are a major source of support for private universities. High estate tax rates make such contributions more or less costless to donors with large estates and thus encourage them to use their funds in this fashion.

As in the case of charitable contributions under the income tax, and perhaps

[30] The permissible chain of life tenants is not unlimited, such limitations as apply being a matter of state law. According to the law of most states, the trust must terminate (the property must accrue to the remainder man) not later than twenty-five years after the death of the last life tenant living when the trust is established. This effectively limits the trust arrangement to a hundred years or so.

[31] Under British law, the trust is included in the estate of the first life tenant and the estate tax is allocated between the property and the trust. Several objections have been raised to this procedure, but it would seem to be the most feasible.

TABLE 14-6
Distribution of Federal Estate Tax Returns, 1969

Size of Estate (Thousands of Dollars)	NUMBER OF RETURNS		*Taxable Estates* (Millions of Dollars)*	*Tax after Credits (Millions of Dollars)*
	Taxable	*Nontaxable*		
0– 100	27,637	26,895	777	126
100– 500	58,245	13,457	5,078	1,042
500– 1,000	5,024	121	2,059	536
1,000–10,000	2,435	47	3,178	1,024
10,000 and over	63		541	271
All	93,424	40,520	11,633	3,000

* Includes taxable returns only.
Note: Items may not add to totals owing to rounding.
Source: U.S. Department of the Treasury, *Estate Tax Returns, 1969, Statistics of Income,* p. 14.

more so, their role under the estate tax poses cultural, social, and political issues which go much beyond the realm of tax policy and which cannot be pursued here. The institution of foundations undoubtedly provides funds for many useful purposes which would not be forthcoming from the public budget, but it also permits a high degree of private control in the use of what are essentially public funds. To deal with these issues, the Tax Reform Act of 1969 places certain restrictions on the use of such funds, especially for political purposes.

In addition, it is necessary to assure that the setting up of tax-free foundations is not used to accomplish essentially private purposes. Thus, a foundation may be set up to maintain family control over a particular business. If the estate tax had to be paid, the business would have to be sold and control would go to the public. If a foundation is established which owns the business, continued control may be maintained via control over the foundation. The Tax Reform Act of 1969 tries to deal with this problem by requiring the broadening of control over time. It also imposes certain restrictions, including a requirement to file tax returns, to pay a 4 percent tax on investment earnings, and to dispose of all earnings.

Rates and Exemptions We have seen that estate tax rates begin at a low rate, rise rather slowly, and reach very high levels at the top end of the scale. This progression raises the question of whether a somewhat higher level of initial rates would substantially increase revenue. As the distribution of the base in Table 14-6 shows, application of even substantially higher initial rates to the base as now defined would not greatly increase revenue and could not render the estate tax a major revenue source in the overall revenue picture.

The next question is whether the revenue potential of the tax could be increased substantially by lowering the rather high present level of exemptions. It is thus important to know the potential size of the tax base. The number of federal estate tax returns for 1966 (the latest year for which such data are available) was 97,000, the value of gross estates (before deductions and exemptions) was $21.8 billion, the amount subject to tax was $9.2 billion, and the tax yield was $2.4 billion. The question is how large a fraction of the potential tax base this reflects.

Unfortunately, there are no very reliable data for answering this question. While estate tax returns for 1966 numbered 97,000 (and taxable returns 67,000), deaths numbered 1.8 million. The total number of estates associated therewith may be estimated at somewhat less than 1 million.[32] Thus, filed and taxable returns were about 10 and 7 percent of total estates respectively. Only a very small fraction of estates was covered. Since the covered estates included the larger estates, this does not, however, tell us what fraction of the potential tax (in dollar terms) was included.

The potential base is given by the amount of wealth which passes through estates each year. While there are no reliable data by which to estimate this amount, some speculation may be helpful to suggest the order of magnitude. The value of privately held wealth (net worth) in 1970 was estimated at $3.1 trillion in Table 14-1. A corresponding figure for 1969 might have been $2.9 trillion. Assuming that about 3 percent of the total passes through estates each year, we estimate the potential base at about $90 billion.[33] This compares with the amount of $27.4 billion actually recorded in tax returns. On the basis of these figures, it thus appears that the value of estates recorded on returns accounts for only one-third of the total and that the actual tax base (after allowing for exemptions and deductions) accounts for only 10 percent thereof. A very substantial expansion in the base would thus be obtained by reducing exemptions, especially if combined with an increase in the lower bracket rates. Nevertheless, even doubling revenue would not render the estate tax a major revenue producer relative to other sources, such as the income, property, or sales tax. The trouble simply is that death is too infrequent an event.

Federal Gift Tax

As noted at the outset, estate taxation and gift taxation are inherently linked. An estate tax without a gift tax could be readily bypassed by inter vivos gifts. The federal estate tax establishes an assumption that gifts made within three years before death are considered to be in contemplation of death, and it includes such gifts in the taxable estate.[34] However, the Treasury must prove its case and the assumption is mostly ineffective. In any case, the need for gift taxation remains with regard to lifetime transfers made well in advance of death.

Ideally, gift and estate taxes should be integrated into a single transfer tax, but such is not the practice now. The United States gift tax is imposed as a separate tax. Like the estate tax, it is payable by the donor, who is permitted an annual exemption of $3,000 per recipient, plus a cumulative lifetime exemption of $30,000. These exemptions are available to husband and wife each. Tax rates range from 2.25 percent on the first $5,000 to 22.5 percent at the $100,000 to

[32] This estimate is based on John C. Bowen, "Transfer Tax Yields," *National Tax Journal,* March 1959.

[33] Based on John C. Bowen, op. cit., who derives the 3 percent estimate from available data on distribution of wealth holdings by age groups and application of mortality rates thereto.

[34] Amounts thus taxed appear as "lifetime transfers" in Table 14-5.

$250,000 range, and 57.7 percent for gifts in excess of $10 million. These rates are somewhat below those of the estate tax, but the rates applicable to gifts made in any one year depend on a cumulated gift total, including gifts made in past years.[35]

It follows that people can obtain tax savings by disposing of part of their estate by gifts inter vivos, rather than by bequests. Given this advantage, it is surprising that only relatively limited use is made of this option. Total gifts in 1966 reported for gift tax purposes amounted to $4 billion, taxable gifts to $2.5 billion, and gift tax liability to $413 million. With reported gross estates of $21.7 billion, evidently only 15 percent of reported transfers were in the form of gifts. People, it appears, are willing to pay for holding on to their wealth to the last day.

Given the limited use of the gift device, integration of gift and estate taxes is not as urgent as it might seem, but would nevertheless represent an improvement in the equity of the tax structure. Under the unified system, there would be only one set of exemptions, the tax would be paid on a cumulative basis on gifts, with the estate at death considered a final gift and treated in the same fashion.

State Inheritance Taxes

Death duties at the state level take various forms. They are applied most commonly in the form of inheritance taxes, imposed on the heir. Such taxes are used in thirty-nine states. Different exemptions and rate schedules apply, depending on the heir's family relationship to the deceased. This approach is illustrated by the following pattern, used under the Minnesota law.[36]

	Rates, %	*Exemption*
Spouse	1.5–10	$30,000
Child or parent	1.5–10	$6,000
Brother or sister	6–25	$1,500
Other than relative	8–30	$ 500

Eight states do not use inheritance taxes but only estate taxes, with rates from 8 to somewhat above 20 percent and exemptions substantially below those at the federal level. Eleven states also impose a gift tax.

Under a law passed in 1926, state estate taxes may be credited against the federal estate tax, up to 80 percent of the federal liability. The purpose of this law was to coördinate estate taxes among states and to avoid unfair competition for wealthy residents. This provision is still in effect, but has lost its significance since it relates to federal liabilities under 1926 rates only. Nevertheless, it enables states to gain revenue through estate taxes for at least this amount. Accordingly, all states, including those which impose inheritance taxes, have a minimal estate tax to pick up this credit.

[35] The tax applicable to a gift made this year is computed as the excess of (1) the tax applicable if all past gifts had also been made this year over (2) gift taxes paid in past years.

[36] See Tax Foundation, *Facts and Figures,* New York: 1973, p. 208.

Conclusion

As follows from the preceding analysis, the present structure of death duties in the United States tax system is hardly satisfactory. If death duties are to play a major role, this has to be accomplished (for reasons similar to those applicable to progressive income taxation) largely at the federal level. An integrated system of federal transfer taxes (including death and gift taxes) is called for. Exclusive reliance on the estate tax approach appears undesirable, since it does not make allowance for the family relationship between testator and heirs. Moreover, the wealth of the recipient, as well as the size of the estate, may be considered relevant. Reform in this area should therefore go beyond narrow estate tax reform and consider a broader approach to the entire issue of federal death duties.

F. SUMMARY

As a general background for wealth taxation, we have noted that:

1. A rationale for wealth taxation may be based on either benefit or ability-to-pay considerations, but neither points to the present type of real property tax.

2. Residential housing accounts for about 40 percent of privately held real property.

3. The distribution of wealth is more unequal than that of income.

The property tax poses many problems of analysis and administration. As the major source of local tax finance, it remains one of the crucial concerns of tax policy:

4. About one-half of property tax revenue is derived from residential property and one-half from business property.

5. A large part of real property is covered by the property tax. However, the property tax base or assessed value is typically only one-third of market value.

6. A distinction must be drawn between nominal and effective rates.

7. The incidence of the property tax burden remains controversial. Viewed as a tax on capital income, it is progressive. When viewed as a tax on housing consumption, it is regressive at the lower end of the income scale.

8. Under the so-called circuit breaker, property tax relief is given to the low-income elderly.

9. An alternative form of wealth taxation would be provided by a personal-type tax on net worth. Such a tax could be applied with exemptions and progressive rates, and would differ sharply from the present type of tax on real property.

Finally, taxes are imposed on estates and gifts at the federal level and on inheritances at the state level.

10. The appropriate type of death duty will depend on what it is intended to accomplish.

11. The federal estate tax applies to estates prior to distribution to the heirs. The tax grants high exemptions, thus applying to large estates only, but combines this approach with sharply rising bracket rates.

12. Effective estate taxation involves numerous technical problems relating to legal arrangements, such as trust accounts.

13. Effective estate taxation must be coordinated with a similar taxation of gifts.

14. State inheritance taxes apply to the heir and are imposed at moderate rates.

FURTHER READINGS

Netzer, Dick: *Economics of the Property Tax,* Washington: Brookings, 1966.

Peterson, George E. (ed.): *Property Tax Reform,* Washington: The Urban Institute, 1973.

Shoup, Carl S.: *Federal Estate and Gift Taxes,* Washington: Brookings, 1966.

———: *Public Finance,* Chicago: Aldine, 1969, chaps. 14, 15.

Tait, Alan A.: *The Taxation of Personal Wealth,* Urbana: The University of Illinois Press, 1967.

Thurow, Lester C.: *The Impact of Taxes on the American Economy,* New York: Praeger, 1971, chap. 7.

Chapter 15

Payroll Tax*

A. Development. B. Coverage. C. Administration. D. Equity Aspects.

It remains to consider the payroll tax. Imposed as *the* source of finance for social insurance, this tax has increased greatly over the last decade. In 1960, it contributed 18 percent of federal tax receipts. By 1970, this share had risen to 26 percent and the payroll tax had become the second most important federal revenue source. By 1974, the payroll tax contribution had come to account for nearly one-third of the total. Payroll taxes as a percentage of personal income rose from 4 to 8 percent over the same period. Payroll taxation is also being used at the local level as an approximation to a local income tax,[1] but our present focus is on the social security tax. Since the payroll tax is an intrinsic part of the social security system, it cannot be properly evaluated without reference to the transfer payments to which it gives rise. Consideration of these broader issues of social security, however, is postponed until later,[2] leaving present concern with the tax side only.

* *Reader's Guide to Chapter 15:* This chapter deals with payroll taxes from the point of view of tax structure only. An evaluation of the payroll tax as an instrument of social security finance follows in Chap. 31 and a discussion of its incidence in Chap. 17.

[1] See p. 282.

[2] See Chap. 31, Sec. C, p. 681.

A. DEVELOPMENT

Old-age and survivors insurance (OASI) was introduced in 1935. Designed to provide retirement payments for the aged, it was to be financed by a payroll tax. Revenue from this tax was to suffice to accumulate reserves and to put the system on a self-financing basis. For this purpose, gradual increases in tax rates were provided for. The initial rate of tax was 1 percent, payable by employees and employers alike and applied to the employee's first $3,000 of wage income. The range of covered employments to which the tax applied was relatively limited. Since then, there have been repeated increases in benefit levels and in payroll tax rates, as well as in the amount of wage earnings subject to tax and in the range of covered employment. Disability insurance was added. The 1974 (OASDI) rate is 4.95 percent on each employer and employee and applies to the first $13,200 of wage income, with the ceiling scheduled to rise automatically with the price level in future years.

The social insurance legislation of 1935 also provided for a system of unemployment insurance. Unemployment insurance is provided under state law and varies slightly among states. However, it is financed by a federally administered payroll tax of 3.2 percent applicable to the employer only, and in most states it covers the first $4,200 of earnings.

The most recent addition to the social insurance system is hospital and medical insurance for the aged (Medicare). The former is financed by a contribution of 0.9 percent from employers and employees each. Combined with the OASDI rate of 4.95 percent, the total social security (OASDHI) payroll tax for each is 5.85 percent. This rate is scheduled to rise to 7.45 percent by the year 2011.

Combining the OASDI, hospital, and unemployment parts of the payroll tax, the total (for both employee and employer contributions) now equals 9.9 + 1.8 + 3.2, or 14.9 percent. If social insurance is expanded in the medical area, which is likely to be done, a substantial further increase to, say, 25 percent may occur. Even this, however, would still leave payroll tax rates below the levels applied in most European countries.

B. COVERAGE

The coverage of the initial social security legislation was relatively limited, but it has expanded greatly since then. Since 1956 the system has covered practically all employees other than some groups, such as federal employees and railroad workers, who are covered by separate systems. Similarly, almost all self-employed workers are included.[3] At the same time, the OASDI tax base falls considerably short of total personal income. This is shown in Table 15-1. The major loss of base (line 2) reflects noninclusion of capital income. Further base loss due to noncovered employment (line 4) is relatively small, but the exclusion of earnings above the ceiling (line 6) accounts for a further substantial reduction.

[3] Self-employed persons pay a combined (OASDHI) rate of 7.9 percent (1974).

TABLE 15-1
OASDI Tax Base, 1973
(In Billions of Dollars)

1. Personal income	944.9
2. — sources other than wages and salaries	318.1
3. Total wages and salaries	626.8
4. — noncovered wages and salaries	14.4
5. Wages and salaries in covered employment	612.4
6. Not reported taxable	129.5
7. Reported taxable	482.9

Notes:
Line 5: Includes self-employed.
Line 6: Includes slab in excess of $9,000 (the 1972 ceiling).
Sources: *Survey of Current Business,* U.S. Department of Commerce, July 1974, p. 22, and *Social Security Bulletin,* U.S. Department of Health, Education, and Welfare, June 1974, p. 56.

C. ADMINISTRATION

The payroll tax is collected from the employer, including the contributions of both employer and employee, the latter's being withheld at the source. Since the tax is on gross earnings and no allowance is made for exemptions, the employee need not be required to file a return. The self-employed, of course, must file a return since there can be no source withholding.

As an in rem tax, imposed on wage income and readily subject to withholding, the payroll tax is an ideal tax from the administrative point of view. It brings in a large amount of revenue while involving a minimum of complexity and compliance cost. Even in the case of the self-employed, compliance can be relied upon since it is in the taxpayer's interest to contribute in order to obtain the resulting benefit claims. The only difficulty arises in applying the taxable wage limit where wage or salary income is received from more than one source. In this instance, the upper limit of taxable earnings is not determined on a global basis, so that a person may be taxed on more than $13,200. Moreover, if more than one member of the family is in covered employment, each will be subject to tax. Somewhat unfortunately, this is only partially reflected in the subsequent benefit structure.

D. EQUITY ASPECTS

Payroll taxes, when introduced in 1935, were thought of as contributions for the purchase of insurance benefits, i.e., retirement income and unemployment compensation. The equity of the system was thus viewed in terms of *net* benefits received, rather than in terms of the tax burden only. Assuming an assignment of individual benefits in line with individual contributions and considering the net impact on lifetime incomes, the distributional results of the scheme would be neutral. Use of a quid pro quo benefit formula, however, did not wholly apply

TABLE 15-2
Distribution of OASDI Payroll Tax Burden among Hypothetical Income Recipients

1. Wage and salary income $	3,000	5,000	9,000	15,000	50,000	100,000
2. Other income $	100	250	900	3,000	15,000	30,000
3. Total income $	3,100	5,250	9,900	18,000	65,000	130,000
4. Tax base $	3,000	5,000	9,000	13,200	13,200	13,200
5. Tax at 9.9% $	297	455	891	1,307	1,307	1,307
6. Average rate on wage income %	9.9	9.9	9.9	8.7	2.6	1.3
7. Average rate on total income %	9.5	8.6	9.0	7.3	2.0	1.0

Notes: Rates and ceiling applicable in 1974.
Line 2: Hypothetical levels of capital income are used for purposes of comparison.
Line 5: Both employer and employee contributions are assumed to be borne by the wage earner.
Line 6: Equals line 5 as percentage of line 1.
Line 7: Equals line 5 as percentage of line 3.

even at the beginning. Redistributional elements were already present in the original benefit formula, resulting in a higher benefit-to-contribution ratio for low-income contributors. Over the years, this element has expanded and has rendered the system increasingly redistributive. This development has led many observers to the view that social security benefits should not be considered in insurance terms, but as an expenditure program forming part of an overall policy of income maintenance, to be provided for (like other expenditures) out of general tax revenue. Looked at in this way, the payroll tax may be judged like any other tax, independent of the benefit side of the social security system.

Whether this is the proper view of the matter we shall consider later, when the problems of social security finance are examined.[4] Here it need only be noted that the payroll tax, *if* considered as part of general revenue and independent of benefits, is a highly inequitable tax. Horizontal equity is offended by the fact that wage income only is taxed, while capital income is excluded. From the point of view of vertical equity, the payroll tax ranks low because it is regressive owing to (1) the exclusion of capital income, an income share whose importance rises with total income; and (2) the exclusion of the slab of wage income above the included level. The ceiling, in fact, inverts the exemption principle as applied under the income tax by providing for a high-income exemption which vanishes as income falls below the ceiling. This is shown in Table 15-2, where line 6 shows tax as the percentage of wage income. The tax is seen to be proportional up to the ceiling, and then it becomes sharply regressive. If hypothetical amounts of capital income are allowed for in the base, the tax (line 7) becomes slightly regressive even from the beginning.

Both patterns are based on the assumption that the entire burden, including the employer's as well as the employee's share, falls on the employee. As we shall see later, this approach runs counter to the legislative intent of splitting the

[4] See p. 688.

burden and is a debatable point.[5] However, it will be seen that the picture is not greatly changed if the employer share is assumed to be passed on to the consumer in the form of higher prices.[6] The ratio of consumption to income, as well as that of wages to income, declines as we move up the income scale, so that fairly similar results are obtained under the two assumptions.

There is no question, then, that the payroll tax—if considered by itself—ranks very low on equity grounds and that the rising share of the payroll tax in the federal tax structure has involved a serious deterioration in its quality. For this reason, recent proposals have suggested introduction of a low-income allowance or exemption calling for possible administrative linkage between payroll and income tax, as well as an upward extension of the ceiling. In this fashion the payroll tax could be made progressive over the larger part of the income range even though a flat rate was retained. This change, however, would involve a further departure from the quid pro quo principle in social security finance; and if this step is taken, the question arises whether it would not be preferable to discard the payroll tax altogether and to substitute increased reliance on the income tax. This again is a question to which we shall return when the general issue of social security finance is examined.

FURTHER READINGS

Brittain, John A.: *The Payroll Tax for Social Security,* Washington: Brookings, 1972.

Pechman, Joseph A.: *Federal Tax Policy,* rev. ed., Washington: Brookings, 1971, chap. 7.

[5] See p. 410.

[6] See Table 16-2, lines 11 and 12, p. 393.

Part Four

Fiscal Incidence

Chapter 16

Tax and Expenditure Incidence: An Overview*

A. Concepts of Incidence: *Statutory versus Economic Incidence; Tax Burden and Resource Transfer; Magnitude of Burden; Types of Tax Incidence; Net Incidence.* **B. Measuring Changes in Distribution:** *Sources versus Uses Side; Distribution among Whom?* **C. The Shifting Process:** *Types of Taxes; Types of Households; Types of Effects; Pattern of Tax Shifting; Expenditure Snatching.* **D. Incidence of the United States Fiscal Structure:** *Distribution of Tax Burden; Distribution of Expenditure Benefits; Net Residue; Scope of Redistribution; Conclusion.* **E. Summary.**

We now turn from the preceding analysis of fiscal structure to a closer view of its economic effects. These include micro effects on the distribution of income and the efficiency of resource use as well as macro effects on the level of capacity output, employment, prices, and growth. All these effects interact. Thus, the distributional effects (or incidence) of particular budget measures depend on their effects on capacity output and employment just as the latter depend on concur-

* *Reader's Guide to Chapter 16:* The determination of tax and expenditure incidence poses complex issues to be considered in subsequent chapters. In this chapter we deal with the general formulation of the problem, and in the concluding section, we give a quantitative picture of the incidence of the United States fiscal structure, including tax burdens, expenditure benefits, and net positions. This chapter presents a basic introduction to the incidence problem, important for the general reader who may wish to bypass the more detailed analysis in Chaps. 17 through 20.

rent changes in distribution. Nevertheless, each type of effect is of interest in itself and must be considered as such in policy formulation. One policy may be superior with regard to distributional results but inferior with regard to its efficiency, growth, or employment effects. Tradeoffs must then be made. Moreover, as a matter of exposition, not all aspects can be dealt with at once. Keeping in mind the general fact of interdependence, Chapters 16 through 20 focus on the effects of budget policy on the state of distribution.

Though only part of the total picture, distributional effects are an important aspect of budget policy. They are key features, especially in the determination of tax and transfer policy. It is these effects which we have in mind when talking about the "incidence" of tax or expenditure policies.

A. CONCEPTS OF INCIDENCE

In discussing tax incidence, certain concepts and issues must be clarified if confusion is to be avoided. Quite apart from the difficulties of measurement, one ought to be clear on just what it is that one wishes to measure.

Statutory versus Economic Incidence

Taxes, according to Justice Holmes, are the price of civilization, but the question is, who pays? As we saw earlier, taxes are not voluntary purchase payments but mandatory impositions, payable in line with whatever tax statute has been legislated. Although these statutes in the end are a reflection (more or less imperfect) of voters' preferences, once legislated they become mandatory levies, imposing burdens which the individual taxpayer will try to avoid or to pass on to others. To determine who pays, we must thus look beyond the tax statutes and the pattern of statutory incidence, i.e., beyond those on whom the legal liability for payment rests. This involves two considerations. First, it must be recognized that in the end, the entire tax burden must be borne by individuals. Though taxes may be collected from business firms, their ultimate burden must be traced to individual households in their capacity as owners of the firms, as employees, or as consumers of their products. Second, the final burden distribution may differ from that of statutory liabilities, whether the tax is imposed on individuals or on firms. Individuals as well as firms may adjust their sales and purchases, thus affecting the position of others.

Suppose first that Mr. Jones is called upon to pay a given amount, say $100 of tax, independently of what he does. Such a tax, referred to as a lump-sum tax, cannot be escaped. Yet, Jones will adjust himself to this loss by cutting back his purchases or savings, or by increasing his work effort. Although he cannot escape payment of the tax, his adjustment thereto will affect the people with whom he transacts and thus will have further repercussions. Moreover, taxes are rarely imposed in lump-sum form. The tax law typically expresses liabilities as a function of some aspect of economic behavior, such as earning income, making sales, or making a purchase. Since such taxes are imposed on economic transactions and since transactions involve more than one party, the transactors on whom the statutory liability rests may avoid tax payments by cutting back on their taxable activity; or they may attempt to pass on the burden to others by changing the terms under which they are willing to trade. Their ability to do so will depend upon the structure of the markets in which they deal and the way in which prices are determined.

Thus, imposition of an income tax may lead to reduced hours of work, thereby driving up the gross wage rate and burdening the consumer. Or, an automobile excise levied on the sellers may cause them to raise their prices, hoping to pass the burden of tax to the buyers, who in turn will attempt to avoid it by substituting other purchases. A tax on the use of capital may lead a firm to substitute labor, and so forth. In each case, the taxpayer's ability to make such adjustments will depend on the willingness of the other transactor to go along. If the seller raises the price, the buyer will fight back by purchasing less, so that the outcome will depend on the response of the two parties. Nevertheless, the resulting chain of adjustments may lead to a final distribution of the burden or *economic* incidence, which differs greatly from the initial distribution of liabilities or *statutory* incidence.

Legislators are quite aware of this. When imposing a manufacturer's tax on automobiles, they do not intend this burden to fall on the manufacturer. If they wished it to do so, they would impose a tax on the manufacturer's profits. Manufacturers merely serve as convenient collection points and are meant to pass the tax forward to the consumer in the form of higher automobile prices. Determining the actual distribution of the tax burden therefore requires an analysis of the economic adjustment process, or the transmission of the burden from its impact point (the place of statutory incidence) to its final resting point (the place of economic incidence). This process is generally referred to as "shifting."

As a matter of ultimate policy concern, it is obviously the distribution of the burden *after* shifting that counts. If this distribution is to be as intended, legislators must choose tax formulas which give the desired result in terms not of statutory incidence but of the economic incidence which ensues after the system has adjusted to the imposition of the tax. This, to say the least, is no simple task, even for the economist who must be called upon to advise what the final incidence of particular taxes will be. As we shall see later, especially tough problems arise with regard to the corporation profits tax and the property tax.

Tax Burden and Resource Transfer

Before considering who bears the burden, we must examine what the concept of burden implies. Here a distinction must be drawn between budget operations which involve a resource transfer to the public sector and others which do not.

In the first case, the government imposes taxes to finance goods and services expenditures. Suppose that the government collects $1 billion and spends it on highway services. As a result, the resources available for private use are reduced by a like amount. This is the opportunity cost of the highway services, the gross burden which their provision imposes on consumers as a whole. Tax incidence refers to the way in which this gross burden is shared among individual households. This burden in turn is accompanied by the benefits of highway services which must be allowed for to derive the net gain or burden (or to determine the net incidence) of the entire transaction.

When budget operations do not involve resource transfers to the public, the government simply collects taxes from the private sector and returns transfers to that sector. There is no shift of resources to public use and no opportunity cost in reduced private resource availability. Some may gain while others will lose, but taxes being equal to transfers, there will be no net change in income available for private use. The problem of incidence is now merely one of tracing the redistribution of privately available income among households.

Magnitude of Burden

Implicit in the preceding argument is the simplifying assumption that the tax burden is equal to the revenue collected. On this basis, the opportunity cost of $1 billion of public resource use equals the $1 billion of revenue that is needed to pay for it. By the same token, obtaining $1 billion in taxes and spending it on transfers leaves private income unchanged and involves no resource cost. This view of tax burden oversimplifies matters and must now be reconsidered.

Excess Burden The total burden may exceed the revenue collected because an "excess burden" results. To illustrate, suppose that $1 billion revenue is collected from a tax on automobiles. The sum total of tax collections from various consumers still equals $1 billion, but the burden imposed on the private sector will be larger. This is so because the tax interferes with consumer choice. Thus, someone may forgo a car purchase because of the tax payable. Therefore, he or she pays no tax but the budget choice is less satisfactory than it was before. This taxpayer therefore suffers a burden which is not reflected in total revenue. Others may reduce their purchases and pay a tax on the reduced amount. In both cases the consumer's expenditure pattern has been distorted by the tax and each suffers a burden which is greater than that which would have applied if they had paid the same amount as a flat charge. Because of this, the overall burden suffered by the private sector tends to exceed the amount of revenue obtained. An additional burden—referred to by economists as "excess burden"—results.

Output Effects There is another reason why tax revenue and total burden as measured by the loss of income available for private use may differ. Imposition of the tax may lead to a change in factor inputs and hence in total output. We may illustrate this case by supposing that the same revenue as in the previous examples was collected under a progressive income tax. As a result, workers may work more or less because the tax is imposed. Let us suppose that they work less and, as a result, their earnings fall. If this decline in earnings is counted as part of the burden, the total burden once more exceeds tax revenue; and the opposite is true if people work harder so that their earnings rise as a result of the tax. Similarly, tax policy may lead to a change in the rate of savings and investment and hence in the rate of output growth. These changes will again be reflected in the level of pretax income, once more causing the change in income to differ from the amount of revenue.

Employment Effects Furthermore, changes in output may result, not because of adjustments in factor inputs in response to changes in after-tax factor rewards, but because of resulting changes in the level of aggregate demand and unemployment. Introduction of a tax may reduce the level of employment, or an increase in expenditures may raise it. This once more complicates the problem of observing the effects of taxation on the distribution of income. As is evident from these considerations, the concept of tax burden is more complex than suggested by the simple formulation in which revenue and burden are set equal to each other. However, this assumption remains a useful approximation when dealing with the problem of burden distribution in an operational way. We shall accept it for purposes of this chapter.

Types of Tax Incidence

Although the expenditure side of the budget should be allowed for, concern with incidence has traditionally focused on the tax side of the picture. There are three ways in which the narrower problem of tax incidence may be viewed, namely as "absolute," "differential," or "budget" incidence.

Absolute Incidence One way is to examine the distributional effects of imposing a particular tax while holding public expenditures constant. Suppose that income taxes are increased without there being a corresponding change in expenditures or an offsetting change in other taxes. In determining the distributional consequences of such a change, one can hardly overlook the macro effects which follow from the resulting decline in aggregate demand. Assuming public policy to pursue a stabilizing course, there will be no burden on consumers as a group, but the question is how the distributional implications of alternative stabilization policies will differ. If no offsetting measures are taken, the tax change, depending upon the state of the economy, may lead to unemployment, a decline in price level, or a reduced rate of inflation.[1] Each result will have its distributional implications which cannot be separated from those of the tax change itself. Any attempt to consider the absolute incidence of a particular tax thus leads one to a much broader set of considerations. The approach is not a satisfactory one.

Differential Incidence To avoid this difficulty, one might examine the distributional changes which result if one tax is substituted for another while total revenue and expenditures are held constant. Thus, the government may replace $1 billion of income tax revenue with a cigarette excise yielding an equivalent amount.[2] This policy change involves no resource transfer to public use and (disregarding the issue of excess burden for the time being) imposes no net burden

[1] A similar problem arises if we consider an increase in public services without a corresponding change in revenue. Deficit finance, no less than tax finance, has its incidence. See p. 570.

[2] As a first approximation, the "equivalent amount" may be defined as the same amount of dollars. But this may be too simple a view. Allowing for changes in relative prices and hence possible changes in the cost of goods bought by government, the equivalent amount is that which permits government to make the same real purchases. Moreover, the equivalent amount should be such as to maintain the same level of aggregate demand. For the latter aspect, see p. 564.

on the private sector. It merely involves a redistribution among households. Households whose income tax is reduced will gain, while others with high cigarette purchases will lose. Going beyond this, tobacco growers and cigarette workers will lose, while others producing the output purchased by former income taxpayers stand to gain. The resulting total change in the state of distribution is referred to as "differential incidence": it measures the difference in the distributional effects of financing a given expenditure by one or another tax. This view of tax incidence is particularly useful because actual tax policy decisions usually involve the choice of raising or lowering revenue by resort to alternative tax increases or reductions.

Budget Incidence Still another way of looking at the problem is to consider the changes in household positions which result if the combined effects of tax and expenditure changes are considered. The income available to particular households for private use will now be affected not only by tax but also by expenditure measures. In the case of transfer programs, private incomes are added to, just as they are reduced by, taxes. In the case of provision for public services, the necessary purchases (whether of the services of civil servants or products) affect the distribution of private income through their effects on earnings. Thus, the expenditure side of the budget has its effects on private incomes as do taxes; and since tax and expenditure effects occur simultaneously, they cannot be separated in this case.

Net Incidence

If we consider not only changes in income available for private use but include benefits from public services as well, we address ourselves to the more comprehensive concept of net burden or gain from the budget transaction as a whole. The problem of budget incidence becomes one of determining the distributional impact of net benefits, combining (1) resulting changes in the distribution of income available for private use, and (2) the distributional impact of the benefits from public services. In the end, it is this net effect (the pattern of net burdens or benefits) that matters. A consideration of tax burdens without inclusion of expenditure benefits remains as one-sided an approach as a consideration of expenditure benefits without allowance for accompanying tax burdens.

If tax revenue is used to provide additional public services, resources are transferred from private to public use and the benefits from public use must be balanced against the loss of reduced private use. Provided that the budget process is planned efficiently, the value of these benefits will, at the margin, equal that of the loss in reduced private consumption; but considering the entire transaction, there will be a net gain. Similar considerations apply if tax revenue is used to finance a transfer payment. In this event, no resource transfer to the public sector occurs, but the distribution of private income is changed. A net gain will result if the additional income of transfer recipients is valued more highly from a social point of view than are the losses of taxpayers.

B. MEASURING CHANGES IN DISTRIBUTION

We return to the strategic case of differential tax incidence and see how resulting changes in distribution are to be measured.

Sources versus Uses Side

Substitution of one tax for another will improve the position of some households and worsen that of others. Changes in the position of any one household may be measured in terms of the resulting change in its real income. Real income may change because disposable income changes or because there is a change in the price of the products which are purchased. Taking a somewhat simplified view of the matter, we note that the disposable real income (DRY) of a household may be defined as

$$\text{DRY} = \frac{E - T_y}{P + T_s} = \frac{DY}{GP}$$

where E is earnings, T_y is income tax, P is the price (at factor cost) of products bought, and T_s is the sales tax addition thereto. DY is disposable or after-tax money income, and GP is the gross (or market) price. We can now see how DRY is subject to both direct and indirect tax effects.

Primary effects of tax changes which operate on the earnings or sources side of the household account will change T_y, while primary effects which operate on the expenditure or uses side of its account will change T_s. Thus an increase in income tax lowers DRY via an increase in T_y and hence a fall in DY. An increase in sales tax lowers DRY via an increase in T_s and hence in GP.

In addition, the general adjustment process may result in secondary changes from the earnings side, or in E; and in secondary changes from the uses side, or in P. While such secondary effects may be of great importance to particular households, chances are that they will not result in a systematic offset to such changes in the size distribution of DRY as have resulted in line with the primary effects.[3] Thus, for taxes on earnings such as the individual income tax, distributional results tend to be dominated by effects from the earnings side, whereas in other cases, such as selective excise taxes, changes on the uses side are of primary importance.

[3] Measuring changes in real income raises considerable difficulties which we are overlooking for the time being.

Thus, the above formulation does not distinguish between changes in E due to changes in the wage rate with hours of work unchanged, and changes in E due to changes in hours worked. In the latter case, the formulation overlooks the gains or losses from resulting change in leisure.

In measuring the implications of price change, there is the problem posed by choice of the proper index. Consider, for instance, the imposition of a tax on product X which raises its price, while the amount purchased declines from Q_1 to Q_2. If the burden is measured by ΔPQ_1, true cost will be overstated, while if measured by ΔPQ_2, it will be understated. The true burden, as we shall see later, would be measured by the lump-sum amount which the taxpayer would be willing to pay instead. These problems and the related issues of excess burden are considered in Chap. 21, p. 461.

Distribution among Whom?

If one wishes to analyze a practical incidence problem—e.g., the distributional changes which result if the corporation tax is replaced by a value-added tax, or if a sales tax is substituted for an income tax—it is not feasible to determine what happens to each of the over 50 million households in the economy. To make the task workable, households must be grouped by categories.

Relevant Groupings Various groupings are possible. The classical economists (Ricardo, for instance) viewed the incidence problem in terms of the impact of tax burdens on capital, labor, and land. For them, incidence theory was primarily an aspect of the theory of factor shares or factor pricing. This was also useful from the point of view of public policy since, in their time, industry, labor, and agriculture did in fact reflect the major social groups. Today the pattern is more mixed, and primary concern—from the viewpoint of social policy—has moved to the size distribution of income. A person receiving only a small amount of capital income and unable to work is poor, whereas a person receiving a large salary is well off. This is also in line with the global income tax approach, where our concern is with the person's level of *total* income, independent of the particular source from which it is derived.

Measure of Change in Distribution When the problem of incidence is viewed in terms of effects upon the size distribution of income, incidence may be measured by comparing the state of distribution before and after a particular tax change. Such a comparison is illustrated in Figure 16-1. Measuring the cumulative percentage of disposable income on the vertical axis and the cumulative percentage of households (ranked from the lowest to the highest) on the horizontal axis, the curve *OAB* shows the percent of income received by the lowest 10, 20, 30, etc., percent of households.[4] Thus the lowest 20 percent of households receives 6 percent of money income and the lowest 80 percent receives 60 percent, leaving 40 percent for the highest 20 percent. If distribution were equal, curve *OAB* would coincide with the straight line *OB*. Given a state of unequal distribution, the ratio of the two areas *OABC/OBC* may be taken as the index of equality. It will equal 1 if the distribution of income is totally equal.

Suppose now that the distributional pattern with the existing tax system is as indicated by *OAB* but that, owing to the change, it becomes *OA'B*. This means that distribution has become more equal—since $OA'BC/OBC > OABC/OBC$ —and in this sense the effect of the tax change has been progressive.[5] Note, however, that this change may have come about in two ways. Thus, the distribution of the initial tax burden might have changed, e.g., the rates of the income tax may have been made more progressive while holding total revenue constant.

[4] To obtain the complete picture and allow for changes from the sources side as well, disposable income would have to be expressed in real terms, i.e., be deflated by the relevant index of consumer prices.

[5] *OA'B* need not lie inside *OAB* throughout but the two curves may intersect. If so, distribution may become more equal over part of the range and less so over another. Social policy, of course, must be concerned not only with the overall state of distribution but also with distribution over particular income ranges. Thus more refined measures of incidence may be devised.

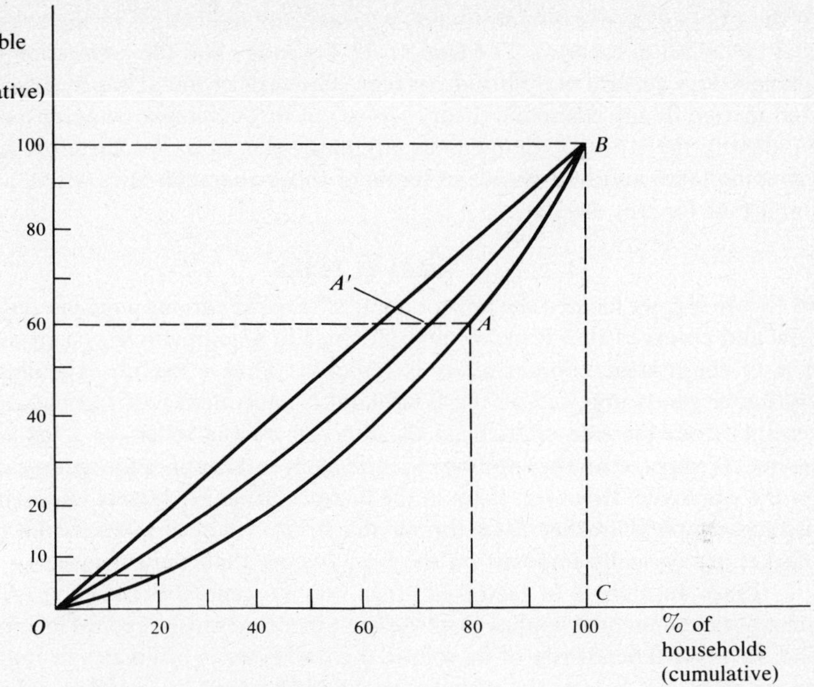

FIGURE 16-1 Measure of Income Equality.

Alternatively, yield may have been increased without changing the progressivity of the rate structure, e.g., by raising all liabilities by the same percentage.

The total effect on distribution, therefore, depends not only on how progressive particular taxes are (i.e., how fast the effective rate or ratio of liability to income rises as we move up the income scale), but also on the overall level of taxation and on the underlying distribution of income. A high but moderately progressive level of taxation may have a greater impact upon the distribution of income than does a low but sharply progressive system.

C. THE SHIFTING PROCESS

The incidence of any particular tax will differ, depending on how the economy responds to it. The responses will depend upon (1) just how the tax is imposed, e.g., whether it is assessed on gross receipts, net receipts, factor payments, or expenditures; (2) how general is the coverage to which the tax applies; (3) the structure of the markets in which the tax is imposed; and (4) the time period allowed for adjustments to occur. Adjustments to a tax will cause factor and product prices to change and these changes will determine the burden distribution among households.

As we have just noted, a household may be affected from the *sources* side of its accounts (i.e., by changes in its net earnings, whether due to changes in gross earnings or in taxes thereon) and/or from the *uses* side (i.e., by changes in the prices of goods which it buys, whether due to changes in the net price or to a tax addition thereto). The final result depends upon the interaction of these changes in a general equilibrium system. The task of incidence theory—or, for that matter, of any economic theory—is to cut through these complex forces and to identify the strategic elements in any particular case. We therefore begin by grouping taxes and households in terms of those characteristics which are most important for this analysis.

Types of Taxes

In Figure 9-2, we located the impact point of taxes at various points in the income flow and observed that it makes no difference in a competitive system on which side of the market counter a tax is imposed. Thus a tax on expenditures on consumer goods imposed on the household is equivalent to a sales tax on gross receipts from the sale of such goods imposed on the seller; or a tax on wage payments imposed on the employer is equivalent to a tax on wage income imposed on the employee. However, taxes in the factor market are largely imposed on the income recipient (rather than the paying firm), whereas taxes in the product market are typically imposed on the firm (rather than the consumer).

Taxes on income or factor earnings may be general or selective. A totally general tax on income applies to all types of income (wages, capital income, rent, and so on) independently of its source (i.e., whether it originates in industry X or industry Y). Selectivity may be introduced either by omitting incomes of certain factors from the tax base (e.g., by applying the tax to capital or wage income only) or income earned (by whichever factor) from certain sources (e.g., taxes which apply to earnings from industry X or from industry Y only).

Taxes on sales of products may similarly be either general or selective. A sales tax may apply to the sale of all products, it may be limited to consumer goods, or it may apply to selected consumer goods only. A distinction may be drawn between:

Income taxes on

1. Labor income originating in all industries
2. Capital income originating in all industries
3. Labor and capital income originating in all industries
4. Labor or capital income only, originating in selective industries

Sales taxes on

5. All consumer goods
6. Selected consumer goods

Type 1 is exemplified by the payroll and type 3 by the individual income tax. The major example of type 4 is found in the corporation income tax, while 5 is aimed at the general sales tax at the state level and 6 reflects the federal and state excise taxes.

Types of Households

The vulnerability of various households to tax-burden incidence depends upon the composition of both the income sources and the uses sides of their accounts.

On the uses side, the household's burden will depend on the share of its income that is derived from factor earnings which are subject to income tax; and it will also depend on the share of its income that is derived from an industry whose product is subject to sales tax. On the uses side, it matters whether a household uses its income for consumption or saving, as its income disposition determines its vulnerability to a general sales tax as distinct from an income tax. Moreover, the household's burden will depend on the share of its consumption that goes into products which are subject to selective sales taxation and the share that goes into others which are not. A final factor is the extent to which the household's wealth is held in the form of assets which are subject to property tax.

While households differ widely in their sources and uses patterns, there are generally applicable relationships between the level of income and the pattern of sources as well as the level of income and the pattern of uses. Since the share of capital income rises as we move up the income scale, a tax on capital income tends to be more progressive than a general income tax, while a tax on wage income only tends to be regressive. Similarly, a tax on luxury products, such as champagne, tends to be progressive, whereas a tax on mass-consumption items—say, beer—tends to be regressive. These relationships, as we shall see in the following chapters, play a key role in dealing with the incidence of various taxes.

Types of Effects

Taxes are initially paid by individual households or firms, and their initial response sets into motion the forces by which the final incidence is determined. This initial response is therefore of great importance. Nevertheless, the resulting adjustments must be viewed within the context of a general equilibrium system. This means that all the forces which bring about the final burden distribution are interdependent, and it is difficult or impossible to say which comes first. However, we shall use the terms "primary effects" and "secondary effects." By "primary effects" we mean the chain of causation which is most strategic in determining the distribution of the burden of any particular tax among families arrayed by income brackets. By "secondary effects" we mean other changes which may be of great importance to particular households but which are not likely to exert a systematic effect on the distributive pattern of the tax burden by income groups. As we shall see, the primary effect of income taxes is likely to operate from the sources side of the household account while the primary effects of product taxes stem from the uses side.

Pattern of Tax Shifting

In the following chapters, the incidence of the major taxes will be examined in some detail, but it will be useful at the outset to sketch the central forces at work.[6] Since the response of the market is easier to predict under a competitive system than under market imperfections, we begin with the former.

[6] This will be especially helpful to the general reader who may wish to skip the more technical analysis of Chaps. 18 to 20.

Competitive Markets: Factor Taxes Taxes on factor transactions (e.g., income taxes) may be general or selective in that all or some factors may be included, and they may be general or selective in that earnings from all or some uses of any one factor may be covered. We thus have these possibilities:

EARNINGS OF	EARNINGS FROM *All Employments*	EARNINGS FROM *Some Employments*
All factors	(1)	(3)
Some factors	(2)	(4)

Beginning with (1), we have the case of a truly general income tax. The tax enters as a wedge between factor earnings (which, in the competitive market, equal the marginal product of the factor) and net income to the factor. If factor supplies are unchanged as a result of the tax, the marginal product is not affected and the burden falls on the taxpayer. If he or she responds by supplying less (i.e., by working less when there is a tax on wage income or by saving and investing less when there is a tax on capital income), further changes may result. If labor supply declines more than capital supply, labor becomes the scarcer factor. As a result, the wage rate will rise while the return to capital falls and part of labor's tax burden will be transferred to capital. If the capital supply declines more than the labor supply, the opposite will result.

Case (2) is illustrated by a general payroll tax on wage income. Here the potential reduction in factor supply initially applies to labor only. If the supply of labor falls, the wage rate will rise while the return to capital will decline, thus transferring part of the burden to capital. The opposite holds for a tax on capital income only. The situation differs, however, for land in fixed supply, so that the tax (even in the longer run) will reduce net rent by the full amount and will stay put with the owner. While some shifting of *general* income taxes is thus possible, especially in the longer run, it appears that the total supply of a factor (in all its uses) tends to be relatively inelastic to the rate of return, so that shifting of the type we have just discussed is not likely to be of major importance.

The situation is more complex for cases (3) and (4), i.e., for taxes on factor earnings in selective uses. Thus, if a tax on capital income were applied to earnings in the steel industry only, capital would move to a tax-free industry. Whereas the supply of any one factor in the economy as a whole may be inelastic, its supply to any one particular industry will be highly elastic. As a result, returns in the steel industry would rise and returns in other industries would fall until net (after-tax) returns in all industries are equalized. Thus the burden of the tax on capital income in the steel industry would tend to be spread among capital in all industries. While we do not have a tax on profits in steel only, a selective tax on capital income is, in fact, applied in the form of the corporation profits tax which is imposed on profits earned in the corporate sector only but which, by similar reasoning, is spread to all capital income. Since the total capital income share rises with income, the result will still be progressive. A tax on wage income from employment in a particular industry similarly would be spread among labor income in general but would remain regressive, since the labor share falls with rising income.

The preceding discussion has focused on changing positions on the earnings side of the household accounts. Further changes may arise on the uses side. Thus, a general income tax may result in a changing pattern of demand with subsequent changes in relative product prices;[7] and a selective tax of type (3) or (4) will raise the prices of products produced in the taxed industry relative to products of the tax-free industries. These price changes will affect household positions from the uses side, but it is unlikely that the nature of the incidence pattern (whether progressive or regressive) as established on the earnings (sources) side will be substantially changed thereby.

Imperfect Markets: Factor Taxes The answer to the incidence problem remains clear-cut for the situation of a pure monopoly, where it may be assumed that the monopolists have maximized their profits before tax; and this being so, it will not be in their interest to raise their prices as the tax is imposed. Net profits, equal to $(1 - t)PR$, will be largest if PR (profits) is maximized. Thus the burden will have to be absorbed by the monopolist. The situation differs, however, if we consider other types of market imperfections, such as a potential monopolist who, prior to tax, has not gone all out in maximizing profits, or the behavior of oligopolists for whom the tax may be a signal to raise prices. Moreover, the firm may not only aim at profit maximization but may have other objectives, such as maximizing sales. In cases such as these, the profits tax or parts thereof may be passed on to the consumer by way of increased prices. A similar situation may arise under the income tax. As tax rates are raised, executives may adjust their salaries upward and collective bargaining agreements may set higher wages. Given imperfect markets, the question of incidence must thus be resolved by empirical evidence rather than by a priori reasoning.

Competitive Markets: Product Taxes We begin again with perfect markets and a general tax on all consumer goods. Imposed at the retail level, this tax enters as a wedge between the net and the gross price. Since the tax is an additional cost, it will push up price and will thus be passed on to consumers. Since the tax is general, applicable to all consumption, low-income consumers will tend to pay a larger fraction of their income in tax than will high-income consumers. The tax will tend to be regressive.

The situation again differs if the tax is imposed on particular products, say, large cars only. The tax now increases the price of large cars relative to smaller ones, and the consumers of large cars will bear the burden. They will do so especially if the demand for the taxed product is inelastic. To the extent that consumers substitute tax-free products (i.e., small cars), and assuming both to be produced under conditions of increasing cost, the price of large cars will fall while that of small cars will rise. Thus part of the burden will be transferred to

[7] Such will be the result because of changes in private demand (differential incidence) or of substituting public for private demand (budget incidence).

other consumers. However, the resulting burden pattern is likely to be dominated by the nature of the taxed product. It will be regressive if outlays on such products as a fraction of income decline as income rises and progressive if this fraction rises.

Although the focus in this connection has been on changes in household positions which result from the uses side of household accounts, earnings positions may also be affected. Thus, earnings in the large-car industry will fall while those in the small-car industry will rise, resulting in a distributional change on the income sources side. But the pattern set on the uses side is now likely to be the dominating factor, as were changes on the sources side in the case of factor taxes.

Imperfect Markets: Product Taxes Once more the result may differ with imperfect markets. An excise tax imposed on a product produced under monopolistic conditions may in substantial part be absorbed by the monopolist. If supply is inelastic, it may come close to acting as a tax on profits.

Expenditure Snatching

The incidence and shifting problem has traditionally been related to the tax side of the budget picture, but analogous considerations may be applied to the expenditure side. As with the case of tax measures, the ultimate concern of policy is not with the statutory incidence of benefits, but with the final distributional results after adjustments are allowed for. Subsidies to firms must once more be traced to individual households and the analysis of tax-burden shifting may be paralleled by one of expenditure or benefit "snatching." Quite similar problems are involved in both instances. In viewing this issue, a distinction is drawn between transfer and purchase payments.

Transfers The incidence of transfers can be dealt with in the same way as that of taxes. Transfers, as we have noted, may be looked upon as negative taxes. Thus the incidence problems of a tax on wages are paralleled by those of a wage subsidy. Just as a payroll tax may be borne by the wage earner or be passed on to the consumer, so may the wage subsidy be enjoyed by the wage earner or lost to the consumer in lower prices. If the transfer is related negatively to income (as with welfare payments), a similar analysis may be applied, the situation in this case being more like that of a positive tax.[8] The results of a subsidy to low-cost housing may be treated in the same way as an excise tax on such housing, and so forth. Related problems also arise with intergovernmental grants. If the federal government makes a "matching grant" to states or localities, it may lead to increased own-financed outlays on their part, or to tax reduction, with the distributional consequences quite different in the two cases.[9]

Purchases In considering the incidence of public purchase expenditures, two aspects must be distinguished.

[8] See p. 676.
[9] See p. 362.

The first relates to the effects of the expenditure policy on private earnings. Thus, increased expenditures on space projects will raise the wages of electronics experts relative to those of textile workers, the demand for whose product falls because of higher taxes. Expenditures on highways will raise earnings in the construction industry, and so forth. Such effects will be of importance for particular industry groups, but as a rule they are not likely to have major bearing on the size distribution of income. There is no presumption that earnings from the production of publicly provided goods are distributed more or less equally than those from the production of privately purchased output. Moreover, the resulting effects on the distribution of earnings is not ordinarily a major consideration in placing public purchases. Incidence considerations, therefore, are of less importance in this connection. Ordinarily, the rule for public purchase policy should be to buy from the cheapest supplier, but there may be exceptions. An order may be placed in a low-income region as a matter of redistribution policy, even though costs are higher than might prevail somewhere else.[10]

A second aspect of expenditure incidence involves the distributional impact of the benefits of the public service itself. Here a distinction may be drawn between public services which are in the nature of final consumer goods (the use of the road for pleasure driving) and those which are in the nature of intermediate goods, i.e., goods which enter as inputs in the production of final goods, such as the use of the road for commercial trucking. In the case of final goods, initial incidence at least will depend on the distribution of the project's uses among income brackets. Beyond this, shifting (or benefit snatching) may again occur. Thus increased highway facilities may lead to increased demand for cars and gasoline, raising their prices and transmitting the benefits to those deriving earnings from these industries.

In the treatment of intermediate goods, the problem is similar to that of a subsidy, except that the subsidy is given in kind rather than in cash. Under competitive conditions, the benefit will be passed on to the consumer of the ultimate product into which the public service enters as an intermediate good. But once more, such need not arise under imperfect market structures.

D. INCIDENCE OF THE UNITED STATES FISCAL STRUCTURE

In the following chapters, we will examine the economics of shifting and incidence as applied to the major taxes in our system. But before doing so, it will be useful to gain an overview of the distributional implications of the United States fiscal structure. The estimates presented here apply to 1968 but the pattern has not changed greatly since then. They are the result of somewhat heroic estimating procedures, the merits and shortcomings of which will be treated briefly.[11]

[10] See our earlier discussion of this issue in connection with cost-benefit analysis, p. 169.

[11] See R. A. Musgrave, Karl E. Case, and Herman B. Leonard, "The Distribution of Fiscal Burdens and Benefits," *Public Finance Quarterly,* July 1974.

Distribution of Tax Burden

The distribution of the tax burden is estimated first. The estimates shown in Table 16-1 involve three stages: (1) Assumptions have to be made regarding the incidence of various taxes. Thus, it may be postulated that the corporation tax falls on shareholders, on recipients of capital income in general, on wage earners in the corporate sector, or on consumers. (2) On the basis of whatever assumption is made, the revenue from each tax is assigned to households in various income brackets, using for this purpose such distributive series as are available. If the corporation tax is assumed to fall on the shareholder, it will be assigned according to the distribution of dividend income; if it is assumed to be passed on to the consumer, it will be assigned according to the distribution of consumer expenditures, and so forth. (3) The effective or average rates of tax are determined by expressing the tax allocation to each income bracket as a percentage of income in the bracket. For this purpose, a broad definition of income, including total corporate-source income (before corporation tax) and imputed income (such as rental income of owner-occupiers), is more appropriate.

Standard Assumptions Table 16-1 shows the results under a set of "benchmark" assumptions. According to these, the various taxes are allocated as follows:

Tax	*Incidence Assumptions*	*Allocated according to*
Individual income tax	Stays put	Tax payments
Corporation income tax	One-half on consumption	Consumption
	One-half on capital income	Capital income
Excises and sales taxes	Consumption	Type of consumption
Estate and gift taxes	Donors	Capital income above $25,000
Property tax		
Residences	Homeowners	Ownership
Rental housing	Tenants	Rental payments
Business	One-half consumption	Consumption
	One-half capital income	Capital income
Payroll tax		
Employer	Consumers	Consumption
Employee	Employees	Covered earnings

The validity of these assumptions will be explored further in the following chapters. Proceeding on this basis, we obtain the results shown in Table 16-1. We find that the federal income tax (line 1) is a distinctly progressive component.[12] The corporation tax (line 3) is regressive at the lower end of the scale

[12] Progression at the upper end is understated somewhat because all brackets over $30,000 are combined. However, as noted before, the effective rate due to capital gains treatment and other reasons does not approach the level suggested by the statutory bracket rate. In comparing these results with those in Table 10-2, note that the present ratios are based on a broader income concept than the one used in the earlier table.

TABLE 16-1
Estimated Distribution of Tax Burdens by Income Brackets, 1968
(Taxes as Percentage of Total Family Income)

	INCOME BRACKETS										
Taxes	*Under $4,000*	*$4,000–$5,700*	*$5,700–$7,900*	*$7,900–$10,400*	*$10,400–$12,500*	*$12,500–$17,500*	*$17,500–$22,600*	*$22,600–$35,500*	*$35,500–$92,000*	*$92,000 and over*	*All Brackets*
Federal Taxes											
1. Individual income tax	2.0	2.8	5.9	7.1	7.9	10.1	10.6	12.7	14.8	18.5	9.9
2. Estate and gift tax	—	—	—	—	—	—	—	0.6	2.0	2.7	0.4
3. Corporation income tax	5.1	6.1	5.0	4.0	4.3	4.6	4.8	5.1	5.3	6.6	5.0
4. Excises and customs	2.5	2.8	3.1	3.0	2.9	2.7	2.1	1.1	0.9	0.6	2.3
5. Payroll tax	5.5	6.3	7.0	6.9	6.7	6.1	5.2	4.2	1.5	0.6	5.2
6. Total	15.2	17.9	20.8	21.6	21.6	23.4	22.6	23.8	24.5	29.1	22.7
7. Total excluding line 5	9.7	11.6	13.9	14.7	14.9	17.3	17.4	19.6	23.0	28.5	17.5
State and Local Taxes											
8. Individual income tax	—	0.1	0.3	0.6	0.7	1.1	1.4	2.3	1.6	1.3	1.0
9. Inheritance tax	—	—	—	—	—	—	—	0.2	0.6	0.8	0.1
10. Corporation income tax	0.4	0.5	0.4	0.4	0.3	0.4	0.4	0.4	0.4	0.5	0.4
11. General excise tax	3.4	2.8	2.5	2.3	2.2	2.0	1.7	1.0	0.5	0.3	1.8
12. Excises*	2.7	3.0	3.3	3.0	2.9	2.5	1.9	1.0	0.8	0.6	2.1
13. Property tax	6.7	5.7	4.7	4.3	4.0	3.7	3.3	3.0	2.9	3.3	3.9
14. Payroll tax	0.2	0.5	0.8	1.0	1.0	1.0	1.1	1.2	0.2	0.1	0.8
15. Total	13.4	12.5	11.9	11.6	11.1	10.6	9.7	9.1	7.1	6.9	10.3
16. Total excluding line 14	13.2	12.1	11.1	10.6	10.1	9.6	8.6	7.9	6.9	6.8	9.5
All Levels											
17. Total	28.5	30.5	32.8	33.1	32.8	33.9	32.4	32.9	31.6	35.9	33.0
18. Total excluding lines 5 and 14	22.9	23.7	25.0	25.3	25.0	26.9	26.0	27.5	29.9	35.3	27.0

* Includes motor vehicle licenses, excises, and miscellaneous revenue.

Notes:
For brief explanation of estimates, see text.
Uneven bracket limits are used for computational reasons.
Items may not add to totals because of rounding.

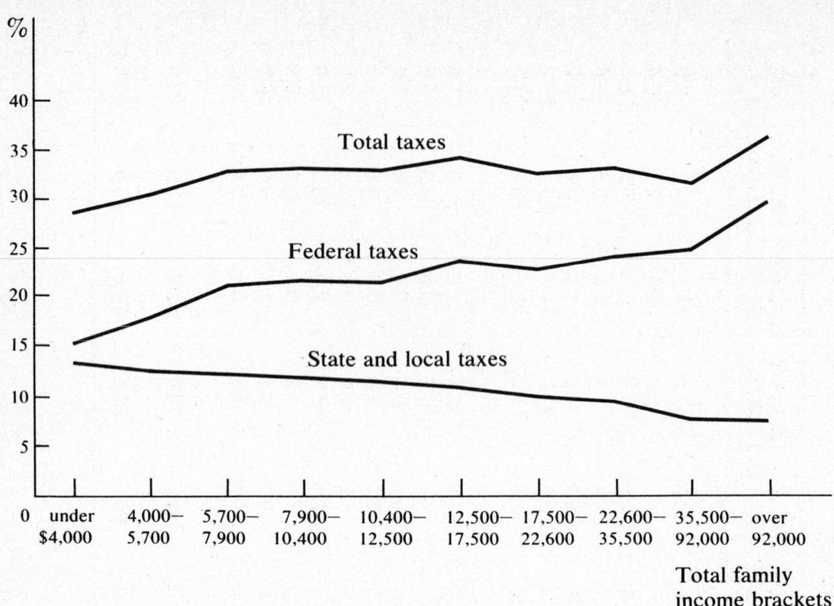

Notes: Total taxes, federal taxes, and state and local taxes are derived from Table 16-1, lines 17, 6, and 15 respectively.

FIGURE 16-2 Total Taxes as a Percentage of Total Family Income.

and mildly progressive thereafter.[13] The estate tax (line 2) is highly progressive but carries little weight in the total picture. Excises (line 4) are regressive, as is the payroll tax (line 5) for all but the bottom end of the scale.[14] The federal system as a whole (line 6 and Figure 16-2) is mildly progressive over most of the range, flanked by sharper progression at both ends of the scale. If the payroll taxes are excluded (line 7), the pattern becomes progressive throughout.

The state and local picture shows a less progressive pattern for the income tax, which in fact turns regressive at the upper end.[15] The regressivity of the general sales tax (line 11) exceeds that of excises and the property tax distribution (line 13) is mildly regressive under the assumptions used here.

The combined pattern, including federal, state, and local taxes (line 17 and Figure 16-2), is the most interesting part of the picture. We find the overall burden distribution to be more or less proportional over a wide middle range—from, say, $5,000 to $30,000—which includes the great bulk of all families. Again we find mild progression at both ends of the scale. If payroll taxes are excluded (line 18), lower-end progression is increased.

Alternative Assumptions We have noted that the choice of the incidence assumptions is the most crucial element in determining the resulting pattern of

[13] These results correspond to the gross burden concept of Table 12-2. Regressivity at the lower end reflects the weight of dividends in retirement income.

[14] The progressive payroll tax burden at the lower end reflects a low share of covered wages in low-bracket incomes, a feature not reflected in the pattern of Table 15-2.

[15] Since bracket rates level off at a moderate level, the increasing share of income subject to preferential treatment results in a decline in the average rate as computed on a full-income base.

TABLE 16-2
Significance of Alternative Incidence Assumptions
(Tax as Percentage of Total Family Income)

	SELECTED INCOME BRACKETS			
	$4,000–$5,700	*$12,500–$17,500*	*$35,000–$92,000*	*$92,000 and over*
Corporation Tax				
1. One-half capital income, one-half consumption	6.6	5.0	5.7	7.2
2. Dividend income	4.7	2.6	8.8	28.2
3. Capital income	6.1	3.7	10.0	13.7
4. Consumption	7.1	6.3	1.4	0.6
5. One-half capital income, one-fourth consumption, one-fourth wages	6.0	5.0	5.8	7.3
*Property Tax**				
6. OR on owner; R on tenant; B—one-half capital income, one-half consumption	5.7	3.7	2.9	3.3
7. All on capital income	4.4	2.7	7.2	9.9
8. OR on owner, R and B on capital income	4.4	3.3	5.4	7.1
9. OR on owner, R on tenant, B on capital income	5.3	3.3	4.5	5.8
10. OR on owner, R on tenant, B on consumption	6.1	4.1	1.2	0.8
Payroll Tax				
11. Employer tax on consumption, employee tax on wages	6.8	7.1	1.7	0.6
12. All on wages	5.6	7.4	1.7	0.4
Total, All Levels of Government				
13. Line 17, Table 16-1	30.5	33.9	31.6	35.9
14. Substituting lines 2 for 1, 7 for 6, 12 for 11	26.1	30.8	39.0	63.2
15. Substituting lines 4 for 1, 10 for 6	31.4	35.6	25.6	26.9

* OR stands for owner-occupied residences; R stands for rental property; B stands for other business property.

† Includes the payroll tax.

burden distribution. This is shown in Table 16-2, where the significance of alternative incidence assumptions is explored. The results are shown for selected income brackets only.

Lines 1 to 5 show a wide variation in the pattern of corporation income tax incidence. Total assignment of the burden to shareholders (line 2) greatly increases upper-end progression as compared with our benchmark of line 1. Total assignment to capital income (line 3) increases progressivity at the lower and reduces it at the upper end. Total assignment to consumption (line 4) would render the tax regressive. In line 5 finally, the consumption component of the benchmark assumption is divided between wage earners and consumers, but we find that this variation does not greatly change the result.

Lines 6 to 10 show alternative assumptions for the property tax. Compared with the benchmark assumption (line 6), imputation of the entire burden to recipients of capital income (line 7) sharply changes the picture and renders the tax progressive throughout the range. This result is not affected greatly if the tax on owner-occupied residences is left with the owner (line 8). Assignment of the entire tax on business property to capital income (line 9) raises progression, and assignment to the consumer (line 10) results in regression.

Lines 11 and 12 compare the benchmark assumption for the payroll tax (line 11) with one which assigns the entire burden to the wage earner (line 12). It appears that the difference is of minor importance only.

In the final part of the table, we compare the overall pattern of the benchmark case (line 13) with corresponding patterns which result if the most progressive (line 14) and least progressive (line 15) assumptions are used. After having gone over the incidence analysis of the following four chapters, readers may wish to construct what they themselves take to be the most likely case.

Limitations Before leaving this survey of tax-burden distribution, some of its shortcomings should be noted:

1. We find that for some taxes the distributional conclusions depend crucially on what incidence hypothesis is chosen.
2. The precise distribution series needed to implement the particular hypothesis may not be available. Thus, the distribution of corporate-source income (which includes retained earnings) must be approximated by the distribution of dividend income.
3. The argument rests on the simplifying assumption that the distribution of earnings before tax will be the same with different taxes. In fact, the distribution of earnings may change in response to changes in the tax structure.[16]
4. The analysis as pictured in Table 16-1 views the problem in terms of absolute incidence and overlooks the difficulties which we have shown to underlie this approach.[17] This difficulty, however, is less serious in Table 16-3, where net benefits or burdens are considered and the problem is viewed in terms of budget incidence.

Having noted these difficulties, it nevertheless remains useful to attempt an estimate of burden distribution. The issue being of such interest and importance

[16] For a critique along these lines, see A. P. Prest, "Statistical Calculations of Tax Burdens," *Economica,* August 1955.

[17] The data provided in Table 16-1 will permit the reader to restate the results in terms of differential incidence, where the prevailing system is compared with the burden distribution under a proportional income tax. As indicated in line 17 of the table, the burden under a proportional tax equals 33 percent in each bracket, i.e., the ratio applicable to the group as a whole. The differential rate for each bracket is then obtained as the recorded rate in line 17 minus 33.0. We find the differential rate slightly negative at the bottom, around zero over the middle range, and positive at the upper end, in line with the previously recorded pattern of effective rates.

to policy makers, the economists can hardly plead complete ignorance in the matter. While the incidence problem is exceedingly complex, as will appear in the following chapters, some hypotheses are more reasonable than others, and even an informed guess at the resulting burden distribution is of some value.

Distribution of Expenditure Benefits

Estimating the distribution of expenditure benefits is similar in some respects to estimating the distribution of tax burdens, but it is more difficult in other respects.

Types of Expenditures In allocating expenditure benefits, we distinguish among (1) goods and services expenditures which permit direct allocation, (2) transfer payments which by their nature lend themselves to allocation, and (3) goods and services expenditures which do not permit direct allocation. It appears that at the federal level, about 40 percent of total expenditures for 1968 lend themselves to direct allocation, with national defense the major item in the other group. At the state and local levels, the share is over 70 percent, and for all levels combined, it equals somewhat less than 50 percent.

Specific Benefits Estimated benefit allocations for certain expenditure categories are shown in lines 1 to 7 of Table 16-3 for the federal level and in lines 9 to 13 for the state and local levels. In making these allocations, it has been assumed that costs incurred on behalf of various groups reflect the value of benefits received.[18] Thus, benefits from education are allocated among households by the distribution of students. In the case of highways, expenditures are divided in line with consumer and business use of facilities. The former are allocated according to household expenditures on automotive products, while the latter, by reducing business costs, are assumed to be passed forward to the consumer. Interest payments are imputed to the holders of public debt with payments to banks imputed to holders of bank shares. Transfers are treated as negative taxes and are assumed to stay put with the recipients.

As shown in lines 6 and 13, the benefit rate from allocated expenditure categories (except for the extreme brackets) falls as income rises, this being so at both the federal and the state and local levels. In the case of transfer payments (lines 7 and 14), much of the highest benefit rate applies in the lowest bracket; then it drops off sharply to the second bracket and continues to decline thereafter. This of course reflects the fact that such payments are largely composed of old-age pensions and welfare payments. Lines 16 to 18 show the picture for all levels combined. Once more the pattern is heavily pro low-income. Indeed, the low-income advantage is much more pronounced in the pattern of benefit distribution than was previously noted for the relative position of low incomes in the tax-burden distribution.

Total Benefits Unfortunately, not all expenditures lend themselves to an attempt at specific allocation. Defense in particular is in this category, but expen-

[18] We are thus not attempting to measure the true value received by any one group, e.g., we do not measure the rate of return which various students will receive from their education, nor do we allow for differences in education costs among locations.

TABLE 16-3
Distribution of Expenditure Benefits
(Benefits as Percentage of Total Family Income)

		SELECTED INCOME BRACKETS						
		Under $4,000	*$4,000– $5,700*	*$5,700– $7,900*	*$7,900– $10,400*	*$12,500– $17,500*	*$35,500– $92,000*	*All*
		I. SPECIFIC BENEFIT ALLOCATIONS						
Federal								
1. Purchases:	Education	0.6	1.1	1.1	1.0	0.6	0.2	0.6
2.	Interest	2.1	2.0	1.2	0.6	0.8	2.3	1.5
3.	Highways	0.6	0.8	0.9	0.8	0.7	0.2	0.6
4.	Agriculture	*	0.2	0.3	0.4	0.4	2.6	0.7
5.	Medical	1.9	1.8	1.0	0.5	0.2	*	0.4
6.	Total	5.2	5.9	4.5	3.3	2.6	5.3	3.8
7. Transfers		78.3	19.8	8.8	4.3	2.1	0.2	6.2
8. Total		83.5	25.7	13.3	7.6	4.7	5.5	10.0
State and Local								
9. Purchases:	Education	5.5	9.9	10.4	8.7	5.4	1.5	5.2
10.	Interest	0.1	0.1	*	*	*	0.1	*
11.	Highways	1.2	1.6	1.9	1.8	1.5	0.5	1.3
12.	Medical	5.7	5.6	2.9	1.5	0.5	0.1	1.1
13.	Total	12.5	17.2	15.2	12.0	7.4	2.2	7.7
14. Transfers		14.5	1.6	0.6	0.2	*	*	0.7
15. Total		27.1	18.7	15.8	12.2	7.4	2.2	8.4
All Levels								
16. Purchases		17.8	23.0	19.7	15.3	10.0	7.5	11.5
17. Transfers		92.8	21.4	9.4	4.5	2.1	0.2	6.9
18. Total		110.6	44.4	29.1	19.8	12.1	7.7	18.4
		II. TOTAL BENEFIT ALLOCATION						
All Levels								
19. Variant A		127.3	61.1	45.8	36.5	28.8	24.4	35.1
20. Variant B		123.7	58.9	45.2	36.3	29.2	24.5	35.1
21. Variant C		180.4	77.0	57.9	40.8	26.2	12.3	35.1

* Less than 0.05 percent.
Notes:
Lines 2 and 10: Interest is included here under purchases although, according to national income accounts, it should appear as a separate category.
Lines 19, 20, 21: For explanation, see text.

ditures going to sustain the general cost of government are also difficult to impute. To complete the picture (and to permit an estimation of net benefits as considered in the next section), lines 19 to 21 show distributions of total benefits, but under three alternative assumptions. Variant A postulates that such general benefits are distributed in line with total family income; variant B allocates such benefits in line with tax burdens; and variant C uses a per capita distribution. The latter, of course, results in the most favorable pattern for the low-income groups. However, in all cases the overall benefit rate declines as we move up the income scale. We also note that the benefit rate in the bottom brackets is substantially above

TABLE 16-4
Distribution of Net Benefits and Burdens
(Net as Percentage of Total Family Income)

	INCOME BRACKETS									
	Under $4,000	*$4,000–$5,700*	*$5,700–$7,900*	*$7,900–$10,400*	*$10,400–$12,500*	*$12,500–$17,500*	*$17,500–$22,600*	*$22,600–$35,500*	*$35,500–$92,000*	*$92,000 and over*
Federal										
1. Specific allocation	76.7	17.7	4.1	−1.9	−4.2	−5.6	−5.6	−5.1	−5.1	−5.1
2. General, variant A	4.3	2.7	1.0	0.7	0.6	−0.4	−0.1	−0.6	−1.0	−3.6
3. Total	81.0	20.5	5.1	−1.3	−3.6	−6.0	−5.6	−5.7	−6.1	−8.7
State and Local										
4. Specific allocation	15.7	8.2	5.9	2.7	0.2	−1.4	−3.2	−3.7	−3.4	−4.4
5. General, variant A	−1.1	−0.8	−0.6	−0.5	−0.3	−0.1	0.2	0.4	1.1	1.2
6. Total	14.6	7.4	5.4	2.2	−0.1	−1.5	−3.0	−3.2	−2.3	−3.2
All Levels										
7. Specific allocation	92.4	25.9	10.0	0.8	−4.0	−7.0	−8.8	−8.7	−8.5	−9.5
8. General, variant A	3.2	1.9	0.4	0.2	0.3	−0.5	0.1	−0.2	0.1	−2.4
9. Total	95.6	27.9	10.5	0.9	−3.7	−7.4	−8.6	−8.9	−8.4	−11.9

Note:
Lines 2, 5, and 8: General expenditures are allocated in proportion to family income levels and tax distributions, as in Table 16-1.

100 percent, meaning that benefits from public expenditures are considerably larger than the earnings received.[19]

Net Residue

We may now put the two sides together and consider the fiscal residue or net benefit (or burden) which the entire fiscal system imposes at various points in the family income scale. In proceeding to this final stage, one is confronted with this dilemma: If we limit the netting-out to the more meaningful part of the benefit analysis, which covers only those expenditures for which specific benefit allocations are feasible, an arbitrary judgment must be made in deciding just what part of the total tax bill should be charged against these particular expenditures. Yet, if the entire tax bill is to be used, total expenditures (including those for which benefits must be allocated more or less arbitrarily) must be included.[20] Neither choice is convincing, yet it *is* of interest to obtain an impression of the overall distributional impact of the fiscal structure.

The residues shown in lines 1, 4, and 7 of Table 16-4 are based on the assumption that each expenditure dollar for programs subject to specific allocation is financed by an average tax dollar. The allocation of general benefits shown in lines 2, 5, and 8 corresponds to variant A in Table 16-3, it being assumed that such benefits accrue in proportion to income. As shown in the table, the net residue is positive at the lower end of the income scale and becomes negative as income rises. The break-even point at the federal level occurs around $8,000, while that of the state and local level is somewhat higher. The overall patterns for the three levels of government and for the entire system are also shown in Figure 16-3.

Scope of Redistribution

Another way of viewing the overall aspect of fiscal redistribution is in terms of Table 16-5, which shows the estimated distribution before and after fiscal intervention. Line 1 gives the distribution of income (including government transfers) before tax. Line 2 shows the distribution of tax liabilities (including all taxes) and line 3 gives the resulting distribution of family income minus taxes. The higher quartiles pay a larger share of taxes but also receive a larger share of income, and comparison shows the distribution of imputed tax burdens to be quite similar to that of income, reflecting the essentially proportional nature of the tax structure. It is not surprising, therefore, that the distribution of after-tax income (line 3) is only very slightly more equal than that of income before tax (line 1).[21]

[19] This result comes about because the numerator includes transfer payments plus imputed benefits from public services, while the denominator of our ratio includes private income plus transfer payments only. If imputed benefits were included in the denominator, the ratio would have to fall short of 100 and the decline in the ratio when moving up the income scale would be less sharp.

[20] Another difficulty arises in the case of deficit finance. However, for the year examined here (1968), budgets were approximately in balance.

[21] For other comparisons of income distribution before tax with distributions after federal individual income tax (but not allowing for other taxes), see E. C. Budd, *Inequality and Poverty,* New York: Norton, 1967. For annual comparisons up to 1964, see *Survey of Current Business,* U.S. Department of Commerce, p. 98, April 1964.

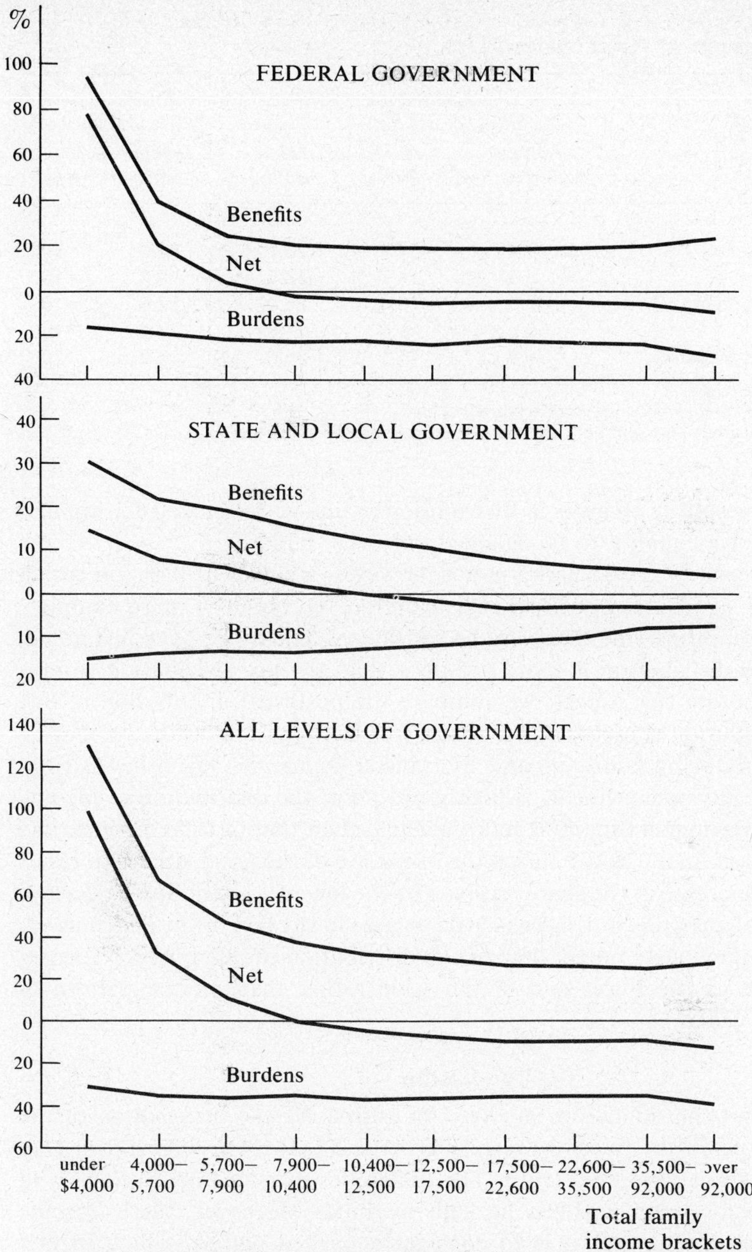

Notes: For *federal* pattern, burdens are based on line 6, Table 16-1; net curve is based on line 3, Table 16-4; and benefits equal line 3, Table 16-4, minus line 6, Table 16-1. For *state and local* pattern, burdens are based on line 15, Table 16-1; net curve is based on line 6, Table 16-4; and benefits equal line 6, Table 16-4, minus line 15, Table 16-1. For *all levels* of government, burdens are based on line 17, Table 16-1; benefits are based on line 19, Table 16-3; and net curve equals line 19, Table 16-3, minus line 17, Table 16-1.

FIGURE 16-3 Tax Burdens and Expenditure Benefits as a Percentage of Total Family Income.

TABLE 16-5
Distributional Aspects of Fiscal System, 1968

	QUARTILES RANKED BY INCOME				
	Lowest 25%	*Next 25%*	*Next 25%*	*Highest 25%*	*All*
1. Income including transfers	6.4	14.9	26.2	52.5	100
2. Taxes	5.8	14.7	26.5	53.0	100
3. Income minus taxes	6.6	15.4	26.0	52.0	100
4. Transfers	56.2	21.0	11.8	11.0	100
5. Income minus transfers	1.9	15.1	28.0	55.0	100

Note: All taxes and levels of government are included.
Source: See Tables 16-1 and 16-3 and the discussions thereof in the text.

Measuring the resulting changes in distribution in line with Figure 16-1, we find the coefficient of inequality to be changed only very slightly.[22]

A comparison of lines 1 and 3 is not, however, a sufficient basis on which to evaluate the significance of fiscal redistribution. To obtain a more complete picture, the expenditure side must also be considered; and as we have just noted, the expenditure distribution is more pro-poor than the tax distribution is anti-rich. To incorporate this aspect, we compare the postfiscal distribution of line 3 with the distribution of income before fiscal transactions. The latter distribution is obtained by reducing family income by transfer payments. Since the distribution of transfer payments (line 4) is highly pro-poor, the distribution of income net of transfer payments (line 5) is more unequal than that of total income (line 1). Comparison of lines 3 and 5 shows the operation of the fiscal system to result in a significant increase in the share received by the lowest quartile and a decrease in that of the top quartile, but there is little change in the rest of the distribution. This reflects a previously noted view of the distribution problem which focuses on the position of the lower end of the scale rather than on the pattern of distribution in general.[23]

Conclusion

It is evident that the difficulties involved in estimating the distribution of tax burdens and expenditure benefits are very great and that the results shown here must not be taken as the final truth. The difficulties in allocating burdens and benefits by income brackets must be kept in mind. Moreover, there is some question of how meaningful it is to consider a burden pattern which in fact compares an average taxpayer in one income bracket with an average taxpayer in another. There are few average people and the position of individuals within each bracket is dispersed. This problem is serious enough if one takes a separate

[22] In similar estimates by J. A. Pechman and B. A. Okner, the pretax ratio *OAB/OBC* in Figure 16-1 equals 0.43, while the after-tax ratio *OA'B/OBC* equals about 0.42. See Joseph A. Pechman and Benjamin A. Okner, *Who Bears the Tax Burden?* Washington: Brookings, 1974, p. 56.

[23] See p. 89.

view of burdens and benefits, with benefits in particular tending to accrue in line with certain characteristics (such as age, employment, and location), not all of which can be shared by the "average" household. The difficulty is greatly compounded if both sides are combined and net benefits are considered. Low-income households which pay payroll tax are typically not recipients of welfare payments or retirement pensions, while others which receive such payments do not pay tax. Thus, the first group may incur a heavy net burden, while the second receives benefits at a rate much in excess of that shown to apply for the average household in the bracket. For these reasons, a more disaggregated approach, in which consideration is given to the position of various subgroups in each bracket, may be in order; or it may be desirable to consider the net pattern for a longer period than a year, say, a lifetime. The problem is obviously a complex one in both conceptual and empirical terms. Yet the need for a global view of the distributional impact of the fiscal system is also evident. Consideration of the tax side only, such as has been the traditional approach, leaves us with a biased picture. In the end, it is fiscal rather than tax equity that matters, and both sides of the budget must be accounted for.

E. SUMMARY

Various concepts of incidence were considered and the following distinctions were drawn:

1. Statutory incidence differs from economic incidence, and it is the latter that matters.

2. The opportunity cost of resource transfer to public use, associated with an increase in public services, imposes a burden on consumers as a group as resources are withdrawn from private use. This transfer is to be distinguished from redistribution among consumers which arises in the case of tax-financed transfers or tax substitutions.

3. Owing to efficiency costs, employment, and output effects, the tax burden may exceed the revenue gain.

4. Net incidence allows for distributional effects of both tax and expenditure policies.

5. In formulating the problem of tax incidence, the differential approach is most useful.

The problem of incidence deals with the effects of fiscal operations on the distribution of real income among households:

6. This problem involves taxation effects on both the sources and uses side of the household account.

7. Distributional changes which result are viewed primarily in terms of distribution among income brackets, but other groupings may also be considered.

8. An overall measure of incidence may be derived by observing the resulting change in the coefficient of inequality.

Tax incidence was shown to depend on a number of factors, including the following:

9. Taxes may be on income or sales, and they may be general or selective.

10. Particular households will be affected depending on the composition of their earnings and the composition of their income uses.

11. The pattern of tax shifting is predicted more readily in a competitive market than in an imperfect one.

12. Selective taxes are shifted more easily than general taxes.

13. In observing the distributional effects of income taxes, the more strategic changes are likely to take place on the sources side of the household accounts, just as the uses side is likely to play the major role in determining the incidence of sales or product taxes.

A survey of the estimated distribution of tax burdens and expenditure benefits in the United States fiscal structure shows the following:

14. The income tax is the major progressive element in the tax structure, just as the payroll tax is the major regressive element. Sales taxes tend to be regressive. The roles of the corporation income tax and of the property tax greatly depend on the shifting assumption which is applied.

15. The distribution of the federal tax burden is progressive, while that of state and local taxes tends to be regressive.

16. Burden distribution for the tax system as a whole is proportional over the larger part of the income range.

17. The distribution of benefits is strongly pro-poor, owing to the role of transfer payments, especially at the federal level.

18. The net effect of tax burdens and expenditure benefits is positive over the lower to middle part, and negative over the middle to upper part, of the income scale.

19. The fiscal system results in a substantial redistribution toward the lowest end of the income scale, but otherwise it has little effect on distribution.

FURTHER READINGS

Hansen, Bent: *The Economic Theory of Fiscal Policy,* London: G. Allen, 1958, chap. 5.

Hicks, Ursula K.: "The Terminology of Tax Analysis," *Economic Journal,* March 1956.

Musgrave, Richard A.: *The Theory of Public Finance,* New York: McGraw-Hill, 1959, chap. 10.

Pechman, J. A., and B. A. Okner: *Who Bears the Tax Burden?* Washington: Brookings, 1974.

Chapter 17

Incidence of the Individual Income and Payroll Taxes*

A. The Individual Income Tax in a Competitive Market: *Tax on Wage Income; Tax on Capital Income; Empirical Evidence on Factor Supply; Price Effects.* **B. The Individual Income Tax in Imperfect Markets:** *Tax on Wage Income; Tax on Capitol Income; Progressive Rates; Conclusions.* **C. Incidence of the Payroll Tax:** *Incidence in a Competitive System; Incidence with Market Imperfections.* **D. Summary.**

Tax incidence is a fascinating but complex problem. In this and the next three chapters, shifting and incidence will be explored with regard to the major taxes, led by the individual income tax and the related problem of payroll tax. In line with our overview of shifting in the previous chapter, the problem will be viewed first under the assumption of perfect markets and then be reconsidered with allowance for market imperfections.

* *Reader's Guide to Chapter 17:* Going beyond the overview of the preceding chapter, the incidence of the individual income tax is now examined in depth, allowing for both competitive and imperfectly competitive markets. Furthermore, the components of tax burden and their relation to revenue are subjected to careful scrutiny. In the final section the controversial issue of payroll tax incidence is considered. This and the following three chapters may be passed over by readers less interested in the theoretical aspects of tax incidence.

A. THE INDIVIDUAL INCOME TAX IN A COMPETITIVE MARKET

The individual income tax applies to earnings originating in all sectors of the economy, and is thus the most general of the major taxes.

Tax on Wage Income

Consider first the case of taxpayers who receive their income from wages. As the tax is imposed, they find their net earnings from any given number of work hours reduced. Since the tax applies to earnings in all employments, workers cannot escape the tax by seeking employment elsewhere. They can only reduce their labor input (by way of reducing either labor force participation or hours worked) for the economy as a whole.

If labor supply to the economy as a whole is totally inelastic to the wage rate, the burden of the tax must be borne by wage earners. This is shown in Figure 17-1, where the vertical axis measures the wage rate while the horizontal axis measures the amount of labor input in man-hours per time period. *SS* is the supply schedule for labor and *DD* is the demand schedule for labor services. In a competitive system, *DD* reflects the value of labor's marginal product for each amount of labor input. Before tax, equilibrium is at *E*, the wage rate equals OW, and man-hours worked equals *OS*. As a tax on labor income at a rate $t = \frac{1}{3}$ is imposed, the *net* demand schedule (showing the net or after-tax wage rate at various levels of labor input) swivels down to *D'D*. Since the *SS* schedule is completely inelastic, labor input remains unchanged and the gross (before-tax) wage remains at OW while the net wage falls to OW_n where $OW_n = (1 - t)OW$. The take-home pay of wage earners declines by an amount W_nAEW, which also equals the government's tax revenue. The entire burden of the tax on labor income is absorbed by wage earners and the magnitude of the burden equals the amount of revenue.

The situation differs if labor supply is variable, or elastic to the wage rate. As shown in Figure 17-2, imposition of the income tax now leads to a decline

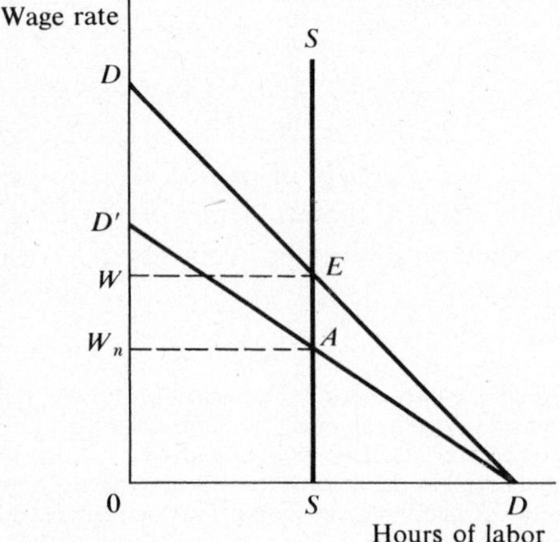

FIGURE 17-1 Tax on Labor Income with Inelastic Supply.

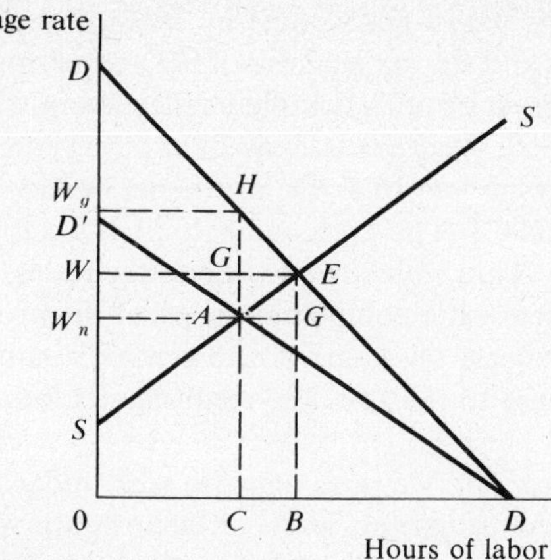

FIGURE 17-2 Tax on Labor Income with Elastic Supply.

in labor input from OB to OC, a rise in the gross wage rate from OW to OW_g, and a drop in the net wage to W_n. Tax revenue equals W_nAHW_g, and W_nAGW is the wage earner's loss of income through payment of tax at the new hours worked. The total loss is less than it would have been had the gross wage rate not risen from OW to OW_g.

In this case, identifying the tax burden is more complex. To trace what happens, the following changes in the position of labor, capital, and the economy as a whole, as expressed by various areas shown in Figure 17-2, may be distinguished:

Labor

1.	Net income loss to labor	$OBEW - OCAW_n = CBEA + W_nAEW$
2.	Leisure gain to labor	$CBEA$
3.	Burden on labor (1 minus 2)	W_nAEW

Capital

4.	Income loss to capital	$WED - W_gHD = WGHW_g + GEH$
5.	Burden on capital	same as 4

Treasury

6.	Revenue gain	W_nAHW_g

Totals

7.	Total income loss to private sector (1 plus 4)	$CBEA + W_nAEW + WGHW_g + GEH = W_nAHW_g + CBEH$
8.	Total income loss to economy (7 minus 6)	$CBEH$
9.	Total burden on private sector (3 plus 5)	$W_nAEW + WGHW_g + GEH = W_nAHW_g + AEH$
10.	Net burden on economy (9 minus 6)	AEH

Beginning with line 1, we show the loss of net income by *labor.* This loss reflects both the change in gross earnings and the tax paid out of the new earnings position. This change in net income, however, is not a complete reflection of what happens to labor. As work-time is reduced, leisure is increased, and this gain in leisure should be deducted from the income loss to arrive at the net burden on labor. The gain in leisure is shown in line 2. The area under the labor supply schedule *SS* may be taken to reflect the value which the worker attaches to the loss of successive hours of leisure and hence the compensation which he or she demands to surrender it. Thus *CBEA* reflects the value of the worker's gain in leisure time as work is reduced in response to the tax. The resulting net burden is shown in line 3.

Turning next to what happens to *capital,* we note that the area under the *DD* curve reflects the value of total output at various levels of labor input, with capital being held constant.[1] Thus with labor input *OB,* total output equals *OBED,* the wage rate (the value of labor's marginal product) equals *OW,* and labor's share in the output equals *OBEW.* This leaves the capital share to be determined as a residual equal to *WED.* As the tax is imposed and labor input falls to *OC,* output drops to *OCHD* and labor's gross share falls to $OCHW_g$, while its net share drops to $OCAW_n$ and capital's share falls to W_gHD. This reflects the fact that with labor supply reduced, capital has become the relatively more plentiful factor so its marginal product has declined. As shown in line 4, the decline in capital income equals $WED - W_gHD = WGHW_g + GEH$. Capital now shares in the burden of the tax. Since we assume the capital stock to be fixed, no adjustment similar to line 2 is needed, and the burden on capital in line 5 is the same as its income loss, shown in line 4.

Finally, the *Treasury* obtains a gain in revenue as shown in line 6, reflecting the difference between labor's gross and net earnings at the new (and reduced) level of work.

Having seen what happens to the various parties in the economy, we may now put the pieces together. With regard to changes in income, we note that total income loss to the private sector comprising both labor and capital (line 7) exceeds the gain to the Treasury (line 6), the difference being equal to the reduction in income for the economy as a whole (line 8). With regard to the burden picture, we note that the total burden in the private sector (line 9) now exceeds the Treasury gain (line 6) by an amount (line 10) which is referred to as the "excess burden," or the efficiency loss which results from the imposition of the tax.[2] The excess burden, however, is less than the income loss of the whole economy (line 8) due to the gain in leisure.

Tax on Capital Income

Precisely the same reasoning holds for a tax on capital income. We need only relabel the axes of Figures 17-1 and 17-2 so as to measure capital input horizon-

[1] Since each vertical block in the diagram under the *DD* curve represents the value of additional output which results as a further unit of labor is added, the total area under the *DD* curve reflects total output.

[2] For further discussion, see Chap. 21, p. 465.

tally and the return to capital on the vertical axis, with labor now held constant. Capital income is now determined directly while labor income follows as a residual. The burden of a tax on capital income, provided that capital input is reduced (capital supply is elastic), now comes to be shared by labor.

Putting the two preceding taxes together, as done with the individual income tax, the input of both factors may decline and the resulting changes in pretax earnings will depend on the relative change in both factor inputs. This modifies the earlier conclusion that the income tax tends to stay put with the taxpayer.

Empirical Evidence on Factor Supply

The outcome, as we have seen, depends on how factor supplies will respond. With regard to labor, we shall find that introduction of an income tax need not reduce hours of work. To be sure, the tax results in a reduction in the net wage rate. This makes work less attractive relative to leisure and induces workers to work less (the so-called substitution effect). But a tax also makes them poorer, so they tend to feel that they cannot afford as much leisure and must work more (the so-called income effect). Depending on which consideration carries more weight, effort may rise or fall. Such empirical evidence as is available gives little support to either hypothesis but suggests that labor supply to the economy as a whole is fairly inelastic to the wage rate.[3]

When we turn to effects on capital input, effects on saving and investment are involved. Since the tax reduces the net return that can be obtained, taxpayers may be expected to substitute consumption for saving and investors may be less eager to invest. This is again the previously noted substitution effect. Moreover, the reduction in disposable income which results as the tax is increased will tend to reduce both saving and consumption, this decrease being again the income effect. Here, however, both effects work in the same direction. As we shall see later, the effects on saving will differ, depending on whose income is reduced as the marginal propensity to consume declines when moving up the income scale.

The final incidence of a general income tax in a competitive system thus depends on (1) the response of factor supplies in the economy as a whole, and (2) the effects of such changes in factor inputs on factor earnings. With regard to labor input, the assumption of fixed factor supply for the economy as a whole is a good working hypothesis, based on the proposition that the income and substitution effects cancel. With regard to effects on saving and the size of the capital stock, this assumption is not acceptable. Nevertheless, we are not too far off the mark in thinking of the burden distribution of the income tax as being in line with the distribution of initial tax payments. Although factor earnings may be affected, such changes as may result are not likely to wash out the distributive pattern set by the structure of tax rates. If the nature of the production function is such, as is widely assumed, that factor shares will be invariant to the contribution of total factor inputs (i.e., if it is of the so-called Cobb-Douglas type), output effects are likely to result in a more or less proportional reduction in pretax earnings of both capital and labor.

[3] For further discussion of taxation effects on factor supplies, see Chap. 22, p. 438.

Price Effects

Looking back over the preceding pages, you will note that our entire concern so far was with effects originating from the income sources side of the household account. While this is where the crux of the problem lies, it cannot be denied that the general adjustment process, with the resulting changes in factor supplies and the distribution of income, will also affect product prices. As relative product prices change, households will be affected from the uses side of their accounts. Such effects may be important for particular taxpayers, but once more the pattern set by the structure of tax rates (and the resulting burden incidence from the sources side) is not likely to be systematically altered. A slight dampening effect may occur,[4] but by and large the distributive pattern will be set from the sources side.

B. THE INDIVIDUAL INCOME TAX IN IMPERFECT MARKETS

It remains to be seen how these results may be modified if imperfectly competitive markets are allowed for.

Tax on Wage Income

It does not take very close observation of the modern economy to conclude that wages are not determined in highly competitive markets, that a large part of the wage structure is set by collective bargaining, and that even wages in nonunionized sectors are influenced by wage rates in the unionized sectors. The question then arises whether the income tax on wage income may not enter into the bargaining decision. Will not the union be able to shift an increase in income tax by demanding higher pay, and will not the employer be able to pass on the cost of higher wages to the consumer?

Much as unions would like to react this way, the question is whether they can do so. The answer is "no" if all parties to the bargain behaved as maximizers prior to tax. Under these rules, unions and employers have already struck the best bargain which they were able to obtain, and imposition of the tax does not change this position. To alter the conclusion, one would have to assume that, prior to tax, unions had asked for less than they were able to obtain. If they had done so, union leaders, under pressure to protect take-home pay, might demand greater wage increases if tax and withholding rates were to rise. This does not seem to have been a major factor in the United States where unions traditionally respond to changes in the cost of living but not to tax-induced changes in take-home pay. Yet, such a response is not impossible. This is shown by countries such as Sweden, which engage in highly centralized collective bargaining and set wage rates as part of a general incomes policy. With income levels viewed in terms of after-tax wages, the income tax comes to be part of the overall wage settlement.

[4] If the tax is less progressive and burdens low-income households more, demand will shift from products bought by low-income households to products purchased by high-income groups. This may reduce the relative prices of low-income products, thus cushioning the real income loss of low-income households.

Turning to the upper end of the income scale, we find the compensation of executives to be determined in a highly administered market. Both the general level of executive compensation and the salaries paid to executives at particular points in the business hierarchy are set in a market where the supply of, and demand for, such services are hard to distinguish and their contribution to output is not readily measured. The compensation pattern for executives depends upon custom and general status considerations rather than upon the precisely measured marginal productivity of their services. In such a market, tax changes may well be reflected in changes in compensation designed to maintain desired patterns of after-tax remuneration. While empirical evidence is difficult to interpret (owing in part to the tax-induced complexity of forms in which executive compensation is given), it would not be surprising to find that the spread of before-tax compensation has widened as tax rates have become more progressive.[5]

Similar considerations hold for fees charged by professionals. Prestigious lawyers or surgeons may find it prudent to charge less than what the market will bear but then allow for changes in their tax burdens in making upward adjustments to their fees.

Tax on Capital Income

Similar considerations arise with regard to capital income. While individual investors will have little influence in negotiating the return on their investments, unincorporated firms (proprietorships and partnerships) may adjust their pricing policy to counter the income tax bite into the return on their invested capital. This problem, being similar to the issue of administered pricing in the corporate sector, will be considered in Chapter 18, where the incidence of the corporation income tax is discussed.

Progressive Rates

Does the fact that the income tax is imposed at progressive rates affect the conclusion that, in a competitive system, the burden stays put with the taxpayer? If progressive rates apply to a truly *global* income base, progression will not affect the taxpayer's choice among alternative sources of income. Assuming factor supplies to the economy as a whole to be fixed, the earlier conclusion still stands. However, the existence of progressive rates may affect the taxpayer's choice between work and leisure and his or her willingness to save and invest. As we shall see later, the existence of progressive rates tends to leave factor inputs at a lower level than would apply if the tax were imposed in a less progressive

[5] For a discussion of changes in before- and after-tax compensation for executives at various levels in the corporate hierarchy, see W. G. Lewellen, "An Intersectoral Analysis of Senior Executive Rewards," *Proceedings of the National Tax Association,* October 1969. The data show that over the period from 1940 to 1963, the percentage increase in the gross receipts of the top executives fell short of that of the next ranking five executives for the sample covered, even though the tax rate increased more sharply for the former group. This particular result does not appear to sustain the shifting hypothesis.

A still different problem arises in the development of forms of compensation which make it possible to reduce or postpone tax, such as deferred payment plans. This, however, is a matter of tax avoidance rather than shifting. See W. G. Lewellen, "Managerial Pay and the Tax Changes of the 1960s," *National Tax Journal,* June 1972.

fashion. Thus the existence of progression may bear on such spreading of the tax burden as may result from changing factor supply and its effect upon total output and factor shares in national income.

However, the income tax as applied in practice is not a fully global tax, since some income sources are given preferential treatment. Such preferential treatment as that extended to capital gains or tax-exempt interest becomes the more valuable the higher is the taxpayer's bracket rate applicable to other income sources. Accordingly, the incentive to choose tax-preferred income sources varies with the taxpayer's total income.

Conclusions

The existence of various types of market imperfections may thus permit some shifting of the income tax through a mechanism other than that of factor supply adjustment which was noted in the competitive system. However, the extent of such shifting is likely to be selective rather than general. The overall conclusion remains that the individual income tax may by and large be taken to stay put. This is also the assumption which underlies the pattern of burden distribution shown in line 1 of Table 16-1.

C. INCIDENCE OF THE PAYROLL TAX

The payroll tax poses problems similar to those of a tax on labor income, but an interesting additional issue arises because of the split of the contribution between employee and employer. Applied at rates of 4.95 and 0.9 percent on employers and employees for the finance of OASDI and hospital insurance and at 3.2 percent on the employer for unemployment insurance, the combined rate is 14.9 percent. Since almost all earnings are now covered, the tax is general in the sense that earnings from all industries are included in the base. However, as noted before, only the first $13,200 (OASDI and hospital insurance) and $4,200 (unemployment insurance) are covered, and of course all capital income is excluded.

Incidence in a Competitive System

Under the assumption of competitive markets, the conclusion of the preceding pages was that a general tax on wage income, applicable to wages in all industries, tends to be borne by the wage earner. Since the tax cannot be avoided by moving to tax-free employment, the only escape is to work less; but with labor supply to the economy as a whole fairly inelastic, this is not likely to be a major factor. Moreover, we have concluded in the preceding chapter that it should be a matter of indifference in the competitive setting whether the tax is collected from employers, from employees, or (as in fact is done) is split between the two. The result should be the same whether we think of the tax wedge as entering between the gross and net wage rate paid by employers or received by employees. The result, as shown in Figure 17-3, is the same in both cases. Before tax, the demand schedule for labor is given by DD and reflects the wage rate, equal to the marginal product of labor at various levels of labor input. OC is the initial labor input and OW is the wage rate as determined by the intersection of DD with the supply

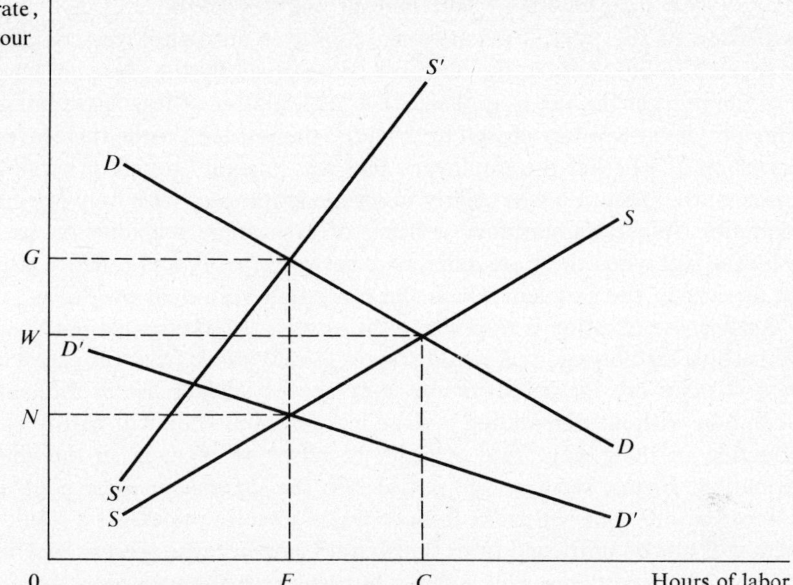

FIGURE 17-3 Alternative Views of the Payroll Tax.

schedule of labor *SS*. Now let a 50 percent tax be imposed on the employers' payroll. They will continue to pay gross wage rates as reflected by *DD* but will deduct the tax in arriving at the net wage. The net demand schedule thus equals $D'D'$, such that the net wage rate available at any given level of labor input equals $(1 - t) W_g$, where W_g is the gross wage rate as offered along *DD*. As a result, the new labor input (as determined by the intersection of *SS* and $D'D'$) is reduced to *OF*, the gross wage rate rises to *OG*, and the net wage rate falls to *ON*.

Alternatively, we may think of the tax as imposed on employees. Since workers must give up part of their gross wage and since their labor supply is related to their *net* wage, they must now ask a higher gross wage for any given labor supply so as to be left with the old net wage. Thus the supply schedule which confronts employers is given by $S'S'$ such that the gross wage W_g, as recorded by $S'S'$, equals $[1/(1 - t)] W_n$, where W_n is the net wage rate recorded by *SS*. Labor input is now determined by the intersection of $S'S'$ and *DD* but again equals *OF*, a result identical with that obtained before.[6] Similarly, the gross wage is again *OG* and the net wage *ON*.

[6] Let the demand for labor be expressed by

$$W = a - bH$$

and the supply of labor by

$$W = c + dH$$

where H is man-hours of work and W is the wage rate. Equilibrium labor input H is then determined by setting

$$a - bH = c + dH$$

Incidence with Market Imperfections

The division of the payroll tax between employer and employee contributions thus appears to be a fiction, the outcome being precisely the same on whichever side of the market the tax is applied.[7] Yet, as a matter of legislative intent, this sharing provision was introduced to "divide" the burden. While this leaves open the question of whether the employer's half was "meant" to fall on profits or on consumers, the intention was clearly to saddle employees with only one-half the contribution. Was this statutory division of rates mere stupidity or, as is frequently the fact when there are differences between theory and practice, are there other aspects to the problem which the preceding argument overlooks?

Raising the question is to point to the answer: Markets need not operate in a competitive fashion and real world responses may differ from the above model. If payroll taxes are increased, unions may accept an increase in the employer contribution without demanding a wage increase, but they will hardly agree to a reduction in their wage rate in order to offset an increase in the employer contribution. Firms, in turn, will not absorb the increase in *their* contribution in reduced profits, but will make it an occasion to raise prices. As a result, wage earners will not be burdened from the sources side because their money income remains unchanged. They will suffer a burden from the uses side, since prices have risen and thus the real value of their money wages is reduced. However, this burden will be less than in the absence of shifting. The reason is that the loss in real income is shared by other consumers who receive income from sources other than covered wages. The payroll tax comes to be translated in part into a product tax which is shared by all purchasers independently of their income source.

This adjustment, to be successful, requires not only that the wage bargain can be adjusted and that prices can be increased accordingly, but also that fiscal and/or monetary policy stands ready to expand aggregate demand sufficiently

---

Now a tax is imposed. Adjusting the demand schedule to

$$W = (1 - t)(a - bH)$$

we obtain an equilibrium H by setting

$$(1 - t)(a - bH) = c + dH$$

Adjusting the supply schedule, instead, to

$$W = (c + dH)/(1 - t)$$

we set

$$a - bH = (c + dH)/(1 - t)$$

The same solution for H is obtained in each case.

[7] The careful reader will distinguish between (1) the conclusion that the division of the tax collected is a matter of indifference, and (2) the proposition that the entire tax falls on the wage earner. The latter is the case only if the amount of labor supplied does not change.

to sustain the same level of real output at a higher money value of GNP. As the nature of labor markets is imperfect and the objective of high employment is a generally accepted target of stabilization policy, these two conditions may well be met. The final answer must again be sought in empirical analysis rather than in a priori conclusions based on the workings of a perfectly competitive market.[8]

However this may be, we noticed in Table 16-2 that the burden distribution by income classes is much the same whether we assume the tax to be borne by wage earners or by consumers. The pattern of payroll tax incidence is regressive in both cases. The rising weight of the payroll tax in the federal tax structure has thus tended to offset the relief from the individual income tax for low-income taxpayers via the rising level of exemptions and of the minimum standard deduction.

D. SUMMARY

The income tax, being a fairly general tax, cannot be easily escaped by changing place of work or type of investment. Its incidence has been considered under the assumptions of perfect and imperfect markets:

1. In a competitive market, a tax on wage income falls wholly on labor if labor supply is inelastic.

2. Capital shares part of the burden if labor supply is elastic to the wage rate.

3. In this case, the combined income losses of capital and labor exceed the revenue collected.

4. The total tax burden equals revenue plus excess burden.

5. Analogous reasoning holds for the income tax on capital income.

6. Empirical evidence suggests that the supply of labor to the economy as a whole is rather inelastic, so that the burden of the tax is likely to stay with the wage earner. The same tends to hold with regard to the response of capital supply to a reduction in the rate of return. However, savings and investment will decline as disposable income is reduced by the tax.

7. Under conditions of imperfect markets, shifting may occur as the wage bargain or the private rate of return on capital is adjusted.

The incidence of the payroll tax presents essentially the same problems as that of a tax on wage income, but certain additional considerations arise:

8. Under conditions of competitive markets, the division of the tax between an employer and an employee contribution is irrelevant, as both parts of the tax have the same burden incidence.

[8] J. A. Brittain (see *The Payroll Tax for Social Security,* Washington: Brookings, 1972, chap. 3) offers evidence in support of the hypothesis that the entire tax is borne by employees. Using cross-section data for over forty countries and interindustry comparisons in the United States, he tests the hypothesis that gross wage rates are a function of productivity and finds little evidence that gross wage rates rise with the payroll tax. For further discussion, see M. S. Feldstein and J. Brittain, "The Incidence of the Social Security Tax: Comment and Reply," *American Economic Review,* September 1972.

9. Under imperfect market conditions, the tax may be passed on. Such shifting is more likely for the employer than for the employee contribution.

FURTHER READING

Brittain, J. A.: *The Payroll Tax for Social Security,* Washington: Brookings, 1972.

Chapter 18

Incidence of the Corporation Income Tax*

A. Incidence in Competitive Markets: *Short-Run Incidence; Long-Run Incidence; Further Aspects.* **B. Incidence in Imperfectly Competitive Markets:** *Incidence with Monopoly; Administered Pricing in Product Markets; Administered Pricing in Labor Markets; Imperfections in Tax Base; Conclusions.* **C. Empirical Evidence:** *Historical Pattern; Econometric Studies.* **D. Summary.**

Perhaps the most controversial issue in tax incidence analysis is posed by the corporation income tax. As shown previously in Table 16-2, the burden distribution under this tax differs sharply, depending on whether it is taken to fall on shareholders, the recipients of all capital income, consumers, or workers. Moreover, the nature of corporation tax incidence has important bearing on various aspects of tax structure design, including the question of integration of the corporation and individual income taxes.[1]

* *Reader's Guide to Chapter 18:* The incidence of the corporation income tax has been the subject of lively debate in recent years. Recent writings have yielded an improved theoretical view of corporation tax incidence in a competitive model, allowing for interactions in a general equilibrium system, as discussed in Sec. A. At the same time, skeptics have continued to point to market imperfections which may alter the results, as examined in Sec. B. Econometric studies of the problem have as yet fallen short of a final answer (Sec. C). The issue therefore remains controversial.

[1] See p. 298.

A. INCIDENCE IN COMPETITIVE MARKETS

The corporation income tax belongs in that family of income taxes which apply to earnings originating in one industry or sector of the economy only, i.e., item 4 in our earlier classification of taxes.[2] Whereas incidence analysis is not greatly complicated when an otherwise general tax is limited to capital or labor income, limitation by industries complicates matters because now wage earners and capital owners may avoid tax by moving from the taxed to the tax-free sector. This tends to be the case with the corporation income tax. Although this tax is limited to capital income originating in a particular form of legal organization rather than in a particular industrial sector, certain activities (automobile production, for one) require the corporate form of organization while others (say, real estate) do not. Thus, the tax tends to be equivalent to one imposed on certain sectors of industrial production.

Short-Run Incidence

Suppose that the tax is limited to profits originating in industry X. In the short run, the amount of capital is fixed, not only for the economy as a whole but also for taxed sector X. The return on capital is thus in the nature of an economic rent, and the owners of capital invested in industry X can do nothing to avoid the tax. The burden, therefore, stays with the owners of capital invested in X. Households, whose capital income is largely from sector X, pay more heavily than do others whose capital income is more largely derived from sector Y.

The conclusion that the owner of capital invested in sector X is stuck with the tax holds true, even though he or she may wish to sell the asset and transfer the investment to tax-free industry Y. This conclusion follows since the owner cannot sell without accepting a lower price for his or her taxed asset, thereby bearing the full cost of the tax. Whatever he or she chooses to do, the loss has been capitalized and is borne by the owner of the asset at the time the tax is imposed. To illustrate tax capitalization, suppose that prior to tax, capital assets in sectors X and Y both yield an income stream of $10 per year. With an interest rate of 10 percent, both have a capital value of $100. Now let capital income originating in X be subject to a tax of 50 percent. The X assets will fall in value to $50 and their owners, if wishing to sell, will have to accept this reduced price. This is the case because the potential buyer will not invest in the taxed asset unless the rate of return net of tax matches that which can be obtained by purchasing a tax-free asset.[3]

Long-Run Incidence

As we turn to the longer run, we will assume first that the supply of capital to industry as a whole is fixed. At the same time, the supply of capital to any one industrial sector will be highly elastic as there is enough time for capital to move from lower to higher yielding sectors.

[2] See p. 387.

[3] We shall encounter this process of capitalization again when considering the incidence of the property tax. See p. 432.

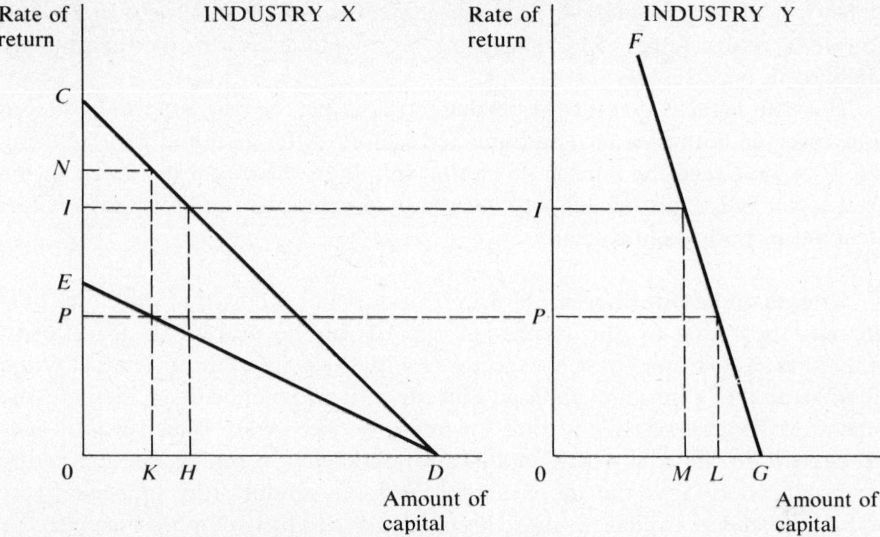

FIGURE 18-1 Tax on Capital Income from One Sector.

Equalizing Net Returns Since the tax is applied to capital income earned in sector X only, net returns in X are reduced and capital will flow from X to Y. As a result, output in sector X will fall, the prices of products produced in X will rise, and the *gross* rate of return on the remaining capital in X will increase. The opposite development will take place in sector Y, with output increased and the rate of return to capital decreased. Assuming perfect capital markets with no obstruction to the movement of capital, this capital flow from X to Y will continue until the net (after-tax) rate of return in X equals the untaxed rate of return in Y. The tax burden on capital income originating in X (on corporate profits in the case of a corporate profits tax) is thus spread between capital invested in both sectors. In the longer run, the burden is thereby shifted in part to capital invested in the untaxed sector.

This is shown in Figure 18-1 where the two panels depict sectors X and Y respectively. Before the tax is imposed, schedule *CD* on the left-hand panel represents the marginal efficiency of capital in sector X. Thus it shows the various rates of return attached to different sizes of the capital stock invested in that sector. A similar schedule, *FG,* is shown on the right-hand panel for sector Y. Before tax, total capital is divided between the two sectors, with *OH* invested in X (the corporate sector) and *OM* invested in Y (the unincorporated sector), where *OH* plus *OM* equals the total capital stock. In this way, the return to capital in both sectors is equated at the margin and equals *OI.*

Now a tax on capital income originating in sector X is imposed. The net return per unit of capital to investors in this sector now equals $(1 - t)r$ where r is the gross rate of return and t the rate of tax. This schedule of net returns is represented by *ED* in the left panel. As a result, capital will move out of the taxed and into the tax-free sector where the rate of return to the investor is higher. This reallocation of capital continues until investment in X falls to *OK* where the net rate of return is *OP*. At the same time, investment in Y rises to *OL* and the rate of return falls to *OP*. Thus, the *net* rates of return to the investor are equalized in both sectors.

It is thus evident that the tax burden on capital in the long run will be shared by investors in both the taxed and untaxed sectors. After an initial period during which we have seen the burden on capital to fall on the owner of capital in the taxed sector only, this burden will eventually come to be shared by the owners of capital in both sectors.

Effects on Factor Shares However, it does not follow that the entire burden must be borne by the owners of capital. In the process of adjustment, production shifts from sector X to sector Y with the price of the X product rising and that of the Y product falling. This shift in production may increase the demand for capital relative to that for labor, or vice versa. Which way it goes will depend on the role which capital and labor play in the production of the two products. If Y is the more capital-intensive product, the increase in its production renders capital the more highly demanded factor; in consequence, the before-tax returns to capital will rise and that of labor will decline. Here, the net rate of return to capital declines by less than the tax, and wage earners will bear part of the burden. Or, if factor demand shifts toward labor, the recipients of wage income will find their returns increased while the return to capital declines. In this case, the net return to capital declines by more than the tax while labor gains. Depending on the circumstances (the nature of production functions), the resulting changes in rates of return may also be reflected in changing factor shares.

Just what will happen depends upon (1) the initial combination of labor and capital in the two sectors, (2) the elasticity of substitution of capital for labor in the two sectors, and (3) the elasticity of substitution of one sector's product for the other's in consumption. Professor Harberger, who originated this analysis, concludes that as applied to the corporation income tax, the relevant magnitudes are such as to result in only minor changes in factor shares, with capital bearing the full burden of the tax.[4]

[4] See Arnold C. Harberger, "The Incidence of the Corporation Income Tax," *Journal of Political Economy,* June 1962; reprinted in Arnold C. Harberger, *Taxation and Welfare,* Little, Brown, 1974, pp. 135-162.

The problem is straightforward if production relationships in both sectors are such that substitution between capital and labor leaves factor shares unchanged, i.e., that the elasticity of substitution is unitary throughout. This is the widely used assumption made in the so-called Cobb-Douglas production function. The flow of capital from the taxed to the tax-free sector then leaves factor shares unchanged. Labor's net income is unaffected and the entire tax falls on capital. Harberger considers this to come fairly close to the actual situation.

Matters are more complex if the elasticities of substitution are other than unity. The burden on capital will then tend to be the greater (and that on labor the smaller) the lower is the elasticity of substitution between labor and capital in X as compared with that in Y. The burden on capital will also tend to be the larger, the lower is the elasticity of substitution in consumption of the two goods. These, however, are tendencies only. The various relationships are interwoven in a complex fashion and no simple conclusion emerges. Moreover, Harberger's analysis holds total factor supplies constant and, as noted in the text, the outcome changes further if factor supplies to the economy as a whole change.

In short, the burden distribution in a competitive system appears to be proportional to total capital income. Since capital income rises as a share of total household income as one moves up the income scale, incidence is progressive. However, the burden distribution, as seen in lines 2 and 3 of Table 16-2, will be less progressive than if it were borne by the owners of corporate shares only, while excluding the recipients of other types of capital income.

Further Aspects

While this is the main part of the story, two further aspects of the problem may be noted.

Effects on Prices The previously noted effects operate on the income *sources* side of the household accounts. As with the income tax, these effects deserve primary consideration, but a set of further secondary effects may enter via price changes operating on the income *uses* side. Some writers have referred to these as "excise effects." As capital moves from sector X to sector Y, the products of X will rise in price while those of Y will experience a price decline. This shift will lower the real income of households that spend a large part of their budget on the X product while raising real income of others that use a large part of their budget to buy the Y product. If corporate products (products of X in our example) weigh more heavily in higher-income budgets, this fact tends to reinforce the progressivity of the corporation income tax arising on the sources side.

Effects on Total Capital Supply In the preceding discussion we have assumed that the tax induces a shift of capital from X to Y while leaving the total capital supply unchanged. If the resulting decline in the net return to capital reduces capital supply as a whole, the output effects (considered previously in dealing with the general income tax on capital income) are superimposed upon the interindustry adjustments which arise under the partial corporation tax. Thus a decline in the size of the capital stock (or in its growth rate) depresses labor income as well as capital income. The rate of income growth in which capital and labor share will be slowed down, and their respective (before-tax) incomes will be reduced. The shares of capital and labor in total income, in turn, may or may not change, depending upon the nature of the underlying production relationships. Further consideration will be given to this aspect when discussing taxation effects on economic growth.[5]

B. INCIDENCE IN IMPERFECTLY COMPETITIVE MARKETS

We now discard the assumption that the corporation operates in a perfectly competitive market.

[5] See p. 505.

Incidence with Monopoly

To begin with, we consider a situation where the firm enjoys a monopolistic position in the product market. Though different from the competitive case in important respects, the situation is similar in that the pure monopolist once more maximizes profits. But if the tax is imposed so as to equal *x* percent of profits, it is evident that the firm will be best off by having the largest possible gross profits. With a tax rate of 48 percent, 52 percent of $100 million is better than 52 percent of $80 million. Therefore, the output and price which give maximum profits without tax will still be the best position after the tax is imposed. In other words, the monopolist finds the corporation's profits reduced by the tax and cannot pass it on to the consumer via higher prices and still remain a profit maximizer.[6]

The result is illustrated in Figure 18-2, giving the familiar diagram for profit maximization of the monopolist. Before tax, profits are maximized at output *OA*, where marginal revenue (MR) equals marginal cost (MC). Price equals *OB* and profits are *CDEB*. As a tax of one-third is imposed, the MR and MC curves remain unchanged but net profits are cut to *CDFG*.[7]

The same is shown in the lower part of the figure where *OPQ* gives total profits at various levels of output, with profits peaking at output *OA*. After the tax is imposed, net profits are reduced by one-third and are given by *ORQ* and *OSQ* showing the amount of tax. Net, like gross profits, peak at output *OA*, which therefore is optimal in both cases.

In the short run at least, the tax is again absorbed by profits in the taxed sector. Moreover, such may remain true even in the longer run. If firms in the taxed sector enjoy monopoly profits, it may be to their advantage, even after their profits are reduced by the tax, to remain where they are rather than to shift to the untaxed sector where they would enjoy a less sheltered position. The earlier conclusion that the tax is shared equally by capital in all sectors must then be qualified.

Administered Pricing in Product Markets

We now turn to a different type of pricing behavior, referred to here as "administered pricing," where firms do not necessarily engage in the economist's rule of

[6] If TR is total revenue and TC is total cost, then profits, P, equal $TR - TC$. Profits are maximized at a level of output where $dP/dQ = 0$, i.e., where

$$[d(TR)]/dQ - [d(TC)]/dQ = 0, \text{ or MR} = \text{MC}$$

After imposition of a profits tax at rate t, the monopolist seeks to maximize $(1 - t)(TR - TC)$. Differentiating this with respect to Q and setting equal to zero gives us

$$(1 - t)\frac{d(TR)}{dQ} - (1 - t)\frac{d(TC)}{dQ} = 0$$

Dividing by $(1 - t)$ again leaves us with MR = MC.

[7] We may also think of monopolists as including their *marginal* tax in marginal cost. This tax is given by *VAW*, as shown in the lower part of the figure. When added to MC in the upper figure, we obtain MC′, which intersects MR at precisely the same point as did MC. The reason of course is that the marginal tax cost is zero where total profits reach their maximum. While such allowance for the *marginal* tax cost is in line with profit maximization, this differs from a procedure by which the *average* tax (tax per unit sold) is added to price and which reduces after-tax profits. This view of the matter was pointed out to us by David Reaume.

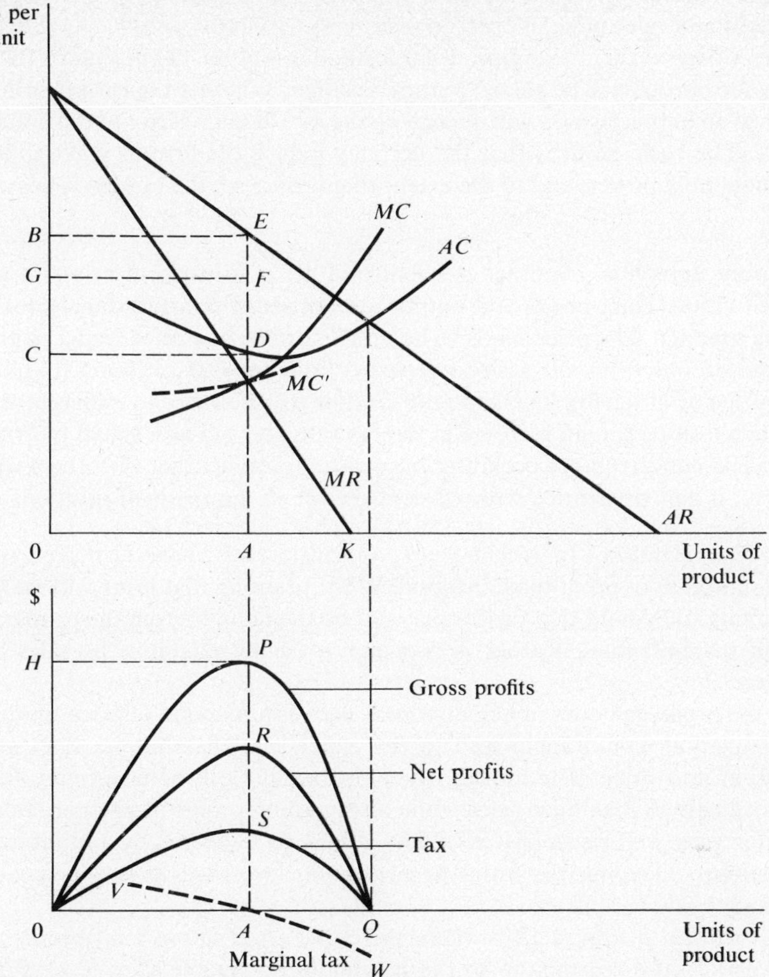

FIGURE 18-2 Profits Tax under Monopoly.

profit maximization. In such cases, the tax may lead to a price adjustment and the final incidence may come to differ.

Restrained Profit Maximization One possibility is that firms may exercise restraint in profit maximization. A firm whose market position is such that monopoly profits can be obtained may choose not to exploit its situation to the fullest. That is to say, it will operate at a larger output and sell at a lower price than it would if profit maximization were its goal. Rather, it may be satisfied with obtaining a target rate of return, say 15 percent, on invested capital. A higher rate of return may be considered "gouging" and socially improper; management may feel that a prudent profit target may help to maintain profits in the long run; or it may fear that excessive returns would invite antitrust action.

As a tax is imposed, the firm finds that its net rate of return has fallen below the target level. It will then be driven to exploit its monopolistic position, to restrict output and raise price in order to restore its net profit position. As it does so, it moves closer to the maximum profit position at output *OA* in Figure 18-2. In this way the burden will be passed to the consumer. Whether the entire burden can be passed on in this fashion will depend on the rate of tax relative to the pretax profit slack. The basic point is that the tax may induce the firm to make fuller use of its monopoly power; and to the extent that it does so, the burden is passed on.

Oligopoly Behavior Another possibility of price adjustment arises in an oligopoly situation. Here prices and output are not set in the traditional profit-maximizing manner. The price tends to be established by the price leader in the industry and no one firm will wish to depart from it for fear of losing its sales if it raises price or of having its competitors follow suit if it tries to undercut the price. In such a situation, an increase in the tax rate may act as a signal to firms to raise price in concert. Since each firm has reason to expect that the others will act similarly, it can raise price without concern for its competitive positions.

Sales Maximization In recent years, various writers have criticized the classical assumption of profit maximization. While granting that firms will maximize something, they hold that profits may not be the only, or even the primary, objective of maximization. Rather, a firm may wish to maximize its sales or market share.

Since the profits tax does not change total sales as a function of price, simple sales maximization would again lead to the conclusion that the tax does not change output and price. The impact, therefore, would still be on profits. But a firm is not likely to maximize sales while disregarding profits altogether. Sales maximization may well be an objective, but it must be tempered by a minimum profit constraint. Defining the latter as net profits, we then have a behavior pattern which leads to shifting.

This is shown in Figure 18-3 where the curve *OCB* shows total profits at various levels of sales receipts up to the maximum obtainable sales level *OB*.[8] For a profit maximizer, the optimal position would call for sales *OG* yielding profits *OD*. But a firm wishing to maximize sales subject to the constraint of minimum profits *OE* will choose sales *OF*. After a 50 percent profits tax is imposed, net profits obtained at various levels of sales falls to line *OKB*. To remain within the minimum profit constraint, minimum gross profits must be raised to *OH* so as to leave net profits at *OE*. Accordingly, sales must be reduced from *OF* to *OI*. Thus imposition of the tax is followed by reduction of sales and hence an increase in price. Once more the result differs from that obtained under full profit maximization, and part of the tax is passed on to the buyers of the products in higher prices.

Other Pricing Rules Economists like to think of business behavior as being rational in the sense of following a maximizing rule. But business executives may

[8] Figure 18-3 traces the sales and profit relationship given by Fig. 18-2 for levels of output to the left of *K*, this being the point where marginal revenue becomes zero and sales are maximized. The sales level *OG* in Fig. 18-3 in turn corresponds to output level *OA* in Fig. 18-2, at which point profits are maximized.

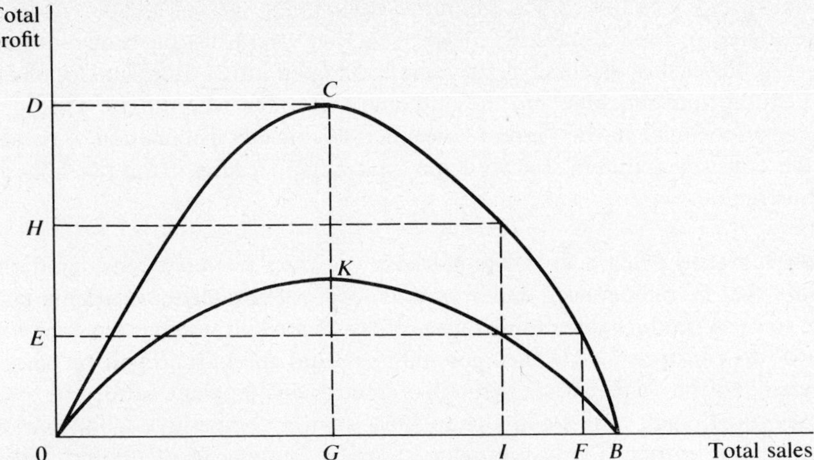

FIGURE 18-3 Profits Tax under Sales Maximization.

not act rationally. They may base their pricing rules upon certain customary criteria which need not follow this pattern.

One criterion is the practice of markup or margin pricing. Under this rule, costs are "marked up" to allow for a customary ratio of profits to costs, or price is set such as to leave profits (i.e., sales minus cost) a customary fraction of sales. Whether this approach gives rise to shifting depends on how costs and margins are defined. Shifting occurs if the tax is included as a cost, or if the margin is defined net of tax.

Another approach is that of average or full-cost pricing. Prices are set to yield a stream of receipts which will recover full cost (including overhead as well as variable costs) within a given planning period. Since the tax reduces this stream, higher prices will be asked and shifting may occur once more.

Both these rules may thus lead to a pricing behavior which *intends* to pass the tax on in higher prices. Whether the firm actually succeeds in so doing is a different matter. The outcome depends on the extent to which it already exercised its market power in the pretax situation.

Who Pays? We have noted a variety of situations where the initial response of the corporation may be to try to raise price in order to maintain its profits. To the extent that the corporate sector succeeds in this effort, the burden is passed on to consumers of the products produced in the corporate sector. The nature of the corporation profits tax in this case is more like that of a rather arbitrary form of excise tax.[9] The general equilibrium adjustment to the tax will be similar to that of an excise tax imposed on the output of this sector, and the primary determination of incidence may occur from the uses rather than the sources side

[9] Since the profit margin (ratio of profits to sales) differs between industries and firms, the implicit rate of sales tax (ratio of price increase to pretax price) will also differ. Thus, the required price change will differ among industries. See Carl S. Shoup, "Incidence of the Corporation Income Tax: Capital Structure and Turnover Rates," *National Tax Journal,* March 1948; reprinted in R. A. Musgrave and C. S. Shoup (eds.), *Readings in the Economics of Taxation,* Homewood, Ill.: Irwin, 1959.

of the household accounts. Since the initial response to the tax is different from that postulated in the competitive model, the long-run adjustment also differs. In terms of our earlier discussion, the coin is dropped into a different slot of the general equilibrium machine and the outcome will differ accordingly. This is of particular importance in the present case since the burden distribution, if passed on to the consumer, differs sharply from that which results if the tax falls on capital income.

Administered Pricing in Labor Markets So far, we have considered the possibility that firms operating under various forms of administered pricing may attempt to raise product price to recoup profits. As a result, the burden is passed "forward" to consumers. Another possibility is that the burden will be passed "backward" to the wage earner through reduction in the wage rate.

Once more, such adjustments cannot occur in a competitive labor market where the wage earner is paid the value of his or her marginal product and is paid the same return by firms which are profitable as by others which are not. If labor markets are imperfect, the situation may differ. If labor is weak and employers are in a monopsonistic position, the wage rate may be set below the value of labor's marginal product. The situation may then be similar to that of restrained monopoly pricing in the product market. Employers in the pretax setting may not fully exploit their position, but the tax may lead them to utilize their market powers more fully, with the result that part of the tax burden is passed to labor.

A similar outcome may result in a quite different setting where labor is in a strong position. Wage rates are set under collective bargaining, but unions in making wage demands may (and frequently do) allow for the profitability of the firm. They may aim to divert a share of monopoly profits to the wage earner while leaving the firm in what they consider an adequate profit position. Since this position depends on corporate profits *after* tax, an increase in the profits tax rate may reduce wage demands. In this way, part of the increase in tax may again be passed "backward" to the wage earner.

Imperfections in Tax Base

A final condition which may account for forward shifting into higher prices is based on imperfections in the definition of the tax base. The profits tax base may diverge from profits as defined in economic theory and include items which in fact are part of a firm's cost. Thus, profits as defined under the tax law do not allow for deduction of imputed interest on equity-financed working capital. Since such interest is a cost of doing business, the tax base is overstated. Part of the tax becomes an addition to cost and may be reflected in output and price. This possibility, however, is not likely to be very important since most deductions from taxable profits are liberally defined.

Conclusions

While economic theory has held traditionally that the short-run incidence of the corporation income tax is on profits, most business owners have maintained that they consider the tax a cost which is passed on. The former view is correct if one assumes that all markets operate in profit-maximizing fashion. But if firms operate as restrained monopolists, if sales rather than profits are maximized, or if other pricing rules apply, firms may well attempt to pass on the tax in higher prices. Moreover, if labor markets are imperfect, higher taxes may be reflected in more limited demands in collective bargaining and thus be passed on to labor.

The outcome, therefore, depends on existing market structures and behavior. The structure of American industry—and especially the larger manufacturing corporations from which the bulk of the corporation tax is derived—is such that administered pricing is likely to occur. Shifting due to administered price adjustments (as distinct from shifting due to factor movements and changing factor supplies in the competitive market) cannot be ruled out on a priori grounds. The same holds for the highly organized labor markets in which these firms operate. Theoretical analysis is inconclusive in such a setting and further empirical investigation is needed to settle the problem.

C. EMPIRICAL EVIDENCE

There have been a number of attempts in recent years to provide such empirical evidence.

The first question is what one should look for. If corporate tax rates differed between industries, the problem would be fairly simple. Insights might be gained from examining resulting price changes and comparing the relative positions of various sectors before and after the tax change. This cannot be done, however, since the tax applies to all incorporated firms at more or less the same effective rate. Nor is a comparison of rates of return on investment in incorporated and unincorporated firms feasible since no adequate data are available for the latter. The remaining possibility is to examine the experience of the corporate sector without the benefit of comparison with tax-free sectors and to explore how various elements of the corporate sector responded to the tax, including such features as rates of return on corporate equity, the share of corporate profits in value added by (i.e., income originating in) the corporate sector, or corporate profit margins.

Historical Pattern

We begin by taking a bird's-eye view of the relevant historical statistics. Some of the key variables are given in Table 18-1. Since the major increases in tax rates occurred during World War II, and since both the thirties and forties were highly unusual periods—one being dominated by the Great Depression and the other by a major war—the best that can be done is to compare the twenties and the decades following World War II.

Comparison of the statutory tax rates and *after-tax* rates of return (columns I and II) for the earlier period with those for the later period supports the shifting hypothesis. In the absence of shifting and assuming no other influences, the 8 percent net return of the later twenties should have fallen to below 5 percent as the tax rose from 12 to 52 percent in the fifties. Actually, no such decline

TABLE 18-1
Corporate Tax Rates and Profits Share
(In Percentages)

Years	*Statutory Corporation Income Tax Rate (I)*	MANUFACTURING CORPORATIONS *After-Tax Rate of Return (II)*	MANUFACTURING CORPORATIONS *After-Tax Profit Margin (III)*	ALL CORPORATIONS: *Profit Share in Income Originating in Corporate Sector (Before Tax) (IV)*
1927–1929	11–13.5	8.0	5.9	21.8
1936–1939	15–19	6.3	4.6	14.8
1955–1959	52	10.9	4.9	22.4
1960–1963	52	9.5	4.5	20.6
1964	50	11.6	5.2	21.9
1965–1967	48	12.7	5.4	22.1
1968–1969	52.8	11.7	4.9	19 8
1972	48	10.6	4.3	18.0

Notes:

Column I: 1968–1969 and 1970 statutory rates include surcharge.

Column II: Profits after tax (excluding inventory valuation adjustment) of manufacturing corporations as percentage of stockholder's equity.

Column III: Profits after tax (as in column II) as percentage of net sales by manufacturing corporations.

Column IV: Profits before tax (excluding inventory valuation adjustment) of all corporations as percentage of all income originating in the corporate sector.

Sources:

Columns I to IV, 1927–1929 and 1936–1939: M. Krzyzaniak and R. A. Musgrave, *The Shifting of the Corporation Income Tax,* Baltimore: Johns Hopkins, 1963, pp. 15, 17.

Columns I to III, 1955–1959 to 1971: *Economic Report of the President,* January 1972, pp. 280–281.

Column IV, 1955–1959 to 1972, *Survey of Current Business* and *National Income and Products Accounts,* table 1.14.

occurred. Instead, the net rate of return rose by nearly 40 percent. To put it differently, the gross rate of return rose by more than was needed to secure full shifting.[10] Similar support for the shifting hypothesis is presented by the more or less constant *after*-tax profit margin, shown in column III. With after-tax margins constant, gross margins rose to reflect the tax. Column IV, however, gives a different picture. Gross profits or profits *before* tax as a share in total income originating in the corporate sector were much the same in the mid-fifties and in the twenties. This runs counter to the shifting hypothesis. If the tax had been passed on to consumers or wage earners to recoup profits, the share of gross profits in national income should have risen accordingly.

The evidence derived from a comparison of the twenties with the fifties and sixties is thus conflicting and is consistent with both the shifting and the no-shifting hypotheses. Nor should one expect this simple-minded appraisal to be very helpful. Many nontax factors were at work over this tumultuous period, so that it is not legitimate to ascribe the entire changes in the profit picture to the

[10] Since these data cover the corporate sector only, it may be noted that some increase in the rate of return might have been expected to result from the flow of capital into the unincorporated sector, being matched by a decline in the rate of return in the unincorporated sector. An increase in the corporate rate of return caused by this adjustment would be compatible with the no-shifting hypothesis, but would have fallen far short of the increase shown in the table.

tax factor. This is also brought out in the later period when substantial fluctuations in the profit picture occurred even though no drastic tax rate changes took place.[11] A more sophisticated approach is needed to permit separating out the effects of the tax changes from those of other changes which came to pass during the period.

Econometric Studies

An empirical measure of shifting thus calls for an econometric approach, designed to isolate the effects of the corporation tax. Various studies of this sort have appeared in recent years, but the issue remains controversial. One type of study has expressed the corporate rate of return as a function of various predetermined variables, such as the level of consumer demand, capacity utilization, government expenditures, and corporation tax rates. By including corporate tax rates, analysts hoped to use the regression coefficient pertaining to this variable to measure the effects of rate changes on the rate of return. Some of these studies have indicated a high degree of shifting, lending more support to a full-shifting, rather than to a zero-shifting, hypothesis. The evidence, furthermore, pointed to fairly rapid responses to tax rate changes, thus suggesting the tax to be shifted via administered price adjustments rather than via capital movement to other sectors.[12]

These studies were criticized by other analysts, who held that the case for such shifting has not been made or that the evidence is against it.[13] Since tax rate changes typically coincide with changes in government expenditures, the effects of the two variables are difficult to isolate. Moreover, tax rate changes typically occur in periods of general economic change. Rate increases are associated with economic expansion and decreases with contraction. The tax variable in these regressions may therefore reflect current economic conditions, so that its coefficient cannot be interpreted as indicating the degree of shifting only.[14] Addition of a variable measuring the current degree of "economic pressure" (such as unemployment or shortfall of actual below potential GNP) reduces the tax

[11] The relative levels of effective tax rates in the later period were, however, lower than indicated in the table since the investment credit and accelerated depreciation are not reflected in the statutory rate.

[12] Marion Krzyzaniak and Richard A. Musgrave, *The Shifting of the Corporation Income Tax,* Baltimore: Johns Hopkins, 1963.

[13] Richard Goode, "Rates of Return, Income Shares and Corporate Tax Incidence," in M. Krzyzaniak (ed.), *Effects of Corporation Income Tax,* Detroit: Wayne State University Press, 1966; J. Cragg, A. Harberger, and P. Mieszkowski, "Empirical Evidence of the Incidence of the Corporation Income Tax," *Journal of Political Economy,* December 1967; M. Krzyzaniak and Richard A. Musgrave, "Corporation Tax Shifting: A Response," and J. Cragg, A. Harberger, and P. Mieszkowski, "Corporation Tax Shifting: A Rejoinder," *Journal of Political Economy,* July–August 1970. These papers are reprinted in A. Harberger, *Taxation and Welfare,* Boston: Little, Brown, 1974. Also see R. J. Gordon, "The Incidence of the Corporation Income Tax in U.S. Manufacturing," *American Economic Review,* September 1967, and response by Krzyzaniak, Musgrave, and Gordon, ibid., August 1968.

[14] In the studies, the economic variables appear on a lagged rather than current basis in order to place the estimating equation in reduced form and to permit prediction of the dependent variable. This is desirable but leaves open the objection that the current tax rate variable stands as a proxy for current economic conditions. It may do so, since the predetermined variables in themselves do not fully reflect other forces by which economic conditions in the current period are determined.

coefficient. Moreover, the experiment shows that the results are sensitive to just how the model is formulated.[15] All participants in the debate would probably agree that results reached so far cannot be considered definitive. Improved data and econometric techniques, combined with the use of less aggregative analysis, should produce better answers in time, but until then, a considerable degree of uncertainty regarding the incidence of the corporation tax remains.

This uncertainty is unfortunate because the incidence issue is of crucial policy importance in assessing the implications of the corporate profits tax. This was shown in Table 16-2, where the burden distribution of the tax was compared for different shifting assumptions. The further significance of these assumptions for the policy problem of integrating the corporation and individual income taxes was discussed in Chapter 12. Yet another aspect which bears on international tax integration will be noted in Chapter 33.[16] Given these uncertainties about the incidence of the tax, the issue of corporate tax shifting remains a major item on the economist's agenda for tax research.

D. SUMMARY

The incidence of the corporation income tax is among the most important and controversial aspects of incidence theory.

1. Under competitive conditions, these conclusions regarding burden distribution may be drawn:

- **(a)** In the short run, incidence would be on the shareholder.
- **(b)** In the longer run, the burden is shared by capital in both taxed and tax-free sectors. Moreover, consumers of products produced in the tax-free sector gain, while consumers of products of the taxed sector lose.
- **(c)** If the tax leads to a reduction in, or a lower growth rate of, the total capital stock, part of the burden may be borne by labor.

2. In the case of monopoly, short-run incidence is again on the shareholder.

3. Other market structures may lead to different results. Oligopoly pricing, sales maximization and other forms of nonprofit maximizing behavior may cause part of the tax burden to be shifted to consumers, whereas labor market imperfections may cause the corporation tax to be reflected in reduced wage rates.

4. Empirical evidence regarding the shifting problem has remained controversial.

FURTHER READINGS

Brown, E. Cary: "Recent Studies of the Incidence of the Corporation Income Tax," in *Public Finance and Stabilization Policy, Essays in Honor of Richard A. Musgrave,* W. L. Smith and J. M. Culbertson (eds.), Amsterdam, North Holland Publishing Co., 1974.

[15] See Cragg, Harberger, and Mieszkowski, "Empirical Evidence of the Incidence of the Corporation Income Tax," op. cit.

[16] See p. 720.

Goode, Richard: "Rates of Return, Income Shares and Corporate Tax Incidence," in M. Krzyzaniak (ed.), *Effects of Corporation Income Tax,* Detroit: Wayne State University Press, 1966.

Harberger, Arnold C.: *Taxation and Welfare,* Boston: Little, Brown, 1974, part III.

Krzyzaniak, M., and R. A. Musgrave: *The Shifting of the Corporation Income Tax,* Baltimore: Johns Hopkins, 1963.

McLure, Jr., Charles E., and Thirsk, Wayne R., "A Simplified Exposition of the Harberger Model, I. Tax Incidence," *National Tax Journal,* March 1975.

Mieszkowski, P.: "Tax Incidence Theory," *Journal of Economic Literature,* December 1969.

Slitor, Richard E.: "Corporate Tax Incidence: Economic Adjustments to Differentials under a Two-Tier Structure," in M. Krzyzaniak (ed.), *Effects of Corporation Income Tax,* Detroit: Wayne State University Press, 1966.

Chapter 19

Incidence of the Property Tax*

A. Incidence in Competitive Markets: *Similarity to Tax on Capital Income; Incidence of a National Tax; Incidence of a Local Tax; Inside versus Outside Burden; Benefit Differentials.* **B. Incidence with Market Imperfections:** *Imperfect Markets; Imperfect Assessment; Conclusions.* **C. Exclusion of Intangibles:** *Private Claims; Claims against Government.* **D. Summary.**

The key characteristics of the United States property tax, as we saw in Chapter 13, are (1) that it is a tax on real property, and (2) that it is a local rather than a national tax, imposed at differential rates by a large number of jurisdictions. This introduces an additional dimension into incidence analysis which is of paramount importance for this tax.

* *Reader's Guide to Chapter 19:* Taxes on rental and business property were traditionally thought to be passed on to tenants and consumers, thus giving a regressive burden incidence. More recently, the tax has been viewed as a tax on capital income and its incidence has been seen as progressive. This change in perspective is of major importance in view of the common concern with excessive property tax burdens. Moreover, the local nature of the tax presents additional problems of incidence, since local tax differentials may induce capital to move from one jurisdiction to another. This in turn poses important issues for the conduct of local government.

A. INCIDENCE IN COMPETITIVE MARKETS

Once more, we begin with a view of the incidence problem as it would apply in competitive markets, leaving market imperfections for later consideration. Moreover, we assume for the time being that the tax is applied to all real capital.

Similarity to Tax on Capital Income

Given perfect capital markets and assessment procedures, a 5 percent tax imposed on the value of an asset may readily be translated into an income tax on the income derived from the asset. Suppose that an asset worth \$1,000 yields an annual income of \$100, in line with a 10 percent market rate of interest. The liability under a 5 percent tax on the asset value is \$50. Expressed as a percentage of the asset's income, it equals 50 percent. The 5 percent tax on the asset value (or property tax) is thus equivalent to a 50 percent tax on the property income (or income tax). Putting it more generally, the value of an asset in a perfect capital market is given by $Y = iV$, so that $V = Y/i$ where V is its value, Y is its annual income, and i is the market rate of interest obtainable on other investments.[1] If the same yield is to be obtained from a property tax at rate t_p and a tax on income therefrom at rate t_y, we must have $t_p Y/i = t_y Y$ or $t_p = it_y$.

Incidence of a National Tax

To begin with, what would be the incidence of a general tax on the value of real capital assets, imposed on a uniform and nationwide basis? It follows from what we have just argued that in a market where capital yields a 10 percent return, the incidence of a general tax on the value of capital assets (property tax) imposed at a rate of \$5 per \$100 of true asset value would be the same as that of a 50 percent tax on capital income. This being so, all that has been said before about the incidence of a general tax on capital income again applies. We have argued that, in a competitive market, such a tax reduces the net return to capital and is absorbed initially by the recipients of capital income. Since such income rises as a share of total income when moving up the income scale, incidence is progressive. In the longer run, this reduction in the net return to capital may depress the capital stock. If it does so, the earnings of labor will decline so that is cannot be said any longer that capital alone is burdened by the tax. However, the pattern of burden incidence set by the short-run effect is likely to be the predominating one.

Incidence of a Local Tax

We must now consider how this conclusion is modified by the fact that the United States property tax is not a national tax but is imposed by thousands of indepen-

[1] This capitalization formula holds for a perpetual income stream. The value of a finite annuity is given by

$$V = Y\frac{1-(1+i)^{-n}}{i}$$

where n is the number of years over which the annual payments extend.

dently acting jurisdictions. If all these jurisdictions were to impose a tax at the same rate, the result would be the same as for the national tax. But they do not. Effective rates vary widely, whether the variation is due to differences in statutory rates or in assessment ratios.[2] To understand how this affects incidence, suppose that a single jurisdiction raises its rate above the national level. What will happen?

Short Run In the short run, capital invested in the high-rate jurisdiction is immobile and its owners must bear whatever higher rates are imposed. This goes for owners of improvements and sites alike. Short-run incidence is on the owners of the local property which is taxed. Moreover, the burden is on the owners who held the property at the time the tax was imposed. They cannot shake off the burden by selling the taxed asset.

To illustrate this, we assume again that the rate of return on capital before tax is 10 percent, so that an asset yielding $100 per year is worth $1,000. Now let a particular jurisdiction impose a property tax of $50 per $1,000 of property value. As noted before, this is equivalent to a 50 percent income tax. Net income is reduced to $50 which, capitalized at 10 percent, lowers the property value to $500. If the initial owner of the asset wishes to sell it, he or she must absorb the tax loss, since the buyer will want to obtain a net return of 10 percent, similar to that available from an investment elsewhere. The burden of the tax thus falls on the initial property owner, i.e., the owner of the property prior to the imposition of tax. Subsequent owners who purchase the old asset will do so at a lower price only and are not burdened by the tax. The loss has been capitalized and stays with the initial owner.[3]

Longer Run In considering the longer-run adjustment, we may distinguish between three aspects of the total picture:

1. That part of the tax base which reflects land or site values is fixed and cannot move. The original owners of land in the high-tax jurisdiction will thus suffer a permanent loss equal to their share in the tax. There is no difference in this case between the short-run and the long-run adjustment. Since income from the ownership of land is more important to high-income than to low-income groups, incidence is progressive.

2. The situation differs with regard to capital. Capital invested in improvements is not caught permanently. In the longer run, it will flee the high-rate jurisdiction and move to jurisdictions where rates are lower. Maintenance expenditures on old assets will be reduced, and new investment in the high-rate jurisdiction will decline. As the capital stock in the higher-rate jurisdiction falls while that in the

[2] See p. 351. We continue to assume for the time being that all forms of real capital are included in the base and are taxed at a uniform rate within any one jurisdiction.

[3] As noted before in connection with the corporation tax (see p. 416), the existence of a *partial* tax is prerequisite to the capitalization process. A truly general tax on property (applicable to all jurisdictions) would not be capitalized. Such at least is the case if government bonds are included in the base. If such bonds are exempted and assuming their supply to be infinitely elastic at the pretax yield, the market rate of interest will remain unchanged. The reduced income from taxed property, being discounted at the unchanged market rate of interest, will then result in a reduced capital value, i.e., the tax is capitalized.

low-rate jurisdiction rises, the gross rate of return on capital in the former goes up while the rate of return in the latter declines. This movement continues until the *net* rate of return from investment in the high-tax jurisdiction equals the rate of return outside. The process ceases when net returns in various jurisdictions are equalized. As was the situation with the corporation tax, a tax imposed upon capital in one sector of the economy comes to be shared by the owners of capital at large. If the tax increase occurs in a small jurisdiction the capital stock of which is only a small part of the total, any outflow of capital will not be enough to greatly affect returns elsewhere. The tax increase will reduce the net return on capital in the nation as a whole by only a small amount. Even capital invested in the high-tax jurisdiction will experience only a slight decline in its net rate of return, although, of course, its share in the total capital stock will have fallen.

The overall result, considering capital income for the nation as a whole, is evidently similar to that which would have occurred had the revenue been derived from a national tax.[4] The net return to capital is reduced and the part of the tax imposed on improvements is borne by the owners of capital in the nation at large. Therefore the burden distribution is progressive since capital income (or ownership) rises relative to income when moving up the income scale.

3. It remains to consider a third factor, namely two-way shifts between groups in the high-tax and low-tax jurisdictions:

- **(a)** As capital leaves the high-tax jurisdiction, less housing will be available to its residents. Rents will rise so that capital invested in housing can obtain the same net return as in the low-tax jurisdiction. As a result, tenants will suffer. At the same time, the supply of housing in low-tax jurisdictions will increase and rentals will fall. The net result will be a transfer in real income from tenants in the high-tax jurisdiction to tenants outside.
- **(b)** The outflow of capital will also reduce business plant. As a result, wage earners who remain in the high-tax jurisdiction will find their earnings reduced since they have less capital to work with, while wage earners on the outside will gain as they will work in better plants. The net result will be a transfer between inside and outside workers.
- **(c)** Finally, a similar transfer will have occurred between the owners of sites in the high-tax jurisdiction and those outside. As residents leave the high-tax jurisdiction, the demand for land declines, just as it increases in the low-tax jurisdiction. Thus the rent income from land falls in the former and rises in the latter location.

It is interesting to note that, whereas the effect shown under 1 results in a net reduction in net income from land and that under 2 in a net reduction in capital income for the nation as a whole, the shifts noted under 3 are between corresponding groups inside and outside the high-tax jurisdiction and do not

[4] This conclusion parallels that reached previously for a tax on capital income imposed in one sector of the economy only, e.g., the corporate sector. But once more the conclusion must be qualified by allowing for changes in factor shares which may result as capital moves from one use (i.e., investment in the corporate sector or high-tax jurisdiction) to other uses (i.e., investment in the unincorporated sector or in the low-tax jurisdiction). In either case, this may lead to a change in the shares of various factors in national income, depending on how capital and labor enter into the output of the two sectors. See p. 418.

imply a net worsening in the position of tenants, workers, or owners of land for the entire nation. The distributional implications of these interjurisdictional shifts are therefore difficult to assess. However, it is likely that low-income tenants and low-income wage earners are in general less mobile, so the incidence of these interjurisdictional shifts will tend to be regressive, thus qualifying the conclusion of progressive incidence noted under 1 and 2.

Inside versus Outside Burden

In the preceding discussion, the incidence of the local property tax was viewed from a national point of view, i.e., the resulting burden distribution within the boundaries of the nation as a whole was considered. But from the point of view of the taxing jurisdiction itself, the more immediate concern will be with that part of the burden which is borne within the jurisdiction as compared with that which is absorbed outside.

Thus, suppose that real property located in jurisdiction A is owned by residents of jurisdiction B. As a result, the short-run burden will be borne by outside individuals while local residents may enjoy a free ride. But they may not fare as well in the longer run when capital can move out. Now local residents find their rents increased and wages reduced while outsiders (as noted earlier under 3) have gained. The greater the outflow of capital, the less will be the revenue obtained and the greater will be the rise in rents and reduction in income suffered by the residents of the high-tax jurisdiction. Not only are local residents unable to export the burden of such taxes as are collected, but they lose to the outside because less capital is available to them. It is not surprising, therefore, if a particular community is hesitant to raise its tax rate much beyond that imposed by rival jurisdictions. Indeed, a community might be tempted to derive net benefits from lowering its tax below that applicable in rival jurisdictions.

Local tax policy thus involves a difficult choice between (1) the gain to be derived by shifting tax burdens to the outside through the taxation of capital owned by "foreigners," and (2) the danger of loss to the local economy from the flight of "foreign" capital. This condition, moreover, does not apply to local finance only. We shall meet it again and on an enlarged scale when examining the coordination of tax policy at the international level.[5]

Benefit Differentials

The preceding discussion has been one-sided in that it has considered the tax side of the picture only, without allowance for the benefits from public services which the revenue may provide. Yet, they must be taken into account when examining the overall effects of an increase in a local property tax.

Just as an increase in property tax rates may reduce property values and induce capital outflows, so may the provision of additional public services raise values and attract capital inflow. Better schools or municipal services may render the town a more attractive place in which to reside or to operate a business. The improvement raises the demand for housing and structures, leading to higher property values, and thus counteracts the effects of increased property tax rates.

[5] See Chap. 33, Sec. B, p. 718.

Thus, expenditure benefits may be capitalized no less than tax burdens, so that the combined tax and expenditure effects may leave housing values reduced, increased, or unaffected, depending on what the revenue is used for.

If all property taxes were imposed in strict conformity with the benefit principle, the two effects should wash out with property values independent of tax rates. Actually, such is not the case. The property tax is used as a general revenue source and goes to finance expenditure benefits not always in close alignment with tax contributions. Nevertheless, empirical investigations show that property values respond to expenditure as well as tax differentials, thus pointing to the importance of considering both sides of the picture.[6] This is a matter to which we shall return later when considering issues in local finance.[7]

B. INCIDENCE WITH MARKET IMPERFECTIONS

Once more, the competitive model must be qualified by allowing for market imperfections and for imperfections in the way in which the tax is imposed.

Imperfect Markets

The conclusion that a general tax on capital value or income falls on the owners of capital rests on the postulate that profits prior to tax were maximized. In this case, which holds for both pure competition and monopoly, introduction of the tax leaves the optimal price unchanged. For shifting to occur, the use of market power prior to the imposition of the tax must have been restrained, or pricing rules other than profit maximization must have applied. These principles have been discussed in connection with the individual and corporation income taxes and need not be repeated here.

However, it is of interest to consider the extent to which the property tax is applied in market structures which may permit departures from the profit-maximizing rule. For this purpose, we return to our earlier discussion of the property tax base in Chapter 14. Based on Table 14-3, the composition of the tax revenue may be estimated as follows:[8]

Types of Property	*Percentage of Revenue*
1. Residential, owner-occupied	31
2. Residential, rental	16
3. Acreage, vacant lots, and farms	8
4. Commercial and industrial	23
5. Public utilities, etc.	8
6. Personal property	14
Total	100

[6] See Wallace E. Oates, "The Effects of Property Taxes and Local Public Spending on Property Values," *Journal of Political Economy,* November–December 1969.

[7] See Chap. 29, Sec. A, p. 614.

[8] See Table 14-3, p. 350. With 61 percent of housing units owner-occupied and 37 percent tenant-occupied (*Statistical Abstract of the United States,* 1973, p. 689), we assume that 66 percent of the revenue from residences, as shown in Table 14-2, is owner-occupied. This makes some allowance for higher housing values in the owner group.

National Tax In viewing the potential for administered price responses in various parts of the tax base, we again return to the case of a uniform national tax on real capital. Beginning with the third of the tax which is assessed on owner-occupied residences (item 1 in the above table), there is little chance that purchasers of houses possess sufficient market power to enable them to purchase residences at a lower price because an increase in their tax rate has occurred. For rental housing (item 2), chances of administered pricing (now in the landlord-tenant contract) are substantially greater. Public concern with rental levels and the constraints of rent control (or threat thereof) may hold down rents below what could be charged, enabling landlords to hike rents as their property tax is increased, thus passing the tax on to the tenant. In this setting, a property tax increase may give rise to increased rental charges. Another instance in which administered price responses may occur is afforded by state-assessed public utilities (included in item 5), where tax changes tend to be reflected in rate setting. Farms and acreage (item 3) and personal property (item 6) are unlikely to offer such options.

The tax on business realty (included under item 4) poses problems similar to those encountered in the corporation tax. Since the tax on business property is more general (extending over the unincorporated as well as incorporated sectors), this source of revenue is less heavily concentrated in large corporations, so that shifting through administered price adjustments will tend to be less prevalent. In all, the parts of the tax imposed on items 2 and 5 are the most likely candidates for administered price shifting, with 4 more questionable and 1, 3, and 6 likely to stay put with the property owners.

Local Tax Regarding a local tax, the possibility of shifting will depend on whether the market pertains to the local economy only, or whether "exports" and "imports" are involved. Thus, a local firm selling in a national market will find it more difficult to shift the tax than a firm selling in the local market only. Similarly, a firm selling in the local market but subject to the competition of imports will have more difficulty in shifting than one which competes with local suppliers only. This means that firms in the high-tax jurisdiction will find it hard to shift their burden unless they operate in a purely local market, say as a grocery store in an isolated area. The market for rental housing, on the other hand, is inherently a local market, since the housing services have to be rendered within the jurisdiction and hence by structures which are subject to the higher tax.[9]

Imperfect Assessment

The ready translation of a general tax on capital into a tax on capital income is based on the assumption that capital values are a precise reflection of the present value of the income streams. This is frequently, or even typically, not

[9] More precisely, the above discussion refers to a firm's ability to shift the excess tax. Thus, if jurisdiction A imposes a rate of 5 percent whereas jurisdiction B imposes a tax of 7 percent, B's excess rate is 2 percent. Firms located in B but subject to competition from firms in A will be unable to shift this "excess" tax of 2 percent. The 5 percent rate, on the other hand, is applicable in both A and B and subject to the shifting conditions which pertain to a national tax at that rate.

the case. For one thing, the market value of an asset may not properly reflect all possible future changes in the prospective income stream to be derived therefrom. For another and more important reason, changes in market value will not immediately be reflected in changes in assessed value. The tax as seen by the firm may thus be in the nature of a fixed charge on the use of capital rather than a tax which varies with the firm's net income. In the short run, such a charge does not enter into marginal cost; but in the longer run, it is equivalent to an increase in the cost of borrowed capital and may come to be reflected in price and passed on to the consumer.

While the property tax is a fairly general tax on most types of real assets, certain types of assets are excluded. Thus, in assessing business property, so-called personalty is frequently left out. The term applies to items, such as inventory and certain types of equipment, which are not fixed in their installation. Since such property can readily be moved (a factory might keep its warehouse in an adjoining low-tax jurisdiction), local taxation of such property is difficult and most experts agree that its exclusion is desirable. Since the types of property which are excluded cannot readily be substituted for fixed (and taxable) property, the exclusion is not apt to distort production methods in order to avoid taxes.

Conclusions

Under competitive conditions, the incidence of a nationwide and uniform tax on real capital would be similar to that of a general tax on capital income. Its burden distribution, at least in the short run, will be in line with the distribution of capital income. This result may be qualified by interjurisdictional shifts which arise in the case of a local tax, but the general conclusion of progressive burden distribution remains.

As market imperfections are allowed for, administered price adjustments may give rise to regressive results. The assumption that the tax falls on the owner remains strongest in regard to residential housing, whereas shifting is most likely to occur in rental housing and in public utility properties. This assumption was reflected in Table 16-1, and the importance of alternative assumptions was tested in Table 16-2. Since the general role of the property tax is now under reconsideration, this is another area where uncertainty complicates the design of tax policy.

C. EXCLUSION OF INTANGIBLES

The property tax, as imposed in the United States, is assessed on real assets and excludes all intangible property. How does this affect its incidence? The answer differs, depending on whether the claims or securities involved originate in the private or the public sector.

Private Claims

Consider first a setting in which there is no public debt or government-issued money. All debt instruments are between private persons. Suppose that there are two individuals, A and B, whose wealth positions are as follows:

	A	*B*	*A+B*
Real property	$100	$50	$150
Debt owed	10	—	—
Debt claims	—	10	
Net worth	90	60	150

We may now consider various ways of imposing a wealth tax. If we collect $15 from a proportional tax on all real property, A pays $10 while B pays $5. If we collect a similar amount from a tax on net worth—i.e., a tax which includes debts claimed and deducts debts owed—A pays $9 while B pays $6. This suggests that A prefers the latter and B the former approach. This reasoning is invalid. If the tax is imposed on real property, borrowers will not be willing to borrow at the same rate of interest as they did before, since the net earnings from their investment in real property is reduced. The lender will have to be satisfied with a lower rate of interest, so that part of the burden is passed from A to B. In the end, the burden distribution will be the same under either tax and in line with the distribution of net worth.

It does not follow, however, that the choice between the two taxes is a matter of indifference. We have noted before that a wealth tax, if imposed on a personal basis and at progressive rates, should be assessed on net worth, since it is net worth that is the measure of ability to pay. Returning to our illustration, a progressive rate tax that is assessed on real property (where A's base is twice that of B) will obviously differ from that assessed on the net worth base (where A's base exceeds that of B by only 50 percent).

Claims against Government

Another reason why use of the real property base differs from use of the net worth base is because of claims against government, whether such claims are in the form of public debt or money backed by Federal Reserve credit and the Treasury. Such claims add to the wealth of one private holder without reducing that of another. Unlike private debt, they are thus an addition to the net worth base for the group as a whole. Suppose, for example, that the above illustration is expanded as follows:

	A	*B*	*A+B*
Net worth from above	$ 90	$60	$150
Claims against government	70	20	90
Net worth, total	160	80	240

In this case, collection of $15 under a flat-rate net worth tax will call for a rate of 6.2 percent, drawing $9.88 from A and $5.12 from B. The result differs from that of a proportional tax on real property above because now net worth includes claims against the government. Moreover, a further difference between the two bases arises if progressive rates are used.

D. SUMMARY

Assuming competitive markets to prevail, the incidence of the property tax is similar to that of a tax on capital income.

1. The short-run incidence of a national tax on real property will be on the owners of property. In the longer run, a reduction in capital stock may result, placing part of the burden on labor.

2. The short-run incidence of a tax will be on the owners of property in the tax jurisdiction. In the longer run, the burden of the tax on mobile capital (but not land) comes to be shared by all capital, including that located outside the taxing jurisdiction. In addition, two-way shifts may occur between various groups of workers and consumers inside and outside the taxing jurisdiction.

3. From the point of view of the taxing jurisdiction, an important distinction arises between those parts of the burden which are borne inside and others which are borne outside.

4. To the extent that the tax-burden differentials between jurisdictions are matched by benefit differentials from public services, house values will remain unaffected and capital will not move.

Under conditions of imperfect markets, administered price adjustments may result in an initial shifting of the burden.

5. Such shifting is more likely to occur with regard to rental property and public utilities and less likely with regard to owner-occupied residences.

6. Firms selling in local markets are in a better position to shift the tax than are the firms selling outside the taxing jurisdiction.

FURTHER READINGS

Mieszkowski, P.: "The Property Tax: An Excise Tax or a Property Tax?" *Journal of Public Economics,* April 1972.

Netzer, Dick: *Economics of the Property Tax,* Washington: Brookings, 1966, chap. 3.

"The Property Tax: Progressive or Regressive?" Symposium by H. Aaron, R. A. Musgrave, H. E. Brazer, Dick Netzer, A. F. Friedlander, E. R. Rolph, G. E. Petersen, *The American Economic Review,* May 1974.

Chapter 20

Incidence of Sales Taxes*

A. Incidence of a General Sales Tax: *Relationship among General Taxes; Sales Tax on Consumer Goods; Who Are the Consumers? Growth Effects.* **B. Selective Sales Taxes: (1) Partial Equilibrium View:** *Changes in Output and Price; Division of Burden; Ad Valorem Tax versus Unit Tax; Adjustment under Monopoly; Maximum Yield.* **C. Selective Sales Taxes: (2) General Equilibrium View:** *Relative Price Changes; Relative versus Absolute Price Changes.* **D. Summary. Appendix: Incidence of Unit and Ad Valorem Taxes.**

Sales taxes are imposed on the gross receipts of firms. As distinct from taxes on net income, they must enter into the determination of price and output and therefore pose quite a different problem of initial adjustment. Sales taxes may again be general or selective; that is, they may be imposed on receipts from the sale of all products or on receipts from the sale of single products only. As noted before, the breadth of coverage is a major factor in determining how taxpayers respond and what the incidence of the tax will be.

* *Reader's Guide to Chapter 20:* The final group of taxes to be considered in our examination of tax incidence are taxes on sales. Beginning with a general tax, the components of tax burden and their relation to revenue are investigated. Subsequently, the incidence of a selective sales tax is explored.

A. INCIDENCE OF A GENERAL SALES TAX

Even "general" sales taxes may differ in their degree of generality. A tax may be imposed on the sale of all current output, including both consumer and capital goods, or on the sale of consumer goods only. In either case, the tax may be imposed at the final (retail) stage or in the form of a value-added tax. The base is the same in both cases and incidence will also be similar. For purposes of this chapter, we shall think of the tax as imposed on the retailer but remember that the same reasoning holds for the value-added type of tax.[1]

Relationship among General Taxes

In an all-consumption economy, a general sales tax on consumer goods would be similar to a tax on all income.[2] With consumer expenditures = sales receipts = factor payments = income, it makes no difference for purposes of the final incidence at which of the four points the tax is imposed. Nor does it matter whether the sales tax, entering as a wedge between the gross receipts of firms and the net outlays of consumers, pushes up absolute prices or reduces the absolute level of factor incomes. Real incomes are reduced in both cases.

The existence of saving and capital formation breaks the equivalence among the four taxes. The base of a tax on the sale (or, for that matter, on the purchase) of consumer goods now falls short of that of an income tax by the amount of saving. Assuming savings to flow into the purchase of capital goods, we see that a tax on income thus equals a tax on the sale of consumer goods plus a tax on the sale of capital goods.[3]

Sales Tax on Consumer Goods

The sales tax on consumer goods is thus a selective tax in the sense that it excludes sales of capital goods. Imposed as a tax on the sale of consumer goods, it enters as a wedge between the net and gross price of such goods. Assuming that wage rates and other costs of production remain unchanged in money terms, we note that price will rise by the amount of tax. The relationship between the old and the new price will be such that $P = (1 - t)P_g$ where P is the old market price and P_g is the new (gross) price. At the higher price P_g, the same level of money wages will purchase fewer consumer goods, so that the real income of consumers is reduced. While the money income of consumers is unchanged, they are able to buy less in real terms. At the same time, the price of capital goods is unchanged, leaving savers (who may be viewed as purchasing these capital goods) unaffected.

Since the impact of the burden is now from the uses side of the household account, the burden experienced by any one household will depend on how its income is divided between consumption and saving. If consumer-good prices rise by 10 percent, a household which consumes its entire income suffers a 10 percent decline in its real income. If only 80 percent is consumed, the decline equals 8 percent.

[1] See p. 337.

[2] See our earlier discussion of the impact points of taxes in the circular flow, p. 224.

[3] More precisely, the equivalence is with a tax on *gross* income. Since the usual income tax is imposed on income *net* of depreciation, it resembles a tax on sales minus depreciation. See p. 338.

People who save all their income, on the other hand, incur no burden. Since they save their income and purchase capital goods, they will find their prices unchanged. Since money wage rates and other costs remain unchanged, the price of capital goods remains unchanged as well. Savers will thus be able to obtain the same amount of capital goods as before.[4]

Who Are the Consumers?

We thus arrive at the conclusion that a sales tax on consumer goods is borne by consumers. The primary determinant in the incidence picture comes from the income uses side; and since the ratio of consumption to income (the average propensity to consume) falls when moving up the income scale, so does the ratio of tax burden to income. This is the basis on which the tax is said to be regressive. Before we accept this conclusion, two queries must be introduced.

Tax Postponement versus Tax Escape Since the tax falls on consumers, a household which saves for purposes of perpetual accumulation will escape tax entirely. But what of a household which merely saves in order to postpone consumption? Such a household must pay tax when dissaving at a later date. It does not escape tax but merely postpones tax payment. Nevertheless, it gains because the present value of its tax burden will be less than that of another household which begins with dissaving and ends up with saving. At a 7 percent rate of discount, a tax dollar payable twenty years hence has a present value of only 26 cents. Confronted with a choice between a tax on consumption and a tax on income, households will differ in their preferences, depending upon the prospective timing of their future income and expenditure flows, which in turn will depend upon their stage in life and their budget plans.

Cross-Section versus Lifetime Pattern The hypothesis that a sales tax on consumer goods is regressive rests on evidence from cross-section data which shows that in any particular year, low-income families will on the average consume a higher fraction of their income than will high-income families.[5] The average propensity to consumer declines when moving up the income scale. By allocating the sales tax burden in line with this distribution of consumption among income classes, the regressive incidence shown in line 11 of Table 16-1 is obtained.

The appropriateness of evidence drawn from a cross-section for any single year may be questioned.[6] Evidence of a falling consumption-income ratio for *any one year* is consistent with a wide range of hypotheses regarding the consumption-income ratios at particular income levels over a *longer period.* Households in any given income bracket will include those whose income is permanently in that

[4] What matters for incidence, here as throughout, is not that the *absolute* level of consumer goods prices rises while that of capital goods remains unchanged, but that the price of the taxed consumer goods rises *relative* to that of the tax-free products.

[5] No such data have been available for recent years, but the Bureau of Labor Statistics Survey for 1961 clearly brings out this fact. See U.S. Bureau of Labor Statistics, *Survey of Consumer Expenditures,* 1960–61, Report 237–93, May 1966.

[6] See also the similar argument in relation to the property tax, p. 355.

bracket as well as others who occupy it only temporarily. In the low brackets, this temporary group will typically consist of units whose income is normally higher. If such households tend to maintain past consumption patterns, they will consume more than do households with permanently low incomes.[7] Because of this, the consumption rates for households in the bottom group (which in the cross-section data includes households whose income is only temporarily low) will be higher than those for households with permanently low incomes. As a result, use of such cross-section data overstates the decline in the average propensity to consume when moving up the income scale and, with it, the regressivity of a sales tax as applied to the more permanent income position of households.

Indeed, if all income were consumed over a person's lifetime, the consumption tax would be proportional in relation to lifetime income.[8] But in fact, not all income is consumed and estates are left; and, though no adequate data are available, it seems likely that the ratio of estates to lifetime income rises when moving up the scale of lifetime income. Viewed in this way, the sales tax remains regressive, although less so than suggested by the evidence drawn from annual cross-section data.

There remains the question of whether tax equity should concern itself with annual or lifetime tax-income ratios. There is merit to the position that an annual base is arbitrary and that a longer period should also be considered. But it would also be unrealistic to argue that the shorter-run relationship between tax liability and income does not matter. Taxes must be paid when they come due, and the more that has to be paid at any one time, the less is left for private use at that time. A time distribution of tax payments which runs counter to expenditure needs is thus more burdensome to the taxpayer.[9]

In all, it is evident that reasoning from annual data is insufficient, but, unfortunately, adequate data on saving-income ratios over longer periods are not

[7] The hypothesis is that an individual's consumption for any one year depends not only on his or her income for that year but also on what the person expects to be his or her more "permanent" (or even lifetime) income. People will thus attempt to maintain consumption at customary levels in any one year, whether their income is normal, unusually high or low. As a result, their consumption-to-income ratio will be high in low-income years and low in high-income years. Applying this to the cross-section picture, we should expect that the lower end of the income scale includes a larger proportion of people whose incomes are temporarily high. Reasoning along these lines helps to explain why the consumption ratio falls as we move up the scale.

The consumption functions used in current econometric models generally make use of lagged, as well as current, income as determinants of current consumption. If past income is interpreted as an indicator of future income, this evidence may be read as supporting the hypothesis that consumption in any one year is a function of expected *lifetime* income. (For a discussion of this issue, see M. Friedman, *A Theory of the Consumption Function,* Princeton, N.J.: Princeton, 1957.) Alternatively, the evidence may be interpreted merely as showing current consumption to depend on past income. In either case, use of cross-section data overstates regressivity of the sales tax as related to more permanent income.

[8] The present value of lifetime consumption taxes at the beginning of a person's working life would still depend on his or her lifetime income and consumption profile. If a larger share of lifetime consumption occurred earlier for low-income (lifetime) families, the distribution of lifetime burden would still be regressive, and in the opposite case it would be progressive.

[9] Even if capital markets were perfect so that a person could readily borrow against future income, timing differences would remain because of interest cost. But in reality, people—especially people with low income—are not readily in a position to undertake such borrowing.

available. In Table 16-1, we have thus accepted the pattern based on cross-section data, but we should remember that the true degree of sales tax regressivity may be less than that shown.

Growth Effects

As in the case of the income tax, the analysis of sales tax incidence must allow for effects on factor supplies and the level of output. Suppose, as is not unreasonable, that the substitution of a consumption tax for an income tax increases saving and investment while lowering consumption. As a result, the future capital stock and level of income will be increased, and this change will benefit the recipients of both capital and wage income. How the gain in income will be split between recipients of wage and capital income (i.e., what will happen to factor shares in national income) again depends on the nature of production relationships in the economy. However this may be, a high-consumption household, while suffering from the uses side of its account, may, in the long run, benefit on the sources side by receiving higher wages.

As we shall see in Chapter 22, this analysis may again be extended to view incidence in the context of an expanding economy, where types of tax policy differ in their effects upon the rate of growth and hence on the future level of income as well as upon its distribution.[10]

B. SELECTIVE SALES TAXES: (1) PARTIAL EQUILIBRIUM VIEW

Turning to a selective tax on a particular consumer good, we must compare not only the position of consumers with that of savers but also that of consumers of the taxed product with that of consumers of the tax-free product.

In terms of our earlier classification, we now deal with a sales tax which is imposed on one product, say the output of industry X, only. This tax corresponds to item 6 in our earlier classification of taxes (see p. 384) and applies to such taxes as excises on automobiles, liquor, cigarettes, or gasoline. Since the sale of X is taxed while that of Y is not, the market price of product X is increased (the tax being added to its factor costs) and rises relative to that of Y. What happens next depends on how consumers and producers respond to this change in relative prices. To simplify matters, we consider a unit tax, e.g., a tax of 10 cents per package of cigarettes. The related case of an ad valorem tax is considered later.

Changes in Output and Price

The resulting changes in output and price in the taxed industry will depend on the elasticities of supply and demand. This is illustrated in Figure 20-1, which shows the industry demand and supply schedules for the taxed product X under various conditions.

If the demand for X is completely inelastic to price, the entire burden of the tax falls on the consumers of X. This is shown in part I of Figure 20-1, where

[10] See p. 505.

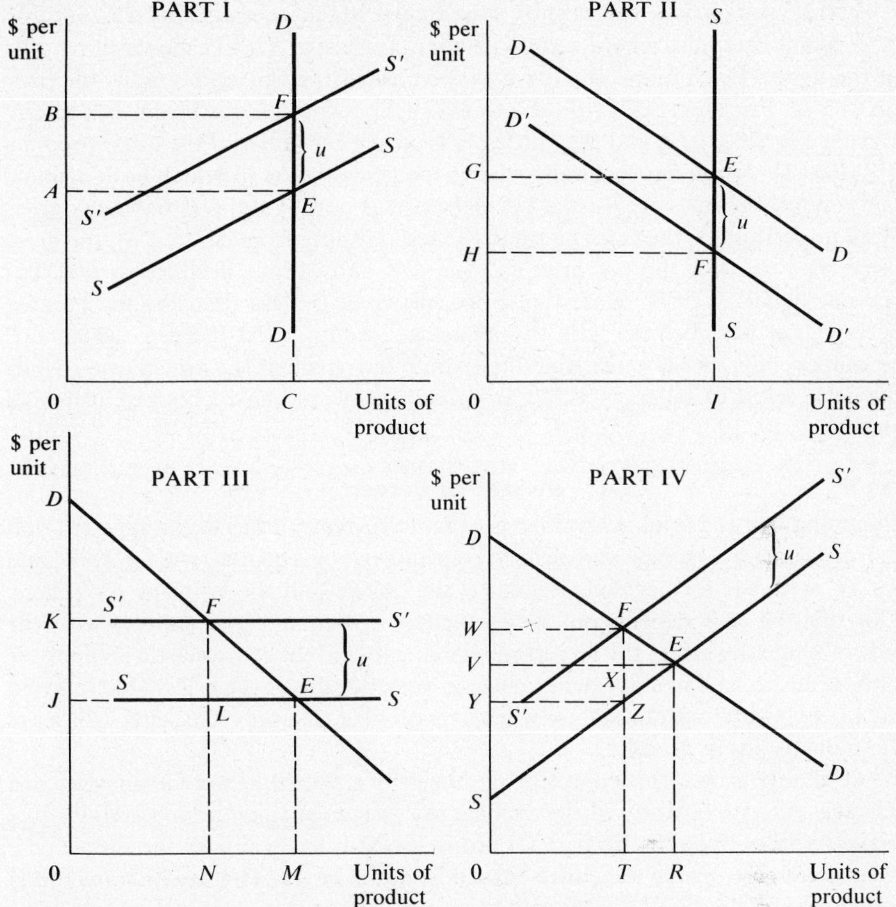

FIGURE 20-1 Effects of Sales Tax in Competitive Market.

SS is the supply schedule prior to tax and *S'S'* is the supply schedule as it confronts the consumer after imposition of a unit tax *u*. The demand schedule is given by *DD* and the pretax price is *OA*. After the tax is imposed, output remains unchanged at *OC*, but the gross price rises to *OB*. Revenue equals *AEFB* and the entire burden is borne by the consumers of X.

Next consider a situation where the supply of X is entirely inelastic. In this case, shown in part II of the figure, the tax is viewed as lowering the net demand schedule from *DD* to *D'D'*.[11] The gross price now remains unchanged at *OG* and output at *OI*, but the net price to sellers is reduced from *OG* to *OH* and their receipts fall by *HFEG*, which in turn equals the government's revenue. The entire burden now falls on the producers of X. The sales tax, in this case of totally inelastic supply, turns out to be similar to a selective income tax on income originating in X.

[11] As shown below, a unit tax may be viewed as either an addition to average cost or a reduction in average revenue.

Next we consider the case of an industry which operates under conditions of constant cost, i.e., where supply is infinitely elastic. This is shown in part III of the figure. Once more, the tax is viewed as raising the supply schedule from *SS* to *S′S′*. Price increases from *OJ* to *OK*, with output reduced from *OM* to *ON*. Revenue equals *JLFK* and the burden falls on the consumer of the taxed product.

Part IV of the figure, finally, shows the general case in which both demand and supply schedules are elastic. *OR* is the pretax output and *OV* the pretax price. With imposition of the tax, the supply schedule shifts from *SS* to *S′S′*, the gross price rises to *OW*, the net price falls to *OY*, and output declines to *OT*. Tax revenue equals *YZFW*. Note that price has risen by less than the tax because average cost has declined with the reduction in output. At the new output *OT*, consumers pay *VXFW* more than they would have paid at the pretax price, while the net receipts of sellers is *YZXV* less than they would have obtained at the old price.

Division of Burden

Assuming that the total tax burden is equal to revenue, it has been suggested that shares borne by buyers and sellers respectively be equated with *VXFW* and *YZXV*, with the former contributed by the buyers and the latter by the sellers. This division will depend on the elasticities of demand and supply, with the buyers' share the larger the less elastic is demand and the more elastic is supply.[12] This stands to reason since, with inelastic demand, the buyer is less able to avoid the tax by switching purchases, whereas with elastic supply the seller will leave the industry more readily.

But this is not the complete picture, since the *total* burden may exceed revenue. As in our study of the income tax, we must trace more carefully just what happens. Referring to part III of Figure 20-1, we deal with the simple case of constant cost, where the entire burden is on the buyer. The situation may then be shown as follows:

Buyers	
1. Pretax satisfaction	*OMED*
2. Pretax cost	*OMEJ*
3. Pretax consumer surplus (1 minus 2)	*JED*
4. Posttax satisfaction	*ONFD*
5. Posttax cost	*ONFK*
6. Posttax consumer surplus (4 minus 5)	*KFD*
7. Burden (3 minus 6)	*JLFK* + *LEF*
Treasury	
8. Revenue gain	*JLFK*
Economy	
9. Net burden (8 minus 7)	*LEF*

[12] It may be shown that $B_b/B_s = E_s/E_d$, where B_b and B_s are the buyers' and sellers' shares of the burden respectively, E_s is the elasticity of supply, and E_d is the elasticity of demand. Thus, referring to part IV of Fig. 20-1, E_d over the relevant range equals $(TR/OR)(VW/OV)$ while E_s equals $(TR/OR)(YV/OV)$. We thus obtain E_s/E_d equal to VW/YV where VW is the buyers' share and YV the sellers' share.

Beginning with the pretax position of consumers, the area *OMED* represents the satisfaction which they derive from the consumption of *OM* units. Viewing the demand schedule as recording the price which they would be willing to pay for successive units of the product, we note that the area under the curve reflects the value of the satisfaction derived from its consumption. At the same time, consumers' pretax cost of obtaining *OM* units was equal to *OMEJ,* which reflects the satisfaction lost by not spending this amount on other products. Consumers therefore derive a "consumer surplus" or net gain equal to *JED.* In lines 4 to 6, the same situation is examined after the tax has been imposed, with consumer surplus now reduced to *KFD.* Their loss of consumer surplus, given in line 7, equals $JLFK + LEF$, this being the burden of the tax on consumers. It exceeds tax revenue, or the Treasury's gain of *JLFK* (see line 8) by the triangle *LEF* (line 9). This is a net loss to the economy which is also referred to as "excess burden." It reflects the efficiency loss to the economy which results from the imposition of the tax, a concept to be discussed further in the next chapter.[13]

Ad Valorem Tax versus Unit Tax

A selective sales tax may be imposed in the form of an ad valorem tax or of a unit tax. In the former case, the tax is set as a given percentage of price. In the latter, it is a fixed amount per unit of the product sold. Although the general incidence problem is the same for both types of taxes, they enter into price determination in a different way. It is interesting to observe why.

The two taxes are compared in Figure 20-2. *DD* is the market demand schedule for product *X, SS* is the supply schedule, equilibrium output before tax equals *OB,* and price equals *OC.* Now an ad valorem tax at rate $t = EF/EB$ is imposed. The net demand schedule shifts to $D'D'$. Output falls to *OG,* the gross price rises to *OH,* and the net price falls to *OI.* Revenue equals *IKLH.*

To obtain the same amount of revenue, a unit tax in the amount $u = KL$ is needed, giving a net demand schedule shown as $D''D''$ on the figure. If this unit tax were viewed as an addition to cost, the supply curve would shift up to $S'S'$. Output is set where *DD* intersects $S'S'$, with gross price again equal to *OH* and net price to *OI.* Moreover, you will observe that the ratio of unit tax to gross price at the equilibrium output must equal the ad valorem rate *t.* At the same time, the ratio of unit tax to initial price or ME/EB exceeds *t.*[14] These matters are developed further in section I of the appendix to this chapter.

[13] While the constant cost case is quite simple, matters are more complex in part IV where costs are rising and the burden is shared by buyers and sellers. The buyer's burden again equals *VEFW* and the seller finds his or her proceeds reduced from *OREV* to *OTZY,* resulting in a cut of $YZEV + TREZ$. By moving factors into other employment, *TREZ* is recouped, leaving a net loss of *YZEV.* The combined loss of buyers and sellers equals *YZEFW* and exceeds revenue *YZFW* by *ZEF,* the new measure of excess burden. In order to designate *ZEX* as an efficiency loss, we must interpret the *SS* schedule as a marginal cost schedule for the industry, reflecting the social opportunity cost of factor use in the taxed industry. For further discussion of this rather difficult aspect, see E. J. Mishan, *Cost-Benefit Analysis,* New York: Praeger, 1971, chap. 2.

It may further be noted that the allocation formula given in the preceding note for the seller's and buyer's share in revenue also holds for the total burden or $YZFW + ZEF$. This follows, since $XEF/ZEX = VXFW/YZXV$.

[14] Note that the unit tax may always be expressed either as an addition to cost (raising *SS* to $S'S'$) or as a deduction from revenue (shifting *DD* downward to $D''D''$). The ad valorem tax is related to price and is therefore introduced as a shift in the demand curve (swiveling *DD* to $D'D'$).

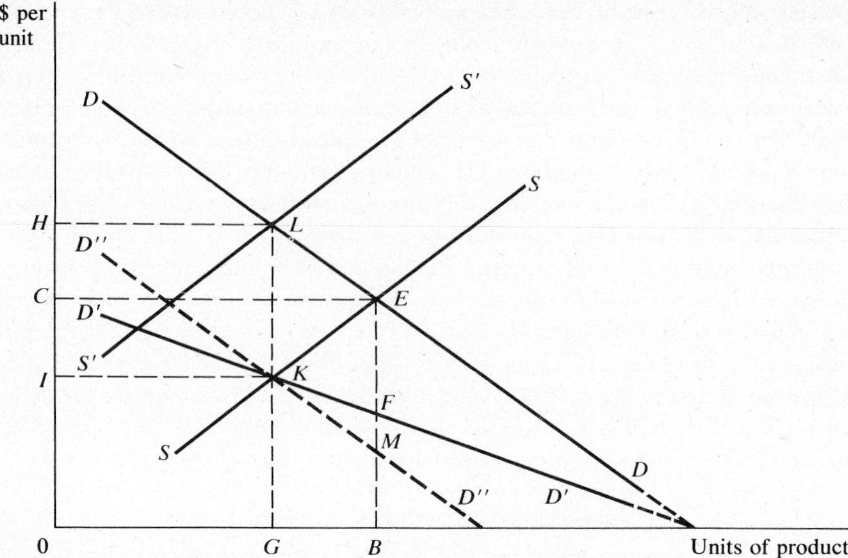

FIGURE 20-2 Comparison of Ad Valorem with Unit Tax.

Under competitive conditions, the outcome is the same for unit and ad valorem taxes of equal revenue. However, it may be shown that in the monopoly case, the price will be higher under the unit tax than under an ad valorem tax yielding equal revenue.[15] As noted before, the ad valorem approach has the further advantage that it permits equal rates to be applied to various products and is thus essential if the tax is to be uniform on all products. Moreover, revenue from an ad valorem tax will respond to price level increase and thus exhibits a greater cyclical built-in flexibility than does the unit tax.

Adjustment under Monopoly

Figure 20-3 shows the adjustment to a sales tax under conditions of monopoly. *AR* and *MR* are the average and marginal revenue schedules before tax. Imposition of an ad valorem tax swivels the net average revenue (demand) and marginal revenue schedules down to the left, with *AR'* and *MR'* the resulting net schedules after the tax is imposed. The pretax price equals *OA*, output equals *OM*, and profits equal *SGDA* (or output *OM* times *SA*, the excess of price over average unit cost). After the tax is imposed, price rises to *OE*, output falls to *ON*, gross profits drop to *FRHE*, and net profits to *FRLK*. Tax revenue equals *KLHE*. Unlike the profits tax, the sales tax is reflected in a shift in the marginal revenue schedule at all levels of output, thus changing the level of output at which profits are maximized. The reader is once more referred to the appendix to this chapter where section II gives a more detailed presentation of the price and output effects of unit and ad valorem taxes under conditions of monopoly.

As inspection of Figure 20-3 shows, the loss of net profits will be the larger

[15] See Richard A. Musgrave, *The Theory of Public Finance*, New York: McGraw-Hill, 1959, p. 304.

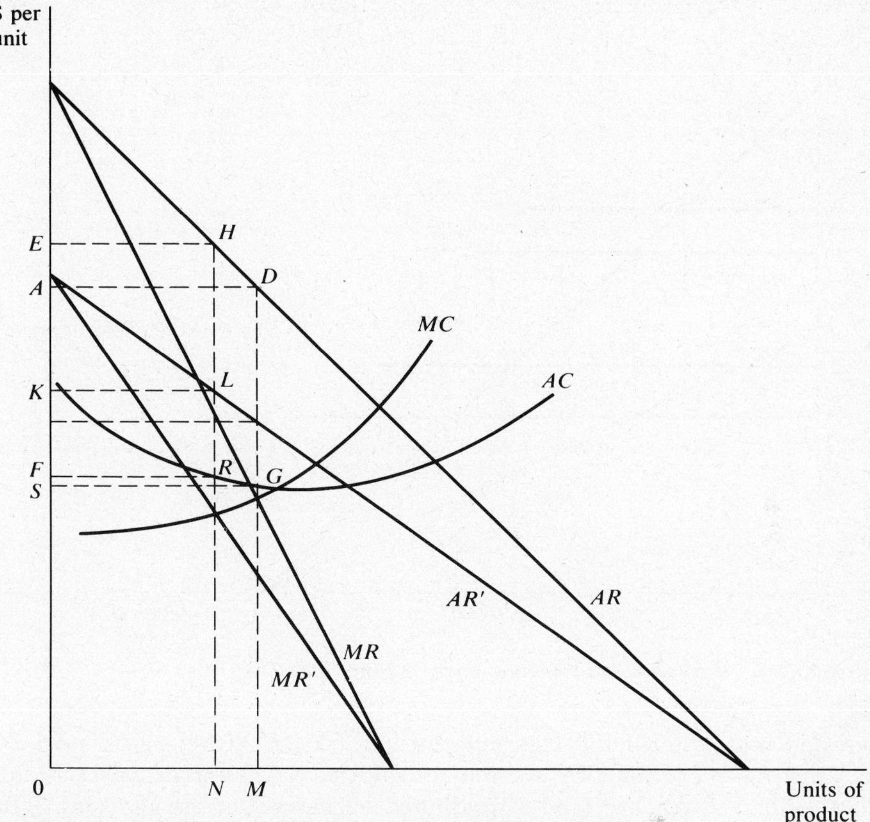

FIGURE 20-3 Effects of an Ad Valorem Tax under Monopoly.

the less elastic is the firm's supply schedule and the more elastic is the demand for its product. In the extreme case where supply is fixed, the excise tax will not affect price but will merely reduce profits, as in the case of a profits tax. This is of special significance during periods of extreme scarcity, such as wartime rationing, when firms, in fact, offer a fixed supply. Under such conditions, the incidence of a sales tax may come to resemble that of a profits tax.

Maximum Yield

In imposing a sales tax, it must not be assumed that by setting a higher rate, revenue can be increased indefinitely. Rather, there is a rate level at which yield is at a maximum, so that a further increase in rates would be counterproductive.

This is shown in Figure 20-4 for the simple case of a unit tax imposed on a good produced at constant cost *OA*. In the absence of tax, *OA* is the price and output is at *OB*. With a unit tax equal to *AC*, output equals *OD*, the price rises to *OC*, and tax revenue equals *AEFC*. As the tax is increased to *AH*, revenue changes to *AKLH*, and with a further increase in tax to *AM*, revenue equals *ANPM*. Tax revenue will be greatest where the excess of consumer expenditures

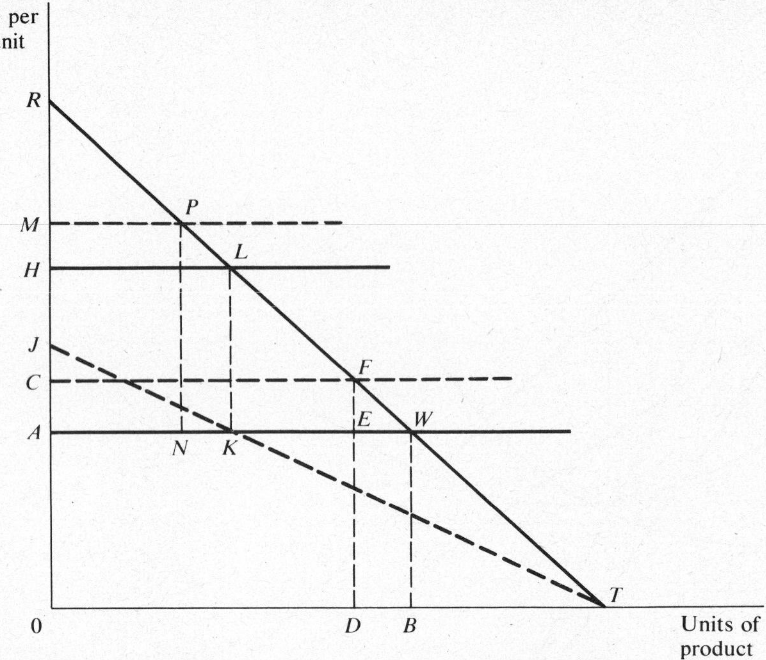

FIGURE 20-4 Maximum Tax Revenue under a Unit Sales Tax.

over cost is at a maximum. This holds for unit tax *AH*, giving a gross price *OH* such that $RL = LW$. This follows from the rule that for a linear demand schedule, unit elasticity is reached (and expenditures are largest) at the midpoint. What matters here is the midpoint *L* of the section *RW* of the demand schedule which lies above *AW*, since it is here the government's purpose to maximize expenditures in excess of cost (which is the same as maximizing tax revenue). This simple answer holds only, however, for a linear demand schedule and constant cost, with a more complicated solution applicable as these assumptions are dropped. An algebraic proof of this is given in the appendix to this chapter.[16]

C. SELECTIVE SALES TAXES: (2) GENERAL EQUILIBRIUM VIEW

So far, we have examined the effects of the tax on the market for the taxed product alone. To obtain a more complete picture, one must take a general-equilibrium view of the adjustment process, including effects on other untaxed markets.

Relative Price Changes

As the tax is imposed, the price of X rises and its output is reduced. The demand schedule for the tax-free product Y shifts to the right and factors will move from

[16] See p. 457. The maximum yield will be the same whether obtained through an ad valorem or a unit tax. While the required rate of unit tax equals *AH*, the required rate of ad valorem tax equals *JR*/*OR*.

the production of X into that for Y. If both X and Y are produced under conditions of constant cost, the price of X will rise by the amount of the tax, while that of Y remains unchanged. The change in relative prices therefore equals the tax. But the change in relative prices will fall short of the tax if both are produced under conditions of increasing cost. In this case, decreased production of X reduces its cost so that the price of X rises by less than the tax. Moreover, increased production of Y raises its cost so that the price of Y rises above its pretax level. For both these reasons, the increase in the price of X relative to that of Y falls short of the tax. Since the price of Y rises as well, the consumers of Y must also pay more for their product and in this way will come to bear part of the burden. If both products are produced under conditions of constant cost, relative prices will change by the extent of the tax wedge only and consumers of other products will not be thus burdened.

Just what happens to the relative prices of the two products will depend on the elasticity of demand and supply in the markets for the two products. More precisely, it will depend upon the elasticity of substitution of Y for X in consumption (i.e., by how much consumers will shift their purchases to Y as the price of X changes) and the elasticity of substitution of Y for X in production (i.e., by how much the relative costs of Y and X change as more Y and less X is produced).

But, though the adjustment may give rise to a complex set of changes in relative prices, it is reasonable to expect that the burden distribution will be dominated by the nature of the taxed product. If the taxed product is of the luxury type (e.g., yachts) which weighs more heavily in the budgets of high-income households, the incidence will tend to be progressive. If the taxed product is in the nature of a necessity (e.g., work clothing) which weighs more heavily in low-income budgets, incidence will tend to be regressive. Other price changes will occur and may affect the position of particular households, but they are not likely to alter the distributional pattern in a systematic fashion.

The same may be said for secondary effects resulting from the income sources side. The shift in production from industry X to industry Y will tend to increase the earnings of households which supply factors of particular importance to production in industry Y while lowering returns to factors which are specific to production in industry X. But, though important for particular households, these changes from the sources side are not likely to affect the regressive or progressive pattern as set by the primary burden incidence from the uses side. There is no presumption that products consumed by low-income groups are produced by high-income households or that products consumed by low-income households generate high-income earnings. Whereas in the case of income taxes the decisive determinant of the incidence pattern is generated from the sources side, in the case of selective product taxes the uses side plays the strategic role.

Relative versus Absolute Price Changes

We have seen that the incidence of a sales tax on a particular product falls primarily upon the consumer of that product. As noted in connection with the general sales tax on consumer goods, it does not follow, however, that the tax must be shifted by way of an *absolute* increase in the price of the taxed product. If factor prices remain unchanged, the insertion of the tax wedge must drive up the price of the taxed product—and the cost and price of the tax-free product remain unchanged.[17] An alternative possibility is for the price of the taxed product to remain unchanged. In this case, insertion of the tax wedge causes factor prices to fall, leading to a decline in the price of the tax-free product. As before, the real income of the consumers of tax-free products will be unchanged while that of the consumers of taxed products is reduced. While an absolute increase in the price of taxed products is the more likely pattern in an economy with downward rigid wages, such as ours, the result is the same in either case. As we have pointed out before, what matters for incidence analysis is the change in *relative* prices, not that in absolute prices.

D. SUMMARY

The incidence of a general sales tax depends on how inclusive the tax base is:

1. If both consumer and capital goods are included, incidence is equivalent to that of a general proportional tax on income.

2. If consumer goods only are included, the burden of the tax falls on consumers.

3. The result is the same whether product prices rise or factor earnings fall as the tax wedge is introduced.

4. The burden on consumers is regressive (relative to income) if based on annual cross-section data regarding the relationship between income and consumption. This result becomes questionable if a longer-term relationship between income and consumption is applied.

The imposition of a selective tax raises the price of the taxed product relative to prices of tax-free products.

5. The price of the taxed product will rise by the amount of the tax if produced under constant cost and by less than the tax if produced under increasing cost.

6. The distribution of the tax between buyers and sellers equals the ratio of the elasticity of supply to that of demand.

7. The burden of the tax on consumers is likely to exceed the revenue gain to the Treasury, the difference being the "excess burden."

8. Imposed on a monopolistic industry, part of the tax burden is absorbed in profits.

9. The revenue which can be obtained from a selective sales tax is limited.

[17] To simplify, we assume that both products are produced at constant cost.

Taking a general equilibrium view, the incidence of a selective sales tax includes repercussions in the markets for tax-free products and in factor prices:

10. The prices of taxed products rise relative to those of tax-free products.

11. The earnings of factors used intensively in the production of the taxed product fall relative to those of factors used intensively in the production of tax-free products.

12. Notwithstanding the resulting changes in the prices of tax-free products and in factor earnings, the pattern of burden distribution by income levels tends to be dominated by the distribution of consumer expenditures on the taxed product.

FURTHER READINGS

Aaron, H.: "The Differential Price Effects of a Value-added Tax," *National Tax Journal,* June 1968.

Bishop, Robert L.: "The Effects of Specific and Ad Valorem Taxes," *Quarterly Journal of Economics,* May 1968.

Brownlee, O., and G. L. Perry: "The Effects of the 1965 Federal Excise Tax Reduction on Prices," *National Tax Journal,* September 1967.

Due, John: "Sales Taxation and the Consumer," *American Economic Review,* December 1963.

Brown, Harry Gunnison: "The Incidence of a General Output or a General Sales Tax," *Journal of Political Economy,* 1939, reprinted in Richard A. Musgrave and Carl S. Shoup (eds.), *Readings in the Economics of Taxation,* Homewood, Ill.: Irwin, 1959.

APPENDIX: Incidence of Unit and Ad Valorem Taxes

I. PRICE AND OUTPUT EFFECTS OF A UNIT AND AN AD VALOREM TAX UNDER COMPETITION

Given a linear demand schedule for product X relating average revenue (AR) or price to quantity sold (Q),

$$AR = a - bQ$$

and a linear market supply schedule relating average unit cost (AC) to Q,

$$AC = c + dQ$$

the industry is in equilibrium where demand and supply intersect at a quantity Q_o such that $AR = AC$ or $a - bQ_o = c + dQ_o$ and

$$Q_o = \frac{a - c}{b + d}$$

with

$$P_o = a - b\left(\frac{a - c}{b + d}\right)$$

Unit Tax

After a unit tax u is imposed, the average net revenue schedule AR_n becomes

$$AR_n = a - bQ - u$$

and the gross price P_t is

$$P_t = a - b\left(\frac{a - c - u}{b + d}\right)$$

The change in the gross price $(P_t - P_o)$ then is

$$\Delta P = \frac{bu}{b + d}$$

Under conditions of constant cost, $d = 0$ and the change in price reduces to $\Delta P = u$.

Ad Valorem Tax

For the case of an ad valorem tax imposed at rate t, the average net revenue schedule becomes

$$AR_n = (1 - t)(a - bQ)$$

and the gross price becomes

$$P_t = a - b\left(\frac{a - ta - c}{b - tb + d}\right)$$

The change in price, therefore, is given by

$$\Delta P = bt\left[\frac{ab + bc}{(b + d)^2 - tb(b + d)}\right]$$

For the case of constant cost, this reduces to

$$\Delta P = \frac{ct}{1-t}$$

We note that for the case of the unit tax, the change in price is a function of the slopes of the demand and supply schedules only, while for the ad valorem tax the intercepts of the two functions also enter as determinants of the price change. Given the value of u or of t, the resulting change in gross price from either tax will be the greater the larger is b (the slope of the demand function) and the smaller is d (the slope of the supply function).

II. PRICE AND OUTPUT EFFECTS OF UNIT AND AD VALOREM TAXES UNDER MONOPOLY

In the case of a linear demand schedule, it may be shown that the increase in price under conditions of monopoly is one-half that of the competitive case. The average revenue schedule AR again is

$$AR = a - bQ$$

while the total revenue schedule TR is

$$TR = AR \cdot Q = aQ - bQ^2$$

Marginal revenue MR is thus

$$MR = \frac{dTR}{dQ} = a - 2bQ$$

The average cost schedule is again

$$AC = c + dQ$$

with total cost TC equal to

$$TC = cQ + dQ^2$$

and marginal cost MC equal to

$$MC = \frac{dTC}{dQ} = c + 2dQ$$

Setting MR equal to MC, we obtain

$$a - 2bQ_o = c + 2dQ_o$$

or

$$Q_o = \frac{a-c}{2(b-d)}$$

and the pretax price is

$$P_o = a - b\left(\frac{a-c}{2(b+d)}\right)$$

Unit Tax

After imposition of a unit tax u, the net marginal revenue schedule becomes

$$MR_n = a - 2bQ - u$$

and the new quantity Q_t is obtained by setting $MR_n = MC$, so that

$$Q_t = \frac{a-c-u}{2(b+d)}$$

Thus, the gross price after tax (P_t) equals

$$P_t = a - b\left(\frac{a-c-u}{2(b+d)}\right)$$

and the change in price becomes

$$\Delta P = \frac{bu}{2(b+d)}$$

which equals one-half the change in the competitive price. For the constant cost case, where $d = 0$,

$$\Delta P = \frac{1}{2}u$$

Ad Valorem Tax

With imposition of an ad valorem tax at rate t, the net marginal revenue schedule now becomes

$$MR_n = (1 - t)\,(a - 2bQ)$$

and the new quantity where $MR_n = MC$ equals

$$Q_t = \frac{(1 - t)a - c}{2(1 - t)b + d}$$

and the gross posttax price then becomes

$$P_t = a - \frac{b}{2}\left(\frac{(1 - t)a - c}{(1 - t)b + d}\right)$$

Thus, the change in price resulting from the tax equals

$$P = \frac{bt}{2}\left(\frac{ad + bc}{(b + d)^2 - tb(b + d)}\right)$$

again one-half that for the competitive case.

III. MAXIMIZATION OF REVENUE UNDER A UNIT TAX

For a competitive industry and using linear schedules, let the demand schedule be defined by

$$P = a - bQ$$

and the supply schedule by

$$AC = c + dQ$$

After imposition of a unit tax (u), the net demand schedule becomes

$$P_n = a - bQ - u$$

with output equal to

$$Q_t = \frac{a - c - u}{b + d}$$

Tax revenue then equals

$$R = uQ_t = u\frac{(a - c - u)}{b + d}$$

Differentiating this expression, we obtain

$$\frac{dR}{du} = \frac{a - c - 2u}{b + d}$$

To maximize tax revenue, we set $dR/du = 0$ and obtain

$$u = \frac{a - c}{2}$$

Given the intercepts of the demand and supply functions, the rate of tax giving the maximum yield is thus independent of the slopes of the schedules.

Part Five

Effects on Efficiency and Capacity Output

Chapter 21

Excess Burden and Efficiency Effects*

A. Tax Distortions in Household Choices: *Conditions for Economic Efficiency; Choice among Products; Choice between Goods and Leisure; Choice between Present and Future Consumption; Multiple Choices and Optimal Excise Rates; Income Tax Progression and Optimal Bracket Rates.* **B. Tax Distortions in Production:** *Single Jurisdiction; Interjurisdictional Differentials.* **C. Measuring Excess Burden. D. Further Aspects of Tax Efficiency:** *Administrative and Compliance Costs; Neutralizing Private Sector Distortions.* **E. Efficiency Aspects of Expenditure Policy:** *Choice among Products: Choice between Income and Leisure.* **F. Tradeoff between Equity and Efficiency:** *Horizontal Equity; Vertical Equity.* **G. Summary.**

As a tax is imposed, consumers, workers, and firms adjust to it. This adjustment not only affects the distribution of the tax burden but also bears upon the efficiency of resource use in the private sector and thereby upon the overall level of the burden.

As explained in our earlier discussion of tax burden, an increased use of

* *Reader's Guide to Chapter 21:* We return here to the concept of tax burden, initially discussed in Chapter 16. Focus now is on those efficiency effects of taxation which may raise the burden imposed on the private sector above what the government receives. The topic is a subtle one and has received much attention in recent years. While challenging to the economic theorist, its importance for applied tax policy is as yet difficult to assess.

resources by the public sector involves the opportunity cost of reduced resources available for private use.[1] As a first approximation, this cost or burden is valued at the price of the resources thus transferred, i.e., by the expenditure undertaken in the process. Viewed in this way, the tax burden is equal to the revenue collected. But this gives only a minimum estimate of the true cost involved. The reason is that a tax which distorts economic decisions in the private sector may introduce an "excess burden" or efficiency cost, so that the total burden exceeds the amount of tax revenue. Our concern now is with the magnitude of this burden, how it can be minimized, and how such minimization can be reconciled with other policy objectives.[2]

The concept of excess burden measures the difference between the total loss of welfare (or the economic cost) of a tax as it is actually imposed and the loss which would result if the same tax revenue had been collected without distorting economic decisions in the private sector. The only tax which can make this claim of a zero excess burden (i.e., of complete neutrality) is a head, or lump-sum, tax. Since the liability incurred is in no way related to economic behavior, the tax can cause no distortion of the latter. Excess burden is thus a measure of differential burden, analogous to our earlier concept of differential incidence.[3]

A. TAX DISTORTIONS IN HOUSEHOLD CHOICES

Any tax reduces a taxpayer's wealth and thus causes the individual to rearrange his or her economic choices. The fact that such rearrangement occurs is not necessarily a cause of inefficiency. Inefficiency results only where the nature of the tax is such as to interfere with efficient choice. The interference may be in the choice among consumer goods, between present and future consumption, or between goods (income) and leisure.

Conditions for Economic Efficiency

Economists consider an arrangement efficient if resources are used in a way which does not leave a possibility of alternative arrangements under which somebody could be better off without anyone's being worse off. As discussed in Chapter 3, economic efficiency involves various requirements, including these central conditions:[4]

1. The marginal rate of substitution (MRS) of any two products in consumption should be equal to their marginal rate of transformation (MRT) in production. Such will be the case in a competitive market where both rates are equal to the price ratio for the two products.[5] Thus,

$$\text{MRS of X for Z} = \text{MRT of X for Z} = P_x/P_z$$

where X and Z are two products.

[1] See p. 377.
[2] See Chap. 1, Sec. E, p. 16.
[3] See p. 379.
[4] See p. 67.
[5] The MRS of X for Z is defined as the amount of Z which the consumer is willing to surrender for an additional amount of X. The MRT of X for Z is the amount by which the output of Z must be cut to produce an additional unit of X.

2. The marginal rate of substitution of leisure for goods (as expressing workers' preferences) should be equal to the marginal rate of transformation of leisure into goods (via work effort), with both rates in a competitive system equal to the wage rate. Thus,

$$\text{MRS of } L \text{ for } Y = \text{MRT of } L \text{ for } Y = w$$

where L is leisure, Y is income (or goods in general), and w is the price of leisure or the wage rate.

3. The marginal rate of substitution of future for present consumption (as valued by consumers or savers) should be equal to the marginal rate of transformation of present into future goods in production with both equal to $1/(1 + i)$, where i is the rate of interest. Thus,

$$\text{MRS of } C_f \text{ for } C_p = \text{MRT of } C_f \text{ for } C_p = 1/(1 + i)$$

where C_f and C_p are future and present consumption and i is the return paid for postponing consumption or the rate of interest.

Whenever any of these conditions is not met, economic welfare can be improved by rearrangement designed to move toward it.[6]

The cause of excess burden may now be viewed in terms of interference with the cited efficiency conditions. Selective excises interfere with condition 1, a general consumption tax with condition 2, and a general income tax with both conditions 2 and 3.

Choice among Products

The problem is straightforward and the efficiency implications of particular taxes can be clearly seen so long as we assume that taxpayers are limited to one type of choice, while holding the others fixed. This assumption is, therefore, a good point of departure. We begin with distortions in the choice between two products, X and Z, while assuming the division of income between present and future consumption, and time allocation between work and leisure, to be fixed.

Comparison among Lump-Sum, General, and Selective Taxes Suppose that a certain consumer has income sufficient to purchase *OA* of X or *OB* of Z,

[6] This may be illustrated with regard to divergence from condition 1 as follows: Consumers will adjust their budget mix so that their marginal rate of substitution in consumption equals the price ratio. Let the price of good X equal $6 while that of good Z equals $3. The rate at which consumers are willing to substitute good X for good Z is therefore 2 (i.e., two units of Z for each unit of X), being equal to the ratio of the price of X to that of Z. Suppose, however, that the rate of transformation of X for Z in production is 3 (i.e., three units of Z must be given up to produce one additional unit of X). In this case, it will be efficient to produce and consume more of good Z and less of good X. This will be so because one additional unit of Z (worth 1/2 unit of X to the consumer) may be gained by giving up only 1/3 unit of X in production. The satisfaction derived from the additional units of Z exceeds that lost through the reduction in X. Hence, there will be a welfare gain. As more Z and less X are consumed, the marginal utility of Z falls while that of X increases, thus raising the marginal rate of substitution of X for Z in consumption. However, as production shifts toward Z, the marginal rate of transformation of X for Z in production tends to fall, thus contributing to the equalization process. The final result will yield a MRS, MRT, and price ratio all equal to somewhere between 2 and 3. This is the best possible position. See also the references given in footnote 26, p. 66.

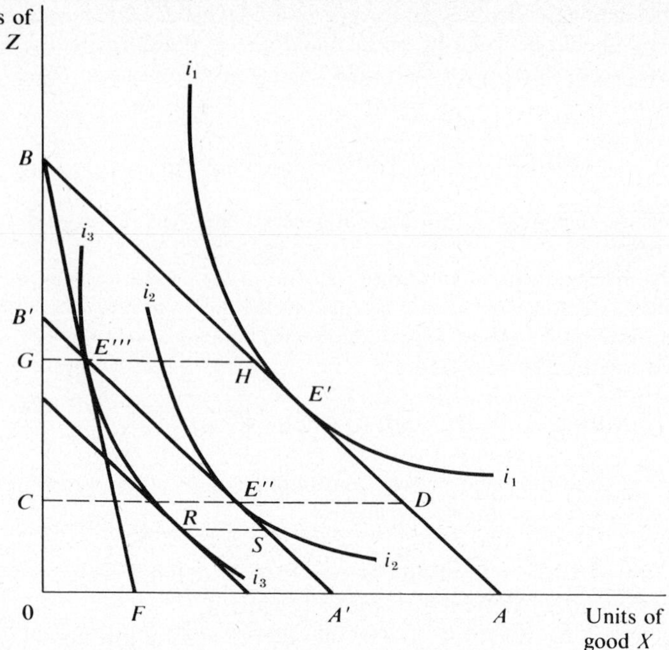

FIGURE 21-1 Adjustment to Selective and General Taxes.

as shown in Figure 21-1 where the horizontal axis measures units of product X and the vertical axis measures units of product Z. *AB* is the price line, and the ratio of prices P_x/P_z equals *OB/OA*. The consumer can then allocate his consumption between X and Z along the price line *AB*, which is his opportunity locus. Given his preference pattern as expressed by his indifference curves i_1, i_2, i_3, he will choose combination *E′* since this places him on his highest possible indifference curve i_1. At this point, the marginal rate of transformation in production, as given by the slope of the price line, equals the marginal rate of substitution in consumption, as given by the slope of the indifference curve.[7]

Now let a tax be imposed. Suppose first that the government uses a *head* or *lump-sum* tax, such that the liability is the same whatever the consumer's economic characteristics and response. As a result, the price line will shift to the left parallel to *AB*. Since relative prices are not affected, the slope of the price line remains unchanged. If tax equals *AA′* in terms of X or *BB′* in terms of Z, the consumer's new price line (opportunity locus) will be *A′B′* and his new equilibrium will be at *E″*. The consumer now retains *OC* of Z, surrendering *BC* to obtain *CE″* of X. *E″D* is the government's revenue in terms of product X. As before, the equality of the marginal rate of substitution, the marginal rate of transformation, and the price ratio is maintained. Resources are allocated efficiently and there is no excess burden.[8]

[7] For an explanation of indifference curves, see Paul A. Samuelson, *Economics*, 9th ed. New York: McGraw-Hill, 1973, pp. 441–445.

[8] The illustration of Fig. 21-1 is helpful but oversimplifies matters by disregarding the possibility that a change in output mix may result in a change in the slope of the original price line *AB*. This

Now suppose that the government obtains the same revenue by imposing a *general* tax on consumption. Applied at the same rate to X and Z, the tax inserts the same wedge between the gross and net prices of both. The price line again moves to $A'B'$, being parallel to AB, with the tax rate equal to AA'/OA or BB'/OB. Equilibrium is once more at E''. The producer remains in equilibrium with the ratio of net prices equal to the marginal rate of transformation while the consumer's marginal rate of substitution equals the ratio of gross prices. Since the tax applies equally to both X and Z, the net and gross price ratios are the same and MRS = MRT.

The situation differs, however, with a *selective* tax, imposed on one product, say X, only. The tax now enters as a wedge between the net and the gross price of X, while there is no such wedge in the case of Z. The ratio of the *net* price of X to the price of Z available to the producer must equal the MRT of X for Z in production, while the ratio of the *gross* price of X to the price of Z available to the consumer must equal his MRS of X for Z in consumption. The two ratios are rendered unequal. Condition 1 is not met and inefficient allocation results.

Returning to Figure 21-1, the government, in order to obtain the same revenue AA' from a tax on X only, must apply a rate equal to FA/OA.[9] The consumer now finds that P_x has risen relative to P_z so that $P_x/P_z = OB/OF$. The price line or opportunity locus swivels from BA to BF and the consumer now purchases less of X than he did under the general tax. His new equilibrium is at E'''. It will be seen that at E''' the slope of BF, or the MRS, exceeds that of $B'A'$ or the MRT. The consumer now surrenders BG of Z to purchase GE''' of X, while retaining OG of Z. Whereas E'' falls on i_2, E''' falls on the lower curve i_3.[10] The burden imposed on the taxpayer by a selective consumption tax is thus greater than that which would have resulted under a lump-sum tax providing equal revenue. It is the movement from i_2 to i_3 that reflects the excess burden.

To put the matter differently, the general tax has an "income effect" only, involving reduced purchases of both X and Z and a shift from E' to E''. The selective tax has in addition a "substitution effect," or replacement of X by Z because of the relative price change resulting in a shift from E'' to E'''. The burden reflected in the move from i_1 to i_2, as caused by the shift from E' to E'', is inevitable if revenue $A'A$ is to be raised. The further burden, referred to as "excess burden," (reflected in the move from i_2 to i_3) is caused by the shift from E'' to E''' and occurs with the selective tax only.

The Magnitude of Excess Burden Consider now the elements which determine the magnitude of the excess burden which is imposed by a selective product

---

implies that government purchases the identical products which are released from the private sector and/or that the transformation schedule for X and Z is linear, i.e., that the MRT and therefore the price ratio are constant.

[9] We know that the new equilibrium must fall on $B'A'$ since the government is to obtain the same revenue of $A'A$. To find the new price line BF, we therefore draw a line through B such that it is tangent to an indifference curve at its point of intersection with $B'A'$.

[10] This follows because (1) E''' lies northwest of E'', and (2) indifference curves cannot intersect. Point (1) holds because at E''', the marginal rate of substitution of X for Z in consumption must exceed the marginal rate of transformation in production, due to the tax wedge.

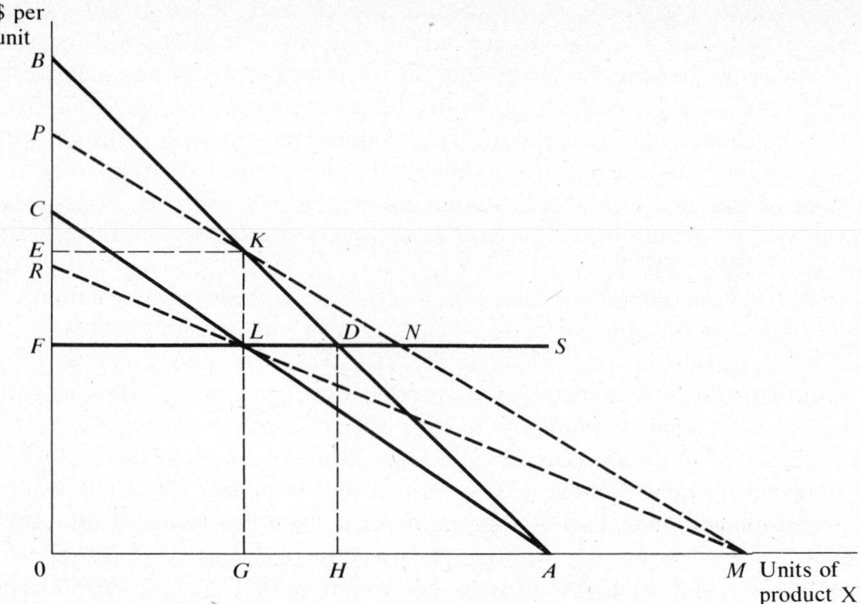

FIGURE 21-2 Excess Burden of a Selective Consumption Tax.

tax. Since the analysis of Figure 21-1 cannot be translated into quantitative terms,[11] we return for this purpose to the concept of consumer surplus as applied in our earlier discussion of income tax and excise incidence. Taking the case of constant cost, we may then view the excess burden as the loss of consumer surplus in excess of revenue obtained by the Treasury.

This concept of excess burden is illustrated in Figure 21-2 which is a partial-equilibrium demand and supply diagram for product X. The demand schedule for product X is shown as *BA,* while *FS* is the supply schedule. The pretax equilibrium is at *D,* the price being *OF* and the quantity *OH.* Now suppose that an ad valorem tax at rate $t = CB/OB$ is imposed. The net demand schedule swivels down to *CA* and the new equilibrium is at *L.* The gross price (inclusive of tax) rises to *OE* while output falls to *OG* and tax revenue equals *FLKE.* Since we are dealing here with a case of constant costs, the consumer (in line with our earlier argument) bears the entire burden.[12] Whereas, prior to tax, he would have paid *OGLF* for the amount *OG,* he must now pay *OGKE,* the additional amount being *FLKE.*

This, however, is not a complete description of the consumer's burden. This total loss is described more properly by the area *FDKE,* with the difference—or the triangle *LDK*—being the excess burden. Prior to tax the consumer paid *OHDF* for amount *OH,* but he would have been willing to pay *OHDB.*[13] Since,

[11] The analysis is similar to that of the unit tax case of Fig. 20-1, p. 445.

[12] See p. 446.

[13] Under certain assumptions regarding the utility function, the demand schedule may be taken to measure the marginal value of consumption applicable to successive quantities. Holding the vertical blocks under the demand curve from *O* to *H,* we obtain the total utility derived from the consumption of *OH.* The necessary assumption is that the marginal utility of income remains constant or changes by the same amount for an additional dollar of income change at any point on the income scale.

under competitive pricing, all units are priced at their marginal value, he received a "consumer surplus" equal to the difference between actual and potential payment, or *FDB*. Under the tax, his consumer surplus has been reduced to *EKB*. He has thus suffered a loss of surplus equal to *FDKE*. Of this, *FLKE* is offset by the government's revenue gain but the triangle *LDK* remains as a net loss or excess burden to the economy.

What determines the magnitude of this excess burden? The area of the triangle is approximated by $\frac{1}{2}(Et^2 PQ)$ where P and Q are the pretax quantity and price respectively, E is the price elasticity of demand, and t is the ad valorem rate of tax.[14] As may be seen from the figure, the triangle will become smaller as demand becomes less elastic at any given initial P and Q. If demand is inelastic, the consumer does not adjust his purchases to price, and the tax cannot interfere with consumer choice. The substitution effect, which is the cause of excess burden, is absent.

We may thus compare the excess burden which results if revenue *FLKE* is obtained from product X, the demand schedule for which is given by *AB*, and from product Y, the demand schedule of which is given by *MP*. In the former case, demand is less elastic and excess burden equals *KLD*, while in the latter, demand is more elastic and excess burden equals *KLN*.

If the choice is between taxing X or Y, X should be chosen. But in effect, several taxes may be drawn upon and the question has to be viewed in general equilibrium terms. Assuming other choices (say between goods and leisure or between present and future consumption) to be fixed, it may be shown that total excess burden will be minimized if tax rates are chosen so that relative prices remain unchanged for all products. A general ad valorem tax applied at a uniform rate meets this requirement. Such a tax exerts no substitution effect and the efficiency criteria continue to be met. A truly general tax on all consumer goods (as noted previously in connection with Figure 21-1) involves no excess burden of this type.

Choice between Goods and Leisure

A similar analysis may be applied to the choice between goods and leisure. To focus on this aspect, we assume that there is only one consumer good (a composite of goods X and Z) which may also be referred to as purchasing power, or income *Y*. We assume further that the choice between present and future consumption remains fixed.

Relabeling the vertical axis of Figure 21-1 to measure leisure and the horizontal axis to measure income *Y* or goods in general, the same argument is repeated.[15] The price line *AB* now shows various combinations of goods (work income) and leisure available for the individual, with the wage rate now equal

[14] The triangle *IDK* equals $1/2(\Delta P \Delta Q)$ where $\Delta P = LK$ and $\Delta Q = LD$. Given $t = \Delta P/P$ and $E = \Delta Q/Q \cdot P/\Delta P$, we substitute and obtain $1/2(Et^2 PQ)$. Using a unit tax u, we obtain the measure $1/2\,(u^2 E \cdot Q/P)$ where, in equilibrium, $u = tP$. See Arnold C. Harberger, "Taxation, Resource Allocation and Welfare," in *The Role of Direct and Indirect Taxes in the Federal Reserve System*, Washington: Brookings, 1964.

[15] The argument may similarly be restated in terms of Fig. 17-1, p. 405, where the consumer-surplus approach was used.

to OA/OB. A lump-sum tax again shifts the wage line to $A'A'$ and equilibrium moves to E'' without excess burden. An income tax (i.e., a tax which taxes goods only but not leisure) again swivels the wage line to BF with equilibrium at E'''. Thus the taxpayer shifts from the higher indifference curve i_2 to the lower curve i_3. An income tax therefore imposes an excess burden and condition 2 is not met, since the tax inserts a wedge between the gross wage rate as seen by the employer and the net wage rate as seen by the worker, or between the MRT and MRS of income for leisure.

How might an income tax be designed to be free of excess burden, as the general consumption tax proved to be when labor supply was assumed to be fixed? Such an income tax would now redefine income to include the value of leisure in the tax base.[16] This would indeed be an ideal tax, not only in the equity context but also from the economic efficiency point of view. Unfortunately, however, such a solution is impractical since it is difficult to measure a person's potential (rather than actual) earnings.

Choice between Present and Future Consumption

The argument may be repeated once more for the choice between present and future consumption. For this purpose, we now hold the choice between work and leisure fixed and deal with one product only. Returning to Figure 21-1, we relabel the horizontal axis to show future consumption C_f and the vertical axis to measure present consumption C_p. OB equals present consumption available if all income is consumed, and OA equals future consumption available if all income is saved. Thus, OA equals $(1 + i)$ OB where i is the rate of interest. BA thus represents all possible combinations of present and future consumption available to the individual, given his or her current income. Pretax equilibrium is at E'.

If a general consumption tax, applicable alike to C_p and C_f and yielding a revenue of AA', is imposed, the price line once more shifts, paralleling BA to $B'A'$, and the new equilibrium is at E''. Since both C_p and C_f are reduced at the same rate, relative prices are unchanged, the MRT and MRS of present for future consumption remain equal, and no excess burden results. The general consumption tax is now neutral and equivalent in its excess-burden aspects to a lump-sum tax.

An income tax, however, reduces the ratio C_f/C_p, since the net interest rate is reduced by the tax and less is gained by postponing consumption.[17] The price line swivels to BF and equilibrium moves to E'''. An excess burden (equal to the loss of welfare in moving from i_2 to i_3) again results. This is the case because

[16] Given our earlier assumption of a full-employment economy, all leisure is voluntary. For a proposal of this sort, see Abba Lerner, *The Economics of Control*, New York: Macmillan, 1944, pp. 231–238. See also our previous discussion of the leisure problem in redistribution policy, p. 95.

[17] Prior to tax, consumers may enjoy their entire income Y in the form of current consumption C. Or the person may save it, earn an income equal to iY, and enjoy a future consumption of $(1 + i)C$. The ratio between present and future consumption is thus: $C/[(1+ i)C]$. With a general consumption tax, present consumption equals $(1 - t)C$ and future consumption equals $(1 - t)(1 + i)C$, with the ratio of the two remaining unchanged at $C/(1 + i)C$.

With an income tax, present consumption is $(1 - t)C$, but future consumption equals $(1 - t)C + (1 - t)(1 - t)iC$, so that the ratio becomes $C/[1 + i(1 - t)]C$.

the tax now destroys the equality between the MRT of present into future consumption as seen by the producer (equal to $1 + i_g$ where i_g is the gross rate of return to capital) and the MRS as seen by the consumer (equal to $1 + i_n$ where i_n is the net after-tax return). While we have argued earlier that the "double taxation of saving" under the income tax does not prove the superiority of the consumption base on equity grounds, there does exist this difference in efficiency cost.[18]

Conclusions The conclusions to be drawn from the foregoing discussion may be summarized as follows, where L is leisure, Y is income, C_p and C_f are present and future consumption, and X and Z are consumer goods:

Choice Fixed between	*Choice Variable between*	*Taxes without Excess Burden*	*Taxes with Excess Burden*
L and Y; C_p and C_f	X and Z	Lump-sum tax Income tax General consumption tax	Selective consumption tax
X and Y; C_p and C_f	L and Y	Lump-sum tax	Income tax Selective consumption tax General consumption tax
X and Z; L and Y	C_p and C_f	Lump-sum tax General consumption tax Selective consumption tax	Income tax

Thus, only a lump-sum tax is neutral with respect to all economic choices. The income, general consumption, and selective consumption taxes all carry excess burdens of one kind or another. Therefore, information regarding the magnitude of the respective excess burdens is needed before the taxes can be compared in their efficiency aspects. But before we turn to the question of measurement, the problem must be restated so as to allow for multiple choices.

Multiple Choices and Optimal Excise Rates

Once multiple choices are allowed for, the clear results obtainable in the single-choice case disappear.

Selective versus General Sales Tax As we allow for flexibility in the choice between work and leisure as well as in that between products, a selective excise on product X need no longer be inferior to a general tax on X and Z. While the selective tax on X discriminates between X and Z as well as between X and

[18] See p. 220.

leisure, it does not discriminate between Z and leisure. The general tax on X and Z in turn avoids discrimination between X and Z but maintains discrimination between X and leisure as well as between Z and leisure. The outcome thus depends on the ease with which X, Z, and leisure may be substituted for one another.

It is no longer true, therefore, that a proportional tax on all consumer goods must be preferable to a selective tax. Since leisure cannot be taxed, the choice of an optimal set of commodity tax rates (i.e., a set which minimizes excess burden) becomes more complex. As far as excess burden which arises from substitution between products is concerned, more general taxes are to be preferred to selective taxes. The reason is that substitutability is greater among particular items within a product group (e.g., among brands of cigarettes) than among all products (e.g., between cigarettes and food). But as far as excess burden caused by substitution between products and leisure is concerned, the situation differs. Here, the assumption is in favor of excise taxes on those particular goods which cannot be readily replaced by (i.e., are complementary to) leisure, such as vacation equipment, television sets, or novels, while exempting others which are complementary to work, such as work clothing or textbooks (such as this one). Combining both sets of considerations, economic theorists might devise an optimal set of selective excise rates which would be best on efficiency grounds, but there is no simple rule that gives the answer.[19]

Income Tax versus Consumption Tax Turning to a comparison of a general consumption tax with a general income tax, we find that both interfere with the choice between goods and leisure, and that the income tax also interferes with the choice between present and future consumption. This does not mean, however, that the excess burden imposed by the income tax must be larger. The outcome depends on the respective substitutability among leisure, present consumption, and future consumption, and there is no simple way of predicting which tax generates the larger burden. The assumed superiority of the consumption tax over the income tax, which follows with a fixed leisure-income choice, now becomes questionable. As in the case of product taxes, a priori judgment becomes difficult once multiple choices are allowed for.

Income Tax Progression and Optimal Bracket Rates

If a given amount of income tax revenue is to be obtained from Mr. Jones, the excess burden will be less if the amount is secured by application of a proportional

[19] In developing this problem, economists have distinguished between three situations, case 1, where there is substitution within the taxable sector only, but not between products and leisure; case 2, where there is substitution between products and leisure but not among products; and case 3, where both substitutions may occur.

Assuming a given revenue to be obtained, the set of optimal tax rates for case 1 should be such as to equalize the resulting percentage change in price for all products, i.e., an across-the-board, equal-rate ad valorem tax is called for. The set of tax rates for case 2 should be such that the resulting percentage changes in prices will be inversely proportional to the own elasticity of demand for the various products. The solution for case 3 involves both types of elasticities of substitution (between products and between products and leisure) and is of more complex form. See W. J. Baumol and David E. Bradford, "Optimal Departures from Marginal Cost Pricing," *American Economic Review,* June 1970, pp. 165–283, which also contains references to an extensive (and in part highly technical) literature on the subject.

rate than by use of a progressive rate schedule yielding the same revenue. This is true because the price ratio at which he considers substitution between goods and leisure (as well as between present and future consumption) is distorted by the rate of tax at the margin, rather than the average rate. Since, under a progressive rate schedule, the marginal rate is higher than the average rate, the excess burden is larger than if the tax were proportional. Unfortunately, this difficulty cannot be avoided if taxation is to be progressive, i.e., if the effective (average) rate is to rise with income. Imposition of an average rate of 20 percent on Jones, whose income is $20,000, and of an average rate of 30 percent on Smith, whose income is $30,000, is equivalent to taxing the latter at bracket rates of 20 percent for the first $20,000 and of 50 percent for the next $10,000.

Nevertheless, economists have recently addressed themselves to the problem of designing a schedule of "optimal" income tax rates. If the government must collect a given amount of revenue, it may withdraw the sum from taxpayers at various points in the income scale. A more progressive distribution will have the disadvantage of calling for higher marginal rates of tax, thereby imposing a heavier excess burden; and it will have the advantage of leaving income where its marginal utility is higher. The problem of constructing an optimal rate schedule essentially is to balance these two factors at the margin, thereby minimizing the total burden. To put it more generally, the problem may be viewed as one of designing a set of negative and positive income tax rates which will secure an optimal solution, allowing for both equity and efficiency aspects.

The solution to the problem of setting the optimal rate schedule depends on a number of considerations, including (1) the distribution of earnings capacities in the population, and (2) the behavior pattern of workers, telling us how much they will work at various net wage rates available to them. In addition, the solution relates to (3) the social welfare function which society wishes to apply. Depending on this function, the objective may be to maximize an unweighted sum of utilities experienced by various individuals, or to maximize a sum of utilities weighted in line with a declining social marginal utility function. Finally, the goal may be to maximize the utility of individuals at the bottom of the scale. This type of analysis, which is still in its early stages, presents a more sophisticated restatement of some of the problems with which we were concerned in Chapter 4. Here, as there, the crux of the problem is to determine the choice of the social welfare function from which the set of optimal rates can be derived.[20]

B. TAX DISTORTIONS IN PRODUCTION

The preceding discussion dealt with distortions in output mix (defined broadly to include leisure) involving the choice among alternative forms of current consumption, goods, and leisure, and between present and future consumption. Another requirement for efficient resource use is that whatever is produced

[20] Among a growing literature in the field, see the basic but difficult paper by J. A. Mirlees, "An Exploration in the Theory of Optimum Income Taxation," *Review of Economic Studies,* 38 (17), 1971. For an application to United States data and further literature references, see Robert Cooter and Elhanan Helpman, "Optimal Taxation for Transfer Payments under Different Social Welfare Criteria," *Quarterly Journal of Economics,* November 1974.

should be produced in the least costly way. Taxes may be a further cause of inefficiency by interfering with this requirement. Illustrations of tax-induced production inefficiencies are easily found.

Single Jurisdiction

In the context of a single jurisdiction, production distortions may arise in a variety of ways, including the following:

1. The corporation tax is a tax on capital income originating in a particular sector or industry only. As such, it leads to a reallocation of capital from the taxed to tax-free industries. We have seen that this flow continues (assuming flexible markets) until *net* rates of return in the two sectors are equalized. In the process, output in the taxed sector is reduced while that in the tax-free sectors is increased, giving rise to the previously discussed type of consumption distortion.

In addition, however, production in the taxed industries will have become less capital-intensive while production in the tax-free industries will have become more capital-intensive than before, thus introducing a distortion in the method of production and a resulting efficiency loss which differs from that imposed by changing the output mix. Thus, if both capital and labor employed in a particular industry were taxed equally, the further distortion in production methods would be avoided.

2. Depreciation rules for the determination of taxable income may interfere with the choice between short- and long-lived capital assets. A neutral policy would apply so-called economic depreciation, where the amount of depreciation allowed each year equals the reduction in the present value of the future income stream during the year. If depreciation is faster, the present value of the tax is reduced. This reduction is greater for long-lived assets, so that rapid depreciation favors the acquisition of such assets relative to short-lived ones. As a result, there will be a bias in technology toward the use of such assets in lieu of assets with shorter lives.

3. Special treatment given to extractive industries in the form of depletion allowances lowers the tax burden on such industries relative to that imposed on others. It thus tends to induce overinvestment therein.

4. Preferential treatment of capital gains offers an inducement for investment in those assets the income from which may be obtained in the form of capital gains.

5. Determination of taxable income permits deduction of interest payments on business debt as a cost of doing business. Yet, no deduction for imputed interest is permitted for the case of equity finance. As a result, the corporation tax gives an incentive to use debt rather than equity finance, which may impose an efficiency cost.

6. Deductibility of expense accounts may distort business expenditures. Entertainment outlays are chargeable as costs to the corporation but are not counted as income to the management on its income tax. Thereby, such expenses are encouraged and various (though unsuccessful) attempts have been made at limiting their deductibility under the corporation tax.

Interjurisdictional Differentials

Another aspect of production distortion arises from the effects of tax differentials on product and factor movements between tax jurisdictions.

Effects on Product Flows Suppose that, before tax, jurisdiction A has a comparative advantage in producing product X while jurisdiction Y has an advantage in producing product Z. As a result, A will produce X and export it to B, while B will produce Z and export it to A. Now let A impose a tax which increases the cost of producing X. As a result, its comparative advantage may be blocked. B may find it no longer worthwhile to import from A, and trade flows will be distorted. Thus, tax policy, much like tariffs, may interfere with international specialization and, as a result, efficiency suffers. This effect has been of central concern to Common Market policy and will be considered more closely at a later point.[21] Similar problems arise among jurisdictions within one nation, but they are usually less severe, since product tax rate differentials applicable at the state and local levels are not very large.[22]

Effects on Factor Flows Differentials in the rate of income or capital taxation induce labor and capital flows among jurisdictions and divert resources from their most efficient regional pattern.

On the domestic scene, the problem involves differentials in corporation tax rates among states and in property tax rates among localities. The latter are of primary importance since corporation tax rates at the state level have remained relatively low, with rate differentials of two or three percentage points hardly a major factor in location decisions. Property tax differentials have been more important and the lure of tax preferences is used by municipalities as a device for attracting investment. However, tax differentials are only part of the picture. Differentials in fiscal positions may arise not only from the tax side of the budget operation but also from the expenditure side. Thus a business firm may be attracted by good schools, roads, and other public services as well as repelled by high tax rates. What matters are the *net* differentials in fiscal burdens or benefits. Nevertheless, net differentials remain and, as we shall see later on, are a cost of fiscal pluralism to be weighed against the disadvantages of a highly centralized structure.[23]

As with product taxes, rate differentials in income and profits taxes are again larger if viewed in the international context. Capital flows in particular are sensitive to international rate differentials; and unless appropriate measures are taken to avoid such effects, the worldwide allocation of capital will be diverted from its efficient pattern. Again, this is a major concern for international tax integration, which will be dealt with further in a later chapter.[24]

C. MEASURING EXCESS BURDEN

Although it is easy to argue that under certain conditions one tax will have an excess burden while another will not, this is not sufficient. Excess burden characteristics are only one aspect in the choice of taxes and must be weighed against other (including equity) considerations. For this purpose, ranking according to excess burden is not enough. A quantitative and operational measure of burden

[21] See Chap. 33, Sec. C, p. 723.
[22] See p. 311.
[23] See p. 629.
[24] See p. 629.

is needed.[25] Estimates of the excess burden for various parts of the United States tax structure have been attempted, based on the technique of Figure 21-2. Thus, for a selective excise tax, the excess burden is measured as the triangle *LDK*, with similar measures applied to other taxes.[26] The results are rough approximations, but they suggest the order of magnitude involved.

Individual Income Tax One might expect the excess burden of the individual income tax to be relatively high since the tax is progressive. However, given the fact that the tax applies to wage income from all sources, response relates to labor supply to the economy as a whole, which is rather inelastic. Moreover, evidence differs for various parts of the labor market. For adult male workers, the labor supply appears to respond positively to a decline in the wage rate but with supply elasticity very low, while for married women, response is negative with supply elasticity substantially higher. Nevertheless, the excess burden of an income tax seems of minor importance for the larger part of the labor force.[27] Marginal tax rates are relatively low for low-income workers while those for high-income earners are higher. However, among high-income earners, the substitution effect is dampened because work effort is more largely related to nonpecuniary considerations, such as concern with status or professional satisfaction. Moreover, the maximum bracket rate on earned income is now limited to 50 percent, so that the problem posed by very high rates has ceased to apply.

The scope for distorting effects on the consumption-saving relationship depends on the interest elasticity of saving. Studies of the relationship between saving and the interest rate differ in their conclusions. Some hold that there is a substantial negative relationship, while others attribute little weight to the rate of interest in the consumption function.[28] However this may be, it is difficult to apply the excess burden argument in this context because *the* market rate of interest, which is said to be distorted, may hardly be claimed as a uniquely efficient value. Interest rates are determined as part of the monetary–fiscal policy mix which is chosen for stabilization purposes, and as such, they tend to be socially set, rather than a competitively set market price determined in line with individual (saver) preferences.[29]

Corporation Income Tax Various estimates have been made of the cost of distortion imposed by the corporation income tax. Since the tax applies to the corporate sector only, capital is diverted to the unincorporated sector.[30] As a result, the prices of products in the unincorporated sector fall while those of the

[25] As noted before, the indifference curve analysis of Fig. 26-1 is of little help in this respect.

[26] This approach has been pioneered by Prof. A. Harberger. See Arnold Harberger, *Taxation and Welfare,* Boston: Little, Brown, 1974, chaps. 1, 2, and 8.

[27] See Marvin Kosters, "Effects of an Income Tax on Labor Supply," in A. C. Harberger and M. J. Bailey (eds.), *The Taxation of Income from Capital,* Washington: Brookings, 1969, pp. 302–325. Kosters does not offer a quantitative measure, but the conclusion appears to be that the wage elasticity of labor supply is generally low.

[28] See Colin Wright, "Saving and the Rate of Interest," in Harberger and Bailey, op. cit., pp. 275–300.

[29] See Chap. 33, Sec. B, p. 718.

[30] See p. 417.

corporate sector rise. This occurrence imposes an excess burden similar to that imposed by selective excise taxes. By estimating the relative price changes which result among corporate and unincorporated enterprises, and by applying estimated demand elasticities, a measure of excess burden may be obtained. The annual cost of distortions in the allocation of capital, based on data from the fifties, has recently been estimated at $2.7 billion. Updated to 1969 levels, the amount totals $11.7 billion. This estimate, however, not only reflects the excess burden caused by differential taxation of capital income due to corporation tax but includes allowance for property taxation and the preferential income tax treatment of owner-occupied housing as well.[31]

This efficiency cost might be avoided in one of two ways. One would be to extend the corporation tax to include profits from unincorporated enterprises as well as corporations. The other would be to do away with the "absolute" corporation tax and to integrate retained earnings into the individual income tax base of the shareholder. As noted previously, the latter solution also has much to recommend it on equity grounds.[32]

Excises Further excess burdens are generated by the set of selective excises imposed at both the federal and the state levels. No direct estimates for this burden are available. It may be speculated that the excess burden imposed by selective excise and sales taxes in the United States is on the order of magnitude of $3 to $4 billion, or from 10 to 15 percent of the excise tax yield.[33] In other words, this is the amount of consumer surplus which would be gained if the existing set of selective excises were replaced by a lump-sum tax or (given the assumption that the choice between products is the only one to be made) by a general tax on consumer goods.

Conclusions Although quantitative evidence is sketchy and underlying procedures are necessarily crude, it appears that the magnitudes involved are more modest than one might expect. While allowance for interdependence of various distortions may affect the total involved, the order of magnitude (for 1970) may range from, say, $10 to $15 billion.[34] Compared with a total tax revenue of $313 billion, this magnitude appears to be small and rather minor compared with the cost of other inefficiencies due to market imperfections, e.g., faulty advertising, monopoly, inefficiencies in the provision for public goods, and

[31] See David J. Ott and F. Attiat Ott, "The Effects of Non-neutral Taxation on the Use of Capital by Sector," *Journal of Political Economy*, July 1973, pp. 972–981.

[32] See p. 291.

[33] A rough guess at the order of magnitude may be obtained as follows: Given consumption expenditures subject to excise tax of about $90 billion (1970) and selective excise tax revenue (federal, state, and local) of $28 billion, the average tax rate is about 33 percent. Assuming $E = 0.80$, the resulting excess burden following this formula would equal about $3.5 billion. Inasmuch as automotive taxes may be considered an offset to the free provision of highways, and as certain other taxes (e.g., tobacco and liquor) contain "demerit" elements, this figure may well be too high.

[34] Interdependence matters because excess burden (in line with the above formula) increases as the square of the differential tax rate. Thus, if product X is subject to a differential corporate rate t_c and again to a differential excise tax rate t_e, the burden becomes $1/2E(t_c + t_e)^2PQ$ and not just $1/2(Et_c^2PQ) + 1/2(Et_e^2PQ)$. On the other hand, the more distortions there are, the greater is the possibility that they will be offsetting.

inefficient regulatory policies, not to mention the cost of involuntary unemployment.

D. FURTHER ASPECTS OF TAX EFFICIENCY

It remains to note two further aspects of tax efficiency, including (1) administrative and compliance costs, and (2) the use of taxes to offset inefficiencies in the private sector.

Administrative and Compliance Costs

Although the preceding discussion has been focused on the economist's concept of efficiency cost or excess burden, two other types of costs involved in the taxing process should be noted. One is the cost of administration, i.e., the budget of the Internal Revenue Service, and the other is the taxpayer's compliance cost. Again, both these costs are directly related to the complexity of the tax system.

The cost of federal tax administration for the fiscal year 1976 is estimated at about $2.7 billion, or less than 1 percent of federal tax revenue. Obviously, this cost will be the higher the more complex are the taxes to be administered and the more vigorously they are enforced. The cost of tax compliance—including the value of time spent by taxpayers in making out returns and fees paid to tax counsel—is substantially larger and may be estimated at from $3 to $4 billion. The total administrative and compliance costs involved may thus be in the neighborhood of $6 billion.

Neutralizing Private Sector Distortions

In considering the distorting effects of various taxes, the implicit assumption has been that such taxes are introduced into an otherwise efficient market. If market imperfections already exist, as of course they do, the evaluation of particular taxes becomes more difficult. Rather than introducing an inefficiency, taxes might then act as correctives to other nontax inefficiencies. Illustrations for this may be readily supplied:

1. Consider two substitute products, X and Z, with X produced by a monopolist and Z in a competitive market. As a result, production of X will be too small relative to that of Z when compared with an efficient solution. This result might then be remedied by imposing a selective tax on Z even though, in a competitive market, taxing both X and Z equally would have been preferable.

2. Or, suppose that in an otherwise perfect market, there already exists a tax on X but not on Z. The excess burden might then be reduced if additional revenue were obtained from a tax on Z rather than from a general tax on both products.

3. Next, selective taxes (or subsidies) may correct for inefficiencies where production or consumption in the private sector involves external costs (or benefits) which are not accounted for by the market. As will be shown later, such is the case with effluent charges imposed to internalize the cost of pollution.[35]

For these and other reasons, potential inefficiencies introduced by particular taxes must be evaluated in relation to other inefficiencies which already exist in

[35] See p. 708.

the system. This evaluation may reduce the resulting excess burden and efficiency may in fact be increased. Yet, in the absence of specific reasons to the contrary, prudent policy will do well to assume that the pretax pattern of prices is efficient.

All this, of course, assumes that efficient allocation is in line with individual preferences. Selective excises may be desirable where it is the explicit purpose of public policy to correct consumer preferences, i.e., in connection with "demerit" goods, or selective subsidies in turn may be desirable where "merit" goods are involved. This presumably is the rationale for heavy taxation of liquor and tobacco. In this case, the usual efficiency argument based on free consumer choice is inapplicable and social preference is substituted for private choice.[36]

E. EFFICIENCY ASPECTS OF EXPENDITURE POLICY

Efficiency problems arise on the expenditure side as well as on the tax side of budget policy. The political process by which public expenditures are determined can only approximate true consumer preferences and may do so but poorly. Less subtly, the execution of public expenditures may involve inefficiencies in that public goods are not provided at least cost. Finally, and of major interest in the present context, reasoning similar to that involved in the excess burden of taxation also applies to expenditure policy. Expenditure, like tax policy, may interfere with the efficiency of choice in the private sector.

Choice among Products

The same reasoning which suggests that a general consumption tax tends to be less burdensome than a selective tax also shows that a general consumption subsidy will be more beneficial than a selective subsidy which reduces the price of a particular product only.[37] This may be shown by repeating the arguments of Figure 21-1 in reverse.[38] A selective subsidy cannot leave the recipient better off than an equal-cost general subsidy, but it may well leave the person in a worse position. The tax concept of excess burden here finds its parallel in that of "benefit shortfall."

Rather than subsidize the purchase of particular products, the government may provide them free of charge, e.g., school lunches or medical services. Such provision will not cause an excess burden if the amount supplied falls short of what consumers would have purchased privately, but an excess burden arises (or a benefit results) if public supply is larger.[39] The fact that relief measures so

[36] See p. 65.

[37] The subsidy may be given to the consumer in cash, with prescribed use; or it may be given indirectly through intermediate expenditures of government which reduce the cost of production for the private firm, such as an access road to its plant.

[38] In line with Fig. 21-1, suppose the consumer is initially positioned at E'' on price line $B'A'$. After a general subsidy of amount $A'A$ is granted, the price line shifts parallel to the right and the new equilibrium is at E'. Now let an equal cost subsidy on X only be applied. The price line remains anchored at B' but swivels around to the right. The new equilibrium is at its intersection with BA, at a point where the new price line is tangent to an indifference curve below i_1.

[39] For a discussion of similar problems arising in the context of intergovernmental grants, see p. 635.

frequently take the form of payments in kind rather than in cash is therefore in need of explanation. As noted before, possible causes may be found in merit-good considerations or the fact that voluntary giving is made more acceptable to the donor if the recipient must use the funds in line with the donor's own preferences.[40]

Choice between Income and Leisure

Income tax effects on the choice between income and leisure are paralleled (if in reverse) by transfer payments, where the amount of transfers is related positively to earnings. This will be the case with a wage subsidy. Such a subsidy imposes an excess burden (or benefit shortfall) as does an income tax, although the substitution effect now works in the opposite direction. As the price of leisure is raised (by the increase in the wage rate), workers substitute work (goods) for leisure. The larger the increase in work effort, the higher will the excess burden now be.

More important for practical purposes are transfer payments which are related inversely to earnings, as, for example, relief payments are. Such payments result in a negative substitution effect similar to that of an income tax, as we shall see in our later discussion of income maintenance programs.[41] Since the marginal rates implicit in a welfare formula are high, this poses a central problem in the design of income maintenance plans.

F. TRADEOFF BETWEEN EQUITY AND EFFICIENCY

Suppose that the federal government, in collecting some $200 billion in revenue, imposes an excess burden of $10 billion, incurs an administrative cost of $1 billion, and causes compliance costs of $4 billion. Total costs would then amount to $15 billion, or 7.5 percent of the total. If the entire revenue were collected in the form of a head tax, these costs might be reduced to, say, $100 million. Is the difference, or $14.9 billion, worth paying for? Or, to put it differently, what is it that the public gets for this payment?

The benefit to be obtained is a more equitable tax structure. There are few who would maintain that a head-tax system is a tolerable way of raising revenue even if there would be a saving of nearly $15 billion. But like all matters of economic choice, the intelligent decision is not made on an all-or-nothing basis but at the margin. The tradeoff between equity and cost considerations should be pushed to the point where the gain is matched by the price in terms of increased efficiency cost. At the same time, any given level of equity should be purchased at the least efficiency cost. Among equally equitable taxes, those should be chosen which carry the least efficiency, administrative, and compliance cost.

Horizontal Equity

Horizontal equity calls for equal treatment of people in equal position which, in the case of the income tax, means a broad-based tax including income from all

[40] See p. 98.
[41] See p. 676.

sources and independent of use. The inclusion of income from all sources is in line with neutrality, or avoidance of excess burden. Failure to define income comprehensively usually offends both equity and neutrality considerations.

But the income tax, by including saving as well as consumption, puts equity ahead of neutrality. Moreover, the very choice of either an income or a consumption base leaves out leisure and thus interferes with the goods-leisure choice. All these problems are avoided by a head tax, but this would be unacceptable on vertical equity grounds. The task, therefore, is to find a set of taxes which would go at least part way in meeting the efficiency objective while being acceptable on equity grounds. Recent efforts to derive an "optimal" system, as noted before, would combine taxes on products with inelastic demand (i.e., cigarettes or basic foodstuffs) so as to reduce the substitution effect, with taxes on goods which are complementary to leisure (such as skis or pleasure boats) so that leisure would be included in the tax base by indirection. Such a combination of taxes would be attractive on efficiency grounds, and less objectionable in terms of equity than a head tax. But horizontal equity would still be offended, as the weight of such taxes in the budgets of households at any given income level might vary widely. A broad-based and uniform tax, such as the comprehensive income tax, may well continue to offer the best compromise, even though it falls short of perfection.

Vertical Equity

Regarding vertical equity, the problem is how to implement a given, presumably progressive, distribution of the tax bill with a minimum of excess burden. Here the conflict must be met head on. We have seen that for any one person, the excess burden involved in paying a given amount of tax will be larger if this amount is paid under a progressive, rather than under a flat rate, schedule. Yet the use of a progressive schedule (with marginal or bracket rates in excess of average rates) is unavoidable if tax liability is to rise as a percentage of income when moving up the income scale. The question then is, up to what point will the equity gain from such taxation be worth the efficiency cost inherent in the higher marginal rates? This is the problem noted previously under the heading of "optimal income taxation."

Posed somewhat differently, the problem is how to secure a given distributional correction with a minimum of excess burden. With labor supply relatively inelastic, chances are that an income tax–transfer approach (as outlined earlier for our distribution branch) remains the best technique. It might be supported by commodity taxes (on the products consumed primarily by high-income taxpayers) and subsidies (to the products consumed primarily by low-income recipients). But even with the best of tax designs, an efficiency cost remains which must be weighed against equity objectives. Neither consideration should be permitted to dominate tax policy, and neither should be neglected.

G. SUMMARY

Private sector adjustments to imposition of a tax not only determine where the burden is placed but also affect the overall level of the burden. An excess burden arises if the conditions of efficient resource use are interfered with. In this connection, we have noted the following:

1. A selective consumption tax interferes with the choice between products, whereas a general consumption tax does not.

2. An income tax interferes with the choice between present and future consumption, whereas a general consumption tax does not.

3. An income tax and a general consumption tax both interfere with the choice between goods and leisure.

4. When all choices are permitted to be flexible, it can no longer be concluded that a general sales tax must be superior on efficiency grounds to a selective tax, or that a general consumption (sales) tax must be superior to an income tax.

5. Only a head tax imposes no excess burden but it is unacceptable on equity grounds, since it is wholly unrelated to economic capacity.

6. Theoretically, a set of excises may be devised which minimize excess burden, but such minimization is difficult to accomplish in practice and may not be acceptable on equity grounds.

7. Similar considerations arise with respect to a redistributive tax-transfer policy. The excess burden imposed by a progressive income tax exceeds that of a proportional tax, as the excess burden depends upon the marginal or bracket rate. The problem of optimal income taxation, therefore, is one of weighing the equity gains of progressive taxation against its efficiency cost.

Among other aspects of the efficiency cost of taxation, the following considerations were noted:

8. Efficiency in production may be interfered with if the use of capital or labor is subject to tax in one particular sector only.

9. Similar distortions may arise between jurisdictions, as the location of production may be affected by differentials in tax rates.

10. Empirical measurement of the magnitude of efficiency costs is difficult, but a recent estimate arrives at a cost of about $10 billion, including the distortions caused by the corporation tax as well as the preferential treatment of homeowners under the income tax.

11. The proposition that taxes should be neutral so as to avoid excess burden is based on the hypothesis that taxes are introduced into an otherwise efficient market. The case for neutrality does not apply where taxes are used to correct for market imperfections in the private sector.

Efficiency costs may result from the expenditure side as well as the tax side of budget policy:

12. There is an assumption that a policy of cash subsidy to households is superior on efficiency grounds to providing free services in kind, or to applying selective product subsidies.

13. Potential interference with the choice between income and leisure poses a major consideration in the design of income maintenance schemes.

The tradeoff between equity and efficiency considerations was considered:

14. Feasible tax policy cannot escape the conflict between efficiency and equity considerations, but must seek to minimize it.

15. Among available alternatives, a broad-based income tax may well remain the superior solution.

FURTHER READINGS

Harberger, Arnold C.: *Taxation and Welfare,* Boston: Little, Brown, 1974, chaps. 1, 2, and 8.

——— and Martin C. Bailey (eds.): *The Taxation of Income from Capital,* Washington: Brookings, 1969.

Little, I. M. D.: "Direct vs. Indirect Taxes," *Economic Journal,* 1951; reprinted in Richard A. Musgrave and Carl S. Shoup (eds.), *Readings in the Economics of Taxation,* Homewood, Ill.: Irwin, 1959.

Mishan, E. J.: See Further Readings for Chap. 7.

Chapter 22

Fiscal Effects on Capacity Output in the Private Sector*

The preceding chapter dealt with the effects of budget policy on the efficiency of resource use in the private sector. Effects on labor supply and the rate of saving were examined with focus on interference with individual choice and the efficiency burden which this may imply. We now turn from effects on efficiency in resource use to effects on the supply of resources themselves. More specifically, we consider effects on the level of *capacity output,* i.e., the level of output or GNP

* *Reader's Guide to Chapter 22:* In this chapter we deal with the effects of fiscal policy on capacity output and growth in the private sector. These effects have been at the center of discussion in the sixties in contrast to the earlier and most recent focus on stabilization policy. Both are important, with growth effects of primary interest for the longer run and stabilization effects for the shorter run. In assessing fiscal effects on growth, we consider effects on factor inputs and the bearing of such effects on the growth of output. More difficult aspects of fiscal effects on the rate of equilibrium growth and its bearing on tax incidence are taken up in the chapter appendix.

which may be reached under conditions of full employment of labor and full utilization of capital stock. We assume for this purpose that the level of full-employment output is reached automatically, i.e., that aggregate demand neither falls short of nor exceeds the value of this output as measured at prevailing prices. Problems which arise if demand is deficient or excessive (thus creating unemployment or inflation) will be considered in the following chapters.

The level of capacity output, or the size of total GNP, is of some interest in itself, but what matters for economic welfare is the level of output or income per person. With any given population size, total capacity output determines the feasible level of per capita income, so that output must grow if the standard of living is to rise. Over the years, per capita output has increased greatly, growing at a rate (corrected for price change) of about 2.5 percent during this century. Reflecting the powers of compound interest, output per head (again corrected for price change) is now about 5 times what it was in 1900. In addition, hours of work are substantially shorter, so that the total welfare gain has been even larger. While the merits of perpetual economic growth have recently come under scrutiny, this skepticism is based on the perspective of an already affluent society.[1] Economic growth remains the only hope for escape from misery for the majority of the world's population in the less developed countries; and if adequate aid from high-income countries is to be forthcoming (as it should be and under the pressure of events will have to be), so must economic growth in the developed countries be maintained.

The major determinants of capacity output are the level of factor inputs—including natural resources, labor, and capital—and the state of technology or productivity with which resources are used. Since the supply of natural resources is more or less given by nature, the major determinants of GNP growth are the rates of growth of labor input and of the capital stock, and the speed of technical improvement. In this chapter, we consider the effects of fiscal policy upon these variables in the private sector.

A. EFFECTS ON WORK EFFORT

The effects of labor supply on economic growth are twofold. An increase in population results in an increase in output; but unless output rises at the same percentage rate as population, per capita income will fall. Population growth, therefore, may depress, rather than increase, per capita output. This outcome,

[1] This criticism involves a number of propositions which are frequently confused and need to be separated to appraise the case for or against growth:

1. A first proposition is that an affluent society should spend more time on creative use of leisure than on increased output of goods. This may well be true but is not an argument against growth properly defined. A proper measure of growth should include both increased leisure time and increased goods.

2. A second proposition is that growth generates cost-externalities such as pollution. This again is an argument not against growth but for a proper measure of growth in which external costs and benefits are accounted for. If growth is to occur, output must rise net of external costs.

3. A third and more difficult proposition is that mankind is not up to living comfortably but needs the discipline of poverty to keep out of trouble, i.e., paradise lost cannot be regained. Judge for yourself.

of course, was the dismal fate which Thomas Malthus predicted some 175 years ago. While economic development in the industrial countries has managed to combine rising per capita income with rising population, the Malthusian specter still darkens the prospects of economic development in the less developed countries.

However this may be, fiscal instruments are not a major factor in population policy. Personal exemptions under the income tax, though related to family size, are hardly sufficient to enter into family planning, and expenditure programs for birth control are hardly within the realm of fiscal economics. Fiscal policy, however, enters the picture via effects on labor input with a given population. Changes in labor input—whether in hours worked or labor force participation —are positively related to the level of both total and per capita output.

Income Tax

Taxation effects on work effort have been dealt with already in our earlier discussions of tax incidence and excess burden.[2] We saw that imposition of an income tax reduces the net wage rate, thereby generating an income effect which increases work effort and a substitution effect which reduces it. There is no a priori basis on which to judge the direction in which the net effect will go, although it is reasonable to assume (as we did in our earlier discussion of redistribution)[3] that effort will decline.

If the labor supply schedule is upward-sloping, as most textbooks draw it, the negative substitution effect outweighs the positive income effect; if the schedule is backward-sloping, the opposite response occurs. Historically, it is evident that rising wage rates have been accompanied by reduced hours of work, i.e., a substantial part of the gains from productivity growth has been directed into increased leisure. Although this does not prove that the short-run supply schedule of labor is backward-sloping (in which case taxation would raise, rather than lower, the amount of labor supplied), it should not be readily assumed that an income tax must reduce effort. While we all seem to know someone who has been discouraged by taxation and has worked less, most of us seem to respond by working more.

As noted before, much depends on the rate schedule. A person will work less under a progressive than under a proportional rate schedule, if the same amount is drawn from him in both cases. Yet, work effort for taxpayers as a group need not be lower under a progressive schedule. The net effect depends on how wage earners at various points on the income scale respond. Earners at the upper end (where rates will be higher than under a proportional tax of equal yield) have more flexibility in hours worked but may also be less responsive to changes in the net wage rate, since other forms of motivation (prestige, interest in work, etc.) may dominate. Employees at the lower end of the scale have less flexibility in their work effort responses and also face lower marginal rates of income tax. The most serious problem of disincentive to work effort may well occur below the

[2] See pp. 407 and 467.
[3] See p. 95.

income tax range where welfare policies are such as to imply high marginal rates of tax on earned income.[4]

There is another aspect of income tax policy which may have important bearing on labor force participation. This is the tax treatment of working wives. In the absence of free child care centers and with inadequate allowance for deduction of child care expenses under the income tax, the net wage rate obtained by the working wife may be exceedingly low or negative so that there is little incentive (other than psychic income or to get out of the house) for entering the labor force. Moreover, the marginal rate of tax applicable under joint returns may be relatively high. Thus tax factors may have an important influence on the role of women in the labor force.[5]

Sales Taxes

Effects on work effort are generated not only by the income tax but also by commodity or sales taxes which raise prices and thereby reduce the real wage rate. Such at least will be the case unless wage earners operate under a "money illusion" and consider their money wage rate only. But will not the disincentive effects be less severe than under an income tax? After all, the worker may escape the consumption tax by saving, thereby avoiding such detrimental effects on work effort as may result from an income tax. Note, moreover, that the comparison must be between taxes of equal yield. Since the consumption base is smaller, the rate of consumption tax must be higher, and there is no ready way of predicting which will be more favorable to work effort. The question is whether leisure is traded more readily for present or for future consumption.

Turning to selective consumption taxes, the work-leisure choice will be affected differently, depending on which types of commodities are taxed. If the tax rests on goods which are complementary to work (such as work clothing), effort will be retarded more than if the tax is on items (such as food) which are relatively neutral to the work-leisure choice. A tax on "leisure products" such as motorboats or vacation trips, on the other hand, will reduce the value of leisure, thereby reducing the opportunity cost of increased hours of work. With rising standards of living, an increasing share of income goes into the purchase of goods the consumption of which involves leisure time, so that taxation of leisure (through the taxation of leisure goods) becomes more feasible. The nature of leisure use thus becomes an important factor in tax analysis, including efficiency as well as output effects.[6]

Expenditure Effects

Work incentives, as noted before, are affected not only from the tax side but also from the expenditure side of the budget policy.[7] Transfer payments may be treated as negative taxes but the income effect now goes to reduce effort. If

[4] See p. 676.

[5] See p. 275.

[6] For an interesting discussion of the economics of leisure, see S. B. Linder, *The Harried Leisure Class,* New York: Columbia, 1970.

[7] See p. 478.

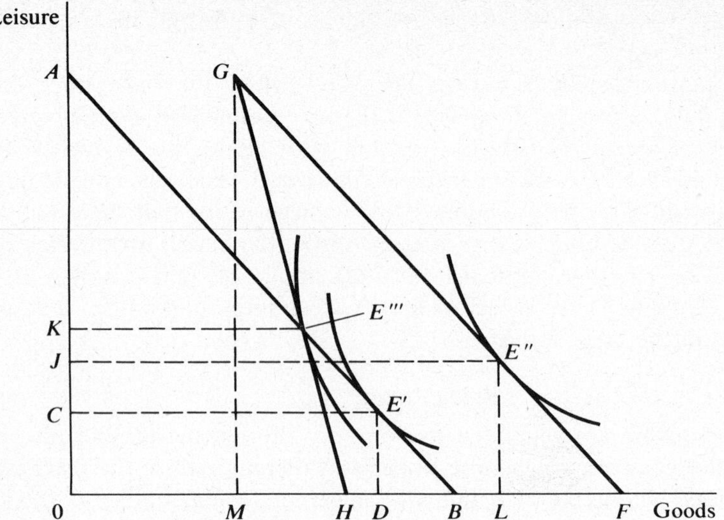

FIGURE 22-1 Effects on Work Effort.

transfers are unrelated to income, this is the entire story. But if the transfer is related positively to earnings (as in the case of a wage subsidy), this income effect will be countered by a substitution effect favorable to work effort. As in the income tax case, the net effect is again in doubt. If, on the other hand, the transfer payment declines with earnings, the substitution effect becomes adverse to work effort. Combined with the adverse income effect, this decline leaves the net effect necessarily one of reduced work effort.[8]

Much the same holds for the "free" provision of public services. If such services were of no use to consumers, we would have to consider only the effect on work effect which results from the taxes collected to finance them. But if public goods are useful, a depressing effect on work effort will result from the expenditure side, as workers will now find it less necessary to exchange leisure for private goods.

This is shown in Figure 22-1 where leisure is measured on the vertical axis and goods are shown on the horizontal axis. The price line, in the absence of budgetary policy, is given by *AB* and the worker is located at *E'*. He or she surrenders *AC* of leisure (i.e., works *AC* hours) to obtain *OD* of goods. Now the government provides *OM* of goods which are available independent of work effort. As a result, the price line shifts parallel to the right without changing its slope. With the new price line at *GF*, the worker moves to *E''*. Since there is only an income effect, consumption of both leisure and goods will be increased. Work effort falls from *AC* to *AJ*. Free provision thus moves the individual to a higher level of welfare at *E''* while reducing his or her work effort.

We now add to this provision the effects of an income tax imposed to finance it. As a result, the price line swivels from *GF* to *GH* and the new equilibrium

[8] See p. 676.

is at E'''. Government revenue equals BF and in turn is used to provide BF free of direct charge. Compared with the prebudget position, work effort is reduced from AC to AK. Assuming that the income tax taken by itself reduces effort, E''' lies north of E''. The combined fiscal transaction then reduces work effort in two ways, the detrimental (income) effect of expenditure policy CJ being added to the detrimental net (income and substitution) effect JK of the tax measure.

Paradoxically, the work incentive effect of the entire package will be more detrimental as expenditures are better designed to correspond to what consumers would otherwise wish to buy.[9] It is only a wasteful expenditure program which does not tend to lower work effort.

Incentives and Social Goods

This, indeed, is the dilemma of utopian communism, where persons should contribute to the community's output according to their individual ability, and compensation (the distribution of goods among individuals) should be according to need. In the absence of a self-interest–oriented economic motivation, another mechanism of work allocation and stimulus to effort would be needed. Ideally, this would be provided by the joys of cooperative effort but whether such attitudes can be developed to deal with the problem is a different matter. Clearly, such has not been the experience in the Soviet Union where the need for compensation in even its crudest (i.e., piecework) form was recognized at an early stage; nor can work participation or job choice in other settings, such as China or Cuba, be considered a voluntary option.

This points to an interesting implication of our earlier distinction between social and private goods. In dealing with the provision for *private goods,* society may choose between a market system and a communist system. In the market system, income is earned as wages and goods are distributed according to consumer purchases. Under pure communism, workers would be assigned to jobs (with income either not paid at all or else taxed away) and goods be distributed directly free of charge to consumers. The second case poses incentive problems which are absent in the first case. With regard to the provision for *social goods,* this choice is not open. The goods must be provided free of direct charge and income must be taxed away to finance them. The incentive problem, therefore, cannot entirely be solved by a market mechanism whatever the system of social organization.[10]

Why Do Effects on Work Effort Matter?

Before leaving the timely issue of taxation effects on work effort, let us consider once more just why these effects matter. The following four reasons may be distinguished:

[9] The depressing effect on work effort, moreover, will be the stronger the more the public goods are complementary to leisure, e.g., ski slopes, marinas, or scenic highways. By the same token, effects will be less depressing if expenditures are work-related (commuting roads) or if taxes are imposed on leisure goods.

[10] See p. 8. For a further discussion of these points, see Richard A. Musgrave, *Fiscal Systems,* New Haven, Conn.: Yale, 1969, chap. 1.

1. As discussed in Chapter 4, substitution of leisure for goods in response to a progressive tax-transfer system may set an effective limit to redistribution.[11]

2. As also shown in Chapter 4, differences in leisure responses greatly complicate the problem of achieving a just distribution.[12]

3. As shown in the preceding chapter, a distortion in the choice between income and leisure imposes an efficiency cost.[13]

4. As discussed here, a tax-induced reduction in work effort reduces output and GNP.

Points 1 and 2 stand by themselves, but points 3 and 4 are easily confused. To avoid this, we note that the substitution of a wage subsidy which raises effort and output is no less burdensome in terms of efficiency cost than is that of an income tax which lowers them. Whereas, in the tax case, a larger reduction in work effort is associated with a higher efficiency cost, the efficiency cost of the subsidy will be the larger the more work is *increased*. High work effort, therefore, cannot be identified with low efficiency cost. Indeed, concern with point 4 in particular appears to be based on the conventional definition of output which excludes leisure. Once leisure is included and properly valued, the distinction between 3 and 4 disappears.

B. EFFECTS ON SAVING

Perhaps the major impact of fiscal policy upon capacity output is through its effect on saving and on capital formation. Since labor is more productive if it is combined with a larger capital stock, capital formation raises productivity. The larger is the share of income which is saved and invested, the higher will the future level of income be. Thus, by influencing this share, fiscal policy has an important impact upon economic growth, i.e., the future level of per capita income. But economic growth has its costs. If the share of income which is currently used for capital formation is increased, that available for current consumption will be reduced. The policy problem, therefore, is one of choosing between present and future consumption. The terms on which this choice can be made have been the subject of much analysis during the past decade, and a brief review of the problem is given in the appendix to this chapter. Here our concern is with the more practical question of how saving and investment in the private sector are affected by fiscal measures.

Household Saving

Effects of tax policy upon saving in the private sector matter (1) because they bear on the division of resource use between consumption and capital formation and hence upon the growth of capacity output; and (2) because they enter into the effects of fiscal policy upon the level of aggregate demand. Our present concern is with item 1 only, leaving item 2 for consideration in Chapters 23 and 24.

[11] See p. 92.
[12] See p. 95.
[13] See p. 467.

TABLE 22-1
Sources of Private Sector Saving, 1973
(In Billions of Dollars)

Personal saving*	74.4
Corporate saving	
Undistributed profits†	25.7
Capital consumption allowances	71.2
Noncorporate capital allowances	39.7
Total private saving	211.0

* Includes retained earnings of unincorporated enterprises.
† Includes valuation adjustment and wage accruals.
Source: See *Survey of Current Business,* July 1974, p. 34.

Private saving in 1973 totaled $211 billion, or 16 percent of GNP. As the data in Table 22-1 show, depreciation charges or capital consumption allowances are much the most important source of saving, and corporate saving alone accounts for nearly one-half the total. The total business share in savings is even higher because personal savings, as reported by the Department of Commerce, include retained earnings of unincorporated enterprises. Purely household saving accounts for no more than one-third of the total.

The division of household income into consumption and saving has received much attention by economists over the past decades. At the heart of Keynesian economics and in the genesis of modern macro theory was the proposition that consumption is a function of disposable income (i.e., income after tax). Since then, this relationship (referred to as the "consumption function") has proven more complex than had been thought initially. Current consumption has been shown to depend not only on the level of current, but also of past, income. Moreover, not only is consumption a function of income, but other factors, such as the rate of interest, consumer wealth, and economic expectations, also enter.

Household Saving as a Function of Income Personal saving as a percentage of disposable income (i.e., personal income after personal taxes have been deducted) has ranged between 6 and 8 percent over recent decades. If all households saved at this same rate, the effect on personal saving of an income tax would be the same no matter how the tax bill was distributed among them. But in fact the fraction saved (the *average* propensity to save) rises as we move up the income scale. Thus, taxes collected from higher incomes may be expected to fall more heavily on saving than do those collected from lower incomes. The difference in the savings impact of more and of less progressive taxes, however, is less than one might think. The reason is that the difference in the consumption-savings impact of a dollar of tax paid by households at the $5,000 and the $50,000 levels of income depends on the differences in their respective *marginal,* and not their average, rates of saving; and though the average propensities to save differ sharply, the respective marginal propensities differ much less.

Line *AB* in Figure 22-2 shows a consumption function (relationship between income and consumption) with a constant marginal, though falling average,

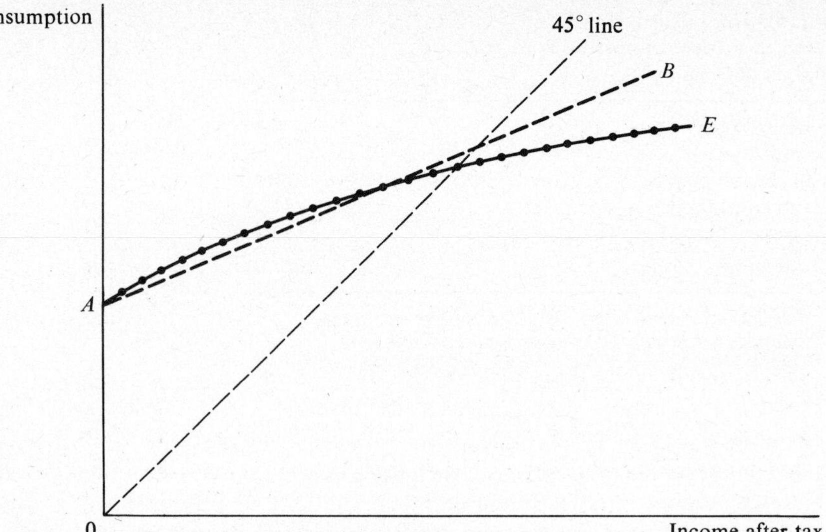

FIGURE 22-2 Income-Consumption Relationships.

propensity to consume.[14] With the marginal propensity to consume constant, all taxes would be divided in the same way between consumption and saving. But actual observation of the consumption-income relationship from cross-section data (i.e., data for a particular year, taken across households at different income levels) shows the consumption function to be slightly curved, as indicated by the dotted line *AE*.[15] This being the case, a more progressive distribution of tax liabilities imposes a higher burden on saving than does a less progressive one. But the departure from a linear function, and hence the difference in effects between alternative tax-burden distributions, is rather slight. Thus, replacement of the present progressive income tax rate structure with a proportional rate tax (leaving exemptions unchanged) might be estimated to raise household saving by less than 10 percent, whereas transition to a comprehensive base (with a proportional reduction in bracket rates to hold yield constant) might reduce saving by 15 percent. Given the modest results of these drastic changes, it appears that tax-structure changes within feasible bounds are not likely to have a major effect on the level of household saving.[16]

[14] Fig. 22-2 shows *AB* as a linear consumption function $C = a + cY$, where a is the intercept and c is the slope, generating an average propensity to consume equal to

$$\frac{C}{Y} = \frac{a + cY}{Y} = c + \frac{a}{Y}$$

which declines as Y increases.

[15] This conclusion is based on annual cross-section data. If allowance is made for the fact that consumer behavior depends on past as well as current income (also referred to as the "permanent income hypothesis"), the average propensity to consume at the lower end of the scale would be lower. This is so because the influence of consumers with temporarily low income would be removed. The consumption function would tend to have a lower intercept and a steeper slope. It is not obvious, however, how the curvature (and hence the marginal propensities at various levels) would be affected.

[16] See R. A. Musgrave, "Effects of Tax Policy on Private Capital Formation," in Commission on Money and Credit, *Fiscal and Debt Management Policies,* Englewood Cliffs, N.J.: Prentice-Hall, 1962, pp. 45–143.

Taxation effects on saving may result not only because the taxpayer's income is reduced, but also because an income tax reduces the net rate of return on saving, thus lowering the rate at which the household can substitute future for present consumption. As a result, one may expect the savings rate to be reduced. The magnitude of the substitution effect is difficult to assess. Since the larger part of personal saving originates in the middle- and high-income ranges where bracket rates are relatively high, the substitution effect may be substantial. Yet, such empirical evidence as is available does not support the proposition that saving is highly elastic to the rate of interest. Indeed, not all households may budget their lifetime consumption so as to save more when the rate of return rises. If their saving is geared to reaching a set level of retirement income, they may, in fact, save less when the rate of return increases.[17]

Effects of Consumption Tax. A consumption tax tends to be more favorable to saving for two reasons:

1. Consumption taxes tend to be distributed regressively, whereas an income tax tends to be progressive in its distribution.[18] With the marginal propensity to consume falling as income rises, the consumption tax (being paid more largely by lower-income households) thus has a heavier impact on consumption and a lighter impact on saving than does the income tax.
2. A consumption tax does not reduce the rate of return on saving and therefore avoids the substitution effect of the income tax, which is adverse to saving.

For these reasons, the use of consumption taxes has been especially advocated in developing countries where a higher rate of saving is held necessary to expedite economic growth.[19] Turning now to tax effects on business saving, our primary concern is with the effects of the corporation income tax.

Business Saving

Depreciation Charges As noted in Table 22-1, much the larger part of business saving is in the form of capital consumption allowances or depreciation charges. Since the profits tax is imposed after the deduction of depreciation, depreciation reserves are not reduced by the profits tax.[20] But their timing may be affected. If the law permits depreciation to be taken at an accelerated pace, tax payments are moved to a later date and depreciation reserves will be accumulated more rapidly. Considering the stream of depreciation generated by a one-shot investment, this will be followed by reduced saving later on. But if a continuing stream of investment is considered, the tax, as we shall note below, may be postponed permanently and corporate saving may be raised on a continuing basis.[21]

[17] See R. A. Musgrave, *The Theory of Public Finance,* New York: McGraw-Hill, 1959, chap. 12.

[18] See p. 391.

[19] See p. 18.

[20] Total depreciation charges might, however, be increased by permitting replacement-cost depreciation in a period of rising prices. See p. 305.

[21] The profitability effects of accelerated depreciation are noted later in this chapter.

Retained Earnings Provided that the profits tax is not shifted, after-tax profits are reduced by the tax. This reduction may in turn reduce corporate saving by lowering retained earnings, or it may be reflected in reduced dividends.

Over the last decade, dividends have been close to 25 percent of corporate cash flow (profits after tax plus depreciation), with retained earnings and depreciation picking up the remaining 75 percent. Empirical studies of dividend behavior show dividends to be a function of current cash flow and past dividend levels.[22] They suggest that the short-run impact of the corporate tax dollar on corporate saving might be as high as 75 percent, while the long-run impact might be of the order of 50 percent. Even on the latter basis, the savings impact of the corporate tax dollar is thus substantially above that of most other taxes.[23] A policy designed to foster growth, therefore, calls for restraint in the taxation of business profits.

Split Rates The division of the corporate tax burden between dividends and retained earnings may be affected by differential tax treatment. Application of a higher rate of corporation tax to retentions than to dividends (also referred to as an "undistributed profits tax") will encourage distribution, whereas favorable treatment of retention will encourage saving. The effects of differential rates will depend on the level of rates applicable at the shareholder level. Both approaches have been used in various countries depending on the particular objectives of economic policy.

Moreover, corporate behavior will be affected by the way in which integration of the corporation tax and the individual income tax is handled. The unintegrated system, in which dividends are taxed at the personal level in addition to the corporate level, favors retention, while neutrality calls for an integrated system.[24]

C. EFFECTS ON INVESTMENT

Saving is a necessary condition for capital formation but it is not a sufficient one. Investors must also be willing to invest. The preceding discussion of fiscal effects on private saving must therefore be followed by an examination of investment effects.

Nature of Investment Function

The nature of the investment function is highly controversial. Theory tells us how investors must behave if they seek to maximize profits, but it does not follow that this describes how real-life investors do in fact behave. They may wish to maximize sales or market shares rather than profits, or they may apply rules of thumb which do not conform closely with maximizing rules. Not only is the theoretical

[22] See John A. Brittain, *Corporate Dividend Policy,* Washington: Brookings, 1966.

[23] In considering the total picture, allowance need be made for the fact that part of dividends will be turned into personal saving. Such, however, may not be the case in developing countries where dividends tend to be consumed or invested abroad rather than returned to domestic investment.

[24] See p. 298.

framework controversial, but empirical testing is equally difficult. Statistical dependence of investment on changes in sales, for instance, may be taken to suggest that investment responds to capacity needs, or the relationship may be interpreted as one in which sales serve as a proxy for profit expectations. Empirical findings support both results, but the distinction is crucial for assessing tax effects.

To assess the investment effects of taxation, a model of investment behavior must be specified. Among major approaches, the following may be noted:

1. Investment is considered a function of past changes in sales and of existing capacity in relation to sales.
2. Investment is expressed as a function of the expected net rate of return.
3. Investment is taken to be a function of the availability of internal funds, including after-tax profits and depreciation charges.

All three hypotheses seem reasonable on a priori grounds and are not mutually exclusive.[25] According to approach 1, investment is undertaken to expand the capital stock, which will be desirable only if existing capacity is not excessive in relation to expected sales. If so, the profits tax has no direct bearing on investment. Fiscal effects enter only via resulting changes in aggregate demand and sales. According to approach 2, investors will invest only if they expect the prospective investment to yield a sufficient return. Here the tax is of direct importance because it reduces the net (after-tax) return, and this is the rate which matters in the investment decision. According to approach 3, investors prefer the use of internal funds, thereby avoiding rigidities inherent in debt service and the diminution of control which may result if funds are raised through equity issues. Once more, taxation is of obvious importance, including now not only effects on profitability but also effects on cash flow. Depreciation charges, as we shall see, enter into both 2 and 3 but in different ways.[26]

Profitability Effects

We begin with tax effects on the profitability of investment or the net rate of return. We further postulate an economy where full employment is maintained automatically. In such a system, the levels of investment and saving are determined by the intersection of the investment and saving schedules, with investment determined as a function of the rate of interest and saving dependent on both income and the rate of interest. The model is illustrated in Figure 22-3, where *II* is the investment schedule showing the available rates of return as investment proceeds at various levels (annual rates) while *SS* shows the supply of saving (out of full-employment income) at various rates of interest. Before tax, the two are equated at an interest rate *OB* and investment and saving equal *OA*.

[25] Much of the recent work on investment functions is based on Dale W. Jorgenson, "Capital Theory and Investment Behavior," *American Economic Review,* May 1963. In this model the tax rate enters by reducing net profits, and the depreciation rate enters by reducing the present value of the tax. For a review of various models, see Dale W. Jorgenson, "Econometric Studies of Investment Behavior: A Survey," *Journal of Economic Literature,* December 1971.

[26] For a general discussion of taxation effects on investment, see Gary Fromm (ed.), *Tax Incentives and Capital Spending,* Washington: Brookings, 1971.

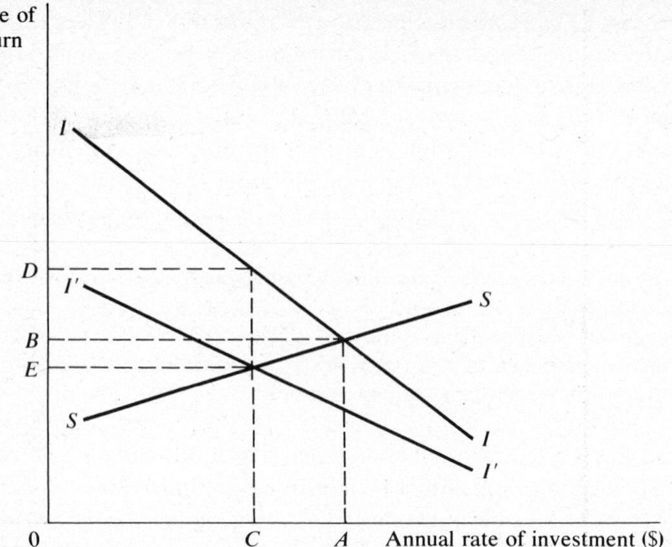

FIGURE 22-3 Tax Effects on Investment.

Now an income tax at rate *DE/DO* is imposed. As a result, the investment schedule expressed in terms of net rates of return swivels downward as shown by *I'I'*. In the new equilibrium, the gross rate of interest has risen to *OD*, the net rate has fallen to *OE* and investment and saving shrink to *OC*. As may be seen from the figure, the decline in investment will be the larger, the more elastic are both the *SS* and *II* schedules.

Loss Offset and the Return to Risk

In the preceding discussion, we took the rate of return (corresponding to various levels of investment) as given by the *II* schedule. We must now note that investment is not a safe bet with a guaranteed return, but rather a risky venture which may or may not pay off. The rate of return as shown on the *II* schedule is thus based upon a range of probable returns, and may be taken to reflect the expected value of this probable distribution.[27]

[27] If $q_1, q_2, \ldots, q_n$ are expected rates of return (positive and negative) and $p_1, p_2, \ldots, p_n$ the respective probabilities of their occurrence, so that $\sum_{i=1}^{n} p_i = 1$, we have

$$y = \sum_{i=1}^{n} q_i p_i$$

where y is the mathematical expectation of the percentage yield. This may be divided into a positive part and a negative part, such that

$$y = g - r$$

where g is the expected value of the positive part of the distribution and r is the absolute expected value of the negative part.

If we think of the return on investment α as a return on risk taking, we may write this as

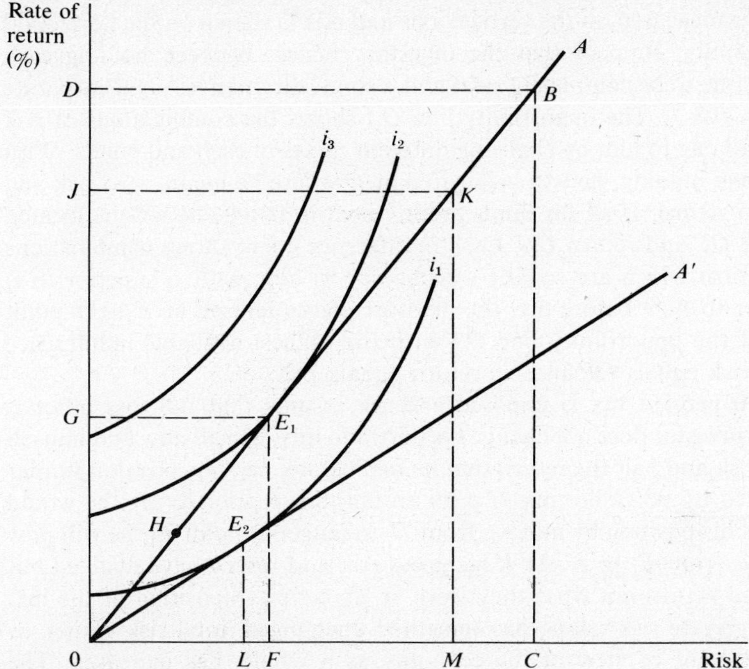

FIGURE 22-4 Taxation and Risk Taking.

An investor in search of income who surrenders his liquidity and purchases real assets (or equity therein by buying shares) undertakes a risk. He may get his money back with a substantial return or he may lose all or part of it. To make an investment means to gamble, and the investor should be interested in the gamble only if the value of probable gains outweighs that of probable losses. Since the investor's marginal utility of income may be expected to decline, an even-money (fifty-fifty) bet is not acceptable. If the tax worsens the odds by reducing the expected return, investment will fall. However, it is not at all obvious that the tax really reduces the odds. A tax will reduce the investor's return if he wins but, provided that loss offset is allowed for, it will also reduce his loss if he loses.[28] Given a proportional tax, both probable gains and probable losses will be reduced at the same rate. Depending on the circumstances of the case, the tax may induce him either to increase or to reduce his risk taking.[29]

The possibility of increased risk taking is shown in Figure 22-4, where the

---

$\alpha = \frac{g-r}{r}$. A tax without loss offset reduces this to $\alpha = \frac{(1-t)(g-r)}{r}$, whereas, under a tax with loss offset, it becomes $\alpha = \frac{(1-t)(g-r)}{(1-t)r} = \frac{g-r}{r}$, thus leaving the return on risk taking unchanged.

[28] See p. 306.

[29] The significance of changes in the level of risk taking may be interpreted in two ways. If reduced risk taking involves the choice of less risky industries while holding total investment constant, the rate of growth may decline, since more risky investments may have a higher potential for raising productivity. If reduced risk taking means the choice of a portfolio with a larger cash component, the effect may be to reduce the level of aggregate demand, thereby stepping outside the "classical" system and causing unemployment.

rate of return is measured on the vertical axis and risk is shown on the horizontal axis.[30] To simplify, suppose that the investor chooses between holding cash (which we assume to be completely safe) and a single alternative, say a corporate bond, of given risk.[31] The opportunity line *OA* shows the combinations of risk and return available to him by choosing different mixes of cash and bonds. With 100 percent cash holding, he will be located at *O* where he incurs zero risk and receives a zero return. If all his funds are invested in bonds, he will be located at *B*, with risk *OC* and return *OD*. Each indifference curve shows combinations of risk and return which are equally satisfactory to him, with i_2 superior to i_1 and i_3 superior to i_2.[32] Before tax, the investor places himself at E_1, the point of tangency of the opportunity line *OA* with the highest available indifference curve i_2. His risk equals *OF* and his return equals *OG*.

Now a 50 percent tax is imposed and we assume that full loss offset is assured. If the investor does not change his portfolio mix, he will now find himself with half the risk and half the return that he had before, i.e., in a position similar to that provided by portfolio mix *H* prior to tax. Since prior to tax, he would have improved his position by moving from *H* to tangency point E_1, he will now choose to move from E_1 to *K*. At *K* his gross risk and return have doubled but his net risk and return are what they were at E_1 before imposition of the tax. Although his private risk taking has remained unchanged, total risk taking, as seen from the point of view of the economy as a whole, has increased. The government has become a partner, as it takes half the return and assumes half the risk. This sequence comes about because loss offset is permitted. Without loss offset, the tax would swivel the opportunity line from *OA* to *OA'* and the new equilibrium would be at a tangency point E_2, with risk taking decreased to *OL*.

This illustration shows that under certain conditions, a tax with loss offset will *increase* risk taking. This somewhat startling result is obtained on the basis of rather simplifying assumptions. Thus the investment choice, as noted before, was limited to cash (assumed to be riskless) and to one risky asset. These simple assumptions may not hold. If we allow for the fact that inflation renders cash far from riskless and if we introduce a choice among alternative risky assets, the conclusion becomes less determinate. The outcome now depends on the precise nature of the investor's preferences or the shape of his indifference curves. The net result may be either to increase or to reduce risk taking, and no simple generalization regarding the outcome is possible.[33]

[30] Figure 22-4 follows James Tobin, "Liquidity Preference as Behavior toward Risk." *Review of Economic Studies,* February 1958.

[31] A convenient measure of risk is the standard deviation of probable gains and losses, but certain other measures of dispersion will do as well.

[32] The indifference curves are drawn so as to show increasing risk aversion. Successive increases in risk call for rising additions to the rate of return if the investor is to remain equally well off. This follows from the assumption that the utility of income schedule rises at a decreasing rate as income increases.

[33] For a further discussion of this topic, see Martin S. Feldstein, "The Effects of Taxation on Risk Taking," *Journal of Political Economy,* September–October 1969, and J. E. Stiglitz, "The Effects of Income, Wealth and Capital Gains Taxation on Risk Taking," *Quarterly Journal of Economics,* May 1969.

Role of Depreciation

In the preceding section we have referred to changes in "the" tax rate. It should now be added that the effective rate of tax (i.e., the percentage reduction in the rate of return) depends upon both the statutory tax rate (e.g., 48 percent under the corporation income tax) *and* the rate of depreciation which is permitted.

When considering an investment, the investor weighs the present value of its net income stream against the cost of the asset. This present value equals the present value of the income stream before tax minus the present value of tax payments thereon. The latter in turn may be viewed as equal to the present value of the gross tax (as it would be if no depreciation were allowed) minus the present value of the tax savings due to depreciation. This negative component will be the larger and the net tax will be the lower, the more rapidly depreciation may be taken. This is so because the present value of the tax savings will be the higher the sooner they are realized.[34] Speeding up depreciation thus reduces the effective rate of tax by postponing the due date of the tax liability.[35] It is equivalent, from the investor's point of view, to an interest-free loan, with the present value of interest savings thereon equal to the present value of the resulting tax saving.

If we consider a single investment, accelerated depreciation does not reduce the total amount of tax that will be paid. The liability is reduced in the earlier years and increased in the later years. The gain results from a once-and-for-all tax postponement, with the Treasury losing revenue in the earlier years and recouping it thereafter. If the case of a continuing investment is considered (i.e., if the asset is replaced as it wears out so as to keep the depreciable base unchanged), the gain from postponement rises over the early years and then levels off. After a while, the loss of revenue ceases but there is no recoupment of the initial loss so long as continuous reinvestment takes place. Recoupment takes place only after reinvestment ceases. Finally, there is the case of a firm with continuing expansion of depreciable assets. If depreciation is sufficiently fast and

[34] Consider an investment giving a constant annual income stream R for n years. Prior to tax, the investor equates the cost of the investment with the present value of its income stream so that

$$C = R_n A_n$$

where C is the cost of the investment and A_n is the present value of an annuity of \$1 for n years, discounted at the market rate of interest.

After tax, we have

$$C = R_n A_n - t(R_n A_n) + t\frac{C}{d}A_d$$

where t is the tax rate and d (assuming straight-line depreciation) is the number of years over which depreciation is spread. A_d accordingly is the present value of an annuity of \$1 over d years. The second term on the right-hand side of the equation is the present value of gross tax, and the third term is the present value of the tax saving due to the depreciation allowance.

[35] A further aspect of the depreciation problem, noted in our earlier discussion of efficiency effects, bears on the relative tax burden placed on different types of investments. Permitting more rapid depreciation is more valuable for a long investment, since the waiting period (until tax relief due to depreciation is obtained) will be reduced by more years. Neutral depreciation between investments of different lengths calls for depreciation rates which parallel the actual economic life of the asset.

expansion sufficiently sharp, such a firm may be able to postpone tax payment indefinitely. All payment is avoided and no ultimate recoupment occurs.[36]

Alternative Investment Incentives

Among alternative measures to stimulate investment are: (1) reduction in the rate of corporate profits tax, (2) accelerated depreciation, and (3) the investment credit. Such a credit is currently provided in the form of a 10 percent allowance on the cost of qualified investments, taken as an offset against tax.[37] For firms whose taxes are sufficient to permit the credit to be offset at once, the investment credit is similar to a cash grant made at the time of investment, and thus it reduces the cost of an asset by 10 percent; for others, the credit may be carried over against future taxes.

Comparing the effectiveness of the three measures is a tricky business. Accelerated depreciation and the investment credit are superior to rate reduction in that they may readily be limited to new investment (or some part thereof), whereas rate reduction has to be applied to profits from all investments, whether new or old.[38] Since it is the profitability of *new* investment that matters for incentive purposes, accelerated depreciation and the investment credit can give a more powerful stimulus than can rate reduction.

An effectiveness comparison between accelerated depreciation and the investment credit is more complex. The outcome depends on how long a view is taken and on how the level of investment behaves. If we consider the revenue cost for the first year of the new policy only, it is obvious that a credit involving a revenue loss of $1 billion will buy the Treasury more incentive than will accelerated depreciation in the form of an initial first-year allowance costing the same amount.[39] Current tax liabilities will be reduced $1 billion in both cases, but with the credit, the reduction is an outright gain, whereas the initial allowance is a loan only. Hence the investor's net rate of return is increased more under the credit. But the situation becomes more favorable to the initial allowance if a longer view is taken. Under the allowance, the Treasury will recoup revenue later as depreciation charges become less than they would normally have been. There is no such recoupment with an investment credit. For the same revenue

[36] An interesting question arises: What happens when depreciation is permitted to be taken in its entirety at the time the investment is made, i.e., when all investment costs may be expensed? Combined with perfect loss offset, this would in fact mean that there is no tax. With a 50 percent tax rate, investment of $100 would yield an immediate refund of $50 which, if reinvested, would yield a refund of $25, and so forth until a total refund of $100 was obtained. The investor would thus combine the initial investment of $100 with an additional $100 advanced by the Treasury, and resulting earnings on $200 net of the 50 percent tax would be the same as the earnings on $100 without tax.

[37] Qualified investments are investments in depreciable assets (other than buildings) which are used in production and with useful lives of at least four years. The 10 percent rate of credit applies for 1975–76.

[38] This is the case because it would be very difficult to impute shares in the total profits of a firm to particular assets.

[39] An initial allowance is an additional amount of depreciation, say 10 percent of cost, permitted to be taken in the first year, with a corresponding reduction in depreciation allowed in subsequent years. This is to be distinguished from the so-called investment allowance which permits a depreciation deduction in excess of cost.

cost incurred over a number of years, the allowance may therefore be set so as to involve a larger initial loss. The comparative results, moreover, depend on what happens to the total capital stock. If the economy expands, the advantage of subsequent revenue recoupment ascribed to accelerated depreciation comes to be postponed and the investment credit approach remains superior even in the long run.[40]

Advocates of the investment credit approach hold that depreciation rates should be set so as to obtain an equitable definition of income, while investment incentives are better given in the more explicit form of an investment credit or an outright investment grant. They also point out that the investment credit performs better as a flexible tool of stabilization policy. Proponents of accelerated depreciation, on the other hand, have preferred the faster write-off method since they view it as a more permanent and stable form of relief. However this may be, both approaches involve nonneutralities. Accelerated depreciation, as noted before, favors long investments, whereas the investment credit favors short-lived assets which permit faster capital recovery and allows a more rapid repetition of the credit benefit.

As an alternative to the investment credit, government may make outright investment grants of the same amount. For a firm which has sufficient tax liability against which to offset the credit, the two approaches are equivalent; but for a firm that does not and that must therefore carry the credit over to future profits tax liabilities, the investment grant makes the relief available more quickly and with greater certainty. This alternative may be of particular importance for small firms. For this and other reasons (the grant is more explicit), Great Britain during the late sixties moved to the grant approach.[41]

Capital Gains Treatment

Preferential treatment of capital gains offers a further approach to the incentive problem. Undoubtedly, the preferential treatment of realized gains and the exemption of unrealized gains has been a major factor in reducing the impact of taxation on property income, especially of high-bracket rates under the individual income tax. But it has also been a costly approach. A blanket preference for capital gains involves a rather arbitrary criterion for types of investments which should and should not be given relief. Not all investments yielding capital gains are worthy of particular support, since gains may be derived from gilt-edged securities and real estate speculation as well as from risk investments in new products and processes which are essential to economic growth. At the same time, profits from such risk capital may not be realized in the form of capital gains but may accrue as ordinary income. In all, there is little support for extending a blanket preference to all capital gains, except perhaps for the proposition that an adequate level of alternative relief, such as a lower but uniform rate of taxation of all capital income, is not politically feasible.

[40] For further comparisons of this sort, see E. Cary Brown, "Tax Incentives for Investment," *American Economic Review,* May 1962; and S. B. Chase, "Tax Incentives for Investment and Spending," *National Tax Journal,* March 1962.

[41] See p. 306.

Effects on Technical Progress

The rate of capital formation is important to growth, but technological improvement is no less significant. Tax policy enters here via its treatment of research and development expenditures. Such expenditures may be expensed, i.e., they may be given the privilege of instantaneous depreciation even though they are basically in the nature of investment outlays. This is a substantial advantage, but further assistance might be given by granting a special tax credit or outright cash subsidy. Such credits, however, are not easy to implement because it is difficult to distinguish between outlays which merely affect the competitive position of a particular firm (e.g., development of minor style or packaging changes) and those which result in genuine technical improvement. In addition, public expenditures can have an important bearing on technical progress, whether through research subsidies to private institutions such as are given through the National Science Foundation or through the technological fallout of government purchases. Development of military hardware has had important spillovers into civilian technology, and direct subsidies to development in certain areas (e.g., a pollution-free automobile engine or mass transport devices) are under discussion.

D. GROWTH AND EQUITY

Raising the rate of investment, so it is frequently argued, should be in everyone's interest because it means that the size of the pie available for distribution would be increased. This view has some merit, but it must not be overlooked that higher future consumption is bought at the price of reduced present consumption and that changes in the rate of growth may affect factor shares and thereby the way in which the increase is distributed. Moreover, the long-run incidence of taxes —as discussed further in the chapter appendix—is closely related to their growth effects.

Fiscal measures undertaken to raise the rate of growth may affect not only the distribution of income before tax but also the distribution of disposable income on the basis of given factor earnings. Thus, measures favorable to growth (including policies aimed at raising the rate of saving and the level of investment) may call for restraint in the taxation of profits and a less progressive rate structure under the income tax. They may thus conflict with equalizing measures.

To the extent that this potential conflict relates to effects on the level of saving, resolution is possible. If savings in the private sector are insufficient to sustain the desired rate of capital formation, the necessary level of savings in the economy may be provided (at least theoretically) by raising taxes and creating a budget surplus in the public sector. The saving thus created may then be made available to private sector investment, whether by public lending, debt retirement, or expansionary monetary measures. But such an alternative approach is not available with regard to investment. Short of substituting public for private investment (with its implicit institutional changes), the net rate of return must be kept at adequate levels to call forth the necessary level of investment, and this approach may present an unavoidable conflict. The best that can be done in this case is to choose investment incentives, such as the investment credit or investment grants, which are more compatible with equity considerations.

Moreover, the growth issue poses a problem in intergeneration equity. A higher growth rate means less present and more future consumption. To some extent, this gain will occur sufficiently early to benefit the present generation, but beyond this, it will mean a transfer to future generations. Since future generations will benefit from technological progress even if they are not left with an increased capital stock, it may be questioned why the present generation should add to this superior position by refraining from consumption. The bearing of such restraint on the future level of per capita income further involves the problem of population growth. Determining an "optimal" rate of growth is thus a complex problem, especially for developing countries where the immediate cost of reduced current consumption is felt most severely.[42]

E. SUMMARY

In this chapter, various effects of fiscal measures on the level of capacity output were considered. They may operate through effects on work effort, saving, and investment. Beginning with effects on work effort, we concluded:

1. An income tax may reduce or increase work effort, depending on whether the substitution effect outweighs the income effect, or vice versa.

2. There is no ready way of telling whether the level of work effort will be higher under an income tax or a consumption tax.

3. Transfer payments which are related positively to income generate income and substitution effects opposite to those of an income tax, with the net outcome again in doubt.

4. Transfer payments related negatively to income reduce effort.

5. The same negative result tends to hold for free provision of social goods.

6. A distinction must be drawn between resulting excess burden and resulting changes in work effort.

In considering effects on the level of saving, a distinction was drawn between household savings and savings by businessess.

7. Household saving as a percentage of income (the average propensity to save) rises with income, but the marginal propensity to save rises less. Since differences in the savings impact of more or less progressive taxes depend on differences in the marginal propensities, they are less important than one might expect.

8. Income taxes may also affect saving because they reduce the net rate of return.

9. A consumption tax tends to fall less heavily on saving than does an income tax.

10. A large part of the corporation tax tends to be reflected in reduced corporate saving.

[42] See p. 745.

The effects of taxation on investment may operate in a number of ways, including their impact on profitability and the availability of internal funds.

11. A profits tax tends to reduce the level of investment by reducing the net rate of return.

12. Such is not the result, however, if loss offset is allowed for.

13. Allowing for depreciation reduces the effective rate of tax, the more so the faster is the permissible depreciation rate.

14. Among other ways of stimulating investment, the investment credit tends to offer the most effective approach.

15. Tax policy may raise the rate of technological progress by preferential treatment of research and development expenditures.

Finally, it was noted that growth policy involves complex questions of equity, regarding both its effect on the distribution of present earnings and the distribution of gains from growth among present and future generations.

FURTHER READINGS

Brown, E. Cary: "Business Income Taxation and Investment Incentives," in *Income, Employment and Public Policy: Essays in Honor of Alvin Hansen,* New York: Norton, 1948.

———: "Tax Incentives for Investment," *American Economic Review,* Supplement, May 1962.

Feldstein, Martin S.: "The Effects of Taxation on Risk Taking," *Journal of Political Economy,* September–October 1969.

Fromm, Gary (ed.): *Tax Incentives and Capital Spending,* Washington: Brookings, 1971.

Goode, Richard: *The Individual Income Tax,* Washington: Brookings, 1964, chaps. 3, 4.

Solow, Robert M.: *Growth Theory: An Exposition,* Fair Lawn, N.J.: Oxford University Press, 1970.

Stiglitz, J. E.: "The Effects of Income, Wealth and Capital Gains Taxation on Risk Taking," *Quarterly Journal of Economics,* May 1969.

Tobin, James: "Liquidity Preference as Behavior toward Risk," *Review of Economic Studies,* February 1958.

APPENDIX: Fiscal Policy and the Rate of Growth

In this appendix, we consider further why the rate of capital formation is important, how it can be affected by fiscal policy, and what options present themselves for public policy. Moreover, consideration is given to the interrelationship between tax incidence and growth.

FISCAL POLICY AND THE ABSOLUTE LEVEL OF FACTOR INCOMES

Assuming an economy with perfectly flexible prices, in which a full-employment level of income is maintained automatically, saving is always matched by a corresponding level of planned investment. An increase in the savings rate thus raises capital formation. An increase in capital formation in turn raises productivity and output. Thus, by increasing today's saving, tomorrow's level of income is raised. The extent of increase, and hence the importance of capital formation, will depend upon the state of technology, the existing capital stock, and the supply of other factors. But a higher rate of capital formation is not costless. It also means a lower level of current consumption. The policy issue is, therefore, how far the present generation will refrain from consumption so as to benefit the future.

FISCAL POLICY AND THE EQUILIBRIUM RATE OF GROWTH

Before considering this question, we must draw a distinction between the effects of fiscal policy upon (1) the absolute level of income at a specified future date, and (2) the future rate of growth of income. Recent developments in growth theory have shown that fiscal policy can raise the absolute level of future income by increasing the rates of saving and investment, but that it cannot thereby affect the equilibrium rate of income growth.

Why should it be that fiscal policy cannot affect the equilibrium rate of growth? The reason is that this equilibrium rate cannot exceed, and indeed must equal, the independently given growth rate of population.[43] Suppose the economy

[43] An initial statement of the basic positions of neoclassical growth theory was given by Robert M. Solow, "A Contribution to the Theory of Economic Growth," *Quarterly Journal of Economics*, February 1956. See also Solow, *Growth Theory: An Exposition*, Fair Lawn, N.J.: Oxford University Press, 1970.

For a further exposition of growth theory, see Thomas F. Dernburg and Duncan McDougall, *Macroeconomics*, 4th ed., New York: McGraw-Hill, 1972, chap. 14; and W. Smith, *Macroeconomics*, Homewood, Ill.: Irwin, chap. 10. In capsule form the argument may be summarized as follows:

The crucial component of the model is the underlying production function showing the relationship between total income and factor inputs. The most commonly used version is the so-called Cobb-Douglas function, or

$$Y = AK^{\alpha}N^{\beta} \tag{1}$$

where Y is output; K is capital; N is labor; and A, α, and β are parameters. Disregarding the limiting factor of fixed natural resources and assuming constant returns to scale (i.e., a situation where doubling of K and N results in a doubling of output), we must have $\alpha + \beta = 1$ so that

$$Y = AK^{\alpha}N^{(1-\alpha)} \tag{2}$$

Equation 2 may, with some mathematics, be restated in terms of rates of growth such that

$$y = \alpha k + (1 - \alpha)n \tag{3}$$

where y is the rate of growth of income, k is the rate of growth of capital, and n is the rate of growth of labor. Since saving and investment are a fixed proportion of Y, it may be shown further that in equilibrium, the rate of growth of capital stock k must approach that of income y. Substituting y for k in equation 3, we obtain

$$y = n \tag{4}$$

That is, the equilibrium rate of growth of income equals that of the labor force.

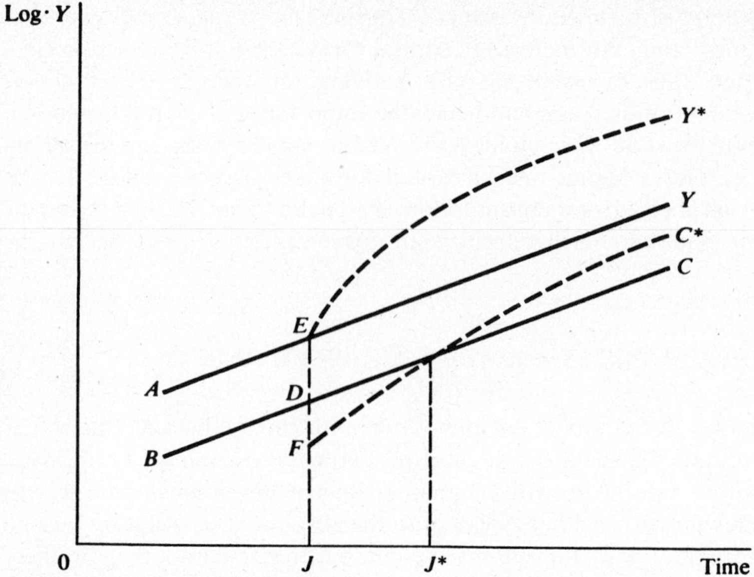

FIGURE 22-A1 Growth Options.

is initially in a position of steady or equilibrium growth, where the growth rate of income, population, and capital stock all equal 2 percent. To simplify matters, the state of technology is held constant. Since population and capital stock grow at the same rate, the capital-labor ratio remains constant and so does the productivity of labor and capital. Suppose also that the savings rate, and hence the share of investment in GNP, is 20 percent. Now fiscal policy measures are taken which cause the savings rate to rise to 25 percent. As a result, the capital stock will increase faster than does the labor supply, and the ratio of capital to labor will rise. Income now grows more rapidly than before, but this increase cannot be maintained indefinitely. The reason is that the rising capital-labor ratio also results in diminishing returns to capital. The increments to the capital stock will become less effective in raising income, and this change acts as a brake on income growth. As income rises less rapidly, the rate of increase in the capital stock also slows down. This is so because the increase in capital stock equals saving, which in turn is a fixed proportion of income.

The process continues until the rate of income growth has again fallen to that of population. At this point, the rate of growth in capital stock again comes to equal that of income and we are returned to the initial condition of equality in the rates of growth of capital stock and labor. Since there is no further change in the capital-labor ratio, diminishing returns cease to operate. We are returned to an equilibrium situation where income grows at the same rate as does population. However, the capital stock is larger than it would have been without the increase in the savings rate and the capital-labor ratio is now higher. Since the growth rate of labor has not been affected, this result means not only a higher absolute level of GNP but also a gain in the level of per capita income.

This development is illustrated in Figure 22-A1, where the vertical axis measures the level of capacity output plotted on a log scale while the horizontal axis shows successive years. The straight line *AY* shows the equilibrium path of income with savings rate *s*. Given the log scale, the slope of each line indicates the growth rate, so that *AY* traces a constant percentage rate of income growth. Line *BC* shows the corresponding path of consumption, such that *DJ* equals consumption and *DE* equals savings at income *JE*, all measured on the log scale. Now suppose that at the beginning of year *J* the savings rate rises to s^*. As a result, income travels the path shown by EY^*. Initially, the growth rate is higher than it was before, but eventually EY^* comes to parallel *AY* and the growth *rate* returns to where it was. However, the *level* of income remains higher throughout. The consumption path is now shown by FC^*, with savings at income *JE* now equal to *FE*. Consumption under the new policy is lower from year *J* to J^* but higher thereafter. Present consumption has been sacrificed for a higher level of future income and consumption.

GROWTH OPTIONS

In choosing between various options, two factors must be considered. The first is that successive increases in the savings rate (and hence in the resulting equilibrium capital-labor ratio) will yield decreasing gains in future consumption. Theorists have shown that there is a savings rate beyond which future consumption will decline rather than rise, as assumed in the diagram. The growth path which yields the highest future consumption is referred to as the "golden rule," a concept which has intrigued theorists with its surprising property of calling for a savings rate equal to the share of capital income in national income.[44] The second consideration is that the future consumption gain must be discounted so as to compare it with the loss of present consumption forgone. It is the present value of future consumption that must be maximized, thus raising once more the problem of what discount rate to choose.[45] With a positive discount rate, the optimal rate of savings or consumption postponement will thus fall short of that indicated by the golden rule.

From a more practical point of view, the equilibrium growth rate is hardly a matter of major concern. Policy makers are not inclined to consider an infinite future, nor can they assume that a policy once set will be continued in perpetuity thereafter. Rather, their concern is with a more limited horizon, and decisions are made and revised on a continuing basis. Consequences for the absolute levels of output and consumption over the immediately ensuing years or perhaps over a decade or two are what matter, and this is still a period during which changes in the savings rate can affect not only the level, but also the growth rate, of income. Since the eventual return to the equilibrium rate of growth is a very slow one, involving a half-century or more, its significance to the policy maker is of questionable importance.

[44] This finding was developed by Edmund Phelps, "The Golden Rule of Accumulation: A Fable for Growthmen," *American Economic Review*, September 1961. Also see, Thomas F. Dernberg and Ducan McDougall, *Macroeconomics*, 4th ed., New York: McGraw-Hill, 1972.

[45] See Chap. 7, Sec. D, p. 170.

GROWTH EFFECTS AND TAX INCIDENCE

In discussing the incidence of various taxes, we have seen that in the longer run, the distribution of the tax burden will depend on the resulting effects on factor supplies, rates of return, and growth. Viewing this problem in terms of "comparative statics," we have shown that a tax on labor income, by depressing labor supply, may result in an increase in the gross wage rate and a decline in the return to capital, so that the net wage rate declines by less than the tax and capital shares in the burden. While this properly describes the direction of adjustment, it does not account for the truly long-run interdependence of capital and labor supply in the context of balanced growth. In recent work, the bearing of this interdependence on incidence has come under consideration.[46]

The nature of this problem is complex, but the general conclusions reached may be described by considering the substitution of a tax on capital income for an equal-yield tax on wage income (the "differential incidence" approach) and examining the results under various assumptions regarding factor supplies and savings rates.

1. Suppose first that the supply of both labor and capital is inelastic to the rate of return and that the savings rates out of wage and capital income are the same. In this case, our tax substitution will not affect factor supplies. The rate of capital accumulation is unaffected as is the capital-to-labor ratio under equilibrium growth. Pretax rates of return to factors, therefore, are unchanged as well. The burden of the tax previously carried by labor comes now to be borne by capital.

2. Next suppose that the supply of labor is elastic, while retaining the other assumptions. As the tax on capital income is substituted for the tax on wage income, labor supply increases. Our earlier discussion, based on a comparative-static approach, suggested that the tax substitution, by increasing the net wage rate, would result in an increase in hours worked. This in turn would reduce the gross wage rate and increase the return to capital, so that part of the burden would continue to be shared by labor. But this will not occur in the context of a balanced-growth model, where there will again be a full transfer of the burden to capital. The increase in hours worked will not affect the long-run growth rate of labor supply, which will still be determined by population growth; and, as we have seen in the preceding summary of growth theory, it is the rate of population growth which determines the equilibrium rate of income growth. Since we assume that the propensity to save is the same for capital and labor income, there will also be no change in the growth of the capital stock. With the capital-to-labor ratio in equilibrium growth unchanged, the pretax rates of return to capital and labor will also be unaffected. With the tax on labor income replaced by a tax on capital income, the burden is thus transferred from labor to capital.

3. The situation differs, however, if the supply of capital is elastic to the rate of return. As a result, the substitution of a tax on capital income reduces capital

[46] See Martin Feldstein, "Tax Incidence in a Growing Economy with Variable Factor Supply," *Quarterly Journal of Economics,* November 1974; and Martin Feldstein, "Incidence of a Capital Income Tax in a Growing Economy with Variable Savings Rates," *Review of Economic Studies,* 1974; and Marian Krzyzaniak, "The Long-Run Burden of a General Tax on Profits in a Neo-Classical World," *Public Finance,* no. 4, 1967.

accumulation. While the growth rate of income remains unaffected (as it is still determined by the growth of population), the equilibrium capital-to-labor ratio will now be lower. Because of this, the pretax rate of return to capital will be increased while that to labor will be reduced. Only part of the tax burden is transferred and labor shares part of the profits tax burden.

4. Finally, consider a situation where both factor supplies are inelastic to the rate of return but where the savings rate out of capital income is higher than that out of labor income. Replacement of a tax on wage income by a tax on capital income now results in a reduced rate of capital formation and similar changes as under situation 3 result. Once more, labor bears part of the burden of a tax on capital income. Putting situations 3 and 4 together, we conclude that the remaining share of the tax burden borne by labor will be the larger, the more elastic the supply of capital is and the higher the savings rate out of capital income is relative to the supply elasticity and savings rate for labor.

Although the tax effects involved in these relationships are complex and depend on the underlying structure of the growth model, it is not unreasonable to assume that, say, one-third of the burden of a tax on capital income comes to be borne by labor. This reasoning, it must be noted, pertains to the very long-run result after the return to balanced growth has taken place. Given the very long time period involved,[47] the more limited approach of the comparative-static type of analysis may be more relevant for policy purposes. In this setting, elasticity of labor supply does matter, and the slower process of different capital accumulation due to different savings rates will be of less importance.

[47] See Ryuzo Sato, "Fiscal Policy in a Neo-Classical Growth Model: An Analysis of Time Required for an Equilibrium Adjustment," *Review of Economic Studies*, February 1963.

Chapter 23

Saving and Investment in the Public Sector*

A. Two Types of Public Saving: *Public Saving in the Classical System; Public Saving in the Keynesian System; Application to Federal Budget; Tax versus Loan Finance; Public Saving and Intergeneration Equity.* **B. Public Investment. C. Summary.**

A. TWO TYPES OF PUBLIC SAVING

Having considered fiscal effects on private saving and investment, we now turn to the direct role of saving and investment in the public sector. For this purpose, two concepts of public saving must be distinguished. The appropriateness of one or the other depends on the nature of the economy in which the budget operates.

Public Saving in the Classical System

In the preceding chapter, we have dealt with fiscal effects on capacity output while assuming that the economy will automatically adjust itself to full employment. This is an economy where the entire income received at full employment is always

* *Reader's Guide to Chapter 23:* This chapter, by focusing on alternative views of budgetary balance, provides a transition to the subsequent discussion of stabilization policy. However, for the time being, emphasis is on the concept of balance in a classical system and on the direct role of public investment. Public saving in the Keynesian system is dealt with very briefly here, and will be understood better after the next chapter has been covered.

respent on either consumption or investment. In this system—referred to as "classical" since it was implied by the British economists from Adam Smith to Marshall—income which is not consumed but saved comes automatically to be channeled into investment. To put it differently, saving will always be matched by a corresponding amount of planned investment.

In such a system, all government receipts—whether in the form of taxes or borrowings—must be reflected in reduced private spending, whether on consumption or investment. A dollar of tax or loan receipts alike reduces private spending by \$1.[1] Government expenditures, therefore, do not affect the level of aggregate demand in this system. But there remains the question of how the pattern of expenditures is affected. Suppose that taxes are paid out of income which is otherwise consumed, while loans are drawn from savings which are otherwise directed into investment. The government's contribution to the withdrawal of resources from consumption and their diversion into investment then equals the excess of tax receipts over government expenditures of the consumption type. We know that total expenditures at full employment (E_f) are the sum of

$$E_f = C + I + G_c + G_i \tag{1}$$

where C and I are private consumption and investment, G_c is government expenditures for consumption, and G_i is government investment. We also know that full-employment income (Y_f) equals

$$Y_f = C + S + T \tag{2}$$

where S is private saving and T is tax payments. By the nature of the classical system $E_f = Y_f$, so that

$$(T - G_c) + S = I + G_i \tag{3}$$

On the left side we have total saving, where the term in parentheses is public saving, while on the right side we have private plus public investment.[2] Government saving, as is shown in (3), is not the same as G_i. Rather, it may be made available to finance either public or private investment. In the latter instance, such savings may be made available to private investors either by government lending or by providing loanable funds to the private sector through debt retirement.

Public saving thus defined equals the surplus on current account in a dual budget system; that is to say, in a system in which the budget is divided into two parts, the current and the capital budget. The current budget includes only

[1] The underlying assumption is that borrowing is from the public, so as to reduce loanable funds available to private investors. If government expenditures are financed by money creation, the argument does not hold and loan finance becomes inflationary.

[2] The equality of E_f and Y_f as postulated here does not reflect a mere identity which follows from the national income accounts (where for any past period E equals Y), but the behavioral relationships which assure maintenance of full-employment income. Note also that $G_c + G_i = T + B$ where B is government borrowing.

expenditures of the consumption type, whereas capital expenditures are entered in the capital budget. Tax receipts are recorded on the revenue side of the current budget. If we assume these receipts to reflect withdrawal from private consumption, the surplus equals the government's net contribution to saving or release of resources for capital formation.

Public Saving in the Keynesian System

A different concept of public saving arises in a model of the economy known as the Keynesian system. Here it cannot be assumed that the private sector will automatically provide for a full-employment level of income. Assuming the level of investment to be given more or less independently, we see that income must settle at whatever level will produce an amount of saving equal to the level of investment. In such a system, the nature of which will be explored in the following chapters, the operation of the budget has an important effect upon aggregate demand. If we assume that taxes come out of consumption while borrowing leaves investment unaffected, the excess of total government expenditures over tax receipts may now be viewed as a measure of the budgetary contribution to aggregate demand.[3] This being the case, the relevant concept of budgetary balance is now given by the excess of expenditures over receipts in the *total* budget. The state of balance in the current budget ceases to be informative in this context since it no longer measures the budgetary contribution to capital formation. This contribution is now reflected in the level of government investment.

Application to Federal Budget

While the federal budget is arranged so that the balance is shown for the budget as a whole, an attempt is made in Table 23-1 to show how a dual budget statement would have looked for fiscal 1975. At the top of the table we show the comprehensive budget including both current and capital expenditures combined. With total expenditures of $313 billion and tax receipts of $279 billion, the overall deficit was $34 billion. But though the total budget showed a deficit, the current budget was in substantial surplus. Estimating current expenditures at $257 billion, we find that the current budget recorded a surplus of $22 billion, while the total deficit reappears as the balancing item in the capital budget. Moreover, note that the surplus in the current budget plus the deficit in the total budget equaled the amount of government investment or $56 billion.

Though the federal budget could be presented in this form, it is not, and the President's Budget Commission recommended against the use of this form for good reason.[3] Since the nature of our economy is not such that full employment is automatically assured by the private sector, budget policy has a major effect on the level of aggregate demand. Tax and loan finance differ in this effect and the choice between them must be used as an instrument of stabilization policy. Since the responsibility for stabilization policy must rest at the federal level, presentation of a dual budget would divert attention from the more important focus on the state of balance in the overall budget. Nevertheless, the contribu-

[3] See *Report of the President's Commission on Budget Concepts,* 1967.

TABLE 23-1
Federal Budget, Total, Current, and Capital
(Estimates for Fiscal 1975, in Billions of Dollars)

	TOTAL BUDGET		
Expenditures	313	Receipts	
		Tax revenue	279
		Deficit	34
Total	313	Total	313
	CURRENT BUDGET		
Current expenditures	257	Tax revenue	279
Surplus	22		
Total	279	Total	279
	CAPITAL BUDGET		
Capital expenditures*	74	Current budget	
Unclassified	−18	surplus	22
		Deficit	34
Total	56	Total	56

* Based on *The Budget of the United States Government, Fiscal Year 1976, Special Analyses,* p. 59. Capital expenditures are defined broadly to include "developmental outlays" as well as acquisition of assets. In a complete system of capital and current budgets, depreciation charges on government assets should appear as an outlay in the current budget, but such charges are in fact not recorded.

tion of the federal budget to capital formation might be brought out more strongly by giving prominent attention to the breakdown of federal expenditures between current and capital items, an aspect now dealt with only in the special analysis section of the budget.

Tax versus Loan Finance

We now return to the setting of a full-employment economy where the double budget system is helpful in pointing out the public sector contribution to capital formation. Our earlier interpretation of the current budget surplus as a measure of government savings implied that all taxes come from private consumption while all borrowing comes from saving, i.e., from funds which are diverted from private investment. Actually, this implication is not correct. We have seen in the preceding chapter that taxes fall on both consumption and saving and that various taxes differ in their impact on these two variables. Furthermore, loan finance may displace consumption rather than investment spending, as savings increase in response to a resulting rise in the interest rate. A more refined measure of the *net* budgetary contribution to saving, therefore, would include only such tax revenue as falls on consumption, while that tax revenue which falls on saving would be entered in the capital budget.

Nevertheless, it is a reasonable first approximation to assume that taxes are drawn largely from private consumption while loan finance draws largely on saving. Tax finance (whether public expenditures are for consumption or capital items) is thus more favorable to economic growth than is loan finance.[4] This conclusion is of considerable importance for development policy, provided again that aggregate demand is sufficient to secure the full utilization of all resources whether in the production of consumer or investment goods.[5]

Public Saving and Intergeneration Equity

So far, we have looked at the surplus in the current budget as the government's contribution to saving. Another application of the double budget bears on fiscal equity in distributing the cost of public services over time. Allowing for the distinction between public consumption and investment, the benefit rule of taxation may be broadened into a benefit rule of finance, calling for each generation to contribute in taxes that part of the cost which corresponds to its share in the benefit stream. This benefit rule means that as a matter of equity, the current budget should be balanced while capital outlays should be financed by borrowing. It also follows that the current budget should include not only current outlays but also depreciation on public assets. Reflecting the current benefit stream, such depreciation should also be paid for by taxation.

As we shall see in our subsequent discussion of the public debt, it is questionable whether this idea can be applied to the formulation of the federal budget, but it clearly has an important place in state and local finance.[6] Indeed, it is the basic reason why a dual budget system is generally used at the state and local levels.

[4] Assuming a uniform propensity to save, this may be demonstrated as follows: With full-employment income given at Y_f, the composition of output is given by the system

$$S = a + s(Y_f - T) + bi$$
$$I = d - ei$$
$$I + G = S + T$$

where S is private saving, T is tax revenue, I is private investment, G is government purchases, and i is the interest rate. Private investment I adjusts itself to match public saving (or $T - G$) plus private saving S out of full-employment income Y_f.

For the case of tax finance, $dG = dT$ and

$$\frac{dI}{dT} = -\frac{s}{1 + b/e}$$

We find that the investment-depressing effect of tax finance is positively related to the propensity to save, s. This follows because a large s means that a large part of tax revenue comes out of saving. We also note that the investment-depressing effect is large if b is small. A small b means that the positive response of saving to an increase in the interest rate (induced in turn by the decline in investment) is weak. Finally, the resulting decline in investment will be greater if e is larger, since a large e indicates a heavy negative response of I to a rise in the interest rate.

For the case of loan finance, we have $dG = dL$, where $L = G - T$ and

$$\frac{dI}{dL} = -\frac{1}{1 + b/e}$$

Investment-depressing effects again vary directly with e and inversely with b, but s now does not enter. The investment-reducing effect of tax finance thus equals s times that of loan finance. If $b = 0$, the entire loan finance is reflected in reduced private investment.

[5] See Chap. 25, Sec. D, p. 569.

[6] See p. 606.

TABLE 23-2
Gross Fixed Capital Formation, 1973
(In Billions of Dollars)

Government	
Federal	
Military	16.9
Civilian	5.9
State, local	36.1
Total	58.9
Private sector, total	194.0
All sectors	252.9

Source: Survey of Current Business, July 1974, p. 32.

B. PUBLIC INVESTMENT

Having discussed the economics of public investment in Chapters 7 and 8, we need not recount it here. At this point we need only note that the role of public investment in economic growth is of obvious importance both in total magnitude and in its strategic role in the development process. The place of public capital formation in the overall picture is shown in Table 23-2.

If public investment is defined narrowly to include construction and equipment only, the total for 1973 amounted to $59 billion, or 29 percent of total government purchases. If civilian expenditures only are included, the total was $42 billion, or 22 percent of civilian government purchases. By comparison, private investment for that fiscal year amounted to $194 billion and equaled 19 percent of total private expenditures. The investment rate in the public sector was thus somewhat higher and 24 percent of fixed capital formation was in the public sector.

This definition, however, reflects a very narrow concept of investment. If developmental expenditures, including investment in human resources such as health and education are added in, the public investment figure becomes over twice this amount.[7] Allowing for a corresponding adjustment in the private investment figure, the public investment share may well reach one-third of the total.

C. SUMMARY

Turning to the role of the public sector in determining capital formation and growth, we have examined the place of public saving and the contribution of public investment.

1. Assuming that taxes are drawn from consumption and that borrowing diverts funds from private investment, we noted that public saving equals the excess of tax receipts over current expenditures.

[7] It is interesting to note that this broader concept is now shown in the United States budget. See *The Budget of the United States Government, Fiscal Year 1976, Special Analyses,* p. 59. See also U.S. Bureau of the Census, *Governmental Finances in 1971–72,* pp. 5 and 15.

2. This is the basis for dividing the budget into a current and a capital budget with focus on the state of balance in the current budget.

3. Although taxes, in fact, tend to fall more largely on consumption than does loan finance, no sharp distinction can be drawn. Much depends on what taxes are imposed.

4. Some argument can be made on equity grounds for balancing the current budget while loan-financing the capital budget, but this is not readily applicable at the federal level.

5. Capital expenditures account for a substantial share of public purchases, especially if investment in human resources is allowed for. The public share then roughly equals the corresponding share in the private sector.

Part Six

Fiscal Stabilization

Chapter 24

Fiscal Effects on Aggregate Demand and Employment*

Having considered in the two previous chapters the effects of fiscal policy on capacity or full-employment output, we now turn to fiscal effects upon aggregate

* *Reader's Guide to Chapter 24:* The effects of fiscal policy upon aggregate demand have been at the heart of Keynesian macrotheory. This and the following two chapters address themselves to the role of fiscal policy in controlling aggregate demand. Section A gives the setting to stabilization policy and its concern with both unemployment and inflation. In Sec. B we examine the effect of expenditures and taxes in a simple system of income determination with only consumption variable. The central argument is given in pages 518 to 528. In Sec. C the system is expanded to allow for a variable level of investment and the role of money. Section D turns to the dynamic aspects of the adjustment process. Price level problems are disregarded in this chapter, with changes in the level of demand reflected in changing output and employment. The problem of inflation will be treated in Chap. 25.

demand and thereby upon (1) the level of actual (as distinct from capacity) output, and (2) the level of prices.[1]

A. POLICY TARGETS AND THE ROLE OF AGGREGATE DEMAND

Leaving aside now the problem of capacity growth, the primary objectives of stabilization policy are the assurance of capacity output and price level stability. We first briefly consider what is meant by these objectives.

Policy Targets

Full utilization of economic capacity is obviously desirable, as underutilization involves waste and inequities. This full utilization includes utilization both of the capital stock and of the labor force. In regard to labor, the objective has come to be described as "full employment." But the level of employment, or rate of unemployment, that implies full employment is not obvious. Economists have defined a situation of full employment as one where all people who wish to work at the going wage rate in the labor market will in fact be able to find a job. But the concept is not easy to interpret in practice. To begin with, labor force participation varies, so that for a given adult population the size of the labor force is, in itself, a problematic concept. Moreover, not all those seeking employment will be employed at any one time because, in a changing economy, some persons will always be between jobs or seeking new employment. Retraining may be needed as the structure of employment changes. Cutting across these difficulties, the custom has developed during the sixties to define the full-employment target as a situation where unemployment does not exceed 4 percent of the labor force.[2]

The target of price level stability is more easily defined. Obviously, it does not imply that there should be no changes in *relative* prices. Rather, concern is with the *average* level of prices as measured by the cost of living or some other price index. In the modern economy, prices tend to be rigid in the downward direction, owing to the behavior of money wage rates and other costs. The problem of price level change, therefore, is in practice one of increase or inflation. Inflation is undesirable because it introduces uncertainty and inequities into the economic system. These defects develop because not all prices (whether of products or factors) rise at the same rate. Moreover, the real value of claims (whether money or debt obligations) declines as prices rise, thus resulting in a loss to the creditor and a gain to the debtor. While few would define the policy target as one of absolute price level stability, an increase in excess of, say, 3 percent per annum is generally considered undesirable. As we shall see later, achievement

[1] The tools of analysis used in this and the following chapters are those of basic macrotheory. For a presentation of the basics, see Paul A. Samuelson, *Economics,* 9th ed., New York: McGraw-Hill, 1973, chaps. 11, 12. For further discussion, see Thomas F. Dernburg and Duncan McDougall, *Macroeconomics,* 4th ed., New York: McGraw-Hill, 1972, chap. 14; and Warren L. Smith, *Macroeconomics,* Homewood, Ill.: Irwin, 1970, chap. 10.

[2] In more recent years the 4 percent line has been questioned. With changes in the structure of the labor force, including a larger proportion of females and young people, it is argued that the full-employment target should be adjusted to permit a somewhat higher rate of unemployment.

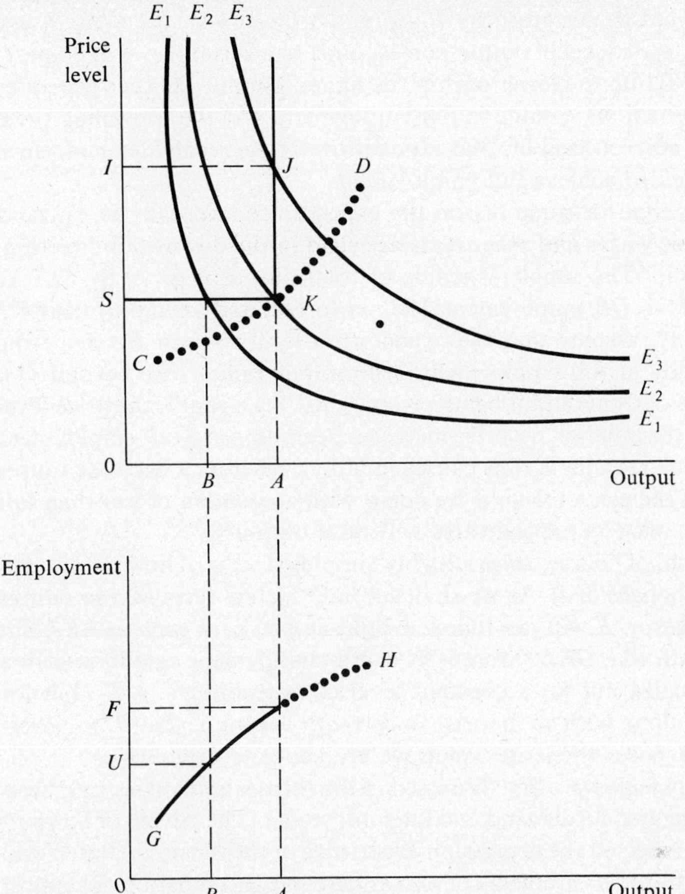

FIGURE 24-1 Aggregate Demand, Output, and Prices.

of the two targets may be in conflict so that a tradeoff between the two has to be considered.

Demand, Output, and Prices

Total expenditures in the economy equal output times prices. Thus we have

$$E = O \cdot P$$

where E is total expenditures or GNP in money terms, O is the amount of goods produced, and P is the price per unit of output.[3] In the upper part of Figure 24-1, where the price level is measured vertically and the output horizontally, this relationship is plotted as a rectangular hyperbola, such as E_2E_2. A higher level

[3] The equation would be self-evident if output contained one product only. Since many different products are involved, O must be thought of as an index of physical output and P as an index of prices.

of expenditures would be described by E_3E_3, and a lower level by E_1E_1. For a given capital stock, each level of output corresponds to a certain level of employment, as shown by *GH* in the lower part of the figure. Output *OA* thus generates employment *OF*, which we assume is full employment. At the prevailing price level *OS*, E_2 is *the* correct level of total expenditure or aggregate demand, since it is the level needed to achieve full employment.

Suppose, now, that for some reason the expenditure level falls to E_1. Also suppose that because wages and other costs are rigid in the downward direction, prices cannot decline. The supply schedule of total output is given by *SK*. As a result, output falls to *OB*, employment declines to *OU*, and unemployment *UF* results. Alternatively, assume that the expenditure level rises to E_3. Since the economy was already at full employment, real output cannot rise beyond *OA*, the supply schedule of total output being given by *KJ*. As a result, the price level rises to *OI*, with *SI* the inflationary price increase. Beginning at a full-employment level of output, an increase in *E* thus causes inflation, whereas a decrease causes unemployment. By the same token, if we begin with a situation of less than full employment, an increase in expenditures will raise output.

This description, of course, gives a highly simplified view of how output and prices respond to changes in *E*. As we shall see later, actual responses in output and prices to changes in *E* will not follow a right-angled path such as *SKJ*, but rather, a curved path like *CKD*. Moreover, a full-employment equilibrium in a growing economy calls, not for a constant level of expenditures at E_2, but for a gradual increase, along with an increase in capacity output beyond *OA*. Nevertheless, Figure 24-1 poses the issue which we are about to examine.

When these problems were first discussed in the thirties and forties, emphasis was upon deficient aggregate demand and unemployment. The advent of Keynesian economics thus reflected the depression experience of the thirties. After World War II, emphasis shifted to problems of excess demand and inflation. The most difficult issue, as economists now see it, is not how to avoid extreme swings in aggregate demand in either direction, but how to deal with "stagflation" and how to steer the economy along a continuous and stable path of high employment with an acceptable degree of price level stability. In pursuing these problems, it would be desirable to deal from the outset with a realistic model of income determination which combines the two contingencies of unemployment and inflation. But this would be too difficult a task. We therefore begin with a setting of substantial unemployment, so that changes in aggregate demand result in a movement along *SK*, being reflected in changing output and employment while leaving prices unchanged. The problem of inflation will be considered in the next chapter.

B. MULTIPLIER MODELS WITH INVESTMENT FIXED

Consider first a simple setting in which consumption is a function of income only and investment is given at a fixed level. We further assume that money wages are downward rigid so that the price level cannot fall, and that there is substantial unemployment of resources so that an increase in aggregate demand will raise

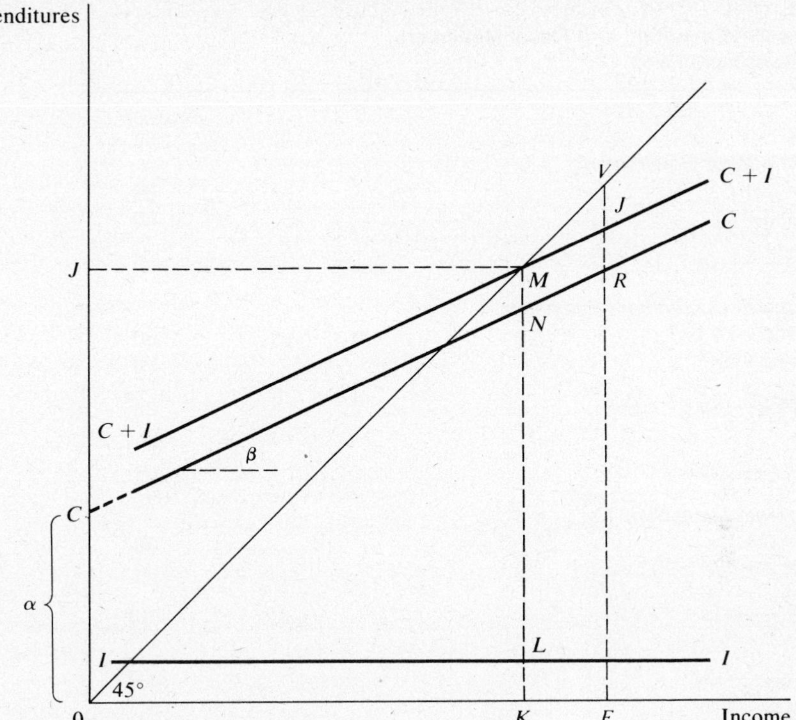

FIGURE 24-2 Income Determination without Government.

real output (income) and employment rather than the price level. Given these assumptions (which will be relaxed later on), we need not concern ourselves with whether the variables under consideration are measured in monetary or in real terms since, without price level change, the two are equivalent.

Income Determination and Budget Policy

We now consider how the equilibrium level of income is determined, first without, and then with, a budget.

Income Determination without Government Income determination, in its simplest form, is shown in Figure 24-2, where income is measured on the horizontal axis and expenditures are measured on the vertical axis. *CC* is the consumption function, showing consumption expenditures to be a rising function of the level of income. Investment expenditures, shown as *II,* are assumed constant and independent of the level of income. By adding *II* to *CC* vertically, we obtain the total expenditure line $C + I$. Equilibrium income is determined where the income received in any one period gives rise to expenditures of an equal amount which, in turn, become the income of the following period. Thus equilibrium income is shown on the diagram where the total expenditure line $C + I$ intersects the 45° line along which expenditures equal income. This point of intersection is at *M,* the equilibrium income level being *OK,* with expenditures equal to *OJ* and

TABLE 24-1
Income Determination and Fiscal Multipliers
(With Investment Fixed)

	Equation No.
System without Government	
$Y = C + I$	(1)
$C = a + cY$	(2)
$Y = \frac{1}{1-c}(a + I)$	(3)
System with Government Purchases	
$Y = C + I + G$	(4)
$C = a + cY$	(5)
$Y = \frac{1}{1-c}(a + I + G)$	(6)
$\Delta Y = \frac{1}{1-c}\Delta G$	(7)
System with Lump-Sum Tax	
$Y = C + I$	(8)
$C = a + c(Y - T)$	(9)
$Y = \frac{1}{1-c}(a + I - cT)$	(10)
$\Delta Y = \frac{c}{1-c}\Delta T$	(11)
System with Income Tax	
$Y = C + I$	(12)
$C = a + c(1 - t)Y$	(13)
$Y = \frac{1}{1 - c(1 - t)}(a + I)$	(14)
System with Government Purchases and Income Tax	
$Y = C + I + G$	(15)
$C = a + c(1 - t)Y$	(16)
$Y = \frac{1}{1 - c(1 - t)}(a + I + G)$	(17)
$\Delta Y = \frac{1}{1 - c(1 - t)}\Delta G$	(18)

$OK = OJ$. At equilibrium income OK, consumption equals KN and saving (or income minus consumption) equals NM. The latter in turn equals investment KL.

In equilibrium, expenditures must equal income so that saving (or income less consumption) must be offset or matched by investment spending. If the level of output (and thus of income) should exceed the level OK, total expenditures will be insufficient to purchase that level of output (i.e., the line $C + I$ lies *below* the 45° line), and output and income will accordingly be reduced to OK. If, on the other hand, the level of output or income should be below OK, total expenditures will exceed the level of current output (i.e., $C + I$ lies *above* the 45° line), with the result that the level of output and income will be increased to OK.

The same story is told in Table 24-1. Equation 1 shows total income to equal

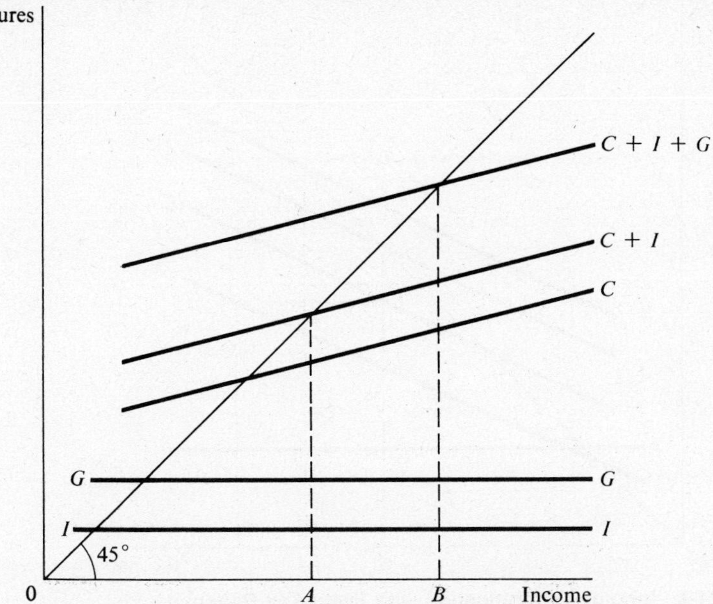

FIGURE 24-3 Income Determination with Government Expenditures.

the sum of consumption and investment, while equation 2 defines the consumption function. The constant term a is the intercept of the CC line in Figure 24-2 with the vertical axis, while the marginal propensity to consume c gives its slope, or tan β. The system is summarized in equation 3 where equilibrium income is obtained by substituting 2 into 1. The fraction $1/(1 - c)$ is the so-called multiplier, and the sum of the constants $(a + I)$ is the multiplicand. If $c = 0.8$, the multiplier is 5, and with a equal to \$50 billion and I equal to \$100 billion, income Y would be equal to \$750 billion.

Returning to Figure 24-2, the resulting equilibrium income OK may be such that at prevailing prices a full-employment output is produced, but this need not be the case. Suppose instead that full-employment income equals OF. If the amount of saving RV which people wish to undertake at this level of income exceeds the given level of planned investment RJ, income must fall until saving is reduced to RJ. Income thus returns to its equilibrium level OK. There is no automatic mechanism in this system which assures that full-employment income is reached and maintained.[4]

Allowing for Government Expenditures We may now introduce government purchases G into our system. As shown in Figure 24-3, these are added to the consumption function along with investment to obtain the total expenditure line $C + I + G$. Introduction of government expenditures thus raises output from OA to OB. An increase in government expenditures, by raising the total

[4] For further discussion, see p. 529, footnote 13.

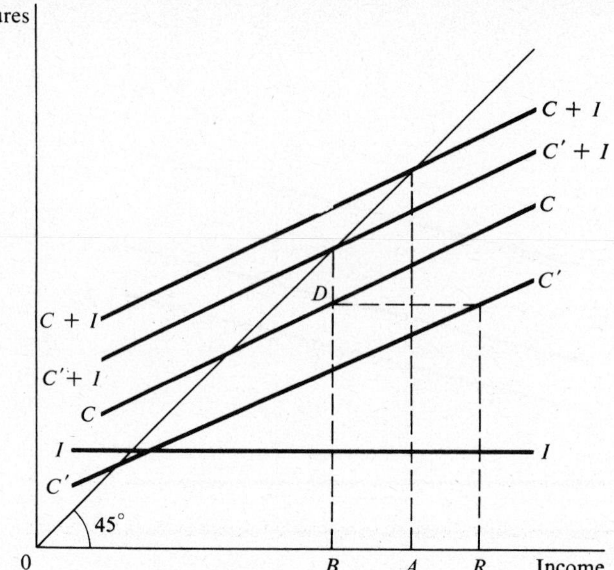

FIGURE 24-4 Income Determination with Fixed Tax Revenue.

expenditure line, may thus be used to raise income. If income is below the level required for full employment, government expenditures may be used to move it there. This is also shown in equations 4 to 7 of Table 24-1. Equations 4 and 5 restate the basic equations, and 6 gives the new income level. Government purchases G become part of the multiplicand. Equation 7, obtained by deducting equation 3 from equation 6, shows the resulting increase in income. With c equal to 0.8, an increase in G of \$1 billion raises equilibrium income by \$5 billion. This increase will be the larger, the greater is the multiplier. The same holds with reversed signs for a decrease in government purchases.

Allowing for Lump-Sum Taxes Next, consider the role of taxes. As shown in Figure 24-4, taxation is first introduced in the form of a lump-sum tax, i.e., a tax of fixed amount, independent of income. Adding II and CC, we obtain the pretax income level OA. Now a tax of revenue BR is introduced. As a result, the consumption function drops from CC to $C'C'$, with the horizontal distance between them equal to BR.[5] Consumption at any level of income falls by the vertical distance between the two. The intersection of the total expenditure line $C'C' + I$ with the 45° line moves down and income falls from OA to OB. A tax reduction in turn, by shifting the $C'C'$ line up to the left, raises the total expenditure line and increases income. Thus taxation, as well as expenditure changes, may be used to adjust the total level of expenditures, and thereby the income and employment levels as well.

The same is also shown in equations 8 to 11 of Table 24-1. In equation 9,

[5] A consumer receiving income OR, after paying BR in tax, has a disposable income equal to OB. His consumption thus equals BD. The new consumption function $C'C'$ is given by $C' = a + c(Y - T)$. While it shows consumption out of before-tax income, it allows for the fact that disposable income is reduced because of tax.

the tax is introduced into the consumption function with the marginal propensity to consume c pertaining to disposable income, or income after tax. In equation 10, we see how the tax reduces the multiplicand. In equation 11, obtained by deducting equation 3 from equation 10 and solving for ΔT, we see how the tax relates to income. Note, however, that the income gain due to a tax cut is less per dollar of tax than was that from an increase in government purchases. While the lump-sum tax does not affect the multiplier, it reduces the multiplicand since the initial change in consumption equals $c\Delta T$ only. Part of the tax reduction is neutralized by its reflection in increased saving rather than in increased consumption. The same argument holds for the effects of a tax increase, which now reduces the level of expenditures less than a corresponding reduction in purchases.

Role of Transfers Transfer payments, as distinct from government purchases G, may, for purposes of this analysis, be viewed as negative taxes. Thus, transfer payments R may be substituted for T in equation 11 but with the sign reversed, showing an increase in R to be expansionary. However, the resulting change in income is again less than for an increase in G. The reason once more is that part of the increase in disposable income due to the transfer payment will be reflected in increased saving rather than in increased consumption expenditures.

System with Income Tax We must now turn to the more realistic case where revenue is obtained from an income tax rather than a lump-sum tax. Introduction of such a tax does not shift the consumption function in a parallel fashion, as occurred with the lump-sum tax, but causes it to swivel downward around its point of intercept. This is so because the tax, and hence the horizontal distance between CC and $C'C'$, increases with income. As a result, the slope of the consumption function, rather than its intercept, is reduced. Expansionary action now calls for a reduction in t.[6] This is shown in Figure 24-5 where CC' is the consumption function before, and CC'' that after tax reduction, with income rising from OP to OF.

This process is shown in equations 12 through 18 of Table 24-1. Note that the way in which the tax enters into the consumption function in equation 13 differs from the case of the lump-sum tax in equation 9, with the result that introduction of the tax now reduces the marginal propensity to consume out of income before tax, and thereby also the multiplier.[7] This result is as one would expect, since tax revenue T now equals tY and is a function of Y. As income rises, so does tax revenue. This depresses disposable income and C, hence checking the

[6] The formula for a change in t corresponding to equation 11 is

$$\Delta Y = -\frac{cY_0}{1 - c(1 - t_1)} \Delta t$$

where Y_0 is the initial level of income and t_1 is the new tax rate.

[7] The relationship between consumption and income as expressed in the consumption function relates to disposable income. With an income tax, disposable income rises by less than before-tax income. As a result, the ratio of incremental consumption to incremental before-tax income is reduced—i.e., the marginal propensity to consume out of income before tax declines.

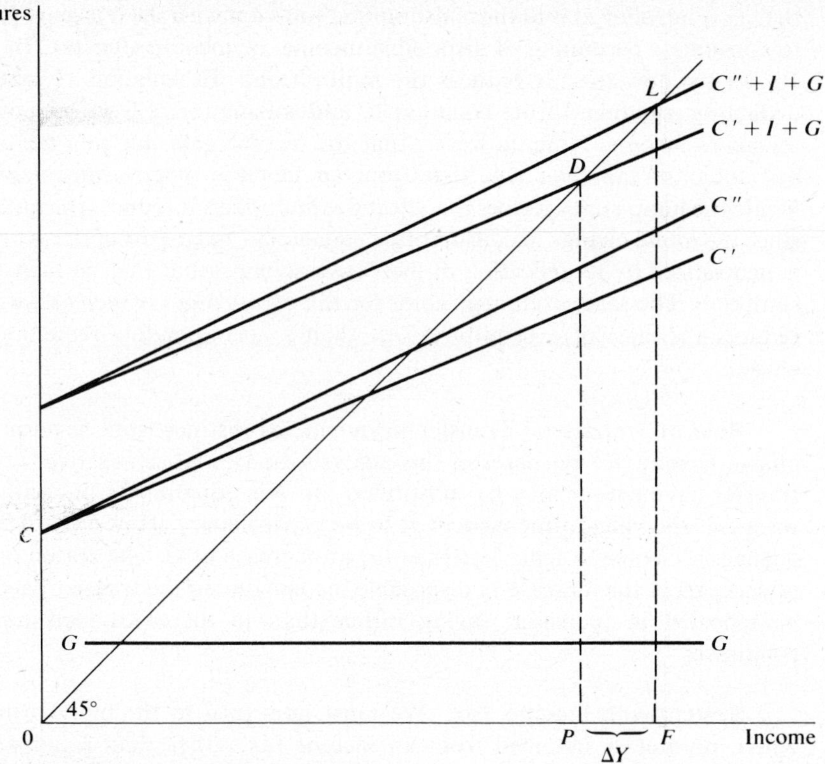

FIGURE 24-5 Tax Reduction with Income Tax.

overall expansionary effect of an increase in G. Thus, with $c = 0.8$, a tax rate of $t = 0.3$ reduces the multiplier from 5 to 2.27. As shown in equation 18, increasing G by \$1 billion now raises Y by only \$2.27 billion. The built-in response of tax yield thus dampens the effectiveness of an expenditure increase.

Balanced Budget Increase Having noted that an increase in expenditures is expansionary while a tax increase is restrictive, we must now consider a balanced budget change such that $\Delta G = \Delta T$. In this case, the gain in income equals $[1/(1-c)]\ \Delta G$, the expansionary effect of increased government purchases, while the decline in income equals $-[c/(1-c)]\ \Delta T$, the restrictive effect of the tax increase. The total effect is $[1/(1-c)]\ \Delta G - [c/(1-c)]\ \Delta G = \Delta G$. The level of income thus rises by just the increase in government purchases and the so-called balanced-budget multiplier may be said to equal 1.0. A balanced increase in the level of the budget operation has an expansionary effect, but on a one-to-one basis only. The enlarging effect of the multiplier is absent in this case.[8]

[8] More detailed analysis will show that this proposition holds only under simplifying assumptions. For instance, the balanced-budget multiplier will differ from 1 if taxpayers' marginal propensities to consume diverge from those of other income recipients. For a further discussion of this and related problems, see Richard A. Musgrave, *The Theory of Public Finance,* New York: McGraw-Hill, 1959, chap. 18.

Differences in Marginal Propensities to Consume

These models help to bring out the nature of expansionary and restrictive adjustments, but they are much too simple. This is true even within the confines of a model in which investment is assumed to be exogenous. Thus we must note that the marginal propensity to consume of various income recipients differs and that saving is undertaken by business firms as well as by households. As we have seen in the preceding chapter, different taxes may depress consumer demand in varying degrees, depending on who pays and how the tax is imposed. While we found the differences in the consumption impact of various personal taxes to be limited, we also noted that the corporation income tax depresses consumption less than do income or sales taxes. But, though differences in the marginal propensity to consume of various taxpayers qualify our argument, they do not change its nature.

Open Economy Aspects

The preceding discussion has viewed the problem in a closed-economy setting. In an open economy, the effectiveness of fiscal policy is reduced substantially by the existence of trade "leakages." This is of particular importance for highly open economies such as Canada or the Netherlands and, as recent years have painfully shown, it also matters for a relatively closed system such as that of the United States. In particular, the open-economy aspect is of importance in developing countries which are highly dependent upon trade.

Expansionary measures, by raising income, lead to increased imports. These increased imports divert purchases from domestic to foreign products, thus adding another leakage from the income-spending stream to that provided by domestic saving and thereby reducing the expansionary effect. Writing E for exports, M for imports, and m for expenditures on imported consumer goods as a fraction of consumption expenditures, c is again the marginal propensity to consume. Letting consumption C include expenditures on imports as well as on domestically produced goods and services, the model underlying equations 15 to 18 in Table 24-1 may be restated as follows:

$$Y = C + I + G + (E - M) \tag{19}$$

$$C = a + c(1 - t)Y \tag{20}$$

$$M = mC \tag{21}$$

$$Y = \frac{1}{1 - c(1 - t)(1 - m)}[a(1 - m) + I + G + E] \tag{22}$$

$$\Delta Y = \frac{1}{1 - c(1 - t)(1 - m)}\Delta G \tag{23}$$

Comparison of equation 23 with equation 18 shows that the multiplier has been reduced by the import leakage.[9] For these and other reasons, including the effects of induced capital movements, it is difficult for a small country with large

[9] To the extent that expansion raises prices, exports (which are here assumed to be unaffected) may decline, thus adding a further cushioning effect.

trade involvement to engage in effective stabilization policy unless cooperative measures are undertaken by other countries operating within the same trading area.[10] Moreover, similar factors explain the inability of state and local governments to undertake stabilization policy and provide the reason why such policy has to be conducted at the central level.[11]

C. MULTIPLIER MODELS WITH INVESTMENT VARIABLE

The next step toward a more realistic view of income determination is to make private investment I an endogenous variable, i.e., determined within the system rather than given from outside. Following the standard Keynesian model, the system of income determination now involves three behavioral relationships: the consumption function, the investment function, and the liquidity preference function.

Income Determination

Such a system is presented in Figure 24-6. The consumption function remains in the same form as was considered in the preceding section, but it is convenient for purposes of this particular diagram to draw it in the form of a savings function, where $S = Y - C$. This is shown by SS in the lower left part of the figure, where saving is measured horizontally and income is measured vertically.[12]

The investment function II shows investment as dependent upon the rate of return or interest. It is drawn in the upper left figure where the rate of return i is measured vertically and the annual amount of investment expenditures is measured on the horizontal axis. The schedule II may be taken to reflect the marginal efficiency of investment as investment proceeds at various annual rates.

In the upper right part of the figure, the liquidity preference function LL is shown, with the interest rate i measured on the vertical axis and the amount of money available for holding as an asset, M_a, measured on the horizontal axis. LL expresses the amount of money which people are willing to hold over and above transactions needs as an alternative to other assets, such as equity and bonds at various levels of interest. The higher the rate of interest or return from investment, the greater is the opportunity cost of holding money balances and the less people will wish to hold. The schedule M_aM_a on the lower right, finally, shows the amount of money which is available for such purposes at various levels of income and a given money supply M. This total may be divided between M_t, or money needed for transactions purposes, and M_a, or money held as an asset to maintain liquidity in the portfolio. Since the need for transactions money M_t rises with the level of money income, the amount left over for M_a declines.

Given these relationships, the equilibrium level of income (here equal to OA) is such that the amount of saving forthcoming from that income, or OB, just equals the level of investment which is made at an interest rate OC. This interest

[10] See p. 571.

[11] See p. 624.

[12] With the consumption function written as $C = a + cY$ and since $S = Y - C$, we have $S = (1 - c)Y - a$.

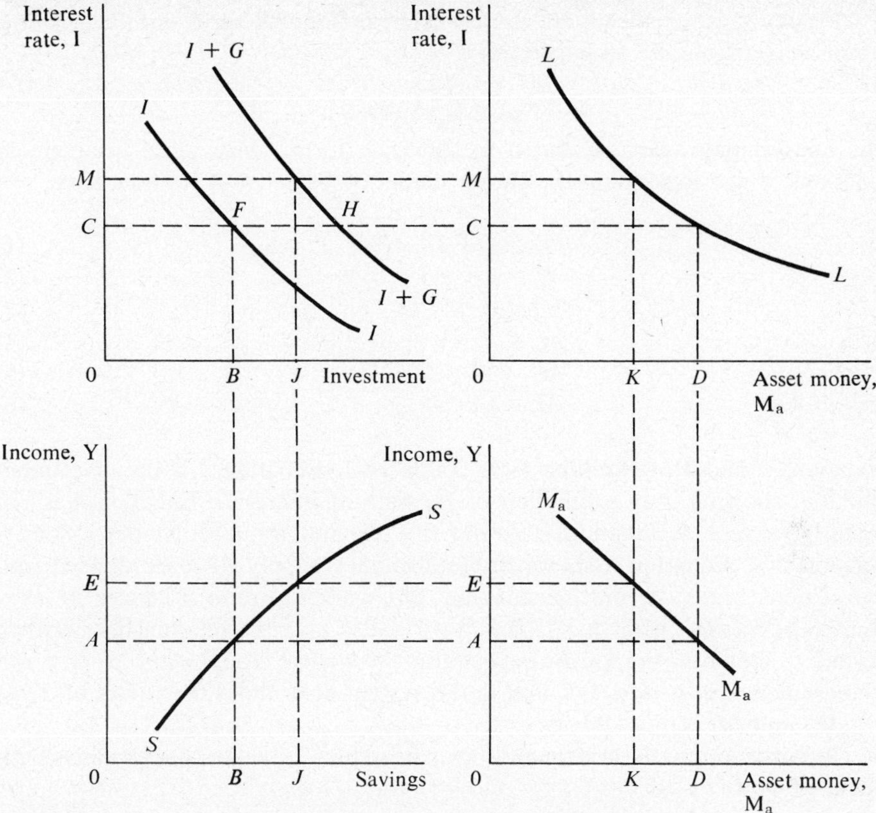

FIGURE 24-6 Income Determination with Investment Endogenous.

rate, in turn, is such that people wish to hold an amount of asset money *OD* which just equals the amount available at income level *OA* and a given money supply *M*. As before, equilibrium income *OA* may fall short of what is needed to purchase the full-employment output at prevailing prices.[13] If this output equals, for instance, *OE*, fiscal measures to raise output and income by an amount *AE* are called for.

We again introduce fiscal variables into the system to see how this can be done. Introduction of government purchases *G* equal to *FH*, when added to the *II* schedule in the upper left figure now permits a level of income with saving equal to $I + G$. Savings rise to *OJ* and income to *OE*, while M_a falls to *OK* and the rate of interest rises to *OM*. The expansion in income in response to government purchases will now be less than it was in the absence of monetary variables. The reason is that the increased need for transactions funds M_t (due to a higher

[13] As explained in the sources given in footnote 1, p. 518, the failure of the system to adjust to a full-employment level of income may be due to various reasons, including (1) an inelastic investment function, and (2) a highly elastic liquidity preference function. Another reason frequently cited is (3) downward rigidity of costs and prices which keep the price level from falling, thereby forestalling a possible upward shift in the consumption function which (provided a wealth term is added to the consumption function) might otherwise result as the real value of money balances rises.

Y) reduces M_a, thus raising the interest rate i and depressing I. The "transaction drain" acts as a brake on expansion.

Fiscal Multipliers

The matter may again be stated in algebraic form. Once more using linear functions,[14] and expanding the earlier model of Table 24-1, we now have:

$$Y = C + I + G \tag{1}$$
$$C = a + c(1 - t)Y \tag{2}$$
$$I = d - ei \tag{3}$$
$$M_a = f - hi \tag{4}$$
$$M_a = M - M_t \tag{5}$$
$$M_t = kY \tag{6}$$

Equations 1 and 2 are familiar from Table 24-1. Equation 3 is the investment function, showing I as a function of the rate of interest i. Equation 4 is the liquidity preference function, showing the demand for asset money M_a as a function of i. Equation 5 shows the total money supply M to be divided into transactions funds M_t and asset money M_a, while equation 6 defines M_t as a fraction of income. Together, equations 5 and 6 give the relationship between M_a and Y shown in the southwest quadrant of Figure 24-6. Given M, G, t and the parameters a, c, d, e, f, h, and k, the system determines the values of Y, C, I, i, M_a, and M_t.

By substitution, the system may again be reduced to multiplier formulas with income defined by

$$Y = \frac{1}{1 - c(1 - t) + ek/h}\left(a + d - \frac{ef}{h} + \frac{eM}{h} + G\right) \tag{7}$$

The change in income due to a change in government purchases G is then given by

$$\Delta Y = \frac{1}{1 - c(1 - t) + ek/h}\Delta G \tag{8}$$

We note that the multiplier in equation 8 is now smaller than in equation 18 of Table 24-1. A large k reduces the multiplier because it makes for a heavy transaction drain as income rises, leading to a fall in M_a, a rise in the interest rate, and hence a decline in investment.

Money Multiplier

By allowing for the role of money, the revised system also offers a further instrument of stabilization policy, i.e., changes in money supply, or ΔM. Returning to Figure 24-5, an increase in M will shift the M_a schedule in the lower right

[14] The functions in Fig. 24-6 are drawn in nonlinear form to give a more general presentation of the Keynesian model.

quadrant to the right. At any given level of Y and transactions demand for money, there will now be more money available for asset holding. At income level OA, more M_a becomes available, so that the interest rate declines in line with the liquidity preference schedule LL. This in turn increases investment and hence the sustainable level of income, i.e., that level at which a correspondingly higher amount of saving is forthcoming.

Returning to equation 7, we may derive a "money multiplier" showing the increase in income with a given increase in money supply. We thus obtain

$$\Delta Y = \frac{e/h}{1 - c(1 - t) + ek/h} \Delta M \tag{9}$$

along with the expenditure multiplier given in equation 8. Monetary and fiscal measures thus offer alternative approaches to aggregate demand control.

As we shall see in the next chapter, the role of money is, in fact, considerably broader than this model allows for. Changes in money supply not only enter via their effect on the rate of interest and investment but also affect consumption expenditures. Moreover, the role of money cannot be appreciated fully until changes in price level and expectations are allowed for. These elements will be taken up in the next chapter.

D. DYNAMIC SYSTEMS

The preceding discussion has traced the effects of fiscal changes upon the level of income by comparing the initial (prechange) level of income with the final (postchange) level. This method—referred to as "comparative statics"—is convenient, but it misses three important aspects of the problem. First, fiscal policy operates in an expanding and not stationary economy. Second, the adjustment process takes time and policy is concerned with how long it takes. If the desired effects come about too slowly, economic conditions may have changed in the meantime and the initial policy may no longer be appropriate. Third, depending on the magnitude of, and lags in, the responses of consumers and firms, a fiscal change may give rise to continuous movement rather than lead to a new static equilibrium of income.

Demand Growth

As we have seen in the preceding chapter, investment results in growth of capacity output. Therefore, the level of aggregate demand must grow as well if full utilization of capacity output is to be maintained. To maintain full employment, fiscal policy must be expansionary to the extent of permitting demand to grow at the same rate as capacity output.

Time Path

To illustrate the time path of adjustment, we return to the simple multiplier model of equations 4 to 7 in Table 24-1. In equation 7, we have seen that an increase in the annual rate of government purchases ΔG raises equilibrium income by $[1/(1-c)]\ \Delta G$. Letting consumption in any one period be a function of income received in the preceding period, we may trace the emergence of this result over successive periods:

Period	*Increase in Income above Initial Level*
1	ΔG
2	$\Delta G + c\Delta G = (1 + c)\Delta G$
3	$\Delta G + c\Delta G + c^2\Delta G = (1 + c + c^2)\Delta G$
n	$\Delta G + c\Delta G + c^2\Delta G + \cdots + c^{n-1}\Delta G$. As n increases, this expression approaches $\frac{1}{1-c}\Delta G$

In period 1, income rises by ΔG only, since consumers have not as yet had time to respend their additional income. In period 2, such respending occurs and adds $c\Delta G$ to the initial increase. In period 3, the additional income received by persons from respending during the second period is also subject to respending so that a further amount equal to $c \cdot c\Delta G = c^2\Delta G$ is added and so forth. Note that the addition becomes less and less as only a fraction c of the additional earnings is respent with $(1-c)$ being saved, thereby becoming a "leakage" from the income stream. Finally, the addition approaches zero and the total gains approach $[1/(1-c)]\Delta G$, as previously shown. In other words, the level of income income rises each period as a lengthening chain of respendings from past periods adds to earnings. But as time proceeds, the spillovers from earlier periods peter out and a higher level of equilibrium income is reached and maintained.[15]

Policy makers need to know how long this multiplier process takes or what fraction of the total gain is realized within, say, a six- or twelve-month period. This depends on the length of the time lags involved. In our simplified model, the only lag considered is that between income receipt and consumption expenditure by the household. In a more complete model, a variety of lags enter, including the lag between receipts and payments by the firm, drawing down and replacing inventory, and so forth. As shown below, the adjustment turns out to be fairly rapid, with a substantial part of the total increase achieved in the first year.

[15] The income determination system may now be rewritten with time subscripts so that (in the absence of taxes)

$$C_t = a + cY_{t-1}$$
$$Y_t = a + cY_{t-1} + I + G$$

In equilibrium,

$$Y_t = Y_{t-1}$$
$$Y = \frac{1}{1-c}(a + I + G)$$

Accelerator

The dynamic nature of the adjustment process was first brought out in connection with the investment function.[16] Whereas in the preceding section investment was shown as a function of the rate of interest, empirical observation has led many observers to depict investment as a function of past changes in income. This is the so-called accelerator type of investment function with investment defined as

$$I_t = b + \beta(Y_{t-1} - Y_{t-2})$$

where n is the time subscript. One interpretation of this formulation is that an increase in GNP or Y calls for increased capacity to produce it, which requires investment.[17] Another interpretation is that investors take the rise in GNP from one year to the next as an indication of future markets and profit prospects and respond accordingly. Adding the accelerator type of investment function to equations 4 and 5 in Table 24-1, we obtain a dynamic system of income change.[18] Not only does an increase in government purchases result in a rise in income due to the operation of the multiplier effects (as derived from the consumption function), but such income increase generates further changes in investment which in turn are subject to the multiplier, giving rise to new consumption and income changes, and so forth. Depending on the values of the marginal propensity to consume and of the accelerator coefficient β, relating investment to income change, the system will move toward a new equilibrium, follow a steady cyclical pattern, or be explosive.

The lag structure is crucial for the behavior of income as determined by this model, and there is no theoretical intuition which tells us just what it should be. This is why theorizing becomes difficult once the dynamic nature of the system is allowed for, and empirical evidence must take over. However, observation tells us that the macroeconomic behavior of the economy is not explosive. Built-in stabilizers exist and income changes tend to level off.

Fiscal Multipliers in Econometric Models

To determine the actual time path of the multiplier effect, one would have to trace out the adjustments over time by use of a model which perfectly describes the

[16] This relationship was first analyzed in a famous article by Paul A. Samuelson, "Interactions between the Multiplier Analysis and the Principle of Acceleration," *Review of Economics and Statistics*, May 1939.

[17] The need for expansion depends upon the size of the existing capital stock and its degree of utilization. Thus a term measuring capacity utilization is frequently added to the investment function.

[18] The model of income determination now reads

$$Y_t = a + cY_{t-1} + b + \beta(Y_{t-1} - Y_{t-2}) + G$$

Depending on the magnitudes of c and β, the accelerator coefficient, the system when disturbed by an increase in G will return to a stable equilibrium, generate a continuing wavelike movement, or become explosive. With $c < 1$ and a small value of β, a change in G produces a fluctuation which tapers off, leading to a new equilibrium level of Y. This is most in line with what actual behavior of the real economy suggests.

TABLE 24-2
Fiscal Multipliers in Econometric Models*

	MULTIPLIER FOR ΔG				MULTIPLIER FOR ΔT		
	Wharton†		*Michigan*	*Dept. of Commerce*	*Wharton†*		*Michigan*
Quarters							
1	1.3		1.4	0.9	0.5		0.6
2	1.6		1.6	1.5	0.7		1.1
3	1.8		1.7	1.9	1.0		1.1
4	2.0		1.7	2.2	1.2		1.2
Years	*(I)*	*(II)*			*(I)*	*(II)*	
1	2.0	1.7	1.7	2.2	1.2	1.0	1.2
2	2.4	1.9	1.4	2.1	1.7	1.4	1.1
3	2.6	1.5	1.1	1.4	1.9	0.9	1.1
4	2.4	1.0	0.9	1.0	1.6	0.5	1.2
5	1.9	0.5	1.1	1.1	1.1	0.2	1.1

* The multipliers show the increase in real GNP as a multiple of a $5 billion increase in real government purchases (ΔG) and a similar reduction in tax yield (ΔT). Results are based on the period 1962–1966 for the Wharton model and on the period from 1962 to 1971 for the Department of Commerce model.

† The quarterly figures and the annual figures under I are based on Wharton quarterly model Mark III, whereas the annual figures listed under II are based on the Wharton annual model.

Sources: Data supplied by Prof. L. Klein. The data are preliminary results from the NSF–NBER Seminar on Comparison of Econometric Models, 1972. See also M. D. McCarthy, *The Wharton Quarterly Econometric Model, Mark II,* University of Pennsylvania, Wharton School of Finance and Commerce, Department of Economics, Economic Research Unit, Studies in Quantitative Economics No. 6, 1972.

workings of the economy. Such an econometric model, alas, is not available, the art of model building and testing still being in a developmental stage. Nevertheless, interesting evidence is available, and comparative data for some of the better known models are given in Table 24-2. While the results for various models are not strictly comparable (since they are not fully standardized with regard to the years on which the models are based), some general conclusions emerge.

The left side of the table shows the multiplier effect of an increase in government purchases, or the ratio $\Delta GNP/\Delta G$ with both G and GNP expressed in real terms to focus on output effects. The various models differ in their speed of adjustment as well as level of response, but it appears that the expenditure multiplier already exceeds 1.0 in the first quarter and that the peak effect is largely reached by the end of the first year. Moreover, we find that the multiplier declines in later quarters. This pattern might be taken as reflecting a developing monetary constraint as well as an increasing absorption into price rise.

The right side of the table shows similar multipliers for a cut in personal taxes. Again, both ΔT and ΔGNP are expressed in real terms. The multipliers are lower and the initial response is somewhat slower, a result one would expect to hold.

Turning now to the magnitude of the multipliers as distinct from their time path, we find that for some of the models the expenditure multiplier is above 2 at its peak, while for others it remains substantially lower. Since these are multipliers which relate the magnitudes in real terms, at least part of this variation is explained by differences in price level responses. Note also that for all the models, the peak multipliers for the tax adjustment are substantially less than for the change in purchases.

In evaluating these ratios, it must be kept in mind that the effects of changes in G or T will depend on the specific economic conditions which prevail, so that the table reflects the conditions of the 1960s on which the data are based. Levels of inventories, capacity utilization, availability of labor, price changes, and accompanying measures of monetary policy all enter and may introduce substantial variations in results.

E. SUMMARY

In considering the general setting of stabilization policy, we have examined its objectives and the key role of aggregate demand.

1. The objectives of full employment and price level stability are readily understood even though some difficulties arise in defining the policy targets precisely.

2. At any given level of prices, a certain overall level of expenditures is needed to secure full-employment output with price stability. An expenditure deficiency results in unemployment while an excess causes inflation.

In order to examine the effects of fiscal policy upon the level of aggregate demand, we begin with a situation of substantial unemployment, where changes in overall expenditures are reflected in changes in real output rather than in prices.

3. Considering first a system in which the level of investment is given and in which there is no government, equilibrium income is determined at a level such that savings which people wish to undertake out of that income equal the given level of investment.

4. Introducing government expenditures and taxes into the system, various multiplier formulas were developed, showing that an increase in expenditures is expansionary, whereas a tax increase is restrictive.

5. Taxes (and in particular, the income tax) the revenue of which moves with income, generate automatic changes in revenue which reduce the multiplier and the expansionary effects of an increase in expenditures.

6. Allowing for differences in the marginal propensities to consume of various taxpayers, the expansionary effect of various tax changes will differ, depending on which taxes are adjusted.

7. In an open economy, the effectiveness of fiscal policy is reduced by import leakage.

The role of fiscal policy was then reconsidered in a setting where the level of investment is itself determined within the system.

8. Fiscal multipliers were shown to be reduced by the monetary transaction drain.

9. Changes in money supply were shown to offer a further instrument of stabilization policy.

10. Investment leads to growth of capacity and thus calls for expansion in aggregate demand over time.

While it is convenient to begin an examination of the effectiveness of fiscal policy by comparing equilibrium positions before and after the fiscal change, a more realistic approach requires one to consider the dynamics of the adjustment process.

11. The effects of fiscal changes on the level of income take time to work out.

12. The magnitude and time path of multiplier effects have been estimated with the use of econometric models.

FURTHER READINGS

Hansen, Alvin: *Fiscal Policy and Business Cycles,* New York: Norton, 1941.

———: *Monetary Theory and Fiscal Policy,* New York: McGraw-Hill, 1949.

Hansen, Bent: *The Economic Theory of Fiscal Policy,* London: G. Allen, 1958.

Samuelson, Paul A.: "The Simple Analytics of Income Determination," in *Income, Employment and Public Policy, Essays in Honor of Alvin Hansen,* New York: Norton, 1948.

Smith, Warren L., and Ronald T. Teigen (eds.): *Readings in Money, National Income and Stabilization Policy,* Homewood, Ill.: Irwin, 1970, sec. 4.

Chapter 25

Aggregate Demand and Inflation*

A. Demand Inflation: *A Simple Model of Demand Inflation; Excess Demand and Money Supply; Implications for Fiscal Policy.* **B. Inflation and Market Structure:** *Bottleneck Inflation; Cost-Push Inflation.* **C. Summary. Appendix: Inflation Model.**

The discussion in the preceding chapter has assumed that changes in aggregate expenditures are reflected in corresponding changes in output and employment. We must now drop this assumption and allow for the possibility of price level change. Since money wage rates are rigid in the downward direction, the possibility of decline in price level (based on falling labor cost) is limited. The problem of price level change is thus primarily one of increase or inflation. But inflation is an ambiguous term, ranging anywhere from a moderate rise in prices of, say, 2 to 4 percent per annum to higher rates of 5 to 12 percent, such as the United States has experienced in recent years, and to still higher levels, such as the 15 to 30 percent experienced in other countries. Beyond this, there is the extreme of runaway inflation where prices may rise by a multiple within a day, such as

* *Reader's Guide to Chapter 25:* This chapter continues the story of aggregate demand effects, now allowing for high employment and resulting inflation. Various types of demand inflation are examined in section A, including the role of money supply and its relation to fiscal policy. In section B, we turn to the more difficult case of market-structure inflation and the recent phenomenon of inflation with unemployment.

occurred in certain European countries following World War I. Our concern here is with the type of inflation which involves an annual price rise of, say, 5 to 10 percent per year. This range falls far short of rampant inflation yet is more than an acceptable price creep.

In tracing the causes of inflation, it is helpful to distinguish between demand (or "pull") and market-structure (or "push") inflation. The former is amenable to restraint by fiscal and monetary measures and indeed may be caused by faulty fiscal or monetary policies. The latter is a difficult problem and is not generally responsive to fiscal and monetary remedies. Although the two causes of inflation interact and cannot be easily separated in practice, a conceptual distinction between the two is useful in formulating policy measures.

A. DEMAND INFLATION

Demand inflation is the most interesting for a study of fiscal policy, because, in both origin and cure, it is related most closely to the fiscal problem.

A Simple Model of Demand Inflation

A first view of the inflation process may be taken using an income determination system similar to that applied in the employment analysis of the preceding chapter. However, we now deal with a situation where the economy is at full employment, i.e., at point K in Figure 24-1, so that a further increase in the level of expenditures leads to a price rise along KJ.

Case I We now assume that government increases its expenditures while holding taxes constant, thus raising the level of aggregate demand. As shown in Figure 25-1, the initial income position is at OY_f, the level where the total expenditure line $C + G$ intersects the 45° line of equality at M. To simplify, we now omit private investment I in the diagram. CC is the after-tax consumption function, and GG shows government purchases.[1] Consumption equals Y_fA and government purchases are $Y_fL = AM$. Let OY_f be the full-employment level of income. Now suppose that the government decides to double purchases from OG to OG', moving the total expenditure line to $C + G'$. Since we assume Y_f to be full employment, any increase in income and expenditures beyond Y_f can be in money terms only, i.e., must be reflected in price rise. Therefore, the resulting expansion in income from Y_f to Y' reflects an inflationary price rise only, with prices going up by Y_fY'/OY_f percent. At the new equilibrium, with income in money terms equal to OY', the government's expenditures have doubled in money terms, but the increase in real terms has been less, since prices have risen. Consumer expenditures have increased in money terms but have fallen in real terms. This is so because consumers are assumed to suffer from a "money illusion," i.e., they fail to allow for price rise and move along their old consumption

[1] These models are based on Arthur Smithies, "The Behavior of Money: National Income under Inflationary Conditions," *Quarterly Journal of Economics,* November 1942. Also see Thomas F. Dernberg and Duncan McDougall, *Macroeconomics,* 4th ed., New York: McGraw-Hill, 1972, chap. 16.

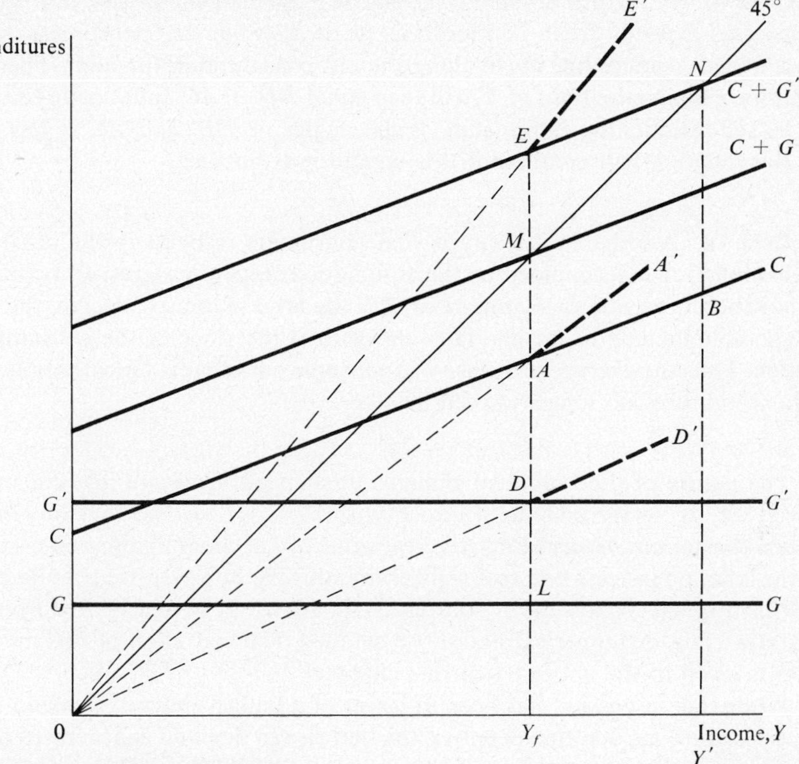

FIGURE 25-1 Inflation Process.

function from A to B. They have suffered an "inflation tax" which has released an increased share in resources to public use.

Case II In the preceding case, inflation was self-terminating because neither the government nor consumers have responded to the price rise. Suppose now that both consumers and government fight back. If government wishes to increase its outlay in real terms from AM to AE and to maintain it there, government expenditures will respond to the price rise and move along DD'.[2] Consumers who experience a rise in money income similarly realize that its real value is unchanged. As a result, the consumption function to the right of Y_f is now given by AA'.[3] The total expenditure line to the right of Y_f, or $AA' + DD'$, thus equals EE'. Note that the slope of EE' is necessarily steeper than that of the 45° line. It will never intersect it, so money income and prices will rise indefinitely in a continuous state of disequilibrium.

[2] Since DD' is the extension of a line from the origin through D, government purchases as shown by DD' are a constant fraction Y_fD/Y_fM for all levels of Y. Since Y remains constant in real terms, so do government expenditures.

[3] The same explanation applies as in footnote 2.

Case III A further possibility is that the government wishes to maintain its increased expenditure in real terms as prices rise, but that consumers do not adjust to rising prices but move along the old consumption function. The total expenditure line to the right of Y_f will then equal $DD' + AC$. Inflation in this case will be self-terminating if the sum of the angles of DD' and AC is less than 45°. But inflation will continue if this condition is not met.

Case IV Another possibility is that consumers respond to the price rise, but that inflation is terminated by the automatic effects of progressive tax rates.[4] As the ratio of revenue to income rises with the level of money income, the ratio of disposable income to income falls and with it the slope of the consumption function. Thus the average propensity to consume out of pretax income falls until total expenditures no longer exceed income.

The nature of the argument remains unchanged if private investment I is allowed for. If, in introducing I into Figure 25-1, we assume that investment remains constant in *money* terms, the real value of I declines as inflation proceeds and the inflation process becomes self-terminating. If, however, we postulate that investment remains constant in *real* terms, inflation will be accelerated from the investment side. A numerical and more detailed demonstration of this inflation model is given in the appendix to this chapter.

While this discussion has been in terms of a budget-induced demand inflation, the same considerations apply if the increase in demand is generated in the private sector. Thus, instead of assuming an upward shift in GG, we may also assume an upward shift in the consumption function (households deciding to save less) or in the investment function (investors' expectations leading them to invest more). Such upward shifts may occur in anticipation of future inflation, thus accentuating the inflation process.

Excess Demand and Money Supply

This description of the inflation process is incomplete. In particular, it does not make adequate allowance for the role of the money supply. This linkage is established by asking how those additional expenditures introduced in the above analysis are to be financed.

The Equation of Exchange There are two ways to finance the additional expenditures—one by making the existing money supply finance a higher volume of transactions, and the other by creating a larger money supply. This is illustrated by the time-honored "equation of exchange," or

$$MV = PQ \tag{1}$$

[4] See p. 379.

where M is the money supply, V is velocity, Q is total output, and P is the price level.[5] Since Q is given by the assumption of full employment, P is a function of MV, or total expenditures. If we assume further that the value of V is also given, then P moves proportionately with M. This is the so-called quantity theory in its crudest form. As such, it is simply a tautology, correct by definition. For the equation of exchange to be of economic interest, it must be shown why V should be constant, or how it is determined.

If the entire money supply were held for transactions purposes, the assumption of a constant V might be acceptable. The velocity of transactions money (previously referred to as M_t) is determined more or less by payments institutions and might be assumed fixed, at least in the short run. But not all money is held for this purpose. Money is also held as an asset, being a component of investment portfolios. The demand for asset money (previously referred to as M_a) is a function of expectations including the outlook for interest rates[6] and, most important in this context, for changes in the price level. Therefore demand is highly volatile, especially in the short run. Since V, as written in equation 1, reflects both the velocity of transactions money and the extent to which the total money supply is used for transactions purposes, it can hardly be assumed constant.[7] Therefore, equation 1 does not explain how the overall level of expenditures will behave as M is changed. Nor does it explain how a change in total expenditures, or MV, will be reflected in a change in either Q or P.

Real Balance Approach In trying to give behavioral content to the equation of exchange, equation 1 has been rewritten in the so-called real balance form, where

$$M = k\,PQ \tag{2}$$

[5] We do not enter here into the detailed questions behind this equation. Since output includes many different products, Q must be understood as an index of physical output and P as an index of prices. There are also the questions of what should be included in M and whether V should be defined as income velocity (as done here) or as transactions velocity, where PQ equals the amount of total transactions involved in producing income (i.e., turnover which exceeds income or value added) plus even those transactions involved in second-hand sales and financial exchanges. An extensive treatment of these problems, basic to much of the modern discussion, will be found in Irving Fisher's noted book, *The Purchasing Power of Money*, New York: A. M. Kelley, Publishers, 1963 (first published in 1911).

[6] Expectations regarding interest rates enter into the explanation of the liquidity preference function (as given in equation 4, p. 530). The demand for money in the context of Keynesian theory is taken to be a function of expected changes in the rate of interest, with interest rates expected to return from the prevailing to a "normal" level. Expectations thus determine the level of interest. However, price level expectations are not allowed for.

[7] This is brought out by rewriting equation 1 as follows:

$$E = V_t M_t$$
$$M = M_t + M_a$$
$$M_a = \alpha M$$

so that

$$E = V_t(1 - \alpha)M$$

where E is total expenditures, V_t is the velocity of transactions money, and α is the fraction of M held as M_a. For any given M, E thus depends on α as well as on V_t.

While k is merely the reciprocal of V, it may be interpreted in a behavioral sense. Rewriting equation 2 as

$$M/P = kQ \tag{3}$$

it may be taken to say that the public wishes to hold a given money supply in real terms (or M/P), the value of which is a fixed fraction k of real output.[8] Suppose that this condition is met to begin with. Now M is increased, so that at a given level of P, the real value of the money supply, or M/P, exceeds kQ. The public, in consequence, will try to get rid of money by spending it, thus driving up P or Q until the value of M/P has fallen to the desired fraction k of Q.

This is a more interesting way of looking at the equation of exchange as it substitutes a behavioral hypothesis for an identity. But the hypothesis of a constant k is too crude a way of describing people's attitude toward holding money. The demand for money is related not only to income but also to wealth; and the fraction of wealth which people wish to hold as money will vary with expectations. Thus the value of k and changes therein, especially in the short run, still remains to be explained. For this purpose, a model such as was used in the preceding chapter is still needed to explain just how expenditures on consumption and investment are determined. However, more adequate allowance must be made for the role of the money supply and the price level. If the model is reformulated accordingly, the formal differences between the Keynesian and the quantity theory models disappear.[9] But the question remains as to which of the underlying relationships [e.g., the size of the multiplier $1/(1-c)$ or the size of velocity V] is more stable and hence more useful for prediction.

The Role of Expectations The problem of inflation, moreover, cannot be understood without making allowance for changing expectations. As prices increase, people will expect them to rise further. Consumers will therefore tend to buy "while prices are still low," thus shifting the consumption function upward. Investors similarly will purchase inventories and equipment to "beat" inflation. This process, if it proceeds at a cumulative rate, leads to runaway or hyperinflation, with velocity taking a sharp, upward turn.

Lenders who expect prices to rise will realize that inflation will erode the real value of their claims. Therefore, they will be willing to lend (to hold debt instruments such as bonds or mortgages) only if the rate of interest is high enough, not solely to yield a normal return but also to compensate for the price rise. Thus, an excessive increase in money supply—by leading to increased ex-

[8] Equation 3 is also referred to as the Cambridge equation, reference being to Cambridge, England. This is the version of the quantity theory which has been developed by British economists, including Marshall, Pigou, and Robertson.

[9] For a modern restatement of the quantity theory which provides a more detailed view of the relation of money supply to the overall level of money expenditures, see Milton Friedman, "The Quantity Theory of Money: A Restatement," in *Studies in the Quantity Theory of Money,* Chicago: The University of Chicago Press, 1956; and Don Patinkin, *Money, Income and Prices,* 2d ed., New York: Harper & Row, 1967.

penditures, price rise, and inflationary expectations—will also lead to an increase in nominal interest rates. If the rate of interest in the absence of price rise is 3 percent and an 8 percent rate of price increase is expected, the nominal rate of interest will rise to 3 + 8, or 11 percent, so as to ensure a real return of 3 percent. This explains what has happened in recent years when rising interest rates coincided with expanding money supply. This pattern sharply differs from our earlier model where, with unemployment and constant prices, an increase in money supply tended to reduce the rate of interest.

Implications for Fiscal Policy

The significance of these approaches for fiscal policy and stabilization is easily seen. If the nature of the economy were such as described in equation 1 with V fixed, only changes in the money supply would matter. Changes in budgetary policy could affect overall expenditures only through their effect on the money supply. This situation would be the very opposite of that visualized in early Keynesian discussion, where the demand for money was assumed to be infinitely elastic, so that a change in money supply was without effect on interest rates and the level of expenditures. While the first extreme is more descriptive of a boom situation and the latter of a severe depression, neither extreme does, in fact, apply. The values of V or k may vary, and both fiscal and monetary policy will be effective tools in the conduct of stabilization policy.[10]

There is, in fact, a close relationship between the two. An increase in expenditures or a tax deduction tends to result in a budgetary deficit which somehow must be financed. This financing may be done by borrowing outstanding funds, thereby drawing such funds away from their use by private borrowers. In this case, the money supply remains unchanged. Or the financing may be handled by increasing the money supply. In so doing, the government may simply resort to the printing press; it may borrow from the Federal Reserve; or it may borrow from the commercial banking system while enabling it (with support of the Federal Reserve) to expand credit. In all these methods, the money supply is increased and policy will be more expansionary. The expansionary effects of fiscal measures thus depend greatly on how the increase in debt is financed. Similarly, the effects of restrictive measures depend on how the surplus is used, i.e., whether to retire outstanding debt or whether to reduce the money supply.[11] In this way a direct link is established between fiscal and monetary policies. In conducting fiscal policy so as to maintain a noninflationary level of aggregate demand, consideration must be given not only to setting an appropriate level of expenditures and revenues, but also to the way in which the deficit is financed or the surplus is disposed of. Moreover, all these factors must be adjusted to the rate at which credit is made available to private borrowers through the banking system.

[10] Thus, neither the fiscalist nor the monetarist approach can be accepted as the only gospel. Historians of economic theory a hundred years hence may be amused, therefore, by the tenacity with which these opposing traditions have continued to influence the thinking of macroeconomists, be it on the Cambridge (Mass.) or the Chicago side of the fence. Vested interests in theories, unlike old soldiers, do not fade away easily.

[11] For further discussion of debt management policies, see p. 594.

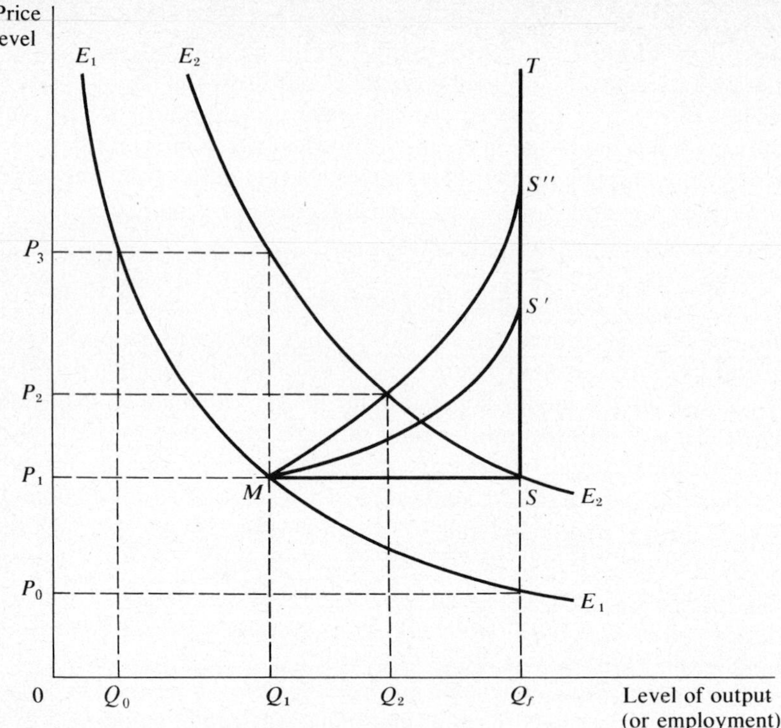

FIGURE 25-2 Expenditures, Prices, and Output.

B. INFLATION AND MARKET STRUCTURE

So far, we have focused on the level of aggregate demand and output without dealing with the role of relative prices. While the inflation problem is concerned with changes in the general price level, the pattern of demand is, nevertheless, an important factor, and changes in relative prices may be the vehicle of price level change. We now turn to the role of relative prices, including prices in the product and the factor markets.

Bottleneck Inflation

A first aspect of this problem may be referred to as bottleneck inflation. It arises while the economy still has potential excess capacity but expansion proceeds at too fast a rate for output to respond adequately and sporadic shortages develop. Such a situation is shown in Figure 25-2. As previously shown in Figure 24-1, the level of output (or employment) is measured along the horizontal axis, and the level of prices is shown on the vertical axis. Line E_1E_1 is again a rectangular hyperbola that represents the various combinations of price level and output which are possible at a given level of expenditures E_1. But a more careful view is now taken of the supply side of the picture. Suppose that with expenditure level E_1, the price level is P_1. Output then equals Q_1, and we are at point M on the E_1E_1 curve. Suppose further that full-employment output equals Q_f, leaving an output and employment gap equal to Q_1Q_f. To raise employment, expenditures must be increased. If the supply schedule of total output were infinitely elastic along *MS*, the appropriate increase in expenditures would be to E_2, as shown by the curve E_2E_2. Unfortunately, this is not the case. As expenditures are raised to E_2, output will move along a supply schedule such as MS'. Thus, output rises to Q_2 while the price level rises to P_2. The reason is that since it takes time for output to respond to the increase in expenditures, the latter will be reflected only partly in increased output, with the remainder going into increased price.[12] The slope of the short-run aggregate supply schedule thus depends on how rapidly expenditures are increased. If MS' reflects the response to an increase in aggregate demand from E_1 to E_2 within one year, the response to the same increase within six months might be reflected by a supply schedule such as MS''. If the expansion in expenditures takes place over a longer period, inventories can be replaced and workers can be moved among jobs, so that the aggregate supply schedule MS' becomes more elastic.

The more gradual the expansion, the more elastic will be the aggregate supply schedule along which the economy moves. If expansion proceeded extremely slowly so that all bottlenecks could be avoided by the necessary shifts in resources, the short-run supply schedule would assume an angular form as shown by *MST*, but in practice it does not do so. Any substantial expansion will involve some rise in prices, but if expansion proceeds at a moderate rate, this is not a serious matter. An excessive rate of expansion, such as developed in the United States economy of 1967–68, on the other hand, generates bottleneck inflation.

Cost-Push Inflation

We now turn to a second type of inflation. It arises not because a "demand pull" is exerted by an excessive level of aggregate demand or too fast an expansion, but because the market structure permits a type of wage and price behavior which results in a "cost-price push." This is a type of instability which, unfortunately, is more difficult to deal with.

Causes of Cost-Push The cost-push type of inflation occurs because the suppliers of factors of production (be it labor or capital) demand, and succeed in obtaining, shares in the national income which add up to more than 100 percent of the total. At high levels of unemployment, unions will be more aggressive in their wage demands and will tend to insist on raises in excess of productivity gains. Employers, similarly, will be more likely to pursue an aggressive price policy and to grant wage demands more readily, feeling that increased costs can be passed on in a sellers' market. Thus, the existence of market power, combined with the knowledge that government will not permit general unemployment to occur, generates a situation in which excess demand is created and perpetuated by subsequent upward adjustments in prices and wages.

Indeed, what appears to be genuine cost-push may simply be the response

[12] To simplify, we overlook the fact that with excess capacity, increased output may reduce average fixed costs, so that over a certain range the aggregate supply schedule may decline.

of the price-wage structure to an initial demand-pull. Thus, an initial increase in government or other types of spending creates excess demand in the product market and pulls up prices. Any attempt to increase output in turn creates excess demand in the labor market and raises wages. This in turn increases demand and the cycle starts anew. Once this process has been set into motion, it is difficult to know whether what one observes is essentially an adjustment to demand-pull or the consequence of an initial cost-push situation.

Phillips Curve In line with these forces, periods of high employment may be expected to be associated with relatively high rates of price increase. This relationship, first demonstrated for the United Kingdom by A. W. Phillips, has come to be known as the Phillips curve.[13] In estimating the Phillips curve, the problem may be formulated in various ways (including, in particular, a distinction between short- and long-run responses) so that its precise shape is controversial. In the very short run, developments are largely determined by recent events, so that no general relationship can be derived. For the longer run, the problem is illustrated by the recent estimates shown in Figure 25-3. These estimates suggest that a 4 percent unemployment rate is associated with an inflation rate of somewhat less than 4 percent, while an unemployment rate of 5 percent tends to go with a price rise of 2 percent only. The steeply rising slope of the Phillips curve to the left of the 4 percent rate of unemployment thus suggests that the 4 percent target itself is precariously close to a position of severe instability.[14] Thus we have come to experience the coexistence of inflation with unemployment and the slow growth of real income, a phenomenon which has come to be known as "stagflation."

The Phillips curve idea, however, should not be overdone. While the data show a negative relationship between price rise and unemployment, this relationship has not been stable. In particular, the pattern applicable to the fifties and early sixties seems to lie to the left (in terms of Figure 25–3) of that applicable to the later sixties and seventies. The curve, it appears, has shifted to the right thus making the task of stabilization policy more difficult.[15]

Stagflation A related phenomenon is the occurrence of "stagflation," a term coined in response to the developments of the seventies. It describes a situation where the economy moves into a recession or depression, while continuing a substantial rate of inflation. Such a development may be explained once more by a complex lag structure, where cost-push pressures for inflation continue even though a recessionary decline in the real level of demand has set in. This decline may be strengthened by rising interest rates, uncertain expectations, and other consequences of price rise. Beyond this, the economy may settle down (i.e.,

[13] A. W. Phillips, "The Relation between Unemployment and the Rate of Change of Money Wage Rates in the United Kingdom, 1862–1957," *Economica,* November 1958. For further discussion, see Warren L. Smith, *Macroeconomics,* Homewood, Ill.: Irwin, 1970, chap. 16.

[14] This estimate, it should be noted, relates to the long-run relationship between unemployment and inflation, with the short-run inflation rate dominated by past cost and price changes rather than by the employment level. See our previous comments on the 4 percent target, footnote 2, p. 518.

[15] For a convenient chart and discussion, see *Economic Report of the President,* 1975, p. 94.

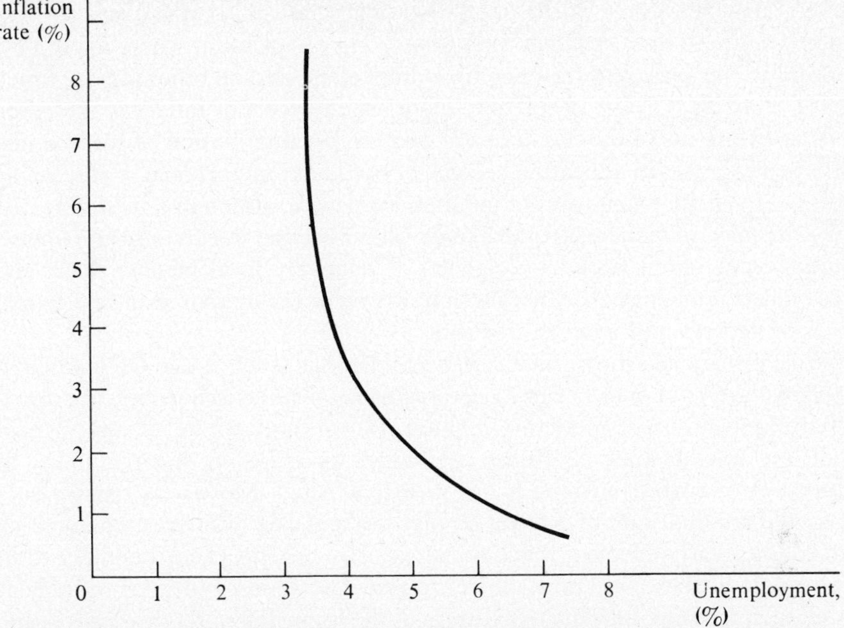

FIGURE 25-3 Long-run Phillips Curve for the United States (1955–72 data base).

Source: Otto Eckstein and Roger Brinner, *The Inflation Process in the United States,* Joint Economic Committee, Feb. 22, 1972, U.S. Government Printing Office, Washington, D.C., 1972. See p. 41, schedule 2.5.

come to stagnate) at a substantial level of unemployment, while retaining a considerable rate of inflation. Such a setting fits neither the classical nor the Keynesian mold, and the appropriate set of policy prescriptions must be reconsidered.

Fiscal Response Given such a situation, what can be done by way of fiscal and monetary policy to meet the dilemma? Suppose now that Q_1 in Figure 25-2 reflects full employment. With expenditures of E_1, the price index equals P_1. Now assume that cost developments push prices to P_3. The policy response can be along various lines. One possibility is to maintain high employment despite rising prices, i.e., to underwrite the cost-push by letting aggregate demand rise to E_2. If this is done, excessive wage and profit demands will be encouraged as the parties are led to expect that there is no danger of pricing oneself out of the market. Thus, faster cost-push may be encouraged. The other possibility is to hold aggregate demand constant so as to choke off the price rise while permitting output and employment to fall to OQ_o. The two evils must be balanced and public policy should choose that point on the Phillips curve which is most compatible with the relative values attached to high employment and price level stability, adjusting aggregate demand accordingly.

The question, then, is how the desirable mix should be determined. On the one side there are the social costs of unemployment and the economic cost of forgone GNP. The latter can be measured fairly easily, but the social costs of unemployment are more difficult to appraise. They depend on where unemployment hits, on the average duration of unemployment, and on other factors which are hard to assess. On the other side, there are the costs of inflation, including distorting effects on resource allocation and on the distribution of income and wealth. Inefficiencies in allocation become of particular importance in developing countries, especially when rates of inflation are severe, although a moderate rate of price rise may, in fact, be favorable to development and the investment climate. Inequities come about because recipients of relatively fixed income suffer and because inflation changes the distribution of wealth (as measured in real terms) in favor of debtors and against creditors.

While history has shown that runaway inflations (such as the German inflation following World War I) can have disastrous social consequences, the distributional implications of moderate inflation (at an annual rate of, say, 3 or 4 percent) are less obvious. As prices rise, wages also rise, so that the ability to consume out of current income is not greatly affected. Moreover, rising prices push up the nominal rate of interest so that the real rate of interest obtained by savers is not greatly affected. Since social security benefits (and the upper limit of the payroll tax base) are now subject to price escalation and since retirement plans increasingly link benefits to earnings in the immediate preretirement years, retirement savings as well have come to be largely insulated against price rise. Furthermore, the option of borrowing (which offers an inflation hedge) has become available to an increasingly broad group through home ownership. For these reasons, the distributional distortions resulting from a moderate rate of inflation may be exaggerated. Nevertheless, a reasonable degree of price level stability remains an essential policy objective; and the severe difficulties encountered in finding ways of combining it with high employment may well prove to be the Achilles heel of decentralized economic systems.

Structural Measures Stabilization policy (whether fiscal or monetary) cannot solve the problem by itself. A solution must be found in measures which will change market structures so as to improve the tradeoff, i.e., to shift the Phillips curve to the left and flatten its slope.

One approach would be to reduce market power by limiting the role of unions and breaking up the dominant position of large corporations. Chances are that this action would not be possible to a sufficient degree. The alternative is to make existing institutions function better by introducing constraints which will narrow down the scope for excessive claims on the national income. This approach might involve a variety of measures ranging from "jawboning" over informal wage-price guidelines and public hearing boards to mandatory wage-price (or wage-profit) regulations of various degrees of comprehensiveness and severity. The basic problem is to reach a consensus on how a fair distribution of the gains in income among factor shares may be accomplished. All these measures pose important and difficult policy problems but they are not primarily in fiscal nature.

C. SUMMARY

Turning to the inflation side of the stabilization problem, we have distinguished between demand inflation and market-structure inflation. Demand inflation is the more important for fiscal policy because it is the type of inflation which may be both caused and checked by fiscal measures.

1. An increase in government expenditures at full employment, followed by a policy of maintaining government expenditures in real terms, generates continuing inflation. But inflation will be self-terminating if consumers continue to spend the same fraction of their income, even though its real value declines.

2. An adequate explanation of the inflation phenomenon calls for fuller consideration of the role of money supply.

3. The equation of exchange, as redefined by the real balance approach, offers a useful insight, but the V or k coefficients cannot be assumed constant, and it remains to be explained how the level of expenditures is determined.

4. Inflation is a process of change and expectations with regard to further price rise, based on past experience, play a major role.

5. Since an increase in money supply raises the level of expenditures, the financing of deficits (or the use of surplus revenue) is of importance for the conduct of fiscal policy; and so is the coordination of fiscal and monetary policies in regulating the supply of credit to private borrowers.

The inflationary effects of an increase in aggregate demand depend upon market structures, and changes in costs and prices generated in imperfect markets may be a causal factor in the inflation process.

6. Inflation of the bottleneck type may arise if the level of demand is expanded too rapidly.

7. Cost-push inflation may arise because claims to income, put forward in an imperfect market, exceed 100 percent of national income. Government is then confronted with the choice between maintaining a high level of employment while permitting prices to rise, or with maintaining price stability while inducing unemployment.

8. The process by which demand inflation is transmitted through the system depends on lags in wage and price adjustments.

9. The relationship between the rate of unemployment and the rate of inflation is described by the Phillips curve.

10. Simultaneous achievement of both high employment and price level stability requires structural measures as well as an appropriate control of aggregate demand.

FURTHER READINGS

Eckstein, Otto, and Roger Brinner: *The Inflation Process in the United States,* Joint Economic Committee, U.S. Congress, Washington: Government Printing Office, Feb. 22, 1972.

Friedman, Milton: "The Quantity Theory of Money: A Restatement," in *Studies in the Quantity Theory of Money,* Chicago: The University of Chicago Press, 1956.

Tobin, James: "Inflation and Unemployment," *American Economic Review,* March 1972.

TABLE 25-A1
Inflation Model with Constant Budget Share

	EQUILIBRIUM $g=0.33;\ c=0.8;\ t=0.17$			INFLATIONARY EXPANSION $g=0.4;\ c=0.8;\ t=0.17$			STABLE EXPANSION* $g=0.4;\ c=0.8;\ t=0.20$
Income Determination	*Year 1*	*Year 2*	*Year 3*	*Year 4*	*Year 5*	*Year 6*	*Year 4 on*
1. $C_n = c(Y_{n-1} - T_{n-1})$	667	667	667	667	738	817	600
2. $G_n = gY_n$	333	333	333	444	492	545	400
3. $Y_n = C_n + G_n$	1,000	1,000	1,000	1,111	1,230	1,362	1,000
4. $T_n = tY_n$	170	170	170	189	209	232	200
5. $D_n = G_n - T_{n-1}$	163	163	163	274	303	336	130
6. $S_n = Y_{n-1} - T_{n-1} - C_n$	163	163	163	163	303	336	130
7. $\Delta Y = Y_n - Y_{n-1}$	—	—	—	111	119	132	—
8. $P = \dfrac{100\,Y_n}{Y_1}$	100	100	100	111	123	136	100
9. Percentage change in P	—	—	—	11	11	11	—

* Based on the assumption that the increase in tax rate from 0.17 to 0.20 is effective in year 3.

Notation: g = ratio of government purchases to income; c = average propensity to consume; t = tax rate; C = consumption; T = tax revenue; G = government purchases; Y = income; S = private savings; D = budget deficit; P = price level index.

APPENDIX: Inflation Model

A numerical illustration of budget inflation, similar to the models of Figures 25-1 and 25-2, is given in Table 25-A1. This particular model, the details of which are given in the first column of the table, is one which generates a continuous rate of inflation. The consumption function (line 1) is now written in lagged form with this year's consumption depending on last year's income. Government expenditures (line 2) are a fixed fraction g and tax revenue (line 4) a fraction t of current income.[16] The deficit equals the difference between this year's expenditures and last year's revenue (line 5). Line 6 defines saving and line 7 the income change. Line 8 is the price index and line 9 gives the change therein. To simplify, private investment is omitted.

Given the values for g, c, and t shown in the equilibrium column, the economy has a stable level of income. Since the propensity to spend for the economy as a whole, or $g+(1-t)c=1$, expenditures in year 2 equal income in year 1 and income remains unchanged at $1,000. Since we assume full employment, this money income equals full-employment output times the price level. At the outset of year 4, the government decides to raise g to 0.4. As a result the total spending propensity exceeds 1, expenditures rise, and hence money income rises. Since prices rise also, government expenditures must be increased further in year 5 to be maintained at 40 percent of total expenditures. An inflation process is under way, with income and expenditures continuing to rise by about 11 percent per year.[17]

This development could have been avoided, as shown in the last column, if the government had raised its tax rate from 0.17 to 0.20 in the third year. In this case, spending propensities, or $g+(1-t)c$, would have been maintained at 1.0.

[16] There being no constant term in the consumption function, the average propensity to consume equals the marginal propensity and is constant so that the previously considered issue of money illusion does not arise. See p. 538.

[17] Money income Y equals Q (real output) times P, the price level. Thus, $P=Y/Q$. But since we are dealing with a constant, full-employment level of real output, the annual rate of price increase is given by the annual rate of increase in money income. Thus the percentage change in prices is given by:

$$\frac{P_n-P_{n-1}}{P_{n-1}}=\frac{Y_n-Y_{n-1}}{Y_{n-1}}=\frac{c(1-t)}{1-g}$$

In our example, during the inflationary years 4 to 6, $c=0.8$, $t=0.17$, and $g=0.4$, and an annual rate of price increase of approximately 11 percent results.

Chapter 26

Applications of Stabilization Policy*

A. Fiscal Leverage: *Level of Leverage; Alternative Policy Mixes with Equal Leverage; Change in Leverage.* **B. The Role of Built-in Flexibility:** *Parameter Change versus Built-in Response; Cushioning Effect of Built-in Changes; Is Built-in Flexibility Desirable?; When Is Fiscal Policy Expansionary?; Effects of Fiscal Expansion on Deficit; Inflationary Gap.* **C. Fiscal Policy Alternatives:** *Policy Lags; Priority for Tax Adjustments?; Choice among Tax Alternatives; Perverse Effects of Tax Changes; Rules versus Discretion; Formula Flexibility.* **D. The Mix of Fiscal and Monetary Policy:** *Policy Instruments and Policy Targets; Domestic Aspects; Open Economy Aspects.* **E. Summary. Appendix:** *Changes in Income, Leverage, and Full-Employment Budget.*

In this chapter we examine a variety of issues which arise in the application of fiscal policy, including the measure of fiscal leverage, the role of built-in flexibility, and the choice among alternative policy instruments.

A. FISCAL LEVERAGE

To develop a realistic measure of fiscal leverage involves all the complexities which determine the response of the private sector to fiscal changes.[1] However,

* *Reader's Guide to Chapter 26:* The framework of fiscal policy analysis developed in the two preceding chapters is applied here to an examination of policy issues. Section A once more makes use of simple multiplier formulas in exploring the concept of fiscal leverage, while the remainder of the chapter is less technical.

[1] For a full discussion, see Bent Hansen, *Fiscal Policy in Seven Countries, 1955–65,* Paris: Organization for Economic Cooperation and Development, 1969. OECD, 1969.

the nature of the problem may be brought out with the help of the simple multiplier formula developed in section A of Chapter 24.

Level of Leverage

In measuring the extent to which the presence of the public sector affects the level of income, we compare the level of income Y_p which prevails with a public sector, with the level of income Y which would prevail without it. The difference, to which we refer as "fiscal leverage," thus equals

$$L = Y_p - Y \tag{1}$$

Substituting for Y_p and Y from equations 3, 6, and 10 in Table 24-1, we have

$$L = \frac{1}{1-c}(a + I + G - cT) - \frac{1}{1-c}(a + I) \tag{2}$$

so that

$$L = \frac{1}{1-c}(G - cT) \tag{3}$$

If we think of Y_p as the full-employment level of income, then L is the level of leverage required to be at full employment. A corresponding definition of leverage may be given for a system with income tax.[2]

To see how the budgetary deficit and surplus enter the picture, we note that

$$D = G - T \tag{4}$$

and, by substituting equation 4 into equation 3, that

$$L = G + \frac{c}{1-c} D \tag{5}$$

Leverage thus consists of two parts, the first corresponding to the balanced-budget multiplier and the second being added because part of G is deficit-financed.[3]

[2] See footnote 11 below.

[3] The concept of deficit as here defined is the deficit in the total budget and thus differs from the previously discussed balance in the current budget. See p. 509. This deficit (or surplus) in turn equals the excess of saving over investment (or investment over saving) in the private sector. Thus

$$Y = C + I + G$$
$$Y = C + T + S$$

so that

$$T - G = I - S$$

The equality of $T - G$ and $I - S$ may be interpreted in two ways. One view is to see it as an identity which follows from the nature of the national income accounts, while the other (used here) views it as an equilibrium condition. In other words, for any given level of income to be maintained, the budget deficit (surplus) must equal the excess (shortfall) of saving out of that level of income over (below) the level of investment in the private sector.

Returning to equation 3, we note that to obtain any given leverage, the appropriate levels of G and T are interrelated. Thus, if G is set, T follows. Moreover, once G and T are given, D follows. Thus, out of all three fiscal variables, G, T, and D, only one can be chosen to satisfy a given level of L and the other two will follow.

Alternative Policy Mixes with Equal Leverage

This relationship is illustrated in the following table. Based on

$$Y = \frac{1}{1-c}(I + G - cT)$$

it shows alternative combinations of G, T, and D which are designed to maintain income Y at 100 while assuming $c = 0.75$ and $I = 10$. Since without budget $Y = 40$, the required value of leverage L is 60. If we want to specify for a system in which the required revenue T is obtained from an income tax, we can substitute $T = tY$, so that both T and t are recorded in the table.[4]

ALTERNATIVE BUDGETS FOR FULL EMPLOYMENT

	(I)	*(II)*	*(III)*	*(IV)*	*(V)*
C	75	70	60	50	30
I	10	10	10	10	10
G	**15**	**20**	**30**	**40**	**60**
Y	100	100	100	100	100
T	**0**	**6.7**	**20**	**33.3**	**60**
D	**15**	**13.3**	**10**	**6.7**	**0**
c	0.75	0.75	0.75	0.75	0.75
t	**0**	**0.067**	**0.20**	**0.33**	**0.60**

In column I, we begin with a zero T or t, with total government purchases of 15 being deficit-financed. As we move to the right, G is raised with the necessary T or t increasing (if you wish, T or t is raised with the necessary G also rising), while the deficit D declines. In the last column, government purchases have increased to 60 and are totally tax-financed, with the deficit down to zero, thus showing the operation of the "balanced-budget multiplier."

Change in Leverage

A more realistic view of the same problem may be taken by considering changes in fiscal leverage, rather than the absolute level of leverage which attaches to the total budget. Thus, if Y is the initial level of income with given values of G and

[4] In this case, the table may be derived from

$$Y = \frac{1}{1 - c(1-t)}(I + G)$$

with T derived from $T = tY$. Since we deal with a fixed level of income and a given level of I, the T and t formulations give the same result.

T, while Y' is the desired income level, the change in leverage required to reach Y' or

$$\Delta L_r = Y' - Y \tag{6}$$

is obtained by rewriting (3) in terms of change, so that for a system with lump-sum tax

$$\Delta L_r = \frac{1}{1-c}(\Delta G - c\Delta T) \tag{7}$$

As before, in order to obtain ΔL_r, the policy maker can set either ΔG or ΔT, but not both. Thus, for a given value of ΔT, we have to set the change in government expenditures so that

$$\Delta G_r = (1-c)\,\Delta L_r + c\,\overline{\Delta T} \tag{8}$$

and with a given value of ΔG, the required change in tax revenue is

$$\Delta T_r = \frac{\overline{\Delta G} - (1-c)\,\Delta L_r}{c} \tag{9}$$

More will be said later in this chapter regarding the more complicated problem of measuring change in leverage in a system with income tax.

B. THE ROLE OF BUILT-IN FLEXIBILITY

In dealing with changes in the values of G and T, an important distinction must be drawn between (1) changes in G and T which reflect changes in expenditure programs or tax rates, i.e., changes in "fiscal parameters" and (2) changes in G and T which are due to built-in flexibility, i.e., automatic responses to changes in the private sector. Changes in the level of Y, resulting from a private sector change such as a change in I, will depend on these responses in G and T. As we shall presently see, the distinction between parameter changes and built-in changes is important in interpreting changes in the budget picture during any given period.

Parameter Change versus Built-in Response

On the expenditure side, an expansionary *parameter* change, also referred to as a discretionary change, is illustrated by the introduction of a new expenditure program or the expansion of an old program. Thus, a new public works program may be instituted or the weekly benefit level of unemployment insurance may be raised. On the revenue side, a parameter change may involve the removal of an old tax or a reduction in tax rates. Corresponding illustrations of restrictive parameter changes include discontinuation of expenditure programs or increases in tax rates.

As distinct from these adjustments, a *built-in* change on the expenditure side is illustrated by a change in the level of benefit payments due to a rise in the number of unemployed. Or, on the revenue side, it is illustrated by a change in tax yield due to a change in the tax base. Thus, income tax revenue rises or falls (at given levels of tax rates) with changes in personal income; profits tax revenue rises or falls with changes in corporation profits, and so forth.

Another way of putting the matter is that parameter changes are "exogenous" to the system of income determination, since they change the fiscal variables such as G or t in the system of expenditure equations by which income is determined. They are thus an initiating source of change in the overall level of expenditures or demand. Built-in changes on the other hand are "endogenous."[5] They do not initiate changes in the economy, but because of their existence the system will respond differently to a change in, say, the level of investment than it would in their absence. Fiscal parameters are part of the response system and affect it.

Cushioning Effect of Built-in Changes

Built-in flexibility or automatic responsiveness of the fiscal system increases the stability of the economy without calling for discretionary action. Thus the very existence of a large public sector is a stabilizing factor since (1) a substantial block of expenditures is rendered more or less independent of changes in GNP or (unlike private outlays) may move counter to such changes; and (2) the built-in response of tax revenue cushions the repercussions of initial changes in private spending levels. To simplify, built-in changes in G are disregarded.

Index of Built-in Stabilization Dampening effects of the fiscal system upon changes originating in the private sector may be measured by comparing the actual resulting change in income with that which would result if there had been no automatic budget response. Comparing ΔY^* (the change in income in response to a change in I with T fixed) with ΔY (the change in income with $T = tY$), we obtain

$$\alpha = \frac{\Delta Y^* - \Delta Y}{\Delta Y^*} = \frac{ct}{1 - c(1 - t)} \qquad (10)$$

where α is an index of "built-in stabilization," measuring the percentage of income change which is prevented due to the cushioning effect of rising tax revenues or the built-in response of the fiscal system.[6] If $c = 0.6$ and $t = 0.3$, α will be equal to 0.43, this order of magnitude being about what may be expected

[5] The reader may object, with some justification, that the government, when changing fiscal parameters, itself responds to economic conditions. By building the nature of this response, including response lags, into the system, the parameter changes themselves might be made endogenous. Some recent work is moving in this direction, but even if this approach is taken, government, in deciding how to respond, will have to distinguish between the consequences of its actions and built-in responses in G or T.

[6] We have

$$\Delta Y^* = \frac{1}{1 - c}\Delta I \quad \text{and} \quad \Delta Y = \frac{1}{1 - c(1 - t)}\Delta I$$

from which we obtain equation 10.

in the United States economy. Thus, about 40 percent of the expansionary effects of raising aggregate expenditures is choked off by the built-in increase in tax leakages.

Flexibility of Major Taxes The magnitude of built-in stabilization, as shown in equation 10, depends on the level of tax rates and hence on the size of the budget relative to income. More specifically, what matters is the change in T in response to changes in Y over the relevant range, i.e., the elasticity of revenue with respect to changes in GNP. The overall elasticity depends on the composition of the tax structure since it differs considerably among the various taxes.

The automatic flexibility of proportional rate taxes is determined by the responsiveness of the tax base to changes in GNP. The built-in elasticity of revenue equals the elasticity of the tax base. For taxes with progressive rates, an additional factor enters. This is the responsiveness of the average tax rate (or ratio of revenue to base) to changes in the tax base. In combination, these factors make for substantial differences in the short-run elasticity of revenue from various taxes.[7]

Even though the tax rate is essentially proportional so that rate variability is absent, the corporation income tax exhibits much the highest elasticity. This characteristic is due to the fact that corporation profits, as a share in national income, fluctuate sharply over the cycle, thus transmitting similar fluctuations to the yield of the corporation tax. Even in a relatively modest recession, corporation profits can readily drop to 25 percent below their full-employment level. The stabilizing effect of the decline in revenue is less, however, than might be expected at first sight. With dividends remaining relatively stable over the cycle, the decline in revenue comes to be reflected in a smaller fall in corporate saving. This helps, but it is not likely, under depressed economic conditions, to result in a substantial increase in the level of corporate investment. Thus there is little immediate effect on the level of aggregate demand.

Among other taxes, the personal income tax leads in built-in flexibility. While personal income varies less sharply than does GNP, the role of exemptions and rate progression makes for a sharper variation in revenue. As income rises, a larger share of personal income falls above the exemption limit and taxable income slides up the rate brackets. Thus, it was estimated that under 1964 rates, individual income tax receipts would automatically increase or decrease by 14 percent for every 10 percent change in personal income. The built-in elasticity of the income tax nevertheless ranks second to that of the corporation tax. Moreover, due to the progressive nature of the tax, the effective rate rises as the average level of income increases, a factor which, as noted before, is of special importance under inflationary conditions.[8] The elasticity coefficient (ratio of

[7] Taking a longer-run view, we find that factor shares and the division of output between consumption and investment show little change. This implies that the base of all taxes varies at more or less the same rate as does GNP. In other words, the GNP elasticity of most tax bases is close to unity. Income tax revenue does, however, show a higher elasticity, owing to the progressive nature of tax rates.

[8] See p. 279 and Joseph A. Pechman, "Responses of the Federal Income Tax to Changes in Income," *Brookings Papers on Economic Activity*, 2, 1973.

percentage change in yield to percentage change in GNP) for consumption taxes is close to 1, and for the payroll tax it is below 1. The short-run revenue elasticity of the property tax also tends to be below 1, but this is due to assessment lags. In evaluating these coefficients, note that a tax will have an automatic stabilizing effect provided its income elasticity is positive. There is no need for it to be unity or higher.

Is Built-in Flexibility Desirable?

In assessing the role of built-in flexibility, we distinguish between short- and long-run aspects.

Short-Run Aspects Built-in flexibility is helpful in that it cushions the amplitude of fluctuations in economic activity. Thus the need for discretionary measures or changes in fiscal parameters is reduced. If the level of expenditures in the private sector falls off and a recession sets in, the decline is dampened automatically. Built-in flexibility is also desirable in an economy which exhibits an inflationary bias. By the same token, however, the built-in response becomes perverse and undesirable if we begin with a position of unemployment. Automatic response now interferes with recovery to full employment and hence increases the burden on discretionary action. Indeed, the magnitude of the required action (e.g., of an increase in government expenditures) is increased because the built-in response dampens the leverage exerted by a given change.[9]

Furthermore, the stabilizing advantages of built-in flexibility pertain to the stabilization aspect of federal finance only. The situation differs at the state and local levels. Such governments do not have control over monetary and debt policy, so that revenue fluctuations can only interfere with continuity of expenditure policy. If revenues are high in the upswing and low in the downswing, expenditures tend to fluctuate in a way which will accentuate the cycle, making for "perverse" fiscal behavior. Moreover, expenditures will be concentrated in high-cost periods. Responsiveness of state-local revenue to cyclical fluctuations is thus undesirable not only from the point of view of state and local government, but also from the point of view of stability in the national economy.

Longer-Run Aspects: Fiscal Drag and Dividend Turning now to the longer-run aspects of built-in response in a growing economy, we find that the need for discretionary action is increased rather than reduced. Given a passive policy which holds tax rates and expenditure programs unchanged, a built-in increase in revenue leads to a rising surplus at a full-employment level of income,

[9] If the desired income change equals ΔY, we have

$$\Delta Y = \frac{1}{1-c}\Delta G = \frac{1}{1-c(1-t)}\Delta G'$$

and

$$\Delta G' = \frac{1-c(1-t)}{1-c}\Delta G$$

where ΔG is the required change in G without built-in flexibility, and $\Delta G'$ the required change in G with built-in flexibility. Thus $\Delta G' > \Delta G$ for any positive tax rate t.

thereby exerting a drag on the economy.[10] The slowdown of the economy in the late 1950s and early 1960s was attributed to this development. A do-nothing policy, which leaves expenditure levels and tax rates unchanged, is in fact a policy of restriction as the economy grows. For policy to be neutral in a growing economy, changes on the expansionary side (rate reduction or expenditure increase) are needed.

The specter of "fiscal drag" thus becomes the bonus of "fiscal dividend." The built-in gain in revenue may be viewed as a "dividend" of economic growth, a dividend which becomes available for the financing of additional expenditures without requiring a raise in taxes, or for tax cuts without program cuts. This aspect offers a pleasant option to the administration in office, but it is also likely to interfere with efficient policy making. The decision on expenditure increase should undergo the explicit test of revenue legislation, and what is considered the proper revenue level should not depend on built-in revenue gain. Such is particularly the case because the burden distribution which lies behind the automatic revenue gain may well differ from the distribution which would be decided upon if there were an explicit step toward increasing revenue.

When Is Fiscal Policy Expansionary?

In the absence of built-in flexibility the effects of expansionary or restrictive fiscal action on the level of income can be measured readily by the change in leverage as defined in equation 5. If the change in fiscal parameters (i.e., in G or T) takes place without a concurrent change in I, ΔL will equal ΔY, the entire change in income being due to the change in fiscal measures. If the change in G or T is made while there are concurrent changes in I, the change in leverage or ΔL will measure only that part of ΔY which is due to the change in G or T.

With built-in flexibility allowed for, measuring the magnitude and direction of fiscal policy change becomes more complex. Our measure of ΔL, when redefined for a system with income tax, no longer singles out the effects of changes in fiscal parameters but also responds to changes in I.[11] How, then, can the effects of the fiscal policy change be separated? Clearly, they are not given by the

[10] See Walter W. Heller, *New Dimensions of Political Economy,* New York: Norton, 1967.

[11] To allow for the role of built-in flexibility, we restate our measure of leverage (given in equation 3 with regard to a lump-sum tax) for a setting with income tax. To simplify, we continue to assume G to be given independent of Y. With leverage again defined as the difference between the level of income as ensues with the prevailing budget and the level which would result in the absence of a budget, we now have

$$L = \frac{1}{1 - c(1 - t)}(I + G) - \frac{1}{1 - c}I$$

As will be seen from this equation, L again rises with expansionary fiscal action, i.e., an increase in G or a decrease in t. But L now also responds to a change in I. If policy changes in G and t are accompanied by concurrent changes in I, the resulting change in L will be a reflection of both sets of changes. If we wish to measure the direction and potency of changes in fiscal parameters in their effect on Y, such effects must be isolated from those of changes in I.

As will be seen from the equation, L declines as I increases. The reason is that an increase in I, by pushing up Y, also results in a built-in increase in T, since $T = tY$. Thereby the dampening component of the budget (i.e., the level of T) is increased, while the expansionary component (i.e., G) is unchanged.

observed change in the level of income or in the actual budget deficit. Y may remain unchanged or even decline while expansionary fiscal action (an increase in G or a cut in t) occurs, if such action is matched or outweighed by a fall in I. Similarly, the actual deficit D may reflect changes in I rather than in fiscal parameters. A sharp decline in I, such as results in a depression, typically increases D even though G and t are unchanged.[12]

Effects of changes in I may be excluded and those of changes in fiscal parameters be singled out if we focus on changes in the level of deficit or surplus at a fixed level of income, say the full-employment level. An increase in G or a reduction in t will raise the full-employment deficit, thus recording expansionary action and vice versa for restriction, quite independent of any concurrent changes in I and their effects on Y. At the same time, changes in the full-employment balance still fall short of providing us with a satisfactory measure of the direction and magnitude of fiscal policy change. The reason is that they fail to record effects of balanced changes in the level of G and T. The "balanced-budget multiplier" effect is left out. A more satisfactory measure of the effects of policy change is given by the hypothetical change in leverage which would have resulted had the policy change occurred while income remained constant at full employment. This measure, and its relation to the other variables, will be explored further in the appendix to this chapter.

Effects of Fiscal Expansion on Deficit

We now consider more closely the effects of automatic revenue response on deficit or surplus. Expansionary changes in fiscal parameters, whether involving an increase in expenditures or a cut in tax rates, raise the level of deficit (or reduce the surplus) at the *initial* level of income. If tax revenue were independent of income, i.e., if a lump-sum tax were used, this would also hold for the future level. But given the fact that revenue rises with income, it does not follow that the *actual* deficit will go up, since income and hence tax yield will rise as well. Thus the deficit-*increasing* effect of the expenditure increase must be combined with the deficit-*reducing* effect of the resulting rise in tax yield. What then will determine the *net* effect of expansionary action on the budgetary deficit or surplus?

Using the simple multiplier model of Table 24-1, it may be shown that the deficit at the new and higher level of income will be larger than before the expenditure increase so long as the marginal propensity to consume is less than 1.[13] While the resulting increase in tax yield cushions the rise in deficit, some increase in deficit must occur. We also find that with $c = 1$, the deficit remains

[12] Even if I remains unchanged, changes in the actual deficit or surplus must not be taken as indicators of fiscal policy action. An expansionary policy, such as an increase in G, will raise the deficit with $T = tY$ measured at the *old* level of Y. But Y increases and so does T. The deficit, as explained in the preceding footnote, may fall rather than rise.

[13] Writing D' for the deficit in the initial period and D'' for the deficit in the subsequent period, we have

$$D' = G' - tY' \quad \text{and} \quad D'' = G' + \Delta G - tY''$$

and obtain

$$\Delta D = D'' - D'$$
$$\Delta D = \Delta G - t\Delta Y$$

unchanged while for c in excess of 1 the deficit declines or a surplus is generated.

While the data show that the average value of c (ratio of consumption to disposable income) for any one year falls short of 1, it is quite possible, for limited periods at least, that the marginal c should exceed 1. Consumers, in anticipation of rising incomes, may take up consumer credit or draw down their balances. Thus a reduction rather than an increase in the deficit may come about even in the simple model in which the effects of expansionary fiscal policy on private investment are omitted. If responses in investment to changes in GNP are introduced and the system is viewed in dynamic terms, the possibility of expansionary fiscal policy leading to a decrease in the budgetary deficit is further enhanced. This is illustrated, as we shall see, by the experience of the late 1950s when restrictive fiscal action operated to increase the actual deficit; and that of 1964 when expansionary measures served to reduce the actual deficit because of an induced increase in investment.

Inflationary Gap

Change in leverage may be positive or negative. Thus, fiscal policy is restrictive if the change in leverage is negative; i.e., if according to equation 11 we have $\Delta G > c\Delta T$. Viewed this way, the preceding analysis can be applied equally well to the case of restrictive budget policy needed to check inflation, as to the case of expansionary policy needed to raise employment. In the one case, the gap to be closed is inflationary and involves excess aggregate demand, while in the other it is deflationary and involves an expenditure deficiency.

But now the question arises whether the gap is to be defined in real or in money terms. Assuming a potential inflationary gap, this difficulty is avoided if the adjustment is set so as fully to close it. In this case, there will be no excess demand, and the price level will not rise. If, however, the adjustment suffices to close the inflationary gap only partially, prices will rise, thus posing the question whether the inflationary gap should be defined in terms of the old or the new prices.

This may be illustrated with reference to Figure 25-1 in the preceding chapter. Referring back to case I there discussed we assumed an increase in G resulting in an upward shift in the total expenditure line from CG to CG' and an increase in money income from OY_f to OY', with a percentage rise in prices equal to Y_fY'/OY_f. The inflationary gap at the old level of prices was equal to $GG' = ME$, while at the new level of prices, it has disappeared. Whereas the

---

and since

$$\Delta Y = \frac{1}{1 - c(1 - t)} \Delta G$$

$$\Delta D = \left(1 - \frac{t}{1 - c(1 - t)}\right) \Delta G$$

The deficit will increase (ΔD will be positive) with an increase in G so long as

$$\frac{t}{1 - c(1 - t)} < 1$$

which will be the case if $c < 1$. But the deficit will remain unchanged ($\Delta D = 0$) if $c = 1$. Finally, the deficit will be reduced ($\Delta D < 0$) if $c > 1$. Note also that a value of $c > 1$ is still compatible with stability (a finite value of the multiplier) provided that $c(1 - t) < 1$.

concept of deflationary gap or demand deficiency may be applied to an equilibrium situation, that of inflationary gap is inherently a dynamic or disequilibrium concept. A neutral policy might now be defined as one which holds full-employment leverage constant in real terms—another way of putting the previously noted case for focusing on the ratio of full-employment leverage to full-employment GNP, rather than on its absolute level.

Finally, the concept of fiscal leverage, like most of the fiscal analysis concepts, is best suited to a setting where changes in aggregate demand will be reflected in changes in either employment or price level. The framework of "stagflation," as we noted in the preceding chapter, renders policies to control aggregate demand less effective and policy concepts such as leverage less meaningful.

C. FISCAL POLICY ALTERNATIVES

We have seen that expansionary or restrictive measures may be taken on both the tax and expenditure sides. Which of the two offers the more appropriate instrument, and on what basis should the choice be made?

Policy Lags

We begin with considerations of timing and of the lags involved in various policies. All fiscal adjustments take time and may be outdated by changing economic conditions before they become effective. This places a great premium on policy measures which minimize the lag involved, including (1) the lag between the time at which the need for action arises and the time at which it is recognized (recognition lag); (2) the lag between the decision to act and the introduction of the actual policy change (implementation lag); and (3) the lag between the introduction of the change and its becoming effective (response lag).[14]

Recognition Lag Early recognition of the need for policy change is essential whether the policy to be undertaken is of a fiscal or a monetary variety. Hence, progress in the art of econometric model building and forecasting is of crucial inportance to the success of fiscal policy and the maintenance of stability in a decentralized economic system.

Implementation Lag This lag involves both administrative and legislative delays. On expenditure policy, the President has limited discretion in adjusting the rate at which appropriated funds may be expended, but the available range may be inadequate. Moreover, changes in the rate of program expansion are not easily applied and require substantial advance planning. On the tax side, the executive branch has no (or very little) control.[15] Tax rate changes, as we saw earlier, must move through a lengthy congressional procedure before legislation

[14] See Milton Friedman, "A Monetary and Fiscal Framework for Economic Stability," in *Essays in Positive Economics,* 2d ed., Chicago: The University of Chicago Press, 1959.

[15] Minor influences may be exerted via administrative measures which change withholding rates or provide for speedups in tax collection. But these are, at best, poor substitutes for a more flexible policy of rate change.

can emerge.[16] This takes time, especially where tax increases are concerned. Unhappily, it is difficult to separate rate changes for purposes of stabilization policy from the more controversial issues of tax reform (as in 1975) or (as in 1963–1964 and in 1968) from disagreements over expenditure policy.

To reduce these delays and to enable the President better to meet the responsibilities assigned to him under the Employment Act,[17] it has been suggested (and recommendations have been made to the Congress by various Presidents) that discretionary authority to change income tax rates be given to the President. To protect the authority of Congress, such changes would be made within limits and patterns prescribed by Congress, e.g., flat percentage increases or decreases in existing liabilities within a 10 percent range. To give further reassurance to Congress, such changes might be made subject to congressional recall and automatic expiration after, say, six months. Congress, however, has been unwilling to grant such authority, holding that it would dilute its constitutional responsibility for control over the government's purse strings. Some solution to the dilemma must be found if fiscal policy is to be given the necessary degree of flexibility. As it stands, such flexibility is available only to monetary policy.

Response Lag The third lag is related to the rate at which changes become effective after they have been introduced. In the case of adjustments in the level of government purchases, the initial impact is when the additional purchases are made or orders are given. Beyond this, effects on output and employment will differ, depending on whether purchases are made out of inventory and how suppliers respond.[18] In the case of tax changes, the initial impact is when the taxpayer adjusts his or her own outlays. For consumption responses, this adjustment may lag by one or two quarters behind the change in disposable income. The change in income, in turn, lags behind the change in tax rates. This lag, however, is greatly reduced by source withholding of tax liabilities.

Lags in Monetary Policy Policy lags arise not only with fiscal but also with monetary policy. The Federal Reserve Board, through decisions made by the Open Market Committee, can act promptly in affecting money market conditions, whether through adjustments in open market policy, changes in discount rates, or reserve requirements. The implementation lag is thus minimal, but the response lag remains and may well exceed that of fiscal measures. A substantial time period is required for changes in monetary policy to work themselves through the money markets and then to affect actual investment expenditures which typically are budgeted and planned well in advance.

Priority for Tax Adjustments?

The logic of our discussion in Chapter 1 suggested that the most appropriate instrument for the functioning of the stabilization branch was provided by increases or reductions in the level of taxation. As was noted there, fiscal policy

[16] See p. 42.

[17] See p. 45.

[18] For an empirical discussion of policy lags, see Albert Ando and E. Cary Brown, "Lags in Fiscal Policy," in Commission on Money and Credit, *Stabilization Policies,* Englewood Cliffs, N.J.: Prentice-Hall, 1963.

should be conducted so as to satisfy potentially conflicting policy objectives.[19] Efficient expenditure policy or resource allocation among private and public uses was to be based on a full-employment level of output while leaving it to the stabilization branch—acting through tax and transfer measures—to assure that this level of output is provided. In the case of recession, this will avoid calling for additional expenditures to generate a higher level of employment, if such use of resources would be undesirable at full employment.[20] Under inflationary conditions, it will avoid cutbacks in programs merely to restrain demand. While the public sector should contribute its share when expansion or restraint in the total level of expenditures is needed, there is no good reason why the entire adjustment should be in that sector. Priority therefore goes to the tax adjustment route.

This pairing of policy instruments with targets has much merit in principle but needs to be qualified in practice. The cyclical sensitivity of various industries differs and the level of unemployment varies regionally. Use of expenditure policy may be desirable because it can be focused locally where unemployment exists, rather than diffused nationally, as is done with tax reduction.[21] Another reason is that tax reduction, by its very nature, can benefit those who receive income but not the unemployed who are not subject to tax. Such at least is so in the absence of a negative income tax or separate transfer programs. There is something to be said for action on both fronts although, in principle, tax rate and transfer adjustments should be given priority over changes in purchase programs.

Choice among Tax Alternatives

The appropriate type of tax adjustment will depend on whether the intention is to influence consumption, investment, or both. In the short-run context, this objective will depend on the prevailing degree of capacity utilization and other structural factors. For the longer view, it will depend on the targets of growth policy.

Consumption Effects Under the present tax structure, changes in income tax rates are the best way of affecting the level of consumption, although it is less obvious just how rates are to be changed. Expeditious legislative response will be easier if the change is "across the board" or "neutral," but it remains debatable how neutrality is to be defined, e.g., whether it entails equal percentage changes in liabilities or equal point changes in bracket rates.[22] For the case of a tax increase, the former is preferable to lower income taxpayers, while for a decrease, the latter is more advantageous, and vice versa for higher incomes. In the temporary tax-change legislation of 1964 and 1969, equal percentage changes

[19] See Chap. 1, p. 16.

[20] Make-work spending was referred to in the thirties as "ditch digging" or "leaf raking." While better than no action, it is inefficient, since the beneficial employment effects could have been obtained also by choosing a more useful initial outlay, including increased private spending induced through tax reduction.

[21] See our earlier discussion of the uniformity rule, p. 28. As noted there, the clause does not apply to expenditure policy.

[22] The two concepts of neutrality correspond to alternative measures of progression. See p. 285.

in liabilities were applied but in 1975 tax reduction was directed more heavily at low-income taxpayers.

Next, there is a question of how effective short-run changes in tax rates will be in affecting consumption. As noted before, such tax changes may be compensated for by consumers through adjustments in their rate of saving. These adjustments will occur if consumption is a function of what consumers consider their more permanent (as distinct from temporary) level of disposable income; or adjustments will be delayed if current consumption depends on *past* disposable income. In either case, the response is weakened and the lag in response to changes in the tax rate is increased.[23] This appears to have been the result with the tax rate increase of 1968, which, initially at least, was followed by a reduction in the savings rate rather than by reduced consumption expenditures.

It is interesting to note, therefore, that temporary tax rate changes would tend to be more effective if applied to a consumption tax. The reason is that a temporary increase in consumption tax will provide a substitution effect and a strong incentive for temporary saving, i.e., for postponement of purchases until rates are reduced. Thus a 10 percent consumption tax, expected to be effective for six months, would imply a return of 20 percent (annual basis) on saving over this period. Some observers have advanced this as an argument in favor of a broad-based federal consumption tax. Since postponement of consumption is most feasible with regard to outlays on durables, the objective might be achieved more effectively, however, by a durables tax, including such items as automobiles and appliances. Also note that the superior effectiveness of the consumption tax will depend largely on rate changes being recognized as temporary and on consumers having a firm expectation of early reversals.

Investment Effects With regard to investment, the most effective approach is through the use of a flexible investment credit. Use of such a device has been widely advocated (most recently by the Board of Governors of the Federal Reserve System), but the credit as first introduced in 1962 was meant to be permanent. While the credit has been suspended, reintroduced, or increased several times (most recently in 1975), there is still hesitation about using it as an outright instrument of stabilization policy. Other countries, such as the United Kingdom and Sweden, have also been using devices of this sort and have adopted them on a flexible basis.[24]

Perverse Effects of Tax Changes

Our general analysis has shown that a tax increase is restrictive and will thus serve to check inflation, while a tax reduction is expansionary and will raise employment. Various exceptions to this rule should be noted.

Perverse Budget Behavior An increase in tax rates will be restrictive provided that the resulting increase in revenue does not induce a rise in public

[23] See p. 532.

[24] As noted earlier, changes in the rate of corporation tax or in depreciation allowances are less suitable for this purpose. See p. 498.

expenditures. This proviso may not hold. If policy behavior is such that a revenue gain in fact leads to a corresponding expenditure increase, the opposite is true.[25] Given such perverse fiscal behavior, a tax increase makes for balanced budget expansion and is thus expansionary rather than restrictive. This applies with regard to built-in revenue gains as well as with regard to discretionary increases in tax rates. The reverse argument holds for tax reduction as an expansionary measure if accompanied by expenditure cuts. While such perverse behavior is anathema to the fiscal theorist, more worldly observers typically expect it to apply in actual practice.

Wage-Price Effects An increase in income tax, moreover, may be counterproductive if it is allowed for in wage bargains or in wage adjustments under a national incomes policy, thus resulting in a subsequent move toward cost-push inflation. While this has not been a significant factor in the United States setting to date, it has been of importance in European countries such as Sweden, where a national incomes policy is applied. Similar considerations arise where an increase in sales or excise taxes is reflected in higher consumer prices which in turn lead to wage escalation. As noted before, the role of aggregate demand control may be vitiated by patterns of price-wage behavior which do not conform with the simple model of a competitive market.

While these considerations introduce an element of caution into the effectiveness of tax increase as an anti-inflationary device, it is not correct to argue, as is frequently done, that a product tax increase contributes to (rather than retards) inflation because it raises costs. While an increase in the sales tax rate may be expected to add to cost and to raise price by the amount of the tax, this is a once-and-for-all adjustment, which is outweighed by the continuing deflationary effect of a reduced deficit or increased surplus. While an increase in income tax is superior to an increase in sales tax in this respect, since the once-and-for-all increase in price is avoided, it does not follow that an increase in sales tax will not have a net deflationary effect.

Rules versus Discretion

Distrust of discretionary measures—fed partly by concern over difficulties in determining the appropriate policy changes and partly by philosophical dislike of government intervention—has led some observers to a search for policy rules by which primary reliance may be placed on automatic stabilization.

Balanced-Budget Rules The time has passed when the balancing of annual budgets was considered the essence of fiscal soundness. It is now generally understood that such a policy would be unacceptable, as it would exclude even the automatic role of fiscal policy in stabilization and would call for procyclical (i.e., perverse) rather than contracyclical measures of discretionary change. At the same time, the desirable scope of fiscal stabilization has remained under debate. This discussion has led to the new rule of "prudent budgeting" which replaces

[25] Expenditure policy would then become an endogenous part of the system, limiting discretionary policy to tax changes. See p. 256, footnote 5.

the old criterion of annual budgetary balance with that of balance at full-employment levels of income.[26]

Defense of this rule as a matter of sound economic policy was advanced in the President's budget message for the fiscal year 1973. It was based on the following reasoning: "The full-employment budget concept is central to the budget policy of this Administration. Except in emergency conditions, *expenditures should not exceed the level at which the budget would be balanced under conditions of full employment.* The 1973 Budget conforms to this guideline. By doing so, it provides necessary stimulus to expansion, but is not inflationary."[27] Similarly, the President's budget message for the fiscal year 1974 stated, "I am proposing to avoid both higher taxes and inflation by holding spending in 1974 and 75 to no more than revenues would be at full employment."[28] Contrary to this dictum, there is no good reason why, as a matter of stabilization policy, a rule of budgetary balance at full employment should be the appropriate solution, certainly not in the short run and even for the average year. There may be sustained periods when to obtain full employment, a full-employment deficit is needed; and there may be other periods when to check inflation, a full-employment surplus will be called for. An economy which does not automatically adjust itself to a stable level of full employment is not likely to be one in which full employment is assured by maintaining a full-employment balance in the budget. By the same token, the statement is in error when claiming that a budget which is balanced at full employment cannot be inflationary. Inflation pressures may well be such that a balance at full employment is inadequate to check excess demand.

But though this case for the "balance at full employment" rule is fallacious, a more valid argument can be made. It rests on the proposition that policy makers are incapable of properly using discretionary measures, so that expenditure or tax changes are as likely to increase instability as to reduce it—or even more so. Given this theory, the budget should be set so as to be balanced at full employment, with departures therefrom limited to the working of built-in flexibility. The same logic is applied to monetary policy where the automatic rule calls for an increase in the money supply equal to that of the rate of growth of capacity output. To us, this view appears excessively pessimistic. Past experience includes successes as well as failures. Substantial advances in econometric analysis and in ability to predict have been made and will continue to be made. Indeed, it would seem essential for the future of market economies that the art of stabilization be mastered.

A final, and perhaps the strongest, argument for the rule is that the use of deficit finance involves a loss of "fiscal discipline," as it invites overallocation of resources to the public sector. Similarly, a surplus policy might result in underallocation. These distortions do not arise with monetary policy, which should

[26] See Committee for Economic Development, *Taxes and the Budget: A Program for Prosperity in a Free Economy,* New York: 1947; and Milton, Friedman, "A Monetary and Fiscal Framework for Economic Stability," op. cit. For a more recent formulation of the CED position, see Committee for Economic Development, *High Employment without Inflation,* New York: 1972.

[27] See *U.S. Budget in Brief, Fiscal Year 1973,* p. 9. Italics added.

[28] See *The Budget of the United States Government, Fiscal Year 1974,* p. 21.

therefore be relied upon for discretionary action. This argument has merit since an efficient separation of allocation and stabilization objectives is not likely to be achieved in practice. The question is, however, whether the loss of potential for effective stabilization, suffered by the absence of discretionary fiscal measures, would exceed the gain in allocational efficiency due to improved budget discipline. Although we think that the loss would outweigh the gain, the argument cannot be rejected lightly.[29]

Formula Flexibility

Another approach, again related to distrust of discretionary measures, is to increase the scope of automatic change by resorting to so-called formula flexibility. For example, legislation might instruct the Internal Revenue Service to lower income tax rates by, say, 10 percent if the unemployment rate exceeds 4.5 percent for two quarters; and to increase tax rates by 10 percent if the annual rate of price increase exceeds 4 percent for such a period. Thus, changes in tax rates would be removed from discretionary policy and be made part of an automatic system.

The basic question, therefore, is not whether automatic revenue changes as now generated by existing taxes are sufficiently large, but whether formulas can be devised which will be superior to discretionary policies in securing appropriate changes in tax rates. One must be skeptical about the superiority of such formulas. The information needed to apply formula flexibility is also available to those in charge of discretionary measures and it appears doubtful whether the sources of instability in the economy are sufficiently unchanging to permit a once-and-for-all solution to the problem by devising a correct set of formulas. The responsibility for discretionary change—and the need to improve its performance—cannot be avoided. Some readers will like this challenge while others would prefer a setting which permits reliance on automatic measures.[30] As happens frequently among economists, technical disputes are but the tip of ideological icebergs.

D. THE MIX OF FISCAL AND MONETARY POLICY

We have seen that the financing of deficits and the use of budgetary surplus establish a direct link between fiscal and monetary policy. Nevertheless, various mixes of fiscal and monetary measures may be used for any given target of income

[29] As a compromise, it has been suggested that new expenditures should be balanced at the margin, while permitting a full-employment surplus or deficit in the total budget if conditions so require. But it is somewhat difficult to see how the average position can be adjusted without affecting the marginal rule.

[30] See Don Juan's eloquent dialog with the devil in G. B. Shaw's "Man and Superman," *Nine Plays,* New York: Dodd, Mead, 1945, p. 646, quoted with permission of The Society of Authors, on behalf of the Bernard Shaw Estate, London:

The Devil: What is the use of knowing?

Don Juan: Why, to be able to choose the line of greatest advantage instead of yielding in the direction of the least resistance. Does a ship sail to its destination no better than a log drifts nowhither? The philosopher is Nature's pilot. And there you have our difference: to be in hell is to drift: to be in heaven is to steer.

The Devil: On the rocks, most likely.

Don Juan: Pooh! which ship goes oftenest on the rocks or to the bottom? the drifting ship or the ship with a pilot on board?

change. A given expansion may be secured by fiscal measures (increased expenditures or reduced taxes), or by monetary measures (open market purchases, reduction in the discount rate, reduced reserve requirements), or by various combinations of the two. Similarly, restriction may be secured by various mixes of policies, and changes in policy mix can be made by adjustments in opposite directions while holding aggregate demand constant. How, then, is the proper mix to be determined?

Policy Instruments and Policy Targets

The choice of policy instruments must be related to the policy targets that are to be met. These targets will include domestic balance (in its double aspect of high employment and price level stability), a desirable rate of growth, and foreign balance. The more targets there are to be met, the more policy instruments must be available to meet them. More specifically, the number of available instruments must match the number of targets to be served. While the usefulness of this rule is somewhat limited by its dependence on how instruments and targets are defined, it offers, nevertheless, a starting point from which to view the problem of policy choice.

Moreover, this framework is much in line with our earlier contention that the three major objectives of budget policy—provision for social goods, corrections in the state of distribution, and attainment of full employment and price stability—can be met by the use of three fiscal instruments as provided by the transactions of the allocation, distribution, and stabilization branches of our hypothetical budget operation. When we add the further targets of growth and foreign balance, the following pairings of policy targets and instruments may be suggested:

Targets	*Instruments*
1. Provision for social goods	**1.** Government purchases and benefit taxes
2. Equitable distribution	**2.** Redistributive taxes and transfers
3. High employment and price stability	**3.** Proportional taxes or transfers
4. Desired rate of economic growth	**4.** Monetary restriction or ease
5. Foreign balance	**5.** Additional instrument required

Having assigned appropriate instruments to the various targets, these instruments must then be applied in a coordinated fashion so as to meet the desired set of targets. Expenditure policy, tax policy, the rate of increase in money supply, and (as will be noted later) balance-of-payments policy must be determined as parts of an overall process of policy formulation. While it is helpful to distinguish among various targets, as well as among various policy instruments, and to assign instruments to targets, it is no less important to realize that the instruments must be used in an interdependent fashion so that the desired mix of targets can be achieved.

Domestic Aspects

Apart from matters of timing which have already been noted, the proper choice of policy mix will depend on the current position of the economy and on long-run growth objectives.

Position of Economy The appropriateness of various policies differs with the current position of the economy. Under conditions of unemployment and excess capacity, expansionary measures are more reasonably directed at consumption than at investment. For this purpose, general fiscal measures, such as tax reduction, will be more suitable than monetary expansion. In a situation of capital shortage, emphasis is more properly on expansion of investment, and for this, monetary expansion is in order. Such at least is the picture if we proceed on the traditional assumption that monetary policy is more effective in dealing with investment, while fiscal policy is more effective in dealing with consumption. Although valid if the comparison is between *general* fiscal and monetary measures, the proposition fails if *selective* measures are allowed for. Selective tax provisions, such as an investment credit, may be used to influence investment, while selective monetary measures, such as consumer credit controls, may be used to influence consumption.

Nor must it be thought that so-called general monetary policy will not be selective in its impact. Monetary restriction, though intended to be general, is most effective in the mortgage market, on housing starts, and on borrowing by local governments, while it has relatively little effect on investment by large corporations. Thus, the selective impact of general measures must be allowed for in policy choice. Moreover, the suitability of various approaches differs depending upon the magnitude of the change that is to be undertaken. Sharp monetary restriction in particular may carry the risk of disorderly money market conditions and thus may indicate relief through supplementary fiscal measures.

Growth Objectives As noted in Chapter 22, economic growth calls for capital formation and capital formation calls for saving. These objectives tend to be favored by a policy mix which combines relatively tight fiscal policy with relatively easy monetary policy. Tightening of fiscal policy by raising income or consumption taxes will reduce private consumption, while easing credit terms will encourage private investment. Thus, a shift in resource use from consumption to investment may be secured at a given level of aggregate demand by varying the policy mix.

Equity Considerations Finally, it should be noted that the choice of policy mix is not without distributional implications. Suppose that a given degree of restriction may be accomplished either (1) by an across-the-board increase in income tax rates, or (2) by monetary restriction. Analogous to our earlier concept of differential incidence among alternative tax measures, the same concept may now be applied to the case of tax versus monetary restriction. Seen in this way, monetary policy has its incidence (distributional implications) no less than does tax policy, a factor which is usually neglected in the monetary policy discussion.

Thus, an across-the-board increase in income tax rates by 10 percent may have the same effect on aggregate demand as a reduction in member bank reserves by, say, $1 billion. Yet, the distributional effects may well differ. Equity considerations should therefore enter into the choice between monetary and fiscal policy as well as into the choice between alternative fiscal measures.

Open Economy Aspects

Measures designed to expand the domestic economy, whether fiscal or monetary, will increase imports and (if prices rise) may tend to reduce exports. In a system with fixed, or only partly flexible, exchange rates, domestic expansion may thus generate a balance-of-payments deficit, and concern over this deficit may become a deterrent to the pursuit of a high-employment policy. This situation developed in the United States in the late 1950s and continued to influence policy throughout the 1960s. Though reduced in importance by a move toward a more flexible system of exchanges in the 1970s, it remains a major policy concern at the present time.

Reconciliation of Foreign and Domestic Balance Considerable attention has been given to the question of how the two objectives may be reconciled by an appropriate mix of fiscal and monetary policies. For this purpose, effects on capital flows are of strategic importance. This is so because capital outflows exert a drain on the balance of payments while capital inflows strengthen it. For instance, the decision of a United States firm to buy a plant abroad means that the supply of dollars abroad is increased. The decision of a foreign investor to purchase securities in the United States means an increase in the demand for United States dollars. Since monetary policy affects the interest rate and high interest rates attract capital inflows and discourage capital outflows, monetary policy has a direct effect on capital flows and hence on the balance of payments. General fiscal measures do not have this effect. Therefore, it is argued that monetary policy should be used to secure foreign balance by acting on the capital account, while fiscal policy should be employed to secure domestic balance.

If domestic expansion is needed, fiscal measures may be used to raise domestic income, while monetary restriction is used to reduce capital outflow or to attract capital inflow. This measure will offset the detrimental balance-of-payments effects of increased imports consequent on the domestic expansion. Since monetary restriction will also affect the domestic economy, a higher rate of fiscal expansion must be applied than would otherwise be needed. The resulting mix of fiscal and monetary policies, however, may not satisfy the further objective of meeting a desired growth rate, so that an additional policy instrument will be needed to meet all objectives. This may involve measures such as a domestic investment credit, differential interest rates on domestic and foreign funds, control over capital exports, and so forth.

Moreover, the suggested reconciliation of domestic and foreign balance may not work equally well in all cases. It will be especially effective if (1) the expansionary effect of fiscal policy is relatively strong, (2) the restrictive domestic effect of monetary policy is comparatively weak, and (3) the effectiveness of monetary restriction in attracting capital inflow or checking outflow is relatively strong. Condition 1 will not be met where the country's trade involvement is high; condition 2 will be met only for countries which are sufficiently large to change their level of interest rates in relation to the rates that prevail in the world market. For small countries which cannot do so, additional policy instruments will be needed to serve both policy objectives.[31] The appropriate roles of fiscal and monetary policies thus depend greatly on how the country's economy is related to the outside world. The higher the degree of trade involvement and the more internationalized the capital market, the more essential does it become for the stabilization policies of various countries to be coordinated.

Stabilization in Common Markets This linkage is becoming of increasing importance in the context of Europe's Common Market where successive removal of economic frontiers calls for increased coordination of stabilization policies. Adoption of a common currency in particular would force unification of monetary policy and would render conduct of separate fiscal policies increasingly difficult. In the end, individual member countries would become unable to conduct their own stabilization policies, just as (and for the same reason) state or municipal governments in the United States cannot do so. The economic logic of the case will call for such policies to be undertaken by a central Common Market authority, thus providing a further step toward political union.

E. SUMMARY

Returning to our earlier multiplier models, we have examined the concept of fiscal leverage as applied to the total budget and to changes therein:

1. Leverage depends on the level of both G and T.

2. The level of deficit or surplus matters, but it must be viewed in conjunction with the level of G.

3. To obtain a given level of leverage, if one of the three fiscal variables (G, T, and D) is set, the other two follow.

A distinction was drawn between (1) changes in expenditures and tax revenue which result because expenditure laws and tax rates are changed (parameter changes), and (2) changes which result as automatic responses to changes in the level of economic activity (built-in changes). The distinction is significant in a number of ways:

4. The operation of built-in flexibility cushions the effect of changes in investment or consumption. It thus increases the stability of the system.

5. In the longer run, built-in flexibility may lead to fiscal drag or yield a fiscal dividend.

[31] This discussion is based on the work of R. A. Mundell. Among other papers of his, see "The Appropriate Use of Monetary and Fiscal Policy for Internal and External Stability," International Monetary Fund, *Staff Papers,* March 1962; and R. A. Musgrave, *Fiscal Systems,* New Haven, Conn.: Yale, 1969, chap. 13.

6. An increase in expenditures with constant tax rates may reduce rather than increase the level of actual deficit.

7. Allowing for built-in response of tax revenue, an expansionary (restrictive) fiscal policy is redefined as one which raises (lowers) the level of fiscal leverage at a full-employment level of income.

8. Mere observation of actual changes in G, T, and D does not tell us how fiscal policy has behaved over a given period. Changes in the actual and the full-employment levels of D may be in opposite directions.

9. Expansionary changes in G or t will increase D at the initial level of Y, but allowing for the response in Y, the level of D may decline.

10. Under conditions of inflation, leverage should be defined in real rather than money terms.

11. One consideration in choosing between alternative policy instruments relates to differences in lags with respect to the rate at which policy changes can be introduced and the rate at which they become effective.

12. While there is a good case for the primary use of tax changes for fiscal stabilization purposes, expenditure changes may be appropriate in certain circumstances.

13. The type of tax change to be used depends on whether consumption or investment is to be affected.

14. Critics of discretionary stabilization policy have argued that reliance should be placed on built-in stabilizers only and that the budget should be set so as to assure balance at a full-employment level of income. While this rule has merit as a means of assuring fiscal discipline, it is not a sound rule for stabilization policy. Formula flexibility, similarly, has its limitations.

Finally, consideration was given to the appropriate mix between fiscal and monetary policy:

15. Where multiple policy targets have to be met, the number of available policy instruments should match the number of targets.

16. In the domestic context, the monetary-fiscal mix has important bearing on the growth rate but also involves equity considerations.

17. In the open-economy context, simultaneous achievement of domestic and foreign balance is difficult, especially for small countries with open economies.

18. When the rate of growth is added to domestic and foreign stability as a policy target, an additional policy instrument (other than general fiscal and monetary policy) is needed.

FURTHER READINGS

Committee for Economic Development: *Taxes and the Budget: A Program for Prosperity in a Free Economy,* New York: 1947.

Friedman, Milton: "A Monetary and Fiscal Framework for Economic Stability," in *Essays in Positive Economics,* 2d ed., Chicago: The University of Chicago Press, 1959.

Okun, Arthur N., and Nancy H. Teeters: "The Full Employment Surplus Revisited," *Brookings Papers on Economic Activity,* Washington: Brookings, 1970.

Ott, David J., and F. Attiat: *Federal Budget Policy,* Washington: Brookings, 1965.

APPENDIX: Changes in Income, Leverage, and Full-Employment Budget

We have seen that it is difficult to measure the effects of changes in fiscal parameters (here dealt with in terms of G and t) once the effects of built-in flexibility are allowed for. The major difficulty is that concurrent changes in investment also affect the level of income and thereby that of revenue. Nonfiscal changes thus interact with fiscal changes, making it difficult to disentangle the one from the other.[32]

One widely followed approach in avoiding this difficulty is to measure leverage as the fiscal contribution to income which results while income is assumed to be at the full-employment level. We thus have

$$L_f = \frac{1}{1-c}(G - cT_f) \tag{11}$$

where L_f is full-employment leverage, Y_f is full-employment income, and $T_f = tY_f$ is full-employment revenue. Equation 11, it will be noted, is similar to our earlier formulation for leverage with a lump-sum tax. With income and hence the tax base held constant, no built-in changes in revenue can occur. The change in full-employment leverage then equals

$$\Delta L_f = \frac{1}{1-c}(\Delta G - c\Delta T_f) \tag{12}$$

with policy for any given period being expansionary, neutral, or restrictive depending on whether L_f is positive, zero, or negative. While this approach has its difficulties[33] and alternative measures may be considered,[34] it has the advantage of focusing on the full-employment position, a position which after all is the target of most policy measures. It is thus worth exploring more carefully how changes in full-employment leverage relate to changes in income and to concurrent changes in the actual budget position.

[32] As shown in footnote 11, leverage (if defined as the difference in income with and without a budget) in a system with income tax depends not only on the fiscal variables G and t but also on I. As noted above, it changes inversely with I.

[33] If income is at the full-employment level prior to the change in fiscal leverage, it may be expected to change with the change in leverage. Measuring the change in leverage at the constant level of income is thus a somewhat artificial procedure.

[34] Alternatively, the change in leverage due to policy changes may be measured as the change in the fiscal contribution to income as would result at the initial income level, such that

$$\Delta L_1 = \frac{1}{1-c}(\Delta G - c\Delta T_i)$$

where T_i is tax revenue at the initial level of income.

Still another possibility, not subject to the difficulty noted in the preceding footnote, is to measure the change in the fiscal contribution to income which results if I is assumed unchanged at the initial level. We then obtain

$$\Delta L_2 = \frac{1}{1-c(1-t'')}(G'' + I') - \frac{1}{1-c(1-t')}(G' + I')$$

where prime and double prime indicate initial and subsequent levels, respectively. Each version is of some interest, there being no single correct way in which to formulate the problem.

TABLE 26-A1
Changes in Fiscal Parameters, Income and Leverage

Variables	*Initial Position* *I*	FINAL POSITION *II*	*III*	*IV*	*V*
Actual					
Y[1]	150	127	169	180	156
C	80	68	90	96	78
I	20	9	29	24	20
G	50	50	50	60	57
T	50	42	56	60	59
c	80%	80%	80%	80%	80%
t	33%	33%	33%	33%	37.6%
B[2]	0	−8	+6	0	+2
ΔB	—	−8	+6	0	+2
Full Employment					
Y_f	210	210	210	210	210
T_f	70	70	70	70	79
L_f[3]	−30	−30	−30	+20	−30
ΔL_f	—	0	0	+50	0
B_f	+20	+20	+20	+10	+22
ΔB_f	—	0	0	−10	+2

[1] The level of income Y is given by

$$Y = \frac{1}{1 - c(1 - t)}(I + G)$$

[2] A balance with deficit shown as (−) and surplus shown as (+).
[3] Computed in line with equation 11.
NOTE: Figures are rounded.

The problem is illustrated in Table 26-A1, where various situations are considered. We begin with the initial position shown in column I, where Y is income, C is consumption, I is investment, G is government purchases, T is tax revenue, B is the state of budgetary balance (− for deficit and + for surplus), c is the propensity to consume, and t is the tax rate. Y_f, T_f, and B_f are corresponding values at a full-employment level of income and L_f is full-employment leverage. We note that the initial position of Y falls short of Y_f, with the actual budget in balance and the full-employment budget in a surplus position.

In columns II and III, we examine the effects of changes in fiscal parameters in conjunction with changes in investment originating in the private sector. In column II, investment is assumed to decline, while fiscal policy as measured by ΔL_f is neutral. Income falls, as does revenue, and the actual budget moves into deficit. It would be a mistake, however, to interpret the latter as an indicator of expansionary fiscal action, as it reflects merely the built-in response of the fiscal system to a private sector change. In column III, fiscal policy is once more neutral, combined now with an increase in investment leading to a rise in income and revenue, and a move of the budget into surplus. Once again this does not reflect fiscal action (expansionary in this case) but merely the automatic response to changes originating outside the fiscal system.[35] A similar point is made in column IV where expansionary fiscal action (a positive ΔL_f) is combined with an increase in I so as to leave the balance in the actual budget unchanged, with the increase in revenue due to the rise in income (reflecting the combined effects of ΔG and ΔT) just enough to match the rise in G. Once more the movement of the state of balance in the actual budget is no indicator of the change in fiscal policy.

Column V serves to illustrate a further point which also has been made before, namely, that a distinction must be drawn between the change in the state of full-employment balance and the change in full-employment leverage, with only the latter being a proper indicator of fiscal policy change. In the case shown here, leverage at full employment is unchanged, but the full-employment surplus is increased. A balanced-budget increase being expansionary, constant leverage must involve an increase in T in excess of that in G, thus raising the surplus at full employment. Finally, column V also shows that a set of changes in G and t, matched so as to hold L_f unchanged, may nevertheless give rise to an increase in the actual level of income Y. This reflects the fact that the increase in t needed to offset the expansionary effect of the rise in G at Y_f will generate a larger increase in revenue than occurs at the lower level of actual income or Y. This is but one of the difficulties in measuring changes in leverage in a system in which built-in responses are allowed for.

[35] The concept of neutrality as defined here relates to the absence of changes in fiscal *parameters* (G and t) but does not exclude built-in responses in T to changes in I. Even though G and t remain unchanged, the response of Y to a change in I differs from what it would be in the absence of a budget.

Chapter 27

Fiscal Policy Experience*

A. Early Record: *The Thirties; World War II; 1946–1960.* **B. Fiscal Indicators:** *1960–1965; 1966–1968; 1969–1974;* **C. Conclusions.**

In this chapter, we complete the discussion of fiscal policy with a brief look at our actual fiscal policy experience. Some of the concepts developed in the preceding chapters will prove helpful in interpreting what has occurred.

A. EARLY RECORD

In surveying United States experience with fiscal policy, we pass quickly over the earlier stages, then take a more careful look at the 1960s and 1970s.

The Thirties

The fiscal policy discussion in the United States dates back to the Great Depression of the 1930s when unemployment rose to the disastrous rate of over 25 percent (1933). While there was much talk about fiscal measures to "prime the

* *Reader's Guide to Chapter 27:* A brief survey of the successes and failures of United States fiscal policy since the thirties and of the new problems posed by operating fiscal policy in a setting of "stagflation."

pump," the principles of fiscal policy were not as yet properly understood, and they certainly had not penetrated to the policy level. While expenditures were increased to provide emergency relief and employment programs such as PWA and WPA, tax rates were raised as well, leaving only a slight net expansionary effect to the economy. Such modest recovery as had been realized by the onset of World War II had been largely a reflection of recovery in the private sector.[1]

World War II

The economic expansion of World War II brought a vast change and provided a powerful demonstration of what massive fiscal policy can accomplish. As federal government purchases increased from $6 billion to $89 billion (1940 to 1944) while the deficit rose from $1 to $52 billion, unemployment rapidly disappeared and GNP climbed from $100 to $210 billion. After allowing for price rise, real output increased by 60 percent. The resulting increase was so large that, even though the war effort came to absorb 40 percent of GNP, an increased output remained available for civilian use. Although wartime conditions differ from those of peace and general price controls permitted a level of deficit finance which otherwise would have resulted in sharp price rise, the experience nevertheless offered an overwhelming testimony to the expansionary potential of fiscal policy.[2]

1946–1960

There was widespread expectation in the councils of economists during the mid-forties that the dismantling of the war budget would reproduce the condition of economic stagnation that had prevailed during the thirties, calling for continued and sustained reliance on a high level of fiscal expansion. This prognosis, however, did not materialize. For one thing, the economic vigor of the private sector proved much greater than had been expected. For another, the responsiveness of the economy to monetary policy measures proved much stronger than it had been during the prewar years. Not only did the need for expansionary action prove more limited, but monetary policy was raised from its state of impotence to become a full-fledged partner of stabilization policy in the postwar period.

To be sure, the share of government in GNP continued at a substantially higher level than had been maintained in the prewar economy. This in itself contributed to the higher level of economic activity. After a drastic cut in defense spending in the immediate postwar years, defense spending again rose and the ratio of total federal expenditures to GNP remained about 20 percent, or twice the pre–World War II level. The unemployment rate, which had risen in the immediate postwar years, declined and remained in the 4 to 5 percent range for the first half of the decade of the 1950s.

The second half of the fifties brought the emergence of rising prices combined

[1] See E. Cary Brown, "Fiscal Policy in the Thirties: A Reappraisal," *American Economic Review,* December 1956.

[2] The inflationary aftereffects caused by large accumulations of liquid assets credited in the course of wartime deficits came to be felt in the late forties. Nevertheless, heavy reliance on deficit finance during the war period was appropriate, since it fueled economic expansion.

with resource slack, a forerunner of the conflict between high employment and price level stability which became such a significant factor in the policy discussions of the late 1960s. The first serious recession occurred in 1958, with unemployment rising to 7 percent. In the ensuing recovery, a sharp increase in full-employment surplus was permitted to develop and contribute to choking off a short-lived recovery. It was this increase in full-employment surplus that became the basis for concern with fiscal drag and played a role in changing policy attitudes during the 1960s.

B. FISCAL INDICATORS

In dealing with the period from 1960 on, we present various relevant data in Figure 27-1 and Table 27-1. They include the actual levels of expenditures, receipts, and budget surpluses or deficits, as well as their full-employment levels, as shown in lines 1 to 6 of the table. In accordance with what we have learned in the preceding chapter, the full-employment levels are more instructive in interpreting and evaluating the conduct of fiscal policy than the actual levels. We have also seen that the leverage of fiscal policy in any one year involves both the level of expenditures and the state of budgetary balance. In line with this earlier formulation, we have combined both these magnitudes into a crude measure of "fiscal leverage" showing the overall contribution to aggregate demand which results from the federal budget. This measure is shown in line 7 of Table 27-1.[3]

Since the level of GNP has risen substantially over the period under consideration, it is helpful, in addition, to relate these magnitudes to the level of full-employment GNP. This relation is shown in lines 8 to 10 of the table. Finally, the direction of fiscal policy in any one year is given by changes in the variables over the preceding years, as shown in lines 11 to 15, with the change in leverage being the more comprehensive measure. Other data pertaining to economic conditions and monetary policy are shown in lines 16 to 20.

In interpreting the movement of the various indices, two comparisons are of particular interest. One is between the actual surplus or deficit (line 14) and the full-employment surplus or deficit (line 13). We find that the two move in the same direction for some of the years but in opposite direction for the 1960–65, 1971–72, and 1973–74 periods. The former years in particular show how a decrease in the surplus at full employment, by raising the level of income, can generate sufficient additional revenue to improve the position of the actual budget.

[3] The leverage measure shown in lines 7 and 15 gives a rough estimate of the contribution of the federal budget to full-employment GNP. Following equation 13, p. 574, and substituting $D_f = G - T_f$, we have

$$L_f = G + \frac{c}{1-c} D_f$$

Assuming that all transfer payments are fully spent, that 80 percent of the average tax dollar is reflected in reduced consumption, and that the marginal propensity to consume for all income recipients (including corporations) equals .67, we use .8 for the value of c in the numerator and .67 in the denominator. We thus obtain:

$$L_f = G + 2.4 D_f$$

TABLE 27-1 Fiscal Policy, 1960–1974

	1960	*1965*	*1966*	*1967*	*1968*	*1969*	*1970*	*1971*	*1972*	*1973*	*1974*
Actual Budget (billions of dollars)											
1. Expenditures	102	124	143	164	181	189	204	221	245	264	299
2. Receipts	98	125	143	151	175	197	192	199	227	259	291
3. Surplus	− 4	1	—	−12	− 6	8	− 12	− 22	− 18	− 6	− 8
Full-Employment Budget (billions of dollars)											
4. Expenditures	100	123	143	164	182	190	203	318	243	263	297
5. Receipts	111	126	139	152	174	198	207	216	232	266	320
6. Surplus	11	3	− 4	−12	− 8	9	4	− 2	− 10	3	23
7. Leverage	74	116	153	193	201	168	193	223	267	256	242
As Percentage of Full-Employment GNP											
8. Full-employment expenditures	17.5	19.8	19.3	20.9	21.6	19.4	18.7	17.9	19.4	19.5	18.0
9. Full-employment surplus	1.9	0.6	—	−1.5	−0.9	0.9	0.4	− 0.2	− 0.7	0.1	1.4
10. Leverage	12.9	18.7	20.6	24.5	23.8	17.1	17.8	19.0	21.2	19.4	16.0
Changes from Previous Column											
11. Full-employment expenditures	*	+23	+20	+21	+18	+ 8	+13	+21	+25	+20	+34
12. Full-employment receipts	*	+15	+13	+13	+22	+24	+ 9	+10	+16	+34	+56
13. Full-employment surplus	*	− 8	− 7	− 8	+ 4	+17	− 5	− 6	− 8	+13	+20
14. Actual surplus	*	+ 5	− 1	−12	+ 6	+12	−20	−10	+ 4	+10	− 2
15. Full-employment leverage	*	+42	+37	+40	+ 8	−33	+25	+36	+34	−11	−14
Other Data											
16. GNP (billions of dollars)	520	685	750	794	864	930	977	1,055	1,155	1,288	1,397
17. Full-employment GNP (billions of dollars)	570	620	740	785	844	980	1,085	1,170	1,260	1,317	1,510
18. Unemployment rate	6.7	4.5	3.8	3.8	3.6	3.5	4.9	5.9	5.6	4.9	5.6
19. Price rise (%)	0.7	1.9	3.4	3.0	4.7	6.1	5.5	3.4	3.4	8.7	6.7
20. Change in money supply (%)	7.0	8.6	4.7	9.8	8.3	2.3	7.9	13.4	13.1	8.7	10.7

Sources: Lines 1 to 3: *Economic Report of the President, 1975,* p. 329.

Lines 4 to 6: For years preceding 1969, see Arthur M. Okun and Nancy H. Teeters, "The Full Employment Surplus Revisited," *Brookings Papers on Economic Activity,* 1970, vol. 1, p. 104. For years from 1971 on, see *Economic Report of the President, 1974,* p. 80, and *1975,* p. 64.

Line 7: Computed from lines 4 to 6 such that leverage equals full-employment expenditures minus (3 × 0.8) of full-employment surplus.

Line 17: See Okun and Teeters, op. cit., for years preceding 1969; figures for 1973 and 1974, unpublished estimates by E. Gramlich, Brookings Institution.

Line 19: Percentage change in consumer prices, December to December, *Economic Report of the President, 1975,* p. 304.

Line 20: *Economic Report of the President, 1975,* p. 310. Reference is to M_3.

ECONOMIC INDICATORS

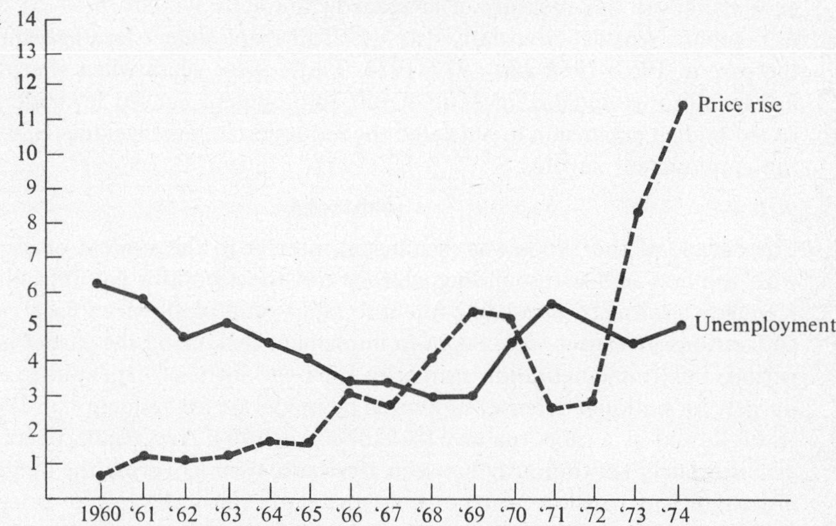

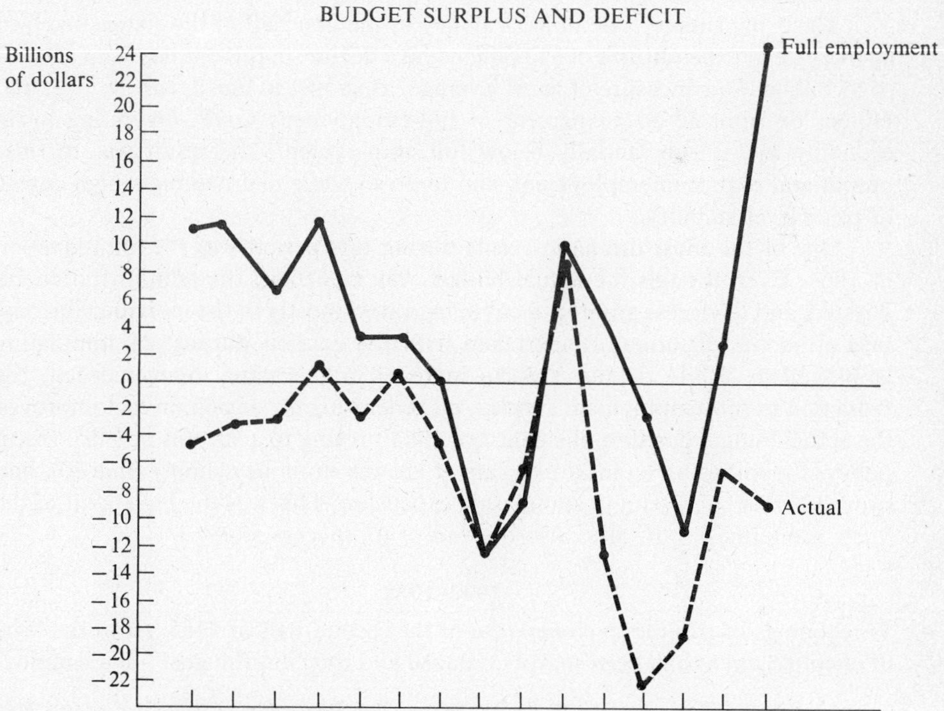

FIGURE 27-1 Fiscal Policy, 1960–74.

A second comparison is between changes in full-employment surplus or deficit and changes in our measure of leverage at full employment (line 15). While the full-employment deficit usually rises with full-employment leverage, this was not the case in 1967–1968 and 1973–1974. Those were years when sharp increases in expenditures and tax revenue at full employment caused leverage from balanced-budget expansion to outweigh the reduction in leverage due to an increased full-employment surplus.

1960–1965

The decade of the 1960s was of unusual interest to the student of fiscal policy, with the first half a resounding success and the second a painful failure.[4] The Kennedy administration had come into office on a platform of fiscal expansion, and various measures were taken to implement it. During the earlier part of the period, this implementation primarily took the form of expenditure expansion (largely for national defense) supported by moderate tax reduction in 1962, which was followed by a more massive tax cutback in 1964. As a result, unemployment declined fairly continuously between 1961 and 1966, covering the longest period of sustained expansion on record. At the same time, the rate of price increase remained modest. Shown in line 13 of the table as well as in Figure 27-1, expansionary fiscal measures resulted in a sharp decline in full-employment surplus while the expanding economy (and with it, built-in revenue growth) turned the actual balance from a deficit to a surplus position.

The expansionary role of fiscal policy in the first half of the sixties involved an increase in expenditures of $23 billion and a decline in full-employment surplus of $8 billion. Our measure of fiscal leverage, as shown in line 7, rose by over $40 billion, or from 13 to 19 percent of full-employment GNP. Operating in an economy as yet substantially below full employment, the result was to raise output and reduce unemployment, and to do so while maintaining a high degree of price level stability.

One of the most dramatic events during this period was the tax reduction of 1964. Even though the actual budget was in deficit, the administration requested, and Congress granted, a cut in tax rates (mostly in the individual income tax) of about $10 billion, undertaken with the explicit purpose of stimulating employment. While risking a sharp increase in the actual budget deficit, the reduction in full-employment surplus, by generating expansion, in fact improved the actual budget position, the deficit of 1964 turning to a surplus in 1965. Fiscal policy, supported by an increased rate of growth in money supply (line 20), had proven highly successful in stimulating expansion. This was the high point of the "new economics" but, alas, also the end of its success story.

1966–1968

Forebodings of trouble to come arose in the second half of 1965. After the level of unemployment had been sharply reduced and the "interim goal" of unemploy-

[4] For further discussion, see Walter W. Heller, *New Dimensions of Political Economy,* New York: Norton, 1967; Arthur M. Okun, *Political Economy of Prosperity,* New York: Norton, 1970; Herbert Stein, *The Fiscal Revolution in America,* Chicago: The University of Chicago Press, 1969; and Charles E. McClure, Jr., *Fiscal Failure, Lessons of the Sixties,* Washington: American Enterprise Institute, 1972.

ment not in excess of 4 percent had been reached, the upswing continued to proceed at a rapid pace. Driven by an investment boom reflecting the stimulating effects of the investment credit of 1962, a rising level of consumption, and sustained increase in government expenditures, the rate of expansion came to exceed a level which could be sustained without inflation. While the speed of price increase still remained modest, proper policy would have called for slowing down the rate of expansion at this point, but a recommendation for tax increase—said to have been advanced by the Council of Economic Advisers late in 1965—went unheeded. Federal Reserve authorities, in trying to go it alone, produced a sharp slowdown in the rate of increase in money supply in 1966, leading to a painful "credit crunch."

Fiscal policy similarly added to, rather than checked, the rising level of excess demand. Federal expenditures rose at a greatly accelerated rate in 1966 and 1967, with half the increase reflecting the rising costs of the Vietnam war. In the absence of tax measures, the full-employment surplus declined sharply in both years (line 13) and the actual budget followed suit, falling from a surplus of $1 billion in 1965 to a deficit of $12 billion in 1967. Since full employment had been reached, the behavior of both budgets—as shown in Figure 27-1—followed the same pattern of decline. Fiscal leverage (line 15) rose sharply, at the very time when the opposite change would have been in order.

Minor restrictive tax measures, including suspension of the investment credit, were recommended and became effective in October 1966, but they remained insufficient. Belatedly, President Johnson called for a more substantial tax increase in his budget message of January 1967. The Congress refused to respond and, moving in the opposite direction, reinstated the investment credit in March 1967. Expenditures continued to rise, and, in view of growing inflationary pressures, the President repeated his request for a 10 percent increase in income tax in a tax message presented in mid-August. Once again, congressional response lagged, and it was not until June 1968 that the tax increase was enacted. In the meantime, the deficit had been allowed to deepen for two years and Federal Reserve policy (line 20) had permitted a rapid expansion in the money supply in 1967 and 1968. In the process, the rate of inflation had accelerated to 4 percent.

Who was to blame for the delay in restrictive fiscal action? Among various factors, the unpredictability of defense outlays offers the best excuse, but it is not a sufficient explanation. While federal expenditures rose sharply from 1966 to 1967, less than half the increase was for national defense. Political hesitation to urge increased tax rates on the part of the White House was another factor, and a rather tardy support for restrictive action by economists did not help matters. The most important single cause, however, was congressional delay in meeting the President's request for a tax increase. Congressional opposition to the Presidential demand for a prompt increase in income tax rates was ostensibly based upon insistence that the tax increase be combined with measures to restrict expenditure expansion, but no doubt this stand was reinforced by the political unpopularity of a tax increase. Notwithstanding uncertainties about budget needs due to the Vietnam war, the economic need for restrictive action was evident. There was little excuse for permitting the buildup of inflationary forces which led to the difficulties of subsequent years.

1969–1974

A marked turn toward restrictive policy, including a sharply restrictive monetary policy and an equally sharp decline in fiscal leverage, did not come until 1969. The latter reflected introduction of the income tax surcharge and suspension of the investment credit in 1969, as well as a decline in the rate of expenditure growth. As a result, both the actual and the full-employment budgets recorded a sharp turnaround from deficit to surplus. This shift served to halt the expansion but also to turn the economy into a recession.

With unemployment rising in 1970 and 1971 and the inflation rate declining, policy turned once more toward expansion. Fiscal leverage increased, reflecting both tax reduction (including suspension of the surcharge, reinstitution of the investment credit in the Revenue Act of 1971, and other tax relief) and a sharp increase in expenditures for civilian programs. In consequence, the full-employment surplus declined, with the actual budget moving sharply into deficit under the impact of a sluggish economy. This shift toward fiscal expansion was accompanied by a sharply expansionary turn in monetary policy. Together, these measures succeeded in retarding the rising rate of unemployment but were less successful with regard to inflation. They were accompanied in late 1971 by a direct approach to the inflation problem through a temporary price and wage freeze. With continued fiscal and monetary expansion in 1972, unemployment leveled off, as did the price rise.

Nineteen-seventy-three brought the dismantling of direct controls, combined with a more restrictive policy stance. The rate of monetary expansion was reduced sharply with fiscal policy also slightly on the restrictive side as full-employment tax receipts (due largely to an increase in payroll tax rates and revenue) outpaced the increase in full-employment expenditure. As a result, the full-employment budget returned to a surplus position, while the deficit in the actual budget declined. With a strengthened private sector, the unemployment rate declined but the inflation rate took a sharp upturn. This was but the prelude to the unhappy developments of 1974 when a two-digit rate of price increase combined with a renewed rise of unemployment.

The course of fiscal policy in 1974 demonstrates what may happen to fiscal leverage under conditions of stagflation. GNP, which must rise in real terms to prevent an increase in the rate of unemployment, did in fact decline. Yet prices rose sufficiently to bring about an increase in GNP in money terms. Tax revenue consequently rose, with the gain about matching the increase in expenditures so as to leave the actual budget with a modest and only slightly changed level of deficit. At the same time, inflation made for a sharp increase in full-employment revenue, reflecting a rise not only in prices but also in real terms. This gain far outpaced the expenditure increase, resulting in a sharp rise in full-employment surplus and a decline in leverage. The role of fiscal policy as measured by our indices was thus distinctly restrictive. Unfortunately, the effect was to contribute to a deepening of the recession rather than a retardation of inflation.

By the end of 1974, the danger of deepening recession had displaced inflation as the primary concern. With unemployment above 8 percent and rising, fiscal policy shifted toward a sharply expansionary position. The Budget Message of

January 1975, which called for a tax cut of $15 billion, was followed by congressional response in April. This legislation provided for a tax reduction of $25 billion, including a refund of $8 billion on 1974 taxes and a reduction in 1975 liabilities of $17 billion. While including an increase in the investment credit, the reduction was largely in individual income tax and focused on low- and middle-income taxpayers. Combined with rising expenditures, the full-employment budget was moved from a surplus of $20 billion in 1974 to a deficit of about $10 billion in 1976. This reflected a swing in leverage of about $80 billion, which, when seen in relation to the level of full-employment GNP, was comparable in magnitude to that introduced in the tax reduction measure of 1964.

C. CONCLUSIONS

Regarding the role of fiscal policy, it is evident that excessive expansion in the second half of the 1960s was the beginning of the trouble and that abrupt and poorly timed policy swings thereafter added to the course of instability. However, it can hardly be concluded that fiscal policy was the major cause of the recent inflation. As shown by Table 27-1, federal expenditures as a percentage of full-employment GNP showed little change in recent years; and as recorded by our indices, the general role of fiscal policy in 1973 and 1974 was restrictive followed by a sharp turn to expansion in 1975. What then was the major cause of failure of stabilization policy over the years from 1966 to 1975?

One explanation points to the complex set of relationships by which economic changes in any one current period depend on how prices, wages, output, and employment have behaved in preceding periods. Because of this complex lag structure, the system once derailed, as happened in the late 1960s, is difficult to return to a stable, full-employment path. The hope is that more judicious policy decisions at an earlier stage can avoid such difficulties in the future, with the burden of proof being on the feasibility of "fine tuning." Another optimistic interpretation is that the policy failure of recent years may be explained by the coincidence of an unusual set of disturbing outside factors, such as the oil crisis, raw material shortages caused by the concurrence of worldwide prosperity, unfavorable harvests, and so forth. Again the implication is that these difficulties will pass, so as to render the task of future stabilization policy more manageable. A less optimistic interpretation is that modern industrial society poses inherent difficulties in securing the dual objectives of high employment and price stability, especially in their implementation through measures of aggregate demand control as are provided by fiscal and monetary policy instruments. While there is no strong evidence for attributing the recent difficulties of the United States economy to a cost-push process, the experience of other countries suggests that this has been a major problem.

FURTHER READINGS

Brookings Institution: *Setting National Priorities, the 1975 Budget,* and issues for earlier years, Washington.

Economic Report of the President. Current discussions of fiscal policy issues may be found in each of the annual economic reports.

Heller, Walter: *New Dimensions of Political Economy,* New York: Norton, 1967.

McClure, Charles E., Jr.: *Fiscal Failure, Lessons of the Sixties,* Washington: American Enterprise Institute, 1972.

Stein, Herbert: *The Fiscal Revolution in America,* Chicago: The University of Chicago Press, 1969.

Chapter 28

Economics of the Public Debt*

A. Structure of the Federal Debt: *Growth of the Federal Debt; Composition of the Federal Debt.* **B. Maturity Mix and Interest Cost:** *Term Structure of Rates; Term Structure and Debt Management.* **C. Further Issues in Debt Management:** *Interest Ceiling; Debt Limitation; Nonmarketable and Special Issues; Inflation-proof Bonds; Refunding Techniques; Agency Debt; Debt Management and Government Lending.* **D. The Market for State and Local Debt:** *Tax Exemption versus Direct Interest Subsidy; Industrial Revenue Bonds.* **E. Debt Burden and Intergeneration Equity:** *Public Debt and Fiscal Solvency; Burden Transfer through Reduced Capital Formation; Burden Transfer with Generation Overlap; Burden Transfer with Outside Debt; Borrowing by State and Local Governments; Burden Transfer in Development Finance; Justification for Burden Transfer.* **F. Summary.**

The public debt in the United States as of December 31, 1974, amounted to about $685 billion, $493 billion of which was federal and an estimated $192 billion state and local. We begin with federal debt and the problems of management which it poses.

* *Reader's Guide to Chapter 28:* The first part of this chapter examines problems of debt structure and debt management, mostly at the federal level. This continues the discussion of stabilization policy and in particular of the interaction between fiscal and monetary policy undertaken in the preceding chapters. The second part deals with problems of debt burden and intergeneration equity. These are of primary importance at the state and local levels. While the public debt has ceased to be the hot issue it was some years ago, it nevertheless continues to be of considerable importance in economic policy.

A. STRUCTURE OF THE FEDERAL DEBT

During the decades of the thirties and forties, the growth of the federal debt and the alleged dangers thereof were a prime issue in public discussion and political controversy. Since then, the debt has become recognized as a relatively minor problem, although its management—i.e., what type of securities to issue and how to conduct refunding operations—continues to be an important factor in stabilization policy. The federal debt provides its holders with more or less liquid claims which in turn affect interest rates and spending behavior. As an instrument of control over liquidity, management of the federal debt is thus closely related to monetary policy.

Growth of the Federal Debt

The growth of the federal debt between 1941 and 1974 is summarized in Table 28-1. We note that this debt rose sharply in the course of financing World War II, both in absolute terms (line 1) and relative to GNP (line 5). But, though the absolute level of this debt nearly doubled between 1946 and 1974, the ratio of debt to GNP fell sharply, and by 1974 had dropped to well below the pre–World War II level. In considerable part this was the result of inflation which accelerated the growth of GNP in money terms. As inflation reduced the net value of debt claims, it acted as a built-in mechanism of debt devaluation. Since the problem of public debt management relates to privately held debt only,[1] excluding debt held by government trust funds and the Federal Reserve Banks, this segment of the debt is shown separately in line 3. The pattern follows that of the total debt for the 1941–1946 period, but the 1946–1974 picture is very different. With about 75 percent of the increase in gross debt between these years absorbed by govern-

TABLE 28-1
Growth of Federal Debt, 1941–1974
(In Billions of Dollars)

	1941	*1946*	*1974*
1. Total gross debt (par value)	58	259	493
2. Held by government agencies*	11	51	222
3. Held by private investors	47	208	271
4. Interest	1	5	19
Ratios			
5. Line 1 as percent of GNP	47	125	35
6. Line 3 as percent of GNP	38	100	19
7. Line 3 as percent of money supply†	63	133	28
8. Line 3 as percent of private debt‡	34	136	13
9. Line 4 as percent of GNP	0.8	2.4	1.4

* Includes holdings by Federal Reserve Banks.
† Money supply includes demand, time and savings deposits, and currency held outside banks.
‡ Private debt includes corporate, noncorporate, and individual debt.
Source: Economic Report of the President, February 1975.

[1] Debt held by the Federal Reserve and the trust funds is subject to government control rather than to decisions by private investors, and therefore does not affect private spending behavior.

ment agencies, privately held debt grew but modestly. As a result, the ratio of privately held federal debt to GNP dropped sharply from 100 to 19 percent (line 6).

A similar pattern emerges if we consider the weight of privately held federal debt in the overall liquidity structure. As shown in line 7, the ratio of debt to money supply grew sharply during World War II but since then has fallen to one-half its prewar level. As seen in line 8, the ratio of federal debt to private debt showed a similar decline. With public debt a greatly reduced fraction of total claims, the task of debt management has been eased accordingly.

As another aspect of the public debt problem, the table also records the changing level of interest payments. As shown in line 4, the absolute amount of interest payments moved up through the three decades, reflecting the rising level of debt as well as of interest rates. Nevertheless, this increase lagged behind that of GNP so that interest as percentage of GNP (line 9) declined sharply from its post–World War II peak, but remained substantially above prewar levels. As we shall see later, this is the ratio which matters in considering the demands of debt service upon the tax system.

Composition of the Federal Debt

The composition of the federal debt by type of issue is shown in Table 28-2.

The total debt is divided into public issues available to private investors and the Federal Reserve System and special issues which are held by government agencies only. As the table shows, public issues constitute 74 percent of the total and are divided into marketable and nonmarketable issues. The former are traded and available to all buyers. The latter are issued to individual holders and can be held only by the initial buyer. They are nonnegotiable and are not transferable to others. Marketable issues include bills, notes, and bonds. The main difference between them is one of maturity. Bills are issued with maturities from three to twelve months, notes from one to seven years, and bonds for longer periods. Notes

TABLE 28-2
Gross Federal Debt by Types of Issues
(Par Values in Billions of Dollars, December 31, 1974)

Public issues	373		
Marketable		283	
Bills			120
Notes			130
Bonds			33
Nonmarketable		88	
Savings bonds			64
Foreign issues			23
Convertible bonds		2	
Special issues	118		
Total gross debt*	492		

* The total includes a small amount of matured debt and debt bearing no interest which is not included in Table 28-3.

Note: Items may not add to totals due to rounding.

Source: *Federal Reserve Bulletin,* January 1975, p. A36.

TABLE 28-3
Gross Federal Debt by Types of Holders
(Par Values in Billions of Dollars, October 31, 1974)

Held by United States agencies and Federal Reserve	218	
United States government agencies and trust funds		138
Federal Reserve Banks		79
Held privately, domestic	206	
Commercial banks		54
Other financial institutions		8
Individuals		84
State and local governments		29
Other corporations and miscellaneous		31
Foreign-held	57	
Total gross debt	481	

Note: Items may not add to totals due to rounding.
Source: *Federal Reserve Bulletin,* December 1974, p. A36.

and bonds are usually issued at a price slightly below par (the redemption value at maturity) and interest is paid periodically in return for coupons attached to the bond. Bills are sold on a discount basis, with the appreciation in value to maturity representing the interest return.

Among nonmarketable issues, the most important item is savings bonds. Sold to individuals at a price below par, these bonds pay in the form of appreciation; bonds may be cashed in prior to maturity but then bear a lower interest rate. Special issues comprise mainly savings notes sold to corporations and special agency bonds.

Distribution of the debt by types of holders is shown in Table 28-3. Of the total, 45 percent is now held by government trust funds and the Federal Reserve Banks. Most important among the former is the OASDI Trust Fund which acquired these obligations in years when current receipts from payroll taxes exceeded benefit payments. Holdings are largely in the form of special issues. Federal Reserve Bank holdings in turn are of the marketable type and are acquired in the process of open market purchases. Given the public nature of the Federal Reserve System (notwithstanding its formally independent status), such holdings are, in fact, part of the monetary base rather than part of the federal debt owed to the public.

Of nongovernment held debt, 73 percent is held domestically while 27 percent is foreign-held, including holdings by foreign central banks. Of privately held debt, nearly 26 percent is held by commercial banks, largely in the form of Treasury bills which, owing to their short-term nature, are more suited to meet the liquidity needs of such investors. Individual investors hold 38 percent, mostly in the form of savings bonds. Financial institutions, such as savings banks and insurance companies, hold 4 percent, largely in the form of longer-term issues. State and local governments hold 14 percent of the privately held federal debt, again largely in the form of bills which serve as investment for their working balances. Viewing the picture as a whole, it appears that the public debt has very largely become an investment medium for short-term funds, while longer-term funds (except for savings bonds holdings by individuals) tend to be invested in private securities or equity. This differs greatly from the pattern which prevailed in the 1930s and 1940s and reflects the upsurge of the private sector in the postwar decades. During those years, private investment outlets resumed their earlier position as preferred investment choices.

B. MATURITY MIX AND INTEREST COST

The major issue in debt management is the choice of maturities. Traditionally, it was held that the public debt should be well "funded," i.e., be in long-term maturities. Thus, the British debt during the nineteenth century was largely in the form of consols or perpetual securities which have no fixed maturity date but can be retired at the government's option provided it is willing to pay the market price. This stipulation would protect the government against the contingency that creditors would demand their money back at an inopportune time. The modern view of national debt and the position of national governments in the debt market is quite different. Debt management proceeds on the assumption that maturing issues can always be refunded. Although the overall level of the debt may be increased at some periods and reduced at others (depending on whether the needs of stabilization policy call for a deficit or a surplus), there is no expectation that accumulated past debts will ever be "paid off." As particular issues mature, they come to be "refunded" into other issues. The shorter is the average debt outstanding, the larger will be the annual volume of refunding operations, but this is of no particular concern and not decisive in determining the maturity structure.

This being the case, what basic guidelines are there to the choice of maturities which the Treasury should offer? One possible answer is that it should select the term structure of the debt so as to minimize interest cost. Since the cost of borrowing tends to differ with the maturity of the debt, those issues should be chosen which investors are willing to absorb at the lowest cost. The same principle of economy which suggests that the government should buy its pencils from the lowest-cost supplier may also suggest that it borrow from the lowest-cost lender. On closer consideration, this proves too simple a rule, but let us first see what it would imply.

Term Structure of Rates

As we look back at the history of interest rates over the course of this century, we find short rates usually have been close to or above long rates. This pattern was reversed during the depression years of the 1930s when the general level of rates declined sharply and short rates fell below long rates. Federal Reserve policy was used to maintain this low level of rates during the war years to permit financing of the war debt at low cost. This required a substantial share of the debt to be absorbed by the commercial banks and a corresponding increase in money supply. Appropriate during the war, this policy was continued until the early fifties. Defended by the Treasury, it came under attack from the Federal Reserve System. The policy proved incompatible with the application of monetary restraint since the Federal Reserve had to stand ready to purchase bonds in the open market when needed to keep their prices from falling and their yields from rising. This constraint proved untenable and the Treasury–Federal Reserve "Accord" of 1951 left the Federal Reserve free to let rates rise. Federal Reserve policy accordingly adopted a "bills only" policy under which all open market operations would be conducted in Treasury bills. After a gradual transition, the securities markets returned to the earlier pattern of higher rates, with short and long rates moving closer together and with short rates occasionally above long rates.

The development of short and long rates since 1960 is shown in Figure 28-1. It will be seen that the general rate level has been rising, with the excess of long over short rates narrowing between 1960 and 1966 and short rates exceeding longs in the later years. A similar development is recorded in Figure 28-2, where yield curves for selected years are shown.[2] We note the upward shift in the yield curve and the change from a rising to a falling term structure of rates.

Theory of Term Structure Economists have tried to explain the term structure of rates on the basis of rate expectations.[3] In a situation where no changes in interest rates are expected, so the argument goes, there is no reason for short and long rates to differ. The yield curve is horizontal. But suppose now that an expectation of rising rates emerges. As a result, lenders (or demanders of debt) will hesitate to commit themselves for a long period as they expect to obtain more

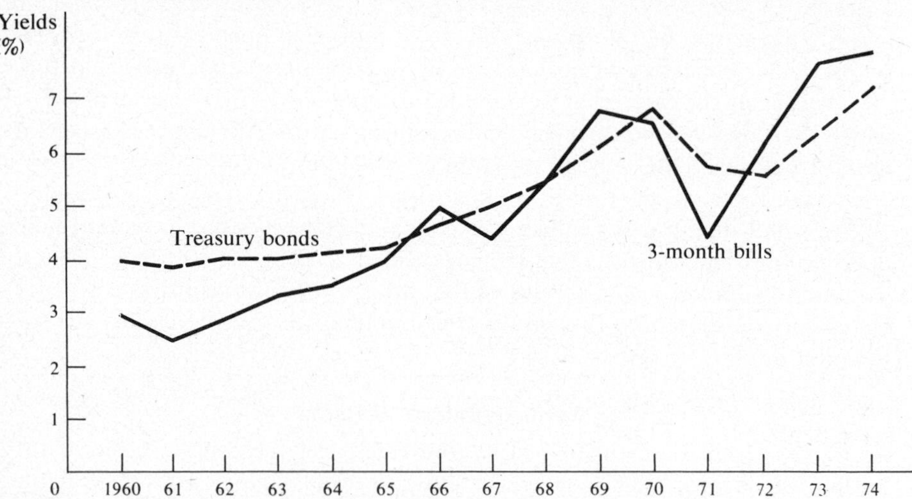

FIGURE 28-1 Short and Long Rates, 1960–1974.
Source: Economic Report of the President, 1974, p. 317, and *Federal Reserve Bulletin,* August 1974.

[2] The yield of a bond is the internal rate of discount at which the present value of the redemption payment plus coupon payment equals the purchase price. If the Treasury issues a bond at par (i.e., its redemption value), the yield equals the coupon rate of interest.

[3] For a convenient summary of this theory, see W. L. Smith, "Debt Management in the United States," Study Paper 19, *Study of Employment, Growth, and Price Levels,* Joint Economic Committee, U.S. Congress, June 28, 1960. For the original presentation, see J. R. Hicks, *Value and Capital,* 2d ed., Oxford: Clarendon, 1946, chap. 11.

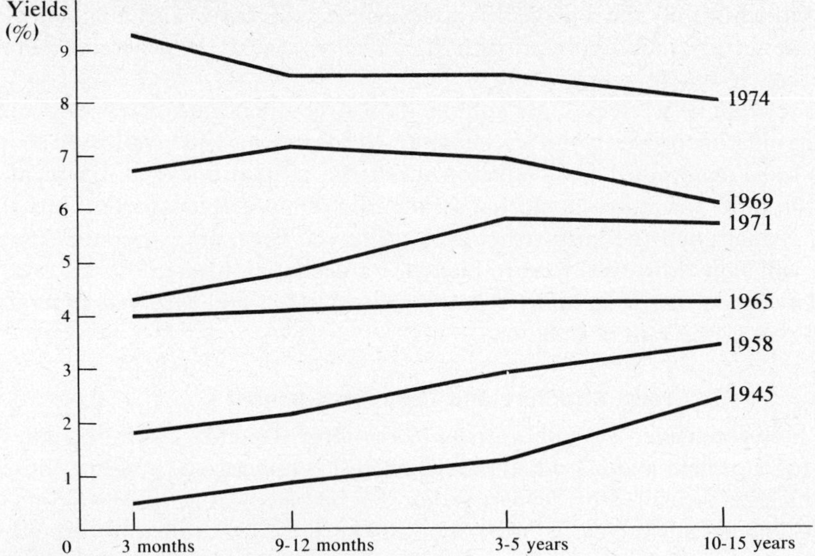

FIGURE 28-2 Yields to Maturity, 1945–1974.
Source: See Figure 28-1.

favorable terms later on. Thus, the demand for debt shifts from the long to the short market. Borrowers (or suppliers of debt), on the other hand, are eager to borrow before costs arise. Thus, the supply of debt shifts from the short to the long market. As a result, demand for debt rises relative to supply on the short end. The price of short-term debt rises and yields decline.[4] At the same time, demand for debt falls relative to supply at the long end. Consequently, the price of long-term debt falls and yields rise. Thus, the yield curve comes to slope upward. The opposite result comes about if declining rates are expected. Long rates, according to this theory, come to reflect the expected level of future short-term rates.

Others have argued that this is too narrow a view of the term-structure problem. While expectations matter, the most important influences at any one time may be generated by developments in various parts of the capital market, resulting in structural changes in the demand for, and supply of, particular debt instruments.[5]

Effect of Inflation Finally, how does inflation enter into the rate structure? The effect of inflation on the general level of interest rates is readily seen. Inflation does drive up rates because lenders wish to protect themselves against a loss in the real value of their claims as prices rise. Thus, if the "real" rate of interest or return in the absence of inflation is 3 percent, while the expected rate of inflation is 6 percent, the nominal rate of interest will tend to be $3 + 6$, or 9 percent. The additional 6 percent is needed to maintain the purchasing power

[4] See Smith, op. cit., p. 92.

[5] See J. M. Culbertson, "The Term Structure of Interest Rates," *Quarterly Journal of Economics,* November 1967.

of the bond while only the 3 percent is a net gain in real terms. This inflationary adjustment accounts for a substantial part of the increase in the general level of interest rates in recent years.

The relation between inflation and the term structure of rates is less evident. As long as inflation proceeds at a *constant* rate, say 4 percent, and investors expect this rate to be maintained, the "inflation surcharge" will also stay at 4 percent, so that the term structure should not be affected. Only if the expected rate of inflation changes will the term structure be affected. Thus, an expectation that inflation will slow down will tend to make for a decline in future nominal rates and hence lead to a rise in short relative to long rates, and vice versa for an expected rise in the rate of inflation.

Term Structure and Debt Management

We can now reconsider the implications of the term structure of interest rates for debt management and ask whether interest cost is minimized by selling those issues which, as measured by current yields, can be placed at the lowest cost to maturity. The answer is clearly "no." Suppose the Treasury can borrow for one year at 5 percent and for twenty years at 7 percent. It does not follow that taking the one-year issue is preferable because by year's end the opportunity to borrow at 7 percent may be lost if the level of rates has risen. Or, suppose that the Treasury can borrow for twenty years at 5 percent and for one year at 7 percent. The former choice is not necessarily preferable since rates may decline before the twenty years have passed.

What matters most is the *direction* in which the Treasury expects rates to change. If debt managers expect rates to rise, the proper choice is to borrow long; if they expect them to fall, the choice is to stay short. The important point is that once a commitment has been made, there is no way of escape. The interest cost contracted for must be carried for the full period even though rates may fall; and the benefits of a low rate will continue to accrue even though the rates may rise.[6] Debt management, therefore, is a fine art which requires a shrewd appraisal of market prospects for a considerable time ahead.

But even if expected rate changes are allowed for, the criterion of minimum interest cost does not offer a sufficient guide. Differences in the behavior of investors who hold long and short debt must also be taken into account. After all, the central government, with its control over money creation, can regulate

[6] Suppose that the Treasury borrows $1,000 in a market in which a twenty-year bond, if selling at par, must carry a coupon rate of 6½ percent. Having sold such a bond, suppose that after one year the market yield on a nineteen-year bond falls to 5½ percent. As a result, the price of the old bond will rise to $1,117, i.e., the present value of $1,000 due in nineteen years plus nineteen annual coupon payments of $65 as discounted at 5½ percent. Thus, if the Treasury were to retire the old bond (assuming that it had a call feature so that this could be done) and to reissue a new nineteen-year bond at 5½ percent, it would have to raise $1,117 rather than $1,000 to replace the outstanding issue. This would leave its position unchanged, since the present values of the two cash flows—i.e., $1,000 in nineteen years plus nineteen annual payments of $65, or $1,117 in nineteen years plus nineteen annual coupon payments of $61.40 discounted at 5½ percent—are the same, and each is equal to $1,117. Similar reasoning applies in a situation where interest rates rise and bond prices fall. Here, nothing would be lost by replacing the old bond with a new one. Even though the former could be retired at a lower price, the latter's coupon rate would have to be correspondingly higher.

the level of interest rates in the market. It can always replace public debt by money, whether crudely through the printing press or more discreetly by borrowing from the central bank. Replacing debt with money would clearly be the cheapest way of handling the matter as it would involve no interest cost at all. Yet, it would not be a satisfactory solution because monetizing the debt would result in greatly increased liquidity, giving rise to an excessive level of aggregate demand and inflation.

Viewed this way, the purpose of issuing debt rather than money (or replacing maturing debt outstanding with new debt rather than monetizing it) is to purchase illiquidity. Investors must be convinced to hold debt rather than money, and the way to do this is to pay them. The question arises whether a dollar of short-term debt is as helpful in reducing liquidity as a dollar of long-term debt. If long-term debt makes the holder less liquid, it might pay the Treasury to issue such debt even if the interest cost were somewhat higher. The principle of minimizing interest costs must thus be restated as one of buying illiquidity on the cheapest terms which are compatible with the objectives of stabilization policy.

Lengthening the debt at the time of refunding will tend to be restrictive, and shortening it will tend to be expansionary.[7] Lengthening will raise long rates relative to shorts. Investors who were willing to hold a given supply of longs and shorts at a certain yield spread must now hold more longs and less shorts. To do this, they will require more favorable terms on longs and will be willing to accept less favorable terms on shorts. The restrictive effect of the resulting rise in long rates on private investment will outweigh the expansionary effect of decline in short rates, since capital expenditures are usually based on long-term financing.[8] Short-term debt being more like money, a lengthening of the debt is thus restrictive.

The same considerations which apply to refunding (or swapping of debt) also apply with regard to choosing the type of issue or addition to the debt with which a deficit is financed, or the type of issue which is to be withdrawn as the surplus is used for debt reduction.[9] In either case, debt management may be used to

[7] A similar problem arises in open market operations of the Federal Reserve. However, such operations involve swaps between debt and money only and not between types of debt. Swaps between debt and money are given increased potency by the nature of fractional reserve banking, where (with a reserve ratio of 20 percent) substitution of $100 of debt for $100 of money may force a $500 reduction in money supply. This multiple effect does not arise with swaps between types of debts. However, even here banks may be induced to utilize excess reserves more fully or to extend their use of the discount window if their liquidity is increased by substitution of short-term for long-term debt, thus increasing the holdings of "secondary reserves."

[8] Consider an investor who is confronted with a choice among money, short debt, long debt, and real investment or equity. The individual will balance his or her portfolio among these assets so as to hold the preferred mix at given yields. For the market as a whole, the demand for, and supply of, various types of assets will result in a structure of yields at which both demanders and suppliers are satisfied. If long debt is substituted for short, the market must hold more of the former and less of the latter. Those who absorb additional long-term debt must discard some other assets, whereas those who reduce their holding of short debt must acquire other assets. It seems likely that the former will want to discard equity holdings while the latter will want to shift toward money. The reason is that long debt, being less liquid, is a closer substitute for equity, while short debt is a closer substitute for money. As a result, the cost at which equity funds are available will rise and investment will decline. The opposite holds if the debt is shortened.

[9] It is easy to see that shortening a given debt is expansionary and that a net addition to the debt in short form is more restrictive (or less expansionary) than a similar addition in long form.

support the expansionary or restrictive effects of current stabilization policy. Consequently, short-run policy objectives, rather than long-run expectations of rate change and their implication for interest costs, may be the decisive factor in determining debt management policy. Long-term refunding may be desirable as a restrictive measure during a boom even though interest rates are high, but this approach will be in order only if alternative and less costly forms of restriction are unavailable. Nevertheless, there arises the further question of what constitutes a "sound" maturity mix insofar as the body of the outstanding debt is concerned. A long debt, as noted before, calls for a smaller volume of refunding operations, but this is hardly a decisive consideration. A debt of given size, if short, will leave the economy in a more liquid position and thus may tend to increase its volatility. As a result, the task of stabilization policy may be made more difficult. On the other hand, too long a debt may introduce rigidities into the financial structure and fall short of providing the necessary liquidity. In either case, much will depend on the size of the money stock. The effect on liquidity in the private sector of a longer debt combined with a larger money stock may be similar to the effect of a shorter debt with a smaller money supply. In the absence of better reasoning, one is left with the view that a "well-balanced" maturity structure up to, say, fifteen years is to be preferred to one which is almost entirely short or almost entirely long.

Whatever the answer, the fact is that the trend in the maturity structure of the debt has been toward a substantial shortening over the last twenty years, as Table 28-4 shows. Whereas in 1950, long-term debt in excess of twenty-five years comprised 16 percent of the total, this ratio has now dropped to 3 percent. Short-term debt, including maturities of less than one year, rose from 27 percent to 51 percent of the total. Average years to maturity fell from eight to two years. Debt management over the last twenty-five years thus produced a substantial shift toward increased liquidity of the debt and thereby contributed to expansionary policy.

A major shift occurred during the 1950s as the long-term bonds sold during the war years were not replaced by similar issues, and a second major shift toward shortening of the debt has occurred in recent years. In an inflationary setting, reliance on short debt permits the Treasury to avoid committing itself to a high-interest cost over a longer period, hoping that inflation will be checked and that nominal interest rates will fall in the future. At the same time, investors feel

---

But it is more difficult to appraise the effects of a net addition of a particular type of debt considered by itself.

Consider a net addition to long-term debt. As a result, the total stock of claims and equity which investors must hold is increased. Since their preferences call for a balanced portfolio, they will not wish to absorb the entire addition in the form of a long debt. They will thus try to substitute other assets. This will increase long-term yields and may thus be expected to be restrictive. However, the addition to long-term debt will not only be reflected in an increased demand for short debt and money, but there may also be some desire to substitute equity. To the extent that this occurs, the cost at which equity funds become available is reduced and investment will rise. While less expansionary (or more restrictive) than the net addition of shorter debt, the effect of adding longer debt, taken by itself, may thus go in either direction. See James Tobin, "An Essay on Principles of Debt Management," in Commission on Money and Credit (ed.), *Fiscal and Debt Management Policies,* Englewood Cliffs, N.J.: Prentice-Hall, 1963.

TABLE 28-4
Composition of Marketable Debt by Maturity

	1950		1960		1965		1974*	
	Billions of Dollars	*Per-centage*	*Billions of Dollars*	*Per-centage*	*Billions of Dollars*	*Per-centage*	*Billions of Dollars*	*Per-centage*
Years to Maturity								
0–1	42	27	70	38	88	42	143	51
1–5	51	33	73	40	56	27	85	31
5–10	8	5	20	11	39	19	28	10
10–20	28	18	13	7	8	4	15	5
20 and over	25	16	8	4	17	8	7	3
Total	155	100	183	100	209	100	278	100
Average Years to Maturity	8.2		4.8		5.3		2.1	

* Figures for November 30, 1974.
Notes: Issues are classified by number of years remaining to maturity. Items may not add to totals due to rounding.
Source: *Economic Report of the President,* January 1974, p. 334, and *Federal Reserve Bulletin,* January 1975, p. A37.

uncertain about the future (inflation may get worse!) and prefer to avoid a long-term commitment. Thus, it is expedient to refund maturing issues short-term, but in so doing, the liquidity of the claim structure is increased.

C. FURTHER ISSUES IN DEBT MANAGEMENT

In addition to the choice of maturities, a number of further issues in debt management will be noted, but cannot be developed in detail.

Interest Ceiling

In the latter part of the 1960s the interest rate ceiling, as noted before, came to interfere with the sale of long-term debt. Toward the close of World War I, Congress had enacted an interest ceiling of 4½ percent on securities in excess of five years, including all Treasury bonds. This ceiling remained largely ineffective until the second half of the 1960s when long-term yields in the market rose above this level. Although the ceiling could have been circumvented by selling bonds with a 4½ percent coupon rate at a price below par, the Treasury chose not to do so, as this would have violated the congressional prohibition. Thus, no long-term bonds could be sold after 1965 when market yields rose above the ceiling. After repeated Treasury requests, Congress in March 1971 authorized the issue of $10 billion in Treasury bonds at above-ceiling yields, but no such bonds have as yet been issued.

The story of the interest ceiling reflects the historical controversy between tight and easy money. It has been a recurrent theme in United States monetary and political history over the last century, witnessed in recent decades by the perpetual feud of the House Banking and Currency Committee (led until recently by Wright Patman) with the Federal Reserve.[10] But whatever one's view of this matter, the issue should not be resolved by a rigid ceiling. The appropriate mix of fiscal, monetary, and debt policies should be determined on its merits and in line with current policy objectives, with bond yields and refunding patterns adjusted to this policy mix. The ceiling placed an undesirable constraint on the conduct of stabilization policy and its removal is thus called for.

Debt Limitation

Another congressional constraint on debt management relates to the size of the debt. Congress annually authorizes a set limit which the Treasury cannot exceed.[11] At the same time, congressional action or inaction with regard to revenue legislation and appropriations often calls for increases in government borrowing beyond the debt ceiling, thus requiring the Secretary of the Treasury periodically to appear before Congress and to beg for an increase in the ceiling. The debt ceiling, as most observers agree, is a roundabout device to secure control over

[10] Tight money and high interest rates are suspect because they mean higher returns for the money lender and higher costs for the borrower, who is held more deserving. This is but one aspect of the problem posed by the differential incidence (or distributional implications) of monetary, as distinct from fiscal, restriction. See p. 570.

[11] See Marshall A. Robinson, *The National Debt Ceiling*, Washington: Brookings, 1959.

expenditure levels which Congress should impose in a more direct and explicit fashion. It should be abolished now that a mechanism for coordinating revenue and expenditure legislation has been provided by the Congressional Budget Act of 1974.

Nonmarketable and Special Issues

Since the preferences of various investor groups for various types of securities differ, debt management may make use of this differentiation and tailor the debt instruments which it supplies to the desires of particular parts of the market. By acting as a discriminating monopolist in selling its bonds, the Treasury may do so for a higher price and hence lower cost in interest payments. Like any discriminating monopolist, it would have to divide the market to prevent arbitrage, and it may do so by selling issues which can only be held by particular groups, e.g., commercial banks, nonbank investors, and life insurance companies. Or this device may be used to give preferential treatment to selected groups. Thus, higher interest rates might be paid on savings bonds held in limited amounts by small investors, so as to encourage savings in that sector. Separation of the market in this fashion was undertaken to some extent during the 1940s, especially by rendering certain issues ineligible for holding by commercial banks, but it has not been relied upon since—at least, not for publicly held debt. Special issues held by trust funds such as the OASDI Trust Fund are used, but this is a different matter.

Inflation-proof Bonds

One proposal, advanced repeatedly over the years and again timely under current inflationary conditions, is for the issuance of a "stable purchasing-power bond."[12] The redemption value of such a bond would vary with the cost-of-living index, thus protecting small investors against the loss of purchasing power from inflation as well as depriving them of a (less likely) gain if prices should fall. While this risk might also be avoided by equity investment, the latter involves stock market fluctuations and failure which the small investor can ill sustain and would be spared if a stable purchasing-power bond were available. The coupon rate on such a bond would be correspondingly lower, since it would carry no inflation premium. Its availability would be of great value to small investors who find it difficult to protect themselves against inflation.[13] Given these advantages, it is difficult to see why such bonds have not been issued. Perhaps the explanation lies in the fact that it is difficult for the Treasury to admit uncertainties regarding the value of the dollar, or because it would generate pressure for similar escalation clauses in the rest of the economy.

[12] For an earlier proposal, see L. Bach and R. A. Musgrave, "A Stable Purchasing Power Bond," *American Economic Review,* December 1941.

[13] If the nominal interest rate adjusts itself to inflation (see p. 593), new investors will be protected thereby. But old investors who purchased the bonds before the inflation was expected are not helped as they do not partake in the rising yield. (Their position is the inverse of the Treasury's position noted in footnote 6, p. 594). Thus, longer-run protection can be given only by a bond whose purchasing power is maintained constant.

Refunding Techniques

Total refunding operations at current levels amount to about $175 billion a year including about $20 billion of maturing notes and bonds and $125 billion of bills, some of which turn over two or three times a year.[14] The smooth handling of these refunding operations requires a high degree of expertise and involves numerous technical problems which cannot be gone into here. Longer-term securities are offered at a fixed price and the cooperation of security dealers and of Federal Reserve policy is needed to assure that the issue is sold smoothly and without disturbing the security markets. Indeed, the Federal Reserve Bank of New York serves as agent for the Treasury in handling these operations. Other devices, such as advance refunding, sales of bonds with call dates prior to maturity, the offering of "tap issues" rather than limited sales at a given date, and the making available of exchange issues to holders of maturing bonds, are employed to assure a smooth functioning of the market. However, with the increasing tendency to issue short-term debt, these problems have become of lesser importance as short-term debt is issued increasingly on an auction basis.

Agency Debt

While the general problem of debt management has declined in importance, an area of growing significance has been posed by federal agency debt. In recent years, debt issues of certain federal agencies have become increasingly important, mainly involving issues by lending agencies such as the Federal National Mortgage Association and the Federal Home Loan Banks. As the importance of such issues increases, there arises a corresponding need to handle their financing in coordination with the Treasury's own debt management policies.

Debt Management and Government Lending

Moreover, government lending (as distinct from spending) enters the scene as an additional instrument of budgetary policy. Lending, like debt retirement, reduces the net debt position of the government. In a perfect capital market, extension of a $100 loan with a ten-year maturity would be equivalent to retirement of a $100 debt issue of similar maturity, assuming the same tax revenue to be used to finance either transaction. But the results of the two transactions may be quite different in an imperfect market. The recipient of the government loan might not have been able to obtain credit elsewhere. Indeed, the very rationale of government lending is to provide funds to creditors who have not been able to obtain them otherwise but who, for reasons of public policy, should be provided with funds. It is thus typically used as an instrument of allocation rather than as stabilization policy, and as such, is particularly important in the context of developing countries where government-supported investment is an important feature of development policy.

[14] For reasons of traditional policy, the Treasury retires outstanding issues only at maturity or call dates. It does not purchase outstanding debt at the market price and replace this debt with new issues. Such a policy, if employed, would greatly increase the flexibility of debt management.

D. THE MARKET FOR STATE AND LOCAL DEBT

The problem of debt management for state and local governments is altogether different from that at the federal level and more like that of private investors attempting to secure funds in the market. The difference holds for both the demand and the supply sides of the picture. On the demand side, the occasion for borrowing by state and local governments occurs primarily when substantial capital expenditures are to be financed. For reasons to be considered in section E, it is prudent that such outlays be loan-financed rather than tax-financed. The rationale for borrowing at the state and local level is thus quite different from that at the federal level where stabilization policy is the primary determinant. On the supply side of the market for funds, a state or local government, unlike the federal government, has no control over the money market conditions under which it must borrow. The best it can do is to obtain funds on as favorable terms as happen to be open to it; and the cost of borrowing differs widely, depending on the fiscal position of the jurisdiction and its "credit rating."

State and local debt now approaches $200 billion and has risen by an average annual amount of about $10 billion over the last decade. It has thus increased more rapidly than the federal debt and at about the same percentage rate as GNP. The debt is largely long-term and may take various forms, including general obligation bonds and special revenue bonds. The latter are issued by particular agencies or public enterprises, such as water or power companies operated by the state, municipality, or other subdivision, and the profits of the enterprise are pledged for the financing of debt service. The cost at which funds are available to various borrowing jurisdictions enters as an important factor into the provision of those state and local services which involve heavy capital outlays, e.g., highways and school buildings. Such outlays are important from the national as well as the state and local perspective, so that state and local borrowing enters as an additional aspect of fiscal federalism.

Tax Exemption versus Direct Interest Subsidy

As we saw earlier, federal policy gives general support to state and local borrowing by excluding interest on such securities from taxable income under the federal income tax.[15] An investor whose marginal tax rate is 50 percent will be willing (other things being equal) to substitute a muncipal bond yielding 4 percent for a corporate bond yielding 8 percent. Currently, AAA-rated state and local bonds may yield 6 percent, whereas corporate bonds will yield 9 percent. Taxpayers whose marginal tax rate exceeds 33 percent will thus have an inducement to hold state and local issues. This tax advantage thus diverts funds into the tax-exempt market, thereby reducing the cost at which state and local governments can borrow.

But this particular form of aid is subject to criticism on two grounds. First, it interferes with the equity of the income tax structure. High-income recipients who receive tax-exempt interest pay less tax than do others with equal income

[15] See p. 251.

from other sources. Moreover, the value of tax exemption rises with bracket rates so that vertical equity is interfered with. On these grounds alone, it would be preferable to provide such assistance as is desired in a way which does not involve tax preferences.

The second objection is that tax exemption results in a smaller gain in terms of interest savings to state and local governments than would be provided by a direct subsidy involving the same cost to the federal government. The reason, as we have noted before, is that the effective rate of subsidy for state and local governments equals the marginal tax rate of the lowest-bracket buyer for whom the incentive is effective, i.e., about 30 percent. Yet, higher-bracket taxpayers are given a benefit (with corresponding revenue losses to the Treasury) ranging from 30 to 70 percent, depending on their bracket rate. This is a further reason why a direct subsidy would be preferable to the interest exemption. Notwithstanding the opposition of state and local officials and high-bracket taxpayers, chances are that a more direct approach will be adopted before long if only because the amount of subsidy available through the exemption route will prove insufficient to attract the required amount of funds. Since at present the investor group for whom the tax benefit matters accounts for only about one-fourth of total savings flowing into the long-term debt market, a more broadly based approach will be needed.[16]

Apart from the question of how support of interest payments is best given, there is the further question of whether general support for interest payments at the state-local level is called for. With state and local borrowing used for capital expenditures, such support is equivalent to a matching grant for capital outlays. Viewed this way, the question is whether capital expenditures as a group are preferable to current expenditures and hence merit a special subsidy, be it on grounds of spillover effects or of merit-good considerations. The answer seems to be in the negative. Aside from matters of politics and constitutional history (with the earlier view that state-local instrumentalities are to be exempted from federal taxation), the very premise of general interest support seems questionable.

Support for state and local borrowing on a more selective basis, parallel to the case for categorical grants, might be more readily justified. In this connection, the creation of a financial intermediary which would itself borrow in the market and then relend to municipalities is under consideration. Such a bank might be instrumental in overcoming the element of arbitrariness now imposed by the system of credit rating, and it would reduce the cost of borrowing for smaller municipalities by spreading risks. On the other hand, it might also introduce elements of political bias into the availability of funds. In other respects, such an institution might be helpful in stabilizing cyclical fluctuations in borrowing costs and in modifying the unevenly heavy impact of changes in monetary policy upon this particular sector of the capital market.

[16] See G. Mitchell, "State and Local Government Borrowing," in M. E. Polakoff (ed.), *Financial Institutions and Markets,* Boston: Houghton Mifflin, 1970, p. 335; and S. S. Surrey and F. Morris, "The Case for Broadening the Financial Options Open to Government," in *Financing State and Local Governments,* Boston: Federal Reserve Bank of Boston, June 1970.

Industrial Revenue Bonds

Finally, notice should be taken of the growth of industrial revenue bonds over the last decade. Such bonds are issued by state and local jurisdictions, the proceeds being used to construct industrial facilities which in turn are leased to private firms. Thus, the cost reduction in financing provided through federal tax exemption is passed on to what constitutes essentially private enterprises. From the point of view of a particular municipality, it is seen as a device to attract firms to its location. But such a policy is not defensible from the national point of view. Congress accordingly provided in 1969 that the tax-exemption privilege on such bonds be limited to issues not exceeding $5 million.

E. DEBT BURDEN AND INTERGENERATION EQUITY

We now turn to quite a different aspect of the debt problem, namely, the proposition that debt finance burdens future generations. If so, this is both a critique of borrowing (since it may be abused by burdening future generations with the cost of services which are enjoyed currently) and an argument for borrowing (since it may be used to secure intergeneration equity by passing on part of the cost of capital outlays to the future). The primary question, however, is: Does such a burden transfer in fact occur, and if so, how?

Public Debt and Fiscal Solvency

The raging debate over debt burden in the thirties and forties was between those who feared that the creation of debt in the course of deficit finance (made necessary in securing high employment) would burden the future, and others who, in defending such finance, argued that it would not do so.

More specifically, the contention advanced by the opponents of deficit finance was that the burden of all public expenditures eventually falls on the taxpayer, with loan finance merely delaying the tax payments to the time when the debt will be paid off. The burden is thus postponed and future generations are born with a chain around their necks, i.e., with the obligation to pay off the national debt. This contention was wrong; there is no need to pay off debt, since it becomes part of the country's claim structure and may be refunded at maturity rather than paid off. Hence, only interest payments create additional tax requirements.

The opposing argument was that such interest payments would impose no burden on future generations since (assuming the debt to be held domestically) the future generation would contain both taxpayers and interest recipients. Gains and losses would therefore wash out, leaving no problem of net burden; there would merely be a transfer from one party to another. Domestic debt imposes no burden since "we owe it to ourselves." This argument was correct in that interest payments involve no loss of resources to the group as a whole, but it overlooked the frictional effects of taxation.[17] As we saw earlier, taxation may

[17] Note that this problem may arise even though interest payments are included in taxable income. The tax rate t required to finance interest is given by $t = idY/(Y + idY) = id/(1 + id)$ where

impose an excess burden and cause deadweight losses. The severity of such effects is likely to rise with the overall level of taxation or ratio of tax revenue to GNP. As the ratio of debt to GNP increases, the ratio of tax revenue (needed to service the debt) to GNP also rises. Conceivably, it becomes so large as to pose a serious tax-disincentive problem, a factor which is overlooked in the "we owe it to ourselves" proposition. Debt accumulation during wars may be so drastic as to lead to fiscal breakdown and debt repudiation in the postwar period. These events occurred in European countries after both world wars.

However, so long as the debt does not grow at a higher percentage rate than does GNP, the debt-to-GNP ratio does not rise and there is little reason why it should rise at a faster rate.[18] Although the finance of World War II resulted in a sharp increase in the ratio of debt to GNP in the United States, the subsequent growth of the economy reduced the ratio (see Table 28-1) within the next few decades to close to what had been its prewar level. Rising interest rates since 1966 have tended to shift up the GNP ratio, but this increase has been more than offset by the inflation-spurred increase in the money value of GNP. The specter of an ever-rising debt-to-GNP ratio which so agitated the public only a few years ago has become of more or less anthropological interest, a striking example of the demise of what once seemed a burning issue.

Burden Transfer through Reduced Capital Formation

Another and more important aspect of the burden problem focuses not on the debt itself but on the effects of loan and tax finance upon growth and the capital endowment passed on to future generations.

Once more we return to the framework of a "classical" system where investment adjusts itself to the level of saving forthcoming at a full-employment level of income. Given such a system, we have seen that $1 of both tax and loan finance reduces private expenditures by $1, but that tax finance is more likely to fall on private consumption, whereas loan finance will tend to fall on investment.[19] For any given set of public expenditures, substitution of loan for tax finance therefore reduces the growth rate of the economy. Future generations will be left with a smaller endowment and hence will receive a lower income. It is this reduction in endowment or net worth which is the vehicle of burden transfer.

This mechanism of burden transfer operates even though the resource withdrawal from private use must occur at the very time when the public expenditure

---

i is the interest rate and d is the ratio of debt to national income Y. With i equal to 5 percent and d equal to 40 percent, t equals 2 percent. If d rises to, say, 100 percent, t increases to 5 percent, and if d rises to 500 percent, t increases to 20 percent. Suppose that the level of t required for the finance of other services were 30 percent. The corresponding total levels of t would then be 32, 35, and 50 percent, respectively. Thus, the need to tax finance interest payments *could* come to absorb a substantial share of the economy's taxable capacity and thereby might displace other outlays.

[18] Suppose that, in order to maintain high employment, a deficit equal to x percent of GNP is needed. The debt then rises by x percent of GNP annually, and as GNP increases, the annual addition to the debt also grows. It may be shown, however, that the ratio of debt to GNP approaches a constant and that, given reasonable values, its level is relatively low. On this matter, see E. D. Domar, "The Burden of the Debt and the National Income," *American Economic Review*, December 1944.

[19] See p. 511.

is made. In this narrower sense, the immediate cost must be borne by the generation that releases these resources. Yet, it makes a difference whether the resource withdrawal is from consumption or from capital formation. In the first case, generation 1, which finances the expenditure, assumes the burden by reducing its private consumption. In the second case, it makes no such sacrifice but reduces the future income and potential consumption of generation 2. Burden transfer, therefore, occurs whenever generation 1, in transferring funds to the government, responds by reducing its capital formation in the private sector. This is the result whether this response is to paying taxes or to buying public debt.

The conclusion that loan finance results in burden transfer whereas tax finance does not reflects the assumption that the former tends to fall on capital formation while the latter does not. This assumption is in the right direction, although, as we have seen earlier, the distinction may be overdrawn.[20] Moreover, the government's ability to choose between loan and tax finance to allocate burdens between generations depends on the assumption that this financing mix does not affect aggregate demand. Under more realistic assumptions, as we noted in the preceding discussion of stabilization policy, tax finance is likely to be more deflationary, i.e., to result in a sharper reduction in private expenditures. In such a system, the combination of tax and loan finance must be set so as to secure the desired level of aggregate demand. Therefore, it cannot also be set so as to secure an allocation of private resources between consumption and investment in line with considerations of intergeneration equity. Unless both targets can be met through appropriate adjustments in the mix of fiscal and monetary policies, the two goals may not be reconcilable. Priority may then be given to demand considerations. Such at least is the situation at the federal level. State and local finance, as we shall see presently, is not subject to this constraint, so that considerations of intergeneration equity may dominate the financing choice.

Burden Transfer with Generation Overlap

When we consider the problem of burden transfer between generations whose life spans do not overlap, then reduction in capital formation is the only mechanism by which a burden transfer to the future can occur. But this is not a necessary condition if the two generations overlap in time. Suppose that generation 1 lives from year 1 to year 50, while generation 2 lives from year 25 to 75.

[20] The reader may wonder whether there is not another aspect to the matter. With loan finance, the lenders of generation 1 receive bonds in return for parting with their funds, whereas, with tax finance, the taxpayers of generation 1 do not receive any such compensation. Therefore, will not the members of generation 1 prefer loan finance, and will they not do so quite apart from their decision to respond by reducing consumption or capital formation?

The apparent conflict between this line of reasoning and that given in the text is resolved once it is noted that loan finance not only results in the handing out of bonds (receipt of which is a gain to the lenders) but also in the assumption of a future tax liability to pay interest on these bonds. Considering generation 1 as a group, these two aspects of bond issue wash out: The present value of future tax liabilities equals the value of the bond, leaving no net gain. Or, to put it differently, additional taxes equal interest receipts. Generation 2, similarly, inherits not only the bonds but also the interest obligation so that the two sides once more cancel out. Disregarding the tax friction burden, each generation does indeed owe the debt to itself. At the same time, it is not a matter of indifference to the two generations whether tax or loan finance is used, provided that the latter falls more heavily upon capital formation in generation 1, thus leaving generation 2 with a smaller capital endowment.

Also suppose that there is no investment in the economy. Now generation 1, in year 25, may be called upon to pay taxes of $200,000 to sustain the cost of a building with a useful life of 50 years. It must do so at the cost of reducing its own consumption by this amount. But it will then be possible, in year 50, to collect taxes of $100,000 from generation 2 in order to refund generation 1, thus involving a shift in private consumption from generation 2 to generation 1. In this way generation 1, while initially assuming the burden of generation 2, may be refunded later on. To implement this mechanism, the government may hand a promise to refund the bonds to generation 1, which will be redeemed later. This procedure, it will be noted, involves a tax system which permits the tax in year 50 to be imposed on generation 2 only, so that generation 1 can be repaid.[21]

Burden Transfer with Outside Debt

Having considered the role of domestic borrowing, we now turn to that of borrowing from outside sources. The mechanism of burden transfer through foreign borrowing differs in several respects. A first difference is that there is now no need for generation 1 to reduce its expenditures. Consumption and capital formation in the private sector can remain intact as the additional resources needed for the public outlay are acquired abroad. Loan finance now imposes a burden on generation 2 not by leaving it with a reduced capital endowment at home but by saddling it with an obligation to service the foreign debt. Taxes must now be paid to finance interest paid to foreigners rather than to domestic holders of the debt. Generation 2 no longer owes the debt to itself. This foreign debt burden replaces the loss of capital income which generation 2 would have suffered had there been domestic loan finance and a resulting reduction in capital formation.

Compare now our three sources of finance—(1) taxation, (2) domestic borrowing, and (3) foreign borrowing. Assuming (1) to fall on consumption and (2) on capital formation, (1) will burden the present generation while (2) and (3) will burden the future. While (2) and (3) are similar in this respect, the choice between them may not be a matter of indifference. The answer depends upon the cost of borrowing at home and abroad. If the cost is the same (if the return on domestic capital is the same as the outside rate of interest), the burden on generation 2 will be the same in each case. But if the domestic return is higher, foreign borrowing will be preferable, and vice versa if the domestic return is lower.

Borrowing by State and Local Governments

The problem of intergeneration equity arises most acutely at the state and local levels where the bulk of public investment expenditures are made and financed.

Suppose that a township is about to construct a school building,[22] the

[21] As we shall see later in connection with social security finance, the tax will in fact be imposed on generation 2 without explicit discrimination if an income tax on wage and salary income is used and if generation 1 is retired by year 50. See p. 688.

[22] The problem does not arise if one considers a steady stream of annual investment with a constant population. Current tax finance will then match the current flow of benefits. Such at least is the case if we disregard both the position of the first generation which is discriminated against and that of the doomsday generation which will benefit.

services of which will extend over thirty years. The expenditures thereon call for a sharp, once-and-for-all increase in the total outlays of the township. If it were to be tax-financed, a sharp if temporary increase in the tax rate would be needed. This would in itself be undesirable, since taxpayers find it easier to live with a more or less stable tax rate. Moreover, and more important, it would be unfair to place the entire burden on those who pay taxes in this particular year. Since the use of the facility will extend over thirty years, it is only fair to spread the burden among the successive "generations" of residents which will benefit from the service.

To accomplish this, the initial cost is covered by borrowing, typically in outside markets. In subsequent years, future generations, present and partaking of the benefits, are taxed each year in accordance with their current benefit share. In the process, the debt is amortized and repaid by the time the facility is used up. Once more, intergeneration equity is secured, with each generation paying for its own benefit share. A township which finances its school building by borrowing and amortizing the debt over the length of the asset life thus provides for an equitable pattern of burden distribution not only between age groups but also between changing groups of residents as the population of the jurisdiction changes in response to in-migration and out-migration.

Burden Transfer in Development Finance

The preceding discussion has an unhappy application to the problems of development finance and economic growth. The mechanism of burden transfer, while it may be used to spread the cost of *public* investment, cannot be used to spread the cost of a development program, broadly defined. The reason is that the very objective of such a program requires that *total* capital formation (public or private) be increased. But no gain is made toward achieving this objective if public capital formation is loan-financed, where this causes an offsetting decline in the rate of private capital formation. Unfortunately, therefore, the mechanism of burden transfer through internal loan finance is inapplicable in the very situation where it would be most appropriate. This does not hold, however, with regard to foreign borrowing, the role of which will be considered further when development finance is examined.[23]

Justification for Burden Transfer

When dealing with the *feasibility* of burden transfer through loan finance, it was best to separate this problem from the expenditure issue. Analogous to the differential view of tax incidence, the problem was to see how the future generation would be affected by alternative methods of finance while holding expenditures constant. When the matter of *justification* for burden transfer is considered, the expenditure side must be brought into the picture. Proceeding on the principle that public services should be financed on a benefit basis, each generation should pay for its own share in the benefits received. Applying this principle to the public capital outlays the benefits of which will extend into the future, it follows that

[23] See Chap. 34, p. 745.

loan finance and burden transfer are called for as a matter of intergeneration equity. Assuming that tax finance falls on consumption while loan finance falls on capital formation, tax finance of current and loan finance of capital outlays is in line with intergeneration equity. Loan finance of current expenditures, on the other hand, places an undue burden on the future and tax finance of capital outlays gives it an undue benefit. This is the rationale for the use of a capital budget (especially at the level of local finance) and for the use of foreign borrowing in the case of development finance.

F. SUMMARY

Over 70 percent of the public debt is federal, with less than 30 percent state and local. Regarding the development and structure of the federal debt, we have observed that:

1. The federal debt as a percentage of GNP is less than it was prior to World War II.

2. About 75 percent of the federal debt is in marketable issues, with 25 percent in nonmarketable special issues.

3. Holding of the federal debt is divided about equally between government agencies (including the Federal Reserve) and private holders.

4. The maturity structure of the public debt has become increasingly short term, with the average length to maturity now only two years.

5. Interest rates have moved up sharply in recent years, especially at the short end of the rate structure.

6. The level of interest rates on long-term debt may be taken to reflect the expected level of short-term rates.

7. The nominal interest rate is increased by inflation, being equal to the sum of the real rate and the expected inflation rate.

Debt management is concerned mainly with refunding the large volume of debt which matures annually. In examining this problem, the following conclusions were drawn:

8. The policy objective is not to minimize interest cost but to purchase illiquidity at the lowest available price.

9. Short-term debt is more like money, so that shortening of the debt tends to be expansionary.

10. Further problems in connection with debt management were examined, including interest ceilings, the debt limitation, the possibility of a stable purchasing power bond, refunding techniques, and government lending.

11. Turning our attention to the market for state and local debt, we have noted that the position of state and local governments is more like that of private borrowers than that of the federal government. We have also observed the important role played by the tax exemption of interest from state and local securities under the federal income tax.

Finally, the problems of debt burden were examined beginning with the implications of servicing the debt.

12. The relationship of the public debt to the solvency of government does not depend on the absolute level of debt but on its level relative to that of GNP.

13. The public debt becomes part of the economy's claim structure and need not be paid off at maturity. The problem, rather, is one of debt service, including refunding and the finance of interest payments. While there is some merit to the contention that such interest payments are not burdensome to the economy as a whole since they involve a transfer from taxpayers to interest recipients, the efficiency costs of a high tax rate must be allowed for.

14. These costs, however, depend upon the ratio of interest payments to GNP. There is little reason to expect it to become excessive in the normal course of peacetime finance.

Turning to the relationship of debt finance to intergeneration equity, we observed the following:

15. In the absence of generation overlap, a burden transfer to the future generation has to take the form of reduced capital formation.

16. In the context of the classical model, loan finance may be expected to fall more largely on investment, whereas tax finance may be expected to fall more heavily on consumption. Loan finance may thus be a means of transferring a burden to the future generation.

17. This argument, however, is not readily applicable to central government in the context of an economy which requires stabilizing measures.

18. Another mechanism of burden transfer may be applied in a situation where the present and future generations overlap.

19. Foreign borrowing permits financing of public programs without placing a burden on the present generation. Applied to public investment, it is particularly important in the context of development finance.

20. Burden transfer is in line with intergeneration equity where the public outlay will result in future benefits.

FURTHER READING

Ferguson, J. M. (ed.): *Public Debt and Future Generations,* Chapel Hill: University of North Carolina Press, 1964. Contains a selection of articles dealing with the problem of intergeneration equity.

Mitchell, G.: "State and Local Government Borrowing," in M. E. Polakoff (ed.), *Financial Institutions and Markets,* Boston: Houghton Mifflin, 1970.

Ott, D.: *Federal Income Tax Treatment of State and Local Securities,* Washington: Brookings, 1962.

Rolph, E. R.: "Principles of Debt Management," *American Economic Review,* June 1957.

Smith, W. L.: "Debt Management in the United States," Study Paper 19, *Study of Employ-*

ment, Growth, and Price Levels, Joint Economic Committee, U.S. Congress, June 28, 1960.

Tobin, J.: "An Essay on Principles of Debt Management," in Commission on Money and Credit (ed.), *Fiscal and Debt Management Policies,* Englewood Cliffs, N.J.: Prentice-Hall, 1963.

Part Seven

Fiscal Federalism

Chapter 29

Principles of Multiunit Finance*

A. Allocation Aspects: *Benefit Regions; Optimal Community Size; A Simplified Model; Differences in Preferences; Differences in Income; Mixed National-Local Goods; Economies of Scale; Congested Goods; Protection of Minority Preferences; Other Aspects of Decentralization.* **B. Distributional Aspects:** *Redistribution as a Central. Function; Intercommunity versus Interindividual Redistribution; Regional Development.* **C. Stabilization Aspects.** **D. Intergovernmental Fiscal Relations:** *Benefit Spillovers; Local Services as Central Merit Goods; Equalization of Fiscal Position; Fiscal Differentials and Distortions in Location; Equity Advantages of Central Taxes.* **E. The Theory of Grants:** *Appropriate Grants; Matching versus Nonmatching Grants; General versus Selective Grants.* **F. Summary.**

So far, most of our discussion has been in terms of a fiscal system involving a unitary form of government. We must now consider the more realistic situation of a multilevel system with fiscal responsibilities vested in both central and lower-level governments (in the United States—federal, state, and local).

* *Reader's Guide to Chapter 29:* The principles of multiunit finance which we consider in this chapter may be viewed as an extension of our discussion of social goods in Chapter 3. The general reader will find the implications of spatial benefit limitation explained in pp. 614–615, and may wish to pass over the more technical discussion of pp. 616–619. The analysis of matching versus nonmatching grants in Sec. E traces the response of jurisdictions to grants, in line with the principles of consumer behavior. The general framework offered in this chapter will be helpful in tackling the more institutional and current policy issues which are to be examined in Chapter 30.

The problems of a decentralized fiscal system, or "fiscal federalism," as it is called, have received much attention in the public finance literature of the past decade. In part, this has been due to an extension of the theory of social goods, initially conceived in terms of national governments, to the problem of state and local governments. It has also reflected certain developments in the United States fiscal structure, including an imbalance in the distribution of resources and needs among jurisdictions, which have called for a reconsideration of the fiscal roles to be performed by various levels of government and of their relations to one another. In this chapter we explore the more theoretical aspects of the problem, leaving the empirical discussion of federal-state-local fiscal relationships for Chapter 30.

While the concrete problems of fiscal federalism are embedded in their historical setting, it is helpful to begin with a normative view. For this purpose, we assume that only national boundaries are given and that political subdivisions may be designed *de novo* so as to secure the most efficient performance of governmental fiscal functions. Considering the basic fiscal functions—allocation, distribution, and stabilization—we inquire whether each function properly belongs to a central government, to lower-level jurisdictions, or to both.

A. ALLOCATION ASPECTS

The allocation function is most directly related to the federal problem and poses the most difficult issues: Should social goods and services be provided on a centralized or a decentralized basis? If the latter, what spatial arrangement of fiscal organization is most efficient in rendering such public services? To begin with and to link up with our earlier discussion of the theory of social goods,[1] we will assume that all publicly provided goods and services are pure social goods, i.e., they conform with the characteristic of nonrival consumption. Let us then ask why the efficient provision of such goods might call for a multiunit system of government.

Benefit Regions

The crucial feature which was noted only briefly in our discussion of social goods is that of spatial limitation of benefit incidence.[2] Some social goods are such that the incidence of their benefits is nationwide (e.g., national defense, space exploration, cancer research, the Supreme Court) while others are geographically limited (e.g., a local fire engine or streetlight). Therefore, the members of the "group" who share in the benefits are limited to the residents of a particular geographic region.

Allocation theory as applied to the public sector has led us to the conclusion that public services should be provided and their costs shared in line with the preferences of the residents of the relevant benefit region. Moreover, given the fact that a political process is needed to secure preference revelation, it follows that particular services should be voted on and paid for by the residents of this region. In other words, services which are nationwide in their benefit incidence (such as national defense) should be provided for nationally, services with local

[1] See Chap. 3.
[2] See p. 58.

benefits (e.g., streetlights) should be provided for by local units, still others (such as highways) should be provided for on a regional basis. Given the spatial characteristics of social goods, there is thus an a priori case for multiple jurisdictions. Each jurisdiction should provide services the benefits of which accrue within its boundaries, and it should use only such sources of finance as will internalize the costs. The spatially limited nature of benefit incidence thus calls for a fiscal structure composed of multiple service units, each covering a different-sized region within which the supply of a particular service is determined and financed. While some services call for nationwide, others for statewide, and still others for metropolitan-area–wide or local units, the argument so far does not call for an ordering of "higher-level" and "lower-level" governments. Rather, we are faced with coordinate units covering regions of different sizes.

Optimal Community Size

The theory of multiunit finance must provide an answer to the question of what constitutes the optimum size of a fiscal community. To deal with this complex problem, we begin with a simple model which allows for one public service only, the benefit incidence of which is limited to all within a given geographical area but vanishes beyond it.[3] To simplify, we also assume that consumers have identical tastes and incomes, so that they agree on the desirability of social-goods provision. The crux of the problem is that the cost to each consumer will be less, the larger the number of consumers who partake of the benefits. Since we postulate a pure social good so that the quality of service received per person is not affected by the number of participants, this means that the efficient solution calls for all consumers to congregate in the same benefit area. The presence of savings from cost sharing due to large numbers leads to a single benefit area and, in fact, to a unitary structure of fiscal provision.

There are, however, other considerations which may pull in an opposite direction, toward a multiunit solution. For instance, one must allow for the fact that people may dislike crowding. Even the number of angels that can dance on the head of a pin is limited. Moreover, as we shall see, the services provided may not wholly meet the definition of pure social goods, so that the quality of service received (from one given overall service level) by any one member deteriorates as numbers rise. This problem, dealt with later in the section called "Congested Goods," is disregarded for the time being. But crowding must be allowed for, and this condition limits the optimal community size.

A Simplified Model

To bring out the nature of the problem, it will be helpful to consider a simplified model in which all individuals are assumed to have the same tastes and incomes.[4] The argument involves three steps.

[3] Instead of assuming that benefits are uniformly distributed within a specific area, it may also be postulated that the intensity of benefits tapers off as one moves away from the location of the service facility. This would be the situation, for instance, with the quality of television reception. Residents would have a tendency to move toward the center, a tendency which would be restrained only by dislike of crowding.

[4] The less technically inclined reader may wish to bypass this section, based on James M. Buchanan, "An Economic Theory of Clubs," *Economica,* February 1965.

Step I The first step involving the choice of *optimum size for a given service level* is shown in Figure 29-1. We assume that a given level of social goods is provided, the total cost of which (the cost to the group as a whole) equals Z dollars. Let us suppose further that each member pays a price equal to the marginal benefit received, which (given equal tastes and incomes) means that the cost is split equally among them. The AA curve then shows the per capita service cost (measured on the vertical axis) for various community sizes (measured on the horizontal axis). This cost decreases as numbers, N, increase. Since the total cost remains equal to Z throughout, the curve AA is a rectangular hyperbola with per capita cost equal to Z/N. It reflects a form of "decreasing per capita cost" with increasing numbers of consumers in the group.[5] The A_mA_m curve, which is derived from the AA curve, shows the marginal saving of (or reduction in) per

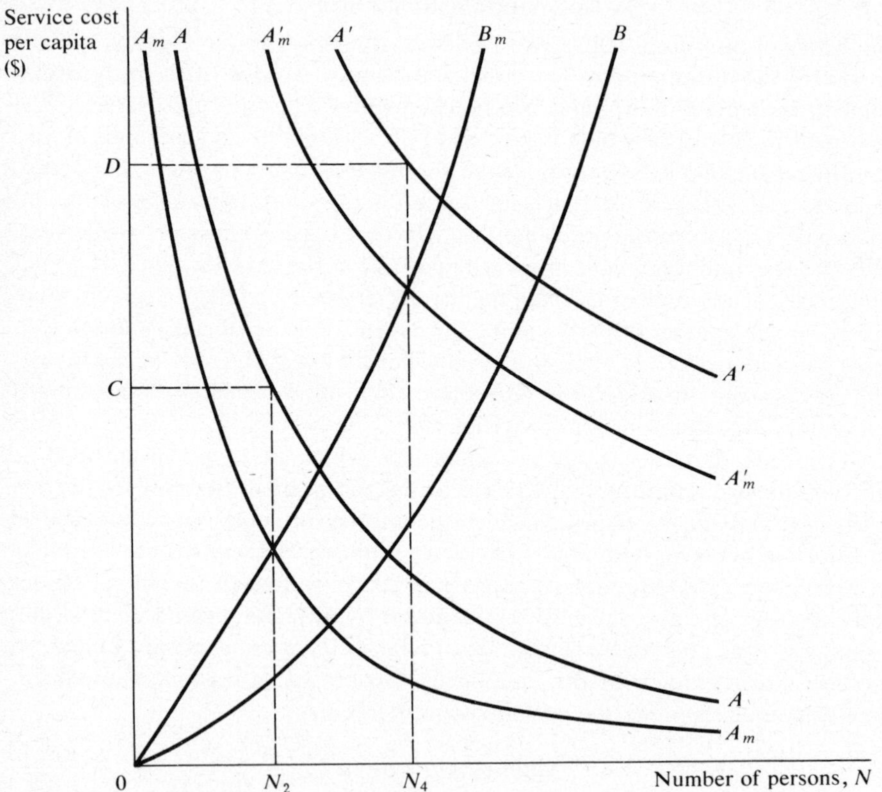

FIGURE 29-1 Choice of Optimum Community Size for Given Service Level.
AA curve: Per capita service cost or *Z/N*
A_mA_m curve: Marginal per capita service cost, or savings in per capita service cost
OB curve: Per capita crowding cost
OB_m curve: Marginal per capita crowding cost

[5] The curve is similar in form to that of decreasing average fixed cost with increasing output as drawn in the usual cost-curve diagram for the individual firm.

capita service cost that results as the group number is increased.[6] If this were all there was to be considered, the optimal group size would be such as to include the entire community. The community would be expanded so long as A_mA_m is positive (i.e., AA is downward sloping), no matter how large the group becomes.

The situation changes if the cost of crowding is allowed for. Let OB trace the per capita cost or disutility of crowding for various sizes of the group while OB_m shows the marginal per capita crowding cost. The optimal size of the community will then be given by ON_2 where OB_m is equated with A_mA_m, calling for N_2 members in this case. The community will be expanded in numbers so long as the extra per capita savings from cost sharing within a larger group exceeds the incremental per capita costs of crowding. Beyond this point, further expansion of the group would reduce total welfare and is therefore not undertaken. Various governmental units of size ON_2 will thus be established with per capita costs for each unit set at OC. With a total population P and given total service cost Z in each community, there will be P/N_2 jurisdictions.

Such is the solution for a service level with total cost Z, but we can readily see from Figure 29-1 what happens if the service level increases. The AA and A_mA_m curves shift up and the optimum size of the group increases. Thus, for a higher service level involving cost Z', the per capita service cost curve rises to $A'A'$ and the marginal curve to $A'_mA'_m$, with the optimal group size increasing to ON_4 at a per capita service cost of OD and with the group enlarged to four members.[7]

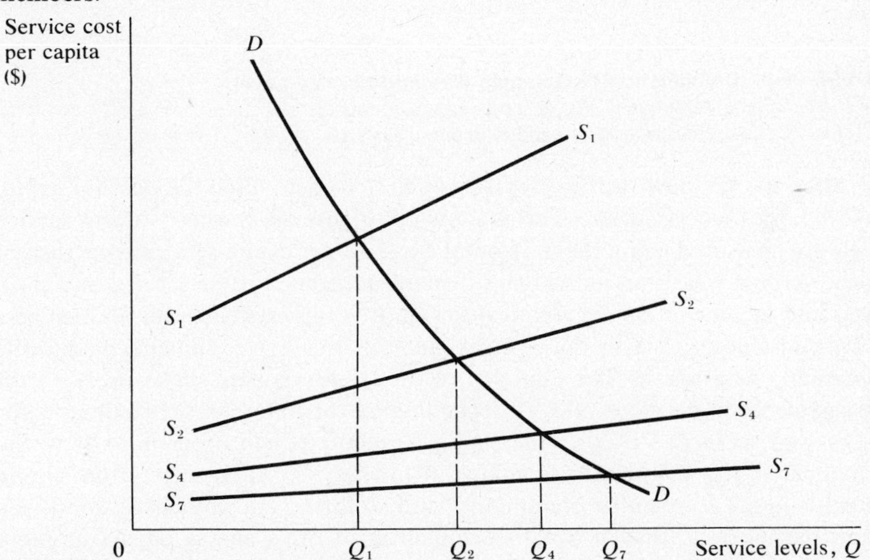

FIGURE 29-2 Choice of Optimum Service Level for Given Community Size.

[6] Mathematically, A_mA_m, the marginal saving in per capita service cost, is equal to $d(Z/N)/dN = -Z/N^2$, i.e., the negative of the slope of the AA curve.

[7] Two features of this presentation should be noted: (1) Up to a certain size, crowding costs may be negative, i.e., additional numbers may be considered a gain (e.g., from increased social contacts) rather than a disutility; (2) since we are here dealing with a pure social good, we assume the OB curve to be independent of the service level. If the "congestion phenomenon" is allowed for

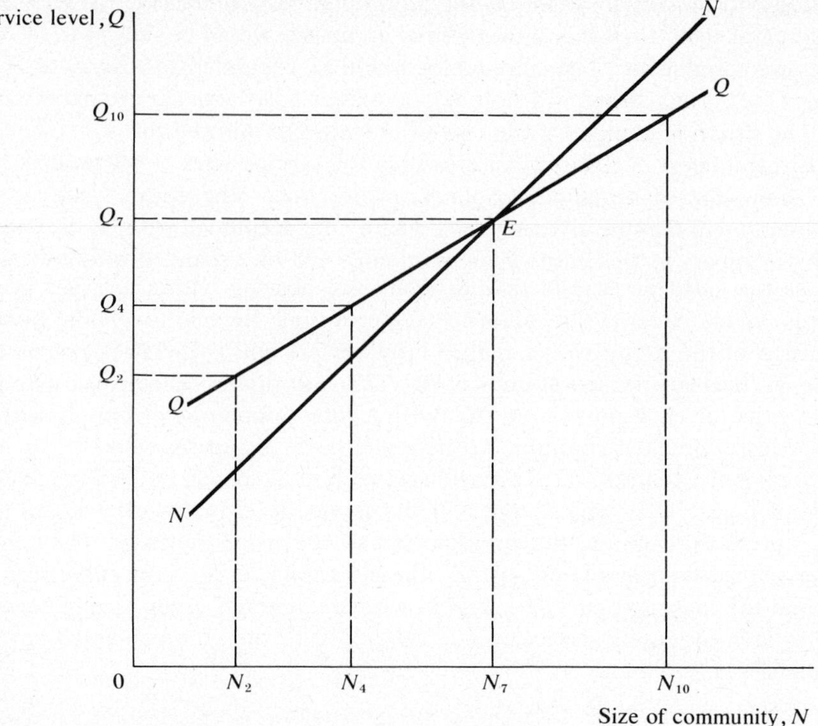

FIGURE 29-3 Combination of Optimum Size and Service Level.
NN line: Optimal community size at various service levels
QQ line: Optical service level at various community sizes

Step II We now turn to step II, which is to determine the *optimal service level for any given group size.* This is shown in Figure 29-2, where various service levels are measured along the horizontal axis and per capita service costs thereof on the vertical. *DD* is an individual's demand schedule for the service, and since tastes and income levels are identical for all, it is representative for all members of the community, S_1S_1 is the cost schedule for the service showing cost to the community as a whole. The unit cost of the facility is here shown to rise with the service level, the slope of S_1S_1 depending on the nature of the facility, factor prices, and so forth.[8] S_2S_2 is the supply schedule which presents itself to the individual if the community contains N_2 members, S_4S_4 reflects the supply schedule in an N_4-member community, and so forth. The vertical level of S_2S_2 is one-half of S_1S_1, that of S_4S_4 is one-quarter of S_1S_1, and so on. Assuming a tax structure which divides total cost equally, all face the same *SS* schedule. Since the same quantity is available to each member of the community, the service level purchased by various sizes of communities will be determined at the intersection of the *DD* curve with the supply curve pertaining to the particular community

(i.e., a decline in service quality with rising numbers), the *OB* curve will swivel down to the right as service levels are increased. In this case, the increase in group size when moving from level *Z* to level *Z'* will be greater than shown in Figure 29-1.

[8] See the section on cost conditions, p. 621.

size. Thus, the service level purchased with N_1 members will be that corresponding to the intersection of S_1S_1 with *DD,* namely OQ_1; the level purchased by N_2 members will be OQ_2 and the level desired by an N_4-member community will be OQ_4, as shown on the diagram.[9]

Step III In the final step, the *two considerations are combined* in Figure 29-3, with community size *N* measured on the horizontal axis and service levels *Q* on the vertical axis. Returning to Figure 29-1, we find that a service level involving a total cost *Z* calls for a community size N_2, that a higher level involving cost Z' calls for size N_7 and so forth. This relationship is traced in line *NN* of Figure 29-3, which shows the optimal community size at each service level (measured in quantity terms), as corresponds to the various cost levels (Z, Z', etc.) of Figure 29-1. Turning to Figure 29-2, we find that community size N_1 calls for service level Q_1, size N_2 calls for Q_2, and so forth. This relationship is traced in line *QQ* of Figure 29-3, showing the optimum service levels for various community sizes. The overall optimal solution is at *E,* where the two lines intersect, the optimal service level being OQ_7, and the optimal group size N_7.

Differences in Preferences

So far, we have assumed that preferences and income are identical. The first step toward greater realism calls for consideration of taste differentials. Obviously, preferences are not the same among individuals, and once we allow for this fact, simple solutions cease to apply. However, we can readily see why taste differentials matter and how they enter into the picture. To focus on this aspect, we still retain the assumption of equal incomes.

Some people will prefer a large share of private relative to social goods in their budgets than will others; and views regarding the desirable mix of social goods will differ. Therefore, an efficient solution will call for people with similar tastes to belong to the same jurisdiction. Thus, some jurisdictions will have a large public sector while others will have a small one; some will emphasize schools and others parks, etc. Each community will do its own thing and everyone will be satisfied.[10] At the same time, hiving off into smaller jurisdictions will be at a cost. As the number of people in any one jurisdiction is reduced, some of its gains (in terms of reduced per capita cost) from large numbers will be lost. This is an offsetting factor which must be taken into account.

Taste differences have another important implication. In our earlier discussion of social goods, we emphasized the difficulties involved in securing revelation of preferences. Now we meet with a situation where voluntary revelation of preferences may occur as people choose to move together with others whose tastes are similar—"voting with the feet," as it has been called. Suburban communities,

[9] Alternatively, the same solution might be obtained by taking S_1S_1 to reflect the supply schedule for the group and by picking its intersection with successive vertical additions of demand schedules as the size of the group is increased. See also p. 53.

[10] It is interesting to observe that this is another respect in which the social-goods and private-goods cases differ. With regard to social goods, since costs are shared it is in a person's interest to associate with others whose tastes are similar. The opposite tends to hold for private goods where a person with unusual tastes (provided that production is subject to increasing costs) will benefit from lower (relative) prices.

for instance, have typical budget patterns; people may choose their location in response to the quality of public schools, and so forth.[11] Multiunit finance has great advantages in this respect, especially where other factors entering into the location decision are more or less equal. One example may be the choice of location within a metropolitan area.

Differences in Income

Differences in income remain to be taken into account. As we shall see, local finances are not capable of dealing with major distributional adjustments. Such adjustments must be made at the central level; i.e., they must be applicable to a more or less closed area. Distributional considerations do, however, enter into our present problem. The price which people are willing to pay for a given supply of social goods will be higher if their incomes are larger. As a result, the gain from association with others not merely is a function of numbers but now assumes an additional dimension. The gain will be larger for a particular individual if others with whom he or she associates and shares public services have higher incomes. By the same token, it will be less advantageous to associate with others whose incomes are lower, since they will be willing to contribute only a small share of the cost. This will be true at least to the extent that taxes are allocated on a benefit basis; obviously, the effect will not occur if taxes are distributed on, say, a per capita basis.

It is interesting to note, therefore, that the tendencies for the wealthy to congregate, for the poor to follow the wealthy, and for the wealthy to exclude the poor via zoning not only are based on gains or losses from redistributional taxation (to be noted later) but hold even in the context of a benefit approach. There is, however, another aspect which works in the opposite direction. Budget decisions are made by majority vote, and preferences with regard to social goods will differ by income groups. The demand will be more income-elastic for some services than for others. As a result, a person is more likely to be dissatisfied with the budget vote if his or her income varies greatly from the average for the community. Because of this, association with others whose incomes are higher need not involve an outcome which on balance is more satisfactory.

Mixed National-Local Goods

While we have so far assumed that the benefits of certain goods are strictly confined to a particular area, they may not be in reality. Some services may yield benefits which are nationwide but which apply with different intensity in various regions. Thus, antimissile defenses are part of a national defense system and therefore are properly provided for on a national basis, but their location on the East or West Coast will result in regional benefit differences. In this sense, such installations are rival in consumption, at least insofar as regional benefit differentials are concerned. The previously noted principle of aligning contributions with benefit areas will then call for regionally differentiated contributions to central

[11] The proposition that optimal local budget patterns will result from location choices of individuals was first developed in Charles M. Tiebout, "A Pure Theory of Local Government Expenditures," *Journal of Political Economy,* October 1956.

finance. Our constitutional provisions which exclude geographic discrimination in federal taxation introduce an inefficiency in this respect.

Economies of Scale

The determination of efficient jurisdictions for the provision of social services is complicated further by the fact that various cost components of a given service may well call for differential scales of operation. Thus, the optimal size for individual schools may be 500 students; the optimal size for the services of a school superintendent may be 5 schools involving 2,500 students; and the optimal size for food purchases to be served in the school cafeterias may be 100 schools involving 50,000 students. Thus, efficient management may call for the combination of various service units to cover particular inputs, making for superstructures of various sizes. This, of course, is a prime factor in efficient arrangement of fiscal administration in the metropolitan area.

Moreover, it is treacherous in this context to speak of "increasing cost" or "decreasing cost" without defining clearly what is meant. In particular, a distinction should be drawn among the following three ways in which the unit cost per individual may vary:

1. Economies of scale which arise with a pure social good if numbers are increased while holding the service level constant.
2. Economies or diseconomies of scale which arise with a pure social good if the level of service is increased while numbers are held constant.
3. Economies or diseconomies of scale which arise (due to crowding or congestion) from changes in numbers while holding the service level constant.

Whereas type 1 refers to the slope of *AA* in Figure 29-1 and type 2 to the slope of S_1S_1 in Figure 29-2, type 3 involves the slope of *OB* in Figure 29-1 and differs greatly for various types of services.

Congested Goods

Up to this point, we have viewed the problem of multiple jurisdictions in terms of pure social goods, i.e., goods the consumption of which is truly nonrival although limited to the residents of a particular geographic area. We must now allow for the important fact that such goods are frequently—or even typically—not of this type. Consider a fire station, a school of given size, a network of city streets, or a sewage disposal plant. They are all goods provided by the municipal government, yet they do not meet the precise criterion of "nonrival" consumption. Rather, the addition of one extra consumer (at least after a certain point is reached) will dilute the quality of service obtained from the given size of operation by the old set of consumers. In other words, there exists a congestion cost to previous users.

Under these conditions, the publicly provided good is no longer nonrival in consumption. But if this is so, should we not consider it a private good and leave it to be provided through the market? The answer is "no," because, unlike the private-good case, there is still the limitation that the same amount must be consumed by all members of the group. Formally, this may be depicted in the same way as was done previously for crowding costs in Figure 29-1. Thus, the OB_m curve may now be interpreted as plotting the marginal cost arising from quality deterioration as additional numbers are added to the group.[12] For any given service level, the problem is again one of balancing the gain from reduced per capita cost as numbers are increased against the resulting disadvantage. Thus, members will be added to the group until the old residents find that the marginal cost of quality deterioration equals the marginal saving (both on a per capita basis) in the form of reduced tax costs needed to finance the service.[13]

Protection of Minority Preferences

It is one thing to view the problem of multiunit finance in normative terms, assuming the provision for social goods within each community to be determined in line with the preferences of its members and costs allocated accordingly, a solution involving the idealized assumptions of an all-knowing referee; but it is another matter to allow for the fact that budget decisions must be made by majority vote and that differing tax formulas may be applied.

It is this fact which previously led us to the conclusion that the provision for social goods involves an inevitable dilemma: Since preferences are not revealed without the pressure of a mandatory voting rule, such a rule is needed; yet, preferences of minority voters are inevitably offended thereby, and this violation involves an efficiency loss. The question here is whether this dilemma can be reduced in severity by resort to decentralized finance, providing for a relatively large number of small units. If the jurisdiction is small enough to include only one voter, no one can be in the minority. At the same time, all the economies of cost sharing are lost. Might it then be argued that numbers in the group should be increased up to a point where marginal gains from cost sharing just offset marginal losses from increased violation of minority wishes?

The argument holds if resort to smaller communities (decentralization) results in a situation in which preferences among members of each jurisdiction become more homogeneous. This may be the case because preferences of residents of different subregions within any existing jurisdiction differ (calling for larger jurisdictions to be divided up accordingly) or because the availability of multiple jurisdictions allows people with similar tastes to move together. Since these conditions may not apply, the assumption in favor of small jurisdictions may not hold. Indeed, minority preferences may be violated more rather than less if we deal with two jurisdictions of four voters each rather than with one jurisdiction of eight voters. Another aspect of the voting problem is that fragmentation into single service districts (e.g., for water or electricity) may render it more difficult to obtain consensus since it will not be possible to form coalitions involving various budget mixes.[14]

[12] As noted before, an increase in service level now not only raises the *AA* or per capita service cost curve in Figure 29-1, but also swings the *OB* or congestion cost curve to the right. See footnote 7.

[13] As noted later, these changes may fall short of the cost needed to provide the facility. See p. 701.

[14] See Julius Margolis, in National Bureau of Economic Research, *Public Finances: Needs, Sources and Utilization,* Princeton, N.J.: Princeton, 1961, and p. 112.

Other Aspects of Decentralization

Other arguments on behalf of decentralization hinge on less tangible propositions, such as greater social integration through citizen involvement in local self-determination, the potential danger to individual liberty of centralized power, and the gain from diversity and experimentation which results from decentralization. All these points have merit but so have the propositions that centralized government involves economies of scale and coordination and that a nation, though made up of diverse elements, is also served by a common sense of national purpose and concern. Nor can one discard the fact that, historically speaking, public policy and administrative initiatives have been generated largely at the central level.

B. DISTRIBUTIONAL ASPECTS

Next we consider how the distribution function is to be performed in the Federalist system.

Redistribution as a Central Function

Policies to adjust the distribution of income among individuals must be conducted on a nationwide basis. Unless such adjustments are very minor, regional differentiation will affect the choice of location for both individuals and businesses and will result in locational inefficiencies. Moreover, regional measures for redistribution are self-defeating, since the rich will leave and the poor will move to the more egalitarian-minded jurisdictions. The present large differentials in public assistance among states in the United States are believed to have contributed to the migration of welfare recipients from the low-benefit rural areas to high-benefit urban states. The tendency for the rich to congregate and to exclude the poor who try to follow—previously noted in the context of the allocation problem—is thus reinforced by decentralized redistribution policies.

Fiscal redistribution—both progressive income taxation applied to the upper end of the income scale and transfers granted to the lower end—must be uniform within an area over which there is a high degree of capital and labor mobility. That is to say, it has to be a function of the national government. As we shall see later, failure to meet this condition in the United States is responsible for much of the fiscal distress experienced by certain local governments in recent years. There is thus a natural link between central finance and redistributive finance, and much of the political debate over fiscal centralization and decentralization must be understood in these terms.

Intercommunity versus Interindividual Redistribution

While it is evident that major redistributional measures can be carried out only at the national level, should national concern be only with adjustments between rich and poor *individuals* or should it also be with adjustments between rich and poor *communities?*

To come to terms with this question, consider a normative setting in which a "proper" state of income distribution among individuals has been provided for by the central government *and* in which capital and labor are free to move among regions. In such a setting, there will still be communities with high incomes and others with low average incomes. Since residents who join with others of high income will obtain public services on more favorable terms (as their neighbors are willing to contribute more), it may be argued that provision for local social goods renders the distribution of real income less equal. It does not follow, however, that intercommunity redistribution is called for. Rather, the conclusion is that this effect should be allowed for in setting the "proper" distribution of income among individuals.

However this may be, the actual state of distribution among individuals can hardly be assumed to be the proper one, and there is a tendency for the poor to be concentrated in particular jurisdictions. Because of this, interjurisdictional redistribution becomes a necessary, if second-best, approach to maintaining viable systems of local finance. We shall return to this point when discussing fiscal equalization.

Regional Development

Another aspect of interregional redistribution relates to economic development and growth. While the responsibility for overall growth policy belongs to the central government, implementation of this policy may involve a regional orientation. Economically backward regions may persist where there are barriers to labor and capital mobility. One solution would be to remove such barriers and to let resources move. Yet this may be politically difficult, or national policy may hold it desirable to support traditionally important regions or to maintain a broader population distribution. At the same time, excessive regional income differentials may be held undesirable, so that redistribution among regions may be called for.

C. STABILIZATION ASPECTS

It is readily seen that the use of fiscal policy for stabilization purposes has to be at the national (central) level. Lower levels of government cannot successfully carry on stabilization policy on their own for a number of reasons. This holds for monetary no less than for fiscal policies.

Since each subunit exists as a completely "open" economy within the national market area, local fiscal measures will meet with large import leakages.[15] While increased public expenditures can be directed at local resources, gains from further respending will be diluted by import leakages, thus resulting in little or no "multiplier effect." Therefore spending and taxing measures by lower levels of government, whether in an expansionary or restrictive direction, would be largely nullified by trade leakages. These leakages do not arise, or are substantially smaller, if such fiscal measures are undertaken at the national level.

Moreover, stabilizing fiscal policy requires periodic budgetary deficits or surpluses with corresponding borrowing and debt repayment. These pose a more serious problem for local governments, which have less ready access to the national capital markets and no control over supporting monetary policy should it be needed. The implications of local government debt, moreover, are different

[15] See p. 527.

from those associated with national debt. Local debt is largely held by creditors outside the jurisdiction, and the use of debt finance at the local level should be geared to secure an equitable burden distribution among generations.[16]

Whereas decentralized fiscal policy for stabilization purposes is largely ruled out by the foregoing considerations, the use of monetary policy by lower levels of government is even less acceptable. Central banking policy is inherently a national function. Not only would decentralized monetary policy be seriously blunted in its effectiveness by the openness of the regional economy, but the power to print money would invite monetary irresponsibility at the state or local level.

In sum, the necessary degree of fiscal coordination is not likely to emerge in a decentralized setting, so central responsibility for stabilization action is required. This is not to say, however, that central government responsibility for stabilization policy need not account for the needs of state and local governments. Thus, levels of spending and taxing at the lower levels of government (in line with their service-providing roles) may be influenced by the central government's stabilization policy. Central banking policy affects the availability and cost of credit for state and local governments, and grants to lower-level units may be varied depending on cyclical conditions.

Just as full employment of resources must be the concern of stabilizing measures at the central level, so must aims of economic growth be implemented by central government policies. The additional resources (such as investment in physical and human capital) required for more rapid economic growth are best generated through policies applied uniformly over the national area. Further, such resources should be put to most effective use without the kinds of distortion which arise from a pluralistic system. As noted before, development policy may be linked to regional problems and may thus call for equalizing resource transfers; but even where this condition exists, such policies must again be a function of the central government.

D. INTERGOVERNMENTAL FISCAL RELATIONS

In the previous section we have discussed the design of an efficient fiscal structure in which the stabilization and distribution functions belong with the central government and the allocation function is performed by jurisdictions defined as "benefit areas," which may be local, regional, or national in scope. In such a normative system, each jurisdiction would carry out and finance (from taxes paid within its borders) its appointed functions without reference to the fiscal activities of others. Any one resident would be within the boundaries of various jurisdictions (or service clubs) and contribute to their respective activities.

Would such a scheme leave any place for "intergovernmental fiscal relations," that is, fiscal transactions and coordinating arrangements among the various communities? The answer is "yes," for various reasons:

1. Intervention by a higher level of government may be needed to correct for spillover of benefits.

[16] See p. 606.

2. The central government may consider local public services as merit goods and wish to subsidize them.

3. The philosophy of fiscal federalism may call for some degree of equalization in the fiscal position of lower-level jurisdictions.

4. Fiscal differentials among jurisdictions may result in inefficiencies in location which need to be moderated.

5. Advantages of central government taxation may lead central government revenue to be substituted for lower-level revenue.

Benefit Spillovers

One major reason for coordinating adjustments among jurisdictions is that existing jurisdictions do not neatly correspond to benefit and tax cost areas. Spillovers result and may be due to a number of factors.

Causes A first cause arises from the complexities of benefit areas. While the spatial model of fiscal structure, which we have examined earlier, has its attractions, it oversimplifies matters unduly. Since spatial patterns differ for various types of public services, the model would call for different but overlapping jurisdictions for each service. A person residing in any one location would be a member of various "service clubs." For some services, the individual would join with close neighbors only, while for others the neighborhood concept would be extended to involve a radius of 10, 100, or 1,000 miles. This system would be exceedingly complex, especially where benefits are not uniform within a region but where extensive spatial "tapering off" of benefits occurs. Moreover, complete separation of services into separate service clubs, as noted before, would render the decision process more difficult, as the bargaining feature of changing budget mix would be lost. The administrative and political costs speak for a more consolidated and simplified system with governmental units performing a variety of functions and departing considerably from our principle of equivalence between taxing and benefit areas.

A further source of nonequivalence may arise because people and businesses are mobile. As a result, public expenditure benefits in one jurisdiction may be carried over to another. For example, benefits from education expenditures embodied in the form of "human capital" get transferred to other jurisdictions with the out-migration of the educated. Other benefits (such as city streets, police, and fire protection) may be currently consumed by suburban residents who commute to the city but have no part in deciding on, and paying for, the services in question.

Finally, and most important, existing jurisdictions are historically given. They were not created on the basis of fiscal rationality alone. State or city boundaries do not neatly coincide with benefit limits; and once established, they are not readily adjusted for purely fiscal reasons. For all these reasons, benefit and cost spillovers from one jurisdiction to another occur.

Interjurisdictional Bargaining with Small Numbers As in other cases of benefit externalities, spillovers must be accounted for and internalized if public service levels are to be efficiently determined. Unless the nonresident recipients of the benefit spillovers pay compensation to the community from which they emanate, there will be an undersupply of the public good in question. In some cases, it may be practicable to redraw boundaries or reassign spending responsibilities. Thus, in recent years there has been a trend in the United States toward the creation of special service districts to carry out certain functions the benefits of which extend across local and state boundaries. Examples are water-pollution abatement programs, sanitation districts, and metropolitan transit systems. In other, and indeed most, instances, intergovernmental cooperation will be needed. In some cases, direct negotiation between jurisdictions may be feasible.

The problem is quite similar in principle to that dealt with in our earlier discussion of benefit-externalities from personal consumption. In particular, it resembles the small-number case of that discussion.[17] If jurisdiction A provides for service X, it may yield not only benefits in consumption for the residents of A but also spillover benefits which are consumed by the residents of jurisdiction B. The latter are not accounted for by A, but should be internalized to yield efficient provision. This may be achieved through bargaining, as jurisdiction B may benefit by paying A for increasing its level of provision and by substituting this for B's own provision. Thus, negotiation tends to lead to some degree of internalization, but, as we concluded before, there is no assurance that an efficient solution will be reached. Nevertheless, bargaining does occur, and interjurisdictional agreements pertaining to such matters as garbage disposal or fire protection are a frequent and useful feature of intergovernmental cooperation.[18]

Federal Intervention with Large Numbers Frequently, the number of interested parties may be sufficiently large to make a bargaining solution difficult. A higher level of government is then called upon to act as a referee or middleman, so as to expedite cooperation and to secure both efficient and equitable solutions. With even larger numbers, a matching-grant system again becomes necessary to provide the called for correction, with a subsidy paid to the benefit-generating lower-level government in line with the value of the benefit to the receiving governmental unit.[19] As a matter of equity, such grants should be financed by charges imposed on the receiving jurisdictions to match the benefit spill-ins.[20]

The significance of such compensatory grants depends on the extent of interjurisdictional spillover and thus on the degree of decentralization. The larger the jurisdictions, the fewer the spillovers. But this fact does not make a decisive argument for centralization, since a highly centralized structure allows little opportunity for differences in expenditure patterns. If community preferences differ widely, it may be better to have more decentralization in public expenditure decisions and to accommodate to the larger spillovers rather than to do the reverse.

[17] See p. 61.

[18] For the role of such agreements at the international level, see p. 727.

[19] See p. 57.

[20] If S_i is a grant or subsidy paid to the ith state, $S_i = a_i X_i - \beta_i X_j$ where a_i is the rate of benefit spill-*out* expressed as a proportion of X_i or public expenditures undertaken by the ith state, while β_i is the rate of benefit spill-*in* to the ith state from expenditures X_j undertaken by the jth state, summed over all states. The matching rates a_i and β_i are weighted averages for various types of public expenditures and thus would vary for each state.

Local Services as Central Merit Goods

Quite apart from spillovers, the central government may wish to influence the fiscal behavior of lower-level governments in order to raise the level of local public services. To put it differently, the central government may view local public services as merit goods. This concern may be directed at local expenditures in general or at selective categories only; and financial support may be independent of the amount spent or may be restricted to assure minimum levels.

In principle, there is no difference between the central government's subsidizing expenditures on social goods by the lower levels of government and its subsidizing private goods purchased by individual consumers. As we have emphasized before, the merit-good characteristic is independent of the distinction between social and private goods.[21] In both cases, the purpose is to redirect consumption patterns, and both fall under the heading of "merit goods." There may, however, be a special argument for interference with consumer (or voter) choice in the provision of social goods at the local level. Where majority decision provides for only a substandard level of public services, the central government may wish to protect the interests of the minority in receiving a minimum level.

Once more, these corrections call for matching grants to reduce the price ratio of public services to private goods, thereby encouraging the local electorate to increase their own taxes and to spend more on public goods. Depending on how general the support is to be, the matching rates will be related to total expenditures or be earmarked for particular uses.

Equalization of Fiscal Position

But grants are also made where there is no intention to interfere with local choice, the objective being one of fiscal equalization. Some jurisdictions—state or local—enjoy a high taxable capacity (the tax rate needed to obtain a given level of revenue is low) and have a relatively low level of need (the amount required to provide certain service levels is small). They are thus in a fiscally strong position, as measured by the ratio of capacity to need. Others are in the reverse position. The central government may then wish to equalize fiscal positions and it may do so in various ways.[22] Here the following distinctions are noted:

1. The central government may wish to equalize the cost—in terms of tax effort or tax rate required—of providing public services in various jurisdictions, while leaving it to the local jurisdiction to decide what service level it wishes to provide. This approach would call for matching grants to jurisdictions which are fiscally weak, i.e., which have low taxable capacity and large needs; and these grants would be financed by taxes on the expenditures of strong jurisdictions, i.e., which have a high taxable capacity and low need. This scheme may be applied to whatever expenditure level a jurisdiction chooses to undertake, or it may be limited to that needed to meet minimum needs.

[21] See p. 65.

[22] Many variants of these schemes, with differing incentive effects, may be developed. See, for instance, Richard A. Musgrave, "Approaches to a Fiscal Theory of Political Federalism," with discussion, in National Bureau of Economic Research, *Public Finances, Needs, Sources and Utilization,* Princeton, N.J.: Princeton, 1961.

2. Alternatively, the central government may wish to equalize actual service levels and for this purpose impose such matching grants (where needed to raise levels) or taxes (where needed to lower levels) as are required to secure equalization.

3. Finally, the central government may wish to secure common minimum levels and adjust its grant policy to secure this objective.

Leaving the details of grant policy for later consideration, we must ask why the central government should apply equalization measures among jurisdictions, rather than directly dealing with equalization of income among individuals? To be sure, such equalization among individuals leaves it to their discretion as to how the additional income is to be used or which outlays are to be reduced. Equalizing the provision of social goods, or of particular social goods, relates the equalization objective to a particular component of consumption. The analogy in the private sector would be to say that even though peoples' overall incomes may differ, they must consume the same amount of bread or some other "basic" goods. The equalization objective comes to be intertwined with the notion of merit goods. But though it is difficult to make a conceptual case for interjurisdictional (as distinct from interindividual) redistribution, two arguments for such measures may be advanced: (1) As distinct from private goods, a person is not free to choose his own provision of social goods, but depends on the cooperation of others. Where this is lacking, central government may step in to provide it. (2) Measures aimed at adjusting the state of interindividual distribution may not be feasible, in which case interjurisdictional redistribution may be the only available if second-best alternative. More will be said about this later on when the finance of welfare is considered.

Fiscal Differentials and Distortions in Location

A case for fiscal coordination arises where fiscal advantages or disadvantages of particular jurisdictions distort location decisions. A particular taxpayer, whether a corporation or an individual, may find jurisdiction A preferable to jurisdiction B because A's tax structure will result in a lower tax bill and/or because the structure of public services is more beneficial. Such differentials affect both product and factor flows and thereby interfere with efficient production.[23]

This gives a further rationale for measures of type 1 above, but the argument goes further. The purpose now is not just to equalize the tax costs which an individual faces in various jurisdictions. What matters here is the net differential or fiscal residue, whether it is the excess of benefits over costs or that of costs over benefits. As we shall develop more fully later, the need for coordination is of particular importance at the international level where fiscal differentials are large; but, to a limited degree, they also arise within a single country such as the United States. Coordination of business taxation at the state level, for instance, has been a subject of congressional concern.[24]

[23] If all taxes in all jurisdictions were imposed on a benefit basis, such differentials would not exist and fiscal factors would not distort location decision. More precisely, this situation would exist only if "benefit taxation" were interpreted to call for equalizing total rather than marginal benefits. Since location choices are all-or-nothing propositions, it is the total benefit that matters.

[24] See p. 310.

Equity Advantages of Central Taxes

Central taxes have the advantage of avoiding distortions in location, but they may also be preferred on grounds of equity. By drawing on the entire economy, the tax base can be defined more comprehensively, as can be done especially with the corporation profits tax. Moreover, progressive taxation cannot be applied effectively by lower-level jurisdictions. This leaves the function of progressive taxation largely at the federal level. Since the burden distribution of the overall tax system is the weighted average of taxes applicable at the federal, state, and local levels, overall progressivity depends upon their respective shares in the revenue total. In the absence of grants, these in turn are determined by the respective levels of expenditures at each level of government.

This relationship can be short-circuited, however, by the use of grants from the federal to the state and local levels. In making grants for this purpose, the federal government would share its revenue (presumably revenue from the income tax) with the state at which the revenue originated. At the same time, this transfer of the taxing function to the higher level would interfere with the requirement, noted earlier in the chapter, that each jurisdiction should determine and pay for those services whose benefits are limited to that jurisdiction. This is one of the dilemmas which have to be faced in order to reconcile the advantages of fiscal decentralization with the disadvantages of resulting distortions in location decisions.

E. THE THEORY OF GRANTS

We have seen in the preceding section that grants may be used to accomplish various intergovernmental objectives. In this section, further consideration is given to the choice of the appropriate grant instrument and to the incentive effects of various types of grants.

Appropriate Grants

For this purpose, it is helpful to distinguish among various types of grants. The main distinctions are: (1) whether the grant is general (also referred to as block grant) or whether it is selective (also referred to as restricted or categorical grant); (2) whether the grant is nonmatching or matching; and (3) whether it is, or is not, related to the fiscal need of the receiving unit. Grouping grants in line with these three criteria, we have the following classification:

		Not Need-related	*Need-related*
General:	Nonmatching	1	5
	Matching	2	6
Selective:	Nonmatching	3	7
	Matching	4	8

Among these grants, the objective of spillover correction is served best by type 4, with the subsidy rate equal to the ratio of external to internal levels of benefits. The objective of support of merit goods will be best served by type 2 or type 4, depending on whether there is to be general support for all local social goods or whether the subsidy is to be selective. Equalization objectives in turn call for grants of type 5, provided the choice between public and social goods at the lower level is not to be affected, or type 6, if it is. A policy combining merit-good and equalization objectives will make use of type 8. A policy aimed at avoiding distortions and efficiency costs which arise from tax structure differentials among lower-level jurisdictions, finally, might call for uniform central taxes while returning revenue to jurisdiction-of-origin in line with type 1 grants. Type 8 might also serve the purpose of substituting central taxes for revenue obtained at the lower levels.

Matching versus Nonmatching Grants

Leaving an examination of actual grant policy to the next chapter, we now take a more careful look at why some types of grants are more effective than others, i.e., accomplish the desired policy objective at a lower cost to the government. We begin with grants which are general in the sense that they do not distinguish among types of public services but may be nonmatching or matching.

Nonmatching Grants The case of a nonmatching grant is shown in Figure 29-4. Social goods are measured on the horizontal, and private goods on the vertical, axis. *AB* is the community budget line, showing various combinations of private and social goods which are available to it. The curves i_1i_1, i_2i_2, etc., are indifference curves recording the community's preferences between the two. The initial equilibrium is at *E*, where the budget line is tangent to the highest

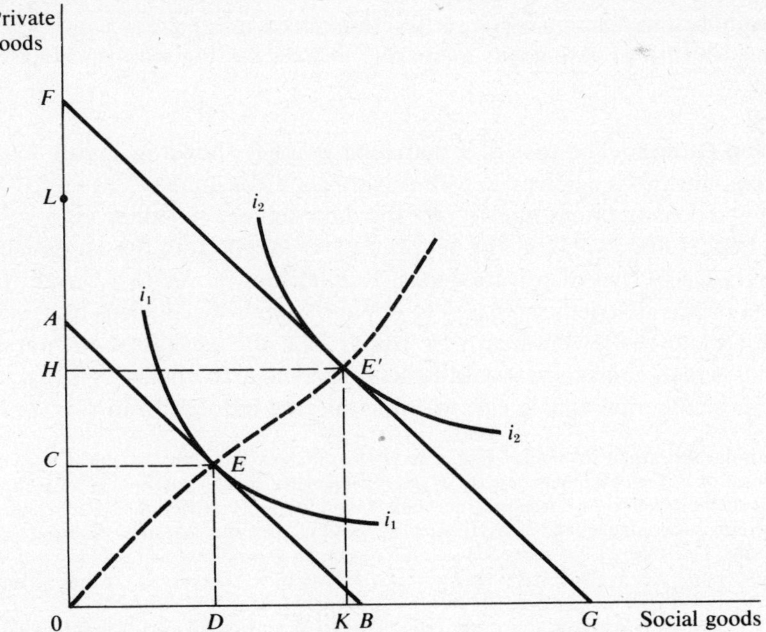

FIGURE 29-4 Response to a Nonmatching Grant.

possible indifference line. Consumption of private goods equals *OC*, and the consumption of social goods equals *OD*. To obtain *OD* of social goods, *CA* of private goods must be surrendered so that the tax rate equals *CA/OA*, where *OA* is income measured in terms of private goods.

Now a nonmatching grant equal to *AF* (measured again in private goods) is given to the community's treasury. As a result, the budget line shifts to *FG* and the new equilibrium is at *E'*. The community now obtains *OH* of private goods and *OK* of social goods. Private-good consumption has risen by *CH* and social-good consumption has increased by *DK*. Part of the grant has leaked into increased consumption of private goods rather than into increased provision of social goods. This is as may be expected. Since use of the grant is not tied in any way, it is equivalent to a general income subsidy. Hence, there is only an income effect which normally may be assumed to be positive and to increase outlays on both social and private goods.

But how can it be said that the grant is equivalent to an increase in income, since it is given to the government rather than to consumers and the government buys social goods only? The answer, of course, is that part of the grant may be made available for private consumption through tax reduction.[25] Consider what happens in Figure 29-4. Since the consumption of private goods rises from *OC* to *OH*, the amount paid in tax falls from *CA* to *HA*. The tax rate, therefore, declines from *CA/OA* to *HA/OA*.[26] Tax reduction equals *HC*. With the cost of the grant to the government equal to *AF* (all measured in terms of private goods), $LF = HC$ passes into tax reduction and only *AL* is added to expenditures on social goods.

The dotted curve *OEE'* finally shows an income consumption path along which the equilibrium position of the jurisdiction moves as the grant is increased, with the leakage into private goods increasing and decreasing with the slope of this line.

Matching Grants The case of a matching grant is shown in Figure 29-5. The initial equilibrium is again at *E*, with private-good consumption equal to *OC* and social-good consumption equal to *OD*. Introduction of a matching grant now swivels the budget line to *AM*, as the net price of social goods to the community has fallen relative to that of private goods. Equilibrium moves to *E'*, with the consumption of private goods increased to *ON* and that of social goods increased to *OP*. The cost to the government now equals *E'S*, the additional amount of private goods which consumers would have to surrender to obtain *OP* of social goods. The tax reduction equals *CN*, with the tax rate reduced from *CA/OA* to

[25] Indeed, the text argument implies that it makes no difference whether the money is given to the government or to the consumers directly. If given to the government, part is used for private goods via tax reduction. If given to consumers, part of it is used for public expenditures via increased taxes. The outcome is the same in both cases. In a realistic setting, the two procedures may well lead to different results, i.e., voting a tax reduction and not voting an expenditure increase may not be symmetrical procedures. See Wallace E. Oates, *Fiscal Federalism*, New York: Harcourt Brace, 1972, chap. 3, app. A.

[26] Note that the tax rate is measured as the ratio of tax to earnings, thus excluding the subsidy to the treasury. If the leakage into private consumption is sufficiently large, taxes may be reduced to zero and a transfer payment (negative tax) may be needed.

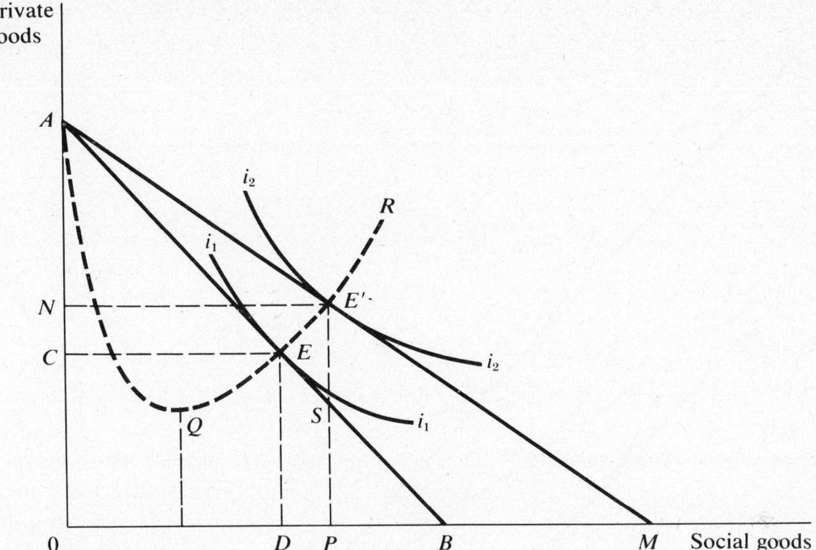

FIGURE 29-5 Response to a Matching Grant.

NA/OA, *CN* being the part of the subsidy cost which leaks into private consumption.

Although the position of *E′* in Figure 29-5 shows that in this instance consumption of both private and social goods has increased, this is not necessarily the case. As distinct from the nonmatching grant where only an income effect was present, we now have a substitution effect as well. Since the price of social goods has fallen relative to that of private goods, the consumption of private goods might decline. The negative substitution effect might outweigh the positive income effect. In Figure 29-5, the dotted curve *AQR* shows the path along which *E* will travel as the price of social goods declines, with the movement from *A* to *R* being caused by increasing matching rates. Up to *Q*, this results in a decline in the purchase of private goods, and beyond *Q* in an increase, with the purchase of social goods rising throughout. In a situation where both *E* and *E′* lie to the left of *Q*, there would be no leakage of grant money, but voters would in fact support the government's effort by voting a tax increase.

Comparison of Grants The two types of grants are compared in Figure 29-6. *E* is again the initial equilibrium, and E_m is the new equilibrium with a matching grant. E_n is the new equilibrium with a nonmatching grant designed so that both grants secure the same provision for social goods, or *OP*. As before, the cost to the government under the matching grant equals E_mS and that under the nonmatching grant equals E_nS. The same objective of securing a social-goods supply of *OP* can thus be secured at a lower cost with the matching grant, the difference being E_mE_n. This is not surprising, since a matching grant is in fact a selective grant which supports provision of social goods only, whereas the nonmatching grant is general, since it may be used to support the purchase of additional private goods by way of tax reduction.

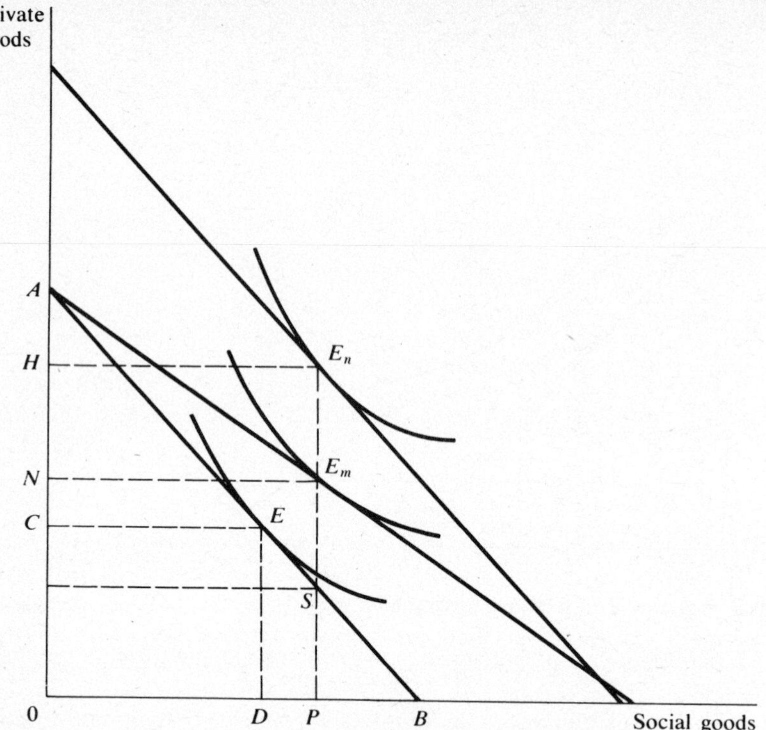

FIGURE 29-6 Comparison of Matching and Nonmatching Grants.

General versus Selective Grants

We now turn to grants earmarked for specific public outlays. If the government wishes to increase expenditures on a particular social good X, a selective grant earmarked for the use of X will be at least as effective in securing increased expenditures on X as will be an equal-cost general grant, and it may well be more efficient.

This is shown in Figure 29-7 for the nonmatching case. Measuring social good Y on the vertical axis and social good X on the horizontal axis, let *BA* be the community's opportunity line prior to the grant with equilibrium at *E.* Now a general grant is given, moving the budget line to *DC.* Equilibrium shifts to *E'*, the purchase of social good X increases to *OG,* and the cost to the government in terms of X equals *AC.* If the government gives a grant of equal amount earmarked for the use of X, only section *FC* of the new budget line will be available to the community, but equilibrium is again at *E'*.[27] Both types of grants secure the same increase in the purchase of X. This conclusion still holds if the government raises its general grant so as to shift the budget line to *HK* and moves

[27] A selective grant earmarked for the purpose of X and costing *AC* = *BF* may be pictured as moving the origin to the right by this distance. *VF* thus becomes the new vertical axis and the effective opportunity line is given by *FC.*

The presentation of Figure 29-7 oversimplifies matters because it shows a choice between two social goods only. We may visualize a third axis showing an option of private-good consumption, in which case a selective matching grant on one social good is subject to leakages in two directions.

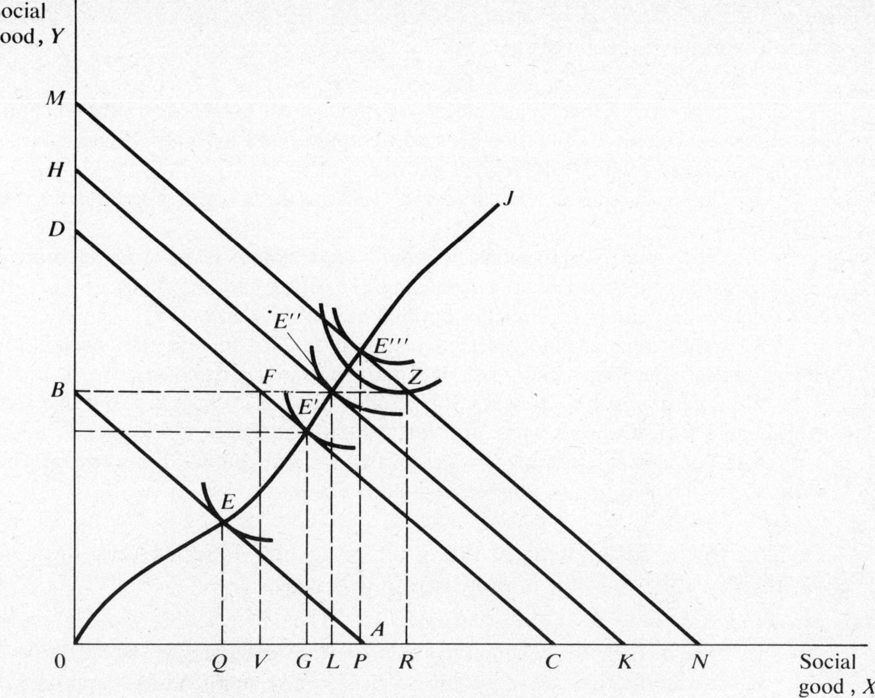

FIGURE 29-7 Comparison of General and Selective Grants.

equilibrium to E'', with the purchase of X rising to *OL*. An equal-cost selective grant, while leaving the community with only the $E''K$ section of the new budget line, again places equilibrium at E''. Up to this point, the two types of grants give the same results in terms of expenditures on X and involve the same cost to the government.

The result differs, however, if a still larger grant is chosen. Suppose, for example, that the general grant is raised further so as to present the community with the opportunity line *MN*. Equilibrium moves to E''' and the purchase of X rises to *OP*. A selective grant, earmarked for the purchase of X and involving the same cost *AN*, confronts the community with the segment *ZN* of the new budget line, with equilibrium now at *Z* and purchase of X equal to *OR*. It will thus exceed purchases of social good X under the general grant by the amount *PR*. The purchase of X will become larger under the equal-cost selective grant once the grant comes to exceed the horizontal distance between *B* and the income-consumption line *OJ*. From this conclusion and that of the preceding section, it further follows that a matching selective grant will be the most effective device in securing increased outlays of a particular social good.

F. SUMMARY

In dealing with the principles of multiunit finance, we have inquired how the allocation, distribution, and stabilization functions of budget policy should be divided among the various levels of government. Beginning with the allocation function, we noted the following:

1. Since the benefit incidence of various social goods is subject to spatial limitation, each service should be decided upon and paid for within the confines of the jurisdiction to which the benefits accrue.

2. This principle of "benefit region" leads to the concept of optimal community size.

3. With pure social goods, it would be desirable to have the number of residents as large as possible, thus reducing per capita cost. At the same time, the cost of crowding enters to limit the optimal community size.

4. Allowing for differences in tastes, it further follows that people with similar tastes regarding social goods will join the same jurisdiction.

5. There is also a tendency for people with higher incomes to move away from people with lower incomes, and for the latter to follow the former.

6. The case for limiting the size of the optimal community is strengthened in the case of mixed goods, where congestion arises.

Turning to the assignment of the other budgetary functions among levels of governments, the situation is more straightforward:

7. The distribution function has to be performed largely at the central level.

8. Redistribution among communities is only a second-best approach to interindividual adjustments in distribution.

9. The stabilization function has to be central because of leakages at the local level.

While these principles suggest a division of the allocation function among levels and placement of the distribution and stabilization function at the central level, they nevertheless leave a place for intergovernmental fiscal relations:

10. Existing jurisdictions are not neatly fitted to benefit areas, so that benefits generated in one area spill over into others. Federal intervention to internalize such benefits may be called for.

11. The central government may consider local public services as merit goods and may wish to subsidize them.

12. The central government may wish to take steps toward equalizing fiscal capacities among lower-level governments.

13. The central government may wish to reduce the distorting effects of fiscal differentials on location decisions.

14. It may desire to substitute central government tax revenue for that obtained at lower levels because central taxes are considered superior.

Consideration was given, finally, to the theory of grants. Here the following conclusions were drawn:

15. Various types of grants may be distinguished and related to various policy targets.

16. For most purposes, matching grants are more effective than are nonmatching grants.

17. If the objective is to encourage particular public services, a selective grant is likely to be more effective than a general grant.

18. Nevertheless, even with selective and matching grants, the revenue gain to the receiving jurisdiction may be partially diverted into other uses.

FURTHER READINGS

Buchanan, James: "An Economic Theory of Clubs," *Economica,* February 1965.

"Federalism," *International Encyclopedia of Social Sciences,* vol. 5, New York: Macmillan, 1968, p. 360.

Musgrave, Richard A.: "Approaches to a Fiscal Theory of Political Federalism," with discussion, in National Bureau of Economic Research, *Public Finances, Needs, Sources and Utilization,* Princeton, N.J.: Princeton, 1961.

Oakland, W. H.: "Congestion, Public Goods, and Welfare," *Journal of Public Economics,* November 1972.

Oates, Wallace E.: *Fiscal Federalism,* New York: Harcourt Brace, 1972.

Tiebout, Charles M.: "A Pure Theory of Local Expenditures," *Journal of Political Economy,* October 1956; and "An Economic Theory of Decentralization," in National Bureau of Economic Research, *Public Finances, Needs, Sources and Utilization,* Princeton, N.J.: Princeton, 1961.

Wagner, Richard E.: *The Fiscal Organization of American Federalism,* Chicago: Markham, 1971.

Wilde, James: "The Expenditure Effects of Grant-in-Aid Programs," *National Tax Journal,* September 1968.

Chapter 30

Fiscal Federalism in Practice*

A. Structure of Fiscal Federalism in the United States: *Historical Development; Governmental Units; Differentials in Fiscal Centralization within States.* **B. Fiscal Capacities and Needs:** *Capacity and Effort: Interstate Differentials; Capacity and Effort: Differentials among Localities; Differentials in Needs and Performance; Position of Cities.* **C. Grants-in-Aid:** *Significance by Level and Program; Categorical Aid; Special Revenue Sharing; General Revenue Sharing; State Grants for School Finance.* **D. Future Directions:** *Assignment of Expenditure Functions; Assignment of Revenue Sources; Redrawing of Jurisdictions; The Role of Grants.* **E. Summary.**

Having examined the general principles of multiunit finance, we now turn to the development of fiscal federalism in the United States and the urgent problems which currently face it.

A. STRUCTURE OF FISCAL FEDERALISM IN THE UNITED STATES

The United States is a federation consisting of a central (federal) government and fifty states and D.C. Each state in turn shares its fiscal tasks with local govern-

* *Reader's Guide to Chapter 30:* Beginning with a brief sketch of the history and current status of fiscal federalism in the United States, this chapter is devoted to an examination of major policy issues, including differentials in fiscal capacity and needs, the role of categorical grants and revenue sharing, and possible changes in the distribution of revenue and expenditure functions.

ments of various types, including cities, townships, counties, school districts, and other special service districts, 18,000 in all. Compared with most other countries, the United States fiscal structure has developed along relatively decentralized lines. At the same time, it has shown flexibility toward changing needs, as evidenced by the expanding role of intergovernmental transfers and the reassignment of fiscal responsibilities.

Historical Development

A look back at the development of fiscal federalism in the United States is needed to understand its current position and trends. The fiscal structure of the original confederation was designed to protect the position of the states and to assure the fiscal weakness of the federal government, with the financing of national expenditures left to contributions by the states. But this structure was short-lived as the Constitution of 1788 strengthened the fiscal position of the federal government and a viable system of federal finances based on customs duties and excises was established. Setting the framework for a decentralized system, the Constitution did not specifically determine what the division of fiscal responsibilities was to be.[1] Nothing was said about the assignment of expenditure functions; and though federal taxing powers were limited by the uniformity and apportionment rules, these rules did not impose severe restrictions and eventually were relaxed further by the Sixteenth Amendment. The taxing powers of the states, similarly, were limited only by the strictures against the imposition of import duties and export taxes. Finally, nothing was said in the federal Constitution about the fiscal role of local governments, leaving its determination for the states to control.

The structure of fiscal federalism was thus left to develop in a flexible constitutional framework, and the relative strengths of the various levels of government have changed over the years. The nineteenth century opened with a great debate between the Jeffersonian view that the function of central government should be minimized and the Federalist position which assigned it a stronger function. Over time, the latter was to win out and the trend of development over the century was toward a stronger federal government. Proceeding slowly at first, this trend toward a stronger federal budget accelerated in the later part of the nineteenth century, driven by the needs of westward expansion and the conduct and aftermath of the Civil War. Federal revenues were dominated by customs proceeds up to the Civil War period, such receipts providing 90 percent or more of total revenue. By the close of the century, however, the contribution of customs duties had fallen below 50 percent. State and local revenues throughout were dominated by the property tax.

At the beginning of the twentieth century, the share of local governments in public expenditures was 52 percent, that of the states 11 percent, and that of the federal government 36 percent. (See Table 30-1, lines 1 to 3.) With the exception of World War I, there was little change in this pattern until the 1930s, when the needs of the Great Depression brought the first major increase in the federal share. State and especially local governments were unable to meet these

[1] See Chap. 2, Sec. B, p. 27.

TABLE 30-1
Distribution of Expenditures by Levels of Government
(As Percent of Total)

	1902	1927	1940	1950	1960	1972
	A. WITH GRANTS INCLUDED AT LEVEL OF ORIGIN					
Total Expenditures						
1. Federal	36.4	33.0	53.0	66.5	64.6	60.9
2. State	11.3	17.7	22.5	17.8	16.4	20.4
3. Local	52.4	49.3	24.5	15.6	19.0	18.6
Total	100.0	100.0	100.0	100.0	100.0	100.0
Civilian Expenditures						
4. Federal	21.2	24.7	47.3	48.4	48.5	49.8
5. State	13.9	19.8	25.2	27.5	23.8	26.3
6. Local	64.9	55.4	27.5	24.1	27.7	23.9
Total	100.0	100.0	100.0	100.0	100.0	100.0
	B. WITH GRANTS INCLUDED AT LEVEL OF RECIPIENT					
Total Expenditures						
7. Federal	35.9	31.9	48.0	62.8	59.6	52.5
8. State	8.5	13.6	17.6	15.2	14.7	18.2
9. Local	55.5	54.5	34.4	22.0	25.7	29.3
Total	100.0	100.0	100.0	100.0	100.0	100.0
Civilian Expenditures						
10. Federal	20.6	23.5	41.7	42.7	41.2	39.0
11. State	10.6	15.2	19.7	23.4	21.5	23.4
12. Local	68.8	61.2	38.6	33.9	37.3	37.6
Total	100.0	100.0	100.0	100.0	100.0	100.0

Sources:
1902–1950: Data based on U.S. Bureau of the Census, *Historical Statistics of the United States,* 1960, pp. 725, 728, 330.
1960: Based on U.S. Bureau of the Census, *Government Finances in 1960,* p. 17.
1972: Based on U.S. Bureau of the Census, *Government Finances in 1971–72,* p. 5.

needs as their tax revenue dwindled with a falling level of national income, and the federal government was called upon to move into a wide range of new programs such as welfare, public works, and farm supports. The late thirties also saw the development of the social security program. As a result, the federal share in public expenditures rose from 33 percent at the close of the 1920s to 53 percent by 1940. This increase was largely at the cost of the local share, which fell from 49 percent to 24 percent. At the same time, total public expenditures rose sharply relative to GNP, climbing from 10.4 percent in 1929 to 17.6 percent in 1940.

After 1940 the rising weight of defense expenditures brought about a second major increase in the total expenditure ratio and in the federal share. Whereas, prior to the 1940s, defense had accounted for 12 percent of total expenditures at all levels of government, this ratio shot up to 90 percent during World War II and settled at around one-third during the fifties and sixties.[2] With defense

[2] The reader should view the changing pattern of shares by level of government in conjunction with the earlier discussion of overall expenditure levels in Chap. 6, especially Tables 6-3 and 6-5.

expenditures almost entirely at the federal level, this led to a further sharp increase in the federal share. Thus, federal expenditures by 1950 had come to account for 66 percent of the total. But the share has declined since then, with the present level at 61 percent. At the same time, the federal share in civilian expenditures (see lines 4 to 6 of Table 30-1) showed little change from 1940 to 1972, standing now at 50 percent.

The preceding expenditure shares included grants at the level of the donor, whereas those shown in lines 7 to 12 of the table include intergovernmental grants at the level of the recipient. As a result, the importance of the higher-level shares is reduced. The federal share drops from 61 to 53 percent of total expenditures and from 50 to 39 percent of civilian expenditures. Both ways of looking at the matter are of interest. If concern is with tax requirements, inclusion of grants at the level of origin is appropriate. If interest lies with what levels control expenditures, inclusion at the recipient level may be preferable, although much depends on the nature of the grants and the extent to which their use is prescribed and controlled by the donor. Assessment of fiscal centralization thus differs, depending on whether concern is with the tax or the expenditure side of the picture. Revenue centralization, as indicated by lines 1 to 3, has been more marked than has expenditure centralization, as measured by lines 7 to 9.

The distinction is of major importance because of the rapidly rising weight of governmental grants. As shown in Table 30-2, the importance of grants in the state and local revenue structure has risen throughout the century and has increased spectacularly over the last decade. This development has provided a means of moving toward increasing centralization of the revenue structure without a corresponding increase in the centralization of expenditures made to the public. With federal grants going largely to the states and state grants to local

TABLE 30-2
Intergovernmental Revenue as a Percentage of Total Revenue*

	Federal Grants as Percentage of State Revenue	*State Grants as Percentage of Local Revenue*	*Federal Grants as Percentage of State and Local Revenue†*
1902	1.6	6.1	0.7
1932	8.7	10.4	3.1
1940	11.6	23.6	8.8
1948	13.9	28.5	9.7
1960	19.4	28.4	12.6
1973	24.0	32.0	15.2

* Excludes revenue from utilities and liquor stores.

† Duplicative transactions between state and local governments are excluded in arriving at total state and local revenue.

Sources:

For 1902–1960: U.S. Bureau of the Census, *Census of Governments, 1962,* vol. VI, no. 4, pp. 38–46.

For 1973: Tax Foundation, *Facts and Figures,* 1975, New York, p. 19.

governments, grants in 1974 provided 24 percent of state, and 32 percent of local, revenue. In turn, they accounted for 15 percent of total federal, and 34 percent of total state expenditures.

Since expenditure and revenue structures differ at various levels of government, the growth of grants had important bearing on the composition of the overall fiscal system. As noted in our earlier discussion of expenditures, national defense and social security occupy a paramount position in the federal budget; education and transportation are the major elements at the state level; and education dominates local budgets, with welfare costs next in line. The capacity to meet the latter functions has been strengthened by the flow of grants. Turning to the tax side, the big revenue producers at the federal level are the individual income tax, the payroll tax, and the corporation income tax. The revenue structure at the state level is dominated by sales taxes, with income taxes providing only 20 percent of the total. At the local level, 80 percent of tax revenue continues to come from the property tax, with various forms of charges the next most important source of revenue. The load borne by the property tax has similarly been eased by grant money.

Governmental Units

The preceding discussion has been in terms of federal, state, and local levels of government, but a word needs to be said about the large array of governmental units at the local level. In addition to one federal and fifty state governments, there are over 80,000 further governmental units, all of which are included under the rubric of local government. The number of units and their estimated role in the fiscal picture is shown in Table 30-3.

TABLE 30-3
Structure of Local Government Finance, 1972

	NUMBER	REVENUE		EXPENDITURES
	(I)	*Own Sources (In Billions of Dollars)* (II)	*Governmental Transfers (In Billions of Dollars)* (III)	*(In Billions of Dollars)* (IV)
Counties	3,049	23.7	10.0	22.8
Municipalities	18,517	35.0	11.5	35.4
Townships	16,991	4.0	0.9	3.9
School districts	15,781	39.3	17.6	38.9
Special districts	23,885	5.2	1.6	5.6
Total	78,218	105.3	39.7	106.5

Notes: Column II: Includes revenue from publicly operated utilities.
Sources:
Column I: U.S. Bureau of the Census, *Statistical Abstract of the United States, 1970,* p. 404.
Columns II, III, IV: U.S. Bureau of the Census, *Census of Governments,* 1972, vol. 1, pp. 26 and 30. Expenditures include direct and general expenditures.

Townships, school districts, and municipalities rank about equal in number, with special districts more and counties much less numerous. There is a great deal of variety in the pattern of local government among the different states. Thus, counties are of major importance in the south, school districts abound in South Dakota, Texas, and Nebraska, and townships are of special importance in the northwestern states.

Municipalities (i.e., cities) rank much ahead of the other units in fiscal importance, with school districts and counties next in line. Special districts and townships, though more numerous, are less significant in terms of the amounts of revenue or expenditures involved.

Differentials in Fiscal Centralization within States

The lack of uniformity in the fiscal structure emerges once more if we compare the degree of fiscal centralization within states. This is apparent in Table 30-4, where the states' share in financing state and local expenditures is given.[3] As shown in column I, the state share in total expenditures ranges from 70 percent for the most centralized quartile of states to 48 percent for the least centralized. We also observe that the degree of centralization differs greatly among functions (columns II to V), with welfare expenditures the most centralized, and school expenditures the least. Welfare costs are largely or entirely state-financed in some states, while in others they are largely local. Highway expenditures, on the other hand, are more centrally financed throughout. At the same time (not shown in the table), there is no distinct relationship between the degree of expenditure centralization and the overall composition of the state-local expenditure structure.

TABLE 30-4
Percentage of State and Local Expenditures Financed by States*

Rankings†	*Total (I)*	*Local Schools (II)*	*Highways (III)*	*Public Welfare (IV)*	*Health and Hospitals (V)*
1. Highest quartile	70.4	72.9	92.0	99.6	89.3
2. Second quartile	60.3	50.8	81.4	94.9	61.7
3. Third quartile	52.5	36.5	66.9	81.2	42.3
4. Lowest quartile	47.8	25.0	49.5	55.2	32.1
5. Highest state	78.9	96.8	94.7	100.0	99.0
6. Average state	52.7	43.3	74.5	76.1	51.5
7. Lowest state	42.9	10.4	51.2	42.1	15.7

* Expenditures financed by state grants are included at the state level; expenditures financed by federal grants are excluded.

† States are ranked differently in each column, in line with the state share in expenditures on the particular function.

Source: Advisory Commission on Intergovernmental Relations, *Significant Features of Fiscal Federalism,* 1973–74 ed., Washington: p. 132, table 84.

[3] Note that the state's share as shown is the share in expenditures financed by state and local sources, excluding federal grants.

TABLE 30-5
Relationship of Tax Structure to Tax Centralization

		PERCENTAGE OF STATE-LOCAL TAX REVENUE FROM SELECTED TAXES			
Ranking	*Percentage of State-Local Taxes Going to State (I)*	*Property Tax (II)*	*Income Tax (III)*	*General Sales Tax (IV)*	*Selective Sales Taxes (V)*
*Ranked by Share of Particular Tax in State-Local Revenue**					
1. Highest quartile	n.a.	34.3	14.4	17.5	15.0
2. Second quartile	n.a.	26.6	8.4	13.4	11.8
3. Third quartile	n.a.	20.6	5.2	11.1	9.8
4. Lowest quartile	n.a.	12.1	0.9	4.6	7.9
5. Highest state	n.a.	39.3	20.4	23.4	19.4
6. Average state	n.a.	26.1	8.2	12.3	10.6
7. Lowest state	n.a.	6.8	0.0	0.0	4.7
Ranked by State's Share in Total State-Local Tax Revenue†					
8. Highest quartile	74.6	11.6	8.2	12.5	10.6
9. Second quartile	67.2	21.7	6.8	13.4	12.1
10. Third quartile	50.0	25.7	6.9	12.2	10.7
11. Lowest quartile	46.1	33.6	6.4	9.4	11.5
12. Highest state	79.7	11.1	19.1	0.0	10.4
13. Average state	54.2	26.1	8.2	12.3	10.6
14. Lowest state	41.2	39.3	0.4	10.3	13.3

* States are ranked differently in each column in line with the particular tax share in revenue.
† States are ranked throughout in line with column I.
n.a.: Not applicable.
Source: Advisory Commission on Intergovernmental Relations, *Significant Features of Fiscal Federalism,* 1973–74 ed., Washington: table 6, p. 28; table 22, p. 35; table 23, p. 36; table 24, p. 37; table 25, p. 38; table 26, p. 39.

Variations in tax structure are shown in Table 30-5. As seen in lines 1 to 7, the share of total state-local tax revenue which is derived from property taxes ranges from 39 percent in the highest state (New Hampshire) to 7 percent in the lowest (Alaska), while the income tax share varies from 20 percent (Maryland) to 0 percent (Nevada). The lower part of the table shows the relationship of differences in the composition of tax revenue to the degree of tax centralization. We note (column I) that the state share in total state-local tax revenue ranges from 80 percent in the most tax-centralized state (Delaware) to 41 percent in the least centralized (New Hampshire). Keeping the same rankings as in column I, columns II to V show the percentage of state-local revenue which is derived from various sources. We now note that the property tax share rises as the degree of centralization falls (column II), whereas the income-tax share rises with centralization (column III). Highly decentralized states, such as New Hampshire, tend to derive a large share of their revenue from the property tax, whereas centralized states, such as Vermont, West Virginia, and Hawaii, derive a relatively small share from this source. However, this pattern again is not uniform. Thus, New York, while below the average in terms of centralization, also has a very low property tax share. The explanation is that "own" finance by large metropolitan areas can draw more readily on local sources other than the property tax, such as local sales or income taxes.

B. FISCAL CAPACITIES AND NEEDS

We now turn to another aspect of fiscal diversity, namely, the differentials in fiscal capacities and needs of various jurisdictions. The ability of a jurisdiction to carry out its fiscal tasks depends on its tax base (its capacity) relative to the cost of rendering public services (its needs). When relatively high-capacity jurisdictions are faced with relatively low needs, a standard level of services can be provided with a relatively low effort (ratio of tax revenue to tax base); and where the opposite holds, a high effort may be needed to provide even a substandard service level. This problem—which arises in comparing fiscal positions both among states and among jurisdictions within states—poses one of the principal issues in fiscal reform. It is of concern both to the federal government, called upon to reduce excessive differentials among states, and to state governments, called upon to deal with excessive differentials among local jurisdictions.

Capacity and Effort: Interstate Differentials

A first approximation to fiscal capacity is given by per capita income. This figure provides a comprehensive measure of ability to pay but does not allow for the fact that the income tax plays only a minor role in state tax structures and as yet hardly any at the local level. Retail sales and assessed property value might be preferable indicators in this respect, or capacity might be measured by combining the various bases with appropriate weights. The latter may be done by applying a "standard tax structure" and measuring capacity in terms of the per capita yield of that structure.

Capacity Table 30-6 shows the range of differentials in fiscal capacity among states. Column I shows per capita income, column II shows the per capita property tax base, and column III shows fiscal capacity as measured by the yield of an average tax structure and expressed as a percentage of the average among states. Both state and local revenues are included. Using the per capita income measure, the range is from over 130 percent of the average at the high end of the scale to 60 percent at the bottom. Using the standard tax system, the range is even wider. As one would expect, the urban states show up better with the income index, and the natural-resource states do better under the property valuation and standard yield measures. This is also shown in column IV, which gives the ratio of standard yield to per capita income.

Column V shows the level of tax effort as measured by the ratio of actual to standard yield. As suggested by the table, there is no close relationship between per capita income and tax effort. The low-income states exhibit an about-average

TABLE 30-6
Interstate Differentials in Tax Capacity and Effort

	INDEXES OF TAXABLE CAPACITY					
Selected States Grouped by Per Capita Income	*Per Capita Income as Percentage of Average (I)*	*Per Capita Assessed Valuation as Percentage of Average (II)*	*Per Capita Yield of Standard Tax Structure as Percentage of Average (III)*	*Column III Divided by Column 1 (IV)*	*Index of Tax Effort (V)*	*Federal Grants Per Capita as Percentage of Average (VI)*
Highest						
District of Columbia	133	123	120	90	85	(334)
Connecticut	125	118	109	87	93	79
Nevada	118	157	169	143	77	145
Alaska	115	96	129	112	106	122
Middle						
Indiana	104	97	98	94	98	62
Colorado	98	102	107	109	107	117
Minnesota	98	89	100	102	116	100
Pennsylvania	100	89	86	86	99	79
Wisconsin	100	74	96	96	116	77
Lowest						
Alabama	76	65	72	94	97	122
West Virginia	73	73	72	99	100	145
Arkansas	68	74	74	108	89	107
Mississippi	60	61	66	110	102	117
Selected Urban States						
New York	118	117	113	95	126	113
Massachusetts	110	93	97	88	112	100
Pennsylvania	100	89	86	86	99	79
Maryland	108	100	98	86	102	85
New Jersey	116	107	104	90	94	69

Notes:
All figures are for 1966–1967 except those in column VI, which are for 1970.
Columns III and V: Both state and local taxes are included.
Sources:
Column I: U.S. Bureau of the Census, *Government Finances, 1966–67.*
Column II: Calculated from Advisory Commission on Intergovernmental Relations, *Measuring the Fiscal Capacity and Effort of State and Local Areas,* Washington: March 1971, tables G1, G2.
Column III: Ibid., p. 120.
Column V: Ibid., p. 126. Effort measured as actual yield as percentage of yield obtained by applying average rates.
Column VI: U.S. Bureau of the Census, *Government Finances, 1969–70.* Data for fiscal 1970.

effort ratio, while among the other states, there exists a negative relationship between effort and capacity. But again, there are significant exceptions such as New York, which combines high income with a high effort ratio.

Capacity and Effort: Differentials among Localities

Comparison among municipalities is more difficult. Jurisdictions differ and fewer data are available. However, a comparison may be drawn in terms of differentials

TABLE 30-7
Differentials in Tax Base and Effort within States
(Distribution across Jurisdictions)

	EQUALIZED VALUATION PER PUPIL (In Thousands of Dollars)			SCHOOL TAX RATE	
	Lowest Decile (I)	*Median Decile (II)*	*Highest Decile (III)*	*Median (IV)*	*Simple Correlation of Tax Rate and Base (V)*
Maine	3.6	7.8	25.6	28.9	−.81
Massachusetts	15.5	27.3	45.2	22.4	−.82
Vermont	16.0	25.9	57.4	12.3	−.71
New Hampshire	13.7	22.6	56.2	18.8	−.88
Rhode Island	23.1	28.9	42.5	17.8	−.73
Connecticut	19.3	29.5	46.8	14.0	−.75

Source: Steven J. Weiss and Robert W. Eisenmenger, "The Problem of Redistribution of Federal and State Funds," in *Financing State and Local Governments,* Boston: Federal Reserve Bank of Boston, 1970, p. 67.

in property tax rates. This is shown in Table 30-7 for the New England states. Based on data for the late sixties, we note that assessed property value per pupil varies sharply across local jurisdictions. Thus, in Maine, the bottom 10 percent of jurisdictions showed an assessed value of $3,600 per pupil as against $25,000 in the highest decile. The variability among jurisdictions within states in most cases is substantially greater than that among states. As also shown in column V, the level of the property tax rate—or index of local effort—is related inversely to the level of tax base per pupil. Moving down column II, the valuation per pupil rises, while the tax rate, as shown in column IV, falls.

Differentials in Needs and Performance

In view of the previously noted differentials in fiscal capacities and revenue effort among states, it is not surprising to find equally sharp differentials in performance levels among states. This is shown in Table 30-8. Total per capita expenditures vary from 64 to 268 percent of the average. The differences are of particular interest with respect to such categories as education and health, with high-income states recording relatively high expenditure levels and low-income states showing low levels. Thus, there exists a strong positive relationship between income and service levels as measured across states.

While comparison between average expenditure levels is instructive, these levels reflect differentials in service levels (relative to an average standard) only to the extent that per capita needs (or costs of standard service levels as measured in dollar terms) are the same in each state. As we have seen, this is not the case. Allowance for cost differentials would dampen the spread for school expenditures. Furthermore, one would want to correct the picture for the share of enrollment in parochial schools. With regard to highways, comparison of per

TABLE 30-8
Per Capita State and Local Expenditures as Percentage of Average, 1971–72

Selected States Grouped by Per Capita Income	*Local Schools*	*High-ways*	*Public Welfare*	*Health*	*Sewage*	*Total*
Highest						
District of Columbia	130	103	192	303	320	178
Connecticut	112	97	89	84	164	103
Alaska	233	426	103	101	277	268
Nevada	115	154	59	147	86	128
Middle						
Oregon	107	133	67	61	99	101
Missouri	91	94	69	78	63	83
Florida	87	89	48	101	63	82
Wyoming	148	251	42	154	27	133
Arizona	107	104	40	73	51	98
Lowest						
South Carolina	79	71	36	99	119	71
Alabama	60	92	73	100	32	75
Arkansas	60	90	71	65	29	64
Mississippi	64	119	82	112	57	79
Selected Urban States						
New York	138	89	138	226	162	155
Massachusetts	107	72	163	107	97	111
Pennsylvania	102	93	95	72	92	92
Maryland	109	83	84	98	151	104
New Jersey	107	105	97	77	127	100

Source: U.S. Bureau of the Census, *Governmental Finances in 1971–72,* table 22, pp. 45–47.

capita expenditures fails to reflect cost differentials of highway services due to geographical differences. Welfare expenditures need to be translated into outlay per recipient, and so forth. While capacity can be measured without too much difficulty, derivation of a measure of aggregate need levels poses a more complex task, which has as yet to be undertaken.[4] But the crude indicators of Table 30-8 suffice to point to the existence of substantial differentials.

[4] To obtain a comprehensive measure of need, it is necessary to postulate a set of service levels—involving such items as education, roads, welfare, health, and municipal services—and to determine what it would cost to provide them in various jurisdictions. To do this, it is necessary to define service levels in "objective terms" and to allow for cost differentials. The definition of service levels in particular is a difficult task. Should service levels be measured in terms of inputs (e.g., teacher hours per grade school child) or in terms of output (e.g., reading proficiency requirements)? How can a meaningful comparison be drawn between the service levels provided by rural and city roads? After these difficulties are met, there is the further problem of costing any particular service, with allowance for the interdependence of costs and service levels.

A final difficulty in measuring needs and capacities relates to the choice of governmental units that are to be compared. As noted before, there are wide differences in governmental organization among states as also within states, which further complicate such comparisons. Yet, such comparisons are important and more work needs to be done to obtain them.

TABLE 30-9
Fiscal Position of Central City and Ring
(Averages for Largest SMSAs in Northeast Region)

	1957		1970		PERCENTAGE CHANGE, 1957–1970	
	Central City	*Ring*	*Central City*	*Ring*	*Central City*	*Ring*
Population*	—	—	—	—	−6.8	22.7
Percentage of population in SMSA*	36.1	63.9	30.6	69.4	−15.3	8.6
Average household income	—	—	$10,325	$13,089	—	—
Percentage of households with income below $3,000	—	—	16	9	—	—
Percentage of households with income above $10,000	—	—	33	46	—	—
Median house value	—	—	$16,200	$27,400	—	—
Per capita expenditure, total	$207	$165	$613	$419	196	153
Per capita expenditure, education	$54	$83	$186	$226	244	172
Per capita expenditure, other	$153	$83	$427	$193	179	132
Per capita tax revenue	$135	$101	$301	$230	123	128
Per capita state and federal aid	$39	$36	$257	$128	559	255

* For years 1960 to 1970.
Note: Missing data were not given in source.
Source:
Advisory Commission on Intergovernmental Relations, *City Financial Emergencies: The Inter-governmental Dimension,* Washington: July 1973, appendix B, tables B1, B8, B9, B11, B14, B17, B19.

Position of Cities

In concluding this survey of fiscal capacities and needs, a closer look is taken at the position of the cities. In 1970, about 69 percent of the United States population lived in metropolitan areas, with 32 percent in central cities and 37 percent in suburbs. Metropolitan finance is thus a large part of the fiscal problem, and the fiscal plight of the central cities has been at the center of recent discussion. While it is difficult to generalize—since metropolitan patterns differ—certain major causes of the problem may be noted.

Major factors affecting the fiscal position of inner cities and the suburban rings around them are given in Table 30-9. These factors are applicable to the eleven largest metropolitan areas in the Northeast region. To begin with, central cities have suffered a population decline in the years from 1950 to 1970, whereas the suburbs have gained. Along with this population shift, the economy of the suburban rings has been expanding ahead of that of the central city. Average household income for the central city in 1970 was well below that of the ring, including a substantially larger fraction of households with incomes below $3,000 and a substantially smaller fraction in the above-$10,000 group. Median house values in the central city were also much below those of the ring.

At the same time, per capita public expenditures in the central city are higher than in the ring and have been rising more rapidly. Notwithstanding the higher level of total expenditures, education expenditures in the central city have been lower, leaving other expenditures very much above those of the ring. This reflects a much higher welfare load, as well as higher costs of operating governmental services. These costs have been pushed up rapidly by rising wage rates of city employees. Although such rates have historically been low, they have now, in many instances, matched or even surpassed rates for comparable private employment. The role of collective bargaining in municipal employment has become a major issue, and the expanding weight of retirement pension obligations will be a major factor in the future.

Turning to the revenue side, per capita tax revenue in the central city exceeds that of the ring. Even though the residential property tax base is lower per capita, it is offset by a larger share of business property, thus resulting in a per capita property tax base equal to, or larger than, that of the ring. However, the increase in the property tax base in the central city has lagged behind rising expenditure obligations. The higher level of tax revenue in the central city typically reflects a larger tax effort, with resort not only to high levels of property taxation but also to the use of income and sales taxes.[5] In addition, the level of per capita aid is substantially higher in the central city.

C. GRANTS-IN-AID

The major link among the fiscal systems at various levels of government is provided by grants-in-aid. As was seen in Table 30-2, intergovernmental grants

[5] For a discussion of urban fiscal problems, see Advisory Commission on Intergovernmental Relations, *City Financial Emergencies,* Washington: 1973; and H. E. Brazer, "Some Fiscal Implica-

TABLE 30-10
Role of Grants in Major Expenditure Programs, 1972
(In Billions of Dollars)

	Federal	*State*	*Local*	*All Levels*
Education				
Total expenditures	13,0	38.3	47.8	*
Direct	5.1	17.2	47.8	70.0
Grants	7.9	21.2	—	29.1
Own finance	13.0	30.4	26.6	70.0
Highways				
Total expenditures	5.5	15.4	6.3	*
Direct	0.4	12.7	6.3	19.4
Grants	5.1	2.6	—	7.7
Own finance	5.5	10.3	3.7	19.4
Welfare				
Total expenditures	15.7	19.2	9.0	*
Direct	2.5	12.2	9.0	23.7
Grants	13.3	6.9	—	20.2
Own finance	15.7	5.9	2.1	23.7

* Total not meaningful because of double-counting.
Notes: To simplify presentation, the entire federal grants are allocated to the states, including a small amount which was, in fact, given to the local level.
Source: Based on U.S. Bureau of the Census, *Governmental Finances in 1971–72,* pp. 7–9.

have become an increasingly important factor in both state and local revenue and promise to remain so in the future.

Significance by Level and Program

The importance of grants in major program areas and by level of government is shown in Table 30-10.

Beginning with education, we note that 41 percent of total direct expenditures (i.e., expenditures to the public) were grant-financed. The federal government played a significant role as grantor but only a minor one in making direct expenditures. The states contributed 72 percent of grants while making only 24 percent of direct outlays. The local level, finally, made 68 percent of direct outlays while contributing only 38 percent of the finance.

Turning to highways, the grant share in total finance for all levels of government was 40 percent. The federal government is now the major grantor, but again only a minor contributor to direct outlays. States now appear as the major agent for direct expenditures, with state grants and direct outlays of local governments of minor importance.

In the welfare field, the contribution of grants to total finance stood at 85

tions of Metropolitanism," and D. G. Davies, "Problems of Urban Finance," both in W. E. Mitchell and I. Walter (eds.), *State and Local Finance,* New York: Ronald, 1970. Also see Robert D. Reischauer, "Fiscal Problems of Cities," in Charles Schultze et al. (eds.), *Setting National Priorities: The 1973 Budget,* Washington: Brookings, 1972, pp. 294, 303.

percent, with the federal government once more the dominant grantor and the states the major locus of direct expenditures. The crucial role of grants in these major expenditure areas is thus readily evident.

Categorical Aid

The traditional approach to federal grants has been in "categorical" form, i.e., as selective grants which are earmarked for particular purposes and which usually involve matching requirements. Recent discussion has questioned this approach. The alternative of "general revenue sharing" was instituted in 1972, is now in full operation, and is likely to grow in importance. However, categorical grants are likely to remain the major component of the system.

Major Programs Major grant categories up to 1975 are recorded in Table 30-11. Grants under the heading of community development and housing are for urban renewal and low-rent housing programs. Under commerce and transportation, nearly $5 billion out of a total of $6 billion are grants made by the federal Highway Trust Fund. These grants go to support the construction of interstate highways, the trust fund being financed from federal automotive taxes. Recently it has been provided that part of these funds be diverted into support of mass transit, but such diversion has so far been very limited. In the education and manpower category, the most important item is support to elementary and secondary education, including a large number of programs directed at specific activities. Next in importance in this category are grants to support manpower development and training activities. Under health, much the most important

TABLE 30-11
Growth of Federal Grants to State and Local Governments
(Fiscal Years, in Billions of Dollars)

	1959	*1970*	*1975*
Categorical Grants			
Community development and housing	0.2	2.6	3.9
Commerce and transportation*	2.7	5.2	6.5
Education and manpower	0.6	3.7	6.5
Health	0.3	3.7	8.5
Income security	1.1	5.0	13.5
Other	1.9	4.3	6.9
Total	6.8	24.5	45.8
General Revenue Sharing	—	—	6.2
Total†	6.8	24.5	52.0

* Includes highway trust fund.
† Includes grants-in-aid in budget accounts and highway trust fund.
Sources:
1959: Tax Foundation, *Facts and Figures, 1971,* New York: p. 77.
1970: Ibid., 1971, p. 77.
1975: Ibid., 1975, p. 85.

items are programs in support of various types of medical assistance programs. Income security grants, finally, are largely for the financing of welfare payments, giving support to assistance payments made under state programs. Reflecting the rising cost of the welfare program, such grants accounted for a large part of the increase in federal aid during the second half of the sixties.[6]

Types of HEW Grants Most of the categorical grant programs are administered by the Department of Health, Education, and Welfare (HEW). While conditional in nature, the tightness of the strings and other aspects of grant design differ for various grants. Most of the grants are so-called formula grants, with the funds available to all eligible jurisdictions. Some grants, however, are given as "project grants," where the recipient must take the initiative and where grants are allotted if the authorities find the project acceptable. Demonstration grants for education or model city grants are of this type. Most grants, finally, involve matching by the recipient governmental unit, but the matching requirements vary. While uniform for some programs, the matching requirement for others varies in relation to the recipient's fiscal capacity. As noted in the preceding chapter, the specifics of the grant formula are important not only for their distributional implications but also for the recipients' responses.

Allowing for these various differences, HEW grants may be grouped as follows:

		MATCHING	
Capacity	*Nonmatching*	*Uniform*	*Variable*
Not allowed for	1	3	5
Allowed for	2	4	6

Group 1 typically takes the form

$$A_i = a_0 + a_1 \frac{P_i}{P_t}$$

with A_i the allotment to the ith state, P_i the size of the "target" population group in the ith state (such as elementary school pupils or welfare recipients), and P_t the total target population for the nation as a whole. The constant a_0 is introduced to allow for overhead administrative costs but is of minor weight. The distribution is thus essentially on a population basis. Though used in the majority of HEW grants, this formula makes no allowance for differentials in capacity and implies a very crude measure of need since it fails to allow for cost differentials and other factors. In other instances, further allowance for need is introduced by relating the grant to average expenditures in the area, but once more, existing expenditure levels may be a misleading indicator of actual needs.

Most HEW grants which call for matching do so with a uniform matching rate. Such rates differ among programs and vary from 33 to 90 percent. Usually,

[6] See p. 641.

a uniform matching rate is combined with a population-based allotment (group 3), but in some programs the allotment (the maximum available amount of matching monies) falls with per capita income (group 4).[7]

In other cases, a variable matching rate is combined with an allotment which does not allow for capacity (group 5). In still others, allowance for per capita income is made in both the allotment and the matching rate (group 6). An illustration is given by the Hill-Burton hospital facilities grant where the allotment is based on the above formula while the matching rate, made a function of per capita income Y, equals

$$F_i = 1.0 - 0.5\ Y_i/Y_t$$

The result is an increased redistributive effect when the allotment is in fact used up.

Without delving further into the details of various grant formulas,[8] we may note the significance of variability in the allotment and matching rate components of the formulas:

1. In the absence of matching, allowance for per capita income in the allotment formulas introduces a need component and renders the grant more equalizing.[9]

2. Introduction of a matching requirement has a substitution effect making for increased "own" expenditures.

3. Relating matching requirements inversely to per capita income exerts a stronger substitution effect on the low-capacity state, thus making for a tendency to equalize service levels.

4. The combination of a variable allotment with a variable matching rate further increases the tendency to equalize service levels.

Special Revenue Sharing

More recently, the traditional structure of categorical grants has come under criticism. Including over 400 programs, most of which differ in matching and other compliance requirements, the system is said to be excessively cumbersome and inflexible, leaving but little discretion to state and local authorities. In response to this criticism, which is widely shared by governors and municipal officials, the President in 1971 proposed a new approach, referred to as "special

[7] This is illustrated by the formula

$$A_i = a_1 \frac{P_i(1.0 - 0.5\,Y_i/Y_t)^2}{\Sigma P_j(1.0 - 0.5\,Y_j/Y_t)^2}$$

as used in allotments under the vocational rehabilitation grants. A_i is the basic allotment to the ith state and a_1 is a constant given by the appropriation. In the numerator, P_i is the population and Y_i the per capita income of the ith state, and Y_t is the average per capita income for the United States. In the denominator, the expression is summed for all fifty states and the District of Columbia. The basic allotment thus determined sets the maximum amount which can be obtained by a state, subject to compliance with a flat matching rate.

[8] For a description of these grant systems, see Selma J. Mushkin and John F. Cotton, *Functional Federalism,* Washington: George Washington University, 1968, chap. 4.

[9] See Chap. 29, p. 623.

revenue sharing."[10] Under this approach, the principle of bloc grants was to be broadened and the proliferation of categorical grants were to be consolidated into a smaller number of grant packages. Six major grant areas were to be defined, with 129 categorical grants folded into six special revenue-sharing programs.[11] The grants made under each program were to be earmarked for use in the general-purpose areas, but without strings *as to their specific application* and without matching requirements.

Congress responded but slowly to these suggestions, but various pieces of legislation have established a trend toward grant consolidation and increased flexibility for the recipient. Thus, an urban renewal and model cities program has recently been combined with five other programs to form a "community development" grant program, and other such consolidations are pending. This new approach meets an obvious need for simplification, and governors and mayors naturally favor increased freedom of action for their jurisdictions. At the same time, increased use of bloc grants and elimination of matching requirements reduce the ability of the federal government to meet particular expenditure needs which are of primary national concern. Moreover, by reducing reliance on matching requirements the grant system is likely to become less efficient in raising the level of public service; and by losing the instrument of variable matching rates, its redistributive impact will be curtailed. The debate over the previously selective grants will continue for many years to come.

General Revenue Sharing

After lengthy debate, a new type of federal aid was enacted in 1972. Referred to as "general revenue sharing," it provided for a new system of unrestricted and nonmatching grants to the states and, via a pass-through provision, to local governments.

Provisions of Act Enacted with strong bipartisan support in 1972 and for an initial five-year period, the legislation, known as the State and Local Fiscal Assistance Act of 1972, is likely to be extended with minor changes. The major provisions of the revenue-sharing program are these:

1. Total grants amounted to $5.3 billion in the beginning year 1972, rising to $7.3 billion in 1976.

2. The grants are to be administered through a trust fund, financed by payments from the Treasury and without requiring annual appropriations or budgetary reconsideration.[12]

[10] For a description and support of this proposal, see Advisory Commission on Intergovernmental Relations, *Special Revenue Sharing: An Analysis of the Administration's Grant Consolidation Proposals,* Washington: December 1971.

[11] The six areas are (1) education, (2) law enforcement, (3) manpower, (4) rural development, (5) transportation, and (6) urban development.

[12] Under the original Heller-Pechman plan, revenue sharing was to be financed by a share in income tax revenue equal to 2 percent of net taxable income under the federal individual income tax. This would have permitted the allotment to grow with the tax base independent of tax rates. Congress, instead, limited the program to a five-year trial period and stipulated the amounts for each year roughly in line with the original proposal.

3. The total is to be distributed among the states on the basis of:

a. A three-factor formula, involving population, tax effort, and inverse of per capita income; or

b. A five-factor formula, adding urban population and income tax revenue. In computing each state's share, the formula yielding the higher allotment applies.

4. One-third of the allotment is retained by the state, with the remainder to be passed through to local governments.

5. Distribution among local units includes all units of general government, i.e., counties, cities, and townships, while excluding school districts and other special-purpose districts.

6. Distribution among local units is to be based largely on a three-factor formula similar to that given in 3(*a*).

7. The states must account for the use of their proceeds and comply with certain administrative provisions, but there are no major restrictions regarding the use to which the funds are put.

These provisions reflect compromises on a number of issues which were debated over the preceding years. Some of these issues, which relate to previously discussed grant functions, will now be considered.

Unrestricted versus Categorical Approach The major innovation in the new program is the largely unrestricted nature of the grant. States are subject to no limitations in their use of the funds except that they must not be used as matching payments for other federal grants. Local governments are constrained to use the funds for "priority expenditures," but the list is broadly drawn so as to cover most current expenditures (except education and welfare) and all capital outlays. Finally, states must not offset the pass-through of federal funds to localities by a net reduction in their own grants.

These restrictions, however, are minimal as compared with the traditional categorical aid approach in which federal support is given to narrowly defined programs. Proponents of the unrestricted approach have argued that the program choice is best left to the receiving units which are thought to be closer to the wishes of the people. Opponents have held that not all state and local uses of funds are equally important from the national point of view and that the donor is entitled to assurance that the funds will be used appropriately.

However this may be, there is the more practical question of whether restrictions can be made to stick. As we have noted earlier, the recipients of nonmatching grants experience only an income effect and may choose to use the funds for tax reduction, or they may shift the use of their own funds from the earmarked category to another outlay. For these reasons, it is difficult to enforce restriction without a matching requirement and detailed supervision.

Outright versus Matching Grants The second innovation is to give large grants without matching requirements like those generally applicable under the categorical grant program. Proponents of outright grants have argued that state and local governments are in general need of fiscal relief and should be permitted to share in the revenue largesse flowing from the superior federal tax source. The objective of the program, as they see it, need not only be higher state-local expenditures but may also be state-local tax reduction, thus permitting increased centralization of the revenue function without a corresponding centralization of expenditure policy.

Critics have questioned whether this approach is compatible with a sound system of fiscal federalism. In particular, they question whether lack of responsibility for raising revenue will not interfere with efficiency in expenditure determination at the state and local levels. Put differently, the question is whether the political process, in determining the use of "gift money," will be as discerning as it would be with the use of "own" funds. Economic rationality would answer "yes" since scarce resources are used in both cases; but human nature may respond otherwise.[13] Another query raised by the critics is whether taxpayers in jurisdiction A should be called upon to support jurisdiction B without the condition that B respond with an adequate effort of its own. While all states and localities share in the grant money, the funds nevertheless must be raised, leaving some as net contributors and others as net recipients. On this basis, a case can be made that matching is in order even though it may not be required to enforce selective use of funds. Although some recognition is given to the need for matching by inclusion of a tax effort variable in the allocation formula, its weight in the overall picture is quite limited.

Degree of Equalization The most lively controversy has centered on how the grants should be allocated among states and how much weight should be given to differentials in their fiscal positions. Consider the first of the two formulas (originally advanced by the Senate), which assigns one-third of the weight each to population, to the inverse of per capita income, and to tax effort. The population weight in itself is somewhat redistributive since equal per capita grants result in a higher grant-income ratio for states with low per capita income. Moreover, this base helps the densely populated urban states. The use of an inverse income variable—defined as the ratio of per capita income for the United States to that in the particular state—directs more funds to the low-income states. The tax effort variable, finally, is more or less neutral since there is no strong relationship between per capita income and tax effort. The additional urban population variable in the second formula (advanced by the House of Representatives) is designed to recognize particular urban needs while the income tax weight is added as an incentive to increased use of income taxation. Given the nature of these weights, it is understandable that the urban Eastern states were primarily concerned with the population and urban weights, whereas the low-income and less populous states favored the income variable as a major factor. The final legislation which permits each state to choose between the two formulas is a compromise solution resulting in a rather ill-defined and not very meaningful pattern.

[13] See footnote 25, p. 632, where the same problem was viewed from a somewhat different perspective.

TABLE 30-12
Ranking of States by Per Capita Income and Aid under Alternative Grant Distributions

State	Per Capita Income (1971) (I)	GRANTS PER CAPITA DISTRIBUTED BY: Population Weighted by Inverse of Per Capita Income (II)	Categorical Grants-in-Aid (III)	Revenue Sharing Act of 1972 (IV)	Column IV, Net (V)
Mississippi	51	1	5	1	1
Arkansas	50	2	20	19	6
Alabama	49	3	9	28	13
South Carolina	48	4	30	21.5	8
West Virginia	47	5	7	12	12
Louisiana	46	6	15	4	4
Kentucky	45	7	19	25	14
Tennessee	44	8	24	32.5	19
North Dakota	43	9	10	3	3
North Carolina	42	10	35	26.5	16
New Mexico	41	11	4	9.5	5
Utah	40	12	18	17	11
Idaho	39	13	26	13.5	7
Maine	38	14	21.5	8	10
South Dakota	37	15	13.5	2	2
Montana	36	16	6	18	15
Oklahoma	35	17	13.5	41.5	24
Georgia	34	18	25	36	25
Vermont	33	19	8	5	35
Texas	32	20	37.5	45.5	32
New Hampshire	31	21	36	44	36
Wyoming	30	22	3	13.5	17
Florida	29	23	50	48	38
Virginia	28	24	37.5	41.5	9
Arizona	27	25	32	23.5	20
Iowa	26	26	47	26.5	21
Missouri	25	27	34	49	39
Wisconsin	24	28	48.5	11	18
Oregon	23	29	12	31	29
Indiana	22	30	51	47	41
Minnesota	21	31	31	21.5	22
Nebraska	20	32	46	29	23
Colorado	19	33	21.5	34	27
Rhode Island	18	34	29	30	31
Kansas	17	35	39.5	40	28
Pennsylvania	16	36	41.5	37	40
Washington	15	37	27.5	43	45
Ohio	14	38	48.5	50.5	46
Michigan	13	39	43	32.5	44
Maryland	12	40	41.5	23.5	43
Delaware	11	41	39.5	15	42
Massachusetts	10	42	27.5	16	37
California	9	43	16	20	34
Alaska	8	44	2	50.5	49
Illinois	7	45	45	35	47

TABLE 30-12 *(continued)*

		GRANTS PER CAPITA DISTRIBUTED BY:			
State	*Per Capita Income (1971) (I)*	*Population Weighted by Inverse of Per Capita Income (II)*	*Categorical Grants-in Aid (III)*	*Revenue Sharing Act of 1972 (IV)*	*Column IV, Net (V)*
Hawaii	6	46	17	9.5	26
New Jersey	5	47	44	38.5	48
Nevada	4	48	23	38.5	50
New York	3	49	11	6	33
Connecticut	2	50	33	45.5	51
District of Columbia	1	51	1	7	30
Average Rank					
Lowest 10 states	47	6	17	16	29
Middle 10 states	27	27	35	33	34
Highest 10 states	6	47	22	47	50
Simple Correlation Coefficients					
With column I	+1.00	−1.00	+0.30	−0.29	−0.78
With column III	+0.30	−0.19	+1.00	+0.23	*

* Not applicable.

Sources:

Column I: U.S. Bureau of the Census, *Statistical Abstract of the United States: 1972,* 93d ed., Washington: 1972, p. 319.

Column II: Ibid., p. 12.

Column III: Ibid., p. 414. Data for fiscal 1971.

Column IV: U.S. Department of the Treasury, Office of Revenue Sharing, *Revenue Sharing Statistics,* Dec. 8, 1972.

Column V: U.S. Bureau of the Census, op. cit., p. 395.

The distribution of the funds among states is shown in Table 30-12. States are ranked by per capita income from the lowest up (column I), and their rank order by per capita grant received under various distribution formulas is given in columns II to IV. Column II shows the ranking for a grant distribution weighted inversely by per capita income.[14] Column III shows the distribution in line with that resulting under categorical grants as a whole, while column IV records the rankings under general revenue sharing as enacted in 1972. An overall

[14] Payments to the ith state equal

$$\frac{P_i \cdot P_i/Y_i}{\Sigma P_j \cdot \Sigma P_j/\Sigma Y_j} \cdot B$$

where p is population, Y is personal income, and B is the total amount to be distributed. Per capita payments, underlying the ranking in column II, accordingly equal

$$\frac{P_i/Y_i}{\Sigma P_j/\Sigma Y_j} \cdot B$$

comparison is given at the bottom of the table where the average rankings for the ten states at the bottom, middle, and top of the scale are compared. The income-weighted population formula is most favorable toward the lowest-income states, while there is little relationship between the grant and per capita income rankings in columns III and IV. A further comparison may be based on the simple correlation coefficients shown at the bottom of the table. We find the distribution of grants under the 1972 revenue-sharing law to be related negatively to per capita income, although the correlation is quite weak. Nevertheless, this differs from the slight positive correlation under the categorical aid program. General revenue sharing is thus more equalizing in its impact as measured in relation to average per capita income, although much less so than it might have been under alternative formulas which would have given more weight to the low-income states. One technique of doing so, as proposed by Senator Javits, would have been to assign a certain share of the total to the lowest-ranking states only.

Increased distribution to the lower-income states would not have solved the problem, however, for two reasons. If the underlying concern is to divert funds toward expenditure programs which benefit low-income individuals, the question is how effectively this can be done by diverting funds to states with low average incomes. Closer consideration shows that to accomplish this objective, direct transfer payments to low-income individuals or categorical grants tied to programs which benefit low-income groups are needed. Without such ties, there is little relationship between (1) the distribution of grants according to average per capita state income, and (2) the distribution of the resulting benefits according to the income of individual beneficiaries. The reason is that high-income states direct a larger share of their total expenditures into programs which benefit low-income groups, a tendency which cancels out the fact that the average expenditure dollar in the higher-income states goes to benefit individuals with a higher average income.[15]

On the other hand, if the objective is to equalize the fiscal position of states, the question is whether there is reason to assume that low-income states rank higher in their need-to-capacity ratios than do high-income states. The urbanized Eastern states in particular have high per capita incomes but also high fiscal needs due to high costs of providing urban services, the poverty problem, and so forth. To meet the objective of fiscal equalization, a much more careful measure of fiscal need is necessary, going beyond the simple proxies of population size and percentage of urban population. Furthermore, the necessary statistical base will have to be established.[16]

Net versus Gross Grants Another view is given in column V of Table 30-12, which shows the ranking of states under the revenue sharing as enacted,

[15] See C. Brown and J. Medoff, "Revenue Sharing and the Share of the Poor," *Public Policy,* Spring 1974.

[16] While extensive work has been done on measuring fiscal capacity (see footnote 4, p. 648), very little has been done on the more complex problem of measuring need. For a rough attempt at grant allocation with allowance for need, see R. A. Musgrave and M. Polinsky, "Revenue Sharing: A Critical View," in *Financing State and Local Governments,* Boston: Federal Reserve Bank of Boston, 1970.

but which now relates to *net* rather than *gross* grants. For this purpose, we assume the grants to be financed by income tax, so that the cost is taken to be distributed among states in line with their contribution to the federal individual income tax. The ranking of 1 is given to the state with the highest per capita net receipts, and that of 51 is given to the state (the District of Columbia is here considered a state) with the highest net payment. We find that 31 states are net gainers while 20 are net losers. As may be expected, the net distribution shows a much higher (inverse) correlation with per capita income than does the gross distribution of column IV, since residents of high-income states pay more income tax. Short of a formula which distributes benefits in line with income tax collection, there must be losing as well as gaining states. While it will be of interest to a senator whether his state falls on the plus or minus side, it does not follow that the existence of the program is a matter of indifference to a state (such as Texas or Rhode Island) with a close to zero net position. Had the federal revenue-sharing program not been introduced, such a state would hardly have collected the same amount and type of taxes as did the federal government to finance its program. Moreover, such additional revenue as the state might have collected could have been used for different purposes than were the proceeds from the federal grant program.

Level of Recipient Another major issue is whether grants should be made to the states only or whether the federal government should deal directly with local jurisdictions. The decentralization thesis favors the latter as does the fact that differentials in fiscal position are frequently more marked among local jurisdictions than among states. Nevertheless, bypassing the states would be politically unacceptable, and direct federal administration of local grants would pose serious administrative problems. In addition, the data base for allocation to localities is as yet inadequate. The course taken by the legislation presents a reasonable compromise in requiring the states to pass through two-thirds of the grants to local governments. After the first year, the states are given some flexibility in the choice of passthrough formula and it remains to be seen what pattern will emerge.

State Grants for School Finance

State grants to local governments cover a wide range of purposes, but grants in support of school finance are much the most important item. Our discussion here will be limited to such grants which, in 1969–1970, provided 40 percent of school finance.[17]

Although school finance was traditionally considered a local function, states have come to assume an increasing share of the cost. The basic reason is that fiscal capacities among local units differ widely. Since local finance is very largely derived from the property tax, even with equal tax efforts, various units would

[17] In a large literature dealing with this problem, see Steven J. Weiss, *Existing Disparities in Public School Finance and Proposals for Reform,* no. 46, Boston: Federal Reserve Bank of Boston, Research Department, February 1970; Paul D. Cooper, "State Takeover of Education Financing," *National Tax Journal,* September 1971; *Financing Public Schools,* Federal Reserve Bulletin of Boston, 1972; and Advisory Commission on Intergovernmental Relations, *Financing Schools and Property Tax Relief—A State Responsibility,* Washington: 1973.

differ widely in expenditure per student; or (which is the same), widely differing degrees of tax effort would be needed to finance similar expenditure levels. The need for equalizing measures thus arose from the desire to avoid both excessive differentials in educational opportunities and excessive differentials in tax efforts needed to provide them.

State aid to equalize expenditures per pupil has taken various forms, with some approaches more equalizing than others. *Flat grants,* involving fixed payments per pupil, were widely used at the outset but provided only a modest degree of equalization. Subsequently, the so-called *foundation grants* became popular and are most widely used today. The purpose of these grants is to assure that the cost (in terms of the required tax rate) of providing a set minimum level of school services is the same throughout. Thus, the grant S_i received by the ith unit equals

$$S_i = e^* P_i - r^* V_i$$

where P_i is the number of pupils, V_i is the equalized assessed property tax base, e^* is a stipulated minimum level of per pupil expenditure, and r^* is a mandatory tax rate. Thus the state will make up for the amount by which the cost of providing the minimum expenditure per pupil exceeds the revenue obtained from the minimum tax rate. The formula may then be modified by introducing weights which allow for wage rate differentials, grade level composition, and other factors determining the cost of providing a set minimum level of services;[18] and to this may be added a more complex measure of fiscal capacity in which per capita income as well as property values is allowed for. In addition, requirements for public services other than education might be taken into account.

But even with these adjustments, the foundation approach has become subject to increasing criticism. The support level is frequently set very low, so that substantial differentials in tax effort remain necessary to support what the communities consider to be adequate standards. Moreover, the foundation formula is not designed to impose negative grants (or tax payments to the state) for high-capacity communities, so that the budgetary cost which the states must carry increases rapidly as the foundation level is raised.

In recent years, interest has developed in so-called *percentage-equalization grants,* also referred to as power equalization. Under this approach, the state participates in local education expenditures at any level of spending, but the matching rate is related inversely to the wealth of the local jurisdiction. As against the foundation approach, it offers support to the education-minded low-capacity unit beyond a more or less arbitrarily set minimum level.

While there is something to be said for this approach, not all objectives can

[18] Even with such adjustments, there remains the more subtle question of how "equal levels" should be measured. Students with different backgrounds may require different inputs to achieve similar outputs, with the responsiveness of "educational achievement" and its measurement a subject of acute controversy. See, for instance, S. Bowles, "Schooling and Inequality from Generation to Generation," *Journal of Political Economy,* May–June 1972.

be met equally well within the confines of a limited budget total. Priorities have to be set up, and a good case can be made for setting higher minimum levels under the foundation formula. This is precisely the same problem which we encountered in connection with revenue sharing and which we shall meet again in the context of the negative income tax: the more broadly based the distribution of scarce funds, the less will be the interference with individual options but the less will be left over to flow to those recipients who are in greatest need. The argument for a relatively simple approach of the foundation type is also supported by the complexity of applying refined measures of educational opportunities and the many interpretations to which this concept may be put.[19]

Given the administrative and political difficulties of legislating a grant system which would achieve a high degree of equalization (not only in tax effort but also in actual levels of education), the Advisory Commission on Intergovernmental Relations has suggested that the states assume the entire cost of education, excepting only the federal share.[20] This is clearly the best approach if total equalization of education within the state is desired. But it is unsatisfactory to those who favor adequate minimum levels while leaving local communities the option of going further.

Which objective is to be preferred poses a major issue in social and educational philosophy. However, it is evident that the problems of grant design will remain even in the case of total state finance. If local autonomy over the expenditure side of school finance is to be maintained, as seems to be generally agreed, it will still be necessary to decide how state funds are to be allocated among communities, i.e., how relative levels of need are to be measured.

Interest in the state role in educational finance has been heightened by recent rulings of state supreme courts that local finance of education is unconstitutional under the equal-protection clause, since it deprives children in low-tax–base communities of an adequate education.[21] While the United States Supreme Court has not endorsed this position, these decisions mirror and reinforce prevailing tendencies toward shifting school finance to the state level. As noted before, this would result in either a substantially reduced reliance on property taxation in the state-local system with a corresponding increase in sales and income taxes, or, more likely, an increased state share in property tax revenue.[22]

D. FUTURE DIRECTIONS

During the sixties, it appeared that state and local jurisdictions were in severe fiscal difficulties. Notwithstanding repeated increases in tax rates, rapidly rising expenditures moved ahead of revenue, with an increasing number of jurisdictions

[19] See H. E. Brazer, "Federal, State and Local Responsibility for Financing," in R. L. Johns et al. (eds.), *Economic Factors Affecting the Financing of Education,* vol. 2, Gainesville, Fla.: National Education Finance Project, 1970.

[20] See Advisory Commission on Intergovernmental Relations, *State Aid to Local Governments,* Washington: 1969, p. 16.

[21] See p. 32.

[22] See p. 356.

going into a deficit position. This trend pointed to a need for the federal government to take steps to relieve the fiscal distress at lower levels of government. Since then, the picture has changed considerably. State and local governments as a whole now show a substantial surplus. This improvement reflects, above all, the drastic increase in federal aid, which rose from $11 billion in 1965 to $24 billion in 1970 and to an estimated $55 billion in 1976. One of the major factors contributing to this increase was the rising level of welfare payments and the federal contribution thereto. At the same time, the rising trend of education expenditures during the sixties has leveled off. But though it is no longer evident that an imbalance exists between the fiscal position of the federal government and that of state and local governments as a whole, severe differentials remain between the fiscal positions of various state and local governments. The problem of imbalance, it appears, is a horizontal rather than a vertical one.

To evaluate the situation, we return to the principles of fiscal federalism as considered in the preceding chapter and ask the following questions:

1. Does there now exist a proper distribution of expenditure responsibilities?
2. Does there now exist a proper distribution of revenue sources?
3. Are existing jurisdictions properly drawn?
4. Is the present system of grants satisfactory?

These questions are now considered in turn.

Assignment of Expenditure Functions

Regarding the assignment of expenditure functions, the preceding chapter concluded that provision for public services should be made by the jurisdiction within which the benefits accrue. The major issue here pertains to the financing of education. In an earlier stage of United States history, local-source finance was appropriate since mobility was relatively low. Now that the degree of mobility has become much greater (relatively few people spend their working lives in the jurisdiction in which they received their public schooling), a broader base is called for. This offers an additional reason for increased centralization of school finance at the state level, quite apart from the previously noted requirement for equal educational opportunities. Moreover, there is a good case for increased federal participation in the financing of higher education.

Another conclusion drawn in the preceding chapter was that the responsibility for distributional adjustments should be at the federal level. This approach makes a strong case for centralization of welfare finance. Poverty should be regarded as a national problem that can be neither left to neighborhood charity nor placed as a tax burden on those who happen to live in jurisdictions or metropolitan areas with large, low-income populations and concomitant heavy welfare needs. As we shall see later, developments of recent years have, in fact, moved steadily in this direction, with the federal contribution to the total welfare cost in 1972 amounting to 66 percent of the total. States contributed 25 percent, leaving only 9 percent to be paid at the local level. This development has been a major source of relief for central city finance, as has been general revenue sharing. If to this were added a higher degree of central participation in elementary school finance, these provisions should go far in relieving the position of fiscally distressed local jurisdictions.

Assignment of Revenue Sources

In determining whether a particular tax is appropriate to a particular jurisdiction, we have applied the criterion that the burden should be borne within the jurisdiction. The reason for this conclusion was that efficient resource use requires that the electorate be confronted with the true opportunity cost involved. Moreover, it would be unfair on distributional grounds for the residents of jurisdiction A to tax those of jurisdiction B. From this point of view, taxes on residential property and retail sales taxes are appropriate. Product taxes imposed on the producer and reflected in increased cost are not, since, when exported, the burden is transmitted to "foreign" consumers. A highly appropriate form of local revenue is the service charge, and increased use of such charges may be a major direction of local fiscal reform.[23]

What, then, should be the role of income taxation at the lower levels of government? Use of the personal income tax is appropriate in that it meets the requirement of placing the burden on residents of the jurisdiction, but its use at the subnational level is subject to the constraint that rates can only be slightly progressive, and that interjurisdictional differentials cannot become too large. Otherwise, higher-income taxpayers will tend to leave the jurisdiction and a loss of tax base will result.

Regarding the corporation tax, we have noted before that profit taxation at the state level poses substantial difficulties of interstate competition.[24] We have also observed that the taxation of corporations on a benefit basis—such as would be especially appropriate at the local level—points to a value-added, rather than a profits or property, tax. When we put together these considerations, it appears that the present state of tax assignments, though not perfect, is reasonably in line with our indicated requirements. The question of whether this approach adds up to a desirable distribution of the overall revenue structure depends on how progressive one wishes the tax structure to be. As noted before, the case for "own" finance by lower-level jurisdictions may come in conflict with what is considered a desirable overall composition of the tax structure.[25]

Redrawing of Jurisdictions

State boundaries in their historically determined form do not correspond to natural economic or fiscal units, but nothing can be done to change this disparity. The states are here to stay, but increasing use can be made of fiscal cooperation among neighboring states and jurisdictions in financing mutually beneficial services. Illustrations range from interstate cooperation in port and transportation facilities to intermunicipal compacts in water supply, fire protection, and garbage disposal.

[23] See Dick Netzer, "Is There Too Much Reliance on the Local Property Tax?" in G. E. Peterson (ed.), *Property Tax Reform*, Washington: The Urban Institute, 1973, p. 23.

[24] See p. 311.

[25] See p. 210.

Another instance in which jurisdictional cooperation is needed arises within the metropolitan area where certain services are beneficial to both city dwellers and commuters and should therefore be financed from a metropolitan-areawide tax base. This case, however, is to be distinguished from the much less evident proposition that the suburbs should be held responsible for the financing of welfare and other low-income services within the city. As argued previously, this situation should be recognized as a national responsibility, to be met out of nationwide fiscal resources.

The Role of Grants

Given such reforms, especially the assumptions of federal responsibility for welfare and of state responsibility for most school finance, what remaining need will there be for grants-in-aid?

1. Even though the bulk of school expenditures would be paid for by state revenues, schools would probably continue to be locally operated, so that state grants to local units would still be needed. In fact, the importance of proper grant design would be increased under such a system.

2. Federal finance of the welfare system, unless combined with federal administration, would continue to call for large grants to the state and local levels.

3. With state assumption of most school finance added to federal assumption of welfare, the fiscal position of municipalities would be greatly improved, thus reducing their need for grants. However, some measure of equalization-oriented general grants might still be needed to reduce differentials in fiscal capacities and needs.

4. In addition, categorical grants for particular functions—designed to adjust for spillover effects and merit-good considerations—would still be needed. In designing these grants, a reasonable compromise between avoidance of excessive proliferation and retention of selective use would be required.

5. If developments should call for an increasing share of expenditures to be made at the state-local levels, maintenance of equity in the overall tax structure might call for increased reliance on general grant finance.

E. SUMMARY

Our review of current problems in fiscal federalism was preceded by a brief review of the present state of our federal fiscal structure:

1. Federal grants have sharply increased in importance, and now provide 24 percent of state, and 17 percent of state and local, revenue.

2. At the local level, nearly 40 percent of revenue is derived from grants, largely coming from the states.

3. Including grants at the donor level, the shares in total expenditures are 61, 20, and 19 percent at the federal, state, and local levels respectively. Including grants at the recipient level, the shares are 53, 18, and 29 percent.

4. The number of governmental units at the local level exceeds 80,000.

5. The degree of expenditure concentration differs among states and by expenditure functions.

6. Differences in the degree of expenditure centralization in various states are also reflected in differences in tax structure.

In examining differences in the fiscal position of various jurisdictions, a distinction was drawn between fiscal capacity, needs, and the effort made to meet these needs:

7. Capacity and effort were shown to vary widely among states, with lower-capacity states generally tending toward a higher effort.

8. Even greater differences were found to exist among localities within states.

9. While need is difficult to measure, per capita expenditures for various major functions were shown to differ widely among states.

10. The fiscal position of cities has suffered from a rapid increase in expenditures and a lagging tax base. However, it has been strengthened by increased grant receipts.

The remainder of the chapter dealt with the role of grants and recent developments in grants policy:

11. Grants (federal and state) now finance over 80 percent of welfare, 40 percent of education, and 39 percent of highway expenditures.

12. The bulk of federal grants is still in the form of categorical aid, but general revenue sharing, introduced in 1972, will gain in importance.

13. A variety of formulas are used in providing categorical grants.

14. General revenue sharing provides bloc grants, largely without strings, at an annual amount rising to $7.2 billion in 1976. Allocation among states is on the basis of a complex formula, and two-thirds of the amount received by states is passed through to local governments.

15. Issues in the debate over revenue sharing involve *(a)* whether the grants should be earmarked for particular uses, *(b)* the degree of equalization to be built into the distribution formula, and *(c)* whether the federal grants should be made to the states or whether there should be direct grants to local units.

16. A grant problem of particular interest arises in connection with state grants for the finance of education, including the so-called foundation approach and percentage-equalization grants.

In viewing the future development of fiscal federalism in the United States, we have dealt with the distribution of expenditure functions, the distribution of revenue sources, rearrangement of jurisdictions, and the future role of grants.

FURTHER READINGS

Break, G. F.: *Intergovernmental Fiscal Relations in the United States,* Washington: Brookings, 1967.

Hirsch, W. Z.: *The Economics of State and Local Government,* New York: McGraw-Hill, 1970.

Joint Economic Committee, U.S. Congress: *Revenue Sharing and Its Alternatives,* July 1967.

Mitchell, W. E., and I. Walter (eds.): *State and Local Finance,* New York: Ronald, 1970.

Mushkin, S. J., and J. F. Cotton: *Functional Federalism,* Washington: George Washington University, 1968.

For a useful collection of data pertaining to state and local finance, see Advisory Commission on Intergovernmental Relations, *Federal-State-Local Finances: Significant Facts of Fiscal Federalism,* Washington: 1973–74 edition or latest volume.

Part Eight

Further Policy Issues

Chapter 31

Welfare, Negative Income Tax, and Social Security*

A. Overview of Income Maintenance Programs. B. Income Maintenance for the Poor: *Present Status of the Welfare System; Critique of AFDC Program; Work Incentives; Negative Income Tax.* **C. Social Insurance:** *Structure of Present System; How Redistributive Is the System? Issues in OASDI; Health Insurance.* **D. Unemployment Insurance. E. Summary.**

The overall impact of fiscal redistribution was considered in Chapter 16 (see especially Table 16-5) and will not be reviewed here. Rather, our concern is with the major transfer programs which contribute to the support of low-income households and retired persons.

A. OVERVIEW OF INCOME MAINTENANCE PROGRAMS

A summary of income maintenance programs by levels of government is given in Table 31-1. In fiscal 1975, total expenditures on income maintenance (broadly

* *Reader's Guide to Chapter 31:* Various transfer programs and techniques of fiscal redistribution are reviewed in this chapter, including the welfare system and alternatives such as the negative income tax and social security finance. They are all issues of considerable current importance. They are examined here from a policy point of view, drawing upon our earlier discussion of the underlying principles.

TABLE 31-1
Income Maintenance Expenditures by Level of Government
(Fiscal Year 1975, in Billions of Dollars)

	Federal		State and Local		Total	
Retirement and Related	99.3		6.5		105.8	
Old-age, survivors, and disability insurance		62.9		—		62.9
Medicare		13.4		—		13.4
Veterans and military benefits		13.1		—		13.1
Civil service retirement		6.9		—		6.9
Railroad retirement		3.0		—		3.0
State and local retirement		—		6.5		6.5
Unemployment	7.1		3.0		10.1	
Unemployment insurance		6.9		—		6.9
Workmen's compensation		0.2		3.0		3.2
Welfare	22.9		10.3		33.2	
Aid to Families with Dependent Children		4.6		3.0		7.6
Supplemental Security Income						
Aged		1.8		0.6		2.4
Blind		0.1		0.04		0.1
Disabled		1.8		0.6		2.4
General assistance		—		0.7		0.7
Medicaid		6.1		5.4		11.5
Other*		8.5		—		8.5
Total	129.3		19.8		149.1	

* Includes housing subsidies, food distribution, and benefits for disabled coal miners.

Sources: U.S. Bureau of the Census, *The Budget of the United States Government, 1975 Special Analysis,* "Federal Income Security Programs," pp. 160–170. State data projected as of March 1974 in *Social Security Bulletin,* July 1974, Tables M–22 to M–27, pp. 56–61.

defined) amounted to $149 billion, with most of the financing coming from the federal level where expenditures for retired persons, veterans, the unemployed, and the poor accounted for 40 percent of total outlays. The largest share of federal expenditures went to finance retirement and related benefits with various forms of welfare programs next in importance. State and local governments spent a total of $20 billion, including $10 billion for welfare, $6 billion for retirement, and $3 billion for unemployment insurance.

The various programs in Table 31-1 have been classified into three main categories. Retirement and related benefits represent much the largest group, accounting for over 70 percent of the total expenditures in fiscal 1975. These programs, among which Old-Age, Survivors, Disability, and Hospital Insurance (OASDHI) is much the most important, provide benefits to covered individuals when they retire or reach a given age, regardless of need. As distinct from these insurance types of programs, the next largest category consists of the welfare programs which are specifically designed to transfer income to needy people and which accounted for a little over one-fifth of the total in fiscal 1975. Next to Medicaid, the Aid to Families with Dependent Children (AFDC) program is the major and most controversial item within the welfare category. The remaining and smallest category is unemployment insurance and workmen's compensation, which amounted to $10.1 billion in fiscal 1975.

B. INCOME MAINTENANCE FOR THE POOR

The problem of how best to provide income support for the poor has received much attention in recent years. But though there is general dissatisfaction with the status quo, very little has been done to improve the situation.

Present Status of the Welfare System

The welfare system in the United States as shown in Table 31-1 consists of four categorical programs financed jointly by federal and state-local governments plus a general assistance program financed solely by state-local governments. In addition, the Medicaid program provides medical services for low-income persons, with slightly over one-half its costs being financed by the federal government.

As shown in Table 31-2, welfare expenditures have grown rapidly in recent years. Total outlays for categorical welfare increased from $3.2 billion in 1960 to $13.2 billion in 1974. The lion's share of this increase was accounted for by AFDC, which rose from $1 billion to $7.6 billion. This increase reflects not so much rise in benefits or in the number of eligible recipients as in the fraction of eligible recipients claiming benefits. Since a high degree of coverage has now been reached, this rising trend should terminate. The coverage of these welfare programs is shown in Table 31-3. In 1974, 14.5 million out of an estimated total of 24.5 million poor people were covered by one or another program. The major groups excluded were non-aged single individuals, non-aged couples without children, and persons in families headed by a full-time worker. These exclusions are explained by the fact that AFDC provides assistance only to families in which the father is dead, incapacitated, absent from the home, or (at the state's option) unemployed.

Critique of AFDC Program

As appears in Table 31-2, the major welfare load is carried by the AFDC program. This program has been subject to severe criticism from many sides. Among the major objections which have been raised are the following:

1. The program is too diverse, made up of fifty-four different state and territorial programs, each plan being separately administered under some broad federal guidelines. Depending on their economic conditions, the states are eligible for federal contributions of 50 to 80 percent. Because of this diversity, there are enormous variations in benefit levels and eligibility requirements. In mid-1972, the nationwide average monthly benefit for a family on AFDC was $188, but a family in New York received $297 while a similar family in Mississippi received $54, or less than one-fifth as much. While this differential has to be adjusted for differences in the cost of living, it nevertheless leaves a large gap in real terms which in turn encourages rural-urban migration.

2. The program is demeaning in the nature of its eligibility requirements and their enforcement. Moreover, it encourages family disintegration since payments are

TABLE 31-2
Growth of Categorical Welfare Programs,* 1960–1974

	NUMBER OF RECIPIENTS (In Millions)		AVERAGE MONTHLY PAYMENT (In Dollars)		TOTAL PAYMENTS (Billions of Dollars)	
	1960	*1974*	*1960*	*1974*	*1960*	*1974*
Aid to Families with Dependent Children*	0.8	3.2	108	197	1.0	7.6
Supplementary Security Income						
Aged	2.3	2.0	59	105	1.6	2.4
Blind	0.1	0.1	67	151	0.1	0.1
Disabled	1.3	1.3	56	153	.2	2.4
General assistance†	0.4	0.5	72	117	.3	0.7
Total	4.9	7.1			3.2	13.2

* Medicaid and "Other," shown in Table 31-1, are not included here.
† Figures refer to families or cases, not to number of recipients.
Source: *Social Security Bulletin,* July 1974, Tables M–22 to M–27, pp. 56–61.

TABLE 31–3
Persons Covered by Categorical Welfare Programs in 1974
(In Millions)

Total number of poor persons	24.5		
Covered by categorical welfare programs		14.5	
Aid to Families with Dependent Children			10.8
Supplementary Security Income			
Aged			2.3
Blind			0.1
Disabled			1.3
Not covered by welfare programs		10.0	
Non-aged single individuals			1.8
Non-aged couples without children			1.4
Persons in families headed by full-time worker			4.0
Other			2.8

Sources: Poverty data from U.S. Bureau of the Census, *Current Population Reports,* Series P-60, No. 91, "Characteristics of the Low-Income Population, 1972," December 1973. For persons covered by welfare programs, see *Social Security Bulletin,* June 1974, pp. 62–63.

generally limited to families in which the male head is absent. Unemployed fathers are eligible for assistance in only twenty-three states.

3. The level of benefits is inadequate for a decent minimal standard of living.

4. Single persons and childless couples are completely excluded from the welfare system unless they are blind or disabled.

5. The working poor are not helped. Families in which the father works full time but who are still poor are excluded from the system. In fact, 40 percent of the poor live in families headed by a full-time worker.

6. The program discourages work because it involves a high marginal rate of tax on earnings. Before 1967, recipients lost \$1 for every \$1 earned, which amounted to a 100 percent tax on earnings. The 1967 amendments to the public assistance laws allow recipients to keep \$30 a month and 33 cents on each \$1 earned, which is equivalent to reducing the tax from 100 to 67 percent. If payroll taxes of 12 percent are added, the total rate rises to 79 percent. It may, in fact, be even higher since certain benefits are also lost as income rises.

7. Welfare payments should not be granted independent of work but should be related to a work requirement, an issue which we have encountered previously in considering the bearing of leisure on distributive justice.[1]

As is evident from the nature of these objections, different views are involved, with point 7 the most controversial. Nevertheless, it is undeniable that dissatisfaction with the present system is widespread. In particular, it is widely agreed that benefits should be extended to the working poor and to poor families without children, and that the disincentive provided by high marginal tax rates should be modified.

In response to this dissatisfaction, a substantial reform proposal was made in 1969 by the incoming Nixon administration. By extending benefits to all low-income families and by permitting a minimum level of earnings without

[1] See p. 95.

penalty, this program would have overcome some of the major shortcomings of the present plan. Nevertheless, it was amended extensively in the course of congressional debate in both House and Senate, and in the end, no new legislation for reform of AFDC was passed. Welfare reform is thus still very much on the legislative agenda.

The only major change which emerged from the discussion was the new federal program for Supplementary Security Income. Beginning in 1974, the former state programs for the aged, the disabled, and the blind were replaced by federal benefit payments paid to all such people without other income. Monthly benefits in 1974 were set at \$140 for single persons and \$210 for couples. The first \$20 of other income (including social security) is disregarded, with benefits reduced \$1 for every \$2 of additional earnings. States are free to pay supplementary benefits to the aged, blind, and disabled persons. Certain provisions in the Tax Reduction Act of 1975, especially the newly instituted earned-income credit, may be taken to offer new approaches to the problem.[2]

Work Incentives

The central dilemma in designing a satisfactory income maintenance scheme is as follows: Given a limited amount of funds available for redistribution, the most effective way of aiding low-income families would be to distribute by filling in income deficiencies from the bottom, thereby assuring as high a minimum level as the available budget permits. But this approach implicitly imposes a high marginal rate of tax over the low-income range and thus reduces work incentives. To avoid the latter effect, the aid has to be extended higher up the income scale, a policy which in turn reduces the amount of aid which can be given where it is most needed.

A number of alternative aid patterns and their implicit marginal rate of tax are shown in Figure 31-1.[3] In the upper part of each panel, earnings are shown on the horizontal axis and income received (after tax and transfers) is measured on the vertical exis. The 45° line *OG* shows income in the absence of transfer and tax. Plan I presents the crudest of all approaches, where a fixed subsidy equal to *OM* is given provided earnings fall short of *OB* = *OM* and where the subsidy is lost once earnings exceed *OB.* As shown in the upper left figure, the subsidy at various levels of earnings is given by the solid line *MAB,* and total income received (or earnings plus subsidy) is given by the dotted line *MDAG.* As shown in the lower figure, this means that the marginal tax rate up to earnings *OB* is zero. But for the first dollar above *OB,* an exceedingly high marginal rate (100 × *OM* percent) applies; then the rate again drops to zero. A person earning *OB* would have to raise his earnings by *BF* only to stay even. While such a scheme may seem absurd, it does in fact apply where eligibility for low-income services is lost once income exceeds a fixed limit, as, for example, in eligibility for Medicaid and, in some state programs, for aid to families with dependent children and an unemployed father (AFDC-UF).

Plan II, shown in the middle panel of Figure 31-1, is more reasonable but

[2] See p. 275.

[3] See also the earlier discussion of incentive effects of transfer payments, p. 486.

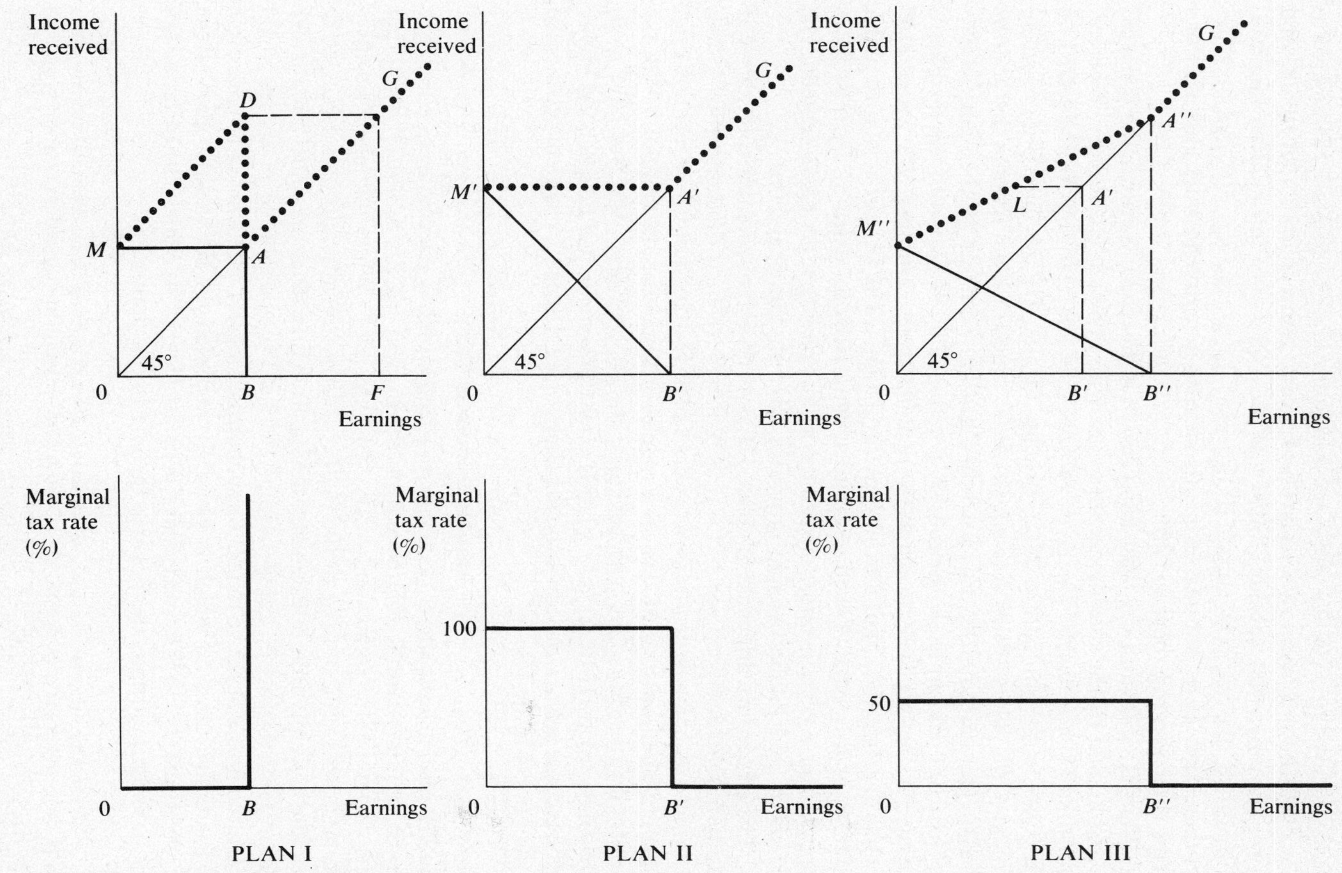

FIGURE 31-1 Alternative Welfare Plans.

still involves a heavy disincentive. This is a plan where the subsidy equals the difference between earnings and a set minimum level of income. If this level is set at *OM′*, the subsidy at various levels of earnings now follows *M′B′*, while total income (earnings plus subsidy) follows *M′A′G*. As shown in the lower diagram, the marginal tax rate now equals 100 percent up to earnings *OB′* and becomes zero thereafter. Thus, subsidy recipients have no incentive to work until they can extend their earnings beyond *OB′*.

Plan III, shown in the right-hand panel, is designed to reduce the disincentive. As in plan II, the subsidy declines as earnings rise but less rapidly. Whereas, in formula II, no subsidy was given to persons whose earnings reached *OB′* (in turn equal to the minimum *OM′*), benefits in plan III are now enjoyed up to earnings *OB″*. The subsidy line equals *M″B″* and the total income line follows *M″A″G*. The marginal tax rate as shown in the lower part of the figure is now less than 100 percent since the subsidy is reduced by only part of the recipient's earnings. As shown here, it equals 50 percent up to earnings *OB″*, where *OB″* is equal to twice the minimum income level *OM″*. The benefit structure under AFDC is of this type. A welfare mother who earns an extra $2 loses $1.34 in support (over a certain range of earnings), thus paying a tax of 62 percent. The food-stamp and public housing programs have similar provisions.

The procedure followed in plan III is thus a compromise solution. The subsidy benefits low incomes and is thus redistributive. At the same time, it does not impose as heavy a disincentive as does plan II. This improvement, however, is accomplished only at the cost of a reduced degree of redistribution. With the same total expenditure for both schemes, the support level *OM* will have to be lower under plan III than under plan II, and the benefits will be extended higher up the income scale. Consequently, the share of total subsidy payments channeled to the poor will be less.[4]

Negative Income Tax

Plan III and variants thereof take an approach which is referred to as a negative income tax, its essential difference from the present welfare approach being that benefit payments are extended to the working poor. While the label "negative income tax" is unappealing to the public, it is technically appropriate since the principle is simply that of extending the positive rate structure under the regular income tax downward, going beyond the zero-bracket range of the personal exemption into a negative range. As such, it is a logical extension of the principle of progressive taxation which is generally accepted for the positive part of the tax. Accordingly, various ways have been considered by which the negative tax may be integrated into the positive income tax structure.[5]

[4] To simplify, suppose that there is one earner at each earnings level. The total subsidy under plan II then equals the area *OA′M′*, all of which goes to families with earnings below the poverty level *OB*. In plan III, total subsidy payments equal *OA″M″*, which is again equal to *OA′M′* in plan II. But of this, only *OA′LM″* accrues to families with earnings below *OB′*.

[5] Integration involves such problems as family size, the definition of income (or absence thereof), the tying in of the tax rate on earnings below the breakeven point with the regular income tax rates applicable above that level, and so forth. See J. Tobin, J. A. Pechman, and P. Mieszkowski, "Is a Negative Income Tax Practicable?" *Yale Law Journal,* November 1967.

In understanding the negative income tax, it is helpful to think of the subsidy received by any one family as

$$s = m - te$$

where s is the subsidy, m is the minimum income, and t is the tax rate (imposed under the negative income tax plan) and applicable to earnings e. The subsidy thus becomes zero where earnings equal m/t, which is also referred to as the breakeven level b. Thus, if the tax rate is 50 percent, b will be equal to $2m$. In designing a negative income tax plan, the interesting variables are m, b, t, and the budgetary cost C. The relationship among these variables is shown in Figure 31-2. Minimum income m equals OA and the total income (earnings and subsidy) line is AE. Breakeven income b equals OD. The slope of the total income line AE or tan α equals HG/AH, or the fraction of earnings which are retained as earnings rise.[6] This fraction also equals $1 - t$ or $1 - m/b$.

The subsidy at each earnings level equals the distance between the total earnings line AE and the 45° line. Assuming an equal number of earners at each level, total C cost may be taken to correspond to the area OGA.[7] It follows that for a given cost C, a higher m can be obtained only at the cost of a higher t and a lower b; or that a lower t can be had only at the cost of a lower m and a higher b. Suppose that m is to be raised to OA'. The new total income line $A'G'$ must then intersect the 45° line at a point below G since the additional cost reflected by the area AKA' must be offset by cost reduction equal to area $KG'G$. Raising

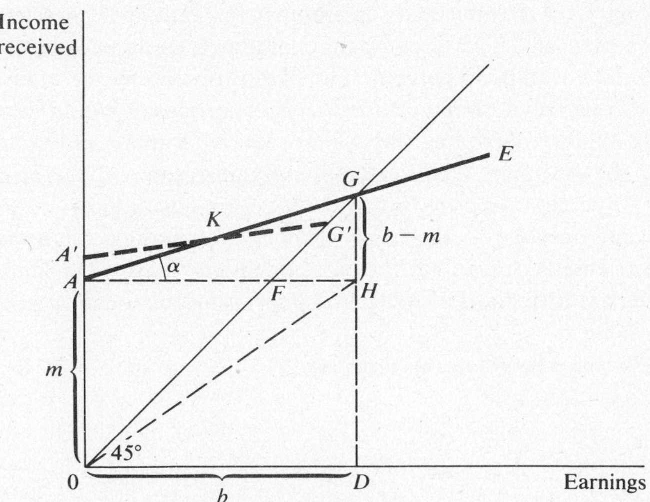

FIGURE 31-2 Structure of Negative Income Tax.

[6] Thus, with earnings OD, total income received equals DG, or the sum of DH (the minimum income allowance) and HG, which is what is left of earnings OD after the tax.

[7] OGA is the *net* cost left after deducting tax revenue ODH (obtained by applying t to earnings up to OD) from gross cost $ODHA$. This net cost remains to be financed by increasing tax rates applicable to income in excess of OD.

m thus raises t by lowering the slope of the total income line and lowers the breakeven point b. Since a high m and low b make for greater redistribution toward the lower end, the desire to redistribute conflicts with the desire to avoid disincentives from a high tax rate.[8]

The choice is thus an unhappy one, and much depends on the weight assigned to the various variables. At 1973 levels, the order of magnitude involved in various policy options may be shown in the following table.

MARGINAL TAX RATE	COST		
	$25 billion	*$50 billion*	*$75 billion*
0.3	m = $2,000 b = $6,667	m = $3,000 b = $10,000	m = $3,700 b = $12,330
0.5	m = $2,500 b = $5,000	m = $3,500 b = $7,000	m = $4,000 b = $8,000

The estimates show that with the lower tax rate of 30 percent, a very high budget is required to let the minimum income (applicable to a family of four) approach the poverty-line level, which for 1973 was estimated at $4,500. The figures also show that by using a tax rate of 50 percent, this objective might be achieved with a substantially smaller (though still large) budgetary cost. The Nixon administration's Family Assistance Program, proposed in 1969, combined a $2,400 floor (including food stamps) with an implicit tax rate of 50 percent, whereas the McGovern plan of the 1972 campaign combined an approximately similar floor with a tax rate of only 30 percent. The plan proposed by the House in 1971 (HR.I) is of a similar order of magnitude. All these proposals would raise minimum benefits only slightly above present welfare levels. A more ambitious plan was proposed by the National Welfare Rights Organization, calling for a floor of $5,500 and a 50 percent tax rate, but the budgetary cost appears to go much beyond what seems feasible at this time. Other combinations might be developed, including variable tax rates, but the basic dilemma remains the same.

Unfortunately, there is little hard evidence for appraising the magnitude of

[8] More generally, the system is defined by two equations:

$$t = m/b \tag{1}$$

$$C = \sum_{i=0}^{i=b} s_i = \sum_{i=0}^{i=b} n_i(m - e_i t) \tag{2}$$

In equation 2, the cost C is defined as the sum of the subsidies s applicable at each level of earnings i times the number at each level of earnings. The subsidy to a family at any one level in turn equals the flat payment m minus the product of tax rate and earnings. Given C, we have two equations with three unknowns, m, b, and t. Substituting, we may write

$$C = \sum_{i=0}^{i=b} n_i t(b - e_i) \tag{3}$$

disincentive effects which result at various levels of tax rates.[9] However, it should be evident that these effects are more important in the case of some recipients (for example, single adults of working age or heads of family with older children) than for others (say, single mothers with small children). By differentiating the treatment of various groups, a higher minimum income can be provided at a given cost and level of disincentive (tax rate) than is possible by applying the same formula to all recipients. This advantage of differentiation must be weighed against the merits of an across-the-board approach which asks no questions except how much earnings are received. A simple across-the-board approach would be ideal if a very large budget were available, but it is costly for those most in need if severe budget constraints apply.

Finally, there is the related question of work requirements or "work-fare." As opponents have pointed out, the bulk of benefit recipients under AFDC are children, and a substantial number of the adult members of the covered families should not be considered part of the labor force. Moreover, work-fare smacks of the mistaken and ugly proposition that the poor are poor because they are lazy. Yet, if purged of these implications, the linkage of income maintenance to employment programs, as applied to those recipients who *are* potential members of the labor force, is a reasonable objective. In the end, such a linkage may prove to be the only way in which an adequate level of income maintenance can be provided without either excessive cost or work disincentive.

As discussed in our earlier examination of the income tax, the recently enacted earned-income credit provides a form of negative income tax as applied to low-income earners. It remains to be seen whether this will become the basis for a more general and extensive acceptance of the negative income tax approach.[10]

C. SOCIAL INSURANCE

The core of the social insurance system is OASDHI. Instituted in 1934 as old-age and survivors insurance (OASI), the program was extended in 1956 to provide benefits for disabled workers. A health insurance plan, giving medical benefits for persons over sixty-five and referred to as "Medicare," was added in 1965 and has become an important part of the system.

Structure of Present System

We begin with a brief description of the system, including its retirement and health components.

Retirement and Disability Insurance Retirement and disability insurance (OASDI) is financed by a payroll tax, half of which is paid by the employer and half by the employee.[11] The original legislation levied a combined rate of 2

[9] For a discussion of experiments to measure work responses, see M. C. Barth, G. C. Carcagno, and J. L. Palmer, *Toward an Effective Income Support System: Problems, Prospects and Choices,* Madison: University of Wisconsin, Institute for Research on Poverty, 1974, esp. chap. 3.

[10] See p. 369.

[11] The OASDI tax for the self-employed usually amounts to three-fourths of the combined employer-employee contribution. See also Chap. 15.

percent on the first $3,000 of wages. However, since 1937 the tax rate has been raised twelve times and the level of maximum taxable earnings has been increased seven times. According to the most recent legislation (1974), the combined tax is 11.7 percent, with 5.85 percent payable by the employer and the same amount by the employee. Of this 5.85 percent, 4.95 percent covers OASDI and 0.9 percent goes to pay for health insurance. These rates now apply to the first $13,200 of wages.

The 1935 social security legislation specified that the old-age insurance program should include all workers under age sixty-five who were engaged in commerce and industry (except railroads) in the United States, with government and railroad employees subject to separate schemes. A major expansion in coverage occurred in 1950 when regularly employed farm and domestic workers were included as well as the nonfarm self-employed (except professionals). In 1965 the latter were added, so that coverage of the working population (except those covered by government or railroad retirement programs) was virtually complete, with covered workers in 1970 comprising over 90 percent of the labor force. Currently, some 27 million people receive benefit payments under OASI and 4 million people receive disability benefits at a total cost of well over $50 billion.

The benefit for an individual worker is derived in two steps. First, an average of the worker's covered earnings over a specified period of time is calculated. Usually, this average is based on earnings since 1950, omitting the five years of lowest wages. Then a table (included in the law) is used to determine, on the basis of the worker's average monthly earnings, his or her primary insurance amount (PIA)—the retirement benefit for a single worker at age sixty-five. If the worker is not married, then the primary insurance amount is the benefit. A married worker receives 150 percent of his PIA. For workers retiring early, the PIA level

TABLE 31-4
Ratio of Old-Age and Survivors Insurance Benefits to Selected Average Monthly Earnings, 1974 Benefit Schedules

		SINGLE WORKER		COUPLE	
Annual Earnings	*Average Monthly Earnings for OASDI Benefit**	*Monthly Benefit*	*Ratio of Benefit to Prior Earnings*	*Monthly Benefit*	*Ratio of Benefit to Prior Earnings*
$ 3,000	$ 250	$194.10	.78	$291.15	1.16
5,000	417	264.90	.64	397.35	.95
7,000	583†	335.50	.58	503.25	.86
10,000	833†	412.40	.50	618.60	.74
13,200	1,100†	469.00	.43	703.50	.64

* Average monthly earnings are calculated as earnings in covered employment since 1950, omitting the five years of lowest wages.

† In 1974 no one could have had average monthly earnings of $583, $833, or $1,000, since the ceiling on annual earnings was increased to $9,000 in 1972, to $10,000 in 1973, and to $13,200 in 1974. For someone working continuously since 1950 and retiring in 1974, the highest "average monthly earnings" would be $542.

Source: Social Security Amendments of 1973, Senate Report No. 93–553, 93rd Cong., 1st Sess., 1973, pp. 97–100.

is reduced by five-ninths of 1 percent for each month between age at retirement and age sixty-five. Potential benefits under 1974 benefit schedules are presented in Table 31-4. Monthly benefits for a couple will range from $291 to $703, depending on average annual earnings.[12]

Benefit levels have risen significantly in recent years. This is the result of two factors. First, benefits for any individual are based on his or her monthly covered earnings since 1951, omitting the five years of lowest earnings. Since average wages have risen steadily, the basis for benefit calculation has also increased. Second, Congress since 1965 has enacted six across-the-board raises in benefit levels, with an 11 percent increase in 1974 being the latest adjustment. As a result, maximum monthly benefits are now 4.5 times their 1951 levels and real benefits have more than doubled.

OASI has been protected against inflation in two respects. The legislation of 1972 provided that the ceiling on taxable wage income is to be raised in line with the price level, as are benefit payments. In fact, over the recent inflation years (1968–1974), benefit levels have doubled, thus well outrunning inflation. Although this does not tell us that benefit levels are adequate, social security beneficiaries have not suffered the fate of fixed income recipients during these years.

Medicare Medicare, which was added to the program in 1965, provides hospital insurance for the aged. As noted before, it is financed by a 0.9 percent payroll tax, payable by employer and employee each. About 21 million persons were eligible for Medicare benefits in 1973 and 16 million are expected to claim benefits. In the ten years since its inception, expenditures for this program have grown to over $6 billion. In addition, a supplementary optional medical insurance is offered to the aged to help pay the costs of physicians' services and other outpatient care. This supplementary insurance is financed half through monthly premiums paid by beneficiaries and half from general revenue. Whereas the system of retirement insurance is fully developed, that of health insurance is still in its inception and extension to the non-aged is a matter of current discussion.

How Redistributive Is the System?

The social security system in its application to the aged was initially looked upon as an insurance plan. Though mandatory and operated by government, it was thought of as more or less similar in nature to the purchase of a private retirement plan. A person would make his or her contribution and then have a contractual right to his or her benefits. As things have developed, this "quid pro quo" nature of the system has given way to some degree of redistribution. The degree of transfer involved may be viewed in various ways, including (1) the distribution of taxes and benefits among income groups arranged on an annual cross-section basis, (2) the relation between average monthly earnings and benefits for particular individuals, and (3) the lifetime rate of return in relation to earning levels as received by particular individuals.

[12] Note that these are the benefit levels which will be available after the higher ceilings for covered earnings have become fully effective. At present, the maximum level is $542. See footnote † to Table 31-4.

TABLE 31-5
Distribution of Social Security Taxes and Benefits, 1966 Law

	FAMILY MONEY INCOME										
Items	*Under $3,500*	*$3,500–5,000*	*$5,000–6,500*	*$6,500–8,000*	*$8,000–10,000*	*$10,000–15,000*	*$15,000–20,000*	*$20,000–30,000*	*$30,000–50,000*	*Over $50,000*	*All*
Percentage by brackets											
Benefits	49.7	14.7	9.6	6.6	5.0	8.6	3.6	1.6	0.3	0.3	100.0
Taxes*	4.6	5.4	8.9	13.2	16.2	29.8	13.1	6.0	2.0	0.8	100.0
As Percentage of Income											
Benefits	54.2	17.8	7.2	3.6	2.1	1.7	1.2	0.9	0.3	0.3	5.2
Taxes*	5.1	6.7	6.8	7.3	6.8	6.1	4.6	3.6	2.0	0.8	5.4
Net	49.1	11.1	0.4	−3.7	−4.7	−4.4	−3.4	−2.7	−1.7	−0.5	−0.2

* The worker is assumed to bear the entire burden of the payroll tax.

Sources: R. A. Musgrave, Karl E. Case, and Herman Leonard, "The Distribution of Fiscal Burdens and Benefits," *Public Finance Quarterly,* July 1974; also see Table 16-1, p. 391.

Distribution by Income Brackets Table 31-5 shows benefits, taxes, and net receipts or payments as a percentage of current income by income brackets. According to this way of looking at the program, it is highly redistributive. The lowest income class pays only 4.6 percent of the taxes and receives almost half of the benefits. Deducting taxes from benefits and computing the net rate as a percentage of income, we find a highly positive rate at the bottom and negative rates at incomes above about $6,000. The lowest income class receives a subsidy equal to 49 percent of its income. Depending on how one looks at the matter, this analysis may be said to overstate the "pro-poor" nature of the program. While the effective tax rate as recorded in the table is progressive up to the fourth bracket, the rate as applied to earners is proportional up to $6,600 (1966 legislation). The recorded rates thus reflect the fact that low-income recipients compose a large share of retired people, with the proportion of earners rising as one moves up the income scale. On the benefit side, the low-income recipients to whom the benefits go are largely people whose incomes are low because they have stopped working. Their lifetime incomes may have been substantially higher and they may possess wealth in the form of homes and financial assets. For these reasons, it may be argued that the redistributional nature of the program is better tested against lifetime, rather than current, incomes.

Average Earnings and Benefits A more satisfactory approach from this point of view is given by returning to Table 31-4, where monthly benefits are related to average monthly earnings. For an individual with annual earnings of $3,000, benefits amount to 78 percent of past wages, or 116 percent if he is married, whereas for high-income earners with maximum earnings of $13,200, benefits equal only 43 to 64 percent of preretirement earnings. The system remains strongly redistributive toward the lower earnings groups, but not as heavily so as under the preceding approach.

Rates of Return Finally, the benefit-tax relationship may be examined in terms of real rates of return, obtained over the lifetime of the individual.[13] The results for a married worker are shown in Table 31-6.[14] Taking the case of a worker who has entered the labor force at age eighteen and whose earnings have risen at an annual rate of 2 percent, we find a return of 5.2 percent at the bottom of the scale and of 3.8 percent at the top. Thus, there again exists a substantial redistributional element toward the lower group, whose return is nearly 40 percent higher.

The results are affected by the growth rate of earnings and the time of entry into the labor force. The rate of return is higher if the individual's earnings grow more rapidly over his or her lifetime, since the later earning years (on which

[13] The real rate of return is defined as the rate which at retirement would equalize the accumulated tax (plus imputed interest) and the present discounted values of real benefits. In other words, it is the rate which would yield a tax-benefit ratio of unity. Individuals were assumed to enter the work force in 1966.

[14] The three basic assumptions of the model are: (1) average earnings are assumed to grow at a fixed rate r (2 or 3 percent); (2) real retirement benefits are assumed to grow at the same rate r; and (3) the social security system will continue to be financed on a pay-as-you-go basis.

TABLE 31-6
Rates of Return on Social Security
(Married Male Worker, 1966 Law)

TYPE OF INSURED		RATES OF RETURN (Percentage)		
		Average Annual Lifetime Earnings:		
Age of Entry	*Growth Rate of Earnings, Percentage*	*$2,000*	*$6,600*	*Mean*
18	2	5.2	3.8	4.4
18	3	6.1	4.7	5.3
22	2	6.1	4.5	5.1
22	3	7.1	5.5	6.2

Note: Analysis is based on the assumption that the worker pays the employer's contribution.
Source: John A. Brittain, *Payroll Taxes for Social Security,* Washington: Brookings, 1972, table 66, p. 170.

benefits are based) are higher relative to the average (on which contributions are based). Moreover, the return will be higher for individuals who enter the working force relatively late, since the tax applies over a shorter period. Both these tendencies favor the higher earning groups. A higher rate of unemployment among low-income workers, on the other hand, favors their rate of return by reducing the contribution period.

The net result of all these factors once more shows redistribution toward the lower end. Put differently, lower earnings receive a subsidy on the return to their old-age investment, whereas higher earners pay a tax thereon. As an offsetting factor, it may be noted, however, that low-income earners tend to enter the labor force earlier and are subject to higher mortality rates.[15]

Issues in OASDI

It remains to consider certain basic issues in the structure of OASDI, issues which have been debated since the introduction of the system and which are still under discussion. They are:

1. Should retirement insurance be compulsory and public, rather than voluntary and private?
2. Should the system be reserve-financed or on a pay-as-you-go basis?
3. Should the system be financed by payroll taxes or a general budgetary contribution?

These questions will be considered in turn, with allowance for recent OASDI developments.

Public versus Private Provision for Retirement The issue here involves both the *compulsory* and the *public* nature of OASDI. In dealing with the compulsory aspect, let us suppose that society has already made such adjustments in

[15] See Henry Aaron, "Demographic Effects on the Equity of Social Security Benefits," Turin, Italy: International Economic Association, April 1974.

the distribution of lifetime income as are considered desirable, so that the case of the aged cannot be viewed as part of a general redistribution problem. Why, then, should not each individual be left to decide how he or she wishes to distribute his or her income use over time? The answer is that while most people will provide for their old age, some will fail to do so. Assuming that society will not permit its imprudent aged to starve, this will impose a further burden on the more prudent. To protect themselves against this contingency, they will impose compulsory insurance.

Having established the need for compulsory insurance, we must ask the further question of why it must be *public*. At first sight, there would seem little difference between requiring the purchase of policies in private insurance companies or in public insurance. The size of private companies is such that they can exhaust the economies of scale in spreading risk. Nevertheless, public insurance can offer a better deal. Under a private system, a reserve must be accumulated that is sufficient in amount to finance the benefits for all insured and to provide the insured with a return equal to the going rate of interest. Under the public system, such a reserve is not required. Each working person can be asked to support the retired population and in turn can be supported by the next generation as he or she retires. Viewing this arrangement as a continuing process which never ceases, the rate of return to the participants will be equal to the combined rates of population and productivity growth and will exceed the rate of interest.[16]

Reserve versus Pay-as-You-Go Finance When the social security system was first established, the intention was to have each generation pay for its own retirement without burdening the generation which would make up the labor force in the future. Short of stowing away food in warehouses, this can be accomplished only by increasing the rate of capital formation. This increase would raise the productivity and earnings of the future generation, thereby permitting it to pay for the support of the aged without a net loss. In line with this intention, the initial plan was to create a large trust fund which would rise until about 1970, when the system would reach maturity. From then on, the reserve would remain constant and a constant payroll tax rate, supported by interest earnings of the fund, would be sufficient to finance the benefits. In the meantime, while the fund was being built up, the surplus receipts would be made available for increased capital formation.[17] This approach was abandoned, however, as early as 1939 when it was decided that payroll tax rates should be set so as to keep the system on a current or pay-as-you-go basis, with the current labor force contributing the amount needed to finance benefits to the current aged. The trust fund came to be considered a contingency reserve only. After reaching $20 billion in 1953, the fund showed little change up to the late 1960s, when it once more

[16] See Henry Aaron, "The Social Insurance Paradox," *Canadian Journal of Economics and Political Science,* August 1966.

[17] The mechanics of implementing this plan would involve substitution of a stabilization mix with tighter fiscal and easier monetary policy. Higher payroll tax receipts would reduce consumption while use of surplus receipts for retirement of debt would permit a higher level of private investment. Thus, debt would be shifted from the public to the social security trust fund, where the growth of interest income would permit financing of future benefits at a lower rate of payroll tax.

started to rise, reaching $39 billion in 1975. However, reserves in relation to current obligations have declined, with the fund now being sufficient to sustain eight months of benefit payments only.

A number of factors contributed to the demise of the reserve approach. For one thing, long-run population estimates are extremely difficult to make and have gone wrong repeatedly. The same applies with regard to productivity gains which must also be allowed for. Since they come to be felt more rapidly on the receipt than on the disbursement side, failure to take them into account means that requirements are overstated. For another thing, Congress has decided repeatedly to raise the benefit structure beyond what had been previously assumed in setting the old tax rates. Most important, however, the very logic of the reserve approach (i.e., that surplus receipts are in fact channeled into increased capital formation) did not prove tenable. As we have noted in the discussion of public debt and intergeneration equity, the setting of the economy proved such that other aspects of stabilization policy had to be given priority.[18]

Somewhat ironically, the very considerations which initially gave rise to the reserve approach are again entering the discussion. As the birthrate declines, the prospect is for a falling ratio of working to retired population. Whereas 38 persons now collect benefits for 100 workers taxed, it is estimated that by the year 2030, there will be 58 supported persons per 100 workers. With pay-as-you-go finance, the average burden on the working population will be 50 percent larger. Pay-as-you-go in an aging population thus poses a serious problem of intergeneration equity, with the required level of payroll tax rates promising to go eventually much beyond the 14.9 percent which the law now contemplates. At the same time, the outlook is not so desperate as this might suggest, since productivity gains will offset or outweigh the higher contribution which will be required of the working population. Consequently, the higher payroll tax rate will not be reflected in a declining level of disposable income.

Payroll Tax Finance versus Budgetary Contribution While Congress has never quite abandoned the reserve idea and the notion of setting payroll tax rates so as to assure a "solvent" system, it has gone far toward accepting the reality of pay-as-you-go finance. At the same time, it has held steadfastly to the idea that benefits should be financed from "contributions" made in the form of payroll taxes. This has been the cornerstone of the continuing contention that social security should be viewed as a contributory or pension system. This position is now under attack, especially since prospects are that, before long, benefits will come to exceed payroll tax receipts, therefore calling for further rate increases to maintain the fund in a balanced position.

Those favoring a contribution from the general budget argue that the payroll tax is highly regressive and that its increased weight in the federal tax structure has been damaging to equity. They hold, further, that exclusive reliance on this tax can be defended no longer by viewing it as an integral part of a contributory social security system. In support of this, they note that the system has lost its

[18] See p. 605.

quid pro quo character in two respects. First, the system is redistributive as between income groups, so that various contributors realize different rates of return on their contributions rather than the same rate, as would be called for on a contributory basis. Second, the system has moved to pay-as-you-go finance, so that it can no longer be said that each generation pays for its own retirement. Rather, the elderly population is at any time supported by the working population of the same period, the only element of quid pro quo being that the latter will expect, or hope, that its children will follow the same practice. Since the contributory nature of the system is thus fictitious, so they conclude, exclusive reliance on a highly regressive tax is no longer defensible. Extended to its logical conclusion, this line of reasoning leads to the position that OASDI should be abolished, and that benefits should be treated as part of a general income maintenance plan (couched in the form of a negative income tax or otherwise) designed to support low-income families regardless of their age.[19]

Those hesitant to move in the direction of budgetary finance must admit that the presumption of a strict quid pro quo scheme is not valid and that it is difficult for any one generation to provide (in real terms) for its own retirement without burdening the future working population. Thus, pay-as-you-go has become more or less inevitable. Nevertheless, the philosophy of contributory finance, so they argue, remains desirable because it is preferable for the aged to receive benefits as a return on their own investment, rather than as a component of an income maintenance scheme. Economists may view this argument as a sentimental point, but from the social standpoint, it is of fundamental importance in dealing with the position of the aged in society. Moreover, it suggests that by relying on a contributory system, benefit payments can be protected against political inroads such as might develop at another date when, owing to an aging population structure, the young may be less willing to support the old.

Given the weight of these considerations, and especially the support of the insurance principle by labor unions, it is unlikely that a drastic revamping of social security and its integration into a broader income maintenance scheme are in the cards. Nevertheless, two possible directions of reform may well emerge. One would be to provide for a matching contribution to payroll tax revenue, to be paid by the general budget and to be earmarked for receipt by the social security fund. Another would be to consider a reform of the payroll tax itself to render it less regressive. Such a change, which may well occur in the very near future, could take the form of allowing an exemption, as under the income tax, or a low-income allowance which would exempt, say, the first $2,000 of wages but vanish as wage income rises above that level. As noted before, the earned-income credit provided by the Tax Reduction Act of 1975 may be taken to serve this purpose.

Changes in the structure of social security financing may come to have a

[19] In 1970, 16.3 percent of persons in families with the head over age sixty-five were poor, while for the nation as a whole, 11 percent lived in poor families. Of unrelated individuals aged sixty-five and over, 47.1 percent—nearly one-half—lived in poverty, whereas the percentage for all age groups was 32.7 percent. See *Social Security Amendments of 1971, Hearings before the Senate Committee on Finance on HR.I,* 92d Cong., 1st Sess., 1971.

major influence on the distribution of the federal tax burden as well as on the extent to which OASDI itself is redistributive. At the same time, changes in the method of financing will not greatly affect the problem of intergeneration equity posed by the prospect of a rising burden on the working population due to a falling worker-to-beneficiary ratio.

Health Insurance

While changes in the structure of OASDI are under consideration, the major concern in the current debate is with proposals for extending government health insurance from the aged and the poor to the remainder of the population. If coverage were extended to disaster insurance only, e.g., to major surgery, the amounts involved would be relatively limited. But if a broad coverage is applied, very large amounts equal to or exceeding those involved in OASDI may be called for. Payroll tax finance of such a program could easily add ten percentage points to present payroll tax rates. Including 11.7 percent for the present OASDHI and 4 percent for unemployment insurance, this approach could push total rates well above 25 percent, a level comparable with those found in European countries but not readily acceptable here. The preferable approach would seem to be direct-fee finance of public health insurance in line with the cost of risks while subsidizing fees payable by low-income contributors out of general budget revenue. The issue of health insurance finance and its claim upon payroll taxes, more than OASDI reform, is likely to be the major factor in the future role of this tax.

D. UNEMPLOYMENT INSURANCE

Unemployment insurance is provided by a set of state systems, while tax collections and the handling of the trust funds (kept separate for each state) are managed at the federal level. Benefits in 1972 amounted to $6.4 billion. The average payroll tax payable by the employer is 4 percent and applies to the first $4,200 of earnings. However, tax rates vary by state and in accordance with the employment experience of particular firms. This principle of experience rating was introduced as an incentive to stabilize employment and as a way not to impose an undue burden on high-employment firms. Congress in 1970 provided for financial support from the federal government to pay benefits for an additional thirteen months beyond the normal benefit period of twenty-six weeks when the unemployment rate exceeds 4.5 percent and for states which show an especially sharp rise in unemployment. Extended further in 1975, this points to a more uniform provision for unemployment benefits in a national system. However this may be, it is generally recognized that unemployment insurance can provide only a temporary solution and cannot take care of widespread unemployment. The only effective approach to unemployment consists of stabilization and manpower policies designed to maintain high employment levels.

E. SUMMARY

Three major components of the transfer system have been distinguished, including welfare programs directed at maintaining the income of the poor, insurance programs directed mainly at retirement, and unemployment insurance.

1. Among the three, the welfare program is the most controversial.

2. Among various components of the welfare program, AFDC is much the most important and has been subject to most criticism.

3. Reform proposals made in 1969 were not enacted. However, the federal welfare system was expanded in 1974 to replace certain state programs and provide relief for low-income families without any other means of support.

4. A major problem with regard to low-income support is posed by its effect on work incentives. With aid related inversely to earnings, the recipient is in effect subject to a high marginal tax rate on his or her earnings.

5. Proposals for a negative income tax have tried to deal with this difficulty. Linkage of aid to work requirements offers an alternative approach.

Much the most important component of the social security system is the old-age, survivors, and disability insurance (OASDI) to which a limited insurance for hospital services for the aged (Medicare) was added in 1965.

6. Combined payroll tax contributions under OASDHI now amount to 4.95 percent on employer and employee each, applicable to the first $13,200 of wage income.

7. While the social security system was planned originally as a system which would function on a quid pro quo basis, it has become redistributive in favor of lower income households.

8. Originally planned on the basis of reserve finance, the OASDI system has moved steadily toward a pay-as-you-go basis.

9. Under current debate is the question of whether the finance of OASDI should be shifted in part to a general budgetary contribution, and whether the payroll tax should be amended so as to make it less regressive.

10. A major factor in the future of the payroll tax will be the emerging development of a national health insurance plan.

11. Unemployment insurance continues as an important and noncontroversial part of the social security system.

FURTHER READINGS

Aaron, H. J.: *Why Is Welfare So Hard to Reform?,* Washington: Brookings, 1973.

Barth, M. C., G. C. Carcagno, and J. L. Palmer: *Towards an Effective Income Support System: Problems, Prospects and Choices,* Madison: The University of Wisconsin, Institute for Research on Poverty, 1974.

Brittain, J. A.: *Payroll Taxes for Social Security,* Washington: Brookings, 1972.

Green, C.: *Negative Income Taxes and the Poverty Problem,* Washington: Brookings, 1967.

Pechman, J. A., H. J. Aaron, and M. K. Taussig: *Social Security: Perspectives for Reform,* Washington: Brookings, 1968.

Poverty amid Plenty: The American Paradox, report of the President's Commission on Income Maintenance Programs, 1969.

Tobin, J.: "Raising the Income of the Poor," in K. Gordon (ed.), *Agenda for the Nation,* Washington: Brookings, 1969.

Chapter 32

Public Pricing and Environmental Policy*

A. Public Sale of Private Goods. B. Marginal Cost Pricing in Decreasing Cost Industries: *The Policy Dilemma; Deficit Paid from General Revenue; Deficit Paid for by User Charges: Two-Part Tariff; Deficit Covered by Price Discrimination; Public Utility Regulation; Public Pricing and Imperfect Markets; Distributional Considerations.* **C. Peak-Load Pricing:** *Given Plant; Variable Plant Size.* **D. Pricing of Social Facilities:** *Uncongested Facility; Congested Facility; New Facilities.* **E. Pricing Pollution:** *Efficiency and Equity Aspects of Pollution; Sources of Pollution and Types of Damage; The Efficient Solution; Lack of Information; Instruments of Control; Equity Aspects; Federalism Aspects; Political Aspects; Current Policies.* **F. Summary.**

Provision for social goods, as discussed in Chapter 3, typically involves situations where sale to particular consumers is either impossible (because exclusion cannot be applied) or undesirable (because consumption is nonrival).[1] In this chapter, various situations are considered where government supplies goods or services

* *Reader's Guide to Chapter 32:* In this chapter, we consider two public-sector activities which, though not purely budgetary in nature, involve problems very similar to those encountered in tax and expenditure policy. These are the problems of public pricing and pollution. The general reader may wish to bypass the two more technical sections dealing with peak-load pricing (pp. 698–699) and pollution abatement with variable technology (pp. 705–707). The remainder is a straightforward application of previously discussed principles to two important policy issues.

[1] See p. 52.

which *can* be sold and where direct payment may be appropriate, and yet where the pricing problem is such that it cannot be readily handled in the market. This may be due to decreasing costs, with subsidies, regulation, or public operation called for; or it may be due to the existence of external costs which are not reflected in price, in which case taxes may be used to internalize such costs and to apply the necessary correction.

A. PUBLIC SALE OF PRIVATE GOODS

The basic rule for efficient pricing is that price should be equal to marginal cost. So long as marginal cost (*MC*) falls short of price or average revenue (*AR*), society gains by producing more. This is so because marginal cost measures the resource cost to society of producing an additional unit while price measures the value of an additional unit to the consumer. The gain from increased output continues up to the point where the two are equal. Beyond this point, additional output involves a net loss to the economy since marginal cost will then lie above price or the value of the marginal unit. This is the rule of "marginal cost pricing" which is central to the discussion of this chapter.

Where private goods are provided through a competitive market, the marginal cost pricing rule is complied with. The selling firms are confronted with horizontal demand schedules since they furnish only a small part of total supply. This being the case, average revenue and marginal revenue (*MR*) are the same. The firms, by equating marginal cost with marginal revenue, also equate marginal cost with average revenue or price. In long-run equilibrium, with the industry operating under conditions of constant or increasing cost, each firm will also operate at a minimum average cost (*AC*) where $AR = AC$ and no losses or monopolistic profits are made.

In an economy such as ours, the government is generally not in the business of producing and selling private goods. This activity is typically left to private firms. However, situations may arise where government does sell such goods. Thus the sale of tobacco is run as a government enterprise in some countries; and the sale of liquor is frequently operated through state liquor stores in the United States. In these cases, the government places itself in the position of a monopolist who is confronted with the entire, and hence declining, market demand curve. Following the behavior of a private monopolist, it could equate *MR* and *MC* so as to maximize profits, leaving $AR > MC$. The efficient solution for the government is not to follow this pattern and exploit its monopoly power, but to provide the competitive industry result. While the determination of this efficient solution might be difficult without competitive markets, once achieved, it will allow for price just to cover full cost, thus permitting the cost to be charged to the consumers of the service.

If the government does not follow this rule but charges a higher price, this practice may be considered equivalent to imposing an excise tax on the product. Imposition of such a tax, as shown previously, distorts resource allocation and involves an excess burden, unless considered justified by "demerit good" considerations.[2] The latter may be the case in the pricing of tobacco and liquor products which are frequently supplied through public sales.

B. MARGINAL COST PRICING IN DECREASING COST INDUSTRIES

More typically, the government supplies goods which cannot be provided efficiently by private firms because production is subject to decreasing costs. This is the case with public utilities such as water and electricity supplies, public transport systems, and the Postal Service. These are situations—also referred to as "natural monopolies"—where a competitive market cannot function because larger firms can produce at a lower cost, and ultimately a single firm tends to supply the entire market. Without government intervention, profit maximizing behavior by the resulting monopolist would entail too little output at too high a price. Although government regulation is one alternative, the existence of decreasing costs implies that the firm would suffer losses if forced to operate where price equals marginal cost. Thus, the government may prefer to render the service itself, and a public enterprise is substituted for regulation of the private firm.

The Policy Dilemma

The situation is explained in Figure 32-1, where *AC* and *MC* are long-run average and marginal cost curves of the industry (which in this case is the same as the firm) and *AR* and *MR* are the average and marginal revenue schedules. Following the $AR = MC$ rule, the efficient price is set at P_{mc} and output equals *OA*. Since *AC* is declining, *MC* must lie below *AC*; and since $AR = MC$ at output *OA*, it

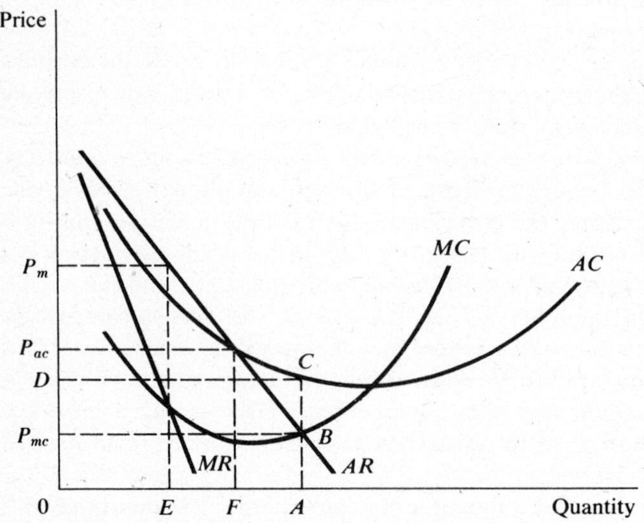

FIGURE 32-1 Marginal and Average Cost Pricing.

[2] See p. 65.

follows that AC is larger than AR. Thus a loss is incurred. In the figure, the unit loss equals BC and the total loss equals $P_{mc}BCD$.

A private firm would avoid this problem by equating MR and MC so as to maximize profits with price P_m and output limited to OE. There is no excuse for public policy to charge P_m unless it is desired to impose what amounts to an excise tax on the product. As a further possibility, might not government avoid the loss by charging an average cost price, thus equating AR with AC? With output OF and price P_{ac}, the firm would break even, but output OF would still be below the efficient level OA. There is no getting around the fact that efficient pricing calls for price P_{mc} and output OA, but this leaves a deficit which must be covered somehow.

Deficit Paid from General Revenue

One way of covering the deficit is to tax the general public, but this poses new problems. If such a tax were imposed in the form of a lump-sum tax, no efficiency cost would be involved, but the solution would be unacceptable on ability-to-pay grounds. If the tax were imposed more equitably, say as an income tax, its imposition would create an efficiency cost. This efficiency cost must be weighed against that which would result if price were equated with average cost (with output reduced to OF) with no outside finance needed. The more elastic the demand for the product, the greater will be the efficiency loss due to setting price above P_{mc}; and the more elastic the labor supply, the greater will be the inefficiency caused by income tax finance. There would seem to be a presumption in most cases that the latter would involve a smaller efficiency cost than the excise tax equivalent of average cost pricing, imposed on the particular service. However, there may be exceptions, especially where demand is highly inelastic.

Deficit Paid for by User Charges: Two-Part Tariff

Moreover, general revenue finance may be held inequitable in terms of benefit taxation since the general public is charged for the financing of a specific service, rather than the users who benefit therefrom. Yet, finance by user charge so as to cover total cost would raise price above the efficient level (where $AR = MC$) and place output below it. To escape or minimize this dilemma, techniques have been developed to recover full costs from users with a smaller efficiency loss than would result from charging a unit price equal to P_{ac}.

One way of doing so is by means of a "two-part tariff." This involves supplementing a charge per unit of service with a flat charge which must be paid if any use is to be made of the service at all. Such a charge or membership fee would be in the nature of a lump-sum tax on the users of the facility. It would have a substitution effect only on the choice between total abstinence or participation; but it would not have a substitution effect on choosing the level of use once the membership fee has been paid. The assumption is that demand for general access to the service will be less elastic than that relating to the level of utilization. If the deficit with marginal cost pricing is small enough and the number of users is large, the required flat fee may be sufficiently low so that very few potential users will be kept from participation. In this case, the efficiency problem is solved without requiring general finance.[3]

Such techniques are in fact used in many instances of public utility pricing. In the case of telephone charges in many areas, local calls are not billed separately but are included in a flat user fee, with only toll calls billed on a unit basis. Electricity and water supply are also typically priced so as to include a flat charge, with additional charges related to the units of consumption. A further example, relating to highway finance, is the combined use of a basic charge and unit tolls, where tolls are reduced for cars which have paid the annual sticker fee.

Deficit Covered by Price Discrimination

Another approach would be to apply price discrimination. Here the consumer would be charged the price P_{mc} for the last unit but would be called upon to pay higher prices for the earlier units. A part of his or her consumer surplus would thus be taxed away to help cover the deficit. Since different consumers have different incomes and tastes, their demand schedules differ. An equitable solution would call for different rate schedules to be applied to the intramarginal units of various consumers. Some elements of this approach are illustrated by the granting of quantity discounts in the pricing of electric power, where intramarginal and marginal units are charged differentiated prices, and in rate differentiation among types of users, such as residential and commercial.

In a situation where the firm sells more than one product, reduction of the deficit by charging a price in excess of MC can be accomplished with a smaller efficiency cost by concentrating the excess charges on the product for which demand is less elastic to price. This stands to reason, since output will be reduced less and therefore the loss of consumer surplus will be smaller. The principle is similar to that previously encountered in considering the excess burden of product taxes which is less for goods with inelastic demand.[4]

Public Utility Regulation

Public utility regulation, in determining allowable charges, typically proceeds on the premise that total costs, including a fair return to capital, should be covered. In determining this return, the usual approach taken is that the return to capital invested in public utilities should be in line with that earned in other industries. If the excess of revenue over necessary costs is such as to provide the utility with a competitive return, an efficient allocation of capital between public utilities and other industries is expected to result. Although this rule seems sensible, it requires determination of necessary costs. If management knows that regulation will permit a higher revenue (whether in the form of higher charges, two-part tariffs, or a larger subsidy) if costs are higher, public enterprise will be encouraged to incur unnecessary costs. The problem is similar to that posed by enterprises

[3] For a local government enterprise, the output of which is consumed by local residents, the use of a general local revenue source may be viewed as the flat-charge component of the two-part tariff, since participation in the service hinges on local residence.

[4] See W. Baumol and D. Bradford, "Optimal Departures from Marginal Cost Pricing," *American Economic Review,* June 1970.

selling to government on a cost-plus basis. Moreover, public utility industries are encouraged to expand capital through debt finance beyond what is needed so as to be permitted larger returns.

Public Pricing and Imperfect Markets

Whenever it is argued that the price of any one product should be set in line with the efficient rule of marginal cost pricing, the assumption is made that other products are also priced efficiently. If this is not so, second-best solutions may call for offsetting departures from efficiency rules.

Thus, suppose that government sells a product, a substitute for which is sold privately at a monopoly price so that price exceeds *MC*. It may then be efficient for the government also to charge a price in excess of *MC* so as to avoid undue substitution of its product for the overpriced private product. If the competing product is complementary to that sold by government, efficiency may call for a public price below marginal cost so as to induce consumers to buy a more efficient package.

By the same token, if the competing product is underpriced, the public price should also be set at less than *MC*; or, if the underpriced private product is complementary to the public product, the public price should be set so as to exceed *MC*. An illustration of this is in the pricing of downtown parking garages. Since downtown use of cars is underpriced (because congestion costs are disregarded), a case can be made for pricing of public parking garages above marginal cost to compensate for this defect. In fact, public downtown garages generally tend to be subsidized rather than taxed, a practice that increases the distortion caused by overuse of cars.

Distributional Considerations

A further qualification to marginal cost pricing may arise where distributional considerations are allowed for in the pricing decision.[5] Since decreasing cost industries, such as public utilities, frequently provide goods which offer "essential" services like water, electricity, or subway rides, the provision of such services at subsidized prices may seem equitable and is frequently the subject of a good deal of political pressure. Nevertheless, the equity case for subsidizing such services is no better than that for subsidizing bread, milk, or low-cost housing. That the services happen to be sold by public enterprise should not be the criterion for deciding whether subsidies are to be granted.

Apart from this, there is again the more basic question of whether distributional adjustments should be made by a frontal attack on the distribution of income or whether they should be implemented by a system of excise taxes and subsidies, depending on whether the products in question weigh more heavily in high-income or in low-income budgets. Our conclusion has been in support of the former approach. However, two exceptions to the rule may be noted.

[5] For a view favoring more general allowance for distributional considerations in public pricing and an approach toward implementation, see M. Feldstein, "Distributional Equity and the Optimal Structure of Public Prices," *American Economic Review,* March 1972.

1. Where a direct approach to adjustments in income distribution is not possible but differential pricing is politically feasible, the latter may be the best available solution, at least for those who accept the distributional objective.

2. The efficiency loss which results from direct measures of income redistribution may exceed that of the differential pricing approach. But even when it does, there is no reason why differential pricing should be limited to products which happen to be sold by public enterprise.

C. PEAK-LOAD PRICING

A major problem in public utility pricing results from the variability of demand for its services. Thus, the demand for power is greater during the day than at night and higher during some hours of the day than at others. How is this variation to be allowed for both in pricing the services of a given plant and in evaluating the investment decision on a new plant? How is the variation in the degree of congestion to be dealt with?

Given Plant

Suppose the capacity of a given plant is such that by charging a price equal to marginal operating cost, the demand during the peak period is greatly in excess of the maximum power supply that can be furnished, whereas in the off-peak period there is a great deal of excess capacity? It will then be necessary to allocate the limited peak-period supply to those who value it most highly. Thus, a price has to be charged to equate the limited supply with demand unless other forms of rationing are used. Consumers who do not find the use of peak-period power at this price worthwhile (or who would choose to use less) will shift their demand to the off-peak period when the service is supplied at the lower price of marginal operating cost only. Off-peak use of the facility will be increased and the consumer surplus derived from its services will be maximized.

This is illustrated in Figure 32-2 where OC is capacity use, D_pD_p is peak-period demand, and D_oD_o is off-peak demand. AB is the marginal operating cost schedule, here assumed constant up to capacity use, at which point the supply schedule becomes totally inelastic. Thus the peak-period price is at OP_p while the off-peak price is OA. Peak-period use is at capacity, or OC, and off-peak use is at OF.[6]

Other illustrations might be given where both the peak and off-peak demands intersect the vertical supply schedule or where there remains excess capacity in both periods but differential prices are charged because of variable operating costs. It is, however, only in the situation of constant operating cost and excess capacity in both periods that a uniform price will be appropriate.

Variable Plant Size

The solution of Figure 32-2 may be the best possible under the circumstances, but it is hardly a satisfactory situation. In the longer run, the problem is how

[6] The careful reader will note that if peak and off-peak services are rather close substitutes, it is not permissible to draw the two demand schedules independent of eath other. We may think of the D_oD_o schedule as it results in the end with the price for peak-time use settled at OP_p and

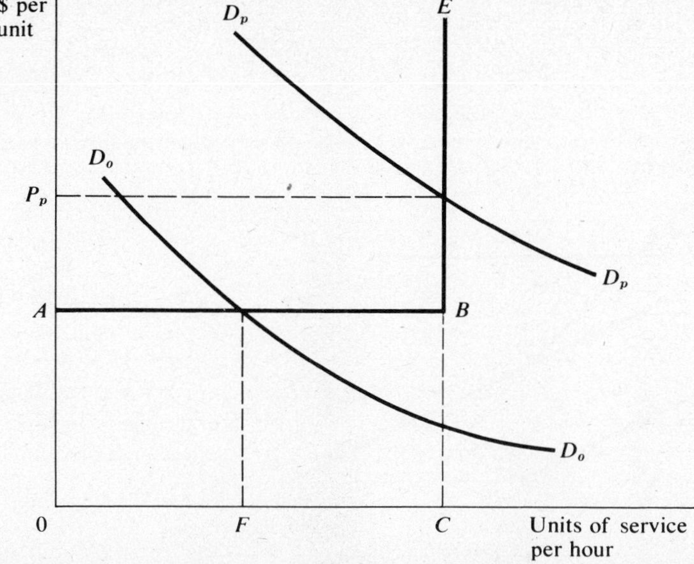

FIGURE 32-2 Peak-Load Pricing with Fixed Capacity.

to adjust the capacity size to the existence of variable demand. The solution to this problem proves of particular interest to the reader of Chapter 3 because we may view peak and off-peak users as joint demanders for the plant's services. Or, putting it differently, we may look on the plant as a social good (of the intermediate-good type) which supplies services to peak and off-peak users who in turn can utilize these services in nonrival fashion. In appraising the profitability of providing a new investment, it is this joint demand which must be considered in applying the rule of equating long-run marginal cost with price.

Such a solution is illustrated in Figure 32-3.[7] The horizontal axis now measures the units of power supplied at capacity operation for various levels of capacity. D_p is the demand schedule for peak-time users and D_o is that for off-peak users, with demand in each case relating to the level of power forthcoming at capacity use. Turning to the cost side, we simplify matters by assuming that marginal operating cost is zero so that only long-run or capacity cost has to be covered. With long-run marginal capacity cost constant at *OA,* the long-run marginal (capacity) cost schedule is thus given as *AS.*[8] Since the two demands relate to different time periods (e.g., peak demand from 7 A.M. to 11 A.M. and

D_pD_p as reflecting the demand schedule for peak-period use after the use of off-peak service has settled at *OF.*

[7] See P. Steiner, "Peak Loads and Efficient Pricing," *Quarterly Journal of Economics,* November 1957; and O. E. Williamson, "Peak-Load Pricing and Optimal Capacity under Indivisibility Constraints," *American Economic Review,* September 1966. The diagram given here assumes that peak and off-peak periods are of equal length and the rate of service use is uniform within each period. If differences in length or rate of service use are allowed for, D_p and D_o must be weighted accordingly in deriving the aggregate demand schedule.

[8] The marginal capacity cost shows the additional cost per unit of output which results as the capacity level of the plant is expanded, assuming each plant size to be used at optimal capacity.

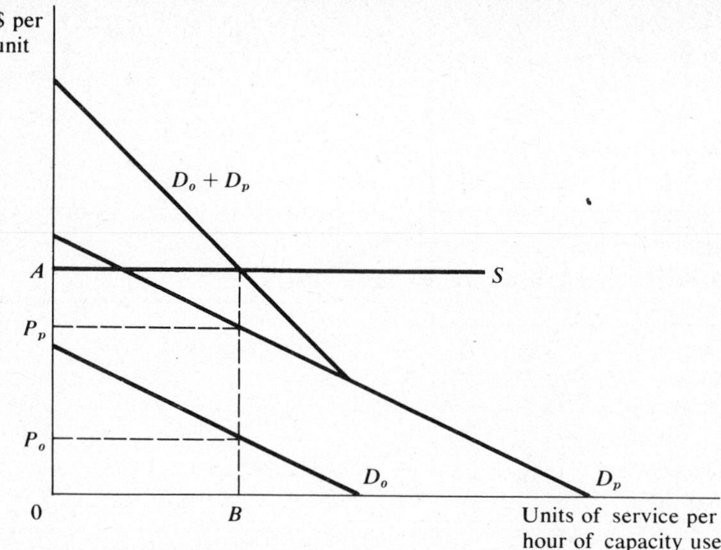

FIGURE 32-3 Peak-Load Pricing with Variable Capacity.

4 P.M. to 8 P.M. and off-peak demand from 11 A.M. to 4 P.M. and 8 P.M. to 11 P.M.), they are noncompeting in their uses of the facility. The demand curves of the two groups of users may therefore be added vertically to obtain total demand for plant capacity. The proper plant size is determined at *OB* where marginal capacity cost *AS* equals price, including OP_p to be charged to peak-period users and OP_o to be charged to off-peak users. At these prices, each group will use the plant fully during its period.[9]

While differential pricing in the case of Figure 32-3 leads to full utilization in both periods, this need not be the result. Suppose that the demand for capacity output in the off-peak period is so low that the D_o schedule falls to zero at a level below that at which D_p intersects the marginal capacity cost schedule. In this case, the efficient solution is to charge the marginal cost price in the peak period while permitting free off-peak use. Since excess capacity remains, it will be inefficient to limit its use by charging a price. This once more raises a question of equity, since peak-period users may feel that off-peak users should not be given a free ride but should contribute to the cost.

The principles underlying this type of analysis are reflected in actual pricing practices of utilities, e.g., in differential pricing of power uses in different parts of the day. In other situations, such differentiation reflects the rationing of deficient peak-period capacity output to its most urgent uses.

D. PRICING OF SOCIAL FACILITIES

Related problems arise in the pricing of social-good facilities. To separate out various issues, we distinguish among (1) the pricing of an existing and uncon-

[9] Since total cost is covered, note that the solution depicted in Fig. 32-3 is not the same as the decreasing cost case of Fig. 32-1, where the efficient solution leaves the firm with a loss.

gested facility, (2) the pricing of an existing but congested facility, and (3) the pricing problem in relation to the construction of a new facility.

Uncongested Facility

Consider a facility, such as a bridge or highway, which is already built. The utilization rate is very low, so that there is no significant crowding cost. Suppose also that there is no wear or maintenance cost involved in its use. In this case, the marginal cost of additional use is zero and efficient pricing calls for free use. If there are use-related maintenance charges, a user charge covering marginal cost is called for.

Congested Facility

Next consider a situation where the existing facility has smaller capacity, so that free use results in congestion. If *DD* in Figure 32-4 is the demand schedule for the service while *OM* is the marginal congestion cost, a charge equal to *OP* will restrict output to the efficient level *OB*. If the charge is lower and the utilization rate is higher, the marginal congestion cost comes to exceed price.

Another application of the congestion problem once more involves the issue of peak-load pricing. Consider a facility, such as a subway or a tunnel, which is used heavily during parts of the day but less heavily at others. The efficient charge to account for congestion cost will be higher during the peak than the off-peak period. This will induce users who can readily substitute off-peak use to do so, thereby rationing out the more valuable peak-time space to those who value it more highly. Therefore the consumer surplus derived from the total use of the facility increases. Many of the peak-load pricing practices address themselves to this problem. Thus charges for toll calls are lower at night when there is less risk of crowding out other calls.[10]

Similar problems arise in setting the prices of several facilities which offer alternative uses to the consumer. Thus, if two bridges are subject to heavy

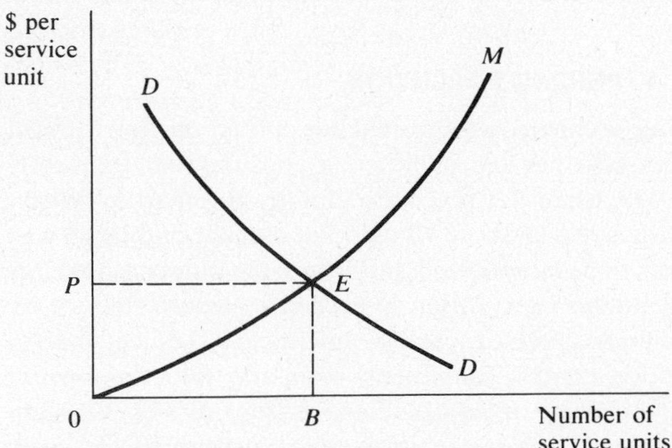

FIGURE 32-4 Pricing with Crowding Cost.

[10] See W. Vickrey, "Responsive Pricing of Public Utility Services," *Bell Journal of Economics and Management Science,* Spring 1971.

commuter traffic, the uses should be balanced so as to equalize price with marginal congestion costs for each bridge. This objective may call for differential charges in line with the respective levels of demand and congestion costs. If, instead, charges are made in line with other considerations, the outcome will be distorted. This mistake is frequently made when charges are applied only to the latest facility in order to recover its capital cost. If such cost is to be recovered, a charge should be applied to both facilities even though this approach once more raises the equity question of who should pay.

New Facilities

Finally, consider the more difficult situation where a new bridge is to be built. In this case, capital cost must be allowed for. Assuming the necessary information to be available, the problem of evaluation is simple enough. In evaluating a given bridge, for example, that is 50 feet wide, we compute the present value of the benefit stream to which it gives rise. In doing so, we assume the bridge to be used at an optimal rate such as will result if the efficient crowding charge is applied. We then compare the present value of the benefit stream with the project cost to see whether it matches or exceeds the latter. Next we apply the same analysis to the incremental costs and benefits of broadening the bridge by, say, 10 feet and proceed until no further expansion is worthwhile. For engineering reasons, it may not be possible to add to the project step by step but only in substantial and discrete amounts. Hence, the optimal size may be one for which a crowding charge is still needed.

This is simple enough conceptually, but the value of the benefit stream is not known. What is worse, imposition of a fee to test the consumer's willingness to pay results in underutilization.[11] The government has to choose between (1) making an investment decision which is not verified, and (2) reducing the usefulness of the investment by imposing charges. Fortunately, the conflict may be eased if the government undertakes many similar projects. Then the information gained from pricing one project may be used in pricing another.

E. PRICING POLLUTION

Another set of public pricing problems arise in making corrections for the cost of pollution. Private activities, whether in production or consumption, frequently give rise to external costs which are not accounted for by the market. Where numbers are small, bargaining between those who do the damage and those who are hurt may cause such costs to be internalized; but where the numbers are large this is not possible, so that public intervention is needed to secure efficient resource use. Such intervention may involve fiscal instruments (e.g., effluent charges or subsidies to install pollution control equipment) or it may take the form of direct regulation (e.g., setting ceilings to permissible pollution). Whichever technique is used, the basic problem is one of accounting for externalities. As such,

[11] Such at least is the case unless the government applies a tax so as to exercise perfect price discrimination, with the amount of tax declining with successive units of use and becoming zero at the margin.

it is a problem in the provision of social goods, as discussed in sections C and D of Chapter 3.

Efficiency and Equity Aspects of Pollution

Consider the case of a chemical factory producing product X and discharging its wastes into a nearby waterway. These discharges reduce the quality of the water and its suitability for other uses, such as swimming. Since water is common property, its services (in this case the service of carrying off wastes) are not sold. The cost in terms of reducing water quality is thus overlooked by the pricing system. The price of product X is too low and inefficient resource allocation results. A similar illustration may be given for air pollution resulting from factory fumes. These external effects pose two problems.

First, failure to account for external costs leads to an oversupply of X and an undersupply of the benefits (good water and clean air) which are reduced by pollution. This is the *efficiency* problem. If the damage cost of pollution were internalized, resource use would become more efficient. The price of X would be higher, less X would be produced, pollution would be reduced, and air and water quality would be improved.

Second, the existence of pollution poses distributional or *equity* problems. They relate most directly to the relative positions of perpetrators and victims. Through the loss of environmental quality, consumers of air and water are forced to subsidize consumers of product X much as they would if a tax were imposed on them and transferred to the latter. This raises the question of property rights to clean air and water. Are the consumers of X entitled to impose this burden on the rest of the community, or should they be made to pay compensation? Moreover, the incidence of pollution damage may fall with different weight upon low-income and high-income families, and this affects the distribution of real income. The same goes for the cost of pollution prevention and the *net* gains to be derived therefrom. In dealing with pollution policy, allowance must thus be made for equity as well as efficiency aspects of the problem.

Sources of Pollution and Types of Damage

It is wrong to think of pollution as being caused by firms and production activities only. Pollution is also caused by households and their consumption activities, where it is use of the product rather than its production that causes the problem. Thus water pollution is caused by the discharge of industrial wastes but also by discharge of domestic wastes into sewers. Air pollution arises from industrial discharges of smoke and fumes but also from consumption activities such as home use of fuel, use of automobiles, or burning of trash and garbage wastes. There are no ready estimates of the relative shares of the total pollution cost based on production and on consumption, but it would surely be wrong to overlook the pollution which results from consumption.

It is not only the perpetrators of pollution which differ, but also the media through which pollution occurs. In most cases, the quality of the natural environment is reduced by the discharge of wastes, but other forms of pollution also exist. The roar of jet engines is a form of pollution no less than engine fumes. Travel time lost by congestion is a form of pollution not dissimilar to that of automobile exhausts inhaled in the process. While deterioration in the ambience or quality of natural resources is an important form of pollution damage, it is by no means the only one. Viewed more broadly, a problem of external costs arises whenever the activities of any one individual harm someone else without being internalized and accounted for.

The Efficient Solution

The formal solution to the problem of pollution is not too difficult to determine provided that all the necessary information is available. Although one of the major obstacles to efficient pollution policy is a lack of information, it is nevertheless useful to consider what the efficient solution would be if the necessary data were known.

Fixed Technology To begin with, suppose that the production of X involves an external cost, e.g., chemicals discharged into an adjoining river. The level of discharge increases with the output of X, as does the cost of damage. Further suppose that nothing can be done to reduce the damage done per unit of output of X. We then have the simple case of Figure 32-5, where *AS* is the firm's supply schedule in producing X, *OC* is the marginal damage cost (i.e., the loss of water quality, valued in dollars per additional unit of X), and AS_t is the summation of the two cost schedules.[12] With demand schedule *DD*, competitive output in the absence of government intervention equals *OQ*, since only private costs reflected in *AS* are allowed for. However, the efficient output would equal *OQ′* and make allowance for external costs as included in AS_t.

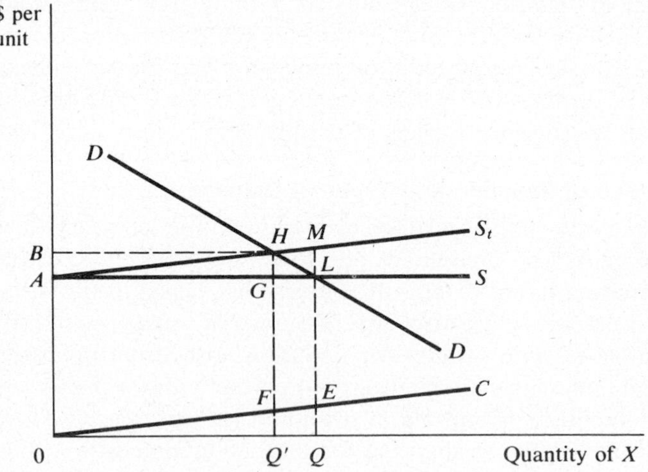

FIGURE 32-5 Pollution Control with Fixed Technology.

[12] The slope of the marginal damage curve *OC* depends upon (1) the level of discharge, and (2) the cost of the damage done thereby. Assuming the rate of discharge per unit of X to be constant, the marginal damage cost may nevertheless rise as the quality of water deteriorates at an increasing rate per additional unit of discharge. This, however, need not be the result. After water has been saturated above a certain level, the additional damage may be constant or declining.

Various policy measures may be taken to achieve the efficient output OQ'. One possibility is a direct regulation requiring the firm to produce OQ'. Another possibility is to impose a tax per unit of output equal to AB, which will bring about the same result.[13] In both cases, output is reduced from OQ to OQ' and the victims of pollution are spared pollution damage equal to $Q'QEF$. As we shall see later, the distributional implications differ depending on which approach is followed. An important point to note is that the efficient solution does not call for pollution to be eliminated. Pollution damage equal to $OQ'F$ still remains. If pollution is cut back further, the gain from reduced pollution falls short of the loss from reduced consumption of X.[14]

This conclusion may not satisfy the naturalist who would like to see totally pure water or air. In the economist's language, this view would set pollution damages so high as to make the OC (marginal damage cost) schedule coincide with the vertical axis, thereby setting the efficient output at zero. As we shall see later, the evaluation of damage cost (or of the benefits of clean air and water) is a difficult matter; but damages are not to be set at an infinitely high level.

Variable Technology The fixed technology case brings out the basic issue of pollution control, but it is much too simple a view. We must now allow for the fact that technologies are not fixed and that the level of pollution can be reduced by changing methods of production. Thus, a factory may install abatement equipment to reduce the pollution content of its discharge. In this case, public policy must provide it with an incentive to do so. Moreover, the firm should be induced to carry treatment to the point where the cost of further treatment begins to exceed the benefits of reduced pollution damage.

The diagrammatics of this adjustment, which the general reader may wish to pass over, are shown in the upper half of Figure 32-6,[15] pertaining to a specified level of output. The level of discharge is recorded on the horizontal axis, and in the absence of abatement efforts, equals OA. Total damage cost TDC is shown for various levels of discharge along the curve OB. Its slope is assumed to increase with rising levels of discharge, an assumption which need not generally hold. Curve CA shows the total abatement cost TAC involved at various levels of discharge reduction. If all pollution is avoided, such cost equals OC. The slope of TAC rises with increasing abatement as it becomes increasingly difficult to reduce pollution further. Curve CFB is the total cost attributable to pollution, obtained by addition of OB and CA. It combines the cost of pollution prevention with that of the remaining pollution and is at a minimum at discharge level OE. This defines the efficient level of pollution prevention for a given level of output.

As shown in the lower part of Figure 32-6, the efficient level of abatement may also be determined by drawing the marginal damage cost curve MDC and

[13] Note that in order to determine the required rate of tax, the supply and demand schedules must be known. Only if the marginal damage cost is constant can the tax rate be set independently.

[14] By cutting back from Q to Q', the pollution damage avoided equals $GLMH$, which exceeds the loss of consumer surplus from reduced consumption of X or GLH. If the reduction in output is pushed beyond QQ', the loss of surplus exceeds the reduction in pollution damage at the margin.

[15] The diagram follows A. M. Freeman III, R. H. Haveman, and A. V. Kneese, *The Economics of Environmental Policy*, New York: Wiley, 1973, p. 85.

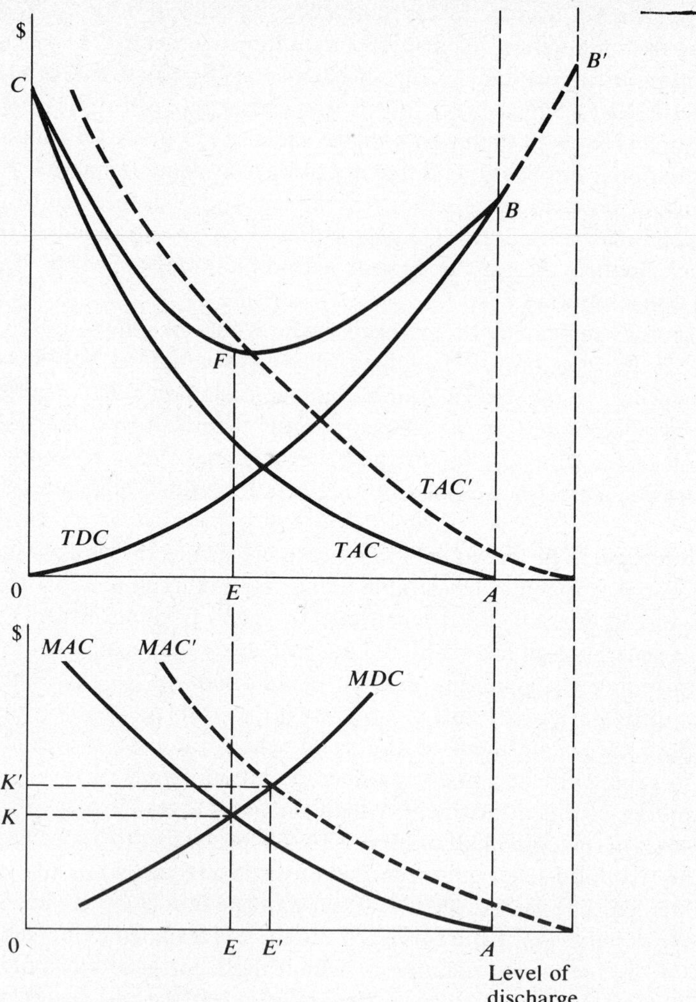

FIGURE 32-6 Pollution Control with Abatement Incentive.

the marginal abatement cost curve *MAC*. The efficient discharge level *OE* is now obtained by equating *MAC* and *MDC*. In order to induce a firm to carry the abatement level to the point where discharge is reduced to *OE*, a tax equal to *OK* per unit of discharge might be imposed. Over the range from *A* to *E*, the marginal abatement cost is less than the marginal tax cost so that abatement will be undertaken. Beyond this point it will be cheaper to pay the tax.

This solution (calling for a tax per unit of discharge of *OK*) applies to this particular level of output only. As the level of output is increased, the total damage cost without abatement will move out along the *OB* curve to, say, *B'*, and the total abatement cost curve will shift to, say, *TAC'*. A similar shift will occur in the marginal abatement cost from *MAC* to *MAC'*. The efficient level of abatement activity will move to *E'*, leaving a higher damage level, while the appropriate tax per unit of abatement will rise from *OK* to *OK'*. Thus, the proper level of tax per unit of discharge varies with the level of output.[16]

The firm, confronted with a schedule of taxes per unit of discharge which varies with output, will then be induced to adjust both its abatement activity and its level of output so as to equate its marginal cost (including tax, abatement, and other costs) with market price. In equilibrium, the tax will again equal the marginal damage cost of the remaining pollution, as was the case in Figure 32-5.[17]

Lack of Information

Unfortunately, the information needed to implement so complex a procedure is rarely available. The major difficulties are as follows:

1. Measuring damage costs (the *TDC* curve in Figure 32-6) or, what is the same, the value of cleaner air or water is exceedingly difficult. In most cases, the simple solution of asking people what they would be willing to pay is not applicable. Where large numbers are involved, evaluation of preferences cannot be obtained either because exclusion (in this case from damage prevention) cannot be applied or because the benefits derived from such prevention are in the nature of social goods and nonrival in consumption, so that exclusion would be inefficient.[18]

Thus, indirect evaluation is necessary. Cleaner air results in better health, the gain from which may be estimated in terms of reduced hospital bills and increased earnings due to a longer working life. While these ways of measuring the gain are feasible and of some value, they are obviously quite inadequate. Improved health means more than just reduced hospital bills; and longer life means more than additional wages. Feeling better, living longer, and the sheer pleasure of breathing cleaner air are overlooked by such "objective" estimates. Similar problems arise with regard to clean water, the gain from which is not fully accounted for by the value of increased catches of fish or willingness to pay bathing fees. As another illustration, how can one value the gain of improved sleep due to reduced jet noise?[19] In some instances, estimates might be based on changes in the value of adjoining real estate, but this is the exception rather than the rule. In most cases, objective evaluation is incomplete or difficult and evaluation by the political process is needed. The difficulties involved in such evaluation of "social bads" are similar to those previously encountered in the valuation of social goods.

2. Although the chemical or biological content of discharges can be measured uniformly across factories, the dollar cost of the resulting pollution may differ greatly depending on the location of the polluting unit. Thus, the damage due to water pollution is greater upstream than downstream, especially if the factory is located above highly populated areas. Similarly, the air pollution cost of air transport in an urban area is greater than that caused by air travel in a rural area, jet noises are more objectionable if close to residential sites, and so forth. Obtaining physical measures of waste discharge is thus only a first step toward the more difficult problem of translating such measures into economic damage cost.

[16] The tax is invariant to the level of output only if the *TDC* function is linear, in which case the *MDC* function is horizontal.

[17] Unfortunately, this result cannot be shown in a simple two-dimensional diagram such as Fig. 32-5 because the tax rate is a function of both the level of discharge and units of output.

[18] See p. 51.

[19] See also the earlier discussion of benefit evaluation, p. 159.

3. The cost of pollution abatement may differ greatly among firms, municipalities, and households. The cost of securing a given total of pollution reduction therefore differs markedly depending on where it is undertaken. Unfortunately, little information is available on this important problem.

4. The most efficient place to reduce pollution need not be with the party which causes the damage. There are always two parties to the pollution problem. If a factory causes air pollution which bothers nearby residents, will it be cheaper to reduce air pollution or to have residents move to less polluted areas? The choice between these two options may have important equity implications, but it must also be looked upon as an efficiency problem.

Instruments of Control

Whether for lack of information or for other reasons, governments do not attempt to implement as refined a solution as Figures 32-5 and 32-6 suggest. Rather, the usual procedure is to decide as a matter of general judgment what overall level of pollution is permitted. If this target level falls, say, 25 percent below the prevailing level, regulations will usually require firms to reduce their pollution by 25 percent on an across-the-board basis. This approach is inefficient because cutbacks should be made where the cost of abatement is lowest. Since the necessary information is hard to come by, the regulatory approach is inefficient in this respect.

This problem may be avoided if effluent charges are used. Thus, the government may impose a tax per unit of discharge and determine experimentally what rates are needed to reduce discharge by the desired degree. By letting each firm equate its marginal cost of abatement with the rate of tax, an efficient allocation of abatement effort will result without requiring information on differential abatement costs.

At the same time, the effluent charge is no cure-all because a uniform charge per unit of discharge would be appropriate only if the damage costs per unit of discharge were the same. As noted before, this is not the fact. Damage costs may differ greatly depending on where the discharge occurs, i.e., the level of the *MDC* schedule in Figure 32-6 or the *OC* curve of Figure 32-5 differs for different polluters. Therefore, the efficient solution requires differential rates of tax for different firms or at least different categories of polluters, depending on location and other characteristics of the watershed or airshed into which discharge occurs.

While the effluent charge involves the "stick approach" to incentive policy, a "carrot approach" might also be offered which would subsidize firms that undertake to reduce pollution. This approach may take the form of outright payment for pollution reduction or of subsidies for the abatement equipment. The latter has the disadvantage that it may bias the choice of prevention technology.

The effluent charge is sometimes criticized as selling the right to pollute, which is considered an immoral way of dealing with the benefits of nature. This, however, is not a well-founded objection. Once it is agreed that the efficient solution does not call for "total" elimination of pollution, some level of pollution remains permissible and the effluent charge is merely a device for allocating emissions in an efficient fashion. A regulatory approach which assigns permissible pollution quotas does essentially the same thing.

Equity Aspects

Assuming pollution to be reduced to its efficient level, there remains the question of distributing its costs in an equitable fashion. Who should bear the costs of abatement measures; and no less important, who should bear the costs of the remaining pollution damage?

The Problem of Compensation Consider the case of water pollution by a paper factory. To simplify matters, assume further that the marginal pollution damage is constant. We then have the situation depicted in Figure 32-7, where *DD* is the demand schedule and *AS* is the supply schedule in the absence of government intervention, with *OG* the corresponding level of output. *MDC* is the marginal damage cost curve, FS_t the supply schedule with damage costs, and *OL* the output if the pollution cost is included in price. We now compare three approaches to securing the efficient output *OL* and see how the various parties involved—including paper factory, readers, the general public, and the displaced bathers—are affected. The results are listed in the following table:

	ALTERNATIVE EFFICIENT SOLUTIONS		
	Regulatory Cutbacks (I)	*Effluent Charge with Tax Cut (II)*	*Effluent Charge with Compensation (III)*
Paper factory	+*ABCF*	0	0
Readers	−*AECF*	−*AECF*	−*AECF*
General public	0	+*ABCF*	0
Bathers	+*LGHK*	+*LGHK*	+*OGHN*

Note: The symbol + indicates gain, and the symbol − indicates loss.

Under the first approach, the government requires the paper industry (which we assume has previously priced competitively) to form a cartel and to cut back output, leaving the resulting profits *ABCF* with the industry. The industry thus

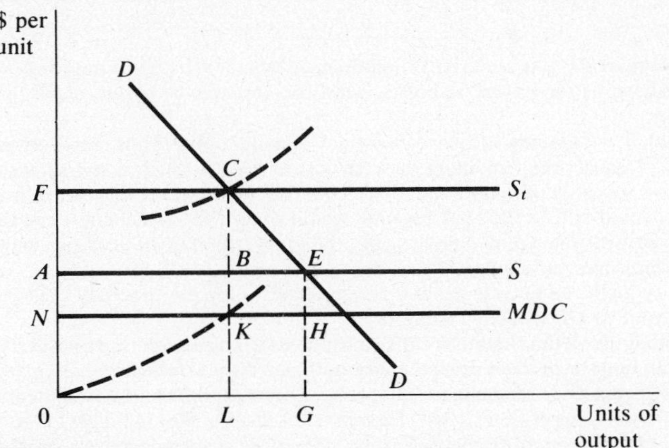

FIGURE 32-7 Equity Aspects of Pollution Control.

gains *ABCF* while the readers who pay more for their books and magazines suffer a loss equal to *AECF* and the bathers obtain a gain in reduced pollution equal to *LGHK*. In the second case, the government imposes a tax equal to *BC* per unit of discharge.[20] It obtains revenue of *ABCF* and uses this for tax reduction. The result for readers and bathers is the same as before, but the gain now accrues to the general public rather than to the industry. In case III the tax is used to compensate the bathers for the remaining damage. Here, the readers pay and the bathers are fully compensated.[21] In all these instances the efficient output *OL* is provided, so that solutions are equally good on efficiency grounds.[22]

At the same time, the solutions differ from an equity viewpoint. Proceeding on the premise that consumers are generally expected to pay a price equal to the marginal cost of the product which they consume, there would seem little reason to reject this principle where the costs involved are of the external type. Nor does it seem reasonable to leave the gain which results from the output correction with the industry or the general public. Rather, it seems fair to compensate the bathers who otherwise would be left with a residual damage cost. To put it differently, they are recognized as having a share in the common property right to clean water and hence are entitled to be compensated for the loss of this share if they should be deprived of it. The equity problem is basically one of entitlement and of the conditions under which society considers such entitlement to exist.[23]

Effects on Income Distribution The problem of equity as just discussed relates to the distribution of gains and losses among polluters and pollution victims. Another aspect of the problem relates to the incidence of pollution and pollution prevention on households grouped in relation to income size. Consider, for example, the additional cost of automobiles caused by engine improvements which are required to reduce emissions. Such costs may well comprise a higher percentage of income for low-income households, so that the cost distribution of damage prevention may be regressive. Another question is how the resulting benefits of improved air quality will be distributed. Since low-income families are likely to live in central parts of the city where pollution is greater, the initial benefit distribution may be expected to be pro-poor. But the ultimate benefit

[20] Assuming competitive markets, it is a matter of indifference whether the tax is imposed on the paper industry, the publishers, or the buyers of books, since the cost will be passed on to the book purchasers in either case.

[21] Matters are simplified if we assume constant marginal damage costs. Thus, revenue as measured by *ABCF* in Fig. 32-7 equals the remaining damage cost or *OLKN*. Such is not so with a variable marginal damage cost schedule. If marginal damage cost rises as shown by the dotted line *OK*, the appropriate unit tax would still be *BC*, but revenue would exceed the remaining damage cost or *OLK*. To equate revenue with remaining damage cost, the tax would now have to rise with successive units of output as measured by the dotted line *OK*.

[22] Still another possibility might be to raise general revenue and to use the proceeds to bribe the industry into reducing output to *OL* without raising price.

[23] It has been suggested that the victim should be entitled to claims if, when acquiring a property (subsequently damaged by pollution), a prudent person could not have been expected to anticipate the development of such damage. See F. I. Michelman, "Property, Utility, and Fairness: Comments on the Ethical Foundations of 'Just Competition' Law." *Harvard Law Review*, **80**:1165–1258, 1966–1967; and H. Demsetz, "Towards a Theory of Property Rights," *American Economic Review, Papers and Proceedings of the A.E.A.*, pp. 347–379, May 1967.

distribution may not be so because real estate values (and rentals) may rise as the smog is reduced, with the benefits accruing to the landlord rather than to the residents. As can be seen from this simple illustration, the problem of benefit and cost incidence is a complex one. In other cases, such as municipal waste treatment, the cost of damage prevention is assumed by the taxpayer and thus depends on the incidence of the marginal tax dollar. The benefit in turn accrues to the consumers of recreational facilities, with incidence depending on the way in which the use of such facilities is distributed. While it is difficult to generalize about the outcome of antipollution measures of various types, there is no simple assumption that the net result will be toward a more equal distribution of real income.

Federalism Aspects

For various reasons, it is difficult to secure an effective solution to environmental problems without intergovernmental cooperation. The reasons are several. Territorial considerations require cooperation because waterways or airsheds frequently extend over more than one jurisdiction. The same applies to traffic problems where transportation systems, such as highways, pass through several jurisdictions. Even where there is no such overlap, cooperation may be essential because the imposition of pollution restrictions and abatement requirements are costly to the industries concerned. The effects of differential requirements on location are thus similar to the effects of differential taxation. Nor is the problem one for the industry only. If tight environmental standards and abatement requirements are imposed in one jurisdiction but not in another, industrial development will be reduced and this curtailment will impose a burden not only on investors but also on those employed in the affected industries. If the application of standards is more general, these impacts will be less severe since the compliance costs cannot be escaped by movement from one jurisdiction to another.

Political Aspects

Nevertheless, pollution controls, even if applied on a nationwide basis, will involve costs for particular industries and hence cause changes in the composition of output and employment. Like all such changes, this one will impose transition burdens on particular groups of investors and workers, groups which will be impressed but little by the proposition that the adjustment is one which will benefit the nation as a whole. The question here, as with other efficiency-increasing policies such as tariff reductions or technological change, is whether the victims of the particular adjustment should or should not be paid compensation. Obviously, failure to compensate increases political opposition to such efficiency measures.

Current Policies

As a result of the growing interest in environmental policies, important pieces of legislation have been passed in recent years to deal with pollution problems. They have resulted in a heavy involvement of the federal government in this field. Some of the more important of these measures will be noted briefly.

Air Pollution Federal legislation in the air pollution field began with the Clean Air Act of 1963, which did not come into its own until the amendments of 1967 and especially the amendment of 1970. The latter established a federal framework for air quality improvement within which local and state governments would have to operate. The country was divided into 247 airsheds or regions, and the Federal Protection Agency (FPA) in 1971 established air quality standards for six major pollutants: sulfur oxides, nitrogen oxides, particulate matter, photochemical oxidants, carbon monoxide, and hydrocarbons. The standards set permissible maximum pollutant concentrations, and states are required to submit plans to meet them, with target levels to be met within three years after the approval of the plan. The particular means to be used in reaching the target is left to the states, but state plans are subject to FPA approval. These techniques are still in the process of development. The controls on stationary-source emissions may include requiring the use of low-sulfur fuel, the installation of specific control equipment, or setting minimum stack heights.

While the details of implementation of these standards were left to the states, the 1970 amendments gave the federal government the initiative to deal with automobile pollution. The standards written into the 1970 legislation apply to all cars sold in the United States, with stepped-up requirements from the 1970 models to the 1975 and 1976 model years. By 1976, automobile emissions must be reduced by 90 percent of the required 1970 level. In response to pressure by automobile manufacturers, FPA has agreed to postpone this schedule until 1976, and it remains to be seen how effective the industry response in reducing emissions will be. Among further controls on mobile sources being considered are emission inspections and other controls on older cars not included under the federal requirements for new automobiles.

Another interesting development is an administration proposal to impose a tax (applicable at higher rates in low-standard areas), beginning in 1976, on emission of sulfur into the atmosphere. This proposal is of particular significance as it makes use of an economic incentive approach which will induce reduction in pollution where it can be obtained at least cost, rather than require such reduction on an across-the-board basis.

Water Federal programs in the field of water pollution are based on the Water Pollution Control Act Amendment of 1956 and further amendments in the Water Quality Act of 1965. The federal government's function under these acts was to make grants-in-aid for the construction of municipal-based treatment plants and to assist the states in regulating water quality. The Water Pollution Control Act of 1972 greatly increased these efforts, setting the ambitious target of stopping all discharges of pollutants into navigable waterways by 1985. For this purpose, the law (which was passed over a Presidential veto) sets up tight new standards and provides for substantial federal finance. This law thus parallels in scope the Clean Air Act Amendment of 1970, with outlays for 1976 of about $3 billion.

Under the new law, grants involving 75 percent of project cost are to be made in support of municipal sewage treatment plants. Industries are required to apply the "best practicable" control technology by 1977 and the "best available" technology by 1983. Moreover, no pollutants are to be discharged except by permission of the Environmental Planning Agency (EPA) or by state authorities, and EPA is not permitted to grant exemptions. Substantial fines are to be imposed for violations. Although the requirements are most ambitious, implementation so far has been slow and there have been increasing pressures, as a result of the energy crisis and other factors, to delay or ease requirements.

Moreover, it is questionable how effectively a program can be implemented which attempts to set specific effluent limits for each of 40,000 sources of water pollution and to determine on an industry-by-industry or even firm-by-firm basis whether adequate efforts toward improving technology have been made. An alternative approach, applying effluent charges on the various pollutants, may very well have been the better solution.

A special problem is posed by municipal sewage treatment plants. Such operations are subject to decreasing costs and, for reasons discussed in the first part of this chapter, are municipally operated. Capital requirements are met out of public funds, including federal and municipal sources. In determining the pattern of charges to finance current costs and debt service, many of the previously noted problems arise, including differentiation between home and industrial users.

Conclusion It is evident that Congress, in recent legislation, has taken major steps in dealing with the pollution problem and in involving the federal government therein. This concern applies not only to the areas of water and air pollution but also to other aspects such as jet noise and (a likely candidate for early legislation) solid waste disposal from household use. Substantial funds have been appropriated in the process, especially in the Water Pollution Control Act of 1972, but the costs of significant improvement are also very large. Thus, it is estimated that by the late 1970s, achieving current goals in water and air pollution might involve annual costs of about \$25 and \$15 billion respectively.[24] However, three-quarters of this total cost should be private sector rather than budgetary cost, with the latter largely directed at abatement of water pollution. Moreover, the allocation of costs will depend on how the necessary abatement is implemented, i.e., whether by regulation, subsidies, or effluent charges. Charges are most attractive from the economist's point of view and also least burdensome to the budget.

F. SUMMARY

In the first part of this chapter, various aspects of public pricing policy were examined. The major conclusions were as follows:

1. When government engages in the sale of private goods, the efficient pricing rule calls for setting price equal to marginal cost.

[24] The costs are in 1972 prices and include operating and annual capital costs after the initial investments have been made. In the earlier years when the new equipment must be installed, outlays would have to be substantially higher. See Ivars Gutmanis, "The Environment," in Charles S. Schultze (ed.), *Setting National Priorities, the 1973 Budget,* Washington: Brookings, p. 374.

2. In the case of decreasing cost industries, this approach involves a loss, and the question is how the deficit is to be covered. Various alternatives were considered, including payment from general revenue, application of a two-part tariff, and price discrimination.

3. The same principles apply to public utility regulations. The widely applied rule that price should allow for coverage of costs plus a fair return to capital is sound in principle but meets with difficulties in application.

4. A major problem in public utility pricing results from variability of demand, with differential pricing called for in peak and off-peak periods. Demand variability also makes it difficult to determine the proper level of plant capacity.

5. The efficiency rule of marginal cost pricing must be qualified if other prices are set in imperfect markets.

6. Further qualifications to marginal cost pricing are introduced if distributional adjustments are to be built into the pricing policy.

7. In pricing social facilities, no price should be charged for existing facilities unless congestion exists.

8. With regard to new social facilities, imposition of a user charge is helpful in verifying past investment decisions and in calculating the profitability of additional investments; but in the absence of crowding, user charges interfere with efficient use.

The second theme of the chapter dealt with the problem of external costs of pollution and the pricing arrangements which might be applied to internalize these costs:

9. Failure to account for pollution costs creates both inefficiencies and inequities.

10. Pollution may result from consumption as well as from production activities.

11. With fixed technology, the efficient solution is provided by a tax which will add the marginal pollution cost to the marginal private cost so that total marginal cost equals price. As a result, pollution will not be eliminated but its level will be reduced.

12. Where changes in technology can be made to reduce pollution, abatement activity should be cut back to where the marginal cost of abatement equals the marginal value of pollution avoidance.

13. Practical problems encountered in the application of pollution control include the difficulties in measuring damage costs as well as the variability of damage and abatement costs among firms and locations.

14. Among various instruments of control, effluent charges are likely to be superior to the setting of standards, but the information needed to formulate an optimal structure of charges remains difficult to obtain.

15. Various techniques will serve equally well to secure an efficient solution, but they may differ in their equity implications.

16. This involves the questions of who should pay for abatement costs and whether or not the victims of remaining pollution should be compensated.

17. Moreover, it is important that compensation be paid so as not to interfere with an efficient solution.

18. In the large-number case, determination of damage cost involves problems similar to those dealt with in the context of social goods, where preferences are not revealed but must be determined.

19. In the concluding pages, recent antipollution legislation, applicable mainly to air and water pollution, was examined.

FURTHER READINGS

Dorfman, R., and N. Dorfman (eds.): *Economics of the Environment: Selected Readings,* New York: Norton, 1972.

Economic Report of the President for 1971, "Safeguarding the Environment," pp. 114–122.

Freeman, A. M., III, R. H. Haveman, and A. V. Kneese: *The Economics of Environmental Policy,* New York: Wiley, 1973.

Friedlaender, A. F.: *The Dilemma of Freight Transport Regulation,* Washington: Brookings, 1969.

Gutmanis, I.: "The Environment," in C. Schultze (ed.), *Setting National Priorities, the 1973 Budget,* Washington: Brookings, 1972.

Roberts, M. J.: "River Basin Authorities: A National Solution to Water Pollution," *Harvard Law Review,* May 1970.

Turvey, R.: "On Divergences between Social Cost and Private Cost," *Economica,* August 1963.

——— (ed.): *Public Enterprise,* Baltimore: Penguin, 1968.

Chapter 33

International Public Finance*

A. Introduction to Tax Coordination: *Interindividual Equity; Internation Equity; Efficiency.* **B. Coordination of Income and Profits Taxes:** *Taxation of Earned Income; Taxation of Capital Income; Evaluation; Balance-of-Payments Aspects; Corporate Tax Burden and International Competitiveness; International Division of Profits Base.* **C. Coordination of Product Taxes:** *Efficiency Aspects; Balance-of-Payments Aspects; GATT Rules; Common Market Policy; Revenue Distribution and Burden Export.* **D. Further Problems:** *Joint Provision of Public Services; International Aid and Redistribution; Stabilization Policies.* **E. Summary.**

Recent years have brought increasing concern with the international aspects of public finance. Various developments have contributed to this interest. The combining of European economies into the Common Market, the increasing role of multinational corporations, the financing of joint efforts such as the United Nations and NATO, and a rising awareness of the international maldistribution

* *Reader's Guide to Chapter 33:* The newest and one of the most interesting aspects of the fiscal problem relates to its role in the international setting. Many of the problems which traditionally have been dealt with only in the confines of national finance are becoming increasingly important in their application to international trade, capital flows, international organizations such as the United Nations, and the relationship between poor and rich countries. A brief survey of these new horizons is presented in this chapter.

of income have all pointed toward the need for international fiscal coordination. In principle, these problems are similar to those previously encountered in the discussion of fiscal federalism within the confines of a single nation, but they differ in magnitude and in the international nature of the cooperative effort which is required.

A. INTRODUCTION TO TAX COORDINATION

Tax coordination has been the most discussed part of the problem, and various techniques have been developed to deal with it. Each country must decide how it chooses to tax the foreign income of its residents and the income of foreigners which originates within its borders. Similarly, it must decide how its product and sales taxes are to apply to its exports and imports. These decisions may be made in conjunction with other countries, and international tax treaties are a means of coordinating some of these matters.

As the sphere of tax policy is extended from a national to an international setting, old problems, such as the requirements of interindividual equity and effects on the efficiency of resource use, must be reconsidered, while new problems such as internation equity are added.

Interindividual Equity

If a person receives income which originates in various countries, he or she will be subject to taxation by more than one authority. Mr. A, a resident of the United States, may spend part of the year in the United Kingdom, and pay a United Kingdom tax on his earnings there. Or he may invest in the United Kingdom and derive dividend income on which a United Kingdom tax is paid. At the same time, he receives United States income and pays United States tax. Does horizontal equity require that he pay the same total of taxes (both domestic and foreign) as Mr. B, who receives the same total income but entirely from United States sources? Or should the United States simply consider taxes paid to other countries as a deduction from income and equalize tax burdens in terms of United States taxes only? In the first case equity is interpreted in an international sense, and in the second case in a national sense.

Internation Equity

A further and distinct equity problem arises in determining how the tax pie is to be divided among the treasuries of the various countries. This problem arises, though in different ways, with regard to both income and product taxes.

In regard to income and profits taxes, it is generally agreed that the country in which the income originates (also referred to as the "country of source") is entitled to tax that income, but the question is, at what rate? The United Kingdom tax imposed on the earnings of United States capital invested in the United Kingdom reduces the net return which accrues to the United States. It differs in this respect from such additional taxes as may be imposed by the U.S. Treasury. The latter do not constitute a loss to the United States but are merely a transfer between United States residents and the U.S. Treasury. The national loss suffered by the United States thus depends only on the rate at which United States capital is taxed in the United Kingdom. One reasonable view of internation equity is that the country of source should be permitted to tax foreign investment income at the same rate that it taxes income received by its own residents but not at a higher rate.

In the matter of product taxes, the equity issue relates to the possibility of burdening foreigners through changes in price. If country A taxes exports, the cost of exports is increased. If the country dominates the export market, export prices will rise and the foreign consumer will pay more. Thus, part of the tax burden may be shifted abroad. Similarly, if imports are taxed, foreign suppliers may find that they must sell their products at a lower net price. Once more, part of the burden is shifted to the outside. If one accepts the criterion that a country should pay its own taxes, such burden shifting may be considered as running counter to internation equity.

Efficiency

Differential profits tax rates or, as pointed out earlier, differential fiscal net benefits or burdens[1] will affect the location of economic activity and tend to draw resources from their most efficient uses. If Mr. D, an investor, finds his taxes lower if he invests in Italy rather than in the United States, he will send more of his capital to Italy than he would in the absence of the tax differential. The question, then, is how to arrange the taxation of international investment income so as not to disturb the efficiency of capital allocation on a *worldwide* basis. But international tax neutrality is not the only possible criterion. The objective may also be to implement a concept of *national* efficiency (to be explored presently), in which case a different arrangement is called for.

Differential product tax rates also cause inefficiencies but in a different way. If such taxes are imposed at the producer stage (rather than at the retail level), they affect the relative costs of producing a given product in various countries. As a result, the location of production is determined not by comparative advantage (or relative resource cost), which is the requirement for efficient trade, but is modified by differential tax costs.

B. COORDINATION OF INCOME AND PROFITS TAXES

With these general principles in mind, we now consider how they apply to the major taxes, beginning with income and profits taxes.

Taxation of Earned Income

The United States (like most other countries) reserves the right to tax the income of its residents no matter where earned. Mr. Jones, who spends six months of the year at a job in the United Kingdom and then returns to the United States, will pay United Kingdom tax on his income earned in the United Kingdom. In determining his United States tax, he will include his United Kingdom earnings

[1] See p. 629.

in his income, but he will credit taxes paid in the United Kingdom against his United States tax liability. His final liability will then be the same as if the entire income had been earned in the United States. Such at least is the procedure so long as his United Kingdom tax does not exceed his United States tax on the same (United Kingdom–earned) income. If it does, no refund is given and his total tax is higher than if his income had all been earned in the United States. Special rules apply regarding the treatment of fellowship stipends, teachers' earnings, and so forth, but the general pattern is to permit income to be taxed in the country of origin with the country of primary residence extending the credit.

This approach is in line with internation equity and is interpreted to mean that the country of income origin is permitted to apply its own rates to the earnings of foreigners; and the granting of a credit by the country of primary residence, though involving a revenue loss to that country's treasury, is in line with the international view of interindividual equity.[2]

Due to the increased labor mobility in postwar Europe, the treatment of migrant workers under social security has become a major problem. The usual policy is to extend social security benefits without differentiation, including payment of family allowances where family members remain in the home country. Differentials in social security benefits among countries have thus become a strong factor in attracting labor to high-benefit countries, the effect having been to widen effective wage differentials.

Taxation of Capital Income

The most important and complex part of the problem concerns the tax treatment of foreign investment income. This includes the treatment of such income received by individuals and corporations, with the latter much the major item.

Present United States Practice The major rules in the treatment of foreign investment income as they now apply in the United States are as follows:

1. An individual investor residing in the United States and receiving investment income from abroad pays individual income tax thereon. The government in the country of income origin typically imposes a "withholding tax" of, say, 15 percent, which in turn is credited against United States tax. In the reverse case, a similar withholding tax is imposed in the United States, the level of withholding rates generally being agreed upon in international tax treaties.
2. A United States corporation operating a branch abroad will find the profits of the branch subject to the foreign corporation tax in the country in which it is located. For purposes of United States tax, the profits of the parent corporation and its branch are considered as a unit. Foreign branch profits prior to foreign tax are included in the parent's taxable profits and the foreign tax is then credited against United States tax. The foreign country usually imposes no withholding taxes when

[2] Note that United States residents will pay under the same bracket rates whether their income is received here or abroad. However, the tax applicable in the United Kingdom will relate to the rate brackets applicable to United Kingdom income only. Some might argue that the United Kingdom is entitled to tax at rates applicable to the foreigner's total income.

the profits are repatriated. Provided only that the foreign profits tax does not exceed the United States tax, it is a matter of indifference to the United States corporation whether profits originate at home or in a foreign branch.

3. Neither of these cases compares in importance with that of the foreign incorporated subsidiary. Though owned by the parent corporation in the United States, the foreign subsidiary is incorporated abroad and is legally a separate corporate entity. Its profits are subject to foreign corporation income tax and the United States tax is "deferred" until the profits of the subsidiary are repatriated by being paid as dividends to the parent company. At that time, such profits become subject to United States corporation tax. Profits gross of foreign profits tax are included in taxable income and the foreign tax is credited against the United States tax due.[3] Provided the foreign tax is not higher, repatriated profits are thus subject to the same (United States) rate as would apply if they had been earned domestically. At the same time, profits which are retained abroad are subject only to foreign tax, with United States tax deferred until such profits are repatriated.

Evaluation

In evaluating these arrangements, we consider the merits of (1) the foreign tax credit, and (2) the deferral provision.

Credit versus Deduction of Foreign Tax Crediting the foreign corporation tax against the United States corporation tax results in tax neutrality. Such at least is the outcome so long as the foreign tax (i.e., corporation tax plus withholding tax) is not higher than the United States tax. Since the United States rate applies whether the capital is invested at home or abroad, tax influences on investment choice are neutralized. Thus the efficient allocation of capital resources on a worldwide basis is not interfered with.

This is an important advantage, but it is not the only way of looking at the matter. While the credit device secures an efficient solution on a worldwide basis, it does not do so from a national point of view. Suppose that investment in both the United States and the United Kingdom yields a pretax return of 10 percent. Suppose further that the corporation tax rate in both countries is 50 percent, thus leaving the investor with a net return of 5 percent. Yet, from the national standpoint, the return on investment made in the United States is 10 percent, with 5 percent going to the investor and 5 percent going to the U.S. Treasury. The latter share is lost to the investor but not to the country as a whole. However, the return to the United States on investment made in the United Kingdom is only 5 percent, the remaining 5 percent share which goes to the United Kingdom Exchequer being lost to the United States as a nation. This suggests that from the viewpoint of national efficiency, capital export should be carried to the point where the return *after* foreign tax abroad equals the before-tax return on domestic

[3] Suppose that foreign earnings of $1 million are subject to a foreign corporation tax of 35 percent of $350,000, leaving $650,000. These earnings are to be repatriated. At the time of repatriation, an additional foreign tax (the "withholding tax") of 15 percent or $97,500 applies, reducing net profits to $552,500. In computing United States taxes, the 48 percent rate is applied to $1 million, giving a gross tax of $480,000. Foreign taxes of $350,000 plus $97,500 are then credited, leaving a net United States tax of $32,500. The investor's total tax equals $350,000 plus $97,500 plus $32,500, equaling $480,000, or 48 percent.

investment. This means a lower level of capital export than is appropriate under the criterion of world efficiency.

The investor will undertake foreign investment up to the point where the *net* return is the same as from domestic investment. Under the crediting approach, this will be the case where

$$(1 - t_{us})r_{us} = (1 - t_{us})r_f$$

t_{us} and t_f being the United States and foreign rates of tax, and r_{us} and r_f the United States and foreign rates of return, respectively. Thus, foreign investment is carried up to the point where

$$r_{us} = r_f$$

and the requirement of world efficiency is met. But suppose now that the foreign tax is *deducted* from United States taxable income rather than *credited* against the United States tax. The investor, in equating the net return from foreign and domestic investment, will undertake foreign investment to the point where

$$(1 - t_{us})r_{us} = (1 - t_{us})(1 - t_f)r_f$$

that is, where $r_{us} = (1 - t_f)r_f$. Thus, the deduction approach meets the requirement of national efficiency.

Which of the two approaches is to be preferred is an open question. From the point of view of United States investors, the credit method is the most favorable since foreign investment income after tax will be larger. In the view of others such as United States wage earners, the deduction approach might be preferred. With more capital staying at home, domestic labor will be more productive and wages will be higher. In the matter of United States foreign investment, there thus exists a common interest shared by U.S. investors abroad and foreign workers (both of whom benefit) and U.S. workers and foreign owners of capital abroad (both of whom lose).

Deferral The deferral provision is based on the somewhat fictitious assumption that the foreign subsidiary is a truly separate entity. Thus it seems to contradict the crediting provision which implies that the subsidiary's tax is in fact the parent's tax. To be sure, deferral makes little difference to the parent corporation if the foreign tax does not fall short of what the United States tax would be, but in fact it frequently does. Western European rates are not greatly below United States levels, but those of developing countries frequently are. Consequently, it has been estimated that, on the average, a dollar of United States foreign investment pays only 70 percent of the tax payable by domestic investment in the United States.[4] Thus corporations are given an incentive not to repatriate and to divert earnings of subsidiaries into investments in low-tax (so-

[4] See P. B. Musgrave, "Tax Preferences to Foreign Investment," in *The Economics of Federal Subsidy Programs,* Part 2, Joint Economic Committee, 92d Cong., 2d Sess., June 11, 1972.

called tax haven) countries. In the 1960s various steps were taken to limit such tax avoidance, but it remains a problem.

Balance-of-Payments Aspects

The tax treatment of foreign investment income may also affect the balance of payments. Given the United States balance-of-payments difficulties over the last decade, this aspect has been much discussed. To the extent that deferral provides a preferential treatment of foreign investment income, capital outflow is encouraged. This flow adds to the balance-of-payments deficit. As foreign capital is built up and earnings come to be repatriated, the tables are turned and the balance of payments is strengthened. Where foreign taxes are lower, this development is, however, retarded by the deferral provision which encourages the reinvestment of earnings abroad.

A more indirect and less readily appraised link to the balance of payments involves effects on commodity trade. On the one hand, exports of machinery and equipment will be stimulated through the creation of foreign subsidiaries. On the other hand, sales by the subsidiaries drawing freely upon United States technology may replace exports by United States–based companies. The net effects are difficult to assess, and they remain a matter of controversy.[5]

Corporate Tax Burden and International Competitiveness

Another view of the problem does not focus on tax advantages which the United States investors may obtain from investing abroad (as compared with home investment). Rather, it compares the relative position of subsidiaries of United States companies with that of other companies operating in the same country, e.g., the relative position of United States subsidiaries and British companies operating in Britain or of United States and British subsidiaries operating in France. Under the deferral rule, both will pay the same tax (that of the country in which the operation occurs) provided that profits are not repatriated.[6] But if profits are repatriated, the final taxes may differ. If they are higher in the United States, do they not reduce the ability of United States companies to compete in world markets?

What is relevant here is the comparison between taxes in the United States and those in other countries which are major sources of foreign investment funds, such as the European countries and Japan. Comparison of the levels of corporation profits taxation among these countries is difficult because allowance must be made not only for differences in tax rates but also for such provisions as depreciation rules and enforcement. Recent estimates suggest that corporate tax burdens in these countries are close to those in the United States although the average level may be somewhat lower by, say, 10 or 15 percent.[7] Because of this, it may be that the United States *share* in total (world) capital formation is less

[5] See P. B. Musgrave, *United States Taxation of Foreign Investment Income: Issues and Arguments,* Cambridge, Mass.: Harvard Law School, International Tax Program, 1970.

[6] A further proviso is that the guest country not discriminate against foreign capital.

[7] See the statement by the Secretary of the Treasury before the Senate Finance Committee, Oct. 7, 1971. Table 1 of that statement shows comparative data for a number of major countries.

than it would be if levels of tax rates were the same; this being so, the United States share of foreign investment may also be somewhat smaller. But beyond these possibilities, the differential tax has no particular bearing on the ability of United States companies to compete abroad. Rather, the basic issue is whether United States policy should be concerned with the relative rate of growth of the United States economy and the bearing which this rate may have on the position of the United States in world politics.

International Division of Profits Base

We have argued that a country should be entitled to tax such profits as originate within its borders; but implementation of this rule renders it necessary, in the case of multinational corporations, to determine the profit shares which arise in different countries. This is not a simple matter. Suppose a United States corporation operates a subsidiary in Canada. Under the rules of internation equity, Canada is entitled to tax the profits of this subsidiary. But how can these profits be separated in a meaningful way from those of the parent company in the United States? If parent and subsidiary sell or buy from each other, profits may be easily shifted from one country to another so as to place them where taxes are lower. The difficulties are compounded where tiers of subsidiaries operating in various countries are involved.

Efforts have been made to formulate rules which will preclude profit shifting, such as the requirement that prices be determined on an "arm's-length" basis, i.e., as they would have been if the dealing had been between independent companies. Given these difficulties inherent in conducting separate profit accounting for interrelated entities, it has been suggested that an altogether different approach might be taken. The profits base of multinational corporations might be allocated among countries not by location of subsidiaries but in line with the national origin of profits earned by the business group as a whole. Such origin might be approximated by a formula including both location of value added and sales in its base. Though attractive as a potential solution, this approach would require an international tax administration to implement it, and it therefore remains a rather far-off alternative.[8]

C. COORDINATION OF PRODUCT TAXES

The case for coordination of commodity taxes may be made on various grounds, including efficiency, balance of payments, and revenue considerations.

Efficiency Aspects

Whereas in the case of income taxes the concern was with effects upon capital flows, attention is now directed to effects of product taxes on product flows. The argument is most readily presented under the assumption of flexible exchange rates.

[8] See P. B. Musgrave, "The Division of Tax Base and the Multinational Corporation," *Public Finance,* Vol. XXVII, No. 4, 1972. See also the analogous problem posed by the allocation of corporation taxes among states, Chap. 12, p. 312.

The case for a free flow of international trade is based on the proposition that all trading countries will benefit if each specializes in the production of those products in which it has a comparative advantage. Suppose that country A has a comparative advantage in producing product X while country B has an advantage in producing Y. Country A will thus export X and import Y, while country B imports X and exports Y. However, with production subject to increasing costs, A continues to produce some of its own Y and B produces some of its own X. Both A and B will be better off than they would be if there were no trade. By exporting X and importing Y, country A obtains a higher real income than if it produced all its Y at home; and vice versa for B.

Now consider how this situation may be affected by various taxes. For this purpose, we distinguish between consumption or "destination" taxes which are imposed where the product ends up and is consumed, and production or "origin" taxes which are imposed where the product originates or is produced. In deciding whether various taxes do or do not interfere with the location of production, the key question is whether the tax affects the relative prices of home-produced and imported goods. If it does, consumers will substitute one for the other and the location of production will differ from what it would be under neutral taxes.

Destination Taxes Destination taxes do not interfere with the location of production unless there is an outright discrimination between home-produced and imported goods, i.e., unless the tax is in the form of a tariff or customs duty.

Suppose that country A imposes a general tax (e.g., a retail sales tax) on the consumption of all X and Y, including home-produced and imported goods. This will have no trade effects since consumers in A find relative prices of imported and home-produced goods unchanged.[9] Next, assume that the tax applies to Y only but again covers all Y whether imported or produced at home. As a result, consumers will increase their consumption of X and reduce their consumption of Y. This adjustment may affect the level of trade, but the location of production for both products (at their new levels) will still be in line with comparative advantage.[10]

The situation differs drastically if the tax applies to imported Y only. The tax now enters as a wedge between the relative prices of home-produced and imported goods, leading A's consumers to substitute home-produced Y for imports. As imports fall, the price of A's currency in terms of B's will rise. Thus, exports of X from A will also decline until a new equilibrium is established at a lower level of trade and with a less efficient division of production of X and Y between countries A and B.

Such taxes or tariffs interfere with efficient trade, and substantial efforts have

[9] Nothing else need be said provided that the general sales tax is added to price, leaving factor costs in A unchanged. If, instead, prices stay unchanged while factor costs decline, there will be an exchange rate adjustment so as to increase the price of A's currency in terms of B's, but trade is again unaffected in real terms.

[10] We do not concern ourselves here with inefficiencies which arise from the distortion of *consumption* choices between X and Y, our only concern in this context being with effects on the *location of production.*

been made in recent years, beginning with the Kennedy Round of the 1960s, to reduce trade barriers of this sort.

Origin Taxes Turning now to the question of origin taxes, we find that distortions may arise though there is no attempt to discriminate against foreign products.

Suppose first that country B imposes a *general* production tax, say a manufacturer's excise tax of 10 percent, on both X and Y. As a result, prices in B rise in line with the tax. B's consumers, finding that the prices of home-produced goods have risen relative to those of imported goods, will import more. A's consumers find themselves in the opposite position. B's exporters will add the tax to their costs, so A's consumers will find import prices increased and will import less. Under flexible exchange rates, the resulting increase in demand for A's currency and decrease in demand for B's currency will cause the price of A's currency to rise relative to that of B's. This will dampen the desire of B's consumers to import more and of A's consumers to import less. Relative prices of exports and imports are unchanged and trade is unaffected in real terms.[11]

The situation differs if B's production tax applies to only one product, say its export good Y. Consumers in A again find the cost of Y increased and will substitute domestically produced Y. As A imports less Y, the price of A's currency in terms of B's rises. B's consumers find the cost of imports increased and B therefore imports less. A new equilibrium is established at a lower level of trade and with a changed distribution in the location of production. Country A now produces more Y and B produces more X than before. Imposition of a selective product tax on Y in country B thus results in a distorting effect similar to that following the imposition of an import duty on Y in country A.

This distorting result would have been avoided if country B had granted a tax rebate on its exported Y. B's move would have forestalled a rise in the price of imported Y in country A, so that there would have been no occasion for substituting home-produced Y. By granting an export rebate B's tax on Y would have been transformed from an origin tax into a destination tax. It would have been made equivalent to a retail sales tax on Y in B, a tax which, as shown before, does not distort the location of production provided only that it covers both imports and home products.

A similar story can be told if B's tax is on X. B's consumers will now substitute imported X, and a corresponding adjustment will follow. In the end, the real level of trade will again be reduced and the location of production will be distorted. More X will be produced in A and more Y will be produced in B than before. The distortion in this case might have been avoided by having B impose a compensating import duty on X. The tax once more would have been transformed into a destination tax (now a tax on all X being consumed in B) without distorting location effects.

[11] To be precise, trade will remain unchanged if government expenditures are similar to those which would have been made privately in the absence of tax; but even if the pattern of demand changes so as to affect trade, the new pattern of trade will remain efficient in responding to the new structure of demand.

Balance-of-Payments Aspects

Similar effects on the location of production result under conditions of fixed exchange rates. However, the equilibrating mechanism of exchange rate adjustments is now absent, and the additional problem of effects on the balance of payments arises. Taxes which worsen a country's balance of trade by raising imports or lowering exports now lead to a payments deficit.[12] Destination taxes are once more neutral, but origin taxes now worsen a country's balance of payments while tariffs improve it. The introduction of export rebates and of compensating import duties now not only forestalls production inefficiencies but also neutralizes the balance-of-payments effects of origin taxes. During the fifties and sixties when current international practices, such as the General Agreement on Tariffs and Trade (GATT) and Common Market policies, were being worked out, the setting was one of fixed exchange rates. Consequently, both efficiency and balance-of-payments considerations entered the picture, with the latter given primary emphasis.

GATT Rules

In line with these objectives, the GATT provides that a country may grant an export rebate against product taxes which enter into the cost of production and may impose a compensating import duty on imported products.[13] Payroll taxes are not considered eligible for credit nor is the corporation tax, which is assumed to be borne by profits and not to be a component of costs.

United States practice complies with the GATT rules. Manufacturer's excises are reimbursed on exports; but this rebating of taxes is limited because United States product taxes are largely imposed at the retail level. Exports are excluded while both imported and home-produced products are subject to retail tax. In European countries, product taxes are typically imposed at an earlier stage or stages, as is the value-added tax. The volume of rebating is correspondingly larger. This has led to the complaint that exporters in European countries are given a competitive advantage because they can credit more tax. The argument overlooks the fact that higher product taxes also increase costs, so that the benefit of the larger credit is needed as an offset. Without it, European producers would be at a competitive disadvantage.

[12] Two further differences between the cases of fixed and flexible exchange rates may be noted:

1. Whereas a general origin tax has no bearing on trade in the case of flexible exchanges, it *does* matter with fixed rates. If country B imposes a general origin tax, the cost of B's products in A will rise and B will export less. At the same time, domestic prices will rise relative to those of imported goods and it will import more. Thus B develops a balance-of-payments deficit, the result being the same as that of currency appreciation.

2. As B imposes a general origin tax, effects on the balance of payments can be neutralized by adding an export rebate and a compensating import duty. This, however, is based on the assumption that prices in B will rise by the amount of tax. If, as is conceivable but not likely, factor prices fall with commodity prices remaining unchanged, no rebate and duty are called for. The GATT rules are based on the premise of rising prices.

[13] See *The General Agreement on Tariffs and Trade,* Part II, Articles III and XVI.

Common Market Policy

The objectives of the Common Market go beyond those of GATT. Although the rebate and compensating duty devices neutralize trade and balance-of-payments effects of origin taxes, they still call for "fiscal frontiers" in order to determine when rebates or duties are due. Yet it was hoped that, with the repeal of internal tariffs, fiscal frontiers could be discarded. To make this possible while maintaining tax neutrality, it has been decided that value-added tax rates should be made uniform across all member countries. This objective, which has not as yet been accomplished, would render export and compensating import duties unnecessary since all products, independent of origin within the market, would pay the same tax.[14] Although this would be accomplished at the price of requiring uniformity in value-added tax rates, countries would continue to set their own rates of retail sales taxes.[15] Some observers who see coordination as a transition to a United States of Europe find the requirement of rate uniformity a desirable step, while others prefer to retain such degrees of freedom for individual countries as are compatible with the achievement of common interests.[16]

Revenue Distribution and Burden Export

In concluding this discussion of product tax coordination, the question of internation equity once more arises. The sensible rule seems to be that a country shall be permitted to tax its own consumers but not those of other countries. This approach renders destination taxes (applicable to both imports and exports) equitable, but not origin taxes. The latter, in the absence of a rebate, may pass part of the burden to foreign consumers if the tax is on exports; or, in the absence of compensating import duties, foreign exporters may benefit if the tax is on import substitutes. Either result runs counter to the rule of self-finance. The rebate and compensating import duty approach is thus in line with internation equity.

D. FURTHER PROBLEMS

While most of the attention in the discussion on fiscal coordination has been directed at the tax side, expenditures also enter the picture. They do so with regard to both government purchases and transfer payments.

Joint Provision of Public Services

Nations, like municipalities, may have common concerns, involving benefit or cost spillovers which lead them to engage in joint projects. The St. Lawrence

[14] Remaining differentials in tax cost with the outside world can then be met by a common border-tax adjustment for trade with the outside world.

[15] See the *Report of the Fiscal and Financial Committee on Tax Harmonization in the Common Market.* This report, prepared under the direction of F. Neumark, is reprinted in *Tax Harmonization in the Common Market,* Chicago: Commerce Clearing House, 1963.

[16] For a discussion of various approaches, see D. Dosser, "Economic Analysis of Tax Harmonization," in C. S. Shoup (ed.), *Fiscal Harmonization in Common Markets,* vol. 1, New York: Columbia, 1967, chap. 1.

Seaway, calling for cooperation between the United States and Canada; NATO, involving a joint defense effort among a score of nations; cooperation in reducing pollution in international waterways such as the Rhine; malaria prevention programs conducted by the World Health Organization; and the operation of the United Nations are cases in point.

In all such situations, a problem of cost sharing arises. Where the number of participants is small, cost shares may be bargained out in relation to the advantages which each partner hopes to obtain. For the particular case of defense, it has been suggested that cooperation proves of greater net benefit to smaller partners since even a slight strengthening in the defense posture of a large ally provides a large increase in the degree of protection obtained by the small partner.[17] Where numbers are large, the problem is similar to that of interindividual budget determination. Some tax or assessment formula has to be used, and ability-to-pay considerations similar to those applied in the domestic context may be employed. If a proportional assessment rate is to be used, each country may be asked to pay the same percentage of its GNP or national income. If progression is to be applied, the question arises whether the rate brackets should be related to the GNP of various countries (with the countries themselves considered the contributors) or whether they should be related to the per capita incomes of the residents in various countries (with individual residents considered the basic units). This problem parallels that of distributing membership votes in a legislative body (e.g., whether the Senate or the House principle of vote apportionment should be followed).

Both types of considerations are involved in determining contributions to the budget of the United Nations. While cost shares are voted upon each year and have been subject to frequent revisions, the procedure is essentially as follows:[18] The total cost is divided among member countries in line with their *contribution base* or GNP. This makes for a proportional tax in relation to GNP, independent of per capita income. This principle is then qualified by three further provisions.

The first provision is for an exemption in relation to per capita income. Countries with very low per capita income may exclude 50 percent of their GNP from the contribution base, with the exclusion percentage declining as per capita income rises and reaching zero at a per capita income of $1,000. This "vanishing exemption" makes for a progressive tax in relation to per capita income at the lower end of the per capita income scale, where the bulk of United Nations member countries are located. The second provision sets the minimum share of any one country's contribution at 0.04 percent of the total budget. This minimum reduces the significance of the exemption provision for small countries with low per capita income. The final provision relates to the upper end of the scale where, it is said, no single country shall contribute more than a certain share. This share,

[17] See M. Olsen, Jr., and R. Zeckhauser, "An Economic Theory of Alliances," *Review of Economics and Statistics,* August 1966; and A. Peacock, "The Public Finances of Inter-Allied Defense Provision," in *Essays in Honor of Antonio de Vito de Marco,* Bari, Italy: Cacucci Editore, 1972.

[18] See John Pincus, *Economic Aid and International Cost Sharing,* Baltimore: Johns Hopkins, 1965; and James E. Price, "The Tax Burden of International Organizations," *Public Finance,* no. 4, 1967.

which limits the contribution of the United States, was until recently set at 33 percent, but has now been reduced to 25 percent. As a result, the United States share is less that it would be under the allocation-by-contribution-base approach. Moreover, it is provided that the per capita contribution of other high-income countries shall not exceed that of the United States.

As a result of these provisions, one would expect the tax rate (defined as ratio of contribution to GNP) to be generally proportional, subject to the qualifications of (1) progressivity in relation to per capita income for the larger countries with low per capita income, and (2) regressivity in relation to GNP for countries with very high per capita income. Some illustrations of the actual burden distributions for large and small countries are shown in Table 33-1. Five pairs of countries are shown, each pair including a small and a large country of about similar per capita income. They are ranked from the lowest to the highest pair. Since these results do not quite conform with the expected pattern, it appears that additional considerations have entered into the allocation of shares.

Other organizations have followed different patterns. Contributions to the International Monetary Fund (IMF) were rendered not on an annual basis, but as purchase of initial capital stock. The quotas were assigned on a "benefit basis," i.e., related to drawing rights which in turn were determined in line with likely needs for IMF credit. A somewhat similar procedure was followed in assigning

TABLE 33-1
Contributions to United Nations, 1971

Selected Member Countries	*Assigned Shares as Percentage of Total Cost (I)*	*Contribution (Thousands of Dollars) (II)*	*GNP (Billions of Dollars) (III)*	*Per Capita GNP (Dollars) (IV)*	*Contribution per Million Dollars of GNP (Dollars) (V)*
Uganda	0.04	63	1.4	136	45
India	1.55	2,355	54.7*	101	43
Singapore	0.05	78	2.2	1,043	35
Argentina	0.85	1,301	20.8	896	63
Israel	0.20	314	5.6	1,860	56
Japan	5.40	9,117	251.9	2,385	36
Netherlands	1.18	1,858	39.8	3,017	47
U.S.S.R.	14.18	22,066	648.8	2,648	34
Denmark	0.62	972	18.1	3,649	54
United States	31.52	56,312	1054.9	5,095	53

* Figure for 1970.
Sources:
Columns I and II: *Yearbook of the United Nations,* 1970, p. 863.
Columns III and IV: United Nations, *Statistical Yearbook,* 1972, table 189, p. 630; and from International Monetary Fund, *Financial Statistics,* August 1974.
Figures for U.S.S.R. based on A. Bergson, "The Comparative National Income of the U.S.S.R. and the United States," in D. J. Dailey (ed.), *International Comparisons of Prices and Output,* National Bureau of Economic Research, 1972, pp. 145–224.

subscriptions to the capital stock of the International Bank for Reconstruction and Development. All these contributions, it should be noted, involve relatively small amounts, so that the stakes for any particular country are not of major importance. Contributions to NATO, which did involve substantial amounts, have not been determined on a fixed formula basis but have been essentially subject to negotiation. The United States has met much the largest share of NATO costs, exceeding what would have been called for if assessment had been made in relation to the levels of GNP.

International Aid and Redistribution

Those considerations, humanitarian or political, that provide the basis for concern with the domestic state of income distribution cannot be limited to the confines of one's own nation. Chances are that aspects of international distribution will become an increasingly important element in the world politics of future decades. But, important though they may be, distribution issues at the international level are even more difficult to deal with than their domestic counterparts. Inequalities are larger and the organizational problem is more complex since there is no "central government" to deal with them and policies must be implemented by transfers among nations. Such measures may be in the form of development aid designed to raise the growth rate of low-income countries, this being the approach which has been followed on a modest scale over the last few decades. Or they might in time lead to redistribution out of the existing level of world income similar in nature to a negative income tax as applied to domestic redistribution. Although this approach is not foreseeable at present, it might someday become a central concern for an international system of public finance.[19]

Magnitude of Transfer Problem In dealing with the problem of distribution on an international basis, is the concern with differentials in average income among *countries?* Or is it with inequalities in the distribution of income among *individuals* on a worldwide basis without regard for national boundaries? To some extent the two problems overlap, since most poor people are in fact residents of the countries with low per capita income; but where they do not overlap, the basic problem is once more that of redistribution among individuals. Little would be gained if redistribution toward low-income countries were to accrue to a small group of high-income residents. The problem, it appears, is quite similar to that previously dealt with in examining the problem of equalization among jurisdictions in the context of fiscal federalism.[20]

The inequality of interindividual income distribution on a world basis is appalling.[21] Domestic inequalities are compounded with inequalities in average incomes across nations. The lowest 50 percent of the world's population receives less than 10 percent of world income, while the highest 20 percent receives 55 percent and the highest 10 percent receives 30 percent. This degree of inequality

[19] For a general introduction to this problem, see D. Dosser, "Towards a Theory of International Public Finance," *Kyklos,* vol. 16, no. 1, 1963.

[20] See Chap. 29, p. 628.

[21] S. Andic and A. T. Peacock, "The International Distribution of Income, 1949 and 1957," *Journal of the Royal Statistical Society,* Series A, vol. 124, 1961.

is much greater than that which prevails within countries, especially higher-income countries. About one-half the world's population, including most of Asia, Africa, and the Middle East and a good part of South America, subsists on a per capita annual income of $250 or less, the average per capita income for the lowest 50 percent being little above $100. This figure compares with an average per capita income for the upper 50 percent of over $1,300. With due allowance for the difficulties inherent in sweeping comparisons of this sort, the degree of inequality is staggering. Moreover, there is reason to expect that per capita income in the developed countries is rising more rapidly than in low-income countries, so that the situation is worsening rather than (as tends to be occurring with domestic distribution) improving over time.[22]

If total world income could be redistributed to achieve complete equalization, a per capita income of $750 could be established. Although such an income would be extremely low compared with the prevailing standards of advanced countries, it would involve a vast improvement for large parts of the world. But obviously, such equalization would be impossible while holding total income constant. Indeed, the contribution rate required from the higher-income countries to achieve even a moderate adjustment would be exceedingly high.

In dealing with the financing of economic aid, suggestions have been made that aid be financed in accordance with a pattern derived by applying, say, the United States personal income tax to the per capita income of developed countries and that shares be related to growth in per capita income.[23] But no internationally determined assessments have been made and the amounts granted in economic aid have been modest. In the mid-seventies, industrial countries contribute annually around $9 billion in official development assistance, or about one-fifth of 1 percent of their combined GNP. It is interesting, therefore, to explore what would be required to secure more substantial transfers.

Redistribution Patterns These relations are illustrated in Table 33-2. The table is based on a fairly comprehensive sample including eighty-six countries and approximately 2 billion people, with the major omission of mainland China.[24] As shown in column II, full equalization at 1966 levels would have put

[22] See G. Myrdal, *Economic Theory and Underdeveloped Regions,* London: Duckworth, 1951; and S. Andic and A. T. Peacock, op. cit.

[23] See P. N. Rosenstein-Rodan, "International Aid for Underdeveloped Countries," *Review of Economics and Statistics,* p. 110, May 1961. A similar procedure is followed by D. Dosser, "Allocating the Burden of International Aid to Less Developed Countries," ibid., May 1963; and D. Dosser and A. T. Peacock, "The International Distribution of Income with Maximum Aid," ibid., November 1964.

For further discussion, see Irving B. Kravis and Michael W. S. Davenport, "The Political Arithmetic of Burden Sharing," *Journal of Political Economy,* August 1963; John Pincus, *Economic Aid and International Cost Sharing,* Baltimore: Johns Hopkins, 1965; and R. F. Taubenfeld and H. J. Taubenfeld, "Independent Revenue for the United Nations," *International Organization,* World Peace Foundation, vol. 18, no. 2, 1964.

[24] Based on population, gross domestic product at factor cost in United States dollars, and per capita GNP of eighty-six countries; United Nations, *Yearbook of National Account Statistics 1965,* New York: United Nations, 1966, table 9A, pp. 493–496. The GNP for the U.S.S.R., not there given, is estimated at $284 billion, with a per capita GNP of $1,144. Table 33-2 is reprinted from R. A. Musgrave, *Fiscal Systems,* p. 316, with the permission of the publishers, the Yale University Press, copyright 1969.

TABLE 33-2
Patterns of World Income Redistribution*

			FLOOR OF $150		FLOOR OF $250	
	Before Equalization (I)	*Full Equalization (II)*	*A Proportional (III)*	*B Progressive (IV)*	*A Proportional (V)*	*B Progressive (VI)*
Per capita GNP, lower 50 percent	$ 118	$751	$ 164	$ 166	$ 250	$ 250
Per capita GNP, upper 50 percent	$1,366	$751	$1,321	$1,320	$1,238	$1,238
Percentage of per capita GNP contributed by (−), or received by (+):						
United States		−74	−3	−3.9	−9	−10.6
United Kingdom		−46	−3	−1.3	−9	−4.1
Sweden		−59	−3	−2.5	−9	−9.0
France		−47	−3	−1.3	−9	−4.2
U.S.S.R.		−34	−3	−0.9	−9	−3.0
Italy		−4	−3	−0.4	−9	−1.7
Japan		+27	−3	−0.2	−9	−0.7
Spain		+59	−3		−9	
India		+816	+83	+82.9	+205	+204.9
Percentage of total subsidy contributed by (−), or received by (+):						
United States		−59	−35	−46.3	−38	−45.1
United Kingdom		−5	−5	−2.1	−5	−2.4
Sweden		−1	−1	−0.7	−1	−0.8
France		−5	−4	−2.0	−5	−2.2
U.S.S.R.		−14	−18	−5.4	−20	−6.9
Italy		−0.2	−3	−0.3	−3	−0.5
Japan		+2	−4	−0.2	−4	−0.3
Spain		+1	−1		−1	
India		+46	+68	+67.6	+60	+60.4

* 1966 data.
Source: R. A. Musgrave, *Fiscal Systems,* New Haven, Conn.: Yale, 1969, p. 315. See also footnotes 24, 25, and 26 of this chapter.

per capita income at about $750. This equalization would involve contributions ranging from 74 percent of GNP for the United States, 46 percent for the United Kingdom, and 34 percent for the U.S.S.R., to 4 percent for Italy. The corresponding shares in total contributions would be 59, 5, 14, and 0.22 percent respectively. At the other end of this scale, India would receive an 816 percent increase in its per capita GNP and 46 percent of total grants.

These magnitudes are startling and would be more so if China were included. Such vast redistribution would, of course, be economically self-destructive and is not useful to pursue. Lesser targets, however, are worth exploring. Columns III and IV show such a target, with grants sufficient to establish a per capita income floor of $150. In column III, we assume these grants to be financed by a proportional tax on countries with per capita income above this level, the required rate being 3 percent. At 1966 levels, this would have involved a United States contribution of about $25 billion, or 3 percent of GNP, and would have amounted to 35 percent of the total transfer. Under the progressive contribution schedule of column IV, the United States contribution would rise to 4 percent of GNP, and its share to 46.3 percent.[25] Columns V and VI show corresponding approaches to the somewhat more ambitious target of setting the income floor at $250. The required proportional rate would now be 9 percent, and the United States share would be somewhat higher.[26]

In the nature of the case, the United States share is very large, reflecting the combination of high per capita income and a large population. This ratio, however, is not very meaningful. What matters are the respective fractions of GNP that would be absorbed in such contributions. These ratios, as shown in the table, are very much larger than current levels of foreign aid, even if the implementation of relatively modest targets is considered. The negative income tax, international model, is a startling concept to contemplate.

Quite apart from the question of how much is to be contributed and received by various countries, implementation of such a plan (like equalizing aid to domestic jurisdictions) raises further problems of internal use and "own" effort. Thus, receipt of aid by a country may be conditional upon its own effort to secure a modicum of internal redistribution and upon assurance that the aid will be used so as to raise incomes at the lower end of the internal income scale. Moreover, the scope of the redistribution problem greatly depends on the number of individuals whose income level is to be supported and hence is closely linked to population policy.

Development Aid As has been pointed out many times, distribution policy must not be considered only as a matter of redistributing slices in a given pie. Effects on the size of the pie, in particular the rate of economic growth, must be studied as well. If this viewpoint holds for the case of national redistribution, it holds especially at the international level where the potential scale of distribu-

[25] The progressive rates used in col. IV are: per capita income up to $500 nontaxable, with rates of 1, 3, 5, and 7 percent applied to successive $500 increments in per capita income.

[26] The progressive rates used in col. VI are: per capita income up to $500 nontaxable, and rates of 4, 5, 9, and 18.2 percent applied to successive $500 increments in per capita income.

tional adjustment is so much larger. Nothing would be gained if the contribution of developed countries were pushed so far as to interfere with their economic ability to render continued aid.

It is generally said in this connection that the best way to render economic aid is to divert capital flows from high-income to low-income countries. In the process, world output might be increased, as capital should be more efficient in countries where the capital-labor ratio is as yet very low; and there would be a redistribution of income from labor in high-income countries (which would then operate with less capital) to labor in low-income countries whose productivity would be increased by the rising capital-labor ratio.[27]

Development aid through capital formation thus contributes to efficient resource use by diverting investment to capital-poor countries. Moreover, it holds out the hope that developing countries, after a successful "takeoff," can continue their growth independently, thus avoiding the "being on welfare" syndrome, which is as disturbing in the international setting as it is in the domestic. Fiscal measures are important in this process not only in extending direct aid or substantial loans, but also in encouraging the flow of private capital through tax incentives. While aid of this sort is limited by the absorptive capacity of low-income countries, available funds have hardly reached this upper limit.

Stabilization Policies

As noted in the earlier discussion of stabilization policy, the task of stabilization is more difficult in an open than in a closed economy. Not only must repercussions on trade and capital flows be taken into account in securing domestic balance, but (given the setting of fixed exchange rates) allowance must also be made for the maintenance of foreign balance. A sustained deficit on trade account is tolerable only if offset by sustained capital inflow, or if there are large exchange reserves on hand.

The constraints which this imposes on the stabilization policy of any one country, especially if its economy is highly open, were noted previously and need not be reexamined here.[28] A word might be added, however, regarding the need for international cooperation. This imperative has been recognized in the monetary field since the end of World War II. With the demise of the adjustment mechanism provided through price level adaptation under the gold standard, a new mechanism had to be provided. This was sought in the liquidity reserves provided by the International Monetary Fund. As recent years have shown, this mechanism proved insufficient, and new approaches are under consideration, approaches which will not only increase the liquidity reserve but also provide some step toward exchange rate flexibility.

Less attention has been given to international coordination of fiscal policies, but it promises to become an increasingly important factor in the Common Market. With rising mobility of commodity and factor flows across borders and

[27] The suppliers of capital in the high-income countries will not lose but gain as larger returns are obtained from investment in low-income countries. Allowance must be made, however, for the greater risks that frequently accompany such investment.

[28] See p. 527.

the broadening of national capital markets into a common pool, it will become more and more difficult for any one country to carry on an independent stabilization policy, whether monetary or fiscal. London, Bonn, and Paris will find themselves increasingly in the position of Albany, Lansing, and Sacramento, and resort to a Common Market (i.e., federal) stabilization policy will become unavoidable.

E. SUMMARY

In this chapter we have dealt with the implications of the fact that there coexist many different fiscal systems which are brought in touch with one another through the international flows of capital and trade. This fact poses problems with regard to both the equity and the efficiency aspects of taxation:

1. With regard to equity among taxpayers, considerations of horizontal and vertical equity may now be extended to include all taxes which a person pays to whatever jurisdiction, as distinct from taxes paid to the individual's jurisdiction of major tax allegiance only.

2. Moreover, there now appears the additional equity question of how the tax base arising from international transactions should be divided among the participating countries, or the problem of internation equity.

3. With regard to efficiency effects, a distinction is now drawn between efficiency as seen from the point of view of worldwide resource use and efficiency as seen from a nation's point of view.

In dealing with the coordination of income and profits taxes, many technical difficulties arise:

4. A United States resident earning income abroad will include such income for purposes of the United States income tax, but he or she may credit foreign tax payments against this tax. This provision applies to both wage and investment income.

5. Foreign branches of United States corporations are taxed abroad, but their income is included in the income of the parent corporation for purposes of United States corporation tax, with the foreign profits tax again credited against the United States tax.

6. Much the largest part of United States direct foreign investment is made through subsidiaries of United States corporations. Their tax treatment differs from that of branches in that the income of the subsidiary is included in the parent's income for purposes of United States tax only when this income is repatriated.

7. An important policy issue is whether foreign taxes should be credited against United States tax or deducted from taxable income. The former is in line with world efficiency, the latter with national efficiency.

8. A second important question is whether the United States tax on subsidiary income should be deferred until repatriation, a problem which also involves tax avoidance through tax-haven operations.

9. A further important policy issue relates to the way in which profits arising from international operations should be divided among the taxing authorities of the participating countries. The so-called arm's-length rule is used in this connection.

In dealing with the coordination of product taxes, our major concern was with potential distorting effects on commodity flows.

10. Destination taxes, e.g., retail sales taxes, do not interfere with commodity flows. They do so only if limited to imported goods, that is, if imposed as tariffs.

11. Origin taxes, or product taxes imposed in the country of production, do interfere with the efficient flow of trade since they affect relative costs of production, thus interfering with the flow of trade based on comparative advantage.

12. Such effects are neutralized, however, if product taxes are rebated at the point of export. GATT rules determine which taxes may be thus rebated.

13. Common Market policy in Europe aims at adoption of a uniform value-added tax, thus achieving efficiency without the need for export rebates.

Among further aspects of international fiscal coordination, the following points were noted:

14. Nations, like states or municipalities, may engage in the joint provision of public services. Such participation poses the problem of how cost shares should be divided among them.

15. Problems of distribution policy similarly may extend across borders, as reflected in economic aid to developing countries. With rising differentials in per capita income, this policy is likely to become a major issue in the future.

16. Highly open economies cannot engage in independent stabilization policy but, instead, policy coordination is called for.

FURTHER READINGS

Dosser, D.: "Economic Analysis of Tax Harmonization, in C. S. Shoup (ed.), *Fiscal Harmonization in Common Markets,* New York: Columbia, 1967, chap. 1.

Musgrave, P. B.: *United States Taxation of Foreign Investment Income: Issues and Arguments,* Cambridge, Mass.: Harvard Law School, International Tax Program, 1969.

Musgrave, R. A.: *Fiscal Systems,* New Haven, Conn.: Yale, 1969.

Chapter 34

Development Finance*

A. Ingredients of Development: *Capital Formation; Technology, Enterprise, and Efficiency; Social and Political Factors; Foreign Exchange; Balance and Bottlenecks; Role of Fiscal System.* **B. Fiscal Policy, Stability, and Growth:** *Revenue Requirements; Taxation, Saving, and the Distribution of Income; Foreign Borrowing; Aggregate Demand, Inflation, and Employment.* **C. Tax-Structure Policy:** *Taxable Capacity and Tax Effort; Tax-Structure Development; Individual Income Tax; Business Income Tax; Land Taxes; Wealth and Property Taxes; Commodity Taxes and Tariffs.* **D. Tax Incentives:** *Domestic Incentives; Capital versus Employment Incentives; Incentives to Foreign Capital; Export Incentives.* **E. Expenditure Policy. F. Summary.**

Public finances, on both the tax and expenditure sides of the budget, play a key role in the process of economic development. Many of the difficulties which obstruct the economic progress of low-income countries call for solution by the public sector; yet the institutional and social settings of such countries complicate

* *Reader's Guide to Chapter 34:* Many of the problems discussed in the preceding chapters, especially Chapters 7, 8, 22, and 23, apply as much to development finance as to the finance of developed countries. However, development finance poses additional problems and some of those previously considered, such as tax structure design covered in Chapters 10 through 15, appear in a somewhat different light. For this reason, the major aspects of development finance are reviewed in this concluding chapter.

and constrain the task of budgetary policy. For these reasons, the problems of development finance deserve special and separate consideration.

A. INGREDIENTS OF DEVELOPMENT

The requirements for economic development in low-income countries include those needed for continued economic growth in the comparatively highly developed countries, but much more besides.[1] To achieve this growth, not only are capital formation (including investment in both physical and human capital) and technological progress needed, but also certain changes are required in the social and institutional settings which have been both cause and effect of a low level of economic development. The public sector has an important part to play in all these ingredients of development.

Capital Formation

A fundamental requirement of economic development is an increased rate of capital formation relative to that of population expansion. Such capital formation should be broadly defined to include all expenditures of a productivity-increasing nature. It may take the form of investment in the public or the private sector. Particularly in the early stages of development, the former is of critical importance since, in the form of so-called infrastructure (power, communications, port facilities, etc.), it sets the framework for subsequent manufacturing investment whether public (in the socialist economies) or private (in the mixed economy case). Furthermore, capital formation includes investment in human resources in the form of education and training as well as in physical assets. Indeed, where human productivity is adversely affected by malnutrition and disease, increased food consumption and provision of sanitation and health facilities take on the aspect of investment in human capital.[2] Thus the use of resources for productivity-enhancing purposes may take a wide variety of forms, and the actual mix must be determined in the process of expenditure and resource planning. Moreover, priorities change over time, and with them, the optimum investment mix.

Leaving aside for the time being the problem of investment planning, let us focus on the sources from which these additional resources for investment can be drawn. Unless unutilized resources can be brought into use or additional resources can be procured from abroad, there has to be a reduction in current consumption to release the necessary resources for investment purposes. To a certain extent, the mobilization of unused resources may be possible. It has been argued, for example, that many low-income economies possess substantial amounts of underutilized labor which may be put to work on simple forms of public capital formation, such as drainage, irrigation, roads, and dams.[3] The

[1] See Chap. 22 for a discussion of budgetary policies to promote growth in the setting of the relatively developed economies.

[2] See C. S. Shoup, "Production from Consumption," *Public Finance,* Chicago: Aldine, 1969, p. 173.

[3] See W. A. Lewis, "Economic Development with Unlimited Supplies of Labor," *Manchester School,* August 1954.

government then enters only as organizer of this improved resource use. But this source of capital formation has its inherent limits; and putting underemployed labor to work may itself require certain supporting investments.

A further possibility is to obtain the needed investment resources from abroad in the form of official loans and grants or as private investment. Neither source, however, is likely to do the whole job, and in any case, will not be forthcoming without supportive "own" effort on the part of the host country. Private investors from abroad, like private investors at home, require the necessary infrastructure investment; and official aid will most likely be conditional upon well-formulated development plans which include provision for substantial tax-financed increases in domestic investment.

Unavoidably, then, a large part of the problem remains one of diverting the needed resources for development from their use in current consumption. In a centrally controlled economy with public enterprise predominating, this shift can be done by holding returns paid to factors of production below their marginal product earnings; but in a decentralized economy, such internal sources of capital formation must come from public or private savings. To some extent, if conditions are rendered congenial, this increased rate of saving may be generated voluntarily in the private sector. Here, the government may be helpful in securing reasonable monetary stability so that savings habits are not discouraged by continuing inflation; also, the government may play a part in facilitating, or itself creating, the appropriate financial institutions to attract household savings and direct them into productive uses. The latter is of particular importance for the small saver for whom few uses for personal savings exist beyond high-risk money lending or the collection of valuables like gold. Taxation, as will be seen, has an important role to play in providing savings incentives and/or disincentives to luxury consumption. Business saving may also be encouraged through a system of business income taxation which encourages the retention and reinvestment of earnings.

Voluntary private saving, while useful and important, cannot be expected to be sufficient in itself, particularly at an early stage of development. An economic climate conducive to private saving takes time to develop, and in the meantime, the less developed country must look to the government budget as the most promising source of finance for development purposes. We again define government savings in the "classical" sense as equal to total revenue minus government consumption expenditures.[4] Thus public sector saving may be increased by raising total tax revenue and/or reducing current expenditures. Tax revenue must be looked on as a precious and scarce resource, hard to come by, and many a development plan has come to grief as a result of the profligate spending policies of the government, which in turn was often acting under political pressure.

Government savings generated by a surplus in the current budget may be used to finance capital formation in either the public or the private sector. In the latter case, the government savings may be channeled into private investment as

[4] This concept of government saving must be distinguished from the surplus in the *total* budget, i.e., total revenue minus *total* expenditures, which is relevant for the management of aggregate demand. See p. 508.

debt or equity capital through the medium of government lending agencies or development banks.

Technology, Enterprise, and Efficiency

Improved technology is another important element in the development process, including both manufacturing and agriculture. The massive improvements in agricultural productivity in a number of developing countries over the past decade attest to the benefits to be derived from improved technology in that sector. A principal benefit of private investment from abroad lies in the improved technologies which it brings, although it is important that these be adapted to the particular conditions and resource endowments of the less developed countries (LDCs) themselves. Tax provisions may be designed to stimulate and encourage the use of improved techniques.

Business enterprise is needed if a flourishing private sector is to develop alongside the public sector. In its absence, government enterprise must fill the gap. As with technology, the tax structure can be designed so as to encourage (or at least not to discourage) the willingness to undertake productive investment.

Needless to say, the issue of efficiency in resource use becomes of critical importance in the resource-scarce LDCs, and in the public no less than in the private sector. This factor involves proper expenditure evaluation on the part of the government as well as a development plan which avoids wasteful bottlenecks arising during the development process. Furthermore, distortions arising in the pattern of taxes and tariffs, which in turn induce an inefficient pattern of production in the private sector, should be avoided.

Social and Political Factors

Some of the most intractable problems associated with economic development include the whole range of social attitudes and organizations which have to be modified if development is to proceed. At the same time, a substantial degree of political stability is also needed to allow individual initiative to flourish, development plans to be implemented, and the necessary economic transformation to take place. It is therefore crucial that the fruits of development be bestowed broadly and that extremes of income inequalities prevalent in many of the LDCs be eliminated. While certain kinds of redistribution (e.g., land reform) can be undertaken without prejudice to the level of output and indeed may be helpful in this respect, conflicts can arise between policies directed toward a more equitable distribution of income and the objective of increased saving and investment. Whereas public saving can be increased by raising the level of taxation, private incentives to invest may have to be traded off against redistributive tax policies.

Foreign Exchange

Foreign trade plays a critical role in many of the less developed economies. With limited internal markets, foreign trade involvement permits greater specialization, economies of scale, and exercise of comparative advantage. In addition, foreign exchange earnings allow the purchase of certain products (such as machinery and equipment) which are needed for the development process but for which the necessary technology is not available domestically. Yet another contribution of exports to development may be the provision of an expanding market around which "linkage" investments may be made, thereby creating an "export-led" nexus of development.

Thus, public policy must be concerned with the division of resources not only between consumption and investment but also between domestic and traded products; and among traded products there are both import-competing and exported goods. The tax structure, again, has a part to play in the general allocation process embodied in the development plan.

Balance and Bottlenecks

As economic development proceeds, various bottlenecks or limitations to the growth rate may crop up.[5] For example, it has been suggested that in the early stage, the rate of internal saving is the controlling factor. As the rate of saving, and with it the growth of the economy, increases (aided, perhaps, by capital inflow from abroad), the absorptive capacity of the economy becomes the limiting factor, i.e., all the supportive factors which are needed to render the investment productive. Finally, the development process begins to create strains in the balance of payments, outstripping the capacity of the economy to earn foreign exchange to meet imports through exports. Thus, the resources made available for development purposes may go to waste because of these bottlenecks. A sound development plan should therefore endeavor to keep the process running smoothly by a policy of balanced growth. Tax policy in particular may be employed to encourage capital inflow as well as to affect the level of imports and exports.

Role of Fiscal System

It is thus evident that the fiscal system plays a multifold role in the process of economic development:

1. The level of taxation affects the level of public saving and thus the volume of resources available for capital formation.

2. Both the level and the structure of taxation affect the level of private saving.

3. Public investment is needed to provide infrastructure types of investment.

4. A system of tax incentives and penalties may be designed to influence the efficiency of resource utilization.

5. The distribution of tax burdens (along with the distribution of expenditure benefits) plays a large part in promoting an equitable distribution of the fruits of economic development.

6. The tax treatment of investment from abroad may affect the volume of capital inflow and the rate of reinvestment of earnings therefrom.

7. The pattern of taxation of imports and exports relative to that of domestic products will affect the foreign trade balance.

[5] See H. Chenery and A. Strout, "Foreign Assistance and Economic Development," *American Economic Review*, September 1966.

B. FISCAL POLICY, STABILITY, AND GROWTH

The role of fiscal policy in securing stability and growth in the LDCs is of fundamental importance. We begin by considering certain macro aspects of this problem.

Revenue Requirements

To begin with, it is helpful to view the problem in terms of a fully employed economy and to focus on the role of fiscal policy as a means of raising the domestic savings ratio. In making a first approximation to the amount of tax revenue needed to achieve a certain target rate of growth, differences between various sources of tax revenue are disregarded. Suppose that the objective is to achieve a 2 percent annual rate of growth in income per head. With, say, a 2 percent annual growth rate of population, national income must then grow at slightly above 4 percent per year. This target rate of growth requires a certain rate of capital formation, or investment expenditures as a percent of national income. This ratio z may be crudely estimated by the use of an incremental capital–output ratio, and is defined as follows:

$$z = \frac{\Delta K}{\Delta Y} = \frac{I}{\Delta Y}$$

K being the capital stock, I the level of annual investment ($=\Delta K$), and Y national income.[6] If g is the desired rate of growth,

$$g = \frac{\Delta Y}{Y}$$

the required investment rate I/Y may be obtained by substitution as

$$\frac{I}{Y} = \frac{\Delta K}{\Delta Y} \cdot \frac{\Delta Y}{Y} = zg$$

Thus, if $z = 3$, and $g = 4$ percent, $I/Y = 12$ percent. This investment ratio must be matched by a corresponding savings ratio to assure economic balance. Therefore, the economy must save 12 percent of national income to grow at the desired rate of 4 percent. We must have

$$S_p + S_g = 0.12\,Y \tag{1}$$

where S_p is private saving and S_g is government saving. The level of private saving is given by

$$S_p = s(Y - T)$$

[6] In reality, macroplanning of this type would proceed on a disaggregated basis in which a weighted average of incremental capital–output ratios for different sectors of the economy is applied.

or

$$S_p = s(1 - t)Y \tag{2}$$

where s is the propensity to save out of disposable income, T is tax revenue, and t the tax rate. The level of government saving equals

$$S_g = tY - \alpha Y \tag{3}$$

where α is current expenditures of government as a fraction of national income.[7] Substituting equations 2 and 3 into 1, we obtain

$$t = \frac{0.12 - s + \alpha}{1 - s} \tag{4}$$

Using a typical value for s of 3 percent and for α of 10 percent, we obtain $t =$ 19.6. That is to say, a tax rate of 19.6 percent is needed to obtain a growth rate of 4 percent.[8] With government current expenditures equal to 10 percent of national income, government saving equal to 9.6 percent of national income may be either used to finance public investment or loaned out to finance additional private investment. Having made this first approximation to its revenue needs, the government must then judge whether such a target is feasible and can be attained under any realistic tax reform program. This decision will depend on the institutional framework, the capabilities of tax administration, and the political will to make the necessary tax assessments stick. But two points should be noted. First, a very large effort is required to raise the revenue-income ratio by even one percentage point. Second, a development plan which is too ambitious to be implemented and requires more than the tax system can reasonably be expected to produce may be worse than no development plan at all, for it invites the waste of uncompleted projects and the danger of inflation, not to mention the social repercussions arising from unfulfilled expectations.

Taxation, Saving, and the Distribution of Income

We must now correct the simplifying assumption of the preceding section that all tax dollars are equally useful in raising the level of domestic savings. Indeed, the central problem of tax policy in developing countries is how to obtain the necessary revenue while at the same time providing some correction for a typically high degree of inequality in the distribution of income, but without interfering unduly with private saving and investment.

In Table 34-1, the setting to this problem is presented in more concrete form. The distribution of income, consumption, and saving is shown as it might apply

[7] Government saving thus defined equals the surplus in the current budget. See p. 511.

[8] Since the required savings rate equals zg, equation 4 may be rewritten as

$$t = \frac{zg - s + \alpha}{1 - s}$$

TABLE 34-1
Distribution Patterns in Less Developed Countries

	PERCENTAGE SHARES IN TOTAL		
Ranking by Income	*Income (I)*	*Consumption (II)*	*Saving (III)*
Top 1 percent	20	18	50
Next 9 percent	25	23	50
Next 15 percent	20	22	0
Lowest 75 percent	35	37	0
Total	100	100	100

Notes: The data in column I reflect a typical pattern among available distribution estimates for Latin American countries. Columns II and III include the authors' best guesses but probably reflect the typical situation.

in a typical LDC, say one of the Latin American countries. We find that the upper 10 percent of income recipients receive some 45 percent of income and the lowest 75 percent receive 35 percent. The corresponding shares in consumption are estimated at 41 percent and 37 percent while the shares in saving are 100 and 0 percent. The degree of inequality is thus substantially greater than in developed countries such as the United States, where the corresponding income shares are 30 and 47 percent.

In addition to the highly unequal distribution of income, two other features stand out. First, a very substantial share of total income goes into "luxury" consumption. Defining luxury consumption as per capita consumption in excess of the average per capita consumption and taking total consumption to be 95 percent of total income, it appears that luxury consumption accounts for about 36 percent of income.[9] This means that luxury consumption provides a substantial potential reserve for additional taxation. Second, such private savings as there are originate largely in the very high income brackets, including corporate savings in which equity shares are owned. This means that highly progressive income taxation as well as high rates of profits tax cut heavily into private-sector saving and thereby retard development.[10] Putting the two features together, we note that the key to development finance appears to lie in progressive consumption taxation.[11]

Ideally, this taxation would be applied in the form of a personal consumption tax, but few if any LDCs could do so effectively. As we have noted before, effective application of such a tax to higher incomes would require balance-sheet accounting as well as the reporting of earnings, which is difficult even for developed

[9] From Table 34-1, it can be calculated that the upper 25 percent of the population partake of 63 percent of consumption. Their luxury consumption (defined as that in excess of average per capita consumption) thus represents 63 − 25, or 38 percent of total consumption. Since consumption as a whole is 95 percent of total income, this "excess" equals .95 × 38, or 36 percent of total income.

[10] For emphasis on the importance of profits in the industrial sector as a source of saving, see W. A. Lewis, *The Theory of Economic Growth,* Homewood, Ill.: Irwin, chap. 5.

[11] See N. Kaldor, "The Expenditure Tax in a System of Personal Taxation," in R. M. Bird and O. Oldman (eds.), *Readings on Taxation in Developing Countries,* 2d ed., Cambridge, Mass.: Harvard Law School, International Tax Program, 1967, pp. 253–273.

countries.[12] Practical policy must therefore make do with a less perfect approach, i.e., a set of excise taxes which impose higher rates on items that weigh more heavily in the outlays of higher-income households. To this may be added a progressive property tax on residences to deal with housing consumption. In this way, revenue can be obtained by drawing on the pool of luxury consumption, thereby reducing consumption inequality while stimulating rather than depressing saving.

Lest the advantages of this approach be overstated, two shortcomings need be noted. For one thing, there still remains the problem of detrimental effects on work incentives. Such effects may be less in the case of consumption taxation than with progressive income taxation, but they are not eliminated. For another, progressive consumption taxes can reduce inequality of consumption but not inequality of income and wealth. Since the distribution of income and wealth is also significant in securing a broad sharing of development gains, progressive consumption taxes cannot entirely replace progressive income and wealth taxation. A proper balance between these forms of taxation is called for, such balance being superior to excessive reliance on the income tax approach.

Foreign Borrowing

Prior consideration was given to the role of loan finance in economic development when discussing public debt, but the problem should be noted once more in the present context.[13] The earlier conclusion was that development requires capital formation and that capital formation requires saving. Public investment which is financed by borrowing does not add to capital formation if it merely diverts funds otherwise available for private investment. This assumption also underlies the preceding model on the basis of which the required rate of taxation was determined.

The situation is different, however, if borrowing is from abroad. In this case, additional resources become available, as borrowing is accompanied by increased imports. This borrowing provides additional resources for investment and permits financing a given growth rate with a lower rate of tax and a higher rate of current consumption. While the net gain to future generations will be less than it would have been with tax finance, their surrender of consumption (to service the foreign debt) will be less burdensome than tax finance would have been to the initial generation. The reason is that other factors of production, such as labor, share in the productivity gain generated by the increased rate of capital formation. Because of this growth, the future cutback in consumption is made out of a higher level of income, and since the marginal utility of consumption declines with rising consumption levels, the resulting burden will be less severe.

It is thus the income gain to domestic factors which renders foreign borrowing such an important instrument of development policy. Other useful functions of capital import include the provision of foreign exchange and the collateral

[12] See p. 333. A particular difficulty in the case of LDCs is tax avoidance by shifting funds abroad, permitting tax-free spending outside the country. Tight exchange controls may therefore be necessary to close this loophole.

[13] See p. 607.

advantages gained from the introduction of advanced technology and managerial know-how.[14]

Aggregate Demand, Inflation, and Employment

In the preceding discussion, we have proceeded on the assumption of a fully employed economy. In this setting, the appropriate level of aggregate demand is given by the available level of output as valued at current prices. The basic rule for fiscal and monetary policy in this case is to let aggregate expenditures rise with the growth in full-employment output, neither faster nor slower. We now consider two ways in which this conclusion may be qualified.

Inflation as a Source of Saving It has been argued at times that some degree of inflation will contribute to development because it may impose forced saving upon consumers. If credit expansion finances increased capital formation (public or private), rising prices reduce the real income of consumers, thus lowering consumption in real terms. In this way, inflation may serve to transfer real resources to capital formation.

Such indeed could be the outcome, but one hesitates to prescribe it as a policy guide. For one thing, inflationary credit creation may be used to finance consumption (especially public consumption) rather than capital formation. For another, the "inflation tax" is among the least equitable of all taxes. Moreover, the inflationary process easily becomes a habit and leads to distortion of investment decisions. Perhaps worst of all, inflationary expectations may lead to a reduction in private saving propensities. For these and other reasons, inflation cannot be recommended as a legitimate approach to development policy.

Underemployment and Unemployment The other side of the coin is whether aggregate demand management may not also be needed to assure full employment of resources. Put differently, the question is whether unemployment in LDCs is of a kind which can be remedied by an increase in aggregate demand, as is frequently possible in developed countries. This problem arises especially in the context of agriculture and migration to urban areas.

It is widely observed in LDCs that there is a surplus of agricultural labor in the sense that labor is only partially employed, except at harvesttime. Cannot such labor be drawn into industrial employment by increased demand based on a higher level of expenditures? The answer depends on the wages which such labor could obtain outside agriculture. If labor productivity is low, the gain might not suffice to offset the increased living costs which are incurred in movement from the farm. The problem may thus be one of low productivity rather than of unemployment; and if this is so, the remedy lies in capital formation and increased productivity rather than in a higher level of expenditures.

The existence of heavy urban unemployment in turn may come about as the

[14] As with all good things in life, there are also disadvantages and dangers. Foreign capital import may bring foreign control and retard the development of domestic managerial talent. For an emphasis on these aspects, see A. O. Hirschman, "How to Divest in Latin America and Why," in A. O. Hirschman (ed.), *A Bias for Hope,* New Haven, Conn.: Yale, 1971, pp. 225–253.

result of out-migration, attracted by what appear to be high wages in the industrial or urban sector; but minimum wage legislation or union demands may place a floor below such wages which in turn may make it impossible to absorb the labor influx. As noted below, a remedy lies in tax provisions which counter the overpricing of labor in the market, with increased aggregate demand again an inappropriate measure.

At the same time, these difficulties do not preclude the existence of genuine "Keynesian" unemployment which can be met by more expansionary demand policy. Some observers have noted that in Latin American countries, existing capital stock is frequently underutilized, so increased employment should be possible. An expansionary fiscal policy, combined with measures to secure the necessary supportive resources, may be helpful in bringing this about.

C. TAX-STRUCTURE POLICY

We now turn to more specific issues of tax policy, beginning with a consideration of tax effort.

Taxable Capacity and Tax Effort

While it is important, in line with our earlier reasoning, to know what overall level of tax revenue is required to secure a given growth target, the feasibility of achieving that level of taxation is an important consideration which must be allowed for when the target is set. Tax policy must be considered along with other aspects of development policy, but it must not be looked at as the "dependent variable" in the system which will automatically respond to the requirements placed upon it.

How, then, can one judge what tax effort a country is capable of, and how can its tax performance be measured? We have noted in our earlier discussion of tax-structure development that the tax-to-GNP ratios in less developed countries are typically quite low, ranging from 8 to 18 percent. Among Latin American countries with per capita incomes below $400, the typical ratio is around 14 percent, with some countries as low as 8 percent. The ratios for African and Asian countries with similar per capita incomes tend to be somewhat (though not much) higher. This compares with developed-country ratios of 30 to 40 percent, as was shown in Figure 6-4 on page 139.

Why is it that the tax effort in developing countries is so much lower? Or does the lower ratio in fact signify a lower effort? The answer depends on what the term "tax effort" is taken to mean. An international lending agency may wish to make its aid contingent on the recipient country's making an adequate tax effort of its own.. The lending agency may then require a country with a higher per capita income to show a higher revenue ratio in order to demonstrate the same level of tax effort.

A low-income country has less scope for the transfer of resources to public use.[15] At a very low level of per capita income, all private income is needed to

[15] See p. 145, where the relationship of "tax handles" to economic structure was discussed.

meet the very necessities of life, such as food and shelter. Unless the public use of funds is to provide equally basic necessities (e.g., minimal health and sanitation programs), the diversion of funds involves an insupportably heavy current burden. This conclusion is modified where a highly unequal income distribution results in substantial luxury consumption. As noted before, this factor is frequently of considerable importance as a potential source of taxation.

Apart from the level and distribution of income, the availability of "tax handles" is related to the economic structure of the country. Thus, the administration of an income tax is much more difficult where employment is in small establishments. Profits taxation is not feasible until accounting practices attain minimal standards, and it is difficult if firms are small and unstable. Product taxes cannot be imposed at the retail level if retail establishments are small and impermanent. Effective land taxation is difficult where food is home-consumed, the agricultural sector is largely nonmonetized, and land surveys are inadequate in providing proper valuations. On the other hand, taxation is simplified in a highly open economy where imports and exports pass through major ports and thus can be readily established by tax authorities.

Finally, the feasibility of taxation depends upon how society views the need for compliance, the extent to which the courts are willing to enforce tax laws, and the availability of a competent and honest staff of tax administrators. Resort to tax farming, i.e., a system where the collector is given a percentage of his tax take as an incentive, may be a helpful short-run device, as may be the assignment of revenue quotas to tax officials, but these are not methods on which a durable and equitable tax structure can be built.

For these and other reasons, a realistic appraisal of tax effort has to allow for such variables as (1) the level of per capita income, (2) the distribution of income, (3) the size of employing establishments, (4) the size of retail establishments, (5) the distribution of profits by firms, (6) the openness of the economy, and (7) the extent to which agriculture is integrated into the monetary economy. In addition, there are the less tangible factors of social mores, legal systems, and administrative capacity, although it could be argued that these are not admissible as excuses for poor revenue performance. Given these complexities, it is hardly possible to devise a simple formula by which tax effort can be measured. Application of a "model tax structure" such as is used in measuring tax effort among municipalities and states also has its difficulties.[16] The weights assigned to particular taxes which are suitable for one country may not be so for another. A highly agricultural country must rely more heavily on land taxation than an industrial one; the accessibility of product taxation is greater in an economy with an urban population permitting large retail establishments than in a decentralized rural economy; and so forth.[17]

[16] See p. 646.

[17] If a meaningful standard system could be devised, the effort ratio might then be measured as $(T_i/T_i^s)/(Y_i/Y_a)$ where T_i is the ith country's actual revenue, T_i^s is the revenue which it would obtain from the standard system, and Y_i and Y_a are the per capita incomes for the ith and the average country respectively. For a discussion of such indices, see R. M. Bird, "A Note on Tax Sacrifice Comparisons," *National Tax Journal,* September 1964; H. Aaron, "Some Criticism of Tax Burden Indices," ibid., March 1965; and Bird, "Comment," ibid., September 1965.

Notwithstanding these differences, it is usually argued that an LDC should be expected to achieve a tax-GNP ratio of at least 18 percent. Assuming one-half of this to be spent for current services and adding a private sector savings rate of 3 percent, an overall savings rate of 12 percent would be achieved. This has been postulated by W. A. Lewis as constituting the desirable minimum level.[18]

Tax-Structure Development

The problems associated with the design and administration of various taxes differ with the structure of the economy in which they are applied and with its climate of public attitudes toward taxation. However, they also differ with stages of economic development, and some general tax-structure characteristics in relation to per capita income may be observed.

Table 34-2 gives tax-structure comparisons for samples of countries at various levels of per capita income. We note the importance of taxes on external trade (mainly customs duties) and of taxes on domestic production and sales for low-income countries, as well as the low share of income taxes. As per capita income rises, the importance of income taxes increases relative to that of customs

TABLE 34-2
Average Composition of Tax Structures for Sample of Countries at Various Levels of Per Capita Income

Per Capita Income in Dollars	*Income Taxes*	*Taxes on Property*	*Taxes on International Trade*	*Taxes on Production and Sales*	*Total, Excluding Payroll Taxes**	*Payroll Taxes*	*Total*
			AS PERCENTAGE OF GNP				
Under 100	1.9	0.5	4.6	3.4	11.6	0.5	12.0
100–200	2.6	0.3	4.4	4.5	12.7	0.5	13.2
200–300	2.8	0.6	5.5	4.3	14.4	1.4	15.8
300–400	3.6	1.0	4.6	5.2	13.4	3.0	16.4
400–500	3.4	1.2	3.5	4.2	12.1	2.1	14.3
500–900	4.8	1.4	2.6	1.7	16.7	2.9	19.6
United States	14.8	5.7	0.3	5.3	25.0	5.7	30.8
			AS PERCENTAGE OF TOTAL TAX REVENUE				
Under 100	16.3	4.1	38.5	28.0	96.7	3.3	100
100–200	19.6	2.0	33.4	33.8	96.3	3.7	100
200–300	17.5	3.9	35.2	27.3	91.3	8.7	100
300–400	22.3	5.9	27.9	30.6	81.8	18.2	100
400–500	23.4	8.4	34.7	29.2	84.9	15.1	100
500–900	24.7	7.5	13.5	8.5	85.3	14.7	100
United States	48.2	11.9	0.9	17.2	81.5	18.5	100

* Includes taxes not previously listed.
Note: Figures shown represent the unweighted averages for countries within each income category.
Sources:
For United States: See Table 9-1, p. 207. Data for 1970.
For other countries: Derived from R. J. Chelliah, "Trends in Taxation in Developing Countries," *International Monetary Fund Staff Papers,* July 1971, table 6, pp. 278–279.

[18] See Lewis, *The Theory of Economic Growth,* op. cit.

duties and taxes on domestic sales and production. Payroll taxes also rise in relative importance as per capita income increases.

In addition to changing shares under the major headings of the table, the nature of the various taxes also is subject to change. Thus, taxes classified as income taxes in low-income countries are frequently capitation taxes which bear little resemblance to the personalized individual income tax of developed countries. Similarly, the so-called business income tax is often closer to a sales tax than to the profits tax as applied in the developed countries, and so forth.[19]

Individual Income Tax

Turning now to particular taxes, we begin with the individual income tax. For various reasons, the individual income tax does not and cannot be expected to occupy the central position in the tax structure of LDCs which it typically holds in developed countries. Nevertheless, the income tax should be established early and strengthened as development proceeds. It is elastic to growth in GNP and therefore a promising revenue source for development finance. Its contribution to total revenue in Latin American countries typically ranges around 20 percent and is thus a significant part of the revenue picture. This is true even though the feasibility of collecting a tax on wage and salary income in LDCs tends to be restricted to government, foreign corporations, and the rather limited group of large local enterprises. Employees of small establishments and the large group of self-employed, especially in agriculture, typically remain outside the orbit of the income tax. In part, this reflects exemption levels which are set high relative to average income, but it is also the result of ineffective enforcement and administration.

Difficulties in reaching capital income are even greater. The principle of self-assessment as followed in the United States is not workable. Official assessments are frequently negotiated rather than objectively based, and there is a substantial lag of final tax payment behind the income year. Use of tax withholding helps to speed up tax collections and is all to the good, but its applicability tends to be limited to the very types of wage and salary income which lend themselves to easy enforcement to begin with. This payment lag enjoyed by capital income is a substantial advantage especially where inadequate interest penalties are charged for delay and the real value of tax debts is eroded by inflation.

Although no reliable estimates are available, it may well be that the taxable income which is in fact reached usually amounts to less than one-half that which should be reached under tight enforcement. There is no magic formula by which these difficulties may be overcome. Source withholding, assignment of taxpayer numbers (especially to high-income returns), computerization and centralized handling of high-income returns, requirements for information returns on interest and dividend payments to be filed by corporations and banks, reduction in assessment lags, and higher penalties for delayed payments are all helpful. Yet they

[19] For further discussion of various taxes in the LDCs, see R. M. Bird and O. Oldman (eds.), *Readings on Taxation in Developing Countries,* Cambridge, Mass.: Harvard Law School, International Tax Program, 1967.

are insufficient unless the courts stand behind strict enforcement of the tax laws, a prime requirement which in the cultural and political context of developing countries is frequently difficult to meet.

Income tax administration, moreover, is bedeviled by the problem of inflation. It is not infrequent for developing countries to experience price level increases between 10 and 30 percent per year. Such, for instance, has been the case in Chile for many years and continues to be so. In adaptation to this, income tax administration may provide for an automatic annual increase in exemption levels and rate brackets as prices rise, so as to keep the relation between marginal rates and real income constant. As a result, the effect of inflation on income tax equity is neutralized, but the built-in inflation check exerted by an unadjusted progressive income tax is reduced.

The problem of capital gains, especially in relation to land real estate, is of considerable importance in developing countries where rapid urbanization gives rise to increasing land values, much as was observed by Henry George toward the close of the nineteenth century in the United States. To meet this problem, a capital gains tax on real estate, i.e., buildings and land, is administered as a separate tax. As noted below, there is a strong economic, as well as equity, case for such a tax, especially if applied only to gains from land (as distinct from improvements).

Business Income Tax

The most difficult problems arise in the effective taxation of business income, whether under a separate corporation profits tax or as applied to partnership and proprietorship income under the individual income tax. Where business accounting has not been developed to a level sufficient to measure profits with reasonable accuracy, other methods have to be applied. Thus, many countries use a presumptive rather than a direct approach to profit determination. This may take the form of a presumptive profit margin on sales, with different margins stipulated for various industries. This method, which is widely used in Asian countries, in fact transforms the profits tax into a type of sales tax. This shift occurs since tax liability is a function of sales and the *presumptive* rather than actual margin.

In still other situations, the presumptive measure of profits is based on such indices as floor space and location by city blocks, a practice also to be found in the tax tradition of European countries, especially with regard to professional income. In the case of agriculture, acreage or head of cattle may be used as the presumptive base. At the same time, "stick and carrot" techniques might be used to reward the conscientious taxpayers by the use of so-called blue returns, while penalizing the laggard payer by penalty rates. Again, the process of improvement must be gradual and cannot run too far ahead of improvement in accounting methods. Tax reformers are frequently tempted to overlook the importance of improving the techniques of presumptive taxation in favor of preoccupation with technical refinements of corporation taxation which, though important in developed countries, apply to only a small part of the business sector in the LDCs.

Furthermore, the legal forms of business organization frequently differ. In Latin American countries, for example, continental European rather than common-law traditions prevail, while in Asian countries, a quite different system of property law may apply; and practices appropriate for a country such as the United States may not be applicable to LDCs, given their traditions and current state of development.[20]

Land Taxes

Since the agriculture sector in most LDCs is large, the problem of land taxation remains of major importance. One basic question is whether the tax should be imposed on the value of land, on actual income, or on the potential income which the land could yield under full utilization. In a perfectly competitive system, the three bases would be interchangeable since land values would equal the capitalized value of its income, and actual income would equal the potential. In reality, such is not the case. Land is frequently underutilized and held for speculative purposes or as a matter of social custom. Markets may be thin and current sales values not readily obtainable. Thus, the three bases yield substantially different results. Moreover, the income tax is rarely applied effectively to the agricultural sector, so that land revenue frequently serves as a combined income and land tax, including not only the rent of land but also labor and improvement (capital) income in its base.

Turning now to the taxation of income from land only (excluding returns to labor and capital improvements), a strong argument can be made for basing such taxation on potential rather than on actual income.[21] This is shown in Table 34-3. Suppose that a parcel of land, at various levels of utilization and in the absence of tax, yields the income shown in line 1 of the table. The difference between actual and potential yield is given in line 2 and reflects the cost of underutilization to the owner. After a 10 percent tax on actual income is imposed, the cost of underutilization as shown in line 5 is reduced. Thus, underutilization is encouraged. This effect is avoided and the cost of underutilization is held at its pretax level if the tax is imposed on potential rather than actual income, with the result as shown in line 8. The reason is that the tax is independent of actual income so that the marginal tax rate is now zero. In line 9, we go a step further and supplement the 10 percent tax on potential income (line 6) with a penalty charge on underutilization. This charge, for purposes of illustration, rises in rate with the degree of underutilization. Thus, the first 25 percent of shortfall of actual below potential income pays a tax of 25 percent. The next 25 percent (i.e., a shortfall between 25 and 50 percent of potential income) pays at a rate of 50 percent, rising to 75 percent on a shortfall between 50 and 75 percent and to 100 percent on a shortfall between 75 and 100 percent. As shown in line 11, the cost of underutilization is now increased substantially above the pretax level, and net income at low levels of utilization becomes negative. The marginal tax rate on

[20] For a discussion of business tax reform proposals, see R. Slitor, "Reform of the Business Tax Structure," in M. Gillis (ed.), *Fiscal Reform for Columbia,* Cambridge, Mass.: Harvard Law School, International Tax Program, 1971, pp. 463–530.

[21] See J. Hicks and U. Hicks, "The Taxation of the Unimproved Value of Land," in Bird and Oldman, op. cit., pp. 431–442; and R. Bird, *Taxing Agricultural Land in Developing Countries,* Cambridge, Mass.: Harvard Law School, International Tax Program, 1973.

TABLE 34-3
Net Income from Land at Various Levels of Utilization and Types of Land Tax

	PERCENTAGE OF UTILIZATION				
	100	*90*	*50*	*20*	*0*
No Tax					
1. Income	100	90	50	20	0
2. Cost of underutilization to owner		10	50	80	100
10 Percent Tax on Actual Income					
3. Tax	10	9	5	2	0
4. Net income	90	81	45	18	0
5. Cost of underutilization to owner		9	45	72	90
10 Percent Tax on Potential Income					
6. Tax	10	10	10	10	10
7. Net income	90	80	40	10	−10
8. Cost of underutilization to owner		10	50	80	100
10 Percent Tax on Potential Income Plus Penalty Tax on Underutilization					
9. Tax	10	12.5	28.75	42.50	72.50
10. Net income	90	77.5	21.75	−22.50	−72.50
11. Cost of underutilization to owner		12.5	68.25	112.50	162.50

additional income turns negative and the tax on deficient income is in fact a tax on idle land.

Whichever approach is taken, the availability of adequate land surveys and their maintenance on an up-to-date basis are an essential requirement for an efficient system of land taxation. Frequently such surveys are not available, so that only haphazard methods of assessment can be applied.

Wealth and Property Taxes

In addition to land revenue, the taxation of urban real estate is an important part of the tax base, especially as urbanization proceeds. As noted before, a good case can be made for progressive taxation of residental property, combining multiple residences in one base so as to supplement the system of commodity taxation on luxury consumption other than housing.

Beyond this, wealth taxation of the net worth type is a frequent component of the tax structure in LDCs. Although such taxes may in the end prove to be little more than part of the system of real property taxation, with intangibles largely escaping the tax base, they are a useful supplement to income taxation as it applies (or rather fails to apply) to capital income. Real capital is visible and, once accounted for under the wealth tax, earnings therefrom may be traced to its owners under the income tax.

Commodity Taxes and Tariffs

The design of commodity taxation involves three major problems: (1) what products should be taxed and at what rates; (2) at what stages such taxes should be imposed; and (3) how taxation of domestic products should be related to import duties.

As noted previously, the twin objectives of protecting savings and of modifying a highly unequal state of distribution point to the taxation of luxury consumption as the most obvious solution. Given that implementation of a personal type of expenditure tax is hardly feasible for LDCs, the situation calls for taxation of luxury consumption. If this view is correct, the basic requirement is not for a comprehensive and flat-rate sales tax but for a system of sales taxation with differing rates.[22] The implementation of progressive consumption taxation by differentiation between products thus depends on the existence of products with sharply different income elasticities, a precondition which appears to be met in developing countries.

The stage or stages at which commodity taxes are to be imposed has to be decided on grounds of administrative feasibility and thus depends upon the structure of the particular economy. With a multiple-stage tax of the value-added type, failure to reach the retail stage involves only a partial revenue loss, not the total loss that would be the result under a retail sales tax. Moreover, use of the invoice method contributes to better compliance.[23] On the other hand, taxation of final products at differential rates tends to be more difficult under the value-added approach. Where products comprising an important part of the tax base originate in relatively large manufacturing establishments, manufacturer excises offer the simplest and most direct approach. In any case, there is no need to rely on one or the other approach exclusively. A combination of methods may be applied, depending on what is most expedient in any particular case.[24]

There remains the need for coordinating domestic excises with import duties. In their desire to impose heavier burdens on luxury consumption, LDCs frequently place higher import duties upon luxury products, At the same time, this measure often goes with a failure to match such duties by corresponding excises on home-produced luxury goods. Thus, luxury tariffs tend to provide protection to domestic substitutes. This is clearly poor policy. If protective tariffs are to be used to permit domestic infant industries to develop, such industries should be chosen according to their development potential and not as a side effect of luxury taxation. The best approach may well be to use largely uniform tariff rates while including luxury imports in the tax base of the domestic excise system.

Another aspect of tariff policy which requires critical review is the practice of excluding domestically used capital goods from customs duties.[25] In a situation where, for various reasons, the cost of capital tends to be undervalued relative

[22] It should be noted that the distinction is not between types of products which, on nutritional or ethical grounds, may be considered as essential (e.g., bread) rather than as frills (e.g., butter) but simply between commodities which weigh more heavily in high-income and low-income budgets.

[23] See p. 339.

[24] J. Due, *Indirect Taxation in Developing Countries,* Baltimore: Johns Hopkins, 1970; and M. Gillis, "Objectives and Means of Indirect Tax Reform," R. A. Musgrave and M. Gillis (eds.), *Fiscal Reform for Columbia,* Cambridge, Mass.: Harvard Law School, International Tax Program, September 1971, pp. 559–573.

[25] Exclusion of domestically used capital goods is to be distinguished from the exclusion of raw materials or intermediate products which in turn enter into exports, this being an unobjectionable policy.

to the cost of labor, this practice accentuates the price distortion, a matter which will be discussed later.

D. TAX INCENTIVES

We have seen that the twin objectives of economic growth and reduction of inequality can be secured best by reliance on progressive consumption taxes; but we have also seen that equity calls for this approach to be combined with the taxation of capital income under a progressive income tax. Given the potential conflict of the latter with investment incentives, it is not surprising that much attention has been given to various devices by which detrimental investment effects can be minimized. It is a matter of policy judgment, transcending considerations of tax policy only, how far a country should go in trading distributional equity for growth gains; but it is the task of tax policy to make sure that additions to growth are bought at the least equity cost. Tax relief for investment which does not pay for itself in generating additional growth not only involves revenue loss without gain but, by giving the relief to high incomes, worsens the state of income distribution.

Judged on these grounds, tax incentives to investment have been generally wasteful and inequitable, so much so that many observers have been led to reject all incentive devices. But notwithstanding the rather dismal experience, total rejection is not justified. Political pressures for tax incentives will prevail no matter what the tax technician may say; and this being inevitable, they may as well be designed as efficiently as possible. Moreover, some concessions to growth may be in order provided they are made in the best way.

Domestic Incentives

In dealing with the incentive problem, it is helpful to distinguish between domestic incentives and the incentive problem as it relates to foreign capital in particular. Domestic incentives might be related to investment in general, or they might be limited to investment in selected industries or regions. Finally, incentives may be designed to stimulate exports and to strengthen the balance of payments.

General Incentives General investment incentives may take the form of investment credits or accelerated depreciation similar to the devices used in developed countries.[26] In addition, LDCs frequently offer tax holidays during which profits from new enterprises are tax-free for an initial period of, say, five to seven years. This method relates the value of the incentive to high initial profitability, which may run counter to the need for stable and more long-run types of investment. For the case of new investment by existing firms, there is the further difficulty of distinguishing between earnings attributable to the new and old components of their capital stock. Once more this problem is avoided by an investment credit or investment grant approach. Moreover, it is a poor policy for government to make long-run commitments to tax subsidies, especially

[26] See Chap. 22, p. 498.

where it is hoped that there will be a declining need for such subsidies in the future.

However this may be, general investment incentives cannot be effective in raising the overall level of investment unless equal attention is given to raising the level of saving. This may be done by encouraging retention of profits as well as by giving tax credits for saving under the individual income tax. The problem, of course, is to reach savings which otherwise would not have been made and to avoid their being offset by dissaving in other parts of the taxpayer's accounts. Thus, many of the same difficulties arise as were noted previously in the context of the expenditure tax.[27]

Growth Industries While the effectiveness of general investment incentives is questionable, there is more reason to expect that incentives limited to particular sectors or industries will be effective in diverting capital to such industries. The big problem here lies in how to select the industries which are to be given preferential treatment.

Presumably, the industries which should be chosen are those which play a strategic role in development and which, without special favor, will remain underexpanded. Undoubtedly there exist external economies in the development process which are not allowed for in private investment decisions; and imperfect capital markets may misdirect investment even without externalities. Wise correction of such investment errors would thus be desirable, but experience has not been encouraging. Frequently the list of eligible industries is so broad as to involve little selection. In other instances, selection reflects political pressure groups, and in still others, incentives are given to sustain the market for public enterprises, such as steel mills, which should not have been constructed in the first place. Although selective use of incentives is good in principle, efficient application is hard to find.

Regional Incentives Another form of selective incentive arises in regional policy. As we have argued previously, a general case can be made for fiscal neutrality in location decisions, whether for labor or capital.[28] Yet, conditions in developing countries may call for departure from this rule. Labor may be immobile, or maintenance of the labor force in particular regions may be preferable either because excessive migration from rural to urban areas is undesirable or because national policy for noneconomic reasons calls for some degree of equalization in regional development rates. Special incentives may then be given to development in such regions.

The question is whether such incentives are given best by subsidizing investment or by subsidizing employment in the target regions. The answer depends upon the policy objective, i.e., whether the focus is on increasing production or value added in the region, or whether the purpose is to increase payrolls and to raise the standard of living of the region's population. With the latter a wage subsidy may well prove more effective, especially if there is a substantial reserve

[27] See p. 333.
[28] See p. 629.

of unemployed (or underemployed) labor in agriculture which can be drawn into industrial employment if labor costs are reduced.[29] Recent evidence on an experiment with a tax credit scheme to develop the Brazilian Northeast, perhaps the most ambitious regional tax credit effort on record, points toward the inability of capital incentives to generate a high degree of labor absorption in the target area.[30]

Capital versus Employment Incentives

The issue of capital versus wage subsidies transcends the regional issue. While incentive policy has been generally directed at increasing the profitability of capital, recent discussion has pointed toward an alternative approach which would increase the profitability of employing labor. This approach reflects dissatisfaction with an emerging pattern of development which involves increased use of capital without a corresponding increase of employment in the industrial sector. This pattern, which results from the use of highly capital-intensive and labor-saving techniques, runs counter to the objective of a broadly based development in which the gains are shared by large sectors of the population.

Use of highly capital-intensive forms of investment is encouraged by price distortions which overprice the cost of labor and underprice the cost of capital. The former tends to result from minimum wage legislation and excessive union demands, while the latter reflects preferential exchange rates, tariff exemptions, and ineffective profits taxation. In order to redress the balance, wage subsidies might be given either directly or through a "wage-bill credit" similar in principle to the investment credit. Alternatively, profits tax relief may be made contingent on the use of more labor-intensive equipment. Such measures might be appropriate in connection with regional incentives where the objective is to raise income levels in backward areas. It might also be appropriate in dealing with unemployment which results from an excessive influx of rural population into urban areas.[31] Another suggestion for inducing more labor-intensive use of capital is to provide tax incentives which reduce the labor cost for night-shift work.[32]

Incentives to Foreign Capital

Foreign capital, as noted previously, plays an important role in development policy, and tax incentives may be helpful in channeling it to the uses which are most desirable for the whole country.

From the national viewpoint, the role of tax incentives to foreign capital differs from that of incentives to domestic capital. While the latter merely involve transfers between the treasury (which loses revenue) and the investor (who gains),

[29] See Charles E. McLure, "The Design of Regional Tax Incentives for Columbia," in Musgrave and Gillis, op. cit., pp. 545–556. See also R. M. Bird, "Tax Subsidy Policies for Regional Development," *National Tax Journal,* June 1966.

[30] For a hopeful early appraisal, see Hirschman, *A Bias for Hope,* op. cit., pp. 124–158. For a less encouraging second look, see David E. Goodman, "Industrial Development in the Brazilian Northeast: An Interim Appraisal of the Tax Credit Scheme of Article 34/18," in R. Roett, *Brazil in the Sixties,* Nashville, Tenn.: Vanderbilt, 1972.

[31] See A. Harberger, "On Measuring the Social Opportunity Cost of Labor," *International Labor Review,* June 1971.

[32] See D. M. Schydlowsky, "Fiscal Policy for Full Capacity Industrial Growth in Latin America," in *Economic Development in Latin America,* Gainesville: University of Florida Press, 1975.

tax relief granted to foreign investors reduces the whole country's share in the profits earned by foreign capital. This loss must therefore be compensated for by the gains from additional capital influx if the tax incentive is to pay its way. The design of incentives may be helpful in directing foreign capital into such uses as are advantageous to the host country. The gains to be derived from foreign capital lie in the increased earnings for domestic factors of production to which the foreign capital gives rise. There is little advantage to the host country in foreign capital which brings its own resources with it and uses the foreign location as a production site only.[33] Tax incentives therefore should be linked to domestic value added which the foreign capital induces. Moreover, they should be designed to encourage reinvestment and permanent operation, while discouraging quick-kill types of investments.[34]

However this may be, the LDC needs the cooperation of the investor's country of origin if effective incentives are to be granted. If the country of capital ownership taxes this foreign-earned income at its own rate while giving a foreign tax credit, lower taxation by the LDC merely results in a transfer to the other country's treasury while leaving no advantage to the investor who repatriates profits. Tax deferral, however, becomes of major importance. It not only serves to attract capital to the LDC which offers a tax incentive but also exerts a continuing incentive to reinvest earnings in the LDC. Therefore there is good reason for maintaining deferral on investment in LDCs while terminating it for investment in the developed countries.

Another device which would render incentives effective to foreign investors who intend to repatriate is the so-called tax-sparing arrangement. Under this provision, the country of capital ownership would extend a credit, upon repatriation, equal to the full tax in the LDC even though a lesser tax or no tax is paid under the incentive arrangements. This approach, however, lacks the incentive for reinvestment; and, as political pressures call for the incentive to be generalized to all domestic investment, taxation of profits in general is undermined.

A final point arises in connection with competition among LDCs for foreign capital. To the extent that one country outbids another by offering larger incentives, LDCs as a group stand to lose. Some degree of cooperation is desirable to avoid self-defeating tax competition. This is one of the important roles of common market arrangements among groups of LDCs, such as are planned for the West Indies.

Export Incentives

Tax incentives for exports are a popular device to assist in the development of foreign markets and to strengthen the balance of payments. Such incentives, to be effective, should not be related to total foreign sales or profits therefrom, as is typical practice, but to domestic value added. It is only the latter component of foreign sales, and not the reexport of imported material or intermediate goods, which add to a country's foreign exchange earnings.

[33] "Tax haven" types of investments which result in office structures but little local employment, for example, offer little advantage to the host country.

[34] See J. Heller and K. M. Kauffman, *Tax Incentives in Less Developed Countries,* Cambridge, Mass.: Harvard Law School, International Tax Program, 1963.

E. EXPENDITURE POLICY

The role of expenditure policy in economic development has been explored less extensively than that of tax policy, and comparative data are more difficult to obtain.[35] However, comparisons of expenditure budgets for a sample of countries in various parts of the world are offered in Table 34-4. In comparing the patterns of African, Latin American, and Asian countries with those of European countries, some evidence regarding the role of per capita income is obtained. Low-income countries direct a higher share of expenditures to education and health services and a lower share to transfers. The higher share for education to some degree reflects the higher cost of educational services in these countries. The higher share of transfers in high-income countries reflects the more developed social security systems.

The strategic role of public investment in economic development has already been noted. This role is based in part on the undeveloped state of private capital markets and in part on local scarcity of entrepreneurial talent; it is also based on the fact that the type of investment needed at the earliest stages of development frequently includes very large outlays, such as those involved in the development of transportation systems or the opening up of undeveloped parts of the country. Moreover, infrastructure investment of this sort carries external benefits which call for public provision.

TABLE 34-4
Average Expenditure Ratios for Selected Countries, 1967

	Africa	*Latin America*	*Asia*	*Europe, United States, and Canada*
As Percentage of GNP				
Expenditures on:				
Education	3.1	3.2	3.2	4.0
Health	1.4	1.3	1.2	2.8
Defense	1.6	2.3	5.0	3.3
Transfers	3.6	4.1	3.2	16.4
Other*	13.0	11.4	7.2	10.7
Total	22.7	22.3	19.8	37.2
As Percentage of Total Expenditures				
Expenditures on:				
Education	13.7	14.3	16.2	10.8
Health	6.2	5.8	6.1	7.5
Defense	7.0	10.3	25.3	8.9
Transfers	15.9	18.4	16.2	44.1
Other*	57.3	51.1	36.4	28.8
Total	100.0	100.0	100.0	100.0

* Equals difference between itemized expenditures and tax revenue.
Note: Items may not add to total owing to rounding.
Source: Based on G. S. Sahota, *Public Expenditures and Income Distribution in Panama*, unpublished manuscript with data based on United Nations, *Statistical Yearbook, 1968*, and *Yearbook of National Accounts Statistics*, 1968. Material used with kind permission of author.

[35] See our earlier discussion of the relationship of expenditure growth to per capita income, p. 138.

It is not surprising, therefore, that the development of public investment performs a major function in the design of development plans in LDCs. In this context, the use of cost-benefit analysis is of great importance. Developing countries can ill afford to waste scarce resources, and yet efficient project evaluation is a difficult task. In one respect, cost-benefit analysis is more readily applied in developing than in developed countries. This is because public investment is typically aimed at the provision of intermediate goods, the value of which may be measured in terms of their effects upon the prices of privately provided goods.[36] Thus the return on transportation or irrigation projects may be appraised in terms of the resulting reduction in the cost of goods as they reach the market. This is a measure which cannot be applied where public outlays go to provide final goods of the consumption type. But in other respects, the task of evaluation is more difficult.

For one thing, the direct benefits thus made available will be accompanied by indirect or external benefits which are harder to assess. For another, costs are more difficult to determine. Since market prices may not reflect the true social costs involved, shadow prices must be used in their place. If capital is undervalued while labor is overvalued, the use of market prices leads to the previously noted distortion toward excessively capital-intensive technology. Further difficulties arise in the context of dynamic development where relative prices which apply when the project is introduced may give way to a quite different set of prices applicable during the years when the services of the project are rendered. Once more, this possibility points to the importance of longer-run planning and the evaluation of individual projects in the context of an overall development plan.

Another factor of obvious importance is proper determination of the discount rate. With private capital markets not fully developed, use of a "social rate" may be more or less inevitable. Considerations suggesting the presence of external benefits indicate that the social rate should be set below the level of rates prevailing in the market, thus pointing to a higher rate of capital formation and the choice of longer-term projects. Pointing in the other direction is the fact that the cost of forgoing current consumption is very high at low levels of income; yet, in the future when the gain from postponement is realized, the margin utility of consumption will be less since income is higher. This fact tends to be overlooked in individual savings decisions but should be allowed for by government. But here, as in other matters of discount rate determination, cruder approaches are likely to be used. In the typical development context, the government may find itself confronted with the practical necessity of determining the politically acceptable minimum path of consumption over the next five or ten years and may derive the discount rate therefrom.

Human investment, as noted before, deserves particular consideration in the development context. Education programs are important not only as a matter of growth policy but also for their important bearing on how the gains from growth will be distributed both among income groups and among various sectors of the economy. Studies have shown exceedingly high rates of return on educa-

[36] See p. 163.

tional investment in developing countries, thus pointing to the particular importance of this form of capital formation, but it is essential that the educational inputs be designed to meet the country's need for specific labor skills.

F. SUMMARY

Fiscal policy in less developed countries differs in important respects from that in highly developed countries. This variation is due to the fact that the economic and social setting in LDCs is different:

1. The fundamental need for capital formation and the difficulty of generating the required level of saving out of a low per capita income are dominant factors.

2. Measures to induce technological improvement, to encourage enterprise, and to develop institutions making for more efficient use of resources are also of major importance.

3. Pursuit of these objectives is made difficult by social and political factors as well as deficient administrative capabilities.

4. Foreign trade is usually of prime importance, as is the need for foreign exchange adequate to secure the necessary imported capital equipment.

5. Sectoral divisions within the economy tend to create bottlenecks and to interfere with balanced growth.

These are but some of the difficulties which arise and which must be considered in the formulation of fiscal policy:

6. Given the target rate of growth, a certain rate of capital formation is needed. The savings rate—public and private—must be set so as to match the needed rate of capital formation.

7. Measuring the contribution of the public sector to overall savings by the surplus in the current budget, this surplus must equal the excess of required total saving over available private saving. From this figure, the required rate of taxation may be deduced.

8. The requirement for a tax structure which secures an adequate level of saving must be reconciled with the requirement for tax equity.

9. While severe taxation of saving and investment by individuals and corporations may be counterproductive because it may retard growth, a substantial tax base is available in the consumption of higher-income households.

10. While the primary concern with growth renders the fiscal policy rules applicable in LDCs more akin to those developed in Chapters 22 and 23 than to those of Chapters 24 and 25, the contingency of deficient demand with underemployment of the labor force and of inflation nevertheless arises.

11. Indeed, inflation generated by budgetary policy is frequently found in developing countries, and it interferes with efficient resource use.

Turning to the problems of tax policy, we have dealt with the general problems of taxable capacity and the composition of the tax structure as well as with the design of particular taxes:

12. The tax-to-GNP ratio of LDCs is much below that of developed countries. This fact reflects lower taxable capacity as well as lower tax effort.

13. At low levels of per capita income, tax "handles" are scarce. The tax structure tends to be dominated by production and sales taxes, especially customs duties, with a low share for profits and income taxes.

14. Effective administration of income and profits taxes is difficult owing to such factors as a high degree of self-employment, the small size of establishments, and inadequate accounting practices. In addition, taxpayer compliance and enforcement tend to be low with large-scale evasion, especially of capital income. Use of presumptive taxes has to be relied on.

15. Agricultural taxation is of major importance in most LDCs because of the relatively large scope of their agricultural sectors. However, effective taxation of land and agricultural income is unpopular and difficult to implement.

16. Wealth and property taxes may be a useful supplement to ineffective taxation of capital income.

17. Implementation of a general sales tax at the retail level is difficult because of the small scale of establishments. Typically, taxation at the manufacturer's level is more feasible and may be combined with use of value-added taxation for some products.

18. As distinct from a flat-rate consumption tax, taxation of luxury products at higher rates, with equal treatment of domestically produced and imported goods, permits a more equitable use of consumption taxes.

19. LDCs tend to make widespread use of tax incentives to investment. Frequently, these are not very effective and create tax inequities.

20. Special problems arise with tax incentives to foreign capital.

21. The incentive structure should be designed to consider effects on employment as well as effects on investment.

Turning, finally, to the role of expenditure policy, we have noted these points:

22. Public investment and public lending play strategic roles in development.

23. The concept of public capital formation should be interpreted to include productivity-increasing investment in human resources.

24. Foreign borrowing increases the current supply of available resources and thus permits development with a lesser burden on the present generation.

FURTHER READINGS

Bird, R. M., and O. Oldman (eds.): *Readings on Taxation in Developing Countries,* Cambridge, Mass.: Harvard Law School, International Tax Program, 1967.

Bird, R. M.: *Taxing Agricultural Land in Developing Countries,* Cambridge, Mass.: Harvard Law School, International Tax Program, 1973.

Hinrichs, H.: *A General Theory of Tax Structure Change During Economic Development,* Cambridge, Mass.: Harvard Law School, International Tax Program, 1966.

Musgrave, R. A., and M. Gillis (eds.): *Fiscal Reform for Columbia,* final report and staff papers of the Columbian Commission on Tax Reform, Cambridge, Mass.: Harvard Law School, International Tax Program, September 1971.

———: *Fiscal Systems,* part 2, Yale, New Haven, Conn.: 1969.

Prest, A. R.: *Public Finance in Under-Developed Countries,* London: Weidenfeld and Nicholson, 1962.

Indexes

Name Index

Subject Index